CRITICAL ACCLAIM FOR THE BERKELEY GUIDES

"[The Berkeley Guides are] brimming with useful infor~ low-budget traveler — material delivered in a fresh irreverent way." —*T~ ~uirer*

"...hip, blunt and lively....these Cal students boogie ~n and tell you where to sleep in a cowboy bunkhouse, get a tattoo and eat cheap meals cooked by aspiring chefs." —*Atlanta Journal Constitution*

"...Harvard hasn't yet met `On the Loose's' pledge to plant two trees in Costa Rica for every one felled to print its books—a promise that, given the true grit of these guides, might well mean a big new forest in Central America." —*Newsweek*

"[The Berkeley Guides] offer straight dirt on everything from hostels to look for and beaches to avoid to museums least likely to attract your parents...they're fresher than Harvard's Let's Go series." —*Seventeen*

"The books are full of often-amusing tips written in a youth-tinged conversational style." —*The Orlando Sentinel*

"So well-organized and well-written that I'm almost willing to forgive the recycled paper and soy-based ink." —*P.J. O'Rourke*

"These guys go to great lengths to point out safe attractions and routes for women traveling alone, minorities and gays. If only this kind of caution weren't necessary. But I'm glad someone finally thought of it."

—*Sassy*

"The very-hip Berkeley Guides look like a sure-fire hit for students and adventurous travelers of all ages. This is real budget travel stuff, with the emphasis on meeting new places head on, up close and personal....this series is going to go places." —*The Hartford Courant*

"The guides make for fun and/or enlightening reading."

—*The Los Angeles Times*

"The new On the Loose guides are more comprehensive, informative and witty than Let's Go ." —*Glamour*

OTHER BERKELEY GUIDE TITLES

the BERKELEY guides

THE BUDGET TRAVELER'S HANDBOOK

MEXICO

ON THE LOOSE 1995

WRITTEN BY BERKELEY STUDENTS IN COOPERATION WITH THE
ASSOCIATED STUDENTS OF THE UNIVERSITY OF CALIFORNIA

MEXICO ON THE LOOSE

Editors: Jessica Blatt, Kora McNaughton
Editorial Coordinators: Laura Comay Bloch, Sharron S. Wood
Executive Editor: Scott McNeely
Creative Director: Fabrizio La Rocca
Cartographer: David Lindroth; Eureka Cartography
Text Design: Tigist Getachew
Cover Design and Illustration: Rico Lins

SPECIAL SALES

Contents

PRESENTING AN INDEPENDENT APPROACH TO TRAVEL.

If you have independent ideas about travel, we specialize in putting you exactly where you want to be. And with over 100 offices worldwide, we'll take care of you when you're there. So when it's time to plan your trip, call us at 1.800.777.0112.

New York: 212-477-7166
Washington DC: 202-887-0912
Philadelphia: 215-382-2928
Boston: 617-266-6014
Los Angeles: 213-934-8722
San Francisco: 415-391-8407

STA TRAVEL
We've been there

What the Berkeley Guides Are All About

Four years ago, a motley bunch of U.C. Berkeley students spent the summer traveling on shoestring budgets to launch a new series of guidebooks—the *Berkeley Guides.* We wrote the books because, like thousands of travelers, we had grown tired of the outdated attitudes and information served up year after year in other guides. Most important, we thought a travel guide should be written by people who know what cheap travel is all about.

You see, it's one of life's weird truisms that the more cheaply you travel, the more you inevitably experience. You're bound to experience a lot with the *Berkeley Guides,* because we believe in living like bums and spending as little money as possible. You won't find much in our guides about how a restaurant prepares its duck á l'orange or how a hotel blends mauve curtains with green carpet. Instead, we tell you if a place is cheap, clean (no bugs), and worth the cash.

Coming from a community as diverse as Berkeley, we also wanted our books to be useful to everyone, so we tell you if a place is wheelchair accessible, if it provides resources for gay and lesbian travelers, and if it's safe for women traveling solo. Many of us are Californians, which means most of us like trees and mountain trails. It also means we emphasize the outdoors in every *Berkeley Guide,* including lots of info about hiking and tips on protecting the environment. To further minimize our impact on the environment, we print our books on recycled paper using soy-based inks.

Most important, these guides are for travelers who want to see more than just the main sights. We find out what local people do for fun, where they go to eat, drink, or just hang out. Most guidebooks lead you down the tourist trail, ignoring important local issues, events, and culture. In the *Berkeley Guides* we give you the information you need to understand what's going on around you, whether it's the latest on NAFTA or the Zapatistas in Chiapas.

The *Berkeley Guides* began by covering Eastern Europe, Mexico, California, and the Pacific Northwest and Alaska. In the course of research our writers weathered bus plunges and landed bush planes above the Arctic Circle. The second year was no different: Our student writers weathered guerrilla attacks in the Guatemalan highlands, motorcycle wrecks in Ireland, and a strange culinary concoction in Belize known as "greasy-greasy." The result was five new guidebooks, covering Central America, France, Germany, San Francisco, and Great Britain and Ireland. This year things were even crazier: One writer lost her skirt on a moped, two crashed their motorbikes, and another spent hours digging through a dumpster to reclaim a batch of "misplaced" manuscript. Bloodied but unbowed, the *Berkeley Guides* brings you four new guidebooks, covering Europe, Italy, Paris, and London, not to mention completely revised and updated editions of our first- and second-year guides.

We've done our best to make sure the information in the *Berkeley Guides* is accurate, but time doesn't stand still: Prices change, and places go out of business. Call ahead when it's really important, assuming, of course, that the place has a phone.

Thanks to You

Putting together a guidebook on Mexico is always an adventure. Our writers pressed on despite derailed trains, buses delayed by army inspections, various gastrointestinal disorders, and the innumerable distractions that stood in the way of getting their manuscript back to Berkeley on time. Throughout Mexico our writers relied on helpful souls for their advice and encouragement, and we'd like to thank the following people—as well as the hundreds of others whom our writers met briefly on the road. Drop us a line—a postcard, a scrawled note on toilet paper, whatever—and we'll be happy to acknowledge your contribution. Our address is 515 Eshleman Hall, University of California, Berkeley, CA 94720.

Alonso Adame (Durango); Luis Ordaz Aguilar (La Paz); Alfredo at the Hostal Internacional (San Miguel de Allende); Gloria G. Alumina (Chihuahua); Nico, Sylvia, and Adolfito Arriaga (Jalapa); Juan José Bretón Avalos (Puebla); Tom Bachmaier and Nahir (Pochutla); Ali Batrus (Guanajuato); Boaz (Isla Mujeres); Bucko (Zipolite); Luis Alejandro Bustamante (Querétaro); the Concha-Balmori family (Mexico City); Jennie Deleskie (Cuernavaca); Don, Mike, and Dave (Ocean Beach, CA); Jan Ellison (Acapulco); Olympia Ortiz Flores (Tijuana); Bridget Gaitan (Casas Grandes); John Gladstein (Indiana); Gonzalo and Jimmy (Jalapa); Erick Herrera (Tapachula); Oscar Herrera (Durango); Hotel Marlowe's entire staff, especially Rita, Abel, Flavio, Julián, Abraham, Araceli, Ana María, Miguel, and Margarita (Mexico City); Katherine and her Aunt Julie (Mazatlán); Francisco Sotelo Leyva (Tijuana); Hortencia Rodriguez Limón (Huatulco); Ronald Loshin (Kensington, CA); Jose and Aurora (Dzibalchén); Gwen Maka (Oaxaca city); James McLaughlin and Margarita (Creel); Gonzalo Medellin (San Miguel de Allende); Andrea Meza (Ensenada); Miguel (Chilpancingo); Mirla (Mazatlán); Amelinda Marroquín Monzón (Tapachula); Liz Murray (Oaxaca city); Alfonso Raul Nader (Tampico); Noodle (Portland, OR); Pablo and Pepe (Tijuana); Teresa Ovando Pascacia (Tonalá); Dr. Luis Palazuelos Platas (Villahermosa); Tracy Perkins (Casas Grandes); Mary Price (Casas Grandes); Octavio Ramos (Chacalapa); Jaime and Inés Rangel (Coatepec); Diego Rhodes and the staff of Paraiso del Oso (Cerocahui); Hugo Antonio Santiago (Oaxaca city); Herbierto Villegas (San Felipe); Michael Werner (San Miguel de Allende); Galinda Worland (Washington, D.C.); and Irma López Zea (San Cristóbal de las Casas).

The editors are especially grateful to the following people, who provided advice, information, and moral support: Jorge Jiménez Aguirre (Berkeley, CA); Ignacio Fernandez (Berkeley, CA); Io McNaughton (Bolinas, CA); Raul (Aguascalientes); Miguel Rivas (Oakland, CA); and copyeditors Frederick Aldama, Loreena Alper-Jones, Jay Dayrit, and Duncan and Eugenia McNaughton.

We are also indebted to the many readers who wrote in with feedback and new information: Brock and Michele (Toronto, Canada); Barbara J. Carter and Marc D. Moskovitz (Toledo, OH); Leonor Ehling (Berkeley, CA); Monica Furness (Indianapolis, IN); Chris Kirk (Navasota, TX); Richard Parker (College Station, TX); Michael Rosenfeld and Vivian Levy (Chicago, IL); and Pamela Walth (Guadalajara).

Berkeley Bios

Behind every restaurant blurb, lodging review, and introduction in this book lurks a student writer. You might recognize the type—perpetually short on time, money, and clean underwear. Six Berkeley students spent the summer traveling around Mexico researching and writing this book. Back in Berkeley two envious editors enjoyed Mexico vicariously at their all-too-stationary computers.

The Writers

Currently finishing her master's degree in Hispanic Languages and Literatures, **Michele Back** has a number of lifetime goals. They change weekly but are always lofty and devoid of money-making potential. Forsaking her first true cultural love—the Caribbean—for the Bajío, Heart-land, and central cities of Mexico, she enjoyed every aspect of her trip—except for 85% of the men she met—and is now mourning her current state of taco and *chilaquiles* deprivation.

Cassie Coleman had to use all her four years of training in anthropology at U.C. Berkeley to maintain her objectivity about the hordes of partying teenagers in the Pacific Coast resorts. (The chance to go mountain-biking in the hills of Jalisco and wander the quiet streets of Taxco helped a bit, too.) She returned to the States to spend two years as a bilingual elementary-school teacher in Oakland's public schools, as part of the Teach for America program.

While swinging in her hammock during her last *Berkeley Guides* assignment in the Yucatán, **Jamie Davidson** hadn't the slightest suspicion that, one year later, she'd find herself thumbing through Baja California and the northwestern states for the 1995 edition. Softening the blow were a few scuba dives, wild desert adventures, and chocolate clams. After graduating from U.C. Berkeley with a degree in philosophy, Jamie plans to abduct a certain U.K. editor for travels far and wide.

Three flat tires and two chicken-filled bus rides into her trip, **Ariana Mohit,** in a dehydration-induced delirium, found herself considering selling her soul—or at least the remains of her worldly possessions (a pair of dirty sneakers and a toothbrush)—for a roll of toilet paper. After spending nine weeks covering Mexico City, Veracruz, and the Northeast, Ariana discovered an affinity for *carne asada* and freak, out-of-nowhere thunderstorms. Ariana is now back in Los Angeles after spending the rest of her summer living and working in Mexico City.

As he passed through the endless army checkpoints in the highlands of Oaxaca and Chiapas, **Ian Signer** often wondered why he was so often singled out for questioning ("What is your mission here?", "Where did you learn to speak Spanish?"). Only later did he realize that his light hair, medium stature, and green eyes matched the government's description of Subcomandante Marcos, the much-sought leader of the Zapatistas. He is especially grateful for the apples, gum, and candy that the soldiers almost always distributed after keeping his bus waiting forever, and to the polite thief in Tapachula who took his backpack but left all the contents (except a pack of gummy bears), a note of apology, and a replacement duffel bag.

Temporarily forsaking an exciting career in tax law analysis, **David Walter** grabbed an old backpack and made his way to the highlands of Guatemala, where he was captured by a small band of revolutionaries with an obscure philosophy and forced to translate the lyrics to Eagles songs. He was finally ransomed by the *Berkeley Guides* and, in exchange for their aid, agreed to write the Yucatán chapter. At one point on his trip, David almost converted to Maya religion after abandoning his mud-caked bicycle to flee from an unidentifiable but unquestionably large and growling quadruped in the ruins of an ancient temple at Hochob.

The Editors

Jessica Blatt and **Kora McNaughton** fused while editing this book and can no longer tell themselves apart. Every day they wondered: "What are two nice Jewish girls like us doing in a place like this?" Jessica, who now questions the wisdom of once riding all over Mexico on a motorcycle, has a degree in anthropology and hopes to move back to Rio de Janeiro and study absolutely nothing at all. Kora, a graduate student in journalism, wants to move to Chile (her *país adoptivo*) and become a ruthless cosmopolite after touring Mexico by second-class bus. Their only regret is that Mexico didn't play Brazil in the final game of World Cup '94.

Finally, we'd also like to thank the Random House folks who helped us with cartography, page design, and production: Bob Blake, Ellen Browne, Denise DeGennaro, Tigist Getachew, Laura Kidder, Fabrizio La Rocca, Tracy Patruno, and Linda Schmidt.

Mexican States and Capitals

CALIFORNIA

Mexicali ★

ARIZONA

NEW MEXICO

BAJA
CALIFORNIA
NORTE

Golfo

de

Hermosillo ★

SONORA

CHIHUAHUA

Chihuahua ★

BAJA
CALIFORNIA
SUR

California

COAHUILA

SINALOA

La Paz ★

Culiacán ★

DURANGO

Durango ★

ZACATECAS

Zacatecas ★

S
P

AGUASCALIENTES

Tepic ★

NAYARIT

Aguascalientes ★

Guanajuato ★

Guadalajara ★

GUANAJUATO

JALISCO

Colima ★

Morelia ★

M

COLIMA

MICHOACAN

To

GUERRERO

PACIFIC OCEAN

N

0 _____ 200 miles

0 _____ 300 km

Mexican States and Capitals

OKLAHOMA

ARKANSAS

TENN.

UNITED STATES

TEXAS

MISS.

ALA.

Rio Grande

LOUISIANA

NUEVO LEON

★ ★ Guadalupe
Saltillo

TAMAULIPAS

Gulf of México

★ Ciudad Victoria

San Luis Potosí

SAN LUIS POTOSI

QUERETARO

VERACRUZ

★ Querétaro

HIDALGO

México City

★ Pachuca

Mérida ★

MEXICO

★ TLAXCALA

Jalapa

YUCATAN

★ D.F

★ Tlaxcala

Campeche ★

Toluca

Puebla

Cuernavaca

PUEBLA

QUINTANA ROO

MORELOS

★ Chilpancingo

TABASCO

CAMPECHE

Chetumal ★

Villahermosa

★ Oaxaca

OAXACA

★ Tuxtla Gutiérrez

CHIAPAS

BELIZE

Caribbean Sea

GUATEMALA

HONDURAS

OKLAHOMA

TENN.

ARKANSAS

MISS.

TEXAS

ALA.

LOUISIANA

Río Grande

Nueva
Laredo

Monterrey

Reynosa

Matamoros

SIERRA MADRE ORIENTE

57

101

Ciudad Victoria

Ciudad Mante

Tampico

Gulf of Mexico

n Miguel
Allende

Querétaro

Poza Rica

El Tajín

Teotihuacán

Mexico City

Veracruz

Mérida

**Chichén
Itzá**

Tizimín

Cancún

Cozumel

Puebla

Campeche

Ciudad
del
Carmen

Uxmal

Cobá

Xel-Há

rnavaca

Bahía de Campeche

Y U C A T Á N

Tulum

hilpancingo

Coatzacoalcos

MADRE DEL SUR

Minatitlán

Villahermosa

Chetumal

186

Monte Albán

Oaxaca

Tuxtla
Gutiérrez

Palenque

San Cristóbal
de las Casas

Caribbean Sea

BELIZE

Tehuantepec

Comitán

Huatulco

*Golfo de
Tehuantepec*

Tapachula

GUATEMALA

HONDURAS

Introduction

By Jessica Blatt and Kora McNaughton

The images of Mexico that circulate outside the Spanish-speaking world are largely those filtered through the media: the mustachioed bandido or wailing mariachi of a Hollywood movie, or the migrant laborer and his hard-working señora about whom the U.S. border patrol are so concerned. There are also counterimages, of course: the downtrodden victims of imperialism, the long-suffering but vibrantly attired Indians, and the fiery, principled revolutionaries. These stereotypes have been circulating with an unusual fierceness of late, as a result of the international attention focused on the signing of the North American Free Trade Agreement, the subsequent rebel uprising in southern Mexico, and the 1994 Mexican presidential elections.

After years of being relegated to the travel section of newspapers, Mexico leapt to the front pages during the debate over NAFTA. Opponents of the trade agreement argued that if it were passed, the movement of U.S. industry and jobs across the border would create a "giant sucking sound," and they conjured up a Mexico where grossly underpaid workers with few rights eke out a squalid living in factories, or scrape it from the unforgiving soil. At the same time, NAFTA's proponents extolled the potential of the huge Mexican market, the country's accelerating industrialization, and its natural resources, all of which were supposed to inject new life into the sagging U.S. economy.

Then, on January 1, 1994, the day NAFTA went into effect, a group of poorly armed but well-organized peasants (mainly of Maya descent) calling themselves the Zapatista National Liberation Army (EZLN) attacked four towns in the southern state of Chiapas with the stated goal of stopping the genocide of southern Mexico's Indian population. In the words of one EZLN spokesman: "The war we declare is a final, absolutely final measure. We have nothing, absolutely nothing. Not a dignified roof, nor work, nor land, nor health care nor education." The apparent leader of this group was a masked soldier known as Subcomandante Marcos, an erudite man who quickly became the preferred object of media attention. He was simultaneously vilified and adored: The Mexican administration said he was probably a foreigner, come to stir up subversion among the poor; for the left, he was a recycled Che Guevara, come to take up the banner of the oppressed.

That all of these events took place in an election year—the first presidential election after 1988, when the ruling PRI (Partido Revolucionario Institucional) was widely thought to have held on to its 60-year rule only by resorting to electoral fraud—raised the stakes riding on all these competing visions of Mexico's present and future. Is Mexico marching into the First World on the strength of free trade and industry? Or is it fundamentally underdeveloped, an authoritarian country whose disenfranchised population can hope for nothing more than a ticket across the border or a low-paying job in a foreign-owned assembly plant? Or is it the last bastion of Latin American communist revolution, a guerrilla-filled jungle resounding with gunfire and calls for justice?

The reality is that all of these visions contain partial truths. Northern Mexico is characterized by vast stretches of desert and a high concentration of *maquiladoras* (foreign-owned factories in duty-free zones) that capitalize on the low wages they can pay their Mexican workers, many of whom live without basic services or health care in shantytowns. The industrialization of the north has also had a significant environmental impact, causing pollution levels to balloon. Much of the country, however, remains agrarian, and Mexico's great *meseta* (central plateau) is some of the most fertile land in the Americas. Geographically, Mexico is incredibly diverse, encompassing scrubby tropical coastland, dense jungle, cool mountain ranges, volcanic plains, temperate forests, huge lakes, and harsh deserts. Regional differences are social and economic, as well as geographical. Wealth is concentrated in the north, largely in the hands of the *criollo* (Spanish-descended) and *mestizo* (mixed-descent) elite. The south is much more indigenous, more agrarian, and poorer. It was in the context of this regional and race-based inequality that the Zapatistas emerged.

The Zapatistas are named for Emiliano Zapata, one of the military leaders of the Mexican Revolution (1910–1917), which continues to have a powerful hold on the Mexican imagination to this day. In many ways, the parallels are striking. In 1910, the Mexican government was in the hands of dictator Porfirio Díaz, whose 34-year rule was characterized by economic modernization, extreme concentration of wealth in the hands of a few *hacendados* (landowners) and foreign investors, the repression of political opposition, and the dispossession and forced relocation of indigenous people. The movement against Díaz was led by Francisco I. Madero, the liberal son of a Chihuahua landowner, and his call of "Effective Suffrage—No Reelection!" Madero was joined by a number of rebel armies, including those of "Pancho" Villa to the north and Emiliano Zapata in central Mexico. Together, they were successful in forcing Díaz's resignation, and Madero was almost unanimously elected in the free elections that followed. As is so often the case with the high ideals of revolutions, however, many of the rebels' goals fell by the wayside during the Madero regime, such as the restoration of Indian lands and agrarian reform in general. Much of the reverence accorded to Zapata today derives from his resistance to this atrophy of revolutionary fervor: When it became apparent that the new government was not committed to land redistribution, he took up arms again.

The Zapatistas of 1994 faced a similar political reality: The PRI has had an almost unchallenged hold on Mexico's federal government since 1929, ruling with authoritarian policies aimed less at enforcing an ideological position than at maintaining their monopoly on power. The two main opposition groups are the right-leaning PAN (Partido de Acción Nacional), which has ties to the Catholic Church, and the left-of-center PRD (Partido de la Revolución Democrática), whose candidate was in the lead in the 1988 elections until a mysterious computer crash interfered with the ballot counting. Both parties have denounced electoral fraud and called for reform for years, but they have had little success in breaking the PRI's hold on

Mexico for Export

While most people don't think of Mexico as having much influence on global culture, Mexican "telenovelas" (soap operas) are popular from Miami to Moscow. Light-skinned actors are the protagonists of simplistic plots dealing with issues of class conflict, gender roles, and of course, love and lust. The dialogue may be melodramatic and the actors chosen for their looks and singing ability rather than any acting talent, but millions of people plant themselves in front of the television every night to soak up idealized images of Mexican life. What many foreign viewers don't realize, however, is that these images are less a reflection of Mexican reality than a vision manufactured by the executives of Mexico's powerful media conglomerate, Televisa.

In this sense, telenovelas represent the selling of Mexican culture by powerful business interests. In fact, much of what Mexico presents to the outside world is such a fabrication, at least in part. Mariachi music, for example, is not as typically Mexican as one would believe: Its predecessor, the "son jalisciense," had been around for a long time before horns were added in the 1940s, when radio stations in Guadalajara decided they needed a more commercially viable sound. So consider carefully what you're buying, or whose version of Mexico you're buying into.

the federal government, and have in many cases been sent not-so-subtle messages to cease and desist (a number of opposition-party workers have been assassinated in recent years).

The Chiapan rebels, however, succeeded in bringing change to the forefront of the political debate. Their leaders began sending communiqués to the Mexican press, explaining that the Chiapan Indians, who for centuries had labored while landowners held all political and economic power, were now resorting to desperate measures to show that progress was leaving them behind. The rebels vowed they would continue to do so until the government was made truly accountable to the people.

The Zapatistas were not looking to replace the government with a pre-packaged ideological program of their own, but were in essence an armed movement for democracy, as strange as that sounds. It was apparent they weren't going to "win" a war with the Mexican army—rather, they effected a sophisticated media coup. The recent elections were far from squeaky clean and resulted in yet another PRI victory, but electoral fraud in Mexico is now an international issue, and elections there have for the first time been opened to outside observers. The new president, Ernesto Zedillo, must deal with the issues of social justice, land distribution, and costs of modernization that the Zapatista uprising brought to the forefront. However, the extent of the PRI's commitment to a more democratic Mexico remains to be seen.

BASICS

If you've ever traveled with anyone before, you know the two types of people in the world: the planners and the nonplanners. You also know that travel brings out the very worst in both groups: Left to their own devices, the planners will have you goose-stepping from attraction to attraction on a cultural blitzkrieg, while the nonplanners will invariably miss the flight, the bus, and the point. This Basics chapter offers you a middle ground, providing enough information to help plan your trip without saddling you with an itinerary or invasion plan. Keep in mind that companies go out of business, prices inevitably go up, and, hey, we're only too human.

Planning Your Trip

WHEN TO GO

The two traditional vacation times in Mexico are Semana Santa (Holy Week, the week before Easter) and the period from Christmas through New Year's. Carnaval is a week-long festival involving costumes, parades, and a great deal of general revelry that takes place in February, during the week preceding Ash Wednesday. During these holidays, hotels in most beach communities, even small ones, are usually booked well in advance, prices may be jacked up, and armies of towel-toting tourists swarm the beaches. Resorts popular with college students (e.g. any place with a beach) tend to fill up in the summer months, when schools are out. To avoid hordes of foreign and local tourists, heavy rains, and high prices, the best times to go are October, March, April, and early May.

CLIMATE The climate in Mexico, from the wet, tropical Yucatán to the dry, hot northwest, is as varied as the country's landscape. Mountains and desert, sea and jungle—there's little room for generalities. The southern region tends to be hot and humid, the north more temperate. Both must contend with the country's long rainy season, which extends from May until mid-October. The south gets a more generous helping of rain—more than 100 inches a year.

HOLIDAYS On public holidays, expect a spirit of celebration and most businesses (especially offices) to be closed. The following are some of the most important Mexico-wide holidays. Regional festivals are listed in individual chapters.

January 1: The **New Year** is celebrated with mariachi music, midnight church bells, and an early morning "rooster mass" (*misa de gallo*). Many agricultural and livestock fairs are also held around this date.

It's easy to remember the dates of important events in Mexican history, as they function as street names in most Mexican cities. For example, you'll find lots of streets named 5 de Febrero—a reference to Constitution Day.

January 6: **El Día de los Reyes** (Feast of the Epiphany or Three Kings Day) is a traditional day of gift-giving. This is also the day when the founding of Mérida is celebrated.

February 5: **Día de la Constitucíon,** or Constitution Day, is a national holiday during which official speeches and ceremonies are conducted nationwide.

March 21: **Natalicio de Benito Juárez** and **Día de la Primavera** celebrates the birthday of Mexico's reformist president Benito Juárez and marks the date of the spring equinox.

May 1: All businesses—even movie theaters—close as **Día del Trabajo** (Labor Day) is celebrated with workers' parades and speeches.

May 5: **Cinco de Mayo** is a national holiday that celebrates the Mexican defeat of the French at the Battle of Puebla.

September 15–16: **Día de la Independencia** (Independence Day) commemorates the speech, or *grito,* by Father Miguel Hidgalgo that called for rebellion against the Spanish in 1810.

November 1–2: On the **Día de los Muertos** (Day of the Dead) dead friends, relatives, and ancestors are honored. People visit the graves of the dearly departed and build altars in their homes with offerings of food, flowers, fruits, and sweets.

November 20: The **Aniversario de la Revolución** recalls the Mexican Revolution with parades, speeches, and patriotic events.

December 12: **Día de la Virgen de Guadalupe** (Day of the Virgin of Guadalupe) honors the patron saint of Mexico with religious rites, processions, and pilgrimages.

The Highs and the Lows

Average daily highs and lows stack up as follows:

City	January: High/Low	June: High/Low
Acapulco	88°F/72°F	91°F/77°F
	31°C/22°C	33°C/25°C
Cozumel	82°F/68°F	89°F/75°F
	28°C/20°C	32°C/24°C
Ensenada	64°F/45°F	75°F/61°F
	18°C/7°C	32°C/24°C
Guadalajara	75°F/45°F	79°F/59°F
	24°C/7°C	24°C/15°C
La Paz	72°F/57°F	95°F/75°F
	22°C/14°C	35°C/24°C
Mexico City	70°F/41°F	73°F/52°F
	21°C/5°C	23°C/11°C
Monterrey	68°F/48°F	91°F/72°F
	20°C/9°C	34°C/22°C
Puerto Vallarta	84°F/63°F	95°F/73°F
	29°C/17°C	35°C/23°C

December 24–25: **Navidad** (Christmas) is celebrated as it is all over the Americas, with dinner and midnight mass on Christmas Eve, followed by mass on Christmas Day.

GOVERNMENT TOURIST OFFICES

Aside from offering the usual glossy tourist brochures, state and local tourist offices can answer general questions about travel in their area or refer you to other organizations for more information. If writing for information, your may want to request brochures on specialized interests, such as boating, horseback riding, or biking, which may not be included in a generic information package.

IN THE UNITED STATES The **Mexican Government Tourism Office** (405 Park Ave., Suite 1400, New York, NY 10022, tel. 212/755–7261; 10100 Santa Monica Blvd., Los Angeles, CA 90067, tel. 310/203–8191; 2707 N. Loop West, Suite 1801, Houston, TX 77008, tel. 713/880–1833; 1911 Pennsylvania Ave., Washington, D.C., 20036, tel. 202/728–1750; 128 Aragon Ave., Coral Gables, FL 33134, tel. 305/443–9160; 70 East Lake St., Suite 1413, Chicago, IL 60601, tel. 312/606–9015) can answer questions and provide maps and travel information.

IN CANADA The **Mexican Government Tourism Office** (2 Bloor St., West, Suite 1801, Toronto, Ont. M4W3E2, tel. 416/925–0704; 1 Place Ville Marie, Montreal, Suite 1526, Que. H3B2B5, tel. 514/871–1052; 1610-999 W. Hastings St., Vancouver, BC V6C2W2, tel. 604/669–2845) has travel information and maps.

IN THE UNITED KINGDOM Mexico **Government Tourism Office** in London is at 7 Cork St., London, England WIX 1 PB, tel. 0171/734–10–58.

BUDGET TRAVEL ORGANIZATIONS

Student Travel Australia (STA) has 120 offices worldwide and offers low-price airfares to destinations around the globe, as well as rail passes, car rentals, you name it. STA issues ISIC (International Student Identity Card) and their own STA Travel Card (about $6) for recent graduates, which proves eligibility for some travel discounts (*see* Student ID Cards, *below*). Write or call one of their offices for a slew of free pamphlets on services and rates.

Council on International Educational Exchange (CIEE) is a nonprofit organization dedicated to the pursuit of work, study, and travel abroad. Through its two subsidiaries, **Council Travel** and

STA Offices

- *UNITED STATES. ARIZONA: Scottsdale (tel. 602/596–5151 or 800/777–0112). CALIFORNIA: Berkeley (tel. 510/642–3000); Los Angeles (tel. 213/934–8722); San Francisco (tel. 415/391–8407); Santa Monica (tel. 310/394–5126); Westwood (tel. 310/824–1574). MASSACHUSETTS: Boston (tel. 617/266–6014); Cambridge (tel. 617/576–4623). NEW YORK CITY: East Village (tel. 212/477–7166); Columbia University (tel. 212/854–2224). PENNSYLVANIA: Philadelphia (tel. 215/382–2928). WASHINGTON D.C. (tel. 202/887–0912).*
- *AUSTRALIA: Adelaide (tel. 08/223–2426); Brisbane (tel. 07/221–9388); Cairns (tel. 070/314199); Darwin (tel. 089/412955); Melbourne (tel. 03/349–2411); Perth (tel. 09/227–7569); Sydney (tel. 02/212–1255). NEW ZEALAND: Auckland (tel. 09/309–9995); Christchurch (tel. 03/379–9098); Wellington (tel. 04/385–0561). UNITED KINGDOM: London (tel. 0171/938–4711).*

Council Charter, CIEE offers discounted airfares, rail passes, accommodations, and guide-books. Council Travel is an international network of travel agencies that specialize in the diverse needs of students, young people, teachers, and other budget travelers. They also issue student ID and youth hostel cards (*see* Student ID Cards, *below*). Forty one Council Travel offices serve the budget traveler in the United States, and there are about a dozen overseas (in Britain, France, Germany, and Japan). **Council Charter** (tel. 212/661–0311 or 800/223–7402) buys blocks of seats on commercial flights and sells them at a discount. Call for prices and availability.

Educational Travel Center (ETC) books low-cost flights (most departing from Chicago) to desti-nations in Mexico and all over the world. ETC claims to beat student and charter fares. For more details request their free brochure, *Taking Off. 438 N. Frances St., Madison, WI 53703, tel. 608/256–5551.*

South American Explorers Club has a great deal of info about Mexico and Central America (notwithstanding the fact that neither of these is in South America). Among other things, mem-bership gets you the quarterly *South American Explorer* magazine, which covers all sorts of off-the-beaten-track activities; access to "Trip Reports" submitted by club members after their travels; and discounts for club maps and brochures. Annual membership is $30. *126 Indian Creek Rd., Ithaca, NY 14850, tel. 607/277–0488.*

Canadian Universities Travel Service, Ltd. (Travel CUTS) is a full-service travel agency that sells discounted airline tickets to Canadian students and issues the ISIC, IYC, and hostel cards. Their 25 offices are on or near college campuses. Call weekdays 9–5 for information and reservations. *187 College St., Toronto, Ont. M5T 1P7, tel. 416/979–2406.*

Council Travel Offices

ARIZONA: Tempe (tel. 602/966–3544). CALIFORNIA: Berkeley (tel. 510/848–8604), Davis (tel. 916/752–2285), La Jolla (tel. 619/452–0630), Long Beach (tel. 310/598–3338 or 714/527–7950), Los Angeles (tel. 310/208–3551), Palo Alto (tel. 415/325–3888), San Diego (tel. 619/270–6401), San Francisco (tel. 415/421–3473 or 415/566–6222), Santa Barbara (tel. 805/562–8080). COLORADO: Boulder (tel. 303/447–8101). CONNECTICUT: New Haven (tel. 203/562–5335). FLORIDA: Miami (tel. 305/670–9261). GEORGIA: Atlanta (tel. 404/377–9997). ILLINOIS: Chicago (tel. 312/951–0585), Evanston (tel. 708/475–5070). INDIANA: Bloomington (tel. 812/330–1600). LOUISIANA: New Orleans (tel. 504/866–1767). MASSACHUSETTS: Amherst (tel. 413/256–1261), Boston (tel. 617/266–1926 or 617/424–6665), Cambridge (tel. 617/497–1497 or 617/225–2555). MICHIGAN: Ann Arbor (tel. 313/998–0200). MIN-NESOTA: Minneapolis (tel. 612/379–2323). NEW YORK: New York (tel. 212/661–1450, 212/666–4177, or 212/254–2525). NORTH CAROLINA: Chapel Hill (tel. 919/942–2334). OHIO: Columbus (tel. 614/294–8696). OREGON: Portland (tel. 503/228–1900). PENNSYLVANIA: Philadelphia (tel. 215/382–0343), Pittsburgh (tel. 412/683–1881). RHODE ISLAND: Providence (tel. 401/331–5810). TEXAS: Austin (tel. 512/472–4931), Dallas (tel. 214/363–9941). UTAH: Salt Lake City (tel. 801/582–5840). WASH-INGTON: Seattle (tel. 206/632–2448 or 206/329–4567). WASHINGTON D.C. (tel. 202/337–6464).

STUDENT ID CARDS

Foreign student ID cards are not universally accepted in Mexico; discounts for museum and theater admission usually apply exclusively to students at Mexican universities. Don't leave your student ID at home, though, because discounts are often left to the discretion of the person working the door. While an ID card issued by a home university or college may be sufficient to prove student status for admission discounts, the following cards have the extra feature of providing insurance in case of accident or other catastrophes.

If purchased in the United States, the $17 cost for the popular **International Student Identity Card** (ISIC) card also buys you $3,000 in emergency medical coverage; limited hospital coverage; and access to a 24-hour international, toll-free hotline for assistance in medical, legal, and financial emergencies. In the United States, apply to CIEE or STA; in Canada, the ISIC is available for C$15 from Travel CUTS (*see* Budget Travel Organizations, *above*). In the United Kingdom, students with valid university IDs can purchase the ISIC at any student union or student-travel company. Applicants must submit a photo as well as proof of current full-time student status, age, and nationality.

The **STA Travel Card** is available to travelers age 35 and under for $6 and is mainly useful for purchasing discounted airfare, though it will often suffice as student ID to get you discounts on admission to museums and other attractions in Mexico. Purchase the STA card at any STA office (*see* Budget Travel Organizations, *above*) before departing.

The **Go 25: International Youth Travel Card** (IYC), formerly known as the FIYTO (Federation of International Youth Travel Organisations) card, is issued to travelers (students and nonstudents) under age 26 and provides services and benefits similar to those given by the ISIC card. The $16 card is available from the same organizations that sell the ISIC.

The $17 **International Teacher Identity Card** (ITIC), sponsored by the International Student Travel Confederation, is available to teachers of all grade levels. The services and benefits you get when buying the card are similar to those for the above cards. Ask a Council Travel or STA office for the *International Teacher Identity Card Handbook*, which has all the details.

PASSPORTS, VISAS, AND TOURIST CARDS

All foreigners traveling for more than 72 hours in Mexico must obtain a tourist card. Although adult U.S. and Canadian citizens technically need only a birth certificate and a photo ID to obtain one, a passport is sure to come in handy in case of a problem. Minors traveling alone must have a passport or a notarized copy of a letter of permission signed by a parent or guardian in order to be issued a tourist card. Legal permanent residents of the United States must present a valid alien registration card, as well. All other travelers must present a passport, but visas are only required of citizens of Hong Kong, South Africa, Brazil, and Taiwan. These can be obtained at any Mexican consular office.

TOURIST CARDS If you intend to visit border towns only, you can do so without a tourist card (called an F.M.T.) for up to 72 hours. Otherwise you must show proof of citizenship (either an original birth certificate and a photo ID, or a passport) and obtain a tourist card. Driver's licenses, credit cards, and military papers will not suffice. A naturalized citizen must carry at least one of the following documents: naturalization papers, a U.S. passport, an affidavit of citizenship, or an armed services identification or discharge card. F.M.T.s are available at Mexican government border offices at any port of entry, on flights into Mexico, any Mexican Ministry of Tourism or consulate in the United States, and travel agencies. No matter where you get it, when crossing the border you must sign the card in the presence of the Mexican immigration official, who may also ask to see proof of citizenship. Be sure to hold on to your receipt, because you are required to fork it over on departure. If you lose it, expect to visit with the border officials for a while.

On the tourist card, you must indicate your destination and expected length of stay: The options are 30, 60, 90, or 180 days. Estimate high, because the process of trying to extend it later is long, arduous, and can involve an ungodly amount of time in an immigration office. Upon leaving Mexico, your card is taken and a new one is issued if and when you return. All questions about tourist-card extensions should be directed (preferably *before* your card expires) to the local **Delegación de Servicios Migratorios.**

If you lose your card, you must also go to the Delegación de Servicios Migratorios. To cut through at least a portion of the red tape involved, it is a good idea to make a photocopy of your card and keep it in a separate place to speed up the creaky replacement process. Carry the original with you at all times; it's required by law.

OBTAINING A PASSPORT

➤ U.S. CITIZENS • First-time applicants, travelers whose most recent passport was issued more than 12 years ago or before they were 16, travelers whose passports have been lost or stolen, and travelers between the ages of 13 and 17 (a parent must also accompany them) must apply for a passport in person. Other renewals can be taken care of by mail. Apply at one of the 13 U.S. Passport Agency offices a *minimum* of five weeks before your departure. For fastest processing, apply between August and December. If you blow it, you can have a passport issued within five days of departure if you have your plane ticket in hand. This method will probably work, but if there's one little glitch in the system, you're out of luck. Local county courthouses, many state and probate courts, and some post offices also accept passport applications. Have the following items ready when you go to get your passport:

• A completed passport application (form DSP-11), available at courthouses, some post offices, and passport agencies.

• Proof of citizenship (certified copy of birth certificate, naturalization papers, or previous passport issued in the past 12 years).

• Proof of identity with your photograph and signature (for example, a valid driver's license, employee ID card, military ID, or student ID).

• Two recent identical, two"-square photographs (black-and-white or color head shots).

• A $55 application fee for a 10-year passport, $30 for those under 18 for a five-year passport. First-time applicants are also hit with a $10 surcharge. If you're paying cash, exact change is necessary; checks or money orders should be made out to Passport Services.

For more information or an application, contact the **Department of State Office of Passport Services** (tel. 202/647–0518) and dial your way through their message maze. Passport applications can be picked up at U.S. post offices, at federal or state courts, and at U.S. Passport Agencies in Boston, Chicago, Honolulu, Houston, Los Angeles, Miami, New Orleans, New York, Philadelphia, San Francisco, Seattle, Stamford, and Washington, D.C.

Those lucky enough to be able to renew their passports by mail must send a completed Form DSP-82 (available from a Passport Agency); two recent, identical passport photos; their current passport (less than 12 years old); and a check or money order for $55 ($30 if under 18). Send everything to the nearest Passport Agency. Renewals take from three to four weeks.

➤ CANADIAN CITIZENS • Canadians should send a completed passport application (available at any post office or passport office) to the **Bureau of Passports** (Suite 215, West Tower, Guy Favreau Complex, 200 Rene Levesque Boulevard West, Montreal, Que. H2Z 1X4, tel. 514/283-2152). Include C$35; two recent, identical passport photographs; a guarantor (as specified on the application); and proof of Canadian citizenship (original birth certificate or other official document as specified). You can also apply in person at regional passport offices in many locations, including Edmonton, Halifax, Montreal, Toronto, Vancouver, and Winnipeg. Passports have a shelf life of five years and are not renewable. Processing takes about two weeks by mail and five working days for in-person applications.

➤ U.K. CITIZENS • Passport applications are available through travel agencies, a main post office, or one of six regional passport offices (in London, Liverpool, Peterborough, Belfast, Glasgow, and Newport). The application must be countersigned by your bank manager or by a solicitor, barrister, doctor, clergyman, or justice of the peace who knows you personally. Send or drop off the completed form; two recent, identical passport photos; and a £15 fee to a regional passport office (address is on the form). Passports are valid for 10 years (five years for those under 18) and take about four weeks to process.

➤ AUSTRALIAN CITIZENS • Australians must visit a post office or passport office to complete the passport application process. A 10-year passport for those over 18 costs AUS$76. The under-18 crowd can get a five-year passport for AUS$37. For more information, call toll-free in Australia 008/02–60–22 weekdays during regular business hours.

➤ NEW ZEALAND CITIZENS • Passport applications can be found at any post office or consulate. Completed applications must be accompanied by proof of citizenship, two passport-size photos, and a letter from a friend confirming the applicant's identity. The fee is NZ$50 for a 10-year passport. Processing takes about three weeks.

LOST PASSPORTS If your passport is lost or stolen in Mexico, file a police report with the local authorities and bring this report and any identification you may have to your home embassy or consulate. If you have a record of the information contained in your passport, the consular officer can probably wade through some red tape and issue you a new one. As a precaution, make two photocopies of your passport identification page and leave one with a trusted person at home. Carry the other copy separate from your passport.

This said, the United States embassy/consulate will *not* issue a new passport except in emergencies (this does not include a desperate desire to see Tierra del Fuego). In nonemergency situations, the embassy or consulate staff will affirm your affidavit swearing to U.S. citizenship, and this paper will get you back to the United States. The British embassy or consulate requires a police report, any form of identification, and three passport-size photos. They will replace the passport in four working days and, in case your tourist card went bye-bye, too, give you a letter to smooth things over with the Mexican government. Canadian citizens face the same requirements as the Brits, but you must have a guarantor with you. A guarantor is someone who has known you for at least two years, lives within the jurisdiction of the consulate or embassy, and belongs to one of the following professions: mayor, practicing lawyer, notary public, judge, magistrate, police officer, signing officer at a bank, medical doctor, or dentist. Since most travelers do not know anyone fitting this description, there is also the option of paying an officer of the consulate/embassy to be your guarantor—proving once again that throwing enough money at a problem usually makes it go away. A replacement passport usually takes five working days. New Zealand officials ask for two passport-size photos, while the Australians require three, but both can usually replace a passport in 24 hours. If you managed to lose your tourist card as well, they may also supply an official-looking letter that will grease the wheels at the border.

GETTING THE BEST AIRFARES

When your travel plans are still in the fantasy stage, start studying the travel sections of major Sunday newspapers: Courier companies, charter flights, and fare brokers often list incredibly cheap flights. Travel agents are another obvious resource, as they have access to computer networks that show the lowest fares before they're even advertised. However, budget travelers are the bane of travel agents, whose commission is based on the ticket prices. That said, agencies on or near college campuses—try STA or Council Travel (*see* Budget Travel Organizations, *above*)—actually cater to this pariah class and can help you find cheap deals.

As a rule, the further in advance you buy the ticket, the less expensive it is. Keep in mind that "advance purchase" to an airline does not mean a week before departure.

Flexibility is the key to getting a serious bargain on airfare. If you can play around with your departure date, destination, amount of luggage carried, and return date, you will probably save money. Options include charter flights, flying standby, student discounts, courier flights, and APEX (Advanced Purchase Excursion) and Super APEX fares; read on to help get through this maze. Another useful resource is George Albert Brown's *Airline Traveler's Guerrilla Handbook* (Blake Publishing Group, 320 Metropolitan Sq., 15th St.

NW, Washington, D.C. 20005, tel. 800/752–9765; $14.95), an in-depth account of how to find cheap tickets, change cheap tickets, and generally beat the system.

If the reservation clerk tells you that the least expensive seats are no longer available on a certain flight, ask to be put on a waiting list. If the airline doesn't keep waiting lists for the lowest fares, call them on subsequent mornings and ask about cancellations and last-minute openings—airlines trying to fill all their seats sometimes add additional cut-rate tickets at the last moment. When setting travel dates, remember that off-season fares can be as much as 50% lower. Ask which days of the week are the cheapest to fly on—weekends are often the most expensive. If you end up biting the bullet and paying more than you'd like for a ticket, keep scanning the ads in newspaper travel sections for last-minute ticket deals or a lower fare offered by desperate airlines. Some airlines will refund the difference in ticket price when they lower fares and you call them on it.

APEX TICKETS If you're not a student, or if you're not the kind of person to spend days scouring newspapers for the lowest fare, an APEX ticket bought directly from the airline or your travel agent is the simplest way to go. If you know exactly when you want to leave and it's not tomorrow (or the next day), ask for the APEX fare when making your reservation—it'll save you a bundle and guarantee you a seat. Regular APEX fares normally apply to tickets bought at least 21 days in advance; you can get Super-APEX fares if you know your travel plans at least one month in advance. Here's the catch: If you cancel or change your plans, you'll pay a penalty, anywhere from $50 to $100.

CONSOLIDATORS AND BUCKET SHOPS Consolidator companies, also known as bucket shops, buy blocks of tickets at wholesale prices from airlines trying to fill flights. Consolidator tickets are often not refundable, and the flights to choose from often feature indirect routes, long layovers in connecting cities, and undesirable seating assignments. If your flight is delayed or canceled, you'll also have a tough time switching airlines. As with charter flights, you risk taking a huge loss if you change your travel plans. If everything goes as planned, though, you'll save 10%–40% on the published APEX fare.

Check out any consolidator's reputation with the Better Business Bureau before starting; most are reliable, but better safe than sorry.

Bucket shops generally advertise in newspapers—be sure to check restrictions, refund possibilities, and payment conditions. One last suggestion: Confirm your reservation with the airline both before and after you buy a consolidated ticket. This not only decreases the chance of fraud, but also ensures that you won't be the first to get bumped if the airline overbooks. For more details, contact one of the following consolidators.

Globe Travel has consolidated tickets to "any place you want," though the best deals are to Europe. *507 5th Ave., Suite 606, New York, NY 10017, tel. 800/969–4562.*

Up & Away Travel offers some decent deals, but good luck getting through on their very busy phone line. *347 Fifth Ave., Suite 202, New York, NY 10016, tel. 212/889–2345.*

STANDBY AND THREE-DAY-ADVANCE-PURCHASE FARES Flying standby is almost a thing of the past. The idea is to purchase an open ticket and wait for the next available seat on the next available flight to your chosen destination. Yet most airlines have dumped standby policies in favor of three-day-advance-purchase youth fares, which are open only to people under 25 and (as the name states) can only be purchased within three days of departure. Return flights must also be booked no more than three days prior to departure. If you meet the above criteria, expect 10%–50% savings on published APEX fares.

There are also a number of brokers that specialize in discount and last-minute sales, offering savings on unsold seats on commercial carriers and charter flights, as well as tour packages. If you're desperate to get to Mexico by Wednesday, try **Last Minute Travel Club** (tel. 617/267–9800).

CHARTER FLIGHTS Charter flights have vastly different characteristics, depending on the company you're dealing with. Generally speaking, a charter company either buys a block of tickets on a regularly scheduled commercial flight and sells them at a discount (the prevalent form in the United States) or leases the whole plane and then offers relatively cheap fares to the public (most common in the United Kingdom). Despite a few potential drawbacks—among them infrequent flights, restrictive return-date requirements, lickety-split payment demands, frequent bankruptcies—charter companies inevitably offer the cheapest tickets around, especially during high season when APEX fares are most expensive. Make sure you find out a company's policy on refunds should a flight be canceled by either yourself or the airline. Summer charter flights fill up fast and should be booked a couple months in advance.

You're in much better shape when the company is offering tickets on a regular commercial flight. After you've bought the ticket from the charter folks, you generally deal with the airline directly. When a charter company has chartered the whole plane, things get a little sketchier: Bankrupt operators, long delays at check-in, overcrowding, and flight cancellation are fairly common. You can minimize risks by checking the company's reputation with the Better Business Bureau and taking out enough trip-cancellation insurance to cover the operator's potential failure.

Council Charter has the scoop on hundreds of different charter and reduced-fare flights. *Tel. 212/661–0311 or 800/800–8222.*

DER Tours is a full-service travel store, with discounted airfares and listings of charter flights. *Box 1606, Des Plains, IL 60017, tel. 800/782–2424.*

Travel CUTS is part of the CIEE umbrella, which means it's a reputable place for Canadian students to book their charter. *187 College St., Toronto, Ont. M5T 1P7, tel. 416/979–2406.*

STUDENT DISCOUNTS Student discounts on airline tickets are offered through **CIEE,** the **Educational Travel Center, STA Travel,** and **Travel CUTS** (*see* Budget Travel Organizations, *above*). Keep in mind that you will *not* receive frequent-flyer mileage for discounted student, youth, or teacher tickets. For discount tickets based on your status as a student, youth, or teacher, have an ID when you check in that proves it (*see* Student ID Cards, *above*).

Campus Connection, exclusively for students under 25, searches airline computer networks for the cheapest student fares to worldwide destinations. They don't always have the best price, but because they deal with the airlines directly you won't get stuck with a heavily restricted or fraudulent ticket. *1100 E. Marlton Pike, Cherry Hill, NJ 08032, tel. 800/428–3235.*

COURIER FLIGHTS A few restrictions and inconveniences are the price you'll pay for the colossal savings on airfare offered to air couriers, the travelers who accompany letters and packages between designated points. The way it works is simple. Courier companies list whatever flights are available for the next week or so. After you book the flight, you sign a contract with the company to act as a courier (some places make you pay a deposit, to be refunded after the successful completion of your assignment, should you agree to accept it). On the day of departure, you arrive at the airport a few hours early, meet someone who hands you a ticket and customs forms, and off you go. After you land, you simply clear customs with the courier luggage, and deliver it to a waiting agent. Don't worry about what you're transporting—we're talking business documents and the like, not drugs or missiles.

The main restrictions are (1) flights can be booked only a week or two in advance, often only a few days in advance, (2) you are allowed one piece of carry-on luggage only, because the courier uses your checked-luggage allowance to transport the time-sensitive shipment, (3) you must return within one or two weeks, sometimes within 30 days, (4) most courier companies only issue tickets to travelers over the age of 18.

Check newspaper travel sections for courier companies, check in the yellow pages of your phone directory, or mail away for a telephone directory that lists companies by the cities to which they fly. One of the better publications is *Air Courier Bulletin* (IAATC, 8 South J St., Box 1349, Lake Worth, FL 33460, tel. 407/582–8320), sent to IAATC members every two months once you pay the $35 annual fee. *A Simple Guide to Courier Travel* gives tips on flying as a courier; Send $15.95 (includes postage and handling) to Box 2394, Lake Oswego, OR 97035, tel. 800/222–3599. Another good resource is the newsletter published by **Travel Unlimited** (Box 1058, Allston, MA 02134), which costs $25 for 12 issues.

Now Voyager connects 18-and-over travelers scrounging for cheap airfares with companies looking for warm bodies to escort their packages overseas. Flights in the summer and over school holidays are in high demand, so try to book two months in advance. Departures are from New York, Newark, Houston, or Miami, and the only desination they serve in Mexico is Mexico City. Most trips are one week in length, with round-trip fares ranging $150 and up. A nonrefundable $50 registration fee, good for one year, is required. Call for current offerings. *74 Varick St., Suite 307, New York, NY 10013, tel. 212/431–1616.*

MONEY

Peso notes come in denominations of 10, 20, 50, 100 pesos. The "no change" dilemma will often confront you: Many shop and restaurant owners don't have change for your purchase even if the note you offer is valued as low as $3.50. In these situations, you'll just have to cool your heels while they run next door to see if anyone else can make change. Enough of these encounters may compel you to request *billetes chicos* (small bills) when you exchange money. Because the value of the peso changes, all prices in this book are given in U.S. dollars.

HOW MUCH IT WILL COST Mexico is still a bargain for travelers used to Western European and U.S. prices; lodging, food, and drink are all much cheaper. Prices vary according to the universal rule, however—the more cosmopolitan the city, the higher the price of a tortilla. Your travel to and from Mexico will probably be your biggest expense, then lodging and transport.

➢ WHERE TO SLEEP • Most travelers to Mexico bed down in hotels, though camping is ususaly a safe option. Hotels ranging from dirt cheap (about $7 per person) to stratospheric. In a typical city, expect to pay $10–$15 for a single, $15–$18 for a double, and a couple of bucks extra for an additional person. A room with a double bed often costs a dollar or two less than a room with two singles. Mexico's few hostels rarely cost more than $5 a night.

➢ FOOD • If you're willing to forgo the tourist fare, you'll be able to spend very little money on food without losing too much weight. One sure cost-cutting strategy in more expensive cities, or whenever you are feeling a painful cash crunch, is to buy fresh fruits and vegetables at the local market (every city, town, and village has one). Most markets also have small *fondas* (covered food stands) offering *comidas corridas* (pre-prepared lunch specials) for less than $5. *Panaderías* (bakeries) sell cheap breads and pastries. More variety and more risk is involved when you buy from street vendors, who sell tacos, tamales, corn soup, and the like for rock-bottom prices. Even the most hygienic-looking stand can sell you a dysentery sandwich, but following the crowds is usually the best strategy for finding well-prepared food.

➢ TRANSPORT • Buses are widely used in Mexico, so fares remain very low. Buses range from antiquated second-class school buses to first-class *especial* coaches with air-conditioning, reclining seats, videos, and meal service. Prices correlate less with the number of hours traveled than with the popularity of the route—heavily traveled routes are served by more classes of service at lower prices than less frequently covered ones. Trains (especially second class) are considerably cheaper than buses, but much slower and often less comfortable. Domestic plane fares will flatten your wallet considerably (*see* Getting Around, *below*).

➢ ENTERTAINMENT • Fun may be free, but entertainment costs can be very high in big cities, where getting a foot in the door of an average club means coughing up anywhere from $7 to $50. Drink prices at an average bar are comparable to those north of the border: a beer runs $1.50–$2, more at popular watering holes. Movie tickets, at least, are a reasonable $3–$4. In many cities, thanks to government subsidies, entrance to some theater, dance, and musical events is free (these bargains are usually cultural events featuring traditional music or dance). If your cash flow has dwindled to a drip, join the locals for traditional, and free, entertainment—an early evening stroll around the town's *zócalo* (main square).

TRAVELING WITH MONEY Cash never goes out of style, but traveler's checks and a major credit card are usually the safest and most convenient way to pay for goods and services on the road. Depending on the length of your trip, strike a balance among these three forms of currency, and protect yourself by carrying cash in a money belt or "necklace" pouch (available at luggage or camping stores) or front pocket; keeping accurate records of traveler's checks' serial numbers; and recording credit-card numbers and an emergency number for reporting the cards' loss or theft. Carrying at least some cash is wise; most budget establishments will accept cash only, and, outside of urban areas, changing traveler's checks may prove difficult. Bring about $100 (in as many single bills as possible) in cash; changing U.S. dollars will be easier than cashing traveler's checks. Credit cards are rarely accepted by budget establishments in Mexico, but they do come in handy at mid-range hotels and restaurants and Visa and MasterCard can be used to obtain cash advances in banks or at ATM machines (*see* Cash Machines, *below*). An American Express card will allow you to cash personal checks at an American Express office (*see* Obtaining Money from Home, *below*), but AmEx is not hooked up to any Mexican ATMs.

CHANGING MONEY You can turn your cash or traveler's checks into pesos at most banks or go to a private exchange office, called a *casa de cambio*. Most banks only change money on weekday mornings, while casas de cambio usually stay open until early evening and often operate on weekends. Bank rates are regulated by the federal government and therefore invariable, but their policies on traveler's checks vary: Some charge a 2%–5% commission. Casas de cambio have more variable rates. Some hotels also exchange money, but they usually do it at extortionate rates. It helps to exchange money early in the day, because after the banks are closed, everybody else's rates tend to worsen. You can buy pesos at your local bank before departing, but this is probably only necessary if you're arriving in the middle of the night, when money-exchange booths are likely to be closed.

You lose money every time you exchange currency, so try to avoid changing so much of your money to pesos that you end up having to change it back as you leave the country.

TRAVELER'S CHECKS Budget establishments in Mexico are extremely unlikely to accept traveler's checks of any sort. They are accepted at most banks, casas de cambio, and some fancy hotels. Most American Express offices change AmEx checks. Some banks and credit unions will issue checks free to established customers, but most charge a 1%–2% commission fee. Members of the American Automobile Association (AAA) can purchase American Express traveler's checks from the AAA commission-free. Buy the bulk of your traveler's checks in small denominations (a pack of five $20 checks is the smallest); many establishments won't accept large bills. Hold on to your receipts after exchanging your traveler's checks; once you're home it's easier to convert foreign currency into dollars if you have the receipts.

Even if you don't have an AmEx gold card, you can still get American Express Traveler's Checks free with an AAA membership. Talk to the cashier at your local AAA office.

➤ LOST AND STOLEN CHECKS • Unlike cash, once lost or stolen, traveler's checks can be replaced or refunded *if* you can produce the purchase agreement and a record of the checks' serial numbers (especially of those you've already cashed). Sign all the checks when you buy them; you'll endorse them a second time to exchange them for cash or make purchases. Common sense dictates that you keep the purchase agreement separate from your checks. Caution-happy travelers will even give a copy of the purchase agreement and checks' serial numbers to someone back home. Most issuers of traveler's checks promise to refund or replace lost or stolen checks in 24 hours, but you can practically see them crossing their fingers behind their backs. If you are traveling in a remote area, expect this process to take longer. In a safe place—or several safe places—record the toll-free or collect telephone number to call in case of emergencies.

GETTING MONEY FROM HOME

Provided there is money at home to be had, there are at least seven ways to get it:

• Have it sent through a large **commercial bank** that has a branch in the town where you're staying. Unless you have an account with that large bank, though, you'll have to initiate the transfer at your own bank, and the process will be slower and more expensive.

- If you're an **American Express** cardholder, cash a personal check at an American Express office for up to $1,000 ($2,500 for gold cardholders) every 21 days; you'll be paid in U.S. traveler's checks or, in some instances, in foreign currency.

- An **American Express** *MoneyGram*^{SM} can be a dream come true if you can convince someone back home to go to an American Express MoneyGram agent and fill out the necessary forms. You don't have to be an AmEx cardholder to send or receive a MoneyGram: simply pay up to $1,000 with a credit card or cash (and anything over that in cash) and, as quick as 10 minutes later, it's ready to be picked up. Fees vary according to the amount of money sent but average about 3%–10%. You have to get the transaction reference number from your sender back home and show ID when picking up the money. For locations of American Express MoneyGram agents call 800/926–9400; from overseas call 303/980–3340 collect or contact the nearest AmEx agent.

- **MasterCard** and **Visa** cardholders can get cash advances from many banks, even in small towns. The bank may charge a commission for this handy-dandy service, and don't forget that your credit-card company will start charging you interest on the amount from the moment you withdraw it. If you get a PIN number for your card before you leave home, you can also withdraw cash at many ATM machines (*see* Cash Machines, *below*).

- Have funds sent through **Western Union** (tel. 800/325–6000). Although this has a certain glamorous ring, it's very expensive. If you have a MasterCard or Visa, you can have money sent up to your card's credit limit. If not, have someone take cash, a certified cashier's check, or a healthy MasterCard or Visa to a Western Union office. The money will reach the requested destination in minutes but may not be available for several more hours or days, depending on the whim of the local authorities. Fees range from 4% to 10% depending on the amount sent.

- In extreme emergencies (arrest, hospitalization, or worse) there is one more way American citizens can receive money overseas: by setting up a **Department of State Trust Fund**. A friend or family member sends money to the Department of State, which then transfers the money to the U.S. embassy or consulate in the city in which you're stranded. Once this account is established, you can send and receive money through Western Union, bank wire, or mail, all payable to the Department of State. For information, talk to the Department of State's Citizens' Emergency Center (tel. 202/647–5225).

CASH MACHINES Virtually all U.S. banks belong to a network of **ATMs** (Automated Teller Machines), which gobble up bank cards and spit out cash 24 hours a day in cities throughout the world. The networks most commonly found in Mexico are **Cirrus** and **Plus**. These bank substitutes are better in theory than practice; ATMs may not always function or even exist outside of big cities. If the transaction cannot be completed—an annoyingly common occurrence— chances are that the computer lines are busy, and you'll just have to try again later. Another problem is that some Mexican ATMs only accept PINs of four or fewer digits; if your PIN is longer, ask your bank about changing it. On the plus side, you get your pesos instantly, at a generally excellent rate of exchange. That said, most banks charge a 1%–3% fee per ATM

Making the Most of Your Parents' Credit Card

Even if you have no job, no credit, no cards, and no respect, you can still tap into fabulous services offered by the Visa Assistance Center if one of your parents has a Visa Gold or Business card and you are a dependent of 22 years or less and at least 100 miles from home. Write down the card number in a safe, memorable place and call the center for emergency cash service, emergency ticket replacement and lost-luggage assistance, medical and legal assistance, and an emergency message service. Helpful, multilingual personnel await your call 24 hours a day, seven days a week. In the U.S. call 800/759–6262; from overseas call 919/370–3203 collect.

So, you're getting away from it all.

Just make sure you can get back.

AT&T Access Numbers
Dial the number of the country you're in to reach AT&T.

ANGUILLA	1-800-872-2881	**COLOMBIA**	**980-11-0010**	JAMAICA††	0-800-872-2881
ANTIGUA (Public Card Phones)	#1	*COSTA RICA	114	MEXICO◇◇◇	95-800-462-4240
ARGENTINA♦	001-800-200-1111	**CURAÇAO**	**001-800-872-2881**	MONTSERRAT†	1-800-872-2881
BAHAMAS	**1-800-872-2881**	DOMINICA	1-800-872-2881	**NICARAGUA**	**174**
BELIZE♦	555	DOMINICAN REP.††	1-800-872-2881	PANAMA	109
BERMUDA†	1-800-872-2881	ECUADOR†	119	PARAGUAY†	0081-800
*BOLIVIA	0-800-1112	*EL SALVADOR	190	PERU†	191
BONAIRE	**001-800-872-2881**	GRENADA†	1-800-872-2881	ST. KITTS/NEVIS	1-800-872-2881
BRAZIL	**000-8010**	*GUATEMALA	190	**ST. MAARTEN**	**001-800-872-2881**
BRITISH V.I.	1-800-872-2881	***GUYANA††	**165**	**SURINAME**	**156**
CAYMAN ISLANDS	1-800-872-2881	HAITI†	001-800-972-2883	URUGUAY	00-0410
CHILE	**00◇-0312**	HONDURAS†	123	*VENEZUELA	80-011-120

Countries in bold face permit country-to-country calling in addition to calls to the U.S. **World Connect**℠ prices consist of **USADirect**® rates plus an additional charge based on the country you are calling. Collect calling available to the U.S. only. *Public phones require deposit of coin or phone card. †May not be available from every phone. ††Collect calling only. ♦Not available from public phones. ◇Await second dial tone. ◇◇◇When calling from public phones, use phones marked "Ladatel." ©1994 AT&T.

Here's a travel tip that will make it easy to call back to the States. Dial the access number for the country you're visiting and connect right to AT&T. It's the quick way to get English-speaking AT&T operators and can minimize hotel telephone surcharges.

If all the countries you're visiting aren't listed above, call **1 800 241-5555** for a free wallet card with all AT&T access numbers. Easy international calling from AT&T. **TrueWorld Connections.**

AT&T

All the Best Trips Start with Fodor's

COMPASS AMERICAN GUIDES

Titles in the series: Arizona, Canada, Chicago, Colorado, Hawai'i, Hollywood, Las Vegas, Maine, Manhattan, New Mexico, New Orleans, Oregon, San Francisco, South Carolina, South Dakota, Utah, Virginia, Wisconsin, Wyoming.

"A literary, historical, and near-sensory excursion."—*Denver Post*

"Tackles the 'why' of travel...as well as the nitty-gritty details."—*Travel Weekly*

FODOR'S BED & BREAKFASTS AND COUNTRY INN GUIDES

Titles in the series: California, Canada, England & Wales, Mid-Atlantic, New England, The Pacific Northwest, The South, The Upper Great Lakes Region.

"In addition to information on each establishment, the books add notes on things to see and do in the vicinity."
— *San Diego Union-Tribune*

THE BERKELEY GUIDES

Titles in the series: California, Central America, Eastern Europe, Europe, France, Germany, Great Britain & Ireland, Italy, London, Mexico, The Pacific Northwest & Alaska, Paris, San Francisco.

The best choice for budget travelers, from the Associated Students at the University of California at Berkeley.

"Berkeley's scribes put the funk back in travel." — *Time*

"Fresh, funny and funky as well as useful." — *The Boston Globe*

EXPLORING GUIDES

Titles in the series: Australia, Britain, California, Caribbean, Florida, France, Germany, Ireland, Italy, London, New York City, Paris, Rome, Singapore & Malaysia, Spain, Thailand.

"Authoritatively written and superbly presented, they make worthy reading before, during or after a trip."
— *The Philadelphia Inquirer*

"A handsome new series of guides, complete with lots of color photos, geared to the independent traveler."
— *The Boston Globe*

Visit your local bookstore, or call 24 hours a day 1-800-533-6478
Fodor's The name that means smart travel.

transaction, so consider withdrawing larger chunks of cash rather than small bundles on a daily basis. **Visa** and **MasterCard** also work in many Mexican ATMs (*see* Obtaining Money from Home, *above*), but **American Express** does not.

WHAT TO PACK

As little as possible. Besides the usual suspects—clothes, toiletries, camera, a Walkman, and a good book—bring along a day pack or some type of smaller receptacle for stuff; it'll come in handy not only for day excursions but also for those places where you plan to stay for only one or two days. You can usually check cumbersome bags at the bus or train station and just carry the essentials with you while you go looking for lodging.

Backpacks are the most manageable way to lug belongings around, but they instantly brand you a foreign tourist. Also, outside pockets on backpacks are especially vulnerable to pick-pockets, so don't store any valuables there. If you want to blend in more with the local tourist population, bring a duffel or large shoulder bag. Like new shoes, fully packed luggage should be broken in: If you can't tote your bag all the way around the block at home, it's going to be worse than a ball and chain in Mexico. Leaving some room for gifts and souvenirs is also wise.

By distributing the weight of your luggage across shoulders and hips, backpacks ease the burden of traveling. You can actually choose among three types of packs: external-frame packs (for longer travels or use on groomed trails), internal-frame packs (for longer travels across rougher terrain), and travel packs (hybrid packs that fit under an airline seat and travel well in cities or the back country). Although external frames achieve the best weight-distribution and allow airspace between you and your goodies, they're more awkward and less flexible than packs with an internal frame. Since an external frame backpack will run you about $100–$225 (internal frames are about $50 more), be sure to have it fitted correctly when you buy it. Check to see that it is waterproof, or bring an extra waterproof poncho to throw over it in downpours. An inside pocket is great for dirty laundry or food storage, and straps for a sleeping mat are good for those who will be roughing it. Straps, zippers, and seams are the most vulnerable points on a bag; check that straps are wide, adjustable, and offer some padding; check the stitching on zippers and seams; and look for a wide zipper. A zipper that can be locked never hurts.

BEDDING If you're planning to stay in hotels, you won't need to bring any bedding. Depending on where you're headed and during what time of year, though, you may want to pack a sheet, a light sleeping bag, or a thermal bag for sleeping on the beach or in a hammock. If you have a backpack, consider a sleeping mat that can be rolled tightly and strapped onto the bottom of your pack; these make train-and bus-station floors a tad more comfy. Sleep sheets often come in handy to make up for skimpy (or scary) bedding.

THE SLEEP SHEET DEFINED:

Take a big sheet. Fold it down the middle the long way. Sew one short side and the long, open side. Turn inside out. Get inside. Sleep.

The Four Rules of Luggage

- *You must be able to carry it at least a mile in steamy hot weather.*
- *You must be able to fit it into a conventional storage locker or be fully prepared to schlep it with you everywhere.*
- *Keep anything you cherish in the middle of your bag. Pack your heaviest stuff in the middle of a pack and whatever you need quick access to (maps, guidebooks, address book) in an outer pocket. Keep money and travel documents on your body if possible.*
- *Attach a clearly marked, water-resistant luggage tag to your bag or write directly on the luggage with indelible ink. Also put some identifying paper or tag inside.*

CLOTHING Smart—and not terribly fashion-conscious—travelers will bring two outfits and learn to wash clothes by hand regularly. At the very least, bring comfortable easy-to-clean clothes. Black hides dirt but also absorbs heat. Artificial fabrics don't breathe and will make you hotter than you'd thought possible, so go with light cotton instead.

Packing light does not mean relying on a pair of cut-off shorts and a tank top to get you through any situation. Shorts will make you awfully conspicuous in small Mexican towns, and women wearing them will attract attention they could probably live without. At resorts and most beach areas, however, shorts are fairly common and locals have become accustomed to seeing lots of foreign flesh. In general, though, you may find that Mexicans dress a little more formally than gringos, and Mexican women generally stay more covered than their northern counterparts.

For maximum comfort, bring cotton pants (two pairs are about right); these will also dry more quickly than jeans. Bring several T-shirts and one sweatshirt or sweater for cooler nights. Socks and undies don't take up too much room, so throw in a couple extra pairs. In jungle areas, you'll need to wear socks and long pants to prevent bug bites and scratches from possibly toxic plants. You'll probably want a swim suit even if you're not headed for the beach—you never know when you'll stumble across a swimming hole, river, or public pool. Rain gear is a must if you're traveling during rainy season; hooded plastic ponchos can be purchased at most sporting goods or Army-Navy surplus stores.

A sturdy pair of walking shoes or hiking boots (broken in before your trip) and a spare pair of shoes (preferably sandals) allow you to switch off and give your tootsies a rest. Plastic sandals or thongs protect feet on hostile shower floors and are also useful when you're camping or beach-hopping. If your feet are larger than size eight or nine, you may be in serious trouble if your shoes give out. In many areas of Mexico, shoe stores don't carry sizes larger than seven for either men or women. Your only option may be asking a marketplace artisan to customize a pair of leather sandals.

LAUNDRY *Lavanderías* (laundromats) exist in all parts of Mexico and usually charge about $1–$3 per kilo. Hotel rooms are often the best (and certainly the cheapest) place to do laundry. A bring-your-own laundry service includes: a plastic bottle of liquid detergent or soap (powder doesn't break down as well), about six feet of clothesline (enough to tie to two stable objects), and some plastic clips (bobby pins or paper clips can substitute). Porch railings, shower curtain rods, bathtubs, and faucets can all serve as wet-laundry hangers if you forget the clothesline. All of these things are, of course, available in stores in Mexico, as well.

Dr. Bronner's Magic Soap is safe for both clothes and your bod, and the label is cool reading material on long train rides.

TOILETRIES You can find almost any toiletry you might need in a Mexican pharmacy—probably even the brand you're used to—at a reasonable price. If you do bring your favorite brands of shampoo, soap, and other necessities, put them in small containers to avoid bulk and weight. Use a separate, waterproof bag for containers that seal tightly; the pressure on airplanes can cause lids to pop off and create moisturizer slicks inside your luggage. Contact-lens wearers should bring all the paraphernalia they need to conduct chemical warfare on their lenses, though saline solution is available at pharmacies. Finally, bring insect repellent, sunscreen, and lip balm from home. **Avon "Skin So Soft"** body moisturizer is the best bug repellent in the world, even if it's not marketed as such. Check the phone book under AVON and make an appointment with your friendly Avon person. Another option is **Green Ban's** environmentally-sound insect repellent: stinky, but reasonably effective.

CAMERAS AND FILM While traveling, keep film as cool as possible, away from direct sunlight or blazing campfires. If your camera is new, or new to you, shoot and develop a few rolls before leaving home to avoid spoiling travel footage with prominent thumb shots or miscalculated f-stops. The smaller and lighter the camera, the better, unless you're an artiste. Pack some lens tissue and an extra battery for cameras with built-in light meters. Consider splurging on a $10 skylight filter to protect your lens and reduce haze in your photos.

On a plane, unprocessed film is safest in your carry-on luggage—ask security to inspect it by hand. (It helps to keep your film in a plastic bag, ready for quick inspection.) The higher the film speed, the more susceptible it is to damage. The effects are cumulative, so you don't have to worry until you pass the five-scan mark. Call the **Kodak Information Center** (tel. 800/242–2424) for details.

MISCELLANEOUS Stuff you might not think to take but will be damn glad to have: (1) extra day-pack for valuables or short jaunts; (2) a flashlight, good for electricity failures, reading in the dark, and exploring caves; (3) Walkman, entertainment for bus and train rides; (4) a pocket knife for cutting fruit, spreading cheese, removing splinters, and opening bottles; (5) water bottle; (6) sunglasses; (7) several large zip-type plastic bags, useful for wet swim suits, towels, leaky bottles, and rancid socks; (8) travel alarm clock; (9) needle and small spool of thread; (10) batteries; (11) books.

CAMPING GEAR Before packing loads of camping gear, seriously consider how much camping you will actually do versus how much trouble it will be to haul around your tent, sleeping bag, stove, and accoutrements in the heat. Also consider climate in choosing what to bring; camping in dry Baja provides different worries than camping in the tropical, humid Landon jungle.

Sleeping bags are a first concern. Synthetic bags run from $100 and up and provide good protection against damp weather. Down bags start at $150, are much warmer, and can be scrunched into a tiny sack, but they're useless when wet. For further protection against cold from the ground, pick up an Ensolite pad or other thin foam pad that can be rolled up and tied to your pack. High-tech sleeping pads like Therma-Rests are a bit expensive, but worth it if you're a serious camper.

Tents come in cotton or synthetic canvas. The synthetic variety is more water-resistant and shelters against wind. Test the weight of the tent and try to visualize yourself packing it around on your back. For camping in damp areas, make sure your tent has edges that can be turned up off the ground to prevent water from seeping in, or bring a plastic tarp along. Also check the tent's windows and front flaps for mosquito-proof netting, and make sure the front flap can be completely zipped shut during rain. In general, the lighter a tent for a given size, the more expensive, but the cost may be well worth the price, especially if you are traveling by bike or backpacking on foot. Expect to pay about $100–$150 for an average two-person tent, much more for a fancy ultra-light model.

You can buy a white-gas-burning ministove that provides one amazingly powerful flame and folds up into a little bag, all for about $35. A kerosene-burning lantern costs about $40. Other handy odds and ends include matches in a waterproof container, a Swiss-army knife, something for banging in tent pegs (your shoe can work if it's sturdy enough), mosquito repellent, a mess kit ($15), a water purifier ($35), and water-purification tablets or iodine crystals ($8).

STAYING HEALTHY

For many people, traveling in Mexico means an extended case of the ever-unpopular Montezuma's revenge, a.k.a. *turista* (tourists' disease). You will experience this, in some form, at least once. Symptoms of turista are obvious: diarrhea and stomachache, sometimes accompanied by fatigue or nausea. If you are severely nauseated or vomiting, have a high, prolonged fever, or there is blood in your stools, see a doctor—you could have food poisoning. Unfamiliar foods and changes in climate and lifestyle can all contribute to diarrhea. Bacteria from contaminated food or drink can cause hepatitis A, giardiasis, and dysentery. Prevention is your best ally. Avoid street food that looks like it's been sitting out for a while, and don't eat any raw fruits or vegetables that you can't peel without washing them well in a solution of purified water and a little bit of vinegar. Bottled water is a good idea, and don't assume that water or fruit drinks sold in nice restaurants is purified. However, if you spend your whole trip consuming only what appears sterile, you'll miss out. The best strategy is to give your immune system a little time to get used to the new challenges it faces by exercising restraint during the first week or so of your trip.

The best treatment for diarrhea is rehydration plus rest. Plenty of liquid remedies are available at Mexican supermarkets and restaurants, including *té de manzanilla* (chamomile tea), *jugo de manzana* (apple juice), and other noncitrus fruit drinks. Avoid carbonated liquids, coffee, milk,

BASICS

The U.S. Centers for Disease Control advises, "boil it, cook it, peel it, or forget it." For up-to-the-minute information about health risks and disease precautions in all parts of the world, call the U.S. Centers for Disease Control's International Travelers' Hotline (tel. 404/332–4559).

cocoa, and alcohol. In severe cases, doctors will suggest an oral rehydration liquid that you can concoct yourself by mixing purified water with a few pinches of salt and a couple of tea-spoons of sugar. If you're hungry, stick to small portions of dry toast, banana, and *caldo de pollo* (chicken broth); avoid greasy, spicy foods. The best cure for diarrhea is to let it pass out of your system, but if you are very uncomfortable or need to travel to your next location, ask a local doctor for prescrip-tion drugs or tell a pharmacist you need something for turista.

IMMUNIZATIONS Use your upcoming trip as an excuse to update routine immunizations if necessary. These include **tetanus-diptheria**, **poliomyelitis** (polio), **measles**, **mumps**, and **rubella** (German measles). A preexposure **rabies** vaccination series is advised for anyone traveling in rural regions or areas with large dog populations. The vaccination provides adequate initial protection, but, if you are bitten by a potentially rabid animal, you will need additional inoculations. Be safe, not sorry, and don't pet stray dogs, cats, or other mammals. **Yellow fever** is an infectious virus transmit-ted by the bite of female mosquitoes. Symptoms, which appear after a three-day incubation period, include headaches, fever, chills, rapid heartbeat, back pain, and severe vomiting. Yel-low fever is a problem in swampy and subtropical regions, and vaccination certificates are required for travelers coming to Mexico from (or having recently passed through) affected coun-tries, including over a dozen in Central and South America—call the International Travelers' Hotline (*see* Resources, *below*) for most recent conditions. To be safe, ask your doctor about yellow fever vaccinations at least six weeks before leaving.

Malaria is a relatively uncommon, yet potentially fatal, hazard in rural areas. According to the CDC, the states with the highest incidence of malaria (in decreasing order) are: Oaxaca, Chia-pas, Guerrero, Campeche, Quintana Roo, Sinaloa, Michoacán, Nayarit, Colima, and Tabasco. Risk of malaria is minimal elsewhere, but **Dengue fever**, also mosquito-borne, affects the northern border states. Reduce exposure to the mosquitoes that carry these diseases by wear-ing protective clothing, sleeping under mosquito netting, and applying insect repellent reli-giously. Many doctors recommend you take chloroquine tablets starting one week before your trip to malaria-infested areas, although the disease has a nasty habit of becoming drug-resis-tant, so ask your doctor if chloroquine is still the way to go. There is no vaccination for Dengue. It's very unlikely you'll have any problems, but keep in mind that if you suffer any flu-like symp-toms, even up to a year after returning home, get yourself tested.

Cholera exists in Mexico, but the World Health Organization discourages vaccination because it is ineffective and short-lived. Few tourists are at risk, but the best way to avoid this poten-tially fatal disease is to completely avoid raw fish and shellfish, and generally take the same precautions that apply against turista.

The International Association for Medical Assistance to Travellers also recommends that any-one traveling outside of touristed areas should vaccinate themselves against viral **hepatitis A** (immune globulin) and **typhoid** before leaving home. Schedule vaccinations well in advance of departure because some require several doses and others may cause uncomfortable side effects.

RESOURCES For up-to-the-minute information about health risks and disease precautions in all parts of the world, the U.S. Centers for Disease Control has a 24-hour **International Travel-ers' Hotline** (tel. 404/332–4559). A comprehensive pamphlet, *Health Information for Interna-tional Travel*, can be purchased for $5 by sending a request to the **Superintendent of Documents** (U.S. Government Printing Office, Washington DC, 20402). The **Department of State's Citizens Emergency Center** (Bureau of Consular Affairs, Room 4811, N.S., U.S. Dept. of State, Wash-ington, DC, 20520, tel. 202/647–5225) provides written and recorded travel advisories.

Diabetic travelers should contact one of the following organizations for resources and medical referrals: **American Diabetes Association** (1660 Duke St., Alexandria, VA 22314, tel. 703/549–1500 or 800/232–3472), **Canadian Diabetes Association** (15 Toronto St., Suite

16

1001, Toronto, Ont. M5C 2E3, tel. 416/363–3373), and **International Diabetes Federation** (International Association Centre, Rue Washington 40, B-1050 Brussels, Belgium, tel. 032/2647–4414 or fax 032/2649–3269). *The Diabetic Traveler* (1596 Washington Blvd., Stamford, CT 06902, tel. 203/327–5832), published four times a year, lists vacations geared toward diabetics and offers travel and medical advice. Subscriptions are $18.95. Available for free is an insulin adjustment card and an informative article entitled "Management of Diabetes During Intercontinental Travel."

HEALTH AND ACCIDENT INSURANCE Some general health-insurance plans cover health expenses incurred while traveling, so review your existing health policies (or a parent's policy, if you're a dependent) before leaving home. Most university health-insurance plans stop and start with the school year, so don't count on school spirit to pull you through. Canadian travelers should check with their provincial ministry of health to see if their resident health-insurance plan covers them on the road.

Organizations such as STA and CIEE (*see* Budget Travel Organizations, *above*), as well as some credit-card conglomerates, include health-and-accident coverage with the purchase of an ID or credit card. If you purchase an **ISIC** card you're automatically insured for $100 a day for in-hospital sickness expenses, up to $3,000 for accident-related medical expenses, and $10,000 for emergency medical evacuation. For details, request a summary of coverage from CIEE (INS Dept., 205 East 42nd St., New York, NY 10017). Otherwise, several private companies offer coverage designed to supplement existing health insurance for travelers; for more details contact your favorite student travel organization.

MEDICAL ASSISTANCE Mexico has socialized medicine, and, happily, travelers can take advantage of this. Nearly every city or town has a **Centro de Salud** (government health center) or **Cruz Roja** (Red Cross) office, where you can receive free emergency medical care. The surroundings may look less than sanitary, but the visit and any drugs you may need are free. English-speaking doctors are found only in larger cities; a list of them is usually available from your embassy, in local tourist offices, or in the phone book. In smaller places, bring your dictionary because English-speaking doctors are rare. If you want to be better informed before you go, or to have an emergency number handy, contact the organizations below.

British travelers can join **Europ Assistance Worldwide Services** (252 High St., Croyden, Surrey CRO 1NF, tel. 0181/680–1234) to gain access to a 24-hour, 365-day-a-year telephone hotline that can help in a medical emergency. The American branch of this organization is **Travel Assistance International** (1133 15th St. NW, Suite 400, Washington, D.C. 20005, tel. 800/821–2828), which offers emergency evacuation services and 24-hour medical referrals. An individual membership costs $62 for up to 15 days, $164 for 60 days.

International Association for Medical Assistance to Travellers (IAMAT) offers free membership (donations are much appreciated) and entitles you to a worldwide directory of qualified English-speaking physicians who are on 24-hour call and who have agreed to a fixed-fee schedule. Also helpful are IAMAT's health pamphlets, such as the frequently updated "World Malaria Risk Chart" and "World Immunization Chart." *Three locations: 417 Center St., Lewiston, NY 14092, tel. 716/754–4883; 40 Regal Rd., Guelph, Ont. N1K 1B5 Canada, tel. 519/836–0102; Box 5049, Christchurch 5, New Zealand.*

Medic Alert offers an internationally recognized identification bracelet and necklace that indicate the bearer's medical condition, drug allergies, or current medication information. It also provides the number of Medic Alert's 24-hour hotline, through which members' medical histories are available. Lifetime membership in the U.S. is yours for the cost of the ID bracelet or necklace, from $35 to $75. *Medic Alert Foundation International, Box 1009, Turlock, CA 95381, tel. 800/432–5378; in Canada, tel. 416/696–0142 or 800/668–1507; in Australia, tel. 09/277–9999 or 08/274–0422; in New Zealand, tel. 05/288219; in the U.K., tel. 0171/833–3034.*

PRESCRIPTIONS Some drugs sold in the States by prescription only are sold over the counter in Mexico. Just to be on the safe side, however, bring as much as you need of any prescription drugs as well as your written prescription (packed separately). Ask your doctor to type the prescription and include the following information: dosage, the generic name, and the manufacturer's name. To avoid problems clearing customs, diabetic travelers carrying syringes should have handy a letter from their physician confirming their need for insulin injections. No matter where you're traveling, most cities have at least one all-night pharmacy, and many that don't actually stay open advertise *servicio nocturno* (night service), meaning that someone sleeps on site and you can ring the doorbell and wake them up at all hours, should need arise.

FIRST·AID KIT For about 97% of your trip, a first aid kit may mean nothing to you but extra bulk. However, in an emergency you'll be glad to have even the most basic medical supplies. Prepackaged kits are available, but you can pack your own from the following list: bandages, waterproof surgical tape and gauze pads, antiseptic, cortisone cream, tweezers, a thermometer in a sturdy case, an antacid such as Alka-Seltzer, something for diarrhea (Pepto Bismol or Immodium), and, of course, aspirin. If you're prone to motion sickness or are planning to use particularly rough modes of transportation during your travels, take along some Dramamine. No matter what your coloring, if you'll be exposed to sunlight for any length of time, pack sunscreen to protect against cancer-causing rays. Women: If prone to yeast infections, you can now buy over-the-counter medication (Monistat or Gynelotrimin) that will save you prolonged grief on the road. However, self-medicating should only be relied on for short-term illnesses; seek professional help if any medical symptoms persist or worsen.

CONTRACEPTIVES AND SAFE SEX AIDS and other STDs (sexually transmitted diseases) do not respect national boundaries, and protection when you travel takes the same forms as it does at home. If you are contemplating an exchange of bodily fluids, latex condoms and/or dental dams are the best forms of protection against STDs. If you're on the pill, be sure to fill your prescription before departure and bring enough to carry you through your trip; you may not be able to get the same dosage or type of pills in Mexico. Birth control in general can even be a touchy subject in this still predominantly Catholic country, and while you can buy it, you're probably better off bringing your own. Pack condoms or diaphragms in a pouch or case where they will not become squashed or damaged.

RESOURCES FOR WOMEN

Foreign commentators (travel guides not least among them) are constantly referring to the chauvinism and sexual aggressiveness of Mexican men. And while this is largely a caricature, it's clear that Mexican *machismo* (probably most accurately translated as sexism) is not completely dismissable as a stereotype. Foreign women traveling alone in Mexico *do* tend to receive plenty of *piropos* (compliments) from total strangers, but there are few places in the world where they don't. Your best resource is common sense, especially where safety is concerned. If you are traveling alone, don't let your gender prevent you from adventuring, but think twice about hitchhiking or camping solo.

PUBLICATIONS *A Journey of One's Own* ($14.95) by Thalia Zepatos is a good resource for general advice for women traveling alone, though it provides little specific information on Mexico. It is published by Eighth Mountain Press. *624 SE 29th Ave., Portland, OR, 97214, tel 503/ 233–3936.*

RESOURCES FOR PEOPLE OF COLOR

Mexico is both racially diverse and very stratified. While exceptions certainly exist, in general the elite is almost entirely white, the middle class is *mestizo* (of mixed descent), and the substantial Indian population lives for the most part in rural poverty. This said, racism is not likely to be a significant problem for travelers. The worst thing you are likely to encounter is curiosity. Black and Asian people are rare enough in some parts of Mexico that they can receive some undue attention. Absurd questions, such as "Why are you black?" may be unsettling, but it is important to realize that it is generally quite harmless and simply stems from unfamiliarity. Keep in mind that other travelers encounter similar situations irrespective of color.

RESOURCES FOR GAYS AND LESBIANS

Gender roles in Mexico are pretty rigidly defined, especially in rural areas. Openly gay couples are a rare sight, and two people of the same gender sometimes have trouble getting a *cama matrimonial* (double bed) even in places accustomed to receiving a lot of tourists. This could be attributed to the influence of the Catholic Church—Mexico is a devoutly Catholic country, and the Church has historically exerted a powerful influence on both Mexican politics and the mores and attitudes of the Mexican people. However, the same rules that apply all over the world apply in Mexico: Alternative lifestyles (whether they be homosexuality or any other bending of conventional roles) are more easily accepted in metropolitan centers such as Acapulco, Guadalajara, and Mexico City. The **International Gay Travel Association (IGTA)** is a nonprofit organization that can tell you about a travel agent in your area who can provide tips for or arrange tours in just about any area in Mexico. *Box 4974, Key West, FL 33041, tel. 800/448–8550.*

PUBLICATIONS The *Damron Address Book* ($13.95 plus shipping) is an excellent resource focusing on gay male travel in a variety of destinations including Mexico, the United States, Canada, the Caribbean, and parts of Central America. The folks at their office can also sell you a copy of *Spartacus* ($29.95), which bills itself as *the* guide for the gay/lesbian traveler, with practical tips and reviews of hotels and agencies in over 160 countries, including info on hotspots in Mexico. *Box 422458, San Francisco, CA 94142, tel. 415/255–0404 or 800/462–6654.*

The guidebook *Places of Interest,* published by Ferrari, includes listings for accommodations and nightlife, as well as general articles about gay/lesbian culture in Mexico and elsewhere. To order, send a check or money order for $19.50. *Box 37887, Phoenix, AZ, 85069, tel. 602/863-2408.*

RESOURCES FOR THE DISABLED

Mexico is poorly equipped for disabled travelers. Most hotels and restaurants have at least a few steps and are not easily accessible. Rooms called "wheelchair accessible" by hotel owners are usually on the ground floor, but the doorways and bathroom may not be maneuverable. There are no special discounts or passes for disabled travelers in Mexico, nor is public transportation, including the Mexico City Metro, wheelchair accessible. Renting or bringing a car or van is your best bet. Roads and sidewalks are often crowded, in poor condition, and without ramps, and people on the street will not usually assist you unless expressly asked.

Whenever possible, reviews in this book will indicate whether establishments are wheelchair accessible. The best choice of accessible lodging is found in resorts like Acapulco and Mazatlán, as well as other tourist-frequented locations. The best strategy is to call ahead to find out what a hotel can offer. Keep in mind, though, that many hotel proprietors don't understand the notion of accessibility. Despite these barriers, disabled Mexicans manage to negotiate places that most travelers outside Mexico would not consider accessible.

ORGANIZATIONS **Twin Peaks Press** specializes in books for the disabled, such as *Travel for the Disabled,* which offers helpful general hints but no information on Mexico. Twin Peaks also offers a "Traveling Nurse's Network," which connects disabled travelers with registered nurses to aid and accompany them on their trip. Travelers fill out an application that Twin Peaks matches to nurses' applications in their files. An application is $10. *Box 129, Vancouver, WA 98666, tel. 206/694–2462 or 800/637–2256 for orders only.*

Mobility International USA (MIUSA) is a nonprofit organization that coordinates exchange programs for disabled people around the world, with frequent programs in Mexico. MIUSA also offers information on accommodations and organized study programs for members ($20 annually). Nonmembers may subscribe to the newsletter for $10. *Box 3551, Eugene, OR 97403, tel. and TYY 503/343-1284.*

WORKING ABROAD

If you have sea legs and happen to be headed where the wind is blowing, head down to the marina and ask about crew jobs. Waterside resorts are always eager to put gringos into the "career of a lifetime"—time shares. Demand also exists for English teachers and for English-speakers to work in posh hotels. Advertisements for such positions appear in newspaper classified ads, especially the English-language newspapers; also try calling language schools or hotels directly. The legal requirements for work are stringent (*see below*).

Students interested in working abroad should contact CIEE's **Work Abroad and Voluntary Service Departments** (205 E. 42nd St., New York, NY 10017, tel. 212/661–1414, extensions 1130 and 1139 respectively). CIEE has work and study-abroad programs all over Latin America as well as in Europe, Asia, and Australia, and publishes several resource books on work/travel opportunities, including *Work, Study, Travel Abroad: The Whole World Handbook* ($13.95 plus $1.50 book-rate postage or $3 first-class postage); *Volunteer! The Comprehensive Guide to Voluntary Service in the U.S. and Abroad* ($8.95 plus $1.50 book-rate postage or $3 first-class postage); and *Going Places: The High School Student's Guide to Study, Travel, and Adventure Abroad* ($13.95 plus $1.50 book-rate or $3 first-class postage).

CIEE's Work Abroad Program is only open to U.S. students; Canadians should contact **Travel CUTS**, which has similar programs for Canadian students who want to work abroad for up to six months. *SWAP, 243 College St., 5th floor, Toronto, Ont M5T 2Y1, tel. 416/977–3703.*

LEGAL REQUIREMENTS By law, a foreigner may legally work in Mexico only if contracted in his or her native country before arriving in Mexico. A Brit, for example, would need a work permit sponsored by his or her employer in England; the employer's affiliate in Mexico would process the permit and pave the way for the newcomer in Mexico. The process is very bureaucratic, and the professions with the best chance of success are those that require specific skills, such as engineering.

STUDYING ABROAD

Many Mexican universities are open to foreigners for Spanish-language programs and general enrollment. Language schools are listed in the Basics sections for the cities where they exist, but the most popular (and consequently the most packed with English speakers) places to study are Cuernavaca and San Miguel de Allende, as well as the more cosmopolitan Mexico City and Guadalajara. For more information on options for study in Mexico, contact **The National Registration Center for Study Abroad** (823 N. 2nd St., Milwaukee, WI 53203, tel. 414/278–0631), or write or call the **Institute of International Education for Latin America** (Londres 16, Piso 2, Distrito Federal, CP, 06600, México, tel. 5/703–10–67 or 5/211–00–42; or Box 3087, Laredo, TX 78044-3089 in the U.S.).

Coming and Going

CUSTOMS AND DUTIES

ARRIVING IN MEXICO If you're bringing any foreign-made equipment with you from home, such as cameras or video gear, it's wise to carry the original receipt or register it with customs before leaving the United States (ask for U.S. Customs Form 4457). Otherwise, you may end up paying duty on your return. When going through customs, a clean-cut appearance goes a long way toward avoiding hassles with Mexican officials. To avoid problems, don't even think about drugs. Being cited for drug possession is no joke, and embassies and consulates often can't do much to persuade country officials to release accused drug traffickers/users (*see* Crime and Punishment, *below*).

If you're arriving in Mexico City, you may be one of the one in 10 people whose luggage is searched. Before passing through customs you'll press a button in front of a small stoplight apparatus. If the resulting light is green, you can pass go; if it's red, officials search your baggage. You will be given a baggage-declaration form to itemize what you're bringing into the country. You're allowed to bring in three liters of spirits or wine for personal use, 400 cigarettes, two boxes of cigars, a reasonable amount of perfume for personal use, one movie camera and one regular camera, eight rolls of film for each, and gift items not to exceed a total of $120. There are no restrictions or limitations on the amount of cash, foreign currencies, checks, or drafts that can be imported or exported by visitors.

RETURNING HOME

➤ U.S. CUSTOMS • Like most government organizations, the U.S. Customs Service enforces a number of mysterious rules which presumably make sense to some bureaucrat somewhere. You're unlikely to have run-ins with customs as long as you *never* carry any illegal drugs in your luggage. When you return to the United States you have to declare all items you bought abroad, but you won't have to pay duty unless you come home with more than $400 worth of foreign goods, including items bought in duty-free stores. For purchases between $400 and $1,000 you have to pay a 10% duty. You also have to pay tax if you exceed your duty-free allowances: one liter of alcohol or wine (for those 21 and over), 100 non-Cuban cigars or 200 cigarettes, and one bottle of perfume. A free leaflet about customs regulations and illegal souvenirs, "Know Before You Go," is available from the **U.S. Customs Service** (Box 7407, Washington, D.C. 20044, tel. 202/927-6724).

➤ CANADIAN CUSTOMS • Exemptions for returning Canadians range from $20 to $300, depending on how long you've been out of the country: for two days out, you're allowed to return with C$100 worth of goods; for one week out, you're allowed C$300 worth. Above these limits, you'll be taxed 20% (more for items shipped home). In any given year, you are only allowed one C$300 exemption. Duty-free limits are: up to 50 cigars, 200 cigarettes, 2.2 pounds of tobacco, and 40 ounces of liquor—all must be declared in writing upon arrival at customs and must be with you or in your checked baggage. To mail back gifts, label the package: "Unsolicited Gift–Value under C$60." For more scintillating details, request a copy of the Canadian Customs brochure "I Declare/Je Declare" from **Revenue Canada Customs, Excise and Taxation Department** (2265 St. Laurent Blvd. S., Ottawa, Ont., K1G 4K3, tel. 613/957-0275).

➤ U.K. CUSTOMS • Travelers age 17 or over who return to the United Kingdom may bring back the following duty-free goods: 200 cigarettes or 100 cigarillos or 50 cigars or 250 grams of tobacco; one liter of alcohol over 22% volume or two liters of alcohol under 22% volume, plus two liters of still table wine; 60 ml of perfume and 250 ml of toilet water; and other goods worth up to £136. If returning from another EU country, you can choose, instead, to bring in the following, provided they were *not* bought in a duty-free shop: 300 cigarettes or 150 cigarillos or 75 cigars or 400 grams of tobacco; 1.5 liters of alcohol over 22% volume or three liters of alcohol under 22% volume, plus five liters of still table wine; 75 grams of perfume and ⅜ liter of toilet water; and other goods worth up to £250. For further information or a copy of *A Guide for Travellers,* which details standard customs procedures as well as what you may bring into the United Kingdom from abroad, contact **HM Customs and Excise** (Dorset House, Stamford St., London SE1 9PY).

➤ AUSTRALIAN CUSTOMS • Australian travelers 18 and over may bring back, duty free: one liter of alcohol; 250 grams of tobacco products (equivalent to 250 cigarettes); and other articles worth up to $AUS400. If you're under 18, your duty-free allowance is $AUS200. To avoid paying duty on goods you mail back to Australia, mark the package: "Australian goods returned." For more rules and regulations, request the pamphlet "Customs Information for Travellers" from a local **Collector of Customs** (GPO Box 8, Sydney NSW 2001, tel. 02/226-5997).

➤ NEW ZEALAND CUSTOMS • New Zealand-bound travelers face a number of restrictions. Travelers over age 17 are allowed, duty-free: 200 cigarettes or 250 grams of tobacco or 50 cigars or a combo of all three up to 250 grams; 4.5 liters of wine or beer and one 1,125-ml. bottle of spirits; and goods with a combined value up to NZ$700. If you want more details, ask for the pamphlet "Customs Guide for Travellers" from a New Zealand consulate.

BY AIR

On your fateful departure day, remember that check-in time for international flights is a long two hours before the scheduled departure.

FROM THE U.S. Airlines serving Mexico with direct flights from major U.S. cities include **Aerocalifornia** (tel. 800/258–3311) from Los Angeles, Phoenix, and San Diego; Aeroméxico (tel. 800/237–6639) from Houston, Los Angeles, Miami, New York, and Tucson; **American** (tel. 800/433–7300) from Dallas/Fort Worth, Miami, and Raleigh/Durham; **Continental** (tel. 800/525–0280) from Houston and Newark; Delta (tel. 800/345–3400) from Atlanta and Dallas/Fort Worth; **Lufthansa** (tel. 800/645–3880) from Dallas/Fort Worth; **Mexicana** (tel. 800/531–7921) from Chicago, Dallas, Denver, Los Angeles, Miami, New York, San Antonio, San Francisco, and San Jose; **Northwest** (tel. 800/225–2525) from Tampa; and **United** (tel. 800/241–6522) from Dulles/Washington, Chicago, and San Francisco.

One of the cheapest ways to get to Mexico from the West Coast of the United States is on a Mexicana Airlines night flight, appropriately nicknamed El Tecolote (The Owl), which flies from San Francisco and Los Angeles to Guadalajara and Mexico City. Other cheap flights depart from southern California and are bound for Tijuana, where travelers grab a domestic flight to their final destination. If you're on your way to Mexico from Europe, it is generally cheapest to fly to a U.S. city first, and then connect to a Mexico-bound flight. When homeward-bound, be prepared to pay a departure tax of $12 (payable in cash only) at the airport.

Flying times to Mexico City from major U.S. cities are: from New York, 4½ hours; from Chicago, 4¼ hours; from Los Angeles, 3½ hours. To Cancún from New York the flight is four hours; from Chicago, 3½ hours; from Los Angeles, five hours. To Acapulco from New York it's six hours; from Houston, two hours; from Los Angeles, three hours.

LUGGAGE You've heard it a million times. Now you'll hear it once again: Pack light. U.S. airlines allow passengers to check two pieces of luggage, neither of which can exceed 62 inches (length + width + height) or weigh more than 70 pounds. If your airline accepts excess baggage, it will probably charge you for it. Foreign-airline policies vary, so call or check with a travel agent before you show up at the airport with one bag too many.

If you're traveling with a pack, tie all loose straps to each other or onto the pack itself, as they tend to get caught in luggage conveyer belts. Put valuables like cameras and important documents in the middle of packs, wadded inside clothing, because outside pockets are extremely vulnerable to probing fingers.

Anything you'll need during the flight (and valuables to be kept under close surveillance) should be stowed in a carry-on bag. Foreign airlines have different policies but generally allow only one carry-on in tourist class, in addition to a handbag and a bag filled with duty-free goodies. The carry-on bag cannot exceed 45 inches (length + width + height) and must fit under the seat or in the overhead luggage compartment. Call for the airline's current policy. Passengers on U.S. airlines are limited to one carry-on bag, plus coat, camera, and handbag (women get a break here). Carry-on bags must fit under the seat in front of you; maximum dimensions are 9 x 45 x 22 inches. Hanging bags can have a maximum dimension of 4 x 23 x 45 inches; to fit in an overhead bin, bags can have a maximum dimension of 10 x 14 x 36 inches. If your bag is too porky for compartments, be prepared for the humiliation of rejection and last-minute baggage check.

Bikes in Flight

Most airlines will ship bikes as luggage, provided they are dismantled and put into a box. Call to see if your airline sells bike boxes (around $10). International travelers can substitute a bike for the second piece of checked luggage at no extra charge; otherwise, it will cost $100 extra. Domestic flights are less gracious and uniformly charge bike-toting travelers a $45 fee.

BY CAR

Bringing a car into Mexico has become seriously complicated. The owner of the vehicle must provide proof of ownership, state registration, and a valid driver's license issued outside Mexico. The owner must provide a credit card number (American Express, Visa, Diner's Club, or MasterCard) or a bond as security against selling the car while in Mexico. All documents and credit cards must be in the name of the owner, who must be driving the car. If your permit runs out or you are found without the proper documents, your car can be immediately confiscated. However, these restrictions only apply for bringing a car into mainland Mexico—Baja is trouble-free motoring. The foreign insurance on your car is not valid in Mexico. Mexican insurance is sold by the day near border crossings. The border officials do not care if you buy any or not, but a cop further south (or anyone with whom you are involved in an accident) very well might.

Compared to bus and train ticket prices in Mexico, renting a car there is outrageously expensive unless you share the cost with other travelers.

A VW is probably your best bet for Mexican car travel. (The Beetle was manufactured just outside Puebla and remains the most popular car in Mexico.) Avoid fuel-injection engines if you have a choice: the simpler the car, the better. Parts and knowledgeable mechanics can be extremely hard to find for European cars such as BMWs, Saabs, Volvos, and Citroens, and high-priced American models. Road conditions in Mexico are variable: Big (and often very expensive) toll roads between most major cities are often in perfect condition, while some areas have only rutted, poorly marked roads and terrible traffic. Two excellent road atlases published in Mexico are Pemex's *Atlas de Carreteras y Ciudades Turísticas* and another put out by Guía Roji. Both of these are widely available in bookstores and at newsstands.

RENTAL CARS If you want to rent in the United States and drive down to Mexico, you'll find rental companies less than obliging. You can rent a car from Avis (tel. 800/331–1084) in Yuma, Arizona, or San Diego, California, and drive it into Mexico, but only in the Baja Peninsula and only for a maximum of 450 miles round-trip. Dollar (tel. 800/800–4000) will allow you to drive 150 miles into Mexico from San Diego or from McAllen, Texas, only as far as Monterrey. Finally, Thrifty (tel. 800/367–2277) allows you to drive from San Diego into Mexico, but only for 70 kilometers.

If your travel dates are fairly rigid, setting up a car rental through an agency in the United States is a cheaper alternative to renting south of the border. You will save at least $10 per day and will be assured of actually getting a car. Check with agencies to see if they have branches in the Mexican city you desire; **Avis** (tel. 800/331–1212), **Budget** (tel. 800/527–0700), **Dollar** (tel. 800/800–4000), **Hertz** (tel. 800/654– 3001), and **National** (tel. 800/227–3876) all rent cars in Mexico, and their prices are basically the same.

In Mexico, rental rates vary according to the make of car, whether it has a manual or automatic transmission, whether the company charges per mile or offers unlimited mileage, and what type of insurance is offered. All rental agencies add a 10% tax to the price. An average rate for a Volkswagen Beetle with stick shift, unlimited mileage, and basic insurance coverage is $50–$60 per day. Most agencies rent only to drivers 25 years old or over, but some have lower age requirements in Mexico than in the United States. For example, you need only be 21 years old at Avis and 22 at National (though you do need two major credit cards). Cash or credit cards are usually accepted as payment.

BY BUS

Unless you're on a tour, such as those run by Green Tortoise (*see below*), you can't get a direct bus into Mexico. Rather, you must trundle down to the border, cross, and then change to a Mexican bus on the other side to continue your journey (*see* Getting Around By Bus, *below*). **Greyhound** (call a local Greyhound number that will connect you to the national switchboard) serves El Paso, Del Rio, Laredo, McAllen, San Antonio, Eagle Pass, and Brownsville, Texas; Nogales, Arizona; and Calexico and San Diego, California. Their sole Mexican destination is

Tijuana. Otherwise, Greyhound will get you to, but not across, the border; you'll have to pick up a Mexican bus on the other side.

Amtrak (tel. 800/872–7245) will get you as far as San Diego, El Paso, or San Antonio. The **San Diego Trolley** (tel. 619/231–8549) will take you from the city to the border for $1.75. Once in Tijuana, you can catch a bus to just about anywhere in Mexico. From San Antonio, you'll have to catch another bus to Laredo, on the border. From El Paso or Laredo, you'll be able to walk across the border.

Green Tortoise Adventure Travel (Box 24459, San Francisco, CA 94124, tel. 415/821–0803 or 800/227–4766 outside CA) is the cheap alternative to humdrum bus travel. From November through April, Green Tortoise buses—equipped with sleeping pads, kitchens, and stereos—offer 14-day trips from the West Coast of the United States to Baja. In November and December, limited space is avaiable for longer trips to Mexico City, Mérida, and Guatemala.

Staying in Mexico

GETTING AROUND

Buses are the most convenient way to get around in Mexico. Hundreds of buses link nearly every city or hamlet, several times a day. Trains are cheaper, slower, offer less frequent departures, but can afford more legroom and spectacular scenery. Car travel grants complete freedom, but a car, especially one that's prone to breaking down, can sometimes be more of a burden than a boon, and gas isn't cheap. Rental-car costs are definitely out of budget range (*see* Rental Cars, *above*). Biking is the cheapest form of transport, but a bad idea for the average or novice rider, as towns are far apart and the roads are ruled by macho drivers. No matter how you choose to travel, make sure you have ample supplies of food, water, and, if necessary, gas since stretches of the country are long, dry, hot, and often desolate.

BY BUS Bus travel throughout Mexico is cheap and easy (*see* How Much it Will Cost, *above*). Buses are basically divided into first and second class, but in reality run the gamut from dilapidated school buses with shrines to the Virgin of Guadalupe attached to the grill and blasting *ranchera* music, to luxury liners with on-board movies. Most of the time, however, second-class means a comfortable bus with no air-condtioning that makes a number of stops, while first-class service consists of a similar bus, chilled beyond reason, and a direct ride. The super-deluxe buses are usually designated *plus* or *especial*. These last can get pretty pricey, but in general the difference in price between first and second class is minimal.

BY TRAIN Of all the forms of transport in Mexico, trains have the worst reputation: notoriously run-down, slow, late, and a haven for thieves. Depending on the type of train and route, they can arrive absurdly late or leave absurdly early, but they are always slower than buses. Buying a ticket is also a uniquely frustrating experience, as ticket offices are often closed most of the day, generally until trains actually roll in. Advantages to train travel include great scenery, a certain romantic air, and a leisurely pace.

The train system includes several routes spanning the entire length of Mexico, not including Baja California. The east–west distances between lines are substantial, however, so if you want to change routes, you'll probably have to pass through Mexico City. There are several classes of service, not all of which are available for any given route. Special first class usually has air-conditioning and functioning bathrooms with water. A limited number of expensive sleeper cars are available on some trains offering special first class. The **Tren Jarocho,** which meanders between Mexico City and Veracruz is one such train. First-class reserved features toilets that function more often than not and reserved seats. One of the many trains offering first-class service is the **Oaxaqueño,** a Mexico City–Oaxaca line. Second class is bottom-of-the-barrel, move-at-a-crawl train travel, characterized by putrid toilets, crowded seats and aisles, no reserved seating—basically double the travel time and half the comfort of first class. Second-class train travel is, however, incredibly cheap (as little as one third the price of a bus ticket), and second-class trains are usually quite lively, with musicians working for donations, food vendors, and lots of action.

BY CAR Go where you want to, when you want to, roll the windows down, and pop in your favorite tape as you cruise down the highway. Sounds heavenly, but be ready for anything: Driving in a foreign country is always an adventure, and the quality of Mexican roads varies substantially. Drivers need a current license and registration, as well as a vehicle permit from border officials for cars not registered in Mexico. *See* Coming and Going By Car, *above*, for the lowdown on permit procedures. Roadside emergency service is available in much of the country from the **Green Angels,** a group of radio-dispatched, English-speaking mechanics. If you break down, pull over and pop your hood up; one will come cruising along if you wait long enough and pray hard enough. Service is free.

The maximum speed on highways is 100 kilometers per hour. Most of the time, however, you'll be lucky to do half that, as many roads, even those connecting major towns, are single-lane routes clogged with smoke-belching trucks. Trucks will often help you out by flashing their turn signals to let you know that it is safe to pass. Driving at night is discouraged, as roads are often poorly marked (i.e. you won't see many signs equipped with those handy reflective stickers so you can see them in the dark), and, in rural areas, animals wandering onto roadways can be a major hazard. If you have an accident, notify the police immediately; take pictures of all cars involved; and, if possible, collect information from the other driver (provided he or she hasn't driven away). Even if the accident wasn't your fault, the rule in Mexico is "guilty until proven innocent," and the police will not necessarily take your word as gospel if the other driver blames you. Photos will strengthen your case.

You are required to stop and show your personal and vehicle documents at *all* roadside customs checkpoints. You are also required to stop anytime a police officer waves you over, but be cautious: Travelers are the favorite targets of robbers who pose as police officers. Highways 1 and 15 in Sinaloa have become infamous due to the high incidence of this sort of robbery. Pemex is Mexico's state owned oil monopoly—all the gas you buy will be Pemex gas. Quality is low, so you may hear some unfamiliar engine knocks. Gas prices are also considerably higher than in the States. Fill up when you see a Pemex station, since the next one may have a broken pump.

The **Associación Mexicana Automovilistica (AMA)**. Mexico's motoring club provides roadside repairs, fuel and tire service, plus free towing (up to 10 km) in Mexico City, Puebla, and Cuernavaca to any tourist in need. *Orizaba 7, Col. Roma, Distrito Federal, CP 06700, México, tel. 5/511–62–85. Emergency tel. 5/588–70–55 or 5/761–60–22.*

BY MOTORCYCLE Motorcycling conditions in Mexico are not ideal. Roads are not always in the best condition, but there are plenty of long stretches to open up the bike and enjoy watching the land whiz by. Small dirt bikes are good for bouncing around the desert. For best results, though, bring your own bike, because rentals are quite expensive. You should know how to do your own repairs and bring plenty of supplies. As with any vehicle in Mexico, avoid driving at night.

BY PLANE Domestic plane travel is expensive. You'll save travel time, but it will cost about four times as much as a first-class bus. **Mexicana** and **Aeroméxico** are government-subsidized and offer similar fares. (Unfortunately, no discounts are available on any flights.) **Aerocalifornia** (in Mexico City, tel. 5/514–6678) flies between Baja California cities and some places in northwestern Mexico. **Aeromar** (in Mexico City, tel. 5/574–9211) flies from Mexico City to Guadalajara. **Aerocaribe** and **Aviacsa** operate in southeast Mexico.

Charter planes fly out of tiny airports to otherwise hard-to-access ruin and jungle sites. Although expensive, prices for charters are negotiable and can be manageable for groups.

BY BIKE Bike travel in Mexico is for the hardy and experienced rider. Some roads have never seen a bicycle, and drivers are unused to bikers. In addition, most Mexican roads lack shoulders and are often pitted. Don't expect to find rental outfits, either; if available, rental bikes will probably be granny-style relics good for short excursions only.

Despite these drawbacks, traveling by bike in Mexico can be fun if you plan ahead. Bikes are especially useful for travel to places where there are only dirt roads or tracks, or where public transportation is scant. In the Yucatán, for example, bikes are a primary form of transportation for locals, and bike-repair shops are common even in smaller towns. When planning your trip, consult an up-to-date AAA, Pemex, or Guía Roji map. Be sure to carry plenty of water and everything you might need to repair your bike. Pack extra patch kits as shards of glass often litter the roads. If you can take your bike apart and fold it up, buses will allow you to store it in the cargo space. Bikers in northern Mexico (Copper Canyon) can transport their bikes on the trains.

Some adventurous cyclists have organized tours of Baja; write to **The Touring Exchange** (Box 265, Port Townsend, WA, 98368) for details. **Backroads Bicycle Touring** (1516 5th St., Berkeley, CA 94710–1740, tel. 800/245–3874) offers trips around Baja and the Yucatán. If you go on your own and plan on biking only part of the way, Amtrak will transport your bike to the border. They provide the bike box, but require you to disassemble the bike. A good book that explores the coastal route from Canada to Mexico is *Bicycling the Pacific Coast*, by Tom Kirkendall and Vicky Spring (The Mountaineers, 306 2nd Ave. W, Seattle, WA 98119; $12.95).

HITCHING Hitchhikers are a rarity in northern Mexico and in densely populated, urban areas. In Baja, near resort areas, and in rural areas in southern Mexico, hitching is more common, and probably safer. Reports of robberies and violence come from all parts of the country, though, so keep your belongings and your wits close by, and don't hitch alone if you can possibly avoid it. Offer gas money and be somewhat flexible, but never accept a ride if you are unsure about the driver. Always be aware of your location and options. Don't hesitate to tell a driver to stop if you feel at all unsafe, and try not to sit in between people, so you'll be free to bolt if necessary.

PHONES

Like some other public services in the country, Mexican phones are a crap shoot. Your experiences with the phones will vary with the phone, the place, the time, and perhaps the alignment of the heavens that particular day. Many different options for making phone calls exist, but none are completely reliable everywhere. Calling out of Mexico can be a challenging, frustrating, and expensive experience.

The country code for Mexico is 52. The city code for Mexico City is 5. Dial 02 for the domestic operator in Mexico; 09 for the international operator (who should speak English or be able to find someone who does); 04 for local information; and 01 for long-distance information. You can dial long-distance calls directly: to the United States, dial 95 + area code + number; direct to rest of world, dial 98 + country code + city code + number; direct to other parts of Mexico, dial 91 + number. Long-distance carriers in the United States often have direct numbers that you can dial to access an operator to place a collect or calling-card call. Ask your carrier if they have an access number *before* departure. **AT&T**'s is 95 + 800/462–4240.

CALLING WITHIN MEXICO Public phones are found all over most Mexican cities. Not so common is a pay phone that works. Calling within cities is pretty cheap, but long-distance calls can add up fast. For local or long-distance calls, another possibility is to find a *caseta de larga distancia*, a telephone service usually operated out of a store such as a *papelería* (stationery store), pharmacy, restaurant, or other small business; look for the phone symbol on the door. Most casetas charge you even to make a collect call, so it's better to call collect (*al cobrar*) from a pay phone, if possible.

INTERNATIONAL CALLS For an international collect or calling-card call, (theoretically) you dial the long-distance operator (09), wait as much as 30 minutes for the bilingual long-distance operator to pick up the line, and give him or her the number you want to call and your name or card number, as appropriate. In some areas, pay phones also accept pre-paid cards, called **Ladatel** cards, that you buy in denominations of 30 or 50 pesos (approximately $10 or $17) from newsstands or pharmacies. To use a Ladatel card, simply insert it in the slot of a silver *Multitarjetas* phone, dial 95 (for calls to the States), and the area code and number you're trying to reach. Credit is deleted from the card as you use it, and your balance is displayed on a small screen on the phone so you can keep tabs on how much you've got left.

Casetas de larga distancia may cost more to use than pay phones, but you have a better chance of immediate success. To make the call, write down the number you'd like to call, and the person on duty will give you a rate and dial for you. Rates seem to vary widely, so shop around. Sometimes you can make collect calls (*al cobrar* or *cobrada*) from casetas, and sometimes you cannot, depending on the individual operator and possibly your degree of visible desperation. Casetas will generally charge from $1 to $3 to place a collect call, and some charge by the minute on collect calls, as well.

MAIL

All cities and most towns have an *oficina de correos* (post office) that sells stamps and has Lista de Correos (poste restante) service (*see* Receiving Mail, *below*). Some post offices also offer telegram, fax, and express mail services.

SENDING MAIL HOME Mail to points beyond Mexico takes anywhere from one to six weeks to arrive, depending on your luck and the size of the city from which you mail the missive. If you're in a hurry, you can send a letter registered mail, which takes about five to seven days, or by Mexpost, the fastest (about two days) and most expensive method. Mailing a package involves buying the necessary paper, tape, box, and string, then visiting the post office and the customs office. Go to the post office first for instructions, as the procedure varies from city to city. Do not attempt to pack up and wrap the goods yourself; the post office worker will rip everything apart to inspect the contents and charge you to rewrap it Mexican-style. They will also charge you duty tax. The whole process can take up to an hour, so be patient.

RECEIVING MAIL You can receive fan mail in Mexico via Lista de Correos, which is basically general delivery service. Mail is held up to 10 days then returned to sender if you don't show up with a picture ID and fetch it. For the Lista de Correos address in any given town, look under the heading "Mail" for that town.

BUSINESS HOURS

Business hours vary from city to city, but most businesses, including banks, open around 9 AM. Everything but restaurants closes between 2 PM and 4 PM for the lunchtime siesta, then

What Did You Call Me?

Travelers who consider themselves well educated in the Spanish language often find themselves befuddled when trying interpret Mexican slang. For example, if someone tells you, "No me mames," don't take it literally (Don't suck on me). You're actually being asked to lay off. The use of the words for mother and father often have nothing to do with the family. If something "no tiene madre" (has no mother) it's absolutely the coolest. "Que padre" (literally, how father) is equivalent to "how cool." "Pinche" (damn) is a word you will hear in every other sentence. "Chingar" is the Spanish verb for "to fuck," and carries the same connotations as it does in English. Variations of the word are used as adjectives, adverbs, nouns; depending on the context, they mean everything from the very best to the very worst. Other handy expressions include "híjole," an exclamation meaning anything from "wow" to "shit" to "uh-oh"; "andale," which means "hurry up," "really," or "go for it"; "güero" or "güera," meaning, basically, "white boy" (or girl); and "wey," which means anything from "dude" to "dickhead" and usually comes at the end of a sentence, as in "Chinga tu madre, wey". For more banal expressions, see the glossary at the back of the book.

reopens until 6, 7, or 8. Banks are open weekdays often close at 1 or 1:30. Banks that offer money-exchange service almost always stop doing so at noon or 1 PM, regardless of when the bank itself closes. Most businesses are closed on Sunday, or open only in the morning; the same goes for holidays.

SHOPPING

Mexico is a bonanza for all sorts of handicrafts and folk art. The best deals are found at outdoor markets, where you can bargain if you think the price is too high. Although this may be an uncomfortable process for haggling-shy travelers, it beats paying the jacked-up prices in the tourist-oriented stores. Many markets are at their best on Sundays. The state of Oaxaca is one of the country's crafts hubs, where you can find hand-dyed and stitched rugs, brightly colored *huipiles* (embroidered tunics), and mats and baskets woven from palm leaves. Puebla is famous for ceramics. Chiapas is known for hand-loomed clothing, a skill of the ancient Maya that has been passed down for centuries. Mérida produces the finest hammocks in the country; a double costs anywhere from $30 to $150 and will last for years. Farther north, the Heartland offers good deals on leather goods, carved and painted wooden sculptures, ceramics, and copper pots and pans. Zacatecas and Taxco, home to silver mines, sell silver jewelry of all sorts.

WHERE TO SLEEP

Mexico offers nearly every type of hotel imaginable, from spotless, sterile rooms, to cozy, colonial houses, to cubicles with bare concrete floors and saggy beds. In general, the more you pay for a room, the better quality you'll receive, though this, like everything in Mexico, is variable. The hotels featured in this book are generally the cheapest we could find, moderately priced ones with character, or more upscale places with budget deals. The price categories in this book typically refer to the cost of the least expensive double room available plus tax.

Check-out time at most hotels is 1 PM. You can usually leave your valuables behind the desk while you roam about during the day. Some places will watch your backpack for several days, usually at no charge, if you take a side trip elsewhere. Hotel/motel chains are not in the budget range, and what most people understand as bed-and-breakfasts are very rare in Mexico, though some budget places will include breakfast in the price of a room. Mexico also has a network of about 16 youth hostels, called *villas juveniles*. No sort of membership card is necessary to stay in the hostels—you can leave that HI card you used in Europe at home. Though they usually cost less than $5 a night, they can be a major hassle to get to.

CAMPING A host of camping opportunities exist in Mexico, but don't expect the typical U.S.-style campground. Mexico's campgrounds are usually nothing more than trailer parks with running water, cooking areas, and room to pitch tents. Tent sites can cost $1–$15. To enjoy more rustic surroundings, you can set up camp off the road or on the beach in relative safety, and save loads of money. Do not camp, however, at archaeological sites or in marijuana-growing areas. For more detailed camping information and humorous camping anecdotes, look to *The People's Guide to Camping in Mexico* by Carl Franz.

ROUGHING IT Along Mexico's coasts, you can usually sleep on the beach for free; just ask a local to make sure it's permissible. Nine times out of 10 it will be just fine. Hammocks are another alternative; lots of beach communities have hammock hooks between trees or inside palapa huts where you can string a hammock for free or for a nominal fee.

Within cities, it's hard to find a place to rough it without being picked up by police. Public parks are rare. You could always dance the night away at a disco, though, or hit the cantina all night. Some bus stations are open 24 hours, though you may be the sole bench occupant.

LODGING ALTERNATIVES Formed in the aftermath of World War II, **Servas** is a membership organization dedicated to promoting peace and understanding around the globe that enables you to arrange two-night stays with host families. Becoming a member makes you eligible for their host list directory for any country you desire. Servas has 204 hosts scattered throughout Mexico, though some regions have only one or two per state. Servas is not for tourists or weekend travelers; peace-minded individuals who want more than a free bed can write or call for an application and an interview. You can arrange a stay with a Servas host or host family in advance or just try your luck when you reach the country. Membership is $55 per year, and a deposit of $25 is required for up to five host lists. *In the United States: 11 John St., New York, NY 10038, tel. 212/267–0252; in Canada: 229 Hilcrest Ave., Willowdale, Ont. M2N 3P3, tel. 416/221–6434; in the U.K.: 83 Gore Rd., London E97HW; in Australia: 16 Cavill Ct., Vermont South, 3133 Victoria, tel. 803–5004; in New Zealand: 15 Harley Rd., Takapuna, Oakland, tel. 594–442.*

World For Free (WFF). WFF helps like-minded people find contacts in foreign cities. The $25 membership fee gets you listed in the WFF Address Book, which means people may start calling or writing you tomorrow to crash at your pad. You are never obligated to house a WFF member, though the whole point is to be nice and to help travelers in need. After joining you also get a copy of the latest *WFF Address Book*, which you can use to contact other members and arrange accommodations by phone or mail. *Box 137, Prince Street Station, New York, NY 10012, fax 212/979–8167.*

FOOD

The first thing many people hear when they tell people they're going to Mexico is "Don't drink the water." However, if you're too cautious, you'll miss out on one of the most enjoyable experiences of any trip: trying all the good stuff there is to eat. Start off slowly, giving your system time to adjust, and follow crowds of locals to find the best (and probably safest) food in town.

Mexican restaurant dining can be a disconcerting experience, at first. When you sit down, a waiter brings you a menu, then returns after about 30 seconds to take your order. He or she expects you to be ready; if you need more time, you'll have to ask for it and you might get a look of surprise. This speediness is balanced by the length of time it takes to actually receive your food—sometimes decades. Choosing a dish gets even more complicated when you try to order and find out that maybe 5% of the items on the menu are actually available, as in this following traveler's experience: "Good morning! I'd like the mixed fruit plate, please, but could I have it without papaya?" "Of course. No papaya." "Uh, excuse me, but this plate has only papaya." "Oh, yes, sir, it's the only kind of fruit we have right now."

Mexicans like meat and eat it for breakfast, lunch, and dinner. Vegetarian restaurants are difficult to find, but with the abundance of beans, tortillas, fresh fruit, vegetables, and nuts, herbivores should do just fine. Be aware lard is often used in the preparation of tortillas. The price categories used in this book are loosely based on the assumption that you are going to chow down a main course, a drink, and maybe a cup of coffee. Antacids are extra. For more info about health risks from food, *see* Staying Healthy, *above.*

TIPPING

Standard practice in Mexico is to tip 10% or a bit higher at sit-down restaurants—there's no need to tip at food stands. Tip taxi drivers if they offer suggestions and don't rip you off (be sure to fix the price first). Tip if you're too lazy to carry your bags yourself and someone helps you out.

LANGUAGE

Although Spanish is the official language of Mexico, different Mayan tongues are also spoken as a first language in a few places, especially in the south, and variants of Nahuatl, the Aztec language, are also common. Knowing even a little Spanish, though, makes your trip more enjoyable, and Mexicans

Thirty-two percent of all adults in the southern state of Chiapas do not speak Spanish

generally appreciate the fact that you're trying. Upper-class Mexicans commonly speak English and/or one or two other European languages, but in general, English is not commonly spoken or understood. See the glossary at the back of the book for some useful phrases.

CRIME AND PUNISHMENT

The moment you step onto Mexican soil, you're subject to the legal theory that you're guilty until proven innocent. The government is cracking down hard on drug trafficking, and police are quick to prosecute anyone found in possession (prescription drugs excluded, of course, though you should carry a doctor's certificate declaring them such and keep the drugs in their original containers). Of all foreign drug prosecutions in the world, those filed in Mexico account for over 20%. Travelers with as little as a third of an ounce of marijuana have been arrested and thrown in jail. Legally, the government can keep you in one of its miserable cells for up to seven years, and since you are not protected by the laws of your native land after you cross the Mexican border, your embassy can do little for you. The situation can be grim, to say the least.

Apart from drugs, police rarely hassle travelers unless they are excessively loud, drunk, or involved in a brawl, in which case the police can keep you overnight in jail and take your money, as well as fine you. Remember, no one will be on your side, so be careful. If you do get into a scrape with the law, you can call the **Citizens' Emergency Center** (tel. 202/647–5225) in the United States, weekdays 8:15 AM–10 PM, Saturday 9 AM–3 PM. After hours and on Sundays, call the emergency duty officer (tel. 202/634–3600). In Mexico you can also call the **Procuraduría de Protección al Turista** (Attorney General for the Protection of Tourists), where English is spoken. The 24-hour hotline in Mexico City is 5/250–01–51, or dial the operator for assistance.

PROTECTING YOUR VALUABLES Money belts may be dorky and bulky, but it's better to be embarrassed than broke. You'd be wise to carry all cash, traveler's checks, credit cards, and your passport in an inaccessible place: front or inner pocket or a bag or pouch that fits underneath your clothes. Neck pouches and money belts are sold in luggage or camping-supply stores. Waist packs (smallish zippered nylon bags that are strapped around your waist or hips) are safe if your keep the pack part in front of your body, safer still if your shirt or sweater hangs over the pack.

When is it safe to take your valuables off your body? Hotel rooms and hostels are not necessarily safe; don't leave anything valuable out in the open. Inside your hotel room, keep your money belt, traveler's checks, airplane ticket, and identification near you at all times. When heading out for the day, hide your backpack out of sight in a closet or behind something. You can sometimes leave valuables in a safe-deposit box at the front desk. And it may go without saying, but *never* leave your pack unguarded or with a total stranger in train or bus stations or any other public place, not even if you're only planning to be gone for a minute—it's not worth the risk. If you're carrying a smaller bag with a strap (or a camera), sling it crosswise over your body and try to keep your arm down over the bag in front of you. Back pockets are fine for maps, but don't keep a wallet back there; you might get the wrong kind of admiring attention.

The best way to avoid theft is to leave expensive jewelry and cameras at home. When packing, ask yourself if you can go on living if a given item is lost or stolen. If not, put that item right back where it belongs—safe at home.

FURTHER READING

PRE-COLUMBIAN MEXICO Good general reference works include: Elizabeth P. Benson's *The Maya World* (Crowell, 1977); Frans Blom's *The Conquest of Yucatán* (Cooper Square Publishers, 1971); Burr Cartwright Brundage's *A Rain of Darts: the Mexica Aztecs* (University of Texas Press, 1972); David Carrasco's *Montezuma's Mexico* (University Press of Colorado, 1992); Michael D. Coe's *In the Land of the Olmec* (University of Texas Press, 1980); Nigel Davies's *The Toltec Heritage* (University of Oklahoma Press, 1980); Richard A Diehl's *Tula: The Toltec Capital of Ancient Mexico* (Thames and Hudson, 1983); Karl W. Luckert's *Olmec Religion* (University of Oklahoma Press, 1980); Sylvanus G. Morley's *The Ancient Maya* (Stanford University Press, 1983); John S. Henderson's *The World of the Ancient Maya* (Cornell University Press, 1981); Mary Miller and Karl Taube's *The Gods and Symbols of Ancient Mexico and the Maya* (Thames and Hudson, 1993); Muriel Porter Weaver's *The Aztecs, Maya, and Their Predecessors* (Academic Press, 1981); and Ronald Wright's *Time Among the Maya* (Henry Holt and Company, 1991).

If you prefer to read about the ancient Mexican civilizations in their own words, a few texts remain and have been translated. *The Destruction of the Jaguar: Poems from the Books of Chilam Balam*, translated by Christopher Sawyer Lucanno and available from City Lights Books and *Popol Vuh* (Touchstone Press,1986) are both based on ancient Maya codices. A translation of the Aztec *Codex Chimalpopoca* is also available from the University of Arizona Press.

COLONIAL AND MODERN HISTORY Many aspects of colonial and modern history are discussed in the following works: Hector Aguilar Camín's *In the Shadow of the Mexican Revolution* (University of Texas Press, 1993); Roderic A. Camp's *Politics in Mexico* (Oxford University Press, 1993); Jorge G. Castañeda and Robert A. Pastor's *Limits to Friendship: The United States and Mexico* (Vintage Books, 1988); Hernán Cortés's *Letters From Mexico* (Yale University Press, 1986); Charles Gibson's *The Aztecs Under Spanish Rule* (Stanford University Press, 1964); Merilee Grindle's *Bureaucrats, Politicians, and Peasants in Mexico* (University of California Press, 1977); Nora Hamilton's *Limits of State Autonomy: Post-Revolutionary Mexico* (Princeton University Press, 1982); John M. Hart's *Revolutionary Mexico* (University of California Press, 1987); Bartólome de Las Casas's *The Devastation of the Indies* (Johns Hopkins University Press, 1992) and *Tears of the Indians* (Oriole Editions, 1972); Michael C. Meyer and William L. Sherman's *The Course of Mexican History* (Oxford University Press, 1991); Lesley Byrd Simpson's *Many Mexicos* (University of California Press, 1971); and Eric Wolf's *Sons of the Shaking Earth* (University of Chicago Press, 1959).

MODERN LITERATURE IN TRANSLATION Mexican literature is obviously a vast and varied field, but the following works are highly recommended: Rosario Castellanos's *The Nine Guardians* (Readers International, 1992), *City of Kings* (Latin American Literary Review Press, 1992), and *Meditation on the Threshold: a Bilingual Anthology of Poetry* (Bilingual Press, 1988); Carlos Fuentes's *Where the Air is Clear* (Noonday Press, 1960), *Aura* (Deutsch, 1990), *Burnt Water* (Farrar, Straus, and Giroux, 1980), and *The Old Gringo* (Farrar, Straus, and Giroux, 1985); Elena Garro's *Recollections of Things to Come* (University of Texas Press, 1969); Gregorio López y Fuentes' *El Indio* (F. Ungar, 1961); Ángeles Mastretta's *Mexican Bolero* (Viking, 1989); José Emilio Pacheco's *Battles in the Desert and Other Stories* (New Directions, 1987) and *Selected Poems* (New Directions, 1987); Octavio Paz's *The Labyrinth of Solitude* (Fondo de Cultura Económica, 1959) and *A Tree Within* (New Directions, 1988); Elena Poniatowska's *Dear Diego* (Pantheon Books, 1986) and *Massacre in Mexico* (Viking Press, 1975); Juan Rulfo's *The Burning Plain, and Other Stories* (University of Texas Press, 1990) and *Pedro Páramo* (Grove Weidenfeld, 1990); and Alan Trueblood's *A Sor Juana Anthology* (Harvard University Press, 1988).

MEXICO CITY AND ENVIRONS

2

By Ariana Mohit

Whatever you've heard about the D.F. (Distrito Federal) is probably not far from the truth. The pollution is staggering, the overcrowding obvious, the city massive and unwieldy. The rest of the country, somewhat resentful of the attention the city receives, refers to D.F. residents as *chilangos,* a slightly nasty label. They are not alone in their reluctance to embrace Mexico City: Even the 20 million-plus chilangos sometimes have trouble loving this city, the world's largest metropolis.

But the problems the city faces are unquestionably overshadowed by its vitality. Visitors to this focal point of government, culture, and education can take advantage of a rich cultural scene and nonstop nightlife unrivaled anywhere else in the country. And while you're likely to shell out more dough here than on the rest of your adventure, the cafés, museums, theaters, and clubs are worth every last peso. The D.F. is the heart of Mexico—the nucleus of this vast and varied country. Tall, shiny skyscrapers loom high above the dark, crumbling shantytowns of the industrial northern sector of the city, a contrast symbolic of the convenience and modernity of city life coming face to face with the slow grind of poverty that still characterizes many other parts of the country.

This capital of several civilizations has been located in the Valley of Mexico since about 1325, when the Aztecs, or Mexicas, founded the city of Tenochtitlán. While the valley itself has always enjoyed a relatively temperate climate, the almost uninterrupted range of volcanic mountains that surround it are one of the main reasons the city is usually blanketed by a thick, brown layer of smog. On top of that, the soft soil upon which the city is built (the site was a lake, but has been gradually filled in by successive civilizations) has caused many of the city's buildings to sink several inches per year. Although the Spanish conquistador Cortés briefly toyed with the idea of moving the capital out of the valley, he ultimately adopted an "If it ain't broke, don't fix it" attitude. But despite all its serious problems, the oldest capital in the Americas has always remained the ultimate seat of political power. During times of violent upheaval, the crucial question—from independence fighter Padre Hidalgo to the revolutionaries Villa and Zapata—has always been, "Did they hold the capital?"

All the warnings about avoiding the suffocating poverty and pollution of Mexico City should be taken with a grain of salt. The gap between the millions of people struggling to make it and the privileged few that have already got it should make you think, not run away.

And who holds the capital today? Mexico City is a complex blend of cultures and classes. Expatriates, political exiles, immigrants, and visitors from around the world mix with Mexicans from

Mexico City

Mexico City

every state in the country. Rural migrants pour into the city daily, looking for work and a better standard of living, draining resources and labor from the countryside. These *campesinos* (peasants) usually end up in slums, each family member working as he or she can, selling gum or shining shoes on street corners and in the Metro. Children peddle roses late at night to the crowds of trendy *fresas* (spoiled rich kids) who club hop in their bright red Jettas and plush Pontiacs complete with cellular phones. It's an unsettling contrast at best, and one that some may find depressing.

You see practically every side, shade, and texture of Mexico and Mexicans in the capital: small-town cantinas and silent church plazas, markets packed with every color and variety of goods, and the tree-lined Paseo de la Reforma, where skyscrapers and 19th-century mansions stand side by side. Within the huge metropolitan area are hundreds of neighborhoods, each with a unique personality and feel. North and northeast of the *centro* (downtown) are the great industrial wastelands, home to destitute chilangos and rural migrants. The affluent classes are cloistered in the south and southwestern districts: the Zona Rosa, Coyoacán, Polanco, and Lomas de Chapultepec. But you don't have to go to the ritzy *colonias* (neighborhoods) to find pretty plazas where people walk, talk, and fall in love in the only privacy they can find in this crowded city. For many, local *fondas* (covered food stands) are an extension of their living room, a place to linger over a long meal or to buy a soda and catch the latest news.

The country and the city go by the same name: "México." Say that and all Mexicans know you mean their capital.

Despite the crowded conditions and gritty pollution, there are still lots of green areas within the city, and **Chapultepec Park** is a favorite retreat. Families spend time together wandering the lush grounds, looking at the mind-boggling collection of artifacts in the **Museo Nacional de Antropología,** or learning about their country's history in the **Museo de Historia Nacional** in the Castillo de Chapultepec. Those with more urban tastes kill time hanging out in the *centro* near the **Zócalo** (Main Square), constantly filled with noisy, giggling schoolchildren on field trips; the mural-covered walls of their **Palacio Nacional;** the **Alameda Central** park; and the massive, marble **Palacio de Bellas Artes.**

Mexico City is a mixed bag; it has a bit of everything, not all good and not pure evil. So how do you answer those kids in the Zócalo who want to know if you like their home? Even if you find the city overwhelming, it does grow on you, and it can even become an addiction. Fans of the city feel the same inexplicable and irrational passion that many feel for their first loves. As a visitor, the places you can go to encounter *lo mexicano* (Mexicanness) depend only on the limits of your curiosity. The majority of the population of the city is polite, to residents and tourists alike. Even on a *pesero* (minibus) during rush hour, when a mass of bodies extends out the front and back doors, the fare is routinely passed through the hands of many a stranger before reaching the driver, the change following the same journey back as each person in the chain gushes with pleases and thank yous. Visitors are granted this same treatment, friendly conversation, and advice. Fair-skinned and/or blond women receive plenty of attention from men in the street, usually in the form of catcalls, though sometimes as up-close-and-personal as an ass-pinch. These unwelcome advances usually don't lead to anything more serious. Still, as in any big city, follow standard precautions and watch your butt.

Basics

AMERICAN EXPRESS This well-equipped AmEx office, one of several in the city, is the main branch and replaces and sells traveler's checks, cashes personal checks for cardholders, receives and keeps cardholders' mail, and provides travel services. Avoid changing money here since the rates are poor. *Paseo de la Reforma 234, at Havre, tel. 5/514–06–29. Open weekdays 9–6, Sat. 9–1. Mailing address: Paseo de la Reforma 234, esq. Havre, Col. Juárez, México, D.F., CP 06600, México.*

BUCKET SHOPS Agencia de Viajes Tony Pérez does a lot of business with the U.S. Embassy across the street and knows about the latest airline promotions. *Río Volga 1, at Río Danubio,* *tel. 5/533–11–48 or 5/533–11–49. Near Ángel de la Independencia monument. Open weekdays 8:30–7, Sat. 9–1.*

Turismo Mirey wins the prize for most honest travel agency in the D.F. They go out of their way to find you the best deals. *Londres 44, in the Zona Rosa, tel. 5/514–57–93. Open weekdays 9:30–6:30, Sat. 11–2.*

Drivers in Mexico City seem to enjoy accelerating whenever they've got pedestrians in the way, perhaps as an unspoken commentary on the five-day-per-week driving limit imposed on every car here in an effort to curb pollution.

CASAS DE CAMBIO All banks offer the same government-set exchange rate (*tipo de cambio*), but they often change money only until noon or 1:30. Several banks have ATM machines, called *cajas permanentes*, that accept Cirrus and Plus cards and also give cash advances on Visa and Mastercard; all ATMs spit out your cash in pesos. **Banamex** is the most accessible bank, with branches on practically every block in the downtown area. If you do decide to exchange money at the banks, be forewarned that they usually require you to run a lengthy bureaucratic obstacle course of signatures and receipts before the financial alchemists will change your foreign currency into pesos.

If time is more important than filthy lucre, however, you'll find several **casas de cambio** throughout the city that are quicker and have longer hours, but offer a lower exchange rate. That said, the casas de cambio with the best rates can usually be found in the Zona Rosa. Try **Casa de Cambio Tíber** (Río Tíber 112, tel. 5/207–61–22), open weekdays 8:30–5, Saturday 8:30–2. Right next door, **Casa de Cambio Consultoria Internacional** (Río Tíber 110, tel. 5/207–99–20) is open weekdays from 8 AM to 8:35 PM and Saturdays from 8 to 2.

EMBASSIES **Australia.** *Jaime Balmes 11, 10th floor, Plaza Polanco, Torre B, tel. 5/395–99–88 for information or 5/404–20–46 for emergencies. Open weekdays 9–1.*

Canada. The embassy also has a library. *Schiller 529, at Tres Picos, Col. Polanco, tel. 5/254–32–88, fax 5/545–17–69. Open weekdays 9–2:30; library open weekdays 9–12:30. Office and library closed Canadian and Mexican holidays.*

New Zealand. *Homero 229, 8th floor, Col. Polanco, tel. 5/250–59–99 for information, 5/445–27–48 or 5/250–16–89 for emergencies. Open Mon.–Thurs. 8:30–2 and 3:30–5:30, Fri. 8:30 –2; closed Mexican holidays.*

United Kingdom. *Lerma 71, Col. Cuauhtémoc, tel. 5/207–24–49 or 5/207–20–89. Open weekdays 8:30–3:30; weekdays 9–2 for visas and registration; closed some Mexican and all British holidays.*

United States. *Paseo de la Reforma 305, Col. Cuauhtémoc, tel. 5/211–00–42, fax 5/511–99–80. Near Ángel de la Independencia monument. Open weekdays 9–5; closed Mexican and U.S. holidays.*

EMERGENCIES The general emergency number is 08. You can also call the **police** (tel. 5/625–74–90 or 5/625–74–91), **fire department** (tel. 5/768–37–00), or the **Cruz Roja** (Red Cross; tel. 5/557–57–57) directly.

The **Procuraduría General de Justicia** (Public Prosecutor) offers emergency assistance to tourists in Mexico City. Police, lawyers, and a doctor staff the two offices 24 hours a day, year-round. If you lose your passport or are a victim of a more serious crime, you can make a report in English, and the staff will translate it into Spanish for you. They'll also contact your country's embassy and assist you in every way they can. *Zona Rosa: Florencia 20, tel. 5/625–70–20 or 5/625–87–61. Centro: Argentina, at San Ildefonso, tel. 5/625–87–62.*

ENGLISH BOOKS AND NEWSPAPERS In a city with more than 30,000 English-speaking expatriates, you'll have very little trouble locating English-language publications. *The Mexico City News* contains summaries of national and international news, entertainment, classifieds, and, most important, horoscopes and Ann Landers. *The Mexico City Daily Bulletin* is full of ads and handy sections like "Bible Digest" and "The World of Science." Published Tuesday–Sunday, it's available free at many hotels. Look beyond the cheesy propaganda for helpful suggestions about hotels, restaurants, and places to shop, and cut out the great city map to carry around with you.

The American Bookstore offers a large selection of books and magazines in English, as well as the *Guía Roji* and the *Guía Pronto,* two good maps of Mexico City. *Madero 25, tel. 5/512–03–06. 4½ blocks west of Zócalo. Open Mon.–Sat. 9:30–7.*

The **Benjamin Franklin Library,** in the U.S. Embassy, is meant to nurture understanding between the two nations. Even mutual understanding has its limits, however: Only Mexico City residents can check out books. The library has a good reference section, numerous novels, and U.S. periodicals and magazines. The English Language Programs' office on the second floor lists institutions looking for English teachers. *Londres 16, tel. 5/211–00–42. Open Mon. and Fri. 3–7, Tues.–Thurs. 10–3.*

The **British Council Library** is a cheerful place to while away a few hours. The library's collection of history and fiction focuses mainly on (you guessed it) Britain. British periodicals—such as *The Times*—and how-to books for would-be English teachers are also available. *Antonio Cazo 127, Col. San Rafael, tel. 5/566–61–44. Open Mon. and Tues. 9–8:30, Wed. 8–7:30, Fri. 9–7:30, Sat. 10–1:30.*

Casa Libros, a used-book store run by the American Benevolent Society, is way out in the boondocks, but since new books in English are prohibitively expensive everywhere else, you should stock up while you're here. The store also has smaller selections of books in Portuguese, Spanish, Italian, and German. *Monte Athos 355, Col. Lomas de Chapultepec, tel. 5/546–51–23. Off Reforma beyond Chapultepec Park. Open Mon.–Sat. 10–5.*

Gandhi, a bright pink-and-lavender coffeeshop/bookstore in San Ángel, has a book selection worthy of acclaim. Most of the titles here are in Spanish, supplemented by gorgeous art books and a handful of English materials. For those who make a hobby of spotting famous literati, Mario Vargas Llosa has been known to browse here among the UNAM students perusing the shelves. *M. A. de Quevedo 134, tel. 5/662–06–00 or 5/661–09–11. ½ block west of Metro M. A. de Quevedo. Open daily 9–11.*

Librerías de Cristal, while not the biggest bookstore in Mexico City, is by far one of the nicest. Although the books here are all supposed to be in *español,* there are quite a few titles in English as well. If you're looking for a particular book, the friendly staff will be more than happy to lead you in the right direction. *5 de Mayo 7, Centro, tel. 5/512–68–96. Open Mon.–Sat. 10–8, Sun. 11–7.*

La Torre de Papel, just around the corner from the telegraph office, is literally a maze of periodicals. Newspapers from all over Mexico make their way here, as well as a few U.S. papers like *The New York Times* and *The Phoenix Sun. Filomeno Mata 6-A, btw Tacuba and 5 de Mayo, tel. 5/512–97–03. Open weekdays 9–5:45, Sat. 10–2:45.*

LAUNDRY **Lavandería Edison** is the laundromat closest to the hotels in the Metro Revolución area, though once you get a look at their prices, you'll realize your clothes aren't so dirty after all. Doing your own dirty work costs $6; letting someone else handle it (same-day service) costs $10. *Edison 91, near Monumento de la Revolución, no phone. Open weekdays 10–7, Sat. 10–6.*

Lavandería San Pablo is close to the downtown area. Three kilos of dirty duds cost $2.50 if you do them yourself, $7.50 if you leave them to be washed (same-day service). *Las Cruces 56, btw San Pablo and Regina, tel. 5/522–67–23. Open Mon.–Sat. 9–7, Sun. 9–1.*

LUGGAGE STORAGE If your hotel won't take your bags, the airport, train station, and all four bus stations have luggage storage (*see* Coming and Going, *below*). If you'll be gone more than a few days, use the service at the airport or at TAPO, the eastern bus station, where you can keep the key to your locker.

MAIL The **Dirección General de Correos** (main Post Office), in a neo-Renaissance building across from Bellas Artes, sells stamps at the *estampillas* windows and distributes mail at the *lista y poste restante* window. Mail sent to you at the following address will be held for up to

10 days: Lista de Correos, Administración 1, Palacio Postal, México, D.F., CP 06002, México. *Lázaro Cárdenas, at Tacuba, tel. 5/521–73–94. 1 block from the Alameda Central. Open weekdays 8–6, Sat. 8–4, Sun. 8–1.*

For fax service, money orders, and telegrams, **Telecom** is just down the street from the post office. *Tacuba 8, tel. 5/512–21–95 or 5/512–59–98. Next to Museo Nacional de Arte. Open weekdays 9–7, Sat. 9–1.*

MEDICAL AID Two private hospitals with English-speaking staff are the **American British Cowdray Hospital (ABC)** (Sur 136, Observatorio, at Las Américas, tel. 5/516–80–77) in Colonia Las Américas, and the **Hospital Español** (Ejército Nacional 613, Col. Granada, tel. 5/531–33–00).

For inexpensive or free medical care, the following hospitals also have some English-speaking staff: **Hospital General Balbuena (DDF)** (Cecilio Robelo y Sur 103, Col. Jardín Balbuena, tel. 5/764–62–17) and **Hospital Juárez 3 (Niños Héroes SS)** (Niños Héroes 151, Col. Doctores, tel. 5/578–61–09 or 5/578–60–42).

For late-night pharmaceuticals, the ubiquitous **Sanborn's** (open daily 7:30 AM–11 PM) is your best bet. There's one in just about every colonia in the city. The pharmacy chain **El Fénix** has several stores throughout the city, including one at Madero 39 (tel. 5/521–98–02), open Monday–Saturday 8–9, Sunday 10–7. For 24-hour service you can always go to **Vyb** (San Jerónimo 630, tel. 5/595–59–83 or 5/595–59–98) in the shopping center Comercial San Jerónimo, near Periférico Sur.

PHONES

➤ LOCAL CALLS • **Local calls** can be made from either the blue or gray Ladatel phones (35¢) or at any orange public phone (these also have a coin slot, but most of them have been free ever since the 1985 earthquake). The real challenge in Mexico City isn't finding a phone per se; it's finding a phone that works. Working phones are identified by the long line of folks waiting to use them; if you don't feel like spending quality queue time with the masses, you'll find that many establishments will let you use their phone for about 35¢. For local directory assistance, dial an operator at 04, but you'll be lucky if you get one.

➤ LONG-DISTANCE CALLS • By far the easiest way to make a long-distance call is with a pre-paid card on a Ladatel Multitarjetas public phone, thereby eliminating the hassle of making change or spending all your cash on the call. You can buy Ladatel phone cards at any Sanborn's (*see* Food, *below*) in 10-, 30-, or 50-nuevo peso denominations; credit is deleted from the card as you use it, and your balance is displayed on the phone screen so you can keep tabs on how much you've got left. To use an AT&T calling card, dial 95/800–462–4240 without depositing money; this connects you with an AT&T USA-Direct operator.

A more expensive option is going to a *caseta de larga distancia* (long-distance telephone office), generally marked with a large, blue sign. Some locations include the **Terminal del Norte** (northern bus station), open daily 5 AM–9:30 PM; **TAPO** (eastern bus station), open daily 7 AM–9:30 PM, and the **train station,** open Monday–Saturday 8 AM–9:30 PM and Sundays 9–3. In each case, you place the call and pay when you're done; the rates are usually higher than if you dial direct.

SCHOOLS UNAM (Universidad Nacional Autónoma de México) makes it very easy for visitors to take classes through the Centro de Enseñanza para Extranjeros (School for Foreign Students). They offer intensive and regular semester courses in Spanish, Chicano studies, art, history, and literature to anyone with a high school degree, and tuition is only about $500 per semester. Most classes are in Spanish, a few in English. Studying here also means that you can use the university's facilities, such as the gyms, swimming pools, libraries, and the campus medical center. The school is on the UNAM campus in Coyoacán. *Mailing address: CEPE, Aptdo. Postal 70-391, C.U. Delegación Coyoacán, México, D.F., CP 04510, México. Tel. 5/622–24–70, fax 5/616–26–72.*

VISITOR INFORMATION Tourist offices in both the international and domestic terminals at the **airport** and in the **TAPO** (eastern bus station) offer help with directions and hotel reservations. The **Asociación Méxicana de Hoteles y Moteles** (Mexican Association of Hotels and Motels; tel. 5/203–04–66) has offices at the airport. Just drop by if you want them to make reservations for you—answering the phone is not a priority for them.

The **Dirección General de Turismo** is centrally located in the Zona Rosa. During peak tourist season (July and August), the office has tons of maps and information on shopping centers, museums and galleries, the Metro, and other cities and regions in the country, but there are plenty of resources available year-round. The staff, although helpful, is probably not as bilingual as one would hope. *Amberes 54, at Londres, tel. 5/525–93–80 or 5/525–93–82. Open weekdays 9–8, weekends 9–7.*

Another good source of information is the **Secretaría de Turismo** (SECTUR), whose English-speaking staff distributes brochures and maps, assists in trip planning, and makes hotel reservations anywhere in Mexico. SECTUR's 24-hour complaint and emergency phone number is 5/250–01–23. They also have a 24-hour, multilingual tourist information number (5/250–01–51) and two toll-free numbers: in Mexico, dial 91–800–9–03–92; from the U.S., dial 800/482–9832. *Presidente Mazarik 172, Col. Polanco, tel. 5/250–85–55, ext. 191 for information; tel. 5/250–62–30 for reservations. Enter on Hegel. Open weekdays 8–8.*

COMING AND GOING

BY BUS Each of Mexico City's four main bus terminals is located at a different cardinal point of the city. The terminals generally service the corresponding section of the country, but, of course, the rule is there is no rule, so don't be surprised to find southbound buses at the northern station. If you're traveling during Christmas, Easter, or during the peak tourist months of July and August, buy your tickets well in advance and be prepared for a mob scene. Tickets for most buses go on sale about three weeks before the departure date. It's best to check your baggage about half an hour before departure and board 20 minutes in advance. Find out the departure point for your bus and stick close by; the boarding announcements are virtually unintelligible, even if you speak Spanish. Each of the stations has luggage storage (about 30¢ per hour), casas de cambio, a post office, a caseta de larga distancia, and Ladatel phones.

If you plan to cross the U.S.–Mexico border by bus, you can purchase connecting tickets for U.S.-bound buses at **Greyhound** (Paseo de la Reforma 27, tel. 5/535–42–00 or 5/535–26–18).

➤ TERMINAL CENTRAL DE AUTOBUSES DEL NORTE • The northern terminal (Av. de los 100 Metros 4907, tel. 5/587–59–67 or 5/587–59–73) is a massive semicircular building across the street from Metro Autobuses del Norte. The bus station is huge and somewhat intimidating, but if you want to go anywhere north of D.F., you'll have to come here. Companies serving this station include: **Tres Estrellas de Oro** (tel. 5/729–07–62), **Flecha Amarilla** (tel. 5/587–52–00 or 5/567–80–33), **Flecha Roja** (tel. 5/689–80–00), **Omnibuses de México** (tel. 5/567–67–58), and **Autobuses del Oriente (ADO)** (tel. 5/587–66–88). Some of these companies also service southern destinations (ADO, for example, will take you to Oaxaca for about $20). From this station, buses leave frequently for Aguascalientes ($23, 7 hrs), Ciudad Juárez ($76, 25 hrs), Guadalajara ($30, 8 hrs), Guanajuato ($15, 5 hrs), Querétaro ($10, 3 hrs), San Luis Potosí ($15, 6 hrs), San Miguel de Allende ($10, 4½ hrs), and Tijuana ($90, 42 hrs). Prices listed here are generally the lowest available—if you want air-conditioning, drink service, or movies, you'll have to pay a higher price. However, the amenities usually don't cost much more, and on long trips they're often worth the extra expense.

Autobuses del Norte is the biggest and best-equipped station in the city. It has a **casa de cambio** (open weekdays 8–8 and weekends 9–4), a Banamex ATM, a **caseta de larga distancia** (open daily 5 AM–9:30 PM), and luggage lockers (a small one is about $3 for 24 hours). A small booth marked HOTELES ASOCIADOS, open weekdays 7 AM–9 PM, offers free help with hotel reservations. You can also call them at 5/587–85–51.

There are no budget hotels near the terminal, but you can easily reach the centro by public transportation. A regulated taxi to a hotel in the centro will cost you about $5; buy a ticket at the taxi booth. Collective taxis are about half that price, but you may have to wait for half an hour and tip whoever found the cab for you. Or, from the bus stop in front of the station, an electric *trolebus* (trolley) takes you right to the Bellas Artes/Alameda Central area for about 30¢. To take a pesero, go down into the Metro and cross under the street. From the other side, catch a RUTA 1 BELLAS ARTES pesero to the Bellas Artes/Alameda Central area or the RUTA 88 METRO REVOLUCION. If you're dying for that first Metro ride, jump on line 5 toward Pantitlán, change at Metro La Raza to line 3 (inconvenient if you have a lot of luggage, since the "Tunnel of Science" connecting the two lines is a thousand miles long), and get off at Metro Juárez. Many budget hotels are near this Metro station.

➤ TERMINAL CENTRAL DEL SUR/TASQUENA • Tasqueña (Tasqueña 1320, tel. 5/544–21–01), as this station is usually called, is easily reached from the Metro station of the same name on line 2. This southern terminal is almost always a madhouse, with huge lines of people carrying armfuls of packages. Service from Tasqueña runs mostly to the south and southwest of Mexico. **Líneas Unidas del Sur** (tel. 5/628–57–38 or 5/628–57–39), **Estrella de Oro** (tel. 5/549–85–20 or 5/549–85–29), and **Autopullman de Morelos** (tel. 5/549–35–05 or 5/549–35–06) are a few of the main carriers. **Cristóbal Colón** (tel. 5/756–99–26 or 5/758–54–12) also offers service to Veracruz from this station. Like the Terminal del Norte, the Tasqueña station has pretty good resources for travelers, but lacks a casa de cambio or ATM. The **luggage storage** (opposite door 3) is open 24 hours, and it costs about $3 to dump your stuff there all day. The **caseta de larga distancia** accepts both Visa and Mastercard, and is open daily 7 AM–9:30 PM. Some destinations include: Acapulco ($20–$45, 7 hrs), Cuernavaca ($4, 1½ hrs), and Taxco ($7, 3 hrs).

The Metro is by far the cheapest transport from Tasqueña to the budget hotels in the centro, but taxis provide a more comfortable alternative. The ticket system mandates a rate of about $7 to the downtown area; purchase tickets at the taxi booth in front of door 3. You can also go out to the street and attempt to bargain with the drivers, although if the meter works, your fare is not negotiable.

➤ TERMINAL AUTOBUSES DE PASAJEROS DE ORIENTE (TAPO) • TAPO (Zaragoza 200, tel. 5/762–59–77) is in a working-class area just east of the city center and is easily reached from the adjacent San Lázaro Metro station (line 1). Buses depart this large, clean, dome-shaped terminal for eastern destinations, although you can catch a southbound bus from here as well. The major bus lines are **ADO** (tel. 5/542–71–92 or 5/542–71–93), **Cristóbal Colón** (tel. 5/756–99–26), and **Autobuses Unidos del Sur** (tel. 5/542–42–15). Luggage storage ($4 for 24 hours), a **casa de cambio**, a **caseta de larga distancia**, a Banamex **ATM**, and a friendly bilingual staff at the **tourist information desk** (open daily 9–9) make this one of the more pleasant terminals to be stranded in. The boarding announcements at TAPO are almost audible (but not necessarily comprehensible). Some of the major destinations served from here include Córdoba ($13, 5 hrs), Mérida ($50–$60, 24 hrs), Oaxaca ($18, 9 hrs), Puebla ($5.50, 2 hrs), and Veracruz ($15, 7 hrs).

There are no budget accommodations near the bus station, but there are several ways to get to the cheap hotels in the centro: The RUTA 22 ZOCALO/BELLAS ARTES pesero or the ALAMEDA bus will pick you up right in front of the terminal; or take the Metro toward Observatorio and get off at Balderas, change to line 3, head toward Indios Verdes, and get off at Juárez.

➤ TERMINAL CENTRAL PONIENTE • If hell were a bus station, this would be it. The terminal (Sur 122 and Río Tacubaya) is huge and dark, and the roof leaks. Of course it's not all bad—there's 24-hour **luggage storage** in room E ($1 per day), as well as a 24-hour **caseta de larga distancia** from which you can call your loved ones and share your misery. Mercifully, buses leave frequently for western Mexico. The main bus lines are **Flecha Amarilla** (tel. 5/271–27–24), **Tres Estrellas de Oro** (tel. 5/271–05–78 or 5/271–36–92), and **Enlaces Terrestres Nacionales (ETN)** (tel. 5/273–02–51), which has its own well-lit waiting room with big chairs. If you're planning on crashing in the station for a night, try to do so here. Major destinations (with cheapest fares) include Acapulco ($25, 7 hrs), Mazatlán ($46, 18 hrs), Morelia ($11, 4 hrs), and Toluca ($3, 1 hr).

Transportation to the station from downtown is easiest by Metro: Take line 1 to Observatorio and follow the SALIDA TERMINAL DE AUTOBUSES FORANEOS signs. To reach the centro from the station, take line 1 to Pino Suárez, switch to line 2, and get off at the Zócalo. Otherwise, get a regulated taxi ticket in the station for about $7.

BY TRAIN The train is slow, and it's not fun. Cancellations and breakdowns are common, so any illusions you had about dashing through the countryside by night (thereby saving money on hotels) should be quickly forgotten. To make matters worse, the **Estación Central Buenavista** is in a rather run-down area of the city—not the best place to be lugging your suitcase around late at night. At least it's a snap to get to; both the Guerrero and Revolución Metro stops are within six or seven blocks of the station. Peseros and buses that stop outside of the Metro stations can take you right to the train station entrance. Even taking a taxi is surprisingly inexpensive—a ride from the Alameda Central/Bellas Artes area will only cost you about $2.50. The train station itself is huge. Why there are only 50 chairs in the entire place is, of course, a mystery, but the floor is clean enough to sit on.

First-class and sleeper-car tickets can be purchased with cash or credit card from any one of the BOLETOS windows. Yes, they're usually almost twice as expensive as second-class tickets, but at least you're guaranteed a seat and won't run the risk of having to stand for 36 hours. Likewise, if you're going on a long trip, the sleeper cars (available only on some routes) are indispensable and well worth the money. The truly organized traveler can purchase a first-class ticket (in person only) up to one month in advance of the departure date; the chronically indecisive can get a full refund for tickets canceled at least 24 hours prior to departure. Trains are packed during the summer and Christmas season, so make reservations in advance if possible.

Second-class tickets (same-day cash purchases only) are sold from a line of windows hidden in the back of the building: Go down the ramp at either side of the main building to find the second-class *taquillas* (ticket counters). Seats are not reserved, so it's best to arrive at least one to four hours before departure; the earlier you get here, the better your chance of getting a seat. You can get refunds for second-class tickets up to three hours before departure.

The friendly folks at the information booth (just to the left of the ticket window) field queries (in Spanish) about rail travel daily from 6:30 AM to 9:30 PM (tel. 5/547–65–93 or 5/547–10–84). For help in English, stop by the **Oficina Comercial de Pasajeros** (next to the caseta de larga distancia). They're open weekdays 10–3 and 5:30–8 and can be reached by phone at 5/547–86–55. **Luggage storage** (down the ramp across from the second-class ticket booth) costs $1 a bag for 24 hours, but they're only open 6:30 AM–9:30 PM. If you show up at 11 PM to pick up your stuff 20 minutes before your train departs, you'll be dismayed to find that your bag is locked up, and the guy who can unlock the door has gone to visit his mother-in-law in Michoacán and won't be back until the next day. The station's **Banamex** ATM accepts Plus and Cirrus cards. The **caseta de larga distancia** is open Monday–Saturday 8 AM–9:30 PM and Sunday 9–3. You can pick up food at the small cafeteria across from the second-class ticket booth, but the selection is poor and the prices high. Instead, try the nearby supermarket (Insurgentes, behind big Suburbia store), which is open Monday–Saturday 8 AM–10:30 PM and Sunday 8 AM–10 PM.

The closest budget hotel area is within walking distance, south on Insurgentes Sur, just below Metro Revolución. To get to hotels south of the Alameda by minibus, take a RUTA 99 ALAMEDA/BELLAS ARTES pesero from Metro Revolución; to get to lodging near the Zócalo, take RUTA 99 TACUBA.

The first-class **Tren División del Norte** leaves daily at 8 PM for Ciudad Juárez ($49, 35 hrs), stopping along the way in Querétaro, Aguascalientes, Zacatecas, and Chihuahua. **Tren Tapatío** leaves daily at 8:30 PM for Guadalajara. First class is $16, first class *especial* (with air-conditioning) costs $27, and $53 will get you a sleeping berth. The **Tren Regiomontano** departs at 6 PM for Monterrey ($17 first class, $37 sleeping berth; 14 hrs), stopping in San Luis Potosí and Saltillo. To Oaxaca, take the **Tren Oaxaqueño** ($14 1st class, $25 1st class especial; 14 hrs), which leaves daily at 7 PM and stops in Puebla and Tehuacán. The **Tren Jarocho** departs daily for Veracruz at 9:15 PM ($11 1st class, $18 1st class especial, $38 sleeping berth; 11 hrs). **Tren 51,** second class only, also goes to Veracruz ($7, 11 hrs) daily at 7:45 AM.

BY PLANE The **Aeropuerto Internacional de la Ciudad de México** is big but manageable and always buzzing with activity. The uncomfortable plastic chairs in the clean but noisy lounges are difficult to nest in, but you can spend a night slumped in one of them without being hassled since flights come and go at all hours. Most major carriers, including Mexicana, American, Delta, Air France, and Iberia, operate from this airport, which connects Mexico with just about every destination in the world.

At the airport, **Bancomer** (open daily 6 AM–10 PM) and **Banamex** (open daily 6 AM to 8 PM) have the same exchange rates, and the latter has an ATM that accepts Cirrus and Plus cards. **Storage lockers** in both the domestic and the international terminals are always open; for about $4 you can stash your gear for 24 hours. The **tourist information office** in domestic terminal A, next to the exit for the Metro, is open weekdays 8 AM–9 PM and weekends 8 AM–10 PM. Their friendly and well-informed staff makes hotel reservations, provides directions and maps, and dispenses advice. The office of the **Asociación Mexicana de Hoteles y Moteles** (*see* Visitor Information, *above*) in the international terminal is open Monday, Friday, and Saturday 8 AM–9 PM, Tuesday–Thursday and Sunday from 8 AM until the last flight arrives. They can recommend accommodations for every budget.

➤ AIRPORT TRANSPORT • The only realistic airport transportation for budget travelers is the **Metro.** It's a cheap but fairly time-consuming (1 hr to the centro) way to travel and probably not the safest late at night, especially since you'll have to make at least one line change to get to or from downtown. **Taxi** service to and from the airport abounds, and drivers aggressively woo tourists at every available opportunity. Service from the airport, however, is regulated, and you must purchase a ticket at the office in the far end of the domestic terminal, where prices are set according to destination and number of passengers. Rates for downtown-bound taxis run from about $10 for one or two people to $15 for three or four passengers. Taxis not officially designated to work the airport offer somewhat lower fares; you'll find them lurking near the fringes of the airport, especially near the Metro Terminal Aérea. If you have an early flight or just plain want to make it there on time, designated airport taxis (tel. 5/571–93–44 or 5/571–92–97) will pick you up anywhere in the D.F. and drive you to the airport for a small fortune (almost $20 from the Alameda), but you must call a day in advance.

If you ask for information and the person you ask doesn't know the answer, he or she may give you wayward directions in a commendable, if misguided, attempt to be helpful. It's best to double- and triple-check your information before you act on it.

BY CAR The main highways approaching Mexico City are 85 from the north, 136 and 150 from the east, 95 from the south, and 15 from the west. A quick count of the roadkill and the memorial crosses on the sides of the roads will help you understand why most Mexicans keep religious figurines on their dashboards or hanging from their rearview mirrors—no doubt you'll want to set up a similar shrine of your own.

GETTING AROUND

Mexico City's size serves to confuse and intimidate. The streets are not all neatly set out in a grid pattern, and their names can change as many as five times as they pass through some of the 350 colonias. You can orient yourself in the downtown area by using the two major arteries, Paseo de la Reforma and Avenida Insurgentes, as guides. Insurgentes runs north–south, intersecting Reforma in the busy downtown area and continuing south through the trendy Zona Rosa. Reforma passes through Chapultepec Park in the southwest of the city and continues north through the downtown, almost touching the Alameda Central. Here Reforma intersects another important street, Avenida Juárez. West of Reforma, Juárez ends in the Plaza de la República and the Monumento a la Revolución; east of Reforma, Juárez runs from the Alameda Central to the Zócalo, becoming Avenida Madero as it runs through the *centro histórico* (historic center) of the D.F.

An intricate web of public transportation connects the neighborhoods of this overwhelming city. While most points of interest are accessible on foot from centrally located Metro stops, exploring the entire city may require a mind-boggling combination of Metros, buses, taxis, and peseros.

An *abono de transporte* (transport pass; $5) is good for 15 days of unlimited travel on both the Metro and the buses. It goes on sale twice a month, about three days before the first and then three days before the middle of the month, at Metro and lottery ticket booths. To make the pass a worthwhile investment, you need to ride either the bus or Metro two or more times per day for 15 straight days.

BY METRO The Metro is by far the fastest and cheapest way to explore Mexico City. It's clean, easy to use, and probably reaches more sights and areas of interest than any other form of public transportation in the city. Modern, French-designed trains run smoothly between clean, brightly lit stations.

The Metro is simple to use: Each of the nine lines is color coded, and stations are named for major sights nearby. If you can't get to an information booth, don't panic—route maps are posted throughout the stations. Free *Red del Metro* maps are available at the information booths at the Balderas, Chabacano, Centro Médico, Chapultepec, Hidalgo, Tacuba, Insurgentes, La Raza, Pino Suárez, and Zócalo stations. To avoid accumulating a pocketful of change every time you buy a ticket (40¢), you can buy five at a time; they don't expire. Transfers don't cost extra, but make sure not to follow the crowds out of the station, because once you pass through the *salida* (exit), you'll need a new ticket to reenter.

Large backpacks or luggage are technically not allowed on the Metro, though it's unlikely anyone will stop you. During rush hours (7 to 10 and 5 to 9), the first car on lines 1, 2, and 3 is reserved for women and children, and guards posted at the gates strictly enforce the rule. Lines 1, 2, and 3 run weekdays 5 AM–12:30 AM. Lines 4–9 run weekdays 6 AM–12:30 AM. All lines run Saturday 6 AM–1:30 AM, Sunday 7 AM–12:30 AM.

If you're hassled or catch someone trying to rob you, making a scene will often scare the offender away. Attempt to remove any wandering hands and say loudly "déjame" (leave me alone).

BY BUS Every day, hundreds of thousands of passengers ride Mexico City's gray, blue, and green buses. Although the system serves the entire city (destinations are marked on the windshields), two routes are particularly useful and run all night long: the principal route between the Zócalo and Chapultepec Park, along the Paseo de la Reforma, Juárez, and Madero; and the route connecting Metro Indios Verdes to University City, passing along Insurgentes through San Ángel. While service is generally reliable and always cheap (about 10¢), the lumbering vehicles absolutely crawl through rush hour (7 AM–10 AM and 5 PM–9 PM). Buses are often extremely crowded during these peak hours, so keep an eye on your pockets, bags, and the people around you; thieves thrive in the close atmosphere and often work in teams. Be particularly wary in heavily touristed areas like the Zona Rosa.

The word "pesero" dates from the days of the old currency, when a ride actually cost one peso. Because of inflation, the price has gone as high as 1000 pesos, but since the conversion to pesos nuevos in 1993, the name is once again almost accurate.

BY PESERO Throughout the D.F., *combis* (old VW vans) and peseros squeeze through impossible spaces, turn left from the far right lane, go from full throttle to dead stop in seconds, and manage to deliver people alive to thousands of street corners all over the city. Peseros cover general zones marked by the number, preceded by the words RUTA NO., painted on the side of the minibus, but individual routes within the zones vary; a good idea is to ignore the ruta numbers and concentrate on reading the destination posted in the window. Corners with stoplights and bus stops are the easiest places to catch peseros, but they generally stop wherever you hail them. Designated stops along Insurgentes and Reforma, however, are indicated by a white-and-green sign. Although the fare varies according to how far you go, it never exceeds one peso.

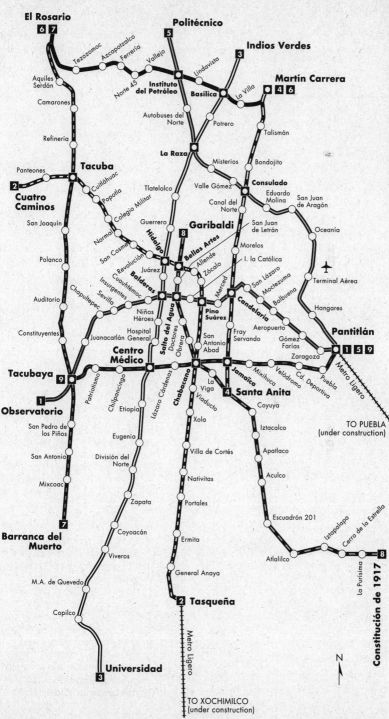

Mexico City Subways

El Rosario 6 7

Politécnico 5

Indios Verdes 3

Martín Carrera 4 6

Tezozomoc
Azcapotzalco
Ferrería
Vallejo
Aquiles Serdán
Lindavista
Norte 45
Instituto del Petróleo
Basílica
La Villa
Camarones
Autobuses del Norte
Potrero
Refinería
Talismán
Panteones
La Raza
Misterios
Bondojito
Tacuba
Cutiláhuac
Valle Gómez
Consulado
Cuatro Caminos 2
Popotla
Tlatelolco
Canal del Norte
Eduardo Molina
San Joaquín
Colegio Militar
Guerrero
San Juan de Aragón
Normal
Garibaldi
San Juan de Letrán
Oceanía
Polanco
Hidalgo 8
Bellas Artes
San Cosme
Morelos
Revolución
Allende
I. la Católica
Auditorio
Chapultepec
Juárez
Balderas
Zócalo
San Lázaro
Terminal Aérea
Insurgentes
Cuauhtémoc
Sevilla
Merced
Moctezuma
Balbuena
Hangares
Constituyentes
Niños Héroes
Pino Suárez
Candelaria
Juanacatlán
Hospital General
Salto del Agua
Doctores
San Antonio Abad
Fray Servando
Aeropuerto
Pantitlán 1 5 9
Tacubaya 9
Patriotismo
Chilpancingo
Obrera
Centro Médico
Chabacano
La Viga
Jamaica
Mixihuca
Velódromo
Cd. Deportiva
Gómez Farías
Zaragoza
Puebla
Metro Ligero
Observatorio 1
Etiopía
Lázaro Cárdenas
Viaducto
4 **Santa Anita**
Coyuya
San Pedro de los Piños
Xola
Iztacalco
TO PUEBLA (under construction)
San Antonio
Eugenia
Villa de Cortés
Apatlaco
Mixcoac
División del Norte
Nativitas
Aculco
Zapata
Portales
Escuadrón 201
Iztapalapa
Cerro de la Estrella
Barranca del Muerto 7
Coyoacán
Ermita
Atlalilco
La Purísima
Constitución de 1917 8
Viveros
M.A. de Quevedo
General Anaya
Copilco
2 **Tasqueña**
Metro Ligero
Universidad 3
TO XOCHIMILCO (under construction)

N

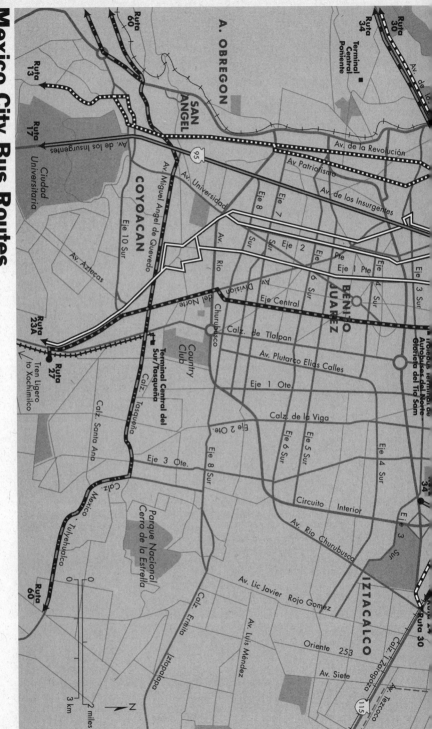

Mexico City Bus Routes

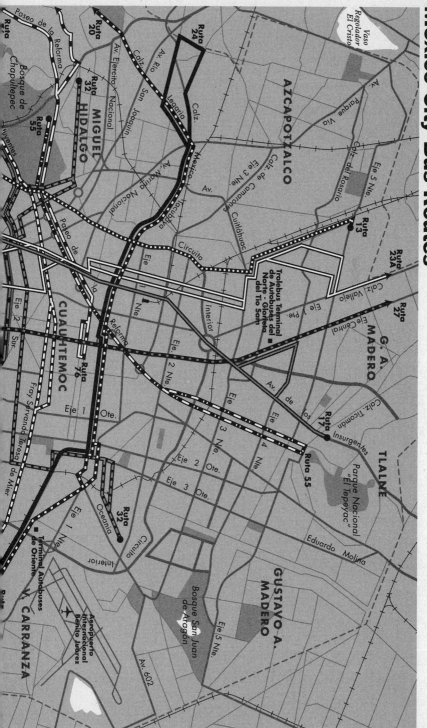

BY TAXI Taxis are easy to come by all over the D.F., especially in the downtown area. Drivers slow down as they pass travelers on the street and wait outside hotels to lure tourists. The big American sedans parked outside most major hotels (and all around the Zona Rosa) are tourist taxis whose English-speaking drivers will gladly take you on shopping tours or off to see the sites. Of course, at the end of your leisurely drive through the city they'll also charge you a small fortune. The cheaper taxis are VW bugs and small sedans. Taxis are available when the sign on the dash says LIBRE. Certified drivers prominently display a government license with a photo and all their stats. If the meter works, the driver will tell you, and the standard, non-negotiable rate will be used. However, if the meter is "broken," you'll have a chance to bargain for your ride before you get in. The green VW bugs usually have meters and are the best way to go since you don't risk being overcharged. The fare goes up by about a third after 10 PM, and drivers tend to be reluctant to venture very far out of the city. Tipping is necessary only when the driver helps you with your bags, drives in a non-life-threatening manner, or otherwise goes out of his way to make your journey somewhat pleasurable.

Physical harassment on the Metro or a crowded bus is fairly common. To avoid being grabbed by a stranger, try to stand with your back to a wall or to a friend. Men are less likely to be hassled, so a woman with her back to a male friend is the safest bet for both parties.

Radio-dispatched *sitio* taxis will fetch you wherever you are. If you have an early flight or bus departure, you can call the night before and request a driver at a specific time, although finding a cab downtown isn't a problem at any hour. It's best to call and remind them half an hour before they're supposed to arrive. Several companies are listed in the phone book under *Sitios de Automóviles,* or try **Servi-Taxi** (tel. 5/529–34–26 in the centro, 5/526–23–00 in the Zona Rosa); **Taxi-Radio** (tel. 5/566–00–77 or 5/566–72–66), with free wake-up call service; or **Servicios Taxi-Mex** (tel. 5/538–49–66 or 5/538–99–37) for airport service only.

BY CAR Only the very brave or very foolish attempt to drive on the D.F.'s streets. Roads are confusing, traffic is hellish, and most other drivers are *totalmente locos.* To add to the confusion, all cars are prohibited from driving two days per week, determined either by a colored sticker on the car or the last digit of the vehicle's license plate number. To figure out which days apply to you, call one of the rental agencies or check with a traffic cop. If you are driving, get a good street map like the *Guía Roji* or the *Guía Pronto* and try to drive like a chilango; fearlessly and with death as your backseat driver.

To rent a car you must have a credit card and a driver's license and be willing to shell out some moolah. Though the minimum age requirement differs from company to company (Hertz will rent to 21-year-olds, but most companies require that you be 25), one thing remains constant: All companies charge a 10% government tax. Rental company offices at the airport are open 24 hours, and there are a slew of branches in the Zona Rosa. Major companies include **Avis** (tel. 5/588–88–88 or toll free 91–800–70–777), **Budget** (tel. 5/566–68–00), **Dollar** (tel. 5/207–38–38), **Hertz** (tel. 5/592–60–82 or toll-free 91–800–70–016), and **National** (tel. 5/525–75–43 or toll free 91–800–90–186).

Where to Sleep

It's impossible to generalize about cheap hotels in Mexico City. You may pay more for a dive than you would for a clean room with a view. At any rate, there are plenty of good double rooms to be found for less than $20. The budget hotel areas listed here are conveniently clustered around Metro stops Pino Suárez, Zócalo, Bellas Artes, and Revolución. Reservations are *always* a good idea, especially during Semana Santa (Holy Week) and the summer months. If you don't make reservations, arrive as early in the morning as possible to stake your claim. Checkout is usually 2 PM, and tax is included in the government-controlled price.

NEAR THE ZOCALO

The huge colonial buildings in the area near the Zócalo have been divided over time to create a densely populated commercial and residential area that also houses dozens of budget hotels. The busy downtown area is also a heavily traveled part of the tourist trail: Step out of your hotel door and you're in the center of everything. At night, however, all the bustle gives way to a virtual stillness, so be cautious about wandering the empty streets, especially alone.

UNDER $15 **Hotel Cuba.** Windows in the lobby of this hotel afford a great view of the garage next door, and management is ambivalent about sharing the planet with you. It's grim and needs work, but at least it's cheap: Singles cost $12; doubles are $13.50 for one bed, $15 for two beds. The bathroom is surprisingly clean (if you ignore the peeling wallpaper), but don't waste your time waiting for hot water. Phones and TVs have been added in an attempt to upgrade the hotel's status and the roomy elevator makes this one of the very few cheap hotels in Mexico City that is relatively wheelchair accessible (there are two steps at the entryway). *República de Cuba 69, tel. 5/518–12–80. From Metro Allende, make a left on República de Chile, walk 1 block to República de Cuba, and turn left. 36 rooms, all with bath. Garage, luggage storage.*

Hotel León. The entrance to this carpeted, relatively clean hotel, right above a bar by the same name, is hidden in a narrow hallway where a *torta* (sandwich) stand is squeezed next to a jewelry shop; climb the stairs to the first floor and you'll find the reception desk. Rooms (singles $10, doubles $12) are about as bare as they come, and although the bathrooms have tubs, the tepid water renders them useless. Women should be especially cautious at night around the República de Peru area just north of the hotel. *República de Brasil 5, tel. 5/512–90–31. From Metro Allende, go east on Tacuba to República de Brasil, then left. 50 rooms, all with bath.*

Hotel Principal. This budget hotel on a busy street near the Zócalo has a dreary entryway, but the rooms are large and comfortable. Without bath, they run $8.50 for a single, $10 for a double. The clean bathrooms come with hot water, soap, and towels. If you'd rather have a bathroom all to yourself, the hotel is still a great deal at $17 for a single and $19 for a double. Guests are mostly Mexican tourists, and there are some permanent residents. *Bolívar 29, btw 16 de Septiembre and Madero, tel. 5/521–13–33 or 5/521–20–32. From Metro Allende, walk 1 block west to Bolívar. 94 rooms, 60 with bath. Luggage storage.*

Hotel Zamora. The entry hall, grimly sporting peeling paint and water stains, sets the tone here. If you have a bathroom, don't bother looking for the toilet seat—it's gone. The señora who runs the place is easily rubbed the wrong way, but many French visitors brave the rooms, which are mostly clean and incredibly cheap. Singles are $10 with bath, $8.50 without; doubles are $17 with bath, $12 without. *5 de Mayo 50, tel. 5/512–82–45. From Metro Allende, go south to Isabel la Católica and right on 5 de Mayo. 36 rooms, 20 with bath.*

UNDER $20 **Hotel Isabel.** The economy rooms in this large, comfortable hotel see hordes of European backpackers. The giant, carpeted rooms aren't that cheap and are almost always stuffy in the summer, and cold in the winter. But after the two-for-one happy hour at the bar, who cares? Singles or doubles with a clean communal bathroom cost $15. Rooms that look out onto Isabel la Católica tend to be noisy. Try to get a room on the fourth floor, which has an out-

Mexico City Lodging

Av. Insurgentes Centro

Gonzales Martinez

Insurgentes

Norte

Maestro Antonio Caso

Monumento a Cristobal Colón

Monumento a la Revolución

Edison

① ②

⑤ ⑦ ⑥ ⑧

⑨

⑩

Av. Juárez

Monumento a la Revolución

J. Terán

REVOLUCIÓN

Av. P. de Alvarado

Javier Mina

Meneses

Aldama

Zaragoza

Donato Guerra

Paseo de la Reforma

Iturbide

Humboldt

eras

JUAREZ

⑫

⑪

Independencia

Av. Juárez

Guerrero

Heroes

Zarco

Av. Hidalgo

HIDALGO

Soto

Alameda Central

⑬ Cjon Tarasquilla

J. Ma. Marroqui

lores

⑭

⑮ Lázaro Cárdenas

SAN JUAN DE LETRAN

Valerio Trujano

Angela Peralta

Mina

Mosqueta

Degollado

Camelia

Sol

gigedo

Moya

Av. Morelos

BELLAS ARTES

⑯

5 de Mayo

Madero

Pensador Mexicano

Tacuba

B. Domínguez

Obispo

Allende

GARIBALDI

Paseo de la Reforma

⑳ ㉑ ㉒

㉓

㉔ Palma

ALLENDE

Donceles

⑰

⑱

Rep. de Chile

Rep. de Peru

Rep. de Honduras

Rayón

16 de Septiembre

⑯

⑯

⑯

Zócalo

Rep. de Cuba

San Ildefonso

㉖

㉗

Rep. de Brasil

Peralvillo

Canal del Norte

ZOCALO

Seminario

Rep. de Argentina

Mayor

s Cruces

Carmen Aztecas

51

door patio facing away from the street. Singles with private bath run $20, doubles $30. *Isabel la Católica 63, tel. 5/518–12–13. 4 blocks north of Metro Isabel La Católica. 76 rooms, 64 with bath. Restaurant. MC, V.*

Hotel Juárez. Tucked away on a little side street right off bustling 5 de Mayo, this budget hotel is hard to find but worth it. The cool, trickling fountain in the Moorish-style lobby sets the tone for this elegant, relaxing hotel. The paneled rooms, with TV, phone, and even piped-in Muzak, are a great deal at $17 for a single, $19 for a double with one bed, and $20 for two beds. *Cerrada de 5 de Mayo 17, tel. 5/512–69–29 or 5/518–47–18. From Metro Allende, walk 1 block south to 5 de Mayo; the hotel is on a small side street btw Isabel la Católica and Palma. 38 rooms, all with bath. Luggage storage. Reservations advised.*

Hotel San Antonio. This quiet hotel on a dead-end alley usually has vacancies even in the afternoon. Persevere until you find it (it's only a block from the Zócalo) and you'll be rewarded with goodies like a TV, a phone, soap, and towels. The small, bright rooms, priced $12–$15 for a single and $14–$17 for a double, have green bedspreads and impeccably clean bathrooms with water that takes a while to get hot. *Cerrada de 5 de Mayo 29, tel. 5/512–99–06. From the Zócalo, walk west on 5 de Mayo to Cerrada. 44 rooms, 40 with bath. Wheelchair access.*

UNDER $25 **Hotel Habana.** The Habana is in a grungy area, down the street from a porn theater, but it's nicely maintained and quiet. Most of the guests who pass through the cool marble entryway are Mexicans traveling on business; there are also some families and a few European students. Singles are $17, doubles $20. *República de Cuba 77, tel. 5/518–15–89 or 5/518–15–90. From Metro Allende, walk 2 blocks north on República de Chile to República de Cuba, then right. 51 rooms, all with bath. Luggage storage. Reservations advised.*

Hotel Washington. The Hotel Washington is popular with backpackers despite the mid-range prices, and there's always someone hanging out in the lobby—probably because the rooms are so damn small. Less claustrophobic, but noisier, are the rooms with French doors that open onto tiny balconies overlooking the street. On the plus side, the water valiantly tries to get hot, and the elevator door is missing so you can watch the floors zoom by on the way up or down. Singles cost $18.50, doubles $20–$22. *5 de Mayo 54, tel. 5/512–35–02 or 5/521–11–43. From Metro Allende, walk south to Isabel la Católica, right on 5 de Mayo. 47 rooms, all with bath. Luggage storage. MC, V.*

UNDER $40 **Hotel Gillow.** A short walk from the Zócalo, this luxury hotel has huge rooms and all the accoutrements: restaurants, room service, TVs, and phones. Bathrooms have a tub and wood-trimmed mirror. The communal area is a relaxing haven, with fountains, plants, and piped-in music. Singles cost $32, doubles $37.50. *Isabel la Católica 17, tel. 5/518–14–40. From Zócalo, walk west on 5 de Mayo, left on Isabel la Católica. 103 rooms, all with bath. Laundry, luggage storage (for nonguests also), travel agency. AE, MC, V.*

UNDER $50 **Hotel Catedral.** If you're feeling used and abused by the smog and traffic, spend a night or two in this very comfortable hotel. Rooms are decorated in unabrasive pastels, and the beds and mirrors are tastefully trimmed in oak. Singles cost $35, doubles $47, and all rooms have TVs, phones, huge closets, and that "new" smell. For a real splurge, get a room

---

Excuse Me, but Do You Have the Time?

If you find yourself on Calle Uruguay (just southwest of the Zócalo), look for number 90. It was the home of Count Juan Manuel Solórzano, an eccentric gentleman with the most disquieting of habits: After dark, he walked in front of his house and asked passersby for the time. If they knew (and were naive enough to tell him), Don Juan killed them on the spot. Legend has it that just before he committed his bloody deeds, he would heartily congratulate them for knowing—with exactitude—the hour of their death.

with a Jacuzzi (singles $53, doubles $60). The large, clean bathrooms have huge showers and rivers of hot water. *Donceles 95, tel. 5/518–52–32. From Zócalo, go north on República de Brasil 3 blocks, right on Donceles. 116 rooms, all with bath. Bar, garage, laundry, luggage storage, restaurant, safe deposit box. Reservations advised. AE, MC, V.*

SOUTH OF THE ALAMEDA CENTRAL

The area just south of the Alameda Central is packed with hotels, restaurants, and stores selling all sorts of odds and ends. Most hotels are just a short walk from the Palacio de Bellas Artes and the Museo Mural de Diego Rivera. The small *barrio chino* (Chinatown) on Dolores is also nearby. While the area is fairly safe and a bit more lively at night than the neighborhoods around the Zócalo, you should use normal precautions when you are out late.

UNDER $20 **Hotel Calvin.** This hotel is right across from the Metropolitan movie theater, whose bright sign makes it a cinch to find at night. Rooms ($15 for one bed, $23.50 for two) are peach colored and equipped with TV and phone. Try to get one facing away from the Metropolitan sign, especially if you plan on turning in early. The large bathrooms are shedding paint and some are missing toilet seats, but they're clean and have warm water. *Azueta 33, tel. 5/521–79–52. From Metro Juárez, walk 1 block east on Independencia to Azueta. 29 rooms, all with bath. Laundry, luggage storage. MC, V.*

Hotel del Valle. Don't be put off by the nondescript lobby or rooms. The location and price (singles $16, doubles $19) are good, and the bathrooms are as clean as they come. The TVs are very new, and each room has a phone. Water, more or less hot, flows readily. *Independencia 35, tel. 5/521–80–67. From Metro Juárez, walk 1 block north to Independencia, then right 4 blocks. 48 rooms, all with bath. Laundry, luggage storage. Reservations advised. AE, MC, V.*

Hotel Toledo. The lobby has a smoky, club atmosphere. Older men sit around teasing each other with the same jokes they've been telling for years. A mint green stairway winds up to rooms with polished wood floors, wood furniture, TVs, and comfy wool bedspreads. The bathrooms are small, but they're clean and have reliable hot water. The hotel's character combined and decent prices (singles $15, doubles $17–$20) make this one of the best budget places to stay in Mexico City. Clients are mostly Mexican and include some permanent residents. *López 22, tel. 5/521–32–49 or 5/518–56–31. From Metro Bellas Artes, go east on Hidalgo to Cárdenas (Eje Central), right to Independencia, and left on López. 35 rooms, all with bath. Laundry, luggage storage (up to 3 days).*

UNDER $35 **Hotel Marlowe.** The beautiful, fully carpeted rooms here have large desks, TVs, and touch-tone telephones, and the impeccable bathrooms have so much hot water the full-length mirrors get steamy enough for you to write notes to the next occupant. Switches on the headboard of each bed control the TV and lights. If you're bored or broke, sit in bed and flip the switches for that *Saturday Night Fever* effect. Singles cost $28, doubles $30. *Independencia 17, tel. 5/521–95–40. 5 blocks east of Metro Juárez. 106 rooms, all with bath. Bar, garage, laundry, luggage storage, restaurant, wheelchair access. MC, V.*

UNDER $60 **Hotel Fleming.** Don't let the vinyl in the '50s-style lobby fool you—this is a posh hotel. Spacious rooms with plenty of mirrors and matching pastel curtains and comforters also have TVs, phones, and other extras. Singles are $40, doubles $50. For 10 bucks more you can get a room with a Jacuzzi. *Revillagigedo 35, tel. 5/510–45–30. From Metro Juárez, go 2 blocks east on Juárez, right on Revillagigedo. 75 rooms, all with bath. Garage, laundry, luggage storage, restaurant. Reservations advised. AE, MC, V.*

NEAR METRO REVOLUCION

Most of the hotels in this area are on quiet, tree-lined side streets with the feel of a true neighborhood. People can usually be found hanging out on the sidewalk, washing their cars, or just shooting the breeze. If suburbia begins to drive you crazy, however, the area is bordered by major thoroughfares—Insurgentes Norte, Puente de Alvarado, and Reforma—providing easy access to all points in the city.

UNDER $20 **Casa de los Amigos.** This Quaker house doesn't cater to the tourist-gone-nuts variety; rather, the people who live and work here welcome travelers who are dedicated to promoting peace and justice. You don't have to pass a test to stay here, but it is a communal situation where cooperation is key. They've got the lowdown on volunteer opportunities and Spanish language classes in Mexico and Guatemala, as well as a library. A huge, healthful breakfast is only $2.50, and guests can use the kitchen. Single-sex dorm beds are $8, but they also have some singles and doubles with private bath (again, $8 a person). An apartment with kitchen and bathroom costs $25 for one person, $28 for two, or $31 for three. Fax them in advance of your arrival to ensure there's space. *Ignacio Mariscal 132, Col. Revolución, tel. 5/705–06–46 or 5/705–05–21, fax 5/705–07–71. 1 block south of Metro Revolución, across from the Gran Hotel Texas. 12 dorm beds, 3 singles and 3 doubles without bath, 2 doubles with bath, 1 apartment. Laundry.*

Hotel Belpra. This hotel is kind of gloomy, but cheap: Singles and doubles with one bed are about $15. The quarters are dark and need to be aired out, but you can thank the deity of your choice for TVs and the minor miracle of hot water. *Ponciano Arriaga 22, tel. 5/566–81–55. 1 block east of Metro Revolución. 33 rooms, all with bath. Luggage storage.*

Hotel Carlton. Across the street from a tree-filled plaza, this is a family-oriented hotel that also welcomes backpackers. The rooms are spacious and clean, as are the bathrooms. Hot water is readily available. The management fumigates the place once a month—the odor is unpleasant, but at least you can rest assured that nothing will slither, crawl, or otherwise find its way into bed with you. Singles cost $15.50, doubles $19. *Ignacio Mariscal 32-B, tel. 5/566–29–11 or 5/566–29–14. From Metro Revolución, walk east on Puente de Alvarado to Ramos Arizpe and right 1 block. 41 rooms, all with bath. Laundry, luggage storage, restaurant. Reservations advised.*

Hotel Paraíso. The new, clean, white-tiled lobby in this small, noisy hotel is deceptive. The rest of the hotel is more run-down, though the rooms themselves aren't half bad, and the bathrooms are fairly clean (some even have bidets). In any event, it's a good deal at $15 for a single and $16 for a double. *Ignacio Mariscal 99, tel. 5/566–80–77. From Metro Revolución, go 1 block east on Puente de Alvarado, south 2 bocks on Ponciano Arriaga, left on Ignacio Mariscal. 45 rooms, all with bath. Laundry, luggage storage, wheelchair access.*

Hotel Pennsylvania. The newly renovated "king-size" rooms in the Pennsylvania (singles $20, doubles $23.50) are done in light peach and baby blue, while the older, cheaper, and mustier rooms (singles $13.50, doubles $17) tend to have a more motley decor. Bathrooms supposedly have hot water, but you have to wait for it. *Ignacio Mariscal 101, tel. 5/703–13–84. From Metro Revolución, walk 1 block east on Puente de Alvarado, right on Ponciano Arriaga, left on Ignacio Mariscal. 50 rooms, all with bath. Wheelchair access.*

UNDER $25 **Hotel Frimont.** If you're one of those people who coordinate their socks and underwear, this is the hotel for you; everything is done in a tasteful light brown and sky blue. The rooms here are spacious and each comes with its own TV and touch-tone phone. Almost-scalding water steams out of the shower. Should you find yourself low on pesos, the friendly staff offers currency exchange. There are also Ladatel phones in the lobby. Mostly business-people take advantage of the reasonable prices: singles for about $23, doubles $24. *Jesús Terán 35, tel. 5/705–41–69. From Metro Revolución, walk east on Puente de Alvarado, right on Jesús Terán. 85 rooms, all with bath. Garage, laundry, luggage storage, restaurant, travel agency. Reservations advised. MC, V.*

Hotel Oxford. The mammoth brown-and-blue rooms in this hotel are big enough to accommodate the entire *Eight is Enough* clan and come with phones and TVs. Big, clean bathrooms have plenty of hot water and soap. Wide, carpeted hallways are bright and airy. Ask for a room overlooking the plaza. Singles here are $17; doubles are $23. *Ignacio Mariscal 67, tel. 5/566–05–00. From Metro Revolución, take Ponciano Arriaga to Ignacio Mariscal. 45 rooms, all with bath. Luggage storage, safe-deposit boxes.*

UNDER $30 **Hotel Edison.** An attractive outdoor courtyard with huge, lush plants is a pocket of tranquility in this otherwise noisy little hotel. The large rooms come with a TV and phone and cost $22 (single) and $25 (double). Bathrooms are completely tiled, clean, and have hot water—if you're patient. *Edison 106, tel. 5/566–09–33 or 5/566–09–34. From Metro Revolución, walk 3 blocks west to J. M. Iglesias and left to Edison. 45 rooms, all with bath. Garage.*

UNDER $35 **Hotel La Joya.** The light pink walls and gray, psuedo-granite furniture in these rooms almost make the place mod. Unfortunately, furniture is scarce (even closets are hard to come by). The very clean bathrooms actually have a tub and bidet. Singles and one-bed doubles are $31. *Ezequiel Montes 35, tel. 5/566–55–33. From Metro Revolución, walk 2 blocks west on J. M. Iglesias, left on Mariscal to Montes. 26 rooms, all with bath. Luggage storage.*

NEAR METRO PINO SUAREZ

The hotels here appeal to traveling salespeople and tourists willing to stay a bit out of the way. There isn't much to see in these few blocks south of the Zócalo, but the hotels are cheap and getting to the major sights is a breeze, thanks to the Metro. During the day, streets are crowded with shoppers looking for bargains on everything from clothing to cashews. At night, however, it's obscenely quiet—great for sleeping, but a bit scary if you're out alone. Since the area is rather far from the Zócalo or the Alameda Central, you're more than likely to find a vacancy, even during the peak tourist months of April, July, and August.

UNDER $20 **Hotel Latino.** The comfortable rooms in this hotel just a 10-minute Metro ride from the Alameda Central all have TVs, phones, and immaculate bathrooms. Both singles and doubles are $19. *Netzahualcóyotl 201, tel. 5/522–36–47. Catercorner to Metro Pino Suárez. 40 rooms, all with bath. Luggage storage, room service. Reservations advised.*

Hotel Monte Carlo. This beautiful, quiet hotel is by far the nicest in its price range. A large, marble staircase winds up from the lobby to the black-and-white tiled second floor. Lofty ceilings and French doors give the rooms a spacious, elegant air. The bathrooms are spotless and have hot water. Rooms without baths have sinks, and all rooms have phones. Doubles and singles cost $15.50, $19 with bath. *República de Uruguay 69, tel. 5/518–14–18 or 5/521–25–59. From Metro Zócalo, walk south on Pino Suárez, left on República de Uruguay. 60 rooms, 36 with bath. Garage, luggage storage, money exchange. Reservations advised.*

UNDER $25 **Hotel San Miguel.** While you may not remember this place next week, at least you won't leave cursing. Interior rooms share a view of large, steel hot-water tanks, but then again, the water in the (relatively) clean bathrooms is hot. Singles are $15, doubles $22. *José María Izazaga 146, tel. 5/522–86–20 or 5/522–86–21. From Metro Pino Suárez, walk north to José María Izazaga; the hotel is bright pink. 40 rooms, all with bath. Luggage storage.*

UNDER $30 **Hotel Roble.** Although both the lobby and the staff at this hotel are unremarkable, the small, earth-colored rooms are tidy. The water in the clean bathrooms gets hot if you give it time. Singles are $20 and doubles are $25. *República de Uruguay 109, tel. 5/522–78–30 or 5/522–80–83. From Metro Zócalo, walk south on Pino Suárez, left on República de Uruguay. 61 rooms, all with bath. Luggage storage, restaurant. MC, V.*

ZONA ROSA

As a rule, hotels in the Zona Rosa are expensive and cater to tourists with money to burn. Still, there are a few comfortable and affordable options in the residential areas bordering the tourist zone. If you're a club hopper, this area is within walking distance of Zona Rosa's bars and discos. The museums and greenery of Chapultepec Park are also close by.

UNDER $30 **Casa González.** Staying at this guesthouse is more like visiting old friends; it's worth taking pains to get a reservation. Once you've made a reservation, you'd best keep it—the Casa is almost always full and, as a result, they require a $42 deposit to guarantee you'll show up. Cancellations must be made at least 10 days in advance to be refunded. The cozy, old-fashioned rooms are immaculate and graced with wood furniture. The baths, complete with tubs, are also spotless, and hot water flows readily from the taps. Singles cost $23, doubles

$27. Señor González, who speaks fluent English, cooks delicious, relatively inexpensive meals (a full dinner is about $10) to order, so let him know if you'll be coming home to eat. *Río Sena 69, tel. 5/514–33–02. From Metro Insurgentes, take Génova across Reforma and Río Lerma. 20 rooms, all with bath. Luggage storage.*

UNDER $35 **Hotel Parador Washington.** The lobby may be somewhat drab, but the friendly staff at this budget hotel livens things up. The bathrooms are roomy, but you may have to fuss with the taps to get hot water. The two "decks" on the roof are perfect for sunbathing and drying wet clothes. Singles are $27, doubles $30. *Dinamarca 42, at Londres, tel. 5/703–08–93. From Metro Insurgentes, go 4 blocks east on Chapultepec, left on Dinamarca. 40 rooms, all with bath. Laundry, luggage storage, restaurant. AE, MC, V.*

ROUGHING IT

For thrill seekers or the incredibly poor, there are always the bus stations. Yes, you can crash at any one of these for the night, but who knows if your stuff will be with you when you awake; stash your valuables in a luggage locker. If you have a late flight or layover (or no money), you can always try sleeping on the extremely uncooperative plastic chairs in the airport lounges.

Food

You can spend plenty of pesos eating your way through Mexico City, which has a wide range of restaurants, both inexpensive and refined. All over the city, but particularly in the Zona Rosa, you can find just about anything to suit your tastes—from sushi to *salpicón estilo puebla* (Puebla-style chopped beef)—but be prepared to pay a pretty penny to satisfy your more exotic cravings.

It is possible to eat for very little money, but only if you're not scared by the myth that eating at tiny mom-and-pop operations or at street stands will send you running for the bathroom. The food in these places is usually cooked to order, so you can tell if it has been sitting out too long or hasn't been cooked well enough. If there's a crowd of local folk at a certain place, you can bet the food there is good. Another budget survival tactic is the *comida corrida* (pre-prepared lunch special), usually beans and rice with meat, plus coffee and sometimes soup or salad for under $5. Look for restaurants advertising their daily comida corrida along Isabel la Católica in the downtown area; you could also try the taco and torta stands on José María Izazaga near Metro Pino Suárez. Cheap fruits and vegetables as well as taco stands can be found at the markets (*see* Shopping, *below*), and for those of you with delicate tummies or sudden, uncontrollable hankerings for a hamburger, there are always **Sanborn's** or **Vip's**, chain restaurants serving a hybrid of American and Mexican cuisines.

Tiny fondas are cheap eating alternatives that provide a slice of Mexican life—don't be surprised to see men in business suits and construction workers side by side, sopping up pozole (corn soup) with fried tortillas.

ZOCALO/BELLAS ARTES AREA

Plenty of restaurants, from humble fondas to elegant tourist-oriented places, crowd the center of the city. Workers eat at the fondas and stands along Motolinia, which is closed to traffic between Tacuba and 16 de Septiembre. If you're closer to the Bellas Artes end, head to Independencia, just a block south of the Alameda. Between Lázaro Cárdenas and Balderas, the street is jammed with restaurants to suit every wallet and palate. Satisfy your sweet tooth at **Dulcería Celaya** (5 de Mayo 39), still located in the same beautiful 19th-century building in which it was founded in 1874. Churro fans crowd into **Churrería El Moro** (Lázaro Cárdenas 42, tel. 5/512–08–96). It's open 24 hours, but there's almost always a line for the sugary fried treats (15¢).

UNDER $5 **Café El Popular.** This restaurant lives up to its name: At breakfast or lunch you'll probably have to wait for a seat. The enchiladas (about $3) and chicken dishes (about $4) are favorites, as are the $3 egg breakfasts, which include fruit, refried beans, and coffee. The waitresses (who aren't exactly famous for their speed) tempt you with pastries while you wait for your food, but try to restrain yourself—they keep tabs and charge for every morsel eaten. *5 de Mayo 52, tel. 5/518–60–81. 1 block west of Zócalo. Open daily 24 hrs.*

La Parrilla Suiza. Diners in this reliable taquería chain are mostly young, hip Mexicans who hang out until the wee hours and tourists who've wandered in, attracted by the irresistible smell of tacos. The *tacos al pastor* (marinated pork, onions, and pineapple on a spit) cost about 60¢ each. The succulent *flautas tirolesas* (fried tortillas with chicken and topped with guacamole and cheese) are $4. *Hidalgo 9, tel. 5/521–30–58. Directly behind Palacio de Bellas Artes. Open Mon.–Sat. 8 AM–1 AM, Sun. 8 AM–midnight.*

Restaurant Café Cinco de Mayo. Come here to slurp delicious soup and soak in the lunch-counter atmosphere (complete with twirling stools). Lentil soup is about $2.50, cream of mushroom about $3. A full menu of Mexican food is also featured, but the soups are the real draw. *5 de Mayo 57, tel. 5/510–19–95. 1 block west of Zócalo. Open daily 7 AM–11 PM. Wheelchair access.*

Super Soya. This health-food store and vegetarian food bar has locations all over Mexico City, but you still have to fight for a seat to enjoy your soy burger ($2) or veggie taco (50¢) at lunchtime. A large fruit salad with yogurt is $3. If you crave ice cream, don't miss the fragrant, homemade waffle cones. *Tacuba 40, no phone. Near Metro Allende. Open daily 9–9.*

UNDER $10 **Café de Tacuba.** Founded in 1912, this expensive but lovely chandelier-lit restaurant is a good place for a splurge. If you can stop laughing at the ridiculously huge bows stuck to the waitresses' heads, you'll enjoy a daring dish of *lengua de res a la vinagreta* (beef tongue in vinaigrette) for about $9. Lighter dishes, such as chicken vegetable soup, cost about $5. The café usually gets pretty full around lunch and dinner, especially Thursdays–Sundays between 6 PM and 10 PM, when there's live music. *Tacuba 28, near Metro Allende, tel. 5/512–84–82. Open daily 8 AM–11:30 PM.*

Sanborn's. The baroque building that houses the downtown branch of Sanborn's—Mexico's version of Sizzler—has had a topsy-turvy history: It started out as the residence of counts, became the elite Mexico City Jockey Club, and, during the revolutionary turmoil, turned into the headquarters of anarchist groups. As far as food goes, Sanborn's has reliable Mexican and American food. *Enchiladas suizas* (enchiladas in cheese sauce) cost about $8, as does a burger with fries. *Madero 4, tel. 5/518–66–76. From Metro Bellas Artes, walk south on Lázaro Cárdenas, left on Madero. Open daily 7:30 AM–11 PM.*

El Vegetariano. You'll have to look carefully to find this hotbed of vegetarianism—it's up a long, narrow stairway squeezed between two jewelry shops. Don't bother looking for the sign—instead, look for the doormat in the entryway. From 1 PM to 7 PM they serve a filling veggie *menú del día* (daily special): fruit or vegetable salad, hot or cold soup, two main dishes, dessert, and *agua fresca* (juice drink) for only $5.50. À la carte dishes, such as spaghetti with mushroom sauce, are $6. *Madero 56, tel. 5/521–68–80. 1 block west of Zócalo. Open Mon.–Sat. 8–7.*

UNDER $15 **Salón Luz.** The place is filled during lunch hour, when local businesspeople come to relax and listen to the live Menudo-meets-Neil Diamond music that's often played outside. The interior could pass for a rowdy cantina, except that the ratio of women to men is about an even one-to-one. The specialty is the Salón Luz ($12), a plate of meat, ham, sausage, pâté, cheese, and fried greens, but you can get a burger for $5. *Gante 23, at Carranza, tel. 5/512–42–46. 1 block south and 4 blocks west of Zócalo. Open Mon.–Sat. 10 AM–11 PM, Sun. 11–7. Wheelchair access.*

ZONA ROSA

The Zona Rosa brims with restaurants, bars, and night spots—most of them beyond a budget traveler's means. Some streets are closed to vehicular traffic, and pedestrians leisurely stroll past street performers and beggars. Copenhague, a tiny block-long street just south of Paseo de la Reforma, has a great variety of restaurants and boutiques. Still, the area around Copenhague, Niza, and Liverpool streets tends to be pricey. If your purse is as empty as your belly, there are a few cheaper joints on Chapultepec near Amberes, right outside Metro Insurgentes. To eat away from the tourist zone, cross Reforma and continue beyond the U.S. Embassy to Río Lerma (or any other street whose name begins with Río) and take advantage of the comidas corridas offered in small restaurants lining the street.

UNDER $5 **Los Cucharones.** Although this little restaurant is about four blocks northwest of the Zona Rosa itself, it still draws a large lunchtime crowd with a $5 all-you-can-eat buffet, making the place look like Insurgentes Sur during rush hour. If you can't stand the crowded push-and-shove atmosphere inside, ask to get your food to go—they'll charge you $4, hand you a large carry-out carton, and let you take anything and everything you can fit inside. *Río Guadalquivir 95, at Paseo de la Reforma, tel. 5/514–28–61. Open weekdays 1–6. Wheelchair access.*

El Gallito Taquería. This taquería serves a variety of hot, delicious snacks sure to satisfy most late-night cravings. The restaurant fills up after 3 AM, when the clubs in the Zona are closed but no one's ready to go home. A filling order of chicken tacos with guacamole costs $4.50. Vegetarians also have it made here: Meatless tacos and quesadillas are available for about $1.50 each. *Liverpool 115, tel. 5/511–14–36. ½ block north of Génova. Open Mon.–Thurs. 10 AM–5 AM, Fri.–Sat. 10 AM–6 AM, Sun. noon–2 AM.*

El Huarache Azteca. Though slightly grimy and yellowed with age, this small, nondescript restaurant lures hungry locals on their lunch break, causing the occasional wait. In the morning, typical Mexican breakfast foods—eggs and rice, *huaraches* (long, filled tortillas), and juice—are served for $3.50. The comida corrida will fill you up for $3. *Chapultepec 317, at Amberes, tel. 5/525–13–04. Open Mon.–Sat. 7:30–7:30. Wheelchair access.*

Kobá-Ich. Once known as El Faisán, this restaurant has recently undergone a change of ownership. The name may have changed, but the good food, reasonable prices, and friendly staff haven't. For those who have never sampled Yucatecan cuisine, it's quite different from typical Mexican food. The *pollo pibil* (chicken baked in banana leaves; $4.50) is so tender it falls off the bone. For the more adventurous, there are *tacos de cazón* (baby shark tacos) for $2.50. *Londres 136-A, btw Génova and Amberes, tel. 5/208–57–91. From Metro Insurgentes, take Génova to Londres and turn left. Open Mon.–Sat. 8 AM–10 PM.*

UNDER $10 **Restaurant Parri.** This bright, airy restaurant all done up in red and white is the place to go for chicken. The *parri tampiqueña* (a quarter of a flame-broiled chicken, an enchilada, guacamole, and refried beans; $6) is especially good. *Hamburgo 154, at Génova, tel. 5/207–07–57. Open Mon.–Thurs. 8 AM–1 AM, Fri. and Sat. 8 AM–3 AM. Wheelchair access.*

Vip's. Although this is where upper-class Mexicans come to flirt, middle-class American culture seems to have inspired the bland food and decor. However, the hamburgers ($3) are more than adequate. While a vegetarian could construct a passable meal here, the menu leans toward meat. *Hamburgo 123, tel. 5/207–70–94. Open Sun.–Thurs. 7 AM–1 AM, Fri.–Sat. 24 hrs.*

UNDER $15 **Fonda El Refugio.** The gleaming white walls, impeccably shined copper pots, and small wooden tables in this elegant little restaurant draw a cosmopolitan clientele. The *sopa de hongos* (mushroom soup; $6) and the *pescado a la veracruzana* (red snapper cooked in tomatoes, onions, capers, peppers, and herbs; $14) go well with the $4 powerhouse margaritas. *Liverpool 166, at Génova, tel. 5/207–27–32. Open Mon.–Sat. 1–1.*

COYOACAN

Although people come to Coyoacán from all over the D.F., the area manages to retain the atmosphere of a small neighborhood, where cozy family establishments and tiny taquerías huddle around plazas. About 1½ blocks south of the plazas on Carrillo Puerto there is a particularly inviting collection of fondas and taquerías.

UNDER $5 **Taco Inn.** Try the delicious beef tacos with cilantro and onions for $2.50, or the unfortuately named *gringas* (pork and cheese sandwiched between two flour tortillas) for $1.50. *Presidente Carranza 106, at Carrillo Puerto, tel. 5/554–02–88 or 5/554–06–73. Open Mon.–Thurs. 1 PM–2 AM, Fri. 1 PM–3 AM, Sat. 1 PM–4 AM.*

El Tizoncito. This taquería chain consistently serves up hot, fresh tacos to please carnivores and herbivores alike. The *no que no* tacos are made with cheese and sliced green peppers and cost $2 each. The place does peak business after midnight, but the ratio of waiters to tables is almost one-to-one, so the service remains swift. Great salsas and guacamole come with each meal. *Aguayo 3, around cnr from Jardín Centenario, tel. 5/554–77–12. Open daily noon–2:30 AM.*

UNDER $10 **El Fogoncito.** Yet another taquería that ends in "ito," this one is famous for its $5 beef tacos with cheese. Vegetarians need not despair, however, because the *enfrijoladas* (beans and cheese rolled in a warm flour tortilla; $5) are great. If it's a nice day, sit at one of their shaded outdoor tables. *Jardín Centenario 9-A, tel. 5/554–75–55. From Metro M. A. de Quevedo, go east along Francisco Sosa to Jardín Centenario; from Metro Coyoacán, take PLAZA HIDALGO pesero. Open daily 11–11.*

Fonda El Morral. Founded in 1967, this bright, Spanish-style fonda has beautiful wrought-iron windows and blue-and-white tiled doorways. The comida corrida here is a reasonable $6, while an order of three chicken tacos with guacamole is $5. *Allende 2, tel. 5/554–02–98. From Metro Coyoacán, take PLAZA HIDALGO pesero to Jardín Centenario. Open daily 8 AM–9 PM.*

Merendero "Las Lupitas." On a narrow, cobblestone street just off sleepy Plaza Santa Catarina, this restaurant is about as picturesque as it gets. The dining area is infused with natural light, earth-colored tiles cover the floor, and thick wooden beams support the ceiling. The food has a *norteño* (northern Mexican) influence, so they use flour rather than corn tortillas. Saturdays are especially busy, and you can expect a short wait for breakfast or dinner (they don't serve lunch). The lightly fried cheese or meat *empanadas* (turnovers) are practically greaseless and cost less than $5. *Jardín de Santa Catarina 4, at Francisco Sosa, tel. 5/554–33–53. From Jardín Centenario, walk west on Francisco Sosa.*

SAN ANGEL

Most visitors avoid the busy Avenidas Insurgentes and Revolución and head up to the quiet cobblestone streets of Plaza San Jacinto to relax and enjoy the serenity of this small, colonial neighborhood. There's a good selection of restaurants along Madero, but even cheaper fare can be found on the side streets near the Pemex station at the base of the Plaza del Carmen. The intersection of Quevedo and Universidad (near Metro M. A. de Quevedo) is another great place to find affordable eats.

La Casona del Elefante. Next to the Bazar Sábado (*see* Shopping, *below*), the entry to this sophisticated and relatively inexpensive Indian restaurant is hidden behind a group of tall potted plants. The reward for your little scavenger hunt is delicious food. A tray of spicy salsas arrives at your table before you know what to order, although service slows considerably after that. All of the meat curries ($10) are recommended, and the curried vegetables make a good meal for about $6. *Plaza San Jacinto 9, tel. 5/616–16–01 or 5/616–22–08. From Metro M. A. de Quevedo, west along Quevedo, left on La Paz; when it forks, take Madero to the plaza. Open Mon.–Thurs. 1–11, Fri. and Sat. 1–midnight, Sun. 1–6.*

Parrilla El Tecolote. This fonda stands out for its incredibly inexpensive food. The waiters are in a constant, frantic rush, and around noon this place is always packed. Despite the frenzy, customers can easily relax in the dark interior with a bowl of *sopa de verduras con pollo* (vegetable soup with chicken) for $1.50 or the filling comida corrida ($2.50). The innocuous-looking light green salsa will have you begging for a glass of water. *M. A. de Quevedo 75, no phone. 1½ blocks from Metro M. A. de Quevedo.*

Queso, Pan, y Vino. This restaurant has pretty Spanish archways, marble floors, soft music in the background, and prompt, polite service. A la carte dishes are a bit out of budget range, but the buffet (weekdays 8–noon and weekends 9–noon) is a steal. Weekdays you can stuff yourself unconscious for a mere $5; on weekends, the buffet is $6. *La Paz 40, in El Globo shopping center, tel. 5/550–75–87. From Metro M. A. de Quevedo, go west on Arenal, which becomes La Paz. Wheelchair access.*

CAFES

Café del Palacio. Hidden away inside the Palacio de Bellas Artes (*see* Worth Seeing, *below*), this quiet café serves relatively expensive salads and sandwiches. Linger over coffee and cake, or have a soup/salad combo for $5. *Juárez, at Lázaro Cárdenas, tel. 5/512–08–07. In Palacio de Bellas Artes, inside bookstore, on 2nd floor. Open Tues.–Sun. 11–9, until 1 AM during late shows.*

Café Gandhi. If you packed a beret, whip it out for an afternoon in this well-known gallery/bookstore/coffeehouse. Strong cappuccino can be ordered with Kahlua or Amaretto ($3.50) for an added kick. Service is about as slow as the chess players who pass entire afternoons brooding over moves while their cigarettes burn low. Non-smokers can rejoice, however; the enlightened management just added a tiny no-smoking section. *M. A. de Quevedo 128, Coyoacán, tel. 5/550–25–24 or 5/548–98–87. Near Metro M. A. de Quevedo. Open weekdays 9:30 AM– 11 PM, weekends 10:30–10.*

Duca d'Este Salón de Thé. This fancy French bakery and tearoom, all done in up in pink, is the perfect place for pastries and old-world lounging. The raspberry and chocolate cheesecakes ($3.50) are heavenly, and the carrot cake ($3.50) is covered with real cream-cheese frosting. *Hamburgo 164-B, at Florencia, tel. 5/525–63–74 or 5/514–05–66. On western edge of Zona Rosa. Open Sun.–Thurs. 8 AM–11 PM, Fri.–Sat. 8 AM–midnight.*

El Parnaso Café. Bliss is sitting comfortably beneath the shady awnings of this popular café/bookstore in the eastern corner of Coyoacán's Jardín Centenario, and smiling smugly at those still waiting for a table. The café is crowded on weekends, but it's quite acceptable to ask one of the cappuccino drinkers to share a table. The waiters are always on the run, so they don't pay much attention to you—order a coffee, and the afternoon is yours. Most coffees are less than $2.50. *Carillo Puerto 2, tel. 5/554–22–25. From Metro M. A. de Quevedo, take PLAZA HIDALGO pesero. Open daily 9 AM–10 PM. Wheelchair access.*

UNAM Café. Stop by if you happen to find yourself south of the UNAM campus or waiting for a show in the Centro Cultural Universitario. Huge windows give a great view of theatergoers meandering past the fountain just outside. Cappuccino and espresso each cost less than $1.50. *Centro Cultural Universitario, UNAM. From Insurgentes, take a TLALPAN-JOYA bus and get off at the 3rd pedestrian overpass on campus.*

La Vienet Café. After a visit to the Kahlo museum, be sure to stop by this little café for some of the sweetest desserts around. A balcony and beautiful wrought-iron chairs almost make you forget that the best of Barry Manilow is playing in the background. A bite of the delicious mocha cake ($2.50) might anesthetize you to "Copacabana." *Viena, at Abasolo, tel. 5/554– 45–23. 2 blocks north and 1 block east of Frida Kahlo museum. Open Tues.–Sun. 8–8.*

Worth Seeing

You could take up residence here for years and still never see all there is to see. The sheer number of museums borders on the ridiculous, so you'll have to be selective when deciding how to spend your time. Worthwhile attractions are clustered in individual districts, making the mammoth Distrito Federal easier to manage. Near the Zócalo you'll want to catch the **Diego Rivera Murals** in the Palacio Nacional, the ancient foundations of the city at the Templo Mayor, and the breathtaking Catedral Metropolitana. The Palacio de Bellas Artes near the Alameda Central houses both the **Ballet Folklórico** (tickets are $30—nobody said culture was cheap), and murals by Diego Rivera (which don't cost anything to see). Amid the chaos of the Alameda Central area, you'll find the **Casa de los Azulejos** on Madero, a colonial house covered entirely in blue and white tiles. It's now a Sanborn's (*see* Food, *above*), but worth a look for the Orozco mural inside. The area around Chapultepec Park is home to more museums than you can shake a stick at, among them the famous Museo Nacional de Antropología. Three museums dedicated to the life and work of Frida Kahlo, Diego Rivera, and Leon Trotsky are in Coyoacán. The Ciudad Universitaria (the huge area encompassed by the Universidad Nacional Autónoma de México) is a great place to spend an afternoon. Murals by Siqueiros, O'Gorman, and Rivera cover many of the buildings on campus, and the scalable Espacio Escultórico (Sculpture Space) peaks over the beautiful, wild greenery of the **Reserva Ecológica** (Ecological Reserve).

The atmosphere in the Zona Rosa seems to agree with upper-class chilangos, kids hanging out after class, hurdy-gurdy men playing music for pesos and, of course, tons of tourists. The district was designed for pedestrians: Wide brick paths weave between well-pruned shrubs and statues. Clean-cut business types take their lunch breaks here, and students wander the streets, ice cream in hand, and ogle the glitzy shops. At night, cars with deafening techno-pop pouring from their open windows crawl along the avenues while disco- and bar-hoppers dressed in black try their best to look cool and mingle outside the doorways of some of the more popular clubs.

ALAMEDA CENTRAL

The Alameda Central was the site of a *tianguis* (market) in Aztec times and the burnings of heretics during the Catholic Inquisition. By the mid-19th century, it had become a park where the rich strolled under the trees, while the poor, who were kept out, looked on. Now everybody meanders through the park, lounging during lunch hour, playing chess, sleeping on the grass, or smooching on the benches. The white marble semicircle on the south side of the park (bordering Avenida Juárez) is the **Monumento a Benito Juárez** commemorating the hero of the Reform period. *Juárez, at Condesa Marconi, next to the Palacio de Bellas Artes; Metro Bellas Artes is opposite.*

MUSEO DE ARTES E INDUSTRIAS POPULARES The bright, Pepto-pink walls of this one-room museum make the place feel more like a *mercado de artesanía* (crafts market) than a museum. Children's toys, ceremonial masks, traditional regional dresses, and weaving from all over Mexico are displayed behind glass. A fairly recent, though unintended, architectural exhibit is also on view through the windows: You can see the massive structural damage endured in the 1985 quake by what was once a bank next door. *Juárez 44, tel. 5/518–30–58. Metro Bellas Artes or Metro Hidalgo. Go down alleyway García Lorca and through doorway labeled EDIFICIO F. Admission free. Museum open weekdays 9–3; gift shop open weekdays 9–6.*

The Hospital de Jesús on Pino Suárez (the entrance is down an alleyway next to Gigo's Pizza) stands on the site where the Aztec Emperor Montezuma II stood face to face for the first time with Hernán Cortés. The hospital itself, the oldest in the Americas, was founded by Cortés in 1524.

MUSEO MURAL DE DIEGO RIVERA Diego Rivera's mural *Sueño de una Tarde Dominical en la Alameda Central* (Dream of a Sunday Afternoon in the Alameda Central) is showcased in its own museum. Despite its apparently uncontroversial subject matter, the work initially caused a stir because Rivera captioned it "Dios no existe" (God doesn't exist). After several incidents of vandalism, Rivera painted over the offending words with "Conferencia de Letrán, año de 1836," a reference to a speech given by the mid-19th century radical congressman Ignacio Ramírez, in which he declared God to be "nonexistent." *Balderas, at Colón, Plaza Solidaridad, tel. 5/510–23–29 or 5/512–07–54. In far western cnr of Alameda Central. From Metro Juárez, go north on Balderas. Admission: $2.50, free students. Open Tues.–Sun. 10–2 and 3–6.*

MUSEO NACIONAL DE ARTE This beautiful stone building, once home to the Communications Palace, now houses an impressive collection of artwork on two floors, each open on alternate days of the week. The 20th-century exhibits on the first floor include some of the more famous works in the post-revolutionary *indigenismo* style. The painters who worked in this style, including Rivera, Orozco, and Siquieros, glorified rural life, the *indígena* (indigenous person), and the *campesino* (peasant), finding in these figures a new understanding of *lo mexicano* (Mexicanness). Nineteenth-century works like those of José María Velasco (famous for his ground-breaking treatment of landscapes) are on the second floor. *Tacuba 8, tel. 5/521–74–61. Near Metro Bellas Artes and Metro Allende. Admission: $3.50, free Sun. Open Tues.–Sun. 10–5:30.*

Mexico City Center

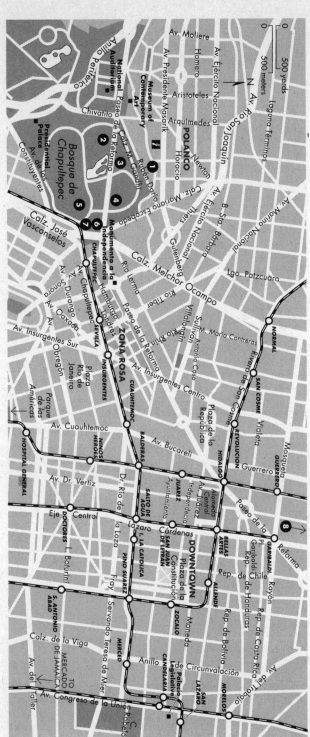

Zócalo and the Alameda Central

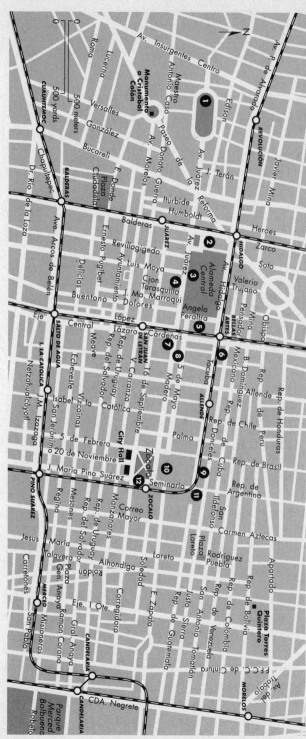

63

MUSEO NACIONAL DE LA REVOLUCION The basement of the **Monumento a la Revolución** now houses the informative National Museum of the Revolution. Newspapers, films, and dioramas carefully document over half a century of Mexican history, from the presidency of Benito Juárez to the signing of the constitution in 1917. *Plaza de la República, tel. 5/546–21–15. From the Alameda Central, walk west on Juárez; from Metro Revolución, follow Ponciano Arriaga to plaza. Admission free. Open Tues.–Sat. 9–5, Sun. 9–3.*

PALACIO DE BELLAS ARTES Construction of the neoclassical Palace of Fine Arts began in 1904 under President Porfirio Díaz. It was scheduled for completion in 1910, the centennial of Mexican independence, but neither Díaz nor Italian architect Adamo Boari took the area's porous subsoil into account. As a result, the heavy building is now sinking. Technical difficulties coupled with the upheaval of the Mexican Revolution delayed completion of the building until July 1932. By then, architectural fads had changed, and the building was given an art deco interior by architect Federico Mariscal, combining geometric shapes, straight lines, and traditional Mexican forms.

The **Ballet Folklórico,** the **Compañía Nacional de Danza** (National Ballet), and the **Orquesta Sinfónica Nacional** (National Symphony Orchestra) perform here. Breathtaking murals by Rivera and Siqueiros grace the walls, and a glistening shower of glass portraying the two volcanoes to the south of the Distrito Federal, designed by Gerardo Murillo (a.k.a Dr. Atl) and put together by Tiffany of New York City, hangs in the main amphitheater. Tickets for performances (*see* After Dark, *below*) can be purchased at counters on the first floor of the palace. Ticket counters are open Monday–Saturday 11–7 and Sunday 9–7.

The top floor of the palace houses the **Museo Nacional de Arquitectura** (National Architecture Museum), whose permanent collection includes plans for the construction of the Bellas Artes. *Lázaro Cárdenas, at Juárez, across from Alameda Central, tel. 5/512–36–33. Metro Bellas Artes. Admission to murals and grounds free; admission to museum: $3.50. Museum open Tues.–Sun. 10–7.*

PLAZA DE LAS TRES CULTURAS/TLATELOLCO At the center of the Tlatelolco District, this plaza is best known for the events that took place here the evening of October 2, 1968.

Frida

Frida Kahlo, probably the most famous Mexican woman artist ever, was born and died in La Casa Azul in Coyoacán. Her image now adorns T-shirts and postcards all over the world, and she has become something of a feminist icon both in Mexico and abroad. Her paintings are as colorful and flamboyant as was their main subject— Frida herself. Born to a Hungarian Jewish father and a Mexican mother in 1907 (though she often claimed that her birth date was in 1910, the year the Revolution began), she was almost killed in a bus accident while she was a teenager; she was in almost constant pain for the rest of her life. She depicted that suffering in her paintings, which often show her bleeding, cracked open, or torn apart and sewn back together. Other themes are political (she was a Communist and a revolutionary who, in spite of her devotion to Stalin, became involved with Leon Trotsky when he lived in Mexico), or concern other aspects of her personal life, such as her stormy marriage to Diego Rivera. Her frank, unapologetic portrayal in art of her own pain, both physical and emotional, represents a public refusal to be a "typical" Mexican woman, a sufrida (long-suffering woman) who bears her sorrow in silence. Her last painting, completed eight days before she died, shows juicy melons, cut open and waiting to be eaten, and is titled Viva la Vida (Live Life).

The preceding week had been one of political protest and riots, including the army occupation of the National University and at least one student's death. Discontent centered around President Díaz Ordaz's anti-activist laws criminalizing "social dissolution," the use of a paramilitary riot squad (the *grenaderos*) against students, and the huge expenses incurred by Mexico's preparations for hosting the 1968 summer Olympics. The evening of October 2, about 5,000 people gathered on the Plaza de las Tres Culturas in a peaceful demonstration to decry the government's failure to meet student demands. They were met by army and police units in tanks and armored cars. The government claims to this day that snipers in surrounding apartment buildings then opened fire, which police returned, killing 43 people. Others claim that the army shot first. At any rate, the government line aside, few today doubt that the death toll was well into the hundreds.

The plaza is named for its symbols of the three main cultures of Mexico—indigenous, Spanish, and mestizo—and is home to the ruins of a pre-Hispanic ceremonial center. The **Iglesia de Santiago Tlatelolco** (1609), amidst a huge complex of apartment buildings around the plaza, is representative of the colonial period, and houses the baptismal font of Juan Diego, the Indian convert to whom the Virgin of Guadalupe appeared in 1531. The church's baroque exterior contrasts with its surprisingly bare and simple interior, quiet except for the sound of the occasional wayward pigeon trying to escape. Mestizo culture is represented on the plaza by the ultramodern Ministry of Foreign Affairs. *From Metro Tlatelolco, go east on Manuel González, right on Lázaro Cárdenas.*

TORRE LATINOAMERICANA Chilangos point proudly at this 41-story tower and insist that they were in the building during the 1985 earthquake. Neither the tower nor the fantastic **Sea World Aquarium** (located on the 38th floor, making it the highest aquarium in the world) suffered severe damage during the quake. The view from the tower is beautiful. *Lázaro Cárdenas, 3 blocks from Metro Bellas Artes. Open daily 10 AM–11 PM. Tower admission: $4. Aquarium admission: additional $3.*

ZOCALO

The spot presently occupied by Mexico City's Zócalo was at the center of the Aztec capital of Tenochtitlán. Sadly, hardly anything from this majestic era remains: Arrogant and anxious to secure a hold on the New World, the Spanish built directly on top of Aztec structures. Beginning in the 16th century, ornate churches and convents, fancy mansions, and other stately edifices were constructed around the plaza, sometimes incorporating the volcanic stone pilfered from Aztec buildings. Toward the end of the 19th century, the upper classes began moving out of the crowded downtown, leaving their mansions to be partitioned and lived in by the working class and the poor. Today the Zócalo, bordered by some of the most beautiful buildings of the colonial era, is a constant buzz of activity. Men in search of employment line the cathedral gate, the small painted signs propped against their knees informing prospective employers of their trade; and busloads of school children on field trips periodically mob the plaza.

The Man Without a Face

Despite Diego Rivera's outspoken opposition to capitalism, in 1933 John D. Rockefeller commissioned him to paint a mural called Man at the Crossing of the Ways for the RCA Building in New York City. Rockefeller was nervous about the first sketches that Rivera showed him. His uneasiness quickly turned to anger when, much to his multimillionaire surprise, the faceless man helping a group of workers that was depicted on the sketches was transformed into Lenin in the mural. Although the tycoon ordered the mural's destruction, Rivera soon found a home for a reproduction of his masterpiece in the Palacio de Bellas Artes (see above).

LA CATEDRAL METROPOLITANA This enormous cathedral on the north side of the Zócalo was built between 1573 and 1813. The first large altar in the center of the cathedral, the **Altar de Perdón**, is a copy of the original that burned in a 1967 fire, the effects of which can still be seen throughout the building. Smaller chapels line both sides of the cathedral. All are beautiful, but a few deserve special attention. The first chapel on the left contains a display with sculpted flowers, each with exactly four petals. This detail, while seemingly insignificant, is an example of the indigenous influence present in the church's architecture. The four petals represent the Aztec view of the universe, each petal symbolizing one of the four principal gods. Toward the back of the church is the third chapel (also on the left), containing **El Señor del Cacoa,** an image of Christ fashioned from corn paste, human nails, and hair. The paintings in the seventh chapel are dedicated to Felipe de Jesús, a martyred saint, and illustrate the story of his journey to Mexico from the Philippines. Apparently his ship was blown off course and wrecked in Japan, where he was condemned to death by the emperor. Legend has it that before his execution he predicted the city where he died (Nagasaki) would go up in flames.

For more information on the history and architecture of the cathedral, ask at the information booth for a guide named Martín Castellanos. For $10 this artist-turned-tour-guide will tell you everything there is to know about La Catedral—or any other place in Mexico City for that matter.

MUSEO DE LA CARICATURA Formerly the Colegio de Cristo (College of Christ), this beautiful building now houses the Latin American Cartoon Museum. The drawings run the gamut from sophisticated political commentary and satire to simple jokes that don't demand any knowledge of Spanish. During restorations of the building after the 1985 earthquake, pre-Columbian artifacts, including the sculpted head of a serpent, were unearthed here. The serpent's head was left as it was found and can still be seen at the back of the museum. Upstairs is the **Salón de la Plástica Mexicana,** with a small collection of 20th-century art. *Donceles 99, tel. 5/789–14–08 or 5/795–11–87. 2 blocks north of Zócalo, btw Brasil and Argentina. Admission to both museums: 30¢. Open Tues.–Sun. 10–4.*

PALACIO NACIONAL The National Palace was built under the direction of Hernán Cortés, on the site where Montezuma's Grand Palace once stood. In fact, the volcanic rock (*tezontle*) now in the facade was taken from the Grand Palace and incorporated into the Spanish design. It was in the courtyard of this impressive edifice that Cortés entertained guests with Mexico's first bullfights. A starving and angry mob tore the palace down in 1692, but it was reconstructed the following year. Today, the bell rung by Padre Hidalgo to proclaim the independence of Mexico in 1810 hangs on the central facade of the National Palace, and the offices of the president, the Federal Treasury, and the National Archive are all housed here.

The second floor of the Palace's main courtyard is covered with over 1,200 square feet of murals that took Diego Rivera and his assistants more than 16 years to paint (1929–45). The series, called *Epic of the Mexican People in Their Struggle for Freedom and Independence,* portrays two millenia of Mexican history. The hero of the pre-Hispanic panels is the plumed serpent god of wind, Quetzalcoatl, whose prophesied return supposedly facilitated Cortés' con-

The Main Pedestal

The Zócalo—officially called the Plaza de la Constitución—is the largest plaza in the Western Hemisphere. The word "zócalo" actually means "pedestal." In the 19th century there were plans to build a monument to Mexican Independence in Mexico City's main plaza. For whatever reason, the monument was never built, and all that remains of those designs is the name for the base of the monument—the "pedestal"—that never came into being. The misnomer stuck and is now the term applied to the main plazas of most Mexican cities.

quest. Also prominent are a man offering a human arm for sale; Spanish soldiers arriving in the not-so-New World; Spanish priests; bell-ringing Hidalgo and reform-writing Juárez; revolutionaries Zapata and Pancho Villa; and even Karl Marx, smiling amid scenes of class struggle. The remaining murals in the corridor, painted from 1945 to 1951, show the capital city of Tenochtitlán and the vibrant market of Tlatelolco before the Spanish Conquest. *East side of Zócalo, tel. 5/512–20–60. Admission free. Open Mon.–Sat. 8:30–5, Sun. 9–5:30.*

TEMPLO MAYOR The Templo Mayor (Great Temple) was the political and spiritual center of the Aztec empire. For more than 400 years, it remained buried beneath the Zócalo. In February 1978, however, while doing routine work behind the cathedral, surprised electric-company workers struck a small section of stone that turned out to be a portion of an eight-ton carving of Coyolxauhqui, goddess of the moon (*see box, above*).

The temple itself was a massive structure, improved and enlarged on more than five separate occasions. Each renovation was a symbolic affirmation of the reigning Aztec's supremacy in the conquered Valley of Mexico. While most temples are typically dedicated to one major deity, the Templo Mayor was dedicated to both Huitzilopochtli (hummingbird god of the sun) and Tlaloc (god of rain and lightning). The Aztecs sacrificed as many as 10,000 humans a year (most of them either tithes from conquered tribes or rival warriors captured in ritual "flower wars") in an effort to appease them and scare the bejesus out of any tribes who dared defy Aztec hegemony. According to Aztec religion, without this sort of divine nourishment the sun god would refuse to move across the sky and Tlaloc would withhold the water for the crops.

Artifacts found during the excavation of the Templo Mayor are displayed in the **Museo del Templo Mayor.** The museum has displays on Aztec history, from the exodus from legendary Aztlán through the Conquest. Included in the exhibit are ceramic warriors, stone knives, skulls of sacrificial victims, the massive stone disk of the moon goddess, and a miniature model of Tenochtitlán. *On Zócalo, at Seminario and República de Guatemala, tel. 5/542–06–06 or 5/542–17–17. Admission: $4.50, free Sun. Open Tues.–Sun. 9–5. Free guided tours in Spanish Tues.–Fri. 9:30–4, Sat. 9:30–1. English-language tours ($1 per person) Tues.–Sat. at 10 and noon.*

BOSQUE DE CHAPULTEPEC

Known simply as "Chapultepec," this park is a haven from all things urban for families, joggers, cyclists, and young lovers. It also harbors many of Mexico's most significant monuments and museums, including the world-famous Museo Nacional de Antropología (*see below*). Outdoor diversions are plentiful: Wednesday through Sunday you can boat on the unsettlingly bright green lake for $2 an hour or traipse around the zoo. Any day of the week, you can see how long that taco you had for lunch stays down on one of the many rides in **La Feria** amusement park (admission $5). Both Metro Chapultepec and Metro Auditorio are located inside the park. Buses and peseros to the park run west from the centro down Paseo de la Reforma.

Dark Side of the Moon Goddess

According to one version of an Aztec story, the moon goddess Coyolxauhqui became furious when her mother, Coatlicue, miraculously became impregnated by a ball of fluff while sweeping at Coatepec, the Serpent Mountain. Coyolxauhqui summoned her 400 brothers and, with their help, slew their mother. Unfortunately for them, the dying Coatlicue gave birth to an adult son, Huitzilopochtli, the hummingbird god of the sun, who avenged his mother's death by dismembering his sister and throwing her remains to the bottom of Coatepec.

MONUMENTO A LOS NINOS HEROES The entrance to Chapultepec Park is guarded by the Monument to the Child Heroes. The six marble columns, shaped like candles (the black tips are supposed to be flames), were erected in honor of six young military cadets who died defending *la patria* (the fatherland) in 1847, during the U.S. invasion. That war may not take up much space in U.S. textbooks, but to Mexicans it's still a troubling symbol of their neighbor's imperialism: The war cost Mexico almost half its national territory, including what are now the states of Texas, California, Arizona, New Mexico, and Nevada.

CASTILLO DE CHAPULTEPEC Chapultepec Castle perches atop a wooded hill overlooking the entire Valley of Mexico. The oldest part of the castle still standing dates to 1785, when Viceroy Bernardo de Galvez built the first fort here. In 1841, the castle was converted into a military academy. Shortly after, at the end of the bloody battle for Mexico City during the U.S. invasion, a young cadet named Juan Escutia (one of the six honored by the Monumento de los Niños Héroes), realizing the battle was lost, climbed to the top of the northern tower, wrapped himself in the Mexican flag, and jumped to his glorious death. A tomb at the foot of the hill marks the place where he landed. Almost 20 years later, Emperor Maximilian, installed by the French, remodeled the place and moved in. Chapultepec Castle would remain the official residence of the head of state until 1944, when President Lázaro Cárdenas moved to Los Pinos, the present-day presidential residence, and gave the castle to the Mexican people as the **Museo Nacional de Historia** (National History Museum). It now houses exhibits on social, economic, cultural, and political history, complemented by murals by José Clemente Orozco and Diego Rivera. *Uphill, beyond Monumento a Los Niños Héroes. Tel. 5/286–07–00. Admission: $4.50, free Sun. and students. Open Tues.–Sun. 10–6; ticket sales stop at 4 PM.*

MUSEO DE ARTE MODERNO Amid the greenery of Chapultepec Park, this museum is dedicated to modern painting, photography, and sculpture. The permanent collection includes work by Frida Kahlo and Dr. Atl (Gerardo Murillo). The annex to the main building houses temporary exhibits of contemporary Mexican painting, lithography, sculpture, and photography, and the surrounding gardens abound with sculpture. *On south side of Reforma, at Gandhi, tel. 5/553–62–11. Admission: $4.50, free Sun. and with student ID. Open Tues.–Sun. 10–5:30.*

MUSEO NACIONAL DE ANTROPOLOGIA Mexico's complex anthropological heritage demands a museum as grand as this one. It is by far the best in the country, with perhaps the finest archaeological collection in the world; each room displays artifacts from a different geographic region and/or culture. Pace yourself—if you try to cover it all, you'll end up hating the place. Make sure to check out stelae from Tula, a town north of Mexico City, with bas-relief carvings showing Maya influence. Guided tours in Spanish, English, and French are available Tuesday–Saturday at 9:30 AM and 5:30 PM. The museum's **Auditorio Jaime Torres Bodet** shows ethnographic films in Spanish daily at 6 PM. *Paseo de la Reforma, at Gandhi, tel. 5/553–62–66 or 5/553–62–43. Admission: $5.50, free Sun. Open Tues.–Sat. 9–7, Sun. 10–6.*

MUSEO TAMAYO DE ARTE CONTEMPORANEO INTERNACIONAL Finding this museum hidden within the dense foliage of Chapultepec Park requires the skill of a 16th-century navigator. Don't give up—it's worth the search. In 1981, Mexican artist Rufino Tamayo and his wife, Olga, donated their personal collection of painting and sculpture to the people, establishing this sleek, granite museum. It contains paintings by Pablo Picasso, René Magritte, Joan Miró, and quite a few of Tamayo's own works. *Reforma, at Gandhi, tel. 5/286–58–89. Walk around Museo de Arte Moderno to Reforma. Admission: $3.50, free Sun. and students. Open Tues.–Sun. 10–6.*

SALA DE ARTE PUBLICO SIQUEIROS Just before his death, muralist David Alfaro Siqueiros (a supporter of Stalin who had been involved in an unsuccessful attempt to assasinate Trotsky) bequeathed his home and studio to the people of Mexico. The interior walls of his workshop are covered with murals, and the house is cluttered with paintings, photographs, and some of the sketches he used to create his most famous works, such as *New Democracy,* currently on display in the Palacio de Bellas Artes (*see above*). *Tres Picos 29, btw Schiller and Hegel, Col. Polanco, tel. 5/531–33–94 or 5/545–59–52. From Metro Auditorio, go north on Arquimedes, right on Rubén Darío, left on Hegel, and right on Tres Picos. Admission: $2.50, free students. Open Mon.–Sat. 10–5.*

SAN ANGEL

The past 50 years have seen this *pueblito* (village) develop into an exclusive suburb for Mexico City's rich. The sprawl of the city, however, impinges upon San Ángel's tranquility: Avenidas Insurgentes and Revolución transect the suburb, bringing traffic, noise, and a lively nightlife. Still, this neighborhood has its share of quiet, cobblestone streets (nice to look at, but tiring to walk on) and colonial architecture, with homes hidden behind high walls.

In the center of San Ángel is the **Plaza San Jacinto,** where artists peddle their wares on lazy Saturday afternoons. It's now a lively spot, but it was the end of the line for about 50 Irish soldiers in 1847. They came to fight in the Mexican–American War on the American side, but later deserted and joined the Catholic Mexicans. Needless to say, the American soldiers who later caught them were none too pleased. Before executing them, they branded the Irish soldiers' foreheads with the letter *D* for deserter. Nearby is the site of the **Bazar Sábado** (Saturday bazaar), where hordes of gawking tourists buy high-quality handicrafts from vendors who accept credit cards. Less expensive goods are sold in the open-air market behind the bazaar. Just off Avenida Revolución sits the **Convento del Carmen,** which houses mummies in its crypt. West of Insurgentes, the **Monumento a Obregón,** in honor of the general of the Mexican Revolution, dominates the corner of La Paz and Insurgentes. Farther north on Revolución is the Museo Carrillo Gil, which includes work by Diego Rivera. **Rivera's studio** is just up the street.

CONVENTO E IGLESIA DEL CARMEN The convent is an interesting example of the simplicity of Carmelite architecture. The mazelike cloister, with its tiled domes and fountains, has been converted into a museum displaying religious artifacts and rotating art exhibits. Those interested in undertaking should check out the mummified corpses on display, and those fascinated by alternative bed accoutrements should see the pillow made of wood in the bedroom on the top floor. *Revolución, at La Paz, tel. 5/548–28–38, 5/548–53–12, or 5/548–75–77. From Metro M. A. de Quevedo, walk west on Quevedo, left on La Paz. Admission: $3.50, free Sun. Open Tues.–Sun. 10–5.*

MUSEO CARRILLO GIL Alvar Carrillo Gil, a doctor and pharmaceuticals producer, set up this spacious museum to house his art collection, which features works by Diego Rivera, Wolfgang Paalen, David Alfaro Siqueiros, Gunther Gerzso, and José Clemente Orozco. Dr. Gil liked slapping paint on the canvas as well, and some of his own creations hang on the gleaming white walls. *Revolución 1608 , at Desierto de los Leones, tel. 5/548–74—67. Admission: $2.50, $1 students, free Sun. Open Tues.–Sun. 10–6. Wheelchair access.*

MUSEO ESTUDIO DIEGO RIVERA Paints are still on the shelves, and his denim jacket and shoes sit on a wicker chair, waiting: The museum that once was home to Diego Rivera appears as if the muralist could return at any moment to continue work or share some tequila with such cronies as Leon Trotsky, Lázaro Cárdenas, or John Dos Passos. Juan O'Gorman, a famous architect and close friend of Rivera's, designed the house in the spirit of functionalism, with large wrought-iron doors, windows framed in industrial steel, and exposed plumbing and electrical wiring. *Diego Rivera 2, at Altavista, tel. 5/616–09–96. Take RUTA 43 ALTAVISTA pesero from cnr of Revolución and La Paz (in front of Pemex station). Admission: $3.50, free Sun. Open Tues.–Sun. 10–6.*

COYOACAN

Coyoacán was a rural village until the '40s, when wealthy chilangos began moving out here to escape the urban madness of Mexico City. Now it's just half an hour by Metro from the center of town and has evolved into one of the many suburbs engulfed by the D.F.'s sprawl. Centuries-old homes, narrow cobblestone streets, an abundance of boho markets and restaurants, and proximity to the Universidad Nacional Autónoma de México (*see below*) attract an affluent and academic elite.

On weekends, there are concerts and handicraft vendors in the **Jardín Centenario** between Puerto Carillo and Tres Cruces. Next door, families wander about **Plaza Hidalgo,** enjoying the karate demonstrations or exercise classes going on outside. The red building on the plaza's north side is the **Palacio de Cortés,** once the conquistador's home and now the administrative

San Angel and Coyoacán

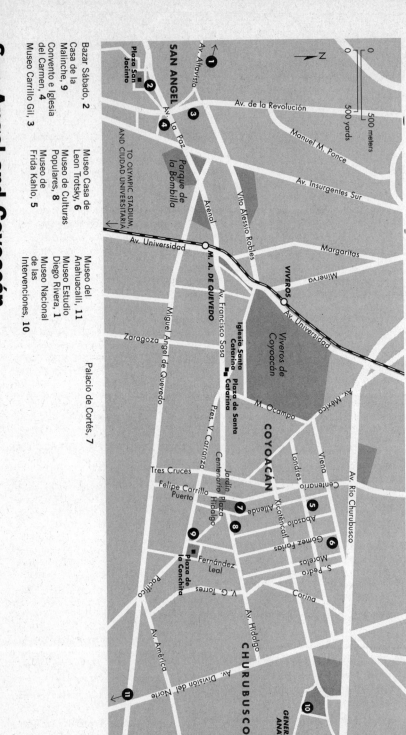

center of Coyoacán. In the back portion of the palace are the offices of the **Foro Cultural Coyoa-canense** (tel. 5/658–48–91), whose friendly staff provides loads of information (ask them to tell you about Cortés' secret tunnel) as well as the scoop on free concerts. The **Casa de la Cultura Jesus Reyes Heroles** (Francisco Sosa 202, tel. 5/658–55–19 or 5/658–52–71) publishes an indispensable monthly calendar of cultural activities in Coyoacán. If you can get a group of about 10 people together, you can call 5/658–55–02 for a guided walking tour of the neighborhood's main attractions. The tour is free and begins at 10 AM on Saturdays and Sundays only. The group leaves from the kiosk in Plaza Hidalgo and wanders through some of the most beautiful sections of Coyoacán—including the **Casa de la Malinche**, the house Cortés built for his Aztec translator and lover; the **Plaza de la Concepción**; the beautiful, tree-filled **Viveros de Coyoacán;** and even the UNAM campus. If you can't get a group together, try crashing one—they usually don't mind an extra pair of feet. Just get there early, bring a comfy pair of walking shoes, and blend in. *From Metro Viveros, go south on Universidad to Francisco Sosa. From Metro Coyoacán, take* PLAZA HIDALGO *pesero.*

> *Diego Rivera says: "Art is like ham. It nourishes people."*

MUSEO CASA DE LEON TROTSKY This lime green house was the home of one of the most important figures of the Russian Revolution. In 1937, after being exiled from the Soviet Union, Leon Trotsky was granted asylum in Mexico by President Lázaro Cárdenas at the urging of muralist Diego Rivera. Upon their arrival, Trotsky and his wife moved to this anonymous and forbidding fortress (whose turrets were manned by armed guards). The first attempt to assassinate Trotsky (involving Siqueiros, a Mexican muralist and Stalinist) left bullet holes that are still visible in Trotsky's bedroom. Unfortunately for Leon, the second attempt was successful. The study where Trotsky was fatally stabbed remains untouched: On the desk lies an article he was going over when Ramón Mercader murdered him with an ice pick on August 29, 1940. The house also contains less morbid memorabilia, from a tin of Colgate tooth powder to cases of books in English, Spanish, and Russian. The guards wandering throughout the grounds are knowledgeable and willing to answer questions, though not all speak English. If you manage to communicate with them, they'll tell you, among other things, how Trotsky's teeth left a permanent scar on Mercader's hand; how he clung to life for 26 hours; what his last words were; and how his ashes are interred in the garden. *Río Churubusco 410, at Viena, tel. 5/658–87–32. From Plaza Hidalgo, walk north on Allende about 6 blocks, then right. Admission: $3.50, $2.50 students. Open Tues.–Sun. 10–6.*

MUSEO DE CULTURAS POPULARES Rotating exhibits of folk art from Mexico and elsewhere are beautifully displayed here, accompanied by plentiful information (in Spanish). Recent shows have included contemporary Haitian painting and sculpture and Mexican photography from the 1940s. *Hidalgo 289, btw Allende and Abasolo, tel. 5/658–12–65. Metro General Anaya. Admission free. Open Tues.–Fri. 9–6, weekends 9–5.*

MUSEO DE FRIDA KAHLO This blue house in Coyoacán is where painter Frida Kahlo (*see box, above*) was born, grew up, lived briefly with husband Diego Rivera, and died in 1954. Now a museum, the building is filled with colorful and sad remnants of Kahlo's life: self-portraits; illustrated journals; love notes; pictures of Mao Tse-tung, Lenin, and Stalin; clunky clay jewelry; and the beautifully embroidered traditional skirts Kahlo favored. Life-size papier-mâché statues and other folk art collected by Kahlo and Rivera adorn the house and lush garden. As a result of childhood polio and a bus accident when she was a teenager, Kahlo spent much of her life in pain, enduring more than 30 difficult operations. Her decorated body cast and her startling paintings convey both her intense emotional and physical suffering, as well as her pride in and passion for Mexican culture. *Londres 247, at Allende, tel. 5/554–59–99. 5 blocks north of Plaza Hidalgo. Admission: $3.50, $2.50 students. Open Tues.–Sun. 10–6.*

MUSEO DEL ANAHUACALLI What *do* you do with all those pre-Columbian artifacts you've collected over the years? If you're Diego Rivera, you design your own museum. The huge black building that houses Rivera's collection was constructed in the 1960s from dark volcanic rock. Even if you're tired of archaeological treasures, visit the building just because it's so strange, like an aboveground tomb that promises (and delivers) echoing footfalls amid eerie silence. The third floor displays sketches from some of Rivera's murals, including *Man at the Cross-*

roads, now in the Palacio de Bellas Artes (*see* box, The Man Without a Face, *above*). *Calle del Museo 150, tel. 5/677–29–84. From Metro Tasqueña, take trolley to Xotepingo stop. Exit to right, where sign says* CALLE DEL MUSEO; *backtrack to intersection and turn left. Admission free. Open Tues.–Sun. 10–2 and 3–6.*

If you're interested in attending religious services of just about any denomination, call the British consulate; they'll be glad to set you on the right(eous) path.

MUSEO NACIONAL DE LAS INTERVENCIONES This museum is housed in the beautifully maintained Ex-convento de Churubusco, the site of a ferocious battle during the Mexican-American War, memorabilia from which is plentiful here. On exhibit are guns, flags, pictures, documents, maps, and other artifacts chronicling interventions by foreign countries, in particular France and the United States. Visitors can also hear regular lectures on subjects related to the museum's theme. *20 de Agosto, at General Anaya, tel. 5/604–06–09. 1 block from Metro General Anaya. Admission: $3.50, free Sun. and students. Open Tues.–Sun. 9–6.*

UNIVERSIDAD NACIONAL AUTONOMA DE MEXICO (UNAM)

The National Autonomous University of Mexico, one of the oldest universities in the Americas, sits on a lava bed in a residential district in the southern part of the city. Originally made up of various *facultades* (schools) scattered throughout the city, the UNAM was consolidated into one huge campus in the 1950s and now has more than 100,000 students. The campus is generally known as the *Ciudad Universitaria* (University City), or simply C.U.

A generation or two ago, a degree from the UNAM was a ticket into political circles and positions of power, but these days the political and business elite tend to come from private institutions. The UNAM is confronted by the severe economic problems that plague most public universities. Professors skip classes when low incomes force them to take on additional jobs, and overenrollment puts pressure on an already populous campus. Despite all its problems, however, the university retains its well-deserved reputation for academic excellence and continues to attract students from around the world. The school year runs from mid-November to the end of March and from mid-May to September. Students choose a major early, and then take the same classes with the same students for all their university years. By graduation, they are often a tightly knit group. Students have clashed with the state before—most famously and violently in 1968, when government tanks occupied the UNAM. The confrontation culminated with the massacre at Tlatelolco in early October that same year (*see* Plaza de las Tres Culturas/Tlatelolco, *above*.)

The university's architects wanted the campus to incorporate the best of traditional and modern design and still harmonize with the natural landscape of cactus and black volcanic rock. They succeeded with the **Estadio Olímpico** (Olympic Stadium). This huge volcano-shaped stadium was the site of the 1968 Olympics, and continues to host university sporting events, including home games of the UNAM's soccer team, the Pumas. The outer ramps of the stadium are covered by yet another Diego Rivera mural, this one titled *La Universidad, la familia mexicana, la paz y la juventud deportista* (University, Family, Peace and Athletic Youth). Murals by Carlos Mérida, David Alfaro Siqueiros, and Juan O'Gorman can be found just about everywhere on the campus, from the **Torre de la Rectoría** (Tower of the Rectory) on the northwest side of campus to the **Vestíbulo de la Sala Nezahualcóyotl** in the south.

An ecological reserve on the southern end of campus contains the **Espacio Escultórico** (Sculpture Space), a giant lava pit encircled by tall, gray triangles of stone. Designed by sculptor Mathias Goeritz, this pool of black, hardened lava is good for climbing, picnics, or cutting class on a sunny afternoon. Just down the street, behind the Biblioteca Nacional (National Library) is another long, winding sculpture, *Las Serpientes del Pedregal*, which seems to slither around the library. Transportation on campus is free, so exploring is easy. *Take* TLALPAN JOYA *pesero south on Insurgentes to 3rd pedestrian overpass on campus, cross street, and head north past*

Biblioteca Nacional. *From Metro Universidad Salida E, take* ZONA CULTURAL *pesero to Espacio Escultórico stop.*

LA VILLA DE GUADALUPE

UNAM tuition costs less than a bottle of Peñafiel (under $1 a year), and any attempts to raise it are met with angry protests by students.

La Villa, with two basilicas dedicated to the Virgin of Guadalupe, is the most revered Christian site in Mexico. Even today, millions flock to the place where the Virgin Mary is said to have appeared to Juan Diego, an indigenous convert to Christianity, in 1531. Unlike the fair Mary of the Roman Catholic tradition, the Virgin of Guadalupe had a brown complexion and spoke Nahuatl, Diego's native tongue. The Virgin instructed Diego to gather a bunch of roses—an impossible task in winter—as a testament of the truthfulness of his vision. When he told his story to a priest, he scoffed, calling him a heretic and claiming that the story was pure fantasy. Yet when Juan Diego opened his cloak, out fell the bunch of roses the Virgin had told him to gather, leaving an image of the Virgin printed on the inside of the cloak.

The museum in the **Basílica Vieja** (the original basilica, dating to 1536) contains exhibits of European and colonial Mexican art. In the hulking, gray mass that is the **Basílica Nueva,** you can glide past Juan Diego's cloak on a moving sidewalk. The new basilica was built in 1976 to accommodate increasing numbers of pilgrims on the Virgin's feast day, December 12 (*see* Festivals, *below*). *Calzada de Guadalupe, near Metro La Villa. Basílica Vieja museum admission: 30¢. Open Tues.–Sun. 10–6.*

CHEAP THRILLS

In colonial times, when literacy rates w ere low, scribes would sit in the plazas and read or write letters for a nominal fee. Today the tradition continues (although in a slightly modernized form) on the **Plaza Santo Domingo.** Modern-day scribes can be found in the local plaza with their typewriters, transcribing everything from term papers to love letters. In a row across from the typists are the printers, who churn out everything from business cards to wedding invitations. Both printers and typists work the plaza daily from about 9 AM to 6 PM. *3 blocks north of Zócalo on Monte de Piedad, which becomes República de Brasil.*

The following museums are free any day of the week with a valid student ID:

- *Museo Mural de Diego Rivera*
- *Museo de Arte Moderno*
- *Museo Tamayo*
- *Museo Nacional de Historia*

Whether you're desperate to replenish your dwindling travel funds, or just woke up feeling really lucky, you can always give the **Lotería Nacional** (National Lottery) a whirl. For $1–$1.50 (depending on the game) you can close your eyes, cross your fingers, and wait for the winning numbers to be announced on Channel 13 or posted on lottery booths around town. Just walk to any lottery ticket booth in Mexico City, hand the ticket seller four pesos, and proudly announce, "Quiero ser millonario/a."

FESTIVALS

Easter (late March/early April): Like everywhere else in Mexico, Semana Santa (Holy Week) is the cause for celebrations and religious processions throughout the city. In Iztapalapa, in the southeastern part of the city (take line 8 to Metro Iztapalapa), devotees reenact the Stations of the Cross, complete with a dramatization of the crucifixion.

September 15 and 16, Independence celebrations: Weeks ahead of time, the city is dressed in the national colors: red, green, and white. The celebrations culminate on the evening of the 15th, when the president steps out onto the balcony at the National Palace to read Hidalgo's *grito,* the call for independence that began 10 years of struggle against the Spanish. The Zócalo is so packed with people that you could faint and still not hit the ground; confetti lies inches thick throughout the centro; and fireworks explode all night long. September 15th is also the anniversary of the 1985 earthquake, and mourners gather at the Ángel de la Independencia monument on Reforma, then walk to the Zócalo, many carrying flowers. As the procession passes sites where the most devastating damage occurred, a moment of silence is observed.

October 2, Anniversary of the Massacre at Tlatelolco: People gather in the black-draped Plaza de las Tres Culturas in the early afternoon and at about 5 PM begin an illegal march through the city streets to the Zócalo. Because the commemoration is not one the government supports—it was responsible for hundreds of deaths here in the 1968 massacre (*see* Plaza de las Tres Culturas/Tlatelolco, *above*)—the marchers' path is periodically blocked by the feared *grenaderos* (riot police). But, as the Mexicans say, "Perro que ladra no muerde" (a dog that barks won't bite), and the police usually only detain the crowd for about a half an hour before allowing the marchers to continue. The event brings together relatives of the victims, students of all ages, workers, and opposition sympathizers who carry banners and sing bawdy songs mocking the government.

December 12, Feast Day of the Virgin of Guadalupe: The celebration of the patron saint of Mexico fills the beautifully decorated city with processions and dances. On this day, the area around the Basílica de Guadalupe is probably the most exciting and most crowded place in Mexico. (*See* La Villa de Guadalupe, *above*.)

December 25, Christmas Day: For Christmas, the entire city is draped with lights, making the evening hardly darker than the December afternoon. The lights on the Zócalo are especially spectacular.

Shopping

Everything can be purchased in Mexico City, from a Gucci bag to the silver and *artesanía* (crafts) for which the country is famous. Those heading out to the wilderness can stock up here on socks, deodorant, or a new pair of shoes, and all sorts of camping gear is available at **Deportes Martí** (Venustiano Carranza 19, Col. Centro, tel. 5/585–02–99). If you're shopping for clothing, boutiques in both the **Zona Rosa** and **Polanco** sell international fashions at high prices. For cheaper clothing, try the area around Metro Pino Suárez, just south of the Zócalo. If for some reason you must go to a mall, take the TLALPAN-JOYA pesero south on Insurgentes to **Perisur,** home to Sears, Guess, and other embarrassing U.S. exports. A good, if somewhat overstimulating, resource for just about anything is the department store/restaurant chain **Sanborn's** (*see* Food, *above*).

MARKETS AND ARTESANIA Handicrafts are generally more expensive in Mexico City than elsewhere in the country. Stalls with all sorts of goodies are set up on the Zócalo, just west of the cathedral, during the height of tourist season (July and August). Even more expensive wares are sold year-round in the Zona Rosa on Génova, before Reforma.

La Lagunilla, once known as the Thieves' Market, overflows with furniture, coins, tacky paintings of the Last Supper, and a spattering of nice old stuff. This market is at its liveliest on Sunday, when curio stalls are set up outside the main building. *Allende, btw República de Honduras and Ecuador, east of Reforma. Open daily 9–7.*

Mercado de Jamaica. The odors of meat, onions, and tacos waft through the corridors of this market where bananas, pineapples, papayas, and mangos sit in enormous heaps. But the market is mainly known for the rows of stalls with huge bunches of roses, carnations, lilies, and birds of paradise. *Morelos (Eje 3 Sur), at H. Congreso. Metro Jamaica. Open daily 8–6.*

La Merced and **Sonora** are two separate markets connected by a small side street, Cabaña. In the huge warehouse of La Merced, where edible goods are sold, the sweet smell of fresh fruits and vegetables pervades. Outside, you can buy just about any useful item: umbrellas, pots, pans, clothes, and even some toiletries. Sonora, just across the way, promises to cure what ails you. Herbal potions guarantee effectiveness against everything from evil spirits to impotency. At the very back, tropical birds, goats, puppies, and other sad caged animals are also for sale: some for pets, and some as food, no doubt. *Mercado de La Merced: Circunvalación, at San*

Pablo. Metro Merced. Mercado Sonora: 2 blocks south of La Merced on Fray Servando Teresa de Mier. Both open daily 8 AM–7 PM.

Anything in the way of consumer goods can be purchased in **Tepito**, a semidisreputable market raided almost daily by police in search of illegal merchandise. The selection is overwhelming; you can find everything from electronics to athletic shoes. But much like a mall full of crazed grandmothers on the last day of Macy's white sale, it's crowded and rough, so leave your valuables at home and bring a *cuate* (buddy) to watch your back. *Eje 1 Norte, at Aztecas. Take TEPITO pesero from Metro Guerrero. Open daily 8–6, except after police raids.*

Tucked away through a doorless, iron entryway, **La Ciudadela** consists of wall-to-wall handicrafts stores. Mounds of beautiful silver jewelry from Taxco, bags and jackets from Chiapas, and even those "My parents went to Mexico City . . ." T-shirts (available in English and *español*) can be found if you look hard enough. Located next to the plaza of the same name, the market is more or less outdoors, with plastic tarps protecting the merchandise from rain. The merchants are tourist-wise—many even accept credit cards—and getting them to lower their prices more than a few pesos will probably be a struggle. *Balderas, at Plaza La Ciudadela. 5 blocks south of Metro Juárez, or 1 long block north of Metro Balderas. Open daily 10–7.*

The **Mercado San Juan** (officially the Mercado de Curiosidades Centro Artesanal) is a conglomeration of tiny shops crowded together into a pink-and-white concrete building that feels more like a huge Mexican shopping mall than a quaint crafts market. However, good-quality artesanía, blankets, hammocks, silver, and mounds of tourist trinkets can be found here. Don't expect too much leeway in the prices—anything short of throwing yourself on the market floor and weeping uncontrollably will probably not move the gringo-wise vendors to compassion. *Ayuntamiento, at Dolores, 4 blocks south of Metro Juárez and Alameda Central. Open Mon.– Sat. 9–7, Sun. 9–4.*

The **Tianguis El Chopo** is a change of pace from the fruits and trinkets of most of the city's markets. This punk-style swap meet features fliers, info on bands, T-shirts, and underground magazines. You may even come away sporting a new tattoo. *Sol, near train station. Metro La Raza. Open Sat. 10–4.*

High-quality, government-approved folk art is available in any one of the several **Fonart** (Fondo Nacional para el Fomento de las Artesanías) outlets in the city. The pieces come from all over Mexico, so you can get just about anything here, though it will probably cost you at least twice as much as it would in that remote highland village. If you'll be traveling on, it's better to use Fonart as a reference for price and quality. *Juárez 89, tel. 5/521–01–71. Other locations: Londres 136, Zona Rosa, and Patriotismo 691, Metro Mixcoac. Open Mon.–Sat. 10–7.*

In June, Tell Everyone Your Name is Pedro

For Mexican Catholics, your Saint's Day is a day on which you receive gifts and the well-wishing of friends and family. Every day of the year is a Saint's Day: For example, if your name were Pedro, you would celebrate on the Día de San Pedro (June 29). June is the Mes de los Santos, a fabrication of the greeting-card companies who capitalize on the fact that the days of the best-known saints, such as Peter and Paul, fall during this month. Even if your name is Moonbeam, you can celebrate the Saint's Day/anniversary festivals held at markets throughout the city, with free food, drink, song, and dance. Ask at the markets about dates.

After Dark

***La movida* (the action) starts late and** keeps going until the early hours of the morning; even after the clubs close at 3 AM, people grab a taco and beer and wait until the more respectable hour of 4 AM to mosey on to bed. The most lively areas at night are the Zona Rosa and Insurgentes Sur in Colonia Juárez. Clubs are the places to be, whether they play disco or *música tropical*, a mix of salsa, merengue, and cumbias. Dance club cover charges are usually quite high, and movies and cafés provide a cheaper alternative. *Tiempo Libre* ($1 at most newsstands) lists places to go and things to see, from tango bars to discos to plays.

For cruising, by car or on foot, and watching the scene, the **Zona Rosa** is always happening. A variety of people—snazzy club-goers in black evening wear, "cool" Mexican teenagers in ripped jeans, and camera-toting tourists—come here to see and be seen. The local **Vip's** and **Sanborn's** (*see* Food, *above*) are central to hanging out in the '90s. At night these chain restaurants fill up with people having a cup of coffee and a cigarette before heading off to a movie or dance club.

A favorite nightspot with locals and tourists alike, **Plaza Garibaldi** (Eje Central and República de Perú) heats up with competing mariachi bands in full regalia, who sing of lost love and cheatin' women. Couples come to be serenaded, and foreigners come to experience "traditional" Mexico. Buying a song can be a bit pricey, but it's simple enough to walk around and listen in on other people's favorite mariachi tunes. If you do decide to buy a ballad, ask for something besides "Cielito Lindo," a song that causes Mexicans to roll their eyes and nod knowingly at one another. Otherwise, you can always escape to one of the cantinas and dance clubs (many of which charge no cover) that line the square.

The **theater** scene in Mexico City offers a wide variety of performances, from musicals to works by Mexican and international playwrights—David Mamet in Spanish is an interesting linguistic experience. Check listings in *Tiempo Libre*.

BARS **Bar Mata.** High up on the fourth floor of a colonial building in the centro, this bar is one of the hottest spots around for the under-30 crowd. This is not a loud, smoke-filled, grind factory; the music is low enough to carry on a conversation, and the atmosphere conducive to mingling and flirting. There's no cover or drink minimum, and the place gets packed after about 10:30. *Filomeno Mata 11, at 5 de Mayo, tel. 5/518–02–37. Open Tues.–Sun. 8 PM–2 PM.*

Caramba. The patrons of this serene bar are usually deeply absorbed in their backgammon games. Tables fill up quickly with mellow older patrons, but they generously share their haunt with the occasional stranger. Strong coffee and a variety of alcoholic beverages are served. *Reforma 264, Zona Rosa, tel. 5/207–24–35. Btw Niza and Copenhague. Open daily 1–1.*

The five best tequilas, according to a bartender at La Guadalupana:

- *Herradura Blanco, Reposado*
- *Sauza, Generaciones*
- *Sauza, Conmemorativo*
- *Cuervo, 1800*
- *Sauza, Hornitos*

La Guadalupana. This Coyoacán cantina dating from 1932 is heavy on atmosphere and local color and is always packed with regulars. Sit at the cloth-draped tables or stand at the bar while you deliberate on which of the eight available tequilas to order. Waiters in white jackets and bow ties, intent on replacing barely used ashtrays and keeping things pristine, negotiate their way around rowdy groups of singing men. The crowd is overwhelmingly male, and unaccompanied women will be the target of quite a bit of friendly attention (and possibly free drinks). If you're harassed, however, the waiters will politely remove the offender from your area and, if necessary, from the establishment. *Higuera 14, tel. 5/554–65–53. Near Plaza Hidalgo. Open Mon.–Sat. noon–midnight, Sun. noon–6 PM.*

La Opera. Porfirio Díaz and his extravagant crowd drank here, and once Pancho Villa, the bandit-hero of the revolution, entered on his horse and shot some holes in the roof. These days the bar is a little quieter and the old-fashioned, carved-wood booths and the ornate ceiling still offer an elegant place to relax without the neon gaudiness of other posh bars. Women can come alone without fear of being hassled every few minutes; in fact, La Opera was one of the first cantinas to admit women. Dinner runs $8–$11, beers cost $2, and you can linger over a drink without ordering food. Beware of the seemingly free snacks that are placed on your table; they'll go on your tab. *5 de Mayo 10, at Filomeno Mata, tel. 5/512–89–59. 5 blocks from Zócalo. Open Mon.–Sat. noon–midnight.*

CINEMAS Most U.S. movies show in Mexico within a few months, so finding a film in English is easy. They're listed in *Tiempo Libre* (see above) by title and theater. The films are generally in poor condition, full of scratches and squiggly lines, and the volume is often low, since most of the audience depends on the subtitles, but for $3 (half that on Wednesdays) it's not too bad. Paseo de la Reforma in the Zona Rosa has quite a few big screens showing recent American and European films; look for **Diana** (Reforma 423, tel. 5/511–32–36), **Latino Plus** (Reforma 296, tel. 5/525–87–57), **París** (Reforma 92, tel. 5/535–32–71), and **Paseo** (Reforma 35, tel. 5/546–58–43). For artsier films (and an artsier crowd), check out the government-run **Cineteca** (Av. México-Coyoacán 389, near Metro Coyoacán, tel. 5/688–32–72).

"You haven't been to Mexico if you haven't been to Plaza Garibaldi by night." — Alberto, a native chilango.

DANCE The Ballet Folklórico de México, which performs in the Palacio de Bellas Artes (*see* Worth Seeing, *above*), is world-renowned for its stunning presentations of Mexican regional folk dances, spectacles that are popular among locals and tourists alike. Performances are Wednesdays at 9 PM and Sunday mornings at 9 AM. Tickets are sold on the first floor of the Palacio Monday–Saturday 11–7, Sunday 9–7 and cost $42 for the first floor, $38.50 for the second, and $30 for the third. Tickets for other concerts and plays held here (listed in *Tiempo Libre*) are sold Monday–Saturday 11 AM–3 PM and 5 PM–7 PM, Sunday 10:30 AM–7 PM.

GAY CLUBS **Bota's Bar.** Smack dab in the center of the Zona Rosa, this new bar is one of the hippest in town, featuring mirrored walls and funky neon lights that pulse in time with the latest rock, rap, and techno. With all that, it should come as no surprise that the bar is a little more expensive than the rest. A reasonable $7.50 cover on Fridays and Saturdays gets you in the door, but there's a two-drink minimum (a beer costs $2.50). *Niza 45, tel. 5/514–46–00. Open Tues.–Sun. 9 PM–4 AM. No cover Tues.–Thurs., and Sun.*

Butterfly. This techno club looks more like a bus terminal than a disco. With five bars, two snack shacks, about 50 tables, and a huge dance floor that's packed to capacity, it's by far the largest gay club in town. The two transvestite shows (11 PM and 1 AM) are rumored to be the best around. Cover is $6.50 Sunday–Thursday, $10 on Friday and Saturday. *Izazaga 9, tel. 5/761–18–61. Open daily 9:30 PM–2:30 AM.*

Spartacus. Dim lights, throbbing techno-pop, and a transvestite show (every night around 10) make this place especially popular with gay men. Cover is $3.50. *Cuauhtémoc 8, Ciudad Neza, tel. 5/558–49–59 or 5/792–44–70. Open Fri. and Sat. 8 PM–6 AM.*

El Taller. There's no sign, only a small, inconspicuous door that marks the entrance to this popular gay bar in the Zona Rosa. Stairs lead down to a dark and grooving disco of men *only* (women are not allowed). Outside, a low profile is maintained so as not to upset the city fathers. The $6.50 cover includes one drink; Monday there's no cover. *Florencia 37, Zona Rosa, tel. 5/533–49–70. 1½ blocks from Ángel de la Independencia monument. Open daily 9:30 PM–3:30 AM.*

According to one traveler, the cutest guys hang out at Bota's Bar.

El Vaquero. You'll have to search a bit for this inconspicuous bar; it's squeezed between a laundromat and a bookstore in a small commercial center. The music here is mostly Latin, and if you like to *cumbia,* this is the place to do it. Management is extremely concerned with keeping things hush-hush, so it may be difficult to get anyone on the phone. Cover is $6.50. *Insurgentes Sur 1231, tel. 5/598–25–95. Open Thurs.–Sat. 9 PM–2 AM.*

MEXICO CITY AND ENVIRONS

➤ JAZZ • **La Mansión.** Although this is also a decent restaurant, you don't need to order food to listen to good live jazz, played Wednesday–Saturday at 8 PM. There's no cover, but drinks are $3–$5. *Taine 322, Polanco, tel. 5/545–43–08. Open Wed.–Sun. 1–11.*

New Orleans. Local groups jam at this smoky bar. The lights are dim and the crowd is laid-back. Music starts around 8:30, and the cover is $8.50. *Revolución 1980, San Ángel, tel. 5/550–19–08. Open Tues.–Sat. 8:30 PM–2 AM.*

➤ ROCK, RAP, AND ALTERNATIVE MUSIC • **La Casa del Canto.** The cheapest place to hear live music is this club atop a Metro station. It's tiny and dark and attracts teenagers and twentysomethings sporting Metallica-wear and thirsting for the live music of bands with names like "Heavy Nopales." Yup, this is *the* heavy metal hangout. The cover is $3 with a $3.50 drink minimum. *Metro Insurgentes, Local CC-04, no phone. Open daily 6 PM–midnight.*

Papa's Bar. It may not be super-hip, but you're not John D. Rockefeller and this ain't the rich and famous guide to Mexico. So the club is small and the smoke machine makes it hard to breathe, but the music is good and women get in free on Wednesday, Thursday, and Sunday. The official cover is $23, but tourists get through the doors for about $8.50, and there's an open bar all night long. Just drink yourself silly and pretend you're somewhere else. *Londres 142, Zona Rosa, tel. 5/207–43–84. From Metro Insurgentes, go south on Génova and left on Londres. Open Wed., Thurs., Sun. 7:30 PM–1:30 AM, Fri. and Sat. 7:30 PM–3 AM.*

Rockotitlán. A casual crowd with oh-so-casually faded Levis and black leather jackets jams into this tiny club, which fills up fast, especially when a popular band plays. Beer and wine are served, and every other Sunday from about 5 to 9 the club hosts *tardeadas* (afternoon dances) with three different groups. Check *Tiempo Libre* to find out who's playing. Cover ranges from $8 to $20, depending on the band. *Insurgentes Sur 953, Col. Nápoles, tel. 5/687–78–93. Take SAN ANGEL pesero south on Insurgentes; it's on the 3rd floor of a small commercial building on a traffic circle. Open daily 10 PM–2 AM.*

Rockstock. Once the most popular club in the city, this place's open-bar days are over, but the drinks, at $2, are still cheap. The $40 cover (gasp!) makes it prohibitively expensive for most budget travelers, but women get in free on Thursdays. Get here before 10:30 PM or you'll have to wait to get in. Or, make goo-goo eyes at the young bouncers who pick and choose among the mass of black-swathed bodies jamming the entryway. The crowd is young, not too dressed up, and there to party. *Reforma 260, Zona Rosa, tel. 5/533–09–06. From Metro Insurgentes, take Génova north to Reforma and turn right. Open Thurs.–Sat. 9 PM–3 AM.*

Tutti Frutti. Despite the cheesy name, this is Mexico City's most underground club. It's also quite far from downtown. People come to the plain and unpretentious darkness to have a beer and dance to the sounds of everybody from the Dead Kennedys to the Pixies. Live bands play some Saturday nights. The cover is $8.50, but women get in free Friday between 10 and 11. Drinks cost $3–$5. *Av. Instituto Politécnico Nacional 5130, tel. 5/368–42–03. From Metro Potrero, walk 3 blocks west and then right. Entrance to club behind the Apache 14 restaurant, under carport. Open Thurs.–Sat. 10 PM–2 AM.*

➤ MUSICA TROPICAL • **Bar León.** The live music at this swanky club lures the cool and goofy alike. Patrons are a mix of students, foreigners from the hotel upstairs, and regulars, who effortlessly avoid wildly gyrating duos practicing the basic steps. Cover is $8.50, with a one-drink minimum. *República de Brasil 5, Col. Centro, tel. 5/510–29–79. Just north of cathedral. Open Wed.–Sat. 9 PM–3 AM.*

Mocamboo. Ask a group of young Mexicanos where you should go to dance salsa and merengue and they'll say the Mocamboo "es padre!" (is cool). Three different orchestras play hour-long sets to a filled-to-capacity dance floor. It's so packed here you don't need to know how to dance salsa to look like a pro—just get in the middle, smile, and let the people around you do all the work. Cover is $16 and worth every dime. *Puebla 191, Col. Roma, tel. 5/533–64–64. From Metro Insurgentes, go west to Chapultepec, right on Puebla. Open Mon.–Sat. 9 PM–4 AM.*

Salón Q. This huge salsa club is one of the more popular places to come and shake your booty. The crowd is young, the music loud, and the drinks are expensive but strong. Cover is $17. *Reforma 169, Col. Guerrero, tel. 5/529–34–95. Open Fri. and Sat. 9 PM–4 AM.*

➤ DANCE HALLS • *Salones de baile* (dance halls) are the essence of working-class popular culture in Mexico City. The dance-hall craze, which began in the late 1920s, reached a peak during World War II, when live bands played mambo, swing, fox-trot, and the ever-popular *danzón* to crowds of eager young dancers. The youth of today prefers the downtown discos, and salones are slowly fading away. The two dance halls listed below attract a crowd of 20- to 80-year-olds whose common denominator is their love of dancing and dressing up.

Salón Colonia. Opened in 1922, Colonia is Mexico City's original dance hall and a favorite with the older crowd. The atmosphere is low-key, and the folks on the dance floor are friendly. This is the perfect place to come practice your moves, because no one seems to mind if you step on their toes. Cover is $5 for men, $3.50 for women. *Manuel M. Flores 33, Col. Obrera. 3½ blocks east of Metro San Antonio. Open Mon., Wed., and Sun. 6 PM–11 PM.*

Salón Los Ángeles. This place attracts a younger crowd that moves to the sounds of salsa instead of the slower *danzón*. The 1930s decor looks as if it came right from an old Mexican movie, with a soda fountain and a huge, open dance floor. The Los Ángeles attracts internationally known musicians about once a month. Cover for those groups is $10, but otherwise they charge $3 for men and $2 for women. *Lerdo 206, near Flores Magon, Col. Guerrero, tel. 5/597–51–81. Open Wed., Fri., and Sun. 6 PM–11 PM.*

➤ PEÑAS • *Peñas* (musical gatherings) appeared in the mid-'60s, when leftists gathered to sing songs of revolution, using the music of rural Latin America then ignored by commercial radio. Dictatorships throughout the Americas imposed *apagones culturales* (cultural blackouts), forcing artists into exile. Thousands of Chileans, Uruguayans, Brazilians, and others made their way to Mexico City, bringing *nueva canción*, the folk music that is still an important element of peña atmosphere. Although these days peñas are less ardently revolutionary, with a feel somewhere between a café and a bar, they function as cultural centers where people relax, listen to music or poetry, or just spend time with friends.

El Condor Pasa. This classic peña with a comfortable, low-key atmosphere is a great place to hear live Latin American folk music. The cover is only about $4, and the drinks are all well under $5. *Rafael Checa 1, Col. San Ángel, tel. 5/548–20–50. Btw Insurgentes and Revolución, at end of SAN ANGEL pesero line; walk back 1 block on Insurgentes, turn left on small road between Mercado de Discos and Mama's Pizza. Open Tues.–Sat. 7 PM–1 AM.*

The management bills El Condor as a place with "family atmosphere, bohemian nights," but what they really mean is "no brawling."

El Hijo del Cuervo. One of the most popular peñas in the city, this old house in Coyoacán is almost always packed with students. The music is a nice blend of everything. There's usually no cover or drink minimum, so you can chill here for just about nothing if you want. But when a live band plays it costs around $10 to get in. Check *Tiempo Libre*, under "bares con variedad," to see who's playing. *Jardín Centenario 17, Coyoacán, tel. 5/658–53–06. From Metro Coyoacán, take pesero Ruta 1 CARRILLO PUERTO to the Jardín. Open daily 1 PM–midnight.*

Hostería El Trobador. This restaurant is probably the least commercial of all the peñas listed. El Trobador offers live Latin American folk music, nueva canción, and sappy romantic music six days a week with no cover charge or drink minimum. *Presidente Carranza 82, at 5 de Febrero, Col. Coyoacán, tel. 5/554–72–47. Open Mon.–Sat. 11 AM–5 PM (restaurant) and 7 PM–1 AM (peña).*

Mesón de la Guitarra. People get dressed up to hear the music at this fancy peña. One look at the crowd and it becomes obvious that this place is for having a good time, not planning revolutions. Under the same management, **Peña Gallos** (Revolución 736, near Metro Mixcoac, tel. 5/563–09–63) is larger, but identical in every other respect. Cover is $7 in both peñas, although women get in free on Thursdays, and everyone gets in free after midnight on Fridays and Saturdays. Reservations are a good idea if you plan to arrive after 9:30. *Félix Cuevas 332, tel. 5/559–15–35 or 5/559–24–35. Take a bus down Insurgentes Sur to Félix Cuevas, ask to be let off at the Liverpool department store, and walk east 5 blocks. Open Thurs.–Sat. 7 PM–2 AM.*

Outdoor Activities

SOCCER Although Mexican *fútbol* (soccer) has rarely distinguished itself at the international level, it is nevertheless a passion shared by millions who gather to play the game in stadiums and open fields just about every weekend. The professional season lasts from September to May or June. You can buy tickets the day of the game, but try to arrive at least an hour before kickoff. The **Estadio Azteca** in the southern part of the city is the biggest stadium in Latin America (in terms of seats, not standing/squishing room; that prize goes to Maracanã Stadium in Rio de Janeiro). One of the most popular teams that plays in Azteca is América, a power-house with lots of fans and rivals. From Metro Tasqueña, catch a *tren ligero* (a sort of trolley) or trolebus straight to the stadium. Tickets for the games (sold at the taquillas outside) cost between $11.50 and $20. The Pumas of UNAM (most players are students) play in the sta-dium at the Ciudad Universitaria (*see* UNAM in Worth Seeing, *above*).

HORSE RACES AND RODEOS You can risk what little money you have at the **Hipódromo de las Américas.** The entrance fee to the track is about 30¢ and, once you're inside, you only need 60¢ to gamble. There are plenty of expensive bars and restaurants at the track that will be happy to help you celebrate your win with a cold $3 beer. The ponies run Tuesday, Thursday, and Friday 5:30 PM–10:30 PM and Saturday and Sunday 2:45–8. *Av. Industria Militar, tel. 5/557–41–00. From Metro Polanco, walk 2 blocks north to Av. Ejército Nacional to catch the DEFENSA NACIONAL pesero.*

Good places for pickup soccer games:

- *Parque Estadio, near Metro Hospital General*
- *General Parque Les Venadas, near Metro División del Norte*
- *Parque Pilares, Col. del Valle*

Rodeos are held Sunday at noon in two locations in the D.F.: **Lienzo Charro de la Villa** (Metro Indios Verdes) and **Lienzo del Charro** (Av. Constituyentes 500; from Metro Chapultepec, take any pesero that passes by). For more rodeo information call 5/277–87–06 or 5/277–87–10, weekdays 9–5.

BULLFIGHTING Brought to Mexico by Hernán Cortés, the tradition of bullfighting continues today. Although the very best matadors perform in the fall, an off-season fight with a novice matador is still worth a trip to the arena, especially if you've never seen a bullfight before. **Plaza México** is the largest bullfighting arena in the world. Fights are on Sundays at 4 PM, and ticket prices range from $1 to $11.50. Seats on the sunny side (*sol*) tend to be cheaper and rowdier than the seats on the shady side (*sombra*). Most large hotels offer $25 bullfighting tours. The ticket window is open Thursday, Friday, and Saturday 9:30–1 and 3:30–7. On Sunday (fight day) it's open from 9:30 until the third bull dies. Get there about an hour before the fight. *Augusto Rodin 241, Ciudad de los Deportes, tel. 5/563–39–59. Take southbound INSURGENTES SUR/SAN ANGEL pesero on Insurgentes Sur.*

JAI ALAI The skill and coordination required to play this lightning-fast Basque handball game (the fist-sized balls have been clocked at more than 110 mph) draws crowds of specta-tors. Of course, they aren't so awestruck so as to forget to place bets which—at about a dollar a match—are as innocuous as they come. You can check out the action at **Frontón México** (NW corner of Plaza de la República) 6 PM–1 AM every day except Fridays and Sundays. Women's matches are played at **Frontón Metropolitano** (Bahía de Todos los Santos 190) Monday–Satur-day 4–10.

Near Mexico City

XOCHIMILCO

More than 700 years ago, the Valley of Mexico was almost entirely underwater. Completely surrounded by high volcanic mountains and lacking a natural subsoil drainage mechanism for rainwater and its plentiful underground springs, the valley was almost completely devoid of dry land upon which to settle. This shortage of *tierra firme* prompted the Xochimilcos to build a series of *chinampas* (floating islands of mud, reeds, and grasses) and anchor them to the lakebed with long poles. As the natural grasses and reeds on the islands began to grow, their roots extended into the water, becoming permanently affixed to the lakebed. As more and more of these floating islands took root, the lake was slowly transformed into a maze of canals. Even now, after six centuries of conquest, colonialism, and change, Xochimilco, which lies 21 kilometers south of Mexico City's Zócalo, remains a testament to this ingenious innovation.

Xochimilco, with its central plaza and market, feels like a small Mexican village rather than a group of drifting islands. The gardens are a favorite picnic spot of middle-class families, but visitors are rare during the week. Sunday is the busiest day, when you'll be squashed by boats on all sides. Enterprising boat owners pick out tourists and try to persuade them to commit to their *lancha* (flat-bottom boat) before they've even seen the water. Although the government sets prices, you can usually negotiate. A float through the gardens lasts about two hours and costs $7–$10 for two or more people. Bring your own lunch, since the canals are perfect for a floating picnic.

COMING AND GOING The easiest way to get to Xochimilco is to take the Metro to Tasqueña (end of line 2). The RUTA 36 pesero goes from the station to the center of Xochimilco, near the market and close to the canals. Alternatively, you can take the tren ligero from the Metro and get off at the last station. After you exit the station, walk south on Cuauhtémoc to José María Morelos; make a left and you'll be in the town center. Either way, the trip from Tasqueña to Xochimilco takes about an hour.

TEOTIHUACAN

By the 12th century, when the Aztecs migrated to the Valley of Mexico, Teotihuacán had already been abandoned for more than 500 years. Awestruck by the massive stone temples jutting high above the lush, green valley floor, the Aztecs named the mysterious ruins "Place of the Gods."

More than a millennium has passed since the Teotihuacanos inhabited the beautiful stone city, and information about the ancient civilization remains scarce. Archaeologists have managed only to divide the history of the site into four distinct stages. What was to become the greatest city of Mesoamerica began in a rather humble way, consisting of a few farming villages in the center of the Valle de Teotihuacán around 900 BC. Gradually the villages grew into larger settlements, increasing their wealth through mining and trading obsidian with the neighboring settlements. By around 100 BC, Teotihuacán was a prosperous, urban society controlled by an ecclesiastic oligarchy.

The powerful union of religious and political authorities made it possible to mobilize a labor force capable of building two massive pyramids: the **Pirámide del Sol** (Pyramid of the Sun) and the **Pirámide de la Luna** (Pyramid of the Moon). By around AD 300, archaeologists believe, Teotihuacán had reached the apogee of its power; its empire spread outward from the valley across Mesoamerica. The Teotihuacanos' expansionist thirst was temporarily quenched, and they turned their attentions to beautifying their capital city. It is from this period that the most impressive artwork dates. Around AD 650, the city began to wane, although no one is quite sure why. Buildings eroded and the city was slowly abandoned. Eventually, Teotihuacán was pillaged by outsiders, forcing the remaining residents to migrate elsewhere and leaving the once-great city to be enveloped by the surrounding vegetation.

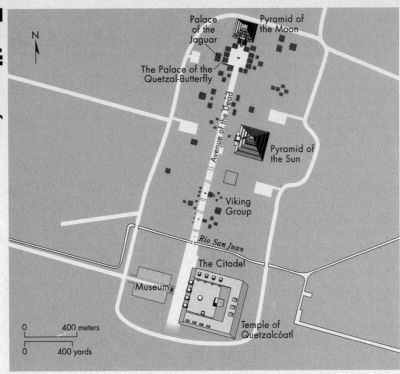

The Palace of the
Quetzal-Butterfly

Palace
of the
Jaguar

Pyramid of
the Moon

Avenue of the Dead

Pyramid of
the Sun

Viking
Group

Rio San Juan

The Citadel

Museum

Temple of
Quetzalcóatl

N

0   400 meters

0   400 yards

Cleared of foliage, the ruins have been groomed for easy tourist access. After you enter the archaeological zone and cross the main thoroughfare, **Avenida de los Muertos** (Avenue of the Dead), you come to the **Ciudadela** (Citadel), a huge square with apartment complexes and tem-

If you're prone to sunburn, bring a hat and sunscreen to Teotihuacán. The sun beams down hot on the valley, and there isn't any smog to filter it. However, even during summer a chilly wind blows, so wear layers. A water bottle is also a good idea, because the climbing is hard work, especially at this altitude.

ples. The detail and workmanship of the artwork here have led archaeologists to speculate that they were once the living quarters of ruling priests. At the far end of the citadel is the **Templo de Quetzalcoatl,** made up of two pyramids; the one on top is a reconstruction of the older pyramid below. The facade of the older one bears bas-relief carvings of the plumed serpent Quetzalcoatl with a lion's mane around his head and the square-faced rain god Tlaloc. To get a better view of the sculptures, go around to the walkway between the two buildings. Halfway down the Avenue of the Dead is the enormous, unmistakable **Pirámide del Sol;** rising more than 65 meters high, it's the third-largest pyramid in the world. The view of lush green mountains and white fluffy clouds, after 248 steps, is breathtaking, and so is the climb. Discovered in 1962, the **Palacio de Quetzalpapálotl** was probably once the home of someone who held great power in Teotihuacán society. The palace has now been almost fully reconstructed. Some of the butterflies

carved into the columns still have their original beady obsidian eyes, which gaze, as they have for centuries, over the beautiful open plazas of the city. Just west of the palace is the **Jaguar Palace,** with reconditioned red-and-green murals showing jaguars dressed in feathers and performing various human activities. These same brilliant reds and greens, as well as blacks and yellows, once covered much of the city. A thorough tour of the ruins would take an entire day, but you can see a lot, if not every pyramid, in three or four hours. *Admission: about $4. Open daily 8–5.*

COMING AND GOING Autobuses Teotihuacán departs from the far north end of the Autobuses del Norte terminal in Mexico City about every hour all day. The bus takes an hour ($2)
and drops you off at the main entrance, Puerta 1.

FOOD Just outside Puerta 1, a series of fondas sell comida corrida for about $2, in addition
to the usual tacos and tortas. Although no food or drink is officially permitted in the archaeological zone (except in the overpriced restaurant inside the complex), no one searches bags at
the entrance, and the garbage cans on the site are filled with food wrappers and drink bottles.
It's doubtful anyone will complain if you pull out some bread and cheese, as long as you take
your trash with you.

TULA

The small city of Tula, known in ancient times as Tollan, is a favorite retreat for day-trippers. If
you stay overnight, you'll escape the frenzy of Mexico City but not the air pollution, which is
still present 70 or so kilometers north of the D.F. Tula's main attraction is the archaeological
site displaying remnants of the Toltec civilization's capital city, complete with ball courts, pyramids, and a palace. Ancient Tula, thought to have been occupied from AD 900 to AD 1150, was
inhabited by as many as 40,000 people at its height. The reigning symbols of the site are the
atlantes—imposing, 4-meter-high warriors, some of which were used for roof supports. Hundreds of these once brightly painted statues and reliefs are dedicated to Quetzalcoatl, the
plumed serpent god. The site itself is on the outskirts of town, some 3 kilometers from the bus
station and best reached by taxi for about $2. Alternatively, you can catch a TEPETITLAN or
ACTOPAN pesero. They leave from Tula's zócalo and zoom by the ruins, so make sure you tell the
driver you'd like to be tossed out near "Las Pirámides." The ruins are open Tuesday–Sunday
9:30–4:30. Admission is about $4.50, free on Sundays.

COMING AND GOING Autotransportes **Valle de Mezquital** departs Mexico City from the
Autobuses del Norte terminal (sala 8) for Tula every 30 minutes. The direct first-class buses
($5) are far more comfortable than the second-class buses, which are only 80¢ cheaper. Sec-
ond-class buses leave twice as often, but they stop so frequently you might as well wait an extra
15 minutes to catch the next direct bus. First-class buses run between 6 AM and 8 PM, while
second-class buses are in service between 4 AM and 11 PM.

WHERE TO SLEEP Directly east of the bus station is the **Motel Lizbeth** (Ocampo 200, tel.
773/2-00-45), a clean, modern, and expensive outfit; singles are $33, doubles $36. Downtown opposite the cathedral is the **Hotel Cuellar** (5 de Mayo 23, tel. 773/2-04-42), a smaller
hotel where singles cost about $14, doubles $18.

CENTRAL CITIES 3

By Michele Back and Cassie Coleman

Many travelers pass through the region south of Mexico City on their way to somewhere else, but it is a destination in its own right for anyone who has an interest in Mesoamerican or Spanish-American history, appreciates colonial architecture, or thrives on hiking or volcano climbing. The early inhabitants of this region came from a number of distinct civilizations, leaving behind evidence of greatness, such as the pyramids of Xochicalco, the murals of Cacaxtla, and the Great Pyramid of Cholula.

Some of Mexico's greatest colonial and ecclesiastic architecture is here, including an abundance of churches dating from the Conquest, such as the grandiose cathedrals of Cuernavaca and Puebla, the Ex-Convento de San Francisco in Tlaxcala, and the baroque cathedral of Acatepec, where the faces of the cherubs painted on the chapel ceiling are sun-bathed brown rather than porcelain white. The War of Independence and the Revolution of 1910 are memorialized throughout the region: Cuautla, in Morelos, was the site of one of the most dramatic battles in the War of Independence, and it was in the town of Ayala that Zapata issued his 1910 declaration of land reform. In 1862, Puebla withstood a decisive battle in the war against the French invaders led by Napoleon III—the battle is commemorated annually by the city's residents on May 5.

Travelers nowadays practice their verb conjugations at the Spanish-language schools that dot the colonial city of Cuernavaca. Tlaxcala's relaxed pace continuously draws urban Mexicans into its sepia-colored hills, but the city isn't boring—the many students attending university in here infuse it with a hip intensity. The outdoorsy crowd is drawn by nearby waterfalls and volcanoes. Puebla is packed with jaw-dropping colonial architecture and tilework as well as fascinating historical sites, and is the home of the famous *mole poblano* (the original chile and chocolate sauce). Mexico's center for silver artisanry is Taxco, a breezy city with a Mediterranean feel. And although Chilpancingo isn't on the must-see list of most travelers, the capital of the state of Guerrero is a pleasant university city, providing a welcome change after the intense tourism of Taxco.

Cuernavaca
The continually flowering trees and sunny climate of Cuernavaca have earned it the nickname "City of Eternal Spring." Only 72 kilometers south of Mexico City, this capital of the state of Morelos has its share of traffic and pollution, but what brings visitors here are the landscaped gardens, cathedrals, colonial plazas, and red-roofed haciendas hidden behind high walls. Wealthy *chilangos*, as residents of Mexico City are called, have been building lavish vacation homes here since the days of Cortés. Most foreign visitors are attracted by the visible traces of Cuernavaca's history or come to study in one of the city's language schools (*see* Schools, *below*). Despite its well-deserved popular-

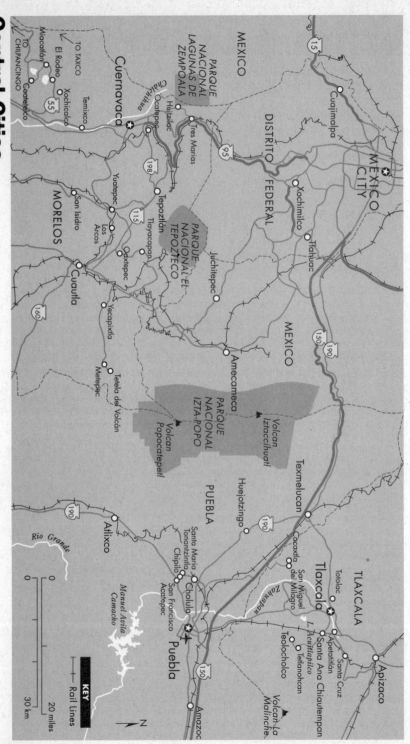

Central Cities

KEY
╫ Rail Lines

86

ity, however, Cuernavaca is not all that expensive. You'll pay more for lodging (only two hotels have decent single rooms for less than $15), but you can eat cheaply if you stick to the lunch specials many restaurants offer.

The original inhabitants of the valley of Morelos, where Cuernavaca is now located, built pyramids within the city and in nearby Tepotzlán. They also constructed a more extensive religious and astronomical center in Xochicalco—both Tepotzlán and Xochicalco can be explored from Cuernavaca. This region was conquered by the Aztecs in the late 1300s, and the Spanish, led by Hernán Cortés, arrived little more than a century later.

The original name for Cuernavaca was Cuauhnáhuac, Nahuatl for "place near the woods," but after the Spaniards burned the city to the ground in the 1520s, they changed the name to the more easily pronounced (for them) "Cuernavaca."

Despite the city's history of foreign domination, Cuernavacans aren't ones to be pushed around. The state of Morelos, where revolutionary leader Emiliano Zapata and his movement for agrarian reform were born, led the southern front of the Mexican Revolution in the early 1900s. Today, the activist students of the University of Morelos in Cuernavaca protest government corruption alongside *campesinos* (peasants) in the city's *zócalo* (main square).

BASICS

AMERICAN EXPRESS The AmEx office is in the **Marin** travel agency, in the Las Plazas shopping center, across Guerrero from the zócalo. They sell and exchange traveler's checks, and cardholders can cash personal checks or have their mail held for them here. *Edificio Las Plazas, Local 13, Cuernavaca, Morelos, CP 62000, México, tel. 73/14–22–66. AmEx services available weekdays 9–2 and 4–6, Sat. 10–1.*

CASAS DE CAMBIO Casas de cambio are scarce in Cuernavaca and most close at 6 PM. **Gesta** (Morrow, at I. Comonfort, tel. 73/18–37–50), near the budget lodging area, is open weekdays 9–2 and 4–6. **Banamex** (Arteaga, at Matamoros, tel. 73/14–04–03) changes money Monday–Saturday 10–noon and has ATMs. The **Hotel Colonial** (*see* Where to Sleep, *below*) changes money at all hours for guests and occasionally for desperate non-guests who grovel well.

EMERGENCIES Dial 06 from any phone in Cuernavaca for police, fire, or ambulance service.

LAUNDRY Only about two blocks from the budget hotel area, **Tintorería Morelos** charges $3 to clean 3½ kilos of laundry and will return your clothes the same day if you bring them in before 10 AM. They also rival the tourist office in providing information about Cuernavaca and surrounding areas. *Matamoros 406, tel. 73/12–44–85. Open Mon.–Sat. 9–8.*

MAIL The post office will hold mail sent to you at the following address for up to 10 days: Lista de Correos, Administración 1, Cuernavaca, Morelos, CP 62001, México. You can send and receive faxes, telexes, and telegrams at the **telecommunications office** (tel. 73/18–58–62) in the same building. *SW cnr of Plaza de Armas, tel. 73/12–43–79. Open weekdays 8–7, Sat. 9–1.*

PHONES Cuernavaca's zócalo is graced with many Ladatel phones. Cash calls can be made from **Caseta Morelos**, which charges about $3 per minute to the States. *Pasaje Galeana 4, tel. 73/18–30–31. In a minimall across the street from Plaza de Armas. Open daily 9–9.*

Conspiracy theories run wild in Cuernavaca's casetas de larga distancia (long distance phone offices), where collect calls are associated with the CIA, national inflation, and Armageddon—no one will place a collect call for you.

SCHOOLS Cuernavaca's many language schools draw students from all over the world. **Cetlalic,** with an emphasis on social justice education as well as language acquisition, stands out. Speakers, films, and trips complement the small, intensive classes, and students can room with local families. *Carranza 10, Col. La Carolina. Tel. 73/13–35–79. Mailing address: Aptdo. Postal 1-201, Cuernavaca, Morelos, CP 62001, México.*

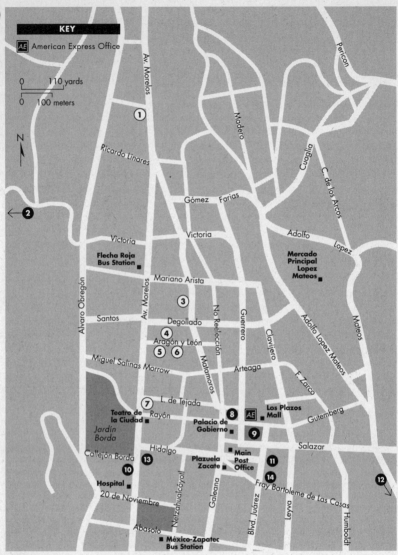

Cuernavaca

KEY

AE American Express Office

0 ——— 110 yards
0 ——— 100 meters

N

Av. Morelos

Madero

Pericon

Cuaglia

C. de los Arcos

Ricardo Linares

Gómez   Farias

Adolfo

Lopez

Victoria

Victoria

**Flecha Roja
Bus Station** ■

**Mercado
Principal
Lopez
Mateos** ■

Mariano Arista

Adolfo Lopez Mateos

Mateos

Alvaro Obregón

Santos

Av. Morelos

Degollado

No Reelección

Guerrero

Clavijero

③

④

⑤ ⑥

Aragón y León

Miguel Salinas Morrow

Matamoros

Arteaga

F. Zarco

Gutemberg

L. de Tejada

⑦

**Teatro de
la Ciudad** ■

Rayón

⑧ AE

**Los Plazos
Mall**

*Jardín
Borda*

**Palacio de
Gobierno** ■

⑨

Salazar

Callejón Borda

⑬

Hidalgo

⑩

Hospital ■

20 de Noviembre

Nezahualcóyotl

Galeana

**Plazuela
Zacate** ■

**Main
Post
Office** ■

⑪

⑭

Fray Bartoleme de las Casas

Blvd. Juárez

Leyva

Humboldt

⑫

Abasolo

■ **México-Zapatec
Bus Station**

Sights ●

Ayuntamiento de
Cuernavaca, **10**
Casa del Olvido, **12**
Catedral de la
Asunción, **13**
Jardín de Arte
Luis Betanzos, **14**
Jardín Juárez, **8**
Palacio de
Cortés, **11**
Plaza de Armas, **9**
San Antón Falls, **2**

Lodging ○

Casa de Huéspedes
la China Poblana, **6**
Hotel América, **4**
Hotel Colonial, **5**
Hotel España, **7**
Hotel
Los Canarios, **1**
Hotel Roma, **3**

Cuauhnáhuac Escuela Cuernavaca is also recommended by students. Classes have no more than four students each, and there is a swimming pool and a volleyball court on the campus. *Morelos Sur 1414, Col. Chipitlán, tel. 73/12–36–73 or 18–92–75. Mailing address: Aptdo. Postal 5-26, Cuernavaca, Morelos, CP 62051, México. U.S. contact: Marcia Snell, tel. 800/245–9335.*

VISITOR INFORMATION The state tourist office has pamphlets about Cuernavaca, the state of Morelos, and some language schools and sells an excellent map of Morelos with a guide book for $5. The staff speaks only Spanish. For tourist information in English, as well as info on day trips and nightspots, talk to Joel or Alejandro at Tintorería Morelos (*see* Laundry, *above*). *Morelos Sur 802, tel. 73/14–39–20. Take* RUTA *4 combi down Galeana to Himno Nacional, then walk west 1 block. Open weekdays 9–3 and 5–8.*

COMING AND GOING

Cuernavaca has four bus stations. The largest station is **Flecha Roja** (Morelos 503, at Arista), two blocks from the budget lodging area. The **Estrella Blanca** line (tel. 73/12–81–90) departs from this station has service to Mexico City every 15 minutes. The ride takes more than an hour and costs about $5. First-class *directo* (direct) buses to Acapulco ($17, 3½ hrs) leave every two hours; more luxury bumps the price up to $21 or $23. The *ordinario* (indirect) buses to Acapulco ($16.50, 5 hrs) leave every hour during the day and stop in Chilpancingo ($10, 3 hrs). Buses to Taxco ($3.50, 2½ hrs) depart every 15 minutes until 10 PM. One bus leaves at 4:15 PM for Nuevo Laredo ($57, 20 hrs). The bus station provides luggage storage.

The **Estrella Roja** station (Galeana 401, at Cuauhtemoczin, tel. 73/18–59–34) has buses to Cuautla ($2, 1 hr) every 10 minutes 6:15 AM–10:15 PM; transfer in Cuautla for Oaxaca. Buses to Puebla ($7, 3½ hrs) leave every hour 5 AM–7 PM. The walk from the station to the budget hotels (seven long blocks) isn't bad, or you can take any CENTRO combi on Morelos to Aragón y Léon.

The remaining two bus stations are less significant. **México-Zacatepec Autos Pullman de Morelos** (Abasolo 106, at Netzahualcoyotl, tel. 73/14–36–50), a few blocks from the zócalo, serves Mexico City, Zacatepec, Xoxocotla, Jojutla, and a few other towns near Puebla. Probably the only reason you'd use this station would be to get to Xochicalco (*see* Near Cuernavaca, *below*); buses to Coatlán or Miocatlán will drop you off at the Xochicalco crossroads. **Estrella de Oro** (Morelos Sur 900, tel. 73/12–30–55) is a *de paso* station, which means buses only stop here en route to somewhere else. As a result, departure times are sketchy. To reach the center of town from here, take any CENTRO combi up Morelos.

GETTING AROUND

Exploring Cuernavaca is not difficult; the budget hotel zone, major sights, and most of the bus stations are within walking distance of each other. The zócalo, at the center of town, is actually made up of two plazas: the Jardín Juárez and the Plaza de Armas. The main streets in Cuernavaca are Morelos, with northbound traffic, and Obregón and Matamoros/Galeana, on either side of Morelos, both of which allow only southbound traffic.

BY BUS Colectivos, also called *rutas* or *combis*, are the major means of daytime travel within Cuernavaca. Drivers of these white, squared-off minibuses cram in as many passengers as possible. The name of the final destination is scrawled in whitewash on the front window of the combi, but routes vary, so ask if it will get you where you want to go before boarding.

BY TAXI You'll have to travel by taxi if you plan to sample Cuernavaca's nightlife; combis don't run after 9 PM. The white Datsuns, VWs, or other small cars can usually be hailed on busy streets, major crossroads, and near tourist attractions. Taxis don't have meters, so fares should be negotiated *before* you get in. Generally the fare within the *centro* (downtown) is a little over $2, about $1 more for outlying neighborhoods. Fares can rise to $5 late at night or when it's raining.

WHERE TO SLEEP

Cuernavaca fills up on the weekends, so make sure to call for a reservation if you plan to arrive on a Friday or weekend. Prices at some hotels (usually only the larger ones) rise above the prices listed here during high season (June–August and December–February), so it's a good idea to shop around during those months. The budget lodging area is along and around Aragón y León, a few blocks south of the Flecha Roja bus station and north of the zócalo. The word "budget" should be taken with a grain of salt—most of the hotels charge between $15 and $30 for a double. If the places below are booked, try **Hotel Las Hortensias** (Hidalgo 22, tel. 73/18–52–65), which has a pleasant courtyard and lumpy beds. A single here is $21 and a double is $28. Many of the city's language schools (*see* Schools, *above*) give students the option of living with a family; you might be able to set up such an arrangement if you're planning an extended stay.

➤ UNDER $15 • **Casa de Huéspedes la China Poblana**. Hidden behind the restaurant of the same name, this hotel is clean and spacious and a bargain at $10 for a single, $12 for a double, both with private bath. The architecture is unspectacular, but that's not what you're here for. Arrive early, because there are only nine rooms. *Aragón y León 110, btw Morelos and Matamoros, tel. 73/12–37–12. 3 blocks north of zócalo and 3 blocks south of Flecha Roja station. Luggage storage.*

Hotel América. This hotel wins an award for prices, but no blue ribbons for the small, dark, musty rooms. The communal bathrooms aren't too bad. Singles cost $9.50, doubles $13. The clientele consists mostly of young men. *Aragón y León 111, tel. 73/18–61–27. About 3 blocks north of zócalo. 40 rooms, none with bath. Luggage storage.*

➤ UNDER $20 • **Hotel Roma**. The sunny courtyard with palm trees is more inviting than the clean and basic rooms, which have tiny bathrooms. Singles and doubles cost $15, and quads are only $22. *Matamoros 405, tel. 73/18–87–78. 1 block east of Flecha Roja station; 4 blocks north of zócalo. 40 rooms, all with bath. Luggage storage.*

➤ UNDER $25 • **Hotel Colonial**. Smack in the middle of the budget lodging area, this hotel is a step above the competition. The large, clean rooms have high ceilings, flowers, and wrought-iron terraces. The staff of young women is friendly and helpful and there is a rule of silence after 10 PM. This hotel is popular with Mexican and foreign travelers alike. Singles cost $15–$20, depending on the size of the room. Doubles go for $23, triples $27. *Aragón y León 104, tel. 73/18–64–14. 3 blocks south of Flecha Roja station; 3 blocks north of zócalo. 14 rooms, all with bath. Luggage storage, wheelchair access.*

➤ UNDER $40 • **Hotel España**. The hotel lives up to its name, with Spanish arches, patterned tiles, and palms. On the first floor are a restaurant serving Spanish food, the reception area, and a small lounge; the second- and third-floor rooms are clustered around a courtyard with potted flowers. The rooms are clean, but the furniture is a bit worn. Singles cost about $22, doubles $32. The noise level can be bothersome in the rooms facing the street. The guests here are mostly Mexican businesspeople. *Morelos 200, at Rayón, tel. 73/18–67–44. 3 blocks west of zócalo; 5 blocks south of Flecha Roja station. 24 rooms, all with bath. Reservations advised.*

Hotel Los Canarios. With 131 rooms in this hotel, you have a good chance of finding a vacancy, even on busy weekends. The rooms, which go for $18 a single, $37 a double, don't compare with those at the Colonial, but the two swimming pools, restaurant, and happy hour at the bar compensate somewhat. Unfortunately, this hotel is further away from the zócalo than the others—a 15-minute walk or a short combi ride. If you're staying for a week, pay in advance and receive a 20% discount. *Morelos 713, tel. 73/13–00–00. 2 long blocks north of Flecha Roja station, just past Virgen de Guadalupe statue. 131 rooms, all with bath. Laundry, luggage storage, wheelchair access.*

FOOD

The cheaper restaurants in Cuernavaca serve a mix of *antojitos* (appetizers) and Euro-American tourist foods like burgers and fries. Most are found on the side streets near the zócalo and close around 5 or 7 PM, so eat early. Later, you can rent a seat in a café on the zócalo for the price of a soda or beer—try **La Parroquia, El Universal,** or **Los Arcos.** Two restaurants in the centro serve vegetarian *comidas corridas* (pre-prepared lunch specials) for about $4: **100/100 Integral** (Hidalgo 208, tel. 73/12–56–18), just south of the zócalo, features the owner's amazing lounge act as well. **Naturiza** (Alvaro Obregón 327, tel. 73/12–46–26) is northwest of the Flecha Roja station, near the corner of Ricardo Linares. The **Mercado Principal** (central market) is the standard place for cheap eats, but this one has a reputation for being particularly unhygienic. Cuernavaca also has several *panaderías* (bakeries), but good luck finding coffee before 8:30 AM.

➤ UNDER $5 • **La China Poblana.** Close to most budget hotels, this restaurant serves a good breakfast and comida corrida. The place is unexciting but clean and breezy, and the staff is friendly. Customers are mostly workers, young families, and the elderly—all of whom appreciate a hearty meal for less than $3.50. *Aragón y León 110, btw Morelos and Matamoros, tel. 73/12–37–12. Open Mon.–Sat. 8–5.*

Pollo y Más. Cheap, tasty, cafeteria-style food is served quickly here. Enchiladas, chiles rellenos, and the specialty, a quarter of a roasted chicken, all come with rice, beans, and tortillas for $2.50. *Galeana 4, across from zócalo, no phone. Open daily 7 AM–9:30 PM. Wheelchair access.*

Restaurante Las Casuelas. This restaurant serves only delicious antojitos. The $4 *menú del día* (daily special) includes dessert, and the chiles rellenos and *jugo de guayaba* (guava juice) are fabulous. Vegetarians will do fine here, too. *Galeana, at Abasolo, tel. 73/14–17–79. Open Tues.–Sun. 10–7.*

La Tarterie. This restaurant serves a $4 comida corrida, espresso, and a large variety of desserts in an umbrellaed outdoor dining area that faces a little plaza. A breakfast of fried eggs or not-too-tender steak with beans, tortillas, fresh-squeezed orange juice, and coffee is $5. Vegetarians will enjoy the $1.50 soups and $2 salads. *Fray Bartolomé de las Casas 103, tel. 73/12–41–52. In Plazuela Zacate (a.k.a. Plaza 2 de Mayo de 1812). Open daily 9–6. Wheelchair access.*

➤ UNDER $10 • **Restaurant El Salto.** "The Waterfall" is a bit off the beaten track. In the village of San Antón near the waterfall for which it's named, this restaurant is filled with *cuernavaquenses* (residents of Cuernavaca) noisily eating and drinking. The menu includes a decent selection of fish, chicken, and game dishes, served in pottery made in the village. The most expensive dish is pigeon for two ($9); recommended are garlic soup ($4), the cactus tamale ($3), and the enchiladas with *carnitas* (rendered pork) and beans ($6). *Bajada del Salto 31, San Antón, tel. 73/18–12–19. Take RUTA 4 combi on Morelos to El Salto de San Antón. Open daily 10–8.*

The bowl-sized rum-and-tequila "Convento" at El Salto in San Antón will set you back $4 and most of your faculties.

➤ UNDER $15 • **Los Pasteles de Vienes.** Continental cuisine and European-style pastries are served in an elegant setting, where lace curtains and jazz music float on the breeze. The restaurant is around the corner from the Teatro O'Campo, which makes it a favorite spot for an after-theater cappuccino. It's also a meeting place for couples and students. The food, especially the breakfast pastries, is excellent and ranges in price from $2 to $12. Recommended dishes include veal cutlet in a wine and mushroom sauce for $9, asparagus stuffed with ham in béarnaise sauce for $7, and spinach crêpes for $6. *Lerdo de Tejada 302, at I. Comonfort, tel. 73/14–34–04. Open daily 8 AM–10 PM.*

WORTH SEEING

The zócalo is the heart of Cuernavaca. It is made up of the **Plaza de Armas,** where you can unwind to the relaxing sounds of the fountain, and the more lively **Jardín Juárez,** the oldest park in the city. It's also near a number of attractions that can easily be seen in one day. Other sites, particularly the Casa del Olvido, San Antón Falls, and the Pirámide de Teopanzolco, are in outlying *colonias* (neighborhoods), so you'll have to plan to take some combis. Keep in mind that many museums and historical sites are closed on Monday.

AYUNTAMIENTO DE CUERNAVACA Also known as the Palacio Municipal, the Ayuntamiento displays murals by Salvador Tarazona that depict Cuernavaca's history and scenes of the Tlahuica civilization. Within the same building is the **Museo Municipal de la Cultura,** which has temporary exhibits by local artists. *Morelos 199, at Callejón Borda. Admission free. Open weekdays 8–8.*

CASA DEL OLVIDO This adobe house once belonged to Emperor Maximilian. It's called the Casa del Olvido (House of Forgetfulness) because there was no room in the house for Carlota, his wife; instead, a small house in the garden was home to his lover, La India Bonita. Today the little house is the **Museo de Medicina Tradicional,** with exhibits about the medicinal and religious uses of plants and herbs in Mexico since pre-Columbian times. Many of the plants described in the museum can be found in the adjoining botanical garden. *Matamoros 200, Col. Acapantzinga. Take RUTA 6 combi from Degollado and No Reelección. Admission free. Open Tues.–Sun. 9–5.*

CATEDRAL DE LA ASUNCION The high walls of the cathedral enclose a convent and three chapels dating from the early 16th to the late 19th centuries. The **Capilla Abierta de San José** is the oldest structure, built by Hernán Cortés in 1523. Its design, which leaves the priest covered by a roof and the faithful exposed to the open air, is said to have been chosen so the indigenous people, used to worshipping outside, would feel more at home. The **Templo de la Asunción Gloriosa de la Virgen María,** the largest structure, was completed in 1552. Newly uncovered remnants of early 17th-century frescoes supposedly painted here by a Japanese immigrant, depict the crucifixion of Christian missionaries in Japan. The **Templo de la Tercera Orden de San Francisco** took 13 years to build, due to the elaborate ornamentation of its carved surfaces. The newest structure is the **Capilla de Carmen,** which dates from the late 19th century. Look for the *retablos* (altarpieces) on the walls. There's a "mariachi mass" (*see box* on Liberation Theology, *below*) on Sundays at 11 AM. *Hidalgo, at Morelos, 3 blocks west of zócalo. Admission free. Open daily 7–2 and 4–8.*

JARDIN BORDA The mansion, landscaped grounds, and botanical gardens here were first built by Manuel de la Borda as a retreat for his father. They became a symbol of imperial Mexico when the estate was turned into the summer retreat of Emperor Maximilian and his wife Carlota in 1865. The original 100 or so varieties of fruit trees and ornamental plants still flourish, and the refurbished front rooms of the mansion now house the **Centro de Arte Jardín Borda,** where you can see the work of local artists. *Morelos, at Hidalgo. Admission: $1. Open Tues.–Sun. 10–5:30.*

MERCADO PRINCIPAL LOPEZ MATEOS The dirty, crowded, and noisy maze that is Cuernavaca's central market offers a glimpse of the people of Cuernavaca and surrounding *pueblos* (towns) engaged in the barter and haggling of everyday life. Mounds of chiles tower over a woman selling *huitlacoche,* a fungus that grows on corn and is considered a delicacy. Of particular interest is the section where eloquent *herbolarios* (herb vendors) guarantee a cure for whatever ails you. *López Mateos. From zócalo, north 4 blocks on Guerrero, right into the covered mall of vendors just before Degollado, and across pedestrian bridge to market below. Open daily about 6–4:30.*

PALACIO DE CORTES This imposing building, built by a conquered people, has been a potent symbol of power throughout Cuernavaca's history. When construction began in 1522, it followed a simple plan, but as Cortés gained wealth, influence, titles—and a wife—the palace grew. It later passed into the hands of the crown and, during the war for independence, was used as a prison for revolutionaries José María Morelos, Ignacio López Rayón, and Nicolás Bravo. It was abandoned during the Revolution of 1910; after the dust cleared, the palace became the offices of the municipal government.

Today, the palace houses a **Diego Rivera mural** and the **Museo Cuauhnáhuac.** The museum traces the history of Morelos from the time of the first pre-Hispanic settlers to today. The mural on the second floor merits a visit, as does the **Jardín de Arte Luis Betanzos,** to the right of the palace, where indigenous artists sell their handiwork. You can buy most anything here, from velvet paintings to beautiful silver work. *Juárez, at Hidalgo, across from SE cnr of the zócalo. Admission: $4, free Sun. Open Tues.–Sun. 10–5.*

PIRAMIDE DE TEOPANZOLCO Pyramid may be an overstatement, and the three flat mounds here haven't been reconstructed, but the trip to these pre-Columbian ruins takes only about 15 minutes. A stone wall surrounds the pyramids, making them seem like animals in a zoo. *Admission: $3.50. Take RUTA 19 combi from east side of Mercado Principal. Open daily 10–4:30.*

SAN ANTON FALLS Despite the fact that this 40-meter waterfall cascades into a brown pool, it's still beautiful. The barrio of San Antón, where it's located, is noted for its terra-cotta pottery, which is shaped into pots and figurines of the Virgin Mary. While you're here, stop for

Liberation Theology in Cuernavaca

The Sermon on the Mount, a lecture on ethics delivered by Jesus, is at the center of liberation theology. This Christian doctrine calls for church involvement in earthly as well as spiritual affairs, specifically in the empowerment of the poor and the struggle for social justice. Many of the principles of the movement were adopted into Catholic dogma at the Second Vatican Council (1962–1965), which instituted mass in the vernacular and stressed greater lay involvement with church services. More recently, Pope John Paul II has condemned liberation theology as smacking of Marxism and justifying priests' involvement in armed rebellion. Nevertheless, a number of Mexican bishops continue to hold to its tenets. Most prominent among them is Bishop Samuel Ruíz of the Chiapan city of San Cristóbal de las Casas, who for many years has supported the demands of indigenous people for land and democracy in that state. Recently, he has played a major role in negotiations between the Zapatista rebels and the Mexican government.

Cuernavaca has a strong tradition of liberation theology as well. In 1957, Bishop Sergio Méndez Arceo commissioned the modification of the city's beloved 16th-century Catedral de la Asunción. The changes moved the figure of Jesus Christ so that, when giving the mass, the priest no longer had to put his back to the faithful in order to face Christ. Concerned about the increasing irrelevance of Catholicism to the lives of the local people, Bishop Méndez Arceo instituted mass in the vernacular (Spanish instead of Latin) five years before the Vatican allowed it. He also began using the music of the people to accompany religious services, and the "mariachi mass" is still held every Sunday in the cathedral.

Today, the Cuernavaca Center for International Dialogue on Development (CCIDD), a nonprofit educational organization, offers one- and two-week programs for those who want to know more about liberation theology and the effects of injustice and economic development on the lives of impoverished Mexicans. Ray Plankey, a Catholic lay minister who worked with Bishop Méndez Arceo, has run the center since 1977. Write to CCIDD at 9297 Siempre Viva Rd., Suite MX, 021–063, San Diego, CA 92173, or call the center in Cuernavaca at 73/12–65–64.

a meal at Restaurant El Salto (*see* Food, *above*), a half block up the street from the waterfall. *Bajada del Salto, Barrio de San Antón. Take* RUTA *4 combi from Morelos. Admission: $1, free Sun. and holidays. Open daily 8–6.*

FESTIVALS

The **Feria de la Primavera** is the biggest in Cuernavaca. Since its inception in 1865 by horti-culturists out to promote the local flower industry, the festival has blossomed every year, usu-ally during the last weeks in April or the first two weeks in May, featuring open-air concerts and other events. In the nearby town of Ocotepec, **Semana Santa** (Holy Week) is celebrated with traditional dances, passion plays, and the presentation of altars to the dead. Also near Cuer-navaca, in Acapancingo, the **Fiesta of San Isidro Labrador** is celebrated every May 15 to bring rain. Oxen wreathed in flowers are paraded through the streets, followed by lots of dancing, drinking, and eating.

SHOPPING

Cuernavaca is popular with tourists, and the prices are jacked up accordingly. However, the area is known for the quality of its *huaraches* (woven leather sandals), and you'll find good deals on ready- and custom-made pairs in the Mercado Principal. **Ayelet** (Plaza Catedral, across from the cathedral on Hidalgo) offers huaraches of better quality at correspondingly higher prices. Another good buy but difficult to find at times is a ceramic chinelo mask, a beautiful and unusual souvenir. Try the artisan's market in the zócalo and on Degollado at the entrance to the Mercado Principal.

AFTER DARK

Cuernavaca is pretty sedate during the week, but when the weekend visitors ooze into the clubs and discos, the scene starts happening, usually at a high price. Women have it made—pretty much every night is "Ladies Night," when women pay half price for admission. Travelers inter-ested in cultural events should check the bulletin board of the **University Cultural Center** (Morelos Sur 136) as well as the booth on the corner of Morelos and Rayón.

BARS The cafés on the zócalo are the most pleasant place to drink a beer or margarita. **Harry's Bar,** where yuppie chilangos and cuernavaquenses hang out, is the first place any young resident will send you. Be advised that it's a meat market. Another trendy hangout for those who thrive on blaring music, flashing lights, and flickering videos is **La Fragua Video Bar, Pizza y Yardas** (Morelos Sur 706, Col. Las Palmas), where the young come to be seen and drink enor-mous beers ($5), and the ill-advised come to eat the so-called pizza (served with Worcester-shire sauce).

CINEMAS/THEATERS Cine O'Campo (across from Jardín Juárez) shows English-language films and is also the home of Cuernavaca's repertory company. Come for a look at the stone fountain in the lobby, the intricately carved wooden ceiling, and the complicated iron grillwork. Admission to live performances is $6 ($3 for students) and about half that for films. **Cine-matográfica Las Plazas**, in the Las Plazas shopping center across from the north side of the Plaza de Armas, shows mostly Hollywood films with Spanish subtitles.

DANCING Cuernavaca has a number of flashy clubs with high cover charges. At **Kaova** (More-los Sur 302, tel. 73/15–43–88), a private club frequented by *juniors* (sons and daughters of the wealthy elite), men are charged a $17 cover, women $7, and Thursday nights feature an open bar. The best thing about Kaova is that it's within a short walk of the zócalo and the bud-get hotel zone. The other popular discos are further away. **Barba-Zul**, north of the centro, charges a $10 cover, with free admission for women on Wednesdays. You can take a RUTA 3 bus on Morelos to get here, but you'll have to cab it home. **Zumbale** (Bajada de Chapultepec, near the Jungla Mágica) plays live tropical music all night long; RUTA 17 and RUTA 20 buses from

Degollado pass right by it. There's also a huge gay disco called **Shadé** (López Mateos, east side of Mercado Principal)—it's probably best to take a cab here.

MUSIC You'll find live music Sundays and Thursdays in the Jardín Juárez, and just about every weekend in the auditoriums around the city. The office staff at the Jardín Borda (*see* Worth Seeing, *above*) is good about giving information on such events. If you want a club atmosphere, you can find jazz on weekends at **Flamingo's Teatro Bar** (Herradura de Plata 102, tel. 73/17–15–54).

OUTDOOR ACTIVITIES

BALNEARIO TEMIXCO This aquatic park with 15 swimming pools, 10 wading pools, water slides, sports fields, and gardens was originally a 16th-century sugar plantation; it was used as a fort during the Mexican Revolution and as a prisoner-of-war camp during World War II. Ruins of the rice mill, the chapel, and the storage bins of the hacienda are still recognizable. On weekends a live orchestra plays dance music and there is a full bar. It takes about 30 minutes by bus to make the 8-kilometer trek from downtown. *Emiliano Zapata 11, Col. Temixco, tel. 73/18–56–94. Take TEMIXCO combi from Matamoros. Admission: $7. Open daily 9–6.*

Near Cuernavaca

TEPOZTLAN

This little town, about an hour northeast of Cuernavaca, was made famous by anthropologists Oscar Lewis and Robert Redfield, who presented it as a prototypical Mexican village. But in the eyes of many Mexicans, Tepoztlán is not typical at all. The nearby village of Amatlán is the legendary birthplace of the feathered serpent god Quetzalcoatl—a place of supernatural powers, of both positive and negative energy. The good vibes are found at the site of the **Tlahuica ruins**, high above the town, while in the caves of the **Cerro del Tepozteco**, *brujos* (witches) supposedly perform their rituals. Unfortunately, entrance to the caves is restricted.

Perhaps because of the site's reputation, the Dominican **Convento de la Natividad** here was built to defy earthly and divine storms, with walls more than 2 meters thick. Situated next to the **Iglesia de la Asunción**, by the plaza, the convent is known for its syncretic *tequitqui* style, in which Christian and indigenous symbols mingle in faded frescoes. In the cloister is the **Museo Arqueológico Colección Carlos Pellicer,** where you can see pre-Hispanic artifacts and photos of the Mexican archaeological sites where they were recovered. They charge a $1 admission fee and are open Tuesday through Sunday from 9 to 5.

The path leading to the Tlahuica ruins is up Avenida Tepozteco past the plaza. The scarred cliffs of the Cerro tower overhead; try to pick out the formation said to look like a flying saucer. The rocky, 45-minute climb up to the ruins can be quite slippery after a rain, with the sound of running water interrupted only by the panting of fellow climbers and the distant clanging of the church bells below. At the top stands the **Pirámide Tepozteco,** dedicated to Tepoztécatl, the Tlahuica god of *pulque* (an alcoholic drink made from maguey). Carved images of figures related to the sky and heavens lead many to believe that the pyramid was an observatory; although the pyramid itself isn't too spectacular, the view from the top is amazing. *Admission: $3, free Sun. Open Tues.–Sun. 9:30–4:30.*

If the hike to the ruins was just a warm-up for you, check out nearby **Parque Nacional El Tepozteco**. Contact the local Boy Scouts' office at **Campamento Meztitla** on the Tepoztlán–Yautepec highway for tips on opportunities for hikers, backpackers, and rappelers. The only hotels in Tepoztlán are far out of the budget range, so unless you have camping equipment, plan to make this a day trip.

COMING AND GOING Buses ($1) leave every half hour until 6 PM from the Mercado Principal in Cuernavaca. On the way back to Cuernavaca you might think of stopping in the town of **Ocotepec**, known for the beauty of its cemetery and its troubador traditions.

WHERE TO SLEEP AND EAT This town does not cater to itinerant students; **Hotel Tepoztlán** (Calle de las Industrias 6, tel. 739/5–05–03) and **Posada del Tepozteco** (Paraíso 3, tel. 739/5–00–10) are both pricey, with double rooms going for about $70. Campers can check out the YMCA-run **Campamento Camohmila** (tel. 739/5–01–10) on the Carretera Autopista a Oaxtepec (Ruta 115); take a Santiago combi from the zócalo in front of Farmacia Villamar and ask the driver to let you off at the campground. The Boy Scouts run **Campamento Meztitla** (Rte. 2, tel. 739/5–00–65) on the Tepoztlán–Yautepec highway; you'll have to take a taxi to get here. There are few restaurants to choose from. Apart from Global Café (*see box*), you might try **Tlacualoyan** (Av. Tepozteco 9), which has a delicious but expensive mole poblano ($8); or, farther down the street, the equally expensive **Los Colorines**. On Sundays, the vendors in the market sell enchiladas, tortas, and such. Look for the **Tepoznieves** stand, which sells a Tepoztlán specialty—tequila ice cream.

XOCHICALCO

The partially excavated ruins of Xochicalco are the most fascinating in Morelos. The ancient city of Xochicalco, which translates as "Place of the House of the Flowers," sits atop terraced hills overlooking a valley. The ruins here display elements of Olmec and Maya architecture, and archaeologists suggest that Toltecs, Mixtecs, or Zapotecs may also have inhabited this site at different points in time. Some say Xochicalco was a ceremonial center where scholars met to correct their calendars.

The site has not been fully excavated, but it is believed that in the early 16th century, when the Spaniards arrived in the region, the people of the valley came from miles around to cover the ancient city with rocks and earth to protect it. The Xochicalco ruins were discovered in the early 1900s by Emiliano Zapata and his troops during a battle, when bullets ricocheted off the hill they were holding.

The center of Xochicalco is the **Plaza Ceremonial** (Plaza 1), located at the city's highest base elevation, where only priests were allowed to roam around what is believed to be the main ceremonial enclosure. The surrounding grounds are thought to have been the site of the local bazaar, where people of the valley gathered to trade goods. The intricately carved **Pirámide de Quetzalcoatl** depicts the alignment of the calendars of several Indian tribes, presided over by Quetzalcoatl, shown as a serpent with two mouths and two tongues, feather headdresses, and a fan of feathers for his tail. If you look closely at the figure, you'll see his left hand discarding a hieroglyph that represents an erroneous date while his right hand pulls in a correct one. The correct date has been identified as Thirteen Monkey, of the 260-day Mesoamerican calendar.

Restaurant Global Café

Opened in 1993 by French/American activist couple Dominique Sepser and Jim Freeman, the Global is a meeting place and information clearinghouse for Tepoztecos and travelers alike. They provide information on everything from hikes to dentists to dry-toilet technology. For a $4 deposit, $3 of which you get back, you can borrow a book from their small but excellent library, which even has a selection of lesbian fiction. The restaurant serves Mexican food as well as chocolate mousse, lemonade, and a mean cup of coffee. Services include telephone, fax, a message center, and a bulletin board of local activities, events, political and environmental activism, and educational opportunities. For more information, write to Avenida Tepozteco 19, Tepoztlán, Morelos, CP 62520, México, tel. 739/5–17–15, fax 739/5–00–46, 800/874–8784 in the U.S. Follow Av. Tepozteco past plaza toward the pyramid.

You can climb the steep staircase of the **Temple of the Stelae**, also on the Ceremonial Plaza, and get a commanding view of the surrounding hills and the valley below.

Down the hill in the **main plaza** (Plaza 2) is the **Two Glyph Stelae Square**, arranged to chart the sun's path through the day. There is also a ball court, one of many found in Mayan ruins throughout Mexico, where two teams of five men attempted to get a small, hard ball through one of the circular stone hoops on either end of the court.

The underground **observatory**, one of 32 interconnected tunnels below the pyramids, was used to trace the path of the sun throughout the year. A small circle of light on the floor of the cavern marks the sun's movement. At noon on the summer solstice (June 21) each year, the sun's rays enter and completely illuminate the chamber's interior. The moment held great religious significance—for one moment each year, the celestial, the terrestrial, and the subterranean were united.

Some archaeologists speculate that team sports originated in the Americas and were brought back to Europe by the Spaniards.

At the ruins, a small snack bar offers nothing substantial to eat; take a picnic lunch or hitchhike toward the village of El Rodeo, about a kilometer past the Crucero de Xochicalco, the intersection of Ruta 166 and the road to the ruins. *Admission: $4, free Sun. and with student ID. Open daily 9–5. Observatory open daily 11–2.*

COMING AND GOING From Cuernavaca, catch a bus bound for Coatlán del Río or Miacatlán from the intersection of Galeano and Hidalgo; ask the driver to let you off at the Crucero de Xochicalco. The ride costs $2 and takes less than an hour. From the crucero it's a 4-kilometer walk uphill to the ruins; taxis charge about $1 on the way up, less on the way down.

CUAUTLA

Cuautla was a revolutionary stronghold during the both the war for independence and the Mexican Revolution, and its main attractions are a source of pride and nostalgia. The statue of revolutionary priest José María Morelos that dominates the Alameda was erected in commemoration of the 1812 Battle of Cuautla. During this battle, Morelos and 3,000 men held the city of Cuautla for 72 days against the attacking Royalist force of 20,000, until starvation drove them out from behind the city walls.

The **Iglesia de San Diego,** across from the statue of Morelos, served as his headquarters. On the other side of the church is the **Convento de San Diego**, now converted into Cuautla's Casa de la Cultura. The graceful building, which also has a collection of antique Mexican rail cars, is not in very good shape. South down Galeana is Cuautla's zócalo with its cream-and-rust bandstand in the middle, the **Iglesia de Santo Domingo** on the west side, and the **Palacio Municipal** on the opposite end. The church served as a hospital during the War of Independence and was defended with four cannons, one in each corner. Across the way, on the southwest corner of the zócalo, is a small house with peeling red paint and a white doorway. This is the **Casa de Morelos,** where the revolutionary leader lived while defending the city. It now houses the **Museo de la Independencia,** open on weekends only from 10 AM to 2 PM and worth a brief visit.

Cuautla boasts a number of hot springs, but they're more like unkempt public pools than all-natural, therapeutic spas.

A 15-minute walk south of the zócalo on Guerrero brings you to the **Jardín Revolución del Sur,** where Emiliano Zapata's body is buried. Zapata, the Mexican revolutionary leader whose image has assumed renewed political meaning with the armed uprising of the Zapatista Army in Chiapas, was assassinated at Chinameca, 31 kilometers away. Facing the Jardín is the **Iglesia Señor del Pueblo**, the señor being Zapata himself.

COMING AND GOING Buses to Cuautla ($2, 1 hr) leave the Estrella Roja station in Cuernavaca every 15 minutes between 6 AM and 10 PM. The two bus stations in Cuautla are **México/Zacatepec/Cristóbal Colón** (2 de Mayo, at Reforma), which serves Mexico City and Oaxaca, and **Estrella Roja** (Costeño, at Vásquez), which serves Cuernavaca, Oaxaca, and Mexico City. **97**

Although Cuautla is the second-largest city in Morelos, it's fairly manageable on foot. The city is shaped roughly like an L, with the centro at the crook. The Alameda is a few blocks north of the zócalo on Galeana. Most colectivos run along the main streets, Zavala/Reforma and Alvaro Obregón. Be prepared for frequent street-name changes and a scarcity of street signs.

WHERE TO SLEEP Hotels here are not the cheapest in the region, but they're still within the range of budget travelers. Right on the zócalo, the **Hotel Colón** (Guerrero 48, tel. 735/2–29–90) has clean, if somewhat run-down, singles and doubles for $12. A five-minute walk north on Galeana and about $15 gets you a well-lit room with a clean bathroom at **Hotel Oasis** (Galeana 21, tel. 735/2–01–01). This hotel is right between the zócalo and the Alameda, so request a quiet room. At the **Villa Juvenil Cuautla** (tel. 735/2–02–18), just past the southern edge of town, single travelers get a dorm bed, communal bathroom, and pool access for $3. From the Cristóbal Colón bus station (about 10 minutes), head toward the IMSS building and turn right just before it. Go over a bridge, then enter the parking lot to your right. For camping information, *see* Outdoor Activities, *below.*

FOOD There's no lack of decent dining establishments in Cuautla. Around the zócalo, the cafeterias **El Cid** and **Colón** sell cheap comidas corridas until fairly late and offer views of the goings-on in the square. More restaurants can be found between the zócalo and the Alameda on Galeana, or try the places on Ingeniero Ramírez just off Galeana, including **Mario, PAN,** and **Cafetería y Jugos Alameda** on the corner. Hangouts at the Alameda are **La Terraza Bar** (a soda fountain) and a burger joint called **Las Tortugas** in the same building as the movie theater. For a more formal dinner, try the restaurant in the **Hotel Colonial** (José Perdiz 18, tel. 735/2–21–64), known for its *cabrito colonial* (specially prepared kid; $14) and paella.

OUTDOOR ACTIVITIES Splashing around in one of Cuautla's several *balnearios* (spa and swimming areas) isn't exactly all that it's cracked up to be, but if you are dying for a swim and a nap in the sun, these are your best options. **Oaxtepec** (Carretera México–La Pera–Oaxtepec, tel. 735/6–12–02) is the showpiece of Morelos's resorts. It has 25 pools, a cable car, lodging, water slides, and other ritzy amenities. Take a blue OAXTEPEC combi. The ride takes half an hour, and admission is $8. **Las Estacas** (Carretera México–La Pera–Tlaltizapan, tel. 734/2–14–44), about 24 kilometers outside town, is also well known. Guests can float down a spring-fed river through a bit of jungle, and the resort has a restaurant and camping facilities. Admission is about $6. If you're too poor for the resorts, there are four pools within the city of Cuautla. **Los Limones** (tel. 735/2–70–02) is smallest and best, with two clean pools and grassy camp sites for $4. **Agua Linda** (next to Villa Juvenil Cuautla) and **El Almeal** (two blocks east of Los Limones, tel. 735/2–17–51) each have a few pools and lots of aqua blue cement. You can camp at El Almeal for $8. Admission to both balnearios is $3. And you can't say you weren't warned about **Agua Hedionda** (tel. 735/2–00–44), a sulphur spring whose name means "stinking water." If you can stand the stench, the water circulating in the pools is fresh.

Tlaxcala

Tlaxcala, meaning "the land of corn," is a tiny state, only about 2½ times the size of Mexico City. The capital city, also called Tlaxcala, is an unexpected mix of cosmopolitan amenities and small-town simplicity. Perhaps this is why in recent years it has become a popular vacation spot for residents of Mexico City, whose urban bones want rest and relaxation without giving up at least an approximation of the constant activity they find at home.

The view from Tlaxcala's hills includes churches and colonial buildings as well as snow-capped volcanoes in the distance, providing a sense of the undisturbed passage of time, but Tlaxcala is hardly frozen and unchanged. Official and unofficial festivals spring up almost every month, if not every weekend, filling the streets with music, dancing, artisanry from around the region, and colorful costumes. The people are proud of both their indigenous heritage and the fact that the city was the first Catholic diocese in Mexico. Tlaxcalans are not without a sense of the irony of the fusion of their cultures. Today, the official name of the city is "Tlaxcala de Xicohténeatl," in honor of the only Tlaxcalteca chieftain who opposed an alliance with the conquistador Cortés.

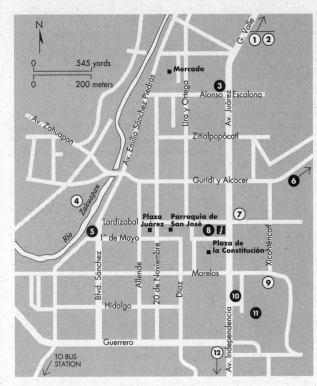

N

0   545 yards
0   200 meters

Mercado

Av. Zahuapan

Av. Emilio Sánchez Piedras

Lira y Ortega

Av. Juárez

Alonso Escalona

Zitialpopócatl

Guridi y Alcocer

Zahuapan

Río

Lardizabal

Plaza
Juárez

Parroquia de
San José

1° de Mayo

Plaza de
la Constitución

Blvd. Sánchez

Allende

20 de Noviembre

Díaz

Morelos

Hidalgo

Av. Independencia

Xicohténcatl

Guerrero

TO BUS
STATION

G. Valle

Sights ●
Basílica de
Ocotlán, **6**
Ex-Convento de
San Francisco, **11**
Museo de Artes y
Tradiciones de
Tlaxcala, **5**
Palacio de
Gobierno, **8**
Plaza
Xicohténcatl, **10**
Sala de Cultura, **3**

Lodging ○
Hotel Alifer, **9**
Hotel Frontera, **1**
Hotel Mansión
de Xicohténcatl, **7**
Plaza-Tlaxcala, **2**
Hotel
San Clemente, **12**
Hotel Zahuapan, **4**

The capital city is an excellent starting point for exploring the state, from the colorful pre-Columbian murals of Cacaxtla and the *pueblito* (small village) of Huamantla to the volcano and surrounding forests of La Malinche.

BASICS

AUTO PARTS/SERVICE Merchant **Zamora Lilia** (1 de Mayo, at Abasolo, tel. 246/2–19–99) sells car parts, and **Reconstrucción y Mantenimiento Automotriz Josué** (Blvd. Revolución 52, tel. 246/2–09–98) handles most mechanical problems.

CASA DE CAMBIO Change dollars or traveler's checks weekdays 9–noon at **Banamex** (Plaza Xicohténcatl 1, tel. 246/2–25–36). Banamex also has ATMs that accept Plus and Cirrus system cards.

EMERGENCIES The phone number for the **police** is 246/2–07–35; for the **Cruz Roja** (ambulance service), it's 246/2–09–20.

LAUNDRY **Lavandería San Felipe** charges $5 to wash 3 kilos of laundry. *Guiridi y Alcocer 30, btw Juárez and Lira y Ortega, no phone. Open weekdays 8–7, Sat. 8–3.*

MAIL The full-service post office on the zócalo will hold mail sent to you at the following address for up to 10 days: Lista de Correos, Tlaxcala, Tlaxcala, CP 90000, México. *Plaza de la Constitución 20, tel. 246/2–00–04. Open weekdays 9–6, Sat. 9–1.*

MEDICAL AID The **IMSS clinic** (G. Valle 64, tel. 246/2–23–44) provides medical services 24 hours a day and has some English-speaking staff. **Farmacia Zahuapan** (20 de Noviembre 1, tel. 246/2–21–56) is also open day and night.

PHONES You'll have to use a pay phone, several of which are located in front of the Parroquia de San José, to make a collect call. For cash calls, the *caseta de larga distancia* (long-distance telephone office) on Independencía across from the Plaza Xicohténcatl is open Monday—Saturday 8 AM—9:30 PM.

VISITOR INFORMATION The Secretary of Tourism has an information desk staffed by eager young people who can arrange for guides with a week's advance notice. *Juárez, at Lardizábal, tel. 246/2–00–27. Open weekdays 9—7, weekends 10–6.*

COMING AND GOING

BY BUS The **Central Camionera** (tel. 246/2–03–62) is eight blocks west of the zócalo. Buses to Mexico City ($6, 2 hrs) and Puebla ($1.50, 1 hr) leave every 15 minutes from 6 AM until about 10 PM, and many other destinations are served as well. To get to the zócalo from the bus station, take any CENTRO or SANTA ANA colectivo. The ride takes about five minutes and costs 30¢. Colectivos marked CENTRAL make the trip in the opposite direction from the corner of Lira y Ortega and Lardizábal.

BY TRAIN There's no train station here, but trains to Puebla and Apizaco (the state's rail center) leave at noon, 2 PM and 7:30 PM from Santa Ana Chiautempan, 10 minutes away. *Tel. 246/2–13–86. Take a SANTA ANA colectivo along Juárez from zócalo.*

GETTING AROUND

Tlaxcala is a manageable size and very easy to get around on foot. The main street running roughly north–south is called Independencia on the south side of Plaza Constitución (the zócalo), becoming Juárez to the north. Past downtown, Juárez changes into Guillermo Valle, which becomes Boulevard Revolución farther on. Most anything of interest lies near or along Independencia/Juárez in the downtown area.

Colectivos (both combis and small buses) go up and down the main drag, as well as to neighboring towns and the Central Camionera. They leave for points north from the stop in front of Plaza Xicohténcatl on Independencia; catch colectivos for points south and west or to the Central Camionera from the northwest corner of the intersection of Lira y Ortega and Lardizábal. Colectivos stop running at about 10 PM.

Taxi stands are in front of the southern porch of the zócalo and the Parroquia de San José. Within Tlaxcala, fares should stay under $3. A ride to the nearby town of Santa Ana is about $5. Unless you have heavy luggage, you probably won't need a taxi; the streets of Tlaxcala are pretty safe at night as long as you stick to the beaten path.

WHERE TO SLEEP

The hotels in Tlaxcala, which are nothing to rave about, charge almost the same price for a single or a double, so solo travelers get the short end of the stick. Even so, it's a good idea to make reservations——hotels fill up fast during fairs in October and May and in the first week of July, when summer sessions begin at the university. If the places below are full, your only alternative is a luxury hotel. The most affordable of these is **Hotel Jeroc's** (Revolución 4, tel. 246/2–15–77), which charges $50 for a single and $73 for a double.

➢ UNDER $25 • **Hotel Frontera.** This is the cheapest hotel in town. The problem is, it's not really *in* town, but 12 long blocks north of the zócalo. On the plus side, the rooms are clean and some have bathrooms. The old woman who owns the place insists on keeping prices low and loves to talk about the "decent people" that have stayed here. Singles cost $10 ($13 with bath), and doubles cost $20, but bargaining isn't out of the question. *G. Valle 82, tel. 246/2–12–26. Take SANTA ANA combi from bus station. 18 rooms, some with bath. Luggage storage.*

Hotel Mansión de Xicohténcatl. This hotel is smack-dab in the middle of town, almost across the street from the tourist office. It doesn't, however, live up to its name. Rooms are clean but drab, though some have small balconies. The owner is too busy watching TV to do anything more than take your money and hand you your keys. The hot water isn't, and you should bring your own towel. Knock at the front door if you arrive after midnight. Singles cost $18, and doubles are $23. *Juárez 15, 1 block north of zócalo, tel. 246/2–19–00. 18 rooms, all with bath. Reservations advised.*

Hotel Plaza-Tlaxcala. Right next door to Hotel Jeroc's sits this quiet hotel, complete with a garden courtyard and restaurant. Guests are mostly families, with a few students during the summer. It's pretty far from the center of town, but a bargain at $17 for a single and $20 for a double. *Revolución 6, tel. 246/2–78–52. Take a SANTA ANA combi from center or bus station; you'll see Hotel Jeroc's sign on left. 12 rooms, all with bath. Laundry, luggage storage. MC, V.*

Hotel San Clemente. Newly remodeled rooms are arranged around a small courtyard with a fountain, roses, and bougainvillea at this hotel, about a 15-minute walk south of the zócalo. The large, carpeted rooms have closets and bathrooms with hot water. Singles for $17 and doubles for $20 make this hotel the best deal anywhere near the zócalo. *Independencia 58, tel. 246/2–19–89. 30 rooms, all with bath. Luggage storage, laundry. MC, V.*

Hotel Zahuapan. This hotel, across the river from the Museo de Artes y Tradiciones, is a little tricky to find, and getting here at night can be hairy, but it's close enough to the center and the market to merit the effort. Large, airy rooms are arranged around a central patio and have TVs and hot water. Singles are $13, doubles $20. *Priv. Río Zahuapan 1, tel. 246/2–59–86. From center, take Guridi y Alcocer until it becomes J. Carillo, cross bridge, and take first left. 24 rooms, all with bath. Reservations advised in summer.*

➢ UNDER $35 • **Hotel Alifer.** Two blocks uphill from the zócalo, the Alifer is close enough to downtown for convenience and far enough away to escape the street noise. The manager likes foreigners and students; they come in droves during the summer. Rooms are comfortable and carpeted, and each has a TV and phone. Singles cost $24, doubles $33. *Morelos 11, 2 blocks east of zócalo, tel. 246/2–56–78. 18 rooms, all with bath. Laundry, luggage storage. Reservations advised. MC, V.*

FOOD

Most of Tlaxcala's restaurants are around the zócalo and Plaza Xicohténcatl. People here seem to favor anything that isn't Mexican, but you'll also find plenty of regional specialties. One of these is *pollo tocotlán,* chicken in maguey salsa cooked in a thin paper bag. For the cheapest food in town, try the taco stands off 20 de Noviembre, near Plaza Juárez, which stay open late: Drinks are at room temperature, the salsa is searing, and you'll probably have to eat standing up, but three tacos only cost about a dollar. Another option is the *rosticerías* (restaurants specializing in roasted chicken), where a whole chicken with a side of tortillas, beans, *rajas* (chile strips), and salsa costs about $2. There are several near the market on Emilio Sánchez Piedras, between Escalona and Lira y Ortega. Try **El Pollo Rey,** open daily until 8:30. The market itself offers prepared food only on Saturdays, when kitchens are set up at the *tianguis* (open-air market).

➢ UNDER $10 • **Café Avenida.** This relatively informal place offers a wide variety of Mexican and American food. *Filete al chipotle* ($6.50), steak covered with a smoked-pepper tomato sauce and cheese on a bed of refried beans, is especially good. The $3 comida corrida includes soup, an entrée, and dessert. If you're eating alone, you can amuse yourself by looking at photographs of Hollywood stars of yesteryear or the coffee menu: There are five different kinds of cappuccino, including Cappuccino Sexi ($3.25) with plum liquor and honey. *Juárez 6, tel. 246/2–63–53. ½ block north of zócalo. Open daily 7 AM–10 PM.*

La Fonda del Convento. On the cobblestone path from the Ex-Convento de San Francisco to Plaza Xicohténcatl is a popular restaurant brightened by the sounds of birds and church bells. The Convento prices most dishes under $5. For a little more than $7, the *carne fonda del convento* is a steak served with an enchilada, rice, fries, beans, and guacamole. Vegetarians should try the quesadillas seasoned with *epazote,* an herb particular to Mexico. *Calzada de San Francisco 1, tel. 246/2–07–65. Open Mon.–Sat. 10–8.*

Los Portales. Across the street from the zócalo, this restaurant serves up traditional food such as *pollo en pipian* (chicken in chile and pumpkin-seed sauce, $5), but you can also choose from a variety of steaks ($8) and exotic hamburgers—try the Hawaiian version with pineapple, cheese, bacon, and lettuce ($4). There's al fresco dining on the porch, but inside or outside, the restaurant is packed with locals of every age. *Independencia 8, tel. 246/2–54–19. Open daily 7 AM–10 PM. Wheelchair access.*

El Quinto Sol. Most vegetarian restaurants in the country serve lots of dieting Mexican women, and this one is no exception. Vegans will rejoice at the presence of soy milk on the breakfast menu—it's served hot and tastes suspiciously like *atole* (a sweet, corn-based drink); at any rate, it's not dairy. Add bread, fruit, yogurt, and some excellent granola, and breakfast is about $3. The lunch menu varies, offering creative dishes such as soy steak. The comida corrida runs $4–$6. *Juárez, at Lardizábal, tel. 246/2–49–28. Next to Hotel Mansión de Xicohténcatl. Open Mon.–Sat. 7:30–7.*

➤ UNDER $25 • **El Mesón Taurino.** This place is next to the Plaza de Toros, and its ambience is marred only by the severed heads of bulls staring down at you as you eat. Try dining outdoors in the garden. Although open for breakfast, this restaurant's forte is dinner, when pasta and fish dishes run $7–$9. For just a bit more you can have fillet mignon in mushroom sauce ($10) or *filete Cacaxtla* ($11), steak topped with *huitlacoche* (a fungus grown on corn) and chile strips. Adding a salad and wine to your meal brings the price to about $20. It's an ideal place to celebrate a special occasion, like having enough cash to eat here. *Independencia 12, at Guerrero, tel. 246/2–43–66. Open daily 8 AM–10 PM.*

WORTH SEEING

Tlaxcala's main points of interest are all within walking distance of the zócalo and can be seen in less than a day. After only a few hours, any traveler will have a sense of how to get around.

The zócalo, known as **Plaza de la Constitución,** is quieter than most Mexican zócalos; goods are only sold here during fairs or the Saturday market. Along the western edge is the **Casa de Piedra,** a colonial-era house with a distinctive stone facade. Legend has it that the doctor who lived here asked his poor patients to pay with a stone of a certain size. In this manner, he went about building his house, stone by stone. Dominating **Plaza Xicohténcatl** is a monument to the cacique of that name, who was hanged by the Spaniards after the successful assault on Tenochtitlán, for refusing to participate in the slaughter of the Aztecs. The plaza is bordered by a number of restaurants and is basically part of the zócalo.

BASILICA DE OCOTLAN This hillside shrine is one of Mexico's national treasures and is considered the best example in the region of the ornate churrigueresque style. The visitor is greeted by a gleaming white plaster facade carved with intricate figures and flanked by two 33-meter-high towers tiled in red and sky blue. Red and white are the colors of the flag of the ancient kingdom of Tlaxcallan, and blue symbolizes the Virgin Mary, in whose honor the shrine was built in 1640. According to church history, the Virgin appeared to a pious Indian in answer to his prayers for water during a drought.

The **Chamber of the Virgin,** where a statue of Our Lady of Ocotlán is housed, took the sculptor Francisco Miguel Tlayoltehuamintzin 25 years to complete, and not an inch remains undecorated. Next door to the basilica is the **Capilla del Pocito de Agua Milagrosa,** which houses a spring of curative water. The chapel walls are decorated with a series of murals on biblical themes related to water, designed by Desiderio Hernández Xochitiotzin (*see Palacio de Gobierno, below*). *From zócalo, north on Juárez, right at Guridi y Alcocer, left at Calzada de los Misterios, and uphill about 2 km. Admission free. Open daily until dusk; closed to visitors during church services (hourly on Sunday 7 AM–2 PM).*

EX-CONVENTO DE SAN FRANCISCO Services were held here before Cortés marched on to Tenochtitlán (present-day Mexico City). The **Capilla Abierta** (Open Chapel) is thought to be the earliest 16th-century construction of its type in New Spain.

Up the stairs and across the courtyard is the **Catedral de Nuestra Señora de la Asunción.** Built in 1526 after Tlaxcala was declared the first diocese in New Spain, it is known for its cedar ceiling, which is carved in the geometric *mosarabe* style. The four *caciques* (chieftains) of Tlaxcallan were converted at the baptismal font, with Cortés and Alvarado acting as godfathers. From the courtyard, there's a bird's-eye view of the Plaza de Toros on the street below. *From zócalo, south 1 block past Plaza Xicohténcatl, left at Calzada de Capilla Abierta. Admission free. Open daily 8–7. Mass daily at 6 PM.*

The atrium of the Ex-Convento is known to locals as el jardín del pulpo (octopus garden) because of all the groping that goes on here in the late evening.

JARDIN BOTANICO TIZATLAN One of the newer attractions of Tlaxcala, this garden sprouts flora characteristic of the *altiplano* (highland) region. You'll learn a lot here—plants are labeled with their scientific and common names and some have descriptions of their medicinal and practical uses. The Jardín is also a good place for picnics and trysts. The **Sala Miguel Lira** theater shows recent American and Mexican films Tuesday–Sunday (tel. 246/2–46–85). *Take SANTA ANA combi from zócalo, get off just before the aqueduct at Camino Real. Admission free. Open daily 9–5.*

MUSEO DE ARTES Y TRADICIONES DE TLAXCALA This living history museum celebrates the traditional Tlaxcalan way of life through handicrafts. In one room, a typical *campesino* (peasant) house is re-created, with Sunday clothes carefully stored in a cardboard box at the foot of the bed. Another room has a fun display of handmade costumes and masks. On weekends, artisans demonstrate weaving and the making of pulque. Guides are available Wednesday–Sunday for tours in Spanish. Ask permission before taking photographs. *Emilio Sánchez Piedras 1, 3 blocks west of zócalo, tel. 246/2–23–37. Admission: $2, $1.50 students, free Sun. Open Tues.–Sun. 10–6.*

PALACIO DE GOBIERNO The interior walls of the municipal headquarters are covered with spectacular, colorful murals painted by Desiderio Hernández Xochitiotzin, who had close ties to Diego Rivera. The palace was built around 1550 for Hernán Cortés. Today the walls of the entire first floor, including the underside of the arches, recount the history of Tlaxcala from the moment the gods gave corn to the Chichimecas (Indians from the north) to the Spanish conquest. The grand murals are filled with symbolic and prophetic figures; the stairwell, for example, pictures the heavens overrun by fantastic creatures, as gods plunge headfirst to the earth. In the background, an inferno swallows the city, while off in the corner a Spaniard mounted on a white horse strikes down the feathered serpent Quetzalcoatl, god of wind. *North side of zócalo. Admission free. Open daily 6 AM–8 PM.*

SALA DE CULTURA This center exhibits contemporary paintings by artists from Mexico and elsewhere in Latin America. There is a bookstore in the basement. *Juárez, at Escalona, tel. 246/2-39-79. Admission free. Open Mon.-Sat. 9–7.*

CHEAP THRILLS

The Río Zahuapan flows through the northwest corner of Tlaxcala; the pedestrian walkway along its bank is known as the **Paseo de la Amistad** (Friendship Walkway). Here you'll find strolling couples, kids on bikes and skateboards, and elderly folks enjoying the sunshine. A bit farther along the paseo is the **Parque de la Juventud,** a good spot for a picnic or a jog.

Couples and families gather on the steep stairway of the **Iglesia del Vecino** (above and behind the cathedral) to enjoy a panoramic view of the city as the sun slips behind the hills. A newly erected monument to Xicohténcatl at the top of the *escalinata* (stairway) where Boulevard Sánchez ends on the south side of town provides yet another sweeping view of the city. Busts of Mexican revolutionary heroes line the stairway and a waterfall running down the middle of the steps diverts your attention from your impending heart attack. Once you get there, all of Tlaxcala is visible, along with several surrounding towns, and you can turn to your loved one and say, "Some day, this will all be yours."

The **IMSS** (G. Valle 115, tel. 246/2-38-00) is a building full of government offices, but it's also got an outdoor pool that's open to the public on weekends 8 AM–2 PM. The pool is wheelchair accessible, and admission is $2. A park across the street from the **Jardín Botánico** is the site of neighborhood soccer games on Sundays.

Music lovers should check out Avenida Muñoz Camargo between Díaz and Allende. Several mariachi bands have small shops here, and in the afternoon they suit up and practice before hitting the lunch and dinner crowds in the zócalo restaurants. The interested should not be shy—the musicians are generally more than happy to answer questions about their art.

FESTIVALS **Late February:** The best festival in Tlaxcala is **Carnaval,** celebrated throughout the week prior to Ash Wednesday. Thousands of people parade through town wearing masks and costumes, and dancers perform in the streets.

July 6: In 1591, a group of 400 Christianized Tlaxcaltecan families left Tlaxcala under orders from King Philip II of Spain and Pope Gregory XIV to colonize the north of New Spain. An impressive reenactment of their departure takes place at the ruins of the Convento de Nuestra Señora de las Nieves in the town of Totolac during the **Celebración de las Cuatrocientas Familias** (Celebration of the 400 Families). The highlight is a candlelight procession down from the hills.

Mid-July: The **Feria del Pan** in Totolac is a typical Tlaxcalan festival with dancing and fireworks. The bread baked especially for this fair is famous throughout Mexico, but the ingredients are kept secret by the participating panaderías.

Mid-August: The **Fiesta de la Asunción** in Huamantla, about a half hour east of Tlaxcala, is a two-week festival celebrating the Assumption and the Virgin of Charity. The highlight is when a figure of the Virgin is paraded through streets carpeted with flowers strewn in symbolic designs. The procession ends when the sun rises and the running of the bulls, à la Pamplona, begins.

Late October: The **Tlaxcala Fair** features bullfights, cockfights, indigenous dances, carnival rides, entertainers, and exhibitions of local handicrafts.

AFTER DARK

Though the cafés are crowded in the early evenings, Tlaxcalans generally go to bed early. During festivals and in July and August, when students from Mexico City descend on Tlaxcala for summer classes, things pick up a bit. As for the rest of the year, if you go out after 10 PM, you've missed whatever action there was. If you just can't stay in, hook up with some youth with a car to *dar una vuelta* (go cruising), the activity of choice among local teenagers.

BARS/MUSIC Although Tlaxcala state is home to the Plains of Apam, where pulque is made, traditional pulquerías are nowhere to be found. A few bars play music; most of the others are seedy cantinas where women are unwelcome. At **El Unicornio** (Plaza Xicohténcatl 8, tel. 246/2–40–73), you can sip drinks ($3–$7) and listen to piano and flute music in the afternoon. **El Frans** (G. Valle 70, tel. 246/2–38–66) plays Mexican and American pop music and occasionally puts on Vegas-style floor shows. They're open until 11 PM.

CINEMAS Both the **Cinema Tlaxcala,** on the south side of the zócalo, and **Cinemas 1 y 2** (G. Valle 113, tel. 246/2–35–44), 6½ blocks north of the center, show fairly recent Hollywood films with Spanish subtitles as well as Mexican films. Shows cost about $3 and play nightly at 4:30, 6:30, and 8:30.

DANCING Most dancing is at weddings, *quinceañeras* (girls' 15th-birthday parties), and festivals. If you haven't been invited to any of these, you don't have much else to choose from. There are two discos in the center of town, one at the **Hotel Arfaze** (Josefa Castelar 20, at Hidalgo, no phone) and **Century** (20 de Noviembre, at Hidalgo, no phone). Arfaze draws an older crowd dancing to Mexican *bailables* (danceables), and Century is popular with students; both close at 10 PM. The late-nighters (generally tourists) party until 2 or 3 AM at **Royal Adler's** (Revolución 4, tel. 246/2–15–77) in Hotel Jeroc's. Mexican and American pop and disco are played here, and drink prices range from $2 to $5. All of the above discos charge an $8 cover.

Near Tlaxcala

About 3 kilometers north of Tlaxcala is **Tizatlán,** once the center of the kingdom of Tlaxcallan. It's now known for carved walking sticks and a Franciscan chapel with a Moorish roof, built on top of the ruins of a pre-Hispanic pyramid. To reach the chapel and its small museum from Tlaxcala, take a combi from the corner of 1 de Mayo and Boulevard Sánchez. **Huamantla,** about 45 kilometers west of Tlaxcala, houses the baroque Iglesia y Convento de San Luis Obispo, and the Museo Taurino, a bullfight museum next to La Taurina bullring that contains posters, costumes, swords, and photographs of the sport. Occasional bullfights are well publicized. To get here, take an ATAH bus from the Central Camionera in Tlaxcala.

If you've seen enough churches and museums, take a break at the **Centro Vacacional La Trinidad,** 15 kilometers northwest of Tlaxcala in Santa Cruz. You can swim and ride horses at this resort on the banks of the Río Tequixquiatl. Rooms in the **Hotel Balneario** (tel. 246/1–03–33) are $50 a night for a double, but you can camp here for $5 a night. Colectivos run between 20 de Noviembre in Tlaxcala and Santa Cruz, and once you're in the town's zócalo, you'll see La Trinidad. Another in place for water sports is **Atlangatepec,** a dammed lake about an hour and a half north of Tlaxcala. To get here, take a bus from Tlaxcala's Central Camionera to Apizaco and transfer to Atlangatepec. **Villa Quinta Olivares** (no phone) has bungalows for $13 a night, or you can camp for free around the lake.

LA MALINCHE

La Malinche is a 4,462-meter volcano named after the woman who was the translator and mistress of Hernán Cortés. The volcano is 43 kilometers east of Tlaxcala and can be reached by bus in about an hour and a half. From the Central Camionera or the market in Tlaxcala, take a bus to Huamantla, and from there to the **Centro Vacacional La Malintzin** (tel. 246/2–40–98). The Centro Vacacional is a government-run resort that rents six-person cabins for $70 a night. You can also pitch a tent here for free if you're relatively discreet. From the Centro Vacacional to the summit of the volcano is a three-hour hike, and getting back down takes another hour. A guide isn't necessary, but they are usually available on weekends. During the rainy season (July–September) it's almost impossible to get to the top, but it's a great hike the rest of the year. The many forests around and on La Malinche make it the most beautiful of the volcanoes to explore near Tlaxcala. There is a restaurant at the Centro Vacacional, but bring food and water for the hike.

CACAXTLA

Cacaxtla, about 16 kilometers southeast of Tlaxcala, is the site of one of the most important Mesoamerican archaeological finds in the past 50 years. In 1975, a series of vivid, polychrome murals were discovered here. The astonishingly well-preserved works are unique in their realistic style and detail. The current theory holds that the murals were painted by the Xicalancas, a group of warrior merchants who arrived in the Tlaxcala Valley about 600 AD. The Xicalancas were descended from the Maya, which explains why the murals contain elements more commonly found in southern Mexico. The figures adorned with blue body paint represent sacrificial victims, and the five-pointed stars are symbols of the goddess of fertility. Cacaxtla means "place where the water dies in the earth," and in the ruins you'll see repeated representations of water and of Tlaloc, a rain god to whom human sacrifices were offered.

The Xicalancas, like the Maya, believed that human beings were made of corn.

The first set of murals, painted on columns flanking the entrance to a small room, depict barefooted blue dancers. Archaeologists refer to this room as the **Star Chamber,** because the dancers are surrounded by five-pointed stars. It may have been here that captives were prepared for sacrifice. The next mural on the right represents water, fertility, and trade. Note that the ears of corn are actually human faces. The **Red Temple** is identifiable by the bands of red paint that run along the bottom of the walls, like a sea of blood. Unfortunately, the general public is not allowed inside the Red Temple: Murals depicting prisoners are painted on the floor of the temple and cannot be walked on.

The **battle mural** for which Cacaxtla is most renowned is found just beyond the Red Temple. The victors wear jaguar pelts and the vanquished wear bird headdresses. One interpretation is that the mural depicts the aftermath of a real-life battle. It is also speculated that it does not represent a battle that actually took place, but rather symbolizes a confrontation between the two ethnic groups, whose union eventually gave rise to the Olmec-Xicalanca people.

A final set of murals is located in **Building A,** to the right of the battle mural. There are five murals—the first to be discovered was the one depicting the black bird-man. The date denoted by the eye of a reptile in indigenous glyphs that appears on the **north mural** corresponds with the supposed birthdate of Quetzalcoatl. Bordering these murals are pictures of various sea creatures, reminders of the Olmec-Xicalanca's origins on the Gulf of Mexico.

A good part of the ruins at Cacaxtla are still undergoing excavation. Below the structures open to the public is another temple, built around AD 200, and it is posssible that yet another lies still further down. In January of 1993, excavation began at **Xochitecal,** the hill opposite the entrance to Cacaxtla. So far, three temples, human remains, and the foundation of a pyramid have been discovered here. Excavation of yet another set of pyramids, believed to be reserved for non-nobles' viewing of ceremonies and sacrifices, began in April of 1994. *Admission: $4, free Sun. Open daily 10–4:30.*

If you make the trek out to Cacaxtla, you might as well visit **San Miguel del Milagro,** 1 kilometer northeast of Cacaxtla, where the archangel Michael is said to have appeared in 1630 to an Indian man named Diego Lázaro de San Francisco. As in Ocotlán, a fountain of healing water bubbled forth, and to this day the **Santuario de San Miguel** is a destination for pilgrims. The **Pocito de Santa Agua** (Well of Holy Water) is in the courtyard outside the church, behind a locked gate. The church itself is filled with 17th- and 18th-century paintings depicting angels and biblical stories. The lacquered **Chinese Pulpit** and the **Cuarto de Exvotos** are of particular interest. Here, pilgrims who have been healed leave offerings—a photograph, a pair of crutches, a handwritten note, and so on.

COMING AND GOING From Tlaxcala, take a NATIVITAS combi from the market or a SAN MARTIN bus from the Central Camionera, and ask to be let off at the *calzada*. The trip takes about 40 minutes and costs 50¢. You'll be dropped off at a crossroads where several combis hang out waiting to take people up to San Miguel and Cacaxtla (about five minutes away). You can also take a SAN MARTIN bus ($1, 1 hr) from Puebla's CAPU terminal.

FOOD The small cafeteria next to the museum in Cacaxtla has a *menú del día* (daily special) for $4, or you can pick up something cheaper from the taco stands in San Miguel, a short walk away. Try the *alegrías,* a honey and millet grain candy native to Tlaxcala.

Puebla
Puebla, Mexico's fourth largest city, is overwhelming at first. Music stores blast the latest Mexican hits onto crowded sidewalks, and taxis and buses weave crazily down narrow cobblestone streets while traffic cops calmly eat ice cream from a safe distance. Your first instinct, once deposited into downtown Puebla, may be to run and hide. But this cosmopolitan city soon seems less chaotic, and its carefully preserved architecture and wealth of historic and religious artifacts lend it a sense of continuity.

Puebla is best explored on foot; as you walk past each building, a peek through the imposing wooden doors reveals extravagant church interiors laden with gilt, exhibitions of folk art and antiques, and steaming platters of *mole poblano* (*see* box Hole Mole, *below*) and other regional dishes. Puebla's popularity among both foreign and Mexican tourists is increasing, but the sheer quantity of things to do means you won't feel as if you're in a tourist trap.

Founded in 1531, Puebla is first and foremost a colonial city, but the ruins in the nearby city of Cholula (*see* Near Puebla, *below*) also reveal the rich indigenous culture that existed long before the arrival of the conquistadors. Puebla was also a key player in the military history of Mexico. In 1862, the city was the site of a major battle, where 2,000 Mexicans defeated 6,000 French troops. Then, in 1910, the massacre of activists by the army gave impetus to the uprising against dictator Porfirio Díaz. Recently, the state university has seen numerous student strikes and protests. Puebla has 14 universities, and students are always busy hanging out in cafés and organizing cultural events.

Almost anything you eat in Puebla, whether it was prepared on a makeshift brazier on the street or in a fancy restaurant, is wonderful. In fact, this is the only Mexican city where a kitchen—La Cocina de Santa Rosa—is considered a tourist attraction.

BASICS

AMERICAN EXPRESS The AmEx office is in the Plaza Dorada shopping center, a five-minute bus ride from downtown. They exchange and sell traveler's checks, replace lost ones, and deliver MoneyGrams. Cardholders can also cash personal checks, replace lost cards, and have their mail held. *Mailing address: Plaza Dorada 2, Local 21—22, Puebla, Puebla, CP 72530, tel. 22/37–55–51. Take PLAZA DORADA bus from Calle 13 Ote., at 2 Sur. Open weekdays 9:30–6, Sat. 9:30–1.*

AUTO PARTS/SERVICE **Sears** auto shop sells parts and does most mechanical repairs. *Av. 3 Pte. 138, tel. 22/42–45–55.*

BOOKSTORES **Librerías de Cristal** (Av. Reforma 511, tel. 22/42–44–20) has an enormous selection of books, magazines, videos, and compact discs. There's a small selection of books in English. *2 blocks west of zócalo, btw Calle 5 Nte. and Calle 7 Nte.*

CASAS DE CAMBIO Exchange cash or traveler's checks at **Bancomer** (Reforma 116, tel. 22/32–00–22) or **Banco Internacional** (Av. 2 Pte. 107, tel. 22/46–40–44, ext. 2128), both open weekdays 9–noon. Many of the banks along Avenida Reforma have ATMs that accept Plus and Cirrus system cards, but those at **Banamex** (Reforma 135) are the most reliable.

EMERGENCIES Dial 06 from any public phone in Puebla for **police, fire,** and **ambulance** service.

LAUNDRY **Lavandería Roly** has both self- and drop-off service. Someone will wash and dry your clothes for $6 per 3 kilos; it costs $4 to do it yourself. *Calle 7 Nte. 404, at 4 Pte., tel. 22/32–93–07. Open Mon.–Sat. 8 AM–9 PM, Sun. 8–3.*

MAIL The main post office is two blocks south of the zócalo. They'll hold mail for you at the following address for up to 10 days: Lista de Correos, 5 Ote. y 16 de Septiembre, Sur C, Puebla, Puebla, CP 72000, México. *5 Ote., at 16 de Septiembre, tel. 22/42–64–48. Open weekdays 8–7, Sat. 9–noon.*

MEDICAL AID The **Hospital Universitario** (Calle 13 Sur, at Av. 25 Pte., tel. 22/43–13–72) has 24-hour emergency service. **Farmacia Carmen** (16 de Septiembre 2107, tel. 22/43–11–88) is the only pharmacy in the city open 24 hours a day, every day of the year. Several other pharmacies around the zócalo offer 15%–30% discounts on prescriptions; try **Farmacia Portales** (2 Norte 5, tel. 22/42–52–71).

PHONES Puebla probably has the highest percentage of functioning payphones in Mexico. You can also make calls from any caseta de larga distancia, found in various stores around Puebla. Just look for a blue picture of a telephone and the initials L.A.D.A. on the side. **Miscelanea Yarida** (4 Norte 408, at 4 Ote.) offers cash calls, and collect calls are free. It's somewhat hard to find, so look for the TIA ROSA PAN DULCE sign. **Helados Holanda** (16 de Septiembre 103) has both long-distance service and a fax machine and is open on Sunday, but you can't make collect calls. Most casetas are open 9 AM–8 PM.

VISITOR INFORMATION The **Oficina de Información Turística,** across from the cathedral and next to the **Casa de Cultura,** is staffed by a knowledgeable and helpful crew. They can provide you with good maps of the city as well as the state. *5 Ote. 3, tel. 22/46–20–44. Open Mon.–Sat. 8 AM–8:30 PM, Sun. 9–2.*

COMING AND GOING

BY BUS Puebla's main bus terminal, **CAPU** (Blvd. Atlixco Nte. s/n), is served by a number of bus lines. **Autobuses Unidos (AU)** (tel. 22/49–74–05) sends buses to Mexico City ($5.50, 2 hrs) every 10 minutes from 5 AM to 11 PM. They also go to Veracruz ($12, 5 hrs) every hour between 6:30 AM and midnight, as well as to Oaxaca ($13, 8 hrs) at 8:30 PM and 11:30 PM. **Estrella Blanca** (tel. 22/49–74–33) serves Acapulco ($33, 7 hrs); buses leave every two hours until 11:30 PM. **Cristóbal Colón** (tel. 22/49–73–27) buses depart for Salina Cruz ($36, 10 hrs) at 9 PM daily. Several other bus companies also go to Oaxaca throughout the day, some of them charging less for buses that make several stops along the way. Besides serving many of the destinations listed above, **Autobuses del Oriente (ADO)** (tel. 22/49–70–42) has buses daily at 9 PM for Mérida ($62, 21 hrs) and Cancún ($67, 24 hrs). Several local companies go to towns closer to Puebla, such as Tehuacán and Tlaxcala. The terminal has luggage storage from 7 AM to 11:30 PM, a tourist information booth, a police station, and a bank that changes money from 9 AM to noon. Several cafeterias, a pharmacy, and shops selling everything from religious ornaments to stuffed animals ensure that you'll be occupied as you wait for your bus.

Unfortunately, the bus terminal is nowhere near downtown Puebla. To get downtown you have to take either a combi or a cab. The authorized taxis (prepay the fare at the booth inside the terminal) charge $3 to the zócalo, where most of the budget hotels are. Take a cab if you can afford it; the combi ride is long (about 20 minutes by a circuitous route) and won't take you all the way to the zócalo. RUTA 48 buses go as close as 11 Norte and Reforma, five blocks from the zócalo.

BY TRAIN Trains pass through Puebla twice a day on their way to Oaxaca from Mexico City and vice versa. They're slower than the buses and cost more, but if you're dying to take that midnight train, this is your chance. Pay the $17 for a first class ticket; it's much more comfortable than second class ($10). The train for Oaxaca leaves at midnight; the train for Mexico City swings through at 7:20 AM. *Calle 9 Nte., at 80 Pte., tel. 22/20–16–64.*

GETTING AROUND

Puebla's streets are confusing at first, but with a little math they can be mastered. Use the zócalo as your compass. Streets are oriented along the cardinal directions: norte (north), sur (south), oriente (east), and poniente (west). The main street, 5 de Mayo, becomes 16 de Septiembre as it goes south of the zócalo. Avenida Reforma

The "directionless youth" of Generation X need not fear— Puebla may be confusing, but most budget hotels and points of interest are within a short walk of the zócalo, and poblanos give helpful directions if asked.

becomes Avenida Ávila Camacho after passing the zócalo from east to west. Otherwise, all streets are numbered. Even-numbered sur and norte streets (calles) are east of the zócalo, odd-numbered are west of it. Even-numbered oriente and poniente avenidas are north of the zócalo, odd-numbered ones south.

BY BUS Puebla has an extensive system of colectivos that run from about 6 AM until 11 PM. However, colectivos and combis don't travel the streets right around the zócalo; the closest they come is Calle 11, about five blocks away. A one-way trip costs about 20¢, and it's usually a bumpy, crowded ride.

BY TAXI Taxi fares within the city range from $1 to about $3.50. As usual, determine the fare before you get in the cab. A ride to the bus station should cost about $2.50.

WHERE TO SLEEP

All of the hotels described below are within a few blocks of the zócalo, in the colonial Centro Historico (historical center) of the city. Clean, livable rooms with a communal bathroom can be found for as little as $7, but most rooms with bath run $13–$15. The only hotel anywhere near the CAPU bus station is the **Hotel Terminal de Puebla** (Carmen Serdán 5101, tel. 22/32–79–80), where a room for one or two people costs $28.

➤ UNDER $15 • **Hotel Avenida.** The management usually hides upstairs in this cavernous hotel, but ringing the bell by the front desk brings them down. Rooms and communal bathrooms are semi-clean, and the walls are painted with fake brick and brown stucco. The best part about this hotel is the price—both singles and doubles without bath are $7 ($13 with bath). Hot water runs between 6 and 11 AM and 7 and 11 PM. *Av. 5 Pte. 336, tel. 22/41–21–04. 1½ blocks west of cathedral. 52 rooms. Wheelchair access.*

Hotel Embajadores. This hotel is spartan at best—most of the windowless rooms share one bath per floor, and the showers are only available from 7:30 to 10 in the morning. However, it's clean and the staff is helpful. Singles cost $7 ($13 with bath), and doubles are a mere $9 ($16 with bath.) *5 de Mayo 603, tel. 22/32–26–37. 4 blocks north of zócalo, at Av. 6 Ote. 90 rooms, 15 with bath. Luggage storage, wheelchair access.*

Hotel Venecia. Established in 1897, Hotel Venecia isn't much to look at, but it's clean, and the clientele consists of friendly Mexican families. None of the rooms have baths, but there's hot water all of the time, which means you won't have to rush through your shower while other guests lurk impatiently outside. Rooms are $8.50 for a single, $10 for a double. *Av. 4 Pte. 716, tel. 22/32–24–69. 2 blocks north and 3 blocks west of zócalo. 24 rooms, none with bath. Luggage storage, wheelchair access.*

➤ UNDER $20 • **Hotel Imperial.** Go out of your way to stay at this hotel. The owner says he'll give anyone carrying this book a 40% discount, putting the ordinarily pricey rooms in the budget traveler's range. From the busy pool table and restaurant on the first floor to the remodeled split-level rooms complete with TVs, telephones, and filtered tap water, you'll feel like you've gone to backpackers' heaven. The owner, Juan José Bretón Avalos (*el Licenciado*), is an expert on Puebla and Oaxaca and loves to chat with students. The discounted prices are approximately $14 for a single, $18 for a double. *Av. 4 Ote. 212, btw 2 Nte. and 4 Nte., tel. 22/42–49–81. 65 rooms, all with bath. Luggage storage, wheelchair access. MC, V.*

Hotel Victoria. The hallways here are dim, but the colorful tile, quirky furniture, and homey comforters make up for it. Hot water is available only from 6 to 10 AM and 6 to 10 PM. Rooms are $15 for a single, $16–$20 for a double. *Av. 3 Pte. 306, tel. 22/32–89–92. 1½ blocks west of cathedral. 35 rooms, all with bath. Wheelchair access.*

➤ UNDER $25 • **Hotel Latino.** The best thing about this hotel is its location on a street redolent with the smell of mole emanating from several nearby restaurants. Green reigns supreme here, from the hallways to the tiled floors. Hot water is only available mornings until noon. Rooms with one bed are $10 ($14 with bath). Rooms with two beds and a private bathroom are $20. *Calle 6 Nte. 8, tel. 22/32–23–25. Two blocks east of zócalo, btw Avila Camacho and Av. 2 Ote. 60 rooms, 50 with bath. Laundry, luggage storage.*

Solo travelers may not want to look for lodging west of Calle 7 Norte. The numerous brothels here make for a seedy atmosphere, and even a brief walk in the area can be uncomfortable.

Hotel Ritz. The standard rooms here are sunny and spacious. The popular rooms with large windows opening onto the street are often unavailable. Singles cost $15, doubles $20. *Calle 2 Nte. 207, tel. 22/32–44–57. 2 blocks north of zócalo. 24 rooms, all with bath.*

Hotel Teresita. The claustrophobic rooms, resplendent with a strange shade of orange, might send you running, but the price is right—$8 for a single ($13 with bath) and $23 for a double with bath. The manager swears there is hot water all the time. *Av. 3 Pte. 309, tel. 22/32–70–72. 1½ blocks west of the cathedral. 58 rooms, 40 with bath. Laundry, luggage storage, wheelchair access.*

➤ UNDER $50 • **Hotel Colonial.** This is a favorite of American and European students taking courses at the university across the street. The entire place is done up in colonial style, with the requisite statues, dark wood, and arches. Rooms are spacious, tiled, clean, and fairly quiet. There's also cable TV, room service, a library, money exchange, and a popular restaurant. Spanish classes are given on a fairly regular basis——ask the management. Both María Luisa Monteyano and Roxana Mendoza speak English and are extremely friendly and helpful. To stay here though, you'll have to cough up $37 for a single, $48 for a double. *Calle 4 Sur 105, tel. 22/46–46–12. 1 block east of zócalo, across from university. 70 rooms, all with bath. Laundry, luggage storage. Reservations advised. AE.*

FOOD

Puebla's nuns had a special gift for culinary creation; *mole poblano* (*see* box Holy Mole, *below*) and *chiles en nogada* (chiles stuffed with beef and covered in a walnut sauce and pomegranate seeds) were both invented in convent kitchens here. Around the university on Avila Camacho and Calle 6 Norte, restaurants serve comidas corridas for $3–$4. Several restaurants serve huge "economical" breakfasts for about $2–$4. **Vip's,** on the corner of 2 Oriente and 2 Norte, serves somewhat expensive American-style breakfasts, but it's about the only place you can get a cup of coffee at 7 AM. If you prefer to eat a little lighter in the morning, bakeries such as **Pan de la Fe** (Av. 2 Ote. 208, tel. 22/32–21–37) have *pan dulce* (sweet rolls) and other pastries for about 25¢ each. Another sweet experience is a stroll down the **Calle de las Dulces** (Av. 6 Ote., btw 5 de Mayo and Calle 4 Nte.), past numerous shops selling Puebla's famous fruit candies. Specialties include *camote* (candied yam) and a meringue concoction called Beso del Angel (angel's kiss). The **Super Churrería** (2 Sur, at 5 Oriente) serves traditional *churros* and chocolate ($2). The twisted, sugary pastries dipped into hot chocolate will send you floating away into ecstasy.

La Pasita on Calle 5 Poniente at Avenida 6 Sur is the only place in the world where they make the drink of the same name, a liqueur made from raisins. The place has been around for three generations and is cluttered with memorabilia. They serve $1.50 shots of La Pasita and other regional liqueurs daily from 12:30 to 5:30.

➤ UNDER $5 • **El Vegetariano.** This plant-filled restaurant in the downtown business district serves only vegetarian fare and non-alcoholic drinks. They make a popular mole poblano with soy chicken ($3). Other dishes, like *enchiladas suizas* (cheese enchiladas; $3) or *rellenos de champiñones* (cheese and mushroom tacos; $3.50), are good, if a bit heavy. The menú del día includes soup, salad, an entrée, and a fruit drink for $4. *Av. 3 Pte. 525, tel. 22/46–54–62. 3 blocks west of zócalo. Open daily 7:30 AM–10 PM.*

Fonda Carolina. This unassuming place with great service, plastic tablecloths, bullfight paintings on the walls, and Mexican pop music in the air is very popular with students. Their chilaquiles, a big, messy plate of tortillas, avocado, shredded chicken, green salsa, and cream, comes with a fruit cocktail and Nescafé or hot chocolate for about $3. For lunch, try the *chalupas poblanas* (Puebla-style tacos; $3) or the comida corrida ($3). *Calle 4 Nte. 5, tel. 22/32–23–39. 1 block east of zócalo. Open daily 8 AM–9 PM.*

La Zanahoria. Bodybuilding waiters flex their muscles at this vegetarian haven with a fairly imaginative menu and a juice bar. Large portions of delicacies such as *nopales* (grilled cactus) stuffed with cheese, crêpes stuffed with spinach, *flor de calabaza* (squash flowers), and *rajas* (chile strips) go for $3–$4. Daily comida corrida specials are $4. *Juárez 2104, tel. 22/46–29–90. 9 blocks west and 3 blocks south of zócalo. Take a RUTA 7 combi from Calle 11 Ote. at 16 de Septiembre.*

San Francisco el Alto Mercado (Garibaldi). What used to be a market has now been turned into the enclosed setting for about 15 fondas (covered food stands). They serve traditional poblano food—about $3.50 for a plate of chicken mole, rice, and beans—in a lively atmosphere. Vendors vying for your business will try to guide you to their fonda, but look and smell around before you decide. On weekends, mariachis play for the working class crowd—upper crust poblanos snub the place. *Calle 14 Ote., at 14 Nte., no phone. 5 blocks north and 6 blocks east of zócalo. Open daily 24 hrs.*

➤ UNDER $10 • **La Concordia.** Though the television and the stereo compete for attention in this small, colorful café, the volume is low enough for a relaxed atmosphere. The extensive menu includes breakfast—juice or milk, coffee, eggs, and *chilaquiles* (tortilla strips doused with salsa and sour cream)—for about $3.50, as well as two types of comida corrida—regular ($3.50) and *ejecutivo* (executive, $5)—served at both lunch and dinner. *Av. 2 Ote. 205-A, at 2 Nte., tel 22/46–68–27. Open daily 8 AM–10 PM. Wheelchair access.*

Restaurant Hotel Colonial. This place is packed for lunch, and the menú del día ($6), served 1:30–5, is enough food to immobilize you for several days. It includes soup, rice with fried plantains, a vegetable dish, an entrée (they always have mole) with black beans on the side, dessert, and coffee. *Calle 4 Sur 105, tel. 22/46–46–12. 1 block east of zócalo. Open daily 7 AM–10 PM.*

Villa del Mar. People wait in line to lunch at this terrace seafood restaurant. The shrimp, octopus, snail, and oyster cocktails ($3.50–$13) are seasoned with cilantro, onion, avocado, chili, and sugar. Another good bet is the shrimp brochette with onion, bacon, and tomatoes ($8.50). *Juárez 1920, in Zona Esmeralda, tel. 22/42–31–04. Take RUTA 7 combi from Calle 11 Ote. and 16 de Septiembre, or walk 8 blocks west from zócalo, then 3 blocks south to Juárez. Open daily 10–5:30.*

➤ UNDER $15 • **Chesa Veglia/Casa Vieja.** This Swiss-style restaurant with an alpine theme serves up treats such as sausage grilled with onions and potatoes ($8.50), scallops "cordon bleu" ($10), and *pollo suizo* (chicken in a mushroom, cream, and paprika sauce; $9). Pastas, soups, and salads are also on the menu. This is one of the few places in Puebla open late at night, and live music starts at 10 PM. *Av. 2 Ote. 208, tel. 22/32–16–41. 1 block north and ½ block east of zócalo. Open daily 10 AM–1 AM.*

Fonda de Santa Clara. This famous restaurant serves typical comida poblana in a setting decorated with *papel picado* (traditional Mexican cut paper) and *lupe muñecas* (papier-mâché dolls) over the bar. This restaurant caters to tourists and the food isn't cheap, but you'd be hard pressed to find their seasonal specials anywhere else. The menu features *gusanos de maguey con salsa borracha* (maguey worms in tequila sauce) in April and May, and *chapulines* (grasshoppers) during October and November. The *café de olla* (coffee flavored wth cinnamon

Holy Mole

Rumor has it mole was invented by the Aztecs as a topping for that tastiest of meats, human flesh, but the more plausible explanation is as follows: Sor Andrea de la Asunción, an 18th-century nun in the Santa Rosa convent, was given the task of creating a special dish for the Archbishop of Puebla. Wanting to combine the best of Mexican and Spanish cuisine, she began with four types of chiles——mulato, ancho, pasilla, and chipotle——for the Mexican element, and almonds as a symbol of Spain. Believing the sauce was too spicy, Sor Andrea added raisins, plantains, and chocolate to sweeten the kick. Sesame seeds and peanuts were thrown in to thicken the sauce, clove and cinnamon for flavor, and anise to make it all go down easily. The finished product had 18 ingredients, and quickly became a standard of Mexican cuisine.

The word mole may be a garbled version of muele (grind, which was what Sor Andrea did with all those ingredients), or the Nahuatl word mollí, which means "hot chile." Today, there are as many different moles as there are cooks, but Pueblan restaurants keep a tight hold on what they claim is the original recipe. Every year in June there is an annual mole festival, when poblanos compete to create the best recipe.

and chocolate; $1) wakes you up from your post-meal coma. *Av. 3 Pte. 307, 2 blocks west of zócalo, tel. 22/42–26–59; open Tues.–Sun. noon–11 PM; wheelchair access. Also at Calle 3 Pte. 920; open Wed.–Mon. noon–11 PM. AE, MC, V.*

Las Buhardillas. This fairly new restaurant has upscale, pleasant service for a decent price, as well as free live music at night and sometimes during the day. Typical dishes such as *pollo en pipian* (chicken in a pumpkin-seed and chile sauce) will set you back $10, but mushroom crêpes, pasta, and several kinds of sandwiches are only $5–$7. *Juárez 2915, tel. 22/30–54–35. In Zona Esmeralda, 1 block from Fuente de la Paz. Open daily 7 AM–midnight. Wheelchair access.*

CAFES Cafés fill up at night with students and artists. Coffee drinks include a shot of alcohol as often as not, and many cafés feature a guitarist or other entertainment.

Café Aroma. The Aroma is a romantic little place with brass lanterns and intimate tables. A cup of coffee here is less than a dollar ($2.50 with alcohol), and appetizers such as *chalupas* (fried tortillas) are available. They also sell coffee beans from the nearby town of Villa Juárez ($5 per kilo). *Av. 3 Pte. 520-A, no phone.*

Café y Arte. This unpretentious, student-staffed café in the Casa de Cultura opens onto a small courtyard and has wicker stools, low tables, and even lower prices. *Av. 5 Ote. 5. Open daily 5 PM–9 PM.*

Teorema. This dimly lit 24-hour café/bookstore has the feel of a literary salon; daily live music and occasional poetry readings take place on the small stage from about 8:30 on. The menu, complete with a poem, includes coffees ($2–$3), desserts (about $3), and beer and wine ($1.50). *Reforma, at Calle 7 Nte., tel. 22/42–10–14.*

WORTH SEEING

Most sights are free, and the ones that aren't reduce admission for students with international IDs. Almost all museums are closed Mondays and free on Sundays, with the exception of the **Museo Amparo**, which is free Mondays and closed Tuesdays. **La China Poblana** restaurant (Calle 6 Nte. 1, no phone) is a must-see for a dose of folkloric overload. Everywhere you look there is papel picado, tiles, painted wood, and other assorted kitsch, topped off by the life-size mannequin dressed in a flashy China Poblana (*see box,* La China Poblana, *below*) costume in the front room.

MUSEO AMPARO This airy, terra-cotta-colored museum—the newest attraction in town—specializes in Mesoamerican art. Signs in English and Spanish guide you through the exhibits, and you can also listen to a recorded audio tour ($3 plus $3 deposit). Interactive computers inform visitors about selected pieces in the museum. On display are beautiful examples of Maya, Olmec, and other artifacts. *Calle 2 Sur 708, tel. 22/46–42–00. 2½ blocks south of zócalo. Admission: $3.50; $3 with student ID, free Mon. Open Wed.–Mon. 10–5. Wheelchair access.*

PALACIO DEL ARZOBISPO This grand, two-story building was once the residence of Juan de Palafox y Mendoza, the Archbishop of Puebla. It now houses the **Casa de la Cultura,** with a concert and lecture hall on the first floor and art exhibits on the second. Also on the second floor is the luxurious **Biblioteca Palafoxiana,** a library that dates back to 1646. Next door to the library is the newly opened **Sala del Tesoro Bibliográfico,** with rotating displays of antique books. The oldest book in the collection is a 1493 history of the world from the beginning of time to the date of publication. Miguel Ramírez Meya, the guy in charge, is hard of hearing, very earnest, and smart as hell. *Av. 5 Ote. 5, tel. 22/46–56–13. Across from cathedral. Admission: free, $1.50 for the library. Open Tues.–Sun. 10–5.*

CASA DE ALFENIQUE Known as the wedding cake house, this 17th-century mansion is now the state museum. First-floor exhibits focus on Puebla's history and archaeology. The second floor is a recreation of a colonial-era residence. A highlight of the museum's collection is the original dress of the legendary China Poblana (*see box* La China Poblana, *below*). *Av. 4 Ote.*

416, tel. 22/41–42–96. 2 blocks north and 1 block east of zócalo. Museum admission: $1.50, $1 with student ID. Open Tues.–Sun. 10–5.

The city of Puebla has been famous since colonial times for its richly decorated and glazed ceramic work; brightly colored tiles decorate many of the city's historic buildings.

CASA DE LOS HERMANOS SERDAN Known as the **Museo de la Revolución,** the house of Aquiles Serdán and his sister Carmen now honors a group of revolutionaries who perished here during a 14-hour gunfight with 500 federal army soldiers and policemen sent to arrest them on conspiracy charges. In the parlor, pierced mirrors still hang on bullet-riddled walls, and broadsheets calling for revolution, published by the Serdán family, are on display. The assassination of Aquiles Serdán and his followers is believed by many to be the event that launched the Revolution of 1910. *Av. 6 Ote. 206, tel. 22/42–10–76. 3 blocks north of zócalo. Admission: $1.50. Open Tues.–Sun. 10–4:30.*

CATEDRAL DE LA CONCEPCION INMACULADA This is one of the largest cathedrals in Mexico, with 14 chapels and two bell towers. Construction began in 1575 and was completed almost two centuries later. One tower is bell-less; according to legend, builders feared that the extra weight would cause the cathedral to sink into the ground like the cathedral in Mexico City. The truth is, the builders simply ran out of money. The massive, gray-blue stone building is an example of the *mudéjar* (Moorish-influenced) style and boasts marble floors and a beautiful altar carved from gray onyx, as well as 300-year-old paintings. Tours in Spanish take place in the afternoon. *On zócalo. Admission free. Open daily 10:30–noon and 4–7.*

EX-CONVENTO DE SANTA ROSA Abandoned during the early 1860s, the convent today is almost completely restored. The centerpiece is a huge, tiled kitchen, the birthplace of mole poblano. Guides (who give tours only in Spanish) are well-versed in its legends. The convent is now the home of the **Museo de Artesanías,** featuring folk art from Puebla state's seven regions: Huochinango, Teziutlán, Ciudad Serdán, Cholula, Puebla, Izucar de Matamoros, and Tehuacán. There's also a great gift shop. *Calle 3 Nte. 1203, tel. 22/46–22–71. 1 block west and 6 blocks north of zócalo. Admission: $1.50. Open Tues.–Sun. 10–4.*

FUERTES DE LORETO Y GUADALUPE A popular destination for both poblanos and tourists, the forts are the main attraction of a hilltop park complex. The Cinco de Mayo celebrations held by Mexicans all over the world honor the Battle of Puebla (May 5, 1862). **Fuerte Loreto** is dedicated to that battle, and the original cannons used to defeat the French army now guard the victorious General Zaragoza's grave. Other aspects of the battle are exhibited in the **Museo de Historia** within the fort, but don't make a special trip just to see the museum. Across the plaza is the **Fuerte de Guadalupe,** which is not as well preserved. The complex features a cluster of museums: the **Museo de Antropología Regional,** which has artifacts from the early Puebla Valley cultures; the **Museo de Historia Natural,** with realistic wildlife scenes; and the excellent **planetario** (planetarium) with has shows for stargazers every hour between noon and 6 PM. Admission prices are separate for each museum, and range from $1.50 for the Museo de Historia Natural to $3 for the planetarium. *Take FUERTES combi from 8 Nte. at 10 Ote., or RUTA 72 combi from anywhere on 5 de Mayo after 8 Pte. Get off at Monumento Zaragoza; museums are to the east.*

IGLESIA DE SAN FRANCISCO Built in the 18th century, this church houses the preserved body of Franciscan Friar Sebastián de Aparicio, who is credited with convincing the Indians to stop carrying heavy loads on their backs and let oxen do the work instead. His skeleton is only partly covered with a monk's robe, and his face wears a mask, because so many people have picked pieces from it. Above the friar's body hangs the famous *Conquistadora*—Hernán Cortés's personal statue of the Virgin Mary. Her bloodstained gown is enough to make you shudder. Both the Franciscan and the Conquistadora are in the chapel, up at the front of the church, to the left of the altar. *Calle 8 Nte., at 14 Ote. 3 blocks east and 5 blocks north of zócalo. Admission free. Open daily 9–7:30.*

CONVENTO SECRETO DE SANTA MONICA It is said that this convent went underground after the constitutional reform of 1857, which provided for the confiscation of church lands and the abolishment of ecclesiastical privileges. Today, guides lead visitors on a tour of the mazelike convent, showing the secret doors where food was supposedly brought to the nuns, peep holes through which they watched mass in the church next door, and the underground crypt where they were buried. The heart of the convent's founder, some 130 years old, is kept on gruesome display here, and religious art fills the twisting and turning hallways. The velvet paintings from the 1850s are startling; as you move from one side of the painting to the other, the faces and feet of the subjects seem to change position and landscapes shift to the other side of the canvas.

Around the corner is the **Señor de las Maravillas.** Crowds of Mexicans visit this statue of Christ made from corn paste, which is believed to perform miracles. According to legend, the statue was fashioned by a fugitive carpenter hiding out in the convent. He and the Mother Superior both dreamed of the Señor on the same night, after which she ordered him to create the figure of the dream or be turned over to the police. *Av. 18 Pte., at 5 de Mayo, 103, tel. 22/32–01–78. 9 blocks north of zócalo. Admission: $1.50. Open Tues.–Sun. 10–5. Mass twice on weeknights, 4 times on Sunday.*

TEMPLO DE SANTO DOMINGO The church dates from 1659 and acquired fame because of the **Capilla del Rosario** (Chapel of the Rosary), a baroque chapel with a surfeit of gold leaf and glitter. The figure of the Virgin is bedecked with precious and semiprecious jewels. Next door is the **Museo Bello Zetina** (tel. 22/32–47–20), which has an interesting display of religious art and antiques. *5 de Mayo 407, 1 block north of zócalo. Admission free. Open daily 10–4; museum closed Mon.*

CHEAP THRILLS

Those interested in Catholic paraphernalia will find plenty in Puebla's stores, including a wide variety of incense, rosaries, and electric "candles" with lights that flicker (for those opposed to the shameless consumption of wax). At **Librería Mariana** (Calles 2 Sur and 3 Ote., across from the zócalo) you can buy prayer cards identifying all those saints you've seen in churches around the city.

FESTIVALS **Cinco de Mayo.** On May 5, the city commemorates the 1862 Battle of Puebla, in which the Mexican army defeated French invaders. It is a day of celebrations and special events, including fireworks, a military parade, sporting events, and performances of traditional music.

Festival de San Agustín. During most of the month of August, Pueblans celebrate with music, dancing, and fireworks. On the 26th (St. Augustine's feast day) it is customary to prepare chiles en nogada (*see* Food, *above*), invented by the nuns of the Santa Monica convent.

Fiesta de San Francisco de Asis-Cuetzalán. The feast day of St. Francis in early October is the annual occasion for two weeks of indigenous dances, a *tianguis* (open-air market), and general merrymaking in the tiny town of Cuetzalán (*see* Near Puebla, *below*). Dancers wear traditional white robes and *tocas de lana* (large, turban-like hats almost 40 centimeters high).

Carnaval de Huejotzingo. Every year before Lent, the residents of Huejotzingo (*see* Near Puebla, *below*) reenact the kidnapping of the daughter of a *corregidor* (magistrate) against the backdrop of the Mexican triumph against the French. The costumes and masks are elaborate, and the festival is noisy and sometimes dangerous—the tradition of shooting colored gun-powder at celebrants often results in injuries.

SHOPPING

The *majolica* techniques developed in Talavera de la Reina, Spain, are used for making tiles and other ceramicware in Puebla. You can learn about the process at **Uriarte** (Av. 4 Pte. 911, tel. 22/32–15–98), a factory and shop devoted exclusively to beautiful Talavera ceramics. Free tours in English and Spanish take place daily from 9 to 6. If the workers aren't too busy, they may even let you sit at the potter's wheel and make your own version. You'll find more Talavera pieces, including dishes and vases, at **El Parian** (Calle 6 Nte., btw Av. 4 and 2 Ote.), a market that's been around since 1796. Nowadays, the more artistic pieces are mixed in with a lot of cheap souvenirs, but it's a fun place to poke around and haggle. Across the street is the **Barrio del Artista** (Calle 8 Nte., at Av. 6 Ote.), where painters and sculptors open their studios to visitors. On Avenida 5 Oriente and Calle 6 Norte you'll find an antiques market known as the **Mercado de Los Sapos.**

AFTER DARK

Unless watching couples in various stages of passionate embrace is your idea of fun, the zócalo is not the happening place to be at night. Less voyeuristic fun can be had in the **Zona Esmeralda,** 10 blocks east of the zócalo on Avenida Juárez. The restaurants, bars, and discos here will swallow you up for a few hours and spit you out, staggering, to the nearest taxi. **Tasaja** (Juárez 2921, tel. 22/49–56–06), **Ovni** (Juárez 2915-B, tel. 22/48–38–53), and **Pagaía** (Juárez 1906, tel. 22/42–46–75) all draw young crowds dancing to techno, hip hop, and the like. Cover is about $5. Call ahead on Fridays, as these places are often rented to student groups for the evening.

For a quieter scene, **Las Buhardillas** (Juárez 2915, tel. 22/30–54–35) has live jazz or chamber music every night. **Antillanos** (Juárez 2109, tel. 22/46–58–47) is a must for Caribbean music lovers, with live salsa bands and an enthusiastic chain-smoking crowd that loves to dance. Cover is a mere $2. If you just want to drink, **María Bonita** (Calle 31 Pte., at 2 Sur), not far from the Plaza Dorada, is filled with college students on Friday and Saturday nights. Weekday nights, everyone heads to coffee bars such as **Teorema** (*see* Food, *above*).

CINEMAS/THEATERS Cinemática Luis Buñuel in the Casa de la Cultura (Av. 5 Ote. 5, tel. 22/46–36–32) has a tiny movie theater that shows international films. New releases from the U.S. are shown at **Cinemas Doradas 1 y 2** (tel. 22/46–83–52) in the Plaza Dorada shopping center. **Cine Continental** (Av. 4 Ote. 212), next to the Hotel Imperial, shows cheesy but entertaining Mexican comedies and adventure movies for $3. Both **Teatro Espacio 1900** (Calle 2 Ote. 412, tel. 22/46–83–53) and **Teatro Hermanos Soler** (Av. 5 Pte. 318, tel. 22/46–98–15) put on live theater and concerts. Teatro Hermanos Soler also has a post-show peña, at which people are invited to play music, sing, recite poetry, and generally make public spectacles of themselves from about 8:30 PM until the last vociferous poet has gone home. The second drink is always on the house. Call ahead to find out if there will be a cover.

OUTDOOR ACTIVITIES

Many people travel to Puebla with the sole purpose of attacking **Volcán Popocatépetl.** Officially, you need to be a registered hiker to climb Popocatépetl. Moreover, it's a hassle to reach without a car. If you're determined, take a bus from CAPU to Chalco, where you can transfer to

La China Poblana

Pueblans still speak of Mirra, the China Poblana (Chinese Woman of Puebla). One version of her legend claims that she was kidnapped as a child from Delhi and later sold to the viceroy of Mexico. Another version insists she was a Mongol princess, captured by pirates from Acapulco. Either way, she was sold to a Puebla merchant and his wife, who adopted and raised her. La China adapted her native dress to that of Mexico, and, according to the legend, the resulting costume was so beautiful and unusual that local women began to imitate her. A modern version of that dress, now elaborately embroidered and sequined, is worn by dancers performing the jarabe tapatío (hat dance). As for Mirra herself, she is said to be buried underneath the altar of one of Puebla's many churches.

Amecameca, and take another one to Tlamacas. The whole trip takes about 3½ hours. In Tlamacas, there's a hostel serving mostly climbers that charges $3 a night for a dorm bed. It's best to get to the hostel in the early evening the day before you plan to climb. Bring food for a couple of days. The easiest route to the summit of the volcano, **La Ruta de las Cruces,** takes you to the top in about seven hours. The climb down should take three hours. Most people climb on the weekends, when there are guides available. For more information, call the **Legión Alpina de Puebla** (tel. 22/32–39–00).

Near Puebla

CHOLULA

Only about 20 minutes by bus from Puebla, Cholula is gringo friendly, with signs and menus in English, and plenty of restaurants that accept credit cards. Best of all, Cholulans are extremely helpful, and much less harried than their Pueblan neighbors. The women of this town are much more open to conversation than in many other places, an aspect of life here that will put female travelers at ease.

Before the Conquest, Cholula was a sacred city that rivaled Teotihuacán as a cultural center. In its heyday, Cholula reportedly had hundreds of temples. It is often referred to as the City of Churches, because, according to legend, conquering Spaniards built a church for each day of the year atop the ruins of Cholulan temples. Although that number is exaggerated, there are approximately 130 churches in Cholula and the surrounding areas today. The view from atop the **Great Pyramid of Cholula** reveals a panorama of steeples and spires. Crowning the pyramid is a blue and white church called **Nuestra Señora de los Remedios.**

The pyramid itself actually consists of three pyramids built on top of on another. The final pyramid would have been the largest in the world if it had been finished; its base is 4,500 square meters. The construction was started by the Choultecas, a mix of people from several regions of Mexico, but was ended around AD 650 when they were attacked and conquered by the warriors of nearby Cacaxtla (*see* Near Tlaxcala, *above*). For a $4.50 admission fee, visitors can explore nearly 8 kilometers of underground tunnels daily from 10 to 4. To get to the pyramid from the zócalo, walk east (away from the volcanoes) along Avenida Morelos for about three blocks. A museum across the road from the pyramid explains what you see in the caverns. Guides, available at the tunnel entrance, charge $9 for an interesting one-hour tour (it's $10 for the English version). Unfortunately, owing to the many flash–toting tourists, the murals depicting a Cholulan drinking party are no longer open to the public.

Down the hill about seven blocks east of the Great Pyramid is Cholula's zócalo, which supposedly has the longest *portal* (porch) in Latin America. Along the portal are several shops, boutiques, and restaurants. Try to visit the zócalo on Sunday (market day), or a saint's day celebration; considering the number of churches in the area, each celebrating at least 10 feast days annually, finding one isn't difficult. Facing the zócalo is the mustard-yellow **Convento Franciscano,** built in 1549 on the site of a temple dedicated to Quetzalcoatl; Cortés's troops and their Tlaxcaltecan allies massacred thousands of Cholulans here. The **Capilla Real** (Royal Chapel) inside the church is unique in that it has 49 domes, inspired by the Great Mosque of Córdoba, Spain.

The Copa de Oro cider factory on Avenida 11 Poniente, 5 blocks south of the zócalo, has been pressing apples for more than 50 years, and winning trophies and prizes for the results. It's open daily 9–1 and 3–3:30 for free tours (in Spanish) and samples.

COMING AND GOING In Puebla, catch a PUEBLA/CHOLULA combi at the bus stop on Calle 11 Norte at 12 Poniente, or catch an **Estrella de Oro** or **Estrella Roja** bus from CAPU (*see* Coming and Going, in Puebla, *above*). Either way, buses leave about every 10 minutes and cost 35¢. The bus stop in Cholula is 3 blocks north of the zócalo.

WHERE TO SLEEP Perhaps because of its proximity to Puebla, Cholula is short on affordable hotels. **Hotel Reforma** (4 Sur 101, tel. 22/47–01–49) is run by a friendly, talkative señora who will urge you to check out her husband's photographic collage of all the churches in the Cholula area. Rooms are $17 for a single or double with bath. **Hotel Las Américas** (14 Ote. 5, tel. 22/47–22–75) charges $17 for a single and $24 for a double. It's close to the nightclub zone, but a 10-minute hike from the zócalo and most bus stops. A pricier option is the **Super Motel** (Av. 12 Nte. 1002, tel. 22/47–15–45), which charges $23 for a single or double—$40 if you want to splurge and stay in a room with a jacuzzi. All three hotels have wheelchair access.

Campsites are available at the **Trailer Park Las Américas** (tel. 22/47–01–34), about five minutes outside Cholula on the road to Puebla; they charge $8 for two people to pitch a tent. There are hot showers and swimming facilities, but it's not the most scenic spot.

FOOD Restaurants are scattered around the city. Right on the zócalo under the portal are several serving Italian food. One of these is **Los Jarrones,** where you can get good pizza, served with salad, spaghetti, and a drink for $5. **Cactus Flautas** (Miguel Alemán 104) serves a huge plate of three *flautas* (deep-fried tacos) smothered in cheese and salsa for only $2. They also have paella on Sundays, but you have to call owner Señora Román 24 hours in advance (tel. 47–73–71) to order. They're open daily noon–10. Two traditional restaurants near the pyramid, **La Lunita** and **La Pirámide,** are popular with locals and serve typical dishes such as mole, pipian, and *filete milanesa* (breaded steak) for $6. Slightly more expensive is **Chialingo** (7 Pte. 113, tel. 22/47–28–31), where you can sit under a big tree amid the bougainvillea and eat pasta, crêpes ($4), or steak ($10). Chialingo is four blocks south of the zócalo and open 1–10 daily.

AFTER DARK Pueblans make fun of the "relaxed" nightlife in Cholula, but it's a happening place, home to, among other places, the gay disco **Keops** (14 Ote., across from Hotel Imperial). A number of discos and bars cater to both locals and exchange students from the **Universidad de las Américas** on the east side of town. Friday or Saturday nights see the best bar hopping. **Enamorada,** under the portal in the zócalo, has live tropical music and no cover charge. East of the pyramid, **Faces** (12 Ote. 1) plays rock and disco for gringos from 10 PM to 4 AM; **Paradise,** across the street, has a more local crowd; and **Le Chat,** up the hill from Keops, is a couples-only joint with live music. All three charge a $9 cover.

NEAR CHOLULA

➤ SANTA MARIA TONANTZINTLA/SAN FRANCISCO ACATEPEC • These villages, less than 3 kilometers south of Cholula, are home to a pair of unique churches. Santa María Tonantzintla's **Iglesia de Tonantzintla** took almost 300 years to build. It's the only church in the area designed and built exclusively by Indians, and is a curious mix of baroque and indigenous aesthetics. The interior is an explosion of bright colors and gilt. Note that the angels and cherubs have Indian features, as does the Jesus on the cross to the left of the altar, and that the statue of the Virgin is framed in neon—wow. The graves of children taken by an early death are marked by the stones in the path leading up to the church.

Acatepec boasts a 16th-century church, decorated on the outside with blue, yellow, and green Talavera tiles and twisting columns on the bell towers. Inside, the newly remodeled interior (the original was destroyed in a fire) rivals that of Santa María Tonantzintla's church in amount of gilt per square inch. You can visit the churches between 9 and 6 daily, unless there's a mass. Red-and-white CHIPILO buses leave from the corner of 5 de Mayo and 6 Poniente in Cholula. Ask the driver to let you off at the churches.

➤ CHIPILO • This town of blond, blue-eyed Italian immigrants was founded in 1882 when Porfirio Díaz brought in a group of Venetians in an attempt to "save the nation" by importing white Catholics. In addition to Spanish, the inhabitants speak an Italian dialect. Chipilo's excellent cheese and other dairy products and Italian restaurants are famous throughout the region. From Cholula, take a CHIPILO bus from 5 de Mayo and 6 Poniente.

TEHUACAN

At one time people from all over Mexico traveled to Tehuacán to "take the waters" and enjoy the warm climate. While still famous for its bubbling waters, Tehuacán is now more of a stop on the way to Oaxaca than a destination in itself. Visitors are rarely seen here, so each new arrival is an object of interest for townspeople.

Northwest of the city are the bottling plants of **Peñafiel** and **Garci-Crespo**. Visitors to the Peñafiel bottling plant are free to drink their fill of the sparkling water gushing out of spigots in a pseudorock cave. Other sights within the city are the **Ex-Convento del Carmen** on Reforma, which houses the **Museo del Valle de Tehuacán** (Reforma, at 2 Ote., tel. 238/2–40–45), open Tuesday–Sunday 10–5. Though there are some interesting pre-Columbian artifacts, the museum consists mostly of stones, husks, and pods, and isn't worth the $2.50 admission.

The **Iglesia del Carmen** and the massive baroque cathedral, both across the street from the zócalo, testify to the symbolic significance of the feminine in Mexican Catholicism. Altars and walls feature paintings and statues of the Virgin Mary and several female saints. Mass is held at the cathedral Sundays every hour from 6 AM to 1 PM. Diagonally across from the cathedral is the **Casa del Gobierno,** a baroque building covered with Talavera tiles. The Casa contains some murals, collaborative efforts of several artists, including Desiderio Xochitiotzin of Tlaxcala, who studied with Diego Rivera.

COMING AND GOING Autobuses del Oriente (ADO) buses leave for Tehuacán ($5, 2 hrs) from Puebla's CAPU every 20 minutes 6 AM–9 PM. Buses go from Tehuacán to Mexico City ($10.50, 4 hrs), Oaxaca ($13, 6 hrs), and Veracruz ($9, 4 hrs). The bus station in Tehuacán (Independencia Nte. 119, tel. 238/2–00–96) is just two blocks from the zócalo, and everything except for the bottling plants is within walking distance. The main streets are Independencia and Reforma.

WHERE TO SLEEP Hotels are numerous in Tehuacán, and several bargains are available. **Hotel Madrid** (Calle 3 Sur 105, tel. 238/2–60–72) has a beautiful courtyard, which makes the $6 singles without bath seem like a steal, even though the communal bathrooms have seen better days. Doubles are $15. The **Casa de Huéspedes San Antonio** (Reforma Nte. 213, tel. 238/2–02–20) has a friendlier staff and is only slightly more expensive—singles without bath are $7 and doubles are $17. Both hotels are wheelchair accessible.

FOOD The regional specialty is *mole de cadera*, a goat-meat stew available only in October because the goats have to be fed a special diet for six months beforehand. Around the 15th, a woman nicknamed La Negrita serves the dish in the patio of the apartment complex next to **Mercería el Botón** (2 Pte. 221, at Carmen Serdán). Plates are about $10—not bad when you compare it with the $17 most restaurants in the area charge. Cheaper food is available year-round at the **Restaurant Mary** (Independencia Nte. 130, no phone). This family-owned restaurant across the street from the bus station sells filling breakfasts for $2. The comida corrida at lunchtime includes soup, rice, an entrée, and dessert for $3.50. They're open 8 AM–9:30 PM. The comida corrida (about $7) at **Hotel Iberia** (Independencia Nte. 217, tel. 238/3–15–00) includes paella every Thursday and Sunday.

ELSEWHERE NEAR PUEBLA

AMAZOC This town 16 kilometers east of Puebla is famous for the intricate silver work created for *charrería* (tack for rodeos). As a result, an abundance of spur-theme souvenirs is available. The second-class bus marked AMAZOC leaves from the corner of 14 Oriente and 18 Norte in Puebla. The fare is less than a dollar.

TEPEACA AND TECALI DE HERRERA The main plaza of Tepeaca was an important stagecoach stop during the colonial era. Architecture buffs will note that the Moorish clock tower is one of only two octagonal structures in Mexico. There is a huge traditional market every Friday.

Nearby onyx quarries give **Tecali,** 10 kilometers from Tepeaca, its name (Nahautl for onyx). The town is home to numerous onyx craftsmen and their workshops. Catch a TECALI or CUAWITANCHAN bus from Calle 11 Sur, on the west side of the Paseo Bravo in Tehuacán. Make sure the driver knows where you're going. Bus rides are 60¢.

HUEJOTZINGO The main attraction of this little village is the imposing **Ex-monasterio Franciscano** on the zócalo. The church was one of the first built by the Spaniards and doubled as a fort. Today it houses a museum. Visit Huejotzingo early on Saturday, when the market is held. If you're in the area before Lent, come for the famous *Carnaval* (*see* Puebla, Festivals, *above*). From Puebla's CAPU, take an **Estrella de Oro** bus.

CUETZALAN Although this town is about four hours from Puebla, it's worth a visit if you've got the time. The indigenous population has preserved many of the customs of past generations. The best day to visit is Sunday, market day, when the Totonacas and Nahoas come down from the *cerro* (hill), dressed in striking costumes of showy *huipiles* (embroidered tunics) matched by the women's elaborate, towering headdresses. Most people attend a Catholic mass given in Totonac, the local language. After mass, there is a traditional dance in the zócalo. On October 4, the feast day of St. Francis is celebrated (*see* Festivals, *above*). A fairly obscure archaeological site, **Yohualichán**, is also in the area. The place to stay here is **Hotel Posada Viky** (Guadalupe Victoria 16, tel. 233/1–02–72), which charges $8.50 per person. Take a bus from Puebla's CAPU terminal to Cuetzalán for about $6.

Taxco

Taxco is a glorious city of twisting cobblestone streets, red-tile colonial houses, silversmith's shops, and, of course, busload upon busload of tourists, most of them hell bent on bringing half of the town's silver supply home in their carry-on luggage. The town, so picturesque it hardly seems real, was built in a small cleft in the Sierra Madre mountains. As the city grows, it creeps higher into the mountains, and now many streets sport steep grades and sharp right-angle turns. Despite its size, Taxco still manages to maintain a small-town atmosphere—see for yourself any evening in the **Plaza Borda**, Taxco's peaceful zócalo, where local families mingle and gossip among wrought-iron benches and well-kept walkways. Overlooking the square is the **Catedral de Santa Prisca**, Taxco's imposing, ornate, pink-stone cathedral.

Taxco, which was first called Tetelcingo (small hill) by the Aztecs, has always been synonymous with silver. The Spanish moved in and made themselves at home in 1522, when Hernán Cortés found silver mines and unleashed a rush. After the Spanish were satisfied that they'd milked the place dry, the town settled into quiet oblivion for about 100 years. All this changed in the 18th century, when José de la Borda, a naturalized Mexican citizen from France, discovered vast, untapped sources of silver. This discovery made Borda extraordinarily wealthy and brought Taxco back into the spotlight. To express his thanks to God for his good fortune, Borda financed the building of the cathedral, and so a local aphorism was born: "If God gives to Borda, Borda gives to God."

Another expatriate drawn by Taxco's silver was New Orleans writer/architect William Spratling, who arrived here in the 1930s. Spratling envisioned Taxco as a center for silver artisanry and established the first silversmith workshops. The jewelry and other silver objects his apprentices soon began to mass-produce earned Taxco worldwide renown.

BASICS

CASAS DE CAMBIO Silver shops usually accept dollars. You can change money at the banks along Cuauhtémoc, the street that connects Plaza Borda with the smaller Plazuela San Juan. **Banco Confia** (Plaza Borda 2, tel. 762/2–01–92) is open for money exchange weekdays 9–noon. **Monedas Continentales** (Plazuela de San Juan 5, tel. 762/2–12–42), open weekdays 9–2 and 4–8, Saturdays 9–2, also changes traveler's checks and dollars. The ATM at **Banamex** (Plazuela del Convento 2, down Juárez from the zócalo) accepts Plus and Cirrus cards.

EMERGENCIES The phone number for the **police** is 762/2–00–07. The **Cruz Roja** emergency number is 762/2–01–21.

MAIL The post office is next to the Estrella de Oro bus station. They will hold mail sent to you at the following address for up to 10 days: Lista de Correos, Taxco, Guerrero, CP 40200, México. *John F. Kennedy 124, no phone. Open weekdays 8–7, Sat. 9–1.*

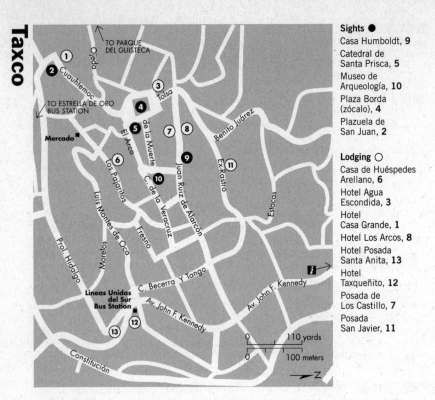

Sights ●

Casa Humboldt, **9**

Catedral de Santa Prisca, **5**

Museo de Arqueología, **10**

Plaza Borda (zócalo), **4**

Plazuela de San Juan, **2**

Lodging ○

Casa de Huéspedes Arellano, **6**

Hotel Agua Escondida, **3**

Hotel Casa Grande, **1**

Hotel Los Arcos, **8**

Hotel Posada Santa Anita, **13**

Hotel Taxqueñito, **12**

Posada de Los Castillo, **7**

Posada San Javier, **11**

MEDICAL AID The **Clínica de Especialidades** offers 24-hour emergency care. *John F. Kennedy, near Hotel Posada de la Misión, tel. 762/2–11–11.*

PHONES There are working pay phones on the zócalo and all over Taxco from which you can make collect or credit card calls. The more expensive option is to place a call from the **Farmacia de Cristo** down the hill from the Plazuela de San Juan. Collect calls cost between $3 and $5. *Hidalgo 18, tel. 762/2–11–19. Open daily 9–8:30.*

VISITOR INFORMATION Taxco's tourist office is run by a helpful, English-speaking staff. *John F. Kennedy 1, tel. 762/2–07–98. Open daily 9–7. From Plaza Borda take ZOCALO combi to gas station.*

COMING AND GOING

BY BUS Taxco has two bus stations, both on Avenida John F. Kennedy. The **Lineas Unidas del Sur** (also called Flecha Roja) station, a few blocks down the hill from Plaza Borda, offers both first- and second-class service (both of which feature air conditioning). *De lujo* (first-class) buses go to Mexico City ($11, 2½ hrs) and Cuernavaca ($5, 2 hrs). *Ordinario* (second-class) service to Mexico City is $9; to Cuernavaca, $3. Only ordinario buses go to Acapulco ($14, 5 hrs) and Chilpancingo ($7.50, 3 hrs). *John F. Kennedy 104, tel. 762/2–01–31.*

The first-class **Estrella de Oro** bus depot (John F. Kennedy 126, tel. 762/2–06–48) is about 1 kilometer south of the Lineas Unidas station. Five buses a day leave for Mexico City: four *plus* ($9, 2½ hrs) and one *primera* ($7, 2½ hrs). The latter leaves at 4 PM only. Take a LOS ARCOS combi to transfer between depots. To get to Plaza Borda from either station, catch a ZOCALO combi (20¢, 10 min), or walk uphill 10–15 minutes, keeping the spires of Santa Prisca Cathedral in sight.

GETTING AROUND

Taxco is fairly accessible by foot, and most sights and budget hotels are clustered around the **Plaza Borda** (zócalo). As you move outward, the twisted, steep streets can become difficult to navigate. If you need to be rescued, hop on one of the many combis roaming the area, if you haven't already been run over by one. The main thoroughfare, John F. Kennedy, traverses the lower part of the city from south to north. Plaza Borda is up the hill from JFK. On the east side of the plaza is **Santa Prisca Cathedral,** whose pink spires are visible from just about anywhere in the city. Another central and busy part of Taxco, the **Plazuela de San Juan,** is about 1½ blocks southwest of Plaza Borda, up Cuauhtémoc.

BY BUS The bus system consists mainly of a fleet of white combis, the ubiquitous Volkswagen buses you'll see careening up and down the hills. Combis labeled LOS ARCOS travel the length of Avenida John F. Kennedy. Those marked ZOCALO run between John F. Kennedy and the zócalo.

WHERE TO SLEEP

Your pack may feel heavy, but your wallet will certainly feel lighter after a night here—hotels aren't cheap. The less expensive hotels are clustered around Plaza Borda and on the hill going up toward the plaza from the Lineas Unidas del Sur (Flecha Roja) bus station. You won't find any real bargains, but the picturesque setting and great views may compensate for the cash drain. Reservations are a good idea on holidays and weekends, especially during Semana Santa (Holy Week) and the months of July, August, and December. If the places below are full, try the **Hotel Taxqueñito** (John F. Kennedy s/n, south of Estrella de Oro bus station, tel. 762/2–06–23), where singles cost $20 and doubles $26. The **Hotel Agua Escondida** (Plaza Borda 4, tel. 762/2–07–26) charges $35 for a single, $46 for a double.

➤ UNDER $20 • **Casa de Huéspedes Arellano.** Only the most determined budget travelers will be able to find this well-hidden hotel, although every Taxco resident knows where it is, so just keep asking and you'll get there. The hotel's decor and standard of cleanliness leave a bit to be desired, and the señora that runs the place isn't too pleasant, but it's the cheapest hotel in town. Singles and doubles with communal bath go for $10 and $15 respectively. *Pajaritos 23, tel. 762/2–02–15. Down alley to right of cathedral, right through market, and 3 levels down. 15 rooms, 8 with bath. Laundry, luggage storage.*

Hotel Casa Grande. Probably the best deal around for the money, this hotel in a large, old, stone building is clean and well-kept. Rooms vary from plain with small grungy bathrooms to nicely decorated with elaborately tiled bathrooms. They're all the same price, so ask to see several. Singles go for about $13, doubles $17. *Plazuela de San Juan 7, tel. 762/2–01–23. From Plaza Borda, 1 block down Cuauhtémoc. 12 rooms, all with bath. Luggage storage.*

➤ UNDER $35 • **Hotel Los Arcos.** This hotel was originally a gift for a viceroy of New Spain, as Mexico was known during the colonial era. Some rooms have lofts, with beds overlooking the sitting area. All of the rooms open to a cool patio of brick, stone, and tile. Singles are $25, and a double will set you back $30. *Juan Ruíz de Alarcón 2, 1½ blocks from Plaza Borda, tel. 762/2–18–36. 24 rooms, all with bath. Laundry, luggage storage. Reservations advised.*

Hotel Posada Santa Anita. The rooms are clean, simple, and large, if hardly stylish. The hotel is next to the Flecha Roja bus station, but not quite as close to the zócalo as some others. Singles cost $18, doubles $25. *John. F. Kennedy 106, tel. 762/2–07–52. 27 rooms, all with bath. Laundry, luggage storage.*

Posada de Los Castillo. This striking mansion, just a few doors from Hotel Los Arcos, has red-tile floors and a fountain in the arched, stone lobby. Rooms are arranged around the interior patio and are simply but beautifully furnished in dark wood. The bathrooms swim in blue tile and are outfitted with tubs and hanging plants. The owner speaks English and is delighted to answer questions. Singles cost about $22, doubles $30. *Juan Ruíz de Alarcón 7, tel. 762/2–13–96 or 762/2–34–71. 14 rooms, all with bath. Luggage storage.*

Posada San Javier. This sprawling establishment has a large, clean pool, a number of pretty little courtyards, bright bougainvillea, and a remarkably hospitable staff. The rooms don't quite live up to the sunny exterior, but they are large and clean. Singles are $22, $29 with a sitting room, and doubles are $29 or $36 with a sitting room. The primarily foreign clientele includes many wholesale silver buyers from the States, so with a little luck you may find out about some bargains. *Ex-Rastro 4 or Estacas 1 (2 entrances), tel. 762/2–31–77. Down stairway across from Palacio Municipal on Ex-Rastro. 18 rooms, all with bath. Luggage storage.*

CAMPING You can camp for about $1 in the **Parque del Guisteco** at the top of the city. There is a store for basic necessities nearby. *Parque del Guisteco, Zona Norte. From the zócalo, north on Ojeda.*

FOOD

Food prices in Taxco reflect the city's popularity with tourists. The cheaper restaurants are on side streets surrounding the zócalo. Taquerías near the Flecha Roja bus station offer decent fare, and cheap meals can also be had in the **market,** down the alley just to the right of the cathedral (*see* Shopping, *below*). Purchase fresh fruits and vegetables here, as well as fresh bread from one of the many panaderías. *Perros calientes* (hotdogs; $1) are sold by vendors that appear magically by the zócalo every evening.

➤ UNDER $5 • **Jugos y Tortas Restaurante Cruz.** This is a family-run budget restaurant with a $5 comida corrida, tacos between $1 and $2, and a $3 burger, fries, and soda special. *Calle del Arco 11, tel. 762/2–70–79. 2 blocks from zócalo. Open daily 8–6. Wheelchair access.*

El Rincón del Abuelo. This café serves a full breakfast of juice, fruit cocktail, coffee, toast, beans, and a choice of egg dishes or pancakes—all for $4.50. It's run by young people and even has a selection of goofy postcards. A hamburger, fries, and salad with a drink will set you back about $5. *Cuauhtémoc 1, btw Plazuela de San Juan and zócalo, no phone. Open daily 8 AM–11 PM.*

Los Taquitos II. Don't come for the atmosphere, but for tacos served at minimal prices with maximum hygiene. Pork, chicken, or beef tacos are a mere $1 each; an egg with a side order of rice is even less. *Hidalgo 13, no phone. 1 block from Plazuela de San Juan. Open daily 1–7.*

➤ UNDER $10 • **Pizza Pazza.** The pungent aroma of pizza and garlic bread waft over the zócalo from this hip place. The view is awesome, and so is the pizza: A large cheese pie for two to three people is only $7, $12 with everything on it. If you're not in the mood for pizza, try the spaghetti ($5), *queso fundido* (cheese fondue; $4), or *pozole* (corn soup; $3). *Plaza Borda, next to cathedral, tel. 762/2–55–00. Open daily noon–midnight.*

Restaurante Cafetería. Scores of beautiful ceramic masks decorate the walls of this funky café. It's a good place to eat breakfast—that is, if the owner remembers to set his alarm and open the place. A fruit salad with coffee goes for $3, and hotcakes with a glass of milk cost $3.50. *Plazuela de Bernal, tel. 762/2–05–58. ½ block from zócalo. Open daily 8–7.*

Restaurant Sante Fé. Ask anyone in Taxco where they spend their precious pesos when taking the family to dinner, and they'll point you toward this colorful restaurant around the corner from the Plazuela de San Juan. The comida corrida includes soup, an entrée such as chile relleno or chicken in garlic sauce, beans, rice, tortillas, and dessert, all for about $6.50. If you're not that hungry, there are sandwiches for $1.50 and enchiladas for $3. *Hidalgo 2, tel. 762/2–11–70. 1 block east of Plazuela de San Juan. Open daily 7:30 AM–11 PM.*

WORTH SEEING

The city itself is the major attraction—which is why the Mexican government declared it a national monument in 1928—but there aren't many individual sights aside from the endless procession of silver shops. If you're in good shape, simply wandering through Taxco's many cramped alleyways and stairs makes for a strenuous but pleasant urban hike.

CASA HUMBOLDT This 18th-century mansion is named after Alexander von Humboldt, a German explorer who stayed here in 1803 and later traveled throughout South America, making maps and conducting scientific surveys. The interior was recently reconstructed, and there's a small, well-kept museum and several small shops selling local handicrafts. *Juan Ruíz de Alarcón 6. Admission: $3.50, $1.50 students. Open Tues.–Sat. 10–5, Sun. 9–3.*

The Catedral de Santa Prisca on Taxco's zócalo is considered one of the best examples of baroque architecture in Mexico.

MONTE TAXCO RESORT A 10-minute ride on the *funicular* (cable car) called the telserico takes you from Los Arcos to the luxurious resort at Monte Taxco, with its swimming pools, gardens, golf course, and spa. It costs $7 to use the pool for the day and $7 to go horseback riding around the grounds for an hour. The incredible view costs only the price of a drink at the bar. The cable car runs daily 7 AM–5 PM, and the fare is $3.50 round-trip. *Monte Taxco, tel. 762/2–13–01 or 762/2–56–09. Combis (20¢) leave from Los Arcos; taxis cost about $2.*

MUSEO DE ARQUEOLOGIA GUILLERMO SPRATLING Just a short walk from the Catedral de Santa Prisca, this museum houses a collection of pre-Columbian artifacts that once belonged to writer William Spratling. The museum is in what was Spratling's house and consists of three galleries, two dedicated to indigenous artwork and artifacts, the third to rotating exhibits of contemporary art. The museum is fairly small, the collection not extraordinary, and the $3.50 admission fairly hefty, so it's really worth a visit only on Sunday or if you have a student ID, in which case it's free. *Humboldt 1, tel. 762/2–16–60. Open Tues.–Sat. 10–5, Sun. 9–3.*

CHEAP THRILLS

Cheap thrills in Taxco are more or less limited to Sunday nights on the zócalo and the eternal search for the most incredible views of town—said to be from the **Monte Taxco Resort** (*see above*) and from **El Mirador,** a lookout high above the city. Think twice about visiting El Mirador alone; there have been several robberies here. Yet if you just can't stand the thought of what you might be missing, catch a PANORAMICA combi at Plazuela de San Juan.

FESTIVALS Aside from the usual festivals (Semana Santa, Las Posadas, Día de los Muertos), Taxco celebrates two special ones: **La Feria Nacional de La Plata** (silver festival), held during the first week of December, and **El Día del Jumil** (Day of the Jumil Bug), held in mid-November. The week-long silver festival hosts cultural events, the crowning of a Silver Queen, and silver exhibitions. El Día del Jumil is held in honor of an insect said to be found nowhere else in the world but the Cerro de Huizteco near Taxco. Traditional healers use them for medicine, while others crush them into a tasty salsa (yum!). In addition, Taxco hosts the **Festival Nacional de Guitarra** in July, with concerts of various styles of guitar music.

SHOPPING

Prices at the shops around Plaza Borda are outrageously high—the shopkeepers have figured out that a good percentage of foreigners are rich and gullible. For a look at the prettiest silver work in Taxco, peek into **Los Castillos** (Plaza Bernal 10, tel. 762/2–06–52). If you're interested in buying silver, stick to the vendors and small, crowded shops located below street level. To get to these stores, head down Cuauhtémoc from Plaza Borda and turn down the small alley at the Banco Mexicano Somex. Also try the stores in the **El Pueblito** complex, down Hidalgo from Plazuela de San Juan, across from the park. Most shopkeepers have two price tiers: *Mayoreo* is the wholesale price given to those who buy at least $100 worth of silver, and *menudeo* is the price per gram for people buying less than that.

You're likely to see three types of merchandise in Taxco's silver shops: alpaca, a silver-colored metal also known as fool's silver; silver-coated alpaca; and solid sterling silver, identifiable by the .925 imprint. Real silver is priced by weight and intricacy of workmanship.

Taxco's extensive **mercado**, extending from the cathedral to John F. Kennedy, is another good place to find less expensive silver, as well as just about anything else. Haggling is common—

two-thirds of the initial price is usually about the best you'll do. The market is held daily, but really heats up on weekends when merchants from nearby towns come to hawk their wares.

AFTER DARK

Most nights the zócalo is the hottest spot around—the place where Taxco youth flirt and local families gather for nightly gossip. Buy yourself a bag of popcorn from one of the street vendors and settle onto a park bench to watch the nighttime spectacle unfold. If you're lucky, you may be surprised by a small parade of adolescents dressed like wedding-cake decorations: This is a party for a girl's *quinceañera,* celebrating her 15th birthday and passage into womanhood.

The town's few drinking-and-dancing establishments close fairly early, and you can forget serious partying during the week. **Taxco Olé** (La Palma 1, facing Catedral de Santa Prisca), a bar popular with locals, is only open Friday, Saturday, and Sunday nights. Your best bet is the bars and restaurants next to the zócalo. **Restaurant/Bar Paco** (Plaza Borda 12, tel. 762/2–00–64) has the best view around and beers for $2.50. At **Señor Costilla's** the same beer costs $2, but the imitation-Hard Rock Cafe atmosphere can be somewhat obnoxious. At the other end of the ambience spectrum is **Bar Berta** (Plaza Borda 9, tel. 762/2–01–72), a hole-in-the-wall, tough-guy drinking establishment. For dancing anywhere close to the center of town your only choice is the **EsCaparArtes Disco** (Plaza Borda 1), a Top-40 place crammed on weekends with gyrating youth, especially the under-18 crowd. The cover is $10. There's also a hopping disco (especially during summer) with a $7 cover at the **Monte Taxco Resort** (*see* Worth Seeing, *above*).

Near Taxco

LAS GRUTAS DE CACAHUAMILPA

The Cacahuamilpa caves, about 30 kilometers outside Taxco, are an amazing expanse of subterranean chambers and crusty rock formations that extend roughly 2 kilometers into the bowels of the earth. The downward trek into this dimly lit world is mildly arduous and sometimes slippery, even though the way is lit and marked by a smooth cement walkway. Guides conduct hourly tours in Spanish, but an English-speaking guide can be hunted up on request. The two-hour group tour is large, slow, and not particularly fascinating—you're better off starting with the tour and then moving on alone through the caves at your own pace. Bring a flashlight if you plan to wander away from the tour, as there are blackouts. The walkway is marked, however, so you'd have to work to get lost. Take a bus ($1.50) from the Flecha Roja station bound for Ixtapán and Toluca—it will pass by Las Grutas, and if you tell the driver where you're going, he'll drop you off at the crossroads about 1 kilometer from the caves. Buses for the return trip pass every half hour or so. You can also catch a LAS GRUTAS combi across the street from the bus station that will take you all the way to the caves—it costs the same as the bus, but is a lot less comfortable. *Admission: $5. Open daily 10–5.*

Chilpancingo
In a green valley between Taxco and Acapulco lies Chilpancingo, Guerrero's state capital and the site of a major university, where stone colonial edifices contrast with modern, abstract sculptures of twisted iron. Despite the pleasant zócalo, well-kept downtown streets, and loads of students hurrying to class or a nearby café, Chilpancingo remains relatively free of tourists. There are no exceptional tourist attractions per se, but if you're in the neighborhood, stop by for a little relaxation and a break from the overtrodden tourist circuit.

The students of the Universidad de Guerrero infuse the town with a lively spirit and ensure an active nightlife, except when school is out (July and August). During the school year, the zócalo is a happening spot at night with bands playing and roaming throngs of people. Next to the white church on the zócalo is the local student center, **Casino del Estudiante** (Guerrero, at Madero, no phone), a great place to hang out; it's full of people, Ping-Pong tables, game rooms, and bulletin boards advertising upcoming dances, concerts, and movies. Although the university itself is a concrete atrocity, it's worth visiting to check out the event notices in the hallways.

The **Instituto Guerrerense de la Cultura,** Guerrero's cultural institute, is housed in a beautiful old building right on the zócalo. Murals depicting Guerrero's history decorate the walls of the interior courtyard. Inside is the **Museo Regional de Guerrero** (tel. 747/2–70–5), a small museum with exhibits of indigenous artifacts as well as relics from the colonial period. It's simple, but worth a visit. Admission is free, and the museum is open Tuesday–Sunday 11–6. Crafts from Guerrero are on sale at **La Casa de las Artesanías** weekdays 9–9. They have sturdy furniture, intricately painted ceramic vases and animals, and decorated wooden boxes of all sizes—fun to browse through, if not particularly cheap. To get here, take the URBANOS or JACARANDA combi from Avenida Insurgentes in front of the market.

At the 1813 Congress of Chilpancingo, Morelos and liberal delegates from all over Mexico drafted a Mexican Declaration of Independence, affirming universal male suffrage and the abolition of slavery, caste systems, and judicial torture.

BASICS

CASAS DE CAMBIO Around the zócalo are several banks that change cash and traveler's checks on weekday mornings. You can also go to the **Casa de Cambio Iguala** (Zapata 10, on zócalo, tel. 747/2–03–82), which takes no commission and has better hours (weekdays 9–4). **Banamex** (Zapata, on NW cnr of zócalo) has an ATM that accepts Cirrus and Plus cards, as does **Banco Serfin** (Guerrero 5, just north of zócalo).

MAIL Chilpancingo's tiny post office is two blocks from the zócalo. They'll hold mail sent to you at the following address for up to 10 days: Lista de Correos, Chilpancingo, Guerrero, CP 39000, México. *Hidalgo 9, tel. 747/2–22–75. Open weekdays 8–7, Sat. 9–1.*

PHONES You can make collect calls from the public phones on the zócalo. For other long-distance calls, go to **Juguería Iris,** one block off the zócalo on the same street as the Estrella de Oro bus station. *Juárez 20-B, tel. 747/2–68–16. Open Mon.–Sat. 9–3 and 4–9.*

Multiservicios de Oficina also has local and long-distance phone service, as well as a fax machine. *Zapata 10, on zócalo, tel. 747/2–54–56. Open Mon.–Sat. 7 AM–10 PM.*

COMING AND GOING

Chilpancingo has two bus stations: the first-class **Estrella de Oro** (Juárez 53, tel. 747/2–21–30) and **Estrella Blanca** (21 de Marzo s/n), which has first- and second-class service. First-class buses are nicer, generally faster, and only a little bit more expensive than second-class ones. From Estrella de Oro, there are buses to Mexico City ($14.50, 5 hrs), Cuernavaca ($9, 3 hrs), Acapulco ($7, 1 hr), Taxco ($6, 1½ hrs), and many other destinations throughout the country. To reach the zócalo from Estrella de Oro, hang an immediate left as you exit the station's front entrance and walk straight for about seven blocks, or catch any bus or combi running up one-way Juárez. Buses to the station run along the parallel street, Guerrero. The Estrella Blanca station is about four blocks farther up Juárez on 21 de Marzo; turn left down 21 de Marzo before the main market and walk one block. A **Sendatur** information office in the Estrella Blanca station (tel. 747/2–06–34 or 747/2–06–38) can direct you through this vast, shiny-clean complex. Second-class buses leave frequently to Mexico City ($12.50, 5 hrs), Acapulco ($5, 2½ hrs), Taxco ($6, 2 hrs), Cuernavaca ($8, 3½ hrs), and Zihuatanejo ($18, 6½ hrs).

WHERE TO SLEEP

Hotel Chilpancingo (Alemán 8, tel. 747/2–24–46) is super cheap (singles $9, doubles $14), but rather depressing. The rooms are reminiscent of prison cells, and the bathrooms are on the far side of clean. **Hotel Cardeña** (Madero 13, no phone), in a former mansion one block off the zócalo, has rooms that open onto a stone courtyard. A smaller courtyard has a few stone washbasins in which you're welcome to scrub your clothes. Rooms are plain, and the bathrooms are only as frightening as the occasional cockroach. Singles cost $14 with bath or $9 without; doubles are about $20 with bath, $13 without.

Hotel Roble. This is the best choice, though it doesn't have much charm. Its brand-new and clean rooms cost $17 with bath or $10 without for either one or two people. The communal bathrooms are a little run down. *Cuauhtémoc 5, tel. 747/2-53-23. From the zócalo, walk east up Hidalgo to Cuauhtémoc. 24 rooms, 20 with bath. Wheelchair access. Reservations advised.*

FOOD

Cheap restaurants and cafés crammed with students are common on the zócalo and the streets surrounding it. Competition and student budgets keep quality high and prices low. For inexpensive fruits, vegetables, bread, and even meat and cheese, go to the huge market on Guerrero near the second-class bus station. For something slightly more upscale than the usual taquerías, try **Restaurant La Parroquia** (Nicolás Bravo 2, tel. 747/2-29-28), a sidewalk café just off the zócalo. Another good restaurant is **El Portal** (on zócalo near Madero and Guerrero, tel. 747/2-46-68), an open-air café with a $4 comida corrida and delicious *aguas preparadas* (juice drinks) for $1. They also serve a big breakfast for $4. **Fuente de Soda Casino del Estudiante** (Guerrero, at Madero, no phone), in the student center on the zócalo, serves up hearty food at rock-bottom prices. The comida corrida includes soup, an entrée, and beans, all for about $2. Milkshakes and sandwiches will set you back about $1.25 each.

AFTER DARK

Partying is pretty much limited to the weekends, when students attend both *tardeadas* (afternoon dances) and *veladas* (parties from about 9 PM to 3 AM). The most popular spot for these is a club called **Sortilegio** (tel. 747/2-83-77), but they only host planned events, so look for postings at the Fuente de Soda Casino del Estudiante (*see* Food, *above*), or ask a student. Sortilegio is on a winding street behind the mercado, so you'll want to take a taxi. The driver will know where it is. Chilpancingo also has its share of video bars, featuring blaring music and videos and plenty of intoxicated youth. **Ton's Que** (tel. 747/2-12-32) is on the zócalo near Guerrero and Madero. **Taco Rock** (Colón 5, tel. 747/2-34-91) is just south of the zócalo. Take Abasolo south and turn right on Colón.

EL BAJIO 4

By Michele Back

The Bajío region is fruitful for those interested in history, architecture, and a change of pace from Mexico's more frequently traveled coastal areas. Encompassing the states of Querétaro, Guanajuato, and San Luis Potosí, the region is a spectacular mix of fertile valleys and dry hills sprinkled with strange cacti and succulents, town centers with cafés clustered around tranquil plazas, and busy industrial zones. Staunch traditionalism and progressive ideals coexist here in a strange harmony, and the result is a region rich in folklore and legends as well as innovative cultural and artistic activity.

The Bajío's mineral wealth attracted empires long before the Spanish happened along. The Olmecs established mines near Querétaro, later exploited by Chichimec people (the nomadic peoples who inhabited this region between the periods of Toltec and Aztec ascendancy) and by the *teotihuacanos*. There is linguistic evidence that the Purépecha people (also called Tarascan) of Michoacán also penetrated this region. At the time of the Conquest, the region was mostly inhabited by speakers of Otomí and hunter-gatherers of other tribes, representatives of which migrated as far south as Michoacán. At first, the relationship between the invaders and indigenous groups was relatively peaceful—Franciscan friars built monasteries and began converting the Otomí people (the more nomadic tribes having in large part escaped to the outskirts once they caught wind of what was going on), while a few wealthy Spaniards raised livestock and crops and established dual governments alongside the Otomí chieftains. All hell broke loose toward the end of the 16th century, when silver was discovered in the hills of Guanajuato and San Luis Potosí. Hundreds of miners poured into the area, took one look at the peaceful Otomís, and told them to get to work. Members of more nomadic tribes were also subdued and forced to work the mines, which provided seemingly endless riches. Extravagant churches, government buildings and private mansions went up during the period of rapid economic development that followed. At the same time, the indigenous people were virtually exterminated— by the height of the mining boom in the 17th century, they had all but disappeared.

The region earned the nickname "Cradle of Independence" when revolutionary leaders Miguel Hidalgo and Ignacio Allende plotted and led the first successful military campaigns of the struggle for independence here in 1810. Both were later executed, but their work was carried on by Padre José María Morelos and others until Mexico was freed of Spanish rule more than a decade later.

Today, the low price of silver has meant decreasing production, and the mines are now mostly tourist attractions. However, the Bajío has much more to offer, including excellent museums and outstanding examples of baroque architecture. Although one of the most conservative regions of Mexico, the population of university students, artists, and bohemians collaborate to

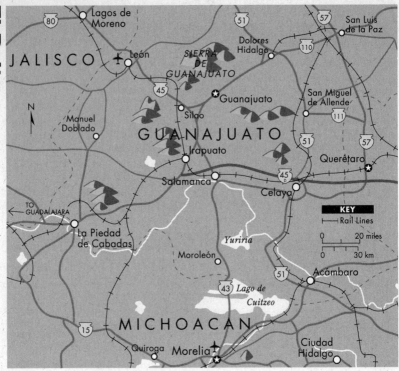

produce an active cultural life. History buffs shouldn't miss Querétaro and the city of Dolores Hidalgo in Guanajuato, both of which contain more than their fair share of historical sites. The best student life is found in the capital city of Guanajuato, and San Miguel de Allende is so darn picturesque and friendly you may want to stay a few years. Finally, the modern city of San Luis Potosí offers easy access to waterfalls, caves, and *balnearios* (swimming areas).

Querétaro

Downtown Querétaro is a great example of the juxtaposition of past and present so common in Mexican cities: Centuries-old colonial buildings now house electronic appliance and women's lingerie shops, and fast-food joints adjoin national monuments. This bustling state capital is a city of more than one million people, but it is worlds away from the pollution and chaos associated with Mexico City, just a three-hour bus trip away. Women can walk alone at night on the well-lit streets with a sense of security, and the universities attract plenty of young students and boho types who hang out or play chess in Querétaro's cafés. And, like other university cities, Querétaro has an active central square and a rocking nightlife.

The heart of Querétaro is an exquisite stretch of tree-shaded cobblestone streets lined with colonial mansions and interrupted frequently by quiet plazas and well-kept gardens. On every city block in this historic center you'll encounter some remnant of the past. The struggle for independence received a push from Querétaro resident Josefa Ortiz, known as La Corregidora, who sent word to conspirators Miguel Hidalgo and Ignacio Allende that their plan to launch a rebellion against Spanish rule had been discovered. Hidalgo acted immediately, sounding the cry for independence in the nearby town of Dolores. The **Plaza de la Corregidora** and **La Tumba de Doña Josefa** commemorate this heroine, who was executed for her subversive activities. Querétaro was also the site of the signing of the Treaty of Guadalupe-Hidalgo, under which

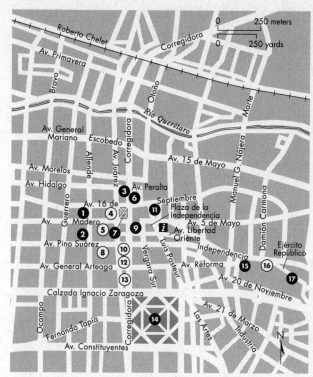

Sights ●

Alameda, **14**

Calzada de los Arcos, **17**

Convento de la Santa Cruz, **15**

Jardín Zenéa (zócalo), **7**

Museo de Arte de Querétaro, **2**

Museo Regional, **9**

Palacio del Gobierno Federal, **11**

Plaza de la Corregidora, **6**

Teatro de la República, **3**

Templo de Santa Clara, **1**

Lodging ○

Hotel Hidalgo, **5**

Hotel Plaza, **4**

Hotel San Francisco, **12**

Posada Academia, **8**

Posada Colonial, **10**

Posada Juárez, **13**

Villa Juvenil (CREA), **16**

Mexico ceded Texas and the California and New Mexico territories to the United States. The **Convento de la Santa Cruz** was the site of Emperor Maximilian's imprisonment before his execution on the **Cerro de las Campanas** (Hill of the Church Bells) just north of town. The signing of the 1917 constitution and the formation of the PRI, Mexico's ruling party, both took place in Querétaro. Today, the city seems wholly dedicated to promoting its historical and modern treasures, which means that travelers are greeted with enthusiasm and an eagerness to discuss all that Querétaro has to offer.

BASICS

AMERICAN EXPRESS Turismo Beverly is a travel agency that provides all American Express services. *Av. Tecnológico 118, Local 1, Querétaro, Querétaro, CP 76030, México, tel. 42/06–15–00. Take any bus on Constituyentes east from Alameda to Tecnológico and walk south 1½ blocks. Open weekdays 9–2 and 4–7, Sat. 9–1.*

AUTO PARTS/SERVICE Several auto parts stores and mechanics are located on Zaragoza between Ignacio Pérez and Montes. **Refaccionaría Capricornio** sells auto parts and can recommend a mechanic. *Calzada Zaragoza 69-A, tel. 42/15–05–09. Open daily 9–7.*

BOOKSTORES Unidad Cultural del Centro sells newspapers and tons of books (in Spanish) on Mexican history, literature, and film. *Andador 16 de Septiembre 10, at Corregidora, tel. 42/14-19-23. Open daily 9–8:30.*

CASAS DE CAMBIO Both **Banamex** (16 de Septiembre 1, tel. 42/12–01–39) and **Bancrecer** (Tecnológico 100, tel. 42/16–55–35) change traveler's checks and cash weekdays 9–noon, have ATMs, and give cash advances on Visa and Mastercard. **Cambio Express de Querétaro** (Madero 6, no phone) is open a little later—weekdays until 3 PM—but only changes cash.

Querétaro

EMERGENCIES The number for the **police** is 42/12–02–06; for an **ambulance,** 42/13–28–04.

LAUNDRY Laundromats are scarce near the center of town, so you'll have to schlep your clothes south of downtown on Avenida Constituyentes. **Lavandería Automática La Cascada,** in the big shopping center on Constituyentes, charges about $6 for a self-service load of 3 kilos or less, or $8 for full service. *In Comercial Mexicana, tel. 42/16–56–96. Open daily 9–8.*

MAIL The post office provides all the usual services, and letters sent to you at the following address will be held for up to 10 days: Lista de Correos, Administración 1, Arteaga 7, Querétaro, Querétaro, CP 76000, México. *From Jardín Zenéa, walk 2 blocks south on Juárez, turn right on Arteaga. Open weekdays 8–7, Sat. 9–1.*

MEDICAL AID **Grupo Médico Zaragoza** (Zaragoza 39, tel. 42/16–76–38) provides most medical services 24 hours a day. **Farmacia Querétaro** (Constituyentes 17, at Ignacio de las Casas, tel. 42/12–44–23) is also open 24 hours.

PHONES You'll find Ladatel pay phones on the Jardín Zenéa and the Plaza de la Independencia. The folks at the *caseta de larga distancia* (long-distance telephone office) charge $1 for collect calls. *5 de Mayo 33. 1 block west of Jardín Zenéa. Open Mon.–Sat. 9:30–2 and 4:30–9.*

SCHOOLS The **Universidad Autónoma de Querétaro** has summer and winter courses in beginning, intermediate, and advanced Spanish. Courses cover all aspects of the language, including grammar, pronunciation, and conversation. For more information, write to: Escuela de Idiomas, Centro Universitario, Cerro de las Campanas, Querétaro, Querétaro, CP 76000, México. *In Centro Universitario, Hidalgo s/n, tel. 42/16–74–66. From Jardín Zenéa, take RUTA R bus.*

VISITOR INFORMATION The **Centro de Información Turística** is staffed by young, enthusiastic people who gladly give out brochures and tell you what is and isn't worth doing around town. *Luis Pasteur, at SE corner of Plaza de la Independencia, no phone. Open weekdays 9–2 and 5–8.*

For more detailed information, you'll need to go to the **Secretaría de Turismo**. Ask for Luis Alejandro Bustamante—he understands budget travel and won't try to coax you into an expensive hotel. *Constituyentes 102 Ote., tel. 42/13–84–83. Open weekdays 9–2 and 5–8.*

COMING AND GOING

BY BUS At press time, Querétaro's bus station was slated to move to Constituyentes near the stadium. However, buses may still be arriving at the old **Central de Autobuses,** on Constituyentes across from the Alameda. To reach the center from here, turn left upon exiting the bus station, walk a block to Corregidores, turn right, and walk four blocks to the Jardín Zenéa. A taxi ride between the bus station and the center will cost about $3.50.

The main bus lines are **Omnibus de México** (tel. 42/12–08–13), which has service to Aguascalientes ($14, 4 hrs); **Estrella Blanca** (tel. 42/12–05–03), which goes to Zacatecas ($15, 5 hrs), San Luis Potosí ($7, 3 hrs), and Mexico City ($9.50, 3 hrs); and **Flecha Amarilla** (tel. 42/12–80–45), which has second-class service to the above destinations and more. Locals say Flecha Amarilla's motto is Better Dead Than Late, though the company is doing its best to convince riders otherwise. However, they offer the only service to some destinations, so you may not have much choice. The bus station has a phone office. Luggage costs 60¢ an hour per bag.

BY TRAIN The small, well-kept train station is roughly 3 kilometers north of the historic center. Taxis between the station and the center cost about $3 each way, but you can catch the RUTA 8 minibus from the station to the Jardín Zenéa (the central plaza). Trains to Mexico City leave three times a day—at 6 AM, 3 PM, and 4 PM, and cost about $8 for first class, $6 for second class. The train for Ciudad Juárez on the U.S. border departs daily at 11:30 PM, and tickets cost about $44 (1st class) and $26 (2nd class). No one has any idea how long the trip takes, which may be an indication of the reliability of the service. *Héroes de la Nacozari, tel. 42/12–17–03. Ticket sales daily 9–11 and noon–5.*

GETTING AROUND

Most of the action you'll encounter during the day happens within walking distance of the **Jardín Zenéa** (the central plaza), also known as the Jardín Obregón. Budget hotels and sights are also in the center. The two main north–south drags, **Juárez** to the west of Jardín Zenéa and **Corregidora** to the east, stem from the Alameda. **16 de Septiembre** borders the Jardín on the north, and **Madero** borders it on the south. Many of the city's streets are closed to cars—these are called *andadores*.

If you want to travel away from the historic center, the white **minibuses** that fill the streets are the easiest and cheapest way to get around. The destination of each bus is painted on the front windshield. Generally, buses on Corregidora are headed north and on those on Juárez go south.

WHERE TO SLEEP

The bargain hotels are near the noisy **Jardín Zenéa,** so expect a fair amount of late-night racket if you stay in one of them. However, the more expensive hotels near the old bus station aren't much better. The cheapest hotels are only semiclean and usually attract couples looking for a place to consummate their affection—if you have the money, stay in a moderately priced place. During December, hotels are booked solid for the **Exposición Ganadera** (a sort of county fair), which is attended by many from outside the city.

➤ UNDER $15 • **Posada Academia.** This is your best bet on the cheap end. Rooms are dark, but relatively clean, and include TVs and hot water all day long. The old woman who runs the place is cheerful, chatty, and oblivious to all the sex going on in her hotel. Singles are $10, doubles $13. *Pino Suárez 23, 1 block south of Jardín Zenéa, no phone. 18 rooms, all with bath.*

Posada Colonial. The lobby here is inviting but deceptive—the extremely small rooms aren't very clean. It is, however, one of the two cheapest places in town, at $6.50 for a single with shared bath and $10 for a single with private bath. Again, amorous couples abound here. Doubles run $9.50 with shared bath, $11 with a private one. *Juárez 19, 3 blocks south of Jardín Zenéa, tel. 42/12–02–39. 16 rooms, 8 with bath.*

Posada Juárez. You get what you pay for here; the rooms are clean enough, but the bathrooms are scary. The staff, at least, is pleasant, and a good number of the guests are actually from out of town. Prices are $9.50 for a single without bath ($13 with bath), and $13 for a double without bath. *Juárez 29, 4 blocks south of Jardín Zenéa, tel. 42/12–32–32. 25 rooms, 18 with bath.*

Many cheaper hotels close their doors by midnight or earlier, so pound hard to wake the proprietors if you get in late.

➤ UNDER $25 • **Hotel Hidalgo.** Huge wooden doors open onto this hotel's sunny courtyard. Rooms have TVs and clean bathrooms, and some have balconies overlooking the cobblestone street. The friendly proprietors speak English, but they aren't around very often. Singles cost $15, doubles $20. *Madero Pte. 11, 1 block west of Jardín Zenéa, tel. 42/12–00–81. 40 rooms, all with bath. Luggage storage, wheelchair access.*

Hotel Plaza. Right on the central square, this is your best option in this price range. Rooms are clean and bright and have TVs and phones. Ask for a room away from the street, as the traffic is noisy at night. Singles are $18.50, doubles $23. *Juárez 23, on west side of Jardín Zenéa, tel. 42/12–11–38. 29 rooms, all with bath. MC, V.*

Hotel San Francisco. On the bustling Avenida Corregidora, this dark and spartan hotel attracts mostly Mexican families and businessmen. Rooms are clean—if the overpowering smell of disinfectant is any indication—and there's always hot water. Rooms are $17 for a single, $20 for a double. *Corregidora 114, tel. 42/12–08–58. 58 rooms, all with bath. Luggage storage, wheelchair access. Reservations advised.*

HOSTEL **Villa Juvenil (CREA).** If you don't mind the 15-minute walk to the center of town, the 11 PM curfew, or the busloads of high school students traipsing in at all hours of the night, this is a decent place to stay. It's clean, cheerful, and cheap at $4 per person. There's a place for hanging hand-washed clothes, and storage for your bags. Sometimes the hostel is filled with student groups, so call ahead if you don't want to take your chances. *Ejército Republicano s/n, tel. 42/23–11–20. From Jardín Zenéa, go south 2 blocks on Corregidora, left on Independencia, right at fork to Ejército Republicano, and go on to crest of hill by church.*

FOOD

There are so many good, cheap things to eat in Querétaro that it can be difficult to know where to begin. You're usually better off at food stands; most food in cheaper restaurants is mediocre, and expensive restuarants cater shamelessly to tourists. However, you can spend less than $5–$6 on breakfast, lunch, and dinner (yes, all three combined) on the streets here. In the morning, vendors work the Jardín Zenéa and Avenidas Constituyentes and Zaragoza around the Alameda, selling 30¢ tamales and *atole* (a sweet corn-based drink, similar to hot chocolate). At lunchtime, you can buy fresh fruit cups doused with lime and chile ($1) and tacos (30¢). Around 6 or 7 PM, at the stands along the pedestrian streets in the center you can buy grilled corn on the cob (30¢) and seafood tostadas ($1).

➢ UNDER $5 • **Café del Fondo.** This restaurant next to a bookstore is beatnik central. Artsy types spend hours here over $2 *cafés exóticos* (cinnamon- or alcohol-spiked coffees). The deliciously sweet cappuccino with nutmeg ($1.50) is one of the better ones. Daily breakfast ($2–$3) and lunch ($5) specials are available, but you're more than welcome just to nurse your coffee, smoke, and sing along with guitar-toting customers. *16 de Septiembre 10, no phone. Open daily 7 AM–10 PM. Wheelchair access.*

Comedor Vegetariano Natura. The decor is decidedly Bradys rec room, complete with wood paneling and wall-sized forest posters, but the food is good, if heavy on the eggs and cheese. Try the mushroom and cheese "burgers" ($2.50), or the soy enchiladas ($3.50). The yogurt

Sola? Solita?

Solo travelers, especially female ones, often encounter incredulous responses from Mexicans after revealing that they are traveling alone. The double request for confirmation—"Sola? Solita?" ("Alone! All by your little self?"), asked by everyone from the grandma at the hotel desk to university students sitting in a café, may give you undue cause for paranoia. But aside from the obvious concerns for your safety, most Mexicans react with surprise because of the close familial bonds that exist in their own culture. Mexican youth travel with family and friends, and, as one female university student explained, "My parents would worry if I traveled by myself."

The influence of family is strong, especially since most people live with their parents until they get married. Bragging about your studio apartment back home usually results not in envy but pity: For many Mexicans, living and traveling alone implies that your family doesn't care much for you. The extended family is a source of economic and emotional support, and any relative, no matter how distant, can show up looking for a meal, a job, or a place to stay. Typical outings, whether a month-long vacation at the beach or a Sunday afternoon in the park, almost always involve the entire family. The bonus of all this group activity is that the solo traveler is rarely at a loss for company: many Mexicans are perfectly willing to expand the family to include a lone gringo for the day.

shakes are made with almost any fruit grown in Mexico. If you happen to be suffering from any gastrointestinal disorders, the restaurant also sells natural remedies, including horsehair tea for dysentery. *Vergara 7, tel. 42/04–22–12. 2 blocks east of Jardín Zenéa on 5 de Mayo, then right on Vergara. Open Mon.–Sat. 8 AM–9:30 PM.*

La Mariposa. This popular café/ice cream parlor has been around for more than 50 years. Delicious milkshakes are $2.50 and light lunches are less than $5. Check out the tempting sweets at the back counter. *Peralta 7, tel. 42/12–11–66. 2 blocks north of Jardín Zenéa. Open daily 8 AM–9:30 PM.*

Restaurant Punto y Coma. This place is filled with students at midday, so conversation is pretty easy to come by. The *menú del día* (daily special) is about $3.50 and includes soup, tortillas, rice, an entrée, and dessert. Meat lovers should try the *hígado encebollado* (liver in onions) when it's available, or the pork chops with apple sauce ($4). The tortillas served here are made fresh in the front of the restaurant. *16 de Septiembre 27, 1 block east of Jardín Zenéa, tel. 42/14–16–66. Open daily 8–6.*

➤ UNDER $15 • **Café Tulipe.** Students, both Mexican and foreign, frequent this pleasant café and restaurant at night. Solo diners can amuse themselves by checking out the art prints on the wall and the prominently displayed dessert cart. Try the *crema conde*, a soup made of black beans, cream, oregano, and *epazote* (an herb particular to Mexico) for $3.50. Other dishes include chicken in orange sauce ($8) and fondue for two ($15). Service is friendly and unobtrusive. *Calzada de los Arcos 3, tel. 42/13–63–91. 1½ blocks west of base of Ejército Republicano. Open Sun.–Wed. 8 AM–10 PM, Thurs.–Sat. 8 AM–11 PM.*

WORTH SEEING

Though Querétaro is a bigger city than you may have expected, most sights are within walking distance of the Jardín Zenéa. **Parque Cerro de las Campanas** is on the northwest end of the city, while the **Convento de la Santa Cruz** is about a half a mile east of downtown. The immense expanses of city blocks stretching out beyond the center are generally residential and industrial areas, with little to attract most visitors.

CONVENTO DE LA SANTA CRUZ This 16th-century convent is one of Querétaro's most intriguing attractions. Still functioning, it's home to about 40 monks who serenely go about their business while tourists traipse through the building. Original furnishings and paintings are on display in several of the rooms, including the cell where Emperor Maximilian awaited his execution. The branches of the famous **Árbol de las Espinas** (Thorn Tree), in one of the convent's many patios, are filled with cross-shaped thorns. According to legend, the tree grows where a friar named Margil de Jesús buried his cane. Nearby is **Calzada de los Arcos,** Querétaro's huge, pink, 19th-century stone aqueduct, the city's emblem. Though the Calzada no longer carries water, it is one of the largest aqueducts ever constructed in the Americas. Look for the charming old gentleman who gives tours daily in English, French, Spanish, and Italian. *From Jardín Zenéa, go 1 block south on Corregidora, then left on Independencia about 6 blocks. Small donation requested. Open Mon.–Sat. 9–2 and 4–6, Sun. 9–4:30.*

MUSEO DE ARTE DE QUERETARO This 18th-century building, once an Augustine monastery, was recently renovated and now houses an interesting and varied art collection. Most of the collection dates from the 16th through the 18th century, but several rooms on the ground floor are dedicated to temporary exhibits of contemporary Mexican artists and photographers, and students from the University of Querétaro. *Allende 14, near Pino Suárez, tel. 42/12–35–23. Admission: $3, free with student ID and on Tues. Open Tues.–Sun. 11–7.*

MUSEO REGIONAL The regional museum is in an ornate building, once a Franciscan convent, that dates from the 17th century. A collection of pre-Columbian artifacts from Querétaro state and an interesting display of items of historical import, including early copies of the first Mexican constitution and the coffin used to bring Emperor Maximilian's body to its final resting place, are housed here. *Corregidora 3, SE cnr of Jardín Zenéa, tel. 42/12–20–31. Admission: $4.50, free with student ID. Open Tues.–Sun. 10:30–4:30.*

PALACIO DEL GOBIERNO FEDERAL Also called the **Palacio Municipal** or the **Casa de la Corregidora,** the palacio now contains municipal offices. During the first rumblings of the war for independence, this was the home of Querétaro's mayor-magistrate (El Corregidor) and his wife, Doña Josefa Ortiz de Domínguez (La Corregidora). In the evenings, anti-royalist conspirators—including Ignacio Allende and Miguel Hidalgo—came here under the guise of participating in the sympathetic Doña Josefa's literary salon. In September 1810, the home of one of the salon's members was raided, revealing the munitions the group had been stockpiling in preparation for an uprising planned for December 8, 1810. Josefa managed to get word of the raid to Hidalgo and Allende in Dolores Hidalgo, warning them of their impending arrest. A few days later, almost three months earlier than planned, Hidalgo gave the speech known as the "Grito de Dolores," regarded as the spark that began the fight for independence. He summoned his parishioners to arms by ringing his church bell, which was later brought here to the palace. Stop by at night when the fountain in the plaza is lit up. *NW cnr of Plaza de la Independencia (Plaza de Armas).*

PARQUE CERRO DE LAS CAMPANAS Morbid though it may be, this park was established on the site where Emperor Maximilian and the royalist generals Tomás Mejía and Miguel Miramón were executed. There is now a chapel in the park dedicated to the three and a small museum, complete with a brief video in English and Spanish about the events leading up to the execution. The park is beautifully landscaped, and a great place for a jog or peace and quiet. The 20-meter monument to Benito Juárez on the grounds is also worth a look, not that you could miss it. *Gómez Farías s/n, tel. 42/15–20–75. From center, west on Morelos 9 blocks. Admission free. Park open daily 6–6; museum open Tues.–Sun. 10–2 and 3:30–6.*

PLAZA DE LA CORREGIDORA This pleasant square is named after the heroine of the Independence movement, Doña Josefa (*see* Palacio del Gobierno Federal, *above*), whose statue graces the plaza. The **Árbol de la Amistad** (Friendship Tree), planted here in 1977 in a mixture of soils from around the world, symbolizes Querétaro's hospitality. Surrounding the square are several outdoor cafés and restaurants. *Corregidora, 1 block north of Jardín Zenéa.*

TEATRO DE LA REPUBLICA This imposing neoclassical building was the site of some of the most important events in Mexico's history, including the passing of Emperor Maximilian's death sentence and the drafting of the new constitution in 1917. Although you probably won't witness anything nearly so momentous, you could catch one of the theater's somewhat infrequent shows. Check at the box office to find out what's going on. *Angela Peralta 22, 1 block north of Jardín Zenéa. Open weekdays 10–2 and 5–8, Sat. 9–noon.*

TEMPLO DE SANTA CLARA This 17th-century church sits in the tree-filled **Jardín Madero.** Exquisite baroque artwork and several intricately carved and gilded altar pieces grace the church's interior. Next to the church, at the corner of Allende, stands the **Fuente de Neptuno** (Neptune's Fountain). The fountain, designed by renowned Mexican architect and Bajío native Eduardo Tresguerra, originally belonged to the monks of San Antonio, who sold the piece (along with part of their land) during tight economic times. *On Madero, near Allende, about 2 blocks west of Jardín Zenéa.*

CHEAP THRILLS

The huge, resplendent **Alameda** park is the best place to collapse after a long day of doing the tourist thing. The nearby **El Molino** bakery (Juárez, at Zaragoza) sells sweet treats you can eat while lounging on the lush grass, or feed to the ducks in the pond. The tranquility is only slightly disturbed by the *tianguis* (open-air market) outside the park, where you can pick up a new belt or the latest Gloria Trevi tape. *At Zaragoza and Corregidora. Park open daily 6 AM–8 PM.*

AFTER DARK

Though there's life downtown during the early evening, most of it fades away by about 9 PM. Serious partiers head off to the bars and clubs on Boulevard Bernardo Quintana on the east side of town. Things get rocking around 11 or midnight, and go until everyone decides they're done, or until dawn, whichever comes first. More conservative nightlife-seekers can head to **Café Tulipe** and **Café del Fondo** (*see* Food, *above*), both of which serve coffee and dessert until 10 PM. The crowd at Café del Fondo draws a bohemian crowd, and Tulipe fills up with students.

BARS Students hang out at **J.B.J. O'Brien's** (Bernardo Quintana 13, tel. 42/13–01–48), **Freeday** (Constituyentes 119 Ote., tel. 42/23–32–12), and **Carlos 'N Charlie's** (Bernardo Quintana 160, tel. 42/13–90–36). The latter features live music Thursday, Friday, and Saturday nights, as well as free appetizers and drinks on the house once you've gotten too drunk to need any more.

CINEMAS Cinema Premier 70 (Corregidora, at Independencia, tel. 42/14–05–10) shows U.S. and Mexican movies for $3. The **Museo Regional** (*see* Worth Seeing, *above*) has regular film festivals with international and avant-garde films; check the billboard in the entryway for details.

CLUBS A newly remodeled disco called **Qiu** (Monte Sinai 103, tel. 42/13–03–61) is an excess of glitter and lights, where they play mostly pop and charge about an $8 cover. *Salsa, cumbia,* and *quebradita* bands play Monday through Saturday evenings at the **Club Dorado** (Blvd. Bernardo Quintana 145, tel. 42/13–45–47). Show time is usually 10:30 PM, and the cover charge is around $10 with a two-drink minimum (and the drinks aren't cheap).

Near Querétaro

SAN JUAN DEL RIO

Some 54 kilometers southeast of Querétaro, this town is full of imposing structures, including the **Parroquia de Santo Domingo,** a 17th-century church whose main draw is a statue of Christ with African features above the main altar. The **Museo de la Santa Cruz** houses pre-Columbian artifacts from San Juan del Río. In addition, Querétaro state is famous for its opal mines and hand-woven items, such as baskets and blankets, plenty of which are for sale in the *artesanía* (crafts) shops here. Don't miss **La Guadalupana** (16 de Septiembre 16, tel. 467/2–09–13), where gemstones are cut and polished. Stands along the *portales* (porches) on Avenida Juárez also sell artesanía. In June, the town hosts a variety of events celebrating the town's patron saint. **Clase Premier** buses depart for San Juan del Río ($1, 30 min) every 10 minutes from Querétaro's Central de Autobuses.

SAN JOAQUÍN

San Joaquín is about 2½ hours from Querétaro by bus. The town's main attractions are two sets of ruins outside the city limits, neither of which has been fully excavated. **Toluquilla,** a 15-minute drive or 40-minute walk from town, is believed to have been a military fortification of the Indians of the Huasteca region, and has several pyramid foundations and ball courts. **Ranas,** a 15-minute walk from the city, was used by Chichimecs as a fortress and ceremonial center, and the remains consist of pyramid foundations and other structures.

You can camp for free here in the **Campo Hermoso** forest reserve—just let the municipal officers (Morelos s/n, tel. 42/2–34–57) know you're there. The camp has showers and a grocery store. Families in San Joaquín also rent out rooms, so ask around once you get there. **Flecha Amarilla** buses leave Querétaro every hour to San Joaquín ($5). Signs direct you to the ruins and campground from the bus terminal.

San Miguel de Allende

It is difficult to explain how San Miguel de Allende seduces new arrivals within a matter of days. Ask any non-native resident, Mexican or gringo, why artists, troubadours, and tourists are lured here and they are usually at a loss for words. Other towns in Mexico, they will assure you, are more picturesque, have better nightlife, and a more liberal attitude, yet people keep coming back to this modest *pueblo* (town) of cobblestone streets and wrought-iron street lamps. The attraction, it seems, lies in a combination of things; the open, honest friendliness of the young artist community, the speed with which you become familiar with the entire town, and the creature comforts provided by the relative affluence here. This is a place where people set down roots, whether to study Spanish at one of the language schools, to paint, sculpt or dance at the **Bellas Artes,** or simply to live their version of the good life.

The gringo population of San Miguel is one of the largest in Mexico, a fact which causes many travelers to ignore it on their way to more "authentic" areas of Mexico. This is unfortunate, not only because the number of non-Mexican residents has dropped considerably in recent years, but also because not all of them are impatient tourists disrespectful of Mexican culture. Many of the expatriates play crucial roles in San Miguel society, whether by helping to maintain the historical integrity of the town or doing social service work. Moreover, the Mexican population considers this *their* town first and foremost.

San Miguel was declared a national monument by the Mexican government in 1926, rendering it next to impossible to make any modern architectural or planning changes to the town; you can thank the government every time you trip over a cobblestone.

The town was named after the Spanish friar Juan de San Miguel, who established a mission on the site because of its proximity to spring waters. Native son Ignacio Allende was a big player in the 1810 Independence movement, plotting the rebellion against Spanish rule. In 1826, the town was renamed San Miguel de Allende in his honor.

Prices are higher in San Miguel because of the large expatriate presence, but that shouldn't scare budget travelers away. Even those trying to avoid gringos should make an exception and stop in San Miguel—you may find your stay of just a few days stretching into a few weeks or more.

BASICS

AMERICAN EXPRESS The AmEx representative, **Viajes Vertiz,** holds mail for cardholders. Traveler's checks are *not* changed, but emergency check cashing is available. *½ block north of Plaza Principal, tel. 465/2–18–56. Open weekdays 9–2 and 4–6:30. Mailing address: Hidalgo 1, Aptdo. Postal 486, San Miguel de Allende, Guanajuato, CP 37700, México.*

BOOKSTORES El Colibrí, in business for 35 years, has an extensive selection of English paperbacks and magazines as well as art supplies. *Diez de Sollano 30, 1 block east of Plaza Principal, tel. 465/2–07–57. Open weekdays 10–2 and 4–7.*

CASAS DE CAMBIO Although the Plaza Principal is surrounded by several banks, **Casa de Cambio Deal** (Correo 15, no phone) is your best bet, because it doesn't charge a commission and is open weekdays 9–2 and 4–5:45, Saturdays 9–1:45. **Banamex** (cnr of Canal and Hidalgo) has an ATM.

CONSULATE In case you hadn't noticed that San Miguel de Allende is practically a U.S. colony, the fact that there's a consulate in this small pueblo should give you a clue. *Macías 72, tel. 465/2–23–57 or 465/2–00–68 for emergencies. Open Mon. and Wed. 9–1 and 4–7, Tues. and Thurs. 4–7, or by appointment.*

EMERGENCIES The phone number for the **police** is 465/2–00–22; for an **ambulance,** 465/2–16–16.

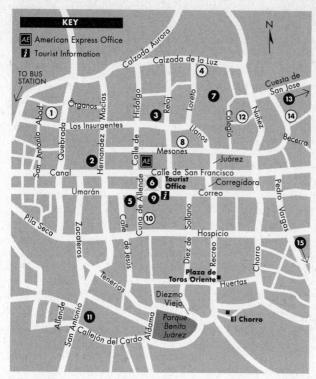

KEY

AE American Express Office

i Tourist Information

TO BUS STATION

N

Sights ●

Bellas Artes, **2**

Biblioteca Pública, **3**

El Mirador, **15**

Instituto Allende, **11**

Jardín Botánico, **13**

Mercado Ignacio Ramírez, **7**

Museo Histórico, **5**

Parroquia de San Miguel Arcángel, **9**

Plaza Principal (El Jardín), **6**

Lodging ○

Casa de Huéspedes, **8**

Hostal Internacional, **1**

Hotel La Huerta, **14**

Hotel Parador de San Sebastián, **12**

Hotel Quinta Loreto, **4**

Posada de Allende, **10**

LAUNDRY **Lava Mágico** has some English-speaking staff and will wash, dry, and fold a load of clothes for $4.50. No self-service facilities are available, but if you drop off your clothes before noon you'll get them back the same day. *Pila Seca 5, tel. 465/2–08–99. Open daily 8–8.*

MAIL The full-service post office will hold mail sent to you at the following address for up to 10 days: Lista de Correos, Correo 18, San Miguel de Allende, Guanajuato, CP 37700, México. *Tel. 465/2–00–89. 2 blocks east of Plaza Principal. Open weekdays 8–7, Sat. 9–1.*

MEDICAL AID **Hospital Unión Médica** provides 24-hour medical treatment and can refer you to an English-speaking physician. *San Francisco 50, 4 blocks east of Plaza Principal, tel. 465/2–22–33.*

You'll have no trouble finding a pharmacy in San Miguel, but Chelo at **Botica Agundis** speaks English and is particularly helpful. The sign says they're open Monday through Saturday 10–10, but Chelo says she's there daily until midnight. *Canal 26, tel. 465/2–11–98.*

PHONES The pay phones in San Miguel are in sad shape. You can make long-distance calls daily 7 AM–11 PM in the **Central de Autobuses** (*see* Coming and Going, *below*). In the center of town, try **El Toro Caseta Larga Distancia,** which charges $1.50 to place a collect call and has good rates for cash calls. *Macías 58-A, at Canal, tel. 465/2–04–11. Open Mon.–Sat. 8–8, Sun. 9–2.*

La Conexión has phone, fax, and mail service, and the staff is good about offering advice to lost newcomers. *Aldama 1, tel./fax 465/2–16–87. Open weekdays 8–8, Sat. 8–3, Sun. 10–2.*

SCHOOLS Although people from all over the world descend upon San Miguel for the language and fine arts classes, they often end up speaking more English than Spanish. By studying during the school year instead of the summer, you'll avoid at least a few conversations in

English. You can also take advantage of the classes in traditional jewelry making, pottery, and sculpture offered by local artisans, as well as dance lessons. If you don't want to commit to an entire course, Spanish classes are also offered at the **Hostal Internacional** (*see* Where to Sleep, *below*).

Academia Hispano Americano offers Spanish language and literature classes from beginner to advanced levels. Scholarships and homestays are available. *Mesones 4, tel. 465/2–03–49.*

Bellas Artes/Centro Cultural El Nigromante is a fine arts school offering classes in dance, art, and music. The director, Carmen Masip de Hawkins, can provide specific information on courses and prices. *Macías 75, tel. 465/2–02–89.*

Centro Mexicano de Lengua y Cultura de San Miguel offers individual or group instruction in Spanish, English, French, and Italian, from basic to advanced levels. *Orizaba 15, tel. 465/2–07–63.*

Instituto Allende is an internationally recognized school of fine arts, but it is rumored to be resting on its laurels. Some say the program doesn't always keep up with the needs of its English-speaking students. *Ancha de San Antonio 20, tel. 465/2–01–90.*

VISITOR INFORMATION Pick up a copy of the local English newspaper, *Atención San Miguel* ($1), for listings of local events, religious services, literary discussion groups, and rental housing. Further information can be found on bulletin boards at cafés, hotels, and **Bellas Artes** (*see* Worth Seeing, *below*). The staff of the **tourist office,** some of whom speak English, will load you down you with maps, brochures, and hotel listings. They also have information on Spanish and art classes. *South side of Plaza Principal, tel. 465/2–17–47. Open weekdays 10–2:45 and 5–7, Sat. 10–1.*

COMING AND GOING

BY BUS San Miguel de Allende's **Central de Autobuses** is about 10 minutes from the center of town. To get to town, hop on any local bus marked CENTRO. The main bus lines here are **Flecha Amarilla** (tel. 465/2–00–84) and **Autotransportes Herradura de Plata** (tel. 465/2–07–05). Buses to Mexico City ($10, 3½ hrs) and Querétaro ($2, 1 hr) leave hourly from 5 AM to 9 PM. Buses leave frequently for Guanajuato ($3.50, 1½ hrs) daily between 7:45 AM and 5:30 PM. Dolores Hidalgo ($1.50, 45 min) buses leave every 20 minutes from 6:40 AM to 10:30 PM. The bus station has long-distance telephone service (open 7 AM–11 PM) and luggage storage (open 7 AM–10 PM).

On Tuesdays, locals set up La Plazita, a market that stretches for four blocks. Pirated cassette tapes, spangly hair baubles, and nylon underwear share space with pastries and fresh fruit. To get here from the Plaza Principal, go three blocks west on Canal and turn right on San Antonio Abad.

BY TRAIN Trains leave at 1 PM for Mexico City ($11 first class, $5 second class) and Querétaro ($4.50 first class, $1.50 second class), and the train to Monterrey departs at 2:30 PM ($23 first class, $10.50 second class). The bus marked CENTRO will take you from the train station to the center of town (Plaza Principal). *Calzada de la Estación, tel. 465/2–00–07. Open for ticket sales Mon.–Sat. 10–3, Sun. noon–3.*

GETTING AROUND

San Miguel is a small town, and most attractions are easily accessible on foot. Though picturesque, the cobblestone streets are impossibly lumpy and at times very steep. Also keep in mind that the town is more than 1½ kilometers above sea level, and it may take time to get used to the altitude (heavy drinking will result in killer hangovers).

San Miguel's central **Plaza Principal** is surrounded by a neat grid of streets. All streets change names at the plaza. Canal, which borders the plaza on its northern edge, turns into San Francisco to the east of the plaza; on the plaza's south side, Umarán goes to the west and Correo to the east. The only buses you're likely to need are those that run up and down Canal to the bus and train stations. Taxi fares from the center to the stations are $2.

WHERE TO SLEEP

Most hotels are near the Plaza Principal, and rooms range from the impossibly expensive to reasonable. Your best bet, however, is the **Hostal Internacional** (*see below*). If you're planning an extended stay, check the bulletin boards in stores and restaurants around town for rental lists. You can also check with **A-1 Real Estate** (Cuna de Allende 11, tel. 465/2–16–30), which lists apartments for rent from $200 to more than $1,000 per month. Discounts for pre-payment and long-term stays are often available. Homestays are another option (*see* Schools, *above*). The prices listed here apply in the low season. During high season (October–January), hotel prices are jacked up as much as 100%.

➤ UNDER $20 • **Hotel La Huerta.** Cheap rooms and peace and quiet make up for the 10-minute walk you'll have to make from the Plaza Principal. The rooms are clean and airy and open onto communal sitting rooms. The staff will also wash your clothes (for a fee) if you ask nicely. Singles are $13, doubles $16.50. *Cerrada de Becerra, tel. 465/2–08–81. From Plaza Principal, 1 block north on Reloj, right on Mesones 5 blocks, right on Cerrada de Becerra. 15 rooms, all with bath.*

➤ UNDER $25 • **Casa de Huéspedes.** The tiled, plant-filled courtyard lends some exoticism to this tiny, friendly guest house. Rooms are large and well-lit, with balconies opening onto the street. The staff is amiable, and there's hot water 24 hours a day. Singles cost $15; doubles, $23. *Mesones 27, 2½ blocks from Plaza Principal, tel. 465/2–13–78. 6 rooms, all with bath.*

Posada de Allende. This is the second-choice cheapy—it's not particularly clean, particularly friendly, or particularly anything. The woman that runs the place is a bit spacey and you'll have to ring the bell hard if you arrive after dark. Still, it's close to the Plaza Principal and the price is right: singles are $16.50, doubles $20. *Cuna de Allende 10, tel. 465/2–06–98. 1 block south of Plaza Principal. 5 rooms, all with bath.*

➤ UNDER $30 • **Hotel Parador de San Sebastián.** Every room here is clean and has antique oak furnishings and a small kitchen, complete with utensils. Don't expect to take a hot shower in the afternoon, though; hot water is only available 8 AM–noon and 8 PM–midnight. Singles are $20, doubles $25. *Mesones 7, tel. 465/2–07–07. 1½ blocks from Plaza Principal. 24 rooms, all with bath.*

Quinta Loreto. Spacious, clean rooms with patios, a large garden, and free use of the pool and tennis court make the Quinta Loreto worth the extra bucks. Rooms upstairs have better views, but those downstairs are cooler. Most guests are foreign tourists. Singles are $23, doubles $29. *Loreto 15, tel. 465/2–00–42. From Plaza Principal, 2 blocks up Reloj, right on Insurgentes 1 block, left on Loreto. 38 rooms, all with bath. Wheelchair access. AE, MC, V.*

HOSTEL **Hostal Internacional.** This hostel gives you so much for your money, there's no reason not to stay here if there's room. For $5 you sleep in single-sex dorm rooms and wake up to free breakfast, as well as coffee and tea all day long. For another $1.50 per day you can use the kitchen facilities. Rooms and bathrooms are cleaner than those of some hotels, and the friendly manager gets rave reviews from his guests. He also pays a local teacher to give Spanish classes Monday–Thursday 4:30–6:30; you can join in for $2. Private rooms are available for $12. *Órganos 34, tel. 465/2–06–74. From Plaza Principal, 1 block west on Canal, right on Macías 3 blocks, left on Órganos 3 blocks. Laundry.*

FOOD

Tourism has hit San Miguel in the belly with some pleasant consequences: An extraordinary number of restaurants cater to a wide range of tastes and price ranges, and a wander through the downtown area will lead you to just about anything you want, from standard tacos and *tortas* (sandwiches) to Lebanese and Italian food. You can get cheap baked goods at **Panadería La**

Espiga (Insurgentes 9, tel. 465/2–15–80), and **Daylight Donuts** (Mesones 79, tel. 465/2–05–82) is an amusing place to watch cranky American retirees attempt to communicate with the Spanish-speaking staff. The **Mercado Ignacio Ramírez** (Av. Colegio, tel. 465/2–28–44) has *comedores* (sit-down food stands) where you can watch the town's culinary masters prepare typical Mexican fare. The prices are very reasonable and the food stands are generally open until dusk.

➤ UNDER $5 • **El Ten-ten Pie.** This restaurant serves up typical Mexican food in a relaxing, fun space filled with works by local artisans. Tacos are a bit pricey at $1, but the manager guarantees the meat is fresh and the vegetables are washed in purified water. Try the poblano chile and cream tacos, or the excellent flan ($2). You can also while away the hours playing chess or backgammon as great music plays in the background. *Cuna de Allende 21, no phone. Open daily noon–midnight. Wheelchair access.*

La Piñata. This unassuming corner diner serves up mountains of cheap food. Scrambled-egg breakfasts, including fresh-squeezed juice and toast, are $2. Tostadas and quesadillas cost less than $1. Try the sugarcane, grapefruit, or carrot juice for $1. *Jesús 1, 1 block west of Plaza Principal, no phone. Open Wed.–Mon. 9–9, Tues. 9–2. Wheelchair access.*

Las Palomas. Tacos, tostadas, and quesadillas with fillings such as chicken mole, *nopales* (grilled cactus), and spicy pork are super-cheap here—three tacos and a drink come to less than $3. The seating area is arranged around the small kitchen so you can watch as your food is prepared. *Mesones 60, btw Hidalgo and Macías, no phone. Open daily 9–9.*

➤ UNDER $10 • **Mama Mía.** Although some sort of Mexican plate is always available, this restaurant serves primarily Italian food. The open-air patio filled with hanging plants, friendly people, great red wine, and live Andean music every night around 8 make this a great place to eat, drink, and be happy. Small pizzas with tons of cheese are $9; other pasta dishes run $6–$9. Breakfasts are cheaper at $1.50–$3. *Umarán 8, ½ block west of Plaza Principal, tel. 465/2–20–63. Open Sun.–Thurs. 8 AM–midnight, Fri. and Sat. 8 AM–1 AM.*

Mesón de San José. Brunch in an interior courtyard overhung with branches and flowers includes fresh whole-wheat bread here. The *quesadilla gourmet*, a flour tortilla stuffed with spinach, mushrooms, and cheese, fills you up for $6. This is also the place to try *chiles en nogada* (chiles stuffed with beef and covered in a walnut sauce and pomegranate seeds; $9), a delicacy usually reserved for holiday meals. *Mesones 38, 3 blocks from Plaza Principal, tel. 465/2–38–48. Open daily 8 AM–10 PM.*

Rincón Español. Don't let the $150 bottles of champagne scare you away from this place—the menú del día, served between 6:30 PM and 9:30 PM, includes soup, an entrée (fish, chicken, or steak), a margarita or soda, bread, and dessert, and costs only $7. Try the *tortilla española* (Spanish omelet with potatoes) on Tuesdays and Fridays, or the *pescado a la veracruzana* (red snapper cooked in tomatoes, onions, capers, peppers, and herbs) on Thursdays. On Saturday nights and Sunday afternoons, live flamenco music accompanies your meal. *Correo 29, 2 blocks east of Plaza Principal, tel. 465/23-27. Open daily noon–10.*

CAFES Cafés in San Miguel de Allende are mostly gringo hangouts where tourists and expats drink cappuccino. **El Buen Café** (Jesús 23, tel. 465/2-58-07) hosts nightly book discussions and poetry readings and has live music from 6 PM to 8 PM Friday and Saturday. Coffee is about $1, and several sandwiches and crêpes are under $5. If you want to escape gringos, try a bar or cantina, identifiable by western-style swinging doors (*see* After Dark, *below*).

A group of old fogey expatriates meets at the Bellas Artes Mondays at 7 PM to share short stories and poetry (inspired, perhaps, by the low cost of retirement in San Miguel).

WORTH SEEING

BELLAS ARTES/CENTRO CULTURAL EL NIGROMANTE
Built in 1765, this former convent now houses a school of fine arts. A peaceful central courtyard and fountain are surrounded by two floors of art workshops and music rooms. Murals by David Siqueiros adorn the interior walls and hallways, and a small

gallery on the first floor exhibits work by local artists. The café serves coffees and light lunches for less than $5. *Macías 75, 1½ blocks west of Plaza Principal, tel. 465/2–02–89. Open Mon.–Sat. 9–8, Sun. 10–3.*

BIBLIOTECA PUBLICA San Miguel's public library has a great collection of books in both Spanish and English. The library's sun-filled courtyard is constantly full of chattering children. English books are on sale and the library stocks current Mexican newspapers and magazines. A bulletin board in the foyer announces upcoming events, and the town's English newspaper, *Atención San Miguel,* is on sale at the front desk. On Tuesdays and Thursdays, people meet in the courtyard from 5 PM to 7 PM for a free English-Spanish exchange. Also on sale is a book in English on San Miguel de Allende's history, but they'll let you take a peek at it for free. To check out books, you must plop down a refundable $30 deposit and supply two passport pictures. *Insurgentes 25, tel. 465/2–02–93. Open weekdays 10–2 and 4–7, Sat. 10–2.*

INSTITUTO ALLENDE Once the country mansion of the Count and Countess de la Canal, this impressive 18th-century building now houses a school of the arts, languages, and social studies. Visitors from around the world study in the lush gardens overflowing with bougainvillea, rose bushes, and ivy. There is also a small gallery with rotating art exhibits. *Ancha San Antonio 20, tel. 465/2–01–90. Office open weekdays 9–1 and 3–5.*

JARDIN BOTANICO EL CHARCO DEL INGENIO One of the best-kept secrets of San Miguel, this 47-hectare area of cacti, succulents, and other flora typical of the region is located in and around a canyon offering hours of hiking and climbing. You'll also find the ruins of a colonial mill, and the view of the city from here is excellent. *Diez de Sollano 21, tel. 465/2–29–90. Take Cuesta de San Jose to Montitlán, go left, and follow road until it becomes unpaved; take right-hand path up hill. Admission: $2. Open daily until dusk.*

MERCADO IGNACIO RAMIREZ This enormous open-air market takes place daily and extends over several city blocks. Be prepared for sensory overload: Squealing pigs and squawking chickens drown out blaring pop music, while the neon colors of cheap clothing compete with the glowing tones of tomatoes and melons. *Behind Plaza Cívica. From Plaza Principal, 1 block north on Reloj and right on Mesones.*

MUSEO HISTORICO DE SAN MIGUEL DE ALLENDE This former mansion, the birthplace of Ignacio Allende, now houses a museum. Exhibits include Allende's clothing and personal effects, as well as pre-Columbian artifacts from Guanajuato state. The placards, posters, and objects tell you more than you ever wanted to know about the history of San Miguel. *Cuna de Allende 1, SW cnr of Plaza Principal, tel. 465/2–44–65. Admission free. Open Tues.–Sun. 9–4.*

PARROQUIA DE SAN MIGUEL ARCANGEL Not only is this church worth seeing, but you'd have to be blind *not* to see it. The original two-towered facade was replaced in the 18th century by the parish priest, who commissioned a local stone carver, Cerefino Gutiérrez, to build it. Apparently Gutiérrez was an Indian with no formal training in draftsmanship, who drew his plans every day in the sand with a stick. The pseudo-Gothic exterior contrasts sharply with the *mudéjar* (Moorish-influenced) interior. On the left side of the entrance is a baptistry. *South side of Plaza Principal.*

Travelers are advised not to go through the hills at the end of Calzada de La Luz in order to get to the Jardín Botánico. Stick to the sidewalks, as several muggings have occurred in these hills, known as the Cerros de las Tres Cruces.

CHEAP THRILLS

The wrought-iron benches on the **Plaza Principal,** also known as *El Jardín* (the garden), are the place to sit and get a feel for the town. The plaza is also the cruising spot of choice among local youth on Sunday nights. **El Mirador** (the lookout), up a steep hill a ways from the center of town, is a popular (and consequently not-too-private) place to view the sunset. Ask a local to set you off in the right direction.

The **Parque Juárez** is a particularly beautiful place teeming with plants, flowers, and birds—a good place for a walk or woolgathering. The walk to get here from the center of town is a pretty one, but a bit complicated: From the Plaza Principal, go east on Correo to Recreo. Then head south on Recreo to Huertas, turn east on Huertas, and go down the hill on the street called El Chorro. After a steep descent, just before the park, you'll reach **El Chorro**, a series of underground springs enclosed by a colonial building. If you peer inside what looks like an old mansion, you'll see the wells that once supplied the town with water. Today, these natural springs function as a "public laundry" where locals gather during the day to wash clothes and occasionally each other.

FESTIVALS The birth of the town's namesake, Ignacio Allende, is celebrated January 21 with a military parade. A comical procession commemorates the **Fiesta de San Antonio de Padua** on June 12. September, however, is the big party month, so be sure to make hotel reservations. September 16 is the **Día de la Independencia**, celebrated with a reenactment of Father Hidalgo's "Grito de Dolores" (which signaled the beginning of the Mexican war for independence) and a marathon. The third Saturday is **Sanmiguelada**, marked by a wild *corrida de toros* (running of the bulls); on the 29th a feast is held in honor of **San Miguel Arcángel**, the town's patron saint. The day is celebrated with a parade of *xóchiles* (huge decorations of flowers, plants, and corn) and *concheros* (shell dancers).

AFTER DARK

Plenty of bars and discos will keep you entertained after the sun sets; San Miguel parties until 5 or 6 AM. **La Cucaracha** (Zacateros 22, no phone) is one of the few cantinas that officially allows women. **Villa Jacaranda Cine Bar** (Aldama 53, tel. 465/2–10–15) is a hopping club that shows movies in English for about $5, which also gets you one drink. If you don't feel like swilling toxic substances, you can always hang out in the Plaza Principal.

BARS AND DANCING Bar Coco. This small bar, frequented mostly by Mexicans, is a great find for those trying to escape gringolandia. They serve food until midnight, have a two-for-one happy hour between 6 PM and 8 PM, and treat patrons to live music starting at 9:30 PM. *Macías 85, at Umarán, tel. 465/2–26–43. Open Tues.–Sun. until the crowd goes home, usually after midnight.*

Laberinto's. They play a mix of Latin and American dance music at this club, which is always crowded with locals on weekends. Cover charge is $3.50, except on Thursdays and Sundays, when it's free. *Ancha de San Antonio 7, tel. 465/2–03–62. Open Tues.–Sun. 10 PM–3 AM.*

Leonardo/Mama Mía Bar. In front of the pizzeria, Leonardo is a small neon-lit bar with thumping music and comfy chairs. Unfortunately, it is something of a meat market. Beers are pricey at $3. Across the hallway is the underground Mama Mía Bar, which gets down and dirty with rock and salsa. Cover is about $3. *Umarán 8, ½ block west of Plaza Principal, tel. 465/2–20–63. Open Fri. and Sat. 7 PM–2 AM; open additional days in summer.*

Pancho y Lefty's. Nightly rock music attracts a lively crowd of Mexicans and some gringos. Unfortunately, the talented bands play only covers, but it's the most popular place for "early evening" (i.e. until 1 AM) partying. *Mesones 99, tel. 465/2-19-58. Open nightly 8–1:30.*

El Ring. One of the most popular nightspots in town, El Ring is a discotheque in the 1978 sense of the word, complete with flashing laser lights and pulsating music. There's no cover for couples—single people in the know simply enter into instant relationships at the door before going in. Otherwise, cover is about $9. *Hidalgo 25. 1 block from Plaza Principal. Open Tues.–Sun. 9 PM–3 AM.*

Near San Miguel de Allende

POZOS

Pozos, established as a mining camp in 1576, is now some-thing of a ghost town, although a few people still live here. The population dropped from 10,000 to 500 in the 19th century, when the mines were abandoned. Today, buildings overgrown with cactus make for excellent exploring in an eerie, dusty atmosphere. Pozos is also famous for its reproductions of pre-Columbian instruments. The museum on Plaza Zaragoza is staffed by friendly folks who like to talk about the instruments, including the *palo de lluvia,* a snake-shaped instrument usu-

Pozos is named for the craters found at the outskirts of town. Drop a rock into one, and it will be seven or eight long sec-onds before you hear it plop to the bottom.

ally decorated with carved figures of corn, cactus, and feathers. The instrument, which repre-sents the feathered-serpent god Quetzalcoatl, is filled with beads that make a gushing sound like water when turned upside down. To get here, take a Flecha Amarilla bus to San José Itur-bide, and from there another bus to Pozos. The entire trip takes about 2 hours.

San Luis Potosí

At first glance, it may seem that the broom- and mop-wielding shopkeepers of San Luis Potosí have swept the downtown clean of life. The immaculate streets, skyscrapers, and occasional Burger King make the city seem like a big Midwestern town in the United States, and the colonial-era plazas and churches in the center of town fail to dis-pel the sterility. But San Luis' development hasn't left rural Mexican culture behind. It shows up in small but insistent ways, in the form of a little boy on the bus singing for a few coins, or the musicians strumming their guitars in the plazas in the evenings.

San Luis also has its share of high culture, with abundant theatrical performances, concerts, and conferences, the majority of which are free. Many fine examples of neoclassical and baroque architecture also serve as elegant reminders of the city's heyday as a colonial capital whose domain once encompassed most of northern Mexico, Texas, and Louisiana. Silver was discovered in the nearby hills of San Pedro in the 16th century, and "Minas del Potosí" was added to the city's name, in the hope that the mines here would yield wealth equal to that found in Potosí, Bolivia. However, the silver was soon depleted, and other minerals and a bur-geoning dairy industry replaced it as the basis for the city's economy. Today the mines in the San Pedro hills still function, but they are fundamentally tourist attractions rather than pro-ducers of silver.

Though there's plenty to see and do in San Luis, probably the best reason to come here is to explore the area beyond the capital city. **Santa María del Río,** a town specializing in the pro-duction of silk shawls, is only a short day trip away, and campers and other adventures will want to head off to **Río Verde,** where they can explore caves and waterfalls. Finally, the ghost mining town of **Real de Catorce** is also worth a visit—take the train for the full 19th-century effect.

BASICS

AMERICAN EXPRESS The AmEx office in the **Agencia de Grandes Viajes** offers the usual services for cardholders. They deliver MoneyGrams, exchange traveler's checks, and replace lost checks for cardholders and non-cardholders alike. *Carranza 1077, San Luis Potosí, San Luis Potosí, CP 78250, México, tel. 48/17–60–04, fax 48/11–11–66. 10 blocks west of Plaza de Armas. Open weekdays 9–2 and 4–6, Sat. 10–1.*

AUTO PARTS/SERVICE Refaccionaria y Rectificaciones Miguel sells and installs most auto parts and does house calls at no extra charge. *Damián Carmona 1565, tel. 48/14-31-77. In front of Jardín de Santiago. Open Mon.–Sat. 9–2 and 4–7.*

BOOKSTORES Librería Cristal (Carranza 765, tel. 48/12–80–15), **Librería Española** (Othón 170, tel. 48/12–57–81), and **Librería Universitaria** (Alvaro Obregón s/n, tel. 48/12–67–49) all have books in English and Spanish. All are open Monday–Saturday 9–2 and 4–7.

CASAS DE CAMBIO Banks on the Plaza de Armas are open weekdays 9–1. **Banamex** changes cash and traveler's checks weekdays 9–noon and has a Cirrus/Plus ATM. *Obregón 355, tel. 48/12–16–56. From Plaza de Armas, 1 block north on Allende to Obregón.*

EMERGENCIES The number for the **police** department is 48/12–25–82; for an **ambulance** it's 48/15–33–26.

LAUNDRY Lavanderías Automáticas Superwash will wash your duds for you at $3.50 per kilo, or you can do it yourself at $2 per load, wash and dry. They offer free pick-up and delivery service, so you don't have to haul your clothes any farther than the front door. *Carranza 1093, tel. 48/13–93–22. 10 blocks west of Plaza de Armas. Mon.–Sat. 8–8, Sun. 9–2.*

MAIL The post office offers all the usual services and will hold mail sent to you at the following address for up to 10 days: Lista de Correos, Morelos 235, San Luis Potosí, San Luis Potosí, CP 78000, México. *Morelos 235, tel. 48/12–27–40. 2 blocks north and 1 block east of Plaza de Armas. Open weekdays 8–7, Sat. 9–1.*

MEDICAL AID The **Beneficiencia Española** (Carranza 1090, tel. 48/11–56–96) and the **Cruz Roja** (Juárez 540, tel. 48/15–33–22) provide 24-hour medical service. **Farmacia La Perla** (Escobedo, at Los Bravo, tel. 48/12–59–22) is open 24 hours a day.

PHONES Computel, near the Alameda, has high-tech long-distance service and charges about $2 for a 10-minute international collect call. You can also make cash calls here. *Universidad 700, tel. 48/18–12–31. From Plaza de Armas, 3 blocks south on Zaragoza, left on Universidad. Open daily 7:30 AM–9 PM.*

SCHOOLS The **Centro de Idiomas** (Zaragoza 410, tel. 48/12–49–55), associated with the Universidad Autónoma de San Luis Potosí, offers two- to six-month Spanish classes beginning in March, June, September, and December. Contact the director, Lic. María Luisa Sánchez Almazán for registration information.

VISITOR INFORMATION The **Centro de Turismo** has a well-informed staff that will weigh you down with maps and brochures, and can even provide guided tours of the city's historical center for $5. Many of the employees speak English. *Carranza 325, 3 blocks west of Plaza de Armas, tel. 48/12–27–70. Open weekdays 8–8, Sat. 9–1 and 4–8.*

COMING AND GOING

BY BUS The **Central Camionera** lies a few kilometers east of the central plaza. To get downtown from the terminal, make a left as you leave, walk two blocks to Avenida de las Torres, and catch the ALAMEDA bus across from the Hotel Central. Luggage storage is available at the station 7 AM–9 PM daily. **Flecha Amarilla** (tel. 48/18–29–23) has frequent service to Mexico City ($15, 6 hrs) and Guanajuato ($8, 4 hrs). **Estrella Blanca** (tel. 48/18–29–63) serves Aguascalientes ($6, 3 hrs) and Zacatecas ($6.50, 3 hrs). **Omnibuses de Oriente** (tel. 48/18–29–41) travels to Guadalajara ($12, 6 hrs) every hour round the clock, as well as to intrastate destinations such as Río Verde ($4, 2 hrs).

BY TRAIN First- and second-class service to Mexico City ($20 and $8.50, respectively, 8 hrs) departs daily at 10 PM. Second-class trains leave for Aguascalientes ($5, 4 hrs) at noon and for Real de Catorce ($5, 3 hrs) and Nuevo Laredo ($10, 12 hrs) at 5:30 PM. The ticket office is open daily 7:15 AM–6 PM. Tickets go on sale 45 minutes before departure, but get in line at least an hour and a half before departure. There's a market nearby where you can stock up with food for a long journey. Buses run east from the station to the Central Camionera and the youth hostel. *Othón, at 20 de Noviembre, tel. 48/12–21–23. Just north of the Alameda.*

GETTING AROUND

The **Plaza de Armas,** also known as **Jardín Hidalgo,** defines the center of town, and most attractions are within walking distance of it. There are four main streets stemming from Plaza de Armas. Carranza runs west–east, changing into Los Bravo as it passes just north of the Plaza de Armas. Madero also runs east–west and becomes Othón as it passes just south of the Plaza. The streets that form the east and west borders of the Plaza are Hidalgo/Zaragoza and Allende/5 de Mayo, respectively. East on Othón from the Plaza is the **Alameda,** near the cheap food, hotels, and train station; the pedestrian shopping area is north on Hidalgo. On the plaza, the cathedral's two bright blue neon crosses form a shining reference point to help you orient yourself at night. The tourist office on Carranza hands out excellent city maps. City buses, which are rarely necessary, stop running at about 11 PM.

WHERE TO SLEEP

The cheapest place to crash is the youth hostel, which is near the bus station. But unless you're looking for a quick place to rest your weary body before catching the next bus out, get the hell out of here—the area is sleazy and far removed from the action. The areas around the Plaza de Armas and the Alameda, offer reasonably priced rooms and more convenience. The desperately poor who want a better location than that offered by the hostel will have to close their eyes, plug their noses, and head to the **Hotel Nacional** (Othón 425, near the Alameda, tel. 48/12–24–50), where singles without bath are $6, doubles are $8.50, and the peeling paint and mildew are free.

➤ UNDER $15 • **Hotel Alameda.** This is the cheapest place to stay in town without having to sacrifice too many comforts—rooms are small and dark but clean, and the management is friendly enough. The nonstop cumbia tunes from bar next door may make your stay a little less pleasant. Singles are $8.50, doubles $10. *La Perla 3, tel. 48/18–65–58. Just off Othón, behind Pemex. 13 rooms, all with bath. Luggage storage, wheelchair access.*

➤ UNDER $20 • **Hotel Jardín Potosí.** Sunny hallways welcome you to spacious rooms, which are slightly nicer than the Alameda location would lead you to believe. The rooms all have bathrooms with dramatically peeling paint. Avoid having your laundry washed here. Singles are $15, doubles $16. *Los Bravo 530, tel. 48/12–31–52. From the Alameda, 1 block north on 20 de Noviembre and left on Los Bravo. 57 rooms, all with bath.*

Hotel Plaza. Although this hotel is well past its prime, its central location and balconies overlooking the plaza make it worthwhile. Large, carpeted rooms with TVs hint at the hotel's former glory, and the staff is extremely friendly and accommodating. Most rooms have bathrooms with hot water that takes a few minutes to kick in. Singles go for $15, doubles $18.50; rooms with balconies and space for two to five people cost $23. *Jardín Hidalgo 22, on Plaza de Armas, tel. 48/12–46–31. 27 rooms, 25 with bath.*

➤ UNDER $25 • **Hotel Anáhuac.** The sunny rooms here are immaculate, and the friendly staff makes up for the traffic, smog, and riff-raff near the Alameda. Singles are $15, doubles $20. *Xochitl 140, tel. 48/12–65–04. From the Alameda go 1 block north on 20 de Noviembre, left on Los Bravo, and right on Xochitl. 45 rooms, all with bath. MC, V.*

HOSTEL **Villa Juvenil San Luis Potosí/CREA.** This state-run hostel packs 'em in to eight to a single-sex room, but at $4 a pop, who can complain? There are baseball and soccer fields and over a dozen basketball courts at your disposal here, but the pool is off-limits. Lack of publicity means that the place is never full; lack of locker keys means you have to check your bags when not in your room. Bring your own towel, soap, and toilet paper. *Diagonal Sur s/n, tel. 48/18–16–17. 1 block from bus station, opposite traffic circle on Diagonal Sur. 72 beds.*

FOOD

San Luis Potosí has a number of regional specialties, including *enchiladas potosinas* (small, fan-shaped enchiladas with cheese and red sauce) and Huastecan pork tamales called *zahacuil*. The ambience at most restaurants is less creative, however—the most popular ones resemble drugstore restaurants or diners, complete with vinyl booths, bright lights, and fake plants. Food stands on the plazas are surprisingly few and far between, but there are several holes-in-the-wall along Carranza and Othón that offer cheap, standard Mexican fare. **Panificadora La Noria** (Carranza 333, tel. 48/12-56-92), offering pastries and fresh breads as early as 6:30 AM, is a good place to start the day.

➤ UNDER $5 • **Café El Pacífico.** This 24-hour café is fairly sterile and mediocre, but cheap and convenient. Enchiladas, *chilaquiles* (tortilla strips doused with salsa and sour cream), and tacos are available for less than $5. Breakfasts including juice, an entrée, and coffee run $4–$5. There's also a phone where you can make free local calls. *Constitución 200, 4 blocks east of Plaza de Armas, tel. 48/12-54-14.*

Tropicana. This semivegetarian restaurant with counter seating is a hidden treasure. Huge fresh fruit drinks ($1–$3) with goofy names like "Tú y Yo" and "Sensual" are made with everything from strawberries and papaya to alfalfa and egg. Quesadillas with avocado are $1.50. Yogurt with honey and granola is $1, as is ginseng tea with honey. *Othón 355-B, tel. 48/12-81-69. NE cnr of Plaza del Carmen. Open Mon.–Sat. 9 AM–10 PM, Sun. 3:30 PM–9:30 PM.*

➤ UNDER $10 • **El Bocolito.** This place benefits a cooperative for indigenous students, and its humble decor gives it a down-home feel. A few tables overlook the Plaza de San Francisco. Unique specialties include *sarape* (sautéed onions, peppers, ham, sausage, and cheese) for $7, and *bocolitos* (thick, tortilla-style bread with cheese, cilantro, and refried beans) for $3. Try the fantastic *café de olla* (coffee flavored with chocolate and cinnamon) for $1. *Guerrero 2, at Aldama, tel. 48/12-76-94. Open Mon.–Sat. 8:30 AM–10:30 PM, Sun. noon–10:30.*

La Corriente. This restaurant pleases with stone- and tile-decorated walls and lots of greenery. Northern Mexican specialties, such as *chamorro pibil* (pork in sweet mole sauce wrapped in banana leaf; $8.50) are served for dinner. A mixed plate of eight typical dishes is $7.50. Breakfast is served from 8 to 11:30 AM, *comida corrida* (pre-prepared lunch special) and the buffet from 1 to 7, and *antojitos* (appetizers) and cocktails after 7 PM. *Carranza 700, 6½ blocks west of Plaza de Armas, tel. 48/12-93-04. Open Mon.–Sat. 8 AM–midnight, Sun. 8 AM–6 PM.*

Restaurante del Portal. The decor here is basic, but locals recommend this restaurant for great *mole poblano* (the original chile and chocolate sauce) and chilaquiles, both for about $4. If you're feeling brave, try the *fiembre potosinas* (pig's feet and tongue in a vinaigrette) for about $5. *Los Bravo 155, tel. 48/12-86-63. In pedestrian mall just off Plaza de Armas. Open daily 7 AM–10 PM.*

WORTH SEEING

All of the sights below are within easy walking distance of the Plaza de Armas. Probably the best day for sight-seeing is Sunday—museums and churches are open, and the numerous plazas often have free theater and puppet shows, as well as early evening concerts. Vendors offer food, drinks, and regional handicrafts, and the streets are filled with families and couples out for their Sunday stroll. For a schedule of most free events, pick up the monthly publication *Guiarte* from the tourist office (*see* Basics, *above*). Upcoming symphonies and theatrical and literary events are also announced on the billboard outside the **Casa de Artesanías** (tel. 48/12-75-21) on the Plaza de San Francisco. The Casa de Artesanías itself is a government-run crafts shop with a decent selection of goods from all over Mexico, but no bargain prices.

CHURCHES San Luis Potosí is divided into seven neighborhoods. Each barrio has its own church, which is the center of social activities. Among the most notable is the **Catedral** in the Plaza de Armas. Built in 1670, the cathedral's baroque facade features Italian marble statues of the 12 Apostles. The interior has been remodeled with neoclassical altars, but some baroque paintings remain. The 1950s neon blue cross atop the cathedral is a hip new addition. The **Templo de San Francisco,** in the plaza of the same name, is another major church and has a pink limestone baroque facade. It was built in 1686 to honor the saint who, according to one story, traveled the world evangelizing until his soul became as clear as the glass of water presented to him by one of God's messengers. When his task was completed, he received the stigmata (bleeding holes in his hands and feet like those of the crucified Christ); several paintings and stone carvings depict the story. The theme of travel, representing Francisco's evengelical journeying, also comes up in strange ways, such as a chandelier in the shape of a boat and a toy truck in the hands of the statue of Sebastián de Aparicio.

Construction began in 1749 on the **Templo del Carmen,** found on the plaza of the same name. The temple represents a mixture of styles, with a churrigueresque facade and neoclassical columns and structures in back. The interior contains an astounding amount of gold leaf, most notably on the gold-covered altar of the Virgin's Chapel. Mass times are posted in church entryways.

CENTRO DE DIFUSION CULTURAL This free museum displays the work of local artists on three floors of rotating exhibitions. The center also has a theater for live performances—ask at the tourist office (*see* Basics, *above*) for a schedule. Tickets go on sale in the center's office the day of the show. *Universidad, at Negrete, on south side of the Alameda, tel. 48/12–43–33. Open Tues.–Sat. 10–2 and 5–8, Sun. 10–2 and 6–8.*

MUSEO NACIONAL DE LA MASCARA This museum holds a collection of more than 1,000 ceremonial and decorative masks from all over Mexico. The written explanations in Spanish give an extensive history and significance of the mask in Mesoamerica, as well as descriptions of the festivals in which they are used. Not to be missed are the eerie exhibit of devil masks and the impressive *gigantes* (giants) of San Luis—eight huge puppets (about 10 feet high) used in the festival of Corpus Christi to represent royal couples from the four parts of the world known to Columbus—Asia, Africa, America, and Europe. *Villerías 2, tel. 48/ 12–30–25. 2 blocks east of Plaza de Armas on Othón, then right 2 blocks on Escobedo. Admission free. Open Tues.–Fri. 10–2 and 4–6, weekends 10–2.*

> "Everything profound loves a disguise, every deep spirit needs a mask."—Nietzsche, as quoted in Museo Nacional de la Máscara.

MUSEO NACIONAL POTOSINO This museum, housed in a former Franciscan Monastery, has one of the largest collections of artifacts from San Luis Potosí's Huasteca region, including a reproduction of a famous statue called the *adolescente huasteco,* said to represent the young Quetzalcoatl. The lower floor also has a small mineral exhibit and an interesting series of early 20th-century photographs of the streets of San Luis, contrasted with current photographs of the same areas. Upstairs is the restored chamber of the Virgin from the monastery, as well as a few 19th-century religious paintings. *Galeana, behind Templo de San Francisco. Admission free. Open Tues.–Sat. 10–4:30, Sun. 10–2.*

CHEAP THRILLS

The **Parque Tangamanga,** a few kilometers southwest of the Plaza de Armas, is the place to escape the smog and traffic of San Luis Potosí. The park is an expanse of lakes, trees, and gardens, with sports fields, museums, a planetarium, and the huge, open-air **Teatro de la Ciudad.** The free **Museo de Arte Popular** displays handicrafts produced in the region as well as a selection of pre-Columbian artifacts. The many cultural events held in the park and the theater are publicized in *Guiarte,* available at the tourist office (*see* Basics, *above*). Catch the PERIMETRAL or RUTA 32 bus from Constitución near the Alameda to get here. To get back into town, you'll have to walk four long blocks up to Diagonal Sur to catch the bus heading back to the Alameda.

For more cultural events and art exhibits, as well as free films in styles ranging from documentary to avant-garde, visit the **Casa de la Cultura** (Carranza 1815, tel. 48/13–22–47), several kilometers west of the Plaza de Armas. The taxi ride costs about $3. Call ahead to find out what's happening, or check the listings in *Guiarte.*

FESTIVALS San Luis Potosí is one of the oldest cities in northeastern Mexico, with a rich tradition of religious festivals and fairs. Mid-January brings pilgrims to the shrine of **San Sebastián** in the barrio of the same name. May brings the 10-day **Festival de las Artes,** with music, theater, and dance, much of it free to the public. In July, contemporary dance troupes come to town for the **Festival de la Danza.** On August 25th, the city celebrates its patron saint, **San Luis Rey,** with a parade and fiesta. The second half of August is also the time of the **Feria Nacional Potosina** (National Fair).

AFTER DARK

San Luis Potosí is dead Sunday through Wednesday, and explosive Thursday through Saturday. One of the more popular bars in town is the weirdly named **Puff!** (Carranza 1145, tel. 451/13–65–53), with Lionel Ritchie tunes at the bar in the early evening and no cover for the discotheque that opens at 11 PM. A whole passel of clubs, most of which rock until about 3 AM, lines Carranza; **Museum** (Carranza 763, tel. 48/12–32–00) caters to a student crowd with disco, house, and tropical music and a $5 cover. **Staff** (Carranza 423, tel. 48/14–70–34) attracts an older crowd with rock and cumbia and also has a $5 cover. **Oasis,** in the Hotel María Dolores (Carretera a México Km. 417, tel. 48/22-18-82), where the cover is about $8.50, is one of the most popular out-of-the-way clubs.

Mariachis practice in the evenings on the Jardín Escontría on Los Bravo, turning the otherwise unattractive plaza into a romantic spot for an early evening stroll.

The gay scene here is also decent, by Mexican standards. Meeting areas include the arches at the Plaza de Armas in the early evening, and in the plaza itself later on. **Cherry's Grill** (Universidad, btw 5 de Mayo and Zaragoza) is a popular, if somewhat divey, gay bar. **Chey's,** best reached by taxi, is a gay disco on Julián de los Reyes.

Near San Luis Potosí

SANTA MARIA DEL RIO This small, unassuming town is famous for its handcrafted cotton and silk *rebozos* (shawls), weaved with techniques that originated in Asia, were passed on to Spain with the Moorish invasion, and then brought to Mexico. You can see how the patterned shawls are woven today in the **Escuela del Rebozo** (tel. 485/3–00–62). To get here, take the Autobuses Potosinos line from San Luis Potosí. Buses leave every half an hour between 6 AM and 11:45 PM ($1.50, 1 hr).

REAL DE CATORCE This town, about 3 hours north of San Luis Potosí, is situated in the *altiplano* (highland) region of the state. Established in 1778 as a mining town, it was at its height through much of the 19th century. By 1910, due to political instability and the low price of silver, the population had dropped from 144,000 to 2,700. Today, less than a thousand people live here, making exploration of the abandoned mines and late baroque architecture a somewhat lonely experience, although the town's popularity with tourists has caused some souvenir shops to sprout up. Huichol Indians from Nayarit and Jalisco visit Real de Catorce every autumn to harvest the peyote in the nearby hills for use in religious rites. Trains go from San Luis Potosí to Real de Catorce ($5), as do **Estrella Blanca** buses. Estrella Blanca offers hourly service to Matehuala ($7, 2½ hrs), where minibuses wait to take travelers into Real de Catorce, as well as one direct bus per day. The latter leaves at 3:30 PM and costs $9.

RIO VERDE Be careful not to blink when you pass Río Verde or you might miss it. It is little, untouristed, and historically undistinguished. Nonetheless, it does offer a small-town experience without making you sacrifice basic traveler's luxuries like hotels, banks, restaurants, and clubs. It also offers ample opportunities for incredible day trips to local lakes, caves, and waterfalls. In the hidden caves—Gruta del Ángel and Gruta de la Catedral—spelunkers will find stalactites and stalagmites in the forms of angels and an altar. The **Laguna de la Media Luna,** a moon-shaped freshwater lake, is fun for snorkeling, with lots of fish, aquatic plants, and fossilized trees under the water. The neighboring town of **Ciudad Valles** offers access to the waterfalls and swimming holes of Tamasopo, El Trampolín, and Puente de Dios. **Omnibuses del Oriente** (tel. 48/18–29–421) serves Río Verde hourly from San Luis Potosí. The 2½-hour trip costs $4.50.

➤ WHERE TO SLEEP AND EAT • You can camp at Media Luna—they charge $3.50 for a tent with two people and $6.50 per vehicle—and at other swimming areas such as **El Charco Azul** (no charge, but no security either) and **Los Anteojitos,** which has the same rates as Media Luna. For more information on camping or other activities in the Río Verde area, contact the **Cámara Nacional de Comercio, Servicios y Turismo de Río Verde.** *Jardín de San Antonio "F," tel. 487/2-08-02. Open weekdays 9:30 AM–2 PM and 4:30 PM–7 PM, Sat. 9:30 AM–noon.*

The Hotel Morelos (Morelos 216, no phone) is cheap, clean, close to the plaza, and the best deal in Río Verde, with singles and doubles at $7. To get here from the bus station, go left on the Carretera San Luis–Río Verde, and then right on Morelos. More upscale lodging can be found at the **Hotel Plaza** (tel. 487/2–01–00) on the Plaza Principal, where singles are $24 and doubles are $27.

Restaurant Rivera (tel. 487/2-01-03), also on the Plaza Principal, is always crowded and serves typical Mexican dishes for under $4 round the clock. The restaurant **La Cabaña** (Carretera San Luis, tel. 487/2–06–25), also open 24 hours a day, adjoins a *discoteca,* making it *the* place to see and be seen.

Guanajuato **If you visit only one city in the Bajío,** make sure it's Guanajuato. Situated in a high valley, Guanajuato is defined by its beautiful architecture. The city's current aspect is the product of silver-driven prosperity in the colonial era, but the region had long been settled by indigenous people at the time of the Conquest. Today, throngs of university students, as well as internationally recognized musicians, artists, and dancers lend the place a playful vitality. The city's winding streets and subterranean roadways are so confusing you could easily lose yourself here, but you probably won't be in any hurry to leave, anyway.

It was in the nearby town of Dolores Hidalgo that Padre Miguel Hidalgo, facing arrest for conspiring against Spanish rule, issued his famous call for Mexican independence, the "Grito de Dolores." Guanajuato itself was the scene of the first major military confrontation between rebel forces and royalist troops on September 28, 1810, and monuments to the city's heroes are everywhere.

In addition to the city's historical importance, Guanajuato is distinguished by a number of unusual points of interest, including the **Museo de las Momias,** a bizarre museum exhibiting well-preserved human corpses, and the home in which artist **Diego Rivera** was born. If you're in town in mid-October, don't miss the **Festival Internacional Cervantino,** when artists, musicians, and dance troupes from around the world come to honor *Don Quixote* author Miguel de Cervantes. The city is overrun during the festival, so make hotel reservations well in advance if you plan to attend.

BASICS

AUTO PARTS/SERVICE **Refacciones Sánchez** has parts for most cars and can recommend a mechanic. *Paseo de la Presa 28-E, tel. 473/2-00-28. Open weekdays 9:30–3 and 4:30–8, Sat. 9–4.*

BOOKSTORES Though there are no English-language bookstores in Guanajuato, the chain store **Librería de Cristal** has a great selection of literature, textbooks, and music in Spanish. *Plaza Agora del Baratillo 4, tel. 473/2-24-48. NW side of Jardín de la Unión. Open Mon.–Sat. 10–9, Sun. noon–8.*

Guanajuato

Sights ●

Basílica, **13**
Callejón del Beso, **8**
Jardín de la Unión, **14**
Mercado Hidalgo, **6**
Monumento al Pípila, **16**
Museo de la Alhóndiga de Granaditas, **3**
Museo de las Momias, **1**
Museo del Pueblo, **10**
Museo Iconográfico del Quijote, **17**
Museo y Casa de Diego Rivera, **7**
Teatro Juárez, **15**
Universidad de Guanajuato, **11**

Lodging ○

Casa Kloster, **12**
Posada de la Condesa, **9**
Posada del Carmen, **5**
Posada El Comercio, **2**
Posada Juárez, **4**

GRITERIA

TO BUS STATION

Jardín del Cantador

Jardín de la Reforma

Plaza San Fernando

Plaza San Roque

Plaza de los Ángeles

Plaza de la Paz

Teatro Principal

San Antonio

Underground Tunnels

Tepetapa
Insurgencia
Insurgencia El Apartado
Insurgencia
Llanitos
La Alhóndiga de Salgado
Reforma
Cine
5 de Mayo
28 de Septiembre
Terremoto
Chililo
Grasero
Santo Niño
Av. Juárez
Juan Valle
Pocitos
Lascuráin de Retana
Ponciano Aguilar
Callejón Truco
Allende
Cantarranas
Alonso
San Miguel
San Antonio
Callejón Calvario
Sopeña
Campanero
Manuel Doblado

0   250 yards
0   250 meters

150

CASAS DE CAMBIO Banamex (Plaza de los Ángeles, tel. 473/2–08–00) changes traveler's checks and cash from 9 to noon weekdays and has an ATM that digests Cirrus/Plus cards, Visas, and Mastercards and spits out cash.

EMERGENCIES In Guanajuato you can access a tourist-specific toll-free number for medical and legal help: 91/800–9–03–92. The phone number of the **police** station is 473/2–02–66; the **Cruz Roja** (ambulance service) is 473/2–04–87.

LAUNDRY **Lavandería del Centro** will wash, dry, and fold your duds for $6 a load (about 4 kilos). *Sopeña 26, tel. 473/2–04–36. West on Juárez from Jardín de la Unión, near Museo Iconográfico del Quijote. Open Mon.–Sat. 9–8.*

MAIL The city's post office is near the University of Guanajuato. They will hold mail sent to you at the following address for up to 10 days: Lista de Correos, Guanajuato, Guanajuato, CP 36000, México. *Ayuntamiento 25, tel. 473/2–03–85. Open weekdays 8–8, Sat. 9–1.*

MEDICAL AID The **Hospital Regional de Guanajuato** (Carretera Guanajuato Cilao, tel. 473/2–08–59) has 24-hour medical service and English-speaking doctors. **Farmacia Santa Fe** (Plaza de la Paz 52, tel. 473/2–01–70) offers discounts on prescriptions.

PHONES Ladatel phones can be found near the Casa Kloster on Alonso (*see* Where to Sleep, *below*) and on the northeast side of the Jardín de la Unión. International collect calls at caseta **Selene Miscelanea** cost $2. *Juárez 110. Open Mon.–Sat. 10 AM–11 PM.*

SCHOOLS The University of Guanajuato has an exchange program with several American universities, but you don't have to be affiliated with any of them to take Spanish language and literature classes at their **Centro de Idiomas.** Programs are in semester units and run from July to December and January to June. Six-week summer sessions are also available. Courses cost about $250. Homestays with local families can be arranged. *Lascurain de Retana 5, tel. 473/2–72–53. For registration information, write to Lic. Patricia Begne, Directora del Centro de Idiomas, Universidad de Guanajuato, Lascurain de Retana 5, Guanajuato, Guanajuato, CP 36000, México.*

VISITOR INFORMATION The staff at the tourist information office is happy to answer all sorts of questions. *Plaza de la Paz 14, near Basílica, tel. 473/2–00–86. Open weekdays 8:30–8:30, weekends 10–2.*

You can also buy an excellent, newspaper-sized map from the **Papelería El Estudiante** across the street from the post office. *Plazuela de la Compañia 2. From Plaza de la Paz, turn right on Ponciano Aguilar and continue to end of street.*

COMING AND GOING

BY BUS The **Central de Autobuses** (Carretera Guanajuato Cilao, Km. 8, tel. 473/2–71–45) is served by four main lines: **Omnibus de México** (tel. 473/3–13–56), **Flecha Amarilla** (tel. 473/3–13–33), **Estrella Blanca** (tel. 473/2–75–63), and **Primera Plus** (tel. 473/3–13–33). Buses to Mexico City ($16, 4½ hrs) leave seven times daily between 5:30 AM and midnight. Buses also leave frequently for León ($3, 1 hr), San Miguel de Allende ($4, 1½ hrs), Dolores Hidalgo ($2.50, 1½ hrs), and San Luis Potosí ($8, 5 hrs). Luggage storage is available daily 7 AM–9:30 PM.

The station is more than 6 kilometers west of the city, so take a city bus marked CENTRO on Avenida Juárez or a taxi (about $3) to the center of town. If you're headed into town and looking for an inexpensive hotel, get off at the busy Jardín Reforma bus stop near the Cine Reforma.

GETTING AROUND

Whoever planned, or rather didn't plan this city was playing a mischievous joke on the uptight proponents of the simple grid system. You're gonna get lost. For those who need order, the most important street to remember is **Avenida Juárez,** the main thoroughfare. As you head east, Juárez turns into **Sopeña** near the main plaza, the **Jardín de la Unión.** Most directions to Guanajuato's sites use the Jardín as a reference point. City buses stop running at 9:30 PM.

WHERE TO SLEEP

Most budget hotels lie along Avenida Juárez between the train station and the Cine Reforma. Conveniently, this area is also near many of the city's attractions and much of the action. As you continue east along Juárez toward the Jardín de la Unión, accommodations become more attractive and more expensive. The **Casa Kloster,** undoubtedly the best backpacker hangout in town, is among the few cheap hotels in this area. During the mid-October **Festival Cervantino** (Cervantes Festival), when hotels are packed, the tourist office (*see* Basics, *above*) provides information on families who will put up travelers for low prices.

➤ UNDER $15 • **Posada de la Condesa.** This posada is much cheaper than most of its neighbors in the Plaza de la Paz area. Rooms are cramped but clean, and all have private baths with round-the-clock hot water. Singles are $10, doubles $13. *Plaza de la Paz 60, tel. 473/2–14–62. From Jardín de la Unión, west on Juárez. 22 rooms, all with bath.*

Posada El Comercio. For now, the rooms here are mildew-scented and depressing, but there has been talk of remodeling. At any rate, the management is always willing to haggle over prices, which are rock bottom to start with at $5 for a single without bath ($10 with bath), or $13 for a double with bath. The 24-hour hot water is a plus. *Juárez 210, near Cine Reforma, no phone. 16 rooms, 10 with bath.*

➤ UNDER $20 • **Casa Kloster.** If you can live with a few house rules, this wholesome hotel is wonderful. Run by the hospitable Pérez family, it has clean rooms, spotless communal bathrooms, and an interior courtyard filled with plants and chirping birds. Couples must be married (time to break out that ring you bought from the street vendor), and you must be quiet at night. Nevertheless, this place is always full of backpack-toting gringos, so be sure to call ahead. Rooms are $10 per person. *Alonso 32, tel. 473/2–00–88. 18 rooms, none with bath.*

Posada del Carmen. Run by a friendly, professional staff, this clean and cheerful place even has a restaurant. Prices go up during the Cervantes festival; off-season prices are $15 for a single and $19 for a double. *Juárez 111-A, tel. 473/2-93-30. 17 rooms, all with bath. Laundry, wheelchair access.*

Posada Juárez. This is the best of the budget hotels near the Cine Reforma. The management is slightly distracted by all the activity on the street, but rooms are clean and smell good, and some even have TVs. Ask for a sunny room on the second floor. Singles are $13, doubles $16. Prices rise $5–$10 during the Cervantes festival. *Juárez 117, tel. 473/2–25–29. 43 rooms, all with bath.*

FOOD

Restaurants are clustered on Avenida Juárez and the surrounding streets. The **Mercado Hidalgo,** on Juárez between Cine Reforma and the Jardín Reforma, also has a number of cheap food stands. For a strange sweet treat, try *momias* (mummies), a hard, sugarcane candy that is shaped into little mummies and sold both at the **Museo de las Momias** (*see below*) and at stores around town. Close to the Jardín de la Unión is the **Pastelería la Paz** (Plaza de la Paz 53, tel. 473/2–18–69), selling scrumptious baked treats as early as 6:30 AM.

➤ UNDER $5 • **La Pasadita Lonchería.** This post-party hot spot doesn't even open until 7 PM. You can satiate your late-night cravings with typical Mexican dishes for a few dollars here while you get the scoop on the evening's action. *Cantarranas 70. From the north end of Jardín de la Unión, right on Allende and right on Cantarranas. Open until dawn.*

El Pingüis. Tucked in the northeast corner of the Jardín de la Unión, this extraordinarily cheap eatery is always full. A breakfast of *huevos a la mexicana* (eggs scrambled with peppers, tomato, and onion), served with beans, bread, and a cup of coffee is $2. Lunch items include enchiladas ($3.50), steak ($4), and sandwiches ($2–$3). The name of the restaurant isn't posted—look for the brown-and-white awnings marked RESTAURANT and CAFETERIA. *Jardín de la Unión, tel. 473/2–14–14. Open daily 8:30 AM–10 PM.*

Restaurant Vegetariano. The name is uninspired, but the food isn't—try the spinach soup ($1) or mushroom tostadas ($2) for a light, healthful lunch. The menú del día includes salad, vegetable, rice, soup, and an entrée for $3. Breakfast is also available. A huge pot of herbal tea is included with every meal. *Callejón de Calixto 22, tel. 473/2–20–62. Upstairs from Plaza de los Ángeles. Open daily 8–6.*

For an evening snack, head for the stand at the southwest corner of the Jardín de la Unión. The proprietor, Daniel, whips up a delicious cup of boiled corn with cream, cheese, and chili powder for $1.

➤ UNDER $15 • **Restaurant El Agora del Baratillo.** This restaurant near the Jardín de la Unión offers patio dining complete with checkered tablecloths and wrought-iron tables. This is probably the only place in Mexico where the comida corrida ($10) is more expensive than any entrée on the menu, but that's because it comes with a glass of wine. Breakfast chilaquiles, a mass of tortillas and eggs with spicy salsa, come with fruit, yogurt, and coffee for about $3.50. For lunch, try the *queso fundido* (cheese fondue) with mushrooms or sausage for $5. *Jardín de la Unión 4, tel. 473/2–33–00. Just past Hotel Posada San José. Open daily 8 AM–9 PM. Kitchen closes at 5:30 PM.*

Tasca de los Santos. This candlelit restaurant near the basilica has tasty Spanish food and attentive waiters. Recommended are the *pollo al vino blanco* (chicken in white wine; $9) and the *tapas* (Spanish appetizers; $4). *Plaza de la Paz 28, off Juárez, tel. 473/2–23–20.*

WORTH SEEING

Getting lost in Guanajuato, where a maze of twisting *callejones* (alleyways) that lead to unknown destinations, is, strangely enough, one of the more enjoyable things to do in the city. As for other attractions, Guanajuato is rich in excellent architecture and museums, most of which are near the center of town and easy to see in a day or two on foot. All musems are closed on Mondays and have limited hours on Sundays.

BASILICA The baroque facade of the **Basílica Colegiata de Nuestra Señora de Guanajuato** is painted a buttery yellow and framed in a brownish-orange, resembling nothing so much as one of the pastries sold at the nearby Pastelería de la Paz (*see* Food, *above*). The basilica, constructed in 1693, houses a bejeweled wooden statue of the Virgin said to be the oldest existing Christian statue in Mexico and is illuminated by sparkling crystal chandeliers. *Plaza de la Paz, near Juárez.*

JARDIN DE LA UNION In keeping with the rest of the illogical layout of the city, Guanajuato's main square is actually a triangle and therefore also known as the "slice of cheese." Surrounded by spectacular buildings and numerous cafés, the plaza is one of the best places in Guanajuato to relax over a cup of coffee or a beer. Evenings here are hopping with locals, students, and tourists. On Thursday and Sunday evenings, musical groups play in the bandstand.

MONUMENTO AL PIPILA High above the city, on San Miguel hill, a huge statue was erected to honor the miner El Pípila, who is said to have set fire to the door of the Alhóndiga de Granaditas (*see below*), where supporters of Spanish rule were making their stand during the battle with rebel forces in 1810. Although the steep, 10-minute climb up the steps will leave you winded, the view from the monument is stupendous. For about 30¢ you can go inside the monument and climb to the top of it. The preferred activity, however, seems to be hanging around outside, looking for love (or whatever). *From Jardín de la Unión, up Sopeña about 1½ blocks, right on Callejón del Calvario, then look for the SUBITA AL PIPILA sign. Monument open daily 9–8.*

MUSEO DE LA ALHONDIGA DE GRANADITAS Grain was stored in this massive stone building in the 18th century. During the first major battle of the war for independence, the local Spanish population congregated here, hoping to hold out until the Royalist forces arrived.

This strategy backfired when the granary's door was set ablaze, allowing the rebel fighters to swarm in and massacre almost all of them. Local tradition has it that an Indian miner known as El Pípila (*see above*) was the one to set the fire. Later in the war, several rebel leaders, including Allende and Hidalgo, were captured and decapitated; their heads were then prominently displayed on large hooks that are still visible on the exterior of the building. Later, under Emperor Maximilian, the building became a jail. Today it's a museum that houses several excellent exhibits on Guanajuato's history. The work of contemporary artists is displayed on the lower level, and huge, colorful murals by José Chavéz Morado, a disciple of Diego Rivera, grace the stairwells. The collection of pre-Columbian clay stamps and seals is also interesting and may give you some ideas for that tattoo you've been thinking of getting. *28 de Septiembre 7, tel. 473/2–11–12. Admission: $4.50, free for students and on Sun. Open Tues.–Sat. 10–2 and 4–6, Sun. 10–2:30. Free guided tours in Spanish Tues.–Fri.*

MUSEO DE LAS MOMIAS About a century ago, greedy bureaucrats decided to dig up the city's graveyards, leaving only those whose descendants paid burial-plot fees; it seems that death is not the great equalizer it's cracked up to be. As it turned out, special properties of Guanajuato's soil lend it a certain preservative effect, and the recovered bodies remained in excellent condition, with remnants of hair and skin (feeling queasy yet?). The cadavers were judged fit for display in a local museum, which now has 108 mummified bodies in various states of undress. If you speak Spanish, be sure to take the guided tour to find out which mummy died from an attempted C-section, which one was hung, and which one was buried alive. *Esplanada del Pantéon, tel. 473/2–06–39. Take MOMIAS bus to end of line. Admission: $2, $1 with student ID, small donation for tour. Open Tues.–Sun. 9–6.*

Like food from street vendors, a visit to the mummy museum is a pleasure for strong stomachs.

El Callejón del Beso

For a few coins, the young men lingering around the "Alley of the Kiss" will tell you the legend associated with this spot. If you don't understand Spanish, just nod your head. You're probably hearing a version of the following: A young woman named Doña Carmen, the only child of a violent father, fell in love with a man named Don Luis. When her father found out about the courtship, he threatened to marry her off to a rich, old Spaniard. Not knowing what to do, Doña Carmen sought the help of her friend Doña Brigida, who, together with Don Luis, devised a plan. The alleyway that separated Doña Carmen's house from the one across the way was so narrow that the houses almost touched, so Don Luis arranged to buy the neighboring house for a steep price. You can only imagine Doña Carmen's surprise when she went out on her balcony one starry night and encountered her lover so near. Just then, they heard the enraged voice of Doña Carmen's father, who proceeded to plunge a dagger into his daughter's heart. Don Luis was only able to lean over and leave a kiss on her lifeless hand. Then, distraught with grief, he took his own life.

Current tradition holds that if you kiss your loved one on the third step up to the balcony on which he died, you'll enjoy seven years of good luck. Lone females need not fear, however—one of the men standing by will undoubtedly offer to stand in as a romantic interest. From the Jardín de la Unión, walk west on Juárez to Plaza de los Ángeles, go up Callejón del Patrocinio, and take Callejón del Beso to the left.

MUSEO ICONOGRAFICO DEL QUIJOTE This shrine to Cervantes features hundreds of depictions of scenes from *Don Quixote* by a number of artists, including Picasso and Dalí. *Manuel Doblado 1, tel. 473/2–67–21. 1½ blocks up Sopeña from Jardín de la Unión. Admission free. Open Tues.–Sat. 10–6:30, Sun. 10–3.*

MUSEO Y CASA DE DIEGO RIVERA Artist Diego Rivera was born and lived the first six years of his life in this brick red house. Now beautifully restored, the house displays some of the original furnishings, including the bed in which Rivera and his twin brother, who died in infancy, were born. The upper floors are devoted to the artist's work, arranged chronologically from his early works through his evolution as a muralist. *Calle de los Pocitos 47, near Plaza de la Paz, tel. 473/2–11–97. Admission: $2. Open Tues.–Sat. 10–1:30 and 4–6:30, Sun. 10–2:30. Free tours in Spanish Tues.–Fri.*

TEATRO JUAREZ The late 19th-century Juárez Theater is one of the most impressive buildings in Guanajuato. The neoclassic exterior features Doric columns, bronze lions, and giant statues of the muses. Inside, opulent decorations and walls hung with red and gold velvet exhibit Moorish and French influences. The theater now serves as the principal venue of the annual mid-October Cervantes Festival, when the city resounds with symphony recitals, plays, and dance performances. Outside the theater, university students gather to gossip and flirt on the steps in the early evening, creating a sort of open-air student union. *Jardín de la Unión, tel. 473/2–01–83. Admission: $1.50, $1 more to take pictures. Open Tues.–Sun. 9–1:45 and 5–7:45.*

UNIVERSIDAD DE GUANAJUATO Founded as a Jesuit seminary in 1732, the school became a state university in 1945. The high walls that rise out of the oldest parts of the building look as if they belong in an old English castle. Students fill the hallways and patios, and notices advertising upcoming events are posted on bulletin boards everywhere. On the right side of the entrance on Lascurain de Retana is a small, free gallery with rotating exhibits of contemporary art. *Lascurain de Retana 5, near Basílica, tel. 473/2–01–74. Closed weekends.*

The university is sandwiched between the **Templo de la Compañía,** the original church from the university's Jesuit days, and the **Museo del Pueblo de Guanajuato.** The museum displays contemporary local art and photography. *Calle de los Pocitos 7, tel. 473/2–29–90. Admission: $1. Open Tues.–Sat. 10–2 and 4–7, Sun. 10–3.*

AFTER DARK

Guanajuato is at its best at night. Crowds fill the streets, laughing, cavorting, pushing, flirting, going somewhere or nowhere. The best public entertainment is on weekend nights at the Jardín de la Unión, where crowds of people, young and old, gather on the steps of the Teatro Juárez to hear the student group Las Estudiantinas strum traditional instruments while dressed in troubador garb. The crowds sing along at the top of their lungs and then follow the Estudiantinas as they make their way through the streets. The busiest time of the year, of course, is during the **Festival Internacional Cervantino**, when cultural events are staged nonstop, and actors, musicians, and dance troupes from all over the world come to Guanajuato to participate.

You can keep abreast of which plays and shows are in town by checking the many bulletin boards found all over the city, as well as at the university and the main theaters, including the **Teatro Juárez** (Sopeña near Jardín de la Unión, tel. 473/2–01–83) or the **Teatro Principal** (Hidalgo, near Allende, tel. 473/2–15–23). The latter has a symphony night every Thursday, when you can hear performances of Bach, Mozart, and other classical greats for a mere $3. Shows start at about 8:30.

BARS AND CLUBS **Café Truco 7.** With big, comfortable wooden tables filled with university students, excellent background music, and good cappuccino, this café is a comfortable spot for intense conversation or romantic letter writing. Though Truco 7 is best at night, you can also grab breakfast or a light lunch here for under $5. *Callejón del Truco 7, tel. 473/2–83–74. Open daily 8 AM–11:30 PM.*

La Dama de las Camelias. Women's dresses and shoes from the first half of the century adorn the walls of La Dama. Be sure to ask the owner about the history of the colonial window in the corner—it's his pride and joy. Drinks are about $2–$3 here, and things generally heat up around 10. *Sopeña 32, east of Jardín de la Unión, no phone. Open Mon.–Sat. 2 PM–dawn.*

Discoteque El Pequeño Juan. Nightlife becomes morninglife here as people rock past 4 AM. The $10 cover includes two drinks at this dress-up, flashing lights, throbbing music kind of club, which always draws a crowd. The best way to get here is by taxi. *Callejón de Guadalupe, at El Pípila, tel. 473/2–23–08.*

Guanajuato Grill. Crowds of scamming students fill this bar, especially on Tuesdays, Thursdays, and Saturdays. The thumping Mexican and American pop music pretty much precludes conversation, but that's hardly the point. Night's end usually sees the crowd singing and dancing on the tables. Beers are about $3. *Alonso 4, tel. 473/2–02–87. From Jardín de la Unión, south on San Antonio, right on Alonso. Open daily 7 PM–3 AM.*

El Rincón del Beso. This dimly lit, intimate bar has a nightly *peña* (musical gathering) with live Latin folk music. Before, during, and after the show, the crowd is enouraged to sing along and even display their own musical and poetic talents. Occasionally, musicians playing for high prices at theaters around town stop in for a spontaneous post-show concert. The owner/emcee José Visoso Septién has himself been known to climb onto the stage and recite his poetry. This is a fun, friendly change of pace from the hormone-driven discos. *Alonso 21-A, tel. 473/2–59–12. Open daily 6:30 PM–2 AM.*

Sí Señor. This bar on the Jardín de la Unión is popular because of its endless two-for-one beer special. The crowd is predominantly Mexican, with a smattering of American students. *Jardín de la Unión, tel. 473/2–51–99. Open daily noon–3 AM.*

Near Guanajuato

DOLORES HIDALGO

Dolores Hidalgo's principal claim to fame is the "Grito de Dolores," the speech given by Padre Miguel Hidalgo in front of the town's main church on September 16, 1810 that set off the armed struggle for Mexico's independence from Spain. However, not much seems to have happened since then.

Points of interest include the **Parroquia de Nuestra Señora de los Dolores** (on the Plaza Principal), Padre Hidalgo's former parish, where the "Grito" was sounded; the **Casa de Don Miguel Hidalgo** (Morelos near Hidalgo), Hidalgo's former house, now a museum; and the **Museo de la Independencia** (Zacatecas 6), which houses a series of impressive paintings depicting the struggle for independence. Admission to the Casa Hidalgo is $4, $1 to the Museo de la Independencia. Both museums are closed Monday. Dolores Hidalgo is also a center for ceramic ware, making it a good place to go bargain-hunting for tiles.

Helados Torres, on Dolores Hidalgo's Plaza Principal, offers corn, avocado, and even chicharrón (pork rind) ice cream for about $1.50 a cone.

Dolores is best visited as a day trip from either San Miguel de Allende or Guanajuato. Flecha Amarilla ($2) buses leave every 20 minutes and take about an hour to Dolores from either city.

LEON

When you think León, think shoes. Think leather goods, such as purses, belts, and jackets, and then start thinking about shoes again. León is the huge, fast-paced, smoggy industrial capital of the state. The most attractive part of the city is the **Zona Peatonal,** where centuries-old buildings and churches are crammed side by side with modern high rises and the omnipresent shoe stores. In this city, rarely frequented by tourists, you may find yourself the object of some incredulous stares, but León is definitely the place to find some fantastic bargains. Buses leave from Guanajuato's Central de Autobuses every 10 minutes or so, and the one-hour trip costs about $3.

THE HEARTLAND   5

By Michele Back

The Heartland is not the place to find picture-perfect beaches, enigmatic ruins, or hordes of camera-toting tourists. Instead, expect cities with cobblestone streets, stately colonial buildings, their fair share of traffic, and a progressive, youthful population. The area encompassing the states of Michoacán, Jalisco, Zacatecas, and Aguascalientes is not easily definable. From the dry hills of Zacatecas to the rich green of Michoacán, the climate is as variable as the characters of each city in this region.

In pre-Columbian Mexico, the Heartland was inhabited by numerous peoples, including the Otomís, Chichimecas, and Purépechas. The Purépechas (Tarascos, in Spanish), who left evidence of advanced metal-working techniques, came to dominate the other groups, forming a vast empire in the 14th century. When the Spanish discovered silver in Zacatecas and in the Bajío, the Heartland was profoundly affected, and every effort was made to supply the mines with labor, often at the expense of Indian lives. Later, independence leader José María Morelos was born here, and his native city was renamed in his honor by the newly formed republic.

The Heartland's historical significance and architectural splendor aren't its only attractions; its cities tend to be exuberant, with many university students, well-known artists, and remnants of indigenous culture. In Pátzcuaro and Uruapan, Purépecha people still speak their own language, and you can get a close look at village life and hike to waterfalls, lakes, and volcanoes. Head north to Zacatecas to admire the works of painter Francisco Goitia and the extensive art collection of Pedro Coronel, as well as to partake of cultural events and reckless mezcal drinking. Finally, Guadalajara, the second largest city in Mexico, gives you a big-city alternative to the capital while retaining an unusual measure of small-town character, not to mention plenty of opportunities to enjoy mariachi music, dancing, and tequila.

Morelia

Morelia's visual appeal is a product of its colonial past. From the gracefully arching walkways to the blocks and blocks of beige stone buildings with plant-filled courtyards, this expanding city manages to retain its dignity despite the crowds, traffic, and multitudes of street vendors hawking jeans and fake flowers on every sidewalk. Although much of Morelia's architecture is from the past, the city lives jubilantly in the present. The capital of Michoacán, Morelia rivals Guanajuato in liveliness, making it one of the most interesting stops in the Heartland. Plaza-side cafés and a progressive arts scene that supports activities such as foreign-film screenings and poetry readings lend it a cultured air. You'll also see relatively few foreign tourists: Although a popular vacation spot for Mexicans, the city remains fairly unknown to the rest of the world.

Every year during Carnaval (February or early March), a group of Morelian musicians and dancers reenact a bullfight, called the toritos de petate, with a fake bull and a man in drag.

Founded in 1541 by the Spanish and given the name Valladolid, the city became the provincial capital in 1580. The city's name was changed to Morelia in 1828, in honor of José María Morelos. Monuments, streets, and the usual hooplah commemorate the city's namesake and make for a good crash-course in early 19th-century Mexican history. Special events include Morelos' birthday on September 30, and the Aniversario de Morelia on May 18, both of which are celebrated with parades and fireworks. The Feria Regional de Morelia, in first two weeks of May, has little directly to do with Morelos, but is a great time to check out a bullfight or any of the many regional dances performed at this time.

BASICS

AMERICAN EXPRESS **Gran Turismo Viajes** is the local AmEx representative in Morelia. They provide all services for cardholders, including holding mail, emergency check cashing, and changing traveler's checks. *Carmelinas 3233, Las Américas, Morelia, Michoacán, CP 58270, México, tel. 43/24–04–84. 1st floor of Bancomer building, across from Gigante shopping center; take RUTA ROJA 1 combi west from downtown. Open Mon.–Sat. 9–2 and 4–6.*

BOOKSTORE **Bazar Ocampo** is a dusty used-book store with a decent collection of English books. Don't despair: somewhere between *The Sensual Woman* and *The Sensual Man* are hidden a few intellectually stimulating paperbacks. Paperbacks run $2–$2.50, or you can exchange yours on two-for-one terms. *Ocampo 242, no phone. From Plaza de Armas, 1 block north on Juárez, left on Ocampo. Open daily 9–8; sometimes closed 2–4 on weekends.*

CASA DE CAMBIO **Banamex** (Madero Ote. 63, tel. 43/12–27–70) changes cash and traveler's checks 9–11:30 weekday mornings and has an ATM that accepts Cirrus and Plus cards. Even bank employees, however, will tell you that better rates are available at the **casa de cambio** around the corner. *Morelos 51, tel. 43/17–01–91. Open Mon.–Sat. 9–3.*

EMERGENCIES If the need arises, call the **police** (Revolución, at 20 de Noviembre, tel. 43/12–22–22) or the Cruz Roja (Ventura Puente 270, tel. 43/14–51–51) for an ambulance.

MAIL Morelia's full-service main post office will hold mail sent to you at the following address for up to 10 days: Lista de Correos, Morelia, Michoacán, CP 58000, México. *Madero Ote. 369, tel. 43/12–05–17. 3 blocks east of Plaza de Armas. Open weekdays 8–7, weekends 9–1.*

MEDICAL AID The **Hospital Civil** (Isidro Huarte, at Fray de Margil, tel. 43/12–22–16), near the Bosque Cuauhtémoc, is open 24 hours a day. **Farmacia Gems** (Blvd. García de León 1711, tel. 43/15–35–76) is far from the center but also is open round the clock.

En Bolsita, Por Favor

Once upon a time, Mexicans were forced to take time out whenever they wanted a soda or mineral water. Instead of paying a hefty deposit on the glass bottle containing the beverage of their choice, most people spent a few minutes inside the corner store, chatting with neighbors and relaxing while they drank. Nowadays, most folks ask for a bolsita (little bag). The drink is poured into a plastic bag, a straw is inserted, and the thirsty person goes on his or her way with the space-age contraption tightly in hand. Few bother to throw their empty bolsitas into a trash can. One look at the littered streets and it's obvious that the bolsitas are more detrimental to the environment, and less sociable, than glass bottles.

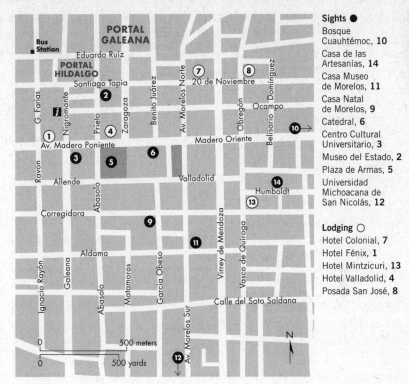

Sights ●
Bosque Cuauhtémoc, **10**
Casa de las Artesanías, **14**
Casa Museo de Morelos, **11**
Casa Natal de Morelos, **9**
Catedral, **6**
Centro Cultural Universitario, **3**
Museo del Estado, **2**
Plaza de Armas, **5**
Universidad Michoacana de San Nicolás, **12**

Lodging ○
Hotel Colonial, **7**
Hotel Fénix, **1**
Hotel Mintzicuri, **13**
Hotel Valladolid, **4**
Posada San José, **8**

PHONES Long-distance phone service is available at the *caseta de larga distancia* (long-distance telephone office) in the bus station (*see* Coming and Going, *below*), but it doesn't allow collect calls. If you need to make a collect call, you'll have to shell out about $2 at the **Computel** office; you pay $6 if your call isn't accepted. *Portal Galeana 157, north side of Plaza de Armas. Open daily 7 AM–9:50 PM.*

SCHOOL You must be affiliated with a U.S. university to take Spanish-language courses at the **Departamento de Idiomas** of the Universidad Michoacana de San Nicolás de Hidalgo, but if you are, make the effort to study here. Options for study includes language, literature, history, and philosophy. The department can arrange for homestays. Semester-long courses in Purépechan, the regional indigenous language, are also offered. For more details, contact Dr. Miguel García Silva at the Departamento de Idiomas, UMSANH, Santiago Tapia 403, Col. Centro, Morelia, Michoacán, CP 58000, México, or call 43/16–71–01.

VISITOR INFORMATION The **Secretaría Estatal del Turismo** is on the south side of the Palacio Clavijero. Here you'll find a friendly English-speaking staff ready to answer questions and give out maps and information about upcoming cultural events. *Nigromante 79, tel. 43/13–26–54. 1½ blocks from Plaza de Armas. Open weekdays 9–2 and 4–8, weekends 9–8.*

COMING AND GOING

BY BUS The busy **Central de Autobuses** (Eduardo Ruíz 526, tel. 43/12–56–64) is four blocks northwest of the Plaza de Armas. **Flecha Amarilla** (tel. 43/12–32–13) takes the prize for most frequent departures and cheapest fares. Their buses go to Guadalajara ($11, 6 hrs), Guanajuato ($6.50, 3½ hrs), Mexico City ($12, 6 hrs), Pátzcuaro ($2, 1 hr), and Uruapan ($5, 2 hrs). For a cushier traveling experience, try **ETN** (tel. 43/13–41–37), which has hourly service to Mexico City ($24, 4½ hrs), as well as frequent departures for Guadalajara ($20, 5 hrs) and a daily 10:30 PM bus to Manzanillo ($33, 8½ hrs). The station also boasts a small post office, a 24-hour long-distance telephone service (no collect calls), several food stands, and a restaurant. Twenty-four-hour luggage storage is available for less than $1 a day. To get to the Plaza de Armas from the station, go left on Ruíz, then two blocks south (right) on Gómez Farías, and finally left on Madero.

BY TRAIN   Morelia's train station is about 2 kilometers west of town. The most comfortable way to get to or from the station is by taxi ($3), but a RUTA AZUL pesero (35¢) is also convenient. Two trains go to Mexico City daily: one at 10:30 AM (2nd class only) and one at 10:55 PM (1st class *regular* and *especial*, as well as 2nd class). The trip takes about 11 hours, and prices are: second class, $6; first class regular, $9.50; and first class especial, $15.50. The train to Uruapan leaves daily at 5:30 AM and 5:30 PM (2nd class only), and the prices are: second class, $2.50; first class regular, $3.50; and first class especial, $6. The trip takes 3½ hours. *Av. del Periodismo, tel. 43/16–39–12. Ticket office open daily 5 AM–6 AM, 10 AM–11 AM, and 10 PM–11 PM.*

GETTING AROUND

Most of the city's points of interest lie within a six-block radius of the Plaza de Armas. The plaza is bordered on the north by the main avenue, Madero, that runs east–west through most of the city, although anything located on the plaza goes by its walkway address, not its street address. The only difficulty is in the change of street names north and south of Madero (and occasionally elsewhere without warning). The newest-looking placard with a street name (out of the three or four on every street corner) usually corresponds to the street name on your map.

Combis (VW buses) have a colored stripe that corresponds to the route they follow. It's easy to master the colors; the hard part is getting one of the combis to slow down for you. Even at designated blue-and-white *parada* (bus stop) signs, you have to wave a hand to let the driver know you're interested. They'll also stop for you on unmarked corners if you wave frantically. Always ask the driver if he's going to your destination, just in case. A ride costs about 35¢.

WHERE TO SLEEP

Hotels here are fairly inexpensive and easy to find; the bus station is surrounded by them. This area is cheap and convenient, but the surrounding streets are constantly busy and it's not the most attractive part of town. The best places to stay are located in the center, on or near the Plaza de Armas. The tourist office has a list of inexpensive hotels, but many of those are *hoteles de paso* (hotels that rent rooms by the hour). You're better off at any of the hotels listed below.

➤ UNDER $10 • **Hotel Fénix.** This hotel is popular with older Mexicans, which at least means it's relatively quiet. Rooms are not exactly loaded with amenities, but they're clean, and the location is a plus. However, the street traffic can be annoying if your room is near the front. The hot water runs all day long. Singles without bath are a steal at $5.50, doubles without bath almost as cheap at $7. One or two people can stay in a room with private bath for about $10. Cheap breakfasts and lunches are served as well. *Madero Pte. 537, tel. 43/ 12–05–12. 3 blocks from Plaza de Armas. 24 rooms, 20 with bath. Wheelchair access.*

➤ UNDER $20 • **Hotel Colonial.** Basic rooms with TVs are made more pleasant by their cleanliness and by the friendly, young staff of this hotel. Ask for a room away from the street; cars and buses go by at all hours. Singles are $13, doubles $16. *20 de Noviembre 15, 43/12–18–97. 2 blocks north of cathedral. 25 rooms, all with bath. Luggage storage. MC, V.*

Posada San José. Huge rooms filled with Brady-era furniture, a light, airy courtyard, and friendly management characterize this hotel. However, the bathroom-less rooms on the bottom smell of mildew. You'll need to ring the bell to get in, as the door is kept locked all day. Negotiable prices are $7 for a single without bath ($10 with bath) and $10 for a double ($13 with bath). *Obregón 226, tel. 43/12–09–79. 5 blocks from Plaza de Armas. 20 rooms, 5 with bath.*

➤ UNDER $25 • **Hotel Mintzicuri.** The main attractions here are the spectacular murals in the lobby and the sauna baths. Rooms are smallish but clean and have telephones, carpeting, and private baths. Singles go for $18, doubles $22. The guy at the desk can be overly friendly with female guests. *Vasco de Quiroga 227, tel. 43/12–05–90. 4 blocks from cathedral. 36 rooms, all with bath. Laundry, luggage storage. Reservations advised.*

Hotel Valladolid. On the Plaza de Armas, the Valladolid is immaculate, and most rooms have stone walls and curtained balconies. One major drawback is the lack of hot water. If steamy showers aren't a priority for you, however, you'll be happy to shell out $20 for a single and $23 for a double here. *Portal Hidalgo 245, tel. 43/12–00–27. 21 rooms, all with bath. Luggage storage.*

HOSTEL **Villa Juvenil.** Unless you're a serious bargain hunter, you might prefer to pay $2-$5 more to stay at a more central hotel. Here, you'll have to sleep four to a single-sex room, be in by 11 PM, and walk about 2 kilometers or catch two combis to most of the attractions in town. On the plus side, the place is clean, the managers are young and hip, and there's a pool out front. The cost is roughly $4 per person. Breakfast is dished up for about $3; lunches and dinners are about $4 each. Sheets and towels are provided, and you get a 10% discount with a hostel card. *Chiapas 180, near Oaxaca, tel. 43/13–31–77. Behind Instituto Michoacano de la Juventud y el Deporte. Take Madero west to Cuautla, turn left, then right on Oaxaca to Chiapas. Or catch RUTA ROJA combi to Cuautla, then RUTA AMARILLA to Oaxaca. 72 beds. Wheelchair access.*

FOOD

Morelia teems with hole-in-the-wall restaurants offering decent fare; most are within several blocks of the Plaza de Armas. The farther away you get from the plaza, though, the cheaper the food—as low as $3 a meal. Stands on Gómez Farías, just outside the bus station, serve up the cheapest eats in town, with *comidas corridas* (pre-prepared lunch specials) for less than $2. Several restaurants serve rich *sopa tarasca* (a tomato-based soup with tortillas, cheeses, cream, and dried peppers), as well as other regional specialties. Sweet-toothed travelers should try *ate*, a Morelian candy made of guava, fig, or pear paste, or *cocada* (coconut candy).

➤ UNDER $5 • **Hindú Vegetariano Govinda.** Judging by the crowd here (or lack thereof) Morelians prefer meat, but that means you can eat your vegetarian meal in peace. Breakfasts of fruit shakes, yogurt, tea, or coffee are $3. The *menú del día* (daily special) is a fairly uninspired repetition of breakfast, with fruit, yogurt, a soyburger or quesadilla, and dessert for $4. *Morelos Sur 39, tel. 43/13–38–86. 1 block east of Plaza de Armas in old Hotel Oseguera building. Open Mon.–Sat. 9:30–noon and 1:30–5:30.*

Restaurant Las Palmas. This place has a warm atmosphere, and the typical Mexican fare doesn't disappoint either. The excellent spicy egg *chilaquiles* (tortilla strips doused with salsa and sour cream), accompanied by juice, coffee, and refried beans make a filling breakfast for $3.50. The afternoon comidas corridas are $3.50–$5.50, depending on the entrée (pork and fish plates are cheaper). *Melchor Ocampo 215, no phone. 1 block north of Plaza de Armas. Open daily 9 AM–9:30 PM.*

➤ UNDER $10 • **Los Comensales.** Tables are arranged around an open-air, interior courtyard filled with plants, flowers, and cages of chirping birds. Two tasty specialties are the *pollo con mole* (chicken in chile and chocolate sauce) for $6, and *paella* (saffron-flavored rice with seafood, sausage, and chicken) for $8.50. The $8 comida corrida includes fruit, soup, pasta or rice, an entrée, coffee or tea, and dessert. *Zaragoza 148, tel. 43/12–93–61. 2 blocks north of Plaza de Armas. Open daily 8 AM–10 PM.*

El Rey Tacamba. This small, pleasant restaurant across the street from the cathedral serves only specialties of Michoacán. The *pollo moreliano* (roasted chicken with red chile and cheese) is served with three enchiladas and costs $8. Enchiladas are $3.50 à la carte. *Portal Galeana 157, tel. 43/12–20–44. Open daily 8:30 AM–11:45 PM. Wheelchair access.*

CAFES **Café Catedral.** This is the place where families and hipsters converge and converse. Coffee here is $1; a variety of teas ($1), from hibiscus to chamomile, are also served. *Portal Hidalgo, next to Hotel Casino. Open daily 9 AM–10 PM.*

Café del Olmo. This café has brick arches and plays soft music in the background, making it a pleasant place for cappuccino ($1) and conversation. The young, amiable staff also serves up a variety of snacks, from cakes and pies ($1.50) to french fries or tacos ($1). *Juárez 95, north of plaza. Open daily 9 AM–9:30 PM.*

Café del Teatro. On the second floor of the Teatro Ocampo, this café is the best and most popular spot in town for a cup of coffee. Wood-beamed ceilings and red velvet curtains make you feel like you forgot your opera glasses. Grab a seat near the balcony overlooking the street and sip a cappuccino ($2) accompanied by a dessert. *Ocampo, at Prieto, no phone. Open weekdays 8–3 and 5–10, Sat. 10–3 and 5–10, Sun. 5–10.*

WORTH SEEING

Just west of the Plaza de Armas is the **Cathedral,** Morelia's main church. This 17th-century architectural marvel took more than 100 years to build and has the tallest bell towers of any church in Mexico—about 61 meters high. The baroque exterior, however, gives way to a somewhat disappointing neoclassical interior, brightened only by warm rose- and gold-colored ornamentation. Works of particular interest include a sculpture of Christ made from cane paste and a fantastic churrigueresque (ultra-baroque) organ.

BOSQUE CUAUHTEMOC The first of the 253 arches of the 18th-century aqueduct frames Morelia's largest park, the Bosque Cuauhtémoc, a 10- to 15-minute walk from the Plaza de Armas. At the edge of the park is the **Museo de Arte Contemporaneo,** with rotating exhibits of contemporary art from all over Latin America, including works by Chilean painters and female graphic artists. *Museum: Acueducto 342. 11 blocks east of Plaza de Armas, down Madero. Admission free. Open Tues.–Sun. 10–2 and 4–8.*

CASA DE LAS ARTESANIAS A wide variety of handicrafts from all over the state of Michoacán, from carved wood to guitars to copper dishes, is housed in this former Franciscan monastery. The collection is on a par with that of the Museo del Estado in terms of variety and detailed explanations. The difference is that everything here is for sale. The Casa de las Artesanías also contains workshops where you can see artisans practicing their crafts. *Vasco de Quiroga, at Humboldt, tel. 43/12–17–48. Admission free. Open weekdays 10–8, weekends 10–6.*

"Dying is nothing when you die for the Fatherland"—José María Morelos (who did).

CENTRO CULTURAL UNIVERSITARIO This is one of the best examples of colonial architecture in Morelia—only it was completed in the 20th century. The cultural center houses temporary exhibits of contemporary art from Mexico's up-and-coming artists, and also has regular film festivals and literary get-togethers. Come to admire the murals on the walls and chat with the staff about upcoming events. *Madero Pte., at Galeana, tel. 43/12–19–09. Admission free. Open Mon.–Sat. 9–2 and 4–8.*

MUSEO CASA DE MORELOS José María Morelos, the city's namesake, once owned this home, which he abandoned to join the fight for independence. The story of his life is interesting, but unless you read Spanish, the displays of his reading glasses and family tree won't do much for you. *Morelos Sur 323, tel. 43/13–26–51. Admission: $3.50, free Sun. Open Mon.–Sat. 9–7, Sun. 9–6.*

MUSEO DEL ESTADO The Purépechas dominated almost the entire region of Michoacán, as this museum chronicles in exhibits of artifacts from pre-Columbian times. Purépechas still populate the area, producing a wide range of handicrafts, some of which you can see here. Rotating shows of regional contemporary art and some artifacts from the Independence movement that you-know-who played such a big part in are also on display. Explanations are in Spanish. *Prieto 176, tel. 43/13–06–29. 2 blocks north of Plaza de Armas. Admission free. Open weekdays 9–2 and 4–8, weekends 9–2 and 4–7.*

CHEAP THRILLS

Pay your homage to Morelos at his birthplace, **Casa Natal de Morelos,** where you can ooh and aah over his signature on documents. The real reason to come here, however, is to meet the students studying and hanging out in the sunny garden. The Cine Club sponsors free foreign films here several times a week, as well as cultural events such as poetry readings. Check the bulletin board. *Corregidora 113, tel. 43/12–27–93. 1 block south of cathedral on García Obeso. Admission free. Open weekdays 9–2 and 4–8, Sat. 10–2 and 4–7, Sun. 10–2.*

The Universidad Michoacana de San Nicolás de Hidalgo is a series of simple, white buildings plopped down in the middle of a field. Though architecturally uninspiring, it is, obviously, a great place to meet students. Hang out in the building that houses the Departamento de Idiomas (A-1, at the end of the campus) and you will inevitably be approached by students wanting to practice their English or discuss their city with you. *Santiago Tapia 403. Take SAN-TIAGUITO bus from east side of Plaza de Armas.*

AFTER DARK

Morelia is at its best at night when the streets and the main plaza are illuminated by soft lights that cast a romantic glow over promenading couples. The Plaza de Armas is a constant hub of activity, with mimes, musicians, dancers, and cotton-candy vendors all vying for attention. Thursdays, Fridays, and Saturdays are the most active throughout the city, but most bars are open seven days a week.

MUSIC AND THEATER The Orquesta Sinfónica performs in the **Teatro Ocampo** Fridays and Saturdays at 8:30 PM. Schedules are seasonal; contact the **Instituto Michoacano de Cultura** (tel. 43/13–13–20 or 43/13–12–15) for info.

The **Cantera Jardín** restaurant puts on theater shows Thursday–Saturday at 9 PM. Programs vary. *Aldama 343, tel. 43/12–15–78.*

If you understand enough Spanish to get the jokes, check out the **Corral de la Comedia** (Ocampo 239, tel. 43/12–13–74), which has comedy shows Thursday–Saturday at 8:30 PM and Sunday at 7 PM.

BARS AND DANCING Those who prefer mindless drinking and shaking won't be disappointed by Morelia. Highly recommended is **Siglo XVIII** (García de León, at Turismo 20, tel. 43/24–07–47), a video bar with a dance floor and a two-for-one special on Thursday nights; all other nights there's no cover but you're required to down $7 worth of the swill of your choice. **Bombay Jungle Bar** (Justo Mendoza 60, tel. 43/12-09–17) attracts the elite with a *barra libre* (open bar) on Wednesday nights. Women pay $3.50 and men $20 to get in the door. Other days the cover is $7, but you've gotta pay for drinks. The only real disco in town is **Xo Club** (Av. del Campestre 100, tel. 43/15–55–14), which charges an $8.50 cover and plays disco, *que-bradita,* and romantic tunes. Drinks are $2-$3. All three places are open every day until 2 AM.

Pátzcuaro

Bordered by a huge lake and green hills, the cool, rainy city of Pátzcuaro is a welcome sight for any traveler. Monuments, churches, and cobblestone streets give this small town a decidedly colonial feel, but the local Purépecha presence is also very strong. Purépecha women hurry to market early in the morning, while men stand around in circles, deep in conversation. The suburbs of Pátzcuaro are expanding rapidly, but the city itself is tranquil, having managed to avoid becoming an overpopulated tourist resort, and 20th-century intrusions mar the colonial setting only slightly. This 19th-century ambience prevails at night, as well: Most hotels have evening curfews, but there's little point in going out, anyway, because the town pretty much shuts down after 10 PM.

A primary reason to visit Pátzcuaro is the surrounding lake region. About 3 kilometers from the town center, **Lake Pátzcuaro** has islands, such as the accessible **Janitzio** (*see* Near Pátzcuaro, *below*), where people of Purépecha descent still live. Not just a great place to relax and enjoy the beauty of the nearby countryside, Pátzcuaro is also home to countless *artesanía* (crafts) shops. Check out the **Casa de los Once Patios,** a former convent where locally made serapes are sold. If you find yourself in Pátzcuaro on the **Día de los Muertos** (Day of the Dead, November 2), you'll see the town come alive with all-night fiestas. **Semana Santa** (Holy Week) in this city and in the nearby town of Tzintzuntzan (*see* Near Pátzcuaro, *below*) are also special. On Good Friday, locals reenact the Stations of the Cross, and on Holy Saturday they mourn Jesus's death with a silent candlelight procession. **The Día de Nuestra Señora de la Salud** (Day of Our Lady of Health) on December 8th honors the Virgin Mary with traditional Purépecha dances including the dance of Los Viejitos (old men). A crafts festival in the first week of November, **Tianguis Artesanal,** draws artisans from around Michoacán.

BASICS

AUTO PARTS/SERVICE Autopartes de Pátzcuaro sells parts for most cars. *Obregón 19, tel. 434/2–08–70. Open weekdays 9–2 and 4–7, Sat. 9–2.*

CASAS DE CAMBIO Banamex (Portal Juárez 32, tel. 434/2–10–31) on the Plaza Bocanegra changes cash and traveler's checks weekday mornings; rates are good, and the lines fairly short. There is also an ATM that accepts Cirrus, Plus, Visa, and MasterCard at Avenida Mendoza 16. **Casa de Cambio Multidivisas** changes cash and traveler's checks and has longer hours. *Padre Lloreda, at Buena Vista, tel. 434/2–3–83. Open weekdays 9–2 and 4–6, Sat. 9–1:30.*

EMERGENCIES For emergency assistance, call the **police** (tel. 434/2–00–04).

LAUNDRY Lavandería Automática will wash, dry and fold your clothes ($4 for 3 kilos). Get here as soon as the place opens if you want same-day service. *Ponce de León 14, tel. 434/2–39–39. ½ block west of Plaza San Francisco. Open Mon.–Sat. 9–2 and 4–8.*

MEDICAL AID The **ISSSTE hospital** (Quiroga s/n, tel. 434/2–12–27), half a block west of Plaza Vasco de Quiroga, has 24-hour service. **Farmacia Guadalupana** (Ibarra 34, no phone) is open round the clock. Other pharmacies take turns doing the night shift: Check the billboard under Portal Hidalgo 1, on the west side of the Plaza Vasco de Quiroga, for current information.

MAIL The full-service post office will hold mail sent to you at the following address for up to 10 days: Lista de Correos, Administración de Correos, Pátzcuaro, Michoacán, CP 61600, México. *Obregón 13, tel. 434/2–01–28. 1 block north of Plaza Bocanegra. Open weekdays 9–2 and 4–7, Sat. 9–2.*

PHONES The two main plazas are surrounded by several casetas de larga distancia, but the best rates are at the **Hotel San Agustín,** where they charge a $2 fee for international collect calls. *Portal Juárez 19, tel. 434/2–00–41. West side of Plaza Bocanegra. Open daily 8:30 AM–10 PM.*

VISITOR INFORMATION The staff at the **Delegación Regional de Turismo** will try to answer your questions, but maps are pretty much the only thing of use they can provide. *Ibarra 2, tel. 434/2–12–14. A few doors west of Plaza Vasco de Quiroga. Open Mon.–Sat. 9–2 and 4–7, Sun. 9–2.*

COMING AND GOING

BY BUS The **Central de Autobuses Pátzcuaro** (Libramiento Ignacio Zaragoza 2600) is about 1½ kilometers south of the town center. City buses and vans labeled CENTRO leave frequently for the center of town (and budget lodging areas) from the station. **Autobuses del Occidente** (tel. 434/2–00–52) goes to Guadalajara daily at noon ($10.50, 5 hrs); Mexico City ($19, 5 hrs) at 9:45 AM and 11:30 AM; and Morelia ($2, 1 hr) on the hour. **Autotransportes Galeana** (tel. 434/2–08–08) has buses to Morelia ($2, 1 hr) and Uruapan ($2, 1 hr) every 15 minutes.

BY TRAIN The train station is about 3 kilometers from the town center, near the Janitzio boating docks. Trains to Lázaro Cárdenas (1st class $9, 2nd class $5.50; 9 hrs), pass through Uruapan ($2 1st class, $1 2nd class; 2 hrs) daily at 7 AM. The train to Mexico City leaves at 9:30 PM and has first-class seats for $18, second-class assigned seats for $11, and you'll-get-one-if-you're-lucky seats for $6.50. The trip takes about 12 hours. Only second-class service is available to Morelia ($1, 1 hr); that train leaves at 9:05 AM. There's a 24-hour restaurant

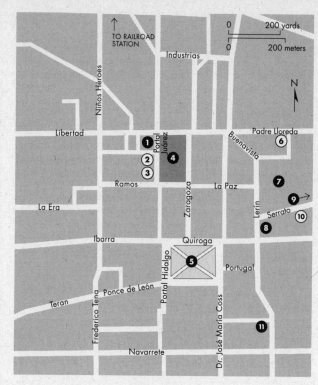

Basílica de
Nuestra Señora, 7
Casa de los
Once Patios, 11
El Humilladero, 9
Mercado, 1
Museo de Artes
Populares, 8
Plaza Bocanegra, 4
Plaza Vasco
de Quiroga, 5

Lodging ○
Posada de
la Rosa, 3
Posada de
la Salud, 10
Hotel
San Agustín, 2
Hotel Valmen, 6

across the street from the station where you can fortify yourself for a long ride. *Paseo Lázaro Cárdenas, tel. 434/2–08–03. Ticket window opens ½ hr before every departure.*

GETTING AROUND

You may have trouble finding street signs in Pátzcuaro, but the central area is small. Most points of interest are within walking distance of the two main plazas, the small and busy **Plaza Bocanegra** (also called Plaza Chica), and the **Plaza Vasco de Quiroga,** one block to the south. Streets change names at both plazas, and around the Plaza Quiroga most businesses use *portal* (walkway) names instead of street names. Several blocks north of Plaza Bocanegra you'll find the train station, a few bars, the dock for boats to Janitzio, and good seafood restaurants.

WHERE TO SLEEP

Prices for clean rooms here are reasonable, and hot water is usually available. Ritzier hotels are on the Plaza Vasco de Quiroga, while the slightly noisier Plaza Bocanegra hosts the budget places.

Hotel San Agustín. This establishment lacks charm but offers tidy, spartan rooms and bathrooms. Advantages of staying here include the great location, the lack of a curfew, and low prices; the bright courtyard is icing on the cake. Singles are $7, doubles with two beds $14. *Portal Juárez 27, tel. 434/2–04–42. 20 rooms, all with bath.*

Hotel Valmen. An extremely friendly owner and a courtyard filled with plants and chirping birds are the main attractions of this modest hotel. Rooms are large, and you have your choice of green or pink walls (ooh). It's the best of the bargain hotels but has a silly 10 PM curfew. Admittedly, there's not much nightlife to keep you out any later. Singles cost around $7, doubles

$14. *Padre Lloreda 34, tel. 434/2–11–61. 1 block east of Plaza Bocanegra. 16 rooms, all with bath. Luggage storage.*

Posada de la Rosa. Squeezed between the shops and hotels of Portal Juárez, this clean and reputable establishment overlooks the Plaza Bocanegra. Randomly furnished rooms—some with tons of furniture, some with none—aren't great, but they'll do. The only drawbacks are the 11 PM curfew and the walk to the communal bathrooms. Bring your own toilet paper and towel. Both singles and doubles cost $10 without bath, $14 with. *Portal Juárez 29, tel. 434/2–08–11. 12 rooms, 3 with bath.*

Posada de la Salud. This cheerful establishment is popular with travelers from the United States. Built in traditional Mexican style with a tiled patio, it's usually quiet, heating up when hotel guests forced to stay in by the 11 PM curfew make their own parties. Rooms are pleasant, with carved wood furniture and large, clean bathrooms. Singles cost about $14, doubles $19. *Serrato 9, tel. 434/2–00–58. 12 rooms, all with bath. Luggage storage.*

FOOD

Among local specialties worth trying are *pescado blanco* (whitefish), caught fresh from the lake, and sopa tarasca. The best of the many fish restaurants are found near the lakefront; **Restaurant Cholita,** near the ticket booth for the boats, is one of the most popular. A huge open-air **market** operates daily on the west side of the Plaza Bocanegra. Stop by **Chocolate Joaquinita** (Enseñanza 38, tel. 434/2–11–04) to buy a huge pack of gritty but delicious homemade chocolate for $5.

➢ UNDER $5 • **Los Equipales.** This tiny, down-home taquería is always full in the evenings. Tacos with beef, sausage, or tripe, and quesadillas are all bargains, at less than $1 each. *Portal Allende 57, no phone. North side of Plaza Vasco de Quiroga. Open daily 6 PM–10:30 PM.*

Hamburguesas y Torti Sam. If you can't handle tiny fish with eyeballs staring at you blankly from your plate, you'll be glad to know there's a humble hamburger joint in town. Get 'em topped with cheese or ham for under $2. French fries are a buck. *Mendoza 12, tel. 434/2–24–06. ½ block south of Plaza Bocanegra. Open daily 10 AM–11PM.*

Restaurant Mery. Set in the front of a private home, this is a cheerful place for an excellent, cheap meal. The rich and filling sopa tarasca is $1.50; other dishes include *corundas* (triangular tamales) and *tortas* (sandwiches) of every combination for $1.50. Egg breakfasts are also available here for $1–$2. The owner is very gracious and makes sure you have everything you need. *Enseñanza s/n, no phone. ½ block west of basilica. Open daily 8 AM–9:30 PM.*

➢ UNDER $10 • **Restaurant Doña Paca.** The wrought-iron and dark wood interior of this restaurant provide an elegant setting, and the *trucha al ajo* (trout in garlic) and other fish dishes for about $6.50 do it justice. You can also simply enjoy a cappuccino Doña Paca for $2 at one of the tables set out on the main plaza. Another good choice is the *churipo de la sierra* (beef with vegetables and herbs), served with corundas, coffee, and dessert for $6. *Portal Morelos 59, in Hotel Mansión Iturbide, tel. 434/2–03–68. North side of Plaza Vasco de Quiroga. Open daily 8 AM–9 PM.*

Restaurante Hotel Posada La Basílica. The enormous windows here open onto an incredible view of Pátzcuaro and the lake. The menú del día ($7) includes soup, rice, blue-corn tortillas, and breaded trout or beef prepared with tomatoes and onions. *Caldo de pescado,* a tomato-based fish soup, is a lighter choice for $5. Be prepared for a leisurely meal—service is slow even when there are few customers. *Arciga 6, tel. 434/2–11–08. From Plaza Bocanegra, east on Padre Lloreda, then up Buena Vista. Open Wed.–Sun. 8–4.*

WORTH SEEING

The bustling *tianguis* (open-air market) is a good place to get a sense of Pátzcuaro's character. It begins on the west side of the Plaza Bocanegra and continues for several blocks. Here you'll find all kinds of fresh food, as well as vendors hawking local handicrafts and cheap, plastic watches and toys. You can get some good deals on handmade woolens, including sweaters, blankets, and serapes. The area is a mass of humanity, so don't expect to go anywhere fast.

CHURCHES Pátzcuaro was the episcopal seat of Michoacán until that honor was moved to Morelia in 1508, and its impressive colonial churches reflect the city's historical importance. Two blocks east of the Plaza Vasco de Quiroga is the **Basílica de Nuestra Señora de la Salud,** built under orders of Quiroga, the first bishop of Michoacán, upon a sacred Purépecha site. The most interesting piece here is the **Virgen de la Salud** (Virgin of Health), made from cornhusk paste and orchid nectar, which Quiroga commissioned from the local Purépechas. At the time it was prohibited to dress holy images with cloth, to keep the *indígenas* (Indians) from hiding their own idols within the Catholic vestments. The basilica is open daily until dusk, and the mass schedule is posted at the side entrance.

In colonial times, young men gathered in the Plaza Vasco de Quiroga for friendly games of correr cañas (running of the sugar cane), in which they conducted mock battles while dressed in full armor and carrying lances made of sugarcane.

El Humilladero (The Place of Humiliation), about 3 kilometers east of downtown on the Antiguo Camino a Morelia, is so named because it is where the Purépecha surrendered peacefully to the Spanish. Inside this plateresque (an ornate Spanish style that mixes Gothic and Renaissance elements) church is a stone cross with a carved image of Christ fashioned in 1553. To get here, catch a bus or van marked CRISTO from the Plaza Bocanegra.

LA CASA DE LOS ONCE PATIOS This convent, built in the 18th and 19th centuries by Dominican monks, now houses several crafts shops. The convent was broken up to make way for streets, leaving only five of the original 11 garden patios, but a hexagonal bath remains in one of them. Prices here aren't too bad, but you can probably find better deals at the markets. The main appeal of the Casa is watching the artisans in action and learning about their work. *Madrigal de las Altas Torres, 2 blocks from Plaza Vasco de Quiroga.*

MUSEO DE ARTES POPULARES This building housed the Colegio de San Nicolás in the 16th century. Today, the aging edifice is the site of Pátzcuaro's crafts museum. On display are a wide variety of local crafts, including ceramic dishes, intricately painted masks, and lacquerware. In the back garden is a traditional Tarascan hut set on a 12th-century stone platform, the heart of the indigenous ceremonial center over which the basilica was later built. *Enseñanza, at Alcantarillas, tel. 434/2–10–29. 1 block east of Plaza Vasco de Quiroga. Admission: $4.50, free Sun. Open Tues.–Sat. 9–7, Sun. 9–3.*

AFTER DARK

Strolling the plaza until about 9 PM or cruising the streets with bored 17-year-olds are about your only options for nightlife. For those who absolutely must find some action, **El Rincón** is *the* bar in town (not the hip bar, just the bar). The mostly young clientele picks up on each other to the accompaniment of thumping music and a loud TV. Drinks are $2–$4. *Open Sun.–Thurs. 7 PM–10 PM, Fri.–Sat. 7 PM—11 PM.*

OUTDOOR ACTIVITIES

The **Volcán del Estribo Grande,** about 4 kilometers west of the center of town, makes a great short hike, with a phenomenal view of both Pátzcuaro and the nearby lake and islands at the end. The walk takes you along cobblestone streets lined with centuries-old homes and towering trees. To reach the lookout, head west on Ponce de León from the southwest corner of the Plaza Vasco de Quiroga. Ponce de Léon turns into Terán, and then becomes Cerro del Estribo.

You can also rent **bikes** from the hotel restaurant Mansión Iturbide (*see* Food, *above*) for $5 an hour. Pátzcuaro's cobblestone streets make for a bumpy ride, but it's a great way to explore the quieter residential areas of town. Ignore the sign that says the bikes are for hotel guests only, since the management does.

Near Pátzcuaro

JANITZIO

The local Purépacha people, who are almost the only inhabitants of the largest of Lake Pátzcuaro's five islands, call their island Xanichu. The meaning of this name is disputed. Some say it means "ear of corn," others say "where it rains," and still others "cornflower," but during the summer rainy season there's no doubt which interpretation is most probable. Most of the islanders' income is generated from fishing and handicrafts produced for the tourist industry. Fishermen here use butterfly nets to catch the whitefish they sell to Pátzcuaro restaurants, but this occupation is neither easy nor particularly lucrative. Many of the houses are run-down, crumbling, and windowless, and many of the children are barefoot, raggedly dressed, and malnourished. On weekends, the island is a classic tourist trap, but if you get out during the week and escape the main shopping and restaurant drag, you will get a better sense of the locals' lifestyle. The Purépecha here still speak, write, and study in their native tongue.

If you're near Janitzio on the first of November, don't miss the Día de los Muertos (Day of the Dead) celebration held here. It is renowned in Mexico for its fantastic dances and candlelight processions to the graveyards.

COMING AND GOING Boats to and from Janitzio run daily 8–5:30. Tickets can be purchased at Pátzcuaro's lakeside dock. Boats leave whenever they're full, so plan to take your time. To get to the lakefront from the center of Pátzcuaro, go to Portal Juárez, which borders the Plaza Bocanegra, and catch a northbound bus or van marked LAGO. The last boat leaves the island around 5:30. Don't miss it: There are no hotels on the island.

TZINTZUNTZAN

This small village, called "Place of Hummingbirds" by the Purépecha, lies about 18 kilometers northeast of Pátzcuaro. Shops selling straw and ceramic handicrafts line the main street. Beside the crafts market is the 17th-century **Templo de San Francisco,** another of Vasco de Quiroga's legacies, which has a newly redone (and consequently somewhat sterile) interior. The olive trees in the front courtyard, planted by Quiroga himself, still bear fruit today. The **Templo de la Soledad** next door is somewhat warmer and more human than the Templo de San Francisco and has original facades and several elaborately clothed statues.

The Purépecha deities were mostly female; important ones included Xaratanga, the goddess of fertility, and Cuerara-peri, the goddess of the sky and mother of all gods and goddesses.

Roughly a kilometer outside Tzintzuntzan are the remains of the religious and administrative capital of the Purépecha kingdom, where Vasco de Quiroga based his evangelical mission. The huge ceremonial platform is topped with circular stone structures known as *yácatas,* and the original altar used for decapitation and other sacrificial acts still stands behind them. There are no guides, but a small museum offers information in Spanish about the Purépecha people. *Museum open daily 10–5. Admission: $3.50, free Sun.*

COMING AND GOING **Autrotranportes Galeana** buses marked QUIROGA ($1, 30 min) leave every 15 minutes 6 AM–8:30 PM from Pátzcuaro's main bus terminal. Let the driver know where to let you off.

Uruapan

Travelers looking for picturesque towns filled with
well-preserved colonial arhcitecure may want to avoid this
small highland city. With few exceptions, Uruapan, with
blocks of dull, modern buildings alongside their run-down colonial ancestors, is difficult to
appreciate. The true lure of Uruapan lies outside the city limits, in the pristine hills of the surrounding area. Highlights include an excursion to the **Parque Nacional Eduardo Ruíz,** a horseback ride up the inactive (you hope) **Volcán Paricutín,** and a visit to the sparkling **Tzararacua**
waterfall.

Otomí and Chontal people took advantage of the rich vegetation and free-flowing waters for
centuries before the arrival of the Spanish in Uruapan. When Father Juan de San Miguel
showed up in 1531, he established a feudal *encomienda* system, reducing the indigenous peoples to serfs upon whose backs agrarian Uruapan grew and prospered. Today it's known as the
world's avocado-growing capital, producing five different varieties. In November, the city trem-
bles with excitement when the annual **Feria del Aguacate** (Avocado Fair) is held. In fact, Uruapan finds some reason to break out the avocados and *charanda* (a local liquor) almost
monthly. Among the biggest festivals is **Semana Santa** (Holy Week), which includes a parade
of people in traditional costumes. On June 30, the **Fiesta de San Pedro** honors St. Peter, an
apostle of Christ, with a parade, band, indigenous dances, and lots of booze. July 23 the **Fiesta
de Santa María de Magdalena** honors the biblical prostitute turned saint with processions and
performances of traditional Moorish and Christian dances. **El Día de San Francisco** commemorates the patron saint of Uruapan on October 4 with a dance by Purépecha women.

Even when there's no festival going on, the people of Uruapan are friendly and the occasional
visitor is received with open-armed hospitality. Surprisingly, there is a sizeable population of
hipster/slacker/artist types, much like you'd find in San Miguel de Allende, with the requisite
alternative attitude, long hair, and recreational drug use.

BASICS

AUTO PARTS/SERVICE Auto Refaccionaria Independencia sells auto parts and can refer
you to a mechanic. *Independencia 37-A, tel. 452/4–30–87. Open Mon.–Sat. 9:30–2 and
4–7:30.*

CASAS DE CAMBIO Banamex (Morelos, at Cupatitzio, tel. 452/3–92–90) changes traveler's checks and cash 9 AM–noon and has an ATM that accepts Cirrus and Plus cards. Inside
the bank, you can get one of those dangerously tempting cash advances on your Visa or Mastercard. On Saturdays, change money at **Compra y Venta de Dólares.** *Cupatitzio 34, tel.
452/4–79–00. 1½ blocks south of Jardín Morelos. Open weekdays 9–2 and 4–7, Sat. 9–2.*

EMERGENCIES For emergency assistance or an **ambulance,** call the **police** (tel.
452/4–06–20).

LAUNDRY Lavandería del Cupatizia charges $4.50 to wash and dry a 3-kilo load. Bring
clothes in before noon to get them back the same day. *Pino Suárez 89, tel. 452/4–28–54. 1
block east and 6 blocks north of Jardín Morelos. Open Mon.–Sat. 8–2 and 4–8.*

MAIL The full-service post office will hold mail sent to you at the following address for up to
10 days: Lista de Correos, Uruapan, Michoacán, CP 60001, México. *Reforma 13, tel.
452/3–56–30. From Jardín Morelos, walk 3 blocks south on Cupatitzio, left on Reforma. Open
weekdays 8–7, Sat. 9–1.*

MEDICAL AID The **Hospital Civil** (La Quinta 6, tel. 452/3–46–60) in front of the Parque
Nacional has emergency service and a 24-hour pharmacy. Other pharmacies in town rotate
night hours on a monthly basis.

PHONES The caseta de larga distancia at the **Restaurant Las Palmas** charges a $2.50 con-
nection fee for a collect call. *Donato Guerra 2, tel. 452/4–65–45. Open daily 8 AM–10 PM.*

VISITOR INFORMATION The town's tourist office provides cheerful attention, maps, and lots of information on where to go and how to get there. *Madero 120, tel. 452/4–06–33. 1 block west and 3½ blocks north of Jardín Morelos. Open Mon.–Sat. 9–2 and 4–7, Sun. 9–2.*

COMING AND GOING

BY BUS The **Central de Autobuses de Uruapan** (Carretera a Pátzcuaro Km. 1, tel. 452/3–44– 05) is about 3 kilometers northeast of Jardín Morelos. Buses marked CENTRO go to the town center; buses to the terminal from downtown are marked CENTRAL. A taxi from the bus station to the center of town should be about $3. **Flecha Amarilla** (tel. 452/4–39–82), the cheapest line, has buses to Aguascalientes ($16, 9 hrs), Guadalajara ($9.50, 6 hrs), Mexico City ($16, 8 hrs), Querétaro ($11, 6 hrs), and San Luis Potosí ($18, 9 hrs). **ETN** (tel. 452/3–86–08), the cushy line, takes passengers to Guadalajara ($19, 4½ hrs), Mexico City ($29, 6 hrs), and Morelia ($8, 2 hrs). For short distances try **Ruta Paraíso** (tel. 452/4–41–54) or **Autotransportes Galeana** (no phone), both of which have service to Pátzcuaro every 15 minutes. The bus station has a caseta de larga distancia and luggage storage.

BY TRAIN The station is about 11 blocks from the center of town, and easily accessible by bus or taxi. Trains to Mexico City leave at 6:35 AM (2nd class) and 7:15 PM (1st class) making stops in Pátzcuaro and Morelia, as well as other cities. The trip all the way to the D.F. costs $13 first class, $8 second class. A train also leaves for the coastal city of Lázaro Cárdenas ($7.50 1st class, $5 2nd class) daily at 10 AM. *Paseo Lázaro Cárdenas, at end of Av. Américas, tel. 452/4–09–81. Ticket office open Mon. and Wed.–Sat. 7:30–7:30, Tues. and Sun. 9–12:30 and 4–7:15.*

GETTING AROUND

Although the city is fairly large, three areas are of most interest to the visitor—the bus station, the **Jardín Morelos** (main plaza), and the strip of bars on Paseo Lázaro Cárdenas. Most buses pass the Jardín Morelos, and routes or destinations are written on the windshield. You'll have to take a taxi to sample the nightlife on Lázaro Cárdenas, since buses stop running around 9. Taxi fare is about $2.

WHERE TO SLEEP

Most of the hotels directly on the Jardín Morelos have seen better days or are out of budget range. Fortunately, there are decent, inexpensive hotels within a short walk of the Jardín.

Hotel Capri. The paint is peeling in these dark rooms, but they're clean and have adequate bathrooms. The friendly owners go to extreme lengths to make you feel at home. Rooms with one bed are $10; with two they're $13.50. *Portal Santo Degollado 10, no phone. 28 rooms, all with bath. Luggage storage, wheelchair access.*

Hotel del Parque. The plain, medium-size rooms here are clean and airy, and couches and a TV in the lobby invite you to hang out with the families who share the place with you. If you don't mind the seven-block walk to the center, you'll appreciate the location in front of the Parque Nacional. Singles are $8.50, doubles $12. *Independencia, at La Quinta, tel. 452/4–38–45. 14 rooms, all with bath.*

Hotel Mi Solar. Patios and large wooden doors give this place a feeling of colonial elegance, and the large rooms have windows opening onto the street. The place attracts foreign travelers, despite the fact that there is hot water only in the early morning and late at night. Singles are $11, doubles $13.50. *Juan Delgado 10, tel. 452/2–09–12. 2 blocks north of Jardín Morelos. 20 rooms, all with bath. Wheelchair access.*

Hotel Villa de Flores. Flowers fill the halls here, accenting the whitewashed walls and black wrought iron. Rooms are large and clean and have balconies, phones, and TVs, making this hotel worth the extra expense. Singles are $22, doubles $25. *Carranza 15, tel. 452/4–28–00. 2 blocks west of Jardín Morelos. 28 rooms, all with bath. Wheelchair access. MC, V.*

FOOD

A picnic lunch from the stands around the Jardín Morelos and behind the Templo de San Francisco (see Worth Seeing, below) won't set you back more than $4. Produce stands in this area sell wonderful fruits and vegetables, and tamales and fresh cheese can also be found here. Grilled meats are a local specialty.

Amazonia. It feels like summer barbecue time at your uncle's house as Zeco, the friendly Brazilian owner, runs in and out of the restaurant waving spears of various grilled meats. From homemade herb sausage to chicken wings, he insists that you try a little of everything. Add plate upon plate of salad, vegetables, and rice and beans and the $13.50 tab is a bargain. Skip breakfast and go nuts here at lunchtime—you'll never have to eat again. *Latinoamérica 19, across from bowling alley, no phone. From Jardín Morelos, east to Justo Mendoza, south to Latinoamérica, then east again. Open daily noon–10 PM. Wheelchair access.*

Cocina Económica Pituka. Food is so cheap and delicious here you may wonder why anyone would eat anywhere else. It gets crowded at lunch with businessmen devouring soups ($1), chicken mole ($2), and chiles rellenos ($2). You can order anything on the menu to go for even less. *Juárez 94, tel. 452/3–21–90. 3 blocks east and 2 blocks south of Jardín Morelos. Open daily 1-5.*

Lonchería La Uno. This tiny kitchen has seating for only about eight people, which makes conversations with your neighbors inevitable. Down-to-earth plates of homemade tacos, gorditas, and tortas are just a few dollars and *licuados* (smoothies) are $2.50. *Independencia 21, tel. 452/3–34–17. Open daily 7–7.*

CAFES **Café La Lucha.** A popular afternoon hangout with a folk-art atmosphere, this comfortable café invites you to do some serious lounging. Musicians often stop by to croon a few pesos out of you. *Café de olla* (coffee flavored with chocolate and cinnamon), espresso, and hot chocolate are a few of the choices (all $1). Pies and pastries are also $1. *García Ortiz 22, tel. 452/4–03–75. ½ block north of Jardín Morelos. Open daily 9–2 and 4–9.*

Café Tradicional de Uruapan. This place has a menu of more than 20 coffees and teas. You can also get just about anything in your coffee, including ice cream ($3) or a stiff shot of brandy ($5). A plain old *café con leche* (coffee with milk) is $1. The menu also includes egg breakfasts ($4–$6), and tamales of all types (50¢ each) are served after 6 PM. *Carranza 5-B, no phone. ½ block west of Jardín Morelos. Open daily 8:30–2 and 4–10.*

WORTH SEEING

The **Parque Nacional Eduardo Ruíz,** on Calzada La Quinta just seven blocks west of the Jardín Morelos, was a private garden in the 16th-century and is now a public park. Here you can see the semi-tropical flora of Michoacán without stepping outside the city limits. Rich vegetation encroaches upon the stone paths that wind their way among streams, fountains, and waterfalls, and the air is heavy with the moist smell of earth, plants, and wet stone. The west side of the park offers the best scenery. Guides will tell you about the legends of the various fountains for about $2, but you may just want to buy the book ($1) and read silently by a creek. If you're able to shake off that hangover on a Sunday morning, come to the *domingo saludable* (healthy Sunday) held in the park, consisting of free martial arts, yoga, aerobics, and ecology classes. The fun starts at 8 AM. The park is open daily 8–6, and admission is 35¢.

Tons of good bargains can be found on everything from juice presses and fresh herbs to camouflage uniforms and wacky jewelry in the open-air market held daily under the portales across from the Jardín Morelos. The market winds around the Templo de San Francisco, ending in the Mercado de los Antojitos, where you can sample regional food for $3–$4 a plate.

DESTILADORA EL TARASCO This distillery gives free tours for those who want to know more about *charanda*, the local firewater. Here you can see the whole process, from the fermentation of sugar cane juice to the distilling and bottling. Tours end with the charanda concoction of your choice. Call before you go. *Pino Suárez 96, tel. 452/4–00–75. 4 blocks NW of Jardín Morelos. Open weekdays 9–2 and 4–7, Sat. 9–2.*

GALLERIES Both **Catharsis** (Américas 48, no phone) and **Temetsi** (Independencia 15-A, tel. 452/4–06–29) display works by local artists. Exhibits change monthly, and if you hang around long enough, you may luck out and get invited to an exhibit opening, where you can drink white wine and schmooze with Uruapan's cool and friendly artistic community. Both galleries are open daily 11 AM–2 PM.

LA HAUPATERA This large colonial structure, founded by Fray Juan de San Miguel as a hospital for indigenous people, is now mainly a hangout for families and couples who toss coins into the wishing well or sit and chat on the moss covered steps. A small museum shows traditional Michoacán handicrafts, and the shop next door has a knowledgeable staff and good bargains on quality crafts. Also nearby is the **Templo de San Francisco**, which has a gorgeous plateresque exterior but a fairly dull, modern interior. *North side of Jardín Morelos. Admission free. Museum open Tues.–Sun. 9:30–1:30 and 3:30–6. Store open daily 9–9.*

AFTER DARK

For a small town, Uruapan has a fairly progressive nightlife. Information on cultural activities such as film and theater is provided by the **Casa de la Cultura**. *García Ortiz 1, tel. 452/4–76–13. Open Mon.–Sat. 8–3 and 4–9.*

There's live blues, jazz, and Latin American folk music at the lesbian-owned **Temetsi** (*see* Worth Seeing, *above*) on Friday and Saturday nights after 9 PM. Cover is about $2–$3, and drinks run $1–$3. In **La Taverna** (Fábrica San Pedro, tel. 452/4–09–91) partiers shoot pool, listen to the occasional band, and shake it on the small dance floor. Once the fun ends at La Taverna (around midnight or 1 AM), most people head next door to **La Caldera** to dance to disco and rock. Cover is $8.50, drinks are $3–$4. **Euforia's** (Madrid 10, tel. 452/3–93–32), off Lázaro Cárdenas, is a video bar with all-you-can-swill nights on Thursdays (free for women, $13 for men) and no cover on the weekend. **La Scala** (Madrid 12, tel. 452/3–02–74), has an $8.50 cover and $3–$4 drinks, but an unfortunate tendency to attract high school students.

Near Uruapan

SAN JUAN PARANGARICUTIRO

A jolting hour-long bus ride will bring you to the small village of **Angahuan**, situated in the midst of a green, mountainous area. The town, with its stone walls, wooden houses with dirt floors, and reticent women in head scarves, feels far removed from city life. The **Paradero Turístico de Angahuan** (on edge of town, tel. 452/5–03–83) rents horses ($9) for the 5-kilometer trek to **San Juan Parangaricutiro**, a town buried by lava when Volcán Paricutín erupted in 1943.

In 1943 the Paricutín volcano burst from the middle of an unlucky farmer's cornfield. Lava spouted for 11 years straight until the volcano suddenly fell dormant. The mysterious beast has been quiet ever since—-though you never know.

Once you arrive, you'll have to clamber over twisted moss- and plant-speckled lava to see the top of a church that is the only visible part of the buried town. If you're interested in a longer trip, you can also rent horses to take you to the source of the destruction: Paricutín itself. Horses come with a guide, and the six-hour round-trip trek should cost about $15 a head. Start out early from Uruapan, pack food and water, and don't worry about finding a guide—he'll find you. From Uruapan, **Autotransportes Galeana** buses go to Angahuan ($1.50, 30 min) about every half-hour. The last bus back to Uruapan leaves around 6 PM, but the Paradero Turístico de Angahuan also rents cabins for about $5 per person and provides free campsites. Local families also rent rooms in their homes; any guide should be able to point you in the right direction.

TZARARACUA

Ten kilometers south of Uruapan is the trailhead for a 2½-kilometer trek through a ravine to Tzaracua, a torrential 43-meter blanket of water that emerges from the dense, tropical vegetation, creating a swimming hole below. You can rent horses ($7) for the trip to the waterfall if you don't want to hike; you'll see them when you get off the bus. This is definitely one of the best day trips to be taken from Uruapan, though its popularity has taken its toll on the site in the form of litter and other icky human residue. **La Tzararacuita**, about 1 kilometer away from the main waterfall, is smaller and cleaner. To get to the trailhead for the waterfalls, catch a TZARARACUA bus (50¢) from the south side of the Jardín Morelos. Buses generally run on the hour, and the ride takes about 30 minutes.

Guadalajara

Despite a population of 5 million, Guadalajara seems like a relatively small city. The anonymity of late 20th-century urban life hasn't made itself felt here: Introduce one Guadalajaran (or *tapatío*, as they call themselves) to another and inevitably they will realize they have a friend or associate in common. Mid-afternoon siestas and promenades around the plazas at night are as common as in any provincial town.

In 1531 conquistador Nuño Beltrán de Guzmán of Guadalajara, Spain, sent one of his strongmen, Juan de Oñate, to establish a city that would connect the coastal territories with the interior. A settlement of Indians whose queen ruled from Tonalá, on the southern outskirts of what is now Guadalajara, rebelled against Spanish rule, and in 1542, the Caxcanes killed Pedro de Alvarado, who had been sent to put down the rebellion. During the colonial era, Guadalajara was the capital of the *audiencia* (administrative territory) of Nueva Galicia, which encompassed the western coast of Mexico from Jalisco all the way up through California. The city has often been characterized as politically conservative, mostly because it was here that the PAN (Partido de Acción Nacional), often linked to the Catholic Church, was organized in the early part of the century. The students of the public Universidad de Guadalajara, however, ensure that the city is constantly infused with new blood, and the gay population here is visible and as "out" as is possible in Mexico.

> *Guadalajara is considered the birthplace of several things "typically Mexican": the woeful love songs of the mariachi, the flirtatious jarabe tapatío (known to gringos as the Mexican hat dance), and charreadas (rodeos).*

Guadalajara has grown quickly in recent decades, especially the 1980s; after the 1985 earthquake in Mexico City, hundreds of thousands of people migrated here. Like any expanding city, Guadalajara is experiencing growing pains that are hard to ignore. Children sleep on the city's sidewalks, and, as in Mexico City, pollution worsens

Paracho

A small indigenous town, Paracho is renowned for its handcrafted guitars; those hanging in Michoacán shops all come from here. The town itself is of no particular interest—the "downtown" area basically consists of shops selling wooden crafts—but if you're in a shopping mood, Paracho merits a visit. If you're in the area in August, however, be sure not to miss the Feria Artesanal de la Guitarra, which attracts folkloric dance groups, luthiers, and the most talented guitarists from around Mexico. The festival lasts one week and is usually held in late August. The tourist office in Uruapan (see above) should have the exact date. Buses to Paracho ($1.50, 45 min) leave from the Central de Autobuses in Uruapan almost every half-hour.

as the city absorbs surrounding suburbs. In 1992 the Mexican oil company, Pemex, leaked gasoline into the sewer system and accidentally exploded a huge section of the city, killing hundreds of people and destroying thousands of homes. The city has also recently been the scene of drug-related violence. In 1993, Catholic Cardinal Juan Posadas Ocampo was killed in a shoot-out between rival dealers at Guadalajara's airport, and in 1994 five people died when a bomb exploded at the birthday party of a girl whose family may have had connections to drug trafficking.

Nevertheless, there's plenty to see in Guadalajara. Several murals by José Clemente Orozco, a native of Jalisco, are at the Instituto Cultural Cabañas and the Universidad de Guadalajara. Mariachi music fills the Plaza de los Mariachis every night, where people pay to hear their favorite songs played especially for them. In the towns of Tlaquepaque and Tonalá (officially independent of Guadalajara, but geographically surrounded by it), you'll find plenty of local handicrafts. Close to the city is Lake Chapala, a favorite getaway for Guadalajarans and retired Americans, while in the nearby town of Tequila, you can take distillery tours that end with free shots.

BASICS

AMERICAN EXPRESS All of the usual services are provided by this AmEx representative—traveler's check exchange as well as personal check cashing and mail holding for cardholders. *Av. Vallarta 2440, Guadalajara, Jalisco, CP 44680, México, tel. 3/615–89–10. West of downtown on Juárez/Vallarta; take PAR VIAL or 500 bus. Open weekdays 9–6, Sat. 9–1.*

AUTO PARTS/SERVICE The main autoparts/mechanic strip is on Calzada Independencia Norte, north of the Mercado Libertad. However, **Autoservicios Rodríguez** does most general mechanic work. *Vallarta 2345, tel. 3/615–64–0. Open weekdays 9–7, Sat. 9–1.*

BOOKSTORES Librería México has a huge selection of popular magazines in English and some paperback bestsellers. *Plaza del Sol, tel. 3/621– 01–14. Open daily 8:30 AM –9:30 PM.*

El Libro Antiguo, 1½ blocks north of the Plaza de la Liberación, is a used-book store that swaps books and sells English paperbacks, though most of what they carry is 1950s pulp fiction with titles like *Impatient Virgin* and *Lovers and Libertines*. Still, a few cheap treasures can be found amidst the junk, and if you read Spanish, there are plenty of choices. *Pino Suárez 86, Col. Centro, no phone. Open Mon.–Sat. 9–8.*

BUCKET SHOP Faculty and students make up most of the clientele at **Agencia de Viajes Universidad de Guadalajara,** so they know about the cheapest plane fares and vacation packages. *Vallarta 976, in the basement, tel. 3/625–85–52. Take the PAR VIAL or 500 bus from downtown on Juárez. Open weekdays 9–3 and 5–8, Sat. 9–1.*

CASAS DE CAMBIO Banamex (Juárez 237, tel. 3/679–32–52) changes traveler's checks and cash weekdays 9–1 and has an ATM that accepts Cirrus and Plus cards. They also give cash advances on MasterCard or Visa. For better hours, try any of the money-changers cluttering up Avenida López Cotilla between Corona and Maestranza. **Cambio de Divisas** has good rates. *López Cotilla 175, tel. 3/614–65–65. Open Mon.–Sat. 9–7:30, Sun. 11–2.*

CONSULATES Canada. *Hotel Fiesta Americana, Aurelio Aceves 225, Local 30, tel. 3/625–34–34, ext. 3005. Near Glorieta Minerva. Open weekdays 9:30–1:30.*

United Kingdom. *Gonzales Gallo 1897, tel. 3/635–89–27. Open weekdays 10–1.*

United States. *Progreso 175, Col. Centro, tel. 3/625–27–00, emergency tel. 3/625–55–53. Open weekdays 8–noon.*

LAUNDRY At **Lavandería Lavarami** you can get about 3½ kilos of your clothes washed, dried, and folded for $6. They'll also pick up and deliver. You can do your own clothes for about $5 a load. *Juárez 1520, tel. 3/657–16–83. Open Mon.–Sat. 9–8, Sun. 10–2.*

MAIL The full-service post office will hold mail sent to you at the following address for up to 10 days: Lista de Correos, Administración de Correo 1, Guadalajara, Jalisco, CP 44100, Méx-

Guadalajara

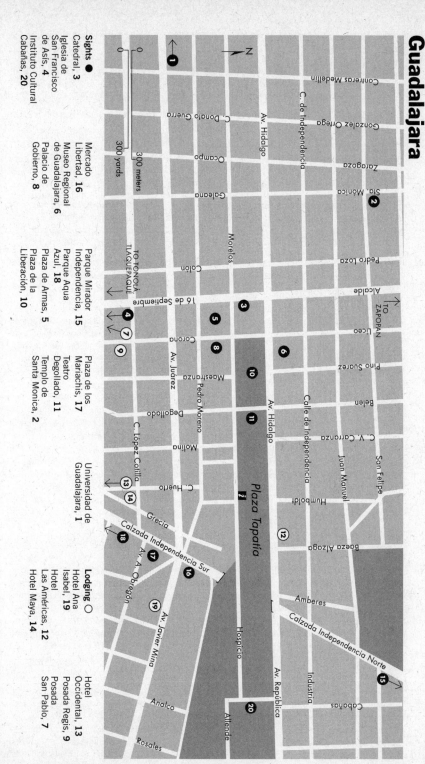

N

300 yards
300 meters

TO TONALÁ, TLAQUEPAQUE

Plaza Tapatía
i

Streets (from image): Contreras Medellín, González Ortega, C. de Independencia, Av. Hidalgo, C. Donato Guerra, Ocampo, Galeana, Sta. Mónica, Zaragoza, Pedro Loza, Alcalde, Liceo, Morelos, Colón, Corona, Av. Juárez, Maestranza, Pedro Moreno, Degollado, Molina, C. Huerto, C. López Cotilla, Grecia, Calzada Independencia Sur, Av. A. Obregón, Av. Javier Mina, Analco, Rosales, 16 de Septiembre, Pino Suárez, Belén, Calle de Independencia, C. V. Carranza, Juan Manuel, San Felipe, Humboldt, Baeza Alzaga, Amberes, Calzada Independencia Norte, Av. República, Industria, Cabañas, Hospicio, Allende

TO ZAPOPAN

175

ico. *Independencia, at Carranza, tel. 3/614–74–25. 3 blocks north of Plaza Tapatía. Open weekdays 8–7, Sat. 9–1.*

MEDICAL AID Both **Hospital del Carmen** (Tarascos 3435, tel. 3/813–00–42) and **Hospital Regional ISSSTE** (Av. de las Américas s/n, tel. 3/633–02–48 or 3/633–02–52) are open 24 hours. The first has English-speaking doctors; the second is closer to downtown.

The **Farmacia Guadalajara** has 24-hour service. *Av. de las Américas 2, near Plaza del Sol, tel. 3/615–85–16.*

PHONES You can make collect or phone-card calls at any working Ladatel phone in the Plaza Tapatía or Plaza de la Liberación. The caseta de larga distancia next to El Libro Antiguo (*see* Bookstores, *above*) charges about $1 for a three-minute collect call. You can pay for direct-dialed calls here, as well. *Pino Suárez 92, Col. Centro. Open weekdays 10–8, Sat. 10–7.*

SCHOOLS The **University of Guadalajara** has five-week courses in Spanish and Mexican culture, literature, and history for foreign students. For more information call Centro de Estudios Para Extranjeros, tel. 3/653–21–50 or 3/653–60–24, or write to Lic. Adriana Ayala Rubio, Guanajuato 1047, Aptdo. Postal 1, Guillón 2130, Guadalajara, Jalisco, CP 44000, México.

The **Casa de la Cultura** offers free classes in Nahuatl (the Aztec language) on the weekends. The classes are open to beginners; call the Casa for the schedule. You can also study art, theater, folkloric dance, and music here. *Constituyentes s/n, tel. 3/619–36–11. Btw Calz. Independencia Sur and 16 de Septiembre (near Parque Agua Azul). Open Mon.–Sat. 10–9.*

VISTOR INFORMATION The helpful, English-speaking staff at the **Secretaría de Turismo de Jalisco** gives out complete maps of the city and information about upcoming cultural events. There are several tourist-information centers dotting the main plazas, but you'll get the most info at the main office. *Morelos 102, Plaza Tapatía, tel. 3/658–22–22 or 3/658–03–05. Open weekdays 9–8, weekends 9–1.*

COMING AND GOING

BY BUS The **Central Camionera Nueva,** the main bus station, is on the Carretera libre a Zapotlanejo (free road to Zapotlanejo) between Tlaquepaque and Tonalá, about a half-hour southeast of downtown. Buses arrive here from destinations over 100 kilometers away. The huge, horseshoe-shaped terminal is divided into seven terminals, each with its own group of bus lines. Each terminal has Ladatel phones, restaurants, and luggage storage—the one in Terminal 1 is open 24 hours. The cheapest way to get downtown is on city Bus 102 or minibus 644. Bus 275 takes you up Avenida 16 de Septiembre to the old bus station. *Colectivos* (collective taxis) from the bus station to downtown cost about $7.50 (buy your ticket at the terminal's booth); the reverse trip, for reasons known only to higher powers, is less than $5.

Leaving Guadalajara should be a breeze, as hundreds of buses depart daily. However, the problem lies in deciding which line to take, since they're spread out over seven terminals stretching for almost a kilometer. Running around to all of them is not a wise idea, so call ahead to several lines. If you're not one to plan ahead, go to **Flecha Amarilla** (tel. 3/600–03–99 or 3/600–00–14) in the first terminal for the cheapest fares and slowest buses. Other lines include **Autobuses del Occidente** (tel. 3/657–64–60), with buses to Morelia ($11, 6 hrs); **Tres Estrellas de Oro** (tel. 3/600–00–83), which has service to Aguascalientes ($11, 3 hrs), Puerto Vallarta ($20, 6 hrs), and Mexico City ($25, 8 hrs); and **Rojo de los Altos** (3/679–04–55), with service to Ciudad Juárez ($57, 24 hrs) and Zacatecas ($13, 5½ hrs). **ETN** (tel. 3/657–43–53) is a good but somewhat pricey first-class line.

The **Antigua Central Camionera** (on 5 de Febrero), the old bus station, sends buses to destinations within 100 kilometers of Guadalajara. Luggage storage is available between 7 AM and 8 PM. **Autotransportes Guadalajara Chapala** (tel. 3/619–56–75) leaves every half-hour between 7 AM and 8 PM for cities around Lake Chapala. **Rojo de los Altos** (tel. 3/619–23–09) leaves for Tequila and Amatitlán ($2.50, 2 hrs) every 20 minutes between 6 AM and 9 PM. **Autotransportes del Sur de Jalisco** (tel. 3/650–23–99) leaves for Tapalpa ($5, 3 hrs) every hour between 6:45 AM and 5:45 PM. To get to the station, take Bus 110 south on 16 de Septiembre.

You can purchase bus tickets for a number of lines from **Global Travel** (Calz. Independencia Nte. 254, under the Plaza Tapatía, tel. 3/617–33–30) for no extra charge. They're open weekdays 9–6:30, Saturday 9–4:30

BY TRAIN The train station (tel. 3/650–08–26) is a little south of downtown, about two blocks from Parque Agua Azul (*see* Worth Seeing, *below*). The train to Mexico City leaves daily at 9 PM and takes 11½ hours. Sleepers with two beds cost about $130, but seats are a steal at $16 first class, $9 second class. The first-class train to Mexicali ($86, 36 hrs) leaves daily at 9:30 AM, with a stop in Mazatlán ($25, 9 hrs) and Sufragio ($41). Much cheaper and slower is the second-class train to Mexicali ($33, 2 days), which leaves daily at noon. All train tickets must be purchased on the day of departure. There is a long-distance telephone office and several stores selling food in the station. *Open daily 7 AM–9 PM. Tickets sold weekdays 9–1 and Sat. 9 AM–11 AM. Take Bus 62 south on Calz. Independencia or Bus 54 south on 16 de Septiembre.*

BY PLANE Guadalajara's airport (tel. 3/688–51–20) is served by **Aerocalifornia** (tel. 3/826–88–50), **Aeroméxico** (tel. 3/621–74–55), **American** (tel. 3/616–40–90), **Continental** (tel. 3/647–46–05), **Delta** (tel. 3/630–35–30), **Mexicana** (tel. 3/647–22–22), and **United** (tel. 91/800–00–307). The cheapest one-way ticket to Mexico City is about $68.

To get to the center of town from the airport by taxi costs $13, but, inexplicably, the ride in the other direction is $17. If you go to the taxi office, you can get better rate—as low as $10. In either case, you should call a day ahead to reserve a taxi. Airport lockers cost about $3 per day. *Taxi office: Enrique Díaz de León 954, at Francia, tel. 3/612–93–37 or 3/612–93–39. Near Glorieta Pila Moderna.*

GETTING AROUND

Although Guadalajara is the second largest city in Mexico, it's easy to get around if you stick to the historic center. Downtown, things revolve around the huge **Plaza Tapatía** and surrounding streets. The plaza is bordered by Hidalgo to the north, Morelos to the south, Avenida 16 de Septiembre to the west, and Calzada Independencia (not to be confused Calle Independencia, a smaller street) to the east. Avenida Juárez heads west from downtown into the university area, crossing the wide, jam-packed Federalismo; after that it becomes Vallarta, crossing Chapultepec and Avenida de las Américas, and ends at a rotary called **Glorieta Minerva.** If you plan to enjoy the nightlife, you'll get to know López Mateos, which takes you south of Minerva to the huge shopping mall, **Plaza del Sol,** and the dozens of bars and clubs nearby.

BY SUBWAY Guadalajara's *tren ligero* (light-rail train) runs both above and below ground, traveling the length of Federalismo between the Periférico Sur and the Periférico Norte stations. At press time, another tren ligero track was being constructed to run east-west along Juárez and Vallarta. For now, the subway is the fastest way to get to northern or southern Guadalajara, but it's useless for travel around the center. It runs 6 AM–11 PM, and the fare is 35¢.

BY BUS Hundreds of buses and minibuses run all over Guadalajara. There is frequent service between 5 AM and 11 PM and fare is 35¢. To get to the Plaza del Sol and the all-important nightlife on López Mateos, take Bus 258 from Calzada Independencia heading south. To get to Tlaquepaque, the Central Camionera, or Tonalá from downtown, catch Bus 275 on Avenida 16 de Septiembre heading south; to Zapopan take the same bus running north. For destinations along Calzada Independencia such as Parque Agua Azul and the train station, hop on Bus 62. The PAR VIAL, which runs west on Juárez/Vallarta to the Minerva and east on Hidalgo to downtown, passes the university. Blue **Tur** buses offer air-conditioned comfort and cost about $1. The 707 runs west on Juárez/Vallarta, while the 706 goes from 16 de Septiembre to Tlaquepaque and Tonalá.

BY TAXI Taxis are the way to get around late at night. Cabs line up in front of expensive hotels, but these charge higher rates than those you hail on the street. A ride from the bar/club area around the Plaza del Sol to the center of town should cost about $5.

WHERE TO SLEEP

Guadalajara has plenty of beds in the $10–$15 range. The nicest inexpensive places to stay are the small *posadas* (inns), which are ususally family run; unfortunately, due to a recent drop in tourism, most in the downtown area have closed. A number of budget hotels are scattered throughout the center of town, generally south of the historic center or near the Mercado Libertad. The cheapest joints are along Calzada Independencia and near the old bus station, but these are pretty sleazy. If you plan to stay a while, *casas de huéspedes* (rooming houses) rent rooms by the month for a little more than $100. Ask for a list from the state tourist office (*see* Visitor Information, *above*). The drawback to nearly all budget hotels in Guadalajara is the noise of street traffic.

DOWNTOWN The best reason to stay downtown is the proximity to sights in the center as well as to the bus lines that will take you elsewhere. The neighborhoods southeast of the Plaza Tapatía have cheap accommodations, but you may not feel safe walking alone here at night. Directly northeast you'll find a similar situation, but as long as you stick to within a five-block radius of the Plaza, you shouldn't encounter anything too scary.

➤ UNDER $15 • **Hotel Occidental.** One of the best of the cheap hotels in the center of town, the Occidental doesn't sacrifice cleanliness for low prices. The hotel is situated in a grungy alley, but the brightly painted halls and rooms are sure to cheer you up once you're inside, if the smell of disinfectant doesn't knock you out first. The *matrimonial* (double) beds were made with a very slim couple in mind. Singles are $11, one-bed doubles are $11.50, and two-bed doubles are $13. *Huerto, at Villa Gómez, tel. 3/613–84–06. 3 blocks south of Plaza Tapatía. 51 rooms, all with bath.*

➤ UNDER $20 • **Hotel Maya.** There's nothing really outstanding about this hotel, but it's decent and clean and has telephones and enormous bathrooms attached to each room. Location—just two blocks away from the Plaza Tapatía and the Mercado Libertad—is a plus. Singles are $15, doubles, $19. *López Cotilla 39, tel. 3/614–54–54. 55 rooms, all with bath. Luggage storage, wheelchair access. Reservations advised Easter week and summer.*

Posada San Pablo. Owner Lili and her family make you feel right at home in the San Pablo's noisy but spacious rooms. A sweeping marble staircase leads up to a courtyard filled with plants and canaries, and the dog is actually friendly. Hot water is scarce in the evenings. Since the place is often recommended by the tourist office, it fills up quickly—call ahead to make sure there's a room available. A single costs $12, doubles $15. A few economical rooms without private bath are decent enough for $7. *Madero 218, at Corona, tel. 3/613–33–12. 2 blocks south of Juárez, next to El Quinto Poder record store. 15 rooms, some with bath. Laundry.*

➤ UNDER $25 • **Hotel Ana Isabel.** Despite its somewhat unpleasant location across from the Mercado Libertad, this hotel is a good choice if you can afford to pay a bit more for comfort and quiet. A long plant-filled hallway leads to peaceful rooms with ceiling fans and small, clean bathrooms. Singles are $17 ($15 if you stay on the top floor and hike up two flights of steps), doubles $20. *Javier Mina 164, tel. 3/617–79–20. South side of Mercado Libertad. 42 rooms, all with bath.*

Hotel Las Américas. The convenient location of this hotel across from the Plaza Tapatía is about all it has going for it. Admittedly, rooms have TVs and phones, but the smell of burnt food can be overpowering. Singles are $17, one-bed doubles are $18.50, and two-bed rooms are $22. *Hidalgo 76, tel. 3/613–96–22. 3 blocks east of Teatro Degollado. 49 rooms, all with bath. Luggage storage, wheelchair access.*

➤ UNDER $35 • **Hotel Posada Regis.** This place has small, carpeted rooms and is popular with middle-class families. It's the place to stay if you are short on cash and need to exercise your plastic; otherwise you'll get a better deal at some of the cheaper places. Singles are $27, doubles $33, but the prices go down if you stay for a week or longer. *Corona 171, at López Cotilla, tel. 3/613–30–26. 1 block south of Juárez. 18 rooms, all with bath. Laundry, luggage storage, restaurant. MC, V.*

NEAR CALZADA INDEPENDENCIA SUR **Hotel Calzada.** This place is right on the bus line to the train station, but if you're not headed that way you might want to find a hotel closer to the center. McDonald's-style red-and-yellow tiles can't quite brighten the small, dark rooms, but the price is persuasive. One or two people in one bed cost $9; two beds in a room are $11.50. *Calz. Independencia Sur 808, at Av. de Paz, tel. 3/614–67–28. A few blocks south of Glorieta Minerva. 74 rooms, all with bath. Luggage storage, wheelchair access.*

HOSTEL **CODE.** The youth hostel, affiliated with a sports complex, has four dorm rooms, with 20 bunk beds stuffed into each one. The facility is clean, with private showers and toilet paper (a real luxury). It's set away from the downtown noise, but access to the city is still quick and easy. The doors close at 11 PM, so if you miss the curfew, prepare to stay out until 6 AM. Beds (including sheets) cost $5. *Prolongación Alcalde 1360, no phone. Take Bus 231 up Alcalde from downtown, and get off ½ block after Instituto de la Artesanía Jalisciense. 80 beds, none with bath. Check-in 8–2 and 3–9. Luggage storage. Closed Christmas and Easter.*

FOOD

It may sound silly, but Guadalajara is a great place to get Mexican food. It's a big city, but the cuisine isn't as international as you might expect. Tourists, foreign and Mexican alike, come here for that "authentic" Mexican experience, so this is a good place to really dig into those tamales *con mucho gusto.*

DOWNTOWN The center of town does not cater to people searching for a fine dining experience, but you'll find lots of cheap fast food here, particularly tortas. During the afternoon on Moreno (1 block north of Juárez), tons of small shops offer specials such as five tacos or three tostadas for less than a dollar. The **Mercado Libertad** has dozens of food stalls with probably the cheapest meals in town, but, as one resident ominously joked, they sell *platillos de cólera* (plates of cholera), so this is one instance when it's best to follow the crowd. For a cheap breakfast, **Croissants Alfredo,** across from the Plaza de la Liberación on Morelos 229, has baked goodies for about 50¢ apiece. It's open daily 8 AM–9:30 PM.

➤ UNDER $5 • **El Convento.** Small, simple, and clean, this eatery whips up comidas corridas at lunchtime for $3.50. Add a drink and dessert and your meal is still under $5. One warning—the chicken mole, smothered in a lot of sauce, is more skin and bones than meat. Happiliy, there are usually three or more entrée choices for lunch. *Moreno 516, tel. 3/658–46–91. 5 blocks west of Plaza Tapatía. Open daily 8–5.*

Gorditas Estilo Durango. Students short on cash come here for *gorditas* (thick corn tortillas) stuffed with sausage, cheese, or shredded beef for $1.50 each. The menú del día (soup, refried beans, an entrée, and a drink) is another filling meal at $4. *Moreno 552, at Díaz de León, tel. 3/626–47–23. Open Mon.–Sat. 8–6.*

Krishna Prasadam. The peacock feathers and pictures of Hindu deities on the wall here might give you the impression that you took a wrong turn somewhere and left Mexico. The delicious comida corrida ($4.50), which includes veggie soup, tofu and peppers in tomato sauce, breaded vegetables, copious amounts of salad and whole wheat tortillas, fruit, and a yogurt drink, will do nothing to dispel that impression. *Madero 694, at Federalismo, tel. 3/626–18–22. Open Mon.–Sat. 6 AM–8 PM.*

Restaurant Panamerican. This is a good place to grab some food while you're near the Plaza de los Mariachis. Though the place itself lacks atmosphere, the food, especially the chicken mole ($4), is excellent. The egg or chicken chilaquiles are the best breakfast deal in town at $2. *Plaza de los Mariachis 47, no phone. Open daily 9 AM–1 AM.*

➤ UNDER $10 • **Café Madrid.** The combination of diner decor and waiters in dress whites and spotless shoes is a little bizarre, but this café is nonetheless popular with local businesspeople lingering to chat with friends or read the newspaper before work. The food costs a bit more than it's worth, but breakfasts are good. *Huevos a la mexicana* (scrambled eggs with tomato, onion, and chiles) are served with refried beans for about $5. Best of all is the *real* coffee ($1), a welcome break from Nescafé. *Juárez 264, at Corona, tel. 3/614–95–04. Open daily 7 AM–10:30 PM. Wheelchair access.*

La Chata. Open for over half a century, this cheerful restaurant serving traditional food is a great choice if you can spare some money. Though you can get some cheaper dishes like *sopes* (fried tortillas topped with beans, salsa, and meat or cheese) for less than $3, you'll probably want to try a specialty such as the *platillo jalisciense* (one-quarter of a chicken, french fries, a sope, one enchilada, and one flauta) for $7.50. Breakfast here is cheaper than at many places downtown, with egg dishes for $3.50. *Corona 126, tel. 3/613–05–88. 2 blocks south of Plaza Tapatía. Open daily 9 AM–10:30 PM.*

AVENIDA CHAPULTEPEC/AVENIDA AMERICAS Restaurants get more upscale the further west you go, and the area between Chapultepec and Américas is no exception. Nevertheless, many restaurants are accessible to the budget traveler. To get here, catch a PAR VIAL bus or take a leisurely walk (25 minutes) from downtown. Food ranges from unique regional specialties to fast food.

➢ UNDER $10 • **Los Itacates.** The Mexican equivalent of the power lunch meeting place, this restaurant specializes in traditional dishes such as *coachal* (shredded chicken and pork with corn). The house specialty is *pollo itacates* (one-quarter of a chicken with cheese enchiladas, potatoes, and rice). Both dishes are about $5. A breakfast buffet is also served for $5. *Chapultepec Nte. 110, tel. 3/625–11–06. A few blocks north of Vallarta. Open Mon.–Sat. 8 AM—11 PM, Sun. 8–7.*

Las Margaritas. A friendly, English-speaking staff and unique vegetarian entrées make this small restaurant a perfect place for lunch *al fresco*. The lentil salad includes cottage cheese, tomato, and onions and is served with bread for $6.50. For a smaller meal, try a peanut-butter-and-banana (or cucumber) sandwich for $4. The comida corrida includes soup, bread, veggies, an entrée, dessert, and coffee for $5. *López Cotilla 1477, at Chapultepec, tel. 3/616–89–06. Open Mon.–Sat. 8 AM–9 PM, Sun. 10–6.*

➢ UNDER $15 • **Los Otates.** Food here is pricey but delicious, and both indoor and outdoor dining is available. Try the *molcajete* dishes ($8–$10), mixtures of meat or seafood, salsa, and spices served in a large stone bowl with tortillas. They also serve cheaper fare such as enchiladas ($5) and tacos ($1 each). *López Cotilla 1835, tel. 3/615–63–01. Open Mon.–Sat. 8 AM–midnight, Sun. 9–7.*

PLAZA DEL SOL Plaza del Sol is a massive open-air shopping mall popular with Guadalajara's nouveaux riches. The neon lights, pulsing rock music, and not-so-subliminal messages to shop like crazy will soon have you longing for the taco stands and grittier life of downtown. On the plus side, the food around here is excellent, if a bit expensive.

Dainzú. In the middle of an upper-class residential neighborhood, this small restaurant introduced Oaxacan cuisine to Guadalajara in 1986. The soups ($2) are fantastic; classic Oaxacan entrées such as *tlayuda con tasajo* ($7), a large corn tortilla cooked with black beans and cheese and a huge slab of marinated meat on the side, easily fills two after a serving of soup. *Diamante 2598-A, tel. 3/647–50–86. From Mariano Otero, east past Expo to Av. Faro, then right on Diamante. Open Tues.–Sat. 1–10:30, Sun. 1–8.*

CAFES **El Café.** If you're going to take in a movie at the **Videosala** (*see* After Dark, *below*), this place next door offers outdoor tables on a lush patio and a bizarre, quasi-Victorian atmosphere indoors, complete with velvet and huge, costumed dolls. Coffee drinks run $1–$3, and they also serve light sandwiches and desserts for $3–$4. *Hidalgo 1292, no phone. Open Mon.–Sat. 9 AM–10 PM.*

Café La Paloma. La Paloma hops every night of the week with a few bohemian types scattered among the Guadalajaran youth, all smoking and looking cool. Coffee is $1.50, beers are $2, and you can fill up with various tacos and tortas for $1–$4. *López Cotilla 1855, tel. 3/630–01–95. 1 block west of Av. de las Américas. Open daily 9 AM–10 PM.*

WORTH SEEING

Most of Guadalajara's sights are on or around the Plaza Tapatía, in what is known as the *centro histórico* (historic center). To tour this area, get a map of the center from the tourist office (*see* Visitor Information, *above*) and hoof it. Although Guadalajara's three important suburbs (Tlaquepaque, Tonalá, and Zapopan) are officially separate from the city, they have been engulfed by the metropolis and are easily reached by city bus.

CENTRO HISTORICO The most important church in Guadalajara is the **Cathedral.** Completed in 1618 after 57 years of work, Guadalajara's religious centerpiece has undergone numerous modifications over the centuries, culminating in an eclectic combination of baroque, Renaissance, Moorish, and neo-Gothic styles. Its twin yellow spires were added in 1854, after an earthquake destroyed the original towers. The cathedral contains an excellent collection of religious art, relics of both the wealth and importance of Guadalajara during the colonial period. King Fernando VII of Spain gave the city 10 silver and gilt altars in gratitude for its financial help during the Napoleonic Wars. Carved out of a single piece of balsa wood, the altar and statue dedicated to Our Lady of the Rose was a gift from King Carlos V in the 16th century. To the right of the main altar are the remains of St. Innocence, brought here from the catacombs in Rome. Over the sacristy is Bartolomé Esteban Murillos's *La Concepción Inmaculada.* The schedule for mass is posted at the entryway. The service is especially beautiful and solemn—don't wander around gawking during the ceremony, as other tourists have been known to do. *Hidalgo, at Alcalde. Open daily 7 AM–9PM.*

➤ CHURCHES • The baroque **Iglesia de San Francisco de Asis** was one of Guadalajara's first churches. Columns with vine-like ornamentation in the entryway lead into the plateresque interior. Note the Santo Niño de Atocha with a homemade sweater and little bears to the right of the main altar. *16 de Septiembre, at Prisciliano Sánchez.*

The **Capilla de Nuestra Señora de Aranzazu** is the only remaining chapel of the five that once surrounded the Iglesia de San Francisco; the others have been demolished. The chapel is unique among churches in Guadalajara because of its three richly detailed wooden churrigueresque altarpieces, considered among the finest in the world. Their physical size and presence overpower the small interior of the church for a fascinating effect. *16 de Septiembre, at Prisciliano Sánchez.*

The **Templo de Santa Mónica** was built in 1773 for the Augustinian nuns who lived next door. The church is considered one of the finest examples of baroque architecture in the city, and residents regard it as one of the loveliest churches as well. In the northwest corner of the building is a statue of St. Christopher with mestizo features. *Santa Mónica, at San Felipe.*

➤ INSTITUTO CULTURAL CABANAS • Built between 1805 and 1810, this place was an orphanage until the 1970s. An important example of neoclassical architecture and full of wonderful courtyards, it now houses the city's cultural center, with art exhibits, a small theater/cinema, and a cafeteria. In the late 1930s, José Clemente Orozco painted a series of murals on the ceiling and walls of the building's main chapel, including what is considered his finest work, *The Man of Fire.* Besides the murals, some of Orozco's lithographs and paintings are on display here. Excellent tours are given in both Spanish and English. *Hospicio 8, east end of Plaza Tapatía, tel. 3/618–81–35. Admission: $3, $2 with student ID, free Sun. Open Tues.–Sat. 10–6, Sun. 10–3.*

➤ MERCADO LIBERTAD (SAN JUAN DE DIOS) • Heavily promoted by the tourism department, this market is just a larger version of markets found all over Mexico. The existing market was built in the 1950s, which explains the architecture, but people have been buying and selling here for more than 400 years. Three stories of jam-packed stalls and shouting vendors are more than sufficient to satisfy the pickiest shopper or cultural anthropologist. There's a large, cheap food area as well. Next to the market is the **Plaza de los Mariachis** (*see* After Dark, *below*). *Javier Mina and Calz. Independencia Sur. Open daily 6 AM–8 PM.*

➤ MUSEO REGIONAL DE GUADALAJARA • The displays of pre-Columbian artifacts here are impressive, and the exhibit tracing the history of Jalisco is interesting if you read Spanish. There's also a collection of colonial paintings, the most interesting of which is the newly-restored *Alegoría del paraíso de las monjas carmelitas.* In this 17th-century painting, a crucified Jesus' spurting blood turns into a field of flowers, plants, and trees at his feet, while a group of Carmelite nuns looks on approvingly. *Liceo 60, north side of Plaza de la Liberación, tel. 3/614–99–57. Admission: $4.50, free Sun. and holidays. Open Tues.–Sun. 9–3:45.*

➤ PALACIO DE GOBIERNO • The governor of New Galicia (a colonial administrative region including what is now Jalisco, Nayarit, and southern Sinaloa) had this stately churrigueresque mansion built in 1643. It was here that independence fighter Miguel Hidalgo decreed the abolition of slavery in 1910, and where Benito Juárez was almost assassinated by his enemies in 1858, before Don Guillermo Prieto stopped the would-be killers with the now-famous phrase, "Los valientes no asesinan" (the brave do not kill). Today, the main attraction is Orozco's dramatic *Social Struggle* in the stairwell on the right. It features a huge portrait of a white-haired Hidalgo jumping out from the chaos of war, fascism, communism, and ecclesiastic oppression. *Corona, btw Morelos and Pedro Moreno. Open daily 9–9.*

Across the street is the **Plaza de Armas.** France donated the wrought-iron kiosk, which is decorated with half-naked women, in 1910. Municipal bands give free concerts here on Thursday and Sunday at 7 PM.

➤ TEATRO DEGOLLADO • One of Guadalajara's most cherished possessions is this neoclassical opera house, modeled after La Scala in Milan and opened in 1866. Above the Corinthian columns that grandly mark the theater's entrance is a relief depicting Apollo and the nine Muses. The interior was exquisitely restored in 1988, and if you don't attend a performance here, make sure to take a look when it's open to the public. The university's renowned **Ballet Folklórico** performs here every Sunday at 10 AM. For some strange reason, the main gringo attraction at the theater is the postcard stand in the lobby. *Av. Belén, at Hidalgo, box office tel. 3/614–47–73. Theater open to the public Mon.–Sat. 10–2.*

➤ UNIVERSIDAD DE GUADALAJARA • The university's administrative offices are in a beautiful turn-of-the-century building. Two famous Orozco murals are on view at the auditorium, one on the dome and another behind the stage. Across the street, take the elevator to the top floor of the university's main building (a big cement block) for a good view of southeastern Guadalajara. The **Cine Foro** in the basement of the same building puts on movies, plays, and concerts; check the billboard at the box office for upcoming events. One block south of the university is the **Templo Expiatorio** (Madero and Escorza), a pseudo-Gothic cathedral that's just been completed after nearly 100 years of construction. It's so dark and imposing that you almost expect to hear Gregorian chants from the choir. *Vallarta, at Enrique Díaz de León. Take PAR VIAL bus west on Juárez.*

SOUTH OF THE CENTRO HISTORICO Guadalajara's premier getaway is the **Parque Agua Azul.** Nine hectares of eucalyptus, pine, and jacaranda entice you onto shady paths, benches, and grassy spots. There's also a huge aviary where you can get up close and personal with parrots, peacocks and other exotic birds, a small orchid greenhouse, and a butterfly house. *Calz. Independencia Sur, just south of Niños Héroes. Take Bus 62 south on Independencia. Admission: $1. Open Tues.–Sun. 10–5:30.*

At the northern end of the park is the **Casa de Artesanías de Jalisco,** a fabulous government-run crafts store, laid out like a museum with examples of crafts from various regions in Mexico. Prices here are generally too high for mere mortals, but it's a good place to check out quality items before buying from street vendors. *Calz. Gallo 20, tel. 3/619–46–64. Next to park cafeteria. Open weekdays 10–7, Sat. 10–4, Sun. 11–3.*

The **Teatro Experimental de Jalisco,** next to the park, performs anything from Shakespeare to Mexican avant-garde. Check the bulletin board near the park entrance or call 3/619–37–70 for information.

The **Museo de Arqueología de Occidente** is small, well organized, and packed with pottery produced by indigenous peoples of western Mexico. *Calz. Independencia Sur, at Calz. Campesino, across from the park. Admission: about 30¢. Open Tues.–Sun. 10–2 and 4–7.*

TLAQUEPAQUE Guadalajara's elite made Tlaquepaque a country retreat, but then Guadalajara's automobiles and city sprawl impinged on its rustic appeal. The town's spacious country homes fell into disrepair and continued to deteriorate until the 1960s, when artists converted the buildings into studios. Today, the central part of town is a shopper's paradise (or hell), as the presence of gallery after gallery indicates, but you don't have to max out your credit cards

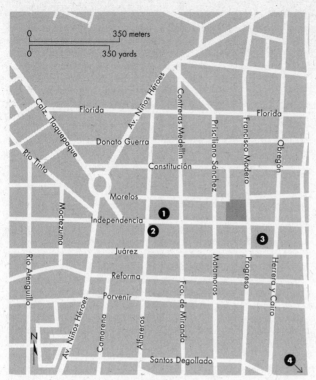

Artmex la Rosa
de Cristal, **1**
El Parián, **3**
Museo Regional
de la Cerámica, **2**
Tonalá, **4**

to have a good time here. Browsing is perfectly acceptable, and, as always, the vendors on the street offer a better deal, and often a better selection, on most items.

The main drag in Tlaquepaque is Independencia, a pedestrian-only street. **Artmex la Rosa de Cristal** (Independencia 232, tel. 3/639–71–80), a glass manufacturer, opens its studio to the public on weekdays 10–2 and Saturdays 10–noon; go for a demonstration of the ancient craft of glassblowing. The free **Museo Regional de la Cerámica** (Independencia 237), housed in an old country estate, exhibits the wonderful work of master potters and operates a small gift shop. Independencia ends in the lively **El Parián** plaza (Independencia and Madero). Named after the Chinese section of Manila, the plaza is a great place to grab a beer and refuse the advances of mariachi bands and portrait artists. Several bars are situated on the outer part of the plaza, while the gazebo in the center features local bands on weekends. For information on festivals, maps, or any other queries, head to the tourist office (tel. 3/635–05–96) at Sánchez 74, right next to the post office. *To Tlaquepaque, take Bus 275 or 275-A south on 16 de Septiembre; after traveling about ½ hour down Revolución, get off at small traffic circle just after passing under brick arches, then walk northwest to Independencia.*

Nearly all of the restaurants here are overpriced, so if you're going to have a sit-down meal, go where it's worth the extra pesos. **Restaurante Sin Nombre** (Madero 80, tel. 3/695–71–68) has excellent food, served on a beautiful patio teeming with plants and peacocks. Soups and salads are $4–$5, main dishes around $12. They're open every day 8 AM–9 PM. Meat lovers can sample a $5 plate of birria (roasted goat or pork in consommé) at **Birriería El Sope** (D. Guerra 142, tel. 3/635–65–38). The restaurant is open daily 9–7.

TONALA This smaller, more humble version of Tlaquepaque is also a famous crafts center. In fact, many of the ceramics and other crafts sold in Tlaquepaque are made here, where prices are cheaper. The simple adobe houses and more down-to-earth feel of the town draw those who tire of the tourist track (although plenty of tourists come here as well). The small tourist-information booth right on the Plaza Principal gives out maps and entertaining brochures, and the staff is quite friendly. Every Thursday and Sunday there is a *tianguis* (market) full of local wares at discount prices, as well as trinkets from Hong Kong. The free **Museo Nacional de la Cerámica** (Constitución 110, tel. 3/683–04–94) displays pottery from different states and eras and has a workshop and small store. Also worth a visit is the **Santuario del Sagrado Corazón,** with its brightly-painted interior and sacred heart sculptures. Behind the altar is a striking representation of Jesus Christ rising from the earth amidst huge, gray clouds. *Take Bus 275 or 275-A south on 16 de Septiembre, past Tlaquepaque.*

> *Tonalá was governed by a woman, Cihualpilli Tzapotzintli, when the Spaniards arrived in 1530. She decided to welcome the newcomers peacefully, despite the opposition of her male advisors. So much for women's intuition.*

ZAPOPAN Another victim of Guadalajara's voracious appetite is Zapopan, about 11 kilometers north of Guadalajara's center. Zapopan is home to the **Basílica de Zapopan,** which has an ornate baroque facade and a tiled dome. The 18th-century basilica is home to the 10-inch **Virgen de Zapopan,** venerated as the source of many miracles and the object of a pilgrimage every October 12, when over one million of the faithful honor the Virgin's return to the basilica after a tour of every church in her diocese. The statuette first achieved fame in 1541, when disorganized Spanish troops were inspired by it while battling an indigenous uprising. Since then she has been regarded as one of the most important sources of miracles in Mexico. The small **Museo Huichol,** at the east end of the basilica, is run by a priest who proselytizes among the Huichol people (*see box, below*). The museum exhibits colorful examples of clothing, beadwork and the unique, elaborate paintings of Huichol myths done entirely in yarn. Most of the items are for sale; proceeds benefit the Huichol people. *To Zapopan, take Bus 275 north on 16 de Septiembre.*

CHEAP THRILLS

On the northeastern edge of Guadalajara, Calzada Independencia comes to an abrupt end at the **Barranca de Oblatos,** a 500-meter-deep canyon. On weekends, the canyon park lures families with its numerous jungle gyms; others are drawn by spectacular views of the canyon and its vegetation. *Take MIRADOR bus north on Calz. Independencia until it turns left on Volcán Zacapu.* Admission: 30¢. Open daily 7–7.

The Struggle of the Huichol

Most Huichol Indians live in northern Jalisco and southern Nayarit, in a 240,000-hectare reservation granted them in 1953. The reservation is only accessible by plane, and often the Huichol will travel for five days to bring their handicrafts to the museum in Zapopan. Although the Catholic Church, specifically the Franciscan order, has made a slight dent in the Huichol's religious beliefs, their primary spiritual leaders are shamans, who have a great deal of political influence in the Huichol community. The Huichol insist on maintaining their traditions, as well as their land, resulting in an ongoing conflict with local landowners. Twenty-two hectares are currently in dispute, and there have been allegations of human rights violations perpetrated by landowners. The government's Human Rights Comission (CEDH) has been investigating the violations since 1993 and has granted some financial and political support to the Huichol, but no resolution has been found. With the PRI governing party facing serious challenges, it's unlikely the Huichol problem will receive much attention in the near future.

A full Sunday, plus some, could be spent browsing the rows of stands in **El Baratillo,** Mexico's second-largest outdoor market. Stretching primarily along Zavala, it branches off periodically to include other streets, forming a huge maze covering some 30–40 city blocks. Just when you think you've seen it all—the shoelaces, cassettes, vegetables, new and used clothes, a new drill press, or live pigs or goats—something else pops up. *Take PAR VIAL bus east on Hidalgo until you see market. Open Sun. early morning–afternoon.*

Still looking for that long-lost Andy Gibb record? Then head on over to **Roxy and Roll** record store, where vinyl is alive and well in a variety of used records, from John Denver and Olivia Newton-John to obscure jazz and classical. The records are $6. *Mezquitan 126, btw Juan Manuel and Independencia. Open Mon.–Sat. 10–8.*

If you didn't get enough dancing on Saturday night, head out to the tardeada (afternoon dance) held outside the arena after the bullfights in the small town of **Santa María Tequisquiapan.** Cowboy culture shows itself in all its glory—men in cowboy hats and boots swing their partners to ranchera music. Admission is only $3.50 (women can usually get in free), and the fun lasts from about 5 to 10 PM. Check with the tourist office to see if there's a bullfight that Sunday. *Take tren ligero south to Periférico Sur stop and ask someone to point you toward Santa María Tequisquiapan; it's not far.*

FESTIVALS Lake Chapala (*see* Near Guadalajara, *below*) is the place to be for **Carnaval** (late February or early March). The **Fiestas de Junio**, from mid-June to early July, celebrate the artesanía of Tlaquepaque with music, dancing, cockfights, and mountains of food and drink.

The **Fiestas de Octubre** is Guadalajara's month-long commercial and cultural fair. If you're not interested in exhibits demonstrating the richness of Jalisco's agriculture and industry, then

In Defense of El Mariachi

Mariachi music has been around since the 16th century, when Mexican bands started playing the son, a type of music from Galicia. At first the bands simply accompanied groups performing popular dances such as the jarabe, but by the 19th century they were gaining popularity and performing without the dancers. It wasn't until the modern age that the insistent trumpets that now dominate the mariachi sound were added—commercial radio stations decided that raising the decibel level would make the music more popular.

Mariachi bands today generally consist of two or more guitars, violins, trumpets, and the occassional harp. A guitar thumps in the background while the other instruments hum along at a rip-roaring pace or slow down to jerk tears from listeners. The songs generally concern heartbreak, heavy drinking, and love for the fatherland and are punctuated by yells and yodels.

Outside Mexico, mariachi music is probably the best known—and least respected— Mexican popular music. The mournful "ay-ay-ay" and the often garish costumes of the musicians have caused many foreigners to condemn it as tacky. Even Mexicans of high society often describe mariachi music as being too de pueblo (lower-class). Today, mariachi ensembles may not be respected by the upper crust, but the music sells, not only in the record stores, but in places like Guadalajara's Plaza de los Mariachis, where listeners shell out up to $8 for a song.

pottery demonstrations, cheese and wine tastings, and musical performances—from folk to experimental—should keep you busy. Smack in the middle of the Fiestas de Octubre, on October 12th, Guadalajara celebrates the **Día de la Virgen de Zapopan** (*see* Worth Seeing, *above*), adding a religious element to the otherwise secular events.

AFTER DARK

Guadalajara has raging nightlife almost seven nights a week, despite the best efforts of city government. Guadalajara once rivaled Mexico City in good times 'til daybreak, but now ordinances require all fun to stop at 2 AM. Of course, it doesn't. Plenty of bars keep going until 3, and there are always taco stands open until dawn.

The beauty of nightlife here is its diversity. The old standbys—bars and discos—are clustered around the **Plaza del Sol** on López Mateos, though you'll need plenty of money and connections for the guy at the door to decide you're cool enough to get in. The alternative scene is also alive and well. *Danceterías,* the Mexican version of raves complete with ecstasy and other Alice-in-Wonderland digestibles, are currently outlawed, but they continue underground. For information on the alternative scene, check with the guys at **El Quinto Poder** music shop (Madero 210, tel. 3/614–05–42).

The San Francisco of Mexico, Guadalajara boasts a substantial gay population and has plenty of happening gay and lesbian clubs. Obregón and Calles 50–60 encompass one of the more popular gay districts, although places are scattered throughout the city.

For a calmer evening, check out *Siglo 21,* a daily paper that lists movies, theaters, galleries, music, and dance. The Friday entertainment section, called "Tentaciones," has the most expansive information. The Sunday edition of *El Informador* also has a good listing of upcoming events.

Flanking the cathedral are three quasi-plazas, **Plaza de Armas, Plaza Libertad,** and **Plaza de la Liberación,** that buzz with frolicking people of all ages during the evening, especially on weekends. Caricaturists and marimba players call out to passers-by, while mimes, puppet shows, and musicians enthrall small crowds. In the bandstand of the Plaza de Armas, the Jalisco State Band gives free concerts (the sounds of which are piped into the Plaza de la Liberación) Thursday and Sunday at 7 PM.

Next to the Iglesia San Juan de Dios and Mercado Libertad, the **Plaza de los Mariachis** is actually a large alley lined with tables and worked by strolling musicians. Songs cost about $7 a piece, but you hardly need to pay for them or understand them to enjoy them. Sit at the first

The $30,000 Cock

If you're interested in learning more about Mexican culture—and the Mexican psyche—drop by Veterinaria Gallero, a store that specializes in fighting cocks. Those for sale are on display, and if you have about $120, you too could be the proud owner of a (cheap) fighting cock. Mexican cocks fight with various types of weapons, from the inch-long arma de filo (blade) to the shorter navaja corta (razor), which are attached to their feet. Cocks of Asian origin are favored, as are those with shorter spurs. The friendly vet will happily answer your questions about the contests and where to find one. Normal wagers for cockfights are about $30–$50, though they can climb as high as $30,000. Losses like this can be a double bummer, for not only are you suddenly destitute, but your favored cock is a heap of dead feathers. Calz. Independencia Sur 500, tel. 3/658–18–40. Open weekdays 9:30–2 and 4–7, Sat. 9:30–2:30.

set of tables near the entrance, grab a $2 beer, and weep loudly as the music tugs at your heartstrings.

BARS **Bar Zelona** is the hip hangout for the monied youth of Guadalajara and is a good place to get wild and maybe even get lucky. There's no cover, but you have to buy a $5 card at the door good for a drink or two, depending on what you want. As the liquor flows and the music gets louder, people start dancing on the tables and chairs, and the waiters don big sombreros and throw confetti at people. *Av. de las Américas 1462, tel. 3/642–75–37. Open Wed.–Sat. 10 PM–1 AM.*

Country Rock Café. They don't play country here, nor much rock, and this is not a café. Getting in is a silly process and up to the whim of the doormen—look as cute and gringo/a as possible and your chances are better. Wednesday and Thursday nights women can drink themselves silly for free, while men pay $20 for all they can drink. Weekends both sexes pay $18.50, with three drinks included. Wednesdays and Thursdays feature live rock and pop bands. *Vallarta 4454, tel. 3/621–97–22. Open Wed.–Sat. 9:30 PM–1 AM.*

Duran Duran. Okay, so the name is super cheesy, but it's a good place to hang out if you're not up to leaving the downtown area. Though it's no big deal, there's a video screen and cheaper-than-usual beer ($1.50). Food is also served: Late night munchies are satisfied here with *queso fundido* (cheese fondue) for $3.50. *Madero 273, tel. 3/614–27–40. Open daily 1 PM–11 PM.*

Vantage. Escape the teenyboppers who dominate other bars. The 25–30 set hangs out here, and gays and lesbians will feel comfortable in the mixed crowd. Wednesday nights are free for women—otherwise everyone pays $7. Drinks are about $3. *Lope de Vega 325, tel. 3/616–88–02. Open Wed.–Sat. 9:30 PM–3 AM.*

CINEMAS Dozens of theaters around the city show fairly recent undubbed American and other foreign films. Current listings are in the daily paper *Siglo 21.* The **Cine Foro** at the Universidad de Guadalajara and the cinema at the Instituto Cultural Cabañas are good places for quality movies (*see* Worth Seeing, *above*).

The University of Guadalajara's **Videosala** (Hidalgo 1296, tel. 36/25–57–23) shows videos of foreign and national art films weekdays for $5. They put out a monthly program guide, available there or at the info booth in the university building on Vallarta. Videosala also has rooms devoted to works made in video, both foreign and national, from video art to TV docudramas.

DANCING Guadalajara has its share of big, flashy, and rather expensive discos. Come here to hang out with the city's hip, upper-middle-class youth and dance to the latest disco sounds. **Dady'O** (López Mateos 2185, tel. 3/622–55–53) elicits rave reviews and lets women in free on Saturdays. Long-time favorites **Ciros** (Mariano Otero 2409, tel. 3/631–62–32), near the Plaza del Sol, and **Osiris** (Lázaro Cárdenas 3898, tel. 3/622–42–70) continue to draw crowds. All clubs charge covers between $5 and $20, depending on the night.

Of the *salones* (dance halls) that host live *bandas* playing traditional Mexican music, **Salón Corona** (López Mateos 2380, tel. 3/647–08–82) is one of the best. Women get in free Monday–Thursday. Also popular are **Guadalajara Grill** (López Mateos Sur 3771, tel. 3/631–56–22) and **Casino Veracruz** (Manzano 486, tel. 3/613–44–22), which has tropical and salsa music. Cover charges are around $5.

GAY BARS AND CLUBS The **Centro Botanero** bar (Javier Mina near Calle 56) is the most popular bar, particularly on Wednesdays and Sundays when the cover is $5 (includes one drink). On weekends, the three main discos heat up: **Mónica's** (Obregón 1713, near Calle 64), with a $5 cover, is mostly for gay men while **La Malinche** (Obregón 1230, near Calle 50), also with a $5 cover, attracts transvestites and lesbians. **S.O.S.** (Av. de la Paz 1413, at Federalismo) is the hottest club for both gays and lesbians, charging a $10 cover.

MUSIC The **Centro Cultural Roxy** (Mezquitan 80, at Hidalgo, tel. 3/658–00–53), in a converted art deco movie theater, is *the* hip, urban/underground hangout in Guadalajara. An art gallery (Galería Margaritte) is in front, while dance, theater, performance art, movies, and live music (everything from rock to reggae) are put on in the gutted theater. Shows take place Friday and Saturday nights at 9 PM. Cover $5–$7.

Peña Cuicacalli is Guadalajara's most popular *casa del canto*. Music is primary here: they play folk music, *trova cubana* (Cuban music), bolero, salsa, nueva canción, and rock. The music is almost always good. Cover is about $5 on weekdays, $8.50 Fridays and Saturdays; beers are $2. *Niños Héroes 1988, tel. 3/625–46—90. At the Glorieta Minerva where it meets Chapultepec. Open Tues.–Sun.; hours vary.*

La Peñita Teccizli is a restaurant with nightly live music similar to that found at Cuicacalli, and a friendly, peña ambience predominates. Sundays are free nights; other nights you pay about $5–$10 to listen to jazz, Afro-Antillian, blues, and Latin American music. The music usually starts at 9 PM (7 PM on Sundays). The tourist office has monthly performance schedules. Beers are $2, wine, $3. *Vallarta 1110, tel. 3/625–58–53. Open daily noon–midnight.*

Near Guadalajara

LAKE CHAPALA

Mexico's second-largest lake is both a weekend retreat for families and home to the largest community of gringos outside the United States. The lily-filled lake, bordered by almost tropical green mountains, is a beautiful place to spend the day.

Chapala is a popular retirement community, and during the week English is frequently heard in the town's restaurants. On weekends, families from Guadalajara take over the boardwalk, and the air is festive with the sounds of vendors hawking ice cream and fried fish. Behind the artisans' market and the lakeshore restaurants, you can rent horses ($7 an hour) and perhaps join one of the impromptu horse races along the lakefront. You can also arrange a boat trip; a ride around part of the lake with seven or eight people costs about $18 and a trip to Scorpion Island costs $30—you'll need to make a few friends to make this a budget-friendly experience.

COMING AND GOING Buses leave from the old bus station (*see* Coming and Going, in Guadalajara, *above*) every half-hour between 7 AM and 8 PM ($2, 45 min). Buses to Guadalajara depart every half-hour until 9 PM from the bus station on the main drag in Chapala.

WHERE TO SLEEP AND EAT The only cheap place to stay in Chapala is the **Casa de Huéspedes Las Palmitas** (Juárez 531, behind market, tel. 376/5–30–70). Basic rooms in this old converted house cost $10 for a single, $13.50 for a double. A number of fairly decent restaurants hug the shore of the lake, and they're not too outrageously priced. **La Playita** (Acapulquito Local 4, tel. 376/5–41–40) serves up big plates of fish and shrimp *al ajo* (with garlic) for $7, but you can get cheaper fare like chiles rellenos for $4. On weekends, vendors sell candy, nuts, and drinks that you can fill up on for even less money. Grab a bag of pistachios ($2 for a ¼ kilo), sit on a nearby bench, and watch a slow Sunday afternoon go by.

TEQUILA

As the name suggests, this is the home of Mexico's national drink, tequila. Nearly everyone here works in the *agave* (the cactus from which tequila is made) fields or in one of the 10 tequila distilleries in town. Cuervo, Sauza, and other companies produce their stuff here, and many offer tours in the late morning. **José Cuervo** (24 de Enero 73, 3 blocks from bus station, tel. 374/2–00–11) gives tours Mondays, Tuesdays and Fridays 11–noon, ending with a free tasting. Groups of more than five people should make an appointment. If you really like tequila, go to the **Herradura** distillery, which makes the best tequila in Mexico in the nearby town of Amatitan.

COMING AND GOING Buses leave from the old bus station (*see* Coming and Going, in Guadalajara, *above*) in Guadalajara every 20 minutes between 6 AM and 9 PM. The trip takes a little less than two hours and costs $2.50. If you want to spend the night, Tequila has plenty of cheap places to stay, most catering to migrant workers.

Aguascalientes

A huge and expanding industrial city, Aguascalientes, capital of the state of the same name, has less colonial charm than other, more popular, Heartland stops. The occasional colonial building raises its weary head from the sprawl, but the city is mostly a tangle of modern buildings and neon, which is just fine by the locals. Even the *aguas calientes* (thermal waters) that originally attracted colonists to the region are no longer very thrilling or even hot for that matter.

The main reason to stop here today is to visit the art museums displaying works by famous local artists Saturnino Herrán, Jesús Contreras, and Enrique Díaz de León. In keeping with the city's artistic legacy, there are at least a dozen art, music, and dance schools that offer a wide variety of classes. These schools, along with the presence of the state university, means

The Spanish dubbed Aguascalientes ciudad perforada (perforated city) because of the catacombs and tunnels built beneath it by indigenous groups before the conquest.

that there are plenty of young, open-minded students around, and most of them are extremely friendly and curious about newcomers. In fact, Aguascalientes is so devoid of tourists that people bend over backward to help you out here. On April 25 the state invites its best artists, musicians, actors, dancers, and poets to participate in a festival that commemorates the feast day of San Marcos. The festival is famous as one of the country's biggest bashes, complete with cockfighting, gambling, bullfighting, and the requisite drinking and dancing.

BASICS

AMERICAN EXPRESS You'd better hope you don't get all your money stolen along with your traveler's checks, because you'll need a taxi to get to **Viajes Chavoya,** the representative for AmEx. They provide all the regular services for cardholders, including cashing traveler's checks and holding mail. *Centro Comercial El Dorado, Local 11, CP 20000, México, tel. 49/13–63–76. Open weekdays 10–2 and 4–7, Sat. 10–1.*

BOOKSTORE **Librería Universal,** in the Centro Comercial El Parián, has books in Spanish of all types. *1 block north of Plaza de la Patria, tel. 49/15—11–84. Open Mon.–Sat. 10–2 and 4–8.*

BANK **Banamex** (Plaza de la Patria, at 5 de Mayo, tel. 49/16–65–70) changes currency weekdays 9–1:30 and has an ATM that accepts Cirrus, Plus, Visa, and MasterCard.

EMERGENCIES You can call the **police** at 49/14–30–43 or 49/14–20–50. The **Cruz Roja** (tel. 49/15–20–55) has ambulance service.

MEDICAL AID The **Hospital Hidalgo,** with some English-speaking doctors, is downtown and open 24 hours. *Galeana 161, south of Plaza de la Patria, tel. 49/15–31–42.*

The **Farmacia Sánchez** has 24-hour service. *Madero 215, east of Plaza de la Patria, tel. 49/15–66–10.*

LAUNDRY **Lavamatic** will wash your clothes for $2 a kilo, or you can do it yourself for $2.50 for a medium load (about 3½ kilos). *Montoro 418-B, east of Plaza de la Patria, tel. 49/16–41–81. Open weekdays 9–2 and 4–8, Sat. 9–8.*

MAIL At the large, pink post office, they'll hold mail sent to you at the following address for up to 10 days: Lista de Correos, Aguascalientes, Aguascalientes, CP 20000, México. *Hospitalidad 108, tel. 49/15–21–18. From Plaza de la Patria, 1 block east on Madero, 1 block north on Morelos, right on Hospitalidad. Open weekdays 8–7, Sat. 9–1.*

PHONES Ladatel public phones are located on the Plaza de la Patria.

SCHOOLS Museums as well as dance and music schools around the city offer courses. Check with the **Casa de la Cultura** (*see* Worth Seeing, *below*) or any of the museums for current course listings.

VISITOR INFORMATION The **Dirección General de Turismo** doesn't have much, but they do have a map of the city and are happy to answer questions. Ask to speak to Raúl, who is especially helpful. *South of Plaza de la Patria, next to Palacio del Gobierno, tel. 49/12–35–11, ext. 132. Open daily 8:30–3 and 5–7.*

COMING AND GOING

BY BUS The **Central Camionera,** open 24 hours, is on the south edge of town, just off Avenida de la Convención. Numerous bus lines have service here, including **Estrella Blanca** (tel. 49/78–20–54), which goes to Guadalajara ($8, 3 hrs), Mexico City ($20, 6½ hrs), and Zacatecas ($3.50, 2½ hrs), as well as other destinations. If you don't want to stop in every town on your way from point A to point B, **Omnibus de México** (tel. 49/78–27–70) offers quicker first-class service to all of the above destinations for a few dollars more. The bus station has a high-tech long-distance phone service and luggage storage. Taxis to downtown should cost $2, or you can take one of the many buses; ask the driver if he goes to el centro.

BY TRAIN The train station (tel. 49/15–21–51) is on the eastern edge of town, some 5 kilometers from downtown. First-class trains depart daily to Ciudad Juárez ($35, 24 hrs) at 7:20 PM, with stops in Zacatecas and Chihuahua, and to Mexico City ($15, 11 hrs) at 10:55 PM, stopping in Querétaro.

GETTING AROUND

Everything you'll want is within walking distance of the **Plaza de la Patria** (the main square). At first, the downtown area seems confusing because the streets fan out from the Plaza, but it's not that tough if you keep in mind that the streets change names at the plaza. Heading south, Juárez and 5 de Mayo change into Colón and José María Chávez, respectively after passing the plaza. Madero, one of the two main drags to the east, becomes Carranza after the plaza. The other main street, Montoro, ends at the plaza. López Mateos, where many bars and nightclubs are, runs east–west.

WHERE TO SLEEP

Downtown is the place for budget travelers to be. The best bargain is the **Hotel Praga** (Zaragoza 214, tel. 49/15–23–57), which has clean rooms for $12 a single, $15 double.

Hotel Imperial. Black, wrought-iron staircases, an inner courtyard, and clean, large rooms, some with balconies, are what this older hotel has to offer. The management is so eager to please that they'll even offer discounts if you stay for more than one day. Singles are $26, doubles $30. *5 de Mayo 106, on north side of plaza, tel. 49/15–16–50. 65 rooms, all with bath. Laundry, luggage storage.*

Hotel Rosales. This hotel might have been the inspiration for an M.C. Escher painting: An endless succession of halls leads to a number of inner courtyards; dizzying tile patterns cover the floor; and spiral staircases lead to single rooms at odd levels. The woman who manages the place seems to have been affected by the strange surroundings as well. Rooms upstairs are small and somewhat quiet, while the first floor rooms are bigger but noisier. The location is prime. Singles are $13.50, doubles $17. *Victoria 104, tel. 49/15–21–65. ½ block north of Plaza de la Patria. 40 rooms, all with bath. Wheelchair access.*

Hotel Señorial. Rooms here have less character than those at Hotel Rosales, but they're also less worn and cleaner, with desks and armoires. The management is extremely accommodating. Singles are $18, doubles $20. *Colón 104, tel. 49/15–16–30. SE cnr of Plaza de la Patria. 62 rooms, all with bath.*

FOOD

➢ UNDER $5 • **Jugos Acapulco.** This hamburger joint is a hangout popular with students. The afternoon comida corrida is $4.50, while a hamburger with fries cost $2.50. Try the delicious all-natural *cerveza de raíz* (rootbeer) for $1. *Allende 106, tel. 49/18–15–20. 1 block north of Plaza de la Patria. Open daily 7 AM–9 PM. Wheelchair access.*

Lonchería Max. If you have the late-night munchies, this taquería operates vampire hours: 8 PM–4 AM or so. Max himself reads minds and will usually have another taco prepared for you just when it's time. Though only a sandwich-and-taco joint, the place is packed on the weekends with drunks, families, and nighthawks. Don't try to hand Max your money personally (he has a cash phobia). *331 Madero, no phone.*

➢ UNDER $10 • **Chicken and Pizza Palace.** A feeding frenzy takes place from noon to 5 at this all-you-can-eat buffet a few blocks south of the plaza. Amid the dizzying array of pasta and salads, the shouting from the kitchen, and the latest video hits blaring through the sound system, you can hunker down in a corner and stuff yourself for only $4.50. *López Mateos 207 Pte., no phone.*

Restaurant Mitla. The classiest bargain in town has service not only with a smile, but in dress whites and ties, no less. This restaurant is a favorite with families, legislators, and cabbies alike. Full meals and drinks are on the expensive side. Try the *tampiqueña tradicional* (beef in salsa with tortillas) for $11. You can get cheaper meals and breakfast ($3–$6) here as well. *Madero 220, tel. 49/16–36–79. East of Plaza de la Patria. Open daily 7 AM–midnight. Wheelchair access.*

Restaurant Vegetariano. Vegetarians swoon over this all-you-can-eat vegetarian buffet. Dishes change daily, but expect to find tasty selections like tofu in tomato and onion sauce, brown rice and broccoli, salads, and spinach soup. Add a pitcher of the daily beverage (made from anything from oats to parsley) and your total is only $5.50. *López Velarde 210, no phone. From Plaza de la Patria, 2 blocks east on Madero, left on Hidalgo (which becomes López Velarde). Buffet served Mon.–Sat. 1:30–5. Wheelchair access.*

WORTH SEEING

The **Plaza de la Patria** is the center of downtown and the site of political demonstrations and concerts, it is partially shaded, full of fountains, and a good place just to hang out. Here you'll find the **Exedra,** a monument to King Carlos IV built in 1807 and later capped with the eagle-and-serpent symbol of revolutionary Mexico. You'll also find the **Palacio del Gobierno,** a fantastic example of colonial architecture with a deep-red hue created from red sandstone and tezontle stones. Inside, 111 arches open onto two inner courtyards. The real highlight of the building, however, is the massive, colorful, and forceful murals by Chilean painter Osvaldo Barra, detailing the history of Aguascalientes. Barra, whose mentor was none other than Diego Rivera, worked on these murals in 1961–62, 1989, and 1991.

CASA DE LA CULTURA Just behind the cathedral and plaza, the Casa is the artistic and social headquarters of Aguascalientes. Built in 1625 as a hacienda for a prominent Spanish family, the building has also been used as a monastery, seminary, and correctional school. Today it hosts rotating art exhibits, films, recitals, and classes of all kinds: dance, music, theater, pottery, and language. The Casa is always the scene of some happening and should be the first place you look for information about upcoming events. *Carranza 101, tel. 49/15–00–97. West of Plaza de la Patria. Admission to exhibits free. Open weekdays 7–2 and 5–9, Sat. 9–2.*

MUSEO DE AGUASCALIENTES Self-taught architect J. Refugio Reyes Rivas undertook the construction of this building at the turn of the 20th century, creating a building in the neoclassical style with a few random details from his other favorite styles thrown in for good measure. Works by the famous local artist Saturnino Herrán are paired with appropriate quotes from Ramón López Velarde, famous local poet and friend of the painter. Other rooms have changing exhibits by contemporary artists. Check the billboard at the entryway for piano concerts held here on Sundays. *Zaragoza 505, tel. 49/15–90–43. Admission $1, free with student ID and Sun. Open Tues.–Sun. 11–6. From Plaza de la Patria, walk 3 blocks east on Madero, left on Zaragoza for 3½ blocks.*

Across the street from the museum is the **Templo de San Antonio,** a bizarre structure with some neoclassical elements and a tall, domed bell tower. The interior is an explosion of colorful murals depicting events in the life of Saint Anthony.

MUSEO DE ARTE CONTEMPORANEO This small but exquisite museum concentrates on local as well as nationally recognized artists of the abstract, surreal, and *arte fantástico* movements. *Montoro 222, tel. 49/18–69–01. 1½ blocks east of Plaza de la Patria. Admission $1, free with student ID. Open Tues.–Fri. 10–2, weekends 11–8.*

MUSEO DE JOSE GUADALUPE POSADA This small museum is dedicated to the artist and journalist whose political caricatures and prints helped stir dissent against Porfirio Díaz during the Revolution. The museum exhibits his art, contains a public library, and offers printing and painting classes. *North side of Jardín del Encino, tel. 49/15–45–56. From Plaza de la Patria, south on José María Chávez, left on Pimentel. Admission $1, 50¢ with student ID. Open Tues.–Sun. 10–6.*

Next door to the museum is the **Parroquia del Encino,** a baroque church with huge oil paintings from the 19th century depicting the Stations of the Cross, and a black statue of Christ. *Open daily 6–1 and 4–9. Mass schedule posted at entryway.*

AFTER DARK

Bars and nightclubs are on the edges of the city, making it impossible to get to the hip spots without shelling out $3 for a taxi; bars and clubs along López Mateos, catering to locals with salsa and quebradita, are a little closer to the center of town. The place to be is **The Station** (Carretera al Campestre 129, tel. 49/12–09–91), which is crowded Fridays and Saturdays with the beautiful people and those who want them. There's no cover. **Alcatraz** (Aguascalientes Norte, near the Pulgas Pandas sports club) is another good bar. For dancing, **El Cabus** (Hotel Las Trojes, Carretera al Campestre, tel. 49/73–00–06) dominates the scene, with an outrageous $12 cover. They're open Thursday–Saturday until 2:30 AM. A quieter early-evening scene can be found at **Café Parroquia** (Hidalgo, just before López Velarde, no phone), attracting bohemians who spend hours over cappuccino and cigarettes. They're open until 9 PM, and coffee is about $1.

Zacatecas

Perched in hilly country at about 2,700 meters, Zacatecas has chaotic *adoquín* (cobblestone) streets, beautiful colonial buildings, a history built on silver mines, and a big university. The art museums are fantastic, and the streets are alive weekend nights. Despite all these attractions, relatively few foreign tourists visit the city.

Although indigenous people knew of the mineral riches of the area long before the conquistadors arrived, it was not until the Spanish forced the mining of local hills that the city of Zacatecas was founded. Legend says that a silver trinket given to one Spaniard brought on the mining fever. The first operations began in the mid-16th century, and by 1728 local mines were producing one-fifth of the country's silver. The silver barons' extravagant mansions bear witness to the prosperity of old Zacatecas.

The buildings in the historic center of Zacatecas are made of a sandstone called cantera rosa, giving it a Miami Beach-pink brightness.

Silver mining tapered off during the fight for independence and declined even further during the Revolution, as political control of the area was hotly contested. Benito Juárez and his troops fought a decisive battle against local insurgents here in 1871, and Zacatecas was again the site of fighting in 1914, when Pancho Villa and his ragtag army routed 12,000 Huerta loyalists.

Amid the mining and fighting, Zacatecas remained a haven for intellectuals and artists, among them renowned artists Francisco Goitia and Pedro Coronel, whose namesake museums are world famous. Other Zacatecan cultural treasures have remained relatively untouched, including perhaps the finest example of colonial baroque architecture in all of Mexico, the **Catedral**

Basílica Menor; a colonial **aqueduct;** and churches and haciendas. Though currently home to a population of almost one million, Zacatecas maintains a small town, traditional attitude in many ways: don't expect to do much here between 2 and 5 in the afternoon, when the whole city shuts down for the siesta. Straw hats and cowboy boots are almost mandatory gear for men of all ages, and women tend to disappear from the streets after 9 PM unless accompanied. However, the presence of the state university here guarantees the existence of open-minded students, who can be found in cafés and plazas around the city. The local economy is now largely dairy-based, giving the city a funny mix of students and farmers with a lot of art thrown in. The drawbacks to Zacatecas are minor: The high altitude requires a period of adjustment, and the city can be chilly, even in summer.

BASICS

AMERICAN EXPRESS **Viajes Mazzocco,** the AmEx representative, offers the usual services for cardholders, including emergency check-cashing and mail holding. *Enlace 115, Colonia Sierra de Alicia, Zacatecas, Zacatecas, CP 98001, México, tel. 492/2–08–59. From cathedral, take Hidalgo (becomes Ortega), right on Enrique Estrada just before the aqueduct, left on Enlace after Museo Goitia. Open weekdays 9–7, Sat. 9–noon.*

AUTO PARTS/SERVICE **Refaccionaria López y Lara** is a huge auto-parts store that actually has people available during siesta. Other auto parts stores and mechanics can be found along López Mateos. *López Mateos 101, tel. 492/2–07–11. Open weekdays 9–7, Sat. 9–2.*

BOOKSTORE **Librería Universal** has a good selection of Spanish-language texts, from books on astrology and botany to literary classics. *Hidalgo 109, tel. 492/4–12–40. From cathedral, walk southwest on Hidalgo 3 blocks. Open Mon.–Sat. 10–2:30 and 4:30–8:30.*

CASA DE CAMBIO **Banamex** changes traveler's checks and cash weekdays 9–noon and has an ATM that accepts Cirrus, Plus, Visa, and MasterCard. *Hidalgo 132, tel. 492/2–58–02.*

EMERGENCIES For medical or legal help call the toll-free tourist line (91/800–9–03–92).

LAUNDRY **Lavandería Aquazac** will wash and dry your clothes for $2 a kilo. Bring your clothes in before noon to get them back the same day. *López Velarde 609, tel. 492/4–01–82. Across from Hotel Colón. Open weekdays 9–2 and 4–6:30, Sat. 9–2.*

MAIL The post office will hold mail sent to you at the following address for up to 10 days: Lista de Correos, Zacatecas, Zacatecas, CP 98001, México. *Allende 111, tel. 492/2–01–96. Open weekdays 8–7, Sat. 9–1.*

MEDICAL AID **Farmacia Issstezac** (Dr. Hierro 512, tel. 492/2-88-89) is open round the clock. **Clínica Hospital Santa Elena** is open 24 hours and has English-speaking doctors. *Guerrero 143, tel. 492/2–68–61. From the cathedral, southwest on Hidalgo, left on Allende, right on Guerrero.*

Clíñica Dental Zacatecas gives free dental exams. *Salazar 338, tel. 492/2–68–03. From pedestrian bridge on López Mateos, ½ block west to Salazar. Open weekdays 9:30–2 and 4–8, Sat. 9:30–2.*

PHONES For collect calls, use the Ladatel phones near the cathedral. You can also make international calls from the caseta de larga distancia (Callejón de Cuevas 103) in the centro. They're open weekdays 9–9, Saturday 9–2 and 4–8.

VISITOR INFORMATION The **Módulo de Información de Turismo,** across from the cathedral, has brochures and a good street map. For tourist information over the phone, call 492/2–66–83. *Hidalgo 603, no phone. Open daily 8–8.*

COMING AND GOING

BY BUS The **Central Camionera** (Terrenos de la Isabélica 1) is on the western edge of town, and the RUTA 8 bus runs to and from downtown until about 9:30 PM. A taxi ride to the downtown area costs about $2.50. **Estrella Blanca** (tel. 492/2–06–84) travels to Aguascalientes

($5.50, 2 hrs); Durango ($11.50, 5 hrs); Guadalajara ($13, 6 hrs); Mexico City ($23, 8 hrs); and San Luis Potosí ($6.50, 2½ hrs) almost every hour. **Omnibus de México** (tel. 492/2–54–95) serves the above destinations and has one bus per day to Guanajuato ($11, 6 hrs), leaving at 5 PM. Luggage storage is available 7 AM–10 PM.

BY TRAIN The train station (tel. 492/2–02–95) is just off Avenida González Ortega, south of downtown. Buses stop near the terminal, but a taxi ride costs only about $1.50 from downtown. Two daily southbound trains leave at about 4:55 AM (2nd class, buy tickets on the train) and 8:15 PM (1st class, buy tickets from 7 PM until the train leaves) for Aguascalientes ($3 1st class, $2 2nd class), León ($7.50 1st class, $5 2nd class), and Mexico City ($18, 1st class only). The trip to Aguascalientes takes two hours, to Mexico City about 13 hours. A northbound, first-class train to Chihuahua ($23) and Ciudad Juárez ($32) leaves at 9:55 AM; tickets are sold between 8 AM and 10 AM.

GETTING AROUND

Although everything you could want to see is in or near downtown, it's easy to get lost here. The pattern of the streets is dictated by topography. There are many side streets, *callejones* (alleyways), and winding thoroughfares. The main street running northeast–southwest is Avenida Hidalgo, which intersects Avenida Juárez. The **Catedral Basílica Menor,** at the heart of town, is a convenient, easily visible landmark.

WHERE TO SLEEP

The hotel strip, López Mateos, just south of the center, has plenty of places to stay in all price categories. The five-minute walk to downtown is pretty entertaining—watch out for speeding buses and candy vendors who take up most of the narrow sidewalk space.

➤ UNDER $15 • **Hotel Conde de Villareal.** Because this hole-in-the-wall hotel is closer to town, they charge more than what the rooms are worth. Nevertheless, it's still budget-friendly, if you don't mind green paint, the pervasive smell of mildew, and keeping company with the mostly single men who stay here. Singles are $10, doubles $13.50. *Zamora 303, tel. 492/2–12–00. From pedestrian bridge on López Mateos, go ½ block west and right on Salazar until it becomes Zamora. 28 rooms, all with bath.*

Hotel Río Grande. Rooms in this three-story hotel overlook either a central courtyard or the city. Medium-size rooms are immaculate, with tiled floors, big comfy beds, and 24-hour hot water. The place is popular with young folks and families, which means it can be pretty noisy at night and early in the morning, but see what your budget has to say about the price: Singles cost about $8.50, doubles, $10.50. *Calzada de la Paz 513, tel. 492/2–53–49. From the pedestrian bridge on Mateos, walk right on Calzada de la Paz; a sign marked HOTEL directs you up the hill. 66 rooms, all with bath.*

➤ UNDER $25 • **Hotel Colón.** This clean and comfy hotel is farther from downtown than many other budget hotels. Rooms are carpeted and have phones, although the location right on López Mateos means the traffic noise will disturb your pleasant dreams. Families on vacation make up most of the guests. Singles are $19, doubles $22. *López Mateos 105, tel. 492/2–89–25. East on López Mateos, 5 blocks past pedestrian bridge. 37 rooms, all with bath. MC, V.*

Hotel Gami. This newly built, three-story hotel is about the same distance south of downtown as the Hotel Colón. Guests and management like to hang out in the hotel's wide halls. Smallish rooms have new red carpeting and small, clean bathrooms. Singles are $19, doubles, $22. *López Mateos 309, tel. 492/2–80–05. About 3 blocks east of pedestrian bridge. 60 rooms, all with bath. Laundry. MC, V.*

➤ UNDER $35 • **Posada de los Condes.** Smack dab in the center of town, this hotel has very large, spotless rooms, some with balconies and French windows. Singles are $27, doubles, $33.50. *Juárez 107, tel. 492/2–10–93. From López Mateos, left on Salazar just before pedes-*

trian bridge, right on Zamora, left on Juárez. 57 rooms, all with bath. Luggage storage, wheelchair access.

FOOD

Zacatecan restaurants cater to a wide variety of tastes, offering everything from Greek to Italian to Chinese cuisine. Tons of small restaurants also serve *menudo* (tripe soup) and tacos made with every meat imaginable. Regional specialties are primarily in the dessert family; among these are *queso de tuna* (a gelatin-like dessert made from the *tuna,* or prickly pear), *dulce de leche* (a candy made from milk that's so sweet it hurts your teeth), and *capirotada* (a sort of bread pudding with raisins and cinnamon).

➢ UNDER $5 • **Los Molocajetes.** Conchita, the owner of this clean, simple kitchen, makes all her food from scratch. She and her daughters are so friendly you'll want to eat all your meals here. The comida corrida is $5, but other traditional dishes like chicken and beef flautas are only $2.50. *López Mateos 409, no phone. Under pedestrian bridge. Open daily 8 AM–11 PM.*

Taquería y Rosticería La Cabaña. The walk past roasting chickens and meat to the clean, wood-paneled dining area here will make you hungry for the meal to come. Service is efficient and attentive, despite the constant crowds. A big plate of roasted chicken with refried beans, salad, homemade potato chips, tortillas, and all the salsa and *rajas* (chile strips) you want is a steal at $3. Tacos are 40¢–50¢ each and come in all types, from carne asada to *sesos* (brains) and *lengua* (tongue). *Aldama 245, no phone. From cathedral, southwest on Hidalgo, left on Juárez to Aldama (also known as Zamora). Open daily 7 AM–1 AM. Wheelchair access.*

➢ UNDER $10 • **El Dragón de Oro.** The new location has less colonial charm than the old one in the center of town, but at least you can order something other than tacos for a change. If you're lucky, the stereo will be playing old American country and western and jazz to accompany your Chinese dinner. The *pollo almendrado* (almond chicken) is about $8.50, while the *sopa fu chuc* (a tofu and noodle soup in a miso-like broth) and wonton soup are perfect light choices for $5. Avoid the *camarones en agridulce* (sweet and sour shrimp) unless paying $10 for four shrimp is your idea of a good time. *González Ortega, at Rayón, tel. 492/4–09–90. From the cathedral, southwest on Hidalgo (which becomes Ortega), 2 blocks past aqueduct. Open daily 2–10.*

La Cantera Musical. This fun, brightly decorated place is popular with local families and tourists. Excellent *ranchera* music and a mini-reproduction of the *teleférico* (tram) strung across the ceiling are amusing. The biggest seller is the *asado de bodajerezano* (pork with chiles, orange, and laurel, served with rice) for $9, but other Mexican fare is available for $4–$5. Try the *platillo ranchero*, a selection of appetizers such as quesadillas, *chicharrón* (pork rind) and guacamole, for $10 for two people. *Tacuba 2, tel. 492/2–88–28. Underneath Mercado González Ortega. Open daily 8 AM–11 PM.*

Restaurant Mesón de la Mina. This downtown restaurant across from the Posada de los Condes is a favorite with *taxistas* (cabbies) and students alike. Bright and noisy, it's open late and offers quick, traditional fare at good prices. The *huevos con chorizo* (eggs with sausage), chilaquiles, and chicken with *mole poblano* (chile and chocolate sauce) are all recommended and cost $4, $4.50, and $6 respectively. *Juárez 15, tel. 492/2–27–73. From cathedral, SW on Hidalgo for 4 blocks, left on Juárez. Open daily 8 AM–11 PM.*

WORTH SEEING

There's no way to see all of Zacatecas in one day; think about exploring one cluster of sights each day. Suggested areas for exploration include all points southwest (the Aqueduct, Enrique Estrada park, and Goitia museum); hilltop sights (the Mina el Edén, Cerro de la Bufa, and teleférico); and the center of town (the two Coronel museums, the cathedral, and the Palacio del Gobierno). The museums are excellent. The weekly cultural paper *Tips* has a listing of upcoming shows, concerts, and exhibits and is available free at the tourist office and around town.

ACUEDUCTO DEL CUBO This colonial aqueduct, constructed entirely of magnificent rose-color sandstone formed into 39 high arches, is a strange and beautiful sight in the middle of the city. Just behind the aqueduct is the old **Plaza de Toros,** which has been refashioned into an incredible luxury hotel—it's worth a look inside, but run if anyone asks if you need a room. **Parque Enrique Estrada** (not to be confused with the hunk from CHiPs), a gorgeous, lush park with fountains, a waterfall, and romantic couples, is across the street from the aqueduct. *From cathedral, SW on Hidalgo (which becomes Ortega) for about 6 blocks.*

CATEDRAL BASILICA MENOR This cathedral is without a doubt the most imposing structure in Zacatecas, and one of the finest examples of Mexican baroque architecture in the country, at least on the outside. The cathedral was built between 1612 and 1752, but the more recently refurbished interior is as powerful in its neoclassical simplicity as the exterior is in its complexity. Just down the street is the state-operated theater, the **Teatro Calderón.** Built in the late 19th century, the theater has beautiful stained-glass windows and is the venue for national and international ballets, operas, and plays. Students congregate on the steps outside the theater.

CERRO DE LA BUFA Thought by the thirsty Spaniards to resemble a *bufa* (wineskin), the mountaintop offers a magnificent view of Zacatecas and the surrounding countryside. You can hike or take the teleférico to the top and explore the **Museo de la Toma de Zacatecas,** a museum dedicated to Pancho Villa's 1914 victory here, with photographs, diagrams, a cannon, and some weapons. Admission is about $1.50 (half that with student ID), and the museum is open Tuesday–Sunday 10–5. Beside the museum is an 18th-century chapel honoring the patroness of Zacatecas, called **La Capilla de la Virgen del Patrocinio.** Just in back of the chapel is the **Mausoleo a los Hombres Ilustres de Zacatecas.** *SW on Hidalgo to Callejón Luis Moya, rightto Calle de la Mantequilla, then left and up, up, and up, across road to path.*

MINA EL EDEN A short trip by tram or a healthy walk straight up Juárez past the huge red IMSS Hospital takes you to another of Zacatecas's star attractions. The tour of this mine is conducted in Spanish and begins with a ride on a miniature train into the middle level of the mine. In the mid-1500s, when the mine was at its peak, an average of eight slaves, responsible for carrying heavy loads through the wet darkness, died here each day. Conditions changed somewhat after independence and again with the Revolution, but mining continued (without electricity) until 1964, when incorrectly placed explosives caused the lower levels to flood. Ironically, the mine is now home to a disco (*see* After Dark, *below*). Bring a sweater for the tour, as it gets pretty chilly in the mine. *Mina el Edén, tel. 492/2–30–02. Admission: about $3.50. From cathedral, SW on Hidalgo 4 blocks, right on Juárez (becomes Torreón). Open daily 11–6:30.*

MUSEO FRANCISCO GOITIA The French-style mansion was built in 1948 for the governor, but now houses works by the Zacatecan artist Francisco Goitia, a 20th-century painter most famous for his *Tata Jesucristo.* Other modern Zacatecan artists are represented as well. The grounds are beautiful, overflowing with well-tended flower beds and fountains. *Just past Enrique Estrada park, tel. 492/12–02–11. Admission: $3.50. Open Tues.–Sun. 10–1:30 and 5–7:30.*

MUSEO PEDRO CORONEL Two blocks northeast of the cathedral is a museum dedicated to Zacatecas's favorite son, artist Pedro Coronel. Coronel was also a prolific collector (in fact, a much better collector than artist), and the works on display here are world-famous. You'll find works by Goya, Miró, Cocteau, Kandinsky, Motherwell, Picasso, Chagall, and Dalí; ancient Greek pottery and statues; Indian, Chinese, Tibetan, and Japanese art; and a large collection of African and Latin American masks. *Plaza de Santo Domingo, tel. 492/2–80–21. Admission: $3.50, $2 with student ID. Open Fri.–Sat. and Mon.–Wed. 10–2 and 4–7, Sun. 10–5.*

MUSEO RAFAEL CORONEL Named for Pedro Coronel's brother, this museum is housed in the former Convento y Templo de San Francisco. The grounds are beautiful enough in their own right, while the collection of character masks used in regional festivals is so enormous that you'll have a problem deciding where to look first. Detailed explanations in Spanish give a historical and cultural background for the masks, and a video provides more information. The museum also has a collection of 19th-century puppets. *Ex-Convento de San Francisco, tel.*

492/2–81–16. From cathedral, NE on Hidalgo (which becomes Juan de Tolosa) around bend to right. Admission: $2, $1 with student ID. Open Mon.–Tues. 10–2 and 4–7, Thurs.–Sat. 10–2 and 4–7, Sun. 10–5.

PALACIO DEL GOBIERNO Adjacent to the cathedral is the 1927 state capital building, originally the mansion of a local silver baron. Inside you'll find a brilliant mural of Zacatecas's history by the noted Zacatecan artist Antonio Pintor Rodríguez. The mural was completed in 1970. *Hidalgo 602. Open weekdays 8–3:30 and 6–9.*

TELEFERICO This Swiss-made tram offers unparalleled views of Zacatecas. The ride is best combined with the Mina el Edén tour, because the west door of the mine is easily accessible via elevator at the end of the tour. Otherwise you'll have to struggle up the massive flight of stairs just to the right of the mine entrance. *Fare: about $3 round trip. Tram runs Tues.–Sun. 10–6, weather permitting.*

AFTER DARK

You'll be at a loss for things to do at night during the week, but Zacatecas picks up on the weekends. Two discos pump out the latest dance mixes and some disco favorites. **El Elefante Blanco** (Paseo Díaz Ordaz 2, tel. 492/2–71–04), near the teleférico station atop Cerro del Grillo, offers great views of nighttime Zacatecas for the steep cover charge of $10. Drinks are $3. **El Melacante,** also known as La Mina, is situated deep in the Mina El Eden. Although you may balk at the $10 cover (more than most miners earned in a year), it's the most popular dance spot. Drinks here also run $3. Both discos are open Thursday–Sunday 9:30 PM–3 AM. **La Terraza** (Centro Comercial El Mercado G. Ortega, tel. 492/2–32–70) closes by 9 PM, but beer is cheap ($1) and you can dine on the balcony. Another bar popular with the younger crowd is **Reina María 2 English Pub** (Tacuba 208, across from Plazuela Goitia). For movies, try **Biblioteca Mauricio Magdaleno,** across from the Plaza Independencia, where a video center shows excellent free Mexican films and dubbed or subtitled foreign films nightly at 5:30. At the entrance is a bulletin board with notices of upcoming local events, or look in the publication *Tips* for more info.

For a night of inexpensive fun, hang out in the Plazuela Goitia (on Hidalgo, ½ block before the cathedral) where bands play on weekends. If you're lucky, you'll run into a private fiesta with music and a donkey with gallons of mezcal on its back.

BAJA CALIFORNIA   6

By Jamie Davidson

The image of a tall, spiny saguaro cactus framed against the cool blue of the Pacific typifies the rugged, surprising landscape of Baja. The bustling, northern cities and southern resorts, both renowned for wild nightlife, offset the sedate, out-of-the-way towns of central Baja. The peninsula's diversity attracts very different types of travelers, including those who do nothing except fry their skin by day and their brain cells by night, and sports enthusiasts who come for the windsurfing, fishing, and scuba diving.

Only in recent years, with the influx of people from all over the country, has Baja become genuinely integrated into mainstream Mexican culture and consciousness. For the past few hundred years, the peninsula had been frontier territory. Although Hernán Cortés officially "discovered" Baja while looking for Amazon queens and pearls, Jesuit missionaries in the late 17th century were the first Europeans to settle Baja successfully. From their original outpost in Loreto, the Spaniards extended the Spanish frontier into what is now northern California. With Mexico's independence and the demise of the missions, Baja withered, leaving a few scattered ranches and mining towns, until tourism briefly boomed in the 1930s. But only in the early 1970s, with the completion of the Trans-Peninsular Highway (Highway 1), did Baja's isolation erode and the region become a popular destination.

Today, Northern Baja is a favorite with tourists, thousands of whom cross the border into Tijuana in search of exotica; most just end up buying trinkets and partying until they drop. The beach towns of Rosarito, Ensenada, and San Felipe attract weekend crowds seeking daytime fun and nighttime parties. Because of the region's tawdry reputation, people interested in an authentic "Mexican" experience often skip Tijuana and its environs altogether. The perversities of tourism taken to extremes aside, northern Baja is intriguing, if you're willing to wander off the tourist track and explore: The region is very diverse, partly because of the migrants who come from all over Mexico to look for work in the region's growing economy.

Baja's economic boom means that prices are often higher here than in other parts of Mexico.

Central Baja is a land for escapists. Tourism here centers around camping, fishing, whale-watching (from January through March), exploring the miles of lonely beaches, and swimming. Highway 1 runs through a number of small towns, which, except for the French mining town of Santa Rosalía, bear the imprint of the Spanish missionaries who founded them as outposts of "civilization"; adobe missions built with Indian labor still survive. Dirt roads criss-cross the Sierra (the mountainous interior), connecting isolated hamlets, ranches, abandoned missions, and small fishing villages.

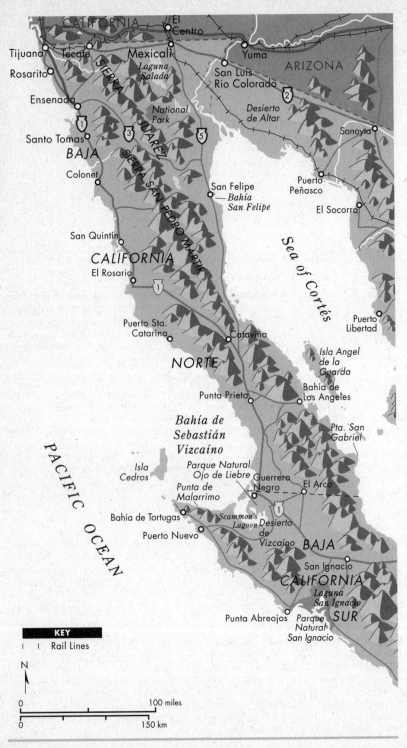

CALIFORNIA

Tijuana
Tecate
Rosarito
Ensenada

El Centro
Mexicali
Laguna Salada

Yuma
San Luis Rio Colorado

ARIZONA

Desierto de Altar

SIERRA

JUAREZ

National Park

Santo Tomas
BAJA
Colonet

SIERRA SAN PEDRO MARTIR

San Felipe
— *Bahía San Felipe*

Sonoyta

Puerto Peñasco

El Socorro

San Quintín

CALIFORNIA
El Rosario

Puerto Sta. Catarina

Cataviña

NORTE

Sea of Cortés

Puerto Libertad

Isla Angel de la Guarda

Punta Prieta

Bahía de Los Angeles

Bahía de Sebastián Vizcaíno

Isla Cedros

PACIFIC OCEAN

Parque Natural Ojo de Liebre

Punta de Malarrimo

Bahía de Tortugas

Puerto Nuevo

Scammon's Lagoon

Guerrero Negro

El Arco

Pta. San Gabriel

Desierto de Vizcaíno

BAJA

CALIFORNIA

San Ignacio

Laguna San Ignacio

Punta Abreojos

Parque Natural San Ignacio

SUR

KEY
ı | ı Rail Lines

N

0 _____ 100 miles

0 _____ 150 km

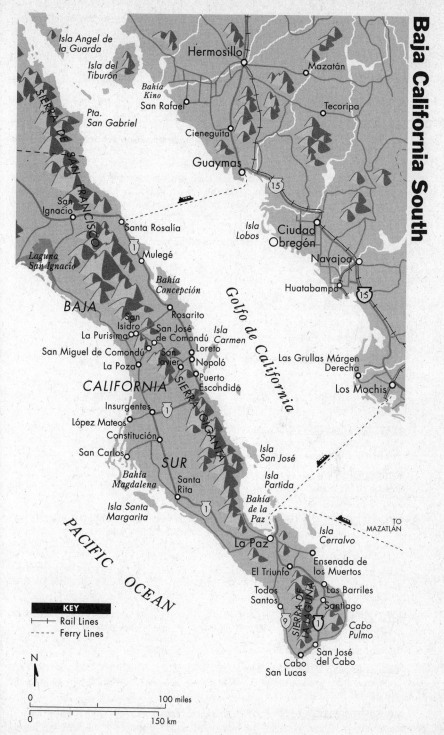

Isla Angel de
la Guarda

Isla del
Tiburón

Bahía
Kino
San Rafael

Pta.
San Gabriel

Hermosillo

Mazatán

Tecoripa

Cieneguita

SIERRA DE SAN FRANCISCO

San
Ignacio

Santa Rosalía

Guaymas

15

Isla
Lobos

Ciudad
Obregón

Navajoa

Huatabampo

15

Mulegé

Laguna
San Ignacio

Bahía
Concepción

BAJA

Rosarito

San
Isidro

San José
de Comondú

Isla
Carmen

Golfo de California

La Purisima

San Miguel de Comondú

San
Javier

Loreto

Las Grullas Márgen
Derecha

La Poza

Nopoló

Los Mochis

CALIFORNIA

Puerto
Escondido

Insurgentes

1

SIERRA GIGANTA

López Mateos

Constitución

San Carlos

SUR

Isla
San José

Bahía
Magdalena

Santa
Rita

Isla
Partida

Isla Santa
Margarita

1

Bahía
de la
Paz

TO
MAZATLÁN

La Paz

Isla
Cerralvo

PACIFIC OCEAN

El Triunfo

Ensenada de
los Muertos

Todos
Santos

SIERRA DE LA LAGUNA

Los Barriles

Santiago

9

1

Cabo
Pulmo

San José
del Cabo

Cabo
San Lucas

KEY

Rail Lines

Ferry Lines

N

0   100 miles

0   150 km

Southern Baja is famous for its white sandy beaches and the vivid hues of its waters. Cabo San Lucas, at the southern tip of the peninsula, is the major resort town where self-indulgence reigns supreme and fishing ranks a close second. San José del Cabo, just to the east, is a quieter city. Tourism still dominates the economy, but it's of a more subdued and relaxed variety. Although Los Cabos, as the two towns are collectively known, are rapidly being built up, there are still miles of infrequently visited coastline along the Pacific and between San José del Cabo and La Paz.

Tijuana

Tijuana is not a pleasant place. It sprawls along what is reputed to be the most heavily crossed border in the world, and its feel and pace are very different from those of other Mexican cities. Popular wisdom among both foreigners and Mexicans from elsewhere in the country has it that Tijuana isn't a "real" Mexican city, but instead an amalgamation of Mexican and gringo cultures, or simply a lawless den of hedonism. In certain respects, these impressions are accurate, as illustrated by the crowds of foreigners, made-for-export *artesanía* (crafts), dollar beers, eyebrow-raising sex shows, and prostitutes on downtown corners. The main drag, Avenida Revolución, is by day a magnet for the middle-age, trinket-buying crowd; by night, it attracts partiers (mostly under 21 and from the United States) who drink, dance, and pass out. Just one block west of Revolución, however, is Tijuana's principal commercial street, Avenida Constitución, lined with pharmacies, hardware stores, and clothing shops. Constitución's buzzing pace, microphone-wielding salesmen, and strolling families with father and son in cowboy hats could be part of any city in northern Mexico.

BASICS

AMERICAN EXPRESS The AmEx office is in the **Viajes Carrousel** travel agency. If you're a cardholder, you can cash personal checks or have your mail held here. Anyone can exchange traveler's checks. *Sánchez Taboada, at Clemente Orozco, tel. 66/34–36–60. Open weekdays 9–6, Sat. 9–noon. Mailing address: Blvd. Sánchez Taboada y Clemente Orozco, Edificio Husa, Zona Río, Tijuana, Baja California Norte, CP 22320, México.*

AUTO PARTS/SERVICE **Serviautos** and **Servipartes** (Revolución 216, at Coahuila, tel. 66/85–97–22) can help you out daily 8–8. The **Green Angels** (tel. 66/23–38–77), a government service, offer free assistance to drivers with car trouble.

BUCKET SHOP **Viajes Victoria Travel** offers good plane fares from San Diego to destinations throughout the United States and Europe, and they speak English. *Centro Comercial Plaza Río Tijuana, tel. 66/34–16–45. Open Mon.–Sat. 9–8.*

CASAS DE CAMBIO Moneychangers abound in the tourist district of Tijuana, but they only deal in cash. The best place to change money is on San Ysidro Boulevard in San Ysidro, just before you cross into Tijuana. To purchase or change traveler's checks, try the AmEx office (*see above*) or **Banamex** (La Juventud, just across the pedestrian bridge, tel. 66/83–52–48). The latter is open for money exchange weekdays 9–5. ATMs accepting Visa and Mastercard are plentiful and can be found at most banks. Try **Bancomer** on Constitución and Calle 5a; **Bital** on Revolución and Calle 2a; or **Serfin** on Constitución and Calle 6a.

CONSULATES **Canada.** Citizens of Australia can also find help at the Canadian consulate. *Germán Gedovius 5–202, Zona Río, tel. 66/84–04–61. Open weekdays 9–1.*

United Kingdom. *Salinas 1500, tel. 66/81–73–23. Open weekdays 9–2 and 4–6.*

United States. In an after-hours emergency, call the San Diego office at 619/585–2000 and an agent in Tijuana will be contacted. *Tapachula 96, Col. Hipódromo, tel. 66/81–74–00. Open weekdays 8–4:30.*

CROSSING THE BORDER U.S. and Canadian citizens do not need tourist cards to travel as far south as Ensenada (including San Felipe); a driver's license or birth certificate is sufficient identification. For travel south of Ensenada, tourist cards are available from the **Delegación de**

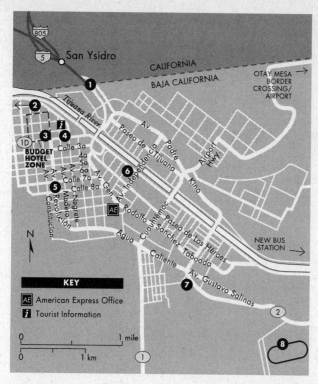

Agua Caliente
Race Track, **8**

Beaches, **2**

Central Viejo
bus station, **4**

Centro Cultural, **6**

El Toreo (downtown
bullring), **7**

Palacio Frontón, **5**

Plaza Revolución, **3**

San Ysidro Border
Crossing, **1**

Servicios Migratorios (immigration office) just over the border, which is open 24 hours a day. It is a good idea to bring your passport if you plan to travel elsewhere in the country, especially southern Mexico. For more information on visas and tourist cards, *see* Chapter 1, Basics.

EMERGENCIES In Tijuana, contact the **police** at 134; the **fire** depatment at 136; the **Cruz Roja** (for an ambulance) at 132.

LAUNDRY Tijuana's laundromats are inconvenient, and you're probably better off rinsing your undies in your hotel sink. But, if you're desperate, try **Lavamática la Limpiecita,** where you can use a machine for $1.50. *L. Portillo 10, at Independencia Ote., tel. 66/23–62–20. Open daily 8 AM–9:30 PM.*

MEDICAL AID Many San Diegans go to Tijuana for dental work, which can cost two-thirds less than in the States—dentists line the streets off Revolución. To find an English-speaking doctor, check the cards displayed at the Chamber of Commerce (*see* Visitor Information, *below*). Plenty of 24-hour pharmacies lie along Constitución, including **Farmacia Regis** (tel. 66/23–14–61), which is at the corner of Calle 5a.

MAIL It's both cheaper and faster to send international mail from the United States than from Mexico. If that's impractical, Tijuana's post office is on Avenida Negrete and Calle 11a. They'll hold mail for you at the following address for up to 10 days: Lista de Correos, Avenida Negrete y Calle 11a, Tijuana, Baja California Norte, CP 22000, México. The **Telecomm** building next door sends telegrams, faxes, and telexes. *Post office open weekdays 8–7, weekends 9:30 AM–1 PM, tel. 66/84–79–50. Telecomm open weekdays 8–8, weekends 8–1.*

PHONES Collect calls are easy to place from Tijuana's pay phones, but it's more expensive to make international calls from Mexico than from the United States. If you want to call from a *caseta de larga distancia* (long-distance telephone office) go to **Helocopias Rubi,** where calls to the States are discounted 50% on weekends. *Calle 7a No. 1906, near Revolución, tel. 66/85–03–11. Open weekdays 9 AM–10 PM, Sat. 9–9, Sun. 8 AM–10 PM.*

VISITOR INFORMATION Tijuana has a number of tourist offices. The most centrally located is run by **CANACO**, the Tijuana Chamber of Commerce, which has a friendly, English-speaking staff, some decent maps, and a public phone and restroom. *Revolución, at Calle 1a, tel. 66/85–16–85. Open daily 8–8.*

Just across the San Ysidro border into Mexico is the **Tourism and Convention Bureau**, which also sells auto insurance. *In building on left just after taxi stand, tel. 66/83–13–110 or 66/83–14–05. Open daily 9–7.*

COMING AND GOING

BY BUS Tijuana has two bus stations, the Central Camionera, which is served by major mainland companies, and the Central Viejo, where you can catch buses for elsewhere in northern Baja. **Greyhound/Trailways** buses to the United States depart from both stations, as well as from the station on the San Ysidro side of the border (tel. 619/428–5277). Buses depart every hour between 5 AM and 6 PM for San Diego ($4, 50 min) and Los Angeles ($18, 3½ hrs), continue on to San Francisco ($62, 12–13 hrs) and Seattle ($106, 34 hrs). There are large, expensive lockers in San Ysidro's Greyhound Bus station, but it's better to lug your gear next door to **UPS**, open Monday–Saturday 9–6, Sunday 10–2, which only charges $1 for 24 hours.

Four bus companies share the **Central Camionera** (tel. 66/26–17–01) on the eastern edge of Tijuana, far from the budget hotel area and most tourist activities. **Tres Estrellas de Oro** operates buses throughout the country, including hourly first- and second-class service to Guadalajara ($78 1st-class, $68 2nd-class; 36 hrs) round the clock. Buses also leave for Mexico City ($100 1st class, $93 2nd class; 48 hrs) every hour between 9 AM and 11 PM. **Transportes Norte de Sonora** and **Transportes Pacífico** also have express buses down the mainland coast to Guadalajara and Mexico City. **Autotransportes de Baja California** serves Baja with hourly first- and second-class buses between 6 AM and 8 PM to Mexicali ($7–$8, 3 hrs), San Felipe ($15–$17, 6 hrs), and Ensenada ($5–$6, 1½ hrs). La Paz ($61, 22 hrs) is served only by first-class buses, with departures at 8 AM, noon, 6 PM, and 10:30 PM.

A taxi will take you down Revolución to the Central Camionera for $7–$10, but your best option is to catch a brown-and-white colectivo marked CENTRAL CAMIONERA from the stop on Madero between Calles 2a and 3a. The colectivo trip takes about 15 minutes and costs less than $1. To get from the bus station to the budget-hotel/tourist area, find a bus that says CENTRO. The station offers luggage storage for 65¢ an hour; the desk is open daily 6:30 AM–10:30 PM. You can also place long distance calls (cash only) from the 24-hour **Computel** booth. Money exchange is available daily 10 AM–9:30 PM.

The **Central Viejo** (Madero, at Calle 1a, tel. 66/88–07–52), serves northern Baja. Buses to Rosarito ($1, 20 min) leave every hour between 6:20 AM and 8 PM. Buses to Ensenada ($4, 2 hrs) leave at 5 AM, 9 AM, noon, 3 PM, and 6 PM. Buses run to Tecate ($2, 1½ hrs) every half-hour from 5:30 AM to 9 PM. The station is within walking distance of both the border and the budget-hotel area. To reach the station from the border, cross over the Río Tijuana pedestrian bridge and continue straight on Calle 1a. To get to the budget-hotel area from the bus station, continue on Calle 1a to Coahuila.

BY TROLLEY The **San Diego Trolley** (tel. 619/231–8549) runs from the America Plaza Transfer Station (C St., btw Kettner and India) in downtown San Diego to San Ysidro and stops right at the border. Trolleys make the 45-minute trip about every 15 minutes from 5 AM to 12:15 AM, except on Saturday night, when hourly service continues from midnight until 5 AM Sunday. Many trolley stations along the line provide free parking, which can save you about $7 in parking expenses at San Ysidro. Be sure to park in a guarded and lighted parking lot. The trolley is wheelchair accessible.

If you're driving, you can save a total of $7.50 on the three toll booths between Tijuana and Ensenada by taking the roads marked "libre."

BY CAR There are two border crossings in Tijuana. The San Ysidro–Tijuana crossing is the busiest; on weekends and holidays, the wait to enter the United States by car can be up to two hours. Lines are shorter at the less central Otay Mesa border crossing near the Tijuana airport (10 minutes east of San Diego), but it's only open 6 AM–10 PM. For more information about the legal and financial formalities involved with taking a car into Mexico, *see* Chapter 1, Basics.

BY PLANE Domestic plane fares in Mexico are no bargain, but they're usually substantially cheaper than international flights into Mexico. If you're in Southern California, you're better off crossing into Tijuana and buying your ticket there. When you leave Mexico, remember that there's a $12 departure tax, payable only in pesos (except in Los Cabos, where you can pay in U.S. dollars).

The **Aerocalifornia** office (Plazería Commercial Center, across from Cultural Center, tel. 66/84–20–07 or 800/258–3311 in the U.S.) is open daily 8:30–8. They serve Los Angeles and Phoenix in the United States; they also fly daily to La Paz and four times per day to Mexico City. **Aeroméxico** (Revolución, at Calle 8a, tel. 66/85–44–01 or 800/237–6639 in the U.S.) and **Mexicana** (Paseo de los Héroes 112, tel. 66/81–72–11 or 800/531–7921 in the U.S.) both offer flights throughout Mexico at comparable prices.

The airport is on the eastern edge of the city by the Otay Mesa border crossing. From the San Ysidro border or downtown a taxi ride costs $7–$10. The city bus marked AEROPUERTO, which you can catch at the traffic circle near the border, makes the trip to the airport in 30–40 minutes.

GETTING AROUND

Tijuana, unlike most Mexican cities, lacks a definite center; there's no principal church or square by which to orient yourself. Avenidas Revolución and Constitución serve more or less as the city's center and heart of the nightlife. Bars, dance clubs, street vendors, and the jai alai arena are all located in this area, which is best explored on foot. Avenidas run north–south; calles, east–west. Address numbers were just changed (for the third time in recent history) in 1993, so many buildings have two, or even three numbers. The ones written in blue are current. If you want to visit the bullring or racetrack on Boulevard Agua Caliente, take a minibus from the stop on Madero between Calles 2a and and 4a, since both sites are far from the center.

The red-light district, in the center just northwest of Avenida Revolución, is frequented by recent migrants drowning their loneliness in tequila and beer, while the sad songs of roaming mariachis remind them of faraway homes and loves.

BY BUS Buses marked 5 or 10 CENTRO go down Agua Caliente, but peseros are faster and come more frequently. The peseros on the Agua Caliente route are red and black station wagons; catch them on Calle 2a near Avenida Revolución. Tan-and-white station wagons go to the Glorieta Cuauhtémoc and the shopping centers along the Río Tijuana; catch them on

Red Cars Are Illegal Today

Any foreigner traveling by car in Mexico stands a good chance of having to deal with the police. Don't be taken in by the popular conception that you can solve all such problems by simply throwing money at the officer in question. While many cops do supplement their meager wages by taking bribes, many don't, and honest cops are not likely to take too kindly to a gringo winking knowingly and waving money at them. Cops looking for a payoff will likely find some way to let you know. If you are in this situation, proceed subtly. Some advise explaining that the legal process in your native country handles the situation on the spot, and would the señor be kind enough to let you pay the "fine" directly to him.

Calle 3a. Buses to the airport and the bus station stop at the traffic circle across from the border crossing and on Calle 4a at Niños Héroes.

BY TAXI Cabs don't have meters, so be sure to negotiate the fare before entering. A trip between the border and downtown should cost about $3, while a ride from the border or city center to the Central Camionera or airport should run $7–$10.

WHERE TO SLEEP

The really cheap hotels are found just northwest of Revolución and around Coahuila. They're only a little darker, dingier, and noisier than hotels on or around Avenida Revolución, which cost $5–$10 more. Women, however, may find the attention they get in the red-light district bothersome and should think twice before staying here. All the hotels listed below have hot water 24 hours a day.

➢ UNDER $20 • **Hotel San Jorge.** Only two blocks from the old bus station and one block from Plaza Revolución, this hotel is great, if a little noise doesn't bother you. Bad backs should beware of the soft beds. Modest singles and doubles with clean bathrooms run $18. *Constitución 506, btw Calles 1a and 2a, tel. 66/85-85-40. 63 rooms, all with bath.*

Tijuana's budget hotels fill up quickly on weekends, so make reservations or come early on Friday to stake out your room.

Hotel y Baños Enva. The small, dark rooms of this hotel face a newly painted courtyard. Rooms, though a bit worn and roach-ridden, have passable private bathrooms. Men who don't like the look of their shower can go next door to the baths and use the sauna, whirlpool, and steam baths for $4, but women are unwelcome at the facilities. Singles cost about $13, doubles $18. *Artículo 123 (Calle 1a) No. 1918, near Constitución, tel. 66/85-22-41. 38 rooms, all with bath. Luggage storage.*

➢ UNDER $25 • **Hotel Nelson.** This five-story hotel on the Plaza Revolución is the cleanest and safest in the area. Some of the large rooms overlook the plaza where mariachis play until the wee hours. Singles and doubles start at $22 and go up to $44 if you want a TV and view. All rooms have phones and clean, private bathrooms, and include secure parking. The hotel's restaurant is open daily 7 AM–11 PM, and the bar is open 11 AM–3 AM. *Revolución 721, at Calle 1a, tel. 66/85-43-02. 92 rooms, all with bath. Luggage storage, wheelchair access. MC, V.*

Hotel San Nicolás. This quiet and safe hotel has a liveable lobby with couches, a TV, and local phones. You can enjoy a picnic on the tables in the rear lot and take advantage of the secure parking area. Monday–Thursday prices are $17 for a single, $20 for a double; Fridays and weekends, they go up to $23.50 and $27. You can change money at the front desk, and make long-distance phone calls 9 AM–3 PM and 5 PM–8 PM as well. Best of all, **Hotel Económico** next door (where sad, dark cubicles run $16 for a single, $24 for a double) has a decent restaurant. *Madero 538, btw Calles 1a and 2a, tel. 66/88-04-18. 28 rooms, all with bath.*

➢ UNDER $35 • **Hotel Catalina.** Clean, quiet, and comfortable, this is the best of the not-too-high-end hotels in the heart of the tourist area. Singles cost $20 and doubles cost $30 (one bed) and $35 (two beds). Some rooms have TVs and all have phones from which you can make international calls. The hotel's cafeteria is open Monday–Saturday 7 AM–10 PM. Reservations are recommended on weekends. *Calle 5a, at Madero, tel. 66/85-97-48. 38 rooms, all with bath. Luggage storage. Reservations by mail: P.O. Box 3544, San Ysidro, CA 92073, U.S.A.*

ROUGHING IT Camping is free on the beaches outside town but it's unsafe. The beaches are dirty and far from downtown, and foot traffic headed north may interrupt your rest. Your best bet is to head south to Rosarito Beach and beyond. People heading out on early buses have been known to crash at the Central Camionera, which has luggage storage and is well lit.

FOOD

Because people move here from all over Mexico, Tijuana is a great place to sample the diversity of Mexican cuisine. Food stalls at the **mercado municipal** (Niños Héroes, btw Calles 1a and

2a) serve dishes from Jalisco, Guanajuato, Michoacán, Guaymas, and other areas for about $3–$5. There's a good selection of inexpensive places along Calle 2a, between Revolución and Constitución, catering to a primarily working-class clientele. Prices on Revolución tend to be higher than on surrounding streets, and Tijuana's more expensive restaurants are along Boulevard Agua Caliente.

La Vuelta. This fabulous place doubles as an all-hours nightclub featuring live mariachi music at 8 PM Monday–Saturday and 6:30 PM on Sunday. The grilled meats ($7–$10) and *antojitos* (appetizers) are delicious. If you can't afford that, just nurse a beer ($2) and plunge into the great atmosphere and free chips and salsa. *Revolución, at Calle 11a, tel. 66/85–72–09. At curve where Revolución changes to Agua Caliente. Open 24 hrs.*

Café Pekín. This Chinese restaurant is popular with locals and serves terrific lunch combos ($3–$5) that meet even the pickiest vegetarian's requirements. Huge dinners range from $8 to $13. You can also get food to go. *Constitución 1435, at Calle 7a, tel. 66/85–24–30. Open daily 11 AM–midnight.*

La Parrilla Suiza. This 24-hour restaurant is hardly Swiss, as its name suggests, but the specials, such as barbecued chicken with salad, beans, tortillas, and salsa for about $4, are generally good. The $2 quesadillas are a good way to refuel after sweating it out at a disco. *Calle 7a No. 1033, off Revolución, no phone.*

Restaurant Los Norteños. Tables outside this small restaurant are a fun place to check out the action on Plaza Revolución. Breakfast here costs less than $3. If you've hit taco overload by lunch and need an alternative, try the meat or vegetarian sandwiches for $2–$3. *Constitución 530, btw Calles 1a and 2a, tel. 66/85–68–55. Open 24 hrs.*

AFTER DARK

Finding something to do at night is not a problem here. Barkers along Revolución lure young, minimally clad revelers into neon-lit dance halls with offers of free tequila. If you feel like getting smashed and grooving to the latest American hits, the following places fit the bill. Happily, none charges a cover, so you can scope out each club until you find your niche or become too drunk to care. Typically, a margarita costs $3–$4, a beer about $2.50. **Tilly's Fifth Avenue** (Calle 5a No. 901, at Revolución, tel. 66/85–72–45) and **People's** (Calle 2a, at Revolución, tel. 66/85–45–72) are both open Monday–Thursday 11 AM–2 AM and Friday–Sunday until 4 AM. Saturday nights are the most popular—so popular, in fact, that they may charge men a $3–$5 cover on holiday weekends.

If you get tired of dancing with the under-dressed and underage, try to keep up with the locals at the restaurant/nightclub **La Vuelta** (*see* Food, *above*). On Friday, Saturday, and Sunday nights, **Disco Salsa** (Revolución 751) plays salsa and merengue, while **La Loa** (Revolución, at Calle 2a) is the place to hear banda.

NIGHTCLUBS **La Estrella.** Packed with locals, this is the place to go if you want dance to cumbia and an occasional salsa tune. Hard-working Tijuanenses come here to let loose. Women without men in tow should be prepared to dance a lot! The $2 cover (for men only) includes a free Tecate. *Calle 6a, tel. 66/88–13–49. Just east of Revolución under star sign. Open daily 10 AM–3 AM.*

Most of the dancing in small bars and clubs in Coahuila is done by strippers. Women walking through the area may feel uncomfortable and should be cautious at night in this neighborhood.

Los Equipales. The main draw at this nightclub with an alternative bent is the nightly shows in which men dress up like famous Mexican actresses and sing torch songs. If you're looking for a way into the gay scene in Tijuana, start here. The cover on Friday and Saturday nights is $4—regardless of gender, refreshingly. You can pick up the newspaper *Frontera Gay* to get an idea of what else is going on around town. *Calle 7a No. 8236, across from jai alai arena. Open daily 9 PM–3 AM, weekends until 5 AM.*

SPECTATOR SPORTS

JAI ALAI This Basque game is played at **El Palacio Frontón** (Revolución, near Calle 7a), a dramatic Moorish-style palace. Something like racquetball played with a curved, wicker basket, three walls, and a balsa-wood, goatskin-wrapped ball moving at about 160 mph, the game stirs the competitive nature. Almost as fun as watching jai alai is betting on it. Next door, you can wager next door on football, baseball, and horse races.

There's elegant seating at the Palacio Frontón, where you can order cocktails as you watch the game. But people in the cheaper seats know a hell of a lot about the game, and they'll help you pick a winner.

DOG RACES Yet another opportunity to play with your money awaits at the greyhound races at **Caliente Race Track**. Races are usually held in the evening at 8, and there are matinees on weekends. *A few kilometers east of town, where Agua Caliente becomes Díaz Ordaz, tel. 66/81–78–11.*

BULLFIGHTING Tijuana has two bullrings, **El Toreo de Tijuana,** the downtown bullring on Agua Caliente, and the preferred **Plaza de Toros Monumental,** the second-largest bullring in the world, known as the "Bullring by the sea." Fights take place May to late September on Sundays at 4 PM. Tickets start at about $7 in the sun, $10 in the shade. The bloodthirsty can purchase $50 seats that are close enough to get splattered. Buy tickets at the caseta on Revolución (btw Calles 3a and 4a, tel. 66/85–22–10), open daily 10 AM–7 PM, or at the ring (Highway 1D, by the ocean).

Near Tijuana

ROSARITO

Rosarito is one big, expensive beach party. This is the first popular beach south of the border, not because it's so great, but because it's easy to get to, and the beaches in Tijuana basically suck. Rosarito is little more than a commercial strip along the highway, about 45 minutes from the border, and is usually packed with drunk American college students who can usually be found at **Papas and Beer on the Beach** (Coronado, at Eucalipto 400, tel. 661/2–04–44), a popular outside bar, volleyball court, and dance club. Cover charge is $3–$10, depending on how busy it is. A margarita will run you $4.50. A good time to show up here is May 14, Rosarito's anniversary/founder's day, when people take to the streets for a fiesta.

About 20 minutes south of Rosarito by car, the town of **Puerto Nuevo** is famous for its grilled lobsters, but it has become so popular that restaurants now charge $15 for a plate of the crustaceans. Forget the food, and come to Puerto Nuevo for the surfing—it has better waves and fewer swimmers than Rosarito.

BASICS You can take medical problems to Dr. Luis Gutiérrez Martinez (Benito Juárez 854, tel. 661/2–28–47), who speaks English. His office is open daily 10–2 and 4–7:30. Conveniently, he shares an office with **GTE**, where you can make collect and credit-card calls with no connection fees. On Sundays, there's a 50% discount on calls within Mexico. The phones are open daily 8 AM–8:30 PM. **Lavamática Moderna** (Benito Juárez, at Acacias), across from Motel Villa Nueva, has washers that cost $2 and dryers for 35¢ a load. The **tourist office** (Benito Juárez 100, tel. 661/2–02–00) has a friendly, English-speaking staff and gives out maps of Baja. They're open Monday–Saturday 9–7, Sunday 10–6.

COMING AND GOING Since there is no bus station in Rosarito, buses leave passengers in front of the **Rosarito Beach Hotel** on the main drag, Benito Juárez. To catch a bus back to Tijuana's Central Viejo station ($1, 1 hr), hail one at this same place—it will usually say TIJUANA on the front. Buses to Ensenada ($3, 1½ hrs) stop four times daily along the main drag, about one block south of the Rosarito Beach Hotel. To reach Puerto Nuevo, take the Ensenada-bound bus and tell the driver where you want to get off. Colectivos also run between Tijuana and Rosarito ($1); catch one across from the Rosarito Beach Hotel. If you want to get back to the hotel zone in Tijuana, make sure you take one marked CENTRAL.

WHERE TO SLEEP The popularity of this beach, especially on weekends and holidays, makes it hard to find a cheap place to crash. Large, expensive, American-owned hotels and resorts have taken over, but **Villa Nueva** (Benito Juárez 97, no phone) provides dingy rooms for about $17 (single or double). The owner speaks some English. Camping on the beach is the cheapest option, but is not recommended for people traveling alone.

TECATE

If you want a break from the hectic pace of Tijuana, head over to its antithesis, Tecate, about one hour east by bus. It's a small, rural town that just happens to be on the United States–Mexico border. No city sits across from Tecate on the American side, and the Mexican government has not developed it for tourism, which accounts for the slow pace and mellow atmosphere. There is nothing to do in Tecate but relax in the tree-shaded *zócalo* (main square). If you plan a couple of days in advance, you can take a free tour of the huge **Tecate Brewing Company** (Guerra 70, tel. 665/4–20–11, ext. 180 *or* 182). The brewery is open 8–noon and 1–5, and tours are given at varying times, depending on their production schedule. Stop by the new **Jardín de Cerveza** (beer garden) on Avenida Hidalgo to try the beer and get more information about tours. People from surrounding ranches and northern Baja descend upon the town July 8–25 for a traditional *fiesta ranchera* (country fair), including food, crafts, music, and dancing.

BASICS Change cash and traveler's checks at **Multibanco Comermex** (Juárez, at Presidente Cárdenas, tel. 665/4–16–94) or across the street at **Bancomer** (tel. 665/4–19–14). Both change money weekdays 9 AM–1:30 PM. Bancomer also has an ATM that accepts Plus and Cirrus system cards. There is a **Computel** phone office in the bus station on Juárez that is open daily 7 AM–10 PM. They accept Visa and Mastercard but won't allow you to make collect calls. **Lavamática Tecate** (Juárez 280, tel. 665/4–15–14) has automatic washers and dryers and is open Monday–Saturday 8–8. For **medical aid,** look for English-speaking Dr. Nestor López Arellano (Presidente E. Calles 56, tel. 665/4–07–39). He's available weekdays 8–8, Saturday 8–6. There's an English-speaking dentist, Dra. Teresa Zazueta (tel. 665/4–45–62), at the same address. **Farmacia del Parque** (Benito Juárez 270, no phone) is open daily 8 AM–11 PM. The **tourist office** (tel. 665/4–10–95) on the zócalo is open weekdays 8–7, weekends 10–3.

COMING AND GOING From either of Tijuana's two bus stations, buses to Tecate ($2) leave about every half hour from 5:30 AM to 9 PM. From Tecate, buses leave for Mexicali ($6) every hour between 6:30 AM and 10 PM. Tecate's bus station is on Avenida Benito Juárez, toward the east side of town. You can store your luggage here for free. As you leave the station, turn left on Juárez and walk about four blocks to the zócalo.

WHERE TO SLEEP AND EAT The cheapest lodging in Tecate is at the skanky **Hotel México** (Juárez 230, near bus station, tel. 665/4–15–04). If saggy beds, a little street noise, and a few drunk hangers about don't bother you, you can get a single for $7 or a double for $8.50 with unpleasant, shared bathroom facilities. Singles and doubles with private bath are $15. Semi-inexpensive lodging is available at the basic **Motel Paraíso** (Alderete 83, at Juárez, tel. 665/4–17–16). Singles cost $15 and doubles are $24. To get to the Paraíso, walk about five

The Surreptitious Guest

While you may not be able to afford to stay in the large resort hotels in Rosarito, that's not to say you can't enjoy their amenities. The patio area in the back of the Rosarito Beach Hotel is a comfortable place to sip a drink and listen to music. And if the ocean isn't enough for you, you may well be able to pass as a guest and use the pool. Heavy bags can hinder this kind of leisure, so ask the remarkably accommodating front desk to hold them for you at no charge.

blocks west of the zócalo on Juárez. **Hotel Tecate** (tel. 665/4–11–16) is on the southwest corner of the zócalo at Libertad and Presidente Cárdenas. It offers singles and doubles with private bath for $22.

To eat well and hang with the locals, try **Jardín Tecate** (south side of zócalo, tel. 665/4–34–53), which serves a menu including chef salads ($4), onion soup ($2.60), and garlic fish ($5) from 7 AM to 10 PM daily. **Restaurant Íntimo** (Juárez 181, no phone) has picnic tables in the front garden and is a nice place for breakfast (omelets and hotcakes cost $3.50). They serve *pescado veracruzano* (red snapper cooked in tomatoes, onions, capers, peppers, and herbs; $6) and a *comida corrida* (pre-prepared lunch special; $3.50).

Mexicali

Huge, poor, and urban, Mexicali is easily stereotyped in familiar border-town terms. It's similar in character to Tijuana, but because of its relative isolation (160 kilometers east of Tijuana), the unbearable summer heat (100°F is the norm), and the absence of tourist diversions, Mexicali is much less visited. The city is trying to shed its tawdry image and recruit more respectable tourists/shoppers, as the downtown shopping center, the hotels and malls under construction, and the new Centro Cívico-Comercial (commercial and civic center) attest. But the fact that Mexicali is the capital of Baja California Norte (Northern Baja) and an important agricultural and industrial center doesn't carry much weight with vacationers. Most tourists spend only as much time here as is necessary to fill the gas tank, but immigrants from rural Mexico flock here seeking work in the *maquiladoras* (foreign-owned factories in duty-free zones), set up near the border.

Mexicali's distinct feature is its large Chinese population, made up mostly of descendants of immigrants brought to Mexico to build the Imperial Canal to the north in 1902. The city has numerous Chinese restaurants and shops, an annual Chinese food fair in June, and even a small Chinese-language newspaper.

For cultural diversions, Mexicali's free **Museo Regional de la Universidad de Baja California** (Reforma, at Calle L) includes exhibits on human evolution, geological photography, paleontology, and the colonial history of Baja California. If you're in Mexicali in October, check out the city's biggest bash, the **Fiesta del Sol** (Sun Festival), featuring live music, drinking and dancing, cockfights, and cultural exhibits. At least one Sunday a month between October and May, Mexicali's **Plaza de Toros Calafia** plays host to some of the best matadors and bulls in all of Mexico; the cheapest tickets, available at the Centro Cívico (Calafia, at Avenida de los Héroes), cost about $10.

BASICS

AUTO PARTS/SERVICE Oasa sells auto parts and repairs cars. *López Mateos 850, tel. 65/52–82–15. Open Mon.–Sat. 8–6, Sun. 9–2.*

CASAS DE CAMBIO Casas de cambio are easy to find near the border crossing and are generally open Monday–Saturday 9–6, but most will change only cash. Nearby banks change traveler's checks and give cash advances on Visa and Mastercard. **Bancomer** and **Serfin,** both on Madero just one block from the border, change money weekdays 9–1:30 and have ATMs.

CROSSING THE BORDER Traveling from the border to Ensenada (including San Felipe), U.S. and Canadian citizens do not need tourist cards; when entering or leaving Baja by land, a driver's license or birth certificate will generally suffice as identification. For travel south of Ensenada, tourist cards are available from the immigration office at the border, which is open 24 hours a day. It's a good idea to bring your passport if you plan to travel elsewhere in the country, especially southern Mexico. For more information on visas and tourist cards, as well as the formalities involved in bringing a car into Mexico, *see* Chapter 1, Basics.

EMERGENCIES From any phone, you can dial 134 for the **police,** 136 for the **fire department,** or 132 for an **ambulance.**

MAIL The post office is a few blocks from the border, but it's cheaper and quicker to send international mail from the United States. They'll hold mail sent to you at the following address for up to 10 days: Lista de Correos 3, Mexicali, Baja California Norte, CP 21101, México. *Madero 491. Open weekdays 8–6, Sat. 8–3.*

PHONES You can make long-distance calls from the caseta at Madero 412 or another one across from the Hotel 16 de Septiembre at Altamirano 380. Both close around 7:30 PM, and all calls must be paid in advance, which means no collect calls.

MEDICAL AID Dr. Juan David Molina Velasco is an English-speaking doctor who provides 24-hour emergency service. *Madero 420, tel. 65/52–65–60. Regular hours Mon.–Sat. 10–3 and 5–8.*

Benavides pharmacy has a helpful staff. *Reforma, at José Azueta, tel. 65/52–29–18. Open daily 8 AM–10 PM.*

VISITOR INFORMATION The tourist office, opposite a statue of General Vicente Guerrero astride a rearing horse, has a cornucopia of maps, pamphlets, and newspapers in English. English-speaking employees are sometimes available. *López Mateos, at Compresora, about 2 km from border, tel. 65/57–23–76. Open weekdays 9–6.*

COMING AND GOING

BY BUS The **Central Camionera** (tel. 65/57–24–20) is in the Centro Cívico-Comercial on Avenida Independencia. Four companies operate from this station and share the same phone number. The counters to your right as you enter the station sell first-class tickets, those to your left sell second-class. **Tres Estrellas de Oro** offers first-class service to Baja and major cities on the mainland, with departures to destinations such as Guadalajara ($72, 32 hrs) and Mazatlán ($55, 24 hrs) every half-hour around the clock, and hourly departures for Mexico City ($93, 42 hrs). **Autotransportes del Pacífico** buses also go down the Pacific coast and over to Guadalajara and Mexico City for about the same price. **Transportes Norte de Sonora** serves the western mainland all the way to Mexico City. **Autotransportes de Baja California** has both first- and second-class service throughout Baja. Buses from Mexicali to Tijuana ($8.50 1st class, $7 2nd class; 2½ hrs) leave about every hour between 6:30 AM and 9 PM, and to Ensenada ($10 1st class only, 4 hrs) between 6 AM and 8 PM. Second-class buses depart for San Felipe ($7, 2½ hrs) at 8 AM, noon, and 3 PM. First-class buses ($8.50, 2½ hrs) leave at 8 PM and 10:50 PM. The station also has a **Computel** office open 24 hours a day for long-distance calls. Use a public phone to call collect. Luggage storage costs 35¢ an hour.

BY TRAIN The train station is at the south end of Ulises Irigoyen, north of the intersection with Boulevard López Mateos. To get here, catch a bus marked FERROCARRIL. One first-class and one second-class train depart daily for Guadalajara, with connections to Mexico City. Both trains stop at all major cities on the way (the second-class train makes many more stops); and you can transfer at Los Mochis for the Copper Canyon train. The first-class train takes about 36 hours to Guadalajara and costs $80 for a comfortable reserved seat. Make reservations in advance. The second-class train to Guadalajara takes about two days and costs only $17. Seats are not reserved, however, so arrive early (about 4 hrs), or you may be standing for a long time. For more information, contact **Ferrocarril Sonora-Baja California** (tel. 65/57–23–86).

GETTING AROUND

Mexicali has two downtown areas on opposite sides of town. The first, **La Frontera** (the border), a.k.a. *el mero centro* (the very center), is characterized by cheap hotels, taco stands, Chinese restaurants, and loads of street vendors. The **Centro Cívico** (civic center) is home to government offices, the city hospital, the Calafia bullfighting arena, and the bus and train stations. Both areas are easily explored on foot, but to get from one to the other you'll want to take a city bus down Boulevard López Mateos, the city's main thoroughfare. Buses to other parts of the city congregate near the border on the west side of Avenida Reforma or on Altamirano, near Avenida

Madero. To get to the budget hotels in La Frontera from the bus terminal, cross the pedestrian bridge and continue about a half block down López Mateos, where you can hail a bus marked CENTRO. Conveniently, their last stop is on Altamirano, near Hotel 16 de Septiembre and Hotel Altamirano. Taxis are not worth the expense ($5–$8) unless you have a carload or it's late at night. If you do take a cab, be sure to negotiate the fare before getting in.

WHERE TO SLEEP AND EAT

The cheapest hotels are clustered in the Frontera area and are accessible on foot from any of the local bus stops on Reforma or Altamirano. Most of the hotels on Reforma are seedy and unsanitary, but cheap. If you have a bare-bones budget and the others are full, **Hotel Capri** and the neighboring **Hotel San Antonio** (both on Reforma, near Azueta, tel. 65/52-02-84) offer tiny, grungy, cockroach-infested rooms for $8.50–$10 single and $12–$14 double. Accommodations near the Centro Cívico are nicer but hard to find and more expensive.

The bathrooms, rather than the rooms themselves, make the **Hotel 16 de Septiembre** (Altamirano 353, tel. 65/52-60-70) a pleasant place to stay; the spacious, tiled shower stalls are among the cleanest in Mexicali and compensate for the dungeon-like windowless rooms. A single is $13, $18 with private bath and air-conditioning; doubles are $18 and $22. The **Hotel Altamirano** (Altamirano 378, tel. 65/52-83-94) has small, basic rooms. Singles and doubles with sinks and communal showers (which aren't all that bad) are only $8.50. Telephones, carpeting, and TVs in each room help make the **Hotel Plaza** (Madero 366, 1 block from border, tel. 65/52-97-59) reasonably comfortable. A single costs $18.50, a double $25, more if you want air-conditioning.

The border area abounds with cheap places to eat, primarily taco stands and Chinese restaurants. Try **Restaurant Maldonado** (Reforma 250), noted for its cleanliness and the *pollo con mole* (chicken in chile and chocolate sauce; $2). **El Nuevo Ken Seng** (Reforma 264, tel. 65/53-46-71) is a dingy downtown restaurant that serves some of the best Chinese food in Mexico, with fresh vegetables at the heart of most dishes ($3–$5). Open 24 hours, it's a hangout for cabbies and drunks; women may not want to linger here after dark. **Nevería Blanca Nieves** (Reforma 503, tel. 65/52-94-85), done in turquoise vinyl, is crowded with old Happys, Dopeys, and Sneezys downing malts ($2.50) and sundaes ($3) at the soda fountain. They've got a great breakfast menu ($2.50–$4) and salads and sandwiches for $2–$4.50. The hours are 7 AM–10 PM daily.

Ensenada
Since the completion of the toll road between Tijuana and Ensenada in 1973, Ensenada has blossomed into one of Baja's most popular resorts. Cruise ships call regularly in Ensenada's port, and passengers tired of shuffleboard head for the fine beaches nearby. Surfers catch waves both north and south of the city, and sport fishers pursue yellowtail and marlin. By night, Ensenada offers a miniaturized version of Tijuana-style nightlife, attracting crowds of hell-raising U.S. college students and Mexicans. But, with a population of about 200,000, Ensenada is considerably smaller than Tijuana, and its pace is less frenetic.

The missionaries who colonized much of Baja skipped Ensenada on their trek north because it lacked fresh water. The city's first major growth period came in the 1870s after gold was discovered to the east in Real de Castillo. Following the discovery, Ensenada became the major supply center, seaport, and, for a while, even the capital of northern Baja. It also enjoyed a brief fling with the Hollywood jet set, serving as a playground for the Southern California elite during Prohibition. With the repeal of Prohibition and the Mexican government's decision to make gambling illegal, tourism in Ensenada dried up. More recently, the loosening of restrictions on foreign ownership of beachside property has spurred a dramatic increase in the number of visitors.

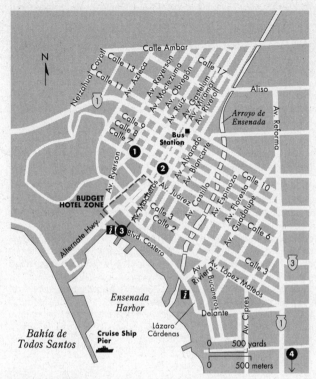

Beaches, **4**
Bodegas de
Santo Tomás, **2**
Fish Market, **3**
Parque
Revolución, **1**

BASICS

CASAS DE CAMBIO Dollars are accepted, and expected, everywhere in Ensenada. **Banco Mexicano** and **Serfin** (Ruíz, at Calle 3a) change cash and traveler's checks weekdays 9–1:30 and give cash advances on Visa and Mastercard; Serfin has an ATM. You can also change cash and traveler's checks at **Cambio de Cheques** (López Mateos 10011, at Blancarte, tel. 617/ 8–14–59), open Sunday–Friday 9:30–7 and Saturday 10–3. They'll allow you to make long-distance calls, including international credit card and collect calls, for a $1 charge.

EMERGENCIES You can dial 134 from any phone for the **police;** 136 for the **fire** department; or 132 for the **Cruz Roja** (ambulance service).

LAUNDRY **Lavandería Panchita** has automatic washers ($2 per load) and dryers (50¢ for 10 min) and will also provide same-day service ($6 per load) if you prefer to leave the dirty work to them. *General Agustín Sangines 245, tel. 617/6–15–16. Open Mon.–Sat. 8 AM–9 PM, Sun. 8–4.*

MAIL The post office, near the Hotel Riviera del Pacífico, will hold mail sent to you at the following address for up to 10 days: Lista de Correos, Administración 1, Avenida López Mateos, Ensenada, Baja California Norte, CP 22800, México. *López Mateos, at Floresta, tel. 617/6–10–88. Open weekdays 8–7, weekends 9–1.*

MEDICAL AID For an English-speaking doctor, contact Dr. Marco A. Molina Collins (Gastelum 731, tel. 617/7–81–14 or 617/4–03–28), who has office hours daily 9–1. For 24-hour emergency service, call Dr. Molina at home (tel. 617/6–90–52). You can pick up whatever he prescribes for you at **Farmacia Regia.** *Gastelum 620-B, at López Mateos, tel. 617/4–05–57. Open Mon.–Sat. 8 AM–10 PM, Sun. 8 AM–9 PM.*

PHONES You can make collect calls from public phones along López Mateos or at the Cambio de Cheques (*see above*).

VISITOR INFORMATION The tourist information booth at the north end of the waterfront has a friendly, English-speaking staff, but they don't know much about out-of-the-way places. *Blvd. Costero, at Gastelum, tel. 617/8–24–11. Open daily 9–7.*

Baja's State Secretary of Tourism, farther south, has fewer pamphlets about local merchants but a more knowledgable staff and better general information about Baja. *Centro de Gobierno, Blvd. Costero 1477, at Las Rocas, tel. 617/2–30–22, ext. 3181 or 3182. Open weekdays 9–7, Sat. 9–3, Sun. 10–2.*

COMING AND GOING

Transportes Norte de Sonora (TNS), Autotransportes de Baja California (ABC), and **Tres Estrellas del Oriente** all serve Ensenada's bus terminal (Riveroll, at Calle 10a, tel. 617/8–66–80). TNS has departures for Guadalajara ($72–$83, 36 hrs) at 10 AM, 11:30 AM, 4:30 PM, and 8:30 PM, with the first three continuing on to Mexico City ($91–$105, 48 hrs). All are first-class buses, but they roll out their shiny, new cruiser (and higher prices) for the 10 AM trip. Ensenada is a major stop on bus routes up and down Baja, and both ABC and Tres Estrellas del Oriente have frequent first- and second-class buses bound for San Quintín ($8.50, 3 hrs), La Paz ($56, 18–20 hrs), and towns in between. Buses depart at 6:30 AM, 8 AM, 2 PM, and 3:30 PM for Mexicali ($13, 3 hrs) and hourly for Tijuana ($6, 2 hrs). To reach the budget-hotel area from the bus station, walk eight blocks to your right as you leave the station. It's a seedy part of town, so be careful if you're walking alone at night. Colectivos take you to the center of town for about 50¢.

GETTING AROUND

Except for the beaches, which lie about 10 kilometers south of town and beyond, Ensenada is easy to cover on foot. The main tourist drag, Avenida López Mateos, a.k.a. Calle 1a, runs more or less parallel to Boulevard Costero and the waterfront. **Riviera del Pacífico,** an elegant old hotel along López Mateos, serves as a good landmark. To reach the **Estero** or **El Faro** beaches, flag down a yellow-and-white van from anywhere along the waterfront on Boulevard Costero. The buses stop within 3 kilometers of the beach. You can also take a red-and-white CHAPULTEPEC bus from the van depot (Calle 6a, at Ruíz) or from Avenida Juárez. Get off at the ESTERO BEACH sign, and walk the 2–3 kilometers to the beach. To get to **La Bufadora,** take the yellow-and-white van all the way to Maneadero and change to a blue van ($1) for the remaining 16 miles.

WHERE TO SLEEP

Ensenada has plenty of cheap rooms, but the low price is often the only thing they have going for them. The budget-hotel area is between Calle 2a and Calle 3a, and on Avenidas Miramar and Gastelum. Miramar is a run-down street lined with bars, so if you arrive after dark, try Gastelum first. The inexpensive hotels are mostly occupied by fishermen and their families, so backpackers get some strange looks. Rooms are usually clean but worn, and communal and private bathrooms are often in need of a good scrubbing. If you're determined to sleep cheap and everything else is full, try **Hotel Río** (Miramar 22, tel. 617/8–37–33), which has 52 rooms with skanky bathrooms for $10 a single and $13 a double; or **Hotel Rosita** (Gastelum, btw Calles 2a and 3a, no phone), another no-frills place where you can get a decent single for $7, $10 with bath, or a double for $13 (private bath). The communal toilets and showers aren't bad at all—as long as the water's working (be sure to ask). There's a clothesline in back for your wash, and the family's enthusiastic (okay, hyper) children assure you'll get an early start in the morning.

UNDER $15 **Hotel El Pacífico No. 1.** These basic rooms are a bit nicer and a lot quieter than those next door at Hotel Rosita, and El Pacífico is a popular stop for European cyclists on their way up or down the peninsula. Singles and doubles are the same price—$8.50 without bath and $12 with. The private baths are surprisingly clean, and the communal ones are nothing you can't deal with. If you ask nicely, the owners may let you use the kitchen facilities. *Gastelum 235, btw Calles 2a and 3a. 30 rooms, 12 with bath. Luggage storage.*

Motel Perla del Pacífico. To compensate for the seedy location, they run a tight ship here, with no alcohol or visitors in the spotless rooms. Even the communal baths are up to *Good Housekeeping* standards, making the $8 singles and doubles with shared bath the best deal in town. A single or double with bath costs $15. Prices rise $2–$5 during holiday weekends and other busy times of the year. *Miramar 229, tel. 617/8–30–51. 72 rooms, 41 with bath. Luggage storage, parking.*

UNDER $30 **Motel 49.** The lingering aroma of disinfectant acts as a constant reminder of how clean the large, modern rooms in this hotel are. Singles and doubles both cost $25. Some have TVs. *Miramar 6, btw Blvd. Costero and López Mateos, tel. 617/4–03–08. 29 rooms, all with bath. Luggage storage, parking, wheelchair access.*

Motel Caribe. Right in the center of the tourist strip, this motel has large, newly carpeted rooms and big windows and beds but doesn't cost the big bucks you'd expect. The bathrooms are a sight for sore eyes, and rooms toward the back get less street noise. Reservations are always recommended but only essential on holiday weekends. Singles cost $20, doubles $25. *López Mateos 627 and 628, tel. 617/8–34–31. 40 rooms, all with bath. Luggage storage, parking.*

CAMPING El Faro Beach has a nice stretch of white sand for camping if you don't mind being 10 kilometers from town. Camping facilities include toilets and showers. A site for a car with two people costs $7, motorcycles $2, and only 50¢ for people without a vehicle. Campsites with no showers or RV hook-ups at La Bufadora cost $5 for a carload of 2, and $2 for each additional person. You can also camp for free on any undeveloped beach between Ensenada and La Bufadora, but you must watch out for trucks and motorcycles in the dunes. For directions to the beaches, *see* Getting Around, *above.*

FOOD

Ensenada's specialty is fish tacos. You can find the best and cheapest ones at the many seafood stalls surrounding the **Fish Market** or in the pink **Plaza de Mariscos** (Boulevard Costero, at Virgilio Uribe). Besides mouth-watering fish tacos, piled high with cilantro, salsa, guacamole, onions, and tomatoes, you can also buy fresh seafood cocktails and *mariscos* (shellfish) prepared in a variety of ways. Cheap restaurants serving Mexican food that will fill you without necessarily dazzling your palate can be found between Calles 2a and 3a and between Miramar and Gastelum.

El Charro. For a break from seafood, El Charro serves excellent spit-roasted chicken, dished up with tortillas and condiments. A log cabin complete with fireplace and dark, smoky atmosphere, this place is right in the heart of the tourist area. Look for the birds turning on the spit in the window. Half a roasted chicken costs about $6. *López Mateos 475, near Gastelum, tel. 617/8–38–81. Open daily 11 AM–midnight.*

Lonchería La Holandesa. No, it's not Dutch, but the man who opened this restaurant over 50 years ago was. These days, it's packed with locals during breakfast and lunch. Popular dishes are pancakes and eggs ($3) or the comida corrida ($4.50). In the evenings, it's a favorite among neighborhood families. No alcohol is served. *Calle 3a No. 443, btw Gastelum and Ruíz, tel. 617/8–19–15. Open Mon.–Sat. 8 AM–9 PM, Sun. 8–4.*

Mariscos de Bahía de Ensenada. Recommended by locals as the best place for fresh and inexpensive seafood (they catch their own), Bahía de Ensenada is great for a long, sit-down meal. The tortilla-maker in the window attracts some tourists, but Mexicans often outnumber foreigners. Anything that's not seafood is expensive, but shrimp ($9), squid ($8), and fresh fish ($6) are good deals. *Riveroll 109, at López Mateos, tel. 617/8–10–15. Open daily 10 AM–11 PM.*

La Embotelladora Vieja. This is a good place to splurge and experience culinary bliss in a gorgeous restaurant. In what used to be a wine aging room, you can dine among wooden casks and choose from a list of 37 wines from Baja California. Start with the cream of garlic soup ($3.50) and continue with the *mantarraya* (manta ray) in sauvignon blanc and green peppper sauce ($12.50), finishing in grand style with chocolate crêpes flambé ($5). *Miramar, at Calle 7a, tel. 617/4–08–07. Open Mon.–Sat. noon–11.*

CAFES La Esquina de Bodegas. The galleries at this café, a new addition to the Bodegas de Santo Tomás (*see* Worth Seeing, *below*), used to be fermentation baths. Now they're the setting for contemporary art. You can buy books on food and wine in both English and Spanish before ordering a light entrée. *Miramar, at Calle 7a, in brandy distillery, tel. 617/4–08–07. Open Mon.–Sat. noon–11.*

El Portal Café y Arte. Aside from the cappuccino napoleon with cognac, whipped cream, and shaved chocolate ($3), the best thing about about this place is the outdoor seating, where people sip away the evenings in the company of lots of bad art. *Ruíz 153, btw Calles 1a and 2a, tel. 617/8–19–70. Open Wed.–Sun. 2–11.*

Pueblo Café and Deli. This is the hippest place in town to mingle with locals and occasional travelers at any hour of the day. It's a great place for breakfast, when omelets are $3 and french toast and eggs are $3.50. Vegetarians will be delighted by their salads—try the Oriental ($5). If paying $3 for an espresso drink doesn't make you feel right at home, the friendly English-speaking bartender will surely do the trick. *Ruíz 96, btw Calle 1a and Virgilio Uribe, no phone. Open daily 8 AM–midnight.*

WORTH SEEING

The waterfront (Boulevard Costero) and the tourist drag (López Mateos) serve as the town's focal points. Avenida Juárez, about six blocks inland, is the main commercial street where locals gather. The **fish market** at the north end of Boulevard Costero displays the richness of northern Baja's coastal waters: tuna, shrimp, squid, marlin, snapper, and much more. Come early in the morning to see fishermen preparing for the day's work, or in the late afternoon when the *pangas* (fishing boats) bring in the latest catch.

The remnants of Ensenada's "frontier" past are still visible in the older neighborhood in the northwest part of the city, especially along Avenida Reyerson. Old clapboard buildings, such as **Hussong's Cantina** (Ruíz, at López Mateos) and Victorian-era, Queen Anne-style wooden homes still stand the test of time, although they're being lost in an expanding sea of modern, upper-middle-class homes. **Parque Revolución** (btw Calles 6a and 7a and Obregón and Moctezuma) is the place to park yourself on a bench in the shade and watch old men chat and young kids play. On the hills surrounding Ensenada live the city's most recent migrants, who have come to look for work in northern Baja's booming construction industry. Terraces of used tires keep the tar-paper shacks from sliding down the steep slopes. For a glimpse behind the scenes at Baja's oldest commercial winery, visit the **Bodegas de Santo Tomás** (Miramar 666, btw Calles 6a and 7a, tel. 617/8–25–09) a legacy of the Dominican fathers of the Santo Tomás mission. Although the grapes are grown about 50 kilometers south of the city, wine production was moved to a large warehouse in the middle of Ensenada in 1934. Half-hour bilingual guided tours of the warehouse end with rewarding wine tasting. Admission is $2, and tours are given daily at 11, 1, and 3.

AFTER DARK

Ensenada's nightlife centers around López Mateos, especially near the corner of Ruíz. Take your pick from a number of dark, neon-lit nightclubs that feature loud American music and huge crowds of college students from Southern California. **Viva Tequila** (López Mateos, at Riveroll, tel. 617/4–04–47) is a new club open weekends 10 AM–3 AM. People head to the second floor to mingle beneath the stars. They also serve antojitos Monday–Thursday 10 AM–6 PM. Beers are a reasonable $1.50 and margaritas are on eternal special at $1. The ever-popular **Papas and Beer** (López Mateos, at Ruíz, tel. 617/4–01–45) provides plenty of beer ($2.50), booze, and boogie 10 AM–3 AM daily. Locals tend to head to the southern end of López Mateos to dance in Latin-style discos like **Hussong's Cantina** (Ruíz 113, at López Mateos, tel. 617/8–32–10), a historic establishment that manages to retain its character despite popularity with tourists. The clapboard building has a long bar, floors sprinkled with sawdust, and lots of drunken Mexicans and Americans shouting over the live mariachi music, though on weekend nights Americans predominate. For an alternative to dancing, check out the row of **billiard halls** along Calle 2a between Gastelum and Miramar. Go by day if you actually want to play billiards (each joint has a few pool tables), or by night to take in the scene. Women are rare in these places at night.

OUTDOOR ACTIVITIES

BEACHES The best beaches, such as **Mona Lisa, El Faro** and **Estero,** are about 10 kilometers south of town. Cleanish sand and moderate waves make them popular with sporting locals and tourists. You can gallop down an empty stretch of beach on rented horses for $8–$10 an hour, though they usually need a good deal of prodding. Between these beaches and Ensenada, four-wheel drives and ATVs plow through the empty sand dunes.

WATER SPORTS Ensenada is an angler's town. Most sportfishing outfitters are located next to the fish market, just off Boulevard Costero. One of those is **Gordo's,** where they'll take you out to sea for about $25 per day. But if you think fish make better swimming companions than entrées, try snorkeling or scuba-diving at **El Faro** and **Estero** beaches or off the **Banda Peninsula.** Mask, snorkel, and fins, though well used, are easy to come by in Maneadero, the area immediately south of Ensenada. Rentals are about $6 a day. Scuba equipment is available at Estero Beach. There's also diving at La Bufadora (*see below*).

Surfing is best just north of Ensenada, but the waves crash on a rocky shore, which could prove dangerous for beginners. The waves aren't quite so vicious near El Faro and Estero beaches. A few places rent old, trashed boards, and prices fluctuate with demand, so smile your darnedest. **Sam's Beach Toy Rentals** rents boards for $10 a day. They also rent boogie boards ($5 a day) and sea kayaks ($20 a day). Sam's is about 1½ kilometers from Highway 1 at the Estero Beach turnoff.

THREE-WHEELING For those who would rather tear up some Baja landscape, the dunes south of Ensenada lead into miles of beach and are prime terrain for off-road vehicles. Around El Faro Beach, Estero Beach, and Maneadero, you can rent ATVs for about $20 an hour; Sam's Beach Toy Rentals (*see above*) has a sizable collection.

Near Ensenada

LA BUFADORA

This dramatic blowhole sprays water and foam as high as 55 meters into the air. Local legend has it that the geyser's real source is a whale that ventured beneath the rocks as a calf and grew too big to escape. The blowhole is at **Punta Banda,** about 45 minutes south of Ensenada, and is easy to reach via public transport (*see* Coming and Going, *above*). The surrounding coastal cliffs are spectacular in their own right, so pack a picnic and make it a pleasant day's outing.

If you're feeling particularly adventurous (and rich), Diego Bernal of **La Bufadora Dive** rents complete scuba equipment ($25) and offers boat dives into the depths of La Bufadora for $20 per person ($50 minimum). Dives begin at 9 AM and noon. You can also rent snorkel equipment for $15. *On the main road at La Bufadora, tel. 617/4–40–71. Open Mon.–Thurs. 8:30–3 or 5 and Fri.–Sun. 8 AM until whenever.*

Diego also rents out a house by the day or week that can sleep up to 15 people for $10 per person per night. Campsites without water or hook-ups at La Bufadora cost $5 per night for a carload of two. Each additional person is $2 extra. Otherwise, you can camp at nearby **La Jolla Beach Camp,** which has showers and a minimart, for $6 for two people.

SIERRA DE JUAREZ

The craggy mountain range of the Sierra de Juárez and the Sierra San Pedro Mártir runs down the spine of northern Baja. The Sierra de Juárez begins just south of the U.S. border and extends south to meet the Sierra San Pedro Mártir where Highway 3 cuts across the peninsula. The Sierra de Juárez range is home to the **Parque Nacional Constitución de 1857,** a great place to escape for some quiet camping. The park is on a plateau covered with ponderosa pines and surrounds Laguna Hanson, a clear, cold mountain lake. Hiking trails are rare or unmarked, so you'll need a compass and topographical maps. There are few formal campsites, but finding a spot shouldn't be a problem except during Easter week, when the park fills up. No buses serve the dirt roads that access the park, so you need to take your own vehicle or hitchhike. The best way to get to the park is from Highway 3: About an hour east of Ensenada, the road forks at a point called Negros, where a dirt road continues for about 48 kilometers to the southwestern entrance of the park, near Laguna Hanson. This can really be no-man's-land, so be prepared. Bring extra water, enough gas, and a spare tire.

Even fewer people visit the rugged, granite terrain of the **Parque Nacional Sierra San Pedro Mártir,** where the **Piacacho del Diablo** (Devil's Peak) soars up to Baja's highest point—around 3,500 meters. Inside the park, you can hike along small mountain paths through *piñon* (nut pine) and oak trees, as well as the very rare San Pedro Mártir cypress. The mountains are also home to mountain goats and puma. Rockclimbers will also find a number of challenging rocks, including the Class 3 ascent up Devil's Peak. Be sure to bring plenty of water, some food, a repair kit, and enough gas to make the round trip; supplies are scarce in these parts. Three routes penetrate these mountains, but you will need a car that can take a beating. The easiest route to the park, but not Devil's Peak, is the 24-kilometer dirt road off Highway 3 at San Matías. This leads to Mike's Sky Ranch at the northwestern base of the park. Otherwise, a dirt road about 16 kilometers south of Colonet along Highway 1 heads about 80 kilometers east through San Telmo to Devil's Peak. From San Felipe, a dirt road runs to Rancho Santa Clara, near Laguna Diablo at the eastern base of the park. For more information on the trails in this park, get a copy of *The Baja Adventure Book* by Walt Peterson (The Wilderness Press, 1992).

San Felipe
Those who love the outdoors flock to San Felipe, on the northern coast of the Sea of Cortez: Fishing, sailing, and off-roading are the big draws here. Although the surrounding desert and extremely hot summers prevented any permanent settlement until the 1920s, saving San Felipe from gross resort development, this small beach town is not undiscovered. With the completion of Highway 5 from Mexicali in 1951, fishermen flocked to San Felipe and were soon followed by other sport-lovers. Sailors from all over Mexico and the United States blow through in April and October to compete in Hobie Cat races, and college students from the States trek down for Spring Break (late March to early April) to test the limits of inebriation. If you don't mind the heat, averaging about 100°F in the summer, you can have the town to yourself in July.

BASICS

CASA DE CAMBIO The **Farmacia San Ángel Inn** on the corner of Mar de Cortez and Chetumal changes traveler's checks and cash. They will give you dollars instead of pesos if you want. *Open daily 6 AM–9 PM.*

MEDICAL AID For an English-speaking doctor, see Dr. Javier Becerra Lira at the **Clínica Médica** (Mar de Cortez 316, tel. 657/7–11–16), who is available for drop-ins daily from 4 to 6 PM and for emergencies 24 hours a day.

You can get whatever drugs you may need at **Farmacia San Ángel Inn.** *Mar de Cortez, at Chetumal, tel. 657/7–10–43. Open weekdays 9–9, weekends 9 AM–10 PM.*

PHONES AND MAIL The **post office** (Mar Blanco) is open weekdays 8–3 and Saturday 9–1. Walk three blocks west of the beach and left at the stop sign. **Farmacia San Ángel Inn** (*see* *above*) charges only $1 for international collect and credit-card calls, and you can also make regular long-distance calls.

VISITOR INFORMATION *Mar de Cortez 300, at Manzanillo, tel. 657/7–11–55. Open weekdays 8–7, weekends 9–3.*

COMING AND GOING

BY BUS Autotransportes de Baja California (ABC) buses leave San Felipe's terminal (tel. 657/7–15–16) daily at 8 AM and 6 PM for Ensenada ($10, 3½ hrs) and Tijuana ($13.50, 5 hrs). Buses leave for Mexicali daily at noon, 4 PM, and 8 PM ($7.50, 2½ hrs). No buses venture onto the dirt roads south of San Felipe, where your best bet is to rent an ATV.

HITCHING The odds of finding somebody headed east from Ensenada (Hwy. 3) or south from Mexicali (Hwy. 5) are good, since San Felipe is one of a small number of destinations along either route. Look for your chauffeur at gas stations on the outskirts of town.

WHERE TO SLEEP AND EAT

Hotels are expensive, so camping is by far the best deal here. At the RV trailerparks along Mar de Cortez, space normally rented to cars ($11) and trailers ($20) costs pedestrian campers about $5, and the managers will usually watch your bags. But if you pitch your tent anywhere along the beach north of the trailer parks, you won't pay anything, and toilets (35¢) and showers ($1) are nearby. If nothing else suits you, Joe Montaro, in the purple house behind the tourist office, rents a modest room for about $20.

If you robbed a bank in Arizona, **El Capitán Motel** (Mar de Cortez 298, tel. 657/7–13–03) can pamper you with clean, air-conditioned rooms, TV, and a swimming pool. Doubles and singles cost $36 on weekdays, $45 on weekends. **Chapala Motel** (Mar de Cortez 142, tel. 657/7–12–40) is one of the nicer hotels downtown, though this doesn't necessarily mean it's worth $40 for a single or double. However, some rooms have kitchenettes and wheelchair access. Reservations for weekend nights should be made two months in advance by writing to: P.O. Box 8082, Calexico, CA 92231, U.S.A.

It's no surprise that the choice meal in this fishing town is seafood. Fish and shrimp tacos, ceviche, and clams are served from picnic tables along the *malecón* (boardwalk) for 65¢–$5. **Restaurant y Mariscos Puerto Padre** (Mar de Cortez 316, tel. 657/7–13–35) opens for good breakfasts (around $3.50) daily at 7 AM and serves seafood entrées for less than $7 from an English-language menu. They close at 10 PM every day. If the sun gets too hot, the air-conditioned **Los Gemelos** (Mar de Cortez 136, near Chetumal, tel. 657/7–10–63) serves seafood, soups, and salads, most costing less than $4, daily 6 AM–11 PM.

OUTDOOR ACTIVITIES

The vast desert that borders San Felipe to the west and the dunes and dirt roads to the south are inviting landscapes for motorcyclists and ATV riders. You can rent the vehicles at **Bahía ATV** (malecón, no phone) for $15 an hour, or haggle for a full-day deal. The calm surf and strong winds of the Sea of Cortez are perfect for windsurfing. You can take off from any beach south of **Punta Estrella**, where sailboards can be rented from Charters Mar de Cortez (*see below*) for $20 an hour. The wide, sandy beach in town is good for catching some rays, joining a game of Frisbee, or swimming.

FISHING Fishing is a way of life in San Felipe. If you're strapped for cash, you might be able to finagle tackle and a boat ride with a local in exchange for beer. Otherwise, **Tommy's Sport Fishing** (Boulevard Costero 176, no phone) and **Pelícanos** (Mar de Cortez 122, tel. 657/7–11–88) organize sport-fishing tours—the catch often includes white sea bass, corvina, dorado, yellowtail, and other sea creatures. Trips require at least four people (five maximum), and cost about $25 per person.

SAILING Charters **Mar de Cortez** (Mar de Cortez 298, at El Capitán Motel, tel. 657/7–13–03) rents Hobie Cats ($25 an hr), kayaks ($15 an hr), paddle boats ($15 an hr) and sail boards ($20 an hr). They run two-hour cruises with unlimited beverages for $30 per person and full-day cruises for $60 per person. Sailing lessons are available for $75–$100, and custom cruises are $50–$100 per person per day.

San Quintín
The twin towns of San Quintín and Lázaro Cárdenas parallel Highway 1 for several kilometers, their ugly cinderblock stores and restaurants doing nothing to attract tourists. Those not immediately scared away will find wonderful, empty beaches and an abundance of fish in the Bahía de San Quintín, just a few kilometers from the towns. San Quintín's beautiful volcanic peninsula juts out to the south, protecting the bay from the wilder and windier Pacific Ocean. The bay attracts vacationers in search of the huge chocolate clams (named for the brown coloring on their edges) that can be found along the shore. Others appreciate the area for its mild, wind-cooled climate. The peninsula, which is populated only by small fishing camps, is both quiet and luxurious for campers: Clams are free if you dig them yourself, and fresh fish and crab can be bought cheaply from local fishermen. South of the two towns is the area's best beach, **Playa Santa María** (near Hotel La Pinta and Motel Cielito Lindo). This long stretch of beach is characterized by small, rolling dunes and constant winds that can make camping a little unpleasant.

BASICS

MEDICAL AID **Farmacia San Carlos** offers long-distance telephone service as well as medicine. *Carretera Transpeninsular (Hwy. 1), tel. 616/5–25–29. Open daily 8–8.*

PHONES AND MAIL The **post office** (Carretera Transpeninsular) is open weekdays 8–5, Saturday 8–noon. They'll hold mail sent to you at the following address for up to 10 days: Lista de Correos, Valle de San Quintín, Baja California Norte, CP 22930, México. You can make both local and long-distance phone calls from **Farmacia San Carlos** (*see above*).

COMING AND GOING

Both San Quintín and Lázaro Cárdenas are major stopping points along Highway 1. Buses stop in San Quintín and at **Marcelo's Restaurant** (Carretera Transpeninsular, tel. 616/5–23–60), at the southern end of Lázaro Cárdenas. If you want to go to the peninsula, get off in San Quintín; if you're bound for the beaches south of town, Lázaro Cárdenas is the best place to stop. Three buses a day head south toward La Paz ($48, 19 hrs) at 1 PM, 5 PM, and 10 PM. You can also take your pick of five buses going north to Tijuana ($14, 5 hrs) at 6 AM, 7 AM, 9 AM, 5 PM, and 7 PM, and four buses destined for Mexicali ($21, 7 hrs) at 7 AM, 10 AM, 1 PM, and 4 PM. They'll do you the kind favor of storing your luggage for free at the station, but there's nothing formal or secure about the setup.

GETTING AROUND

San Quintín and Lázaro Cárdenas are separated by a bridge and about 3 kilometers of highway. Unless you walk, taxis ($1) are the only way to travel between the two. From Lázaro Cárdenas you can catch an AZUL Y BLANCO microbus across from Mercado Avigal to Playa Santa María for about $1. These buses run every half-hour and will let you off about 5 kilometers from either Hotel La Pinta or Motel Cielito Lindo, where you'll find nice beaches. If you're driving, look for the HOTEL LA PURITA sign along the highway. The walk from San Quintín to the shoreline at the beginning of the peninsula is about 5 kilometers. You can hitch a ride with local fishermen, but it'll be hard to distinguish between you and the day's catch by the time you get off.

WHERE TO SLEEP AND EAT

Because there's nothing of interest in San Quintín or Lázaro Cárdenas, and because they're both a few miles from the beach, staying in town is a rather dismal prospect. **Motel Uruapan** (Hwy. 1, near church in San Quintín, no phone) is the cheapest place in town, but be prepared for sagging beds, insufficient wattage, and somewhat grungy bathrooms. However, the friendly management makes this a passable place for a night. Singles cost $15, doubles $20. Unfortunately, the few beachside hotels aren't geared toward the budget traveler. Your best bet for lodging around San Quintín is your own tent. Miles of open and often isolated coast offer lovely free camping, but there's little protection from the wind. **Playa Santa María** is the easiest to reach—pitch your tent around Hotel La Pinta or anywhere else up or down the beach.

If you are unprepared to camp, **Cielito Lindo** (south of San Quintín, 5 km west of Hwy. 1, no phone) is a great place close to the beach. The rooms are expensive but large enough to accommodate four people in the two queen-size beds. Doubles cost $40. **Motel Chavez** (Carretera Transpeninsular (Hwy. 1), at the south end of San Quintín, tel. 616/5–20–05) is the best deal in town. Spotless rooms for $25 (singles) and $29 (for up to four people) are reasonable by northern Baja standards. Though a far cry from beach-front property, the **Motel Romo** (Hwy. 1, tel. 616/5–23–96) is close to the bus station and has nice rooms with spotless baths for $18 (singles and doubles). Their popular restaurant is open daily 7 AM–10 PM.

San Quintín specializes in clams. White shells litter the ground near the roadside food stands that sell the tasty, tight-lipped critters. **Palapa El Paraíso** (300 meters before Pemex in San Quintín, no phone) offers shady outdoor seating while you enjoy delicious, huge steamed clams for $2 a plate. Lázaro Cárdenas has several cheap restaurants. Near the bus station, fill up on tacos with all the fixings at the unmarked white shack next to Hamburguesas Doña Magui, open 7 AM–8 PM. **El Turista Restaurant** (east side of the highway in Lázaro Cárdenas, tel. 616/5–20–54) has a great menu and prepares delicious *pollo ranchero* (chicken with tomatoes and onions) for $4 and shrimp in garlic sauce for $9.

Guerrero Negro

Guerrero Negro sits on the Pacific coast halfway between Tijuana and La Paz, just south of the dividing line between northern and southern Baja (a giant, rusting eagle, adorned with birds nests, looms over the highway as you approach Guerrero Negro, marking this division). Every year from December to March, thousands of gray whales migrate some 6,000 miles from the Bering Sea to the tip of Baja, stopping in the warm, calm waters of Scammon's Lagoon, 27 kilometers south of town, to birth their calves and put on a show for the whalewatchers. Scammon's Lagoon, also known as **Laguna Ojo de Liebre** (Hare's Eye Lagoon), is within the bounds of **Parque Natural de Ballena Gris** (Gray Whale Natural Park). Bring binoculars to better admire the spouts of water shooting high into the air and the huge 12-foot-wide flukes thundering against the placid waters. Farther south, in **Laguna de San Ignacio**, you can hire a boat from local fishermen to get a spectacularly close view of these massive mammals. The whales sometimes swim so close to the boat that you can reach out and touch their barnacle-encrusted backs. Aside from the brief deluges of whale-watching tourists, Guerrero Negro lives off its saltworks. South of town is the ultrahot and arid Vizcaino Desert. If evaporative salt-production techniques don't turn you on, there's no reason to stop in this town outside whale-watching season, unless you want a halfway point to break up your journey through Baja.

No public transportation goes to the lagoon. If you decide to hitchhike, look around the western part of town in the morning for tourists who can give you a ride back as well (you don't want to get stuck out at the lagoon). You can also join an organized tour in town. **Cabañas Don Miguelito** (*see* Where to Sleep, *below*) runs day-long trips (including lunch) for $30 per person. **Agencia de Viajes Mario's** (Emiliano Zapata, tel. 115/7–10–88) does whale watching trips and also arranges two-day trips to the cave paintings of San Francisquito (*see* Near San Ignacio, *below*; $35 per person), 10-hour trips to Bahía de Los Angeles ($35 per person), and three-hour visits to the salt mine ($12 per person). However, these trips happen only when the whales are around, because Mario visits his kids in California the rest of the year.

BASICS

AUTO PARTS/SERVICE Boulevard Zapata is loaded with mechanics, each with their own specialty. **Autopartes Sandy** has English speakers. *Zapata, tel. 115/7–00–51. Open Mon.–Sat. 8–8, Sun. 8–1.*

CASA DE CAMBIO Banamex changes cash and traveler's checks and gives cash advances on credit cards weekdays 8:30–1. *Av. Baja California, just past saltworks, tel. 115/7–05–55.*

MEDICAL AID Farmacia San Martín not only has everything you need for scrapes and bruises, but long-distance telephone service as well. However, they don't allow credit card or collect calls. *Zapata, tel. 115/7–09–11. Open Mon.–Sat. 8 AM–10 PM, Sun. 9–4.*

PHONES AND MAIL Finding a place to make a phone call is more difficult than it should be since all of the pay phones on the street have been ripped out. Both **Hotel Brisa Salina** and the **IMSS** clinic have public phones from which you can make international, collect calls. Otherwise, try **Farmacia San Martín** (*see above*) for cash calls paid on the spot.

The **post office** is in a round, beige-colored building on an unnamed street in the old section of Guerrero Negro. To reach it, walk past the square and turn left at the Lion's Club and elementary school. It's open weekdays 8–8. They'll hold mail sent to you at the following address for up to 10 days: Lista de Correos, Guerrero Negro, Baja California Sur, CP 23940, México.

COMING AND GOING

Autotransportes de Baja California (ABC) and **Transportes Norte de Sonora (TNS)** serve the **Terminal de Autobuses** (near highway on motel strip, tel. 115/7–06–11). Six northbound buses pass through Guerrero Negro daily, making stops in San Quintín ($19, 7 hrs), Ensenada ($25, 10 hrs), and Tijuana ($30, 12 hrs). Seven buses head south daily, stopping in San Ignacio ($7, 2 hrs), Santa Rosalia ($10, 3 hrs), Mulegé ($12, 4 hrs), Loreto ($18, 6 hrs), and La Paz ($32, 10–12 hrs).

GETTING AROUND

Guerrero Negro is divided into two very different halves: the old section around the square and the new commercial and tourist strip on Zapata near the highway. The only way to travel between the two is by taxi, on foot (a 20- to 30-minute walk), or in the back of some kind soul's truck. To get to the attractions near Guerrero Negro, you need your own transportation (unless you're with a tour). Gravel and dirt roads lead from town to Scammon's Lagoon and Bahía Tortugas. The latter has an airstrip, and chartered planes (tel. 115/7–00–56) can take you there from Guerrero Negro in a half-hour for about $30 daily at 10 AM. You might also be able to scam a ride from the mailman who leaves the post office between 7 and 8 AM.

WHERE TO SLEEP AND EAT

The hotels near the bus station in Guerrero Negro look cheap, but in fact only some are within the budget traveler's reach. The more reasonable include **Hotel San José** (across from bus terminal, tel. 115/7–15–20), **Motel Las Ballenas** (behind El Morro, tel. 115/7–01–16), and **Motel Brisa Salina** (Zapata, tel. 115/7–13–25). All have well-kept singles for about $20 and doubles for $22. Of the three, Motel Brisa Salina is the most desirable. To your right as you exit the bus station, look for **Malarrimo** (tel. 115/7–02–50 or 115/7–00–20), which has beautiful, clean, quiet rooms in modern bungalows for $22 (single) and $25 (double). Malarrimo is run by the same management as **Cabañas Don Miguelito,** an RV park that costs $8 per space for two people (additional persons $2 each). If the above hotels will break your budget, try one of the following.

The **Motel Dunas** (Zapata, next to market) has decent rooms, though they're somewhat dark and overdue for a good scrub. Check the bathroom before accepting a room because some are awful. Singles cost $14, doubles $16. In one room, they'll let you cram up to six people for $23. Call the market (tel. 115/7–00–57), and they'll connect you with the hotel office. The best deal for the single traveler is the **Motel Gámez** (Zapata, tel. 115/7–03–70). Singles are $10, doubles $12–$13.50. Be sure yours has a full set of sheets, and try to avoid getting your toenails caught in the disintegrating bedspread. *12 rooms, all with bath. Luggage storage.*

If you're just passing through Guerrero Negro, you don't have to wander far from the bus terminal to eat well. Just next door, **Cocina Económica** comes highly recommended by locals and has great typical Mexican dishes for $4–$6 from 7 AM to 10 PM daily. Around the first bend in Zapata, you can forage among a string of cheap places. At **Cafetería Johana,** just past the first Pemex station, you can slouch over your morning eggs ($3.50) as early as 6 AM or munch on a plain ol' burger ($3) until 10 PM. Their comidas corridas are especially good at $3.50. In the evenings, sandwich shops and ceviche and taco stands that you hadn't noticed during the day pop up, and hot dog vendors hit the streets, selling dogs smothered in beans and chile for $1.

Near Guerrero Negro

THE LONELY COAST

Everything—from huge whale bones to bottles stuffed with rescue notes—eventually drifts ashore at Playa Malarrimo.

Twenty-two miles southeast of Guerrero Negro is the hot, dry **Vizcaíno Desert,** which juts out into the Pacific Ocean. Although as arid as Death Valley, it's no barren wasteland—a few amazing and often weird plants, such as *tillandsia recurvata* (ball moss) and *datillo* (a.k.a. *yucca valida,* resembling the Joshua tree) manage to live in this extremely harsh environment. Ejido Vizcaíno, a small spice-farming community, thrives in the midst of the desert due to deep wells. Toward the end of the peninsula, on its northern edge, is a junk collector's dream come true: **Playa Malarrimo,** otherwise known as Scavenger's Beach. Because the beach lies perpendicular to the currents moving down Baja's Pacific coast, it acts as the junkyard for ocean debris. The southern side of the peninsula, from **Bahía de Tortugas** southeast to **Punta Abreojos,** is an empty stretch of coastline. From January to mid-March, you can see whales calving in **Laguna Ojo de Liebre**, and sea turtles laying their eggs in the small Bahía de Tortugas.

San Ignacio

The verdant town of San Ignacio bakes in the middle of the desert about halfway between Guerrero Negro and the Sea of Cortez. An underground stream surfaces near the town and brings the desert to life: Birds sing, insects buzz, flowers bloom, and fruit trees thrive. Date palms, introduced by Jesuit missionaries, dominate the landscape. This is a good departure point for whale-watching in **Laguna de San Ignacio** or exploring precolonial cave paintings in the **Sierra de San Francisco** and **Sierra de Santa Marta.** If you arrive from northern Baja, San Ignacio is the first town you'll encounter that is laid out in the traditional Mexican fashion, with a zócalo at the center of everything. Life for San Ignacio's residents takes place around this tree-shaded square and the adjacent **Misión San Ignacio de Loyola.** Jesuits began constructing the mission's four-foot-thick walls out of volcanic rock in 1716, but construction wasn't completed until the Dominicans took over and finished the job in 1786. A particularly beautiful mass is held on Sundays at 11 AM.

Many of the buildings around the square, shaded by Indian laurel trees, are more than a century old, their adobe walls sometimes peeking through new layers of plaster and paint. Fall is the time to pick dates and grapes and make homemade wine, another legacy of the missionaries. Try to sample some of the local wine, goat cheese, and *cajeta* (a sweet made from goat's milk) from the ranches in the surrounding Sierra. The residents of San Ignacio used to live off the land, but the town is now primarily a supply center for the ranches in the area, and many residents have migrated to the coast to earn their living fishing. Many return in the last week of July, though, for San Ignacio's five-day fiesta. For information about the town and surrounding area, ask the policeman in the plaza (he's always there).

COMING AND GOING

The bus station consists of two shaded benches on the highway, less than 3 kilometers outside town. The one next to the Pemex station is the stop for buses going north; cross the street for southbound buses. The only way to ride from the bus stop into town is by taxi ($2), but during the day, the walk is pleasant, if sweaty. Seven buses go south to La Paz ($23, 6 hrs) every day between 6 AM and 1 AM. Buses headed north to Tijuana ($32, 14 hrs) and Ensenada ($28, 12 hrs) pass through town six times a day. The people at the store next to the Pemex station can tell you about changes in the schedule, but you buy your ticket on the bus. The Pemex station is also an easy place to hitch a ride.

WHERE TO SLEEP

San Ignacio may be restful, but unless you're prepared to camp, it's not a cheap place to spend the night. Running water is sporadic, so check the sink before you sign in for the night. **Motel Posada** (Carranza, tel. 115/4–03–13) offers clean rooms with the most reliable water supply in town for about $20 for a single, $25 for a double. To get here, walk along the curving road that runs along the front of the mission and beyond. If you prefer to stay in a local home, two families rent a couple of rooms. **Lonchería Chalita** (Hidalgo 9, west side of zócalo, tel. 115/4–00–18) has two rooms ($17 single or double), but they're small and stuffy. Although there's a private entrance, the friendly family encourages you to walk through their kitchen and backyard gardens. They also serve the best meals in town. **Pablo Cordán Vega**, a.k.a. Lupita's (Hidalgo, tel. 115/4–00–66), is a family-owned place where small cottages ($17 single or double) have front porches, but often lack water.

CAMPING For its size, San Ignacio has quite a few campgrounds, and they're all fairly cheap. The best one is also the cheapest: At **Las Candelarias**, a few hundred meters from Hotel La Pinta, you can camp for $3 in a well-maintained grove of date palms, but the bathrooms are simple outhouses without showers. If you're not driven into an hysterical frenzy by watersnakes, they've got the best swimming hole around. **Trailer Park El Padrino** (1 mile south of Hwy. 1, near Hotel La Pinta) provides campgrounds, toilets, and showers for $6 per tent. Other campgrounds have backbreakingly hard ground or are infested with insects. You may be able to camp for free just past Hotel La Pinta, but the persistent braying of a burro is a hefty price to pay for a free night.

FOOD

Take your pick from among the few restaurants in town. The best is **Lonchería Chalita** (Hidalgo 9, west side of zócalo, tel. 115/4–00–18), where the elderly owners have turned their living room into a small restaurant. The comida corrida costs $3.50, while the typical Mexican à la carte menu runs $4–$6. The thatch-roofed **Restaurant Tota** (Hidalgo 39, tel. 115/4–00–42) has a wonderful variety of breakfasts, from clam cakes ($5) to oatmeal ($2). Or come by in the evening for fish ($6) or shrimp ($10) dinners.

Near San Ignacio

Gray whales stop in the **Laguna de San Ignacio** from January through March on their migration from Alaska to the tip of Baja. The lagoon is two hours southwest of San Ignacio, about 46 miles along rough dirt roads, so you'll need to drive a sturdy car, hitch (and expect to get stranded for a while), or hire a guide (*see below*). Once there, hire a local fisherman for about $20 to take you out on his boat to see the whales.

To reach the cave paintings in the Sierra from San Ignacio, you need to make a mule-back trek through the high desert of Baja's mountains. The trip is spectacular in its own right, and the caves are just the finishing touches of one of Baja's most incredible experiences. The now-faded paintings in the Sierras of San Francisco and Santa Marta depict giant men, fish, deer, and hunting scenes. When the missions in the area declined, many of the original Baja Californians fled to the Sierra de San Francisco, where their descendants remain, living off their gardens, goats, and, more recently, fees from guiding visitors to the caves. To get here on your own, you'll need to drive or hitch 74 kilometers of poorly maintained dirt roads. Finding a guide at the caves is no problem, however—they foist themselves on visitors with enthusiasm. Entrance to the caves, including guide, is $10, and mules to get you from cave to cave run about another $10 per day.

If you don't have your own transportation and don't want to hitch, a last resort is Oscar Fisher of San Ignacio's Motel Posada (*see* Where to Sleep, *above*). Oscar takes up to six people on the day-long tour to the cave paintings for $120, which includes transportation (car and mule) and a guide. He'll also make the two-hour drive and two-hour boat ride to the Laguna San Ignacio (and then back again) for $45 per person.

Santa Rosalía

Traveling south down Highway 1, Santa Rosalía is the first town on the Sea of Cortez, but there's very little wind here, so you won't get much relief from the heat and dust of the interior. Founded by El Boleo, a French copper-mining company in the mid-1800s, Santa Rosalía looks unlike any other town in Baja or in Mexico. French-style buildings constructed with imported European wood have long sloping roofs hanging over small, fenced porches. Santa Rosalía was laid out in a regimented fashion, with rows of identical houses corresponding to various ranks within the company, and the old residences of the French mining officials sit high above the canyon in which the town is laid out. Some local people have blond hair or East Indian features, testament to the varied ancestry of the town's original workers, who included native Californian, French, East Indian, and Chinese people.

Santa Rosalía is home to the Iglesia Santa Bárbara, a pre-fabricated iron church designed by Alexandre Gustave Eiffel (of Tower fame) and imported from Europe by the mining company that founded the town.

When the mining company pulled out in the early 1950s, Santa Rosalía's economy hit a slump from which it has never quite recovered. Today, most residents make their living from the sea or by working in plaster mines on nearby Isla de San Marcos. Santa Rosalía is one of Baja's poorer towns; its unkempt central square, houses in need of repainting, street lamps lacking bulbs, and rusting copper works contrast with the more touristed towns farther south. There are no good beaches in Santa Rosalía proper. Explorer types can go 3 kilometers north of town to **Playa Santa María** for sun, surf, and chocolate-clam digging. **El Morro Hotel,** south of town, also has a nice beach. Unsociable beach-goers can travel a little further to the more isolated shoreline near the fishing village of **Punta Chivato.**

BASICS

AUTO PARTS/SERVICE **Autopartes Plaza**. *Constitución, east side of zócalo, tel. 115/2–01–67. Open daily 8 AM–9 PM.*

CASA DE CAMBIO **Bancomer** changes cash and traveler's checks weekdays 8:30–1. They also give cash advances on Visa and Mastercard. *Obregón, at Altamirano, tel. 115/2–02–65.*

LAUNDRY **Lavamática Shylusa's** has automatic washers for $2.50 and dryers for $3. *Obregon 24, no phone. Open daily 8–1 and 3–8.*

MEDICAL AID **Farmacia Central** sells drugs and has long-distance telephone and fax service. *Obregón, at Plaza, tel. 115/2–20–70, fax 115/2–22–70. Open Mon.–Sat. 8 AM–10 PM, Sun. 9–1 and 7–10.*

PHONES AND MAIL Not only are there are no pay phones along the streets of Santa Rosalía, nobody wants to let you make a collect call. **Farmacia Central** has a caseta de larga distancia, but it's cash only. The **Hotel Real** (Montoya, near the park) also has a caseta. The **post office** (Constitución, btw Calle 2 and Altamirano) is open weekdays 8–3 and Saturday 8–noon. They'll hold mail sent to you at the following address for up to 10 days: Lista de Correos, Avenida Constitución, Santa Rosalía, Baja California Sur, CP 23920, México.

COMING AND GOING

BY BUS Autobuses de Baja California (ABC) (tel. 115/2–01–50) buses run from the terminal just south of town on Highway 1, a quick 10-minute walk from downtown. Eight buses a day head south, with stops in Mulegé ($3.50, 1 hr), Loreto ($9.50, 3 hrs), and La Paz ($25, 8 hrs). Seven buses a day go north to Tijuana ($38, 14 hrs), stopping in Guerrero Negro ($10, 3 hrs) and Mexicali ($46.50, 16 hrs). To get to the beach at Punta Chivato, hop on any of the southbound buses and ask the driver to let you off. You can also try to swing a ride at the Pemex station on Highway 1 just before the bus terminal.

BY FERRY Sematur offers biweekly ferry service from Santa Rosalía to Guaymas in the state of Sonora. Ferries to Guaymas leave Wednesday and Sunday at 8 AM. A seat costs $15, while a bed in a four-person cabin costs $30. If you want to bring a car to the mainland, you'll have to have a car permit from the **Delegación de Servicios Migratorios** offices next to the ferry office (for more information, *see* Chapter 1, Basics). The office opens sporadically; the best time to catch them is around 3 PM on Tuesdays and Fridays, when the ferry arrives from Guaymas. *Pier south of town, tel. 115/2–00–13 or 115/2–00–14.*

WHERE TO SLEEP AND EAT

The **Hotel Central** (Obregón, at Plaza, tel. 115/2–20–70) above the Farmacia Central, which has decent singles for $10 and doubles for $14; or **Hotel Olvera** (Plaza 14, tel. 115/2–00–57), where $14 gets you a clean, single room with TV, $19 a double, and $22.50 a double with air-conditioning.

The clean, well-worn rooms at the **Hotel Blanco y Negro** (Sarabia 1, at Calle 3a, tel. 115/2–00–80) are a magnet for American budget travelers. To get a room, you may have to rouse the owner, who lives on the second floor of the bright yellow building. Singles with bath go for $10. Doubles cost $10, $12 with bath. And until the owner burns down the **Hotel Playa** (Calle 1a No. 2, no phone) with his eternally lit cigarette, this is the cheapest hotel in Santa Rosalía. Rooms are run-down, dirty, and adorned with faded calico curtains and are $5 for a single without bath, $7 with bath. Doubles are a mere $10.

Don't expect to feast royally in Santa Rosalía. Expensive restaurants that cater to passing tourists are concentrated along Obregón, while cheap restaurants are scattered throughout town. If you put off lunch too long, the entire town mysteriously runs out of comida corrida and shuts itself down, so plan ahead. **Cenaduría Gaby** (Calle 5a, at Progreso, tel. 115/2–01–55) is the best place in town. For breakfast, they'll serve your eggs any way you like them for $3. In the evening, huge meals of chicken or fish are just $5. Unfortunately, they're closed Monday and Tuesday. **Lonchería Martha** (Montoya 8, no phone) is another popular spot for $3 comida corrida. Be sure to stop by **Panadería El Boleo** (Revolución, at Calle 4a), a bakery founded by the French mining company to supply the town with baguettes. Thirty years later, their French bread and pastries are still delicious. If you're an early riser, peek inside the doors around the side to watch the bakers loading bread and pastry dough into brick wood-burning ovens.

CHEAP THRILLS

Other than poking around the rusty old locomotives and copper-works near the harbor breakwater (which are officially closed to the public), there's not much to do here but read in the shade, sweat in the sun, or fish. For the latter, you can ask Pino Beltri, a good-natured man with 13 kids, to help; he says he'll take tourists fishing for free on his days off (Friday, Saturday, Sunday) and in July. Finding him might be a chore, but they may know at the Hotel Playa or near the lake where the fishermen hang out. Bring him a present to show your thanks (U.S. baseball paraphernalia goes over well). Other fisherfolk may also be open to such an arrangement—try bringing a bottle of tequila down to the shore to break the ice.

Mulegé

The Santa Rosalía River courses through Mulegé, watering the small forest of date palms and creating a seaside desert oasis, just 18 kilometers north of the spectacular beaches and warm water of the **Bahía de Concepción**. Here, the calm and soothing waters, in a wide spectrum of blues, contrast sharply with the surrounding harsh, semidesert landscape. Mulegé's own rocky beach lies at the mouth of the river, about 2 kilometers east of town along the main road, and although the beach is not as white-sand spectacular as those farther south, it's a pleasant walk and okay for swimming; best of all, you can camp here for free.

Mulegé proper is a quiet town that lives comfortably off the heavy tourist trade. But the simple life co-exists here with the garishly commercial: The hardware store is located alongside T-shirt and curio shops in the same cracked adobe-style building. The plain but impressive **Misión Santa Rosalía de Mulegé**, built in 1766 and reconstructed in the early 1970s, overlooks the town, and date palm fields perch on the hilltop on the opposite bank of the Río Santa Rosalía. Mulegé does not have a hopping nightlife scene; the large community of retired North Americans play cards and dominoes at **Grannie's Goodies** (under the highway bridge over Río Santa Rosalía), the local codger hangout.

BASICS

AUTO PARTS/SERVICE Refaccionaria Mulegé sells parts and can recommend a mechanic to suit your needs. *Zaragoza, tel. 115/3–00–41. Open daily 8–1 and 3–8.*

CASAS DE CAMBIO Servicio de Cambio (Moctezuma 7, no phone) changes cash only Monday–Saturday 9–1 and 3–7. Most places in town also accept U.S. dollars.

LAUNDRY Lavamática Claudia has $2.50 washers and 50¢ dryers. *Moctezuma, tel. 115/3–00–57. Open Mon.–Sat. 8–6.*

MEDICAL AID The staff at the **Farmacia** can offer advice about minor medical problems. *Madero, next to post office, tel. 115/3–00–42. Open daily 8–1 and 3–10.*

PHONES AND MAIL The **post office** (Madero, on the plaza) is open weekdays 8–3. They'll hold mail sent to you at the following address for up to 10 days: Lista de Correos, Fte. Jardin Corona, Col. Centro, Mulegé, Baja California Sur, CP 23900, México. The drugstore on Zaragoza around the corner from the post office has long-distance telephone service.

VISITOR INFORMATION The tourist office is run by the owner of **Hotel and Restaurant Las Casitas** (Madero 50, tel. 115/3–00–19). You can trade English books at **Grannie's Goodies** (underneath highway bridge over Río Santa Rosalía).

COMING AND GOING

At the entrance to town (the "Y") is a shaded bench that functions as the bus station. Seven north-bound buses pass through with stops at Santa Rosalía ($3.50, 1 hr) and Tijuana ($41, 15 hrs). Eight buses per day go south to Loreto ($6, 2 hrs) and La Paz ($21, 7 hrs). Ask a taxi driver when the buses are expected to pass. Be prepared to wait because schedules are rarely kept. Buy your tickets on the bus.

Mulegé is small and easy to navigate. If you don't have a car, it's about a 30-minute walk to Mulegé's beach. The better beaches of Bahía de Concepción are too far away to reach on foot, but it's easy to hitchhike. You can also catch a southbound bus from town to the beach; flag down one heading north to get back to Mulegé.

WHERE TO SLEEP

Most beds for rent in Mulegé start at $20, but three guest houses offer cheaper, simpler rooms. At **Casa de Huéspedes Manuelita's** (Moctezuma, tel. 115/3–01–75) the facilities are spartan and the private baths somewhat dirty, but you pay only $7 for a single, $9 for a double. Next door is the even cheaper **Casa de Huéspedes Nachita** (Moctezuma, tel. 115/3–01–40), where $5 per person gets you a pleasant room within earshot of the friendly owner's exotic bird collection, plus a fan. Unfortunately, the common bathroom becomes the land of the king-size cockroaches once the sun sets, so plan ahead. A couple of elderly ladies run the **Casa de Huéspedes Canett** (Francisco, at Madero, tel. 115/3–02–72), where singles with rickety beds and acceptable baths are just $5, doubles $10. **Hotel Suites Rosita** (Madero 2, no phone) is a deal if you're traveling with friends. The huge apartment-style rooms come complete with kitchenette, living room, two separate bedrooms, and air-conditioning and go for $27 for up to four people. Laundry service is also available.

CAMPING Camping is free on Mulegé's beach (the southern end is less rocky), about 3 kilometers east of town. **Orchard RV Park Resort** (south side of river, tel. 115/3–03–00), a half-kilometer walk from town, is the closest and most deluxe campground, with clean, white-tiled bathrooms, a volleyball court, bonfire pit, and shady fruit trees. Roberto, the extroverted manager, speaks English and can be persuaded to show you his favorite clam-digging spots at Bahía de Concepción. One person in a tent costs $6, two people in a tent runs $7, and space for an RV costs $15.

FOOD

Mulegé is short on inexpensive restaurants. Take your pick from the places near the bus stop on Highway 1, or join the crowds waiting for great guacamole around **Taquería Danny's** (closed Wednesday) on Madero. If you have a sudden, uncontrollable craving for chocolate-chip cookies, there's a delicious, expensive, American-style bakery at **Villa María Isabel RV Park**, south of town on Highway 1. **La Cabaña** (Madero, across from bus station, no phone) has a good egg-and-tortilla breakfast for $3, as well as typical Mexican lunch and dinner plates ($3.50–$5). On Fridays, head for **Las Casitas** (Madero 50, tel. 115/3–00–19) for the mariachi buffet ($8.50). Mexican and seafood dishes of all kinds are served for $6–$10, and they've even got a vegetarian plate for $5. The restaurant is open daily 7 AM–10 PM.

OUTDOOR ACTIVITIES

Baja Tropicales at the Hotel Las Casitas (Madero 50, tel. 115/3–00–19) rents boats ($25 per day) and kayaks ($30 per day) so you can paddle along the river among the date palms. Tours of Bahía de Concepción can also be arranged for $30.

The warm waters here usually have very good visibility and teem with colorful aquatic life. The best diving spots are just off the Santa Inez islands and accessible only by boat. **Mulegé Divers** offers snorkeling trips for $20 ($25 with gear) and scuba diving forays, which cost anywhere from $30 to $50 per person, depending on how much equipment you rent. *Gral. Martínez s/n, tel. 115/ 3–00–59. Open Mon.–Sat. 9–1 and 3–6.*

Near Mulegé

BAHIA DE CONCEPCION

Without a doubt, the most beautiful bays in Baja lie along Highway 1 just south of Mulegé. The highway runs along 40 curvy kilometers of coastline, where hidden coves open onto white-sand beaches and electric-blue water. The water is excellent for snorkeling, scuba-diving, windsurfing, kayaking, or just swimming, but Windsurfers are hard to come by at these beaches or in Mulegé. The first beach you'll hit heading south is **Playa Punta Arena** (20 km from Mulegé on Highway 1), popular among sailboarders. **Playa Santispac,** about 24 kilometers south of

Mulegé, can turn into RV-camper hell overnight, but for the most part, it's a beautiful, mellow stretch of beach with good facilities. Local entrepreneurs provide tourists with palapas ($4 per night), showers ($1), and a fairly inexpensive restaurant. Sign up with **Baja Tropicales** (near palapa 17, tel. 115/3-00–19) for a $30 kayaking excursion, complete with a guide knowledgeable about the birds, fish, and shells of the area. Snorkeling gear is more affordable at $5. The beautiful beaches just a few more kilometers to the south—**Playa Tordilla, Playa Los Cocos, Bahía Los Burros,** and **El Coyote**—remain unexploited, with more modest facilities (i.e. pit toilets and scattered palapas). There's a sunken airplane about 200 meters offshore and 10 feet down at Los Burros that makes for an eerie snorkel. **Playa Requeson,** 14 kilometers south of El Coyote, surrounds a bay so shallow that you can walk across the sand bar to a small volcanic island.

Loreto

Life in Loreto revolves around fishing and not much else. For many years, Loreto was accessible only to the wealthy or adventurous who flew in on private planes or arrived by yacht. Today it plays host to a somewhat more diverse crowd that comes for dolphin fish, marlin, and sailfish. The beaches in Loreto are small and grungy—you can swim, but it's more fun to go out in a panga. Fonatur, the tourist-development arm of the Mexican government, has elected a 38-kilometer stretch of coastline just south of Loreto, around **Nopoló** and **Puerto Escondido**, as the luxury beach resort area. Development began in 1982, but enthusiasm and funds drifted elsewhere before Escondido was completely adulterated. A rocky shore complete with yachts, a parking lot where you can car-camp for free, and man-made canals surround a hotel frozen in mid-construction. The beaches of Nopole are much nicer than those in Loreto, but no budget lodgings exist. The reefs around **Isla del Carmen, Isla Coronada**, and **Isla Danzante** make diving and snorkeling another popular diversion.

Stingrays are known to lurk in the sand off Loreto's beaches; as you walk though the water, shuffle your feet in the sand as you walk to scare them off.

Loreto is also the oldest permanent settlement in the Californias. Founded by 1697, this was the "heart and brains" of the chain of Jesuit, Dominican, and Franciscan missions that colonized Baja and California Alta (present-day California). The **Misión de Nuestra Señora de Loreto**, built in the late 1600s in the shape of a Greek cross, was the first of Baja's missions and is still the town's social and religious center. Beautifully restored in the early 1970s, the chapel is impressive for its masonry, wood ceiling beams, and gilded altar bearing the figure of the **Virgen de Loreto**, famous throughout Baja for her miraculous powers. Every September 8, the statue is paraded down from her mountain shrine to Loreto, where a fiesta, with music, dancing, eating, and drinking, is held in her honor.

BASICS

CASA DE CAMBIO **Bancomer** is open weekdays 8:30–1, but they'll only change money (both cash and traveler's checks) until noon. *Salvatierra, at Madero, tel. 113/5-00–14.*

LAUNDRY Full service laundry is $3 a load at **Lavandería El Raymonjon** (Salvatierra 79, no phone). They're supposed to be open Monday–Saturday 8–8, Sunday 8–2, but if no one's around, they're probably across the street at the artesanía/junk-shop/tourist information tent that they also run.

MEDICAL AID **Farmacia Misión** has basic medical supplies and a knowledgeable staff. *Salvatierra 66, tel. 113/5-03–41. Open daily 8 AM–11 PM.*

PHONES AND MAIL The **post office** is located just off the west end of Salvatierra, near the Cruz Roja building, and is open weekdays 8–3, Saturday 9–1. They'll hold mail sent to you at the following address for up to 10 days: Lista de Correos, Loreto, Baja California Sur, CP 23880, México. Loreto's one and only working pay phone is in **Supermercado El Pescador** (NE end of Salvatierra), open daily 7 AM–10 PM.

COMING AND GOING

BY BUS The bus station (tel. 113/5–07–67), served by **Autotransportes de Baja California (ABC)** and **Águila,** is at the beginning of Salvatierra and Paseo Tamará, about a 10-minute walk east of the town center. Six buses a day travel south to La Paz ($15, 5 hrs) between 8 AM and midnight. Northbound buses that go all the way to Tijuana ($47, 18 hrs) leave at 1 PM, 3 PM, and 9 PM; three others going only as far as Santa Rosalía ($9.50, 3 hrs) leave at 2 PM, 5 PM, and 10:30 PM. Morning buses heading in both directions are often so crowded that it's hard to find a seat, but after a stop or so, there's more room.

BY PLANE Aerocalifornia has one flight per day at 8:20 AM from Loreto's small international airport (tel. 113/5–05–55) to Los Angeles ($66 one-way). You can catch connecting flights in La Paz to San Diego, Phoenix, and other cities on the Baja Peninsula and the mainland. Yellow-and-white vans irregularly shuttle people from (and only *from*) the airport to Loreto for about $5. The alternative is a $10 taxi ride. Taking a taxi (or hitching) is the only way to get to the airport from town.

WHERE TO SLEEP AND EAT

Most hotels in Loreto are geared toward anglers who have a slightly larger lodging allowance than the average budget traveler. Your only cheap alternative is camping at **Loremar** (Madero, south of town) or **El Moro RV Park** (closer to the center, on Rosendo Robles). Loremar is much nicer and only about 1 kilometer from the town plaza, offering toilets and showers for $10 (two people). If you can forgo the facilities, camp for free on Loreto's beaches. Those north of town are more private, but if you're feeling a little nervous, ask at the army post if you can pitch your tent on the beach opposite the post. The guards should protect you from any unwanted guests (at least those not in uniform).

Although the **Hotel Salvatierra** (Salvatierra 125, tel. 113/5–00–21) is not the cheapest place in town or the closest to the water, the rooms are clean and air-conditioned, with large, sliding-glass doors that look out over the Pemex station. The singles ($20) and doubles ($23) have great bathrooms. The walk to the town plaza is only 5–10 minutes, and the bus station is almost next door. The **Hotel San Martín,** (Juárez 4, at Davis, tel. 113/5–04–42) long considered the best backpacker hangout of the area, caters to young travelers from all over the world. Singles and doubles with fans are the best deal in town at $13 and $20. Be sure to pick a mango off the tree in back if they're in season.

The cheapest restaurants in Loreto are on Hidalgo, at the fork in Salvatierra. Of these, **Restaurant Acapulco** (open daily 7 AM–8:30 PM) takes the cake with its enormous comidas corridas ($3.50) and friendly clientele. **Cafe Olé** (Madero, near zócalo, tel. 113/3–04–96) serves breakfasts ($3.50–$4.50), appetizers ($4–$5), and banana splits ($4) beneath the palapa and at sunny outdoor tables daily from 7 AM to 10 PM. For seafood, follow the fisherfolk to **Embarcadero** (Calle de la Playa, up from Hotel La Misión, tel. 113/5–01–65). Steamed clams are $6, and a fish dinner is $7, slightly cheaper if you bring your own fish. Embarcadero is open 6 AM–9 PM but often closed Wednesdays.

OUTDOOR ACTIVITIES

Prices for fishing trips vary, so shop around. Try asking the fishermen coming into the marina in the afternoon, or, befriend some tourist with a private boat.

Fishing enthusiasts ready to splurge should do it here— sportfishers claim Loreto's waters are some of the richest in the Sea of Cortez.

Alfredo's Sport Fishing (Calle de la Playa, tel. 113/5–01–32) offers excursions costing a hefty $100 for two people plus $8 per rod. Included are the boat and fishing licenses, and they'll negotiate during the low season. Alfredo's also offers an earful of self-promoting "tourist info" and rents cars.

Islas del Carmen, Coronada, and **Danzante** are popular destinations for scuba divers. Snorkeling is popular at the beaches around Nopoló and Puerto Escondido. Snorkeling in the shallow waters around the islands is wonderful. **Deportes Blazer** rents complete scuba equipment for $24 and snorkeling gear for $7. You can also rent just the tanks ($7). They don't offer any guided underwater tours, but are a good source of advice if you're going on your own. *Hidalgo 23, tel. 113/5–09–11. Open Mon.–Sat. 9–1 and 3–7:30.*

Near Loreto

SAN JAVIER

The tiny village of San Javier is up in the mountains, some 32 kilometers from Loreto. The main reason to make this trek is to see the beautiful **Misión de San Javier**. This well-preserved mission was built in Moorish style, with domes, great attention to detail, and exquisite stone carvings. The town and surrounding ranches are much more modest—most people here live by growing their own food and herding goats. The houses consist of large palapas with a small adobe building for cooking and storing belongings. Days in this mountain desert are hot, and the sunlight is strong and punishing, but the evenings are quiet and beautiful. The road from Loreto to San Javier is rough, and while taxis from Loreto do make the trip for a pricey sum, it's best driven in a high clearance car or a jeep. If you don't have a car, or don't want to drive, hitchhike up in the late afternoon and descend in the morning. There's just one restaurant in town. You can camp for free near the dam, or rent a room from Doña Elena; just ask around. Bring your own bottled water, because they don't sell any up here. If you're in the area December 1–3, be sure to come for the big fiesta, which resounds with music, dancing, drinking, and horse races.

La Paz

Although it sits on the water, and beautiful desert beaches are only 15 minutes away by bus, La Paz is not a beach town. Rather, this capital of southern Baja is a sophisticated city with a university and a good museum. Tourists do come here, but the new airport outside Los Cabos is causing many to bypass La Paz altogether. Mainland-bound travelers are most likely to pass through on their way to pick up the ferry to Mazatlán or Los Mochis.

La Paz was founded by Cortés during his search for pearls (diving for pearls continued until the 1940s) and was developed by Jesuit missionaries. More recently, the center of social life has shifted from the mission/cathedral and zócalo to the malecón, lined with restaurants and bars. On weekend evenings, after the older residents have finished their promenade along the water, the malecón is transformed into a hangout spot for local youth.

BASICS

AMERICAN EXPRESS The travel agency **Turismo La Paz** provides AmEx services, including changing and selling traveler's checks and keeping cardholders' mail for about two weeks. *Esquerro 1679, La Paz, Baja California Sur, CP 23000, México, tel. 112/2–76–76 or 112/2–83–00. Behind Hotel Perla. Open weekdays 9–2 and 4–6, Sat. 9–2.*

CASAS DE CAMBIO **Banco Mexicano** (Puerto, at Esquerro) has shorter lines than **Bancomer** (16 de Septiembre, at Obregón), but the latter has an ATM that accepts Visa. Both banks change cash and traveler's checks weekdays 9–noon.

EMERGENCIES You can dial 06 from any phone in La Paz to reach the **police, fire** department, or an **ambulance**.

MAIL The post office is one block from the main plaza. They'll hold mail sent to you at the following address for up to 10 days: *Lista de Correos, Centro La Paz, Baja California Sur, CP 23000, México. Revolución, at Constitución. Open weekdays 8–7, Sat. 9–1.*

MEDICAL AID **Farmacia Baja California.** *Madero, at Independencia, on plaza, tel. 112/2–02–40. Open Mon.–Sat. 7 AM–11 PM, Sun. 8 AM–10 PM.*

TO PICHILINGUE

Bahía de
La Paz

N

BUDGET
HOTEL
ZONE

TO
AIRPORT

Carretera
Transpeninsular

| 0 | 1000 meters |
| 0 | 1000 yards |

Sights ●
Biblioteca de las
Californias, 1
Cathedral, 3
Cultural Center, 5
Main bus station, 6
Mercado
Municipal, 2
Museo de
Antropología, 4

Lodging ○
Villa Juvenil, 7

PHONES There's a **Computel** caseta in the bus terminal, and many of the businesses along the malecón have phones you can use to make collect and credit-card calls. The bookstore on Obregón at Arreola has long-distance phones and is a good place for a private conversation, especially because they don't charge a connection fee.

VISITOR INFORMATION The staff of the tourist office is knowledgeable, but be prepared to ask lots of questions, because they don't offer information voluntarily. Pick up good maps and southern Baja's free English papers here. *Obregón, at 16 de Septiembre, tel. 112/ 2–59–39. Open weekdays 8–8, weekends 9–1.*

COMING AND GOING

BY BUS The main bus station (Jalisco, at Héroes de la Independencia, tel. 112/2–64–76 or 2–42–70) has **Autobuses de Baja California (ABC)** and **Águila** buses and is a 30-minute walk from downtown. City buses marked IMSS from downtown let you off about three blocks from the terminal. To go downtown from the terminal, take any city bus and get off at the municipal market (Revolución, at Degollado). Buses for Tijuana ($61, 22 hrs) and destinations on the way depart La Paz at 10 AM, 4 PM, 8 PM, and 10 PM. Eight buses also depart between 7 AM and 8 PM for Cabo San Lucas and San José del Cabo ($8.50). The Pacific route through Todo Santos ($3, 1 hr) takes 2½ hours to Los Cabos, an hour less than the route via San Bartolo. Águila buses headed toward the beaches and **ferry terminal** in Pichilingue ($1.50, 20 min) depart the **Terminal Malecón** (Obregón, near tourist office, tel. 112/2–78–98) eight times daily between 8 AM and 6 PM. The last bus back to La Paz departs Pichilingue at 6:30 PM.

BY FERRY **Sematur** offers passenger and vehicle service from Pichilingue to Topolobampo (near Los Mochis) and Mazatlán. Boats for Topolobampo depart Pichilingue daily at 8 PM, arriving at 6 the following morning; the ride costs $14.50 for a seat, $29 for a bed. The trip to Mazatlán leaves at 3 PM and lasts about 18 hours; it costs $21.50 for a seat and $43 for a bunk. To catch the Sematur ferry you need to go to Pichilingue, about a half-hour south of La Paz (*see* Coming and Going By Bus, *above*). Ideally, you should arrive at the ferry station about an hour before departure. Reserve your ticket as far in advance as possible, especially during vacation periods. Ticket lines form quickly and move slowly, so it's much easier to buy your ticket from a travel agency downtown for the same price.

If you want to take a vehicle over to the mainland, get a car permit from the **Delegación de Servicios Migratorios** (Obregón, at Juárez), open weekdays 8–3. Bring your passport and registration or ownership papers. With permit in hand, go to the Sematur office to reserve a place; then, on the day of travel, buy your ticket between 8 and 11 AM. The price varies according to the size of the vehicle, but an average car costs about $100. Try to arrive at the ferry terminal four hours prior to departure. *Sematur office: 5 de Mayo, at Guillermo Prieto, tel. 112/ 5–38–33. Open daily 8–1.*

BY PLANE At the airport, your choices are limited to **Aerocalifornia** (tel. 112/5–10–23) and **Aeroméxico** (tel. 112/2–00–91). A one-way flight to Mazatlan runs about $85, to Mexico City about $235. They also have reasonable fares to the States, such as $180 for a round-trip ticket to Los Angeles. Unfortunately, taxis are the only transportation to and from the airport, 8 kilometers from town, and their monopoly is reflected in the price ($10).

GETTING AROUND

Most sights in La Paz are concentrated in the downtown area and within easy walking distance. Obregón (the boardwalk, or *malecón*) runs along the water and is a major point of reference. The downtown area does not follow the rest of the city's grid pattern. Get your bearings from the cathedral and market, both on Revolución, which mark the limits of the downtown area. If you want to go to the main bus station, youth hostel, or cultural center, catch a bus at the municipal market on Revolución at Avenida Degollado. The Pichilingue beach and the Sematur ferry terminal are about a half-hour south of La Paz and are easily reached by bus from the Terminal Malecón (*see* Coming and Going By Bus, *above*). From the ferry terminal, walk south (left on the highway) for about five minutes to reach Pichilingue beach—an easy place to kill a few hours until your ship comes in. To get to any of the three beaches south of Pichilingue (Playa de Balandra, Playa el Tecolote, and Playa el Coyote), take the bus to Pichilingue and hitch or catch a cab for about $3.

WHERE TO SLEEP

La Paz boasts a number of budget hotels with a lot of character. Most inexpensive lodgings are in the downtown area. If you're traveling with several people and can spend a little more money, **Suites Misión** (Obregón 220, tel. 112/2–00–14) offers a great deal. Small suites ($45) fit up to four people and feature a living room, kitchen, bedroom with two double beds, balcony with a sea view, and a retro atmosphere. Reservations are necessary. The office is open 9–2 and 4–7:30; when it's closed, go to **Curios Mary** (downstairs, tel. 112/2–08–15). Camping isn't really worth it, considering the availability of decent hotels in the center of La Paz for about the same price. Campsites are at least 2 kilometers southwest of town and cost about $10 for two people with an automobile. Cheaper rates may be offered to walk-in tent campers.

A few hotel owners in La Paz, banking on the appreciation of budget travelers for anything idiosyncratic, have made creative use of weird knickknacks in their decorating schemes.

Hotel Posada San Miguel. For a couple extra bucks, you can take your siesta in a large room close to the malecón. Rooms are simple, but the bricks, tilework, wrought-iron railings, colored glass, and central courtyard with flowers and fruit trees create an amiable, refined atmosphere. The bathrooms are generally clean, and portable fans make the heat bearable. Singles are $10, doubles $13. *Belisario Domínguez 1510, tel. 112/2–18–02. Near old municipal palace. 15 rooms, all with bath. Luggage storage.*

Hotel Yeneka. You can find cheaper places, but probably not with rooms this large and well furnished. The lobby resembles an artfully tended junkyard, with a rusty Model A and other pieces of discarded machinery. A chained spider monkey lives on the roof. Singles cost $15, doubles $19, and all have clean bathrooms. Long-term stays ($450 for a month) include laundry service. *Madero 1520, btw 16 de Septiembre and Independencia, tel. 112/5–46–88. 20 rooms, all with bath. Laundry, luggage storage, wheelchair access.*

Pensión California. This classic budget traveler's abode offers nothing beyond a mattress on a cement bed, a ceiling fan, buzzing fluorescent lighting, and a primitive bathroom. The lobby is bizarre, crammed with weird paintings, overgrown plants, and once-plush couches huddled around a TV. You can use the communal stove and laundry area, although unattended bras have been known to disappear. Singles cost $9.50, doubles $13. The owners also manage **Hostería del Convento** around the corner; prices are the same. *Degollado 209, ½ block from market, tel. 112/2–28–96. 25 rooms, all with bath. Luggage storage, wheelchair access.*

HOSTEL Villa Juvenil (CREA). In a sports complex outside the center of town, this hostel offers standard bunks in excessively air-conditioned single-sex dorms for $7. The communal baths are well kept. Although you're perfectly likely to have an entire room to yourself, this may not be the best place to stay given its location and the availability of cheap hotels downtown. However, there are a laundromat and grocery store across the street. Be sure to let them know if you'll be staggering in after 11 PM so they can leave the gate open for you. *5 de Febrero, at the Carretera al Sur (Hwy. 1S), tel. 112/2–46–15. From bus station, down Jalisco and left on Camino a las Garzas, or take 8 DE OCTUBRE bus. 70 beds. Reception open 7 AM–11 PM. Luggage storage, meal service, no alcohol.*

FOOD

The nicest places to eat in La Paz are those overlooking the water. Apart from sidewalk vendors, however, restaurants along the malecón are pricey. Cheap food is easy to find throughout the downtown area. A section of the **market** (Revolución, at Degollado) is devoted to *loncherías* (snack bars) that serve comidas corridas for about $4. As you enter, the cooks yell out their offerings to draw your attention. Try **Conchería Colonial** for an amazing $4 seafood feast.

➢ UNDER $10 • **El Camarón Feliz.** This reasonably priced restaurant on the malecón serves fish ($8.50), stuffed crab au gratin ($10), and shrimp ($13). The thrifty should stick with typical Mexican dishes or just order a margarita ($3), fill up on chips and salsa, and enjoy sitting on the patio. *Obregón, at Bravo, tel. 112/2–90–11. Open daily noon–midnight.*

El Quinto Sol. La Paz's vegetarian restaurant and health-food store sells granola, wheat germ, vitamins, and other health items. Traditional Mexican dishes ($4–$7) are made with tofu or wheat gluten as a substitute for meat. Wheat bread is also available. *Belisario Domínguez 12, at Independencia, tel. 112/2–16–92. 1 block from plaza. Open Mon.–Sat. 7 AM–9:30 PM.*

Restaurant de Mariscos Mar de Cortez. If you don't mind eating in an out-of-the-way restaurant near a busy road decorated with dead, dried things, come here for the $8 marlin or $10 shrimp dishes. *5 de Febrero, at Guillermo Prieto, tel. 112/2–29–08. From market, take either 8 DE OCTUBRE or 5 DE MAYO/5 DE FEBRERO bus, and get off at stone church with 2 towers. Open daily 9–9.*

WORTH SEEING

The modern **centro cultural** (Altamirano, at Encinas, tel. 112/5–03–76) presents folkloric dance, music, and theater performances. Buy tickets weekdays 8–3. **Biblioteca de las Californias** (across from cathedral, in old Municipal Palace) is a unique library with an extensive collection of material on Baja in both English and Spanish. The small **Museo de Antropología** (5 de Mayo, at Altamirano) provides information on the history and people of the peninsula, and the docent speaks English. The museum is open weekdays 8–6, Saturday 9–2; a donation is requested.

OUTDOOR ACTIVITIES

The beaches in town are small and lousy for sunbathing; the farther you get from La Paz, the better. Just north-west of town lie **Playas Hamacas** and **Comitán.** Heading in the opposite direction (toward Pichilingue) are the gorgeous sands and free camping opportunities at (in order) **Playas Palmira, El Coromuel, Caimancito, Punta Colorada, Tesoro,** and **Pichilingue.** The last is just a five-minute walk from the ferry terminal. To get to the others, take a bus toward Pichilingue and ask the driver to let you off. The best beaches, **Balandra, El Tecolote,** and **El Coyote** lie beyond Pichilingue and can be reached by cab or thumb. El Tecolote is a popular beach, with a restaurant, bar, and restrooms. Puerto Balandra, a beautiful cove with white sandy beaches and weird rock formations, was once a pirate's refuge.

The waters around La Paz offer prime **scuba diving.** The most popular dive sites are around **Espíritu Santo** island, where clear waters offer excellent visibility almost year-round. For $85 per person, **Viajes Palmira** (Obregón, btw Rosales and Allende, tel. 112/2–40–30 or 112/5–72–78) offers a two-tank dive including equipment, guides, lunch, and a boat ride. Certification will set you back $300. They also offer snorkeling trips to the same island for $40. Full-day fishing trips including rods, licenses, a boat, and guide are also available and cost $160 for two people. Whale-watching trips are $90 per person in season. **Baja Diving Service,** (Independencia 107-B, tel. 112/2–18–26) offers the same deal on scuba, snorkeling, and whale-watching tours and sells fishing tackle and rods. You can also simply rent equipment here if you're not keen on a package deal. About 30 minutes southwest of town, the calm waters are protected by bizarrely shaped rock formations, making the area perfect for kayaking. The agencies above have information on kayaking and kayak rentals.

Ask at **Hotel Yeneka** (*see* Where to Sleep, *above*) for **mountain bike** ($10 per hour, $30 per day), horse ($20 per hour) and boat ($60 per person per day) rentals.

Los Cabos
San José del Cabo, Cabo San Lucas, and the stretch of beach between them make up the peninsula's primary tourist destination. In 1982 the Mexican government decided to propel Los Cabos into tourist consciousness, marketing the towns to high heaven. Their plans have largely succeeded, especially in Cabo San Lucas, which now has far too many resorts. San José del Cabo has managed to avoid becoming hotel hell, and retains a certain modicum of charm and local identity. Even if you are normally turned off by places that get this kind of hoopla, the beauty of Los Cabos justifies the attention, and you may even get sucked into the Cabo spirit. If that fails, you can always retreat back up the peninsula to the quiet town of Todos Santos. People come to this region in droves to enjoy the miles of white, desert beaches and warm, turquoise waters that swell into good surfing waves. For the time being at least, a few gorgeous, isolated, and unspoiled places remain here—but you'd better hurry.

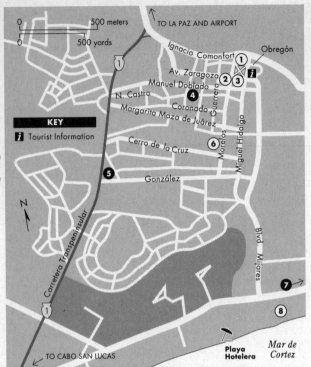

Sights ●
Bus station, **5**
Estuary, **7**
Mercado Municipal, **4**

Lodging ○
Casa de Huéspedes Sr. Mañana, **1**
Hotel Ceci, **2**
Hotel Colli, **3**
Hotel Consuelo, **6**
Hotel Stouffer Presidente, **8**

KEY
ℹ Tourist Information

San José del Cabo

Until recently, San José del Cabo dominated the tip of the peninsula. Jesuits founded the town in the 1800s, taking advantage of an underground stream that surfaces nearby to create a large natural estuary. The mission, zócalo, and other buildings erected during that period give San José del Cabo a sense of history, making it feel more like a real Mexican town than a tourist playground. The center of town is about a kilometer from the water. The primary tourist zone—major hotels, condos, time-shares, and a golf course—lies between the town and the water.

Just north of San José you can drive or hitch (there is no bus service) along the coast on a nameless dirt road that passes through **Cabo Pulmo, Cabo Frailes,** and **Punta Gorda,** among other desolate places, before it hooks back up with Highway 1 at the town of La Cueva. The dirt road is graded, but expect a slow and bumpy trip. A few resorts are scattered about, but most of the country is empty beach and prime for camping. Cabo Pulmo, 46 kilometers northeast of San José del Cabo, has the peninsula's only coral reef. Hundreds of brightly colored fish are visible in the clear water just offshore. Pepe's Dive Center offers dive tours daily at 10 AM—ask at Hotel Señor Mañana (*see below*).

BASICS If you're willing to spend some time in line, you'll get the best rates for traveler's checks at **Bancomer** (Zaragoza, at Morelos) on weekdays 8–1. Rates at the exchange booth farther up Zaragoza, which is more efficient, are slightly worse. They're open weekdays 10–6 and Saturday 10–3. Almost all the restaurants, hotels, and shops accept Visa, Mastercard, and American Express as well as traveler's checks. The long-distance **telephone office** (Morelos, at Zaragoza) is open daily 8 AM–10 PM. They charge $1 to make international collect calls. **La Botica** (Mijares 33, tel. 114/2–35–66) has a public phone and fax and sells a good selection of English books, magazines, and newspapers as well as Haägen Dazs ice cream. It's open Monday–Saturday 9–6. The **post office** (Mijares, at Margarita Maza de Juárez, tel. 114/2–09–11) will hold mail sent to you at the following address for up to ten days: Lista de Correos, Blvd.

Mijares, San José del Cabo, Baja California Sur, CP 23400, México. You can pick up and send mail weekdays 8–6, Saturday 9–1.

The phone number for the **police** is 114/2–03–61; for the **Cruz Roja** (ambulance service), it's 114/2–03–16. English-speaking mechanics provide parts and service at **Refaccionaria California** (González, near bus station, tel. 114/2–31–30), open weekdays 8–7, Sat. 8–1. **Lavandería VERA** (González, east of bus station) sells suds and has self-serve washers for $1.50; dryers are $2. It's open Monday–Saturday 8–1 and 3–8. The new tourist office (Zaragoza, at Mijares, tel. 114/2–04–46), open weekdays 8–3, is next to the zócalo carries mostly resort brochures. However, the English-speaking staff is eager to help.

COMING AND GOING The bus station (tel. 114/2–11–00) is on González near Highway 1, on the southwest edge of town. From here, it's about a 10-minute walk east down González and north up Mijares to the center of town. Eleven buses leave daily between 6 AM and 7 PM for La Paz ($9, 3 hrs). Eight buses head to Cabo San Lucas ($2, 30 min) between 7 AM and 8 PM. You can catch a bus to Todos Santos from Cabo San Lucas, but for other destinations you'll need to transfer in La Paz.

➤ BY PLANE • The **Aeropuerto International Los Cabos** is served by **Aerocalifornia** (tel. 114/3–08–48), **Mexicana** (tel. 114/2–06–06), **Alaska** (tel. 114/2–10–15), and **United** (tel. 95/800–00–30–07). Vans charging $10–$20 shuttle people between the airport and Los Cabos. Otherwise, you can try to get a free ride from one of the time-share sellers. The bus from San José to the airport departs from Manuel Doblado, near the municipal market, and costs about $2 for the 12 kilometer trip. By taxi, the 15-minute ride costs about $10.

Surfing the Coast Road

The highway from Cabo San Lucas to San José del Cabo has a number of good surf spots. Monuments (in front of the Condos Misiones, just off the road between the Cabos) is the place to go when there's no swell—if there are waves anywhere, it will be here (after a six-foot swell, though, it's out of control). Farther towards San José, you'll come to Chileno and Boca de Tule—you'll know you're there when you see the bridge and sign reading Royal Tule Puente. Both are rights with killer tubes. Approaching Costa Azul farther on is Killer Hook Surfshop, a board rental and repair shop along the beach. Surfboard rentals are $15 a day, boogie boards $8 a day. Costa Azul is also a pretty easy place to bum a tabla de surf (surfboard). There are three good rights here; Old Man's, a mushy long-boarders' ride; The Rock; and Zippers, the best and fastest wave. The competition for waves at all of these can be a bit aggressive, though. The places listed above can all be reached on any bus between the Cabos.

If you continue onto the dirt road that hugs the coast north of San José (you'll have to drive or hitch, because there's no bus service), you'll come to East Cape followed by Y Mesa—hard-core, big-wave spots with lots of rocks. Further on there are tons of hard-to-find "secret spots"—Nine Palms is the spot for long boarders, Punto Perfecto has Hawaii-size waves, and La Bocana is a walk-in freshwater estuary filled with with territorial local kids when heavy rains open up the river mouth, creating giant tubes. These places don't appear on maps, but once you're in the vicinity, ask anybody with long hair and a tan to point you in the right direction.

WHERE TO SLEEP If you've got camping gear, you'll want to use it here, because hotels are relatively expensive and beautiful beach sites are plentiful along the coast in either direction from San José. Otherwise, the **Hotel Consuelo** (Morelos s/n, above Cerro de la Cruz, tel. 114/2–06–43) is the cheapest place in town ($10 a single and $13 a double), probably because it's far from the center of town. The friendly family who runs the place will be pleased to have you rest your head on a freshly washed Star Wars pillowcase and eat in their small restaurant. Clean, well-ventilated **Hotel Ceci** (Zaragoza 22, near church, no phone) has a pleasant back patio with rocking chairs. Singles here are $17, doubles $18.50.

Casa de Huéspedes Señor Mañana. Look out—Robinson Crusoe has gone art-deco and opened a mini-zoo. Watch for falling mangos and guavas as you hang your hammock under a palapa for $5. Groovy jungle rooms start at $10 a single, $18 a double. For $30 a night, you can be picked up at the airport and come back to a posh suite, complete with refrigerator. Monthly rates in these run $230 single, $250 double. The common cooking and dining facilities include dibs on whatever's ripe on the premises. Watch out for mosquitoes. *Obregón 1, tel. 114/2–04–62. 1 block from central plaza. 13 rooms, 11 with bath. Laundry, luggage storage.*

Hotel Colli. This super-clean hotel offers quiet, secure singles for $25 and doubles for $30. Prices are $28 and $33 with air-conditioning and go up even more during tourist season. *Hidalgo, near Zaragoza, tel. 114/2–07–25. 12 rooms, all with bath. Luggage storage.*

➤ CAMPING • You can pitch your tent anywhere along the beach near town (though it's best to avoid staying near the big hotels or the mosquito-ridden estuary) as long as you set up camp late, don't build a fire, and leave in the morning. A few kilometers down the road toward Cabo San Lucas you can set up at a more permanent surfer camp next to the **Costa Azul Hotel.** There are also a couple of trailer parks, **Brisas del Mar** and **Montanes de Palmillas,** outside town on the highway toward Cabo San Lucas. Both are expensive ($15 for two people in a tent), but they have showers, flush toilets, a pool, laundry, and a restaurant.

FOOD Food stalls serve fresh, seasonal food and comidas corridas (about $3) at the **mercado municipal** (Castro, at Green). For a decent cup of coffee (and a chance to practice your English), **El Café Fiesta** (Mijares 14, tel. 114/2–28–08) has endless refills and lots of opportunities for checking out the local populace on a nice patio. They have real food, too, but it's overpriced. **Restaurante Calafia** (Mijares 34, no phone) offers better value, with witty service and a pleasant rear courtyard hung with ripening mangos. Try the pollo en mole ($7.50) or shellfish chiles rellenos ($7.50). For something different, try **Restaurant-Bar Canton** (Zaragoza, tel. 114/2–04–03). A combination dinner with eggrolls, rice, and an entrée (vegetarian dishes available) is $5 per person, and lunch is even cheaper.

AFTER DARK For real disco action, head to Cabo San Lucas. If you can't get motivated, the **Eclipse** on Mijares is the local disco. Beers are $1 during happy hour (6 PM–10 PM), but this doesn't quite make up for the blaring TVs, obnoxious karaoke, and the crowd of louses who pay the $8.50 weekend cover charge to hang out here and bother women.

OUTDOOR ACTIVITIES The water in front of most of San José's beach hotels has strong currents and swimming can be dangerous, so both residents and tourists head to Hotel Palmilla's **Playa Palmilla,** about 7 kilometers west of town. For surf spots and beaches between and around Los Cabos, *see* box, *above.* Surfboards ($15 a day), boogie boards ($8 a day), snorkel gear ($8 a day), fish tackle ($9 a day), and bicycles ($11 day) are available for rent Monday–Saturday 9–7 from **Killer Hook Surfshop** at Costa Azul (*see above*). They've also got a shop (but no rental gear) in town (Hidalgo, near church, tel. 114/2–24–30), if you want more information. If you'd rather swim in a pool, you can try sneaking into any major hotel in the area.

Cabo San Lucas

Cabo San Lucas was originally a small fishing village where a few hardy or rich sportfishermen flew or boated in to go after huge marlin and sailfish. Over the past decade, however, spectacular growth has turned Cabo into a tourist nightmare and a drunkard's dream. The small town

is congested, claustrophobic, and expensive; L.A. shopping-mall architecture and prices reign supreme. One compensation for this over-development is the availability of all sorts of water-sports equipment (for a small mound of cash). The beaches, happily, are still beautiful and free. On the street, English is the lingua franca, U.S. dollars are expected, and, in typical SoCal fashion, the major hotels water the desert green. Stray a few blocks north of the tourist track to the dirt roads and taco stands, however, and you'll discover Cabo as it existed before the landscape architects arrived.

There seem to be a higher percentage of Anglos in Cabo San Lucas than in California.

BASICS Moneychangers line Lázaro Cárdenas between Hidalgo and Matamoros, but U.S. dollars are actually preferred in most places. Credit cards and traveler's checks are also widely accepted. If you do need some pesos, **Bancomer** (Cárdenas, btw Hidalgo and Guerrero, tel. 114/3–19–50) is open for money exchange weekdays 8:30–noon. The **Union Bank** just across the street has an ATM that accepts Cirrus cards as well as Visa and Mastercard. The Cabo San Lucas **post office** (Lázaro Cárdenas, at 16 de Septiembre, tel. 114/3–00–48), open weekdays 9–6, will hold mail sent to you at the following address for up to 10 days: Lista de Correos, Av. Lázaro Cárdenas, Cabo San Lucas, Baja California Sur, CP 23410, México. Public phones are common downtown, but can also place calls from most resort hotels in the area. For cash calls, the **Casa de Larga Distancia** (Lázaro Cárdenas, at San Lucas, tel. 114/3–00–80) is your best bet, but they'll charge a $1 connection fee if you make a collect call.

The phone number for the **police** is 114/3–00–57; for the **Cruz Roja** (ambulance service), it's 114/3–33–00. **Farmacia Sinaloa** (Madero, near Marina, tel. 114/66-4–17) has an English-speaking counter person who can recommend a good hangover regimen or refer you to a doctor, should the need arise. It's open Monday–Saturday 9–2 and 4–10, Sunday 5 PM–8 PM. **Libros** (Plaza Bonita, on Marina, tel. 114/3–31–71), open daily 9–9, has an adequate supply of best-sellers in English, as well as a fair selection of magazines and newspapers in both English and Spanish. The local **lavandería** (San Lucas, btw 5 de Mayo and Constitución, tel. 114/3–20–25) is full-service and charges $6 for up to 4 kilos. They're open Monday–Saturday 8–8.

COMING AND GOING The **bus station** (Zaragoza, at 16 de Septiembre, tel. 114/3–04–00), served by the **Autobuses de Baja California (ABC)** and **Águila** bus lines, is two blocks from downtown and 10 blocks from the youth hostel. Frequent buses leave daily for La Paz ($10.50, 3 hrs), between 6 AM and 6:30 PM, and 15 buses depart daily for San José del Cabo ($2, ½ hr) between 7 AM and 10 PM. Buses also leave daily for Todos Santos ($6, 1 hr), at 1 PM and 3:30 PM. For other destinations, take a bus to La Paz and transfer.

➢ BY PLANE • There is one airport for both Cabos (*see* San José del Cabo, *above*). The trip to the airport from Cabo San Lucas takes about an hour, and you have to take a taxi. A shuttle will bring you directly to Cabo San Lucas from the airport for about $20, or you can take a cheaper shuttle to San José and then take the bus to Cabo San Lucas (*see above*).

WHERE TO SLEEP Lodging here is generally expensive. Your cheapest options are the youth hostel (*see below*) and camping on the beach. If you want to camp, head out of town because you're likely to be hassled if you try to sleep in front of the big hotels. The hotels listed below are pretty expensive, but they're the best and most convenient of the bunch.

Hotel Dos Mares. This place is relatively clean and quiet, given that it's right in the center of things. Rooms have fans, but about $5 more will get you air-conditioning, and the algae-green pool is available to any guest who braves it. Singles or doubles are $20; rooms with kitchen are $30. Weekly and monthly rentals ($120–$350) are also available. *Zapata, near marina, tel. 114/3-03-30. 42 rooms, all with bath. Luggage storage.*

Hotel Mar de Cortez. One glance at the tropical courtyard, stately registration desk, and inviting swimming pool here convinces most budget travelers they couldn't possibly afford to stay here, but they just might be wrong. A basic, well-maintained room with one bed and air-conditioning costs $28 for one person and $31 for two. A third person costs $4.50 extra. *Lázaro Cárdenas 11, at Guerrero, tel. 114/3-00-32. 72 rooms, all with bath. Laundry, luggage storage, wheelchair access.*

Siesta Suites Hotel. If you are planning to stay for a few days and can split the cost with someone, these suites are the way to go. Each of the fairly new and spanking-clean suites has a private kitchen. Doubles run $41 ($50 with air-conditioning) and are big enough to squeeze in several additional bodies (for $10 per person). The weekly rate is $250 ($300 with a/c). *Zapata, next to Hotel Dos Mares, tel. 114/3-27-73. 12 rooms, all with bath. Luggage storage.*

➤ HOSTEL • **Villas Juveniles (CREA).** The youth hostel is the cheapest place to stay in Cabo San Lucas, though you may have to ask them to turn on the water and electricity for you. In any case, bring your own toilet paper. The inconvenient walk from the center of town is compensated for by the prices only if you're traveling alone. A night in a single-sex dorm (which you're likely to have to yourself) costs $7; pay $10 and be assured of a private room with your own bath ($7 per person if you share it with the mate of your choice). *Av. de la Juventud, 3 blocks east of Morelos, tel. 114/3-01-48. Walk 15 minutes up Morelos from downtown. 176 beds. Luggage storage, no alcohol.*

➤ CAMPING • There are several RV parks in Cabo San Lucas, but the following have nicer facilities. **Club Cabo** (tel. 114/3-33-48) is a good deal at $5 for two people in a tent, $12 in an RV, and $40 for a little house. **Vagabundos** (tel. 114/3-02-90) is $16 for two persons regardless of whether they're in a 50-foot Winnebago or a four-foot tent. Both are 3–4 kilometers east of town along Highway 1. Hotel owners don't like it if you crash on the beaches in town or near them. The beaches a few kilometers outside town are gorgeous, secluded, and definitely the way to go if you've got the gear and are not traveling alone.

"Why, Yes, I'm a Trust Fund Baby"

Interested in buying a time-share? Even if you aren't, play the part while chatting with the salespeople who work on commission for major hotels and time-share companies. If you're at least 25 years old (or look it) and have a major credit card, take advantage of the free trips and meals that time-share companies offer to lure you into listening to an hour-long spiel, which usually includes breakfast or lunch. If you pretend to be interested for about 15–20 minutes, the person who sent you gets paid as well. Just remember who's hustling whom, or you'll be the proud new owner of a suite in Cabo for two weeks each year.

FOOD Surprisingly, Cabo San Lucas features a number of good, decently priced restaurants, mostly on or north of Niños Héroes. The simplest and arguably the best meal in Cabo San Lucas is a $3.50 plate of fresh chocolate clams at the stand on the corner of 16 de Septiembre and Leona Vicario. Get here early—they close at 7 PM every day. **Café Cabo** (Morelos, near Lázaro Cárdenas, no phone) has a cheery staff and serves big breakfasts for $3.50, as well as an afternoon comida corrida. If you're nostalgic for neo-hippie California culture or cuisine, **Mama's Royal Café** (on the beach, near all the rental stands) delivers on both scores. Omelets, salads, and sandwiches here are all about $5.

Mariscos Mocambo. This spot is the undisputed favorite among locals, who spend their afternoons over red snapper ($9.50), crab in garlic sauce ($11), or seafood soup ($8.50). The fresh-squeezed king-size lemonade ($1) is also good. *Morelos, at 20 de Noviembre, tel. 114/3–21–22. Open daily 9–9.*

The One that Got Away. This second-floor restaurant across from Cabo Wabo club offers good, cheap grub and a mellow atmosphere where you can play pool while digesting your food. Mexican and fish dishes cost $6, or bring your own catch and have it prepared for $4. *Guerrero, at Lázaro Cárdenas, no phone.*

AFTER DARK Cabo San Lucas is *the* center for nightlife in southern Baja. The crowd starts at **Río Grill** for $1 margaritas until 9 PM, then makes its way to the **Giggling Marlin**, where drunk gringos are rumored to be hung up by their feet and weighed like the day's catch. The last stop is at **El Squid Roe**, where the by-then sufficiently inebriated dance themselves silly to the greatest pop hits of the eighties; food and beer are served, but tequila shots are more popular. All of these bars are on Boulevard Marina (the main drag), which turns into Lázaro Cárdenas. None charges a cover.

Cabo Wabo (Guerrero, near Lázaro Cárdenas) is owned by members of Van Halen. Well-known acts often play here on weekends, and any fool who's got about $20 burning a hole in his pocket (and that's just the cover) can come here to look for aging rock stars. If you get tired of tourists, head up to **El Toro Bravo** (16 de Septiembre, off Morelos), a macho drinking establishment (complete with show gals) where unaccompanied women are as welcome as they are rare.

OUTDOOR ACTIVITIES Cabo San Lucas's waters are ideal for almost any water sport. You can rent everything from a waterbike to a catamaran, a Windsurfer to a wave runner. Try **Plaza Las Glorias Beach Club** for these toys, but travelers with tight budgets may be stuck renting more economical equipment such as snorkel gear ($10 a day), surfboards ($15 a day), or boogie boards ($9 a day) at **Cabo Sports Center** (Madero, near Guerrero, tel. 114/3–07–32). The Sports Center is open Monday–Saturday 8–6. You can enjoy many of these expensive activities for free or half-price by listening to a time-share sales rap for a few hours (*see box, above*). And for the very daring, **Baja Bungee** has recently begun sending people attached to a big rubber band off an 80-foot tower for $35 per jump. Contact Alex Darquea at Siesta Suites (tel. 114/3–27–73). You can get a $10 discount on your jump if you purchase it along with a $30 parasail at **The Activity Center** (by Las Palmas Restaurant on Medano Beach, tel. 114/3–30–93), which basically serves as a ticket outlet for all of Cabo San Lucas' water sports and activities.

Los Arcos and **Lover's Beach** sit at the tip of the rocky peninsula south of town. It's here that the Pacific Ocean and the Sea of Cortez meet, the waves sculpting weird formations and tunnels in the offshore rocks. Many people will try to lure you onto their boats for trips to Lover's Beach, but the 30-minute hike is easy and offers spectacular views. Currents in the water here send a cascade of sand spiraling to a depth of about 30 meters. You can view the top with snorkeling equipment, but to get the full effect of the diversity of the marine life here, scuba diving is the way to go.

Cabo Acuadeportes (Hacienda Beach at Km.1 or Chileno Beach at Km. 14, tel. 114/3–01–17) arranges trips to the sand waterfall, as well as to Pelican Rock, Los Arcos, and Cabo Pulmo (Baja's only coral reef). If you're a certified diver, this isn't a place you want to miss, and if you aren't certified, it's a great place to start. Trips cost about $80 for certified divers (if you don't have your PADI card with you, they can call to get your number). Diving certification courses cost $400, and resort courses are about $90 with equipment. **Dive Adventures** (Plaza Bonita, tel. 114/3–26–30) and **Cabo Diving Services** (Marona, at Hidalgo, tel. 114/3–01–50) both have similar prices and trips to the same sites. It's a matter of deciding where you'd like to dive and then calling around to see who's going where on the day you want to go.

Near Los Cabos

TODOS SANTOS

Good (but sometimes dangerous) surf, free camping, and the absence of obtrusive hotels make Todos Santos the perfect place to retire at 20. Founded by Jesuit missionaries in 1734, and subsequently abandoned because of resistance from the local Pericú people, Todos Santos was finally permanently settled by sugar-planting mestizos in the 19th century. Today, despite the substantial number of elderly resident Americans, Todos Santos remains a small town that revolves slowly about its shady zócalo.

BASICS **Bancomer** (Juárez, at Obregón) exchanges cash and traveler's checks weekdays 8:30–noon. The **post office** on Colegio Militar is open weekdays 8–1 and 3–5. For a small connection fee (less than $1), you can make collect and credit-card calls at the *caseta* (phone office) in **Pilar's O.G. Fish Tacos** (Colegio Militar, tel. 114/5–01–46), which also serves as the bus station. The caseta is open daily 7 AM–8 PM. **Farmacia Todos Santos** on Juárez is open daily 7 AM–10 PM, but you can knock at the door at any hour for emergency service. **El Tecolote** bookstore (Juárez) doubles as a source of tourist information and the hub of the resident gringos' social network.

COMING AND GOING Buses depart Pilar's (*see above*) for Los Cabos ($5.50, 1 hr) every couple of hours from 8 AM to 9 PM. Buses for La Paz ($5, 1 hr) leave every half-hour between 7 AM and 8:30 AM, and every few hours until 7 PM. You can store a few bags for free at Pilar's.

WHERE TO SLEEP AND EAT If you didn't cruise down in a Winnebago, you'll probably want to camp on the sandy stretch of beach about 2 kilometers south of town. There's also good camping at **Playa San Pedrito**, 6 kilometers to the south. The only affordable place to stay in town is **Hotel Miramar** (Mutualismo, at Pedrajo, tel. 114/5–03–41). This tranquil retreat at the edge of town is wheelchair-accessible and has parking, a laundromat next door, and a swimming pool. Single rooms are $15.50, doubles $19.

Pollo Asadero on Colegio Militar serves roasted chicken for less than $4, or you can eat at either of the nameless ceviche stands next door for about the same price. **Restaurant El Puente** (Randel, at Colegio Militar) has patio tables and a varied menu, with most meals between $5 and $10. **Lonchería Karla** (Colegio Militar, opposite the park) has $3.50 plates of tacos, tamales, and other antojitos.

SONORA AND LOS MOCHIS

By Jamie Davidson

Travelers often overlook the northwest corner of Mexico because of the terrain: It's primarily desert country with harsh weather and temperatures that reach over 100° during the blistering summer months. Although the state of Sonora bills itself as *una ventana al mar* (a window to the sea), the coastal towns along the Sea of Cortez are none too accessible for the visitor of limited means. Yet to dismiss the area entirely would be a major injustice. The towns of Puerto Peñasco, Bahía Kino, and Guaymas have fairly unspoiled beaches; Nogales is renowned for the arts and crafts trucked in from all over Mexico; and Hermosillo, the capital of Sonora, is simply a lively place to be. South of Hermosillo, mountains give way to the Sonoran desert, where the sandy tans of the flatlands take on tinges of ochre and yellow. Agribusiness, the region's economic mainstay, still irrigates the desert with waters from dammed rivers, making Sonora the second-richest state in the Republic.

The small colonial town of Alamos, with narrow cobblestone streets and elegantly restored haciendas, recalls a time when this sleepy settlement was the prosperous mining center of the northwest. Los Mochis, south on the coast in the state of Sinaloa, was founded by an American sugar entrepreneur. Today, it's an essential stop if you plan to take a ferry to Baja or the train through the Copper Canyon (*see* Chapter 14). Ferries to Santa Rosalía on the Baja peninsula leave from the harbor city of Guaymas.

The Sonoran Yaqui people are famous for fierce resistance to outside domination. Porfirio Díaz set the army against them in the 1890s when they objected to his selling their land to private investors, and thousands of prisoners were sent to work building railroads in southern Mexico. Even so, the Yaqui were not fully "subdued" (that is, they kept killing settlers) until the late 1920s.

Nogales

The unimpressive town of Nogales, Mexico crowds against the border across from Nogales, Arizona. Like Tijuana to the west, but on a much smaller scale, Nogales is famous (or infamous) for its shopping, which attracts hordes of Arizonans bargaining for tacky knickknacks—this is the place to find that stuffed armadillo that's been eluding you back home. Blue glass from Guadalajara, silver from Zacatecas, and burnished pottery from Oaxaca are also available, though you'll find all these at lower prices farther south. Nogales boasts a decent bullfighting arena, which is the hot spot during **Cinco de Mayo.** This festival, including bullfights, cockfights, horse races, and *artesanía* (crafts) exhibitions, celebrates Mexico's defeat of the French in the battle of Puebla and lasts from the end of April until May 5.

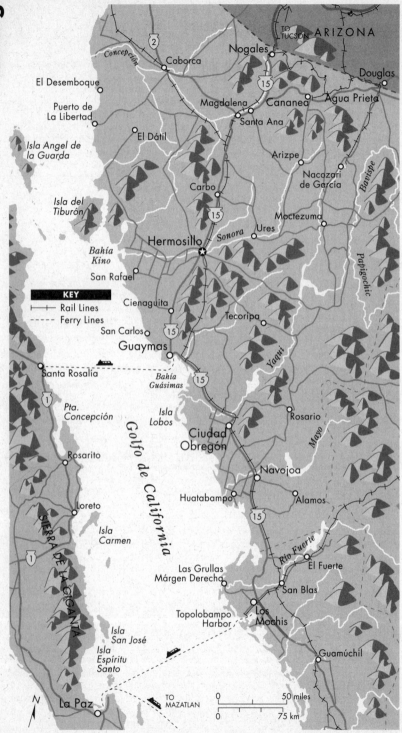

TO
TUCSON ARIZONA

Nogales

Douglas

Coborca

2

Concepción

El Desemboque

Magdalena Cananea Agua Prieta

Puerto de
La Libertad

Santa Ana

15

El Dátil

Isla Angel de
la Guarda

Arizpe

Carbo

Nacozari
de García

Bavispe

Isla del
Tiburón

15

Moctezuma

Hermosillo Sonora Ures

Bahía
Kino

San Rafael

KEY

Cienaguita

Rail Lines

Ferry Lines

Tecoripa

Papigochic

San Carlos 15

San Carlos

Guaymas

Yaqui

Santa Rosalía

Bahía
Guásimas

1

15

Pta.
Concepción

Isla
Lobos

Rosario

Rosarito

Ciudad
Obregón

Golfo de California

Mayo

Navojoa

Loreto

Huatabampo Alamos

Isla
Carmen

1

15

SIERRA DE LA GIGANTA

Río Fuerte

Las Grullas
Márgen Derecha

El Fuerte

San Blas

Isla
San José

Topolobampo
Harbor

Los
Mochis

Isla
Espíritu
Santo

Guamúchil

N

La Paz

TO
MAZATLAN

0   50 miles

0   75 km

244

Nogales ("walnuts" in English) serves as a major export depot for Sonora's rich agricultural produce. But, like many of its border cousins, Nogales has been affected by important economic changes over the past decade. The town hosts an ever-increasing number of industrial parks and *maquiladoras* set up by foreign (mostly U.S.) companies in special duty-free zones in order to take advantage of cheap Mexican labor. Poor workers' *colonias* (neighborhoods) overlook the town, with shacks and small houses sloping perilously on the hillsides.

BASICS

CASAS DE CAMBIO It's best to change money at the banks on the U.S. side of the border, where exchange rates are pretty good. **Bank of America** is on the east side of the street, about one block into the States. On the Mexican side, you'll find several money-exchange offices along Campillo, one block from the border. **Bancomer** (López Mateos, 5 blocks south of border crossing) exchanges money 9–noon and has an ATM that accepts Visa cards.

CROSSING THE BORDER Both the U.S. and Mexican customs offices at Nogales are open 24 hours a day. Americans and Canadians who plan to stay in Mexico longer than 72 hours or go south of the border towns need a tourist card. Present proof of citizenship at the Mexican government tourist offices or at the Mexican government border office in Nogales. Bringing a car can be a little tricky (*see* Coming and Going, *below*).

EMERGENCIES Bilingual operators staff the emergency telephone service run by the national tourism office 24 hours a day; dial 91/5–250–0123 or 91/5–250–0151. There are also direct numbers for the **police** (tel. 631/6–15–64) and **fire** and **ambulance** service (tel. 631/4–07–69).

MAIL The *oficina de correos* (post office) will hold mail sent to you at the following address for up to 10 days: Lista de Correos, Benito Juárez y Calle Campillo, Nogales, Sonora, CP 84000, México. *Benito Juárez, at Campillo, 2 blocks from border crossing. Open weekdays 8–7, Sat. 8–11 AM.*

MEDICAL AID Several reputable, English-speaking medical offices are found in the first few blocks of Obregón. **Roberto Belches Vasques, MD** (tel. 631/2–37–21) and **Rene Romo De Vivar, DDS** (tel. 631/2–05–00) have offices in Nogales.

Farmacia San Xavier is open 24 hours. *Campillo 73, 2 blocks from border crossing, tel. 631/2–55–03.*

PHONES Working (yes, working!) Ladatel pay phones can be found along major streets, and there is a *caseta de larga distancia* (long-distance phone office) in the bus terminal. Downtown, **Farmacia San Ángel** offers long-distance and local service but no collect or credit-card calls. *Ochoa, off López Mateos. Open Mon.–Sat. 8 AM–10 PM, Sun. 8–7.*

VISITOR INFORMATION The unhelpful tourist office, on the right just across the border, hands out a bite-size city map. Fortunately, Nogales is easy to navigate. *López Mateos, at Internacional, tel. 631/2–06–66. Open weekdays 8 AM–2 PM, weekends 8 AM–3 PM.*

COMING AND GOING

Almost everything you could need or want to see is near the border crossing area and easily accessible on foot. Local buses run to other parts of town from López Mateos. Taxis will charge you roughly $1 per kilometer, but be sure to set a price before getting in.

BY CAR Bringing a car into Mexico is complicated. You'll need to present either a $5,000 cash deposit or a credit card at the border. You'll also need Mexican auto insurance, available for as little as $10 per day at the border. Have your car registration and driver's license with you at all times. Driving in the Sonora area is not difficult. Highway 15 is well maintained, and the smaller roads branching off the highway are generally in pretty good shape. You can ask at the border if weather has caused any road damage.

BY BUS There is a new bus station in Nogales, but it's a good 6 kilometers from the center of town on Highway 15. Local buses labeled CENTRAL CAMIONERA run along López Mateos to the station. Three bus companies use the station: **Transportes Norte de Sonora** (tel. 631/3–17–00) and **Tres Estrellas de Oro** (tel. 631/3–02–33), serving Baja as well as mainland Mexico; and **Transportes del Pacífico** (tel. 631/3–16–06), serving the western mainland. Buses headed south leave at least every hour, and four leave for Mexico City each day—the 1½-day journey costs $98 first class and $71 second class. Tres Estrellas and Transportes Norte de Sonora each have a daily evening departure for Mexicali ($23 1st class, $20 2nd class, 9 hrs). Or you can take any bus headed south to Santa Ana ($4.50 1st class, $3.50 2nd class); Santa Ana is a major transport hub, and many buses leave for Mexicali from its station. From Nogales there are buses to Tijuana ($30 1st class, $24.50 2nd class, 12 hrs), Hermosillo ($10 1st class, $8.50 2nd class, 5 hrs), Guaymas ($14.50 1st class, $13.50 2nd class, 7 hrs), Los Mochis ($30 1st class, $24.50 2nd class, 12 hrs), Mazatlán ($50 1st class, $43 2nd class, 17 hrs), and Guadalajara ($71 1st class, $61 2nd class, 31 hrs). The terminal has phones, luggage storage (35¢ per bag per hour), and a money exchange booth.

On the Arizona side of the border, **Greyhound** (tel. 800/231–2222) has frequent, direct service to Tucson ($6.50, 1½ hrs) and scheduled connections throughout the States. You can cram your luggage in a locker here for $1. Collective taxi/vans go directly to the airport in Tucson from here for $10 per person.

BY TRAIN The train station (tel. 631/3–02–05) is across from the bus station, about 6 kilometers outside town off Highway 15, and can be reached via any local bus marked FERROCARRIL or CENTRAL CAMIONERA. Daily first- and second-class rail service is available to Benjamin Hill ($6 1st class, $4 2nd class); Hermosillo ($11 1st class, $6 2nd class); Sufragio (transfer point for the Copper Canyon; $30 1st class, $15 2nd class); Mazatlán ($47 1st class, $24 2nd class); and Guadalajara ($70 1st class, $35 2nd class). You can change trains for Mexico City in Guadalajara, or for Mexicali in Benjamin Hill. The second-class train leaves at 7 AM; the first-class train at 3:30 PM. Tickets can be purchased at the station; be sure to arrive about 30 minutes prior to departure.

WHERE TO SLEEP

If you're traveling on into Mexico, you may be better off avoiding a night in one of Nogales's overpriced hotels by taking an overnight bus straight out of town. If you do stay, the wheelchair-accessible **Hotel Holandia** (Morelos, no phone), on a walkway just off Campillo, is the cheapest place in town. The decent rooms with private bathrooms and hot water are worth the $17 for a single or double, if you can tolerate the saggy beds and lack of ventilation. **Hotel Orizaba** (Juárez 29, near Campillo, tel. 631/2–58–55) has similar conditions at similar prices ($17 single, $18.50 double), except they give you a fan in place of your own bathroom. The communal baths get pretty nasty when the place is full, but they do have hot water.

Hotel Olga. You can get fairly well-kept singles and doubles without bath here for $20. For $23, you get air-conditioning and a private bath with hot water, but if you've got that much money, you'd do better at the Hotel Pasaje (*see below*) anyway. *Juárez 17, near Campillo, tel. 631/2–35–60. 13 rooms, 7 with bath. Luggage storage, wheelchair access.*

Hotel Pasaje. Though relatively expensive, this hotel is still the best deal in town. The small rooms ($23 single or double) are very clean and cozy, with private baths, hot water, and air-conditioning; some even have TVs. It also offers luggage storage and a nice restaurant. *Obregón 75, near Campillo, tel. 631/2–00–18. 25 rooms, all with bath.*

FOOD

The Nogales restaurant scene is pricey unless you get off of the main boulevard. Taquerías and push-cart vendors, found on almost every corner, are an inexpensive alternative at $2–$3 a meal. Cheap eateries can be found along Ochoa. Of these, the 24-hour **Restaurant Café Río Sonora** (Ochoa, near Hidalgo, no phone) serves the best and cheapest multi-course *comida corrida* (pre-prepared lunch special; $3.50). **Café Olga** (Juárez, at Campillo, tel. 631/2–16–41) is a popular breakfast spot where hot cakes and eggs are just $4. **La Fábula** (Vásquez, at López Mateos, tel. 631/2–20–48), near the local bus terminal in the center of town, serves up good Chicago-style pizza (starting at $6 for a small, $9 for a large) from noon until 11 PM daily.

AFTER DARK

Except for weekends, when Arizonans cross the border to whoop it up Mexican style, Nogales's night life is pretty mellow. **El Salón Regis** (Obregón, opposite Café Olga) is packed on weekends. Drinks are $1–$3, but lone women are likely to be hassled. **Harlow's Discotheque** (Elías 21, no phone) has all the latest in lasers, lights, and hip-hop music, all for a $5 cover. On Fridays and Saturdays, locals head to **Monaro** (Colonia La Loma) to drink and dance to cumbia and salsa. The cover here is $3.50.

Near Nogales

PUERTO PENASCO

This relatively undeveloped tourist trap sits on the lonely northern coast of the Sea of Cortez. Vacationing Arizonans in search of the sea congregate on the southern side of town in the summer with their RVs, dune buggies, and Jet Skis. The town is surrounded by the **Desierto de Altar**, where the temperature often soars to more than 100° in summer. The best time of year to visit the area is late spring, when temperatures are mild, and the cholla, saguaro, organ pipe, barrel, and other cacti and desert vegetation bloom into red, yellow, and white flowers. Other than heading to the beach, there is little to do or see here, but nature lovers will appreciate the desert for its simple beauty; nights are clear and starry, and sunsets are glorious.

Jesuit Father Eusebio Kino, who established a number of missions in northwestern Mexico in the late 17th century, reportedly drew a parallel between the Desierto de Altar and his vision of Hell.

COMING AND GOING Tres Estrellas de Oro buses serve Puerto Peñasco, but you have to take a bus to Caborca ($9, 4 hrs) and transfer. Puerto Peñasco is also served by the train, but you'll need to go to Benjamin Hill and change lines.

WHERE TO SLEEP AND EAT Check out the quiet **Hotel Villa Hermosa** (Calle 13, at Armada Independencia, no phone), which offers well-maintained singles and doubles overlooking the beach for $15–$18. **Restaurant Los Arcos** (Eusebio Kino, at Tamarindos, tel. 638/3–35–97) has a breakfast special for just $2 and is open daily 7:30 AM–10 PM. You can also head for one of the many seafood stands near the end of Boulevard Kino.

Pick Your Poison

Like tequila, mezcal comes from the fermented heart of the maguey plant (a large succulent). The more expensive tequila, however, is from only one species of maguey, whereas mezcal is a mixture. It comes in several different classes. The cheapest is called pechuga or minero and is not as smooth as mezcal de cordon or mezcal de punto, both of which consist of only the first and finest drops to fall from the distillery. All mezcal is originally clear, but if stored in wood, it will take on a distinct color and flavor. The infamous "worm" (a beetle larva that lives in the maguey) also imparts its own distinctive flavor. On special occasions, look for pechuga especial, distilled with apples, oranges, and chicken for an extra flavorful brew.

Hermosillo

The capital city of Sonora, Hermosillo is about 230 kilometers south of Nogales. With a state university and a population of almost half a million, this is a prosperous city. You might expect such a place to be dynamic and exciting, but it's basically big, hot, dirty, crime ridden, and exhausting. If you're stuck here, at least you can still see traces of Hermosillo's colonial history in residential architecture along boulevards lined with orange and palm trees and in grand public buildings such as the **Catedral de la Asunción** and the **Palacio de Gobierno** on the central **Plaza Zaragoza**. You can visit the **Centro Ecológico de Sonora** (southern outskirts of town off Hwy. 15) to see exhibits on the flora and fauna of the local desert. At the eastern base of **Cerro de la Campana** (Bell Hill), the **Capilla del Carmen** occasionally holds a "mariachi mass"—a loud, colorful trumpet- and guitar-accompanied Sunday mass that's worth getting out of bed to attend (*see box* on Liberation Theology, in Chapter 3). Near the Capilla del Carmen, the free **Museo de Sonora** holds a fine collection of pre-Columbian artifacts. Special annual events include **La Fiesta de la Vendimia** (the grape harvest celebration) in July, and Yaqui Indian dances, held during **Semana Santa** (Holy Week). Most visitors, however, prefer to head south to beach resorts such as the Bahía Kino towns on the Sea of Cortez, and, farther south, Mazatlán on the Pacific.

It cools off in Hermosillo between October and February, but not by much.

BASICS

AMERICAN EXPRESS The AmEx office in **Hermex Travel** sells traveler's checks, insurance, and plane tickets. They also hold mail for card holders and cash their personal checks. *Rosales, at Monterrey. Open weekdays 8:30–1 and 3–6:30, Sat. 9–1. Mailing address: Edif. Lupita, Hermosillo, Sonora, CP 83000, México.*

CASAS DE CAMBIO A number of banks line Rosales, in the downtown area, and Eusebio Kino, in the northwest corner of town. **Bancomer** (Sonora, at Matamoros) changes traveler's checks weekdays 9–noon and has a *caja permanente* (ATM) that takes Visa cards. More ATMs can be found downtown, on Serdán between Juárez and Jesús García.

CONSULATE United States. The consulate has an answering machine that is checked every hour when the consulate is not open. *Monterrey 142, behind Hotel Calinda, tel. 62/17–23–75. Open weekdays 8–4:30.*

EMERGENCIES Police (tel. 62/13–40–46); fire (tel. 62/12–01–97); ambulance (tel. 62/4–07–69).

MAIL The post office downtown will hold mail sent to you at the following address: Lista de Correos, Blvd. Rosales, Hermosillo, Sonora, CP 83000, México. You can send or receive telegrams and faxes at the office next door. *Post office: Rosales, at Serdán, tel. 62/12–00–11. Open weekdays 8–6, Sat. 8–noon.*

MEDICAL AID There are two 24-hour clinics on Norberto Aguirre between Juárez and Jesús García. You'll also be happy to know that, if the need arises, there's a 24-hour funeral home right around the corner. For simpler problems, **Farmacia Margarita** (Morelia, at Guerrero, tel. 62/13–15–90) is open 24 hours.

PHONES There are pay phones along the streets, but finding one that works could take you all day. It's quicker to head to **Café Monte Carlo** (*see Food, below*), which has working ones. Otherwise, long-distance calls and faxes can be placed at **Farmacia Margarita** (*see above*).

VISITOR INFORMATION The **Secretaría de Fomento de Turismo** (Secretary of Tourism), in the Palacio de Gobierno, usually has someone on hand who speaks English, but anyone can load you down with brochures and maps, some in English. *Tehuantepec, at Comonfort, tel. 62/17–29–64. Open weekdays 8–3 and 5–7, Sat. 10–1.*

COMING AND GOING

BY BUS Three main bus companies serve Hermosillo's **Central Camionera** (Transversal 400): **Transportes Norte de Sonora** (tel. 62/13–24–16), **Transportes del Pacífico** (tel. 62/17–05–80), and **Tres Estrellas de Oro** (tel. 62/13–24–16). To get to the Central Camionera from downtown, take any bus marked TRANSVERSAL or PERIFERICO. Taxis will attempt to charge you about $7 from the station to downtown, but if you walk away from the station, you can flag one down and pay about $5. Buses run north to Tijuana ($31, 12 hrs), stopping in Nogales ($10, 3½ hrs) and Mexicali ($23, 10 hrs); and south to Mexico City ($60, 31 hrs), stopping in Guaymas ($5, 2 hrs), Los Mochis ($18.50, 7 hrs), Mazatlán ($35, 12 hrs), and Guadalajara ($43, 26 hrs) every hour, all day. Luggage storage and money exchange are available at the terminal.

BY TRAIN The train station (tel. 62/15–35–77) is about 3 kilometers north of town, just off Highway 15. First-class trains leave for Mexicali ($27, 10 hrs) and Nogales ($11, 4 hrs) daily at 5 PM. Second-class service to those same destinations leaves at 1 AM, takes somewhat longer, and costs about one-third the price of first class. First-class trains for Guadalajara ($63, 22 hrs) leave daily at 8 PM. Second-class trains to Guadalajara ($23, at least 27 hrs) leave daily at noon. If you're Mexico City bound, you'll need to change trains in Guadalajara. Buses marked EST. FERR. will take you from the market in central Hermosillo to the station; a cab from the center is $5.

BY PLANE **Mexicana** (tel. 62/16–78–86 or 62/17–11–03) and **Aeroméxico** (tel. 62/16–82–06) serve Hermosillo with several daily flights from Tucson and Dallas in the United States, as well as from other parts of Mexico. The airport lies about 10 kilometers from town on the road to Bahía and Nuevo Kino. Taxis ($12–$15) are the best way to get to the airport.

GETTING AROUND

With several hills to orient you, it's difficult to get lost in Hermosillo. The most prominent hill downtown is **Cerro de la Campana.** Highway 15 runs through Hermosillo and on to Nogales to the north. Boulevard Transversal transects the city northwest–southeast. The bus and train terminals are a fair distance from downtown, but local buses are cheap and dependable, if not always fast. Taxis charge roughly a dollar per kilometer, often twice or thrice that at night or from the bus station.

WHERE TO SLEEP

There are a number of clean, comfortable budget hotels in the downtown area directly north of the Cerro de la Campana, near Plaza Zaragoza. Because drugs and prostitution were running rampant, the government shut down most of the flophouses along Sonora and Juárez, thus limiting options for budget travelers. Spared from the sweep was **Casa de Huéspedes Hotel Carmelita** (Sonora, btw Revolución and Gonzáles, no phone), where singles and doubles are $13. The ugly communal bathrooms are a disadvantage, but the staff is truly amiable, and there are fans in the rooms. Women (and even some men) may get hassled in this area after dark.

Hotel Monte Carlo. Ignore the drunks hanging around outside this older hotel, because inside you'll find clean private bathrooms and good air-conditioning. Singles are $23, doubles $25, and a room for four is $35. *Juárez, at Sonora, opposite Plaza Juárez, tel. 62/12–08–53. 28 rooms, all with bath.*

Hotel San Andrés. Hermosillo may not be the place for a big splurge, but the travel-weary can head for security and relative opulence at this hotel near the Plaza de Zaragoza. The big rooms here have TVs, phones, heat, and air-conditioning. Singles cost $40, doubles $50. *Oaxaca 14, tel. 62/17–30–99. 83 rooms, all with bath.*

Hotel Washington. The Washington offers clean, oddly shaped, old rooms, all with private bath and big shower stalls with warm water. On the down side, the plumbing is leaky, mornings can be noisy thanks to the local bus depot out front, and the heat and air-conditioning are weak.

Singles cost $20; doubles are $22.50 for one bed, $25 for two. *Noriega 68, at Matamoros, tel. 62/13–11–83. 28 rooms, all with bath.*

FOOD

The downtown area is loaded with cheap taquerías and street vendors selling everything from fruit to hot dogs. You can go out to dinner here with $5 in your pocket and come back with a full belly and some change. Fresh, cheap fruits and vegetables are sold at the **mercado municipal** (Matamoros, at Roberto Elías Calles). For basic, fast, and cheap Mexican food downtown, **Cenaduría Yañez** (Yañez Sur 7, tel. 62/14–18–72) serves up spicy tacos or *burritos de machaca* (chopped-beef burritos) for about $2, from noon until midnight daily. **Café Lydia** (Sonora, at Gonzáles, no phone) opens bright and early for decent breakfasts (about $3).

Cafe Monte Carlo. Baseball paraphernalia all over the walls adds ambiance to this eclectic place. Try a tongue omelet ($5.50) and pineapple juice ($1.50) for breakfast. Their extensive dinner menu includes chicken in green sauce ($7) and liver and onions ($6). *Juárez, at Sonora, tel. 62/12–22–59. Open Mon.–Sat. 7 AM–10 PM.*

La Huerta. This restaurant is a bit out of the way, but worth the trip for delicious seafood at reasonable prices. The *pescado a la veracruzana* (red snapper cooked in tomatoes, onions, capers, peppers, and herbs; $10) is a welcome relief from tacos and beans. *San Luis Potosí 109, tel. 62/14–82–88. From Plaza Zaragoza, take MORELOS, KINO, or HUERTA bus to San Luis Potosí. Open daily noon–7 PM.*

Jung. The wholesome fare at this vegetarian restaurant includes salads, sandwiches, and entrées, all fashioned from fresh fruits and vegetables and whole-wheat breads. Breakfast, lunch, and dinner each run $6–$10. *Niños Héroes 75, tel. 62/13–28–82.*

CHEAP THRILLS

Hermosillo is short on diversions, but on a nice afternoon you can go play at the **Parque Madero** (Jesús García, btw P. Elías and Norwalk), not far from the eastern base of the Cerro de la Campana. The long, fast slides, jungle gyms, merry-go-rounds, and swings here send the local kiddies wild, and you might as well join them. On hot days, watch out for the bratty children who jump into the fountain, emerge dripping and jubilant, and proceed to embrace anyone not quick enough to get out of the way.

AFTER DARK

Because downtown Hermosillo (especially the Plaza Juárez and surrounding streets) is unsafe at night, most will want to stay in. For diehards, there's **Blocky'O** (Rodríguez, at Juárez, tel. 62/15–18–88), a huge disco with frequent bar specials. A little farther south, just off Rodríguez, you'll find **Nova Olimpia** (Frontera, at C. L. de Soria, tel. 62/17–30–13), where cumbia and salsa play on Friday and Saturday nights. Both clubs charge a hefty $8 cover charge for men, about $3 for women. A few blocks farther south you'll stumble onto **Marco 'n' Charlie's** (Blvd. Rodríguez 78, tel. 62/15–30–61), a popular bar and grill frequented by young, middle-class Hermosillans.

Near Hermosillo

BAHIA KINO

The two towns of Kino Viejo and Kino Nuevo share the Bahía Kino on the Sea of Cortez, and both are blessed with beautiful beaches. They are also both easily explored from Hermosillo, about 120 kilometers away. Otherwise, they'd be hard-pressed to be more different. The sleepy fishing village of Kino Viejo was established by the Jesuit priest Eusebio Kino some 200 years ago as a mission for Seri Indians and today consists of a few stores, restaurants and fishermen's houses strung along a dusty road. Kino Nuevo is a haven for American retirees who have created a secluded, sanitized version of the States behind a fenced-in, faux-villa facade. As you amble through town or along the beaches, you may encounter Seris selling the ironwood sculptures for which they are known. The small **Museo de los Seris** in Kino Nuevo serves up historical and cultural information on these indigenous people. Local hustlers may try to persuade you to visit the Isla del Tiburón (Shark Island), home to Seri Indians until they were forcibly resettled in the 50s. The island is now a fragile wildlife refuge; please don't visit.

Summer is the best time to visit the Kinos: The resident Americans stay indoors to avoid the blistering heat, and the sea is exquisite.

COMING AND GOING Ten buses a day leave Hermosillo for the Kinos between 5:40 AM and 5:30 PM. Buses depart from the old **Transportes Norte de Sonora** station (Sonora, btw Revolución and Gonzáles), not the Central Camionera, and the two-hour trip costs $4. The same buses pass through both Kinos, and hitching between towns is easy.

WHERE TO SLEEP In the off-season various RV parks in the Kinos rent tent spaces for $10–$15, including use of their pools. Try **Trailer Park Kino Bay** (tel. 624/2–02–16) or **Islandia Marina** (tel. 624/2–00–81). Beach bungalows with kitchen facilities rent for about $20 at **Islandia Trailer Park** (just outside of Kino Viejo, toward Hermosillo, no phone). You can also string a hammock or plop your tent for free under one of the many *palapas* (thatched huts) along the 18-kilometer beach in Kino Nuevo. Camping here is generally safe, but you need to watch your stuff. Avoid camping on the beach in Kino Viejo; there's a lot of foot traffic on the beach at night.

FOOD Kino Viejo has worthwhile restaurants and a number of fish and taco stands. **Restaurant Costa Azul** (Blvd. Kino, near the water, no phone) is a friendly spot to relax over a fish ($5) or lobster ($12) dinner, or sit into the night drinking a beer ($1.50) after a rough day at the beach. They also serve good breakfasts for about $4. **Restaurant Dorita,** just opposite the police station/post office/Red Cross building on the main drag, serves good, cheap food (lunches about $5) amid bustling families from 7 AM to 7 PM daily. They've also got a public Ladatel phone. **La Cabaña de Pepe** (Santa Rosalía, at Acapulco, tel. 624/2–00–44) serves spicy tamales and chiles rellenos (about $4) from 8 AM to 9 PM daily.

OUTDOOR ACTIVITIES Water sports in the bay are too inviting to pass up. If you have your own equipment, pick any spot and dive in; if you don't, you'll find rental equipment available primarily in Kino Nuevo. Check with **Villas del Mar** (tel. 624/18–70–45) for snorkel gear ($8 per day), Windsurfer ($15 per day), or Jet Ski rentals ($20 per ½ hour)—you'll see the shop right off the highway. Better yet, head down to the water in Kino Viejo in the early morning when the fishermen push their *pangas* (fishing boats) off the sand and see if you can go along (you'll probably be expected to help with the nets).

LA PINTADA

Also accessible from Hermosillo is an archaeological site known as La Pintada, some 60 kilometers to the south off Highway 15. Once a refuge for Pima and Seri Indians fleeing the Spanish, the area is now filled with vibrantly colored rock paintings. Catch a bus toward Guaymas and ask the driver to let you off at La Pintada or join a research group from Hermosillo's university during the school year. Contact the tourist office in Hermosillo (*see* Visitor Information, *above*) for more information.

Guaymas

The port city of Guaymas provides a welcome respite from the sweltering heat inland. There's not much to see here, but it's fun to wander along the docks, watching the fishing boats and checking out the people. Another reason to visit is strictly practical: There is twice-weekly ferry service from Guaymas to Santa Rosalía, on the Baja Peninsula.

Guaymas seems more concerned with commerce and fishing than tourism. An extensive shrimp- and sardine-fishing fleet operates from here, and seafood processing is one of the

Locals head to the uninspiring Playa Miramar in summer, but the best beaches by far are in nearby San Carlos.

main local industries (check out the town's **Monumento al Pescador,** an enormous fisherman battling a huge fish). The town's **Plaza de San Fernando** is a good place to sit back, enjoy a *refresco* (soda), and watch the kids run around in the midday sun.

BASICS

AUTO PARTS/SERVICE **Auto Partes Ibarra, S.A.** sells parts and can recommend mechanics according to your specific problems. *Serdán 251, tel. 622/2–01–36 or 622/2–31–36. Open Mon.–Sat. 8–noon and 2–6.*

CASAS DE CAMBIO There are a number of banks along Avenida Serdán. **Bancomer** (at Calle 20) changes cash weekdays 8:30–noon, and travelers checks until 1 PM. Their 24-hour ATM accepts Visa. The **Banamex** ATM, down the street, accepts Plus and Cirrus.

EMERGENCIES **Police** and **fire** (tel. 622/2–00–30); **ambulance** (tel. 622/2–55–55).

LAUNDRY **Guaymas Superlava** has automatic washers for $2 and $5 and dryers for $4. They will also do up to 3 kilos for you for $7. *García López 884, tel. 622/2–54–00. Open Mon.–Sat. 8 –7.*

MAIL The post office will hold mail sent to you at the following address for up to 10 days: Lista de Correos, Av. 10, Guaymas, Sonora, CP 85400, México. *Av. 10, at Calle 20. Open weekdays 8–5, Sat. 8–2.*

MEDICAL AID There are several doctor's offices in the plaza between Calles 18 and 19 on Serdán. **Dr. David Robles Rendón** is a general practicioner. *Serdán, at Calle 17, tel. 622/2–83–13 and 2–16–69. Open weekdays 8–1 and 5–8, Sat. 8–1.*

Farmacia Benavides. *Serdán, at Calle 18, tel. 622/2–30–44. Open daily 8 AM–9:30 PM.*

PHONES The public phones along the streets often don't work. You can make local, long-distance, and international calls from the caseta at the **Farmacia Santa Martha**, but you'll have to pay cash, because collect and credit-card calls are not allowed. *Calle 19, at Serdán. Open Mon.–Sat. 8:30 AM–9 PM, Sun. 9–3.*

VISITOR INFORMATION The local tourist office is on the second floor of a gray building, above a paint store. *Serdán, at Calle 12, tel. 622/4–29–32. Open weekdays 9–2 and 4–7 (if they feel like it).*

COMING AND GOING

In Guaymas, Highway 15 becomes García López. Avenida Serdán runs from García López on the east side of town, is central to everything but the beaches, and is served by rickety but well-marked local buses. Buses marked SAN CARLOS make the 15-minute trip out to the beaches of San Carlos for 65¢.

BY BUS Three bus lines, **Transportes Norte de Sonora** (tel. 622/2–12–71), **Tres Estrellas de Oro** (tel. 622/2–12–71), and **Transportes del Pacífico** (tel. 622/2–30–19), operate from terminals on Rodríguez near Calle 13, two blocks south of Serdán. Buses depart hourly, heading south to Mexico City ($77, 29 hrs), with stops in Los Mochis ($15, 5 hrs), Mazatlán ($30, 10 hrs) and Guadalajara ($50, 24 hrs); and north to Tijuana ($40, 17 hrs), stopping in Hermosillo ($4.50, 1½ hrs), Nogales ($15, 5 hrs), and Mexicali ($30, 15 hrs). Transportes del Pacífico goes to Navojoa ($7, 3 hrs), the transfer point for Alamos, frequently between 5 AM and midnight.

BY TRAIN The train station (tel. 622/3–10–65) is 10 kilometers south of Guaymas in a town called Empalme. Get here via a red and white TNS (Transportes Norte de Sonora) bus marked EMPALME from any bus stop on Serdán or from the Transportes Norte de Sonora station. Northbound first- and second-class trains depart daily between 7 and 8 AM for Mexicali ($32, 12 hrs

1st class; $12, 15 hrs 2nd class), Nogales ($16.50, 6 hrs 1st class; $6.50, 8 hrs 2nd class), and Hermosillo ($6, 1½ hrs 1st class; $2.50, 2 hrs 2nd class). Southbound trains depart daily at 2:30 PM (2nd class) and 9:40 PM (1st class). The first-class trip to Guadalajara (the transfer point for Mexico City) costs $53 and takes 24 hours. Second class costs only $20 and takes (at least) four hours longer.

BY PLANE Aeroméxico, which serves most of Mexico, flies into the Guaymas airport, 13 kilometers north of town. One-way fares to La Paz are about $120; to Mexico City, about $135. You can buy tickets at the **airline office**. *Serdán, at Calle 16, tel. 622/2–01–23. Open weekdays 8–1 and 2–4:30, Sat. 8–1.*

BY FERRY The **Sematur** ferry terminal (tel. 622/2–23–24) is at the east end of town, just off Serdán. Ferries to Santa Rosalía, on the Baja coast, run on Tuesday and Friday at 8 AM ($15, $30 tourist class). You can put a car on the ferry, as well, but it's expensive—they charge by size, and the smallest car costs about $110. You can buy tickets at the ferry terminal Mondays and Thursdays 8–3 or the morning of departure 6 AM–7:30 PM.

WHERE TO SLEEP

There are plenty of clean, reasonably priced hotels on and near Serdán. **Casa de Huéspedes Lupita** (Calle 15 No. 125, tel. 622/2–84–09), only a few blocks from Serdán and the bus terminals, is a bargain. Singles with bath go for $12, doubles $15. Without bath the prices drop to $9 and $12, respectively, and you might as well save your dough, because the communal baths aren't bad at all, and the lukewarm water doesn't get any warmer in the pricier rooms. Behind the city market, the **Motel del Puerto** (Yañez 92, tel. 622/2–34–08 or 622/2–24–91) has basic, clean rooms complete with fresh sheets, curtains, clean bathrooms, hot water, and air-conditioning, and the lobby has a long-distance telephone. This area is a bit seedy at night. Singles are $17, doubles $23, and they take AmEx and Visa cards. For a bit more, the same levels of cleanliness and comfort can be found at the **Hotel Santa Rita** (Serdán, at Calle 9, tel. 622/4–14–64 or 622/2–81–00). Small rooms with TV and air-conditioning, a short walk from the center of town, are available for $28.50 (single) and $35 (double). They take traveler's checks and AmEx and Visa cards and have some wheelchair-accessible rooms.

FOOD

Serdán is lined with reasonably priced restaurants, bars, *loncherías* (snack bars), and taquerías serving fresh local seafood and typical Mexican dishes. Buy fresh fruits and veggies at the **mercado municipal,** in a long building one block south of Serdán, near the intersection with Yañez. If you prefer to splurge, **Del Mar** (Calle 17, at Serdán, tel. 622/2–02–26) prepares high-quality cuts of beef to order and serves excellent fresh seafood dishes such as shrimp flambé ($13) and lobster burritos ($10) in a cool, dark refuge from the sun.

Restaurant Las Cazuelas. This restaurant serves a traditional Mexican breakfast ($3) with eggs, rice, and beans, as well as a tasty comida corrida ($5) and fried fish ($6). *Av. 12, at Calle 15, no phone. Open Tues.–Sat. 8 AM–10 PM.*

Restaurant Todos Comen. This spot has a good selection of breakfast dishes, just about all of them less than $4. Later, they serve fish fillet ($7), *bistec ranchero* (steak cooked with chiles, tomatoes and onions; $14), and your standard tacos and enchiladas (combo plate $6). *Serdán, at Calle 15, tel. 622/2–11–00. Open daily 7 AM–12:30 AM.*

Tío Juan's. "Uncle Juan's," a favorite with both the local and tourist crowds, serves traditional Mexican food in a log cabin setting. The food here isn't particularly cheap, but portions are big and the service is great. Good deals include the enchiladas (about $6) and the *caldo* (soup) for $4. *Serdán 394, tel. 622/2–57–00. Open daily 8 AM–10 PM.*

Near Guaymas

SAN CARLOS

Despite the golf courses, Club Med, and a resident jet set who charter fishing boats and take scuba lessons, San Carlos, on a beautiful bay about 21 kilometers northwest of Guaymas, is a wonderful place to spend the day. The town itself is still relatively undeveloped, locals still swarm the beaches and walk the streets, and the summer heat still sends most tourists scrambling indoors in search of climate control.

COMING AND GOING Buses marked SAN CARLOS stop along Serdán in Guaymas every half-hour. The 15-minute ride costs under $1, and the last bus returns to Guaymas from San Carlos at 9 PM.

WHERE TO SLEEP Unless you've got a tent, you'll want to make San Carlos a day trip; the cheapest hotels here are the **Hotel Fiesta** (tel. 622/6–02–29) and **Motel Creston** (tel. 622/6–00–20), but both charge more than $40 for double rooms. The Creston has a pool, long-distance phone service, and accepts Visa and Mastercard. Both are on the main road off Highway 15. For about $8 a night you can camp at **Teta Kawi Trailer Park** (tel. 622/6–02–20), just outside town toward Guaymas, or next door at **Totonaka Trailor Park** and take advantage of the swimming pools and nearby laundry. RV camping costs $14 for two people. The beaches get a lot of foot traffic at night, so beach camping is best avoided.

FOOD Food stands along the main street are the cheapest way to fill your belly. If you want to have a real sit-down meal, though, try **Rosa Cantina** on the main drag, where the specialty is baby goat ($8.50). There is also a branch of the **Carlos 'n' Charlie's** chain at the turnoff to the marina, serving up decent lunches accompanied by frosty margaritas.

OUTDOOR ACTIVITIES You can rent anything from windsurfing equipment (about $15 an hour) to banana boat rides (you're pulled behind a boat on a rubber float) on the main beach. Diving is the big sport in San Carlos: **El Mar Diving Center** (263 Creston tel. 622/6–04–04), **Gary's** (near the marina), and **Cortes Explorations** (near the marina) all rent gear and organize trips. Two-tank dive trips to sites off nearby islands go for about $60; add another $30 if you need equipment. Resort courses are $70. Gary's also organizes fishing trips.

CIUDAD OBREGON

About 130 kilometers southeast of Guaymas, Ciudad Obregón is surrounded by fields of corn, cotton, and flowers. There isn't much to do or see in Obregón, but if you want to be able to boast to the kids back home that you spent the night in the garbanzo capital of the world, or if you just have to get off that damn bus for a day, Obregón isn't the worst place to end up. There's a movie theater down the street from the bus station, and the **Biblioteca Pública Museo de los Yaquis** (Allende, at 5 de Febrero) holds an extensive collection of Yaqui crafts.

COMING AND GOING Obregón is on Highway 15, and most buses headed north and south make a stop here. The **bus station** (tel. 641/2–12–71) is in the southeast corner of town, near the junction of Rodolfo Elías Calles and California. You can find public phones and luggage storage ($2 a day) here. Daily trains depart for the north and south from the **train station** two blocks north on Alemán, between Avenidas Hidalgo and Guerrero.

WHERE TO SLEEP When looking for a place to lay your head in Obregón, remember that you get what you pay for. There are some cheap places, but they aren't pretty. If you have to spend the night, you'll find most of the hotels near the bus station or in the center of town along Avenida Miguel Alemán. The **Casa de Huéspedes Nayarit** (5 de Febrero 771, at Rodolfo Elías Calles, tel. 641/6–75–59) is clean and air-conditioned. Singles run $17, doubles $27. The friendly family who runs **Restaurant Lonchería Ruíz** (in front of bus station, tel. 641/6–50–92) will set you up in a run-down but comfortable, air-conditioned single for $13; doubles cost $17. If worse comes to worst, **Casa de Huéspedes Bien Estar** (California 511, near Zaragoza, no phone) can put you up in one of its 11 cells (all with access to a grimy communal bath wanting for privacy and hot water) for $8.50 double or single.

FOOD Sit-down restaurants are few and far between, but taquerías and other fast-food stands crowd the streets, especially near the bus terminal. **Restaurant Lonchería Ruíz** (tel. 641/6–50–92), in front of the bus station, serves a more-than-decent plate of *pollo asado* (grilled chicken) for just $3. **Carnitas La Central** (Rodolfo Elías Calles, at Hidalgo, tel. 641/2–03–12) has ceviche tacos, tostadas, and tamales, each for only $1.50. **Merendero La Reja** (Nuevo León 532 Sur, at Niños Héroes, tel. 641/3–46–01), about four blocks from the bus terminal, specializes in *cabrito* (kid; $13), but less expensive fare is also available.

ALAMOS

This small city 53 kilometers east of Sonora Highway 182 is one of the oldest in northern Mexico. Alamos may be a bit complicated to reach, but once you get here, the narrow cobblestone streets, horseback ranchers in cowboy hats, and secluded haciendas with elegant inner courtyards may charm you into staying longer than you had planned.

Entertainment in Alamos comes in the form of exploring the crumbling adobe buildings: Especially noteworthy sites include the **Hotel Mansión de la Condesa Magdalena** on Obregón, worth peeking into even though you probably can't afford to stay. The **Iglesia de la Purísima Concepción** has a towering three-tier bell tower and impressive architecture. The **Museo Costumbrista de Sonora** (open weekdays 9–1 and 3–6) at the north end of the Plaza de las Armas also merits a visit (especially since it's free) for its displays on Sonora's history. The **Plaza de las Armas** is a beautiful park that starts hopping with kids, couples, and people-watchers as soon as the sun dips below the horizon.

BASICS You can change cash or traveler's checks mornings at the **Bancomer** at the south end of the Plaza de las Armas, but there's no ATM. The **post office** is next to the police station on Zaragoza. There are no public phones on the streets here, but Polo's Restaurant (open daily 7 AM–9:30 PM), at the far end of Zaragoza, has a small **caseta** (telephone office) that doesn't charge a commission on collect and credit-card calls. The **tourist office** (tel. 642/8–04–50) below Hotel Los Portales, is, theoretically, open weekdays 9–2 and 4–7, Saturday 9–2. **Farmacia Botica Económica** (Rosales 20, in front of park) is open Monday–Saturday 8:30 AM–9 PM, Sunday 8:30–2.

COMING AND GOING The only way to get to Alamos is by car or a local bus from the town of Navojoa. A **Transportes del Pacífico** bus from Guaymas will let you off in Navojoa at the corner of Revolución and Guerrero. You'll have to walk about 10 minutes down Guerrero (toward the center) to a small terminal at the corner of Rincón where buses leave for the hour-long journey to Alamos ($2) about every 40 minutes between 6:30 AM and midnight. From Alamos, buses make the return trip to Navojoa almost every half-hour between 4 AM and 6:30 PM from the station on Morelos, at Plaza Alameda.

WHERE TO SLEEP Rooms in Alamos are not cheap. By far the best deal in town is the quiet **Motel Somar** (Madero 110, tel. 642/8–01–95). The short walk to get here from the center of town is more than compensated for by the reasonable prices ($20 a single, $22 a double) and comfortable, wheelchair-accessible rooms with fans and clean, private bathrooms. If you're in the mood for a major splurge, try the beautiful **Hotel Mansion de la Condesa Magdalena** (Obregón, tel. 642/8–02–21), which rents $50 singles and $60 doubles.

Hotel Casa de los Tesoros. This former convent has been beautifully restored with air-conditioning, fireplaces, large, tastefully furnished rooms, an inner courtyard with a pool, and a restaurant serving Mexican and Puerto Rican food. They've also recently begun restoring newly discovered murals from the 1700s, when music and painting were taught at the convent. In summer, singles cost $55 and doubles, $66. From mid-October to mid-May, rooms are $88 and include breakfast. *Obregón, behind cathedral, tel. 642/8–00–10. Luggage storage, wheelchair access.*

Hotel Enríquez. The high-ceilings and glorious courtyard here basically fail to make up for the disgusting communal bath (which has no hot water) and the annoying practice of charging per person ($12) rather than per room. The lone single room with a private bath is $15. *Plaza de las Armas, no phone.*

➤ CAMPING • The **Dolisia Motel** (Hwy. 182, 1½ km west of Plaza Alameda, tel. 642/8–01–31) has a trailer park out back where you can pitch a tent ($8.50 for 2 people), or park an RV ($13). There are also a few RV parks where $13 will get you a tent site for two people with showers and a swimming pool; **Trailer Park Acosta Ranch** (tel. 642/8–02–46), just over a kilometer from town near the cemetery, and **Los Alamos Trailer Park** (tel. 642/8–03–32), at the entrance of town on the highway, are two of the better ones. RV spots at either cost $20–$25.

FOOD Vendors clustered around Plaza Alameda serve tacos and such for about $1. You can also hit the **mercado municipal,** at the east end of the plaza, for locally grown fruits and vegetables, as well as meats and cheeses, but you can eat almost as cheaply at a number of restaurants here. **Taquería Blanquita** (Antonio Rosales, next to the market, no phone) is packed with locals from the time it opens at 5:30 AM. Long, get-to-know-your-neighbor tables are generously stocked with chile and guacamole to dress up the $3 comida corrida. The air-conditioned **Restaurant Bar María Bonita** (Rosales 36, tel. 642/8–04–92) overlooks a garden and serves terrific, reasonably priced food. Good breakfasts are $4, and fish or shrimp comes with rice, beans, and salad for $9. Plates of tostadas or enchiladas are $6. **Las Palmeras** (on Plaza de las Armas) has outdoor patio seating with a view of the church, $3 vegetable salads, and real coffee.

Los Mochis

Just over the Sonora-Sinaloa border on Highway 15 is the agricultural boomtown of Los Mochis, surrounded by farmland and located some 20 kilometers from the sea. The city was founded in 1893 by Benjamin Johnston, who managed to buy up huge quantities of land during Porfirio Díaz's massive land grab just before the turn of the century, during which almost one fifth of the entire Republic was turned over to Díaz's friends and foreign investors. He turned the area into a sugar-producing and refining region and brought the Chihuahua al Pacífico railroad across the Sierra Madre Occidental mountains to Los Mochis. Today, most tourists pass through only to catch that train for the famous Copper Canyon ride or to board a Baja-bound ferry. Los Mochis and its environs boast a few points of local interest, however. You can see what remains of Johnston's opulent estate, with its pleasant botanical garden, or visit the town's lively Sunday morning market.

BASICS

AMERICAN EXPRESS The AmEx representative in **Viajes Krystal** will change traveler's checks if they have enough cash on hand, as well as provide the usual services for cardholders (mail service, advances on AmEx cards, and personal check cashing). The travel agency also sells plane, bus, and train (1st class only) tickets. *Alvaro Obregón 471-A Pte., Los Mochis, Sinaloa, CP 81200, México. Tel. 681/2–20–84 or 681/2–41–39. Open weekdays 8:30–1 and 3–6:30, Sat. 8:30–2.*

BOOKSTORES **Librería Los Mochis** has a wide selection of literature in Spanish, as well as a few newspapers and magazines in English. *Leyva, at Madero, tel. 681/5–72–42. Open daily 8 AM–10 PM.*

CASAS DE CAMBIO A number of banks and several casas de cambio line Calle Leyva downtown. **Servicio de Cambio** (Leyva, near Juárez, tel. 681/2–56–66) changes both cash and traveler's checks Monday through Saturday from 8 AM to 7:30 PM. If you get going early, you can change money at **Bancomer** (Leyva, at Juárez)—the money-exchange window is open until noon, but try to be in line by 11 AM.

EMERGENCIES You can reach the **police, fire department** or **ambulance** service by dialing 06 from any public phone.

LAUNDRY The self-serve **Lavarama** is around the corner from the bus terminals on Juárez, near the corner of Juárez and Guillermo Prieto. Automatic washers cost $2, dryers $3, and they'll do it all for you for another $1 per load. *Juárez 225, tel. 681/2–81–20. Open daily 8–7.*

MAIL The post office is a few blocks east of the municipal administration building, near the corner of Ordoñez and Guillermo Prieto. They will hold mail sent to you at the following address for up to 10 days: Lista de Correos, Los Mochis, Sinaloa, CP 81281, México. *226 Ordoñez Pte. Open weekdays 9–6, Sat. 9–1.*

MEDICAL AID The **Centro Médico de Los Mochis** is open 24 hours. *Rosendo G. Castro, btw Allende and Guillermo Prieto, tel. 681/2–74–26 or 681/2–01–98.*

Farmacia Tecolote is open 24 hours. *Hidalgo, at Rosales, west of downtown, tel. 681/5–45–43.*

PHONES Most of the public phones on the streets seem to be just for show, but if you'd like to make a collect or credit-card call without paying a connection fee, use the functional public phone in the lobby of **Hotel Hidalgo** (*see* Where to Sleep, *below*). For cash calls, the **Computel** office is quiet and convenient. *Independencia 474, near Flores, tel. 681/5-17-34. Open weekdays 7:30 AM–9 PM, weekends 10–6.*

VISITOR INFORMATION The small tourist office in the **Unidad Administrativo** building is intimidatingly disguised as a private office, behind dark, reflective windows. Don't be deterred: The English-speaking staff is happy to help you with transportation schedules and prices and load you down with pamphlets on Sinaloa. *Allende, at Cuauhtémoc, tel. 681/2–66–40. Open weekdays 8–3 and 4–7.*

COMING AND GOING

BY BUS The **Tres Estrellas de Oro** (tel. 681/2–17–57) terminal is on Juárez, at Degollado. The **Transportes Norte de Sonora** (tel. 681/2–04–11) and **Transportes del Pacífico** (tel. 681/2–03–41) terminals are a few blocks north of downtown, side-by-side on Avenida José María Morelos between Avenidas Leyva and Zaragoza. All have luggage storage and are open 24 hours. Buses depart from the Tres Estrellas terminal on Juárez for main destinations throughout Mexico, but you're more likely to find an immediate departure from the busier terminal on Morelos. The latter also has more buses to smaller towns in Sinaloa and Sonora. First- and second-class buses run to Mazatlán ($16–$18, 6 hrs), Guadalajara ($34–$39, 11 hrs), Mexico City ($57–$66, 24 hrs), Nogales ($25–$30, 10 hrs), Mexicali ($42–$48.50, 22 hrs), Tijuana ($49–$56.50, 24 hrs), and Navojoa ($6–$7, 3 hrs).

BY TRAIN The railroad station (tel. 681/2–93–85), 2 kilometers from downtown on the southeastern outskirts of town, is the southwestern terminus of the famous **Chihuahua al Pacífico** iron rooster that winds its way through the Copper Canyon region (*see* Chapter 14). If you only take one train ride in Mexico, this should be it. Two trains depart from Los Mochis in the morning, arriving in Chihuahua ($36, 13 hrs 1st class; $10 2nd class) some 12 hours later: the first-class *Vista,* departing at 6 AM with stops in the Copper Canyon towns of Bahuichivo ($14, 6½ hrs), Divisadero ($16.50, 7½ hrs), and Creel ($20, 9½ hrs).; and the second-class *Mixto* (also called *pollero* or *burro*), departing at 7 AM and costing about $5, $6, and $7 for the same stops. The amount of time the Mixto train will take to arrive in any given destination is anybody's guess, but you can be sure it won't be fast.

Buy tickets a day in advance if you can; travel agencies and most hotels sell tickets for the Vista train, but Mixto tickets are available only at the train station. Although buses marked COL. FERR. go to the train station, they don't operate in the early morning and are therefore useless to most travelers, since early morning is precisely when the trains leave. Instead, look for taxis in front of the Hotel Santa Rita on Leyva and Hidalgo. If you're taking the slower Mixto, it's best to begin your Copper Canyon trip from Los Mochis in order to see the most spectacular scenery before nightfall. Travelers heading north toward Mexicali ($34 1st class, $10 2nd class) or south to Guadalajara ($31 1st class, $9 2nd class) need to depart from the Sufragio station on the **Ferrocarril del Pacífico** line (tel. 681/5–77–75), which departs from El Fuerte, about 52 kilometers northeast of Los Mochis. To reach Sufragio, you can take a bus headed for El Fuerte.

BY FERRY You can buy tickets for a Sematur ferry to La Paz on the Baja Peninsula at **Viajes Paotam** (Serapio Rendón 517 Pte., tel. 681/5–19–14) in Los Mochis. Second class (a hard seat) is $14, tourist class (a cushy seat) $28, a cabin $40. Be sure to buy tickets at least 24 hours in advance if you're determined to leave on a specific day. The agency office is open 8–1 and 3–7 Monday through Saturday. Ferries leave Tuesday through Saturday from the dock in Topolobampo, 25 kilometers west of Los Mochis, at 9 AM (more or less), and the trip takes about nine hours. Buses marked TOPOLOBAMPO leave from behind the Hotel Santa Anita (Leyva, at Hidalgo) and stop along Boulevard Rosendo G. Castro on the way out of town. They also leave from the Alianza de Transportes de Norte Sinaloa on Calle Zaragoza.

BY PLANE The Los Mochis airport, 20 kilometers south of town, is served primarily by **Aeroméxico** (tel. 681/5–25–70 or 681/5–25–80) and **Aerocalifornia** (tel. 681/5–21–30 or 681/5–22–50), which provide limited service to major Mexican cities such as Guadalajara ($149) and Mazatlán ($108), and to Tucson ($159) and Los Angeles ($190) in the United States. You can catch a PLAN DE GUADALUPE bus (about $1) to the airport from the corner of Guillermo Prieto and Cuauhtémoc; it beats a $15 taxi ride.

GETTING AROUND

Los Mochis is easily navigated, and everything but the train station, airport, and ferry terminal is accessible on foot. Calles Allende, Guillermo Prieto, Zaragoza, and Leyva run parallel to each other and are where you'll probably spend most of your time, with hotels, drugstores, restaurants and just about anything else you could need clustered between Boulevard Castro and Avenida Madero. People congregate at the **Plaza Fiesta Las Palmas** and the nearby **Parque Sinaloa,** at the corner of Avenida Obregón and Boulevard Antonio Rosales. City buses are easily hailed all around town, and many originate at the **mercado,** at Calle Guillermo Prieto and Avenida Cuauhtémoc.

WHERE TO SLEEP

Look in the downtown area for budget accommodations. Above Bar Apache, **Hotel Los Arcos** (Allende 534 Sur, btw Castro and Obregón, tel. 681/2–32–53) features lousy air-conditioning, self-service laundry in the form of a clothesline on the roof, and grimy communal bathroom sinks with hot water. The tiny rooms need painting, but the price is right, and the management is always cheery. Singles go for $10, doubles $13. The interior of the **Hotel del Parque** (Obregón 600, tel. 681/2–02–60) is better than exterior would lead you to believe, but not by much. This wheelchair-accessible hotel close to Plaza Fiesta offers basic rooms with fans for $17 (single) and $20 (double), but there's no hot water in the bathrooms. The **Hotel del Valle** (Guillermo Prieto, at Independencia, tel. 681/2–01–05) needs a good spring cleaning but is fairly modern, and those with cash-flow problems will be happy to find that they accept Visa and MasterCard. Rooms are shabby but comfortable enough, with fans and bathrooms with hot water. Singles start at $17 ($20 with TV and phone); doubles are $20 and $25, respectively. The colonial-style **Hotel Montecarlo** (Independencia, at Ángel Flores, tel. 681/2–18–18) is tucked between a restaurant and a noisy bar in the downtown area, not far from the cathedral. Rooms on the second story have small balconies, and all are comfortable, with air-conditioning, TV, and clean bathrooms with hot water. Singles are about $25, doubles $31 and $37 (the more expensive doubles are wheelchair accessible). As a last resort, try the noisy, overpriced **Hotel Hidalgo** (Miguel Hidalgo 260 Pte., tel. 681/2–34–56), where the showers are cold, and run-down singles go for $17, doubles $22.

CAMPING **Los Mochis Trailer Park** (1 km west of Hwy. 15, tel. 681/2–00–21) charges as much as the cheapest hotel ($15 for two people) and is almost 2 kilometers out of town. In addition to the communal bath facilities, there are coin-op laundry machines and a recreation room.

FOOD

The downtown area teems with fish, taco, and fruit stands. The **mercado municipal** (Guillermo Prieto, at Cuauhtémoc Pte.) has excellent fresh vegetables and fruits, a huge fish and meat market, and several decent *comedores* (sit-down food stands).

Restaurant Chic's (Plaza Fiesta, Rosales, at Obregón, tel. 681/5-47-09), a few blocks west of downtown, seems at first like a characterless, upscale version of Denny's, but once the families start strolling in after mass, it's a good place to people-watch. The food is surprisingly good; try the combination breakfast ($6) of tamales, *chorizo* (spicy sausage), and beans, or the fresh fruit plate ($4.50). The restaurant is conveniently open every day from 6:30 AM to midnight. **El Farallon** (Obregón, at Ángel Flores, tel. 681/2-14–28), specializing in fresh, spicy, seafood is a favorite of Los Mochis businessmen. Dishes such as calamari ($10) and ceviche ($5) come with tortillas and beans. **Restaurant/Bar Miramar** (Obregón 145 Pte., tel. 681/5-00-80) serves large breakfasts with eggs ($3.50) and lunches such as seafood soup ($6), octopus cocktail ($6), and *camarones rancheros* (shrimp sautéed with tomatos and onions; $7). Women are graciously allowed to hang out at night, when customers turn their attention to the bar rather than the menu. Look for the door painted CAME IN, CONDITIONED AIR.

Minors, women, and uniformed men aren't allowed in most cantinas in Los Mochis. If you qualify for entrance, you'll see men letting loose their repressions, fighting, hugging, caressing, crying, and, finally, stumbling home wrapped in each other's arms.

CHEAP THRILLS

If you happen to be here on a Sunday around 11 AM, be sure to head to the downtown shopping area for the *tianguis* (open-air market), on Leyva, just across Rendon. All of Los Mochis seems to flock here once church services are over; the shops and stalls are packed with residents furiously haggling, their voices competing with the blare of radios and car horns. Come early, though—everything is closed down and quiet by 2 PM.

The **Parque Ecológico de Sinaloa** occupies the grounds of sugar baron and town founder Benjamin Johnston's former estate. This park is home to trees imported from around the world, such as towering palms from Cuba and fuzzy cypress from Arizona. Near the entrance, a giant tree bears Indian carvings of an eagle, a bear, a snake, deer, and other animals, including Mr. Johnston himself. There's also a children's playground right in front of the gardens, where, if you're lucky, you may be able to join an impromptu soccer game. *On Rosales, behind Woolworth shopping center. Open daily.*

Near Los Mochis

Clearly marked buses headed for the towns of Topolobampo and El Fuerte depart Los Mochis from the **Alianza de Transportes de Norte Sinaloa** station on Zaragoza between Cuauhtémoc and Ordoñez, just west of the post office. Buses to Topolobampo leave about every hour 7 AM–8 PM and cost about $1 for the 30-minute ride. Don't get off at the bus station in Topolobampo—the bus will continue on to the ferry dock. Buses to El Fuerte ($2) depart a little less often, also between 7 AM and 6 PM, for the hour-long journey.

TOPOLOBAMPO

Some 25 kilometers west of Los Mochis is the town of Topolobampo, founded at the end of the 19th century by a bunch of Americans looking to set up a socialist utopia. This dream was soon squashed, however, when the colonists began fighting among themselves and Los Mochis sugar baron Benjamin Johnston managed to scoop up the water rights to the area and evict everybody. Today, the harbor town is largely dependent on shrimping and industry, and sea lions frolic in the deep bay, using Isla El Farallon, just off the coast, as a breeding ground. You are most likely to come here only to get on or off the ferry, but if you do stay a day or two you can take advantage of the spectacular natural surroundings of this less-than-spectacular town. Although the harbor itself lacks swimming or sunning beaches, shell collectors will have a ball here. Sun- and wave-seekers can head to **Isla Venados, Isla Santuario,** and **Playa Hamacas.** Short boat trips from Topolobampo can be arranged through the office of the **Sociedad Cooperativa de Servicios Turísticos Mazocahui,** next to the customs building. One of their guides,

Guadalupe Elguezabal or Teodolfo Cital, will take you fishing ($50 per person) or on a tour of the islands ($40 per person) on a yacht, or to the beaches in a boat for about $3. They don't have a telephone, but they're usually around the office in the mornings. **Playa Miramar** is about 2 kilometers to the north—you'll have to hoof it if you don't have a car. Topolobampo makes a nice day trip, but lodging here is scarce and expensive, and camping is unsafe. If you're stuck, you can get a bed in a dorm for $12 at **Pensión Paotam** (at the ferry dock), or pay $17 for a single or $33 for a double.

EL FUERTE

This small colonial town 75 kilometers east of Los Mochis is not enormously exciting, but it's nicer than spending the day in Los Mochis. El Fuerte is dotted with colonial buildings built around central patios, and has a pretty, though often nonfunctional, fountain on the *zócalo* (main square). The **Hotel Posada de Hidalgo** is is one of the nicer colonial buildings, and although you probably can't afford to stay here (it's over $50 a night), peek inside the inner courtyard anyway for a look at the murals. Stop for food at **Restaurant Anita** near the entrance of town.

THE PACIFIC COAST 8

By Cassie Coleman

The Pacific Coast states of Sinaloa, Nayarit, Jalisco, Colima, and Guerrero contain major resorts, deserted beaches, farmland, big cities, and mountainous Huichol and Cora communities. Mazatlán marks the beginning of what the cruise-ship industry terms the Mexican Riviera, which stretches south along the coastline for 1,450 kilometers and includes some of Mexico's best-known vacation spots. Mazatlán itself is two towns rolled into one: a thriving port city, home to an important shrimp fleet, and a hedonistic beachfront strip where tourists, mostly foreign, offer their oiled bodies to the sun. Puerto Vallarta and Acapulco are more of the same, except in lusher, more tropical settings. Ixtapa/Zihuatanejo is more relaxed by far, while still offering all the conveniences of a major resort. Step outside of any of these developments, though, and you'll find jungly hills and crescent-shaped stretches of beach, much of which you can have all to yourself. Wherever you go, the best time to do it is summer, the off-season for tourists, when lodging rates can fall by as much as 50%.

The state of Nayarit has kilometers of fantastic coastline and no major resorts. The hippie-ish town of San Blas would be another developer's dream, were it not for the ferocious mosquitoes that keep it tolerant, cheap, itchy, and famed as the budget traveler's village. The northern coast of Nayarit offers the most isolated beaches—82 kilometers of smooth sand not yet touched by chain-hotel glitz. Farther south, budget travelers flock to the Bahía de Navidad, where the twin towns of Barra de Navidad and San Patricio Melaque offer lounge-friendly sand and waves of every size. Nayarit's landlocked Cora and Huichol towns are also worth a detour for the fresh climate and interesting culture. Apart from Mexcaltitán, the town of Santiago Ixcuintla, accessible from San Blas or Nayarit's busy capital city of Tepic, is most noteworthy, largely because of the cultural center for Huichol artisans and cultural survival that is here.

Mexcaltitán, a small island in a saltwater lagoon in Nayarit, is reputed to be the site of Aztlán, the original home of the Aztecs.

The coast of Jalisco stretches far south of Puerto Vallarta, including miles of beaches along the Bahía Chamela that see more vacationing Guadalajarans than foreigners. Along the border of Jalisco and the tiny state of Colima, the twin Colima Volcanoes await intrepid hikers (the really intrepid can tackle the Volcán de Fuego, which erupted as recently as the summer of 1994). Guerrero is the namesake of Vicente Guerrero, Morelos's most brilliant field commander in the struggle for independence. It's an appropriate name, really, as Guerrero has always been a tumultuous and revolution-torn state; as recently as 1972, the federal government sent troops here to quell a local rebellion that was sparked by economic problems and outrage with the authoritarian Echeverría regime. In Guerrero's popular coastal cities of Ixtapa/Zihuatanejo and

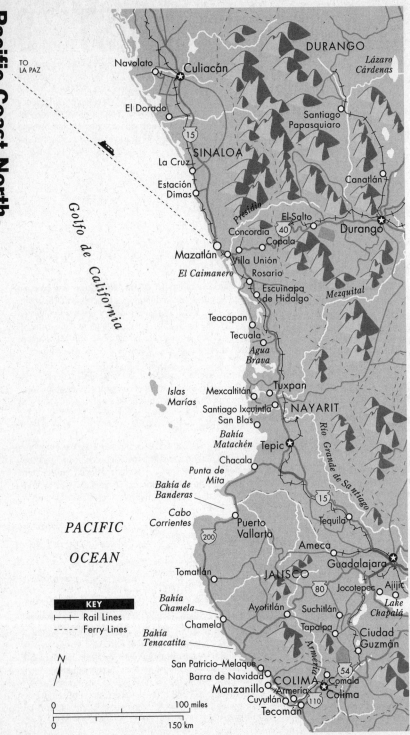

Pacific Coast North

TO
LA PAZ

DURANGO

*Lázaro
Cárdenas*

Navolato

Culiacán

El Dorado

Santiago
Papasquiaro

15

Canatlán

SINALOA

La Cruz

Estación
Dimas

El Salto

Presidio

Concordia
Copala

40

Durango

Golfo de California

Mazatlán

Villa Unión

El Caimanero

Rosario

Escuinapa
de Hidalgo

Mezquital

Teacapan

Tecuala

*Agua
Brava*

*Islas
Marías*

Mexcaltitán

Tuxpan

Santiago Ixcuintla

San Blas

NAYARIT

*Bahía
Matachén*

Tepic

Río Grande de Santiago

Chacala

Punta de
Mita

*Bahía de
Banderas*

15

*Cabo
Corrientes*

Puerto
Vallarta

Tequila

200

PACIFIC

Ameca

Guadalajara

OCEAN

Tomatlán

JALISCO

80

Jocotepec

Ajijic

*Bahía
Chamela*

Ayotitlán

Suchitlán

*Lake
Chapala*

Chamela

Tapalpa

Ciudad
Guzmán

*Bahía
Tenacatita*

KEY

Rail Lines

Ferry Lines

San Patricio—Melaque

Barra de Navidad

COLIMA

Comala

54

Armería

N

Manzanillo

Armería

Colima

Cuyutlán

110

0   100 miles

Tecomán

0   150 km

262

Acapulco, however, little of this restiveness remains to be seen: You can expect a gracious welcome, if occasionally accompanied by a bit of hard sell.

Mazatlán

Mazatlán has something of a split personality. On the southern tip of the peninsula, it's a bustling port and shrimping city, referred to as Mazatlán Viejo (Old Mazatlán). In this area is Olas Altas, once the premier resort area, now a pleasant, sleepy strip since the hard-core tourism moved north to the Zona Dorada (Golden Zone). Visited by over a million people a year, the Zona Dorada is just the monstrous conglomeration of huge hotels and overpriced, sterile restaurants that such a figure would lead you to expect. Connecting Mazatlán's two contrary halves is the *malecón,* Mazatlán's boardwalk, which, stretching more than 11 kilometers, is the longest in Mexico.

In summer, Mazatlán becomes the hot and humid playground of throngs of high school and college students from the States, as well as Mexican tourists. In winter, when the mercury drops from the scorching 90s to the comfortable 70s, Mazatlán hits its high season, when older people from the United States and Canada trade their down parkas for leisure suits and flock to Mazatlán's expensive hotel rooms. Although the party atmosphere prevails year-round, **Carnaval,** celebrated just before Lent (usually February), is Mazatlán's biggest fiesta. Thousands of tourists, both domestic and foreign, descend on the town for six days and nights of music, dancing, fireworks, parades, drinking, and carnal lust.

At **Playa Sábalo** and **Playa Las Gaviotas,** the main Zona Dorada beaches, you can do all your souvenir shopping without leaving your towel. Locals share these beaches with both foreign and Mexican tourists, but they dominate at the less crowded **Playa Norte.** Mazatlán Viejo's downtown streets and markets are other places to escape the glitz of the hotel zone and feel like you're in a real city. If you tire of traffic, people, and commerce, wander Mazatlán Viejo's quiet residential streets with their colorful, colonial-style buildings, or attend one of the folk dance, music, opera, and theater performances that take place throughout the year in the historic Teatro Ángel Peralta on the Plaza Machado in the heart of the old city.

The palapa (thatched-hut) restaurants along Playa Norte sell fresh seafood at much lower prices than you'll pay in the Zona Dorada.

BASICS

AMERICAN EXPRESS This staff here is used to catering to the package tourists of the Zona Dorada, and is consequently a bit lame, but they do change traveler's checks and deliver MoneyGrams, and cardholders can have mail sent here or cash a personal check. *Camarón Sábalo s/n, 1 block south of Dairy Queen, tel. 69/13–06–00. Open weekdays 9–5, Sat. 9–1. Mailing address: T. Diagonal H, Av. Camarón Sábalo s/n, Centro Comercial Balboa, Local 4, Mazatlán, Sinaloa, CP 82000, México.*

CASAS DE CAMBIO The Zona Dorada teems with casas de cambio, but downtown they're scarce, so if you're here try the **Casa de Cambio Camiga** in Plaza Concordia. *Belisario Domínguez 2, at Flores, tel. 69/85–00–03. Open Mon.–Sat. 9:30–1:30 and 3:30–7.*

Banamex (Flores, at Juárez, tel. 69/82–77–33) exchanges cash and traveler's checks weekdays 8:30–4:30 and has ATMs that accept Cirrus and Plus cards. Banamex has another location (with ATMs) on Camarón Sábalo in the Zona Dorada, just south of the Dairy Queen, but they stop changing money at 2 PM.

CONSULATES United States. Mazatlán doesn't have a full-fledged U.S. consulate, but you can visit Geri Nelson, the consular representative, here. In an after-hours emergency, call 62/17–23–75 for the consulate in Hermosillo. *Loaiza 202, tel. 69/16–58–89. In Zona Dorada, in front of Hotel Playa Mazatlán. Open weekdays 9–1.*

Canada. *Loaiza 203, tel. 69/13–06–00. In Zona Dorada, next to Hotel Los Sábalos. Open weekdays 9–1.*

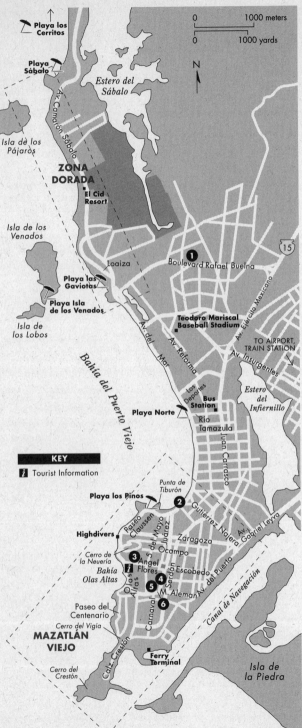

Mazatlán

Playa los
Cerritos

Playa
Sábalo

Estero del
Sábalo

Isla de los
Pájaros

**ZONA
DORADA**

El Cid
Resort

Isla de los
Venados

Loaiza

Playa las
Gaviotas

Playa Isla
de los Venados

Isla de
los Lobos

Bahía del Puerto Viejo

Boulevard Rafael Buelna

**Teodoro Mariscal
Baseball Stadium**

TO AIRPORT,
TRAIN STATION

Los
Deportes

**Bus
Station**

Playa Norte

Río
Tamazula

Estero
del
Infiernillo

KEY

i Tourist Information

Punta de
Tiburón

Playa los Pinos

Highdivers

Cerro de
la Nevería

*Bahía
Olas Altas*

Paseo del
Centenario

Cerro del Vigía

**MAZATLÁN
VIEJO**

Cerro del
Creston

Paseo
Claussen

Zaragoza

Angel
Flores

Ocampo

Escobedo

M. Aleman

Canal de Navegación

**Ferry
Terminal**

Isla de
la Piedra

Monumento al
Pescador, **2**

Museo
Arqueológico, **3**

Plaza de Toros, **1**

Plaza Machado, **5**

Plaza Revolución
and Basílica de
la Inmaculada
Concepción, **4**

Teatro Angel
Peralta, **6**

0   1000 meters

0   1000 yards

N

Av. Camarón Sábalo

Av. del Mar

Av. Reforma

Av. Ejercito Mexicano

Av. Insurgentes

Juan Carrasco

Gutiérrez Nájera

Av. Gabriel Leyva

Av. del Puerto

Serdán

Carnaval

Olas Altas

Calz. Creston

Paseo del Mayo Juárez

15

EMERGENCIES The number for the **police** is 69/82–18–67; they can get you an **ambulance,** should need arise.

LAUNDRY For about $5 a load, **Lavandería Romo** will wash, dry, and fold your dirty duds. *Hidalgo, near 5 de Mayo, no phone. Open daily 8 AM–9 PM.*

MAIL The post office will hold mail sent to you at the following address for up to 10 days: Lista de Correos, Administración Postal No. 1, Centro, Benito Juárez y 21 de Marzo, Mazatlán, Sinaloa, CP 82000, México. You can send or receive telegrams at the office next door. *Juárez, at 21 de Marzo, tel. 69/81–21–21. Open weekdays 8–6, Sat. 9–1.*

MEDICAL AID Miguel Ángel Guzmán Elizondo (Nelson 1808, tel. 69/81–21–64) is a locally respected, English-speaking doctor. He sees patients Monday–Saturday 10–2 and 5-8, and charges between $26 and $30 for a consultation. For minor problems or prescriptions, **Farmacia Cruz Verde** (Gutiérrez Najera 901, at Obregón, tel. 69/81–22–25) is open 24 hours.

PHONES You'll find pay phones on just about every other block throughout the Zona Dorada and Mazatlán Viejo. To place cash calls or send faxes, try **Computel** (Serdán 1512, near Belisario Domínguez), open 24 hours a day.

VISITOR INFORMATION The massive federal tourist office has a helpful English-speaking staff. *Olas Altas 1300, at Escobedo, tel. 69/85–12–20. Open weekdays 9–1.*

The smaller state-run tourist office has brochures and maps. *Loaiza 100, Centro Commercial Los Sábalos, tel. 69/83–25–45. Open weekdays 9–4.*

COMING AND GOING

BY BUS The bus station is on Calle Río Tamazula, near Avenida Ejército Mexicano (which becomes Highway 15), in a large, semicircular building divided into sections: One part is devoted to first-class buses, and, across the bus parking lot, another to second-class buses with service to nearby towns. **Transportes Norte de Sonora** (tel. 69/81–38–46) buses stop here hourly on their way to Guadalajara ($18, 8 hrs), Mexico City ($41, 17 hrs), Tijuana ($67, 25 hrs), and Nogales ($49, 20 hrs). At the same TNS ticket counter you can buy **Transportes Escoinapa** tickets to Santiago Ixcuintla ($7, 3½ hrs). **Autotransportes Transpacífico** (tel. 69/81–38–00) also has service to Monterrey, Mexico City, Guadalajara, Tijuana, and Nogales, as well as a direct bus to San Blas ($11, 4 hrs), which leaves daily at 11 AM and 5 PM. **Estrella Blanca** (tel. 69/81–53–81) goes to Durango ($12.50, 7 hrs) five times a day; to Monterrey ($33, 17 hrs) three times a day; and to Zacatecas ($23, 13 hrs) daily at 6:30 PM. **Tres Estrellas de Oro** (tel. 69/81–36–80) serves the coast as well as most of Mexico. One daily first-class bus to Acapulco ($58, 28 hrs) with stops in Puerto Vallarta ($20, 8 hrs) and Manzanillo ($32, 12 hrs) leaves at 9:45 PM, and buses to Tepic ($12, 4 hrs) leave every hour. To get downtown or to the market from the bus station, catch any bus marked INSURGENTES on Avenida Ejército Mexicano, or walk over to the malecón and take a southbound CAMARON SABALO bus. The same bus going in the opposite direction will take you to the Zona Dorada. Luggage storage is available at the station.

BY TRAIN Mazatlán lies on the Pacific line, which runs from Mexicali ($62, 24 hrs 1st class; $24, 26 hrs 2nd class) to Guadalajara ($24, 12 hrs 1st class; $9, 14 hrs 2nd class). Major stops to the north are Culiacán ($9, 4 hrs 1st class; $3.50, 5 hrs 2nd class), Sufragio ($17.50, 6 hrs 1st class; $7, 8 hrs 2nd class), and Nogales ($47, 20 hrs 1st class; $18, 26 hrs 2nd class). The Guadalajara-bound train stops in Tepic ($12.50, 6 hrs 1st class; $5, 7 hrs 2nd class). The first-class northbound train leaves daily at 7 PM and fills up quickly, so reserve your seat the morning of your departure. The second-class train for the same route leaves at 12:30 AM. The southbound trains leaves daily at 8 AM (1st class) and 4 AM (2nd class). The train station (tel. 69/84–67–10) is northeast of Mazatlán Viejo, on Avenida Ferrocarril in the Colonia Esperanza.

BY PLANE Mazatlán's airport is a good 40-minute drive from town. Taxis make the trek for around $20, as do *pulmonías* (literally, pneumonias; in this case, golf carts). Cheaper still are Volkswagen colectivos that charge roughly $10 between the airport and Mazatlán's major hotels. Carriers that serve Mazatlán from Los Angeles, San Francisco, or Denver include **Aeroméxico** (Camarón Sábalo 310, tel. 69/14–11–11), **Alaska Airlines** (in airport, tel. 69/85–27–30), and **Mexicana** (Paseo Claussen 101, tel. 69/82–73–81). Domestic carriers include **Aerocalifornia** (tel. 69/13–20–42) and **Aviación del Noroeste** (tel. 69/14–38–33), both with offices in the El Cid Hotel on Camarón Sábalo.

BY FERRY **Sematur** takes passengers on the 18-hour ferry crossing to La Paz, Baja, at 3 PM every day except Thursday. An uncomfortable reclining seat costs $23, and a berth in a four-person cabin is $43. A two-person cabin with a bathroom is $58 a head. You can also put a vehicle on the ferry, but the price varies according to size. Make reservations a few days in advance, even sooner during Easter holidays. Take the PLAYA SUR bus from the market to the ferry terminal, and arrive about an hour before the boat departs. The terminal has luggage storage, but there are no markets nearby, so stock up on edibles and water before you come. The boat has a high-priced restaurant and a snack bar on board. You can reserve and buy tickets in the office at the ferry landing on Playa Sur (Prolongación Carnaval, tel. 69/81–70–21), which is open daily 8–2:30. Or, for the same price, you do the same at the travel agency **Turismo Coral** (5 de Mayo 1605, tel. 69/81–32–90), open weekdays 8–2 and 3–7, Saturday 8–2.

GETTING AROUND

Mazatlán has two primary neighborhoods: Mazatlán Viejo, including the malecón and Playa Norte; and the Zona Dorada. Mazatlán Viejo, the southern end of the city, is the civic and commercial center. This easily walkable area centers around **Plaza Revolución** (the zócalo, or main square) and the **Basílica de la Inmaculada Concepción,** Mazatlán's main church, on Avenida Benito Juárez. **Olas Altas,** a relatively quiet strip of beach that used to be the main resort area, lies along the waterfront in Mazatlán Viejo, about seven blocks east of the basilica along Avenida Ángel Flores. Avenida del Mar, which connects Old and New Mazatlán, runs north along Playa Norte to Valentino's Disco, where its name changes to Camarón Sábalo. The Zona Dorada, the primary tourist area, begins here.

Because the newer area of Mazatlán is so stretched out, walking can take a long time. Fortunately, you can get a bus from the central market to just about anywhere in town. The SABALO-BASILICA bus gets you from the downtown market to the Zona Dorada. Golf carts driven by maniacs cruise the streets of Mazatlán, and charge less than taxis. Arrange the fare (and say your prayers) before boarding.

If you're feeling adventurous, you can rent a scooter ($6.50 an hour, $25 a day), complete with helmet. A number of rental shacks are located at the south end of the Zona Dorada. Try **Hot Wheels Moto Rent** (Camarón Sábalo 35, no phone) near McDonald's.

WHERE TO SLEEP

For a popular resort town, Mazatlán has a surprising number of decent, cheap hotels. You'll find budget lodging downtown, behind the Monumento al Pescador; and even in a few pockets of sanity within the Zona Dorada. Prices listed below are for the low season—if you're in town around Semana Santa or the Christmas and New Year holidays, expect to pay a bit more. If you're only in town for a night or so, the best of the hotels near the bus station is the **Hotel Emperador** (Calle Río Panuco s/n, tel. 69/82–67–24), where each room has a color TV and air-conditioning and costs $20 a night for one or two people.

OLD MAZATLAN

➤ UNDER $15 • **Casa de Huéspedes El Castillo.** This old but well-maintained home in the center of town has huge, comfortable rooms. There are only two shared baths, however, which might present a problem if the place is full. Singles are $7, doubles $10. *Teniente Azueta 1612 Nte., tel. 69/81–58–97. Btw Canizales and 21 de Marzo, a few blocks from basilica. 9 rooms, none with bath. Laundry, luggage storage.*

Hotel del Río. This family-run place feels very safe, and the rooms and bathrooms are clean. The quality of the rooms varies, so ask to see a few before you choose. A single or double costs

$10. *Juárez 2410, at Quijano, tel. 69/82–46–54. 27 rooms, all with bath. Luggage storage, wheelchair access.*

➤ UNDER $25 • **Hotel del Centro.** What the Hotel del Centro lacks in atmosphere, it makes up for in big, clean, air-conditioned rooms, all with private bath. Each floor has a small lobby with potted plants and rocking chairs. A single room is $12, a double $16. *Canizales 705 Pte., tel. 69/81–26–73. ½ block from basilica. 19 rooms. Luggage storage.*

Hotel Santa Bárbara. The Santa Bárbara is run by a hip, young sister-brother team. The rooms are tidy, as are the bathrooms, and each floor has a bright, breezy patio. Singles cost $13.50, doubles $15 for one bed or $17.50 for two. *Juárez 2612, at 16 de Septiembre, tel. 69/82–21–20. 21 rooms, all with bath. Laundry, luggage storage.*

➤ UNDER $30 • **Hotel La Siesta.** This is the best—though not the cheapest—place to stay on the aging tourist strip of Olas Altas. The clean, air-conditioned rooms open onto a lush courtyard. Unfortunately, the courtyard connects with that of the touristy Shrimp Bucket restaurant, so expect some noise. They occasionally have specials on rooms without sea views. Generally, singles are $20, doubles $25, and you can pay about $4 more for TV. *Olas Altas 11 Sur, tel. 69/81–26–40. 58 rooms, all with bath. Luggage storage. AE, MC, V.*

ZONA DORADA

➤ UNDER $15 • **Apartamentos Ibis.** Rooms with kitchenettes and clean bathrooms are $13 for one or two people at this family-run place. Some rooms are small, so ask to see several. *Camarón Sábalo 1666, at Calle Río Ibis, tel. 69/13–59–38. Across from Balboa Towers. 40 rooms, all with bath. Luggage storage.*

➤ UNDER $25 • **Hotel Bugambillas.** This charming place hidden in the heart of Zona Dorada has medium-size, clean rooms for $17 (single) and $20 (double). Apartments with kitchenettes for two people are $33, with an extra charge of $7 for each additional person. *Camarón Sábalo, at Costa Azul, just south of Costa de Oro Hotel, tel. 69/14–00–29. 10 rooms, all with bath; 11 apartments. Luggage storage.*

Hotel San Diego. The rooms here are decent but very dark—stay here if being near the Zona Dorada is important to you. Bring an alarm clock because no morning sun will shine on your sleepy face. The most basic singles are $17, doubles $20. *Rafael Buelna, at Av. del Mar, tel. 69/83–57–03. 50 rooms, all with bath. Luggage storage, wheelchair access.*

CAMPING The Zona Dorada has a few trailer parks, but they're all expensive ($13–$17 per night for a tent space). The best of the bunch is **Mar Rosa** (Camarón Sábalo, near Holiday Inn, tel. 69/13–61–87), which is right on the waterfront. Prices vary according to the desirability of your spot. You can also camp on the beach on **Isla de la Piedra,** across the old marina from Mazatlán Viejo. Catch the ferry ($1) on Avenida del Puerto near Gutiérrez Najera. Ferries depart every 15 minutes, 24 hours a day.

FOOD

Like cheap hotels, inexpensive eateries are scattered throughout town. The **mercado municipal** (city market) at Avenidas Serdán and Melchor Ocampo, open daily 7 AM–8 PM, is, as always, your cheapest option. Mazatlán is known for its shrimp. For an afternoon meal of delicious, relatively cheap seafood, head for one of the palapas on Playa Norte.

Restaurants in the tourist zone aren't cheap, but the food is good and the drinks are concocted with creativity. It can also be fun to kick back on the patios and scope out the packs of college students, if you're in the mood. **Club Natural** (Camarón Sábalo, near Loaiza) serves fresh-squeezed versions of everything from pineapple to papaya 24 hours a day. They also have tasty sandwiches ($4) and a salad bar.

➤ UNDER $5 • **La Casa de Ana.** Soy-beef burritos ($3), soups ($4), salads ($3), and a $3 vegetarian *comida corrida* (pre-prepared lunch special) are served here on a patio overlooking the plaza. *Plaza Machado, at Constitución, no phone. Open Mon.–Sat. 10–5, Sun. 11–6. Wheelchair access.*

Cenaduría El Túnel. This dinner place on the Plaza Machado across from the Teatro Ángel Peralta serves $2.50 orders of three tacos or three *gorditas* (thick corn tortillas) with beans and cheese, as well as other standard fare. *Carnaval 1207, no phone. Open Thurs.–Tues. 7 PM–11 PM or later.*

➢ UNDER $10 • **Cenaduría El Velorio Feliz.** This tiny sidewalk eatery on the Plaza Machado is usually packed with local actors, drama teachers, and directors eating great food and hanging out with the owner, Mirla, and her sisters. You can get everything from tacos or quesadillas to *aguas frescas* (juice drinks) for less than $1, and there are often specials such as steamed almond fish or beef in *mole* (chile and chocolate sauce) costing $5–$7. If Mirla remembers, there'll be desserts too. *Constitución 507, no phone. Open daily 6 PM–midnight.*

Jungle Juice Restaurant and Bar. Despite the dumb name, this place is worth your time for the selection of juice drinks (around $2); the $4 soy burger platter with fries, beans, and rice; or hearty egg, potato, and toast breakfasts ($3). You might even splurge and pay $7 for a stir-fry or a big slab of meat, both of which are also delicious here. *Calle de Las Garzas 101, btw Loaiza and Camarón Sábalo, tel. 69/13-33-15. Open daily 7:30 AM–10:30 PM; bar open until 2 AM.*

Karnes en su Jugo. "Meat In Its Juice" is the name of this restaurant, and the cook is very serious about living up to it. A hefty order of beef comes with onions, beans, bacon, and homemade tortillas for $6. *Av. del Mar, near Playa Norte, tel. 69/82-13-22. Open daily 1 PM–2 AM.*

Restaurant Joncol's. This diner-esque place with wood paneling and silly, fake streetlamps is served by an efficient army of uniformed waitresses. *Carne asada* (steak) and a fish plate are both $5—be sure to ask for all the extras (tortillas, chips, and bread) you want, as there's no charge. *Ángel Flores 608, near Palacio Municipal, tel. 69/81-21-87. Open daily 7 AM–10 PM. Wheelchair access.*

Royal Dutch. Started as an in-home bakery, this place has expanded into a café with courtyard dining and a fairly expansive menu. Two eggs, hashbrowns, and toast run $3, sandwiches run $3–$5, and soups go for $2. Breads and deserts are still made on the premises, and the coffee ($1) and cappuccino ($2) are good and strong. *Juárez 1307, at Constitución, tel. 69/81-20-07. Open Mon.–Sat. 8 AM–9 PM.*

WORTH SEEING

The best way to see Mazatlán Viejo, with its mix of crumbling old mansions and smaller homes, is on foot. The center of town is the **Plaza Revolución**. The blue-and-gold spires of the adjacent **Basílica** rise above the downtown buildings, making them a convenient reference point. A few blocks away is the former center of town, **Plaza Machado** (Constitución and Carnaval), around which a number of elegant colonial-style buildings have been turned into cafés and restaurants with outdoor seating. On Sunday evenings, the plaza fills up with everybody from gray-haired grannies to giggly children who come to listen to music, stroll around, or sit on park benches and make out. As Avenida del Mar meanders north toward the Zona Dorada, you'll pass the very strange **Monumento al Pescador** (Fisherman's Monument), an enormous statue of a voluptuous nude woman reclining on an anchor, her hand extended toward a fisherman, also naked, hauling his nets. The malécon ends at the beginning of the Zona Dorada (marked, appropriately enough, by the white, pseudo-Moorish monstrosity that is **Valentino's** disco) giving over the prime waterfront space to the hotels.

ACUARIO MAZATLAN Halfway between Zona Dorada and Old Mazatlán is this aquarium/zoo offering close-up views of tropical fish, turtles, and crocodiles, as well as an aviary swarming with chirpy birds. Visitors can also observe fish in a feeding frenzy daily at 3:30 PM, or a sea-lion show half an hour later. A film on sharks follows; although the film is in Spanish, Anglophones won't have a hard time following the sharks chomping on bloody meat. *Av. de los Deportes 111, 2 blocks off Av. del Mar, tel. 69/81-78-15. Admission: $5. Open daily 9–7.*

MUSEO ARQUEOLOGICO One of the few nods to pre-Columbian Mexico you'll encounter in Mazatlán, this museum features a permanent display of local artifacts. It also hosts temporary exhibits by local painters, sculptors, and ceramicists and is well worth a visit, especially since it's free. *Sixto Osuna, west of Plaza Machado. Open Tues.–Sun. 10–1 and 4–7.*

PLAZA DE TOROS Bullfights are held here most Sundays between Christmas and Easter. You can buy tickets in advance at Valentino's disco or most big hotels on the strip as well as at the bullring the day of the fight. The cheapest tickets are about $7; fights start at 4 PM. *Rafael Buelna s/n, near the Zona Dorada.*

TEATRO ANGEL PERALTA This striking theater, built in 1860 and declared a historic monument in 1990, has recently reopened after a two-year restoration and is once again host to the various music and dance performances of Mazatlán's active dramatic arts community. You can find out what is playing at the office just to the right of the main entrance. *Sixto Osuna, at Carnaval, tel. 69/82–44–47. Box office open daily 8:30–2 and 4–7.*

AFTER DARK

Most of Mazatlán's many nightclubs and discos are in the Zona Dorada and frequented by young, energetic types. Most also have a cover charge, but, at clubs located on the beach, at least, it's often possible to take advantage of the mayhem and slip in through a back entrance. Best of the froufrou clubs on Avenida del Mar are **Señor Frog's, Valentino's,** and **Bananas Ranas** (frog bananas—go figure). Neither Señor Frog's nor Bananas Ranas charges a cover, and both open daily around noon and stay open until 2 AM. Valentino's gets started at 10 PM and stays open until 4 AM, but charges $10 at the door. For a more mellow bar scene, try **Jungle Juice Restaurant and Bar** (*see* Food, *above*).

CHEAP THRILLS

If you've had enough of the party scene, you could try to grab a moonlight swim in the small saltwater pool built into the rocks at the base of the **Cerro de la Nevería** (Icebox Hill), off the malecón along Paseo Claussen. If you want something more strenuous (or need to work off a newly acquired beer gut), you could try climbing *up* the hill or taking one of the short hikes listed below. You'll be rewarded for your clambering about with some awesome views.

CERRO DEL VIGIA Just south of Olas Altas, about halfway down the peninsula, sits Lookout Hill, used by the Spanish to keep watch for pirates (hence the rusty cannon you see today). It's a steep climb up the Paseo del Centenario to the top, but there are a number of vista points along the way where you can recover while pretending to take in the stunning views.

EL FARO Further down the peninsula from Olas Altas is the **Cerro del Crestón,** where you can climb to the *faro* (lighthouse), said to be the second-highest in the world, after Gibraltar. It takes about 30 minutes to hike to the top of the hill.

OUTDOOR ACTIVITIES

Playa Sábalo and **Playa Las Gaviotas** are worked by vendors of everything from boogie boards to Jet Skis to five-minute parasail rides. To get away from the crowds, take a boat tour to the three empty islands facing the Zona Dorada—**Isla de los Venados** (Deer Island), **Isla de los Pájaros** (Bird Island), and **Isla de los Lobos** (Wolf Island)—for about $7 round-trip. There are no facilities here, but if you want to swim or snorkel with your own equipment, the tiny slices of sand that skirt each island are pleasant. North of the Zona Dorada are some quieter beaches, such as **Playa Bruja** and **Playa Cerritos**. To reach these, take a CERRITOS bus from the Zona Dorada.

As you might imagine, you can rent just about any kind of watersports equipment in Mazatlán, provided you're willing to pay through the nose for it. Surf and boogie boards are often rented by vendors on the beach near Valentino's disco for about $5 an hour. At the **Aqua Sports Center** (tel. 69/13–33–33), next to El Cid, you can rent a Waverunner (like a Jet Ski) for $33 per half hour, a Hobie Cat ($25 for 3 hrs), a boogie board ($3 an hr), or snorkeling gear ($8 for 2 hrs). One-tank scuba dives for certified divers include equipment and transportation for $50.

Non-certified divers can participate if they first take a $30 resort course. Guided snorkeling trips to Isla de los Venados leave every two hours during the day and include equipment for $17. They also offer eight-hour sportfishing trips for five or six people that include boat, guide, and all equipment for $200.

Near Mazatlán

CONCORDIA AND COPALA

The foothills east of Mazatlán offer a great day trip in the form of **Concordia,** a small city known for its wood, leather, and cane furniture as well as its brown clay pottery. Overlooking the zócalo is the 18th-century **Iglesia de San Sebastián,** considered the only truly baroque church in Sinaloa. Second-class (school) bus fares to Concordia from the main bus station in Mazatlán are $3; the journey takes 45 minutes.

About 24 kilometers past Concordia is the mining-cum-tourist center of **Copala,** whose cobblestone streets, colonial homes, and quaint air attracts an annoying quantity of tour groups from Mazatlán. After the hordes leave, you can enjoy the peaceful streets, the cool mountain air, and, during the rainy season, the lushness of the surrounding hills. On the square is the pleasant and reasonably priced **Hotel San José.** The second-story wood balcony, full of chairs and hammocks, overlooks the square, the church, and the hills beyond the town. Buses run every hour and a half or so to Copala from the main thoroughfare in Concordia.

San Blas

San Blas is the budget traveler's resort. Between Mazatlán and Manzanillo, this small fishing village of about 6,000 clings to the edge of a mangrove swamp in the tropical lowlands of the Pacific Coast. Although San Blas is visually uninteresting, its beaches are unspectacular, and its biting insects are endemic, there is something appealing about this relaxed, friendly town. Plenty of facilities serve the traveler, and most hotels and restaurants are family-operated. San Blas does not segregate locals and tourists—everybody eats, drinks, swims, and hangs out in more or less the same spots.

During the summer, locals lock themselves indoors at sunset, or sit around a dry coconut fire to protect themselves from the mosquitoes and gnats. Follow their lead, and be sure to bring toxic bug repellant to this otherwise inoffensive little beach town

San Blas wasn't always the epitome of tropical lethargy. From the 1500s to the 1800s it was an important Pacific port with a peak population of over 30,000. It was soon eclipsed by Mazatlán and Manzanillo, but the ruins of an old stone cathedral, fort, and accounting house remain. One plausible reason for San Blas's downfall are the vicious biting insects that plague it during the rainy season, from mid-June through October. The logs kept by Spanish explorers remark on the number of mosquitoes, and how the local people took cover at dusk. More recently, Japanese businessmen, who were interested in buying some land for resort development, sent a team to investigate the situation. The team planned to set up two mosquito-counters, but the first one was full before they could put up the second, so they quickly discarded the whole idea.

So you, some surfers, and a few hippies have got the beaches to yourselves. **Playa Borrego** is the main beach, about a kilometer from the center of town. Beach restaurants line the first few hundred yards of sand, after which the hustle and bustle subsides. Near the lighthouse in San Blas is the other town beach, **Playa del Rey,** with tangled vegetation, pelicans, and, in the summer, carnivorous insects. Even quieter beaches await to the south, at the **Bahía de Matachén.** Besides basking on the sand or waiting for a kilometer-long wave to surf, you can trek or take a boat trip through the jungle and mangrove swamps to **La Tovara,** a freshwater swimming spring. As a last resort, you can ponder the chemical reaction between suntan lotion and insect repellant: "Will they neutralize each other, leaving me unprotected, or will I simply burst into flame?"

BASICS

AUTO PARTS/SERVICE The three brothers who run **Servicio Mecánico Sandoval** will deal with your car troubles at any time of day or night—just call if the office is closed. *Juárez s/n, near gas station, tel. 321/5–04–05. Open Mon.–Sat. 7–7, variable hrs on Sun.*

BANK Banamex (Juárez, off zócalo) changes cash and traveler's checks weekdays 8 AM–10 AM, but lines are often long and they sometimes charge unwarranted commissions or run out of cash altogether. The adjoining ATM, fortunately, graciously accepts Cirrus and Plus cards.

MAIL The post office is on Sonora, at Echevarría, one block up and one block left from the bus station. They'll hold mail sent to you at the followng address for up to 10 days: Lista de Correos, San Blas, Nayarit, CP 63740, México. The office is open weekdays 8–1 and 3–5, Saturday 8–noon. The younger of the very kind *dueñas* (proprietors) of **Casa de María** (*see* Where to Sleep, *below*) also sells stamps and will mail letters for you if asked nicely.

PHONES There is a public Ladatel phone in the Palacio Municipal on the zócalo. You can also place cash calls from the *caseta de larga distancia* (long-distance telephone office) on the zócalo or pay a $2 commission there for long-distance collect or credit-card calls.

VISITOR INFORMATION Rosa, who greets visitors at the bus station, is extremely knowledgeable about the area, and Frederico, at **Bungalows Portola** (*see* Where to Sleep, *below*), can also be very helpful. Manuela Córdova Delgado runs the **Delegación de Turismo Municipal,** across the street from McDonald's restaurant (*see* Food, *below*). She or a member of her staff can direct you to wherever you want to go. *Juarez s/n, tel. 321/5–02–67. Open daily 9–3 and 6–8.*

COMING AND GOING

The bus station (tel. 321/5–00–43) is on Sinaloa, just off the zócalo. Two buses a day travel to Guadalajara ($11, 6 hrs), leaving at 8:30 AM and 4 PM. There are also three daily buses to Santiago Ixcuintla ($2, 1½ hrs). Buses that stop at beach towns along the route to Santa Cruz ($1.50, 45 min) leave every two hours between 8:30 AM and 4:30 PM from the corner of Sinaloa and Paredes, next to the market. Buses for Puerto Vallarta leave at 7 AM and 4:30 PM; the 3½-hour trip costs $7. Buses to Las Varas ($3.50, 2 hrs) leave at 7 AM, noon, and 2 PM.

WHERE TO SLEEP

If you arrive in San Blas by bus, you will invariably be greeted by Rosa, who offers to guide road-weary travelers to a hotel. Take advantage of her services; it won't cost you any money—she receives a commission from practically every hotel in town. Just don't let her pressure you into staying somewhere you don't like. Wherever you stay, if you're here between June and October, inspect the windows, screens, and door for any possible entryways, lest you get sucked dry by voracious mosquitoes. Hotel prices vary depending on the season. Prices listed below apply during summer and fall, but expect to pay a few more dollars in winter and around Easter.

Hotels in San Blas are oriented toward budget travelers who like to cook their own food and wash their own clothes.

➤ UNDER $15 • **Casa de María.** This place is made up of two casas, each run by half of a mother-daughter team (both named María). The places are similar, so pick one and knock—you'll find a kind owner and modest lodgings with kitchen facilities. Basic, clean doubles are $13 with bath, $10 without. *Batallón 52 and 108, tel. 321/5–06–32. 2 blocks from zócalo, at Michoacán. 11 rooms, 8 with bath. Laundry, luggage storage, wheelchair access.*

Hotel Playa Hermosa. About 1 kilometer south of town is what remains of a regal ocean-front hotel that was built in 1951 and has since fallen into disrepair. The empty pool, overgrown garden, and mostly vacant rooms are decidedly eerie. Don't listen to Rosa at the bus station when she says this hotel is closed, however. It lives on, looking like a hallucination you'd get from eating too many agave worms. Hippie-types will feel right at home amongst the bats and the few year-round residents. A single costs $10 and a double $13. Ask about weekly and monthly rates. Try to arrive between 9 and 4:30 to check in. *Walk 15 min south on beach, past restaurants and two sets of rocks jutting into water. Kitchen, luggage storage.*

Posada Azul. This modest guest house is quiet and close to the beach, and the prices are great: Small rooms cost $9 for one or two people, while larger rooms cost $13 for up to three people. Kitchen facilities are available. *Batallón 126, near beach, tel. 321/5–01–29. Laundry, luggage storage, wheelchair access.*

➤ UNDER $25 • **Bungalows Portola.** Each of the bungalows here has a large kitchen and living/dining room separated from a good-size bedroom. The gregarious owner will gladly rent you a bike or make you a plane reservation—and if you happen to get sick, chicken soup would not be out of the question, either. A single costs about $17, a double $24. Peso pinchers should ask for the cheap apartment above the office. *Paredes 118, just past Yucatán, tel. 321/5–03–86. From church, 1 block down and a few blocks right. 7 bungalows, all with bath. Laundry, luggage storage, wheelchair access.*

La Quinta California. These newly restored bungalows are the nicest in town. Alma Rita and Chris are the groovy owners who double as tenders of the noisy bar nightly until 2 AM. Summer prices are $20 for one to two people, $27 for three to five. Winter rates are higher at $27 and $40, respectively. Ask about long-term rates. *Matachén s/n, no phone. 5 bungalows, all with bath. Behind Bar Los Panchos on Batallón. Laundry, luggage storage, wheelchair access.*

CAMPING The palapa restaurants on the beach will often let you use their facilities to string a hammock after closing. Prices range from free to $4, depending on how much money you spent at the restaurant during the day and, of course, the proprietor's mood. **Ramada La Palapa** is a good bet, as the owners live there and will keep an eye on you. They also have a few hammocks they have been known to loan.

For tent camping with all the facilities, **Trailer Park Coco Loco** is not unreasonably priced for what you get. It's conveniently near the beach and inconveniently near the mosquitoes. Facilities include decent bathrooms with hot water and an overpriced bar. Whether you're in an RV or a tent, the fee is $5 for one person and $7 for two. *Teniente Azueta, tel. 321/5–00–55. Down Batallón toward the beach. 100 sites. Wheelchair access.*

FOOD

San Blas is a fishing town, and its seafood is fresh and not too expensive: During the day you can get fried fish at the beach restaurants for about $6. San Blas is also proud of its *pan de plátano* (banana bread). A group of local surfers called Team Banana supports its competitive surfing by selling some of the best in town. You can buy the sweet-smelling loaves for $2–$3 at storefronts on Batallón, or on **Playa Las Islitas** (*see* Near San Blas, *below*) from the surfers themselves.

Cocina Económica. Come early during mealtime or this super-cheap eatery might run out of food. And don't expect your own table—there are only two. Most patrons get their beans, rice, and tortillas ($3 a plate) to go. One sad note: No beer is served here. *Sinaloa, at Salas, no phone. Open 8–3 and 6–10.*

La Hacienda. The talk of the town, this traditional restaurant has delicious food and an atmosphere approaching elegant. Try their specialty, *pescado gaviota* (fillet of sea bass stuffed with shrimp in a cheese sauce; $8.50) or the economical *sincronizadas* (sandwiches made with tortillas instead of bread; $1.50). *Juárez 41, tel. 321/5–07–72. Open daily 2 PM–10 PM, bar open until midnight. Wheelchair access.*

McDonald's. No, gringo fast food has not infiltrated this sleepy town. As they say in San Blas, this is the *Mexican* McD's, with no golden arches or heat lamps in sight. A fruit platter is $2.50, as is a standard plate of huevos rancheros, and the dinner specials (e.g. grilled chicken with enchiladas, guacamole, french fries, beans, chips, salad, and tortillas) will immobilize you for $6. *Juárez 75, ½ block from zócalo, no phone. Open daily 7 AM–10 PM. Wheelchair access.*

Rosy's. A fried-fish plate costs about $3 at Rosy's, and a *bistec ranchero* (steak with tomatoes and onions) about $3.50. If you're not very hungry, try the *sopa de arroz* (rice soup) for less than $1—make a point of asking for garlic and chiles. *Batallón 43, on zócalo, no phone. Open daily 9–8.*

CHEAP THRILLS

The roof of the Hotel Playa Hermosa (*see* Where to Sleep, *above*) is the right place to drink a few beers and admire the San Blas sunset. Also, look for the aging hippie, Kearney, who's been hanging out in San Blas for over 15 years and often plays his guitar and sings the blues at night. He only lives in San Blas for six months out of the year, but no one is quite sure which six months. He frequents **Mike's Bar** (*see* After Dark, *below*).

For an historical look at San Blas and a fantastic view of the area, make the 15-minute hike from town up to La Contadoría. Here you'll find the ruins of **Nuestra Señora del Rosario,** a fort built in 1769, now garrisoned only by sun-loving iguanas. The adjoining structure was built in 1770 to house Spanish bureaucrats. The hill itself, conveniently near one of Mexico's most prosperous Pacific ports, was later used by pirates to hide the riches they seized. To get here, walk on the main road out of town; before the bridge, veer right past the restaurants and follow the stone road up the hill on your right.

AFTER DARK

The bars in town are all easy to find. The restaurant **La Familia** (Batallón 16, tel. 321/5–03–58) has a bar and often shows videos at night. **Viejano's Bar** (Batallón 9, just off zócalo, tel. 321/5–03–90) is open until 2 AM, showing music videos (mostly the Doors) on their laser-disc player. **Mike's Bar,** above McDonald's (*see* Food, *above*) plays slightly more contemporary music. On Saturdays people head to **Disco La Fitte,** a block down from McDonald's, which charges a $3 cover. Keep an eye out for **Los Bixaneros,** a local band led by a Jamaican that plays salsa, merengue, and other tropical sounds at parties and other events. Warning: Compared to the heady high season (December–May), the summer months see only very mellow nightlife.

OUTDOOR ACTIVITIES

Bike rentals are available at **Bungalows Portola** (*see* Where to Sleep, *above*) for $2 an hour, even if you're not a paying guest. You can also ask for Toño Palma, who will be happy to take you out on a boat to watch whales or fish for tuna and red snapper. His fees vary according to the season, and perhaps how much he likes the look of you.

LA TOVARA San Blas's famous jungle boat ride through thick mangrove swamps full of birds, insects, turtles, and crocodiles brings you to this freshwater spring. Boats leave from the bridge just outside of San Blas; the trek costs about $30 for up to four people. If you take the SANTA CRUZ bus to Matachén and leave from the embarcadero where the bus ($1) drops you, it costs about $23 for four. The boats fit more people, but the price increases with additional passengers. Take the first boat at 8 AM and you'll have an hour to swim in the spring before the bulk of tourists arrive. For an extra $20 you can also visit the new crocodile research center, **El Centro Reproductor de Cocodrilos,** where, if you're lucky, you can watch the birth of baby crocs. If you don't want to pay for a boat trip, or are feeling somewhat masochistic, you can hike to La Tovara during the dry season (November–early June), but it takes two hours and the rocks are slippery. Two kids, Leonardo and Javier, will competently guide any size group for about half of what the boats charge. Ask for them at Bungalows Portola (*see* Where to Sleep, *above*).

Near San Blas

Just south of San Blas are a number of beaches along the **Bahía Matachén.** The first and best is **Playa Las Islitas** (also called Stoner's Beach), which is famous for the kilometer-long wave that occasionally appears in summer or fall, depending on some fortuitous conjunction of equinoctial and lunar forces. Team Banana rents surfboards and boogie boards for $3 an hour and $8 a day here, in addition to selling their banana bread. Farther south along the bay the beaches are rockier but less infested with mosquitoes in summer. The oyster-harvesting town of **Aticama** has a small beach that runs into **Playa los Cocos,** a beautiful spot with lots of coconut trees. The trailer park here isn't that attractive, but it does offer cheap, secure tent camping for about $5. The teeny town of **Santa Cruz,** at the extreme south end of the bay, is almost totally untouristed and has a few inexpensive hotels. Buses run along the bay from the stop at the corner of Sinaloa and Paredes in San Blas, leaving for Santa Cruz every two hours between 8:30 AM and 4:30 PM.The last returning bus sets out from Santa Cruz at 4 PM, so be sure to keep an eye on the time if you don't want to spend the night outside San Blas.

Tepic

The capital of the agricultural state of Nayarit, Tepic is not a city to linger in if you're short on time or have the beach and an ice-cold coconut drink on your mind. There are, however, a few reasons to visit this city. The bus station is a hub for transportation throughout western Mexico, so your travels between Puerto Vallarta and San Blas or Los Mochis might make Tepic a required stop. Tepic is also a base for some interesting excursions to rural towns (*see* Near Tepic, *below*), where you can learn about Huichol and Aztec culture. Even if you don't make a day trip from here, you'll meet some Huichol and Cora people, who come down from the hills to buy supplies in Tepic, or to travel to work on the coast. You'll also see geriatric men in cowboy hats, their faces darkened and wrinkled from labor in the sun, chatting on street corners and shopping in small stores that sell leather goods, tools, ammunition, seeds, and chemical fertilizers.

If you're going to be in Tepic for more than a few hours, head for the free **Museo Regional de Nayarit** (México 91, at Zapata, tel. 321/2–19–00) near the zócalo, where you'll find a fine collection of pre-Columbian clay figurines. **The Ex-Convento de la Cruz de Zacate** (México, at Calzada del Ejército), also downtown, was built to guard a grass cross that, legend has it, miraculously appeared nearby in 1540. The building now houses the offices of the state tourism department and a progressive theater group. To escape Tepic's general drabness, commerce, and noise, take a stroll through **Paseo La Loma** (Insurgentes and Colegio Militar), a large park full of pine and eucalyptus trees with a rideable miniature train.

The gray buildings of Tepic stand in marked contrast to the colorful Huichol embroidery and yarn paintings sold in the town's many markets.

BASICS

AUTO PARTS/SERVICE **Taller Mecánico Mana** is near the main bus station and can help with most mechanical problems. *Insurgentes 328, no phone. Open weekdays 9–noon.*

CASAS DE CAMBIO Casas de cambio and banks are downtown along Avenida México. **Banamex** (México, at Zapata) has an ATM that accepts Plus cards. For traveler's checks and dollars, casas de cambio give slightly better rates, but banks don't charge a commission, so it's a toss-up between the two. Hours may be the deciding factor: Banks change money only between 9 AM and noon. The **Casa de Cambio El Rublo,** (México, at Zapata, tel. 321/2–73–88), on the other hand, is open Monday–Saturday 8:30–2 and 4–7.

EMERGENCIES The number for the **police** is 321/2–01–63; they can get you an **ambulance.**

MAIL A joint post and telegram office in the bus station is open weekdays 8–1:30. The main post office (Durango 33 Nte.) is open weekdays 8–7, Saturday 8–noon. The latter will hold mail sent to you at the following address for up to 10 days: Administración de Correos, Durango 33 Nte., Tepic, Nayarit, CP 63000, México.

MEDICAL AID You can get advice about minor medical problems as well as basic first aid at the **Farmacia de Descuento** near the zócalo. *México 65, tel. 321/2–17–17. Open Mon.–Sat. 9–7:30, Sun. 9–2.*

PHONES The best place to make long-distance calls in Tepic is the bus station. You can place collect or credit-card calls from the payphones at the station. There's also a 24-hour telephone office in the first-class side of the bus station, but they won't let you make collect calls.

VISITOR INFORMATION The Nayarit regional tourist office can provide maps of Tepic and the state as well as handfuls of tourist brochures, most of which are in Spanish. *México 32 Sur, tel. 321/2–95–45. Open daily 9–2:30.*

COMING AND GOING

BY BUS The bus terminal is on Avenida Insurgentes, about six blocks east of Avenida México. To get downtown from here, take an ESTACION FRESNOS bus. **Transportes del Pacífico** (tel. 321/3–23–13) has buses to Mazatlán ($12, 5 hrs), Guadalajara ($12, 4 hrs), Los Mochis ($29, 12 hrs), Mexicali ($72, 28 hrs), and Tijuana ($72, 30 hrs). Service to Puerto Vallarta ($7, 4 hrs) leaves on the half hour, 24 hours a day. The Puerto Vallarta bus will also let you off at Rincón de Guayabitos and other beaches on the way, if you ask the driver. **Transportes Norte de Sonora** (tel. 321/3–23–15) serves San Blas ($3, 1½ hrs) hourly between 6 AM and 7 PM. **Omnibus de México** (tel. 321/3–13–23) has one bus leaving at 4:30 PM daily to Cuidad Juárez ($77, 28 hrs). They also have hourly service to Guadalajara ($12, 4) round the clock, and evening service to Mexico City ($39, 12 hrs). In both Guadalajara and Mexico City you can transfer buses for just about any other major city in the country.

BY TRAIN To reach the train station, hop an ESTACION FRESNOS bus, which passes the train station on its way between the bus station and downtown. Trains go north from Tepic to Mexicali ($75, 32 hrs 1st class; $29, 38 hrs 2nd class), with stops in Culiacán ($15, 8 hrs 1st class; $6, 10 hrs 2nd class); Sufragio ($25, 10 hrs 1st class; $10, 12 hrs 2nd class); and Nogales ($60, 23 hrs 1st class; $23, 28 hrs 2nd class). The southbound train goes as far as Guadalajara ($8, 5 hrs 1st class; $3.50, 6 hrs 2nd class). The first-class northbound train leaves daily at 2 PM. The second-class train for the same route leaves at 5 PM. The southbound trains leave at noon (2nd class) and 4 PM (1st class). *Tel. 321/3–48–13. Ticket office open 10 AM–about midnight.*

GETTING AROUND

Central Tepic, including the downtown area, the park, and the bus station, is walkable, if not tiny. The bus station and park are on Avenida Insurgentes, which crosses Avenida México, the main commercial street. Near the intersection of Avenidas Insurgentes and México you'll find casas de cambio, restaurants, hotels, most of Tepic's points of interest, and the zócalo. You can travel down both main avenidas in Volkswagen buses for about 35¢.

WHERE TO SLEEP

Tepic has a few inexpensive hotels right by the bus station—convenient for weary travelers but also noisy. Turn left out of the bus station, take an immediate left, and walk one block. Here, diagonally across from the back of the bus station, is the **Hotel Nayer** (Martínez 439, tel. 321/3–23–22). It's not a bad choice considering the price: Singles are $8.50, doubles $11. The bathrooms are clean and have hot water. In the same area, **Hotel Tepic** also has clean rooms and bathrooms, but it's noisier. Singles cost $11, and doubles are a deal at $12. For a better night's sleep at Hotel Tepic, request a room on one of the upper floors. In the morning come downstairs for a decent $3 breakfast. **Hotel Abasolo** (Abasolo 207, at Sánchez, tel. 321/6–19–86) is cheap and basic—you won't get a lot for your pesos, but you won't have to surrender too many of them, either. A room for one or two people, decorated in faded pink cement, costs $7 without bath, $10 with bath. Considering the noise problem at the these places, you're better off sleeping downtown if you plan to stay more than one night.

The **Hotel Sarita** (Bravo 112 Pte., tel. 321/2–13–33), close to the zócalo and second-class bus station, has a tiled lobby, furnished with potted plants and colonial-style furniture, is a welcoming introduction to the clean, fan-cooled rooms. Rooms with one bed cost $17; with two beds the price is $20. The **Hotel Altamirano** (Mina 19, tel. 321/2–10–31), just off the zócalo, is quiet, calm, and wheelchair accessible. Singles and doubles are $20.

FOOD

Food is generally cheaper in Tepic than in the seaside resorts, and better than you might expect. Fresh seafood comes straight from San Blas, and vegetarian restaurants pop up with surprising frequency. Grill joints stretch along Avenida Insurgentes below the park. Super-cheap grub is also sold near the second-class bus station on Avenida Vitoria, below the central square.

Tacos at **Antropós** (México 73 Nte., near Zapata, no phone) are kind to your wallet (they're less than $1) and come with all the trimmings—cilantro, tomatoes, guacamole, salsa, and grilled onions. Heftier dishes, from carne asada to *queso fundido* (cheese fondue) run $5–$6. For tasty vegetarian food in a great location, try **Girasol** in Paseo La Loma park, where soy burgers are $2 and veggie *pozole* (corn soup) overflowing with mushrooms is about $5. The owner's brother runs a similar place, **Restaurant Vegetariano Quetzalcoatl** (León, at Lerdo, no phone) on the fringe of downtown. Carnivores in the mood for a real meal can head for the **Restaurant Altamirano** (México 109 Sur, tel. 321/2–13–77), near the Palacio Municipal. High ceilings stone walls, and the sound of frying tortillas create an "authentic" atmosphere here, and *lengua en salsa* (beef tongue) or *pollo en mole* (chicken in chile and chocolate sauce) will cost you $5.

SHOPPING

Tepic has a number of stores that sell Huichol and Cora artwork. Prices may be good compared to those at the tourist resorts, but they're not quite the deal you'd expect: Store owners prevent the indigenous people from selling their work on the street, so you're still paying a middleman. Time allowing, visit the worthwhile **Centro Cultural Huichol** in Santiago Ixcuintla (*see below*) to do your souvenir hunting.

Centro Cultural Huichol

Huichol artisans supposedly tap into the metaphysical world and then translate the knowledge thus acquired into meticulous beadwork, embroidery, yarn paintings, and weaving. Susana and Mariano Valadez, an American anthropologist and a Huichol artisan, respectively, founded this nonprofit center in Santiago Ixcuintla to provide local Huichol people with an alternative to working in chemical-ridden tobacco fields. The center provides medical care, shelter, legal aid, and training in art and farming techniques, as well as a place where Huichols can congregate while working on the coast—all to help the Huichol become economically self-sufficient through the practice of traditional art forms and sustainable agriculture. The center supports itself through the sale of the high-quality artesanía (crafts) produced here. Although the prices are not always lower than in Tepic's stores, the work is often better, and the proceeds go back into the project and to the community. There is also a small museum on site. People who are committed to learning about and participating in this sort of social venture, especially those with valuable skills to share (such as doctors or carpenters) are welcome to come and stay for a while in exchange for labor. If you are interested, call 323/5–11–71, or fax 323/5–10–06 for more information. The center is located at Avenida 20 de Noviembre 452, at Constitución.

Near Tepic

Several indigenous communities make easy day trips from Tepic. If, however, all you want is nice scenery and good food, travel an hour by bus to get to the **Laguna de Santa María del Oro.** This deep, cold lake is the heart of a low-key resort area frequented by families from Tepic. It's a relaxing place to camp, fish, and swim. The lakeshore is lined with restaurants, most of which serve the area's specialty, *pescado dorado,* literally "golden fish," served grilled with a variety of sauces. **Transportes Noroeste Nayarit** buses leave Tepic for Santa María hourly ($3) from the Terminal Centro at Avenidas Victoria and México.

SANTIAGO IXCUINTLA

This midsize city is in the center of Nayarit's tobacco fields, 63 kilometers northeast of Tepic. Far off the tourist track, it's a good place to soak up the atmosphere of rural Mexico, especially if you're feeling shell-shocked from a visit to Mazatlán or Puerto Vallarta. A small museum in the Municipal Palace displays archaeological pieces from the area, but the main attraction of this city is the **Centro Cultural Huichol** (*see box, above*). Susana of the Huichol Center is a great resource for information about the region. The easiest way to get to here is to take a cab from the plaza and ask for the Centro Huichol or *la gringa Susana.* Cheap hotels surround the plaza; try the reasonably priced **Hotel Santiago** (tel. 323/5–06–37), where all the rooms have TVs and those little refrigerators; singles are $18, doubles $20. Buses to Santiago Ixcuintla leave regularly from Tepic and thrice daily from San Blas.

MEXCALTITAN

This small village 21 kilometers northeast of Santiago Ixcuintla is decidedly peculiar. It sits on an island in the middle of a saltwater lagoon and is laid out like a wheel, with a central hub out of which radiate numerous spokes that connect to a street that runs around the circumference. Because of the village's shape, some believe it to be Aztlán—the mythical first city of the Aztecs. During the rainy season, the streets are underwater, so locals use boats to get around. You can reach Mexcaltitán from Santiago Ixcuintla by taking one of the two buses per day that travel to Embarcadero Batanga and then taking a boat to the village. Mexcaltitán has restaurants but, as of yet, no hotels, so make sure you board a boat in time to catch the last bus back to Santiago at 4 PM. Otherwise, you'll have to take a taxi ($5–$7) to nearby Tuxpan, where there is a hotel.

Puerto Vallarta

Puerto Vallarta is famous for its beaches and its cobblestone streets and whitewashed, red-roofed buildings. Unfortunately, many of the latter are condos and timeshares. Like most of the resorts on the Pacific Coast, the city has a gringo-ized hotel zone (the *zona hotelera*) that stands separate from the "Mexican" part of town—staying here would be like living at your local shopping mall. The downtown area around the Río Cuale is more residential, with several cafés, a number of good restaurants, lots of beach to play on, and plenty of opportunities to rent snorkel gear or get out on the water.

Puerto Vallarta's zona hotelera is climate and ambience control taken to the extreme.

So yes, Puerto Vallarta is a big, often ugly resort—but there are reasons people come here. The natural setting, between lush tropical hills and a coastline worth ogling, is spectacular. Some credit for making Puerto Vallarta such a popular destination also belongs to *The Love Boat,* some to John Huston's *The Night of the Iguana,* or more specifically, the romance between Richard Burton and Liz Taylor that blossomed here during the filming of the latter. Mexicana also had a hand in it all. The airline "discovered," developed, and promoted the resort town in the early 1950s to combat Aeroméxico's monopoly on flights to Acapulco. For the budget traveler, summer is the ideal time to visit since hotel rates are much lower. The surrounding coast is also worth visiting and easily accessible from Puerto Vallarta.

Puerto Vallarta

El Eden, **7**

Iglesia de
Nuestra Señora
de Guadalupe, **4**

Malecón, **1**

Mercado
Municipal, **5**

Palacio
Municipal, **3**

Plaza Lázaro
Cárdenas, **6**

Plaza Principal, **2**

TO AIRPORT,
PLAYA NORTE,
PUNTA DE MITA

Bahía de Banderas

Díaz Ordaz

Allende

Pípila

L. Vicario

Miramar

Morelos

Aldama

Corona

Galeana

Juárez

Iturbide

Libertad

Rodríguez

Encino

Río Cuale
Island

Río Cuale

Aquiles

Serdán

Suárez

Ignacio

Madero

Av. Lázaro

Venustiano

Av. Vallarta

Av. Insurgentes

**BUDGET HOTEL
ZONE**

Cárdenas

Carranza

Aguacate

**Playa de
los Muertos**

Olas Altas

Frac.

Rodríguez

Púlpito

Amapas

Cafeto

Av. Insurgentes

Amapos

Av. Insurgentes

N

**Playa
Mismaloya**

TO LAS ANIMAS, YELAPA

0   500 meters

0   500 yards

BASICS

AMERICAN EXPRESS The office sells traveler's checks and changes them at a good rate. Cardholders can cash personal checks and have their mail held here. *Centro Comercial Villa Vallarta, Local H-6, Puerto Vallarta, Jalisco, CP 48300, México, tel. 322/2-68-77. On road to airport. Open weekdays 9-2:30 and 4-6, Sat. 9-1.*

AUTO PARTS/SERVICE **Multi Servicio y Auto-Baño Refer** can help you with car troubles or direct you to someone who can. You can also get your car washed here. *Insurgentes 333, at Badillo, tel. 322/2-41-57. Open weekdays 9-6, Sat. 9-3.*

CASAS DE CAMBIO Puerto Vallarta has many casas de cambio, usually in tiny storefront booths with caged-in employees. The rates are no better or worse than in other cities, and all change cash and traveler's checks, but nary a one is open on Sundays. **Casa de Cambio** (Díaz Ordaz 866, no phone), at the north end of the malecón, is open Monday through Saturday 9–8:30. The **Asociación Cambiaria** (Morelos 480, tel. 322/2-40-77), at the south end of the malecón, changes all sorts of currency Monday–Saturday 9–9. The **Banamex** on the south side of the Plaza Principal has ATMs that accept Plus and Cirrus cards.

CONSULATES Canada: *Hidalgo 226, tel. 322/2-53-98. Open weekdays 9-noon (until 1 in winter).*

United States. The consulate answers its phone at all hours. *Parian del Puente 12-A, behind Restaurant Fuente del Puente, tel. 322/2-00-69. Open weekdays 9-1.*

EMERGENCIES The number for the **police** is 322/2-01-23. They can get you an **ambulance**.

LAUNDRY The amiable staff at **Lavandería Blanquita** will wash, dry, and fold three kilos of clothes for $3. *Madero 407-A, no phone. Open Mon.-Sat. 8-8.*

MAIL The post office is half a block above the malecón, at Juárez. They offer the usual services and will hold mail sent to you at the following address for up to 10 days: Lista de Correos, Calle Mina 188, Puerto Vallarta, Jalisco, CP 48300, México. *Mina 188, tel. 322/2-20-33. Open weekdays 8-7:30, Sat. 9-1.*

MEDICAL AID The **CMQ** clinic (Badillo 365, ½ block east of Insurgentes, tel. 322/3-19-19) has English-speaking doctors and attends patients 24 hours a day. Prices start at $30 for an appointment, and walk-in emergency care is also available. **Farmacia CMQ** (Badillo 367, tel. 322/2-29-41), next door, is open 24 hours.

TELEPHONES Both the **Autotransportes del Pacífico** (Insurgentes 282) and **Tres Estrellas de Oro** (Carranza 322) stations have casetas de larga distancia, open 6:30 AM–midnight. Both charge a flat $3 for collect calls. Save your precious pesos by calling from a pay phone—the Plaza Principal is lined with them, as is the malecón, and most are in good condition.

VISITOR INFORMATION The only real tourist office is the **Delegación Federal de Turismo**—the rest are out to sell you something. They have a fair number of brochures and free copies of a decent English-language newspaper. *In Palacio Municipal, tel. 322/2-02-42. Open weekdays 9-9, Sat. 9-1.*

> *If you're 25 or older and have a major credit card, you can get a free meal and discounts on tours, rentals, and discos by taking one of the tours offered by the time-share people who line the malécon. But beware: They are conditioned not to hear the word "no."*

COMING AND GOING

BY BUS Puerto Vallarta does not have a central bus station. Instead, each bus line operates an individual office, all of which are south of the Río Cuale on or near Avenida Insurgentes. **Tres Estrellas de Oro** (Badillo 11, at Insurgentes, tel. 322/3-11-17), which also operates **Elite** buses, leaves for Hermosillo ($62, 16 hrs) at 2:15 PM with stops in Tepic ($8.50, 3 hrs) and Mazatlán ($18, 8 hrs). Buses leave for Manzanillo ($13, 5 hrs) at 6:30 AM and 8 AM. The 6:30 bus continues on to Acapulco ($35, 19 hrs). They also send three buses a day to Mexico City ($38, 14 hrs). **Transportes del Pacífico** (Insurgentes 282, tel. 322/2-10-15) has hourly service to to Guadalajara ($18, 6 hrs) between 7 AM and 1 AM as well as frequent Tepic-bound buses. Slightly more expensive *plus* service is also available to the same destinations. **Transportes Norte de Sonora** (Carranza 322, btw Insurgentes and Constitución, tel. 322/2–66–66) goes to San Blas ($7.50, 3 hrs), as well as Mazatlán and Tepic. Luggage storage is available at this depot. **Transportes Cihuatlán** (Madero, at Constitución, tel. 332/2–34–36) has frequent service to Manzanillo ($10.50, 6½ hrs) and to intermediate points such as Bahía Chamela ($6, 4 hrs) and Barra de Navidad ($8.50, 5 hrs).

BY PLANE Puerto Vallarta's international airport is 6.4 kilometers north of town and not far from the major resorts. **Mexicana** (Centro Comercial Villas Vallarta, in zona hotelera, tel. 322/4–89–00) and **Aeroméxico** (on Plaza Genovesa, tel. 322/4–27–77) have daily flights to Guadalajara (about $80 one way), Mexico City (about $150 one way), and Los Cabos (about $130 one way). Both carriers also have service from Los Angeles and Dallas, as do U.S. carriers **Continental, Delta, Alaska Airlines,** and **American.** City buses marked AEROPUERTO, IXTAPA, or JUNTA drop you off on the highway a hop, skip, and a jump from the terminals. You can also take an airport taxi from the center of town for a whopping $10.

GETTING AROUND

Puerto Vallarta is divided into three parts: the northern zona hotelera (a long stretch of hotels, shopping centers, and overpriced restaurants); the pedestrian-friendly downtown area (also called Viejo Vallarta), centered around the banks of the Río Cuale; and, to the south, Playa de los Muertos, the most popular beach in Puerto Vallarta proper. The **malecón** begins at Díaz Ordaz and then runs south along the bay, past the **Plaza Principal** (also called Plaza de Armas). Near the plaza is the **Iglesia de Nuestra Señora de Guadalupe**, whose most distinctive feature is the large crown, a copy of the one worn by the empress of Mexico in the late 1860s, atop its bell tower.

To reach the zona hotelera from the downtown area, hop a bus marked HOTELES, AEROPUERTO, or MARINAS VALLARTA on Avenida Insurgentes or Avenida Juárez. The buses return along Morelos and, south of the Río Cuale, along Avenida Insurgentes.

WHERE TO SLEEP

Nearly all the budget hotels are just south of the Río Cuale. The good news is they are close to the bus stations and a short four–seven blocks from the beach. The bad news is that most have cramped hallways and rooms overlooking noisy interior courtyards. Remember that hotel prices jump as much as 30% between October and March.

➤ UNDER $15 • **Hotel Azteca.** An airy outdoor courtyard makes this the best of the cheapies. Singles cost $9, doubles $11. Rooms with kitchenettes are $15. *Madero 473, tel. 322/2–27–50. 46 rooms, all with bath. Luggage storage.*

Hotel Villa del Mar. This hotel is a steal during summer, when the clean exterior rooms with balconies and fancy beds cost $13 for a single ($11.50 for an interior room), $17 for a double ($14 interior). For $22 you can have an apartment-style room for two with a kitchenette. *Madero 440, 3 blocks east of Insurgentes, tel. 322/2–07–85. 49 rooms, all with bath. Luggage storage. MC, V.*

Posada El Real. Hidden behind a store is a long entranceway that takes you to clean, decent-size rooms, whose only major drawback is a lack of light. The management is more personable than most, despite the bars they hide behind to protect themselves from who knows what. Singles are $10, doubles, $14. *Madero 287, tel. 322/2–05–87. 8 rooms, all with bath. Luggage storage, wheelchair access.*

➤ UNDER $20 • **Hotel Posada Don Miguel.** This posada has a tiny pool and spacious rooms that cost $13 for one person and $17 for two. Some beds are lumpier than others, so check a few rooms before you choose. One problem is that it's on the noisiest street in town; another is that prices *double* in winter. *Insurgentes 322, just south of Carranza, tel. 322/2–25–40. 50 rooms, all with bath. Luggage storage. MC, V.*

Hotel Yasmin. A lush courtyard, clean rooms, and a fine location (one block from Playa de los Muertos) make this place well worth the few extra dollars. It's also a skip, hop, and stumble from the Cactus Club disco, and the fabulous Café de Olla (*see* Food, *below*) is downstairs. In summer, singles cost about $17, doubles $20, but again, prices double for the winter season. *Badillo 168, tel. 322/2–00–87. 33 rooms, all with bath. Luggage storage, wheelchair access.*

➤ UNDER $30 • **Hotel Belmar.** Easily the nicest of the reasonably priced hotels, the Belmar has clean, freshly painted walls, tile floors, and brightly striped bedcovers. The bathrooms are clean, and rooms ($13 single, $20 double) open either to a balcony on the street or the court-yard hallway. You can get a TV for $3.50 extra. *Insurgentes 161, at Serdán, tel. 322/2–05–72. 29 rooms, all with bath. Luggage storage.*

Hotel Rosita. You'll pay a bit more here, but you'll be where the action is (near the beach and malecón), in a nice room with a balcony overlooking the beach and access to a pool. In low sea-son, a small single costs $18, a larger one $22; double occupancy costs $26 regardless of the size of the room. If Puerto Vallarta has put you in a mood to splurge, go for a "suite"—a high-ceilinged room with brick walls, air-conditioning, carpet, a beautiful tiled bathroom, a sofabed, and a comfy, new king-size bed for $29 for two–four people. Prices here jump a bit earlier than in other hotels, generally in August. *Díaz Ordaz 901 (north end of malecón), tel. 322/2–10–33. 112 rooms, all with bath. Luggage storage. AE, MC, V.*

CAMPING Hotels don't look favorably upon (and sometimes even hassle) people sleeping on hotel beaches. If you're set on beach camping, it's better to crash at the south end of **Playa de los Muertos.** During Semana Santa, temporary campgrounds are set up here to accommodate the crowds.

FOOD

There's a huge variety of food here, including many French and Italian restaurants, but prices are often exorbitant. You can even try Aztec food, with, if you're lucky, maguey worms, for $25 a plate at **Mogambo** (Díaz Ordaz 644-D, tel. 322/2–64–96). For simpler food at low prices, go to the **market,** just north of the Río Cuale, where good comidas corridas are about $3. You can get fresh juice ($2) or a quick espresso a few blocks away at **Café Malibu** (Morelos, at Guer-rero). Cheap eats are also available along Insurgentes, on the other side of the Río Cuale.

➤ UNDER $5 • **Café de Olla** has delicious, inexpensive food. Tamales are $2 each, and a plate of chiles rellenos with rice, beans, tortillas, and tons of cheese is $5. The coffee is damn good, too. *Badillo 168, btw Olas Altas and Pino Suárez, tel. 322/2–0–087. Open Wed.–Sun. noon–10.*

Cenaduría el Campanario. This unmarked restaurant is usually packed with locals and tourists in the know who appreciate the excellent pozole ($4). Tamales are a buck each. *Hidalgo 339, at Independencia, tel. 322/3–15–09. Open Mon.–Sat. 7 PM–11 PM. Closed first 2 weeks of Aug. Wheelchair access.*

Cenaduría Doña Chela. The pozole ($3) is made with lots of chicken and pork here, making for a satisfying meal. A plate of four tacos is $2.50. Wash it all down with an *agua fresca* (juice drink) for 50¢. *Serdán 255, at Vallarta, tel. 322/2–24–32. Open Tues.–Sun. 6 PM–11 PM.*

➤ UNDER $10 • **Café Sierra.** There is a decent selection of good, not-too-expensive food here, and you can wash it all down with a variety of espresso drinks ($1–$3). Breakfasts run between $4 and $6, and they also serve sandwiches ($5–$7). Italian sodas with ice cream cost $4. *Insurgentes 109, just south of Río Cuale, tel. 322/2–27–48. Open daily 8:30 AM–10:30 PM.*

La Dolce Vita. If you've been craving pizza, indulge yourself. The oven-baked pies ($8) are nothing like the pale imitations served in most Italian restaurants in Mexico, and one feeds two hungry people. *Díaz Ordaz 674 (north end of malécon), tel. 322/2–38–52. Open Mon.–Sat. noon–2 AM, Sun. 6 PM–midnight.*

➤ UNDER $15 • **Archie's Wok.** Founded by Archie Alpenia, once John Huston's private chef, this restaurant dishes out the best, most varied Asian food around. Choose from Hoisin ribs ($9) and Thai coconut fish ($10), or get your fix of stir-fried vegetables ($6). *Rodríguez 130, tel. 322/2–04–11. Near pier at Playa de los Muertos. Open Mon.–Sat. 2 PM–11PM. Closed Sept.*

CAFES **Café Europa.** Espresso drinks are $1–$3 here, and a light menu is also served. A spinach-and-cheese crêpe ($5) comes with juice, coffee, and toast for breakfast; salade niçoise is $6. *Badillo 252, at Vallarta, tel. 322/ 3–19–25. Open daily 9 –2 and 6–10.*

Café San Cristobal. This coffee shop roasts its own beans, which they supply to restaurants and other cafés around the city. They also have a small menu (a cheese and fruit plate is $3.50) to accompany the coffees and deserts. *Corona 172, btw Juárez and Morelos, tel. 322/3–25–51. Open Mon.–Sat. 8 AM–10 PM.*

OUTDOOR ACTIVITIES

Most of the things to do in Puerto Vallarta involve getting wet, but if that's not to your taste, or you've simply had enough, you can go mountain biking with a group organized by **Bike Mex** (Guerrero 361, 1 block north of market, tel. 322/3–16–80). Trips are divided into beginner, intermediate, and advanced, and range from four-hour trips costing $40 to $600 week-long adventure tours. All equipment and food is included.

Playa de los Muertos is the most popular beach in Puerto Vallarta. The gloomy name (Beach of the Dead) is derived from a battle with the Spanish that took place here—it's not a reference to unlucky tourists. At sunset, people congregate here to watch the horizon turn persimmon red. You can go parasailing for a painful $25, or ride a banana boat for $10. You can rent snorkel gear ($9 for 24 hrs) or arrange guided snorkel or dive trips ($45 and $50 respectively) through **Chico's Dive Shop** (Díaz Ordaz 770-5, tel. 322/2–18–95).

Los Arcos (the Arches) are a set of large rocks under which caves have been formed by wave erosion. Chico's and other dive shops will take you scuba diving in these protected waters, which are full of tropical fish. To save yourself big bucks, however, rent your own snorkel gear, take a RUTA 2 combi from Plaza Lázaro Cárdenas (near Playa de los Muertos) to **Playa Mismaloya**, get off at the Arcos Hotel, walk down to the rocky beach, and swim out yourself. Playa Mismaloya is also a good sunning/swimming beach. John Huston's classic film *Night of the Iguana* was shot here, though the massive Arcos Hotel that now looms over everything hadn't been built at the time. If you walk inland from Playa Mismaloya along the dirt road, you'll find **El Eden,** where the movie *Predator* was filmed. You'll be rewarded for your 90-minute, uphill walk with a user-friendly waterfall where you can swim, slide down rocks, or swing on ropes into the water. To refuel, stop at either of two restaurants along the way.

The more isolated beaches of **Las Animas** and **Yelapa** are on the southern side of the **Bahía de Banderas,** past Playa Mismaloya, and are accessible only by boat. Las Animas is less developed than Yelapa, which has a small colony of expatriate gringos who pretend they never left home. Yelapa has pricey and often full cabanas, but you can camp for free on the beach in either place. There's a small waterfall 15 minutes from the beach in Yelapa. When the tide is low enough, you can walk along the shore from Boca de Tomatlán to Las Animas, though you might get wet negotiating some pretty daunting rocks. The cheapest way to reach these beaches is on the **Autobus Acuático** (tel. 322/3–03–09). Two of these water shuttles leave daily at 10:30 AM and 11 AM from the pier at Playa de los Muertos, returning at 3:30 PM. Fares are $5 one way to Las Animas, $8 one way to Yelapa.

AFTER DARK

There are a million discos here, but most either extort an outrageous cover or charge scandalous prices for drinks. Fortunately, you can sometimes get free or discounted passes by playing up to the oh-so-friendly time-share people, and once you're inside a club, you can often get free passes to return. **Cactus Club** (Vallarta, at Diéguez) and **Zoo** (Díaz Ordaz 630, tel. 322/2–49–45) are the hip hangouts, and anything from a bathing suit to an evening gown is considered suitable attire. The Cactus Club, designed as a giant cave sprouting a few fluorescent cacti, opens at 11 PM and charges a $10 cover. The Zoo is an after-hours club (open midnight to 6 AM) that charges no cover and features go-go dancers in cages, as well as waiters dressed as gorillas. For a slightly more familiar scene, try the always raging (and, happily, cover-free) **Carlos O'Briens** (Díaz Ordaz 786, tel. 322/2–14–44), open 11 AM to 2 AM, or one of the more pretentious clubs: **Christine's** (Hotel Krystal, Carretera al Aeropuerto Km. 4.5) or **DIVA** (Vallarta 266, btw Carranza and Ardenas).

Christine's doesn't charge a cover on Monday, and women get in free on Thursday—otherwise it's 15 buckaroos. DIVA charges $10 at the door, no matter what. **Los Balcones Bar** (Juárez 182, 1 block south of Plaza Principal) is a popular gay hangout, open 9 PM to 4 AM; the $3.50 cover gets you a drink. Cruise over to **Cielito Lindo** in the zona hotelera if you prefer live salsa and *música tropical*, a more Mexican crowd, and no cover.

Sunday nights around sundown, there's usually a free dance or theater performance on the malecón.

To avoid the dance scene altogether, **Le Bistro**, on Río Cuale island, is one of the sleekest restaurant/bars in town. Sit at the classy black-and-white bar or in the dimmer lounge and listen to the gurgling of the Río Cuale while the DJ plays CDs of your favorite jazz artists. Sip your drinks slowly because they cost dearly. Another option is to go shoot a game of eight ball with some local pool sharks at the **Pool Hall** (Madero 279). Unaccompanied women are certain to get hassled here, however.

Near Puerto Vallarta

North of Puerto Vallarta, off Highway 200 in the state of Nayarit, are a number of golden, sandy beaches not frequented by tourists, at least in summer. **Rincón de Guayabitos,** a family resort filled with bungalows and restaurants, is the most developed beach in these parts. **San Francisco, Lo de Marco,** and **Chacala** are some of the nicer ones. On all the beaches you'll find palapas selling fresh seafood at decent prices, and all except Chacala (where you can camp on the beach relatively undisturbed) have small hotels and/or bungalows in a range of prices. With the exception of Chacala, all are also within fairly easy walking distance from the highway, and can be reached on any Tepic-bound bus (*see* Coming and Going, *above*). To reach the more isolated Chacala, get off the Tepic bus at Las Varas and take a colectivo along an unbelievably bumpy road for 8 or so kilometers. Theoretically, the colectivos pass by the beach until just after sunset, but you may find it faster to hitchhike back to the highway.

PUNTA DE MITA

On the northern tip of the Bahía de Banderas, Punta de Mita has both glassy water that's perfect for swimming and, around the point, waves for surfing. The landscape here is drier than what you find along most of the Pacific coastline, but the views of the bay and mountains are fantastic. The beach is often crowded, especially around the restaurants and banana boats, but a short walk along the coast in either direction brings you to solitary stretches of sand. There are no hotels here, but you can camp for free. You can also hire a boat to visit **Isla Marietas,** home to many seabirds. If you want to camp on the island, arrange a pick-up time with the boat captain. The round trip costs $40, and the boat fits five. Along the north shore of the bay are great beaches, such as **Cruz de Huanacaxtle**, **Arena Blanca**, and **Destiladeras,** all served by local buses. Just past Cruz de Huanacaxtle is a restaurant, **Las Amapas,** that serves iguana, armadillo, snake, and other such dishes for $6–$8.

Transportes Medina (Nicaragua 349, at Brasil, tel. 322/2–19–42) in Puerto Vallarta has service to Punta de Mita every half hour between 6 AM and 7 PM. The trip takes 1 to 1½ hours and costs $2. Keep in mind when thinking about bus schedules that the time zone changes at the airport, so 2 PM in Punta de Mita is 3 PM in Puerto Vallarta.

Bahía de Navidad

Two towns have sprouted around the Bahía de Navidad in the southern corner of the state of Jalisco: San Patricio-Melaque and Barra de Navidad, 6 kilometers apart. If simple living and soft, sandy beaches entice you, then look no further. Many who knew these towns 10 years ago lament the way increasing tourism has marred their natural beauty. Nevertheless, both still offer something of a beach-bum paradise, if only because the sandy beaches are clean, the prices reasonable, and the pace decidedly laid back.

Melaque is popular with vacationers from Guadalajara, many of whom own beach homes that sit idle most of the year. Canadians and people from the States also roost here for several months in the winter. But, in general, Melaque has fewer tourists than Barra does, and is more accessible to the budget traveler. Melaque also feels more like a real town, especially in the evening when people gather in the square under the green, neon glow of the church cross. When the sun shines, the only thing to do is lounge on the sloping, golden-sand beach that gently curves around the three-quarter moon bay, and play in waves that vary in intensity in relation to their proximity to the open sea.

The calm, unhurried pace of both towns is imperiled by the internationally financed, deluxe resort and 18-hole golf course being built on Isla Navidad.

In **Barra de Navidad**, about 6 kilometers down the beach, the unfinished Church of Christ is separated from the square, leaving the town somewhat centerless. Most action happens at the hotels and restaurants along the bay side of the sand spit that stretches toward Isla Navidad. Avenida Veracruz, where locals and tourists mingle, is a pleasant place for a stroll at any time of day.

The annual fiesta in Barra, celebrated June 5–11, honors the town's patron saint, San Antonio de Padua. Melaque's patron saint is, of course, San Patricio, and the merrymaking in his honor begins on March 10, ending on his feast day, March 17. During this time, there is a week-long party at **Los Pelícanos** (*see* Food, *below*), including a solemn mass and blessing of the fleet, folk dancing, and cake-eating contests. On any Saturday night, you might catch a boxing match at the ring on Morelos, half a block north of the post office.

BASICS

CASAS DE CAMBIO There is just one casa de cambio on the Bahía, and it hides behind Farmacia Nueva in Melaque. They change both traveler's checks and cash. *Gómez Farías 27-A, tel. 333/7–03–43. Open Mon.–Sat. 9–2 and 4–7, Sun. 9–2.*

If you absolutely need a bank, make the trek to Cihuatlán (*see* Near Bahía de Navidad, *below*) where there's a **Banamex** (Obregón 58, tel. 333/8–20–47) with an ATM.

EMERGENCIES The number for the **police** in Melaque is 333/7–00–80; in Barra, the number is 333/7–03–99.

MAIL In Melaque, the post office will hold mail sent to you at the following address for up to 10 days: Lista de Correos, Melaque, Jalisco, CP 48980, México. *Morelos 44, on zócalo. Open weekdays 9–1 and 3–6.*

For the same service in Barra, the address is Lista de Correos, Barra de Navidad, Jalisco, CP 48987, México. *Guanajuato 100, 1 block from zócalo. Open weekdays 9–1 and 3–6, Sat. 9–1.*

PHONES Pay phones are hard to come by on the Bahía. There is one, however, in Barra in front of the Delegación Municipal (Veracruz 179). There is a caseta de large distancia in Melaque at Corona 65. Collect calls cost about $2. You can place collect and cash calls for similar prices in Barra at the long-distance caseta at Miguel López de Legazpi 117.

VISITOR INFORMATION If you need a question answered in Melaque, drop by **Los Pelícanos** (*see* Food, *below*) and strike up a conversation with Phil, the owner, who knows everything there is to know about the area.

COMING AND GOING

The bus station in Melaque is on the corner of Gómez Farías and Carranza. Second-class buses leave for Guadalajara ($16, 7 hrs), Puerto Vallarta ($12, 5 hrs), and Manzanillo ($4, 1 hr) just about every hour, all day and most of the night. For the longer trip to Guadalajara or Puerto Vallarta, it's definitely worth laying out an extra $3 to take a faster *plus* bus, with videos and chilling air-conditioning. All the above buses also stop at the bus station in Barra de Navidad on Avenida Veracruz, about a block south of the zócalo.

Green-and-white minibuses connect the two towns with each other and with Cihuatlán. The fare is 50¢. In Barra, you can flag buses to Melaque and Cihuatlán headed north on Veracruz. From Melaque, buses run south along Juárez. Hitchhiking between the Bahía towns is also easy.

WHERE TO SLEEP

It's possible to crash on the beach basically wherever you want. The tourism office suggests camping in front of a hotel where the beaches are illuminated, so you won't be hassled by drunks tripping over the sand (or you) at night. In Melaque, join the RVs on a vacant lot turned makeshift campsite on the beach north of the palapas. You can pay for a shower a few blocks south, but if you're nice to Phil at Los Pelícanos (*see* Food, *below*), she might let you use hers. If you want a solid roof over your head and have no luck with the places below, in Melaque try the **Posada San Patricio** (Gómez Farías 413, tel. 333/7–02–44), where rooms with private bathroom and ceiling fans cost $14 for a single, $20 for a double. Prices listed here are in effect in low season; expect them to rise by $5–$10 in summer and around the Christmas and Easter holidays.

MELAQUE **Bungalows El Márquez.** These bungalows are a great deal for a group (up to six people can stay in one of them), especially one that likes to cook. A large railroad-car style apartment with a kitchenette, dining room, two sleeping areas, and a large bath costs $40 in low season, $85 in high season. *Gómez Farías 407, btw Guzmán and Orozco, tel. 333/7–02–13. 5 bungalows, all with bath. Laundry, luggage storage.*

Bungalows Villa Mar. Happily, two people can stay here in a bungalow that fits up to eight and pay a reduced amount. The facilities are spacious and clean, and the bedrooms are separate from the bungalow. A double with kitchenette and bathroom is $23; singles are $17. *Hidalgo 1, at Gómez Farías, tel. 333/7–00–05. Laundry, wheelchair access.*

Hotel Hidalgo. Rooms in this hotel facing the beach are clean and well kept, making it a popular place with vacationing families. Singles are $15, doubles $18. *Hidalgo 7, tel. 333/7–00–45. 14 rooms, all with bath. Laundry, luggage storage, wheelchair access.*

Posada Clemens. The teal-and-yellow rooms here are equipped with clean but run-down bathrooms. Because this place is somewhat farther away from the action than other hotels, it's cheaper: Singles cost $13 and doubles $16. Speak loudly if you want any response from the elderly woman who works the desk. *Gómez Farías 370, at Guzmán, tel. 333/7–01–79. 4 blocks from bus station. 14 rooms, all with bath. Luggage storage, wheelchair access.*

BARRA DE NAVIDAD **Casa de Huéspedes Caribe.** This is the cheapest place to stay in the entire area ($7 for one person, $10 for two), and it's in good condition to boot: The spartan rooms are generally clean and comfortable, all the mattresses are new, and the private bathrooms were recently redone. The friendly owner sweeps the pigeon poop out of the hallway at every opportunity. *Sonora 15, btw Legazpi and Veracruz, tel. 333/7–02–37. 10 rooms, all with bath. Luggage storage.*

Hotel Delfín. The immaculate rooms and managerial efficiency account for the high prices here. Large rooms open onto a shared balcony, and guests have access to a pool, fitness room, and restaurant. Singles are $19 and doubles $24. *Morelos 23, tel. 333/7–00–68. 24 rooms, all with bath. Luggage storage. Reservations advised in winter.*

Hotel San Lorenzo. The orange color of the stucco walls give the San Lorenzo the look of a new shopping mall. Still, the rooms are good-size and generally clean, if sparsely furnished. Rooms cost $13 for a single and $17 for a double. *Sinaloa 7, at Mazatlán, tel. 333/7–01–39. 25 rooms, all with bath. Luggage storage, wheelchair access.*

Posada Pacífico. Veteran travelers consider this the best budget hotel in town. Each room is different, reflecting the owner's intent to treat every guest like a member of the family. His son, Ernesto, is into ecology, and if you ask, he'll show you pictures of an untouched Barra de Navidad from 10 years ago. Singles cost $13 and doubles $17. *Mazatlán 136, at Michoacán, tel. 333/2–03–59. 22 rooms, all with bath. Laundry, luggage storage.*

CAMPING If you prefer not to take your chances on the beach, try **Trailer Park La Playa.** This well-maintained parking lot/campground in Melaque is crowded with RVs in winter. It's rather expensive at $12 for a tent space, but the bathrooms are decent and have hot water. *Gómez Farías 250, tel. 333/7–00–65. 1 block from bus station. 45 sites. Wheelchair access.*

FOOD

For cheap eats in Melaque, the **market** on López Mateos, near the zócalo, is a good place to start. The beach is also sprinkled with palapas that serve seafood at moderate prices. In Barra, Avenida Veracruz is lined with inexpensive food stands and restaurants. The atmosphere is pleasant, and can even get boisterous at night. Only some of these restaurants are open during the day, but those that are serve full breakfasts for about $3. The more expensive seafood restaurants along the bay provide orchestra seats for the setting sun.

If you like coconut, try an atole de coco, a sweet, corn-based drink with coconut water. It's sold at stalls on Avenida Veracruz in Barra.

MELAQUE **César and Charly.** This place has a patio that spills out onto the beach, and although it's a little more expensive than Los Pelícanos and has less character, you can get a delicious meal here without having to walk as far. Grilled fish costs about $7. *Gómez Farías 27-A. Past casa de cambio towards water. Open daily 7 AM–10 PM.*

Los Pelícanos. The best of Melaque's palapas is run with motherly care by Italian-born ex-New Yorker Philomena "Phil" García. Her ham and eggs would make Dr. Seuss green with envy, and rumor has it that Robert Redford flies in for breaded octopus ($8). Apparently, the San Francisco 49ers have discovered this place, too. Two regulars, Trini and Francisco, are happy to talk your ear off—they can tell you a lot about the Bahía. *5th palapa from end of beach. Open daily 9–7.*

BARRA DE NAVIDAD **Hotel Delfín.** Inside the hotel is a palapa where you can treat yourself to a great breakfast: A buffet of fresh fruit, bread, rolls, and coffee costs $4; with eggs or banana pancakes, $6. Later in the day, they serve dessert and "the original Bavarian grill sausage" ($4). *Morelos 23, tel. 333/7–00–68. Open daily 8:30–10:30 and noon–7.*

Memo's Restaurant. Here you can get a $4 fish breakfast, or eggs any style with tortillas, beans, and coffee or juice for $3.50. A few tacos and a drink run $4–$5. The atmosphere is fun—Memo's friends and relatives are constantly stopping by. *Veracruz 146, tel. 333/7–05–51. Open daily 7–2 and 6–11.*

Restaurant y Café Crêpes Ámbar. Run by a French-Mexican couple, this second-story palapa serves refreshing salads ($3) and a large variety of delicious sweet and savory crêpes ($2.50–$6.50). Half the menu is vegetarian. Good coffee, too. *Veracruz 101-A, tel. 333/7–00–21. Open daily 3 PM–11 PM.*

OUTDOOR ACTIVITIES

The main diversions here (apart from bayside margarita-sipping) are swimming, surfing, splashing, or just plain gawking at the sunset. Barra's beaches are a little rougher than Melaque's, where there are few waves, and you can sit peacefully with nothing but the dry, rocky peninsula to look at. **Colimilla,** sometimes called **Isla de Navidad,** is another peninsula that starts near the Manzanillo airport. For $10, somebody from the **Barra tourist-boat cooperative** (Veracruz 40, tel. 333/7–02–28) will ferry you to Colimilla and its first-rate beachfront restaurants. You could also head to the rougher, more beautiful, less touristed **Playa de Oro,** on the Pacific side of Colimilla. Take a bus from Melaque or Barra to Naranjo and walk 15 minutes to the beach. Another option is fishing: the Barra cooperative charges $20 per hour for up to eight people, equipment included, to fish the coastal waters for marlin, tuna, and sailfish. Unlike most outfits, they don't set a minimum number of hours for a trip, so you can give it a shot without breaking the bank.

Near Bahía de Navidad

South of Puerto Vallarta, Highway 200 turns inland and doesn't meet the coast again for 150 kilometers, until it touches the **Bahía Chamela.** The coast between Bahías Navidad and Chamela is developed in isolated patches, some of them self-contained, deluxe resorts such as Careyes, El Tecuan, and Club Med's Playa Blanca. Bahía Chamela itself, however, has plenty of empty beaches for the less well heeled. Winter brings the older RV crowd down from the States, and Mexican holidays (August, Christmas, and Easter) signal the arrival of Guadalajaran families. For the rest of the year, you can expect relative seclusion in this dry coastal area.

BAHIA CHAMELA

From the rocky point at **Punta Perula,** a sweeping crescent of white sand curves south to such beaches as **Playa Fortuna** and **Playa Chamela.** This area is great for camping; supplies are available in Chamela, at the south end of the bay. **Villas Polinesia Camping Club** (Carretera 200 Km. 72, tel. 36/22–39–40 in Guadalajara for reservations), about 2 kilometers outside Chamela, has tent spaces for $10 a night per person. Their thatched, Polynesian-style, two-story huts with bathrooms are at least a better value for your money at $30 for a double or $50 for three to four people. The camping club provides barbecue pits, where you can cook your own food, and a kitchen where they will prepare meals for you with advance notice. Second-class buses from Barra de Navidad (2 hrs) or Melaque (1½ hrs) to Puerto Vallarta drop you off at Chamela ($3). The buses leave almost hourly and let you off at a dirt road leading to the beach (a 15-minute walk).

South of Chamela is **Bahía Tenacatita,** where 8–10 kilometers of somewhat narrow beach is backed by small dunes and coconut plantations. The beach is a 15-minute walk from Bahía Chamela; you'll see a sign after walking up the path to the highway. On the northern side of Bahía Chamela, **Boca de Iguanas** is a wider beach. There are a few campgrounds here, a pricey hotel, and one small restaurant.

CIHUATLAN

Cihuatlán is the largest and most important commercial center in southern coastal Jalisco, but it isn't much to speak of. One reason to be here is the **Banamex** (Obregón 58, tel. 333/8–20–47), which has an ATM that accepts Plus, Cirrus, Visa, and Mastercard. The bank changes cash and traveler's checks weekdays 9–noon. While you're there, you can cruise down Cihuatlán's main commercial street, which has some interesting farm-supply stores. To get here, take a green-and-white bus from the bus station in Barra de Navidad (*see* Coming and Going, *above*). Buses leave every 15 minutes, and the trip takes 20–30 minutes.

Manzanillo
Manzanillo, as the area encompassing the Bahías de Manzanillo and Santiago is known, seems to be trying for a happy medium between larger Pacific resorts such as Acapulco and relaxed beach towns like Barra de Navidad. Unfortunately, it doesn't succeed as either very well, perhaps because it's also the busiest seaport in Mexico. Ritzy hotels are clumped around beaches along the Península de Santiago and farther north on the Bahía de Santiago, while the hotels, motels, and "suites" that line the highway along the beaches of both bays cater to tourists on a tighter budget. The town is quite spread out, so unless you've got your own vehicle, you have to take buses almost everywhere, and the

only place to relax quietly is the **Jardín Alvaro Obregón,** a good distance from any decent beach. Dirt and sweat hover in the air, and "heinous" is the only word to describe the water lapping at the docks. Somehow, though, the fish in the area flourish, as Manzanillans claim the area is the sailfish capital of the world.

Foreigners are enough of a novelty here that they get a genuine, hospitable welcome. If you strike up a conversation with the guy sweeping the street, he'll probably invite you home for dinner. Most tourists go to the beaches along the two bays—those on the Laguna San Pedrito and near the neighborhoods of Santiago, Salahua, Las Brisas, and Burocrática are better than those in Manzanillo proper. They're all accessible, but most are unexceptional—the sand tends toward dirty, the scenery toward boring, and they're bordered by a highway rather than a malécon. One claim to fame here is **Las Hadas,** an ultradeluxe resort complex on the peninsula that separates the bays, notorious as the setting for the Bo Derek flesh fantasy *10.*

BASICS

AMERICAN EXPRESS The office is in the travel agency **Bahías Gemelas** in Salahua. They cash personal checks and hold mail for cardmembers. You can also receive MoneyGrams here. *Blvd. Costero Miguel de la Madrid 1556, Manzanillo, Colima, CP 28200, México, tel. 333/3–10–00. Near IMSS building. Open weekdays 9–2 and 4–7, Sat. 9–2.*

CASAS DE CAMBIO Banamex (México 136, in Manzanillo, tel. 333/2–04–08) changes money weekdays until noon, and has ATMs that accept Plus and Cirrus cards, as well as Mastercard and Visa. There is another branch on Plaza Manzanillo on the Boulevard Costero in Salahua. The **Farmacia Americana** (México 218) also changes money and is open daily 9–9.

EMERGENCIES For any kind of emergency assistance, dial 06.

MAIL The post office in Manzanillo proper will hold mail sent to you at the following address for up to 10 days: Lista de Correos, Manzanillo, Colima, CP 28200, México. *Juárez, at 5 de Mayo. Open weekdays 8–7, Sat. 9–1.*

MEDICAL AID The **Hospital General** (tel. 333/2–19–03), off the Carretera a Santiago as you leave Manzanillo proper, charges on a sliding scale. The **Hospital Naval** (on naval base, Col. San Pedrito, tel. 333/3–18–44) seems to have better facilities, but is more expensive. You can get all the drugs you need at **Farmacia Americana** (*see* Casas de Cambio, *above*).

PHONES Phone and fax service is available daily 8 AM–10 PM on Madero, just off Manzanillo's Jardín Obregón. Collect calls cost $2.

VISITOR INFORMATION The **tourist office** has crude brochures and nothing else of much use. The staff is friendly, but their English is limited. Better information is available from the hotels and the local AmEx agent (*see above*). *Blvd. Costero Km 9.5, tel. 333/3–22–77. Open weekdays 9–3:30.*

COMING AND GOING

BY BUS The **Central Camionera** is east of the town center; it's not an easy walk to the town center from here. A taxi to the center costs $1.50, or cross the street and hop on any ROCIO bus, which will leave you at the corner of México and Cuauhtémoc, a four-block walk from the Jardín and most of the budget hotels. Buses leave frequently for San Pedrito, Las Brisas, and Santiago from the back of the station, all the way to the left.

Autotransportes del Sur de Jalisco (tel. 333/2–10–03) serves Tecomán and Armería, the jumping-off points for El Paraíso, Cuyutlán, and Boca de Pascuales (*see* Near Manzanillo, *below*); buses leave every 15 minutes, and the cost is $1.50 for the half-hour ride. They also send buses to Colima ($3, 1½ hrs) every half hour until 7:30 PM. **Tres Estrellas de Oro** (tel. 333/2–01–35) gets you to Acapulco ($30, 12 hrs), with buses leaving at 11 AM and 6:30 PM. **Autotransportes Cihuatlán** (tel. 333/2–05–15) has second-class buses to Guadalajara ($13, 7 hrs) and Puerto Vallarta ($10, 6½ hrs) every hour between 3 AM and 9 PM.

Manzanillo

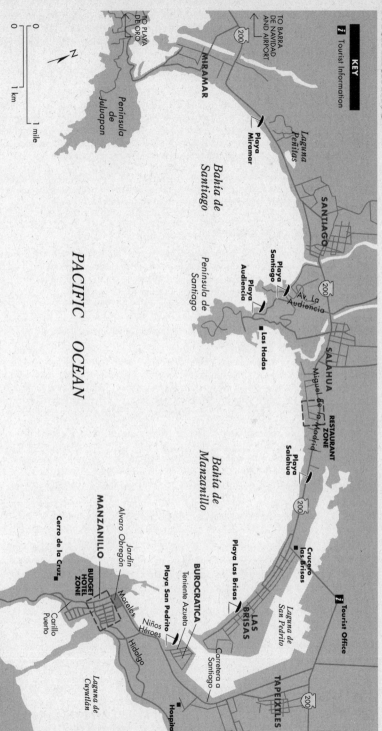

KEY

i Tourist Information

0

0   1 km

0   1 mile

N

TO BARRA
DE NAVIDAD
AND AIRPORT

TO PLAYA
DE ORO

Península
de
Juluapan

MIRAMAR

Laguna Peñitas

Playa
Miramar

*Bahía de
Santiago*

SANTIAGO

Península de
Santiago

Playa
Santiago

Playa
Audiencia

Av. La
Audiencia

Las Hadas

PACIFIC OCEAN

SALAHUA

Miguel de la Madrid

**RESTAURANT
ZONE**

Playa
Salahua

*Bahía de
Manzanillo*

Crucero
las Brisas

i Tourist Office

Laguna de
San Pedrito

Playa Las Brisas

**LAS
BRISAS**

TAPEIXTLES

MANZANILLO

Cerro de la Cruz

Jardín

Alvaro Obregón

**BUDGET
HOTEL
ZONE**

Carilo
Puerto

Morelos

Hidalgo

Niños
Héroes

Playa San Pedrito

BUROCRATICA

Teniente Azueta

Carretera a
Santiago.

Hospital

*Laguna de
Cuyutlán*

289

BY TRAIN The train station (tel. 333/2-00-40) is on Avenida Niños Héroes, three blocks from the zócalo. Same-day tickets are sold here. Train 91 to Guadalajara ($6, 8 hrs) leaves Manzanillo at 6 AM. The train stops at Colima ($2) 2½ hours into the ride. Buy your ticket on the train.

GETTING AROUND

Manzanillo winds its way around steep hills and along the waterfront. The main commercial street is Calle México, which hits the Jardín. The waterfront road, Avenida Morelos, goes out to Playa San Pedrito, about 1 kilometer from the Jardín. This is about as far as you want to walk in Manzanillo. Fortunately, frequent bus service makes it easy to reach the beaches of the Bahías de Manzanillo and Santiago. **Playa Las Brisas** is the first decent beach you'll hit.

Buses to Miramar and Santiago leave frequently from the train and bus stations. Buses also frequent Las Brisas and Las Hadas. If you find yourself in Salahua or Santiago in the late evening and need to be back in Manzanillo, you'll have to take a taxi (about $7).

WHERE TO SLEEP

Cheap hotels are concentrated in Manzanillo proper, near the train station and around the Jardín, but only a few rise above the sweatbox level. Most hotels outside central Manzanillo and near the water are more expensive, especially in Santiago—if you're feeling wealthy, stay at Santiago's wheelchair-accessible **Hotel María Cristina** (8 de Agosto 36, btw Morelos and Hidalgo, tel. 333/3-09-66) which has a pool and nice rooms. The cost is $28 for a single or $35 for a double. As a last resort in Manzanillo itself, try the not-so friendly **Hotel Emperador** (Balbino Dávalos 69, tel. 333/2-23-74), where a single is $10 and doubles are $15 for one bed or $20 for two.

MANZANILLO **Casa de Huéspedes Petrita.** The small rooms here—basically wooden boxes with floor fans—overlook a courtyard filled with washing machines and clothes hanging out to dry. Friendly owners and generally clean rooms and bathrooms (most of them communal) make this a decent place to stay. Rooms are $8.50 per bed. *Allende 24, tel. 333/2-01-87. 5 blocks from Jardín. 19 rooms, 3 with bath. Laundry, luggage storage, wheelchair access.*

Hotel Flamingos. The generally clean but muggy rooms at this standard, multilevel hotel would be spacious were it not for the useless china cabinets stuffed into them. Assorted other oddities include what seem to be medieval lighting fixtures. Be sure to get a room with a window, or you might melt. Singles cost $13.50, doubles $17 for one bed, $20 for two. *Madero 72, at 10 de Mayo, tel. 333/2-10-37. ½ block from Jardín. 32 rooms, all with bath. Luggage storage.*

Hotel Miramar. The rooms here are small and plain, but the huge balconies and odd staircases compensate. Third-floor rooms are breeziest. Singles cost $11 and doubles $17. *Juárez 122, ½ block from Jardín, tel. 333/2-10-08. Look for FANTA sign. 25 rooms, all with bath. Luggage storage.*

SAN PEDRITO **Hotel Magisterio.** This hotel is a short walk from the Jardín in Manzanillo, and not nearly as cramped as others downtown. Basic, decent-size rooms surround a large swimming pool—since swimming in the nearby ocean is a health hazard, this is a real plus. Prices fluctuate with the tide, so be prepared to haggle when you arrive, but the latest quotes were $10 a single, $17 for a double. *Teniente Azueta 7, tel. 333/2-11-08. ½ block from San Pedrito bus stop. 35 rooms, all with bath. Luggage storage.*

LAS BRISAS **Posada del Pacífico.** Big rooms with two double beds—for as many people as you can fit in them—cost about $20 here. It's often full and there's no way to make reservations, so you might want to drop your stuff in another hotel while you find out if there's anything available. *Francisco Villa, at Zapata, no phone. 12 rooms, all with bath. Laundry, luggage storage, wheelchair access.*

CAMPING You can set up camp on the beach in San Pedrito, Las Brisas, or Playa Miramar. San Pedrito is probably safest, and the local supermarket rents showers for a few pesos.

FOOD

Manzanillo has restaurants for all budgets. The cheapest place to eat in town is the **market** (Cuauhtémoc, at Madero), preferably at lunch, when the food is fresh. Budget restaurants in town are located around the Jardín, and you can always get a hot dog with everything for $1 from one of the stands. There are more reasonably priced restaurants on Boulevard Costero, near the IMSS building in Salahua.

MANZANILLO **Chantilly.** Of the restaurants that surround the square, this is the cheapest and most popular. The menu is standard and the food just okay, and you'll have to beat your waitress over the head with a menu to get her to take your order. Once she does, though, there's hardly a wait for your food. Chicken costs about $4, fish or shrimp about $6. *Juárez, at Madero, tel. 333/2-01-94. Open Sun.–Fri. 7 AM–10 PM. Wheelchair access.*

Eloy's Gourmet Café. Popular with a young, hip crowd, this hangout between downtown Manzanillo and Salahua serves the best marlin, shrimp, shark, and fish tacos in the tourist zone. The best deal is the plate of tacos with your choice of fillings that serves two for about $10. The $4 shrimp burgers, which come with a salad and french fries, are also good. Fresh banana chips are also on the menu. *Blvd. Costero Km. 9.5, no phone. Next to Chrysler dealership, just after after IMSS. Open daily 10 AM–midnight.*

If you bring this book to Eloy's Café, the owner promises a free round of beers with lunch for everyone in your group.

Plaza La Perlita. This restaurant has outdoor seating around wrought-iron tables and features live music Thursday through Sunday. A regular shrimp cocktail costs $3, a huge one, $6. A fish fillet, cooked to your liking, is $4. *Morelos, in front of train station, tel. 333/2-27-70. Open daily 10 AM–midnight. Wheelchair access.*

La Pollería. This tiny hole-in-the-wall serves a fabulously tasty whole, grilled chicken with rice, tortillas, soup, and salsa for just $5. Eat it here or take it to go and have a picnic on the beach or in a park. Don't confuse this place with **Servi Pollo** or **Pollo Feliz** nearby. *Jesus Alcaraz s/n, btw Morelos and Hidalgo, no phone. Open Mon.–Sat. 11–9 , Sun. 11–7*

Restaurant Roca del Mar. This restaurant serves a filling, satisfying comida corrida consisting of soup, rice, an entrée, and tortillas for $5. Breakfasts of eggs, beans, and tortillas are $3. Vegetarian soups are $2, and an order of meat or vegetarian quesadillas with tasty guacamole is $4. *21 de Marzo 204, on Jardín, tel. 333/2-03-02. Open daily 8 AM–10:30 PM.*

SAN PEDRITO **El Ultimo Tren.** When you order a drink here you get *free* snacks—tacos, ceviche, guacamole—all salty and often hot. The theory is, the more you eat, the more you drink: Most people leave here smashed. Clanging beer-bottle toasts, live mariachi music, and the drunken singing create what an ad calls "Real Macho Atmosphere." If you're careful, you can eat for cheap; if not, you probably won't be in a state of mind to care. *In Centro Botaneros, Blvd. Costero 22680, just past San Pedrito, no phone. Take SANTIAGO or MIRAMAR bus. Open evenings, variable hours.*

SANTIAGO **Restaurante Savoy 2.** Young locals fill the tables here for the $5 comida corrida and for the wide selection of desserts. They've always got a movie on the VCR (usually in English with Spanish subtitles), and if that fails to entertain you, you can browse through the odd lamps sold in the back corner. *Plaza Santiago, across from zócalo, tel. 333/3-07-90. Open daily 7 AM–midnight. Wheelchair access.*

AFTER DARK

Manzanillo has one happening disco, **Vog,** on the Boulevard Costero in Salahua—cover is $10. There's no cover at the **Bar de Félix,** a little up the road from Eloy's (*see* Food, *above*), and the place is pretty fun, with music and movies going almost all night. It wouldn't be a Mexican resort without **Carlos 'n Charlie's** (Blvd. Costero Km. 6.5, tel. 333/3-11-50), a beach-side restaurant/bar. To get here, take a MIRAMAR, SANTIAGO, or LAS HADAS bus to the Unidad Deportivo and cross the highway.

OUTDOOR ACTIVITIES

Manzanillo's biggest (and really only) attraction is its beaches. **Playa San Pedrito,** the beach nearest downtown, is heavily frequented by locals, especially on Sundays when the sandy soccer fields are filled with people kicking balls between cases of beer. However, woe the person who actually swims in the water; his feet would probably disintegrate before his knees got wet. To get to the beach, walk 1 kilometer down Niños Héroes, or take a Santiago or Miramar bus from the train station.

Playa Las Brisas is Manzanillo's most popular beach, though it may be too close to the port for your comfort. Centered around the Las Brisas crossroads, this dirty-gold beach is lined with hotels, houses, and restaurants, shielding it from highway traffic. To get here, take a MIRAMAR or SANTIAGO bus to the *crucero* (crossroads) for Las Brisas, or a LAS BRISAS bus all the way into town.

Playa Audiencia, on the peninsula dominated by the Las Hadas resort, is best beach in Manzanillo. It's small and can get rather crowded, but green hills on both sides create a cove with a feeling of seclusion that is absent in Manzanillo's other beaches. Take one of the minibuses provided by Las Hadas (they have dolphins on them) from Niños Héroes or from the Las Brisas crossroads and ask the driver to stop at the turnoff for Playa Audiencia. While you're here, take a self-guided tour of the fantastical Las Hadas hotel, which looks like something out of *Arabian Nights*. To avoid a charge at the entrance, say you're going to one of the shops or restaurants.

Playa Miramar's sand is marbled with black and gold, but it appears more dirty than pretty. It's long enough to have some quiet areas, but the entire beach is smack up against the freeway. You can rent boogie boards for $2 an hour and surfboards for $10 an hour on the beach from a very friendly guy named Abraham. He and his brothers also rent horses for $10 an hour and offer $8 banana boat rides. To get here from the train or bus station, take a bus marked MIRAMAR and get off wherever the beach looks appealing.

Near Manzanillo

South of Manzanillo lies a stretch of coast dotted with black-sand beaches, testament to the activity of Colima's volcanoes. Life is cheaper and more tranquil here than in Manzanillo, though the beaches couldn't exactly be described as tropical paradises. The sand is more gray than black, and the water sometimes turns an unappealing brown, especially during the summer rainy season. The isolated beaches do face the open sea, so surfers or anyone mesmerized by crashing waves will enjoy the isolated beaches of Cuyutlán, El Paraíso, and Boca de Pascuales (*see below*). Although there are hotels in the area, beach camping is free and encouraged. If you've got a hammock, most beachfront restaurants will let you string it up for a couple of bucks. To reach Cuyutlán or El Paraíso, you'll have to catch a local bus in the town of Armería. Buses leave Manzanillo for Armería ($2, 40 min) every 15 minutes (there is also frequent service to Armería from Colima). The transfer point for Boca de Pascuales is **Tecomán** (the transfer depot is one block to the right as you leave Tecomán's main bus terminal). The bus to Tecomán from either Manzanillo or Colima takes one hour and costs $2.

CUYUTLAN

The most developed of the three beach resorts fills up with Mexican vacationers during August, Christmas, and Easter. During the rest of the year, the town is almost deserted, taking on that sad, lonely, run-down feel of Coney Island in winter. But Cuyutlán is a real town, with more hotels, restaurants, and services than other nearby beaches. It is also the home of the *ola verde* (green wave). No one quite agrees on what this is, but they certainly do talk about it a lot. Rosario at the Manzanillo bus station swears that it was a tidal wave that wiped out the entire town of Cuyutlán in 1942. A tourist brochure claims that the ola verde happens every April and May, when the sun shines on the waves at a certain angle, making them look green. Still others believe it's just a local name for phosphorescent algae that glows a sparkly green in the water. Buses leave Armería for Cuyutlán every 40 minutes between 6 AM and 8 PM, and the fare is about 50¢.

WHERE TO SLEEP AND EAT In addition to great camping, Cuyutlán has a good selection of beachfront hotels, many of which are affordable. **Hotel Tlaquepaque,** at the northern end of the boardwalk, has decent rooms off a long hall cooled by sea breezes. Singles are $8, and doubles are $17, but you can negotiate with the owner if you stay a while. Five of the rooms at **Hotel Morelos** (2 blocks north of zócalo, tel. 332/4–18–10) have a kitchen/dining room for no extra cost—prices are exactly the same as at the Tlaquepaque. The hotels are also the best place to look for food. The **Hotel Morelos** serves a decent, filling breakfast for $4, lunch for $4.50, and dinner for $4; otherwise, try the **Hotel Fénix.**

EL PARAISO

Smaller and less developed than Cuyutlán, El Paraíso has one short road that runs the length of the town, passing hotels and restaurants overlooking the ocean. The town is wondrously small, and the beaches are more often than not yours and yours alone, but don't expect to find diversions beyond the sound of the waves. Buses to El Paraíso from Armería leave approximately every 45 minutes between 6 AM and 6:45 PM. The fare is about 50¢.

WHERE TO SLEEP AND EAT There are three hotels in town. The nicest, **Hotel Paraíso,** charges $20 for a double. **Hotel Villa del Mar** has claustrophobic rooms that cost $15 for up to three people. **Posada Ramírez** has basically clean rooms with lumpy beds and tiny showers for $11. Pick a restaurant, any restaurant, in El Paraíso—they all serve fresh fish for around $4.

BOCA DE PASCUALES

The smallest of the beach resorts isn't really a town, but a collection of palapa restaurants clustered on the beach where the Río Pascuales empties into the sea. Boca de Pascuales is famous for its huge waves. Swimming, therefore, is a potentially perilous activity (look out for the red "do not swim" flags). Nevertheless, Boca de Pascuales is also a year-round hot spot for kamikaze surfers, called *surfos*. They're known to survive here on only a few dollars a day, which means that you can, too. Indeed, the only people who will really want to visit Boca de Pascuales are surfers, admirers of surfers, or those looking for an inexpensive, somewhat isolated beach upon which to do nothing.

Boca de Pascuales is protected from the sea by a figure of the Virgin of Guadalupe that was found wet, with sand on her feet, after the town was almost destroyed by waves. The locals decided that she came down to the beach to save them. For that reason, every February a procession goes from Tecomán to Boca de Pascuales, carrying the statue high overhead.

WHERE TO SLEEP AND EAT The only hotel in Boca de Pascuales, **Estrella del Sur Hotel** (the sign says Surf Hotel), has small cement rooms with fans for $10 (single) and $17 (double). **Restaurant Hamacas del Mayor** (tel. 332/4–21–36) is more expensive than the other palapas, but it's something of an institution here: They've been serving delicious seafood on white-clothed tables under a huge palapa since the 1950s. People come from Manzanillo and Colima for the crayfish ($13), but if you're pinching pesos try the octopus ($7) or fish ($9). Other palapa restaurants here serve fresh seafood for a few dollars less.

Colima
Colima is the quiet, easy-going capital of Colima state. Well-maintained colonial buildings make the town visually appealing, and the friendly residents make you feel welcome. Although Colima's climate is tropical, the temperature is cooler than in Manzanillo, and for very little money, you can actually live it up here rather than just survive.

Colima was the third city founded by the Spaniards in Mexico, but its history reaches much further back. Archaeologists have discovered tombs filled with ceramic figurines that point to the existence of a complex indigenous culture. Many of the figurines are on display in museums here, except for some titillating phallic ones that were whisked away to museums in Mexico

Colima is best explored on foot. To truly appreciate this city's charm, be a Peeping Tom and peek surreptitiously through the doors that open onto the flowered inner courtyards of the city's colonial residences.

City. In addition to the museums, events such as poetry readings and performance-art pieces are frequent. People at the University of Colima put out 10 local newspapers and are constantly publishing new books of poetry and prose. There's even a table of philosophers—the **Mesa de Despelleje**—at Los Naranjos Restaurant (Gabino Barreda 34, tel. 331/2–00–29). Colima is also gleamingly clean. Half the residents work for the government, and there's a concerted effort to keep the streets clean and safe. To top things off, this city boasts more parks per capita than any other in western Mexico.

BASICS

AUTO PARTS/SERVICE If the mechanics at **Taller El Nieves** can't help you, they'll refer you to someone who can. *Gómez 149, no phone. 5 blocks SW of Jardín Principal. Open weekdays 9–2 and 4–7, Sat. 9–noon.*

BOOKSTORES **Las Palmeras** is a small magazine store next to Hotel Ceballos on the Jardín Principal. They carry *Time, Newsweek,* and *National Geographic,* as well as many Mexican magazines. *Portal Medellín 14, no phone. Open daily 8 AM–11 PM.*

Galería Universitaria, just off the Jardín Principal, carries books in Spanish, including those published by the university. *Torres Quintero 62, tel. 331/2–44–00. Open daily 9–2 and 3–9.*

CASAS DE CAMBIO **Casa de Cambio Majaparas** offers better rates than banks for cash, but not for traveler's checks—they cash those into U.S. dollars only. *Juárez 200, at Madero, tel. 331/4–89–98. Open weekdays 9–2 and 4:30–6:30, Sat. 9–2.*

Several banks on Madero have ATMs, but most only accept Visa and Mastercard. The ATM at **Banamex** (Hidalgo 90, tel. 331/2–26–29), two blocks north of the Jardín, accepts Plus and Cirrus cards, and the bank itself changes cash and traveler's checks weekdays 9–noon.

EMERGENCIES For assistance, call the **police** (tel. 331/2–18–01) or **fire** department (tel. 331/2–58–58).

LAUNDRY La Lavandería washes and dries three kilos of clothing for $3. Service is same-day. *Rey Colimán 14, no phone. Open Mon.–Sat. 8–8.*

MAIL The full-service post office will hold mail sent to you at the following address for up to 10 days: Lista de Correos, Colima, Colima, CP 28001, México. *Madero, at Nuñez, tel. 331/2–00–33. Open Mon.–Sat. 8–7, Sun. 9–noon.*

MEDICAL AID The **Hospital Civil** (San Fernando, tel. 331/2–02–27) is open 24 hours. For minor problems, try the **Farmacia Colima,** which also has a telephone caseta. *Madero 1, at Constitución, on Jardín Principal, tel. 331/2–00–31. Open Mon.–Sat. 8:30 AM–9 PM.*

PHONES There are public phones on all four corners of the Jardín Principal. You can place cash calls at **Computel,** on the south side of Parque Nuñez. The connection fee for collect calls here is $2. *Morelos 239, tel. 331/4–59–01. Open daily 7 AM–9 PM.*

VISITOR INFORMATION If you speak Spanish, ask about upcoming events at **Livornos Pizza** (*see Food, below*). For official information about Colima, city or state, talk to the immensely helpful staff of the air-conditioned **tourist office.** *Portal Hidalgo 20, west side of Jardín Principal, tel. 331/2–83–60. Open weekdays 8:30–3 and 5–9, weekends 9–1.*

COMING AND GOING

BY BUS The **Central de Autobuses de Colima** is at the northeast edge of town. To get downtown catch any 4 CENTRO bus just outside the terminal, or take a taxi (buy a ticket at the booth) for about $1.50. **Tres Estrellas de Oro** (tel. 331/2–84–48) and **Flecha Amarilla** (tel. 331/4–80–67 or 331/4–80–27) are the major bus lines. Buses leave for Guadalajara ($13, 3 hrs) almost every hour. Buses to Manzanillo ($4, ½ hr) leave every hour, and there is service to Mexico City ($32, 10 hrs), as well as other cities both in and out of state. You can also store your luggage here.

The **Central de Autobuses Sub-Urbana** (Carretera Colima-Coquimatlán, tel. 331/2–04–35) serves smaller, in-state destinations. Buses bound for Tecomán ($2), Armería ($2), and Manzanillo ($4) depart every 20 minutes between 4:30 AM and 10 PM. Buses for nearby towns and villages such as Comala (50¢), Suchitlán (50¢), and San Antonio/Laguna La María leave frequently during the day. The bus station is a 20-minute walk southwest on Cuautéhmoc from the Jardín Principal. Taxi rides to the station cost $2.

BY TRAIN The train station (Colón, tel. 331/2–92–50) is open daily 7:30–11:30 and 2:30–5. The one bus that passes by the station goes to the center of town. A taxi ride to or from the station costs about $1. Colima is a stop on the Manzanillo–Guadalajara route. The train to Guadalajara ($3, 5 hrs) leaves at 8:20 AM, and the Manzanillo train ($2, 2½ hrs) leaves at 3 PM.

GETTING AROUND

On a clear day, you can orient yourself by the volcanoes to the north of Colima. Even when it's cloudy, however, parks laid out along Avenida Madero are landmarks that make downtown Colima easy to navigate. The **Jardín Libertad** (also known as the zócalo or the Jardín Principal) is at the corner of Avenidas Madero and Reforma. This is the center of town, where families and friends gather in the evening. One block east is the **Jardín Quintero,** with a splashing fountain and more benches. Three blocks further east is the massive **Parque Nuñez.**

In keeping with its clean and efficient image, Colima has a modern fleet of microbuses, which cost about 35¢ to ride. Most buses stop at the corner of Reforma and Díaz, on Medellín along the Jardín Quintero, or on Avenida Rey Colimán near the southwest corner of the Parque Nuñez. A taxi ride anywhere in the city shouldn't be more than $5.

WHERE TO SLEEP

Colima doesn't have a huge selection of hotels, but it's not exactly a tourist mecca, so finding a room isn't a problem. All budget hotels are near the center of town. If the places below are full, try the **Gran Hotel Flamingos** (Rey Colimán 18, tel. 331/2–25–25), where singles cost $17 and doubles $20.

➤ UNDER $15 • **Casa de Huéspedes Familiar.** Slightly worn but clean rooms are above the house of the friendly manager, Señora Sauceda. Singles cost $8 and doubles $13. Let her know when you want hot water and she'll light the boiler. *Morelos 265, tel. 331/2–34–67. Just east of Parque Nuñez, near Pemex. 12 rooms, all with bath. Luggage storage.*

Hotel Impala. The best bargain in town, this hotel has rooms with pink walls and quilts embroidered in blue and white. Some have fans, but all have windows and clean bathrooms with hot water. The downside is that it's the hotel farthest from the center. Rooms with one bed cost $12, single or double occupancy. *Moctezuma 93, tel. 331/4–30–97. 22 rooms. Luggage storage.*

Hotel Nuñez. Rooms surround a courtyard in this converted colonial house overlooking the park of the same name. Rooms are small and lack personality, but the communal baths are spic and span. Rooms (single or double) without bath are $9; with private bath, they're $13. *Juárez 88, tel. 331/2–70–30. 32 rooms, 16 with bath. Luggage storage, wheelchair access.*

➤ UNDER $35 • **Hotel Ceballos.** This grand hotel facing the Jardín isn't cheap, but at $30 for one or two people, it makes a decent splurge. The large halls and courtyards flanked by stone columns are more impressive than the smallish rooms—the nicest have windows opening to the patio or street. The price goes up with amenities such as TV, phone, and air-conditioning. *Portal Medellín 12, tel. 331/2–44–44. 63 rooms, all with bath. Laundry, luggage storage. Reservations advised in summer.*

FOOD

Colima prides itself on its *antojitos* (appetizers) such as enchiladas with sweet sauce and pozole. Restaurants are scattered throughout the city, but there are tons of cheap ones near the Jardín Libertad.

Ah Que Nanishe. For a change of pace, try the Oaxacan specialties at this downtown eatery. Chicken tamales with Oaxacan mole (chile and chocolate sauce) are $2 each, and a *huarache* (corn-fungus turnover) is $3. They also have an assortment of soup specialties ranging from $3 to $7. Sweet tamales are $2. *5 de Mayo 267, 4 blocks west of Jardín Libertad, tel. 331/4–21–97. Open daily 1:30–midnight.*

Cafetería Las Palomas. Surrounded by plants, a waterfall, and caged doves, the inner courtyard of this restaurant is a quiet retreat. A standard egg or pancake breakfast with juice and coffee costs $4.50, the daily special is $6, and *tortas* (sandwiches) are $3. *Portal Medellín 12, in Hotel Ceballos, tel. 331/2–44–44. Open Mon.–Sat. 7:30 AM–10 PM.*

La Fonda de San Miguel. In an old colonial building, this tastefully decorated restaurant is popular with better-off locals. Try their delicious regional dishes, such as enchiladas and pozole (both $4) and grilled steaks ($8). Breakfasts of hotcakes ($2.50) or eggs ($4) come with orange juice. *27 de Septiembre 129, tel. 331/4–48–40. 3 blocks north of Madero. Open daily 8–6.*

Livornos Pizza. At this pub-like pizzeria you can get a small meat or veggie pizza and a drink for $5. Have a beer and strike up a conversation with the manager for information about cultural events and the causes of *la ilusión óptica* (*see* Cheap Thrills, *below*). *Andador Constitución, near cathedral, no phone. Open daily noon–midnight.*

Restaurant Familiar El Trébol. This place is cheap, busy, and clean, but you have to be aggressive to give your order to the harried waitresses. An egg breakfast with beans, tortillas, and juice is $3, and a fried chicken dinner with beans, french fries, and a drink is about $5. *Degollado 39, at 16 de Septiembre, tel. 331/2–29–00. SW corner of Jardín Libertad. Open Sun.–Fri. 8 AM–11 PM. Wheelchair access.*

WORTH SEEING

The **Jardín Libertad** has served as the center of the city since its founding and is a good place to begin your exploring. On the south side of the Jardín is the free **Museo Regional de Historia de Colima,** where you'll find a few exhibits of pre-Columbian pottery and local crafts. Across from the Jardín is the neoclassical **cathedral,** which is unlike many of Mexico's churches in that all the ornamentation is saved for the lavish interior. Next door is the **Palacio de Gobierno,** a beautiful building built at the turn of the century. Its mural portraying the history of Mexico was painted by Coliman artist Jorge Chávez Carrillo in honor of Independence leader Padre Miguel Hidalgo.

MUSEO DE LAS CULTURAS DEL OCCIDENTE This excellent museum is dedicated exclusively to pre-Hispanic ceramicware from the Colima area. On display are a collection of figurines, among them the famous Colima dogs, supposedly the product of a culture in which dogs were believed to mirror human personalities (and to be a source of food, as well). *Galván Norte, at Ejército Nacional, tel. 331/2–31–55. Take NORTE bus toward university from Rey Colimán. Admission free. Open Tues.–Sat. 9–7, Sun. 9–4.*

CASA DE LA CULTURA Next to the Museo de las Culturas del Occidente, the **Casa de la Cultura** shows a permanent collection of works by Coliman artists as well as rotating exhibitions. They also give free classes in arts and crafts, music, and regional dance and have a cinema club that shows foreign and national art films on Thursday or Friday. The gallery is open daily 10–8 and admission is free. The café is a good place to stop for a drink and listen to live music, featured daily 8 PM–11 PM. *Galván Norte, at Ejército Nacional, tel. 331/2–31–55.*

MUSEO UNIVERSITARIO DE CULTURAS POPULARES This university crafts museum is not particularly impressive, but it has a wonderful gift shop. Outside the museum, under a giant banyan tree, an artisan makes reproductions of pre-Columbian ceramics Monday–Saturday 9–3. Go to Room 30 in the museum building to find out about cultural events at the university. *Gallardo, at 27 de Septiembre, tel. 331/2–68–69. Admission free. Open Tues.–Sat. 9–2 and 4–7.*

The Parque de la Piedra Lisa (Park of the Smooth Stone) is near the university. Legend has it that if you slide down its big rock, you will soon be wed.

CHEAP THRILLS

If you've got a car or access to one, you can experience a truly strange phenomenon on the road from Suchitlán to Comala (*see* Near Colima, *below*), just past Restaurante Los Pinos. Some say it's caused by an optical illusion (they call it *la ilusión óptica*), others say it's a magnetic field. Whatever the cause, bring the car to a dead stop where the road is level, just before the hill. Keep your foot off the gas and, somehow, your car will climb all the way to the top.

AFTER DARK

Café Colima (Jardín Corregidora s/n, tel. 331/2–80–93) is Colima's version of a *peña*, in which spectators participate in performances by folk musicians, and the music often takes on a political tone. The seats are outdoors in the Jardín Corregidora, under an awning where patrons eat somewhat pricey food and sip a variety of coffees, a beer, or a glass of wine. The music begins around 6 PM. To get here, take a RUTA 9 bus from Medellín, at Jardín Quintero. Closer to the center of town, on Jardín Quintero, is **La Taba,** an Argentinian restaurant/bar with live music and dancing. La Taba gets crowded around 11 PM and closes at 3 AM Thursday–Sunday. For technopop, there's **Cheer's** (Zaragoza 521, tel. 331/4–47–00), a disco with a $5 cover charge that gets going around 10:30 and stays open until 3 AM.

Near Colima

Just north of Colima are two volcanoes, known as the **Volcanes de Colima**—despite the fact that one of them is actually just across the Jalisco state line. The taller, at 4,335 meters, is the **Volcán de Fuego** (Fire Volcano). The **Volcán Nevado de Colima** (also called the Volcán de Nieve, or Snow Volcano) rises 3,900 meters. The former has been living up to its name of late, with a massive eruption in July of 1994. It can, obviously, be dangerous to visit, and there are no buses to the trails or facilities for hikers. If you're determined to set out on your own, you'll need to drive or hitchike to the town of Atenquique, and get permission from the military there. Ask at the tourist office in Colima (*see* Visitor Information, *above*) about current safety conditions. The Volcán Nevado, on the other hand, is a hikers paradise. About two-thirds of the way up the volcano is a shelter called **La Joya**, where you can stay for free in a cabana that fits at least 20 people. The cabana has a fireplace and nothing else, so bring food, drink, and gear. From La Joya, it's a three- or four-hour hike up to the snowy peak of the volcano. Bring layers of clothes to keep you warm at night and cool during the day. Buses going to Guadalajara from the Central de Autobuses de Colima stop in Ciudad Guzmán, where you can catch another bus to the the town of Fresnito, at the base of the volcano. From here, you'll need to either find someone willing to drive you up to La Joya (it's about 37 kilometers) for a fee, or hitch a ride—because of the number of hikers who make this trip, this shouldn't be too difficult. Plan on a three-day trip, at least: It will probably take you the better part of a day to reach La Joya, another to climb and descend, and a third to get back to Colima. If this sounds too ambitious for you, there are a number of small towns nearby that make considerably milder day or overnight trips and are frequently served by buses from the Colima's Central de Autobuses Sub-Urbana.

COMALA

A 15-minute bus ride north of Colima, this picturesque village of white adobe houses with red-tile roofs is a pleasant place to spend an afternoon. Explore the town and the surrounding farmland, then come back for a meal in one of the *botaneros* (bars serving appetizers) on the zócalo.

At **Restaurante Bar Comala,** a $2 beer or alcoholic punch comes with guacamole, ceviche, tacos, and other snacks. Each drink brings forth another round of food. A 10-minute walk south of the main plaza is the **Escuela de Artesanías Comala** (Carretera Colima Km. 6, tel. 331/2–56–96), where they make and sell painted furniture and ironwork.

LAGUNA LA MARIA

Laguna La María is a vacation retreat for Colimans at the edge of the **Parque Natural Nevado de Colima.** The verdant lakeshore offers great camping, and you can swim and fish to your heart's content here. Camping fees are $3 per night, or you can stay at one of the cabanas or hotels nearby. It's wise to make reservations, so get in touch with the tourist office in Colima (*see* Visitor Information, *above*)—they'll do it for you. To get here, take the SAN ANTONIO bus from the **Central de Autobuses Sub-Urbana** in Colima. Buses leave Colima in the morning and evening, and return in the afternoon. You'll be dropped off at the entrance to the park, where you can get information about camping.

Ixtapa/ Zihuatanejo

If only one resort on the Pacific Coast is worth visiting, it's Ixtapa/Zihuatanejo. A four-hour drive up the coast from Acapulco, this twin-town resort is less expensive than its big brother to the south and has nicer beaches. **Zihuatanejo,** once a fishing village, is the base for budget travelers. By some miracle, affordable hotels are right on the waterfront here—some rooms even have views—and the seafood is great and not that expensive. Playas **La Ropa** and **Las Gatas** on Zihuatanejo Bay are two of the nicest beaches in the area. The surf in the bay isn't very challenging, but more exciting waves are an easy 5-kilometer bus ride away in Ixtapa.

Ixtapa is now one long strip of pavement, manicured lawns, and clunky buildings lining the beach. As is par for the course in areas targeted by Fonatur (the federal tourism department) for development, you'll find plenty of luxury hotels and air-conditioned mini-malls featuring the same stores you'd find in New Jersey. You'll also find rough surf and a nightlife that is quickly adopting a party-till-you-drop attitude. With Ixtapa/Zihuatanejo, you get the best of both worlds—dip into Ixtapa's liveliness, then beat a retreat to peaceful Zihuatanejo.

BASICS

CASAS DE CAMBIO Banks seem to be on every street corner in Zihuatanejo. **Banco Mexicano Somex** (Juárez, near Mango, tel. 753/4–24–16) is open weekdays 9–11:30, and there are ATMs at **Banamex** (Cuauhtémoc, near Nicolás Bravo) and **Serfin** (Juárez, at Nicolás Bravo). The casas de cambio don't have the greatest exchange rates, but they have better hours than the banks. The one by the waterfront (Galeana, near Nicolás Bravo, tel. 753/4–35–22) is open daily 8 AM–9 PM for both cash and traveler's-check exchange.

EMERGENCIES Fire **department** (tel. 753/4–20–09); **police** and **ambulance** (tel. 753/4–23–66 or 753/4–31–22).

LAUNDRY **Lavandería Super Clean** in central Zihuatanejo charges $2.50 per kilo. *González 11, at Galeana, tel. 753/4–23–47. Open Mon.–Sat. 8–8.*

MAIL The post office in Zihuatanejo is hard to find: Walk up Vicente Guerrero away from the water and turn right onto Morelos. When Morelos forks, go to the left but stay on the right side of the street. Three blocks past the Pollo Feliz restaurant is a dirt road. Halfway down, you'll find the post office, a white building marked by a small TELECOM sign. They'll hold mail sent to you at the following address for up to 10 days: Lista de Correos, Domicilio Centro SCT, Zihuatanejo, Guerrero, CP 40880, México. There is no post office in Ixtapa. *Tel. 753/4–21–92. Open weekdays 8–8, Sat. 9–1.*

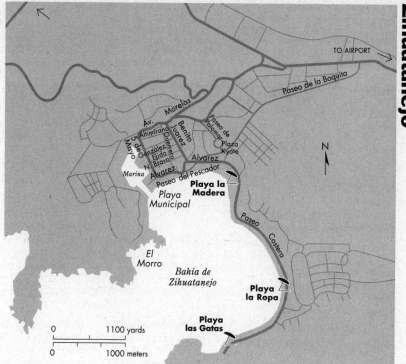

MEDICAL AID The **Centro de Salud** (Paseo de la Boquita, at Paseo del Palmar, tel. 753/4–20–88) in Zihuatanejo charges $2 for a consultation. There are no 24-hour pharmacies in town, but **Farmacia del Centro** (Cuauhtémoc 20, at Nicolás Bravo, tel. 753/4–20–77) is open daily 8 AM–9 PM.

PHONES There are two pay phones in front of Zihuatanejo's Palacio Municipal on Álvarez, and two catercorner from the **Caseta Larga Distancia**. The caseta will charge you a $2 connection fee for a collect or credit-card call, and you can pay cash for long-distance calls here, as well. *Altamirano 6, at Guerrero, tel. 753/4–39–70. Open Mon.–Sat. 8 AM–9:30 PM, Sun. 8–2 and 5–9.*

VISITOR INFORMATION Don't be misled by the booths advertising tourist information—they are really fronts for time shares and offer next to no information. The real tourist office is next door to Zihuatanejo's Palacio Municipal. *Álvarez, near Cuauhtémoc, tel. 753/4–20–01. Open weekdays 9–3 and 6–8, Sat. 9–2.*

COMING AND GOING

BY BUS The new bus station is on the highway on the outskirts of Zihuatanejo. To reach downtown Zihuatanejo from here, take any bus or VW combi marked ZIHUATANEJO or CENTRO. You'll be let off on either Juárez or Morelos, in either case just a few blocks from most of the cheaper hotels in town. To return to the station, head to the corner of Juárez and Ejido and board a combi marked CORREO.

Estrella Blanca (tel. 753/4–34–77) operates out of the Zihuatanejo station. Direct buses to Acapulco ($11, 4 hrs) run on the hour. The bus to Huatulco ($39, 13 hrs) leaves at 7: 30 PM and 9:30 PM and stops in Puerto Escondido along the way. Three buses a day also head for

Mazatlán ($52, 9 hrs). A first-class bus to Mexico City ($30, 10 hrs) leaves daily at 8:45 PM. Three fancier buses leave for Mexico City later in the evening for about $10 more.

BY PLANE The international airport (tel. 753/4–22–37 or 753/4–26–34) is 11 kilometers east of Zihuatanejo on the Carretera Costera (Hwy. 200). **Aeroméxico** (tel. 753/4–20–18), **Mexicana** (tel. 753/4–22–08), and some U.S. carriers serve the airport, which is accessible only by taxi. The ride to or from Zihuatanejo costs $19 in a private taxi or $5 in a shared one.

GETTING AROUND

Zihuatanejo is easily walkable; you'll find budget hotels, restaurants, shops, and the beach all near the center. This area is marked by Álvarez along the town beach to the south; Juárez to the east; 5 de Mayo to the west; and Morelos to the north. Ixtapa has one main thoroughfare, the Paseo Ixtapa; this is essentially a 3-kilometer strip of hotels and malls. To get to Ixtapa from Zihuatanejo (a 15-minute trip), catch one of the blue-and-white buses on Morelos at Juárez. Catch the bus back to Zihuatanejo anywhere along Ixtapa's Paseo de Ixtapa.

WHERE TO SLEEP

Downtown Zihuatanejo is packed with fairly inexpensive hotels, many of which are near the waterfront. Unfortunately, budget hotels in Zihuatanejo are generally reluctant to let lots of people pack into a room for low rates: Some even charge by the person, rather than by the room, so groups may have a harder time than usual getting a break. There are plenty of hotels around Playas La Madera and La Ropa, if you don't care about being right in town. The prices listed below apply in the low season. Expect to pay a bit more from November to February.

➤ UNDER $20 • **Casa Elvira.** The cheapest acceptable indoor sleep in town, excepting the youth hostel, can be found here, two steps from the beach. The sweet, elderly proprietor keeps the no-frills rooms very clean. She charges $12 for a single, $19 for a double, but you might try to negotiate for a cheaper rate if the place doesn't look full. *Álvarez s/n, near 5 de Mayo, no phone. 8 rooms, 5 with bath. Luggage storage.*

➤ UNDER $25 • **Hotel Casa Aurora.** The narrow entryway of this hotel is hidden by souvenir shops and grocery stores. Once through it, you'll find a tiled interior patio decorated with sprawling plants. Most of the clean rooms have stone walls and floors, and those on the second floor rooms have huge, shaded decks with comfortable lounge chairs. You can keep food in the refrigerator on the first floor. Rooms are $10 per person. *Nicolás Bravo 27, near Juárez, tel. 753/4–30–46. 15 rooms, all with bath.*

Hotel Casa Bravo. A pretty interior courtyard welcomes you into this hotel, where each room has a small TV, a balcony, and a tiled bathroom. Singles cost $17 and doubles $20. *Nicolás Bravo 11, near Juárez, tel. 753/4–25–48. 10 rooms, all with bath. Laundry, luggage storage.*

Hotel Lari's. The burnt orange rooms here are well worn, as are the bathrooms, and there is no hot water. This hotel is also farther away from the beach than the others, but it's pretty cheap: Singles cost $13, doubles $20. *Altamirano 1843, near 5 de Mayo, tel. 753/4–37–67. 4 rooms, all with bath. Luggage storage.*

Hotel Raúl Tres Marías. This hotel on a hillside overlooking Zihuatanejo Bay is the best in its price range. Each floor has a plant-decorated communal deck with chairs and tables and a great view. The cement rooms (singles $13, doubles $20) are ample, clean, and have ceiling fans. The same management runs a slightly more expensive ($20 single, $27 double) hotel with the same name on Álvarez. *La Noria 4, tel. 753/4–21–91. Cross footbridge over lagoon at west end of Álvarez. 15 rooms, all with bath. Luggage storage.*

Hotel Rosimar. This clean, breezy hotel has sitting areas on every floor, each overlooking the street. This is the cleanest, newest hotel for the price. Singles cost $13, doubles $20. *Ejido 12, btw Galeana and Guerrero, tel. 753/4–21–39. 12 rooms, all with bath. Luggage storage.*

➤ UNDER $40 • **Bungalows Pacífico.** Walk over to Playa La Madera (*see* Outdoor Activities, *below*) and treat yourself to one of these first-rate bungalows. You can lounge in a hammock, cook yourself a fish dinner and eat it on the deck outside your backdoor, or descend the vine-draped stairway for a walk on the beach. Each bungalow has four beds, a kitchen, a view, and a breeze. Doubles are $35 in low season, $50 in high season, and there's a $10 charge for each additional person. *Cerro de la Madera s/n, tel. 753/4–21–12. 6 bungalows, all with bath. Luggage storage.*

HOSTEL **Villa Juvenil.** This friendly, crowded place is just outside town, less than a mile from the waterfront. It's always full, so if you plan on coming during high season, reserve way in advance. Facilities are rudimentary but clean, and this is a good place to meet other travelers. A single bed in one of the single-sex dorms costs $5 and there is a $6.50 deposit for sheets. Breakfast costs about $2; lunch and dinner are each $3. Be careful if you're going out at night—the doors lock at 11 PM. *Paseo de las Salinas, tel. 753/4–46–62. West on Morelos until it becomes Paseo de las Salinas, left at fork. 62 beds. Open 7 AM–11 PM. Luggage storage.*

CAMPING You can pitch a tent at the hostel (*see above*) and use their bathrooms and showers for $2.50 a night. Camping on the beach is also allowed at **Playa La Ropa,** south of Playa La Madera in Zihuatanejo, and **Playa Linda,** west of the hotel zone past Playa Quieta in Ixtapa. You might want to get a permit (free) at the tourist office to show to waterfront restaurant owners in case they hassle you.

FOOD

The restaurants in Ixtapa tend to be fancy and overpriced. Zihuatanejo, however, has a good selection of reasonable eateries, the best of which are listed below. Not surprisingly, seafood is an excellent choice here. If you order fish, it's best to order a whole one, rather than a fillet, because the latter are often not as fresh. For quick snacks, try the **Panadería Francesa** (González 15), a warehouse-size bakery with a wide selection of *pan dulce* (sweet rolls) and breads.

➤ UNDER $5 • **Cafetería Nueva Zelandia.** Shiny wooden tables and hanging plants make this restaurant look like a health food store, but it's really more of a breakfast place and café. Hotcakes cost $3 and fruit salad is $2. Eggs any style go for $4, and the cappuccinos ($2) are large. *Cuauhtémoc 23, tel. 753/4–23–40. Open daily 7 AM–10:30 PM.*

Fonda Susy. Friendly Fonda Susy serves incredibly cheap meals. Your choice of entrée is served with rice, beans, and freshly made tortillas for about $2.50. This is a family-run place, so be prepared for an onslaught of giggling children. *Nicolás Bravo 33, at Galeana, no phone. Open daily 8–5.*

➤ UNDER $10 • **Restaurante Bar Aquarium.** This place is cheaper than the decor—dark blue ceramic tableware and an aquarium with multicolored fish—would lead you to expect. Their upscale comida corrida costs $5 and includes soup, a soda, and a choice of entrées such as chicken mole, steak in wine sauce, or grilled fish. *Ejido, at Guerrero, no phone. Open Mon.–Sat. 10 AM–midnight.*

La Sirena Gorda. Seafood tacos are the specialty at this waterfront restaurant. The name means "the fat mermaid," and ceramic mermaids and other knickknacks adorn the tables and the busy wooden bar. The tasty smoked-fish tacos are $3 for an order of two. Octopus tacos are steeper at $6. *Paseo del Pescador s/n, by pier, tel. 753/4–26–87. Open daily 7 AM–10 PM. Wheelchair access.*

Tamales Atoles Any. This place specializes in tamales of all varieties, including sweet ones. They also have soups, queso fundido, and vegetarian selections. A meal will run you $3–$5. *Nicolás Bravo 33-B, tel. 753/3–27–09. Just east of Galeana, next to Fonda Susy. Open daily 7:30–1 and 4:30–midnight.*

➤ UNDER $15 • **La Bocana.** This popular spot near the beach on offers tasty, fresh seafood dishes as well as standard Mexican fare, accompanied in the evenings by live marimba music. Prices are high: The fish grilled in garlic is $10, while a plate of enchiladas (the cheapest entrée on the menu) costs $7. An order of beans with cheese and tortillas will get you a table to listen to the music and serve as a decent snack for $2. *Álvarez 13, tel. 753/4–35–45. Open daily 8 AM–10 PM. Wheelchair access.*

Restaurant Bar Tata's. This is a happening spot with excellent food and lots of atmosphere. Tables are right on the beach, shaded by palm fronds, and the super-hip waiters bop to the beat of the Top-40 pumping from loudspeakers. Breaded red snapper with rice and tortillas costs about $10. Another great $10 dish is the *filete a la tampiqueña*, a steak served with enchiladas, beans, and rice. They run a two-fer special during happy hour (5 PM–9 PM). *Paseo del Pescador, tel. 753/4–20–10. Open Wed.–Sun. 8 AM–midnight.*

AFTER DARK

You won't party as hard in Ixtapa/Zihuatanejo as you could in hedonistic Acapulco, but don't get ready for bed yet. Most of the action is where the dollars are: Ixtapa. If you crave a pulsating beat, try the local representative of the ubiquitous **Carlos 'n Charlie's** (tel. 753/3–00–85), on Paseo del Palmar at the northwest end of the hotel strip. Next to the Hotel Kristal in Ixtapa are **Christine's** and **Magic Circus**, both of which charge a $12 cover. Over in Zihuatanejo, the only night club/disco is **Roca Rock** (5 de Mayo, at Nicolás Bravo, no phone), which is open Thursday nights and weekends 9 PM–3 AM and features a nightly transvestite show. The happy hour at **Restaurant Bar Tata's** (*see* Food, *above*) is also pretty rocking. For a more sedate evening, catch a flick at the theater on Cuauhtémoc near Nicolás Bravo in Zihuatanejo, which usually shows movies in English with Spanish subtitles.

Sunday nights around 9 PM, the basketball court on Playa Principal fills up with locals who've come to watch their friends and family perform traditional dances and music.

OUTDOOR ACTIVITIES

The beaches at Las Gatas and Isla Ixtapa are both well-known scuba-diving spots. Shops along the waterfront in Zihuatanejo, Playa Las Gatas, and Isla Ixtapa rent diving equipment, but at $40 an hour it's only for aficionados. The NAUI-certified **Zihuatanejo Scuba Center** (Cuautémoc 3, near Álvarez, tel. 753/4–21–47) offers beginner's pool lessons for $45, followed by guided reef dives for another $45. Also available are fun, functional plastic kayaks for $5 an hour or $25 a day. A half-day snorkeling excursion runs $25 with equipment and includes a lesson on how not to kill coral. Deep sea fishing is also popular, but also costs an arm and a leg: The **Cooperativa de Pescadores** (Paseo del Pescador, at 5 de Mayo, tel. 753/4–20–56) rents charter boats for $120–$200 a day. More affordable is parasailing (a 10-minute ride costs $10). At most of the beaches, you can also rent snorkels, fins, and other equipment for $5 a day. Boogie boards are currently hard to find, but, at press time, the Zihuatanejo Scuba Center was trying to import a few for rental, so check with them.

ZIHUATANEJO The **Playa Municipal** in Zihuatanejo, with its many restaurants and surf shops, is the easiest to reach from the hotels listed above, but it's not nearly as impressive as other beaches around the bay. **Playa La Madera**, a pretty stretch of sand with inviting water, is the next beach to the east. To get here, follow Álvarez for about half a mile, until you reach a set of stairs leading over a canal; cross over and continue east toward the water. When you hear surf pounding, cut down to the right past one of the big hotels.

Past Playa La Madera is **Playa La Ropa,** with clean, calm waters perfect for swimming and waterskiing. Make the sweltering trek from Zihuatanejo's downtown on foot, or take a taxi for $2–$3. If you're walking, follow the route to Playa La Madera, but keep to the right on the main road (the Paseo Costera), always heading up. As the road descends and the ocean comes into view, cut through the nearest hotel, or follow the road until it winds down to the beach. You can also get here by walking 15 minutes north from Playa Las Gatas (*see below*). Public fresh-water showers are available next to La Perla restaurant.

The last beach at the southern end of the Paseo Costera is the clean, pretty **Playa Las Gatas.** Unfortunately, the inviting waters here hide a rocky bottom that is hard on naked toes. Las Gatas is, however, perfect for snorkeling because the flippers protect your feet, and visibility is good. Walk south along the beach for about 15 minutes from Playa La Ropa, or take a pleasant 10-minute boat ride from the *muelle* (pier) in Zihuatanejo. Round-trip tickets cost about $3, and the boat runs 8:30–5.

IXTAPA **Playa del Palmar** is a long, sandy stretch bordering the Ixtapa hotels where rough surf pounds the shore. To the northwest are several more pristine beaches, including **Playa Quieta, Playa Linda,** and Ixtapa's **Club Med.** To get to Playa del Palmar, take the white minibus northeast from the intersection of Morelos and Juárez in Zihuatanejo. Get off at any of the towering hotels and cut through to the beach.

Isla Ixtapa, off the shore of Playa Quieta, has two beaches for swimmers and sunbathers and one for divers. Snorkeling is popular here and allowed on all three beaches. There are a few restaurants on the island, but there's no place to stay. The best thing about Isla Ixtapa is the hour-long boat trip from the pier in Zihuatanejo. Boats leave at 11 AM, return at 4 PM, and cost $10 round trip.

Near Ixtapa/Zihuatanejo

If even mellow Zihuatanejo is too touristy for you, make a midweek trip to the slow-paced seaside village of **Barra de Potosí,** where the main activity consists of hanging out between swims in one of several rustic beachfront restaurants. Red snapper with rice and tortillas will set you back about $5 here (much less than in Ixtapa/Zihuatanejo). At night, visitors are welcome to sleep free of charge in the hammocks slung beneath the restaurants' eaves. The 30-minute bus ride from Ixtapa/Zihuatanejo takes you through beautiful tropical countryside. During the week, there's absolutely nothing to do in Barra de Potosí but relax, enjoy the fine weather and food, and chat with the locals—in a word, it's paradise. Weekends, however, are a different story: The little town fills with teenagers whose boom boxes and car stereos pound away.

COMING AND GOING Catch either a VW combi or one of the white minibuses that run along Juárez (heading away from the water), checking first with the driver to be sure he is stopping at **Los Achotes** (50¢, 30 min), where you can find a *camioneta* (small, flat-bed truck) to shuttle you to Barra de Potosí; they run every half hour or so, and the trip takes 10 minutes.

Acapulco
Acapulco is, to steal a phrase from Dorothy Parker, not a city to be tossed aside lightly. It should be thrown aside with great force. The air hangs thick with grime, and the water is not as pristine as it used to be. Once the crowning star of the Pacific Coast, this city is now in many ways a fortyish bachelor, still partying the night away but desperately pushing his thinning hair back to conceal an ever-growing bald spot. The luxury-hotel architecture is as hideous as luxury-hotel architecture the world over, and the main draw continues to be the discos, which are expensive, crowded, and rock through the night with special effects to rival *Jurassic Park*'s. Less sensory overload can be found in the quieter town of Pie de la Cuesta, within a 45-minute bus ride of the center of town.

People have inhabited the area around Acapulco Bay for over 2,000 years. The Spanish showed up in the 1530s, settling where the downtown area (Acapulco Viejo) and the zócalo are located. Both Acapulco Viejo and the newer luxury hotel strip are bustling and amazingly alive with people, stores, street vendors, and flashy entertainment. The smells of the ocean and the freshly grilled fish and sweet fruit in the marketplace compete with heavy exhaust fumes, open sewers, and piles of garbage, which you'll sometimes see in the middle of the sidewalks. All of this coexists with the incredible natural beauty of the setting, and the highly contrived beauty of the rich and tanned who come to the fancy hotels and clubs to strut their stuff.

BASICS

AMERICAN EXPRESS The main office is in the heart of the luxury-hotel strip. They change traveler's checks, deliver MoneyGrams, and replace lost or stolen AmEx cards and checks. Cardholders can cash personal checks or receive mail here as well. *Costera Miguel Alemán 709-4, Acapulco, Guerrero, CP 39300, México, tel. 74/84–68–87 or 74/84–55–50. Open weekdays 9–2 and 4–6.*

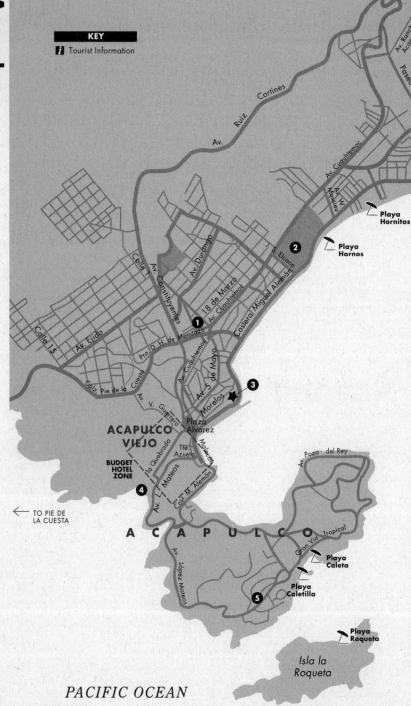

KEY

i Tourist Information

Av. Rancho Acapulco

Paseo del R

Av. Ruiz Cortines

Av. Cuauhtémoc

Av. W. Massieu

Fu
Di

Playa
Hornitos

Calle 1

Av. Constituyentes

Av. Durango

J. S. Elcano

Costera Miguel Alemán

2

Playa
Hornos

18 de Marzo

Av. Cuauhtémoc

1

Calle 15

Av. Ejido

Pro. D. H. de Mendoza

Av. Cuauhtémoc

Av. 5 de Mayo

3

Cplz. Pie de la Cuesta

Av. V. Guerrero

Morelos

Plaza
Alvarez

**ACAPULCO
VIEJO**

Tte.
Azueta

Malecón

Av. Pozo del Rey

**BUDGET
HOTEL
ZONE**

la Quebrada

Av. J. Mateos

Cast. M. Alemán

4

← TO PIE DE
LA CUESTA

A C A P U L C O

Gran Vía Tropical

Playa
Caleta

Av. López Mateos

Playa
Caletilla

5

Playa
Roqueta

*Isla la
Roqueta*

PACIFIC OCEAN

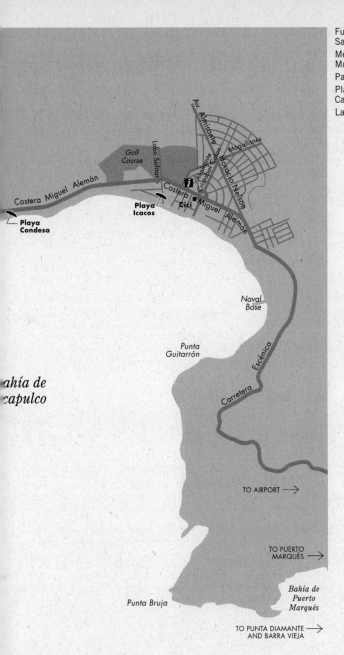

Fuerte de
San Diego, **3**

Mercado
Municipal, **1**

Parque Papagayo, **2**

Plaza de Toros
Caletilla, **5**

La Quebrada, **4**

Av. Almirante Magallanes

Golf
Course

Lobo Solitario

Costera Miguel Alemán

Almirante Cristobal Colón

Horacio Nelson

Costera Miguel Alemán

i

CiCi

**Playa
Icacos**

Costera Miguel Alemán

**Playa
Condesa**

Naval
Base

Punta
Guitarrón

Escénica

*ahía de
capulco*

Carretera

TO AIRPORT →

TO PUERTO
MARQUÉS →

Bahía de
Puerto
Marqués

Punta Bruja

TO PUNTA DIAMANTE →
AND BARRA VIEJA

N

| 0 | 880 yards |
| 0 | 800 meters |

AUTO PARTS/SERVICE **Taller Mecánico Ramiro Vargas Solís** in Acapulco Viejo is run by Señor Vargas himself, who speaks English and has fixed many tourist's car. *18 de Marzo 135, tel. 74/85–01–04, or 74/85–23–84. From Costera, 4 blocks up Niños Héroes, right on 18 de Marzo.*

BUCKET SHOPS The dozens of travel agencies along the Costera offer local tours and travel packages as well as international flight services. **Las Hamacas,** in the hotel of the same name, is one easy-to-locate, established agency. *Costera Miguel Alemán 239, tel. 74/82–48–92. Near Comercial Mexicana, btw Old Acapulco and the strip. Open weekdays 9–2 and 3–6, Sat. 9–2.*

CASAS DE CAMBIO There are tons of casas de cambio on the luxury-hotel strip. Near the zócalo in Acapulco Viejo, **Ventanilla de Cambio** (Costera Miguel Alemán 207, no phone) changes cash and traveler's checks weekdays 9–5. Also in the zócalo area is **Banamex** (Costera Miguel Alemán 211, tel. 74/82–57–50), where money is changed weekday mornings and the ATM accepts Plus and Cirrus cards.

CONSULATES The **United States** and **Canada** have consulates at the Club del Sol Hotel (Costera Miguel Alemán, tel. 74/85–66–00, ext. 4873) that are open weekdays 10–2. The **United Kingdom** consulate is at Las Brisas Hotel (Carretera Escénica, tel. 74/84–16–50) and is open weekdays 10–4.

EMERGENCIES The number for the **police** is 74/85–04–90; they can get you an **ambulance.**

MEDICAL AID The tourist office can recommend an English-speaking doctor, or call **Servicio Médico Especialista** (in Hotel Club del Sol, opposite Plaza Bahía, tel. 74/85–80–66); they charge $30 for a consultation and make house calls anywhere in Acapulco for the same price. You can also try the **Cruz Roja** (tel. 74/85–41–00) or the adjacent **Hospital General** (tel. 74/85–17–30), both on Ruíz Cortines. To reach them from the zócalo, follow Constituyentes north until it become Ruíz Cortines—the hospital and clinic are on the 600 block.

You can fill prescriptions or buy over-the-counter remedies at **Farmacia Emy** 24 hours a day. *Costera Miguel Alemán 176-C, in front of Hotel Acapulco, tel. 74/84–53–33.*

MAIL The huge main post office is on the Costera, a few blocks east of the zócalo. They will hold mail sent to you at the following address for up to 10 days: Lista de Correos, Costera Miguel Alemán 215, Acapulco, Guerrero, CP 39300, México, *tel. 74/82–20–83. Open Mon.–Sat. 8–8, Sun. 9–1.*

PHONES There are pay phones on the zócalo, or you can place calls from the convenient **Caseta Alameda,** hidden in an alleyway off the west side of the zócalo. They charge a $2 fee for collect and credit-card calls. *Calle La Paz 8, tel. 74/83–82–58. Open weekdays 9–8, Sat. 9–3, Sun. 9–1.*

VISITOR INFORMATION Only in Acapulco, where the streets are patrolled by tourist police, would the tourist office be open from 9 AM to midnight daily. The staff is extremely helpful and will send you off with an armful of reading materials, much of it in English. *Costera Miguel Alemán 4455, tel. 74/84–45–83. In luxury hotel area, one block west of CiCi.*

COMING AND GOING

BY BUS The **Central de Autobuses Lineas Unidas del Sur** (Ejido, btw Calles 6 and 7), commonly called Estrella Blanca, is in Colonia La Fábrica and can be reached from the zócalo area on any bus marked EJIDO or CENTRAL. Buses labeled CALETA or CENTRO make the trip in the opposite direction. A taxi ride costs about $3 each way. Tourist information is available at the **Sendatur** booth in the station. A number of companies serve the station, but **Estrella Blanca** (tel. 74/69–20–30) has both first-class and *ejecutivo* (deluxe) service to most common destinations. First-class buses to Mexico City ($22, 7 hrs)—usually with stops in Chilpancingo ($7.50, 2 hrs), Taxco ($13, 4 hrs), and Cuernavaca ($17, 5 hrs)—leave every hour between 11:30 AM and midnight. Direct, luxury buses to Mexico City ($29, 5 hrs) leave on the same schedule. First-class buses also run to Zihuatanejo ($12, 4 hrs) and Huatulco ($24, 9 hrs), with stops in Puerto Escondido ($19, 7 hrs) and Pochutla ($22, 8 hrs). You can also catch buses from a number of other companies to far-flung destinations such as Guadalajara, Monterrey, and Tampico.

The **Central de Autobuses Estrella de Oro** (Cuauhtémoc 751, Fracc. Las Anclas, tel. 74/85–93–60) is served only by Estrella de Oro. To reach the zócalo from here, cross Cuauhtémoc and catch any westbound bus. To go from the zócalo to the station, catch a bus labeled CINE RIO on the corner of 5 de Mayo and Constituyentes. Estrella de Oro has three routes only: north to Mexico City with stops in Chilpancingo, Taxco, and Cuernavaca; west to Zihuatanejo; and east to Huatulco, with stops along the Oaxaca coast. Service is comparable to Estrella Blanca's, and prices are a few pesos higher. Luggage storage is available at the station.

BY PLANE Acapulco's airport is about 30 kilometers east of the city on the coast highway (200). There's no public transportation to the airport, and taxis average $17. If you're alone, a cheaper alternative is **Transportaciones Aeropuerto** (Costera Miguel Alemán 284, tel. 74/85–23–32 or 74/85–60–15), a shuttle service that costs $10 per person. If you call 24 hours in advance, they'll pick you up at your hotel.

GETTING AROUND

Acapulco can be divided roughly into two sections, the city itself, known as Acapulco Viejo (Old Acapulco), and the strip, where all the fancy hotels are. Most of the budget hotels in Acapulco are in Acapulco Viejo, around the zócalo, also called **Plaza Álvarez.** Bordering the zócalo to the south is the Costera Miguel Alemán, an 8-kilometer thoroughfare that runs along the bay. As you move east along the Costera, away from the zócalo, you'll encounter the **Fuerte de San Diego, Papagayo Park,** several beaches, the **Fuente Diana** traffic circle, and finally the tourist zone that stretches from the tunnel on the Costera to the naval base, including the decadent **CiCi** water park.

Tourism 101: A Crash Course in Resort-Town Economics

In the 1960s, the Mexican government decided that tourism was the ticket out of Debt City. Tourism means an influx of foreign currency, and for Mexico, that was supposed to translate into a painless way of repaying foreign debt. A department of tourism, Fonatur, was formed, and after careful consideration, five sites were singled out to become megaresorts: Acapulco, Cancún, Ixtapa, Los Cabos, and the Bahías de Huatulco. These billion-dollar babies have enjoyed varying success: Cancún, a paradise carved out of the Yucatecan landscape, reigns supreme, while Huatulco, in Oaxaca, is still in the development stages.

No one can argue with the fact that increased tourism has ushered in a flood of foreign dollars. The question is, just how much of that stays in the country? Sure, construction money stays, since the law says Mexican labor must be used to build these megaresorts. And fees for water and electricity stay here, as does money spent by tourists in Mexican-owned businesses—and did we forget to mention taxes? Still, the costs have included some pretty radical environmental degradation, and "Hyatt" and "Sheraton" don't sound particularly Mexican to this observer—when did they get in on the act? And here's an interesting statistic to chew on while you reapply that sunscreen: More than half of all the profit made on tourism in developing countries manages to find its way back to the rich north.

BY BUS Buses are by far the cheapest way to get around; fares average 35¢. Buses marked LA BASE and HORNOS run in both directions along the Costera from 6 AM to midnight. Yellow aluminum structures are bus stops.

BY TAXI Taxis are expensive, about $2 even for short distances. Even if you see a meter, set a price before getting in, and don't be afraid to haggle—remember that if the first *taxista* (cabbie) doesn't give you a price you like, another will be along in about 30 seconds.

WHERE TO SLEEP

Don't even think about staying on the strip unless some relative has just died and left you a sizeable inheritance. You needn't lose heart, however: Budget lodging is easy to find, and competition keeps prices down, although couples may be frustrated by the common policy of charging by the person, rather than by room or bed. The best places are clustered around the zócalo in Acapulco Viejo. This area is generally safe, but, as always, you should be alert walking on the streets at night. There are even a few budget options a bit farther toward the strip, several blocks past the Fuerte de San Diego and within binocular-view of the ritzy part of town. Another option is a hotel at one of the beaches on the outskirts of Acapulco. Pie de la Cuesta (*see* Near Acapulco, *below*), a 30-minute bus ride from town, has several respectable hotels and restaurants. Wherever you stay, expect prices to jump substantially in the high season (Semana Santa and around the Christmas and New Year holidays).

NEAR THE ZOCALO The best deals are on the west side of the zócalo. If everything listed below is full, try the **Hotel Sacramento** (Carranza 4, tel. 74/82–08–21), where double rooms are $17.

➤ UNDER $25 • **Hotel Añorve.** The rooms at this hotel are run-down but very clean and cool, and most have balconies. The shady courtyard is lined with plants, and the place is generally homey and comfortable. Singles cost $13, doubles $20. *Juárez 17, 3 blocks west of zócalo, tel. 74/82–40–93. 18 rooms, all with bath. Luggage storage.*

Hotel Lucía. This hotel has recently remodeled its clean lobby and rooms, but it can be loud on weekends. Bathrooms are small but tidy, in keeping with the rest of the establishment. Rooms cost $10 per person. *López Mateos 33, tel. 74/82–04–41. From zócalo, SW on Hidalgo, which converges with Mateos. 16 rooms, all with bath. Luggage storage.*

Hotel Paola. The above-average rooms here are clean and decorated completely in white, but there is no communal space aside from the teensy pool on the roof. Singles cost $10, doubles $20. *José Azueta 16, tel. 74/82–62–43. From zócalo, 4 blocks west on Hidalgo, left on Azueta. 36 rooms, all with bath. Luggage storage.*

➤ UNDER $30 • **Casa Mama Helene.** Without a doubt, this slightly worn hotel is Mama Helene's house. Upon entering, you see a cement courtyard with a Ping-Pong table, bookshelves, plants, and Mama Helene sitting around with her friends. The price per person is $13. The hotel has a restaurant and laundry service, but it's cheaper to go elsewhere for these services. *Juárez 12, 3 blocks west of zócalo, tel. 74/82–23–96. 20 rooms, all with bath. Luggage storage.*

Hotel Asturias. The Asturias has a pool and yard where it's easy to meet fellow guests. The environment is generally friendly and laid-back, and the small rooms have working fans, comfortable beds, and clean bathrooms. A plus is that La Quebrada, of cliff-diving and sunset-watching fame, is only a five-minute walk away. Singles cost $13, doubles $25. *La Quebrada 45, tel. 74/83–65–48. 4½ blocks west of zócalo. 5 rooms, all with bath. Luggage storage.*

Hotel Misión. This place has the most charm of any budget hotel in Acapulco. The atrium is filled with philodendrons, mango trees, and wicker rocking chairs. Rooms are clean (except for a few stray cockroaches) and have high ceilings with wooden beams, powerful fans, and colorfully tiled bathrooms. Singles cost $15, doubles $27. *Felipe Valle 12, 3 blocks west of zócalo, tel. 74/82–36–43 or 74/82–20–76. 28 rooms, all with bath. Luggage storage, wheelchair access.*

NEAR THE STRIP Acapulco never sleeps, and you might not either if you choose to stay in this noisy area, near the western beaches and within walking distance of the strip. Traffic pours past at all hours, and prices tend to be a bit higher for the same sort of rooms that you'll find near the zócalo. The hotels listed below are the best of the bunch.

Hotel Playa Suave. A reasonable place to stay if you want to be as close to the beach as possible, this hotel is across the street and west of the luxury hotel strip. Rooms are dark but clean, as are the bathrooms. The hotel has a swimming pool, parking, and a restaurant. Singles are $20, doubles $26. *Costera Miguel Alemán 253, just west of Hotel de Brasil, tel. 74/85–12–56. 16 rooms, all with bath. Luggage storage.*

Hotel Sevillano. Alfredo, the Sevillano's manager, successfully enforces high standards of cleanliness and service and sees to it that his pink decor is unsullied by nasty crawling things by staging regular fumigations. Rooms smell of insecticide but have fans, TVs, and phones. Several restaurants and the Comercial Mexicana supermarket are within walking distance. Singles cost $17, doubles $22. *Tadeo Arredondo 7, tel. 74/83–83–58 or 74/83–83–59. 65 rooms, all with bath. Luggage storage, wheelchair access.*

CAMPING According to the tourist office, it's illegal to pitch a tent on the beach in Acapulco or Pie de la Cuesta. During high season, camping is allowed on the beach at Puerto Marqués (*see* Outdoor Activities, *below*). The **Playa Suave Trailer Park** (Niñez Balboa, behind Hotel de Brasil, tel. 74/85–14–64) is right between Old Acapulco and the strip, a block away from the beach. You can pitch a tent here for $13 in the low season, $18 in high season.

FOOD

The deals are around the west side of the zócalo in Acapulco Viejo, especially on Juárez, where you'll find literally hundreds of small, clean establishments frequented by locals. **Restaurante Ricardos** and **Restaurante San Carlos** may lack atmosphere, but they're two of the best in the area. For about $2 you can eat at one of the *fondas* (covered food stands) in the mercado—try **Fonda Christie.** To reach the market, take a HOSPITAL bus going inland from the zócalo. If you want to stock up on snacks for the beach, three warehouse-size grocery stores on the Costera between Acapulco Viejo and the strip are good places for cheap yogurt, fruit, deli meats, and freshly baked bread. Otherwise, prices skyrocket as soon as you get anywhere near the high-rise hotels.

NEAR THE ZOCALO

➢ UNDER $5 • **Cafetería Astoria.** This little outdoor café tucked away in a secluded corner of the zócalo is the place to sit and relax for hours with a cappuccino ($1.50) and some pan dulce. *Chilaquiles rojos* (tortilla strips and chicken in red sauce; $3.50), meat enchiladas ($4), and club sandwiches ($2.50) are also served. *Plaza Álvarez, tel. 74/82–29–44. Open daily 7 AM–10 PM.*

Restaurant Goyo's. A favorite with locals, this tiny open-air restaurant serves large portions of wholesome, tasty food. A breakfast of eggs, toast, juice, and coffee costs $3; hotcakes with fruit and coffee are $3.50. After breakfast, the best deal is the ample $4 comida corrida. *5 de Mayo 33, near 2 de Abril, no phone. Open daily 8 AM–10 PM.*

➢ UNDER $10 • **El Amigo Miguel.** A few blocks west of the zócalo you'll find about four seafood restaurants that all look the same: airy and comfortable, with starched tablecloths and solicitous waiters. This one has the freshest seafood and a second-floor balcony that overlooks Acapulco Bay. Fish quesadillas are $2, and a fillet of sole comes with vegetables, rice, and warm bread for $4.50. Rice with seafood is $7. *Juárez 31, at José Azueta, tel. 74/83–69–81. Open daily 10:30–8:30.*

ON THE STRIP Don't come to the strip to find a cheap meal—you won't. Do come to see what's happening and, of course, to see and be seen.

➢ UNDER $10 • **100% Natural.** Acapulco's biggest health-food chain has several outlets that serve green salads, steamed vegetable dishes, and soy burgers. (Warning: The branch on the zócalo is an imitation and not worth your time). Main dishes range $5–$8. All their restaurants are open 24 hours, so, if you're in overdrive, come here for a bit of sanity and a green salad. If salad doesn't appeal to you at 4 AM, try **Bob's Big Boy** down the street for greasy fries. *Costera Miguel Alemán 4864, 1 block past CiCi, tel. 74/81–08–44. Wheelchair access.*

El Fogón. Thursdays in Acapulco are called *jueves pozolero,* because almost everyone eats the corn-based soup with pork called pozole ($4), and this is the place to come for it. Vegetarians can request a meatless version. *Costera Miguel Alemán 188-A, tel. 74/85–14–13. Open 24 hrs.*

➤ UNDER $20 • **Suntory.** This spotless, elegant, and air-conditioned Japanese restaurant serves an assortment of sushi for $13 and a set meal of several courses is $16. Lighter fare includes miso soup ($1) and fried rice with vegetables ($2). Most of the discos are within walking distance. *Costera Miguel Alemán 36, tel. 74/4–80–88 or 74/4–87–66. A few blocks east of CiCi. Open daily 2–11.*

El Zorrito. Large crowds of young people flock here in the afternoon. The food is good and not too expensive for the area—hearty eaters should try the *filete a la tampiqueña,* a steak served with a chicken taco, a chicken enchilada, guacamole, and beans, all for $13. The menu also includes hamburgers ($5), onion rings ($2), and fried chicken ($7). *Costera Miguel Alemán, just east of Ritz, tel. 74/85–37–35. Open Wed.–Mon. 9 AM–6 AM, Tues. 3 PM–6 AM. Wheelchair access.*

DESSERT/COFFEEHOUSES **Cafetería Astoria** (*see above*), on the northeast corner of the zócalo, is where most coffee-sippers relax for the afternoon, reading the newspaper or playing dominoes. **Café Los Amigos** (La Paz, tel. 74/83–65–85), on the west side, serves ice cream, fresh juice drinks, and a mean cappuccino ($1). Around the corner at the **Fat Farm** (Juárez 10, tel. 74/83–53–39), coffee goes well with a banana split ($3) and cheesecake ($2). These last two establishments also serve good breakfasts (about $4) and comidas corridas (about $5).

WORTH SEEING

Most points of interest lie within a Frisbee's throw of the Costera. Check out the **mercado municipal** (near Cuauhtémoc and Mendoza), where you'll find produce, freshly butchered animals, shell earrings, and Guatemalan vests and backpacks. Or head to the zócalo, where the entire city seems to gather around sunset.

FUERTE DE SAN DIEGO This fort, so well restored it imparts absolutely no sense of history, sits on a waterfront hill just east of the zócalo and consists of huge walls of beige stone encircling manicured lawns and a museum. The original fort, built in 1616, was destroyed by an earthquake; the present structure dates from the 18th century when it was used to protect Acapulco from pirates. Among the few artifacts in the museum are chests, swords, and some Chinese goods left from Acapulco's days as Mexico's principal port for the Asia trade. *Costera Miguel Alemán, near Palacio Federal, tel. 74/83–97–30. Admission: $3.50, free Sun. Open Tues.–Sun. 10:30–4:30.*

PARQUE PAPAGAYO This huge park on the Costera—complete with such kid thrillers as a roller rink and skating park, rowboats in a murky, scum-covered lagoon, and an aviary—is a five-minute walk west of the Ritz Hotel. It's primarily a hangout for local youth and, on weekends, for families, but it also makes a nice break from the beach scene for tourists. Free musical performances take place Sunday at 6 PM in the auditorium. Entrance is free, but the amusements will cost you up to $1 each. *Open daily 6 AM–8 PM; some attractions open until 11 PM.*

PLAZA DE TOROS CALETILLA Bullfights take place almost every Sunday between Christmas and Easter at this bullring just a few minutes' walk northwest of Playa Caletilla (*see* Outdoor Activities, *below*). The cheapest tickets, available at the bullring, are $5. *López Mateos, Península de las Playas.*

LA QUEBRADA About a 10-minute walk northwest of the zócalo, these beautiful cliffs offer a breathtaking view of the ocean and surrounding landscape. Acapulco's famous divers risk their lives daily, plummeting approximately 60 meters into the rock-filled waters below. To get to the cliffs, walk straight up La Quebrada, the street that begins directly behind the zócalo's main church. This being Acapulco, you have to pay an admission charge of about $1.50 for the best viewing spots. The divers also accept (expect?) small gratuities. Dives take place daily at 12:45 PM and once an hour 7:30 PM–10:30 PM; at night, divers fling themselves into the water bearing flaming torches.

AFTER DARK

The legendary disco scene of Acapulco is mind-boggling in its excess of mirrored walls, strobe lights, disco music, and laser beams; however, it does slow down during low season (spring—except Semana Santa—and fall). Covers average $15 year-round, and in many cases drinks are as high as $5. The deal to look for, assuming you lack a company expense account, is a *barra libre* (free bar). This means there's a hefty cover (up to $30), but all drinks are included in the price. There are even discos on ships that cruise around Acapulco Bay—**Bonanza Cruise** (tel. 74/83–18–03) leaves at 4:30 and 7:30 nightly from the pier at Caleta Beach; $40 tickets include dinner and music.

As at any beach resort, the gay bars in Acapulco are both active and about as seedy as the rest of the clubs. **TaBares,** on the Costera across from the Diana fountain, has a pretty mixed, though mostly male crowd. Cover is $10.

BARS There are almost as many bars along the strip as there are fast-food places. **Carlos 'n Charlie's** (Costera Miguel Alemán 999, tel. 74/84–00–39) is usually a guaranteed rockin' good time; get there early or you'll wait in line. Another fun place is the restaurant **El Zorrito** (*see* Food, *above*), which stays open until 6 AM.

DISCOS WITH NO COVER CHARGE You gotta love these places. **Disco Beach** (Costera Miguel Alemán, tel. 74/84–70–64) is an outdoor disco in the middle of the strip, overlooking the ocean. Expect lots of young muscle men and bleach blonds. Equally rowdy is **Iguanas Ranas** (Costera Miguel Alemán s/n, tel. 74/85–27–03), on the beach near the tunnel. Music runs the gamut from Top-40 to world beat here, and the place is open from 9 PM until the last stragglers stumble home, at which point you can hop a taxi to **Faces** (Juan de la Cosa 32, tel. 74/84–76–01), an after-hours club open from 1 AM to 8 AM.

DISCOS Besides those mentioned below, the up-and-coming hot spot at press time was **Atrium** (Costera Miguel Alemán 5040, tel. 74/84–19–00). The club gets going at 10:30 PM, and the cover ($17 for women and $23 for men) includes drinks.

Baby O. Probably the most popular spot with the 18–30 age group, this club is packed almost every night of the week during high season. The jungle decor appears to bring out the animals, and there's little chance of going home alone unless you're so inclined—try using a tranquilizer gun to stall for time while you escape from the herd. The club is free for "girls" Monday–Thursday; otherwise the cover is $13. Beers are $5. *Costera Miguel Alemán, near Nelson, tel. 74/84–74–74. Opens at 10:30 PM.*

B&B. On the first floor you'll hear American music from the '60s and '70s; on the second, romantic Mexican pop. Cover is about $15, drinks $3–$5. This club is a ways from the zócalo, so you're best off taking a cab if you come. *Gran Vía Tropical 5, tel. 74/83–04–41. Opens at 10:30 PM.*

D' Paradise. This a huge disco is decorated entirely in black with tables set in tiers around a circular dance floor. The laser-light show begins at midnight, so don't be late. Women enter for free, men pay $10, and no one will be well received in sandals, shorts, or T-shirts. *Costera Miguel Alemán, near Yucatán, tel. 74/84–88–15. Opens at 10:30 PM.*

LIVE MUSIC AND DANCING **Ninas** (Costera Miguel Alemán 41, tel. 74/84–24–00), a dance place with live tropical and salsa music, is one of the few alternatives to disco hell. They're open from 10 PM every night except Monday, and the $20 cover includes drinks. **Cats** (Juan de la Cosa 32, tel. 74/84–72–35), next to Faces (*see above*), is a similar salsa saloon with a $24 cover that includes all the (domestic-only) alcohol you can drink. Cats opens nightly at 10 PM, there's a drag show at 1:30 AM, and the bar closes at 3 AM.

OUTDOOR ACTIVITIES

The beaches lining Acapulco Bay, in clockwise order, are: **Hornitos** and **Hornos**, frequented primarily by Mexican tourists; **La Condesa**, on the most populated part of the strip; and **Icacos**, a quieter stretch of sand that runs from the El Presidente Hotel to the naval base. Before diving into the deceptively beautiful water, remember that the bay is quite polluted—mostly with sewage. An alternative is to sneak into a hotel pool.

Lots of watersports are popular here, though you may want to choose one that requires the least amount of contact betweeen you and the less-than-pristine water. Deep-sea fishing is a good bet: **Barracuda's Fleet** (Costera Miguel Alemán 147, at Martínez, tel. 74/83–85–43) charges $60 per person (plus $7 for a fishing permit) for three hours of marlin, shark, sailfish, and tuna fishing, all equipment and round-trip transportation from your hotel included. Sailing is available at Puerto Marqués for about $20 per hour. There's waterskiing at Puerto Marqués for $50 an hour and windsurfing at Caleta and Caletilla for $15 an hour. Scuba diving is also expensive: **Mantarraya** dive shop (Gran Vía Tropical 2, tel. 74/82–41–76), near Playas Caleta and Caletilla, has reasonable deals: Two-hour resort courses and longer dives for certified divers are both $40, and snorkel trips are $20. Prices include equipment as well as round-trip transportation from your hotel. On any of Acapulco's beaches, $5 will get you a 15-minute banana boat ride, and $40 an hour will rent you a Jet-Ski. Don't worry about finding these services—the salespeople roaming the beach will find you.

BEACHES The main draw to the beaches closest to the center of Acapulco Viejo, **Caleta and Caletilla,** is the big waves that crash in, tossing banana-hauling speed boats, paddling tourists, boogie-boarders, and swimmers like a big, wet, dirty salad. Formerly the hot spots of Acapulco, Caleta and Caletilla were left in the dust by the strip and now cater more to Mexican tourists than foreigners. While here, you can take a trip in a glass bottom boat ($8.50) to see the **La Virgin Sumergida,** a one-ton statue of the Virgin of Guadalupe placed at the bottom of the sea by a group of scuba divers some 35 years ago. Unfortunately, cloudy water means that visibility through the bottom of the boat is limited. The ticket hawkers for the **aquarium** ($7 and only worth it if you're with small children) and the various rides are very aggressive. Across the bay you can see **Isla Roqueta**, which is accessible from either beach by boat. The island itself has little to offer besides scrub brush, roaming tourists, a small beach, and a view from the lighthouse. The boat ride ($5 round-trip, 10 min) is pleasant, however. Buy a ticket from the offices marked ISLA ROQUETA near the wharf, or from a roaming seller on the beach. To get to the dock, board a bus marked CALETA heading west along Costera.

Acapulco's cleanest beaches lie on the **Bahía de Puerto Marqués,** east of the city near the airport freeway. The water here is cleaner than in Acapulco Bay, making the spot popular with water-skiers and skin-divers. On weekends the more developed **Playa de Puerto Marqués** usually fills up with Mexican tourists. Buses marked PUERTO MARQUES (50¢, 45 min) leave from the Costera across the street from Sanborn's. A bit farther on is the pristine **Princess Beach,** named for the hotel that looms over it. The waves are big but not too frightening. To get here, you'll need to take a cab ($1.50) or hitch a ride from Puerto Marqués.

Near Acapulco

PIE DE LA CUESTA

This short stretch of sand about 15 kilometers northwest of Acapulco has waves so powerful that residents don't swim here at all. The nearby **Laguna de Coyuca** is better for swimming. The lagoon, completely surrounded by wild vegetation and twittering birds, is an incredible shade of blue. To get to Pie de la Cuesta from Acapulco, catch a PIE DE LA CUESTA bus headed east on Costera, across the street from Sanborn's or the main post office. Bus fare is about 50¢ and the trip takes 30 minutes.

WHERE TO SLEEP Bungalows María Cristina. The best thing about these homey bungalows is their location, directly on the beach and just across the street from the tranquil lagoon and its towering palm trees. The small central porch has wooden rocking chairs and hammocks to lie in while you enjoy the cool breeze and the sound of the pounding surf. Three of the bungalows have kitchens. The cost is $17 for one person, $23 for two, and $50 for a bungalow for four with a kitchen. *Playa Pie de la Cuesta s/n, tel. 74/60–02–62. 8 bungalows, all with bath. Luggage storage.*

Villa Nirvana. The Nirvana villas are right on the ocean, surrounding a small plaza. The rooms are simply furnished and clean, with fans and terraces, and there is a pool. Although only one room has a kitchen, everyone has access to the large kitchen—ask nicely and owner Roxana will let you keep some stuff in the fridge. Singles cost $17, doubles $26. *Playa Pie de la Cuesta 302, tel. 74/60–16–31. 6 rooms, all with bath. Luggage storage, wheelchair access.*

➤ CAMPING • Pitching tents on the beach is frowned upon here. The **Acapulco Trailer Park** (Playa Pie de la Cuesta 200, no phone), charges $10 for one or two people in a tent.

FOOD **El Zanate.** During low season at this small store-front restaurant, the standard fare is the $3.50 comida corrida, which includes rice, beans, salad, tortillas, and your choice of anything from fish to steak to chiles rellenos. In the high season, referred to by owner Berta as "the time of the gringos," they have a wide selection of fresh fish and "whatever else the gringos want." For a big group, they will even prepare a feast, such as roast pig. The other owner, Hector, thinks he is captain of the port of Pie de la Cuesta and will be happy to give information about excursions on the Laguna de Coyuca. *Playa Pie de la Cuesta, no phone. Open daily 6 AM–11 PM. Wheelchair access.*

OAXACA 9

By Ian Signer

Travel in Mexico can be a commercialized, packaged affair with the same mini-
malls, fast-food restaurants, and smog you'll find anywhere in the world. Oaxaca comes closer
to the Mexico of dreams, where 10,000 years of tradition has not been relegated to museums,
but continues to bring people together in markets, churches, and *zócalos* (main squares).

The landscapes of this mountainous southern state vary enormously, with cacti-carpeted
deserts and sunset-colored canyons giving way to tropical jungles and scrubby coastland. For
centuries, the Sierra Madre del Sur mountains have afforded a certain protection for the
region's Zapotec, Mixtec, Mixe, Huave, Triqui, and other indigenous people. Within Oaxaca's
seven regions more than 17 distinct Indian languages continue to be spoken, and in smaller
villages, Maya rites and ceremonies, complete with tambourines, flutes, and traditional
dress, still mark the passage of girls and boys into adulthood. The agricultural techniques
used in many mountainside fields are also the same as they were centuries ago, as is the staple crop, corn.

Oaxaca de Juárez, or Oaxaca city, the state's capital, sits at the confluence of three river valleys. Here the region's Indians, mestizos, and expatriates meet in the shady, café-filled zócalo.
Monte Albán, Mitla, and other pre-Columbian sites are easily accessible from the capital, as
are many small towns filled with artisans and craftspeople. South of Oaxaca city, the Sierra
Madre del Sur drops sharply to the sea, forming at their base a long stretch of Pacific Coast
beaches ideal for those seeking sun and relaxation. Puerto Escondido is *the* surfer mecca, and
Puerto Angel is a cliffside fishing village where you can swim, snorkel, or just laze about. Near
Puerto Angel is Zipolite, the favorite beach of international hippies in the know. Even Huatulco,
which the Mexican government is promoting as the next Cancún, still has some untouched
coves and good places to camp.

The Isthmus of Tehuantepec is a neglected destination, usually viewed as a dull gateway to
Chiapas and Tabasco. This is partly because much of the region, largely Zapotec in population, has adapted to the modern world in its own way, choosing to embrace its old traditions
and customs, rather than attract tourists with fancy hotels. Here, the pleasures are simple:
You can simply watch the world go by, eat boiled iguana eggs, or whiz around in a moped-
propelled chariot. It's not for everyone, though—travelers who want to know more about
Zapotec culture without the tourist trappings will find plenty; otherwise, it's hot, flat,
and dusty.

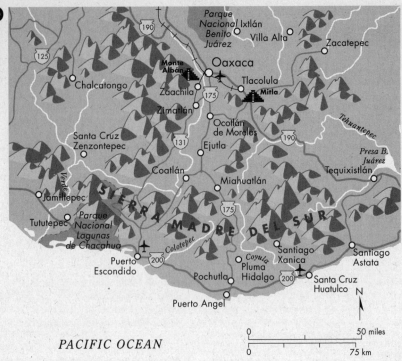

PACIFIC OCEAN

Oaxaca de Juárez

The Zapotecs began building ceremonial centers near what is now Oaxaca city around 500 BC. Today, five important archaeological sites are less than an hour away by bus from Oaxaca city: Monte Albán, Mitla, Zaachila, Dainzú, and Yagul. At the time of the Conquest, both Mixtecs and Zapotecs were paying tribute to the expanding Aztec empire. But the Spanish demanded more than just territory and tribute; they also began a bloody campaign of religious and cultural conversion. The missionaries who accompanied, and in some cases preceded the conquistadors, erected grandiose monasteries and churches, many of them, not coincidentally, near or atop ancient ceremonial centers. Now, those monasteries and convents decay alongside the crumbling temples of the Oaxacan landscape.

Despite its increasing popularity with tourists, Oaxaca de Juárez has managed to maintain a certain grace, dignity, and timelessness.

The zócalo of Oaxaca city is a microcosm of the complexity and cultural richness you'll find throughout the entire region. Triquis selling weaving from their high mountain villages sit alongside Tehuana women from the isthmus, with children clinging to their long, colorful skirts. The fluid sounds of Spanish mingle with Zapotec, French, and English, and shoe-shine boys chat with university students. Demonstrations are common in the zócalo, whether they be for the rights of students and Indians, or better pay for school teachers. Tacky commercialism is also present—don't be too surprised if you find giant helium-filled Teenage Mutant Ninja Turtles floating over the whole scene. It is this meeting of worlds that energizes the city and fuels its people, who continue to innovate while respecting their traditions.

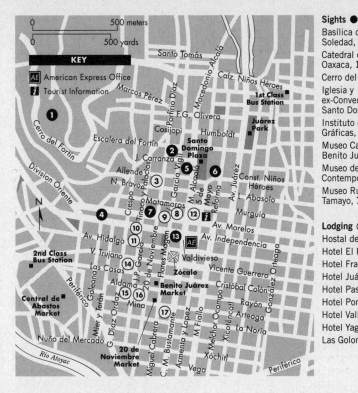

Sights ●

Basílica de la
Soledad, **4**

Catedral de
Oaxaca, **13**

Cerro del Fortín, **1**

Iglesia y
ex-Convento de
Santo Domingo, **6**

Instituto de Artes
Gráficas, **5**

Museo Casa de
Benito Juárez, **2**

Museo de Arte
Contemporáneo, **12**

Museo Rufino
Tamayo, **7**

Lodging ○

Hostal del Centro, **8**

Hotel El Palmar, **15**

Hotel Francia, **10**

Hotel Juárez, **11**

Hotel Pasaje, **16**

Hotel Pombo, **9**

Hotel Vallarta, **14**

Hotel Yagul, **17**

Las Golondrinas, **3**

BASICS

AMERICAN EXPRESS The American Express office is inside the travel agency **Viajes Micsa** on the northeast corner of the zócalo. They exchange all traveler's checks with no commission, replace lost checks, and deliver MoneyGrams. They also cash personal checks, hold mail, and replace Amex cards. *Valdivieso 2, Oaxaca, Oaxaca, CP 68000, México, tel. 951/6–27–00, fax 951/6–74–75. Open weekdays 9–2 and 4–6, Sat. 9–2.*

AUTO PARTS/SERVICE **Refacciones y Partes La Central** offers parts and service on most vehicles. *Hidalgo 407, 3 blocks west of the zócalo, tel. 951/6–24–45. Open daily 9–2 and 4–8.*

BOOKSTORES **Librería Universitaria** has a good selection of secondhand books in English, as well as a fair number of tourist and cultural guides. *Guerrero 104, 1 block east of zócalo, tel. 951/6–42–43. Open Mon.–Sat. 9:30–2 and 4–8.*

Provedora Escolar is the largest bookstore in central Oaxaca. Most of the books are in Spanish, but they do sell a few new English-language novels and tourist guides. Downstairs is a full stationery and art-supply store. *Independencia 1001, at Reforma, tel. 951/6–21–23. Open weekdays 9–1:30 and 4–8, Sat. 9–2 and 4–8.*

CASAS DE CAMBIO **Cambio La Estrella** (Alcalá 201, Apt. 101, tel. 951/4–53–65) is near the American Consulate and has decent exchange rates. For ATM service—Plus, Cirrus, and credit cards—try **Bancomer** (García Vigil 202, tel. 951/6–76–43).

CONSULATES **Canada and United Kingdom.** *Hidalgo 817-5, Oaxaca, Oaxaca, CP 68000, tel. 951/6–56–00. Open weekdays 9–1.*

United States. *Alcalá 201, Rooms 204 and 206, Oaxaca, Oaxaca, CP 68000, tel. 951/4–30–54. Open weekdays 9–1.*

EMERGENCIES In an emergency, dial 06 from any phone for the **police**, the **fire** department, or **ambulance** service. Oaxaca also has a tourist-specific police unit (tel. 951/6–38–10).

LAUNDRY The most economical option is to ask someone at your hotel if they would do your laundry for a small fee (usually $1–$2). If this fails, **Azteca Lavandería** will wash and deliver your clothes in under two hours, but they charge $5 for the first 3½ kilos. *Hidalgo, at Díaz Ordaz, tel. 951/4–79–51. Open Mon.–Sat. 8–8, Sun. 10–2.*

MAIL The main post office is just off the zócalo, facing the front of the cathedral. They will hold mail sent to you at the following address for up to 10 days: Lista de Correos, Administración 1, Oaxaca, Oaxaca, CP 68001, México. *Tel. 951/6–26–61. Open weekdays 8–7; Sat. 9–1.*

Telecomunicaciones de México provides telegram, money order, and fax service. *Next to post office, tel. 951/6–42–55. Open weekdays 8–8, Sat. 9–2.*

MEDICAL AID The **Cruz Roja** (Armenta y López 700, tel. 951/6–44–55) offers 24-hour free medical service and emergency care. **Hospital San Antonio del Carmen** (Abasolo 215, tel. 951/6–26–12) has English-speaking doctors on call 24 hours a day. If you need a dentist or specialist, the tourist office (*see* Visitor Information, *below*) at 5 de Mayo and Morelos can refer you to someone who speaks English. **La Farmacia Guadalupana** (Hidalgo 340, tel. 951/6–53–82) is open 24 hours daily.

PHONES You can make local and international collect calls from the orange phones scattered across town. The blue phones on the zócalo accept major credit cards, but not international calling cards. **Computel,** a private long-distance phone and fax office, provides the fastest and most expensive international calls. *Trujano 204, tel. 951/4–73–19. Off zócalo btw Cabrera and 20 de Noviembre. Open daily 7 AM–10 PM.*

SCHOOLS Oaxaca has a number of reputable language schools, most of which will arrange for you to share the home of a local family while you study. The **Instituto Cultural de Oaxaca** (Juárez 503, tel. 951/5–34–04) offers intensive Spanish courses, as well as classes in Mexican cooking, ceramics, textiles, history, and archaeology. The **Instituto de Comunicación y Cultura** (Alcalá 307, No. 12, tel. 951/6–34–43) offers classes in Zapotec, as well as all levels of Spanish. The **Centro de Idiomas de la Universidad Autónoma "Benito Juárez"** (Burgoa, btw Armenta y López and Bustamante, tel. 951/6–59–22) offers college credit (ask at your school about requirements) for intensive courses in Spanish, Mixtec, and Zapotec. Prices at all schools are flexible and vary with the number of students per class. Don't be afraid to shop around, bargain, and specify what kind of course you want.

VISITOR INFORMATION Stop by the **Oficina de Turismo** for bus schedules, maps, and a list of local families with rooms to let. You can also leave notes for fellow travelers here for up to a month. If you read Spanish, be sure to pick up a copy of the monthly *Guía Cultural*, which lists free films, art exhibits, and music and theater performances taking place throughout the city. *5 de Mayo, at Morelos, tel. 951/6–48–28. Open daily 9–8.*

A second Oficina de Turismo in the Palacio Municipal also provides free maps and bus schedules. *Independencia, at García Vigil. Open Mon.–Sat. 9–3 and 6–8, Sun. 9–3.*

Also check out the bulletin board in the back of the **Biblioteca Circulante de Oaxaca** for listings of everything from ceramics classes to acupuncture to house rentals. You're also free to browse through their extensive collection of English-language reading materials, including more than 50 different magazines, but only members can take them out. *Alcalá 205, no phone. Open weekdays 10–1 and 4–7, Sat. 10–1.*

COMING AND GOING

BY BUS Oaxaca's crowded and noisy first-class bus terminal (Calzada Niños Héroes 1306) is about 11 long blocks north of the zócalo—a 20-minute walk from downtown or about $2 by cab. **Autobuses del Oriente (ADO)** (tel. 951/5–17–03) and **Cristóbal Colón** (tel. 951/5–12–14) buses serve most of Mexico out of this station, including frequent daily service to Mexico City

($20, 9 hrs) and Puebla ($15, 8 hrs), two buses daily to Veracruz ($21, 10 hrs) and Salina Cruz ($10, 4½ hrs), and one bus daily to San Cristóbal de las Casas ($21, 12 hrs).

The second-class station is south of the railroad tracks across from the Central de Abastos market, on the corner of Trujano and the Periférico expressway. The many bus companies based here serve outlying towns, as well as Mexico City ($15, 9 hrs), Tapachula ($19, 12 hrs), and other major cities. For service to the coast, look for **Estrella del Valle** (tel. 951/4–57–00), which goes to Puerto Escondido ($9.50, 7 hrs), Santa Cruz Huatulco ($9.50, 7 hrs), and Pochutla ($8, 6½ hrs). One bus also serves Puerto Escondido daily for about the same price from the **Hotel Mesón del Angel** (Mina 518, tel. 951/6–53-27).

BY TRAIN The Oaxaqueño train goes (slowly) to Mexico City from the station on Madero (tel. 951/6–22–53) once a day at 7 PM. Tickets cost $8 second class, $12 regular, and $25 first class.

BY PLANE The **Aeropuerto Nacional de Oaxaca-Zozocatlán** (tel. 951/6–23–32) is about 8 kilometers south of town. Two daily flights go to Mexico City; the cost is about $80 (one-way) and the trip takes one comfortable hour. Tickets can be purchased at the airport or from agencies downtown—try **AVIACSA** (Porfirio Díaz 102 No. 2, tel. 951/3–18–01) for the widest variety of destinations. For $3.50 **Transportación Terrestre Aeropuerto** (tel. 951/6–27–77) will shuttle you between the airport and downtown Monday through Saturday, 9 AM to 8 PM. For tourist information at the airport, head for the desk inside the main terminal.

HITCHING While hitching is always risky, people who wouldn't hitchhike elsewhere in Mexico will do so in these parts, and it's fairly easy to get rides from here to the rest of the state and beyond. The best places to stand are on the main roads leading in and out of the city—try Calzada Niños Héroes and the Periférico.

GETTING AROUND

Oaxaca city is walker-friendly; you can cross it in 45 minutes. At the heart of it all is the **zócalo,** bordered by the mammoth cathedral and the **Parque Alameda de León.** North of the zócalo is the posh part of town, where you can find (or avoid) luxury hotels with tourist-oriented discos. The southern rim of the city proper is edged by the **Periférico.** It's here you'll find the huge **Central de Abastos** market, the second-class bus station, and the red-light district. The hill that overlooks Oaxaca, **Cerro del Fortín** (Fort Hill), is about a 20-minute walk northwest from the zócalo. Keep in mind that most streets change names as they cross Avenida Independencia going north–south and Bustamante/Alcalá going east–west.

Buses are hardly used—or necessary—in the downtown area. Taxis are best for getting to and from the bus stations after dark, when the southwest corner of town gets a bit dicey. Standard fares within downtown are $3–$5, but you should agree on a price before getting in.

WHERE TO SLEEP

There are two main areas to crash in Oaxaca, one north and one south of the zócalo. The north side is the quiet, residential, and colonial part of the city, and you'll pay more to stay there. The south side, near the markets and second-class bus station, caters to working-class Mexicans and shoestring travelers. If you plan to stay a while, consider the **Posada San Pablo** (Fiallo 102, tel. 951/6–49–14), which offers furnished apartments with kitchens and private baths in a beautifully maintained ex-convent for about $430 per month for two people.

The **tourist office** on 5 de Mayo at Morelos (*see* Visitor Information, *above*) provides lists of local families with rooms to let; the rates ($5–$15 per night) often include laundry service and meals. Oaxaca's Spanish-language schools (*see* Schools, *above*) can also arrange family stays for their students.

SOUTH OF THE ZOCALO

➤ UNDER $15 • **Hotel El Palmar.** The simple, clean rooms here are $8.50 for a single and $10 for a double ($13.50 and $15, respectively, with private bath). Rooms facing the street are brighter but noisier than those in the interior. Be sure to shower in the morning, because the hot water is shut off in the afternoons. *J. P. García 507, btw Aldama and Mina, tel. 951/6–43–35. 30 rooms, 8 with bath. Luggage storage.*

➤ UNDER $20 • **Hotel Pasaje.** A courtyard with blooming tropical foliage, festive tiles, and a gregarious green parrot make the Pasaje a favorite among budget travelers. The clean, comfy rooms have desks and private baths with hot showers. Doubles are $15, singles $12. *Mina 302, tel. 951/6–42–13. ½ block west of 20 de Noviembre market, btw J. P. García and 20 de Noviembre. 18 rooms, all with bath. Luggage storage. No check-in 2 AM–6 AM.*

Hotel Vallarta. The gracious owner of the Vallarta is very proud of her clean and well-kept hotel. The freshly painted rooms are plain but blessed with amenities: private bathrooms, purified water, towels, soap, and desks. Doubles with one bed cost $18, with two beds $23. Singles fetch $14. *Díaz Ordaz 309, tel. 951/6–49–67. 3 blocks SE of zócalo, btw Trujano and Las Casas. 30 rooms, all with bath. Luggage storage.*

Hotel Yagul. In the heart of the bustling market district, the Yagul offers quiet rooms that open onto a spacious courtyard. Singles go for $14, doubles for $17, and all have baths with hot water. You're welcome to use the kitchen to fix your own meals, and drivers can pull their cars into the courtyard and park them for free. *Mina 103, at Bustamante, 3 blocks south of zócalo, tel. 951/6–27–50. 30 rooms. Luggage storage.*

NORTH OF THE ZOCALO

➤ UNDER $15 • **Hotel Pombo.** This sprawling hotel with peeling paint and cracked mirrors is full of character, close to the zócalo, and a great place to meet Oaxacan university students. As added bonuses, you're right next door to the best cappuccino in town at Morgan's (*see* Food, *below*), and you get to light a fire in your water heater before you take a shower. Ask at the desk for a small roll of newspaper and wood chips. Be careful. A double room costs $12, with private bath $17. Singles without bath are the cheapest in town at $5; with bath they jump to $12. *Morelos 601, tel. 951/6–26–73. 30 rooms, 25 with bath. Luggage storage. Reservations advised for July and Dec.*

➤ UNDER $20 • **Hostal del Centro.** The large, carpeted rooms and a super-clean communal bathroom with 24-hour hot water make this place a bargain at $12 a single, $17 a double. The friendly management will let you use the small kitchen to fix yourself a cup of hot tea, which you can sip in the quiet, plant-filled courtyard. Ask for Room 7, which has direct access to the rooftop patio. *Matamoros 206, btw Porfirio Díaz and García Vigil, tel. 951/6–84–16. 7 rooms, none with bath. Luggage storage. AE, V.*

➤ UNDER $30 • **Las Golondrinas.** "The Swallows" offers quiet, clean, tastefully decorated rooms, and a number of patios overflowing with roses and tropical flowers. Sun worshippers are welcome on the roof. Doubles cost $29, singles $22. A triple with a tiny living room is a great deal at $33. *Tinoco y Palacios 411, 5 blocks north of zócalo, tel. 951/4–21–26. 27 rooms, all with bath. Laundry, luggage storage.*

Hotel Francia. The Francia is where writer D.H. Lawrence stayed during his 1925 visit to Oaxaca. Mexico's colonial past is recalled in the dramatic rooms of the old wing, with high ceilings and tiled floors. The past is lost in the new wing, where rooms have modern furniture and bigger bathrooms. Ask to see a few before you choose. Doubles cost $26, singles $19. *20 de Noviembre 212, tel. 951/6–48–11. 1 block west of zócalo, btw Hidalgo and Trujano. 45 rooms, all with bath. Luggage storage, wheelchair access. MC, V.*

Hotel Juárez. This hotel presents stiff competition for the Francia, its more famous next-door neighbor. A cobalt blue-tiled archway opens onto a sunny, palm-lined courtyard. The rooms are spacious, and each has a clean private bath. Doubles cost $25, singles $19. *20 de Noviembre 208, tel. 951/6–46–16. 32 rooms, all with bath. Restaurant, laundry.*

FOOD

Oaxacan cuisine is spicy, delicious, and famed throughout Mexico (*see box, below*). The 20 de Noviembre, Benito Juárez, and Central de Abastos markets offer a gastronomical extravaganza where you can sample some of the many local specialties without breaking the bank.

Restaurants on the south side of the zócalo are generally cheap and cater to a mostly Mexican crowd. More gringo-oriented fare can be had on Avenidas Morelos and Independencia, just north of the zócalo. For *donas de chocolate* (chocolate doughnuts) and other artery-clogging treats, head to **Bamby Panadería** (cnr of Morelos and García Vigil). If that doesn't fill you up, you can try a delicious sandwich ($1–$2) from the adjoining **Tortas Bamby** for dessert.

SOUTH OF THE ZOCALO

➤ UNDER $5 • **Cafe Alex.** This popular restaurant near the second-class bus station offers a variety of Oaxacan specialties. Share the back patio with cages full of chattering parrots and parakeets as you sample the hearty chicken mole ($4). Their breakfast specials are also a good deal, with juice and granola for less than $2. *Díaz Ordaz 218, at Trujano, tel. 951/4–07–15. Open Mon.–Sat. 7 AM–9 PM, Sun. 7–noon.*

Cafetería Tayu. The tranquil green patio of this restaurant is just steps away from the action on 20 de Noviembre. Kids frolic in the play fort out back, and they serve a filling *comida corrida* (pre-prepared lunch special) for only $2.50. This place is very popular, so be prepared to share your table with Oaxacans who know a good value when they see it. *20 de Noviembre 416, tel. 951/6–53–63. Open Mon.–Sat. 7–7.*

Restaurant Montebello. A meal here will be accompanied by loud ranchera music and a view of the action on Calle Trujano. You can chow down a huge breakfast, including *bistec* (steak), bread, beans, salsa, tortillas, and a huge glass of fresh-squeezed O.J. for less than $3. Their comida corrida is about the same price. *Trujano 305A, 3 blocks SW of zócalo, tel. 951/6–50–47. Open daily 7 AM–11 PM.*

NORTH OF THE ZOCALO

➤ UNDER $5 • **Nutritortas Gigantes.** This hole-in-the-wall has a variety of sandwiches priced $2–$3. The ones with tangy chapulines (*see box, below*) are crunchy, yummy, and perfect for late-night munchies. *Nicolás Bravo 216, tel. 951/6–64–69. 4 blocks NW of zócalo. Open daily 9 AM–10 PM.*

Quickly. This restaurant challenges the heartiest appetites with *chilaquiles* (tortilla strips doused with salsa and sour cream), a big portion of which costs less than $3. Also worthwhile

Eat This!

Modern Oaxacan food continues to be based on local ingredients and traditional recipes, elements of which predate the Spaniards' arrival. Oaxaca's three markets are the best places to sample any of the following regional specialties without paying tourist prices.

- *Chapulines are tangy fried grasshoppers prepared with chile and lime. They go down a bit easier if you pull off the legs first. According to local folklore, one taste will charm you into never leaving Oaxaca.*
- *Jicuatote is a wiggly, sweet, white gelatin made with milk, cloves, cinnamon, and cornmeal. It's served in tubs and usually colored red on top.*
- *Mole Oaxaqueño is Oaxaca's dark, rich version of the famed sauce made with fruit, chiles, nuts, and chocolate. Tamales oaxaqueños, filled with mole and chicken, are sold in the markets.*
- *Tejate is a beverage made from the flowers and roasted seeds of the cacao tree, corn, coconut milk, sugar, water, and spices. Look for huge bowls of white paste and watery, brown liquid.*
- *Tlayudas are huge, flat tortillas spread with refried beans and topped with salsa, fresh vegetables, and guacamole.*

is the dubiously named but tasty "gringa" hamburger ($3.50), loaded with ham, bacon, cheese, and tomato. Tlayudas (*see box, above*), at $4 apiece, are popular with locals. *Alcalá 100B, ½ block NW of zócalo, tel. 951/4–70–76. Open weekdays 8 AM–11PM, weekends 2–11.*

Señor de la Salud. The "Lord of Health" lives up to its title, offering nutritious vegetarian and meat dishes in an open, clean setting. Try their veggie chilaquiles with beans, tortillas, juice, and coffee for $3.50. *Juárez 201D, btw Morelos and Murgia, no phone. Open Mon.–Sat. 8–8.*

Super Torta Fiesta. Despite the name, this place has a classy atmosphere and wide variety of typical Oaxacan dishes. Try their *pozole* (corn soup) for $2 or *tasajo* (marinated beef) at $5. They offer excellent *cenas económicas* (cheap dinner combinations) for only $2–3. *Porfirio Díaz 208, btw Morelos and Matamoros, no phone. Open daily 7 AM–10 PM.*

➤ UNDER $10 • **Flor de Loto-Plaza Gourmet.** Not to be mistaken for the adjoining vegetarian Flor de Loto-Sureste (whose owner "borrowed" the original's name and reputation), this groovy little lavender eatery offers a tantalizing array of vegetarian and meat dishes. The emphasis here is on health—the amiable owner personally shops for the fresh fruit, vegetables, fish, and meats every day. Breakfast specials cost $4, the comida corrida $5. *Morelos 509, tel. 951/6–91–46. Next to Museo Rufino Tamayo. Open Wed.–Mon. 8 AM–10 PM, Tues. 8–6.*

CAFES The tourist scene in Oaxaca revolves around the cafés on the zócalo, but those wrought-iron tables crowded with gringos are far from the last word on the city's café culture. The following are a couple of out-of-the-way spots recommended by Oaxacans.

Antojitos de los Olmos. It's easy to miss their tiny black sign on touristy Alcalá, but pass through the small doorway and you're welcomed into the patio of the private home of Antonia Olmos Guebarra. She serves the best *atole* (a sweet, corn-based drink, similar to hot chocolate) in town to her festive crowd of loyal customers for only 60¢. Delicious tamales, tacos, and tostadas are cooked up before your eyes for $1. *Alcalá 301, tel. 951/6–44–10. Open Mon.–Sat. 7:30 PM–11:30 PM.*

Café Hipótesis. The Hypothesis features shelves and shelves of eclectic literature and, occasionally, live guitar music. So pick an interesting title, sit back, and work on a *yarda* (a tall glass, literally a yard) of beer or sangría for less than $3. They also offer quesadillas, tostadas, and excellent sandwiches on whole-wheat bread. *Morelos 511, no phone. Open Mon.–Sat. 1 PM–2 AM.*

Cafetería Morgan. Their bulletin board claims they serve "the best coffee for 4000 miles," and it may well be true. Morgan's breakfasts ($2–$3) include a cup of their famous cappuccino. *Morelos 601B, no phone. Open Mon.–Sat. 7:30–1 and 5:30–10.*

WORTH SEEING

Oaxaca city has a wealth of Roman Catholic churches, convents, and monasteries dating from the colonial period, only a few of which are mentioned below. Some have been converted into government offices and museums, but many remain active places of worship, where rituals have changed little in the past century. The city offers much more than colonial edifices, however, and the life of the city is in the zócalo, markets, and busy southside streets, where old men gossip on street corners, and Zapotec vendors hawk their handmade crafts.

BASILICA DE LA SOLEDAD This 17th-century baroque church, which took 60 years to build, holds a black-draped figure of the Virgen de la Soledad (Our Lady of Solitude) to which believers ascribe healing powers. On December 18, the **Danza de la Pluma** (Feather Dance; *see* Festivals, *below*), a dramatization of the Conquest, is performed here as part of the festival in her honor. Behind the church is the **Museo Religioso de la Soledad** (tel. 951/6–75–66), which displays art dedicated to the Virgin. *Independencia 107, at Galeana. Admission: 35¢. Museum open Mon.–Sat. 9–2 and 4–7, Sun. 11 AM–2 PM.*

CATEDRAL DE OAXACA Construction of the cathedral began in 1553, but was interrupted by earthquakes, and the church wasn't completed for another 200 years. The beautifully carved baroque facade depicts the ascension of the Virgin, and the huge wooden clock on the south wall chimes faithfully every 15 minutes. The centerpiece of the cathedral is a bronze altar imported from Italy. The cathedral also houses the Señor del Rayo, a giant gold and silver crucifix which, legend has it, miraculously survived a fire begun by a bolt of lightning. The charms hanging behind the cross are offerings from the faithful. *On the zócalo, facing the Alameda. Masses held daily and in English Sun. at 10 AM.*

CERRO DEL FORTIN The hill dominating the city has been a site of festivals and celebrations since pre-Columbian times. A long flight of stairs leads up to the Cerro from Avenida Crespo, about 2 kilometers uphill northwest of the zócalo. Crowning the Cerro is an open-air auditorium used for the festivities of **La Guelaguetza** (*see* Festivals, *below*), as well as a planetarium and an observatory, both of which are unfortunately accessible only for large groups by special appointment. The lookout point has an awesome view of the city and a huge bronze statue of Benito Juárez, captioned by his famous phrase: "El respecto al derecho ajeno es la paz" (Respect for the rights of others is peace). *Walk due north from the zócalo along Díaz Ordaz.*

IGLESIA Y EX-CONVENTO DE SANTO DOMINGO Santo Domingo, built in the 16th century, is one of Oaxaca city's most ornate houses of worship. The rose-colored exterior is striking but pales in comparison to what is found inside. The ceiling of the entryway is decorated with an amazing tree sprouting depictions of church benefactors, and busts of saints and martyrs observe you from every corner and archway.

The adjacent monastery, built in 1619, now houses the **Museo Regional de Oaxaca,** where Mixtec artifacts from the tombs of Monte Albán are artfully displayed, including skulls encrusted with jade and turquoise, gold earrings and ornaments, and elaborately carved jaguar bones. The pieces are exquisite, and the setting is equally impressive. *Alcalá at Gurrión, 5 blocks NW of zócalo. Admission: $4.50, free Sun. Open Tues.–Fri. 10–5:30, weekends 10–5.*

INSTITUTO DE ARTES GRAFICAS This splendid, little-known museum, library, and art gallery features rotating exhibitions with an emphasis on graphic art prints. *Alcalá 507, near Santo Domingo, tel. 951/6–69–80. Donations encouraged. Open Wed.–Mon. 10:30–8.*

MARKETS With their colorful mix of handicrafts, unfamiliar fruits and vegetables, and thick air filled with sweet, ripe, rank, stomach-churning, and tantalizing smells, the markets of Oaxaca present an adventure for all the senses. The **Central de Abastos** market, across from the second-class bus station, is a labyrinth of hanging bags, shoes, hammocks, fruit, witchcraft stores, and gory meat stands. The **Benito Juárez** market, hemmed by 20 de Noviembre, Las Casas, Cabrera, and Aldama, offers a smaller selection of the same just one block from the zócalo, and is ringed by *artesanía* (crafts) vendors. The **20 de Noviembre** market, directly across Aldama from the Mercado Benito Juárez, contains mostly food and cheap *comedores* (sit-down food stands).

MUSEO CASA DE BENITO JUAREZ Benito Juárez (1806–1872), born in the town of Guelatao, remains the only Mexican president to have been of pure indigenous (Zapotec) descent. Skip the three-hour bus ride to Guelatao and pay homage to him at the house where, for two years, Juárez worked for a Franciscan friar who taught him Spanish. The study, dining room, kitchen, and bedroom are open for viewing. Also on display are some personal letters, documents, and Juárez's death mask. *García Vigil 609, tel. 951/6–18–60. Admission: $2.50, free Sun. Open Tues.–Sun. 10–7.*

MUSEO DE ARTE CONTEMPORANEO DE OAXACA This excellent museum is dedicated to contemporary Oaxacan artists, both mestizo and indigenous, but occasionally features big-name European exhibits as well. The outdoor café in back serves respectable coffee and cool juices in a tropical garden setting, and free films are shown on Friday, Saturday, and Sunday nights. *Alcalá 202, tel. 951/6–84–99. Donations encouraged. Open Wed.–Mon. 10:30–8.*

MUSEO RUFINO TAMAYO Pre-Columbian artifacts from all over Mexico are displayed in this beautifully restored colonial mansion. The collection belonged to Rufino Tamayo, one of Mexico's premier artists, who amassed it over 20 years and then donated it to the people of his native Oaxaca. Pieces are arranged chronologically to give an idea of the artistic development that preceded the Conquest. *Morelos 503, tel. 951/6–47–50. Admission: $3. Open Mon. and Wed.–Sat. 10–2 and 4–7, Sun. 10–3.*

CHEAP THRILLS

The **Casa de la Cultura Oaxaqueña** (González Ortega 403, tel. 951/6–18–29) features free films, dance, theater, art, and musical events. You can stop by weekdays between 9 AM and 9 PM or Saturday early in the day to find out what's going on. The **Teatro Juan Rulfo** (Independencia, at Mier y Terán) has nightly musical performances as well as frequent cultural events, most of which are free. Wednesdays there is live music, usually in the nueva canción style, and Fridays are devoted to issues affecting women. Another freebie is a look at the beautiful murals by Arturo García Bustos depicting Oaxaca's pre-Columbian and revolutionary history in the **Palacio del Gobierno** on the south side of the zócalo, where the guards will happily let you in to take a peek.

FESTIVALS

La Guelaguetza. The most famous Oaxacan festival, also called *Lunes del Cerro* (Monday of the Hill), is celebrated on the two Mondays following the Fiesta de la Virgen del Carmen (July 16). Thousands of people from all over Mexico gather to perform folk dances and exchange gifts. A pineapple dance is performed by Papaloapan women and the Feather Dance is enacted by Zapotec men. Dances are in the amphitheater atop the Cerro del Fortín. The preceding week is filled with music, parades, and cultural events. A highpoint is the dramatic portrayal of the martyrdom of the Zapotec princess Donaji, who was decapitated by the Mixtecs for spurning her Mixtec lover in favor of her people. Legend has it that when her corpse was found, lilies of the valley were growing from her severed head. Donaji remains an important symbol of regional pride, and the image of her head now graces the Oaxacan state seal.

Christmas. Festivities include a two-day feast commemorating the Virgen de La Soledad (December 16–18), nightly *posadas* (reenactments of Joseph and Mary's search for lodging), and the ringing of church bells on Christmas Eve. On December 23, also known as *La Noche de los Rabanos* (The Night of the Radishes), radishes carved into elaborate shapes are displayed in booths around the zócalo.

SHOPPING

Oaxacan artisans are famous for the quality and inventiveness of their work. If you only want to browse, explore the expensive boutiques along the Andador Turístico and the shops north of the zócalo. Pesos are better spent in nearby villages (*see* Near Oaxaca, *below*) and at the Central de Abastos Saturday market, said to be the largest indigenous-run market in Mexico. Regional crafts include black and green ceramics, gold filigree jewelry, *alebrijes* (brightly painted wooden animals), *rebozos* (shawls), engraved knives, and *huipiles* (intricately embroidered tunics).

AFTER DARK

At the heart of Oaxaca's nightlife is the zócalo, which bustles with action long into the night. At dusk you can check out the passersby, look for love, or just sip an icy Corona with lime. After the sun sets, head for a café (*see* Food, *above*) for some live music and conversation, take in a film, or hit the disco scene.

CINEMA A number of movie theaters often show subtitled or dubbed American movies. Right off the zócalo is the **Plaza Alameda** (Independencia, at 20 de Noviembre, tel. 951/6–11–99), where admission is $3.50. **The Museo de Arte Contemporaneo** (*see* Worth Seeing, *above*) offers free films, usually with political or cultural themes, on Friday, Saturday, and Sunday nights.

DANCING Candela (Ignacio Allende 211, tel. 951/6–79–3) heats up with live salsa and Caribbean rhythms Monday through Saturday 9:30 PM–1:30 AM. A shot of mezcal is less than $2, and gay couples, rhythmically impaired gringos, and even lone women feel at ease jumping about on the dance floor. Depending on the band, the cover charge fluctuates between $3.50 and $5.

If you prefer to swim through smoke and flashing disco lights to the sound of technopop, go to **Eclipse** (Porfirio Díaz 219, tel. 951/6–42–36). It's as packed with young people as it is with attitude, and is open Thursday through Saturday 10 PM–2:30 AM and Sunday 7 PM–midnight. There's a hefty cover charge for men, about $10 Thursday through Saturday; women pay the same on weekends but get a break Thursday nights. Sundays, everybody pays $3.50.

How do you tell a good mez-cal? Shake it. If bubbles form, it's good; if not, it's been watered down.

MUSIC Sunday, Tuesday, and Thursday nights, the town band plays in the zócalo's central gazebo. On Fridays and Saturdays, mariachi bands roam the zócalo serenading anyone who'll buy a song. Some of Oaxaca's cafés also feature live music (*see* Food, *above*). **Los Tres Patios** is the place to chill out and sip a mixed drink while listening to live jazz. The cover is usually about $3.50. *Cosijopi 208, btw Porfirio Díaz and García Vigil, no phone. Open Mon.–Sat. 8 PM–2 AM.*

Near Oaxaca

Within 50 kilometers of Oaxaca are a number of important pre-Columbian ruins, most notably Monte Albán and Mitla, and indigenous communities that maintain distinct languages, customs, folklore, as well as ties to the sacred ruins. (When archaeologists discovered the tombs in Zaachila, townspeople insisted on being involved in the excavations because, after all, it was the burial site of their ancestors.) Visiting the ruins and the indigenous communities on their market days is an unobtrusive way to gain an appreciation of the culture of this region.

The Valles de Oaxaca are dot-ted with small towns, whose inhabitants have lived for gen-erations largely from a single craft, such as pottery, carving, or weaving. Oaxacan artisans have earned a national and, in some cases, international reputation.

MONTE ALBAN

High on an artificially leveled plateau overlooking Oaxaca city lie the ruins of the greatest ceremonial center in the Valley of Oaxaca, Monte Albán. The Zapotecs began building Monte Albán as early as 500 BC, which at the height of its power had a population of over 40,000—more than the largest city in Europe at the time. The indigenous name for the city is not known—it had been abandoned more than 500 years before the Spaniards arrived. Monte Albán (White Mountain) is the name they gave it.

The site covers an area of more than 40 square kilometers, but the most impressive structures are in the **Gran Plaza.** At each end of the plaza are ceremonial platforms aligned along a north–south axis. The acoustics here are such that sound carries clearly from one platform to the other. The square openings bored into the pyramids and platforms were made by archaeologists.

Clockwise from the monument to Dr. Alfonso Caso, the Mexican archaeologist who began excavations in 1930, you find first the **Juego de Pelota** (ball court). Its capital *I* shape and sloping side walls are distinctive to the region.

Next is an open-air structure known as **Edificio P.** The columns once supported a roof, but no walls were ever built. An inner stairway connects one corner to a tunnel whose mouth is at the central altar. Zapotec priests may have used the tunnel to appear, as if magically, during ceremonies. Next door is **El Palacio,** apparently the residence of a high-status Zapotec. Its patio is circled by 13 chambers, some with sleeping ledges. A tomb was found in the middle of the patio. Not much of the **Plataforma Sur** (South Platform), which looms above the palace has been excavated, so little is known about its construction.

Edificio L, the oldest building at the site and more commonly known as the **Edificio de los Danzantes** (Building of the Dancers), is covered with carvings of human figures. Originally the fig-

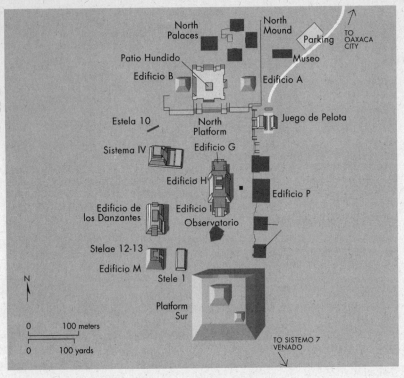

North
Palaces

North
Mound

Parking

TO
OAXACA
CITY

Patio Hundido

Museo

Edificio B

Edificio A

Estela 10

North
Platform

Juego de Pelota

Sistema IV

Edificio G

Edificio H

Edificio de
los Danzantes

Edificio I

Edificio P

Observatorio

Stelae 12-13

Edificio M

Stele 1

N

Platform
Sur

0   100 meters

0   100 yards

TO SISTEMO 7
VENADO

ures were thought to represent swimmers, acrobats, or dancers (hence the name); the current theory is that the building once served as a medical school and the carvings show various medical conditions. Others say that the figures represent tortured captives—though the figure of a woman in childbirth seems to rebuff this claim.

In **Sistema IV,** the next building over, archaeologists constructed a tunnel that lets you view an enormous *talud* (altar) of large stones. Some are carved with *danzante*-style figures, indicating that later inhabitants may have stripped older buildings and recycled the stones.

The massive **Plataforma Norte** (North Platform) completes the circle. A path behind the platform leads to the entrances of a number of tombs. **Tomb 4** contains some of the site's best-preserved carvings and murals.

The **Observatorio** and **Edificios 1, H** and **G** are in the middle of the plaza. The arrowhead-shaped structure close to Plataforma Sur is the Observatory. Unlike the other buildings, it's aligned with the pathway of the sun, not along the cardinal points. Its danzante figures are often upside down or placed on an incline, suggesting that they may have been recycled from older buildings.

On the descent from the ruins to the visitor center are various paths leading to the remains of **Tumbas** (tombs) **7, 72,** and **105.** These tombs were not built by the Zapotecs, who originally inhabited Monte Albán, but by their conquerors, the Mixtecs, who used the city as a necropolis. Tomb 7 contained one of the richest art finds in the world. Its treasures are now on display in the **Museo Regional de Oaxaca** (*see* Worth Seeing, *above*).

COMING AND GOING Buses from **Hotel Mesón del Angel** (Mina 518, tel. 951/6–53-27) in Oaxaca city offer $3 tourist service to Monte Albán. Departure times vary according to the season but are typically every hour beginning at 9:30 AM. The trip takes 20 minutes. If you don't mind walking, you can catch a bus to Colonia Monte Albán (the town) from the second-class bus station for 40¢. From the colonia, it's a 15–20-minute steep but beautiful walk to the ruins. The ruins are open from 8 AM to 5 PM daily, and no matter how you get there, you'll have to pay the $4.50 entrance fee (except on Sundays and holidays, when it's free).

MITLA AND THE EASTERN VALLEY

While most visitors head in this direction just to see the ruins of Mitla, there are a number of worthwhile stops on the way, including less well-known archaeological sites, and little towns where traditional crafts are still produced (if not for the traditional clientele). If you would like to make more than a day trip out of Oaxaca city to explore this region, consider staying in one of the newly built **YU'U** cabanas set up by the tourist office in Teotitlán del Valle, Tlacolula, Santa Ana del Valle, or Hierve el Agua. They offer comfortable dorm-style beds, kitchens, and super-clean bathrooms for just $10 per night. Ask at the tourist office in Oaxaca city for details on renting cabanas in the different towns before you head out.

THE ROAD TO MITLA All buses for Mitla (*see below*) pass the places listed below—just let the driver know where you'd like to get off, and sit close to him so he doesn't forget you. The first stop out of Oaxaca city on your way east is the 2,000-year-old **El Tule** tree in tiny Santa María del Tule. El Tule is supposedly the largest cypress in the world; it is 51 meters high and 40 meters of spectacularly gnarled trunk in circumference. Further on, you'll come to the crossroads for the partially unearthed Zapotec ruins of **Dainzú.** From there, walk about 20 minutes to the site, whose main attraction is its many carved bas-reliefs, some depicting ball players in full costume. You'll have to pay $2.50 unless you go on a Sunday or holiday, when admission is free.

After Dainzú, you can hop off the bus at the crossroads for **Teotitlán del Valle,** or, shortly thereafter, the town of **Tlacolula,** which is also the crossroads for **Santa Ana del Valle.** Teotitlán is a small village whose inhabitants specialize in woven serapes, some still colored with homemade dyes from the dried carcasses of insects and the ink of sea snails. Monday is market day. Tlacolula provides yet another incentive to take this trip on a Sunday (when admission to all the ruins is free), in the form of its lively Sunday market. Santa Ana (also called "Shan-dany," Zapotec for "at the foot of the mountains") is known for its Tuesday market as well as the locally funded **Zapotec museum.** The museum holds a modest and carefully guarded collection of historical and archaeological pieces, including a uniform that supposedly belonged to Hernán Cortés. The church across the street also has a wildly painted interior worth a peek. You'll need to walk about 20 minutes or catch a colectivo from the crossroads to get to Teotitlán; it's also about a 20-minute walk from Tlacolula up the road to Santa Ana.

Somewhat more spectacular than Dainzú are the ruins at **Yagul,** the bus stop for which is about halfway between Tlacolula and Mitla. Yagul is believed to have been a residential area for high-status Zapotecs, such as priests and aristocrats. It features a grand **Palacio de 6 Patios** (Palace of 6 Patios) and a completely restored **Juego de Pelota.** A scramble up the path to the right of the entrance will give you a panoramic view of the ruins, tomb, and fortifications. As at Dainzú, admission to Yagul is $2.50 unless you go on a Sunday or holiday, when it's free.

MITLA The name Mitla (Mictlán) is Nahuatl for "place of the dead" or "place of rest." Mitla's Zapotec name is *Leobaa.* Here, 34 kilometers southeast of Oaxaca, the Zapotecs established a massive burial ground in 100 BC. The Mixtecs conquered the site in 1250 and it remained important up to the time of the Spanish invasion.

Of the five groups of structures at Mitla, only two have been fully excavated and restored. The **Conjunto de Columnas** (Group of Columns) was part of an official's private home. Inside the north structure is a room covered from stone floor to wooden ceiling with three distinct patterns of *greca* (mosaic), unique to Mitla, composed of thousands of bits of well-cut

Many place names in Southern Mexico and Guatemala are Nahua, some because they were once part of the expanding Aztec empire, others because the conquistadors traveled with Aztec guides who gave place names in their own language.

327

stone set in clay to form geometric patterns. These particular grecas represent air, earth, and water and at one time were coated with stucco and painted red. Some believe that this room was a library, and that the patterned greca hold coded knowledge. Also in this group you'll see what is popularly referred to as the **Columna de la Vida.** According to legend, you can tell how many years you've got left by embracing the column and calculating the space left between your outstretched hands. Presumably, the longer your arms the sooner you can expect to die. The site, open daily 8–5, is directly in front of the Iglesia San Pablo, far from the center of town. Admission is $3.65, but free on Sunday and holidays.

Downhill from the ruins, beyond the mezcal stands and shawl vendors, close to the center of the modern village of Mitla, the **Frissell Museum** exhibits beautiful pottery and other pieces recovered in Mitla and nearby sites. It's open 8–5 every day except Saturday, and donations are encouraged.

COMING AND GOING Buses leave Oaxaca for Mitla every 20 minutes from the second-class bus station and every hour from **Hotel Mesón del Angel** (Mina 518, tel. 951/6–53–27). The ride to Mitla costs about $1 and takes just over an hour.

SOUTH OF OAXACA

In the valley to the south of Oaxaca city you can meet the personalities behind the green-and-black pottery, embroidered blouses, and painted wooden beasties that fill the city's open markets. All the villages listed below are within a 20-minute to half-day second-class bus ride from Oaxaca city. Arrazola, Cuilapan, and Zaachila all lie on one road, and together make an enjoyable day trip. San Bartolo Coyotepec, San Martín Tilcajete, and Ocotlán de Morelos together can also be visited in a day. Special markets are held on Thursday in Zaachila and on Friday in Ocotlán de Morelos.

ARRAZOLA Five kilometers off the main road between Oaxaca city and Zaachila is the small village of Arrazola, internationally famous for its wood carvers who create fantastic animals, called alebrijes, out of copal wood (also valued for its resin). The town's best-known artisan is Don Manuel Jiménez, who delights in chatting with anyone interested in his work. His son and grandson are carrying on the Jiménez tradition; all of their hand-crafted creatures bear the tripartite family signature. To get here, take a bus bound for Zaachila and get off at the crossroads, then wait for a colectivo to take you to the town. The whole trip takes about 30 minutes.

CUILAPAN DE GUERRERO This village, 10 kilometers south of Oaxaca city, is home to the 16th-century Dominican monastery **ex-Convento de Santiago Apóstol,** distinctive for its huge, open, Renaissance-style chapel. Inside, there are tiny monks' quarters, later used as jail cells. Vincente Guerrero, a liberal general in the struggle for Mexican independence from Spain, who was also made president for a brief period, was held and executed here by his political enemies in 1830. The chapel holds a grave believed to be that of the legendary Zapotec princess Donaji. The monastery is open daily 8–5 and charges an entry fee of $2.50, except on Sundays and holidays, when it's free. To reach Cuilapan de Guerrero from Oaxaca, hop on any bus headed for Zaachila.

Hierve el Agua

After you've seen Mitla, consider trekking out to Hierve el Agua, a group of spectacular, bubbling, turquoise, mineral springs (their name translates as "the water boils"). You can clamber around the cliffs, swim, and camp out or stay in the newly built YU'U cabanas (see above). If you're driving, follow the road to San Lorenzo and keep your eyes peeled for signs, but be advised that it's a rough road and it's easy to get lost. The best bet for those without their own vehicles is to get a group together and hire a taxi from Mitla, being sure to set round-trip fare (about $35) before leaving.

ZAACHILA Eighteen kilometers south of Oaxaca, Zaachila is the site of an archaeological find that was never looted, thanks to the townspeople's devotion to their ancestors' graves. One tomb is empty, but all the artifacts it once held are now in museums. The other tomb has tiny grecas similar to those found in Mitla (*see above*), and depictions of two figures. One figure, wearing a long alligator mask, represents the god of death. The other carries a bag of *copal* (resin used for ceremonial incense), suggesting that it represents a priest. The ruins are open 8–5 daily. Admission is $2.50, except Sundays and holidays, which, as always, are free.

More fun than the ruins is Zaachila's Thursday market, which feels a bit like a country fair, with dozens of bulls, rabbits, chickens, sheep, and goats being hauled from one prospective buyer to another. The bus ride to Zaachila from the second-class bus station in Oaxaca city takes about half an hour and costs 35¢.

SAN BARTOLO COYOTEPEC This village, 15 kilometers from Oaxaca city, is known for its black pottery. The clay here takes on a metallic sheen when polished, as a local woman named Doña Rosita discovered in 1934. Rosita is gone, but you can still visit the workshop run by her son to see how the pottery is made, or buy some if you wish. To reach the village, take a bus for Ejutla de Crespo and ask the driver to let you off in San Bartolo. It'll cost you about 50¢ for the 20-minute ride.

SAN MARTIN TILCAJETE In this tiny town, you will be invited into private homes to see fantastical painted animals, the sale of which supports entire families. It is well worth the half-hour bus ride and 20-minute walk it takes to find it. You will be warmly welcomed as you visit each house to admire different versions of the craft, and it's best to buy here, where you can be sure the money goes straight to the artist. To get to this hospitable town, ask the driver of any bus headed to Ejutla de Crespo to drop you off at the road leading to San Martín Tilcajete, and walk or hitch the rest of the way.

OCOTLAN DE MORELOS This wonderful little town is home to the famous Aguilar Sisters: Guillermina, Josefina, Irene, and Concepción, all of whom are skilled pottery painters. You can visit their adjoining homes and workshops on Continuación de Morelos, near the entrance of town. The best day to come is Friday, when Ocotlán holds its small market. It takes about an hour on the Ejutla del Crespo bus to get here, and costs $1.

Oaxaca Coast

The Sierra Madre del Sur mountain range looms over almost 240 miles of sunny Oaxacan coastline, including many, many deserted beaches. Because so much of this region is undeveloped, most visitors do their frolicking around three main tourist destinations: Puerto Escondido, Puerto Angel, and the Bahías de Huatulco.

Sporting opportunities abound here. In Puerto Escondido, surfers from around the world congregate to ride the Mexican Pipeline at Playa Zicatela. Snorkelers head out to the calmer waters nearby at Puerto Angelito and Carrizalillo, or to Estacahuite near Puerto Angel. Scuba enthusiasts make their way to Roca Blanca off the shores of Cacoletepec. Most travelers, however, come here to kick back and enjoy the ocean breezes. Zipolite beach, near Puerto Angel, is famous for the hippies who come to commune with nature and each other, get sunburned (and otherwise baked) on the beach, and do very little else. Santa Cruz Huatulco is the Mexican government's latest target for development; fortunately, the planned megaresort is still in its infancy, and nearby beaches remain undisturbed campers' paradises.

Puerto Escondido

The touristy part of Puerto Escondido actually consists of two separate but coexisting resorts: one for the surfers drawn to the area by the famous Mexican Pipeline, the other for Mexican families on vacation. High seasons for tourism are the summer and Christmas holidays. Puerto Escondido also plays host to two championship surfing contests, a local one in August, and an

You can eat for less than half the price of the restaurants on the Andador Turístico in the real downtown on the other side of the Carretera Costera.

international one in November. If you decide to visit during these months, be prepared for the *pachanga* (party) that ensues.

Puerto Escondido is much less flashy and pretentious than most of Mexico's other coastal hot spots. Out-of-towners come here to hang out, relax, surf, or play in the waves and do little else. The same cannot be said of the inhabitants of the "other" Escondido, which lies to the north away from the resort areas, on the other side of the Carretera Costera (the Coast Highway). This is where the locals live, and where you'll find the post and telegraph offices, the bus stations, and a typical Mexican town atmosphere with cheap food, busy streets, and friendly people.

BASICS

➤ CASAS DE CAMBIO • The only casa de cambio in town is on Pérez Gasga, near the hotel Rincón del Pacífico; it's open weekdays 9–2 and 5–8. **Bancomer** (Pérez Gasga s/n, tel. 958/2–03–37) changes cash and traveler's checks and is open weekdays 9 AM–1:30 PM.

➤ MEDICAL AID • Emergency medical care is available 24 hours a day at the **Centro de Salud** (Pérez Gasga 409) or the **Comisión Nacional de Emergencia** (Tlacochahuaya s/n, at Fracc. Bacocho). Dr. Luis Flores at the Centro de Salud speaks English.

➤ PHONES AND MAIL • You can make collect and cash calls at the **caseta de larga distancia** (long-distance telephone office) on Pérez Gasga by the Andador Revolución, a stairway connecting Pérez Gasga to the Carretera Costera. There are also public phones that accept credit cards in front of the pharmacy at the west end of Pérez Gasga. The **post office** (Calle 7 Norte, at Oaxaca, tel. 958/2–09–59) is a long, hard uphill walk on the inland side of the highway. They will hold mail sent to you at the following address for up to 10 days: Oficina de Correos, Puerto Escondido, Oaxaca, CP 71980, México. You can send or receive telegrams, money orders, and faxes at the **telegraph office** (tel. 958/2–09–57) next door.

➤ VISITOR INFORMATION • The Puerto Escondido **tourist office** is at least a half-hour walk from town, but they do provide maps, semi-useful information on local hotels, and an earful of warnings about theft. *Calle 5 Pte. s/n, at the highway, tel. 958/2–01–75. Walk west out of town toward the airport. Open weekdays 9–2 and 5–8, Sat. 9–1.*

COMING AND GOING
The town is split in two by the Carretera Costera. To the north is the untouristed part of town. The street that snakes south down the hill from the highway and then east along the coast is Pérez Gasga. Where it runs parallel to the beach and only pedestrian traffic is allowed, it is known as the **Andador Turístico** (tourist walkway). Many of the town's hotels and restaurants are here. **Zicatela**, the town's most famous surfing spot, lies to the east of the main beach area.

➤ BY BUS • The **Estrella del Valle-Oaxaca Pacífico** bus station is uphill from the beach, on the corner of Hidalgo and 16 de Septiembre, a good 15-minute walk from the beachfront. Destinations include Oaxaca city ($9.50, 7 hrs) at 8:30 AM and 8 PM; Pochutla ($2.50, 1½ hrs) every hour between 5:30 AM and 7:30 PM; and Acapulco ($9.50, 7 hrs) at 6 AM, 8 AM, 8 PM, and 11 PM. **Transportes Oaxaca-Istmo** and **Transportes Galeca/Lineas Unidas Del Sur** (both on Hidalgo, at 5 de Mayo) offer frequent service to Pochutla, Oaxaca city, Salina Cruz, and Acapulco. You can also flag down a bus for Pochutla along the highway—there's one every 15–20 minutes.

➤ HITCHING • You can hitch most anywhere along the highway, but it's a good idea to stay close to the intersection with Pérez Gasga, where you can always hail a microbus in case no one offers you a ride.

➤ BY PLANE • The national airport is at Kilometer 3 of the Carretera Costera. **Mexicana** (tel. 958/2–04–22) flies daily to Mexico City ($100 one way), while **Aeromorelos** and **Aerovías Oaxaqueñas** fly small planes daily to and from Oaxaca City ($85 one-way). **Transportes Aeropuerto y Turístico** (tel. 958/2–01–23) will take you into town for about $2 in a Volkswagen van; look for their signs at the airport.

WHERE TO SLEEP Puerto Escondido's hotels and cabana villages charge up to three times their normal prices (listed here) during the summer, surfing championships, and around the Christmas and New Year holidays. The cabanas on Zicatela are fairly simple and cater to a surfcat's lifestyle, with an emphasis on convenience (i.e., proximity to the water) rather than comfort. Most supply essentials such as sunscreen, leashes, and board wax.

➢ UNDER $10 • **Neptuno.** Forty quite run-down cabanas are scattered over a fairly large area by Playa Marinero; each has a cement floor, a bare bed (no sheets), and a stool. Electric lights are provided at night; mosquito netting is not. Communal bathrooms are none too clean, and the toilets don't always have seats or paper. A cabana costs $6.50 for one or two people. You can also camp here for a negotiable $3.50–$6.50 per tent. *Pérez Gasga s/n, tel. 958/2-03-27.*

➢ UNDER $15 • **Cabañas Aldea Marinero.** Not to be confused with Cabañas Marinero across the way, this small cluster of huts just off Playa Marinero surrounds a small garden. A wall of graffiti attests to the satisfaction of former guests. The brick-floored cabanas have cots, electric lights and outlets, and mosquito netting and rent for $10 double occupancy, $6.50 single. The semi-clean *sanitarios* (bathrooms) are communal. Hammocks and fans can both be rented for $2 per night. *Calle del Morro s/n, no phone.*

Rockaway Surfer Village. A wall encloses this well-kept, inexpensive, beachfront cabana village, where guests lounge and drink beer on the porch of the surf shop. They also have a clean freshwater pool. All cabanas have ceiling fans, mosquito netting, and private bathrooms and cost $12 a night. *Playa Zicatela, just past Bruno's, tel. 958/2-06-68. 12 cabanas, all with bath.*

➢ UNDER $20 • **Bungalows/Cabañas Acuario.** The cabanas here have refrigerators and simple furnishings; some of the larger ones (called bungalows) have full kitchens. The friendly, laid-back management can provide info on excursions and scuba lessons, and arrange for airport pickup and medical services. A two-person cabana is $18, a two-person bungalow (with kitchen) about $35. *Calle del Morro s/n, Zicatela, tel. 958/2-03-57. 14 cabanas, all with bath.*

➢ UNDER $30 • **Flor de María.** Half a block from Playa Marinero, this hotel has comfortably furnished rooms with private baths and hot water, as well as a pool and restaurant. More to the point, there's an out-of-this-world bakery across the street. Singles cost $16.50, doubles $27. *Playa Marinero s/n, next to Cabañas Aldea Marinero, tel. 958/2-05-36. 24 rooms, all with bath. Luggage storage.*

Hotel San Juan. The clean rooms here have fans and private baths with hot water for $17 a single, $20 a double. Ask for an interior room; those facing the outside catch lots of highway noise. *Felipe Merklin 503, tel. 958/2-05-18. 26 rooms, all with bath. Luggage storage. MC, V.*

➢ CAMPING • It's illegal to plop your tent down on the beach, and good spots are hard to find, anyway. You can pitch a tent at **Neptuno** (*see above*) or pay too much (about $12 per spot) to stay at the **Puerto Escondido Trailer Park,** on the cliff overlooking Playa Carrizalillo.

FOOD The seafood is always fresh here, and probably your best bet. There are also a number of Italian restaurants in town. Pasta is usually safe, but you'll likely be disappointed with the local version of pizza. Apart from Bruno's (*see below*), the restaurants on Playa Zicatela serve little besides hamburgers, fries, and *cerveza* (beer) because—so say the cooks—their clientele will accept nothing else.

➢ UNDER $5 • **Bruno's.** Zicatela surfers who appreciate good food, good music, and each other's company fill this place regularly. They've got a happening bar and a message board advertising everything from massages to long-term rentals. A killer vegetarian stir-fry costs $4. *Playa Zicatela, no phone. Open daily 7 AM–11 PM.*

➢ UNDER $10 • **San Angel.** Shellfish is a specialty at this small, unpretentious eatery. Try the shrimp tostadas ($5) or the shrimp-filled pasta ($6.50). *Pérez Gasga s/n, tel. 958/2-07-26. Open daily 7 AM–midnight.*

Las 7 Regiones. Tables on the second floor overlook the action on the Andador Turístico, and the fondue, pastas, salads, and soups are all excellent here. Particularly good are the shrimp

It's too expensive to rent a room at the Santa Fe Hotel between Playas Principal and Zicatela, but come here at sunset to have a drink on the balcony

with chile and bacon ($7.50) and the daily fresh fish special ($7) cooked in cream and garlic. *Pérez Gasga s/n, tel. 958/2-05-51. Open daily 7 AM–11 PM.*

➢ UNDER $15 • **Sardina de Plata.** The Silver Sardine (as its name translates) welcomes diners with a cool, open, brick-and-adobe interior. The seafood and Mexican dishes are ample and fairly priced: The daily fish special ($10) comes with beans, rice, and tortillas, and the dinner special ($10) includes ceviche or fish soup, rice, a fish fillet, coffee, and dessert. *Pérez Gasga 512, tel. 958/2-03-28. Open daily 7 AM–11 PM.*

BEACHES The beaches around Puerto Escondido offer a variety of sporting opportunities. If you want to snorkel (best at Puerto Angelito and Carrizalillo), boogieboard (best at Playa Principal and Carrizalillo), or surf (best at Zicatela), you're better off renting your equipment in town for the entire day, rather than hourly on the beach. **Mango Club** (Pérez Gasga 605A, tel. 958/2-00-05) rents snorkel gear ($7 a day), inflatable rafts ($10 a day) and boogieboards ($10 a day). If you'd like to explore further afield, they also rent motorcycles ($50 a day) and bicycles ($17 a day), but only with a deposit or a credit card. They're supposed to be open daily 9 AM–8 PM, but often close down for a while in the afternoon.

➢ PLAYA PRINCIPAL • This beach, which runs parallel to the Andador Turístico, is a favorite spot for strolling and taking in the sun. You can also go sailing ($10 per hour), rent horses ($8.50 per hour), or hire a boat to Puerto Angelito or Carrizalillo or out to sea to frolic with the sea turtles ($10 per hour). The eastern section of the beach, called **Playa Marinero,** is separated from the rest by a lagoon. It's ideal for learning to surf, clambering on the rocks, swimming, and exploring tidepools.

➢ ZICATELA • To the east of Playa Marinero lies this famed and perilous surfing spot. Considered one of the top surf beaches in the world, Zicatela's waves roll in with impressive force. If you're not a surfer, you can also rent horses or dune buggies, as well as the ubiquitous boogie boards and snorkel gear, from vendors who set up tents on the sand. The top of the rock, marking the boundary between Zicatela and Playa Marinero, affords a good view of the perfect tubes of the Mexican Pipeline. When you do venture into the water, be careful of the currents—they're notoriously deadly.

➢ PUERTO ANGELITO • It's about a 20-minute walk or a $3 taxi ride to this small inlet and the neighboring beach of **Manzanillo.** The calm water attracts families with young children. It's a great area for swimming and snorkeling, and, sure enough, young boys rent out the necessary gear for about $4 an hour. If you'd prefer something sedentary, you can rent a hammock and take a nap, or have a meal or drinks at one of the many palapa (thatched hut) restaurants. To get here on foot, walk west along Pérez Gasga until it curves uphill toward the highway. Here you'll see the Camino a Puerto Angelito, which leads to a set of cement stairs down to the beach.

➢ CARRIZALILLO • This isolated beach is relatively free of the hordes of families that crowd Puerto Angelito, its neighbor to the east. The U-shaped cove does draw snorkelers and strong swimmers (the currents can be tricky). It's a ways out of town and lies at the bottom of a rocky cliff. You can make the dusty trek on land, or take a boat ride from Puerto Angelito or the Playa Principal. **Bacocho,** the most westerly beach, is good for swimming, but has a resort development.

AFTER DARK During the summer, the November surfing championships, and around Christmas time, the Andador Turístico itself is the party, with locals checking out the tourists, surfers mingling with sightseers, and everybody out to have a good time. It's also lined with quite a few bars and clubs, which range from absolutely dead in the low season to hopping and jammed when everyone's in town. At the western end of the Andador, **Bananas** offers canned pop music along with Ping-Pong and table football. **Tío Mac,** a video bar across the street, has juicy burgers and pounding rock music. A more out-of-the-way spot for American music is **El Tubo.** It's down a flight of stairs on the beach side of Pérez Gasga (look for the sign with a surfer riding a tube) and rocks from 11 PM until about 3 AM.

Karaka (Pérez Gasga, s/n, no phone) is the hottest new place to boogie down to live Latin and Caribbean music. They're open nightly 9:30 PM–2 AM. **El Son y La Rumba** (Andador Mar y Sol, above Pérez Gasga, no phone), features dancing to live salsa, jazz, or reggae on a minuscule dance floor after 10 PM nightly. They often charge a cover during the high season.

NEAR PUERTO ESCONDIDO

Trying to organize the following trips on your own can be frustrating, because once you get where you're going, you still need to negotiate horse or boat rentals (boat trips are the best way to see these places). This is one time when working with a guide will save you time, money, and hassles. Contact Ana Márquez at the Hotel Rincón del Pacífico (Pérez Gasga 900, tel. 958/2–01–93). She's a native Mixteca who understands the needs of budget travelers and can arrange or at least provide information on all of the following excursions.

MANIALTEPEC This briny lagoon 18 kilometers northwest of Puerto Escondido is home to a remarkable variety of wildlife, including wild geese and herons. You can rent a boat from **Isla del Gallo** to explore the lagoon. To get here from Puerto Escondido, take a bus heading toward Acapulco and get off at the signs for Manialtepec. If you take a taxi, don't let the driver charge you more than $4. A guided tour with Ana Márquez takes half a day and runs about $27.

ATOTONILCO The attraction of the town of Atotonilco, about 35 kilometers from Puerto Escondido, is the nearby thermal springs, accessible only on horseback after a difficult ride through dense vegetation. If you hire a guide, you're home free. If you hazard it alone, take a bus from Puerto Escondido toward Acapulco; 30 minutes down the road, ask to be let off along the Río Manialtepec. In Atotonilco, a short walk away, you can rent horses ($12 per person) for the 2½-hour ride to the springs.

CACALOTEPEC About 1 kilometer offshore from the picturesque village of Cacalotepec is **Roca Blanca** (White Rock), a little-known diving area with extraordinary coral. From Puerto Escondido, take a bus heading toward Acapulco and get off at the village. Residents in the area don't seem that friendly toward foreigners, so you may prefer to make arrangements through Ana Márquez (*see above*) or another locally based guide. Contact Maurizio Mendici at the Hotel Aldea del Bazar (Benito Juárez L7, tel. 958/2–05–08) in Puerto Escondido to rent diving equipment.

ZAPOTALITO AND PARQUE NACIONAL LAGUNAS DE CHACAHUA About 74 kilometers west of Puerto Escondido is a tropical park encompassing two lagoons—**Chacahua** and **Pastoría**—deserted beaches, and much wildlife. The town of Zapotalito, many of whose inhabitants are descended from African slaves, sits close to the entrance of the park. You can rent a boat here, or hire a guide to take you around the park.

You can swim in the lagoon, lunch on grilled fish and bananas sold by local women at **Playa Chacahua**, or visit the alligator hatchery in the village for which the beach is named. Morolette alligators are bred here to safeguard the survival of this threatened species in Mexico. The hatchery workers can show you small bathtubs full of tiny, squirming alligators, their eyes still shut but their jaws already snapping. It takes about an hour to cross the lagoon in a boat, and you need a guide. Slightly closer to Zapotalito (about a 45-minute boat ride down the river) is **Playa Cerro Hermoso,** an isolated lagoon beach, ringed with mango trees and black orchids and separated from the sea by only a narrow ridge of sand.

If you go with a guide from Puerto Escondido (about $30 for a full day with Ana Márquez) your transportation to and within the park is arranged. If you prefer to hire a guide in Zapotalito, catch an early bus heading toward Acapulco and ask to get off at the road leading to the park. It's about a 10-kilometer hike to the town. Park admission is free, but boat rentals run $50–$75. Go with a group and allow a full day for the excursion to make it worth your while.

Puerto Angel

Puerto Angel, 11 kilometers off the main highway, is touted as an unspoiled beach paradise, but reality and reputation do not exactly match. Still, Puerto Angel is far more laid-back than either Puerto Escondido or Santa Cruz Huatulco, with little commerce and no posh hotels. Nor is there direct bus service—to get here, you need to take a bus to the nearby town of **Pochutla** and catch a colectivo or a cab. Pochutla is also the place to go when you need to change money, send a letter, or make a long-distance call. In Puerto Angel, you can join the locals for a swim in the blue-green bay off the main beach, or arrange for a day of snorkeling or sightseeing by boat from one of the coves on either side of town.

Puerto Angel is a cliffside fishing village where the nightlife consists of hiking up to the lighthouse to catch the sunset and then strolling down to the main street with a paleta *(popsicle).*

Playa Panteón, in a sheltered cove just west of town, is where local families splash around in gentle waves, and where, among other things, you can rent snorkel equipment or arrange a boat trip. In the opposite direction (about a 20-minute walk from town), you'll find **Estacahuite,** where you can rent snorkel gear on the beach and explore the offshore coral reef. After Estacahuite, the next beach is **La Mina,** an undeveloped, palm-shaded lounger's paradise. Puerto Angel also serves as a comfortable base for trips up into the sparsely visited towns of the green Sierra Madre del Sur mountains that loom to the north.

COMING AND GOING The bus to and from Pochutla runs between 6 AM and 8 PM and costs about 35¢ each way. Colectivos do the same route frequently for about 70¢; a private taxi shouldn't cost you more than $3.50.

GETTING AROUND Puerto Angel is a tiny town, but finding places can be somewhat complicated because very few have street addresses. Just consider the faded signs pointing down twisting alleyways part of the town's charm, and you won't get frustrated. The highway from Pochutla turns into Avenida Principal at the entrance to town, and later turns into Boulevard Virgilio Uribe (though few make this distinction). The bus will drop you off or pick you up at *el árbol* (the tree), on the main street (officially Virgilio Uribe at this point) just before the naval base. Further on, the road crosses a dry creek bed and then forks just after the navy store—the high road leads to Zipolite, the low road to Playa Panteón.

WHERE TO SLEEP Most of Puerto Angel's hotels are planted high atop rocky cliffs, and reaching them often requires climbing a healthy number of stairs. The rewards for your efforts will be unobstructed ocean breezes and a tremendous view of the cove. The prices listed below apply to the low season; typically, room prices jump about $5 when the gringos roll in during the summer and around Christmas vacation. Cheaper accommodations, usually along the lines of a hammock and maybe some mosquito netting, are to be had at nearby Playa Zipolite (*see below*).

➤ UNDER $15 • **Casa de Huéspedes Gundi y Tomás.** The simple, stone-walled rooms in this clean, basic guest house come outfitted with a foam pad on a wooden pallet, a table, and screened windows. During the low season, $13.50 buys a double and $8.75 a single. The owners will let you hang a hammock on the porch for $3.50 year round. *Up the stairs just west of el árbol. 8 rooms; none with bath. Safe-deposit boxes.*

➤ UNDER $20 • **Pensión Puesto del Sol.** This multilevel, red-roofed pension is perched amid a profusion of hibiscus flowers and lemon and pomegranate trees. The rooms are simple and clean, though not very breezy; the bathrooms, both private and communal, are spotless and have cold water 24 hours a day. Harold, the proprietor, will share his maps and bus schedules (and perhaps a beer) with you in the open-air lounge. Doubles without bath are $17, with bath $20; add $1.50 for a fan and $2 for a small terrace and private entrance. *Follow the road from el árbol toward Zipolite. The pension is to the right just beyond the navy store. 13 rooms, 8 with bath.*

Posada Cañon de Vata. This posada is spread out over a tranquil valley just behind Playa Panteón. Rooms at the bottom of the valley run $15 a single, $18.50 a double ($17 and $20 with private bath). Private cabanas higher up, as well as rooms in *el cielo* (literally "the heavens," but in this case a small building with a stunning view of the bay atop the hill), run $23.50 for a single and $27 for a double with bath. The owners, a transplanted Californian named Suzanne and her artist husband Mateo, offer day-long snorkel trips ($6.50) and fishing expeditions ($5). They also rent snorkel equipment ($5 a day) and give advice on all Puerto Angel has to offer. Their small restaurant offers vegetarian fare. *Playa Panteón. 20 rooms, 17 with bath. Luggage storage. Closed May–June.*

Posada Rincón Sabroso. This inn has a communal garden and lots of colorful tile work, and there are two big beds, a fan, and a private bath in every room. Unfortunately, not only is there no hot water, there's no water at all, except 7 to 10 AM and 6 to 8 PM. Singles cost $13.50, doubles $17. *From el árbol, backtrack along the main road toward Pochutla and look for signs and a steep stairway. 8 rooms, all with bath. Luggage storage.*

➢ UNDER $30 • **La Buena Vista.** This hotel allows you to appreciate the tranquility of this small fishing town without being too far from what little action there is on the main drag. The rooms ($18.50 a single, $25 a double) are simple but tastefully furnished; top corner rooms have small terraces and spectacular views. *Take the main road across the bridge; it's to the left. 12 rooms, all with bath. Luggage storage.*

FOOD Everything except seafood must be trucked into Puerto Angel, so plan on spending a bit more than usual. Even so, prices are not unreasonable, and you'll find a handful of simple restaurants and, in the evenings, a few taco stands along the main road. For a more substantial meal, head to a guest house or hotel restaurant, where dinner is often shared with the proprietor's family. If you manage to catch something at sea, somebody at your guest house will likely prepare it for a nominal charge.

La Buena Vista. This hotel restaurant is more Tex-Mex than Mexican, but the food is great. Try the delicious barbecued chicken ($5) with a piña colada ($2.75). *Take the main road across the bridge and it's to the left. Open Mon.–Sat. 7–11 and 6–10.*

Gundi y Tomás. The restaurant at this guest house offers a limited selection of basic fare. They serve a good fruit salad for $2.50. *Up the stairs just west of el árbol. Open daily 7 AM–9 PM.*

El Tiburón Dormido. This open-air palapa on the main beach dishes up grilled fresh fish and shrimp for less than $6.75 à la carte. Fish tacos ($1.75) and garlic-and-onion soup ($2) make satisfying light meals, and the margaritas are $2.50. *Open daily 7 AM–10 PM.*

NEAR PUERTO ANGEL

The green mountains of the Sierra Madre del Sur hide villages that seem worlds away from the beach towns on the coast. San José del Pacífico and Chacalapa are both in the foothills north of Pochutla and can be reached from any Oaxaca city-bound bus from there. You can make a day trip of it, but if you decide to spend the night, both towns have small, well-furnished *hospedajes* (guest houses) that charge about $17 double occupancy. A local family may very well ask you to stay or invite you to hang a hammock on their front porch—you might be the most exciting thing that's happened in a long time.

CHACALAPA This quiet town, set in a green valley surrounded by a forest, is just 12 kilometers from Pochutla. Here you'll find Tom Bachmaier, an artist who etches Oaxacan landscapes on small bamboo beads. Even if you're not interested in buying, stop by his beautiful home to admire his work and garden. Across the path is **Alberca El Paraíso**, a swimming pool filled with turquoise mineral water from a nearby natural spring. Octavio Ramos, who owns the pool and surrounding ranch, will happily guide you through the forest and show you how those unfamiliar tropical fruits you see in the markets grow. There's a $1.50 charge to use the pool for a day, or, if you're drawn in by the warmth of the Ramos family, you can enjoy free use of the pool and stay in one of the brand-spanking-new cabanas with hot water, private baths, and ceiling fans for only $17. The pool is emptied and cleaned every Tuesday.

SAN JOSE DEL PACIFICO This small village is off Route 175, about an hour from Pochutla. It is the jumping-off place for the trails of the nearby cloud forest. It's also a favorite destination of foreigners who, after being transformed into beach bums in Zipolite, come in search of the hallucinogenic mushrooms rumored to be found here. As with anything that might get you in trouble with the Mexican police, caution is the watchword.

Zipolite

A sweaty 30-minute walk from Puerto Angel brings you to Zipolite (Beach of the Dead), and another world. The feeling here is 1970s—Led Zep, Marley, scruffy gringos, and lots of dope. Nudity is the rule on the beach, and the southern section, known as **Playa del Amor,** has a pretty active gay scene. Be *extremely* cautious about swimming here: Zipolite's name refers not, as some seem to think, to the Grateful Dead, but to the many lost to its currents every year.

When night falls, go to Zipolipas, a palapa bar with taped reggae and rock music; it's the closest thing to a nightclub in these parts.

Just past Zipolite are the beaches of **San Agustinillo** and **Mazunte.** Just before the first you'll find a hammock-making co-op (*see box, below*); the second is home to an abandoned turtle slaughterhouse and the El Mazunte Sea Turtle Protection Program (*see Near Zipolite, below*) that replaced it.

COMING AND GOING It's about a 30-minute walk from Puerto Angel to Zipolite. Buses (35¢) run between Zipolite and Puerto Angel and Pochutla every half hour between 6 AM and 8 PM. You can also catch a colectivo to or from Pochutla for $1.70. If you arrive in Pochutla at night, you'll need to take a private taxi for about $5. Boats from Puerto Angel also run irregularly to Zipolite; the going rates are $5–$10.

WHERE TO SLEEP You can rent a hammock in a communal palapa for about a dollar; double that amount if you want a little privacy. Don't expect much as far as the communal bathrooms are concerned, and you won't be disappointed. Also keep in mind that theft is common, so you might do well to ask a hotel in Puerto Angel to store the bulk of your gear while you're

Hammocks That Won't Let You Down

In San Agustinillo, just beyond Shambhala, you'll find the workshop of a cooperative association of highly skilled hammock makers. The following are some of their tips on how to tell a good hammock from what could become a tangled, uncomfortable ball of string:

First, stretch out a section and look at the cross weave. Most Oaxacan hammocks are made of heavy cotton or thick nylon thread (the latter lasts longer but is a little less comfortable), and good ones have a double weave.

Next, grip the material near the loop where the rope is attached to get an idea of the amount of material in the hammock. An average-size gringo needs at least a fistful of threads. You'll probably want a matrimonial (double) or familiar (family size). Single-size hammocks may look big, but try to sleep in one and you'll decide to take it home for your baby sister.

Now look at the number of threads attaching the loop to the cross weave. In the best hammocks, each thread coming out of the loop anchors only one cross weave. (Two or three is also okay.) This allows better flexibility and weight distribution.

Finally, check the edges to be sure there are a large number of straight threads before the cross weave begins. These will keep the hammock from breaking if you sit on the edges (and ensure that it's strong enough to support a moment or two of passion).

here. Some people never swerve from the beach, but the *posadas* (inns) up in the hills merit the diversion. The coolest one is **Shambhala,** also known as Gloria's, up on the hill at the northern end of the beach. Sprawling over half the hillside, it has meditation altars and a patio restaurant with a spectacular view of a hidden bay. Drugs are a no-no here. Gloria, the transplanted Californian who owns the place, offers a variety of lodging options: Run-down cabanas on the beach with a bed and private bath run about $12; huts with locking doors are $7; rooms with a hammock or "bed" (a straw mat on a raised platform) cost $5, as do the palapas with hammocks; and a simple campsite costs $1. Bed linen and sleeping mats are not provided, but luggage storage and a safe-deposit box are. **Lo Cósmico,** right next to Shambhala, offers clean, cool palapas complete with two hammocks for $5.

FOOD Zipolite has no market, so you're stuck with the posadas and beachfront palapas, which serve mostly seafood and tortilla dishes. **Gemini's** is indistinguishable from all the other palapas except that it serves a decent pizza. **Lo Cósmico,** with board games and rock music to keep you entertained, is a groovy place to nurse a beer and sample the specialty crêpes ($2–$4). You can get a California-style granola breakfast in **Shambhala's** hilltop restaurant, or try their tasty chicken mole or some vegetarian turnovers (each about $2.50) over candlelight for dinner.

NEAR ZIPOLITE

MAZUNTE As you ride past San Agustinillo, you'll notice a cluster of dilapidated, rusty buildings on the far end of the beach. These were once centers for processing turtle meat and shells. Today, just past them in Mazunte, is a center for the turtles' protection. The **Centro Mexicano de la Tortuga** offers educational tours in Spanish and English Tuesday through Saturday from 10:30 AM to 5 PM and Sundays between 11 AM and 3 PM. You can watch all the species of sea turtles that inhabit Mexico's coastal waters swim in huge tanks. Individual turtles are only kept on display a short time, after which they're released or used in conservation research. The $3.50 entrance fee goes toward conservation and education projects. Buses come here from Zipolite (35¢), Puerto Angel (70¢), and Pochutla ($1).

Bahías de Huatulco

The area often simply referred to as Huatulco in fact consists of nine bays spread out over 20 miles of coast. The heart of it all is Santa Cruz Huatulco, which just 10 years ago was a small fishing village of simple adobe huts on a pristine bay. That was before the Mexican government chose it as the site of a luxury tourist development meant to duplicate Cancún's success in attracting foreign sun seekers and their money. Now, wide, palm-lined boulevards with new electric lights and grassy dividers, rolling golf courses, and huge, white hotel complexes make it seem closer to Santa Barbara or Palm Beach than to Oaxaca city.

However, while this area is certainly set up to cater to a five-star clientele, it actually still has a lot to offer the traveler of more limited means. Due to the government's policy of "responsible ecodevelopment," the outlying bays and the forests that ring them remain relatively unspoiled. It's even a lot more convenient to visit these places now that the brand-new Ladatel phones and air-conditioned banks of Santa Cruz are within easy reach.

Huatulco's bays, from west (closest to Puerto Angel) to east are: San Agustín, Chachacual, Cacaluta, Maguey, Órgano, Santa Cruz, Chahué, Tangolunda, and Conejos. Along with Santa Cruz, Chahué and Tangolunda are the most developed, while Órgano, which can only be reached by foot or water, is the most pristine. Camping is officially allowed only on Chahué, but you can camp for free on Órgano, or in a quiet corner on any of the other bays except for Santa Cruz and Tangolunda. The town of **La Crucecita** (about five minutes inland from Santa Cruz) is where most of the people who work in Santa Cruz's boutiques and hotels live, shop, and eat, and is the budget traveler's base for the area.

BASICS **Bancomer, Banamex,** and **Comermex** are all next to each other on the main road in Santa Cruz, and all have ATMs and change traveler's checks between 9 AM and 1:30 PM. The post office is in La Crucecita, just off Benito Juárez where it turns toward Chahué. You can find maps and helpful English speakers in Santa Cruz at the **Asociación de Hoteles y Moteles** (Monte Albán, at Santa Cruz, tel. 958/7–08–48).

COMING AND GOING There is direct bus service between Santa Cruz Huatulco and Oaxaca city ($9.50, 7 hrs). Buses also run between Pochutla and La Crucecita every 15 minutes. The ride takes one hour and costs $1.25. There are daily flights from the local airport to Oaxaca city and Mexico City; tickets and airport transportation can be arranged at any of the travel agencies in Santa Cruz or La Crucecita.

GETTING AROUND The bays are extremely spread out, and though they're now accessible by paved roads, it's a bit of a haul to get from one to the other. The rich tourists overcome this obstacle by touring by boat. The rest of us, however, can reach the three central bays—Tangolunda, Chahué, and Santa Cruz—by *urbano* (city bus) from La Crucecita (35¢). They leave from the road that leads out toward Chahué from the main square.

Colectivos ($2) leave early in the morning from Santa Cruz and La Crucecita to take workers out to Conejos, Maguey, and Cacaluta. You can try to catch one of these, or take a cab for $5. To get to Órgano, you'll have to walk over the hill on the east end of Maguey; it should take about half an hour.

To get to San Agustín and Chachacual, you need to catch any bus toward Pochutla and get off at the crossroads for Santa María Huatulco. From there it's a $5 taxi ride or $2 colectivo (if you're lucky enough to get one) to the bay of your choice. Another option for all the bays is to show up at the marina in Santa Cruz bright and early and try to hitch a ride with someone boating out to one of the beaches to work. If you luck out and someone's willing, expect to pay between $2 and $7.

WHERE TO SLEEP AND EAT Camping is the way to go in Huatulco. It's officially allowed only on Chahué, but you'll find deserted beaches and forest galore if you venture farther afield, and slinging a hammock or pitching a tent is no problem. Órgano is the most deserted; it has no palapas or tourist facilities, so you'll have to bring food and fresh water if you're going to stay the night. Most of the other beaches have some palapas. These, however, close by late afternoon, and the beaches are deserted in the evenings. If you prefer not to camp, **Hospedaje Gloriluz** (Pochote, btw Gardenia and Bugambilias, tel. 958/7–01–60) in La Crucecita rents simple, clean rooms with fans and private baths for $17 a single and $27 a double.

In La Crucecita, comidas corridas and 35¢ tacos abound. Avoid the touristy restaurants on the zócalo (you'll know 'em when you see 'em), and you'll find no shortage of cheap eats. **Antojitos Oaxaqueños** (Palo Verde, at Gardenia) offers hearty Oaxacan specialties for less than $4.

The Isthmus of Tehuantepec

The Isthmus of Tehuantepec stretches a mere 215 kilometers from the Caribbean to the Pacific, and encompasses parts of both Oaxaca and Tabasco. Most tourists do not consider it a destination in itself. Rather, they stop here while traveling along the gringo trail between Oaxaca and Chiapas to switch buses, to refuel, to break down, whatever. From that vantage point the isthmus can seem particularly unattractive—dusty, hot, provincial, and boring, especially after the Oaxacan coast or the Chiapan highlands. If, however, you're interested in Zapotec culture you'll find the region fascinating. The large Zapotec population here has resisted being "Mexicanized" and instead identifies with the isthmus itself. You'll see this in the teaching of Zapotec poetry in the cultural centers, and in the distinctive local costumes and foods.

The three main cities of the Oaxacan part of the isthmus are Salina Cruz, Tehuantepec, and Juchitán. Despite the fact that they are all within 32 kilometers of one another, they have developed in very different ways. Salina Cruz has the most modern conveniences (such as

ATMs). Tehuantepec, the area's namesake, is the smallest and prettiest of the three, while Juchitán, recognized as the cultural center of the isthmus, is where the Zapotec presence can be most strongly felt.

Calls in Zapotec announcing geta tzuki (small, dense breads) and geta bingi (shrimp-filled tortillas) for sale resound in the zócalos and marketplaces of the isthmus towns.

BASICS

BANKS **Bancomer** on Camacho in Salina Cruz exchanges currency weekdays 10–noon. **Banamex** on 5 de Septiembre in Juchitán does the same weekdays 9–noon.

MEDICAL AID There's an IMSS Clinic (tel. 971/4–15–72) on the Carretera Transístmica on the outskirts of Salina Cruz. The name of **Farmacia 24 Horas** (Camacho 503, tel. 971/4–14–06) in Salina Cruz tells you when it's open.

PHONES For a surcharge of $3, **La Pasadita** (Camacho 603A, tel. 971/4–01–73) by the waterfront in Salina Cruz lets you make international collect calls weekdays between 7 AM and 6 PM. For a similar commission, **El Paraíso** (5 de Mayo 1, tel. 971/5–02–12) in Tehuantepec provides long-distance and collect service from 8 AM to 10 PM. In Juchitán, you'll find two new, blue Ladatel phones across from the telephone office at 20 de Septiembre 66.

COMING AND GOING

BY BUS In all three towns, locals catch second-class buses along the highways instead of at the established stations, especially for rides up and down the isthmus. Second-class bus drivers will stop for a waving hand.

➢ SALINA CRUZ • If you don't want to flag down a second-class bus on the highway, first-class **Cristóbal Colón** (tel. 971/4–02–59) buses leave from the station at 5 de Mayo 412, two blocks from the zócalo. Destinations include Tapachula ($11, 9 hrs), Tuxtla Gutiérrez ($8, 6 hrs), and San Cristóbal ($10, 8 hrs) in Chiapas; Huatulco ($5, 4 hrs) and Puerto Escondido ($6, 7 hrs) on the Oaxacan coast; and Mexico City ($30, 15 hrs). Micros and second-class buses also depart daily from the railroad tracks for Puerto Escondido and Santa Cruz Huatulco, as well as other villages on the isthmus.

➢ TEHUANTEPEC • First- and second-class buses operate out of the station (tel. 971/8–57–52) on kilometer 20 of the Carretera Transístmica.

➢ JUCHITAN • The **Cristóbal Colón** (tel. 971/2–00–22), **Fletes y Pasajeros** (tel. 971/1–04–19), and **Alas de Oro** (tel. 971/1–04–69) bus lines operate out of the station next to the Pemex station on the road to Salina Cruz. This is also a good place to hitch a ride.

Salina Cruz

There's not much in Salina Cruz to distinguish it from other industrial port cities, but it's got the highest concentration of services like banks, phones, clinics, and so forth in the area. For those desperate for a beach, **La Venta** is a clean, windswept stretch of coast just before you hit the city. Unfortunately, the smell of petroleum is pretty strong here.

WHERE TO SLEEP Hotels in Salina Cruz cater to businessmen and tend to be expensive. **Hotel Fuentes** (Camacho 114, tel. 971/4–02–43) has clean rooms with color TVs; a double with fan is $18.50, with air conditioning, $27. A few doors down and a bit cheaper is the **Hotel Posada del Jardín** (Camacho 108, tel. 971/4–01–62), where doubles with fans cost $15.

FOOD You'll find taco stands and women selling dried fish and seafood around the market on 5 de Mayo, and stands near the zócalo offer hot tacos and terrific fresh seafood cocktails. **Café Istmeño** (5 de Mayo 305A, tel. 971/4–17–40) is directly across from the zócalo and serves the best coffee in town, as well as $2 *tortas* (sandwiches), 24 hours a day. **Jugos Hawaii** (Camacho, 1 block from the zócalo) offers a good selection of tropical fruit *licuados* (smoothies).

Tehuantepec

Sixteen kilometers north of Salina Cruz is Tehuantepec, on the river of the same name. It feels the least modern of the main isthmus towns, and the most common form of transportation here is a heavily decorated and fringed motorcart (basically a moped with a wagon on the back). You can start exploring at the **Casa de La Cultura,** housed in a crumbling former convent with a small garden and fountain. The Casa sponsors cultural events and sells books about isthmus history and tapes of traditional music.

Tehuanas still wear their unique costume—a brightly patterned cotton skirt, a hand-embroidered huipil, and, on special occasions, a headdress of starched lace called a bidainiró or olan.

WHERE TO SLEEP One block past the zócalo is the **Hotel Oasis** (Ocampo 8, tel. 971/5-00-08), which has two sad-looking monkeys chained to a tree and some parrots in its courtyard. Doubles with private baths and ceiling fans are $17; singles are $13.50. The three-story **Hotel Donaji** (Juárez 10, tel. 971/5-00-64) is built around a peaceful, ivy-covered courtyard, though rooms that face the street can be a bit noisy. A double with private bath costs about $22; a few dollars more gets you air conditioning, as well. For the simplest and cheapest sleeping arrangements, head down the street from the Oasis toward the railroad tracks to the **Posada Hasdar** (Ocampo 10, tel. 971/5-02-07), where slightly rumpled rooms with private baths and ceiling fans are $8.50.

FOOD **El Portón** (Juana C. Romero 54), off the zócalo near the Oasis and Donaji hotels, sells simple, fresh regional food. The beer ($1.25) is kept cold and they'll turn on the fan and stereo on request. Soups are 50¢ a bowl, and big plates of enchiladas, chiles rellenos, or tacos are all a steal at $2.75. Two blocks from the zócalo is **Café Colonial** (Juana C. Romero 66, tel. 971/5-01-15). The thing to order here is *huevos motuleños,* a messy but yummy concoction of sunny-side up eggs, tortillas, ham, cheese, and salsa for about $5.

Juchitán

Juchitán's dusty, potholed streets give the town a grubby feel, but it buzzes with activity and is worth a visit. The **Mercado 5 de Septiembre** is the place to people watch or find cheap food. The **Casa de la Cultura** (Colón, at Juárez, tel. 971/1-13-51) is a regional art center with a focus on artists from Juchitán itself. It's housed in a former convent, part of the 15th-century **Iglesia San Vicente Ferrer,** and has a small museum and an all-Spanish lending library. About 10 kilometers outside of town an estuary called **Mar Muerto** (Dead Sea) because of the stillness of its waters is good for fishing and boating. To get there, take a morning bus labeled 7TH SEC. from behind the market in Juchitán.

In Juchitán's market, vendors sell iguana eggs as well as live iguanas with their mouths sewed shut and legs tied behind their backs. The little leathery eggs are eaten by biting off the top of the shell and sucking out the yolky, slightly salty contents. The iguanas are also tasty, especially entomado (cooked in tomato sauce).

WHERE TO SLEEP Your best choice on the zócalo is **Hospedaje Echazarreta** (Juárez 23, tel. 971/1-01-82). It's run by a friendly family who stocks the clean rooms with fresh towels daily. A double is $10, $12 with private bath. The **Hotel Gonzanelly** (16 de Septiembre 70, tel. 971/1-13-89) offers large rooms with private baths. A fan-cooled double runs $20; for air conditioning you pay $3 more.

FOOD Juchitán is regionally famous for its seafood. The popular **Mariscos Sylvia Juchitán** (2 de Abril, btw Aldama and Hidalgo, tel. 971/1-22-35) serves an enormous *vuelva a la vida* (back to life) cocktail ($8), crammed with chunks of octopus, shrimp, conch, oysters, avocado, onion, and cilantro. **Restaurant Casa Grande** (Juárez 12, tel. 971/1-34-60), on the zócalo, has linen tablecloths and a cool courtyard; their pungent garlic soup is well worth $2.50.

CHIAPAS AND TABASCO

10

By Ian Signer

The states of Chiapas and Tabasco share a narrow strip of land between the Gulf of Mexico, the Pacific Ocean, and Guatemala, emcompassing mountains, swampy lowland, desert, volcanoes, cloud forests, and thick jungle. This region, at the heart of the great Olmec and Classic Maya empires, was an important area of contest and communication for many Mesoamerican civilizations. Despite their close geographical proximity and shared history, however, the contrast between these states couldn't be more striking. The oil boom of the 1970s left Tabasco a a relatively prosperous, largely mestizo state of many modern, air-conditioned buildings, massive cement expressways, and huge hotels. In Tabasco, one almost never hears Mayan languages spoken, and Indians are a rare sight. The larger and more mountainous Chiapas, on the other hand, is rich in indigenous culture—Spanish is the second language of much of the population—and colonial history, but little else. It is the poorest state in the country, with "Third World" standards of living, literacy rates, and infrastructure. It was partially in response to this type of regional inequity that, in January 1994, the Zapatista National Liberation Army invaded the historic Chiapan city of San Cristóbal de las Casas, effectively placing some of the chronic problems of this long-overlooked state into the political limelight.

Even before the uprising scared off all but a small mob of journalists, relatively few tourists had explored these two states. Tiny Tabasco has put lots of money into tourism in the past few years, printing glossy pamphlets about its extensive museums and attractions, such as the Yumká ecological reserve. The wonders of Chiapas have received less fanfare but are mind-blowing to even the most worldly of travelers. The state contains a large tract of endangered rain forest and is home to vital indigenous cultures unlike any others in the country.

Tuxtla Gutiérrez, the capital of Chiapas, is a busy, basically unattractive city, of interest to most travelers only as a transportation hub, although the zoo and regional museums on the fringes of town are the best in the state. Just two hours from hot and humid Tuxtla rises the now-famous San Cristóbal, where a cool climate and pine forests provide the setting for one of the country's best-preserved colonial cities. Although the Zapatistas occupied the city for just a few days, their presence can still be felt in the form of army checkpoints dotting the countryside and hotels and cafés that are now relatively empty of travelers. The hilly terrain near San Cristóbal is the living fabric of Maya culture, with over a score of indigenous groups speaking several Mayan languages.

The coffee- and cacao-growing region of southern coastal Chiapas is almost never visited by the package tour crowd. The town of Tapachula is a gateway to Guatemala for backpack-toting adventure seekers as well as a lively city in its own right. From here, you can hit a few undeveloped beaches or head for the cool mountain air in the beautiful town of Unión Juárez,

Bahía de Campeche

Ciudad del Carmen

Laguna de Términos

Frontera

Paraíso

Comalcalco

Río Grijalva

Río San Pedro

CAMPECHE

186

Villahermosa

180

TABASCO

187

Catazajá

186   199

Palenque

Teapa

195

Palenque

Agua Azul

Misol-Ha

Tenosique

Pomoná

Río Usumacinta

Sumidero Canyon

Pantelho

199

Toniná

Nahá

Ocosingo

Yaxchilán

Tuxtla Gutiérrez

San Andrés San Juan Chamula

Chenalho

Tenejapa

Oxchuc

Lacanhá

Bonampak

Río Lacantún

Zinacantán

Chiapa de Corzo

San Cristóbal

Río Lacantún

SELVA LACANDONA

TO ARRIAGA & TONALÁ

CHIAPAS

190

Amattenango del Valle

Parque Nacional Lagos de Montebello

Comitán

Chinkultik

La Trinitaria

190

SIERRA MADRE DE CHIAPAS

Presa de la Angostura

Ciudad Cuauhtémoc

200

GUATEMALA

Motozintla

Escuintla

Acapetahua

Huixtla

Volcán Tacaná

KEY

Rail Lines

Las Palmas

N

Golfo de Tehuantepec

Tapachula

Unión Juárez

Talismán

Puerto Madero

Ciudad Hidalgo

0   20 miles

0   30 km

on the Guatemalan frontier. On the side of the Tacaná volcano, Unión Juárez offers access to great hiking in the wilderness around the volcano and among the foothills dotted with coffee plantations. Further inland is Comitán and the Parque Nacional Lagos de Montebello, with more multicolored lakes than one person could ever swim in. It is also a major Maya archaelogical site.

The eastern region of Chiapas is mostly rain forest, though more and more acreage is being lost to cattle ranching as Mexico pushes to colonize the untouched land and relocate people from the overpopulated highlands. The famous ruins of Palenque and Toniná are here, and rivers and waterfalls course through the land, offering luxurious escapes from the heat. Agua Azul, an oasis of waterfalls and swimming ponds in various shades of brilliant blue near Palenque makes a rewarding day trip. The southeast corner of Chiapas is the Lacandón rain forest, which hides the remote ruins of Yaxchilán and Bonampak. It is also home to the Lacandón Indians, whose culture and religious practices are considered by many to be more closely related to the ancient Maya than those of any other living group.

Tabasco's humid swamplands are rarely traveled, and some of its beaches are hidden paradises where you can dine on seafood and cool off with tropical fruit concoctions for less than most places in Mexico. The 1970s brought radical changes to this state: The discovery of oil caused the contamination of some of the Gulf coastline and spawned modern malls and highrises in the capital, Villahermosa. Oil money also created a relatively high standard of living for Tabascans, and paid for the draining of the basin containing La Venta, the largest Olmec archaeological find in Mesoamerica.

Tuxtla Gutiérrez

"The new ugly capital of Chiapas," declared Graham Greene in 1939, "is like an unnecessary postscript to Chiapas, which should be all wild mountain and old churches and swallowed ruins and Indians plodding by." You may not agree with him, but he has a point: Tuxtla is not set in a lush rain forest where brightly dressed indigenous people sell their wares. Rather, it's a busy administrative and university city with a long, brightly lit strip that evokes Las Vegas at night. The city is popular with travelers mainly because it offers bus connections to surrounding states and nearly everywhere within Chiapas. In the midst of all the cement islands and superexpressways, however, you'll find a great zoo, botanical gardens, and cultural museums worth at least one day of exploration. A short trip outside the city takes you to the colonial town of Chiapa de Corzo, the departure point for a boat ride through the deep, narrow Sumidero Canyon.

This part of Chiapas gets a lot of rain from the end of May until as late as October. The rest of the year it hardly rains at all.

Demands for land reform in southern Mexico have been in the international spotlight of late because of the Zapatista uprising, but they are far from new. The conservative city of Tuxtla became the capital of Chiapas in 1892 after a bloody battle with liberal forces at the old capital of San Cristóbal de las Casas. Tensions soon arose because of Tuxtla's support of dictator Porfirio Díaz's land policy that favored a few *ladino* (Spanish-descended) families over the indigenous *campesinos* (peasants). To this day, Chiapas's fertile land is concentrated in the hands of a tiny, powerful fraction of the population.

BASICS

AMERICAN EXPRESS American Express operates through **Agencia de Viajes Marabusco.** Cardholders can cash personal checks, receive advances on AmEx cards, or have their mail held here; anyone can change money, receive a MoneyGram, or have their lost traveler's checks replaced. *Av. Central, at 15a Pte., tel. 961/2–69–98. Mailing address: Pl. Bonampak, Local 14, Colonia Montezuma, Tuxtla Gutiérrez, Chiapas, CP 29030, México. Open weekdays 9–2 and 4–7, Sat. 9–2.*

CASAS DE CAMBIO **Bancomer** (Av. Central, at 2a Pte., tel. 961/2–04–33) and **Banamex** (1a Sur Pte. 141, tel. 961/3–52–64) both change traveler's checks on weekdays 10–noon. Bancomer also changes cash and offers cash advances on credit cards.

You can change cash or traveler's checks or get a cash advance on your Visa, Mastercard, or AmEx card after hours or on weekends at **Cafetería Bonampak**. *Blvd. Belisario Domínguez 180, tel. 961/3–20–50, ext. 127. Open daily 7 AM–midnight.*

EMERGENCIES For an ambulance, call the **Cruz Roja** at 961/2–00–96. For any other emergency, call the **police** (961/2–16–76).

LAUNDRY **Lavandería La Burbuja** will wash and dry 3 kilos for $5. *1a Nte. Pte., at 3a Pte. Nte., tel. 961/2–52–34. Open weekdays 9–2 and 4–8, Sat. 9–4.*

MAIL The post office (tel. 961/2–04–16) on the northeast corner of the *zócalo* (main square) will hold mail sent to you at the following address for up to 10 days: Lista de Correos, Tuxtla Gutiérrez, Chiapas, CP 29002, México. They are open weekdays 8–7 and Saturday 9–1. The **telegram office** (tel. 961/2–02-81) is next to the post office and is open weekdays 9–8 and Saturday 9–1.

MEDICAL AID The **Centro de Salud** (9a Sur Ote., at 2a Ote. Sur, tel. 961/2–03–15) is open Monday–Saturday 7:30–noon for walk-in appointments. Round the clock medical attention is available at no cost through the **Cruz Roja** (5a Nte. Pte. 1480, tel. 961/2–00–96).

PHONES Blue Ladatel phones are found in front of the movie theaters near the zócalo. Cash calls can be made from *casetas de larga distancia*, (long-distance telephone offices), as can collect calls, which generally cost $4. There are a number scattered around town, but there's a convenient one, open 9 AM–10 PM, at 5a Oriente Sur 122.

VISITOR INFORMATION Tuxtla Gutiérrez has a small underground visitor information center beneath the zócalo where you can pick up maps, restaurant and hotel guides, and information on everything from taxi fares to boat rides up the Sumidero Canyon. *2a Nte., at Calle Central, tel. 961/3–76–90. Open weekdays 9–3 and 6–9, Sat. 9–1.*

The **federal tourist office,** in a modern building among other federal agencies, is staffed by helpful young people fresh out of college. While you're here, try to get your hands on *La Cartelera*, a monthly publication that lists theater performances, local festivals, exhibitions, readings, and lectures taking place in Tuxtla and other Chiapan cities. Photocopied brochures with maps and practical information about other towns in Chiapas are also available. The tourist police unit *Los Angeles Verdes* (Green Angels) has an office in the same building. Travel related thefts or other criminal activity can be reported to these green-banded guys through the tourist office. *Blvd. Belisario Domínguez 950, tel. 961/2–45–35. Open weekdays 8 AM–9 PM.*

COMING AND GOING

BY BUS The first-class **Cristóbal Colón** station (2a Nte. Pte. 268, tel. 961/2–51–22) is two blocks northwest of the zócalo. Buses to San Cristóbal ($4, 1½ hrs) leave every hour 5 AM–9 PM. Two regular first-class and two "Servi-Plus" buses to Mexico City ($49, $51 for Servi-Plus, 12 hrs) leave daily. Buses leave to both Puebla ($43, 10 hrs) and Córdoba ($31, 9 hrs) at 4:30 and 9:30 PM. For luggage storage, try the small store right next to the station.

The **Autotransportes Tuxtla Gutiérrez** station (3a Sur Ote. 712, tel. 961/2–02–30) near the market offers both first- and second-class service, with a wide variety of departure times and prices. Second-class buses go to (among other places) Ocosingo ($4, 3½ hrs), Palenque ($7.50, 6 hrs), and Villahermosa ($9, 8½ hrs).

Small **regional buses** leave the dusty terminal at the corner of 2a Oriente Sur and 2a Sur Oriente for Chiapa de Corzo every 15 minutes 4 AM–10:30 PM. The ride takes twenty minutes and costs 50¢.

BY PLANE Tuxtla's federal airport (Carretera Panamericana, tel. 961/3–01–03), 35 kilometers west of Tuxtla, is served by **Aerocaribe** (tel. 961/2–20–32), with daily flights to Oaxaca,

Guadalajara, Monterrey, Tijuana, Villahermosa, Mérida, and Cancún; and **Mexicana** (tel. 961/2–00–20), with twice-daily flights to Mexico City. Colectivos ($4) leave for the airport from Hotel Humberto (Av. Central, at Calle Central) until the last flight (around 4 PM). A taxi ride will set you back about $15. Allow 40 minutes if traveling by colectivo, 25 minutes for a taxi.

There is another, closer airport (Aeropuerto Terán) on the Carretera Panamericana, 10 kilometers west of Tuxtla (tel. 961/2–15–24). **AVIACSA** (tel. 961/2–06–01) has flights from here to the Yucatán, Oaxaca, and Mexico City. There is no money exchange, luggage storage, tourist information, or food available at the airport. Taxis are the only available transport to Terán; the cost is about $5.

GETTING AROUND

Though Tuxtla is a large, sprawling city, it's fairly easy to navigate. Two main thoroughfares (the east–west Calle Central and north–south Avenida Central, also referred to as Avenida 14 de Septiembre) intersect at the zócalo and divide the city into four quadrants. All the other streets are named and numbered according to their position relative to the center. To reach the American Express office, main tourist office, and discos from the center you'll need to take a colectivo down Avenida Central until it turns to Boulevard Belisario Domínguez toward the western outskirts of town.

Learning the Spanish names for the cardinal directions will help you find your way around Tuxtla Gutiérrez: Norte (Nte.) = North; Sur = South; Oriente (Ote.) = East; and Poniente (Pte.) = West.

BY BUS Colectivos run throughout the city between 6 AM and 9 PM. Destinations are plainly marked on the front windshields, and stops are indicated on the street by blue signs. Unlike those in many Mexican cities, the colectivos here pick up passengers only at marked stops; waving your arms elsewhere won't do you a bit of good. Microbuses are bigger and run to Tuxtla's outlying sights, such as the zoo and botanical gardens. They can be hailed on most main streets and their destinations are clearly marked on the front windows.

BY TAXI Taxis, necessary if you want to return from one of the discos late at night, run 24 hours. Don't let them rip you off—the most you should pay anywhere within the city limits is $2.

WHERE TO SLEEP

Most hotels in Tuxtla are modern, lacking the patios, wrought-iron furniture, and plants that give character to many establishments in other Chiapan cities. The up side, however, is that relatively clean and inexpensive rooms are easy to come by. Rather than ambience, look for a working fan and clean sheets—if you've seen one hotel here, you've pretty much seen them all.

➤ UNDER $15 • **Casa de Huéspedes Muñiz.** The dusty upper rooms of this guest house have a view of the surrounding urban poverty, but for $6 a single and $10 a double with communal bath, one shouldn't expect to be insulated from reality. The water's not hot here, but there are fans and a nice family runs the place. *2a Sur Ote. 733, no phone. 32 rooms, 13 with bath. Laundry, luggage storage.*

Hotel Casablanca. The Casablanca features a pleasant courtyard filled with plants, and its rooms all have ceiling fans. The bathrooms even have blue tiling, towels, soap, and toilet paper. With communal bath, singles are $6, doubles $11. Rooms with private bath are $11 for a single and $15 for a double. The showers in both the communal and private bathrooms have hot water 24 hours a day. *2a Nte. Ote. 251, 1 block NE of zócalo, tel. 961/1–03–05. 52 rooms, 37 with bath. Luggage storage.*

Hotel La Catedral. A maze of stairways and corridors lead to sparkling clean, quiet guest rooms. All rooms have ceiling fans and private bathrooms with hot showers. A single goes for $10, a double for $12. *1a Nte. Ote. 367, at 2a Ote. Nte., tel. 961/3–08–24. 30 rooms, all with bath.*

Hotel San Antonio. This hotel is like a breath of fresh air on the busy streets near the second-class bus station. With only 15 exceptionally clean rooms, all with fans and private bathrooms, this place is usually full, but it's worth a try. Singles cost $10, doubles $13.50, and triples $18. *2a Sur Ote. 540, tel. 961/2–27–13. Around the cnr from 2nd-class bus station.*

➢ UNDER $20 • **Hotel Plaza Chiapas.** This fairly new hotel offers very clean rooms complete with fans and color-coordinated bathrooms with hot water and towels. Singles are $12, doubles $15, and triples $18.50. *2a Nte. Ote. 299, 2 blocks NE of zócalo, tel. 961/3–83–65. 34 rooms, all with bath.*

HOSTEL **INDEJECH Youth Hostel.** Located in a youth-sports center, this clean hostel provides single-sex dorm-style accommodations complete with clean sheets, pillowcases, and towels for $4 a night. Three meals a day are available, each for about $2. It's an excellent deal, even with the cold showers and 11 PM curfew. *Av. Central, at 18a Ote., tel. 961/3–54–77.*

CAMPING **La Hacienda Trailer Park.** If you are determined to camp, you can pitch a tent for $12 a night plus $2 per person and use all bathing and pool facilities here. *Blvd. Belisario Domínguez 1197, tel. 961/2–79–86. 2 km from the tourist office.*

FOOD

Because people from all over the state come here to shop, sell their products, or do other types of business, Tuxtla offers a chance to sample cuisine from almost anywhere in Chiapas. The center swarms with eateries and cafés; look for the striped umbrellas off the zócalo. Most restaurants serve local favorites, including crumbly Chiapan cheese, tamales, and spicy tacos top-heavy with chiles. The city's prosperity has also bred a substantial middle class, which, like its counterparts worldwide, has time and money to spend worrying about things like whether meat is good for them. The result: Gyms and health-food stores are scattered about town, and most restaurants have a selection of vegetarian dishes—there's even a place to find a killer soy burger.

In the morning or early afternoon, look for people sitting around stands drinking out of gourd bowls. These are filled with posol, a cold, corn-based drink flavored with sugar and/or cacao, with chewy cornmeal at the bottom.

➢ UNDER $5 • **Restaurante Imperial.** This central restaurant serves tasty and inexpensive local fare such as *entomatadas de pollo* (chicken in tomato sauce). The ample daily menu includes soup, a meat entrée, tortillas, a drink, and dessert for $4. The same management runs **Restaurante Tuxtla,** across the street, where food and prices are comparable. *2 Nte. Pte. 106, at Calle Central, no phone. Open daily 7 AM–6:30 PM.*

Restaurante Vegetariano Nah-Yaxal. Vegetarians are in for a treat here. Tasty *tortas* (sandwiches) made with soy beef on whole wheat, or chilaquiles with gluten are both $2.50, and the mammoth Energética Nah-Yaxal (fruit salad smothered in yogurt and granola) is $3.50. While you eat, you can browse through the book collection: Titles include *The Power of Respiration* and *Sprouts: The Most Perfect and Complete Natural Food. 6a Nte. Pte. 124, tel. 961/3–33–16. Open Mon.–Sat. 7:30 AM–9 PM.*

➢ UNDER $10 • **Las Pichanchas.** The menu here includes *tamales chiapanecos* (with mole sauce, olives, raisins, and meat and wrapped in banana leaves) for about $3.50 and *milanesas de ternera* (breaded cuts of veal) for the same price. Come for coffee and dessert to enjoy the cheesy but fun show put on by regional dancers and musicians every evening. *Av. Central Ote. 838, tel. 961/2–53–51. Open daily 8 AM–midnight.*

Trattoria San Marco. Of the tourist traps on the zócalo, this place wins the prize for variety, with one of the largest menus in Tuxtla. Try such house specialties as spaghetti bolognesa ($5), crepes ($6), or pizza topped with anything from avocado to *salchicha* (sausage) for $5–$9. Come here at night to join the crowd of regulars, including a cadre of chess players, for a $1 cappuccino or a $2.50 beer. *Off zócalo, tel. 961/2–69–74. Open daily 7 AM–midnight.*

WORTH SEEING

Tuxtla's main attractions lie in three distinct areas of the city: The **Parque Madero** is in the northeast part of the city; the **Parque Zoológico** is to the southeast; and the **zócalo** and **cathedral** are in the center. To reach the zoo from the center you will need public transportation from the town center, but the other two attractions can be easily reached on foot. The **market,** just two blocks south of the zócalo, is a dimly lit maze of giant papayas and other fruits, local cheeses, costume jewelry, and crisped *chicharrón* (pork rind).

PARQUE MADERO Just a few years old, the Parque Madero complex brings together a variety of indoor and outdoor Chiapan wonders, all within easy walking distance. Its attractions easily offer more than an afternoon's diversion for travelers with a yen for archaeology, botany, or cheesy amusement parks. The park begins at the intersection of 5a Norte Oriente and 5a Oriente Norte, about nine blocks northeast of the zócalo. Immediately outside the Parque Madero is the **Teatro Bonampak,** an open-air theater for cultural events. Consult *La Cartelera* (*see* Visitor Information, *above*) for a list of special performances.

➢ TEATRO EMILIO RABASA • The park's central landmark is the Teatro Emilio Rabasa, a huge modern theater that hosts frequent cultural events. *La Cartelera* (*see* Visitor Information, *above*) provides information on performances. Two tree-lined walkways extend from the theater. The western path, lined with bronze busts of famous Mexican leaders, winds its way to the museums and botanical garden, while the eastern path cuts through the children's recreational park.

➢ MUSEO REGIONAL DE ANTROPOLOGIA E HISTORIA • This sleek museum in a modern glass, brick, and marble structure provides a look at the Chiapan past and present. Exhibits trace the growth of early indigenous civilizations and are packed with Olmec, Maya, and Aztec artifacts. Look for oddly shaped Olmec skulls: Cosmetic cranial deformation was performed on noble Olmec children. Across the courtyard and upstairs is an exhibition on the Spanish invasion. Interspersed with huge colonial paintings of the Virgin Mary, ornate clocks, chests, guns, swords, crowns, and other Spanish artifacts are historical narratives and images of the enslavement and displacement of indigenous people. The contrast is effective. Musical instruments and crafts are also displayed. *Admission: about $2. Open Tues.–Sun. 9–4.*

➢ MUSEO Y JARDIN BOTANICO • Farther down the esplanade is a botanical museum run by the Chiapan Botanical Institute. Displays include native trees, flowers, and medicinal plants and provide a sense of the scope of preservation efforts being undertaken across the state. Across the esplanade from the museum is the botanical garden, founded by Faustino Miranda, who was, until fairly recently, the sole documentor of Chiapan fauna. Winding paths that crisscross the garden are filled with kissing teenagers walking through canopies of bamboo, mango trees, and twisting vines. *Admission free. Museum open Tues.–Sun. 9–3; garden open Tues.– Sun. 9–6.*

The Chiapan rain forest is home to representatives of 40% of all species found in Mexico, yet it's rapidly disappearing as a result of the government's eagerness to sell the highly marketable wood.

➢ CENTRO DE CONVIVENCIA INFANTIL • You don't have to be traveling with children to enjoy this kiddie park on the east esplanade, which features giant renditions of a demented Mickey Mouse. There are also pony rides, a little train, and piped-in music. *Admission free. Open Tues.–Fri. 10–9, weekends 24 hrs.*

PARQUE ZOOLOGICO The Parque Zoológico, one of the best in Latin America, features a selection of the spectacular and diverse wildlife of Chiapas. Concrete paths climb through cool, lush tropical canopies ringing with the songs of birds and insects. More than 100 species of native Chiapan creatures, many of them endangered, wander here in an approximation of their natural surroundings. There's an environmental education center, aviary, and even an insect zoo filled with giant roaches and huge, hairy spiders. The zoo affords rare glimpses of tapirs, a black panther, *guacamayas* (macaws), and the spectacularly plumed quetzal. Roaming free are *guaqueques* (rabbit-size rodents with tiny ears and no tail) and two species of turkey-like fly-

Bits of eco-inspiration around the zoo encourage conservation and respect for Mother Earth. Cleverest is the reflective glass with a sign that reads "This is the most dangerous species of all, responsible for all destruction and probably, eventually, its own destruction as well."

ing birds, the *pavil* and the *paron. SE of town, off Libramiento Sur. Take* CERRO HUECO *bus, which leaves every half hour from 1a Ote. Sur, btw 6a and 7a Sur Ote. Donations encouraged. Open Tues.–Sun. 8:30–5:30.*

AFTER DARK

For a reputedly hum-drum town, Tuxtla has a number of late-night surprises. In addition to the movie theaters near the zócalo, you'll find a wide variety of nightlife options that range from Budweiser monster-truck rowdiness to candle-lit melancholy. The music of street performers is common in the zócalo, especially on Sundays. Anything from a marimba ensemble or romantic-ballad crooner to a military band may be the performance of the day. *La Cartelera* (*see* Visitor Information, *above*) provides the rundown on more folkloric cultural events, and rock concerts are advertised in record stores.

BARS The clientele at the bars and cafés tends to change as the evening passes. In the early evening, cafés and bars attract a college-age crowd that congregates to find out where the real action will be taking place later that night. Next, middle-aged regulars come around to listen to live bands and/or watch *fútbol* (soccer) on TV. Check out **Obsession** (3a Ote. Nte. 142) and **Bar El Nucu** (Hotel María Eugenia, Av. Central Ote. No. 507) for throaty Mexican ballads from about 9 PM until 3 AM.

DANCING Tuxtla's discos attract a young crowd and tend to host events like bikini and "best legs" contests. The cover is generally about $5–$8 (usually a little less for women), and music ranges from Mexican pop to tropical and American Top-40. Worth checking out on weekends are **Sheik** (Hotel Flamboyant, Blvd. Belisario Domínguez Km. 1081, tel. 961/5–00–95), **Colors** (Hotel Arecas, Blvd. Belisario Domínguez Km. 1080, tel. 961/5–11–21), and **Freeday** (Blvd. Los Laureles, at Blvd. Belisario Domínguez). All are too far from the zócalo to walk. You can take a colectivo down Avenida Central until 9 PM, but after that you'll need to take a taxi ($2). Closer to the center is **Úngalo** (Av. Central Ote., 3 blocks east of the zócalo), which is packed with teeny-boppers rockin' to reggae and American pop on weekend nights. The cover here is $3.50.

Near Tuxtla Gutiérrez

CHIAPA DE CORZO

You might not guess that a quiet, friendly riverside town awaits you only 20 minutes by bus from Tuxtla. In the early morning you'll hear crowing roosters and the early bells of mass rather than cars, which only make rare appearances on these stone-paved streets. Nearly every Tuxtlan you meet will ask if you've taken the boat ride through the **Cañon del Sumidero** from Chiapa de Corzo. The locals' opinion of the place is exalted but justified: Gliding between the kilometer-high canyon walls is an experience not to be missed.

The fountain in the zócalo is connected to an abundant underground water source that helped townspeople to survive the epidemics that swept through much of Mexico in colonial times.

Chiapa de Corzo was an important pre-Columbian and colonial center because of its strategic location on the Río Grijalva. Today, its main sights are clustered around the **zócalo,** with its colonial clock tower and 16th-century fountain representing Queen Isabella's crown in the Moorish-influenced *mudéjar* architectural style. The **Palacio Municipal**, just off the zócalo in the arched **Plaza de Ángel Albino Corzo,** has murals depicting scenes from local and national history, including portrayals of the Chiapa Indians, who threw themselves into the Sumidero Canyon to escape enslavement by the Spanish. Handicraft shops around the plaza sell lacquerware, leather goods, and regional clothing. The free **Museo de la Laca** (Lacquerware Museum), on the top floor of the 16th-century **Ex-convento de Santo Domingo,** behind the cathedral, has an extensive collection of bowls, boxes, masks, and crosses from all over Mexico and Guatemala. Adjacent is a tiny shop with a meager selection of locally made bowls and masks. Behind the museum you can watch lacquer artisans teach young apprentices their craft. If you're lucky, you can catch a weekend class and learn the basics of this complex art.

You can also take a taxi from Tuxtla or Chiapa to any of four *miradores* (lookouts), which afford a bird's eye view of the Sumidero Canyon. The best way to enjoy the canyon, though, is by taking a two-hour boat ride along the Río Grijalva. The canyon is full of birds, alligators, and iguanas, and your pilot will maneuver into caves and close to shore to point them out. In July and August, heavy rains create four waterfalls, the largest of which is the **Árbol de Navidad,** a conical plume of water that cascades down the green canyon wall in the shape of a giant Christmas tree.

Expeditions originate from Chiapa's embarcadero and from Cahuaré (about five minutes up the road toward Tuxtla). To get to Chiapa's embarcadero from the zócalo, head past the cathedral and down the hill on Calle 5 de Febrero for two blocks. The fare is $7–$12, depending on the number of people. Trips run daily, from early morning until around 4 PM. Come in the morning if you're alone and want to to get in on a group deal.

Cascada El Chorreadero is a waterfall and swimming hole 7 kilometers east of Chiapa, toward San Cristóbal. The site is most beautiful in the rainy season (June–August), when the waterfall is strongest. Go on a weekday if you want some solitude. Take a bus from Chiapa toward San Cristóbal or pay $4 for a taxi.

COMING AND GOING Microbuses leave from 3a Oriente Sur between 2a and 3a Sur Poniente in Tuxtla every five to 10 minutes and go directly to Chiapa for 50¢. The buses run 6 AM–8 PM, and the ride takes about 20 minutes. Chiapa's bus station is one block east of the zócalo on 21 de Octubre, but you can always jump on a bus as it passes the zócalo. Taxis between Tuxtla and Chiapa are also readily available and cost about $5.

WHERE TO SLEEP Chiapa is an easy day trip from Tuxtla and even from San Cristóbal, so few visitors stay the night. **Hotel Los Ángeles** (Julián Grajales 2, tel. 961/6–00–48) is on the zócalo, near the fountain. The colonial-style building has somewhat grimy but spacious rooms with desks, fans, and French doors that look out onto the town and mountains. In high season (December and January, Semana Santa, late summer), it's best to call ahead and make reservations. Singles are about $12, doubles $18.

FOOD Chiapa's center has a number of food stands and small restaurants. For a little extra money and a lot more ambience head down the hill to one of the restaurants at the embarcadero and try the *mariscos* (shellfish). You'll also get a view of the river and perhaps some live marimba music. On a corner just outside the Museo de la Laca, a local family sells some of the best posol in Chiapas. You'll see a crowd of locals on the corner slurping, chewing, and scooping it out of the gourd bowls. It's only served before noon, so come early.

You Get What You Pay For

Lacquerware is made in Chiapa de Corzo by a labor-intensive process in which a gourd is rubbed with fat, then with a natural colorant (such as charcoal or earth), and buffed. This process is repeated at least four times before the gourd is ready to be painted. Most of the so-called lacquerware sold in the shops is in fact simply coated with oil paint and decorated. How do you tell the difference?:

- *Oil paint is slick and shiny and has a distinguishable odor, even when dry.*
- *Because lacquerware is repeatedly buffed, the surface is relatively blemish-free, resembling smooth pottery. Imitations will have a less uniform surface.*
- *If it's really cheap, it's not real.*

El Ausente. A favorite of locals, this restaurant serves a whopping plate of prawns fried in garlic with tortillas and condiments for $5.50. *Embarcadero, no phone. Open daily 8–6.*

Jardines de Chiapa. Just off the zócalo, Jardines costs more than most local places and caters to tourists, but it serves tasty and unusual local specialties unavailable elsewhere. *Sopa fiestera,* the hearty soup typically served on religious holidays, will fill an empty stomach with shredded chicken, avocado, hard-boiled eggs, tomatoes, onions, cheese, and noodles for $2.50. Also try *chipilín con bolita* (balls of corn paste, tomato sauce, and cheese cooked with a local tarragon-like herb). Average prices for a complete meal are $6–$10. Don't confuse this restaurant with another one of the same name on the zócalo. *Francisco I. Madero 395, tel. 968/6–01–98. 1 block from the zócalo, towards the pier. Open daily 9 AM–8 PM.*

FESTIVALS January is a month of folklore and festivals in Chiapa. A series of dances—including the **Las Chuntá** dance, in which men dress as women, and the **Parachico,** in which street dancers mimic Spanish conquistadores—begins on January 9 and runs throughout the month. The **Feria de San Sebastián** takes place January 15–22.

San Cristóbal

On January 1, 1994, the hilly colonial town of San Cristóbal, long a favorite of the international backpacking set, made headlines abroad when the Zapatista National Liberation Army (EZLN), made up mostly of Tzeltal and Tzotzil speakers, rushed in and took over the main square and municipal palace. The Zapatistas (so named in honor of the great Mexican revolutionary and champion of Indians' rights Emiliano Zapata) timed their uprising to coincide with the signing of the North American Free Trade Agreement. Their stated objective was to focus international attention on their demands for national democratic reform as well as land redistribution and improved education and health care for the region's desperately poor indigenous population.

Contrary to the impression created by the international press, however, the real action of the uprising in Chiapas took place around Ocosingo and in the Lacandón jungle, not in San Cristóbal. The Zapatistas were only here for three days. Nonetheless, the impact of the uprising can still be seen. Declining tourism has brought hotel prices down and quieted cafés, and masked dolls bearing sticks inscribed "EZLN" are now sold on the zócalo.

A masked, green-eyed EZLN spokesman calling himself Subcomandante Marcos emerged as a cult figure shortly after the January uprising. His witty communiqués and astute use of the media prompted some observers to call him the first postmodern guerrilla.

While you will not find a revolution in progress here, you will see Chiapan highlanders in traditional dress arrive in town every morning bearing home-grown produce, woven clothing, and handicrafts to sell at the market. The remaining European expatriates and backpackers still hang out and sip cappuccino in the cafés and bookshops downtown, and yogurt and granola are as common as beans and tortillas on restaurant menus. For a good view of the city, take a walk east of the zócalo and up the stairs to the yellow-and-white **Iglesia de Guadalupe**. You can see for miles around from the **Iglesia de San Cristóbal de las Casas,** at the top of the stairs leading up the Cerro de San Cristóbal. Cerro de Santa Cruz, the city's third vista point, requires a hike up a steep hill, but you'll be rewarded by the view from the **Iglesia de Santa Cruz**.

BASICS

AUTO PARTS/SERVICE **Refaccionaria La Aguilar** (Carretera Internacional, btw Insurgentes and Crescencio Rosas, tel. 967/8–42–26) offers parts and service for a wide variety of cars weekdays 8–7 and Saturday 8–6.

BOOKSTORES **Librería La Quimera** (Real de Guadalupe 24-B, tel. 967/8–59–70) is run by Lucas, a friendly Frenchman who carries a wide selection of Spanish, English, French, and German literature. Books on Maya culture and history are featured. La Quimera is open Mon-

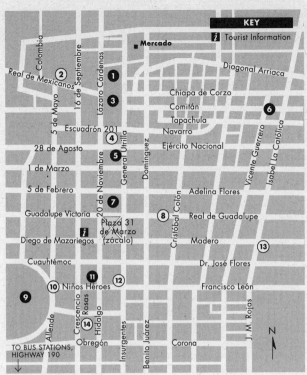

KEY

i Tourist Information

■ **Mercado**

Sights ●

Arco del Carmen, **14**

Casa de las Artesanías de Chiapas, **11**

Catedral, **7**

Centro de Estudios Científicos Na-Bolom, **6**

Ex-convento de Santò Domingo, **3**

Iglesia de San Cristóbal de las Casas, **9**

Museo Cultural de los Altos de Chiapas, **1**

Museo del Ambar, **5**

Lodging ○

Casa Margarita, **8**

Hospedaje Bed and Breakfast, **13**

Posada Caridad, **4**

Posada El Candil, **2**

Posada Morales, **10**

Posada San Cristóbal, **12**

day through Saturday 9–2 and 4–8. **Soluna** (Real de Guadalupe 13-B, no phone) has an equally impressive selection and is open weekdays 9:30–8:30.

CASAS DE CAMBIO Bancomer, Banamex, and Serfin, all clustered around the zócalo, exchange currency in the mornings. Banamex offers advances on both Visa and Mastercard between 10 AM and noon. For after-hours or weekend currency exchange go to **Casa de Cambio Lacantún** (Real de Guadalupe 12-A, tel. 967/8–30–63), half a block from the zócalo. It's open for cash and traveler's-check exchange Monday–Saturday 8:30–2 and 4–8, Sunday 9–1.

EMERGENCIES The **police** can be reached at 967/8–05–54. For an ambulance, call the **Cruz Roja** at 8–07–72.

LAUNDRY Lavorama (Guadalupe Victoria 20-A, tel. 967/8–35–99) is open Monday through Saturday 9–7, Sunday 9–2. Your clothes are washed and ironed in a couple of hours for about $2 per kilo.

MAIL The post office will hold mail sent to you at the following address for up to 10 days: Lista de Correos, San Cristóbal de las Casas, Chiapas, CP 29200, México. *Cuauhtémoc, at Crescencio Rosas, tel. 967/8–07–65. Open weekdays 8–7, Saturday 8–1.*

MEDICAL AID The **Hospital Regional** (Insurgentes, at Santa Lucía, tel. 967/8–07–70) offers 24-hour emergency care. **Cruz Roja** (Prolongación Ignacio Allende, tel. 967/8–07–72) does the same, and it's free. **Farmacia Regina** (Diego de Mazariegos, at Crescencio Rosas, tel. 967/8–02–41) is open day and night; after 10 PM, knock on the metal door for service.

PHONES There are public phones in front of the Palacio Municipal. **Pakal Yakaltic** (Adelina Flores 3, tel. 967/8–51–01), open daily 9–2:30 and 4–10, offers collect and cash long-distance service.

SCHOOLS The cultural center **El Puente** (Real de Guadalupe 55, tel. 967/8–22–50) offers one-on-one or group Spanish instruction at negotiable rates and can arrange homestays.

TOURS AND GUIDES Privately run tours to ruins and the surrounding indigenous communities are cheaper than those arranged by travel agencies. See Moisés at **Casa Margarita** (Real de Guadalupe 34, tel. 967/8–09–57) for information about trips to Toniná, the Sumidero Canyon, Palenque, Agua Azul, and the Lacandón jungle. Prices may seem steep to budget travelers ($170 to see the Lacandón jungle, Yaxchilán, and Bonampak; about $35 for all the others), but keep in mind that the cost includes a bilingual guide, transportation, and several meals. For a guided visit to nearby villages, meet Mercedes Hernández Gómez on the zócalo at 9 AM (*see* Near San Cristóbal, *below*).

VISITOR INFORMATION The **tourist office** in the Palacio Municipal can answer most questions. Although brochures are in short supply, they have stamps and maps and post information on buses and live music. *Off the zócalo, tel. 967/8–07–15. Open weekdays 9–8, Sat. 9–2.*

COMING AND GOING

BY BUS The first-class **Cristóbal Colón** bus terminal (tel. 967/8–02–91) is on Insurgentes, about eight blocks south of the zócalo. Buses depart daily for Mexico City ($47, 21 hrs) at 2:15 PM and 5:30 PM, with luxury service ($57) at 4 PM. Buses leave for Oaxaca city ($21, 12 hrs) at 5:15 PM; Ocosingo ($2.50, 3 hrs) at 10 AM, 5 PM, and 8:15 PM; Palenque ($6, 7½ hrs) once at 9 AM, and frequently in the evening; Tapachula ($12, 9 hrs) at 6 AM and 6 PM; Tuxtla Gutiérrez ($3, 2 hrs) and Comitán ($4, 1½ hrs) hourly from 7 AM to 9 PM; Mérida ($33, 15 hrs) at 9:15 AM and 8 PM; and even Cancún ($48, 21 hrs) at 7 PM. It's wise to book ahead since buses fill up quickly. No luggage storage is available at the station.

Second-class service is available from the **Transportes Tuxtla Gutiérrez** station (tel. 967/8–48–69), half a block up Allende from the Carretera Internacional (the Pan-American Highway). Ten buses daily serve Palenque ($5, 8 hrs), with a stop in Ocosingo ($2, 3 ½ hrs). There is hourly service to Tuxtla Gutiérrez ($2.25, 2 hrs) and Comitán ($2, 2 hrs) during the day. Buses for Tapachula ($8, 9 hrs) leave at 5:30 AM and 12:30 PM.

School buses and microbuses run by **Transportes Lacandonia** (Pino Suárez, at the Carretera Internacional, tel. 967/8–14–55) leave for Ocosingo ($2, 3½ hrs) and Palenque ($6, 8 hrs) seven times daily; Villahermosa ($9, 9 hrs) at 7 AM; Mérida ($21, 18 hrs) at 6 PM; and Chetumal ($20, 15 hrs) at 8 PM. To reach the station from the zócalo, walk eight blocks down Insurgentes to the Carretera Internacional, then head two blocks to your right.

HITCHING Hitching to the villages surrounding San Cristóbal is fairly easy, but once out of town you may have to wait a while before a vehicle passes by. If you're going to a remote locale, don't wait until evening to come back, because the roads are infrequently traveled even during the day. Drivers will let you ride for free, but it's acceptable and appropriate to offer some money.

GETTING AROUND

Most sights are within easy walking distance from the center, and the farthest are only a 20- or 30-minute walk away. The hub of the town is the zócalo, otherwise called the **Plaza 31 de Marzo,** bordered on the north by the cathedral. The streets off the square are loaded with budget eateries and hotels. Although the streets are clearly labeled, remember that all streets change name as they come level with the zócalo. (For example, Insurgentes becomes Utrilla as it passes through the center going north).

BY BUS Crowded colectivos run frequently. Major routes are north to south along Insurgentes/Utrilla from the Carretera Internacional to the market and east to west along Real de Guadalupe/Guadalupe Victoria. The fare is about 35¢. To get a ride, flag down one of the always-attentive drivers at any point on the road and pay him directly. To make it known that you would like the driver to stop, shout "se baja!" ("someone's getting off").

BY TAXI Taxis await passengers in front of the cathedral on the north side of the zócalo. Rates within the city are standardized; without baggage the cost is about $2, with baggage $2.50. Rates to surrounding sites and villages are negotiable. Coming from the Cristóbal Colón station, taxis other than those recruiting passengers to Tuxtla or Comitán are hard to find. Take a colectivo or walk a few blocks west to the Transportes Tuxtla Gutiérrez station, where taxis are more plentiful.

BY CAR **Budget Rent A Car** (Diego de Mazariegos 36, tel. 967/8–18–71) will rent you a VW bug for a hefty $65 a day including insurance and 100 free kilometers. In the rainy season (summer), the roads are dangerously slippery where the pavement ends. Try to start out early in the day to avoid getting caught in the torrential afternoon rains.

WHERE TO SLEEP

Loads of hotels—many touched up with colonial flourishes—have sprung up here in the last two decades. Competition keeps prices low and cleanliness standards high. Anywhere you stay, make sure the hot water is in working order; the morning air in San Cristóbal can be chilly. If all the places listed below are full, try **Posada El Candil** (Real de Mexicanos 7, tel. 967/8–27–55).

➤ UNDER $10 • **Hospedaje Bed and Breakfast.** The prices at this guest house make up for the walk it takes to get here from the center of town. Doubles without private bathrooms are $9.50. Singles and doubles with private bath are $5 and $12.50 respectively, and a bed in one of the dorm rooms is $3.50; the prices include a generous breakfast. Weekly and monthly rates are also available. None of the rooms is luxurious, but the proprietor is kind, and hot water is available early in the mornings. *Madero 83, 8 blocks east of zócalo, tel. 967/8–04–40. 25 rooms, 9 with bath; 9 dorm beds. Luggage storage.*

Posada Caridad. This inn is clean and comfortable, if a bit drab, and offers a great location. Rooms are $8.50 without bath or $10 with private bath for both single and double occupancy. The tap spouts hot water all day. *Escuadrón 201 No. 6, 4 blocks north of the zócalo, no phone. 14 rooms, 7 with bath. Luggage storage.*

➤ UNDER $20 • **Casa Margarita.** At this former private mansion, rooms have high ceilings and triple-blanketed beds, and the courtyard has comfy chairs for reading. Singles are $8.50, doubles $12, and dormitory beds $4. Everyone shares the clean communal bathrooms, and the showers are hot all day. This is a great place to meet other travelers or make contact with lost companions via the bulletin board. You can also arrange horseback riding and excursions from here (*see* Tours and Guides, *above*). *Real de Guadalupe 34, 3 blocks east of the zócalo, tel. 967/8–09–57. 26 rooms, none with bath. Luggage storage, wheelchair access.*

Posada Morales. Ten private cabanas, each a big bed, antique dresser, desk, fireplace, and stove, rrent for $18 a night, regardless of the number of occupants. *Allende 17, at Niños Héroes, tel. 967/8–14–72. 10 cabanas, all with bath. Luggage storage.*

Posada San Cristóbal. The huge rooms in this grand old building have high ceilings, white walls, dark plank floors, antique furniture, and tall, heavy French doors that block all light and sound. Newly remodeled bathrooms and balconies off every room are a plus. Singles are $15, doubles $19, triples $23, and quadruples $25. *Insurgentes 2, 2 blocks south of zócalo, tel. 967/8–38–42. 10 rooms, all with bath. Luggage storage.*

➤ UNDER $60 • **Na-Bolom.** This colonial home (*see* Worth Seeing, *below*) once belonged to Gertrude and Frans Blom, who turned it into a cultural center devoted to the study and preservation of the Lacandón Maya and their rain forest. It also features 12 luxurious guest rooms, each decorated in the style of a different indigenous village. Singles are $43, doubles $50, and the price of the room includes meals eaten with the center's staff and other guests. Fireplaces, books, bathtubs, art, and access to the garden and educational events are extra perks. With Gertrude's death in 1993, however, the place has changed ownership, and may be turning into more of a resort than a cultural center. *Vicente Guerrero 33, tel. 967/8–14–18. From Santo Domingo, walk 8 blocks east on Comitán. 12 rooms, all with bath. Luggage storage. Reservations advised.*

CAMPING **Rancho San Nicolás Camping and Trailer Park** (tel. 967/8–00–57), just under a kilometer east of town at the end of Francisco León, has tent spaces and cabins. Facilities include kitchens, electricity, and hot water for showers. Camping for two people costs $5; a room for two is about $9. If you don't mind going without the amenities, you can bypass the park and camp for free a short ways downriver.

FOOD

The large expatriate presence has had a decisive influence on San Cristóbal's cuisine. In addition to Chiapan fare, many restaurants and cafés serve yogurt, whole-wheat bread, green salads, and pizza. Budget eateries abound on the streets around the center, ranging from 50¢-taco stands to sit-down restaurants that serve five-course meals for $5. If you're broke, try some corn on the cob at the zócalo, or shop at the market, just north of Santo Domingo. If you have $8 to spend, **Na-Bolom** (see Worth Seeing, below) serves lunch at 1:30 and dinner at 7 PM at a communal table where you can eat with the staff and other travelers. Reservations for meals at Na-Bolom must be made at least two hours in advance.

➢ UNDER $5 • **Comedor Familiar Normita II.** Norma herself presides benevolently over this comfortable spot, where the enchiladas in red mole ($3.50) are especially tasty. A fireplace takes the bite out of the cold mountain air. *Benito Juárez 6, at José Flores, no phone. Open daily 8 AM–10 PM.*

Restaurante El Mirador II. This hole-in-the-wall cafeteria has a wide variety of Mexican food at rock-bottom prices. Try the *huaraches* (long tortillas filled with refried beans and topped with cheese, lettuce, meat, and salsa) for less than $1 each, followed by a mug of *atole* (a sweet, corn-based drink similar to hot chocolate) for $1. *Madero 14, no phone. Open daily 9 AM–11 PM.*

Restaurant Las Estrellas. Tangy brown rice with veggies and salad sets you back about $3 at this unpretentious eatery. A heaping plate of spaghetti with meat sauce is $3.50, and the filling quiche ($3), followed by a goblet of creamy hot chocolate ($1.50), primes you for a deep sleep. The pies ($1.50), especially the lemon chiffon, are also wonderful. *Escuadrón 201 No. 6-B, no phone. In front of Santo Domingo. Open daily 9 AM–10 PM.*

➢ UNDER $10 • **Casa de Pan.** This bakery/restaurant is run by baker extraordinaire Kippy Nigh. Fresh bread, the best bagels in Mexico, organic salads, and veggie empanadas with curry ($3.50) are served on the comfortable patio. There's live music Thursday and weekend nights, so you can salsa to your heart's content after dinner. *Navarro 10, at Domínguez, tel. 967/8–04–68. Open Mon.–Wed. 7 AM–9 PM, Thur.–Sun. 7 AM–midnight.*

Madre Tierra. "Mother Earth" sells fresh yogurt with fruit and granola, big bowls of lentil soup ($2.50), and vegetarian or chicken entrées ($6 and $7, respectively). Homemade whole-wheat bread comes free with your meal. *Insurgentes 19, 3 blocks south of the zócalo, tel. 967/8–42–97. Open daily 8 AM–9:45 PM.*

Restaurant Tuluc. The daily offering here changes regularly, but it's always a bargain. A four-course dinner might include: an aperitif of milk, rum, and nuts; spicy vegetable potato soup; pasta; chicken bathed in olive oil, garlic, onions, and mushrooms; and flan with coffee, all for $6.50. Breakfast begins as early as 6 AM, but lunch and dinner are the best reasons to come. *Insurgentes 5, 1 block south of the zócalo, tel. 967/8–20–90. Open daily 6 AM–10 PM.*

El Teatro. Jazz plays in the background as you dine on French and Italian food in this elegant restaurant. The daily special ($6.50) includes a filling plate of spaghetti. The crêpes with chicken and mushrooms ($5) are so good that even the competition raves about them. Come here to linger over a long meal of good wine, satisfying food, and, of course, chocolate mousse for dessert. *1 de Marzo 8, 2 blocks north of the cathedral, tel. 967/8–31–49. Open daily 11–11; closed Tues. off-season.*

DESSERT/COFFEEHOUSES Espresso, cappuccino, tea, and pastries are always at hand in San Cristóbal. The places below are good for lively conversation, reading, writing, or spacing out, and you can nurse one hot beverage for hours with no hassle.

Cafetería/Restaurante Palenque. Though a bit out of the way unless you're coming from or going to the bus station, this friendly place features five specialty coffee drinks, including the *beso del ángel* (angel's kiss) with Kahlua and rum. A good-sized cappuccino costs under $1. The dessert selection is limited, but the fried plantains ($1) will definitely make you happy. *Insurgentes 40, no phone. 2 blocks north of Cristóbal Colón station. Open daily 8 AM–9 PM, but closes early when business is slow.*

Cafetería San Cristóbal. Coffee is about all they serve in this crowded café where locals spend hours bent over chess boards and newspapers. "American" coffee and espresso are 50¢, and the excellent cappuccino is $1. *Cuauhtémoc 2, at Insurgentes, tel. 967/8–38–61. Open Mon.–Sat. 9 AM–10 PM, Sun. 10–2 and 4–9.*

La Galería. The upper level of this popular café, art gallery, and handicrafts shop is a spacious parlor. The French doors facing the street allow good light for reading or writing. Locals and foreigners alike are lured here by the excellent pies and cakes that sell for less than $2 a slice. Come after 8:30 PM for live music. *Hidalgo 3, south of the zócalo, tel. 967/8–15–47. Open daily 8 AM–11 PM.*

WORTH SEEING

San Cristóbal is a conglomeration of many neighborhoods, each with its own church and patron saint, but the center of town is the **Plaza 31 de Marzo**, the zócalo. The **Hotel Santa Clara** on the south side of the zócalo was conquistador Diego de Mazariegos' house and is adorned with stone sirens and the royal lions of Castille, Spain. On the north side of the zócalo is the **Catedral**. It was first constructed in 1528 as a run-of-the-mill church, but, ten years later the pontiff declared it a cathedral, and paintings, altars, and an ornate facade were added. San Cristóbal's **market** (about eight blocks north of the zócalo, on Utrilla) is eight square blocks of vegetables, tropical fruits, medicinal herbs, poultry, and more. The produce comes from the small plots of land farmed by local Tzotzil and Tzeltal people, who carry it into town each day.

During the colonial period, the native people were required to bring goods to the zócalo as tribute to the king of Spain.

ARCO DEL CARMEN This tower is an example of the Moorish-influenced *mudéjar* architectural style, which incorporates elements of Islamic art. Begun in 1597, the tower was nearly destroyed in 1652 in one of the city's worst floods and was rebuilt by 1680. However, bad luck struck again in 1993 when a fire raged through the tower and church, destroying many early 18th-century religious paintings. It's still worth a look, if only to appreciate the efforts of locals attempting to rebuild a structure that is supposedly the only one of its kind in Latin America. *Hidalgo, 3 blocks south of the zócalo.*

CASA DE LAS ARTESANIAS DE CHIAPAS This store/museum is run by a government program meant to encourage handicraft production while improving the quality of life in the indigenous villages. The handicrafts for sale are quality-controlled, and the museum of local costumes is free. *Hidalgo, at Niños Héroes, tel. 967/8–11–80. Open Mon.–Sat. 9–2 and 5–8.*

CENTRO DE ESTUDIOS CIENTIFICOS NA-BOLOM This cultural center, museum, library, garden, home, and guest house is devoted to the study and preservation of the culture and rain forests of the Lacandón Indians, whose culture is considered closest to the pre-contact Maya than that of any other contemporary indigenous community. It was established by the late Frans and Gertrude Blom, a Danish/Swiss couple who dedicated much of their lives to the study of and advocacy for the Lacandón people.

The house has a comfortable library with 2,500 books on Chiapan culture, not to mention travel guides, the Bloms' writings, and other books on Mexico. Frans' collection of religious art is on display in the chapel, an exhibit of Lacandón artifacts fills the museum, and Gertrude's black-and-white photos of Chiapan Indians decorate the halls of the house. The bookstore carries books of Gertrude's photography and Frans' map of the Lacandón jungle, supposedly the best available. Hour-long tours take place twice a day and are followed by a film about the

Lacandón Maya and their rain forest. You can stay the night here (*see* Where to Sleep, *above*), or come for a meal featuring fresh produce from the garden (*see* Food, *above*). Things may be changing here, however—the person who took over since Gertrude's death in late 1993 seems more interested in Na-Bolom's money-making potential than in its social mission. *Vicente Guerrero 33, at Comitán, tel. 967/8–14–18. Admission to museum (including tour): $3.50. Tours Tues.–Sun., in English at 4:30, Spanish at 4:40.*

EX-CONVENTO DE SANTO DOMINGO The 16th-century former monastery of Santo Domingo houses **Sna Jolobil** (tel. 967/8–26–46), or "Weaver's House" in Tzotzil. It is the outlet store of a weaver's cooperative made up of about 800 Tzotzil and Tzeltal women. The cooperative's aim is to preserve Mayan techniques of weaving on the back-strap loom, and to ensure that the artisans receive a fair price for their work. The group derives its main income from the store, where fine *huipiles* (embroidered tunics), wool vests, brocade shirts, and ribboned hats characteristic of the surrounding villages are displayed and sold. If you haven't yet heard Tzotzil or Tzeltal spoken, listen discreetly here. The store is open Monday–Saturday 9–2 and 4–6. The **Templo de Santo Domingo,** with an interior of Chiapan cedarwood plated with gold, is next door. **J'pas Joloviletik** (Utrilla 43, tel. 967/8–28–48), another weaver's cooperative store across the street, is open weekdays 9–1 and 4–7, Sunday 9–1. *Santo Domingo is just above Escuadrón 201, btw Lázaro Cárdenas and Utrilla.*

MUSEO CULTURAL DE LOS ALTOS DE CHIAPAS This small museum focuses on local history and culture. All posted explanations are in Spanish, but you'll get the gist even if you can't read them. There are exhibits on the *encomienda* system by which the conquistadores were awarded the right to exact tribute from certain groups of Indians, and on the quantities of gold, natural resources, and agricultural products the Spanish sent back to Europe. Textiles from surrounding indigenous communities are displayed upstairs. Look closely—some of the symbols woven into the fabric are like those found in ruin carvings and murals. There is also a library around the back. *Next to Santo Domingo. Admission free. Open Tues.–Sun. 10–5. Library open weekdays 9–2 and 4–7, Sat. 10–1.*

MUSEO DEL AMBAR DE LOS ALTOS DE CHIAPAS Amber, a yellow-brown fossil tree resin, is on display and sold at this tiny museum. Nearby Simojovel Valley is one of the few areas in Mexico where amber is still mined. It's then polished and set in earrings, necklaces, and other ornaments and sold at a moderate price, especially when you consider that some sediment and bugs trapped in amber have been carbon-dated to the Jurassic Age. Be sure to check out the display of ants, beetles, butterflies, and mosquitos trapped in amber, as well as the carvings of Maya figures. *Utrilla 10, 2 blocks north of the zócalo, tel. 967/8–35–07. Admission free. Open weekdays 10–8.*

CHEAP THRILLS

A relaxing treat, particularly if your hotel doesn't have hot water, are the **Baños Mercedarios,** where you can choose between a steam or dry-heat sauna followed by a shower. The whole hour-and-a-half ritual comes to less than $3.50. Soap, towels, razors, and refreshments cost extra, about 65¢ each. *1 de Marzo 55, tel. 967/8–10–06. Open Mon.–Sat. 6 AM–7 PM, Sun. 6 AM–2 PM.*

FESTIVALS With its many neighborhoods and their patron saints, San Cristóbal celebrates something almost every week. The five-day **spring fair,** following Easter Sunday, is the biggest festival of the year, with street artists, music, and food. On July 25 is the **Fiesta de San Cristóbal.** On November 22 the **Fiesta de Santa Cecilia,** honoring the patron saint of musicians, is held. December 12–14 is the **Fiesta de la Virgen de Guadalupe.** For a comprehensive list of smaller festivals, ask at the tourist office (*see* Visitor Information, *above*).

SHOPPING

San Cristóbal is known for its woven and leather goods and amber jewelry, most of which are handmade by people from local villages. Shops crowd Real de Guadalupe and Utrilla. You can also buy Guatemalan goods in many of these shops, but they cost a lot more than they would across the border. The finest weaving is to be found in the weaving cooperatives of Sna Jolobil and J'pas Joloviletik, and the government-run Casa de Las Artesanías de Chiapas (*see* Worth Seeing, *above*). Don't buy amber off the street—it could easily be plastic or glass.

AFTER DARK

On Sunday night, everyone congregates on the zócalo. Stroll with a coffee or some popcorn from the numerous stands and soak in the scene. You can also head to one of the many restaurants in San Cristóbal that feature live music around dinnertime (about 8), usually without a cover charge. Whatever you do, come out early because the town, Cinderella fashion, shuts down at midnight sharp.

San Cristóbal's one real movie house is **Cinemas Santa Clara** (16 de Septiembre 30, tel. 967/8–23–45), showing mostly films of the sex-and-violence variety. Cultural center **La Puente** (Real de Guadalupe 55, tel. 967/8–22–50), run by California expatriate Bill English, offers an extensive array of services including a language school, art workshops, a ride and message board, and a new and used book collection in addition to evening presentations and occasional films. Best of all, they're usually free! Call or stop by to see what's up.

For the best salsa and nueva canción, try **La Galería** and **Casa de Pan** (*see* Food, *above*), where the music starts around 9 PM. **Restaurante Pizzeria La Taberna** (Real de Guadalupe 73, tel. 967/8–16–28) and **El Circo** (Crescencio Rosas 7, no phone) also feature a variety of bands from about 7:30 PM to midnight. If you prefer more of a party scene, **Disco Palace** (Crescencio Rosas 59) is the hot spot. The cover is $6.50.

OUTDOOR ACTIVITIES

Trails abound in the mountains surrounding San Cristóbal. You can hike around or rent a mountain bike from **Pingüinos** (5 de Mayo 10B, no phone). They're open daily 10–2 and 3–6, and the price is 75¢ per hour or $10 for the day. You can also take horseback-riding excursions to Chamula or the **Grutas de San Cristóbal**, a dank, stalactite- and stalagmite-filled cave about 11 kilometers southeast of town. Two-hour riding trips from Casa Margarita (Real de Guadalupe 34, tel. 967/8–09–57) cost $20–$25 per person. Others leave from Hotel Real del Valle (Real de Guadalupe 14, tel. 967/8–06–80) and cost $25–$30 per person. You can also head out to the Grutas on your own by hopping on any Comitán-bound bus and telling the driver where to let you off.

The **Huitepec Ecological Reserve,** just 3 kilometers out of town, is alive with hundreds of birds, bright flowers, and 600 plant species, including, in the rainy season, lots of deadly mushrooms. There's a 4-kilometer loop trail that affords a quiet, 1½-hour hike up through the cloud forest on the side of the Muktevitz volcano. The reserve is run by Pronatura, a conservation group that buys land and establishes parks to preserve the wildife for educational and scien-

Sergio Castro's Private Museum

A longtime resident of Chiapas, Sergio Castro has dedicated most of his life to preserving local indigenous cultures, working particularly with the Tzotzil community of Chamula. He has a beautiful collection of indigenous textiles and a detailed photographic record of local community development projects. Sergio works 7–5 every day in local indigenous communities and entertains small groups in his house after 6 PM. You need to get some friends together and call in advance for an appointment (be persistent, there's often nobody home). Sergio speaks French and English as well as Spanish. The tour is free, but donations are encouraged. Guadalupe Victoria 47, tel. 967/8–42–89.

tific purposes. To get to the reserve, take a colectivo bound for Chamula or Zinacantán from the market and ask to be let off at Huitepec. Guided tours are offered on Tuesdays, Thursdays, and Saturdays 9:30 AM–11 AM; sign up in advance at the Pronatura office at Adelina Flores 21 (tel. 967/8–40–69). Admission to the park is free, and it's open Tuesday through Sunday 9–5.

Near San Cristóbal

Several indigenous communties, each one-half to two hours from San Cristóbal, can easily be visited on day trips. Sundays, when local Tzotzil and Tzeltal people congregate in the markets to sell livestock, fruits, vegetables, and textiles, are the best days to go. Wonderful tours to Chamula and Zinacantán are led by Mercedes Hernández Gómez, who grew up in Zinacantán. The tour group meets daily (except for major holidays) at 9 AM at the zócalo's kiosk in San Cristóbal; look for Mercedes' umbrella. The tour is well worth it at $14, transportation included. If you're not sure you want to spend that much, go to the zócalo and listen to her introductory spiel, then decide.

All villages listed below are accessible by infrequent bus service or colectivo, with the exception of Zinacantán and Chamula, which are served frequently. If you do choose to go on your own, dress conservatively, don't take pictures without permission (it's also appropriate to pay your model), and stick to the main public areas—injudicious wandering will not be appreciated.

SAN JUAN CHAMULA Chamula's wood-and-mud houses and cornfields spread out into a small valley. Residents are recognizable by their dark-blue shawls and shirts, with ribboned braids for women and wool serapes and leather belts for men. The best time to visit is during the Sunday-morning market, when vendors expect visitors as well as locals and display their trademark cloth dolls, handmade clothing, and bracelets in addition to everyday items. Sunday mornings are also when the town's ruling body, called the *cargo*, holds an *audiencia* (public question-and-answer period) for villagers on the benches outside the church.

Evangelical Christianity is viewed with such suspicion by Chamulan elders that families who join Evangelical churches are expelled from the community.

Whenever you visit, however, don't expect an over-friendly welcome here—outsiders are treated with detached suspicion. Photography is an especially sensitive issue. You can enter Chamula's church, where the floor is covered with pine needles and shamans heal sick villagers, but you will be closely watched. Show respect, keep your distance, and put your camera away when you enter the church. Colectivos to Chamula ($1, 20 min) leave from the San Cristóbal market.

ZINACANTAN The men of Zinacantán wear elaborate, hot-pink serapes; the women wear beautifully embroidered huipiles and colorful shawls with red borders. The quiet town's main industry is the cultivation and sale of chrysanthemums and gladiolas. Sunday morning brings a small market (come early for the freshest flowers) and religious services. If you're lucky you may also catch the town's elders as they exit the church playing handmade guitars, harps, and drums and wearing ceremonial white shorts with high-backed Maya sandals.

To get here, take a colectivo ($1, 20 min) from the San Cristóbal market. There is also a path between Zinacantán and Chamula, but it has been the site of several assaults and should be avoided.

SAN ANDRES LARRAINZAR The Tzotzil village of San Andrés is about half an hour north of Chamula by bus. The people are friendly, and the Sunday market is interesting mainly for the brocade shirts sold here. There are no hotels, so make sure you leave early to catch a colectivo back to San Cristóbal. The major festivals are the Fiesta de Santiago Apóstol (July 24–26), the Fiesta de la Virgen de Guadalupe de Santa Lucía (December 12–13), and the Fiesta de San Andrés (November 30). Colectivos ($1, 45 min) leave from the San Cristóbal market.

CHENALHO Chenalhó lies about an hour's bus ride north of San Cristóbal, through tiny settlements and dramatic mountain scenery. The Sunday market fans out from the Iglesia de San Pedro in the center of town. Enter the church on Sunday and you'll find yourself in the midst of candles and thick, pine-fragrant incense. Carbonated drinks, such as Coca Cola, are used in ceremonies here as in other highland villages—the burp clears the body of evil spirits. Chickens and eggs are also passed over the body to absorb evil spirits and sickness, then killed or broken.

The major festival here honors San Pedro on June 29. The town has a hotel; if the none-too-receptive management feels like letting you stay, it's $3.50 per night for a scary room and tolerable communal bath. If you don't plan to stay over, plan a morning visit since colectivos become scarce in late afternoon. Buses depart from San Cristóbal's market.

AMATTENANGO DEL VALLE This Tzeltal town, about 39 kilometers south of San Cristóbal on the road to Comitán, is known for its pottery. Once a year the people dig for their annual supply of red clay. Black or white sand is mixed with the clay, depending on its density, and a

The Father, Sun, and Holy Ghost

While pre-Hispanic religions are still practiced in various forms throughout Mexico, the beliefs of many indigenous people today combine the symbols and deities of their ancestors with the Catholicism brought by the Spaniards and the Protestantism of more recent missionaries. The conventional exteriors of Catholic churches in Indian pueblos of southern Mexico often give way to pine-strewn, candle-lit interiors redolent with the fumes of copal, an incense sacred to the Maya. The sun god of the Maya pantheon has been recast in the figure of Jesus Christ, who has taken on many of his attributes, and San Juan Bautista is worshipped with many of the ritual elements once reserved for Chaac, god of rain and lightning. The most famous example of this sort of syncretism is the cult of the Virgin of Guadalupe, the brown-skinned Mary who first appeared in 1531 in a vision to a converted Indian on the hill of Tepeyacac, where the local people had traditionally worshipped the mother of the gods.

Other uniquely Mexican "Christian" traditions include Día de los Muertos, or the Day of the Dead. This ritual honoring dead friends and relatives is celebrated on November 2 throughout Mexico. The beginning of November was an important Aztec festival in honor of the glorious deaths of warriors and children, now combined with All Souls Day, a Catholic holiday of remembering the dead. Families sprinkle the graves of loved ones with marigolds, then eat an honorary meal in the cemetery, while children eat candy skulls painted with their names in bright icing, a reminder that death is not something to fear.

Even before the Spanish arrived in Mexico, however, the groundwork was laid for a union of Christian and native religions. The symbol of the cross, for example, was a potent one for ancient Mexico: It is said that just before he disappeared from the Earth, the feathered serpent god Quetzalcoatl planted a giant wooden cross on the beach at Huatulco that resisted all efforts to pull it down. The cross symbolized the ceiba tree that held up the Mesoamerican world, and life itself. The stone covering the sarcophagus of Lord Shield Pakal, 7th-century ruler of Palenque, depicts his descent into the underworld with a giant cross, representing life, emerging from his body. Today, pine branches (another symbol of life) are tied to crosses overlooking highland towns, a testament to the blending of Mesoamerican and European beliefs.

ground rock called *bash* is added to help the pottery harden. The clay is then worked into huge round-bottom stoves, bowls, urns, platters, cookware, and water vessels by local women. The work is done entirely by hand, without the aid of a pottery wheel (incredible, given the uniformity of the pieces). The town will seem deserted at first, but soon a child may approach and ask you to look at her clay animals. People work out of their houses and are likely to invite you in to look at their wares. The major festivals are the celebrations of the village's patron saint, San Francisco, from April 28 to 30; of San Pedro Mártir, on October 4; and of Santa Lucía, on December 13. Any Comitán-bound bus will get you here in about 40 minutes.

Ocosingo and Toniná Ruins

Ocosingo is a medium-size Tzeltal town in the green foothills of the Sierra Madre, at a confluence of valleys that run from the Chiapan highlands to the Lacandón jungle. It was here, in January 1994, that the Zapatista rebels confronted the Mexican army in one of the biggest battles of the uprising, and that the photographs of bloodied bodies that got so much international press were taken. The dead were peasants suspected of rebel activity, executed by the army in Ocosingo's central plaza.

The Zapatistas weren't the first to appreciate Ocosingo's strategic location. Just seven miles from town are the impressive, but little known, ruins of Toniná, a Maya city that was at its height from AD 500 to 1000. The ruins are tough to get to, but well worth the effort. Passageways wind through the imposing seven-tiered pyramid and descend into tombs complete with stone sarcophagi and still-discernible depictions of jaguars, skeletons, and decapitated ball players. A small museum displays a fair selection of Toniná statuary; many of these pieces were also decapitated, supposedly by the invading forces of a rival city. The site and museum are open daily 9–4, and the entrance fee of $3.50 gets you into both. Sundays, admission is free.

The people of Ocosingo are still feeling the tension of *el conflicto* ("the conflict," as people here refer to the recent violence), and you can expect army checkpoints, nervous villagers, and some suspicious looks if you venture into the boonies. Still, this may be your best chance to get a glimpse of the reality behind the news stories, and you're in no real danger here, unless things have changed radically for the worse—just keep an eye on the news.

COMING AND GOING

Frequent buses connect Ocosingo with San Cristóbal and Palenque. First-class buses depart from the **Cristóbal Colón** station (Carretera Ocosingo–Palenque Km. 2, tel. 967/3–04–31). The station is about a 20-minute walk from the zócalo along 1a Oriente Norte. Buses leave for Palenque ($4, 3 hrs), Puebla ($41, 13 hrs), and Mexico City ($46, 16 hrs) at 4 PM; for Tuxtla Gutiérrez ($5, 5 hrs) at 11:30 AM; and for Villahermosa ($8.50, 5½ hours) at 2 PM and 10:30 PM.

From the zócalo in Ocosingo, walk 3½ blocks up the gentle hill on Avenida 1a Norte Poniente for the departure point of the second-class lines. **Autotransportes Ocosingo** has second-class service to Tuxtla Gutiérrez ($4.50, 4 hrs) and San Cristóbal ($2, 2½ hrs) frequently between 5 AM and 3:30 PM daily. **Transportes Fray Bartolomé de las Casas**, which locals criticize as unreliable and dangerous, serves Agua Azul at 2 PM for $3.50. To get here, walk up the hill from Autotransportes Ocosingo and turn left on 1a Norte. The most reliable second-class bus service is offered by **Transportes Tuxtla Gutiérrez** (Carretera Ocosingo–Palenque, across from Las Casas), which goes to Tuxtla ($4.50, 3 ½ hrs), Comitán ($2.50, 2½ hrs), San Cristóbal ($2, 2 hrs), and Palenque ($3, 3 hrs). **Transportes Lacandonia** (near the Tuxtla station) runs second-class buses into the Lacandón jungle, including the village of Nahá (*see* Near Palenque, *below*). The cost is $8 for the six-hour ride.

There is no public transportation to Toniná, so unless you have a car or want to hire a taxi ($14–$25 for the trip), you'll need to go to the market in the morning, and ask around until you finally get on a truck that will pass the road that leads to the ruins. Your best bet is someone headed to Guadalupe, a town just past the ruins, but make it clear that you're headed for the ruins, because trucks don't always go that route. Don't be fooled by the signs for Toniná—the first is a good three-hour walk from the site. With luck, you'll be let off at the last cross-roads, a 20-minute walk from the ruins. Be sure to head out early to hitch a ride for the return trip, as traffic is light and you may be in for a 3 ½ hour walk back to town. If it's late, you might be able to scam a ride home with the people who work at the site and museum. You'll be expected to pay 50¢–$1 for the ride.

WHERE TO SLEEP

Ocosingo has few hotels, and the ones that exist tend to have delightful little extras like cockroaches and smashed mosquitos on the walls. It's possible to make a day trip here from San Cristóbal or Palenque, but if you do decide to stay the night, these are your options:

Hospedaje San José. The cheapest beds in town are simple and dark, but fairly clean. A room with two beds and a bath runs $10. They claim there's hot water, but don't count on it. *1 Ote. Nte. 9, tel. 967/3-00-39. 22 rooms, 21 with bath. Luggage storage.*

Hotel Bodas de Plata. The big rooms are stocked with towels and soap as well as some creaky old furniture and floral-patterned curtains. Best of all, the fans in every room cool things off during the midday heat, and there is piping hot water for cool Ocosingo mornings. Singles are $10, doubles $14, triples $17. *1a Sur, at 1a Pte., tel. 967/3-00-16. Just south of the Palacio Municipal. 15 rooms, all with bath. Luggage storage.*

Hotel Central. This hotel provides small, quiet, comfortable rooms. All have tiny black-and-white TVs with cable and bathrooms with plenty of hot water. The restaurant/café downstairs offers a vantage point above the action on the zócalo. Singles are $15, doubles $23. *Calle Central 5, tel. 967/3-00-24. 12 rooms, all with bath. Luggage storage.*

FOOD

Ocosingo's market offers cheap fruit, bread, fresh tortillas, and locally made cheese; to find it, walk downhill on 2a Avenida Sur Oriente and turn left just before the dusty lot. Good, cheap tacos are cooked up in front of you at **El Buen Taquito** (967/3-02-51) on Avenida Central near the zócalo. There are also a few tiny, reasonably priced food stores around the zócalo.

La Michoacana. This pink-and-white-striped restaurant outshines the other budget eateries clustered around the zócalo. Fill up on quesadillas of locally made cheese for 35¢ each; order *sincronizadas* (sandwiches made with tortillas instead of bread) and you're in for a concoction of cheese, ham, onions, chiles, and avocados for only $2. With a wide selection of *licuados* (smoothies) for $1, you can afford to indulge in banana, *guanábana* (custard-apple, similar to cherimoya), and oatmeal smoothies. *Av. Central Ote. 3, in front of zócalo, tel. 967/3-02-51. Open daily 6 AM–9 PM.*

Restaurante La Montura. This is the kind of place where you arrive famished and leave absolutely stuffed with bread, wine, coffee, and dessert for $6–$10. A platter of spicy chicken *chilaquiles* (tortilla strips doused with salsa and sour cream) is $4, and filling fried bananas with cream are $1.50. Choose your preferred pick-me-up; order a foamy cappuccino ($1) or head for the full bar. *Off zócalo, beneath the Hotel Central, 967/3-05-50. Open daily 7 AM–11 PM.*

Palenque
The ruined Classic Maya city of Palenque is magical. As you watch the morning mist rise over the temples and listen to the howler monkeys call through the jungle, it's hard not to be awestruck. The nearby town of Palenque doesn't have quite the same effect. It's dusty, small, relatively expensive, and basically uninteresting. Get out as fast as you can and head for the ruins and surrounding rain forest and waterfalls.

Luckily, many of the big tour buses have cancelled their stops at the Palenque ruins until the conflict in Chiapas calms down to the satisfaction of your average package tourist. So, for the moment, you can enjoy the ruins unmolested by the hordes that usually descend on major archaeological sites. Because Palenque normally crawls with tourists, however, restaurant and hotel owners are accustomed to charging top dollar for meager services. Plan to spend long days exploring the ruins and rain forests or lying in your hammock and hanging out with hippies at the nearby Mayabell campground to ensure that you escape from this tourist trap with a few pesos left in your wallet.

BASICS

AUTO PARTS/SERVICE The **Centro Refaccionario Automotriz** offers parts for a variety of mechanical monsters. *Juárez 180, tel. 934/5–03–05. Open Mon.–Sat. 7:30–3 and 4–9.*

CASAS DE CAMBIO At **Bancomer** (Juárez 25, tel. 934/5–01–99), several blocks west of the zócalo, expect to wait up to two hours to exchange traveler's checks and receive Visa advances. It's open weekdays 10–noon for traveler's-check exchange. There are also ATMs here. **Viajes Yax-ha** (Juárez, at Aldama), as well as most other travel agencies, will change cash and traveler's checks, although the exchange rate drops after the banks close. *Open daily 9–2 and 5–9.*

LAUNDRY **Lavandería Automática Palenque** washes clothes and returns them the same day for $1.50 a kilo. *Allende, at 5 de Mayo, next to ADO bus station. Open Mon.–Sat. 8–1 and 4–7.*

MAIL The post office has the usual services and will hold mail sent to you at the following address for up to 10 days: Lista de Correos, Palenque, Chiapas, CP 29960, México. *Independencia, at Nicolás Bravo, 1 block south of zócalo, tel. 934/5–01–43. Open weekdays 9–1 and 3–6, Sat. 9–1.*

MEDICAL AID The **Centro de Salud** (Juárez, tel. 934/5–00–25), at the west end of town, is open weekdays 7 AM–8 PM and charges $2.50 for a general consultation. The **Hospital Regional** (Prolongación Juárez, tel. 934/5–07–33) has expensive 24-hour emergency service. **Farmacia 24 Horas** (Juárez, at Allende) is the place for reckless late-night self-medication.

PHONES The blue Ladatel phones around the zócalo often suffer the abuses of vandalistic kids. If they're in working order, they're your best bet. Otherwise, you'll have to pay a service charge of about $2 for international collect calls at a long-distance phone office. **Caseta Levis** (Juárez 13, tel. 943/5–08–56), open daily 7 AM–11 PM, is the best in town.

TRAVEL AGENCIES A number of travel agencies offer charter flights and other package deals to Bonampak, Yaxchilán, and the Lacandón jungle that will make your wallet go limp. Two-day trips to Yaxchilán and Bonampak include transportation, meals, lodging, and guides for $100 per person. Day trips to Yaxchilán (van and boat) and Bonampak (van and a two-hour hike) cost about $75 and $65 per person, respectively. Most require a minimum of four people. The one-day plane trip to both places costs $600 for one to four people. Other options include jungle tours and horseback and fishing trips. Travel agencies are clustered around Avenida Juárez and Aldama and coordinate with each other in putting together tour groups (usually four to six people are needed). Travelers who have taken the trips advise you to establish a big group (don't get suckered into a "private tour") and haggle. Agencies known to wheel-and-deal on prices include **Viajes Misol-Ha** (Juárez 48, tel. 934/5–04–88), **Viajes Toniná** (Juárez 105, tel. 934/5–03–84), and **Viajes Yax-Ha** (Juárez 123, tel. 934/5–07–98).

VISITOR INFORMATION The somewhat disorganized but friendly staff at the tourist office hands out business cards for the travel agencies and has a message board to reconnect lost friends and traveling companions. A map of the city, with a brief explanation in Spanish of the Palenque ruins, is also available. *Jiménez, at 5 de Mayo, tel. 934/5–08–28. Around the cnr from the Palacio Municipal. Open Mon.–Sat. 8 AM–9 PM.*

COMING AND GOING

BY TRAIN Absolutely pick some other way to travel to and from Palenque unless you've got lots and lots of time and/or very, very little money; the train that passes through Palenque offers ridiculously cheap and ridiculously slow third-class service only. A ticket to Mexico City costs $10.50, for example, but the trip can take up to three days. The trip in the opposite direction is notoriously unsafe, but if you want to try your luck it will get you to Mérida for $6—whether your luggage will arrive with you is another question. The train station is several kilometers north of town, so you'll have to take a taxi (about $2) to get there.

BY BUS First-class, air-conditioned **ADO** buses (5 de Mayo, at Juárez, 5 blocks from zócalo, tel. 934/5–00–00) go to Mexico City ($44, 14 hrs) four times daily, Mérida ($20, 8 hrs) twice daily, Campeche ($14.50, 6 hrs) three times daily, and Villahermosa ($6, 2 hrs) six times daily. **Cristóbal Colón** (past the Maya statue on main road to Palenque ruins, tel. 934/5–01–40) also offers first-class service: The fare to Mexico City is $39, and the bus leaves at 6:30 PM. Other destinations are Campeche ($19, 6 hrs), with a departure at midnight; Villahermosa ($5, 2 hrs), with departures at 1:30 PM and 5 PM; and San Cristóbal ($6.50, 5½ hrs) and Tuxtla Gutiérrez ($9, 7½ hrs), both with departures at 9:30 AM and 11:30 AM.

Roomy second-class **Transportes Tuxtla Gutiérrez** (tel. 934/5–03–69) buses leave regularly from the end of Avenida Juárez for Tuxtla Gutiérrez ($7, 8 hrs) and San Cristóbal ($6, 6 hrs). The station offers luggage storage.

GETTING AROUND

Palenque is easy to cover on foot. The town centers around the zócalo, which is three to five blocks from most hotels, restaurants, and bus stations. In typical Chiapan fashion, calles run north–south and avenidas run east–west. Most of the town's hotels, restaurants, pharmacies, travel agencies, juice bars, and other shops are on the main drag, Avenida Juárez. Taxis congregate on the east side of the zócalo. They're good for getting to the train station and to the Mayabell campground after the combis stop running, but they're a rip-off to the ruins or Agua Azul.

Microbuses and colectivos run by **Transportes Palenque** (20 de Noviembre, at Allende, 3 blocks SE of zócalo) and **Transportes Chambalu** (Allende, at Juárez, 3 blocks NE of zócalo) go to the ruins, Misol-Ha, and Agua Azul. Both offer service to the ruins every 10 minutes from 8 to 5 daily for about 50¢. Package plans to Misol-Ha and Agua Azul leave at 10:30 AM and noon, spending half an hour at Misol-Ha, then moving on to a three-hour visit at Agua Azul. The whole deal lasts about six hours and costs about $6.50, which is a bargain since it costs almost $5 to get to these places on your own, and you can't count on front-porch delivery to the sites on local buses.

WHERE TO SLEEP

Prominent on the list of gringo destinations, Palenque caters to both budget and luxury travelers. You can find fairly cheap dives as well as the purest air-conditioned luxury, although most places fall in the middle to upper price range. To save a few bucks, camp out at Mayabell (see below) or rent a hammock in Agua Azul (see Near Palenque, below) for $1. If money is tight and you're willing to let basic sanitary and aesthetic standards slide, check into either **Posada Charito** (20 de Noviembre 15-B) or **La Posada** (behind Hotel Maya Tulipanes, down a dirt road just across from the Maya statue) for $10 singles and $12 doubles. One final consideration is the time of year you're in town: The months of April, July, August, November, and December unfortunately bring about a 15% price increase for rooms. Don't be afraid to haggle—the recent depression in tourism should make the hotel managers a bit more flexible.

➤ UNDER $15 • **Hotel Posada San Juan.** On a dirt road off the tourist track, San Juan feels like it's in a cooler climate than the rest of Palenque. It's a deal for its pleasant, airy rooms and its proximity to transportation to the ruins. Singles are $10, doubles $13.50, and triples $17. Off Allende, near the cnr of 3a Av. Sur, tel. 934/5–06–16. From zócalo, walk up Juárez to Allende, then head left 4 blocks. 18 rooms, all with bath. Luggage storage.

➤ UNDER $20 • **Hotel Lacroix.** This unusual place has been an institution since 1956, when archaeologists began to frequent the ruins. On the lobby walls are painted replicas of letters written by famous archaeologists. The letters are addressed to Señor Lacroix, the late French archaeologist who owned Palenque, and illustrate interesting and varied views of the ruins. It's pricey for what you get, but the place is always full. Singles are $14, doubles $18, and triples $21. *Hidalgo 10, tel. 934/5–00–14. To left of zócalo when heading from bus stations. 6 rooms, all with bath. Luggage storage, wheelchair access.*

Hotel Misol-Ha. Straightforward lodging in the heart of the city, Misol-Ha is surprisingly quiet and neat. The kind staff cleans the rooms daily, leaving you a fresh towel and soap for the cold-water showers. The price would be high in other areas of Chiapas, but by Palenque standards, it's a good deal. Singles are $14, doubles $18 during the low season, but they jump to $22 and $25 respectively during the high season. *Juárez 14, tel. 934/5–00–92. 28 rooms, all with bath. Luggage storage.*

➤ UNDER $25 • **Hotel Vaca Vieja.** On a quiet street beyond Avenida Juárez's dusty hubbub, this hotel offers plenty of clean rooms and a jovial staff. The hotel's Restaurante Yunyuén, (*see* Food, *below*), is highly recommended. Singles are $14, doubles $22, and triples $25. *Av. 5 de Mayo 42, at Chiapas, tel. 934/5–03–77. 28 rooms, all with bath. Luggage storage.*

CAMPING **Mayabell.** This place is known worldwide to the hip, burned-out, and curious who come here to camp in overgrown surroundings and get the score on the 'shrooms. Avoid loose talk; locals have turned traveling *jipis* over to the police. Stringing your own hammock or pitching a tent costs about $2.50 per night. They'll rent you a hammock for another $2.50. Cabanas with two big beds and a private bath are $20. The communal bathrooms lack hot water but are super-clean, and there's a restaurant across the street. The campground is on the road to the ruins, several kilometers out of town. Take a colectivo headed for the ruins for about 10 minutes; simply tell the driver to let you off at Mayabell.

FOOD

Though Palenque is expensive and touristy in general, the prices at the many restaurants along Avenida Juárez and around the zócalo are moderate. For a simple, cheap meal, try the snack stands on the upper side of the square, where you can find tacos, tortas, licuados, and corn on the cob. Buy cheap bread and cheeses of every color at the small market four blocks south of the zócalo.

➤ UNDER $5 • **Restaurante "El Rodeo."** The Rodeo serves a decent, ample *comida corrida* (pre-prepared lunch special) for $4.50. The homesick can opt for a U.S.-style "rodeo burger," with ham, cheese, bacon, and all the trimmings ($3.50), and vegetarians will appreciate the selection of soups—the cream of mushroom ($2.50) is especially good. *Juárez 10, tel. 934/5–02–03. Open daily 7 AM–11 PM.*

Restaurante Girasoles. Of the cheap restaurants in town, this is one of the best and cleanest. An added bonus is its proximity to the ADO and Tuxtla bus stations, making it the spot for a snack while you wait for a bus and a good place to meet fellow travelers. Breakfast begins at 7 AM and runs about $1–$4. A hamburger piled high with bacon, cheese, and avocado comes with fries for just $2.50. *Juárez 189, tel. 934/5–03–83. Open daily 7 AM–11 PM.*

Restaurante Yunyuén. This restaurant in Hotel Vaca Vieja (*see* Where to Sleep, *above*) serves generous appetizers for $3 or less and light meals of yogurt and fruit for just $2. A monstrous goblet of chocolate milk is $1.50. The entertaining bilingual menu advertises tantalizing "sparrow gas" (asparagus) and the ancient Mayan delicacy, "pouches" (peaches). *5 de Mayo, at Chiapas, tel. 934/5–03–77. 3 blocks east of zócalo.*

➤ UNDER $10 • **Restaurante Maya.** Popular with Mexican and foreign tourists, this place is a bit pricey but serves quality local food. The best deals are the sandwiches ($2.50–$4) and breakfast specials ($3.50–$5.50). These breakfasts include fruit, bread and jelly, eggs, black beans, a stack of tortillas, and enough *café con leche* (coffee with milk) to drown a person. The pleasant atmosphere and view of the zócalo invite you to sip cappuccino ($2) and write post-cards after dinner. There's also a full bar. *Independencia, at Hidalgo, tel. 934/5–00–42. Open daily 7 AM–11 PM.*

Restaurante Mero-Lec. Live music and starlight seating are extra perks here, but the real attraction is good food at good prices. A shrimp cocktail is only $4, a hearty order of tacos just

$3.50. After dinner you can have a drink or play a game of Ping-Pong. *Merle Green s/n, in Centro Turístico La Cañada, no phone. Follow dirt road near Maya statue and turn right at Hotel Maya Tulipanes. Open daily 4 PM–midnight. Live music Wed.–Sat. 9:30–midnight.*

WORTH SEEING

The ruins of Palenque, a great Classic Maya center, are a sure stop for any traveler in the area, and for good reason—they are not only spectacular, but truly beautiful. The city, which is thought to have been founded in the 3rd century AD and abandoned for unknown reasons in the 9th, was at the height of its glory in the 7th century AD under the rule of the clubfooted Lord Shield Pakal. He is represented in numerous bas-reliefs and is most remembered for his tomb, one of the most important archaeological finds of the century.

You should allow a couple of hours to see everything, or more if the heat makes you sluggish. Guidebooks to the ruins are not sold on the premises, but you can buy a pamphlet with a blurb on each major structure. The English version is $2, the Spanish, $1. For more in-depth explanations, a private tour, arranged by a local travel agency or at the entrance to the ruins, costs about $24 per group. A cheaper and more flexible alternative is to simply blend in with another tour group and fade out when the explanations or tourists become tiresome. The ruins are open daily 8–5, and the entrance fee is $4.50, free on Sunday. Be prepared to slap down an additional $8.50 if you're toting a video camera. Colectivos shuttle frequently between the town and ruins (*see* Getting Around, *above*).

Palenque's rulers did not often marry outside the dynasty, and the physical deformations that resulted were considered marks of divinity. Zak-Kuk, mother of Pakal, had a massive head and jaw. Pakal, who was clubfooted, may have married both his mother and his sister. His son, Chan-Bahlum, had six toes on each foot and six fingers on one hand.

TEMPLE OF THE INSCRIPTIONS This wins the Building-You're-Most-Likely-to-See-on-a-Postcard contest. For the vertigo-free, the view from the top of the 26-meter pyramid is spectacular and provides a sense of the vast lands once under Palenque's domain. It is also a good vantage point from which to see the surrounding buildings' roof combs, vertical extensions that are characteristic of southern Maya architecture.

From the top of the pyramid you can descend to Pakal's tomb, in a chamber 1½ meters below ground. The six-toed Chan-Bahlum, Pakal's son, buried his father here in AD 683 and then had the entire 38-meter space above the tomb filled with debris. Mexican archaeologist Alberto Ruz uncovered the tomb in 1952 after spending four years plowing through the rubble, thwarting Chan-Bahlum's efforts to deter grave-robbers and nosy academics. Ruz found Pakal's body wrapped in red cloth and decorated with jade jewelry, an obsidian death mask, and other items to ensure his comfort in the next world. These are now exhibited in Mexico City's Museo Nacional de Antropología. At the site, you can see the tomb's five-ton lid, intricately carved with a likeness of Pakal as a young man, descending through the gateway to the afterlife. The enormous crypt is comparable to the huge tombs found in Egypt. The tomb, open daily 10:30–4, is definitely worth the sweaty, narrow, downward trek.

PALACE Next to the Temple of the Inscriptions, in the center of the site, is a cluster of buildings constructed over a number of years. Structures include steam baths, latrines, dwellings supposedly inhabited by priests, and rooms for religious ceremonies. From the center tower you can see walls of stucco friezes and masks in relief, many depicting Pakal and his dynasty.

THE THREE TEMPLES To the right of the Temple of the Inscriptions, these three pyramids were constructed by Pakal's son. The **Temple of the Cross** holds an image of a cross, representing the ceiba tree; the **Temple of the Foliated Cross** has a depiction of the monster of the underworld; and in the **Temple of the Sun** is a depiction of a shield, the sign of the sun god. Present-day Maya culture is certainly far removed from that of the Classic period, but such

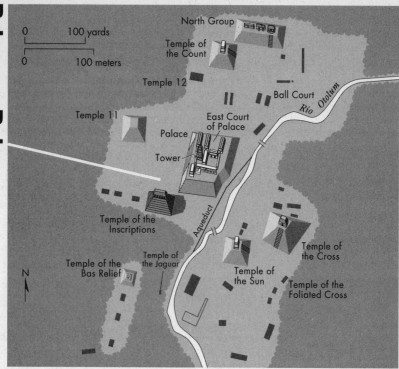

0   100 yards

0   100 meters

North Group

Temple of the Count

Temple 12

Temple 11

Ball Court

Río Otolum

East Court of Palace

Palace

Tower

Temple of the Inscriptions

Aqueduct

Temple of the Jaguar

Temple of the Bas Relief

Temple of the Sun

Temple of the Cross

Temple of the Foliated Cross

N

symbols retain their significance. In contemporary indigenous villages, for example, crosses decorated with pine branches still mark sacred places of worship.

TEMPLE OF THE JAGUAR This tiny temple is hidden up a short trail to the left of the Temple of the Inscriptions—follow the dirt path into the jungle alongside the Otolum River. The temple features a slippery stairwell leading to an exposed chamber. The trail continues on to some other smaller ruins amid dense jungle.

MUSEUM The brand new museum features bits and pieces from the site's digs as well as a general overview of the religious, social, and political structures of the Maya. Most notable are the stone slabs covered with hieroglyphics and the carved sculptures of Maya faces, which illustrate the Maya custom of cranial deformation for aesthetic ends. The photographs of Maya descendants, including Lacandón and Tzotzil people, are reminders that the ruins aren't just a pile of rubble from a forgotten, "ancient" civilization. Colectivos from the ruins come here for 35¢. *1 km down the hill from ruins on main highway. Admission: $4. Open Tues.–Sun. 10–5.*

QUEEN'S BATHS Pakal's wife reportedly dipped her queenly body into the various small waterfalls and swimming holes that dot a 3-kilometer trail leading to the ruins from the museum. You can refresh your aching bones in these pools set against the rain forest, but good luck trying to sneak into the ruins along this path—the guards are wise to that trick. If you just want to cool off before entering the ruins legally, the guard will let you splash around the first bathing pool for free. *Take a colectivo to the museum (1 km after the ruins) and walk across the street to the tiny path leading through the dense vegetation; it's about 100 m to the first swimming hole.*

Near Palenque

MISOL-HA AND AGUA AZUL

Rivers snake through the Chiapan rain forest, forming crashing waterfalls and deep swimming holes. Misol-Ha and Agua Azul are two such spots, both popular tourist stops which have yet to become completely overrun. Eighteen kilometers down Route 199 from Palenque, the single towering cascade at Misol-Ha thunders into a deep, cold, green pool. You can swim, sun on the rocks, and scramble and slide on the slippery boulders in the misty regions behind the falls.

Twenty-three kilometers farther south toward Ocosingo is Agua Azul. The lower swimming areas are often crowded with families and aggressive souvenir vendors, but it's still a treat to float down the river or play on the rope swing. For a more secluded experience, walk up the trail from the main swimming area, along the cascades for just under 2 kilometers to the calm pools. The colorful pools alternate with waterfalls in a steplike pattern. You can continue up the trail or climb from one level to the next in the water. It's safe to climb in this spot but deadly elsewhere, as is clearly marked with skulls and crossbones and multilingual warnings.

Crosses by the riverside mark the spots where people have perished. The marker for a German traveler named Franz reads: "He always loved the water."

COMING AND GOING You can choose from a number of ways to get here, depending on how much time you have and how much you like to walk. Microbuses from **Transportes Chambalu** and **Transporte Palenque** (*see* Getting Around, in Palenque, *above*) run directly to both spots from Palenque, stopping at Misol-Ha for 30 minutes and then spending three hours at Agua Azul. The round-trip fare is $6.50 to both places, and the journey takes about two hours one-way. If you prefer to go at your own pace, all buses bound for Ocosingo or Yajalón pass the *cruceros* (crossroads) for Misol-Ha and Agua Azul. The Misol-Ha crossroads is about 3 kilometers from the falls, and the ride will cost you $1. The 1½-hour ride to the crossroads for Agua Azul from Palenque costs $2, and the bus lets you off about 5 kilometers from the river. The walk is on a narrow, hot, paved road; watch out for microbuses swerving around corners. When you enter Agua Azul, you may be asked to pay an entrance fee of around $2, depending on how attentive the guards are.

WHERE TO SLEEP At the base of the Misol-Ha waterfall are several cabanas with all the modern amenities, like refrigerators, stoves, ovens, and cooking utensils as well as giant beds, hot water, and fans. Best of all is the private access to the spectacular falls and surrounding rain forest. The tourist industry hasn't discovered Misol-Ha yet, so you're in for a tranquil respite in these cabanas, which are a much better deal than accommodations in Palenque. All nine cabanas have private baths with hot water and mosquito screens. Get a group of four friends and rent the *familiar* (family-size) for about $40 during low season, $60 during high season. Cabanas for one to two people cost $20 during low season and $30 during high season.

You can hang your own hammock at Agua Azul for $2, or rent one for $2 more. Tent spots are also $2. Another alternative is to head toward the upper falls, where the people who run the *comedores* (food stands) may let you hang your hammock for free and offer you shelter if the rain sets in. Wherever you sleep, you'll need to bring some food, because lunch is the only meal sold here.

THE LACANDON RAIN FOREST

The Lacandón rain forest is not always as people imagine it, especially where humans have encroached, stripping it of its precious wood and razing the land for cattle ranches and farms. A road built smack-dab through the center of the forest, connecting Palenque with Nahá, has effectively done away with the natural and cultural isolation of the region. It is still home, however, to the Lacandón Indians, considered to be the living indigenous group most similar to their Maya ancestors, and it contains two important Maya archaeological sites, Bonampak and Yaxchilán.

NAHÁ AND LACANHÁ Most Lacandón people now live in or around the two main towns of Nahá and Lacanhá. Neither town offers hotel lodging, but local families will often let visitors sling hammocks in their homes. Bring your own provisions, and delicacies such as sugar and salt are appreciated as gifts. If you go to Nahá, mayonnaise is a favorite of Chan K'in Viejo (*see box, below*). Most of the southern Lacandón live in Lacanhá, and until very recently, most of them worshipped at Yaxchilán; the northerners worshipped at Palenque. These days, the northerners worship at Yaxchilán, and most of the southerners have converted to Christianity. Nahá is more isolated than Lacanhá. Many, especially those living in Lacanhá, now speak Spanish, but some speak only Mayan. Crafts, including bows and arrows and seed jewelry, are for sale in both places.

The best road into the Lacandón jungle runs straight to Lacanhá, a six-hour trip from Palenque. Nahá is farther, on a worse road, and takes about nine hours to reach from Palenque, or six from Ocosingo. You should bring a tent or hammock, and locals will tell you where you can spend the night. Transportation is available from Palenque or Ocosingo by second-class bus and through travel agencies in San Cristóbal and Palenque. Before venturing off into the jungle, it's a good idea to pick up a map of the rain forest, available in bookshops and at Na-Bolom (*see* Worth Seeing, in San Cristóbal, *above*), because many of the towns don't appear on most maps of Chiapas.

BONAMPAK In the grand scheme of things, this small ceremonial center played only a minor role during the Late Classic Maya period. What's notable about Bonampak, built between AD 400 and 700, are the colorful frescoes that depict people socializing, unlike most surviving Maya carvings that show religious rituals and high-ranking functionaries. The first white explorers to the region were on a 1946 National Fruit Company expedition looking to build a road through the rain forest. They stumbled upon this tiny palace, its murals strangely preserved in living color by a thin coating of limestone. Excavations took place soon after (National Fruit footed much of the bill), and several partially destroyed buildings and a plaza were uncovered.

The Lacandón Maya

The arrival of the Spanish in Chiapas induced many diverse Maya groups to band together and flee into the jungle. The Spaniards (wisely) didn't follow them into the treacherously unfamiliar territory. These Maya called themselves Hachack-Winick (the True People) and lived in isolation, scattered throughout the rain forest, until this century, when they were first contacted by anthropologists.

Currently, the physical existence of the Lacandón people is not in jeopardy, but they are becoming assimilated in greater numbers. Phillip Bayer, a Baptist missionary, spent 12 years trying to convert the people of Nahá with meager results. When he heard the last two elders of Lacanhá had died, he rushed in and successfully converted virtually all of southern Lacandón to Christianity in just a couple of years. The 104-year-old patriarch of Nahá, Chan K'in Viejo, has taken upon himself the task of preserving Lacandón social and cultural traditions.

To the many who have turned away from tradition, Chan K'in warns that to "cut the umbilical cord connected to one's traditions" means to "be denied the key to the heavens." Some predict that traditional Lacandón culture will fall apart when Chan K'in Viejo dies. Chan K'in has had three wives, one of whom has passed away; two still live with him. Together, their children (the youngest of which is said to have been conceived when Chan K'in was 102) are estimated to comprise 35% of the population of Nahá.

The colors are rather faded, and some claim that seeing the reproductions in Mexico City's anthropology museum will save you a lot of time and unnecessary effort. But the real thing in its original context, plus the adventure of getting to the site, is exciting. Just don't expect comic-strip clarity on the walls. Admission to the site is $5, free on Sundays.

Buildings 1, 2, and 3 are clustered around the south side of the plaza. Building 1 contains the murals. The scenes depict an everyday religious ceremony, with people enjoying themselves, interacting with one another, and changing expressions from frame to frame. The royal figures are dressed in capes, and the main lord wears quetzal feathers. Another mural depicts royal women practicing ceremonial bloodletting by pricking their tongues.

➤ COMING AND GOING • Transportation to the ruins is most easily set up through a travel agency (see Travel Agencies in Palenque, or in San Cristóbal, above). If you're coming by car, drive past Lacanhá until the road ends and then hike the 9 kilometers to the ruins. You can also get here by bus. From Palenque, take a **Transportes Montebello** second-class bus down the winding road to Lacanhá (6 hrs) and walk 13 kilometers to the ruins.

YAXCHILAN The Yaxchilán ruins lie on the shores of the Usumacinta River, 32 kilometers north of Bonampak, at the Guatemalan border. This ceremonial center, built between AD 500 and 800, was considerably more important than Bonampak and is still considered sacred by the present-day descendents of the Maya. For several years, the Lacandón people were prevented from worshipping at Yaxchilán and Palenque by the National Institute for Anthropology and History (INAH), because it was feared they would damage the temples. Access has been restored, and inhabitants of the northern Lacandón once again perform their ceremonies here. They used to worship at Palenque, but according to Lacandón elder Chan K'in Viejo, "the spirits have left there now," to retreat to their last home in Yaxchilán.

The site was ingeniously landscaped around the twisting Usumacinta River; the ruins remain accessible only by boat. The highlight is the series of high temples, many with stelae and glyphs. Carvings depict the two most important rulers: Jaguar Shield, in power in the seventh century, and Bird Jaguar, who ruled a century later. You'll probably have to fork out a tidy sum for a visit here, so try to see everything you can. Transportation is arranged by travel agencies. Or, you can try to arrange boat transportation with a local resident in Lacanhá for about $20. Boat trips also leave the border town of Frontera Echevarría, called Corozal on the Guatemalan side, for $120 each way, for up to eight people.

There's a large palapa for sleeping in Yaxchilán, but no facilities. You can bathe and fish in the river, and have your catch or any other food prepared by the woman who cooks for the guards. Any gifts of cigarettes, liquor, or fresh food are well appreciated. You'll pay a $4.50 fee to enter the ruins, except on Sundays. Spanish-language guided tours are free and mandatory (i.e. your guide also makes sure you don't ruin anything).

Comitán and Lagos de Montebello

Though usually used only as a stop-over for those traveling to and from Guatemala, Comitán is a pleasantly cool city with some unusual little museums and a pretty zócalo complete with ceiba trees, bougainvillea, flowers, and white benches. The real draw to this area, however, is the Parque Nacional Lagos de Montebello, comprised of over 2,000 acres of pine-forested hills dotted with lakes in brilliant shades of blue, green, and gray.

Comitán was originally a Maya, Tzeltal-speaking community called Balún-Canán, meaning "Place of the Nine Stars." Its current name is derived from the name given by the Aztecs, Comitlán, which translates from Nahuatl as "Place of the Potters." You can see remnants of Maya civilization dating back as far as AD 900 near the Lagos de Montebello at Chincultic (see Near Comitán, below), at Tenam Puente, and in the archaeology museum (see below) in the library adjoining the Casa de la Cultura.

The Maya ruins of Tenam Puente are 8 kilometers from Comitán, off the road to the Lagos de Montebello. The ruins, comprised of a number of buildings and stelae, are set on a hill affording a view of the green valley below.

BASICS

CASA DE CAMBIO Bancomer (Av. 1 Ote. Sur 10, tel. 963/2-02-10), near the zócalo, has an ATM and is open weekdays 9:30 AM-11:30 AM for cash and traveler's-check exchange and advances on Visa cards.

CONSULATE The **Guatemalan Consulate** (1a Calle Sur Pte. 26, at 2a Av. Pte. Sur, tel. 963/2-26-69) is open weekdays 8-4:30. For specific information on visas and border crossings, *see* box Going to Guatemala, *below.*

MAIL The post office provides the usual services and will hold mail sent to you at the following address for up to 10 days: Lista de Correos, Comitán, Chiapas, CP 30000, México. *Av. Central Belisario Domínguez Sur 45, tel. 963/2-04-27. Open weekdays 8-7, Sat. 9-1.*

PHONES There are Ladatel phones on the zócalo in front of the Palacio Municipal. **Caseta Maguis** charges a 35¢ per minute commission on international collect calls. *2a Calle Sur Pte. 6, at Av. Central Belisario Domínguez. Open Mon.-Sat. 8 AM-9 PM, Sun. 9-2 and 5-8.*

VISITOR INFORMATION The tourist office in the Palacio Municipal is stocked with an excellent selection of brochures, as well as good maps of the city, the Lagos de Montebello and nearby ruins, and the villages around Comitán. The staff is well versed in local history, geography, and transportation options, but doesn't speak English. *On the zócalo, no phone. Open Mon.-Sat. 9-2 and 4-8, Sun. 9-2.*

COMING AND GOING

BY BUS The first-class **Cristóbal Colón** station (Blvd. Belisario Domínguez Sur 43, tel. 963/2-09-80) is on the highway about 12 blocks southwest of the center. Buses for Tuxtla Gutiérrez ($6, 3½ hrs) with stops in San Cristóbal ($3, 1½ hrs) leave frequently every day between 11:30 AM and 7:30 PM. Buses leave for Ciudad Cuauhtémoc on the Guatemalan border ($3, 1½ hrs) six times daily, and for Villahermosa ($15, 8½ hrs) at 6:30 PM. Three buses leave daily for Mexico City (about 22 hrs); it's $50 for regular first class, and $59 for a more luxurious version with extra-comfortable seats, TV, and beverage service.

Second-class **Transportes Tuxtla Gutiérrez** (tel. 963/2-10-44) and **La Angostura** (same phone) buses leave from the station at Boulevard Belisario Domínguez Sur 27. To get here, walk six blocks west of the zócalo on Calle Central Benito Juárez, then left 1½ blocks down the highway. They serve Tuxtla Gutiérrez ($4, 3½ hrs) and San Cristóbal ($3, 2 hrs) from 5 AM to 7:30 PM. Buses for Ciudad Cuauhtémoc ($3, 2½ hrs) also leave several times daily. Buses to Tzimol (75¢, 30 min) and La Mesilla ($1, 45 min) leave about every half-hour between 8 and 5.

GETTING AROUND

Comitán is hilly, and the walk from the bus terminals with a loaded pack seems endless—it's better to take a colectivo (35¢) to the center. The town itself, however, is easy to navigate once you master the grid system. Calle Central Benito Juárez runs east–west, Avenida Central Belisario Domínguez north–south. The two divide the city into four quadrants. All calles run east–west, all avenidas north–south. The two cardinal directions (Ote. for east, Pte. for west, Nte. for north, and Sur for south) in each street name indicate which of the four quadrants the street is in. The number in each street name indicates how far it is from either Avenida Central Belisario Domínguez or Calle Central Benito Juárez. For example, 2a Calle Sur Pte. runs east–west two blocks south of Calle Benito Juárez in the southwestern quadrant of the city. As the street crosses Avenida Central Belisario Domínguez into the southeastern quadrant of the city, it's called Calle 2a Sur Ote. Got it?

The bus terminals are on the highway (called Boulevard Belisario Domínguez or Carretera Internacional), west of the center, and can be reached via the colectivos marked CARRETERA INTERNACIONAL that leave from the east side of the zócalo.

WHERE TO SLEEP

Many of Comitán's budget hotels are near the center of town. The climate here is cooler than in most other areas of Chiapas, so hot water should be more of a consideration than fans or air-conditioning when it comes to choosing a room. If there's no room at the places listed below, try **Posada Las Flores** (1 Av. Pte. Nte. 17, tel. 963/2–33–24) or **Posada San Miguel** (1 Av. Pte. Nte. 19, tel. 963/2–11–26) next door; double rooms at both are $8, but an hourly rate is also available. Head to the Lagos de Montebello to camp.

➢ UNDER $15 • **Hospedaje Montebello.** An amiable young couple runs this clean, traveler-friendly place, which is always full. The hot water is erratic in some of the private bathrooms, but the communal showers are reliable. Singles are $6 with communal bath or $8 with private bath; doubles are $10 with communal bath, $13.50 with private bath. *1a Calle Pte. Nte. 10, tel. 963/2–35–72. 14 rooms, 8 with bath. Luggage storage.*

➢ UNDER $20 • **Hospedaje San Francisco.** When the stained-glass and wood doors swing open and the gates are parted, you'll enter two huge courtyards that give this hotel the air of a palace rather than a pension. The rooms, unfortunately, don't live up to this first impression. Although quiet, they're musty and lack the hot water you crave on a chilly morning in Comitán. Singles go for $8.50, doubles $17. *1a Av. Ote. Nte. 13, tel. 963/2–01–94. 30 rooms, all with bath. Luggage storage, wheelchair access.*

Pensión Delfín. With clean, plain rooms and a dingy courtyard facing the zócalo, this inn is unspectacular but perfectly acceptable. The hot-water supply is dependable, at least. Singles cost $15, doubles $18.50, triples $22, and quadruples $25. *Av. Central Belisario Domínguez Sur 21, tel. 963/2–00–13. 21 rooms, all with bath. Luggage storage.*

➢ UNDER $30 • **Hotel Internacional.** Just one block south of the center, this spacious hotel with perfumed, spotless rooms and plentiful hot water is a luxurious bargain for two or more. For better or worse, it's crawling with jovial Mexican businessmen in suits. Singles are $22, doubles $25, triples $30, and quadruples $35. *Av. Central Belisario Domínguez Sur 16, tel. 963/2–01–12. 28 rooms, all with bath. Luggage storage. MC, V.*

FOOD

The affordable restaurants lining Comitán's zócalo serve international dishes and regional specialties, particularly soups and coffee made from locally grown beans; try **Restaurant Nevelandia** (tel. 963/2–00–95) for tacos and quesadillas (under $3) or breakfast specials of eggs, tortillas, beans, fruit, and coffee for $2.50. The **market,** in a huge yellow building one block east of the zócalo, has a good selection of fruits and vegetables, fresh tortillas, pottery, and some woven baskets, and, as always, is the place to find the cheapest food. It is open until late afternoon.

Café Gloria. This family-owned restaurant features locally grown coffee and tasty *sopes* (fried tortillas topped with beans, salsa, and meat or cheese) at two for $1. Other dishes are similarly priced, and all come with four kinds of homemade salsa. Little boys sometimes serve as waiters here, and they'll introduce each dish to you as if it's a person. *Av. Central Belisario Domínguez Nte. 22, tel. 963/2–16–22. Open daily 6 PM–11 PM.*

Restaurant Alis. This is the place to go for typical Comitecan food. Their *platón chiapaneco* (Chiapan platter; $10) includes *butifarras* (beef sausage) and *cecina* (dry, salted beef) and is enough for two. They also offer a wide selection of breakfasts and sandwiches at $3–$4 a meal. *Calle Central Benito Juárez Pte. 21, tel. 963/2–12–62. Open daily 8:30 AM–9 PM.*

WORTH SEEING

Comitán has some fine examples of colonial architecture and interesting, well-curated museums. The 16th-century **Templo de Santo Domingo** on the zócalo displays elements of the Moorish-influenced *mudéjar* style. Just off the northeast corner of the zócalo stands the **Iglesia del Calvario,** unusual because of its columns and gables.

IGLESIA DE SAN CARALAMPIO The festival honoring San Caralampio (*see* Festivals, *below*) is one of the biggest religious events of the year in Comitán. Caralampio was a pious Christian who was burned to death by nonbelievers in his native Greece. Years later, a Comitán rancher named Raymundo Solís, inspired by a book about Caralampio, commissioned a statue of him for his ranch. At the time, a cholera epidemic was devastating Comitán. When no one on Don Solís's ranch was affected, townspeople attributed this to Caralampio's protection. The statue was then brought to town and installed in the 17th-century church. *1a Calle Nte. Ote., at 4a Av. Ote. Nte.*

MUSEO ARQUEOLOGICO DE COMITAN This new museum and library displays Maya artifacts from the sites near Comitán. Especially notable is the display of bones and ornately decorated pottery found in the caves of Cam-Cum and Los Andasolos. *1a Calle Sur Ote., just behind the Casa de la Cultura. Admission free. Open Tues.–Sun. 10–5.*

MUSEO DE ARTE HERMILA DOMINGUEZ This museum two blocks south of the center features modern works by Mexican artists, including Rufino Tamayo. Many of the pieces deal with mystical themes, depicting mestizo and indigenous people and their connections to the earth, sky, and water. *Av. Central Belisario Domínguez Sur 53. Admission: 35¢. Open weekdays 10–1:45 and 4–6:45, Sat. 10–1:45.*

MUSEO DR. BELISARIO DOMINGUEZ Dr. Domínguez was a statesman and proponent of preventive medicine who represented Chiapas in the Senate under President Francisco Madero just after the Mexican Revolution. After Madero was ousted from power, arrested, and shot by U.S.-backed General Victoriano Huerta in 1913, Dr. Domínguez publicly denounced Huerta as a brutal tyrant. Predictably, Domínguez was then murdered. This museum, once his home, displays his pharmaceuticals, ominous-looking medical instruments, photographs, letters, and other personal effects. *Av. Central Belisario Domínguez Sur 35, tel. 963/2–13–00. Admission: 35¢. Open Tues.–Sat. 10–6:45, Sun. 10–12:45.*

AFTER DARK

There seems to be a band on every block in Comitán, and there are plenty of places to relax and hear live music at no charge. **Helen's Enrique** (Av. Central Belisario Domínguez Sur 19, tel. 963/2–17–30), just across the street from the zócalo, is the prime hangout; a cappuccino is $1.50. They have live music Thursday through Saturday after 8 PM. The bar in **Restaurant Nevelandia** (see *Food,* above), with live music nightly, is an equally mellow scene. More alcohol-driven, smoky, and male-dominated is **El Rincón de la Guitarra** (1st Calle Sur Ote. 13, no phone), which has live music every night from 7 PM to 3 AM. They offer some funky drinks, like the Muppet (tequila with Squirt) or the Cucaracha (tequila, anise, and Kahlua) for $4 each.

FESTIVALS

Comitán has many festivals, some barrio-specific and others citywide. The most important citywide events are the **Festival de San Caralampio,** featuring floats, flowers, music, and processions from February 8–22; **Semana Santa** (Easter); and the **Feria de Agosto,** a 10-day festival of Comitecan agriculture, theater, and cuisine in honor of Santo Domingo that takes place in early August.

Near Comitán

The main draw to the area surrounding Comitán is the lake country, but there are some other nice swimming spots and interesting towns that you may want to check out if you're around for a while. In a green valley 8 kilometers west of Comitán is the town of **Tzimol,** where sugar is grown with the same farming methods that have been used for hundreds of years. The town is known for its *panela* (cakes of hardened sugar-cane juice used in Chiapan pastries); you can purchase sugarcane syrup and raw sugar here. A 15-minute bus ride past Tzimol brings you to the town of **La Mesilla,** from which a 5-kilometer path leads to great swimming at an isolated waterfall called **El Chiflón**. **Transportes La Angostura** buses serve both towns (*see* Coming and Going, *above*).

Twenty five minutes northwest of Comitán is the pretty town of **Las Rosas**. From here, it's a 2-kilometer hike to a freshwater spring called **Manantial el Vertedor,** where you can take a cool dip. Las Rosas is served by buses from the **Transportes Cuxtepeques** station (Blvd. Belisario Domínguez Sur 12, at 1a Calle Nte. Pte., tel. 963/2–17–28) in Comitán. The ride costs $1.

LAGOS DE MONTEBELLO

Set among a forest of pine trees, blackberry bushes, and maples, the 60-odd blue, gray, and green lakes of the Parque Nacional Lagos de Montebello provide a spectacular setting for wonderful hikes and swimming. The most popular lakes are those close to the road: Esmeralda, Ensueño, Agua Tinta, La Encantada, and Bosque Azul. A 45-minute walk on the unpaved road from the park gates leads to **Lago Montebello,** the larger **Laguna Tziscao,** and a dozen tiny lakes. The bus continues past this junction and parks at **Lago Bosque Azul.** Two dirt paths lead out into the forest from here. The one to the left takes you to a riverside picnic spot called **El Paso del Soldado.** The other takes you to **San José El Arco,** a natural limestone arch and cave. Bring a flashlight to explore the cave. Little boys will offer to be your guide; it's probably not necessary, but they can be fun to have along. Tip them a few pesos if you accept. At Bosque Azul, older boys will also offer to take you to more isolated lakes on foot or horseback. Be sure to agree on a price before setting out ($3 an hour is reasonable), and wear a watch, since most guides aren't too concerned about getting you back in time for the last bus. The **Lagos Peinita** and **Bartolo,** surrounded by white cliffs that offer spectacular views of the surrounding farmland and mountains, are best reached accompanied by a guide. You can pick up a useful map of the lakes at the tourist office in Comitán (*see* Visitor Information, *above*).

Just at the edges of the park are the Maya ruins of **Chincultic.** This site has a number of stelae, a ball court, and pyramids from which you can admire the surrounding lakes and the deep *cenote* (spring-fed water hole) from which Chincultic gets its name (it means "terraced well"). The ruins are a half-hour hike from the main road that leads to the the lakes, and buses between Comitán and the park pass the turnoff; ask the driver to let you off at Chincultic. The ruins are open every day 8:30–4, and an admission fee of $3.50 is collected Monday through Saturday.

COMING AND GOING Colectivos from **Transportes Comitán-Montebello** (2a Av. Pte. Sur 17, at 2a Calle Sur Pte., tel. 963/2–08–75) let you off at Lago Bosque Azul; they leave every half-hour from 5:45 AM until 4:45 PM daily. The trip takes about an hour and costs $2. The last bus back to Comitán leaves Bosque Azul around 4 PM.

WHERE TO SLEEP You can easily stay in Comitán and make day trips to the lakes, but if you want to stay overnight, bring warm gear and expect a chilly evening. Camping is officially permitted at Bosque Azul, La Encantada, and Tziscao, all of which are outfitted with palapas, fire pits, and restrooms. Throngs of Mexican families congregate around Tziscao, but once you get beyond them, the pristine wilderness is wide open.

Tapachula

The southernmost city of any size in Mexico, Tapachula is the center of the Soconusco region, extending from the Chiapan mountains to the coast and down into southwestern Guatemala. Modern-day Tapachula is home to a diverse population. Significant numbers of European and Asian immigrants, many fleeing World War II and the Communist Revolution in China, were attracted to the area by its coffee- and cacao-driven prosperity. Guatemalans come here to shop, do business, find work on the plantations, or escape political persecution, and budget travelers are attracted by its relative development and proximity to the Guatemalan border. All this activity has rendered Tapachula a relaxed, cosmopolitan town with better-than-average budget hotels and good cappuccino in the zócalo. The area also has much to offer outdoorsy types: The nearby beach towns of Puerto Madero and Las Palmas are pleasant places to cool off in the gentle ocean waves; and the Izapa archaeological

*Tapachula, which means
"Place of Sour Prickly Pears"
in Nahuatl, originally designated an administrative, trib-
ute-paying region of the Aztec
empire. The Aztecs demanded
colored feathers, jade, jaguar
pelts, and cacao as tribute from
their southern subjects.*

zone, where easy hikes through cacao fields lead you to infre-quently visited ruins, lies close to the city. A bit farther away, at the foot of the Tacaná Volcano, the cool mountain town of Unión Juárez offers limitless camping, hiking, and swimming.

BASICS

AUTO PARTS/SERVICE Gloria Cordova (Colonia 5 de Febrero, Calle 45 Pte. 12, tel. 962/6–88-92), on the outskirts of town, offers parts and service for cars.

CASAS DE CAMBIO Banco Internacional (2a Av. Nte., at 1a Calle Pte., tel. 962/5–05–01) changes traveler's checks and cash weekdays 10–noon. Your best bet for good exchange rates for not only American traveler's checks, but also Guatemalan quetzales, Honduran lem-piras, and Salvadoran colones is the **Casa de Cambio** (4a Av. Nte., at 3a Calle Pte., tel. 962/6–51–22). It's open Monday–Saturday 8–7, Sunday 8–1.

CONSULATE You can get a visa for travel into Guatemala (*see box,* Going to Guatemala, *below*) at the Guatemalan consulate. *2a Calle Ote. 33, tel. 962/6–12–52. Open weekdays 8–4:30.*

LAUNDRY Lava Ropa (Av. Central Nte. 33, tel. 962/6–35–25) will wash and dry 3 kilos of clothing for $3.50.

MAIL The post office is a seven-block trek from the center. They offer all the usual services and will hold mail sent to you at the following address for up to ten days: Lista de Correos, Tapachula, Chiapas, CP 30700, México. *1a Calle Ote. 32, at 7a Av. Nte., tel. 962/6–39–22. Open weekdays 8–7, Sat. 9–1.*

MEDICAL AID Farmacia 24 Horas (8a Av. Nte. 25, tel. 962/6–24–80) offers Pringles and Cokes as well as medication round the clock.

PHONES There are two blue Ladatel phones on the southwest corner of the zócalo and some in a quieter area just a block north of the zócalo on 1a Calle Poniente, at 6a Avenida Norte. If for some reason these aren't working, you can make international collect calls at **Tel. Fax** for a $3.50 service charge. *9a Pte. 7-C, tel. 962/5–51-91. Open Mon.–Sat. 8 AM–9 PM, Sun. 8–2.*

VISITOR INFORMATION The tourist office has three wonderful employees, Enrique, Magui, and Amelinda, who are very proud of their region and will help you arrange treks into the countryside or provide information on crossing into Guatemala. *4 Av. Nte. 35, on the sec-ond floor, tel. 962/6–54–70. Open weekdays 9–3 and variable evening hours.*

COMING AND GOING

BY BUS The first-class bus terminal (17a Calle Ote., at 3a Av. Nte., tel. 962/6–28–80) is a good 12 blocks from the center. To get here, take a colectivo (about 35¢) down Avenida Central Norte or a taxi (about $1). **Cristóbal Colón** and **ADO** offer first-class direct service to San Cristóbal de las Casas ($12, 10 hrs) with six departures a day. Four buses a day go to Salina Cruz ($15, 8 hrs) and Mexico City ($45, 24 hrs), and two leave daily for Oaxaca city ($23, 14 hrs).

If your next destination is San Cristóbal de las Casas or Comitán, second-class **Transportes Casa Lombargo** (9a Calle Pte. 63, at 11a Av. Nte.) offers the most frequent service, with about 10 departures to each city daily. It's $7 to San Cristóbal, 10 hours away, and $5 for the six-hour trip to Comitán.

Autobuses General Paulino Navarro (7a Calle Pte., at Av. Central Nte., tel. 962/6–31–02) offers two second-class buses a day to Tuxtla Gutiérrez ($10, 7 hrs) and frequent service to nearby towns and border crossings. **Unión y Progreso** (5a Calle Pte., tel. 962/6–33–79) buses serve Talismán and Unión Juárez infrequently between 5:30 AM and 8 PM for about $1. Colec-tivos also depart from the bus stations and near the market along 10a Avenida Norte for Ciu-dad Hidalgo and Talismán.

BY TRAIN The train station (Calle Central Sur, at 18a Calle Pte., tel. 962/5–21–76) is far from the center but accessible by colectivo or taxi. Trains depart for Juchitán, Mexico City, and Veracruz. Service in this area is slow and uncomfortable—opt for the bus. If you do decide to take the train, head to the station early in the morning and buy your tickets in advance, since the office often closes capriciously.

BY PLANE Aeroméxico (tel. 962/6–20–50), Aviacsa (tel. 962/6–31–47), and **Taesa** (tel. 962/6–37–32) serve the airport (tel. 962/6–22–91), at kilometer 22 on the Carretera Puerto Madero. All three companies fly directly to Mexico City, but fares vary dramatically, from $70 during low season (February, April, May, and October) to as much as $219. The airport is about 18 kilometers from the city and is accessible by taxi for about $10 or by airport bus for $4. Call or stop by the airport bus office (2 Av. Sur 40, tel. 962/5–12–87) in advance to make arrangements for a hotel pick up.

GETTING AROUND

The city's main sights and many budget establishments are clustered around the zócalo, at the intersections of 3a and 5a Calles Poniente and 4a and 6a Avenidas Norte. Most of the city is easily walkable, but colectivos and taxis crowd the streets and can take you around cheaply. Two long boulevards, Avenida Central Norte/Sur and Avenida Central Poniente/Oriente, divide the city into four parts. Calles run east–west and avenidas run north–south. Even-numbered calles are south of Avenida Central Poniente/Oriente, and odd-numbered calles are north of it. Even-numbered avenidas are west of Avenida Central Norte/Sur, and odd-numbered avenidas are east of it.

WHERE TO SLEEP

Many better-than-average budget hotels are concentrated around the center. If you lack the means for anything more than the bare minimum, **Casa de Huéspedes Yuli** and **Hospedaje La Mexicana** (both at 8a Av. Nte. 60, near 2nd-class bus stations) offer fairly clean, padlock-secured double rooms for $5 a night.

➤ UNDER $10 • **Hospedaje Las Américas.** This hotel is just steps away from the market and second-class bus stations. The quiet, clean rooms open onto a tree-filled central courtyard and are a terrific deal at $7 a single or $8.50 a double. *10a Av. Nte. 47. tel. 962/6–27–57. 20 rooms, all with bath. Luggage storage.*

➤ UNDER $20 • **Hotel Cervantino.** Four blocks from the center, this exceptionally clean hotel is a big score. All rooms have fans, rocking chairs, and tables. The management is friendly and extremely helpful. Singles are $10, doubles $15, triples $18, and quadruples $25. *1a Calle Ote. 6, tel. 962/6–16–58. 21 rooms, all with bath. Luggage storage, wheelchair access. MC, V.*

Hotel Colonial. This downtown hotel is overflowing with plants and character. "Hanging herbs keep the bats away," according to the kind owners, and the beautiful gardens keep the guests happy. It looks like a hole-in-the-wall from the street, but it's actually a pleasant, tranquil spot to spend the night. Singles are about $9, doubles $15. *4a Nte. 31, tel. 962/6–20–52. 10 rooms, all with bath. Luggage storage.*

➤ UNDER $25 • **Hotel Puebla.** This four-story hotel right next to the Palacio Municipal offers spacious rooms overlooking the action on the zócalo. All rooms have fans and hot water. Singles are $17, doubles $20. *3a Pte. 40, tel. 962/6–14–36. 40 rooms, all with bath. Luggage storage, wheelchair access.*

FOOD

Perhaps because of the many Guatemalan migrant workers who work on the coffee and cacao plantations here and have no place to go for the night, Tapachula has a number of restaurants open around the clock. Most of them are around the zócalo. **La Parrilla** (on the zócalo, tel. **375**

962/6–51–98) offers cheap sandwiches and breakfasts, as well as filet mignon with a baked potato for $7.50. **La Michoacana** (6a Av. Nte., at 7a Calle Pte., no phone), is filled with Guatemalan workers watching TV and slowly sipping $1 licuados into the wee hours. If you're looking for something more exotic, you won't be disappointed, either. Thanks to Tapachula's large Chinese and European immigrant populations, as well as its proximity to both the mountains and coast, the city offers a surprising variety of great food.

El Mandarín. Just a block from the zócalo you'll find a restaurant that could fool you into thinking you're in San Francisco's Chinatown. Ascend a narrow flight of stairs and you'll emerge in their elegant dining room, with wood paneling, red tablecloths, and even a carp-filled pool stalked by a Siamese cat. Try the *cha siu agridulce* (sweet and sour pork) for $6 or broccoli in oyster sauce for less than $2. The vegetables are crunchy and not drowned in the salt and grease you'll encounter in most Chinese restaurants in Mexico. *8a Av. Nte., at 7a Calle Pte, tel. 962/6–20–12. Open Mon.–Sat. 1–10, Sun. 1–7.*

Ostionería El Pulpo Jarocho. After you get past the name (it translates as the "Veracruzan Octopus Oyster Bar"), the small patio of this unassuming seafood restaurant is a fun place to eat. It's always packed, and the family who runs the place scrambles to keep up with demand. Seafood cocktails with conch, oysters, octopus, squid, and shrimp are only $4–$6 and come with crackers and crunchy fried tortillas. *5a Privada Sur, tel. 962/6–73–03. In an alley just south of Calle Central Ote., about 6 blocks from zócalo, near post office and Guatemalan consulate. Open Mon.–Sat. 11–5.*

WORTH SEEING

The labyrinthine **Mercado Sebastián Escobar,** on the side of a steep hill next to the zócalo, is a two-block indoor/outdoor market where tropical fruits, vegetables, live birds, and every trinket you can imagine are sold. The indoor part is open in the morning only, and the fruit selection is best before midday.

Also worth a visit is the **Museo Regional del Soconusco**, inside the splendid Art Deco **Palacio Municipal** just off the zócalo. The museum displays bits of stelae and other artifacts from nearby ruins. There are also photos of the excavation sites. *Tel. 962/6–35–43. Admission: $3.50, free Sun. Open Tues.–Sun. 10–5.*

FESTIVALS

About 7 kilometers out of the city on the road to Puerto Madero is the site of the **Feria Internacional,** Tapachula's big yearly bash in celebration of the agricultural, artistic, and commercial richness of the area. Another big event is the **Feria de San Agustín,** which takes place August 20–28.

Near Tapachula

While Tapachula is attractive enough to tempt you to stay put for a while, there are a number of towns easily visited on day trips from here. The seaside town of **Puerto Madero,** 27 kilometers southwest of Tapachula, is the closest place to breathe some sea air, although its little beach, **Playa San Benito,** is a bit dirty. The water is pleasant and warm, and iguanas bake themselves on the boulders that line the beach. If you decide to stay the night, the village has one hotel of dubious quality, and easy beach camping. Microbuses from Tapachula's **General Paulino Navarro** bus station (*see* Coming and Going, *above*) leave about every half-hour until 5:30 PM and charge about $1 for the 20-minute ride. A better beach a bit farther away (45 minutes north up the coast) is the gloriously quiet, palm-fringed **Las Palmas.** To get here from Tapachula you need to take a General Paulino Navarro bus (*see* Coming and Going, *above*) to Acapetahua or Escuinala where you can catch a colectivo to Las Palmas. If you're not camping, plan on catching a bus back by afternoon or you may end up sleeping on a towel at a deserted beach.

Also easily accessible is the impressive **Izapa** archaeological zone, only 15 minutes away on the road to Talismán. Closest to Tapachula are ruin groups A and B, about 20 minutes down a jungly path marked by a sign at the highway. Group A is sadly uncared for. Continue farther along the path and through the cacao fields to Group B, where you'll find a huge pyramid and some better-preserved stelae. The largest and most impressive ruins (Group F) are visible from the highway less than a kilometer farther along to the left. This fully restored ceremonial center, complete with pyramids, a ball court, altars, and stelae, enjoyed its heyday around 300–200 BC. To reach the sites, take one of the frequent colectivos from either of Tapachula's second-class stations toward Talismán and ask the driver to let you off at Izapa. Buses ($1) run 5:30 AM–8 PM. The sites are officially free, but you might want to give a donation to one of the three families who maintain the ruins.

UNION JUAREZ

Whatever you do, if you're going to be in the area for any length of time, do not fail to visit Unión Juárez. This coffee-growing town clinging to the base of **Tacaná Volcano,** 30 kilometers northeast of Tapachula, offers great swimming and hiking, and good food and places to stay. Its steep cobblestone roads wind through coffee plantations and cool, lushly forested valleys crisscrossed by rivers. The **Cascadas de Muxbal** (Muxbal Waterfalls) have a deep pool for swim-

---

Going to Guatemala

Mexico has three official border crossings into Guatemala: Talismán and Ciudad Hidalgo (both near Tapachula) and Ciudad Cuauhtémoc (near Comitán). Boats also navigate the Río Usumacinta from the town of Tenosique in Tabasco to Guatemala's Petén region, but there are no immigration offices on this route, so you'll need to obtain a visa before setting out or risk being arrested as an illegal alien once you arrive in Guatemala. Because of the ongoing civil war between rebel forces and the Guatemalan government centered in the Petén region, such considerations may end up being the least of your worries if you take this trip. More convenient, to say the least, is Talismán, where all the customs offices are near one another and the border itself; military types keep a low profile to avoid scaring the tourists; and frequent buses make the four-hour trek to Guatemala City.

When you reach the border you will be shuffled from office to office and charged a number of small processing fees. Cash can easily be changed at the border, but change just what you need because rates are generally poor. It's also a good idea to bring some U.S. currency in small bills to help you through any "formalities." To enter Guatemala you must have a valid passport and either a visa (obtainable at the Guatemalan consulates in Tapachula and Comitán) or a tourist card (available at the border). U.S. citizens are eligible for free, 30-day, multiple-entry visas. Canadian, British, Irish, and Australian citizens are given 30-day single-entry visas. These are free for Canadians but cost $10 for everyone else. Tourist cards ($5 regardless of nationality, payable in cash only) are available at all three border crossings and allow for a stay of 30–90 days, depending on the mood of the immigration officer or your brownnosing skill. You'll want to keep your passport and tourist card handy at all times—buses traveling along border routes routinely stop at immigration checkpoints, where officers sometimes mysteriously single out passengers, demanding to inspect their papers and/or baggage.

ming and are situated in a narrow canyon hung with gargantuan ferns. There are also pools for bathing on the **Río Mala.** Two vantage points are each about an hour hike out of town. **Pico de Loro** (Parrot's Beak) is an outcropping of rock overlooking the jungle that resembles (what else?) a parrot's beak and affords a beautiful view of Guatemala and the ocean. **La Ventana** (The Window), the other vista point, is on a hill overlooking a forested valley. Ask for directions and maps at the Palacio Municipal in Unión Juárez. The climb to the top of Tacaná is a day-long enterprise; if you brave it, you'll have to spend the night on the summit. Don Humberto Ríos at **Restaurante La Montaña** or Roberto Moody at **Posada Aljoad** (*see* Where to Sleep and Eat, *below*) provide guide service for Tacaná and elsewhere. Whatever you choose to do, head out early in the morning, since the fog and rain arrive like clockwork in the afternoon.

COMING AND GOING Direct buses between Tapachula and Unión Juárez are hard to come by. The simplest way to get here is to catch a minibus or combi from Avenida 12 Norte in Tapachula to the town of Cacahuatán ($1.50, 40 min), where you can squeeze into one of the always-crowded VW buses that run frequently to Unión Juárez.

WHERE TO SLEEP AND EAT Kicking yourself because you didn't pack camping gear? Don't fret—this tiny mountain town offers two solid lodging options. Pay about $24 a night for a double room or $40 for a private chalet at the A-frame **Hotel Colonial Campestre** (Hidalgo 1, no phone) and enjoy hot water, TVs, telephones, and even a disco. The other option is to join nature enthusiasts and groups of young hikers at the **Hotel Posada Aljoad** (Mariano Escobedo s/n, right off zócalo, no phone). The hot water is temperamental, but rooms are slightly cheaper, with the most basic double at $20.

For such a remote town, Unión Juárez has remarkably good food. **La Montaña** and **Restaurante Carmelita,** both on the zócalo, offer tasty regional entrées at shoestring prices. Don't leave without trying the *plátanos fritos* (fried plantains) at La Montaña for less than $2.

Villahermosa

Villahermosa is largely the product of the 1970s, when the region's rich oil reserves brought prosperity and expansion to the city. Huge luxury hotels; the massive Tabasco 2000 complex with its modern apartments, shopping mall, fairgrounds, municipal palace, and tourist office; and active cultural centers and museums were among the additions. The city that resulted lacks the natural beauty of the verdant highlands and forests outside its boundaries, but it does have a certain human-made appeal—there are lots of parks and pedestrian-only streets.

The city was originally established farther north, but was relocated after British, French, and Dutch pirates repeatedly looted the area for cacao and *palo de tinta* (a tree used for making dyes) during the 16th and 17th centuries. The city moved south, away from the river connecting it to the pirates' sea route, and was renamed San Juan Bautista. King Felipe II of Spain changed the name once again (to Villahermosa) and gave it a new coat of arms in the late 1700s. The area disappeared from the world market until the Mexican Revolution in the early 1900s, when exports of bananas and cacao began to flourish. Then, of course, came the oil boom. At its worst, Villa is an excessive jumble of streamlined '70s cement architecture, expressways reminiscent of Southern California, and stores filled with cheap neon clothes. At its best, Villa is an oasis of culture with museums, a beautiful archaeological park, an ecological reserve that puts SeaWorld to shame, and many affordable hotels to serve as a base for exploring the nearby coast, as well as Comalcalco, Teapa, and even Palenque. At any rate, do be prepared for a brief bit of culture shock, especially if you've been tramping around the remote Chiapan highlands.

BASICS

AMERICAN EXPRESS Turismo Nieves runs a full-service American Express desk that will hold mail, replace lost cards, and cash personal checks for cardholders, as well as deliver MoneyGrams and exchange traveler's checks (or replace lost ones) for anyone. *Sarlat Incidencia 202, tel. 93/14–18–88. From the Zona Luz walk down Carranza a block past Parque Juárez* *and turn left. Mailing address: American Express, Turismo Nieves, Sarlat Incidencia 202, Villahermosa, Tabasco, CP 86000, México. Open weekdays 9–1:30 and 4–6, Sat. 9–noon.*

AUTO PARTS/SERVICE Refaccionaría Automotriz "Miguel" offers just about any auto part you could want and is always crowded with bus and taxi drivers. *Pino Suárez 416, tel. 93/12–92–00. Open weekdays 8–2 and 4–6:30, Sat. 8–2.*

BOOKSTORES Books in English are hard to come by, but if you read Spanish, **Librería Fondo de Cultura** (27 de Febrero 603, Plazuela la Aguila, tel. 93/12–24–24) has a large selection of novels and books on Tabasco's natural and cultural heritage. **Librería El Alba** (Madero 616, tel. 93/12–22–24) also has a wide selection of novels (in Spanish), as well as textbooks and crafts.

CASAS DE CAMBIO At last count, there were nine banks squeezed in among the shops and budget hotels of the Zona Luz area. All major banks (Banamex, Bancomer, and Banco Internacional) will change U.S. dollars and traveler's checks 10–noon. The lines are surprisingly short, but budget a little extra time just to soak up the air-conditioning.

For longer hours, head to **Blahberl** (27 de Febrero 1537, tel. 93/13–34–19), open weekdays from 8:30 to 6:30 and Saturday 8:30 to 4. Take a cathedral-bound bus down 27 de Febrero and ask to be let off at *el reloj con tres caras* (the clock with three faces). They change Canadian dollars as well as cash from most major European countries. For a commission, you can also cash personal checks written in U.S. dollars.

EMERGENCIES For help in an emergency, dial 06.

LAUNDRY **Lavandería Automática** (Reforma 502, tel. 93/14–37–65), just out of the Zona Luz toward the river, will wash 1 kilo for about $2. Same-day service is 50¢ more.

MAIL The most convenient post office is in the Zona Luz. They'll hold mail sent to you at the following address for up to 10 days: Lista de Correos, Villahermosa, Tabasco, CP 86000, México. *Sáenz 131, tel. 93/12–10–40. Open weekdays 8–7, Sat. 9–noon.*

MEDICAL AID The **Centro de Salud** (Pepe del Rivera, at Choco Tabasqueño, tel. 93/14–21–01) is in the center of town, across the river from the Zona Luz. It's open for general consultations (about $3) daily 7 AM–2 PM and offers 24-hour emergency service. Pharmacies abound in the Zona Luz, but all close at 9 PM. **Farmacia Mariana** (27 de Febrero 626, tel. 93/14–23–66), a few blocks up 27 de Febrero from the Zona Luz, is open 24 hours a day.

PHONES You can't walk 10 paces in the Zona Luz without running into a blue Ladatel phone, and you shouldn't have to wait long to get through to an international operator. If you want to make a cash call, or call anywhere besides the United States collect, you can use the caseta in the **Café Barra** (Lerdo 608). It's open Monday–Saturday 7 AM–10 PM and charges a service fee of only $1 for a collect call. There is also a 24-hour caseta across from the ADO station (*see below*).

VISITOR INFORMATION The federal tourist office (Paseo Tabasco 1504, Tabasco 2000 Complex, tel. 93/16–36–33), open weekdays 8–4, offers a few brochures on various local sights, as well as a map of the city and information on Tabasco. Some members of the well-informed staff speak English. The office is in an ultra-modern cement monstrosity across from the Palacio Municipal. Ask the guards out front for *la oficina de turismo* and you'll be pointed to an unmarked interior office up the stairs and to the right. To get here, take the TABASCO 2000 or PALACIO MUNICIPAL bus from the *malecón* (boardwalk). Also helpful is the tourist booklet *Amigo Tip's*, which comes out bi-monthly and is available at the Amigo Tip's office (Zaragoza 516, tel. 93/14–35–26).

COMING AND GOING

BY BUS The first-class bus station (Francisco Javier Mina 297, at Lino Merino) is big and efficient, with computers at the ticket windows. It's served by many of the major first-class bus companies, including **ADO** (tel. 93/12–14–46), **Cristóbal Colón** (tel. 93/12–29–36), and **UNO** (tel. 93/14–20–54). Unfortunately, the lines are long morning, noon, and night, and seats sell out, so be absolutely sure to buy your ticket in advance. Service is frequent to destinations like Chetumal ($21, 9 hrs), Mérida ($24, 10 hrs), Mexico City ($36, 16 hrs), Oaxaca city ($27, 16 hrs), Palenque ($6, 2 hrs), Tapachula ($28, 16 hrs), Teapa ($2, 1½ hrs), and Tuxtla Gutiérrez ($10, 6½ hrs). Luggage storage at the station is available 7 AM–11 PM daily for about 25¢ an hour per bag. To get to the city center, walk a good 12 blocks southeast, or take a bus marked PARQUE JUAREZ. Buses marked CENTRO will take you to the Palacio Municipal; those marked CENTRAL will take you to the Central Camionera.

The huge **Central Camionera** (Ruíz Cortinez, east of the intersection with Javier Mina) has ticket sellers from 19 different bus companies sitting in cages even smaller than the ones holding animals at La Venta's zoo. Buses range from clean and plush to sticky and grimy but serve a dizzying array of destinations more frequently than the first-class buses and at lower prices. You can get to Mexico City for $32, to Puebla for $27, to Jalapa for $20, to Veracruz for $16, to Palenque for $2.50, and to Teapa for $2. To get here from the malecón, take any bus marked CENTRAL.

Buses to the coast and Comalcalco leave from the **Transportes Somellera** terminal (Ruíz Cortinez, at Llergo, tel. 93/14–41–18). There is service to Comalcalco ($2, 1½ hrs) every half-hour and to Paraíso ($3, 2 hrs) every hour. The easiest way to get here is to take a bus to the Central Camionera, cross the bridge over the highway, and walk down Cortinez towards the Hotel Maya Tabasco. You'll see the station a block or so past the hotel on your left.

BY PLANE The airport (tel. 93/12–43–86) is served by **Aeroméxico** (tel. 93/14–16–75), **Aviacsa** (tel. 93/14–47–55), **Mexicana** (tel. 93/12–11–64), and **Aerolitoral** (tel. 93/14–36–14). No public transportation goes to the airport. Taxis charge about $12, but you might be able to bargain. Luggage storage is available at the airport.

GETTING AROUND

Villahermosa can be difficult to navigate, even with the faded map given out at the tourist office. Have no fear, however: A few prominent landmarks, abundant city buses, and cheap taxis will help you visit all the sights without too much walking in the blazing heat.

The center of town is bordered by three avenues, along which lie many of the major points of interest. The main highway is Ruíz Cortinez, a huge expressway with fast and deadly traffic. The Central Camionera (second-class bus terminal), Transportes Somellera, and the biggest food **market** are all here. Cortinez turns south at the **Parque Museo La Venta**—you'll see the *mirador* (viewing tower)—where it intersects with another main avenue, Paseo Tabasco. This street runs from the **Tabasco 2000** complex, with its huge, black mushroom of a water tower, to the **malecón** (boardwalk), which runs along the bank of the Río Grijalva. CICOM (*see* Worth Seeing, *below*) is on Carlos Pellicer, which is the name the malecón takes on just past the roundabout where it hits Paseo Tabasco.

Within this ring, the streets that will be most important to you are Francisco Javier Mina, which heads up to Cortinez and the first-class bus station; Méndez, which runs from Llergo to the malecón, crossing Mina; and Madero, which runs five long blocks from Cortinez to the malecón, parallel to Mina. Follow the one-way flow of traffic north on Madero and you'll pass the **Parque Benito Juárez,** at the northeast corner of the **Zona Luz.** The Zona Luz is a largely pedestrian-only area bordered by Madero on the east, Zaragoza on the north, Castillo to the west, and 27 de Febrero to the south. This is where you'll find the best budget lodging and restaurants.

The bus system in Villa can be confusing—so confusing, in fact, that you'll probably see more than one local anxiously asking the bus driver for reassurance about the route. You would be wise to follow suit.

BY BUS Destinations are usually marked on windshields, but routes are often very roundabout. To reach the tourist office or La Venta, take either the TABASCO 2000 or PALACIO MUNICIPAL bus from Madero, one block north of Parque Juárez. From the same stop, you can catch buses for CICOM (*see* Worth Seeing, *below*). For buses to the second-class bus station or market, take either the CENTRAL or MERCADO bus from the malecón.

BY TAXI Because drivers pack their tiny Nissans with passengers, taxi rides are cheap ($1–$2 within the city). Wait in line at a taxi stand and an attendant will shuffle you into the proper taxi. There are taxi stands in front of the first-class bus station and on Madero near Reforma.

WHERE TO SLEEP

Villahermosa has a number of three- and four-story hotels with standard rooms and competitive prices ($10–$17 for a double). Many hotels have permanent residents, so you may have to check a few before you find space, but most hotels will store your luggage for you while you look. The best time to search is noon–1, the usual checkout time. Budget hotels are clustered in the Zona Luz on Madero and its side streets such as Lerdo de Tejada, where the hotels overlook the pedestrian walkways, affording the quietest rooms.

If none of the places listed below is available, try **Hotel Tabasco** (Lerdo de Tejada 317, tel. 93/12–00–77) for singles ($10) and doubles ($13.50) of middle-of-the-road quality; or **Hotel San Francisco** (Madero 604, tel. 931/2–31–98), which is expensive in comparison with neighboring hotels ($20 single, $23.50 double), but affords little extra luxury.

➢ UNDER $15 • **Hotel Oviedo.** Because it's one of the cheapest places in town that still maintains reasonable standards, you'll have to scramble for a room (but if you're lucky enough to secure one, you'll save enough for three tacos around the corner). The basic rooms with fans vary dramatically in quality and noise level, so check a few if possible before checking in. Singles are $9.50, doubles $12, and triples $13.50. *Lerdo de Tejada 303, no phone. 45 rooms, all with bath. Laundry, luggage storage.*

➢ UNDER $20 • **Hotel Madero.** The conscientous proprietor has seen to it that this is one of cleanest, most comfortable inexpensive hotels in the city. The rooms are decorated in various tranquil shades of blue, the bathrooms have hot water, and the staff is more than eager to help you find your way around town. Singles are $13.50, doubles $17, and triples $20. *Madero 301, tel. 93/12–05–16. 29 rooms, all with bath. Luggage storage.*

Hotel Oriente. On a busy section of Madero under the arched awning, this modest, fairly clean (although somewhat dark) hotel is a decent value. Request the penthouse rooms (Nos. 43 and 44), with cross-ventilation from three sets of windows. Singles are $12, doubles $15. *Madero 425, tel. 93/12–11–01. 22 rooms, all with bath. Luggage storage.*

Hotel San Miguel. The proprietor cares about his city and his hotel and wants visitors to leave with a favorable impression of both. The clean, orange-toned rooms have phones and floors decorated with orange-and-white circus stripes. This is one of the more popular budget places and is consistently full. Singles are $13, doubles $15, and triples $20, $23.50 with air-conditioning. *Lerdo de Tejada 315, tel. 93/12–15–00. 45 rooms, all with bath. Luggage storage.*

➢ UNDER $30 • **Hotel Palma de Mallorca.** All the rooms here are sunny and clean. With fans, singles are $18.50, doubles $25; with luxurious air-conditioning, singles and doubles run $30. *Madero 510, tel. 93/12–01–45. 36 rooms, all with bath. Luggage storage.*

ROUGHING IT If you're absolutely broke, you could try crashing at the **Parque de la Choca**, the city fairgrounds, where (unless some event is taking place) you'll find lots of empty palapas, large lawns, and abandoned, creepy-looking, rusty amusement park rides. Drivers have also been known to park their cars in the lot here to crash for the night.

FOOD

Variety is not a problem here. The large, enclosed **Mercado Pino Suárez** (Bastar Zozaya, 2 blocks west of the Río Grijalva) is open mornings and has good fruit and bread selections and a bunch of 5¢-taco stands, some of which look much cleaner than others. You can also cool off with a ladle of juice from the many *agua fresca* (juice drink) shops, open-air places with rainbows of *paletas* (popsicles) and icy vats of tamarind, lime, pineapple, horchata, and other flavored drinks. Try *jamaica,* a hibiscus-flower drink that quenches your thirst like a soda never could. **Mini-Leo** (Juárez 504) is a citywide chain with burgers, fries, tacos, quesadillas, and the like. Frozen-yogurt shops, bakeries, and supermarkets fill the Zona Luz, so the makings of a good snack or picnic are always close at hand. **Las 2 Naciones** (Juárez 533, tel. 93/12-12-22) has temptingly fresh baked goods from 7 AM to 9 PM every day except Sunday.

➤ UNDER $5 • **El Torito Valenzuela.** Tender beef tacos on fresh, handmade tortillas with lots of cilantro and onion (four for $3) are the specialty here, but the *queso fundido* (cheese fondue) and quesadillas ($1) are excellent as well. Their comida corrida ($4.50) is more than one person should ever eat in one sitting, with soup, tortillas, a wide choice of entrées, french fries, beans, rice, fried plantains, a drink, and dessert. Also good are the breakfast specials ($3) with eggs, tortillas, beans, chiles, and plenty of coffee. *27 de Febrero at Madero, tel. 93/14-18-89. Open daily 8 AM–midnight.*

Tortillería Chetumalito. In addition to fabulous $1.50 quesadillas, this place serves up plenty of comfortable neighborhood cheer. You can chat with the jovial owner while you eat, or watch him joke with schoolkids and friends who come to buy sodas and candy from the counter. *Madero 804, tel. 93/12-04-87. Open Mon.–Sat. 8 AM–9 PM.*

➤ UNDER $10 • **Aquarius.** You'll find vegetarian sandwiches, soups, and yogurt, as well as medicinal herb teas and vitamins at both Aquarius locations. A filling, hot sandwich with beans, cheese, avocado, alfalfa sprouts, and more is about $2. Wheat breads are also sold in the adjacent health-food store. *Two locations: Zaragoza 513, in the Zona Luz, tel. 93/12-05-79, open Mon.–Sat. 8 AM–9 PM; and Javier Mina 309, 2 blocks from ADO bus station, tel. 93/14-25-37, open daily 8 AM–10 PM.*

Birbiri's. This teal-and-pink restaurant is a bit pricey and out of the way, but locals swear by the fantastic seafood. Shrimp in garlic will set you back about 10 well-spent dollars, and you can linger after dinner, sipping a drink from their full bar and listening to the singer who performs in the evenings. *Madero 1032, tel. 93/12-61-45. Open Mon.–Sat. 10–8.*

WORTH SEEING

Villahermosa is rich with places to stroll—along the river's malecón, through Benito Juárez Park, above the river at the end of Aldama, and around the Zona Luz. Sunday is the big beach day, when families excitedly pack market food, bags of chips, and bottles of cola and head for the bus station. **La Feria del Desarrollo** (Development Fair) during the last week of April celebrates the diversity of culture in Tabasco, and each municipality showcases its typical dances, arts, and music. There's also a parade of decorated boats down the Grijalva, with fireworks and general revelry. The main action takes place in the **Parque de la Choca,** past Tabasco 2000. In February, **Carnaval** is especially big here, with music, dance contests, and processions.

MUSEUMS Most of Villa's museums offer free guided tours in Spanish. Olmec art and artifacts are on display at La Venta and the Museo Regional de Antropología. The museums in the Zona Luz are small hole-in-the-wall operations worth a look mostly because they're cheap (or free) and only a short walk from the budget lodgings. If it's Monday, go to Teapa, Comalcalco, or the beach, because every museum in town is closed.

➤ PARQUE-MUSEO LA VENTA • Perhaps Villa's biggest attraction, this sprawling park displays all the major finds from La Venta archaeological site (on the border with Veracruz), which was threatened by oil drilling in the '70s. The jungly park has dirt paths that wind past 20 or so Olmec carvings, mosaics, and stelae. Characteristic are sculptures of naked people with pudgy arms and giant heads with full lips and wide noses. Also common are depictions of half-jaguar/half-human creatures. Free guided tours in Spanish leave every half-hour from the entrance, and tours in English can be arranged for a price. Warning: Without bug repellent, the 30- to 40-minute walk through the steamy jungle could leave you with itchy battle scars. Before you enter La Venta, you'll have to pass through a dismal zoo, the **Centro de Convivencia,** with small cages and lonely animals. When you buy your ticket, you'll also have the option of getting a ticket to the **Museo de Historia Natural,** just across the parking lot from the zoo. Unless you're dying to see a Tyrannosaurus Rex skeleton and a fake rendition of the jungle that surrounds you at La Venta, don't waste your time or money. *Ruíz Cortinez s/n, tel. 93/15-22-28. Take a TABASCO 2000 bus from Parque Juárez, get off at the cnr of Paseo*

Tabasco and Ruíz Cortinez, and walk along the lakeshore to the entrance. Admission to the zoo only: 15¢; to zoo and La Venta: $1; to everything: $2. Open Tues.–Sun. 9–5.

➢ MUSEO REGIONAL DE ANTROPOLOGIA CARLOS PELLICER CAMARA • This museum in the CICOM cultural center (*see below*) emphasizes Olmec influence on the cultures that succeeded them, particularly the Maya to the south and the Huasteca to the north. There are a few well-worn Olmec heads, altars, and stelae, and a number of pieces from as far away as Nayarit, Chihuahua, and the Yucatán. *CICOM, Carlos Pellicer 511, tel. 93/12–18–03. Take any bus marked CICOM. Admission: $2. Open Tues.–Sun. 10–4.*

➢ MUSEUMS IN THE ZONA LUZ • Just around the corner from the budget lodgings are three museums, each worth a quick peek. The small, free **Casa-Museo Carlos Pellicer** (Sáenz 203, tel. 93/12–01–57) has memoirs, desks, pens, wedding pictures, and other miscellanea that once belonged to this famous Tabascan poet who funded the excavation of La Venta and helped save its pieces from destruction. Be sure to check out the gruesome metal cast of his face taken at his death. The **Museo de Cultura Popular** (Zaragoza 810, tel. 93/12–11–17) has mannequins dressed in local costumes, as well as a collection of Tabasco's famous carved gourds. In the back is a dusty "typical" hut and a small pond with a *pejealargato* (alligator gar), a large, toothy freshwater fish popular in regional dishes. Admission is free here, too. The largest of these museums is the **Museo de Historia de Tabasco** (Juárez, at 27 de Febrero, tel. 93/12–49–96), which has a maze of displays chronicling the history of Tabasco from pre-Hispanic times through the modern industrial age. It houses mostly posters and illustrations, but there are also a few old books, colonial uniforms, pieces-of-eight, weapons, and medals. The interior is covered with beautiful changing patterns of tiles, in honor of which the museum is also known as the Casa de los Azulejos (House of Tiles). Admission is $1.50. Sprinkled among the museums are art galleries and cultural centers (*see below*). All three museums are open Tuesday–Sunday 10–4.

CULTURAL CENTERS

➢ CICOM • The Center for the Investigation of Olmec and Maya Cultures lies along the malecón, above the Río Grijalva. Of main interest is the Museo Regional de Antropología Carlos Pellicer Cámara (*see above*). Near the museum is the **Teatro Esperanza Iris,** a modern, plush, red-curtained center for national and regional events. The Instituto de la Cultura sponsors shows here. Major events, such as performances by the National Ballet, tend to be jam-packed and cost $5–$10, although frequent lesser-known attractions, such as local dance and folk-music performances, are often free and usually only half full. The **CEIBA** arts center offers classes in music, dance, theater, and graphic arts. They have a small gallery and information on upcoming exhibits, poetry readings, and the like.

CICOM also houses the mammoth **public library** (open Monday through Saturday 9–9), where you'll find air-conditioned relief from the heat, as well as an impressive and varied collection of books in both Spanish and English (look in the shelves upstairs and to the right for English). University students punch away at calculators downstairs, where there is also a cafeteria. On Sundays, free movies are shown three times a day in the auditorium to the left of the main library entrance. On weekdays, videos are shown at 7 PM. The bookshop here is also worth checking out. *Av. Carlos Pellicer, south of Paseo Tabasco. From Parque Juárez, take a CICOM bus. Open Tues.–Sun. 10–4.*

➢ CENTRO CULTURAL DE LA UNIVERSIDAD AUTONOMA DE TABASCO • Just steps away from the Zona Luz, this cultural center has two galleries showcasing local artists and sponsors a wide variety of events. There are free films Wednesday nights, and "cultural Thursdays" feature music, dance, or performing arts. Every couple of Saturdays they hold *paseos culturales* (cultural outings) to nearby towns and archaeological sites. Sign up in advance to be sure you'll get a spot. It usually costs $5–$7 for an all-day outing that includes transportation and a knowledgeable guide. *27 de Febrero 640, tel. 93/12–45–57. Open weekdays 8 AM–9 PM.*

➢ CENTRO CULTURAL DE VILLAHERMOSA • Across from the Zona Luz, this brand-new center has wonderful art exhibits from all over Mexico, foreign films, concerts, a shop dedicated to Tabasco's crafts, and a good café. All performances and exhibits are free. *Madero s/n, at Zaragoza, tel. 93/14–55–52. Open Mon.–Sat. 10–9.*

ART GALLERIES Calle Sáenz in the Zona Luz features two small art galleries. In an old house in the Zona Luz, the **Galería Tabasco** (Sáenz 122, tel. 93/121–43–66) features exhibits by local artists Tuesday–Saturday 3 PM–10 PM. Styles range from your basic still-life oil painting to surreal dreamscapes. Just up the street is **Galería El Jaguar Despertado** (Sáenz 117, tel. 93/14–12–44), a combination café, art gallery, and bookshop.

YUMKA: CENTRO DE INTERPRETACION Y CONVIVENCIA CON LA NATURALEZA

The recently opened Yumká, named for a magical dwarf who looks after the jungles, is a 250-acre ecological park featuring tropical rain forest, savanna, and a lagoon, each with all the corresponding flora and fauna. Nature freaks from around the world join Mexican family vacationers on the two-hour guided quest that ventures through rain forest by foot, savanna by open-air tram, and lagoon by raft—all, of course, in the most environmentally friendly manner. Yumká was set aside as a nature reserve in 1984, but not developed until 1992. The guides are professional biologists, gifted at instilling in visitors a deeper appreciation of (and hopefully a desire to preserve) the natural beauty and diversity of Tabasco. Dr. Luis Palazuelos, who oversees the operation, can provide further details for those interested. *Take a YUMKA bus from the Las Blancas Mariposas restaurant, next to La Venta ($1.50). Admission: $5. Open daily 9–5.*

Yumká's brochures highlight the imported African animals that draw Tabascans into the park. But don't be fooled—this is no packaged wild-animal safari. The main focus of the park is actually the Tabascan rain forest and lagoon ecosystems, and the African animals act mainly to draw in local visitors, who wouldn't otherwise come to see the amazing things living in their own backyard.

AFTER DARK

For a modern and apparently cosmopolitan city, Villahermosa goes to bed early. Around dinner is the prime time to be out and about, as this is when street bands entertain crowds, dancers fill the plazas, and old men gossip over heated games of dominoes. **Café Casino** (Juárez 531) and **Café Barra** (Lerdo de Tejada 608) both offer cappuccino, espresso, and the buzz of heated conversation. Come nine o'clock, however, all grinds to a sudden halt. By 10, the Zona Luz is a virtual ghost-town, with used napkins and empty cups rolling in the soft breeze. The cultural centers (*see above*) put on the occasional event, but otherwise, if you're determined to party, you'll have to content yourself with one of the not-too-hopping bars or head to a ritzy disco elsewhere in town.

DANCING The young and trendy spend their weekend evenings at **Tequila Rock,** a modern, neon-lit extension of the Holiday Inn in Tabasco 2000 (tel. 93/16–44–00). **Ku Rock House** (Prolongación de Saudino 548, tel. 93/15–94–31) and **Snob** at the Hyatt Hotel (Juárez 106, tel. 93/13–44–44) are also popular. Cover charges are stiff (usually $10–15), but the action starts about 10 and lasts until one or two in the morning.

BARS For live Latin music, you can hit the bar in **Hotel Don Carlos** (Madero 518, tel. 93/12–24–99), just across from the Zona Luz. The band starts about 9:30 PM and keeps swingin' until 1:30 in the morning. There's no cover, no minimum, and drink prices aren't too outrageous ($2.50 for a beer, $3 for a margarita). **Baccarat "Ladies Bar"** (Sánchez Marmol 410, across from Parque Juárez, tel. 93/14–17–50) with soft lights, wood paneling, and velvet seats, has live soft jazz from 8 to 11 on weekend nights. Most of the clientele seems to be single and male, but the atmosphere is relatively relaxing and classy.

Near Villahermosa

COMALCALCO

One of the easternmost Maya sites, Comalcalco is best known for the fired brick with which all of its lasting edifices were constructed. Because the jungle in these whereabouts had no rock, the Chontal Maya who lived here made a mixture of clay, sand, and ground conch shell to form thin reddish bricks that were fired and used for 282 buildings covering an area of 10 square kilometers. The city was built in the 7th century, and its sloping roofs (suited to the heavy rains) and stucco figures show evidence of the influence of Palenque.

Comalcalco has two major groups of buildings and many unexcavated mounds. **Temple I,** the main pyramid, is on the large plaza. Farther along are the **Great Acropolis** and **Temples IV–VII.** Temple VII features a huge stucco mask representing the sun god. From the hill of the Acropolis you can enjoy the cooling winds and a view of the emerald-green mounds and the thick jungle canopy interrupted by plantations of some of Tabasco's finest cacao. The **museum** displays a mummy from the site, stucco etchings, and an exhibit on Maya life. *Admission to site: $4.50, free on Sundays. Open daily 10–5.*

COMING AND GOING Buses to Comalcalco leave every half hour from **Transportes Somellera** in Villahermosa (*see* Coming and Going, *above*). Buses for Villahermosa leave their station in Comalcalco (Méndez 411, tel. 931/4–00–27) until around 6 PM. From Comalcalco city you can take a microbus (30¢) directly to the ruins or to the highway drop-off point for the ruins, a 15-minute walk away. Microbuses leave from the highway and Avenida Gregorio Méndez, right across from the roundabout with the small brick pyramid in the center. Comalcalco has modest hotel and food offerings, but it's easier to commute from Villahermosa. The Tabasco coast is only 21 kilometers from the Comalcalco ruins; you can catch a bus marked PARAISO at the intersection of the highway and the road from the ruins.

THE TABASCAN COAST

Although once pristine, Tabasco's beaches don't enjoy the most favorable reputation these days. The '70s oil boom brought black death to some of the coastline, and nowadays swimmers complain of resin-coated pebbles washing up on shore. But whatever ecological destruction ultimately results from the drilling, right now the effects aren't readily apparent in some places, and the most visible uncleanliness stems from humans too lazy to pick up their trash. Few foreign travelers pass through, and, other than on weekends and during Semana Santa (Holy Week), the beaches are often empty. The beaches generally do not have lodging apart from palapas with hammock hooks, but most are within day-trip distance of towns with hotels and restaurants, such as Villahermosa, Comalcalco, and Paraíso.

The beaches at **Laguna de Mecoacán** and **Limón** are all within a short bus ride of the medium-sized city of **Paraíso.** Both have long stretches of white sand and pleasant water with little waves. Laguna has lots of palapas for sleeping or avoiding the sun and a few restaurants, including **La Posta,** which offers tasty seafood caught fresh from the lagoon and nearby sea, and whose friendly staff gives out information on boat rentals and hooks to hang hammocks for about $3 a night ($5 if you need to rent one). Limón has many palapas and endless stands of coconut trees, which makes it fairly easy to hang your hammock for free. Be sure to hit the beaches on a weekday or be prepared to share your retreat with the entire state of Tabasco.

Colectivos leave for the beaches fairly frequently from Paraíso's central bus station, about six blocks from the market. Colectivos also run between Paraíso and the beach at **Puerto Ceiba,** which is quieter and a bit farther away. Second-class **Transportes La Somellera** buses run between Paraíso and Villahermosa ($3.50, 1½ hrs), and microbuses make the trip from Comalcalco (65¢, 15 min).

TEAPA

Tabasco is not all oil fields and muggy wetlands. The air feels remarkably clean and fresh in the city of Teapa, just one hour's worth of banana fields from Villahermosa. The pretty **zócalo** is forested with enormous trees and houses a community library at one end, and the Río Teapa runs right through town. You can swim in the river here (the best spot is just off the main street as it approaches the zócalo on the way into town) or take excursions out of town for a cooling swim, a healing sulfur bath, or some subterranean exploration.

The Puyacatengo River in **Tacotalpa,** a short bus ride away, has rapids and is a popular place to play among locals. You can also camp here; there are no real facilities, but you're safe if you're not alone. A 6-kilometer bus ride toward the town of Pichucalco and a $3.50 entrance fee will buy you almost unlimited hedonism at **El Azufre Spa,** where the clean pool and bubbling sulfur spring are known for their healing properties. Once you've paid the entrance fee, you're free to store your stuff in the administration office and camp on the soft green lawns of the gorgeous valley for free as long as you like, enjoying use of the pools, palapas, and picnic tables. If you'd rather have a room, the adjoining **Hotel Azufre** rents huge ones with fans and bathrooms for $34. The kicker is that the two beds and hammock hooks in each room mean that they sleep up to eight people for the same price.

If you prefer something a bit less lazy, you can tromp around inside the **Grutas de Coconá,** a set of spectacular caves out in the country. A bus marked MULTIGRUTAS leaves for the caves every half-hour or so from the side of the church in Teapa. To walk here, go down Méndez to the Pemex station and turn right—a green sign alerts you—and follow the road a ways until it turns to countryside; you'll find the grutas shortly thereafter. Once here, pay the $1 fee and enter the still darkness, where you'll hear only the squeaking of tiny bats and the dripping of water. The caves may be lighted, but maybe not: Bring a flashlight and see if you can make out the figures of King Kong and his family, a giant peanut, a cow's tongue, a headless chicken, and, of course, Jesus Christ in the rocks. The caves are open daily 10–4.

COMING AND GOING Autotransportes Villahermosa Teapa (Méndez 218, tel. 932/2–00–07) has hourly buses to Villahermosa between 5 AM and 5 PM. First-class fare is $2.50, second-class, $2. The station can be hard to find—look for a small, tree-filled square with lots of red taxis parked outside. It's about five blocks from the zócalo where the island in the middle of the main road begins. You'll need to arrive a bit in advance of your intended departure time, as these buses fill up quickly.

Those headed farther afield can take advantage of the Córdoba–Mérida **train** that passes through town. The station (Ignacio Zaragoza s/n, tel. 932/2–01–65) is at the very end of the main drag, a 20-minute walk from the zócalo. If you're headed for Veracruz or Mexico City, you'll have to take the train to Córdoba ($9.50, 16 hrs) that leaves between 6 AM and 8 AM, and transfer there. The train leaves for Mérida ($10.50, 14 hrs) every day sometime between 7 PM and 9 PM, passing Palenque ($2, 2 hrs), Tenosique ($3, 4 hrs), and Campeche ($8, 10 hrs) on the way. In this direction, however, the trains are infamously dangerous and slow.

GETTING AROUND Teapa has one main street that stretches from the train station (about a kilometer from the center) to the zócalo. It begins as 21 de Marzo, changes to Carlos Ramos at the Pemex station, and changes again to Gregorio Méndez as it approaches the zócalo. Many of the city's side streets are pedestrian walkways, and the town is definitely manageable on foot. Buses and colectivos to the grutas and other attractions leave from the zócalo and from the lime-green clock on the outskirts of town.

WHERE TO SLEEP In addition to the places listed below, you can camp around Teapa if you keep a low profile. No formal camping facilities exist, but the area along the river is rife with opportunity, and there's always **El Azufre Spa** (*see above*) just a few kilometers away. The worst hazard you're likely to face is mosquitoes.

Casa de Huéspedes Miye. The rooms here are small but clean and the hallway is green with plants. With communal bath, singles run $8.50 and doubles, $10; rooms with private baths for one or two people are $12. None of the showers has hot water, but you probably won't need it anyway. *Méndez 211, tel. 932/2–04–20. 2 blocks from the zócalo. 16 rooms, 8 with bath. Luggage storage.*

Hotel Jardín. The rooms are painted a cooling pastel blue, and the lobby is guarded by the friendly owner's collection of porcelain animals. All the rooms are well ventilated and have bathrooms with cold showers, and the screened doors overlook the patio. Singles are $13.50, doubles $17. *Plaza Independencia 123, tel. 932/2–00–27. At top of Méndez, just past zócalo. 11 rooms, all with bath. Luggage storage, wheelchair access.*

FOOD Food in Teapa tends to be either greasy or expensive. It's better to stick to sandwiches from any of the many hole-in-the-wall restaurants rather than test your digestive system exploring more ambitious fare. **Restaurant El Jacalito** and **El Mirador** are both rather expensive for mediocre food. Another safe option is the market, right across from the lime-green clock.

THE YUCATAN PENINSULA

11

By David Walter

At the heart of the ancient Maya city of Chichén Itzá stands El Castillo, a soaring 27-meter pyramid honoring the god Kukulcan. Every year at the spring and autumn equinoxes, the sun casts a shadow on the temple that makes it appear as if the serpent god is slithering down the pyramid to the city's sacred well. In its way, this monument of astrological precision embodies everything that attracts visitors to the Yucatán today: the ingenuity of the ancient Maya, whose ruined cities dot the peninsula, and an emphasis on the sun that manifests itself today in the form of pale gringos immolating themselves on the beaches of Cozumel, Cancún, Playa del Carmen, and Isla Mujeres.

Encompassing the states of Yucatán, Campeche, Quintana Roo, Belize, and part of Guatemala, the Yucatán peninsula covers 113,000 square kilometers. Much of the peninsula is vast, scrubby desert covering porous limestone ("one living rock," as an early Spanish priest put it) with a smattering of *cenotes* (spring-fed water holes), jungles, and tell-tale mounds hiding unexcavated ruins. The eastern coastline has everything you could ask for—clear Caribbean waters, a tropical climate, unbroken stretches of beach, and stunning coral reefs. Developers are doing their best to pave this coast to accommodate the stream of winter tourists (November through April is prime time for sun seekers; May through September brings torrential downpours). So far only Cancún has been transformed into an obscene tourist complex. Isla Mujeres, Playa del Carmen, and Tulum remain laid-back havens for budget travelers, and some of the most beautiful beaches along the coast are still undeveloped.

Often overlooked in the sprint for the beaches, though, are the towns of the Yucatán. The peninsula was one of the first areas of the New World to be settled by the Spanish, and the legacy of the colonists lives on in towns such as Mérida and Campeche. Huge baroque churches, old mansions, and winding cobbled streets give these towns a distinctly European look, albeit softened by age and tropical heat.

But most visitors to the Yucatán are attracted by the Maya ruins, ancient cities dating back as much as 4,000 years. Hundreds of Maya sites dot the Yucatán, only a handful of which have been excavated. Chichén Itzá is the best known, and other

Kukulcan is the Mayan name for Quetzalcoatl, the feathered serpent god of the Toltec (and Aztec) pantheons. Evidence that Kukulcan took on added importance after Toltec incursions into the Yucatán is found in architecture of the post-classic period, most prominently at Chichén Itzá.

major ruin sites are Uxmal, near Mérida, and Cobá, within easy reach of Caribbean beaches. If you're prepared to forgo the most famous Maya ruins in favor of less spectacular or unexcavated sites, you can wander through entire cities with no company but the jungle and iguanas.

Golfo de México

Parque Natural
Ría Celestún

Punta Baz

Sisal

Progreso
Yucalpetén

Chelem

Chicxulub
Puerto

Telchac
Puerto

Santa
Clara

Chabihau

D
d

Telchac

Te

Hunucmá

Dzibilchaltún

Mérida

Motul

Tixkokob

Izam

Celestún

Punta Nimun

Umán

Kanasín

Hoctún

Holca

Maxcanú

Acanceh

Telchaquilo

Calcehtok

Muna

Mayapán

YUC

Oxkintok

Xpukil

Santa
Elena

Ticul

Santa
Cruz

Uxmal

Oxkutzcab

Kabah

Loltún

Tekax

Sayil

Bolonchén
de Rejón

Labná

Xlapak

Chacmultún

Tzucacab

Grutas
Xtacumbilxunaan

Tenabó

Tinúm

Campeche

Punta
Seybaplaya

Hopelchén

Vicente
Guerrero

Edzná

QU

La Joya

Dzibalchén

Champotón

Hochob

Chunchintok

CAMPECHE

Río Champotón

Sabancuy

Francisco
Escárcega

Xpujil

Becan

Río Bec

Río

The Yucatán Peninsula

Parque Natural Ría Lagartos

Santa Teresa
Sinaí
Cabo Catoche

ue Natural San Felipe

San Felipe
Río Lagartos

Holbox
Isla Holbox

Chiquilá

Punta Sam
Isla Mujeres

am ravo

El Cuyo

Cancún
Puerto Juárez

295

Yucatán

Kantunilkin

180

176

Sucilá

Tizimín

307

x

Tunkas

X-Can

Puerto Morelos

re ón
Piste
Chichén Itzá

Valladolid

Punta Bete

Molas

lankanché

180

Dzitnup

Chemax

Playa del Carmen
Xcaret
Paamul

xcabá

Cobá

Cozumel

Santa Pilar

TÁN

Akumal
Chemuyil
Xel-Ha
Xcacel

Palancar Reef

Tihosuco

Parque Natural de Quintana Roo

Tulum

Punta Sur

295

307

Santa Rosa

Punta Allen

Caribbean Sea

Sian Ka'an Biosphere Reserve

Punta Pájaros

184

Polyuc

Felipe Carrillo Puerto

Tupak

Punta Herrero

NTANA ROO

293

Limónes

307

Punta El Placer

Laguna de Bacalar

El Cocal

Puerto Bravo
Punta Río Indio
Majahual

Bacalar
Cenote Azul
Ucum

Bahía de Chetumal

Cayo Centro

N

condito

Nicolás ravo

Chetumal

unlich
Palmar

Bahía de Corozal

Río Hondo

BELIZE

Xcalak

0   30 miles

0   40 km

The Maya cities now lie in ruins, but the Maya themselves and their way of life are very much alive, despite the best efforts of the original Spanish colonists. Indeed, traveling into the Yucatán from elsewhere in Mexico is like entering another country. The people are visibly different. Most of the population is mestizo (mixed Maya and Spanish blood), and a fair amount are pure Maya, identifiable by their broad faces, dark skin, and short stature. Mayan, not Spanish, is the predominant language in many country towns and villages.

It is still common for the Maya to make annual offerings of corn to Chaac, the god of rain.

Christianity for many yucatecos is a mix of Catholicism and traditional animism, a belief that the sun, the earth, the plants, the animals, and the rain are gods. This melding of the ancient and the new is actually the result of a particularly bloody and cruel period of colonization. Since Hernan Cortés' landing on the shores of the Yucatán in 1519, the Maya have battled for their land and their freedom. The Spanish burned religious texts, including astronomical works, and destroyed stone idols. Disease and forced labor decimated the Maya population, but the Spanish never really succeeded in breaking their resistance. In the 1840s, after losing much of their lands, the Maya captured much of the peninsula during the War of the Castes, but they failed to follow through and take the principal city, Mérida. The inevitable retaliation of the *hacendados* (landowners) resulted in the extermination of nearly half the Maya. Not until 1935, when the Chan Santa Cruz people signed an accord with the government, did the fighting cease.

Here, as in much of Mexico, poverty is the enemy, aggravated by the peninsula's thin, parched topsoil. Increasingly, yucatecos are turning away from agriculture to more lucrative jobs in the oil industry, tourism, and at fish-processing plants. After oil, tourism is now the second-biggest industry here. Development continues apace, particularly along the Caribbean coast—a boon to the local economy and a scourge for those travelers who jealously protect their quiet tropical retreats.

Campeche

Campeche is a way station for travelers headed north to the Caribbean beaches or to the ruins of Campeche state. However, there's no reason to hurry away from this fort city. Most of the city's 250,000 residents are oblivious to tourists—they're polite but won't talk to you unless approached. Campeche has all the trappings of Spanish colonialism: fortified churches, mansions, Moorish arches, and winding narrow streets. As its surviving forts and ramparts attest, however, Campeche was once much more. It was through this port that the gold and silver of Mexico were shipped to Spain during the 16th and 17th centuries. Not surprisingly, the city's wealth attracted the attention of pirates, who preyed continually on the city and its ships. Finally, in 1663, a brutal pirate attack resulted in the massacre of almost the entire population of Campeche. Five years later, construction began on fortifications, and Campeche remains one of the few walled cities in the Americas. These days, Campeche tends to be more cosmopolitan, and a little less colorful, than the traditional Maya villages nearby. Unfortunately, the oil industry has ruined the beaches, and the fish you catch may be marinated already.

To become a policeman in Campeche, candidates need only show proof of a high school education and fill out an application; there is no training involved. Locals complain that officers aren't even given driving tests.

BASICS

AMERICAN EXPRESS Cardholders can pick up mail and everyone can replace lost traveler's checks at the American Express office run by the travel agency **Viajes Programados**. Unfortunately, you can't change money or cash personal checks here. *Prolongación Calle 59, Edificio Belmar, Apartado Postal 82, Campeche, Campeche, CP 24000, México, tel. 981/1–10–10. Open daily 9–2 and 5–7.*

AUTO PARTS/SERVICE **Servicio Pitocha** provides parts and service for American and foreign cars. *Madero 242, tel. 981/6–59–08.*

CASAS DE CAMBIO You can change money any time at the **Ramada Inn** (Ruíz Cortines 51, tel. 981/6–22–33). For a better rate, endure the long lines at **Bancomer** (16 Septiembre 120, tel. 981/6–66–22), which changes money daily from 9 to 12:30. **Banamex** (cnr of Calle 10 and Calle 53, tel. 981/6–06–29) has ATMs that accept Visa, Mastercard, and Plus. They change money 9–noon.

EMERGENCIES The **police** station is open 24 hours a day. *Calle 12, btw Calles 57 and 59, tel. 981/6–21–11.*

LAUNDRY **Lavandería y Tintorería Campeche** charges $3 per load (about 2 kilos) for same-day service. *Calle 55 No. 22, tel. 981/6–51–42. Open Mon.–Sat. 8–4.*

MEDICAL AID The **IMSS** clinic has 24-hour ambulance service. *López Mateos, at Baluartes, tel. 981/6–52–02 or 981/6–18–55.*

Farmacia Canto. *Calle 10, at Calle 55, tel. 981/6–52–48. Open daily 8–2 and 5–9.*

PHONES AND MAIL There are **Ladatel** phones at the Parque Principal and on sidewalks throughout the city. At **Computel** you can place international collect calls. *Calle 8 No. 255, fax 981/1–01–29. Open daily 7 AM–10 PM.*

The **Oficina de Correos** is the joint post/telephone office, offering fax, long-distance phone, telex, and mail services. They'll hold mail sent to you at the following address for up to 10 days: Lista de Correos, Oficina Urbana 1, Campeche, Campeche, CP 24000, México. *16 de Diciembre, 2 blocks east of Parque Principal, tel. 981/6–21–34. Open Mon.–Sat. 9–1.*

VISITOR INFORMATION The **state tourist office** has a knowledgeable and enthusiastic staff that provides brochures, hotel lists, bus schedules, and information about local events. *Calle 55 No. 25, btw Calles 12 and 14, tel. 981/6–67–67 or 981/6–60–68.*

COMING AND GOING

BY BUS The main terminal is on Gobernadores, about a kilometer from Parque Principal, just outside the city walls. **Autobuses del Oriente** (ADO, tel. 981/6–28–02), the principal first-class carrier, offers regular service throughout the peninsula. Sample fares include Mérida ($8, 3 hrs), Veracruz ($36, 5 hrs), and Mexico City ($52, 18 hrs). The second-class bus station, serving mostly destinations on the peninsula, is behind the ADO station on Calle Chile. You can catch a bus to Hopelchén ($2, 2 hrs) or Uxmal ($4.50, 3½ hrs), among other destinations. Baggage handlers store your luggage for a tip, and passengers with tickets can crash in the lounge area. To reach town from the ADO terminal, turn left onto Gobernadores; the first fort you reach marks the beginning of the old town. Otherwise, catch a bus across the street and ask to be left near the Parque Principal.

BY TRAIN Train travel in the Yucatán is fairly grim. Second-class service was once notoriously unsafe, but theft has diminished since the trains were lighted. In addition to daily first-class service to Mexico City ($20, 30–40 hrs), three trains leave every day for Mérida ($3, 4 hrs). *Héroes de Nacozari, tel. 981/6–51–48. 3 kilometers from downtown; take the CHINA bus, which runs frequently between the station and the market.*

BY PLANE **Aeroméxico** (tel. 981/6–66–56) has flights from Campeche's small airport to cities all over the country, most with a stopover in Mexico City. To the D.F., the fare is about $120. The airport, about 10 kilometers southeast of downtown, is accessible only by taxi ($5).

HITCHING The best place to get a ride out of Campeche is the gas station at Santa Lucía, on the outskirts of town. Cars going in all directions must pass by here. To get to the gas station, take the PLANCHAC bus from downtown.

GETTING AROUND

Virtually everything of interest lies inside the walls of the *villa vieja* (old city) and is easily accessible by foot. Even-numbered streets run parallel to the waterfront, and odd-numbered streets run perpendicular. All buses stop at the **market** and at the **Palacio de Gobierno** (Malecón, at Calle 61). The fare is about 35¢.

BY CAR Hertz rents VW bugs for $100 a day, including mileage. *Hotel Baluartes, Ruíz Cortines, at Calle 61, tel. 981/6–39–11.*

WHERE TO SLEEP

The lodging situation in Campeche is fair. Hotels aren't packed with tourists, but rooms fill up with businesspeople instead. If you arrive at the bus station in the wee hours, you're better off paying the cab fare (about $2) to any of the following hotels, all located in the old city, rather than staying in one of the noisy, overpriced holes near the station.

➢ UNDER $15 • **Hotel Campeche.** This rambling colonial mansion was a single-family home during the colonia era. Just visit the lobby to taste the owner's *jamaica* (a hibiscus-flower drink). The assistant manager speaks excellent English. Small rooms, which smell slightly of toilet cleanser, are a bargain at $12 for a single, $15 for a double. *Calle 8 No. 2, by Parque Principal, tel. 981/6–51–83. 42 rooms, all with bath. Luggage storage.*

Hotel Castelmar. A friendly family keeps the gigantic rooms in this airy, colonial-style hotel fairly clean. Some rooms have balconies with sea views, while others face onto a noisy street. The beds must have made good trampolines once, because they're uncomfortable now. Slightly dingy bathrooms are separated from the rooms by curtains and don't afford much privacy. Singles and doubles cost $15. *Calle 61 No. 2, tel. 981/6–28–86. 18 rooms, all with bath. Luggage storage.*

Hotel Reforma. Though a bit grimy on the lower floors, this hotel improves as you climb upstairs. Unfortunately, hot water is rare here, and the toilets seem like relics from colonial times. Hotel Reforma is under the same ownership as Hotel Campeche, and you can call the latter to make reservations at either place. Singles cost $11.50, doubles $13.50. *Calle 8 No. 257, no phone. 20 rooms, all with bath. Luggage storage, wheelchair access.*

➢ UNDER $25 • **Hotel Colonial.** The often-full Hotel Colonial has bright white sheets and spotless bathrooms. The management accepts reservations between 7 AM and 3 PM. Singles are $20, doubles $22, and additional guests cost $5.50 each. The rooms do get stuffy, so if you're feeling large, you might want to pay the extra $5.50 for air-conditioning. *Calle 14 No. 122, btw Calles 55 and 57, tel. 981/6–22–22. 30 rooms, all with bath. Luggage storage.*

Hotel López. Whoever designed this hotel was obsessed with cruise ships. It's built around a rectangular courtyard, above which rise two stories of portholes and wildly curving balconies. The rooms, all with fans or air-conditioning, have matching film noir furniture. All of the rooms are doubles costing $23, $30 with air-conditioning. Bathrooms are clean. *Calle 12, btw Calles 61 and 63, tel. 981/6–33–44. 39 rooms, all with bath. Luggage storage, restaurant.*

La Posada del Ángel. Facing the cathedral on Parque Principal, this place is convenient but noisy. The narrow corridors smack of fresh white paint, and the bathrooms are a vision to behold. Early check-in is advised, because rooms rent out fast—the hotel is popular among salesmen. All rooms are doubles ($22), though single travelers receive a small discount. Rooms with air-conditioning cost $5 more. You have to knock to be let in after 9:30 PM. *Calle 10 No. 309, btw Calles 55 and 53, tel. 981/6–77–18. 15 rooms, all with bath.*

HOSTEL **Villa Deportiva de Campeche.** This hostel is 3 kilometers from the old city, but well worth the bus fare—it's an amazing deal at about $3.30 per bed. Guests share small, well-kept quadruples cooled by fans. Clean sheets are available with a $7 deposit. The communal showers are bright and clean and even have semi-hot water. Rooms are segregated by sex, but couples may be able to share if there's space. Call ahead if you're going to be late; there's an 11 PM curfew. The hotel fills up fast in July and December. *Agustín Melgar s/n, tel. 981/6–18–02.*

18 rooms, none with bath. Take DIRECTO/UNIVERSIDAD bus to or from ADO station; ask driver to let you off as close to hostel as possible. Meal service, wheelchair access.

FOOD

Campeche's seafood has a well-deserved reputation throughout Mexico. Local specialties include *pan de cazón* (baby shark wrapped in a tortilla) and *camarón chiquito* (an ultra-small shrimp). Many of the city's better restaurants, as well as a handful of small sandwich shops, line Calle 8 across from the Parque Principal. If you're pinching pennies, go to the huge, frenzied market on Avenida Gobernadores just outside the city wall. There you can buy loads of luscious fruit, or take your chances at a taco stand.

➤ UNDER $5 • **Puerta Del Mar.** The decor is impressively tacky—the booths are carpeted and portraits of fish stare down from the linoleum walls. Locals sit around the plastic replica of Uxmal and discuss politics over a beer ($1.50) and sandwich ($1.50). Dinner specials (shrimp and rice or fillet of pómpano) are about $4. *Calle 8 No. 261, facing Parque Principal, tel. 981/6–23–28. Open daily 7 AM–10 PM.*

Restaurant La Parroquia. A great place to hang out and listen to old men gossip, La Parroquia features a huge menu, daily specials, and low prices. The *pollo adobado* (baked chicken) is exquisite. The daily specials, served with beans, tortillas, and a tiny salad, are less than $4. It's open 24 hours and serves freshly brewed coffee all day and night. *Calle 5 No. 8, 1 block west of Parque Principal, tel. 981/6–80–86.*

Tortas Colón. You can sate yourself with yummy tortas (sandwiches) for $2 and huge bowls of fresh fruit and yogurt ($1.50–$2) and wash it all down with a *licuado* (smoothie) for $1.50. You'll spend next to nothing in this long, narrow joint with stools. *Calle 10, btw Calles 57 and 59, no phone. Open Mon.–Sat. 8–2 and 6–10.*

➤ UNDER $15 • **Marganzo.** For some truly fabulous regional dishes served by suave waiters in festive costumes, count your pesos and head for Marganzo. Seafood specialties range from $7 to $13, but *antojitos campecheños* (Campeche appetizers) are only $5.50–$6.50 and equally good. Pan de cazón ($6), the regional specialty, is outstanding. There's live music some nights. *Calle 8 No. 268, tel. 981/1–38–98. Open daily 7 AM–midnight.*

WORTH SEEING

A walk through Campeche is like a trip through the military and commercial history of the Spanish colonies. Forts that protected the city from marauding pirates still stand, as do centuries-old churches and homes. Most of the interesting colonial buildings in Campeche are within the old city, and all are easily accessible on foot.

CIRCUITO DE BALUARTES Five years after much of the city was wiped out by pirates in 1663, the first stones of a new defense system were laid. The fortifications consisted of a 10-foot-thick wall running around the city, protected by seven *baluartes* (forts). Even ships had to pass through the four gates that controlled access to the city. The construction took more than 35 years, but effectively ended Campeche's role as the Yucatán's 90-pound weakling. Today, it's possible to follow the Circuito de Baluartes around the various forts, many of which are government buildings.

Closest to the market, the **Baluarte de San Pedro** (Calle 51, at Gobernadores) houses a couple of *tiendas de artesanías* (handicraft stores) selling *huipiles* (embroidered tunics) and other local wares. Across the street is the **Iglesia de San Juan.** Built in 1675, it still has its original stone exterior, which has been renovated. White flowers adorn the altar, and birds fly freely through the church. The Baluarte de San Pedro is open weekdays 9–1 and 5–8, Saturday 9–1. If you continue southeast around the circuit, you'll come to the **Baluarte San Francisco** (Calle 18, at 57). Only part of the original fort stands; the rest was destroyed to make room for a cable car. Inside is a small **Sala de Armas,** filled with old swords, axes, and guns. Admission is free, and it's open weekdays 9–1 and 5–8, Saturday 9–1.

Baluarte San Carlos (Calle 8, btw Calles 61 and 65) was the city's first fort, completed in 1676. Today the baluarte is the site of the **Museo de la Ciudad,** a collection of photos, maps, and models illustrating the history of Campeche. The museum features various artifacts, such as a golden key to the city, 18th-century silverwork, and a saber that belonged to Montejo the Younger, conquistador of the Yucatán. The real attraction, however, is the fort itself: Standing in its turrets, you can imagine yourself fending off pirates and other vermin. A mere 25¢ gets you in, and the museum is open Tuesday through Saturday 8–8, Sunday 8–1. Farther along on Calle 8, the **Puerta de Mar,** now in ruins, once controlled access to the port from the sea. Nearby, at the **Baluarte de Soledad,** some poorly preserved Maya stelae and columns are on display.

At the northern corner of the old city is the small **Baluarte Santiago,** demolished at the end of the last century and reconstructed in the 1950s. Today it houses the beautiful **Jardín Botánico** (botanical garden), where you can check out the flora of the region. *Calle 8, at Calle 49. Admission: $1. Open Tues.–Fri. 8–2, Sat. 9–1 and 4–8, Sun. 9–1.*

CHURCHES Facing the **zócalo** (main plaza), the beautiful **Catedral de la Concepción** dates from the 18th century. Inside, note the illustrations of the Stations of the Cross, and the small but brilliant stained-glass windows under the cupola at the front of the church. Other beautiful churches in the old city include the **Iglesia de San Francisquito** (Calle 12, btw Calles 59 and 61), which dates from the 18th century. The **Iglesia de Jesús El Nazareno,** on Calle 55 at Calle 12, features dramatic, elaborate icons standing on ostentatious altars.

MUSEO REGIONAL DE CAMPECHE Campeche has consolidated its most important historical pieces in the former mansion of the royal governor. Pre-Conquest artifacts on the first floor include the skull of a child whose head had been flattened with boards, thought to be a mark of beauty. Some of the small statues from the classical period are quite detailed and marvelously preserved. Low-relief stelae and jade work complete the collection. Spanish artifacts include a full-size cabriolet and the usual assortment of swords, guns, and armor. *Calle 59, btw Calles 14 and 16. Admission: about $4.50. Open Tues.–Sat. 8–8, Sun. 8–1.*

AFTER DARK

Like most cities on the peninsula, Campeche goes to sleep early. On weekends the **malecón** (boardwalk) is the happening place to be. Bars and discos, including **Atlantis** (Ramada Inn, Ruíz Cortines 51) and **Jet Set Bar** (Ah-Kim-Pech shopping center), are frequented by well-off locals and tourists staying at the expensive hotels on the waterfront. Both have a cover charge of $8.50. There is free music in the Parque Principal, usually on Thursday and Sunday nights. The light show at **Puerta de Tierra** (Gobernadores, toward the Old City from the main bus station) rehashes Campeche's history of pirate invasions. The spectacle is performed by local musicians and dancers at 8 PM on Fridays. The performance, mostly in Spanish, costs $2.50, $1.50 with student ID.

Near Campeche

EDZNA

Evidence suggests that this large site 60 kilometers southeast of Campeche may have been settled as early as 600 BC, but the city thrived during the late Classic Period, from AD 600–900. The beauty here lies in the overall building scheme rather than in the ornamentation. Later styles of architecture (as seen at Uxmal, for example) may be more elaborate but according to some, they signal the decline of the Mayan unity and autonomy that produced grand achievements in science and art. The classic style is also characterized by the superb stelae (carved stone slabs) found all over Edzná. Many of these are still on the premises, although they have been moved to a roped-in, palapa-covered gallery outside the ruins.

The main attraction here is the **Temple of Five Stories,** an example of early Puuc architecture situated on the large Plaza Central. The temple on the top story is capped with a 7-meter roof comb, once decorated with a mask of Chaac that seemed to change expression as the sun rose and fell. The mask is believed to be the origin of the name Edzná, meaning *Casa de los Gestos* (House of the Expressions). Several other excellently restored buildings cluster around the **Gran Acrópolis**—including the **House of the Moon,** the **Temazcal** (sweat house), and three additional structures. Edzná can also be translated as House of Echos, probably referring to the amazing acoustics among the principal buildings—standing in the doorway at the top of the pyramid, you can hear the voice of someone at the far end of the Gran Acrópolis. On the first day of the Maya year, the sun reaches its zenith over Edzná, leading to speculation that the amazingly accurate Maya calendar was devised here. The most recent work in reconstructing the Gran Acrópolis has been carried out by Quiché Maya refugees from Guatemala. Vicious mosquitoes breed in surrounding swamps and stagnant waterholes, so bring repellant. *Admission: $4.50, free Sun. and holidays. Open daily 8–5.*

COMING AND GOING Servicios Turísticos Picazh (Calle 16 No. 348, tel. 981/6–44–26) in Campeche has organized tours, departing at 9 AM and 1 PM, for about $17 per person. Admission and lunch are included. But there are cheaper ways to get there. Take a **Camioneros de Campeche** bus from behind the ADO station to **Hopelchén.** Ask to be let off at **Cuyal.** From the crossroads at Cuyal, it's not difficult to hitch a ride to Edzná. Walking the 19 kilometers to the ruins is not advised—robberies and assaults along this route have been reported. An excellent alternative for early risers is the direct bus to Edzná between 7 and 7:30 AM, leaving from Avenida Gobernadores in Campeche, one block up from the Pemex station. An old white-and-blue bus marked PICK, it runs every day and costs $4. On the return trip, the bus passes the ruins at about 11:30 AM; if you go on a Sunday, the bus will probably be packed with Jehovah's Witnesses on their way to church. Otherwise, it's easy to hitch or flag down a bus at the crossroads (if you're going toward Campeche). The last bus bound for Campeche ($2) passes Cuyal around 5 PM.

CHENES RUINS/XTACUMBILXUNAAN

Any comprehensive tour of Maya archaeology in the region should include the Chenes ruins. The sites aren't included in most package itineraries, which is a bonus if you're tired of dodging tour buses. The remote ruins at Hochob and El Tabasqueño are rarely visited, in part because reaching them is tough, even if you have a car. Those who persevere will discover that their solitude is interrupted only by the occasional animal. Hochob displays one of the purest styles of Chenes architecture, which is characterized by elaborate decoration. The Xtacumbilxunaan caves are naturally ornate and more accessible than the ruins, lying just off Highway 261. **Servicios Turísticos Picazh** (Calle 16 No. 348, Campeche, tel. 981/6–44–26) arranges pricey trips.

COMING AND GOING It's virtually impossible to make the bus odyssey to any of the Chenes ruins and return to Campeche in one day. It's best to stay the night in Hopelchén, and leave early in the morning for the ruins. Six buses leave Campeche daily for Hopelchén, 53 kilometers east of Campeche, before continuing on to Mérida. In Hopelchén, take one of four daily buses ($1.50) 41 kilometers south to Dzibalchén, which serves as the crossroads to the ruins. Also, a pickup truck carries passengers from the park in Hopelchén to Dzibalchén and Iturbide

The Mennonites of Hopelchén

Hopelchén is home to a community of tall, blue-eyed people who look like they just stepped off the set of Little House on the Prairie. As their overalls, boots, and utility shirts might suggest, they're farmers—very good ones, as townspeople will tell you. Throughout the states of Campeche and Yucatán, the Mennonites establish tightly-knit, insular farming communities. The Mennonite residents of Hopelchén speak excellent Spanish, many are fluent in English, German, Dutch, and their homemade cheese is delicious.

($1.50, about 15 kilometers further south) every day at 7 AM. The last bus back to Hopelchén ($1.50) leaves Iturbide at 5 PM, passing through Dzibalchén at about 5:30 PM. To get to Mérida from Hopelchén, wait for the bus in front of the store facing the park, a half block from the town's sole hotel (you can inquire there about bus schedules). Campeche-bound buses leave from the opposite side of the park.

WHERE TO SLEEP The only hotel in the area is **Los Arcos** (tel. 981/2–00–37) in Hopelchén, which offers huge, sunny, clean rooms and bathrooms with hot water for $10 (single), $13.50 (double), and $17 (triple). If you are left high and dry at any of the sites, you can pitch a tent or string a hammock, but the mosquitoes will drive you stark raving mad. Several open-air loncherías (snack bars) line the avenue beside the hotel, where you can eat like a king (two fat tamales and a Coke) for about $2.

WORTH SEEING

➤ DZIBILNOCAC • Among the scattered dirt mounds hidden in the thick vegetation are two buildings which, until a few years ago, were unrecognizable. Recently, however, the western pyramid has been excavated and reconstructed and now stands in almost perfect condition. Masks of Chaac cover the uppermost temple, and the curled pattern of his nose is repeated in relief on all sides. A neighboring structure, as yet unrestored, houses the remains of beautiful red and green frescoes. Don't mistake the primitive-looking black graffiti in one of the chambers for ancient cave painting—it's more contemporary. To get to Dzibilnocac, walk 1 kilometer west of Iturbide on the dirt road leading out of town.

➤ HOCHOB • Reaching this site deep within the rain forest is not easy, but Hochob's appeal lies in its splendid isolation. There is little to suggest that you aren't the true discoverer of a long-lost civilization, a sensation that is heightened if you camp overnight. Only the central plaza has been excavated. Countless other buildings lie unexplored under the thick vegetation. The main building is the **Temple of Chaac,** a rectangular building 40 meters long and 7 meters high. Look carefully at the facade to see a giant image of Chaac: The motifs on the lintel above the entrance to the temple are his eyes, and the open door represents his mouth.

Although he recommends visiting Hochob, writer David Walter suggests you avoid going on a bicycle during the rainy season (June–August)—gallons of water pour down, and rattlesnakes come out of their holes to avoid drowning. And don't go alone, because if you fall down one of the many hidden chultunes *(underground cisterns), you'll be food for the birds. He broke both these rules, but ignorance is bliss.*

Getting to Hochob is difficult, even if you have your own car. There is no public transport, so your only option is to walk or bike the 13 kilometers from Dzibalchén. Take the Campeche road north for 1 kilometer, then turn left onto a dirt road leading to the tiny village of Chencoh. The 8 or so kilometers to Chencoh are clay, sand and rock—not ideal for traversing on a bike. They're even worse if it's raining—bicycles (and cars) will slowly grind to a stop after 25 pounds of instant pottery has glommed onto the tires.

When you reach Chencoh, turn left again and head another 4 kilometers into the rain forest. José William Chan (tel. 982/2–01–06), the self-appointed guide and bushwhacker in Dzibalchén, rents bikes for $5, and he is more than happy to show you the way as well; his services cost $10–$20, depending on the number of people and your means. If you miss the last bus out of Dzibalchén at 5:30 PM, José and his family sometimes allow visitors to pass the night in hammocks in their back room. Bring your mosquito repellent and anticipate a pre-dawn wake-up call from roosters, insects, and birds. To find José, walk straight out of town on the road to Iturbide. You can't miss his large signs reading TOURIST INFORMATION.

➤ EL TABASQUENO • If your Indiana Jones ambitions have not been satisfied by Hochob, El Tabasqueño, a.k.a. Xtabas, may be just the place for you. Seven kilometers from Dzibalchén and 2 kilometers off the road, El Tabasqueño is completely hidden in the forest. The trek through the jungle to reach it is probably the most interesting part of the trip. The site has only one building, a temple featuring masks of Chaac and the face of Itzamná. Decorations include the double-headed serpent, the symbol of Kukulcan. The only way to get to El Tabasqueño is through the paid services of José William Chan (*see* Hochob, *above*); there is no sign indicating where to begin your hike and no discernible path leading to the ruins. In the rainy season, you may be especially glad to have José trailblazing through the jungle with his machete. He charges $10–$20 to accompany you on this trip.

➤ XTACUMBILXUNAAN CAVES • Near the town of Bolonchén, 34 kilometers north of Hopelchén, are the Grutas Xtacumbilxunaan (Caves of the Hidden Girl). Legend has it that the Maya lost a young girl here when they arrived searching for water. The colorful caves are unbelievable, especially if you see them before heading on to the Loltún Caves, which spoil you for anything else. Seven underground wells, each of a different color, lie deep beneath the main caverns and are accessible only to those with climbing equipment, lanterns, and a sense of adventure. The surreal two-day excursion is rarely attempted. You'll need to negotiate the price for a guide—you'll find them hanging around during open hours. You may also camp for free at the sight, but be prepared to share your flesh with thirsty mosquitoes. An attendant charges 65¢ to visit the site daily from 8 to 5. At other times, bring your own flashlight. Xtacumbilxunaan lies on Highway 261 between Hopelchén and Bolonchén. Take the Mérida-bound bus from Hopelchén and ask the driver to drop you at the *grutas* (caves).

The Puuc Region

The southwestern part of Yucatán state is one of the richest archaeological zones in the world. The Puuc Hills, a low-lying mountain range covering about 156 square kilometers, contain six major sites and some of the most distinctive Maya architecture on the peninsula. You'll want to dedicate at least three days to the region: one to see the main site at Uxmal; another for the surrounding Maya ruins of Kabah, Sayil, Labná, and Xlapac; and a third to explore the spectacular caves at Loltún and the surrounding towns, where many of the residents speak only Mayan.

Maya civilization reached its zenith in the Puuc cities during the late Classic Period (about AD 800–1000), when Uxmal was the center of a community that included the surrounding towns of Kabah, Sayil, Labná, and Xlapac. At one time as many as 20,000 people lived in the area, but the cities were abandoned before the Spanish arrived. No one knows for sure why the Maya left, but drought is a reasonable guess. This part of the Yucatán is extremely arid, with none of the cenotes common elsewhere on the peninsula. Instead, the Maya relied on chultunes to catch and store rainwater. These chultunes, scores of which dot the region, held as much as 7,000 gallons each. The strong emphasis on water is also evident in the attention given to Chaac, the rain god, in the region's architecture. Images of Chaac, with his unmistakable hooked nose, are everywhere.

Considered the most beautiful of all Maya building styles, Puuc architecture is characterized by finely shaped limestone veneers applied to lime-base concrete. The lower facades of Puuc buildings are typically smooth and plain, contrasting with elaborate upper facades decorated with intricate mosaics. Among the most common motifs are X-shape lattices, geometric designs, serpents, and masks. It is a highly complex architectural style that nonetheless draws on a simple idea: that of the *choza*, or one-room thatched hut, common in the region. Stylized representations of the choza appear on the greatest works, such as the archway at Labná. Later Puuc architecture, with its profusion of mosaics, serpents, and masks, displays a Toltec influence that is somewhat top-heavy with decoration.

Even if you just pass through on a bus, it's impossible not to see the large, moss-covered Spanish-colonial churches at the heart of even the smallest towns in this region. Most of these small towns—Muna, Tijul, Oxcutzcab, Maní, and Santa Elena—have a market, a few scattered loncherías, a hotel, and a bar. If you get stuck waiting for a bus, just do what everyone here does. Hang out, take a nap on a bench, and enjoy the quiet.

BASICS

VISITOR INFORMATION Admission fees to the archaeological sites can quickly destroy your budget, but there are ways to get around them. Your best bet is to schedule your visit to Loltún and the Puuc towns for a Sunday or holiday, when admission is free. If you want to buy a guidebook to the Puuc Hills, get it before you leave Mérida or Campeche, or you'll pay through the nose. Otherwise, Uxmal has a large tourist center, which runs half-hour documentaries on the archaeological, cultural, and environmental riches of the Yucatán. A small museum also displays a few archaeological remains with descriptions printed in Spanish. But apart from small tourist shops selling crafts and soft drinks, smaller sites have no amenities, not even bathrooms.

COMING AND GOING The Puuc route snakes its way from Campeche to Mérida, and many travelers take in the sights on their way between the two towns. The main attractions, Uxmal and Kabah, are about 25 kilometers apart along Route 261. From Campeche, follow 261 to the ruins; buses from Campeche to Uxmal cost $4.50. From Mérida, take Highway 180 south to Umán and Highway 261—the journey is only about 97 kilometers. Seven second-class buses make the 1½-hour trip daily from Mérida ($3), or you can take the daily direct bus that leaves Mérida at 8 AM and returns from Uxmal at 2 PM ($6 round trip). To return to Mérida or continue on to Kabah from Uxmal, flag down a bus along Highway 261—north to Mérida or south to Kabah. The problem is getting them to stop when you want to come back. Some of the bus drivers consider passengers an unnecessary nuisance and won't stop even if you are waving your arms madly.

Exploring the other sites on the Puuc Route, such as Labná, Xlapak, Sayil, and the Loltún Caves, is not so easy. There are few buses and little traffic. If you have the bucks, rent a car in Mérida or Campeche. Otherwise, the easiest way to reach these Puuc towns is to take the **Tura Puuc ADO Bus** (ADO station, Calle 69, no phone), which leaves Mérida daily at 8 AM and returns at 3 PM. It passes through Santa Elena's plaza every day between 9 AM and 9:30 AM. Unfortunately, if you only go for the day, the unguided tour only allows you 40 minutes at Labná and Kabah, 20 minutes at Xlapak and Sayil, and one hour at Uxmal. The tickets are $10, and you should reserve a day in advance.

A less reliable option is to hitch to the sites, though it would be foolish to try it at night. During the day, the road is not regularly traveled, but you can usually get a ride. Just be patient and bring lots of water; it could take a couple hours. The best places to pick up rides with tourists are in Kabah or Loltún (see Oxkutzcab and the Loltún Caves, below).

WHERE TO SLEEP Many people visit as a day trip from Mérida, since lodging options in the Puuc region are severely limited. But if you want to explore the area in depth, it doesn't make sense to keep commuting back and forth from Mérida. Staying in the small towns of **Santa Elena, Ticul,** or **Oxkutzcab** (see below) is a more convenient option. You'll still have to take a bus or hitch to get anywhere, but it's no more than 56 kilometers to any of the sites.

Of the Puuc sites, only Uxmal has accommodations, most of which are expensive hotels. If you insist on staying in the area, head for **Rancho Uxmal,** a hotel 4 kilometers north of the Uxmal ruins. Singles are $25; each additional person is $5. However, you can pitch a tent or hang a hammock (and still have use of bathrooms, hot showers, and an enticing swimming pool) for only $3.50 per person. *Hwy. 261, tel. 999/2–02–77. Walk, hitch, or flag-down a Mérida-bound bus. 20 rooms, all with bath. Laundry, luggage storage, restaurant.*

It makes more sense to stay at the **Sacbé Campgrounds,** just outside of Santa Elena along Highway 261. It's halfway between Uxmal (to the north) and four other major archaeological sites (to the south). The couple that owns the place has gone all out to create a clean and cheerful campground where you can sling a hammock or pitch a tent ($3). They have three bungalows, as well; the two smaller ones cost $8.50 for one person, $11 for two; the larger goes for $9.50 and $12, single and double. The owners also cook breakfast or dinner for guests ($3 per meal). They know the local bus schedules and offer inside information about free activities, shortcuts to sites, and local wildlife. *¼ of a kilometer south of the road to Santa Elena. Take any bus from Mérida or Campeche that travels down 261 and ask the driver to let you off at the campo deportivo. From Ticul, take a combi to Santa Elena. No phone.*

FOOD If you're coming from Mérida, consider bringing a picnic lunch. The restaurants around Uxmal are horribly expensive, and most of the other Puuc sites offer little more than junky, over-priced snacks. If you are coming by bus or car, you might want to stop off for a meal or stock up on fruit at one of the area's transport hubs: Muna, Santa Elena, Ticul, or Oxkutzcab.

UXMAL AND THE PUUC ROUTE

Although the carefully kept lawns and hordes of plaid-clad tourists at Uxmal (pronounced oosh-mahl) provide an unfortunate reality-check, the beauty and scale of the buildings are such that you will soon forget the manicured surroundings. The Chilam Balam, a chronicle of the Maya of this region, says that Uxmal was founded in the mid-6th century. Uxmal means "built three times," but the structures were apparently reconstructed at least five times. No one knows exactly who used these buildings, but one theory suggests that the Xives, a people from the central Mexican plain, occupied Uxmal briefly in the 10th century. Some evidence of this remains in inscriptions, but their paucity suggests that the Xives's stay was relatively short. Whatever the case, the city was abandoned soon afterward.

The satellite Puuc towns of Kabah, Sayil, Labná, and Xlapak are not as large or as historically impressive as Uxmal. However, their remote setting in the Puuc Hills adds to their appeal. Many of the temples and pyramids remain hidden by the low vegetation, and tropical birds flit among the ruins. The ruins may not be in the best condition, but few tourists will interrupt your musings, except in Kabah. If aesthetics are more important to you than nitty-gritty archaeo-logical details, you will love these sites. Apart from Kabah, the towns lie along the 48-kilometer back road that runs from Highway 261 to the town of Oxkutzcab and Highway 184. If you do travel this road, plan to visit the Loltún Caves along the way (see Oxkutzcab and the Loltún Caves, below).

UXMAL The archaeological ruins are open daily 8–5. Admission is $6.50, except on Sunday, when it's free.

The magnificent **Pyramid of the Magician** is the first thing you'll see when you enter the archaeological site. The pyramid has an unusual oval base and stands 39 meters tall. The first stage of its construction dates to the 6th century, and five temples were added during the next 400 years. To get to the fifth temple, you'll have to climb 150 narrow steps at a 60° angle. If the vertigo hasn't done you in, climb down the west side to the temple just below it. The entrance is framed by the mouth of a huge mask of Chaac. Most impressive is the careful stone-by-stone construction and the incredible way the shape of the pyramid seems to change when viewed from different perspectives.

According to legend, the pyramid was constructed in a single night by a dwarf with magical powers who was hatched from an egg by a witch.

Behind the pyramid is the **Nun's Quadrangle**, an imposing complex of four long, narrow buildings around a central courtyard. Flocks of tropical birds flutter in and out of the evenly spaced

The Road Best Traveled

Several roads connect Campeche with Mérida, the shortest and fastest being a bland stretch of Highway 180. If you are at all interested in Maya civilization, past or present, take a more leisurely and circuitous route along Highway 261. Any road trip should include Mayapán (see Maya Ruins, in Near Mérida, below) and some of the smaller Puuc Hills ruins. Highway 261 puts travelers in prime position for visiting the remote ruins of Dzibilnocac, Hochob, and El Tabasqueño (see Near Campeche, above). Bring a hammock and mosquito net, and you won't be dependent on bus schedules or hotels.

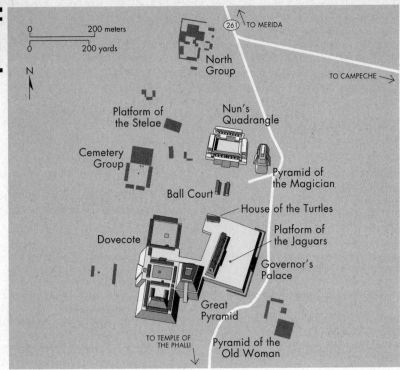

North
Group

TO MERIDA

TO CAMPECHE

Platform of
the Stelae

Nun's
Quadrangle

Cemetery
Group

Pyramid of
the Magician

Ball Court

House of the Turtles

Dovecote

Platform of
the Jaguars

Governor's
Palace

Great
Pyramid

TO TEMPLE OF
THE PHALLI

Pyramid of the
Old Woman

0   200 meters
0   200 yards

N

doorways and across the courtyard. The complex received its name from the Spanish, who thought the layout and the 74 small rooms inside resembled a European convent. Its real purpose remains unclear: Red handprints covering one wall have led to speculation that the building was associated with Itzamná, the god of sun and sky. However, images of Chaac, the rain god with the distinctive hooked nose, are also prevalent. Many walls are decorated with geometric patterns and animal carvings, including images of a two-headed serpent. Facing the Nun's Quadrangle is a four-building complex called the **Cemetery Group.** Now badly decayed, the structures were once decorated with carved skulls and bones.

Head southwest from the Nun's Quadrangle to reach the **juego de pelota** (ball court). The badly deteriorated complex used to have stone bleachers from which spectators watched players put balls through stone rings (*see box, below*).

Close to the ball court and the Governor's Palace is the **House of the Turtles**, a simple structure typical of Puuc architecture. The upper half of the building, which consists of a series of rooms, is most interesting: A series of columns supports a cornice sculpted with small turtles. The Maya believed that turtles would appeal to Chaac on behalf of drought-stricken humans.

Set on a large raised platform, the **Governor's Palace** is one of the finest examples of pre-Hispanic architecture in Mesoamerica. Its 107-meter length is divided by three corbeled arches, creating narrow passageways or sanctuaries. The friezes along the uppermost section of the palace are as intricate as any in Maya architecture, with carvings of geometric patterns overlaid with plumed serpents and Chaac masks. These mosaics supposedly required over 20,000 individually cut stones.

Southeast of the Governor's Palace is a badly deteriorated pyramid with a rectangular base and the remains of a temple on its top. Now covered by vegetation, the whole complex is known as the **Pyramid of the Old Woman,** referring to the witch who hatched the dwarf magician. The latter is said to have imprisoned her here. Continuing south from the Pyramid of the Old Woman, you reach the small **Temple of the Phalli.** Suspended from the cornices, the phalli were used to channel rain into storage containers. Most phalli have been destroyed or stolen, but you can see one in the museum at the tourist center.

Southwest of the Governor's Palace are the remains of the **Great Pyramid**. The structure is in poor condition and cannot compare with the Pyramid of the Magician, but the view from the 33-meter mound is rewarding and the climb up the reconstructed stairway is relatively easy. Inside the temple at the top is a shrine to Chaac. Small bowls are carved into parts of the mask, presumably to hold water or a small offering.

Behind the Great Pyramid is the **Dovecote,** a long building topped by eight triangular belfries perforated with what appear to be pigeonholes, hence the name of the building. No one has a clue as to what the place was actually used for. About half a kilometer south from the Dovecote is a small building half-covered by dirt and vegetation. The ruined structure had two stories, an oddity in Puuc architecture. The geometric carvings on its facade look like a centipede, giving the building the name *chimez* (centipede in Mayan).

KABAH Highway 261 from Mérida to Campeche splits Kabah in two. About 25 kilometers south of Uxmal, Kabah is among the most impressive sites in the Puuc region and dates from AD 850–900. The most interesting structures uncovered so far lie on the eastern side of the road, while the ruins on the western side remain partly hidden beneath dense vegetation.

The **Codz-Pop** is the principal structure at Kabah. The fantastic western facade is decorated with nearly 300 masks of Chaac, the god of rain, to whom the building was dedicated. The name Codz-Pop means "coiled mat," possibly a reference to the noses, which curl like rolled-up mats. The noses may have been used as supports for lanterns, in which case the wall would have been brilliantly lit and visible for miles. Some archaeologists have suggested that the building had a legal or military function.

Behind the Codz Pop are two structures built in the plainer, more traditional Puuc style: **El Palacio,** a palace that featured over 30 chambers, half of which still remain; and the **Temple of the Columns,** which boasts some well-preserved columns at the back of the building.

On the other side of the road are several more magnificent structures, still largely unexcavated. Over hundreds of years, the roots of jungle vines and trees have transformed the **Great Pyra-**

Ball Courts

Ball courts, found in virtually all the ruins of Maya ceremonial centers, are laid out in the shape of an H. The object of the game was for players on two opposing teams to knock a rubber ball through a stone ring mounted on the wall using only their hips, elbows, and knees. The game resembled present-day soccer, albeit with greatly reduced salaries.

The games celebrated the creation of the cosmos and mankind by the great Progenitors. The movements of the players and the ball reenacted the tests that ancient heroes faced, as well as the movements of the stars and planets. The planetary cycles, in conjunction with each other, were the cause of peace and strife, fertility and infertility, life and death. The walls of the courts were often elaborately decorated with mosaics depicting beheadings and other bloody rituals, presumably performed upon the defeated team. Though subject to debate, some archaeologists believe the losing team's captain was sacrificed, and the defeated players turned into the victors' slaves.

mid, once the most important temple in Kabah, into a mound of rubble. Traces of a stairway appear on its southern side. The **Arch of Triumph** marks the end of a *sacbé*, a raised road leading from Kabah to Uxmal. Southwest of the arch is the newly excavated **Templo de las Manos Rojas** (Temple of the Red Hands), which features small red hands imprinted in the northern wall of the first chamber. The handprints have been variously interpreted as the signatures of the ancient architects and the marks of Itzamná, the spiritual guide of the Maya. *Admission: $3.50, free Sun. and holidays. Open daily 8–5.*

SAYIL Meaning "the place of the ants" in Maya, Sayil, 10 kilometers from Kabah, is best known for its magnificent **palace.** Built in AD 730, the palace is 65 meters long, with more than 50 rooms sprawling over three levels. The second level is decorated with columns similar to those found in Greek temples. The sculpted frieze above these columns features masks of the rain god, as well as images of the Descending God, an upside-down figure, and the Blue Lizard, a snakelike figure. Both the walls and the frieze of this level are decorated with closely-spaced vertical "columnettes" which imitate, stylistically, the joined bamboo or wooden rods of the choza, or hut. South of the palace is the badly decayed **El Mirador,** which features the rooster-comb roof and a **ball court.** Don't leave Sayil without getting a good look at the city from a distance—the view from the hill across the road from the entrance is the best. *Admission: $3.50, free Sun. and holidays. Open daily 8–5.*

XLAPAK About 6 kilometers east of Sayil is Xlapak, the smallest and least important site on the Puuc Route, with only one partially restored palace. The smooth-wall structure is typical of Puuc style, featuring geometric designs and masks of Chaac. *Admission: $2.50, free Sun. and holidays. Open daily 8–5.*

LABNA Probably the oldest of the Puuc cities, Labná (4 kilometers from Xlapak) is thought to have been built during the early Classic Period (about AD 500). Labná means "The House of Old Women" in Mayan, but it probably received this name after the city was abandoned. Only a few structures have been uncovered at Labná, but they are exquisite. The best-preserved site is the **arch**; once part of a larger building, it now stands alone except for two surviving rooms leading off the passageway. The corbeled passageway is richly decorated with geometric patterns, mosaics, and small columns. Over the two flanking passageways, two large choza designs stand in relief. The **palace** is the other major ruin at Labná. The largest complex in the Puuc Hills, it sits on a huge platform more than 150 yards long. Despite its size, the palace isn't nearly as inspiring as the palace at Sayil. However, the decoration of its facade is noteworthy. Although no one knows exactly what the palace was used for, it seems to have been built some time in the 9th century. Another impressive structure at Labná is **El Mirador,** a pyramid with a temple on top. The pyramid is little more than rubble today, but the temple has survived better. *Admission: $3, free Sun. and holidays. Open daily 8–5.*

OXKUTZCAB AND LOLTUN CAVES

Sixteen kilometers southeast of Ticul, the small town of Oxkutzcab is seldom explored by tourists. Although some people come here to get a bus or taxi to the nearby caves at Loltún, few bother to walk around it. During the morning, Oxkutzcab is in a state of pandemonium, filled with people and trucks. The huge **market** (Calle 51, btw Calles 48 and 50) draws people from throughout the region who come to buy produce. Prices are as low as you're likely to find in Mexico. If you decide to spend the night, try **Hospedaje Trujeque** (Calle 48 No. 102A, btw Calles 51 and 53, tel. 997/5–05–68), which has pleasant rooms with private bathrooms and hot water for about $10 single and $14 double.

The Grutas de Loltún are the largest and most spectacular on the peninsula, and definitely deserve your time. About 19 kilometers east of Labná and 10 kilometers west of Oxkutzcab, Loltún consists of a maze of underground labyrinths filled with enormous stalagmites and stalactites. Archaeologists have had a field day here, unearthing evidence about the Maya and their ancestors, who inhabited these caves for more than two millennia. Religious ceremonies were held in the **Cathedral,** a vast chamber crowded with stalagmites and stalactites. Some formations in the center of the chamber resemble an altar. In another cavern you can see the soot from cooking fires and the remains of *metates* (stones used for grinding corn). The caves contain several carvings of figures and hieroglyphs, some of which date back to 2000 BC, as well as black ink paintings. The entire place was once under water, which gives the rocks a smooth, liquid quality. Since the caverns dried out thousands of years ago, dripping water has carved the rocks into bizarre shapes. Tour guides find no end of amusing resemblances, including the Virgin of Guadalupe, a dolphin's head, a camel, a jaguar, and an eagle. Especially interesting are two semihollow rock formations extending from the ceiling to the floor. If you tap them the right way, they produce musical tones. According to legend, only virgins can produce this sound, so think twice before you strike. The floor of the dark caves is slippery and uneven, so bring a sturdy pair of shoes. Guided tours are led daily every 1½ hours from 9:30 to 3. Guides expect a tip—a dollar or two each is about right. *Admission: $6, $2.50 on Sun.*

COMING AND GOING Combis (tarp-covered trucks) for Oxkutzcab leave from the Parque San Juan in Mérida whenever they're full; ADO buses leave from the terminal (Calle 62, btw Calles 65 and 67) every half-hour. Combis and buses both cost around $3. From anywhere besides Mérida, you'll have to go to Ticul first and catch a combi from Calle 25, between Calles 26 and 28. The ride from Ticul to Oxkutzcab takes about 30 minutes and costs 65¢.

To get to Loltún from Oxkutzcab, you'll have to wait until one of the trucks carrying workers to the fields fills up—generally wait in front of the market. The 11-kilometer trip costs only about 50¢. If you don't want to wait around, you can hire one of the many taxis or combis to take you to the grutas for about $5. From Loltún wait (and hope) for the truck to come back, or hitch a ride. During the day, hitching is neither dangerous nor difficult in these parts. From Oxkutzcab, combis leave for Ticul from Calle 52, between Calles 51 and 53, or from the northwest corner of the park (the last leaves at 7 PM). Buses leave for Mérida from Oxkutzcab every half hour until 9 PM.

TICUL

The small town of Ticul, 86 kilometers south of Mérida, is a convenient base from which to explore the region. The town itself has little to offer, but shoe fetishists will have a fine old time: Ticul is a major shoe-manufacturing center. Some of the finest huipiles in the Yucatán are made here as well. Apart from watching the bicycles go by, there is little to do, except on Sunday, which is drinking day. Everything but the liquor stores is closed, and the police patrol the streets, carting off the obviously drunk. Probably the most interesting feature of Ticul is the extent to which Mayan is spoken—you are likely to hear Mayan as often as Spanish.

BASICS Banco Atlántico (Calle 23, tel. 997/2–02–48), diagonally across from the plaza, changes money 9–1:30. Twenty-four hour medical aid is available at the **clinic** (Calle 23, at Calle 30, tel. 997/2–09–44).

COMING AND GOING From Campeche and Hopelchén, you'll have to take the Mérida bus via Highway 261 and change at Santa Elena—combis await incoming buses to take passengers on to Ticul from about 5:30 AM to 6 PM. Combis leave Mérida for Ticul ($3) from the Parque

Some Helpful Phrases in Mayan

B'ish ka' ba?	**What is your name?**
Im ka' ba . . .	**My name is . . .**
Baax a kajal?	**What is your town?**
In kajale' (Berkeley),	**I live in (Berkeley)**
nadz' ti' (San Francisco).	**near (San Francisco).**
Bis a wool?	**How are you?**
Jach kimac in wool,	**I'm content./I'm dancing.**
tin o'k'ot.	

San Juan whenever they are full. Buses also make the 80-minute trip from the main bus station for about the same price.

To reach Uxmal and Kabah, take a combi for Santa Elena from the plaza or from the combi station at Calle 30 No. 214, three blocks away. In Santa Elena, catch the Campeche-bound bus to Kabah (65¢) or the Mérida-bound bus to Uxmal ($1.50). To reach Loltún, your best bet is to take a combi to Oxkutzcab. They hang out near the plaza at Calle 25, between Calles 26 and 28. The ride only takes 30 minutes and costs about 65¢.

WHERE TO SLEEP AND EAT The little old man who runs the **Hotel San Miguel** (Calle 28 No. 213, btw Calles 21 and 23, tel. 997/2–03–82) speaks Mayan, but his Spanish is rough. At least the clean rooms have hot water and fans. Singles are $8.50, doubles $12. The woman who works at the **Hotel Sierra Sosa** (Calle 26 No. 199, tel. 997/2–00–08) in the afternoons speaks excellent English. The simple rooms have comfortable beds, fans, and hot water. Street noise can be annoying in the front rooms, so request a room in the back. Singles are $8.50, doubles $12. There are laundry facilities and you can store your luggage here.

Unlike the Puuc sites, Ticul has plenty of places where you can eat cheaply. For breakfast, head to the **market** (Calle 23, btw Calles 28 and 30) for fruit or food from one of the many *fondas* (covered food stands). For lunch or a snack, **Lonchería Mary** (Calle 23, btw Calles 26 and 28, no phone) serves licuados for 60¢. If you need a break from Mexican food, head for **Cafetería y Pizzería La Gondola** (cnr of Calles 23 and 26, tel. 997/2–01–12), open daily 7–1 and 6–midnight. They serve spaghetti for $5 and even deliver pizzas with all the toppings for $4–$8. If you're in a spending mood, try **Restaurant Los Almendros** (Calle 23, btw Calles 26 and 28, tel. 997/2–00–21), open daily 9–7, where they serve excellent Yucatecan dishes. Expect to pay about $10 for a meal.

Mérida

Mérida is the biggest and hippest city on the Yucatán Peninsula. From aging, elegant neighborhoods to frenzied commercial districts, each sector of the city has a distinct ambience. The Paseo de Montejo is a broad street with restored mansions, sidewalk cafés, and ritzy hotels. Fumes from buses that roar endlessly in and out of the city clog the air near the market, and in the Parque Central, students, tourists, and locals hang out near the cathedral and the Palacio de Gobierno, monuments to the 500-year struggle between European and Maya culture. With all this going for it, it's a wonderful place to dawdle and a good base from which to explore the Gulf Coast and the ruins of the Puuc Hills. If you do only have one day to spend in Mérida, try to make it a Sunday, when the central streets are closed off and the whole city turns out for festivities like Yucatecan folk dancing and an especially grand market. The best time to visit is generally during the dry season, November–April.

Founded in 1542, Mérida has long enjoyed prosperous trade with Europe, much of it based on henequen, a hemp used to make twine. The city is built on the site of the Maya settlement of T'hó, where temples and columns reminded the Spanish of the Roman ruins at Mérida in Spain, hence the name. The colonists forced the Maya to dismantle their temples and used the masonry to create new buildings, churches, and mansions. Like its buildings, Mérida's residents are the result of a merger of indigenous and European cultures: Maya aesthetics and tradition flavor the opulence and formality of Spanish colonial culture.

BASICS

AMERICAN EXPRESS AmEx offers emergency check cashing as well as lost-card and lost-check service. They will hold clients' mail for a month. *Paseo de Montejo 494, btw Calles 43 and 45, Mérida, Yucatán, CP 97000, México, tel. 99/28–43–73 or 99/23–31–91. Open weekdays 9–2 and 4–5, Sat. 9–noon.*

AUTO PARTS/SERVICE The **Ángeles Verdes** (Green Angels), a government-funded road service agency with a small office in Mérida, answer questions about service, tolls, and other car-related matters. *Calle 14 No. 102, btw Calles 73 and 75, Circuito Colonias, Col. Morelos Oriente, tel. 99/83–11–84. Open 7 AM–8 PM.*

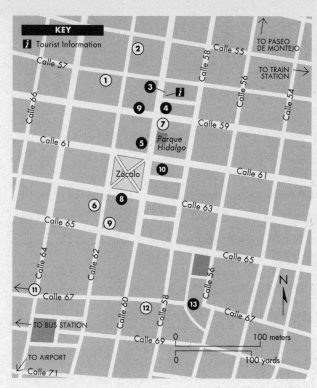

Sights ●

Casa de Montejo, **8**

Catedral, **10**

Iglesia de la Tercera Orden, **4**

Mercado Municipal, **13**

Palacio de Gobierno, **5**

Teatro Peón Contreras, **3**

Lodging ○

Casa de Huéspedes Penicci, **6**

Hotel América, **12**

Hotel Caribe, **7**

Hotel Casa Becil, **11**

Hotel Montejo, **1**

Hotel Sevilla, **9**

Hotel Trinidad, **2**

BOOKSTORES **Librería Dante** (Calle 59 No. 540, at Calle 68) and **Teatro Peón Contreras** (Calles 60 and 57) have a limited selection of English titles.

CASAS DE CAMBIO Most banks are on Calle 65, between Calles 60 and 64, and change money weekdays 9–12:30. But lines are long and exchange rates slightly worse than at casas de cambio. A **Banamex** ATM on Calle 56 at the corner of 59 accepts Visa, Mastercard, Cirrus, and Plus cards. **Agencia de Cambio Money Exchange** (Calle 56 No. 491, btw Calles 57 and 59, tel. 99/28–21–52) is open Monday–Saturday 9–5.

CONSULATES **United Kingdom.** *Calle 58 No. 450, tel. 99/28–61–52. Open weekdays 9–noon.*

United States. *Paseo de Montejo 453, at Colón, tel. 99/25–50–11. Open weekdays 7:30–4.*

EMERGENCIES The **police** station (tel. 99/25–25–55) is on Calle 72, between Calles 39 and 41.

LAUNDRY **La Lavamática Lafe** charges $4 to wash and dry 3 kilos of clothing; they'll return your clothes the same day. *Calle 61 No. 518, btw Calles 62 and 64, tel. 99/24–45–31. Open weekdays 8–7, Sat. 8–4.*

MEDICAL AID The **Cruz Roja** offers 24-hour ambulance service. *Calle 68, btw Calles 65 and 67, tel. 99/28–53–91 or 99/83–02–43.*

Farmacia Yza (Calle 71, at Aviación, tel. 99/23–81–16) is open round the clock.

PHONES AND MAIL The **post office** will hold mail sent to you at the following address for up to 10 days: Lista de Correos, Administración Urbana 1, Mérida, Yucatán, CP 97000, México. *Calle 65, at 56, tel. 99/28–54–04. Open weekdays 7–7.*

You can find **public telephones** on the zócalo, at the Palacio Municipal, and in parks around the city. Dial 09 for international collect calls. You can only call direct from casetas—there's a **Computel** on Calle 59 (at Calle 58). They charge $3.50 a minute for calls to the U.S.

SCHOOLS The **Academia de Cultura e Idiomas** offers beginning through advanced Spanish classes, including classes geared toward scientists and businesspeople. Regular courses entail four hours of class per day and cost about $115 a week for a four-week course. The school arranges affordable homestays for students. *Calle 13 No. 23, tel. and fax 99/44–31–48. Mailing address: Aptdo. Postal 78-4, Mérida, Yucatán, CP 97100, México.*

TRAVEL AGENCIES Shop around for tours to the Maya ruins near Mérida—prices of day trips fluctuate widely. Trips to Uxmal and Chichén Itzá should cost about $25. Reliable agencies include **Ceiba Tours** (Calle 60 No. 495, tel. 99/24–44–77) and **Eco-Turismo Yucatán** (Calle 3 No. 235, btw Calles 32 and 34, tel. 99/25–21–87).

VISITOR INFORMATION The **tourist information center** at Teatro Peón Contreras has a knowledgeable staff that speaks English fairly well. They also have copies of *Yucatán Today*, with general information and some maps. Information booths at the airport and the bus station stock similar material. *Calle 60, at 57, tel. 99/24–92–90. Open daily 8–8.*

COMING AND GOING

BY BUS The main bus station, the **Unión de Camioneros del Yucatán** (Calle 70, btw 69 and 71), is three blocks west of the zócalo and three blocks south, and has service on **Autobuses del Oriente (ADO)** (tel. 99/24–86–10) and **Peninsulares** (99/24–92–63), among others. First-class buses leave frequently during the day for Cancún ($6, 6 hrs), Campeche ($8, 2 hrs), Mexico City ($60, 24 hrs), and Villahermosa ($27, 8 hrs). Buses also run to Palenque ($24.50, 9 hrs), San Cristóbal de las Casas ($24.50, 9 hrs), and Chetumal ($16, 6 hrs). A **Banpaís** at the station changes money weekdays between 9 and 1. Buses leave for the nearby beaches of Progreso and for the Maya ruins at Dzibichaltún every 20 minutes from the station at Calle 62, between Calles 65 and 67.

BY CAR Avoid the evil toll road ($12 to Valladolid, another $12 to Cancún) by veering to the right at Kilometer 67 of Highway 180 out of Mérida. The *carretera de cuota* (toll road) and the *carretera libre* (free road) go through the same places, but you can't get off the toll road (which, admittedly, is a hell of a lot faster) until Valladolid.

BY TRAIN The **Estación Central de Ferrocarriles** (Calle 48, at Calle 55, tel. 99/23–59–44) serves Córdoba ($19.50, 30 hrs) at 6:15 PM every day. The train makes many stops, including Campeche ($3, 5 hrs) and Palenque ($8.50, 14 hrs), but you're much better off taking the bus. Robberies on trains are common. Strap all important papers onto your body, and never let your baggage out of sight. The station is six blocks east and three blocks north of the zócalo, where most of the budget accommodations are located. It's open 24 hours, but the ticket office is open only from 5 PM until the daily train departs; buy tickets the day you intend to travel.

BY PLANE The Mérida airport is 7 kilometers west of the city's central square. **Aeroméxico** (Paseo Montejo 460, tel. 99/27–90–00) has nonstop service from Cancún, Mexico City, Villahermosa, and Miami; **Mexicana de Aviación** (Cnr of Calles 58 and 61, tel. 99/24–66–33) flies nonstop from Cozumel, Havana, and Mexico City. Additional service is provided by **Aerocaribe** (Paseo Montejo 500-B, at Calle 47, tel. 99/28–67–90) and **Continental** (Mérida airport, tel. 99/46–13–07).

The airport has no currency-exchange office, but the taxi drivers outside will change small amounts of U.S. dollars at lousy rates, so change just enough to get to town. The tourist office at the airport is open weekdays 8–8. It's fairly easy and cheap to get to town: Just take the Autobus 79 (AVIACION) to the corner of Calles 67 and 60 downtown. The half-hour trip costs about 35¢. An airport taxi (usually a VW combi) to your hotel costs $5 for up to four people.

GETTING AROUND

Despite its size, Mérida is easy to figure out; most of the interesting buildings and budget hotels are around the zócalo. Streets are numbered, not named. Streets running east–west are odd numbers, and north–south streets are even numbers. The zócalo is bordered by Calles 60, 61, 62, and 63.

BY CAR Most rental agencies are on Calle 60, between Calles 57 and 59. **Executive** (Calle 60 No. 486, tel. 99/28–17–94) rents VW Bugs for $36 a day, which includes 400 free kilometers and insurance. **National Inter Rent** (Calle 60, across from Executive, tel. 99/28–63–08) charges $43 a day with unlimited mileage and insurance. Most companies will bargain if you tell them someone else offered you a better price.

BY BUS You won't need to use the bus to see the sights in the center of Mérida. If you want to go beyond the area around the zócalo, however, bus travel is a cheap option; city buses run daily 5 AM to midnight. Some buses stop earlier than that, so be sure to ask the drivers. Buses leave from Calle 59 between Calles 58 and 56, and from Calle 56 between Calles 59 and 67, around the market area. Destinations are marked on the windshields.

BY TAXI Avoid the regular taxis, which are very expensive. Instead, look for *colectivos,* or shared taxis ($1), which have fixed routes throughout the city. Tell the driver where you want to go before you get in, and he'll tell you if it's on his way. Colectivos leave from the zócalo, the market area, and the Parque San Juan at Calles 67 and 62.

WHERE TO SLEEP

Mérida has two good areas for lodging: near the bus station and around the zócalo. If you must stay near the bus station, try the **Hotel Alamo** (Calle 68 No. 549, at Calle 71, tel. 99/28–62–90), which rents boxes with breathing-holes and private bath for $10 and nicer doubles for $12.50; or the much nicer **Hotel Casa Becil** (*see below*).

➤ UNDER $15 • **Casa de Huéspedes Penicci.** Rooms at this colonial mansion are in various stages of disrepair. They're huge and decorated with rickety antique furniture and cobwebs; rooms on the second floor facing the central patio are the best. The shared bathrooms are not for the squeamish, and the water is cold and smells like gasoline. Rooms don't have locks, but the manager will loan you one. Singles cost about $8, doubles $10.50 ($12 with bath), and additional persons cost about $1 each. *Calle 62 No. 507, btw Calles 63 and 65, tel. 99/28–55–18. ½ block south of zócalo. 30 rooms, 2 with bath. Kitchen, laundry, luggage storage, wheelchair access.*

Hotel América. The simple rooms here have private bathrooms (most with hot water), but the beds are a bit uncomfortable. A couple of blocks from the zócalo, the hotel is popular with families. Singles and doubles without hot water are $8.50 for one or two people. With hot water, single rooms cost $13, doubles $14. *Calle 67 No. 500, btw Calles 60 and 58, tel. 99/28–58–79. 43 rooms, all with bath (30 with hot water). Laundry, luggage storage, meal service, wheelchair access.*

Hotel Trinidad. These funky hotels (two locations) are conceptual art pieces gone berserk. Every room has its own unique character, from antiques to avant-garde Mexican art. Some rooms even have waterbeds. Bring your own papier mâché and finger paints. The second hotel, the **Trinidad Galería** (a couple blocks farther from zócalo), has a swimming pool and coffee bar open to guests at both hotels. Room prices vary wildly but start at $13.50 for a double with shared bath, $17.50 with private bath. Ask to see a few rooms before you choose one. *Two locations: Cnr of Calles 51 and 60, tel. 99/23–24–63; and Calle 62 No. 464, btw Calles 55 and 57, tel. 99/21–30–29. Laundry, luggage storage, meal service, parking, wheelchair access.*

➤ UNDER $20 • **Hotel Casa Becil.** Close to the bus station and the zócalo, this place attracts an over-30 American crowd and features a sun deck with oh-so-tasteful plastic flamingos and a garden with white iron chairs. The bathrooms are clean. Breakfast and lunch cost $2.50; room service is free. Singles and doubles are $17.50. *Calle 67 No. 550-C, btw*

Calles 66 and 68, tel. 99/24–67–64. 12 rooms, all with bath. Laundry, luggage storage, kitchen, wheelchair access.

Hotel Sevilla. Vast archways, a beautiful patio, and small but airy rooms give this well-kept hotel a cozy atmosphere. All rooms have ceiling fans and hot water. Those facing the street tend to be a bit noisy. Singles are $15, doubles $16, and triples $17. *Calle 65 No. 511, at Calle 62, tel. 99/28–24–81. 32 rooms, all with bath. Luggage storage, wheelchair access.*

➢ UNDER $30 • **Hotel Montejo.** A gorgeous courtyard, stout columns, and colonial-style arches are what you'd expect in a hotel of this caliber in Mérida. The beautiful dark wood furniture in every room gives it an elegance that merits the extra bucks. Singles cost $25, doubles $28.50. Air-conditioned rooms are $2.50 more. *Calle 57 No. 507, btw Calles 62 and 64, tel. 99/28–02–77. 22 rooms, all with bath. Laundry, luggage storage, restaurant, wheelchair access.*

➢ UNDER $50 • **Hotel Caribe.** If you want to splurge, Hotel Caribe at Parque Hidalgo is the place to do it. This beautiful hotel occupies an old school and has a neatly kept garden with a fountain and a swimming pool. The "high class" rooms are well worth the extra bucks; singles cost $38.50, doubles $42, and triples $45. Cheaper rooms are also available, but aside from access to the pool, they aren't worth the expense. *Calle 59 No. 500, at Calle 60, tel. 99/24–90–22. 56 rooms, all with bath. Laundry, luggage storage, meal service, wheelchair access.*

FOOD

Eating well is one of the highlights of any trip to Mérida. Yucatecan food is delicious, and nowhere is it better prepared than in this city. Unfortunately, eating out can be downright expensive. However, many small loncherías and street stands around town sell *antojitos* (appetizers), tortas, and *panuchos* and *salbutes* (both variations on the taco); all cost less than $1. Vegetarians should head for **Antojitos San Juan de Dios** (Calles 62 and 67), in the Bazar San Juan, where you can get pea sandwiches, oat sandwiches, and soups. The second floor of the **mercado municipal** (Calles 65 and 67, between Calles 54 and 56) has more than 20 simple loncherías offering full lunches for under $3, where customers share the single, long table. The municipal market is also a wonderful place to buy fresh fruits and vegetables, brought daily from the villages.

➢ UNDER $5 • **Amaro.** This vegetarian restaurant set in a shady courtyard near the zócalo offers the traveler blessed relief from greasy lonchería food. Specialties include cream of zucchini soup ($2.50) and eggplant curry with cheese (or soy) and rice ($5). If you're dining really cheaply, a plate of brown rice and steamed veggies is just $2.50. Beware the "green salad," though, which is nothing but an overturned pack of sprouts. *Calle 59 No. 507, btw Calles 60 and 62, tel. 99/28–24–51. Open daily 8:30 AM–10 PM.*

Café y Restaurante El Louvre. There's nothing French about Mérida's answer to the American coffeeshop. Stout waiters with little black bowties and white shirts patrol the brown-tiled restaurant yelling orders to the cook, who stands behind a glass counter hacking at a pot-roast. If you're still up before sunrise try the pancakes ($2) or eggs ($1–$3). Soups ($1–$2) and daily specials ($3.50) are especially good and cheap. *Calle 61, at Calle 62, on the zócalo, tel. 99/24–50–73. Open 24 hrs.*

Cafetería Pop. This "concept" cafe is brilliantly decorated with orange and lavender pop-art designs. It is often crowded and always a good place for conversation. A standard breakfast (eggs, beans, fruit, coffee, and meat) is $3–$4. Corn-tortilla soup costs $2.50. Also good is the Cuban sandwich (ham, roast beef, and cheese) for $3.50. *Calle 57 No. 501, btw Calles 60 and 63, tel. 99/28–61–63. Open daily 7 AM–11 PM.*

➢ UNDER $10 • **Pizza Bella.** This wanna-be-Italian restaurant with its checkered tablecloths and waiters in red berets has little tables out on the patio facing the park, making it a great place to kick back, meet people, and savor the lovely aroma of exhaust from passing cars and buses. The menu features spaghetti for $3 and good pizzas (including a vegetarian one) for

$7.50–$10. Espresso and cappuccino go for about $1.50. *Calle 61 No. 500, btw Calles 60 and 62, tel. 99/23–64–01. Open daily 8 AM–midnight.*

Restaurant Express. The food here is quite good and servings are abundant, but plan to spend $5–$7 for typical Yucatecan dishes. The specialty is pollo pibil (chicken baked in banana leaves; $7). Try some *chilaquiles* (tortilla strips and chicken doused with salsa and sour cream) for $5. *Calle 60, at Calle 59, tel. 99/28–16–91. Open daily 7 AM–11 PM.*

El Trapiche Restaurant y Juguería. Get your day started with an omelet, toast, and coffee ($3.50) or a vegetarian omelet ($3.50). Lonzado, the owner, has produce organically grown especially for his restaurant. Licuados of various fruits (ask for samples) cost about $1.50. In the evenings, spaghetti ($2.50) and pizza ($3–$8) are served, as well as cheap sandwiches (under $2). *Calle 62 No. 13, btw Calles 59 and 61, tel. 99/28–12–31. Open daily 7:30 AM–10:30 PM.*

WORTH SEEING

Since Mérida was founded, wealthy residents have invested an enormous amount of money and pride in their city, and the government continues to dole out generous handfuls of dough to keep the city's colonial heritage in good shape. Museums, galleries, and stores are stocked with antiques and artwork from ancient, colonial, and contemporary times, and every week new listings of dance, theatrical, and music performances appear; ask at the tourist office about upcoming events.

The sites listed below are only part of what makes Mérida interesting. It's best to take your time and really look around. On every block in the zócalo area you will find old mansions, churches, and theaters. Some restoration jobs are better than others, but even if you walk into a run-down hotel, you're likely to see beautiful stained glass, decaying hardwood furniture, oil paintings dating back one or two hundred years, columns, marble and ceramic tiles, and beautiful courtyards.

CASA DE MONTEJO On the south side of the zócalo stands the old Montejo family palace, built between 1543 and 1549 by Francisco de Montejo, the destroyer of the Maya city T'hó and founder of Mérida. The bas-relief on the facade depicts Montejo (the younger), his wife and daughter, and a number of Spanish soldiers standing on the heads of the vanquished Maya. The house has been converted into a Banamex branch and is open to the public weekdays 9–1. *Calle 63, btw Calles 60 and 62. Admission free.*

CATEDRAL The splendid twin-spire cathedral stands austerely at the front of the zócalo. It looks more like a fort than anything else and is a subtle reminder of how difficult the Spanish found it to convert the Maya to Christianity. Built in 1561 entirely of stone (much of which came from razed Maya buildings), the cathedral was indeed designed for defense—gunnery slits, not windows, stare out onto the square. The interior is rather bleak, having been ransacked during the Mexican Revolution and never restored. However, the pillagers did not touch **El Cristo de las Ampollas** (Christ of the Blisters). Legend has it that a local peasant once claimed he saw a tree burning all night, but that the tree was not consumed by the flames. A statue of Christ was carved from the tree and placed in a church in a nearby town. Later, the church burned down, but the statue survived, albeit covered in blisters. *Calle 60, at Calle 61. Open daily 7–noon and 5–8.*

IGLESIA DE LA TERCERA ORDEN The Church of the Third Order, across from Parque Hidalgo at Calles 60 and 59, was built by Jesuit monks in the 17th century. The stones of the facade come from the great pyramid of T'hó; if you look carefully, especially on the Calle 59 side, you can still distinguish Maya designs on them. This is the "in" place to get married in Mérida, and every Friday and Saturday night you can invite yourself to the wedding ceremony of some member of the city's upper crust.

MERCADO MUNICIPAL Probably the most interesting place in Mérida is the gargantuan municipal market, occupying the area between Calles 65 and 67 and Calles 54 and 56. The market is considered by many travelers to be the best on the peninsula. If you're hunting for a hammock, hold out for the fine ones sold here (*see* Shopping, *below*). There's even a saint-repair shop, in case your traveling icon has been damaged. The market is open daily from 6 to about 5.

MUSEO DE ANTROPOLOGIA E HISTORIA The museum is about a kilometer from the zócalo, but it's worth visiting, despite the $5 admission fee. Exhibits are mostly Maya arti-facts—including figurines of the Maya messenger between the gods and man, Chac Mool, and artifacts retrieved from the sacred cenote at Dzibilchaltún. There's a reconstruction of a burial chamber, as well as deformed skulls: The Maya flattened their children's skulls with boards for cosmetic reasons. *Paseo de Montejo, at Calle 43. Admission: $5, free Sun. and holidays. Open Tues.–Sat. 8–8, Sun. 9–2.*

PALACIO DE GOBIERNO Built in 1892 on the northern side of the zócalo, the Governor's Palace is a beautiful example of neoclassical architecture, with Doric columns topped by arches. Inside, murals by Fernando Castro Pacheco, a Yucatecan painter, depict the tumul-tuous history of the Yucatán, including the Caste War (*see box, below*), when Maya fought against Mexicans of European extraction. *Calle 61, btw Calles 60 and 62. Admission free. Open 8 AM–9 PM.*

PASEO DE MONTEJO The Champs-Elysées in Paris was the inspiration for this avenue (Calle 47 between Calles 56 and 58), built when Mérida enjoyed extensive trade links with Europe and was home to many French merchants. Sidewalk restaurants (open for dinner only) and expensive hotels and discos line the wide avenue, and stately old homes, many of which were built with profits from the henequen trade, line the side streets. *From the zócalo, walk north on Calle 60 and left on Calle 47 (about 8 blocks); or, take a bus up Calle 60 to Calle 47.*

The Caste War

While indigenous communities in central Mexico were slowly being crippled by Spanish rule, the Yucatán Peninsula remained a fierce outpost of Maya resistance. The Yucatán offered the conquerors neither gold nor fertile land, but it was to become an important administrative and military foothold. As in other regions of Mexico, the indigenous peoples were used as slave labor and their religion was condemned.

When Mexico earned its independence from Spain in 1821, the Maya had no reason to celebrate, as their situation changed little. They had lost much land, including access to precious water sources. In 1847, a Maya rebellion began in Valladolid. Not only did the Maya win control of the town, but within a year, they conquered all of the Yucatán except Mérida and Campeche. Europeans in the capital appealed for help from Spain, France, and the United States, but none was forthcoming. The outnumbered Europeans made plans to evacuate. Just as the Maya prepared for a final, decisive assault, the winged ant (symbolic of coming rains) made an early appearance. The Maya took the insects' arrival as an omen, packed up their weapons, and returned to the fields to plant the sacred corn, without which they could not survive.

Help for the Spanish settlers then arrived with a vengeance from Mexico City, Cuba, and the United States. The Maya were mercilessly slaughtered until their population dropped from 500,000 to 300,000. Survivors escaped into the jungles of Quintana Roo, and held out against the Mexican government until 1974, when the region officially accepted statehood with Mexico.

TEATRO PEON CONTRERAS In front of the Iglesia de la Tercera Orden is the Teatro Peón Contreras (Calles 60 and 57), another city landmark. The building was originally a Jesuit school, built in 1618, and later a university. It was eventually converted into a theater that burned down in 1813. The current building dates from 1877, but it has undergone several transformations, the most drastic in 1905, when Italian artists gave it a neoclassical design. The theater hosts classical music recitals and ballets on Tuesdays at 9 PM. Ballet tickets usually run $9. Check local newspapers for current shows.

SHOPPING

Mérida is the best place on the Yucatán Peninsula to buy a hammock, but the experience can be like looking for a used car. Salesmen are aggressive and will tell you anything, so visit at least two shops. Don't buy from street vendors, because you'll have less of an opportunity to compare prices and quality, and don't be afraid to bargain.

Hammocks come in several sizes—single, double, matrimonial, large matrimonial, and family. Judge the size for yourself by comparing the weights of different hammocks—don't trust a salesman's claims. Light cotton and nylon weigh about the same, while stronger cotton hammocks weigh much more. You'll probably have to ask in the stores to see the stronger hammocks, since merchants make less profit from them and don't display them prominently. Yucatecans like to sleep in big hammocks; they allow you to sleep diagonally, which is better for your back. Cotton-nylon hammocks are the most comfortable, but nylon ones last twice as long and the colors don't fade—the nylon hammocks are consequently more expensive. Prices vary, but the smallest ones should be no more than $10 for the cotton-nylon, $15 for the nylon. Matrimonial hammocks cost about $25 for cotton-nylon and $35 for the nylon. Whether you buy a cotton or a nylon hammock, the end-strings should be nylon for greater strength. Also, several long, straight strings should run along each side of the hammock for stability. Ask the salesman to hang the hammock for you, and see how closely it's woven.

AFTER DARK

The bar and disco scene in Mérida could be more exciting, and residents seem to prefer strolling around the zócalo, where mariachis dressed in white eagerly serenade the strollers for tips. Things livens up a bit on the weekends, when the city goes all out, staging huge cultural events and folkloric shows, and most are free.

BARS **Natzú.** Though the doorman insists that this is not a gay bar, it is, nevertheless, where homosexuals tend to congregate. It's something of a strip bar, but not too sleazy. Drinks are a bit pricey—beers are $3.50, margaritas $5. Cover is $3.50. *Calle 60, at Calle 53, tel. 99/23–80–79. Open Mon.–Sat. 8 PM–3 AM.*

Panchos. This festive indoor–outdoor restaurant/bar is hardly a secret kept from tourists. Still, there's no cover, and some lively bands take the stage, so it remains a favorite among locals. Waiters in giant sombreros carry drinks (beers or piña coladas, $3) to patrons at intimate wrought-iron patio tables. There is a small dance floor. *Calle 59 No. 509, btw Calles 60 and 62, tel. 99/23–09–42. Open daily 6 PM–2 AM.*

El Trovador Bohemio. Come here to watch white-haired and wealthy Meridians toasting long life while lounging about under dimly lit chandeliers. The exclusive bar features three live bands that entertain nightly with romantic ballads. Drinks are expensive: beers are $3.50 and margaritas go for $5.50. There's a $3 cover. *Calle 55 No. 504, btw Calles 60 and 62, tel. 99/23–03–85. Open daily 9 PM–2:30 AM.*

DANCING The really slick discos popular among the upper-class youth are on Prolongación Montejo. The bus situation is sketchy at night though, and a taxi from Mérida costs about $5. The most popular is **Bin-Bon-Bao** (Calle 29 No. 97, at Calle 18), open Friday–Saturday 9–3. Downtown, a somewhat older crowd dances to salsa at **Estelares** (Calle 60 No. 484, btw Calles 55 and 57, tel. 99/28–28–58). There's live music after 10:30, and no cover. It's open Thursday–Saturday 9 PM–3 AM. The **Sala de Fiesta Montejo** (Calle 62, at Calle 65, in front of bus station, tel. 99/24–90–36) is a parking lot during the week, but on Saturday and Sunday nights between 8 PM and 3 AM, it's where working-class Mexicans come to dance to live tropical music and drink $2 beers. Admission is $7 for men and free for women, who should think twice about coming here alone.

Near Mérida

Yucatán state is home to some of the most exciting sites in Mexico, from beautiful caves and impressive ruins to deserted fishing villages. Mérida is a convenient base from which to explore the surrounding area, but in your rush to visit places, don't overlook the inhabitants. Scattered around Mérida are numerous *pueblos* (villages) that provide travelers a window on the real Yucatán. Although most Yucatecan towns have historic churches that will interest fans of colonial architecture, it would be impossible to see them all. However, you can see some of the largest and most elaborate cathedrals at **Umán,** 18 kilometers southwest of Mérida, and at **Hunucmá,** 29 kilometers west of Mérida.

CALCEHTOK AND OXKINTOK

The spectacular caves at Calcehtok (Mayan for "Bleeding of the Deer's Throat") are unknown to all but the most ambitious travelers because they aren't easily accessible. Although they are only 70 kilometers southwest of Mérida and about 15 kilometers from Maxcanú, you have to wait an eternity for transport to the village of Calcehtok and then hike 3 kilometers on a dirt road to the caves. Just when you think the heat and the monochromatic vegetation will drive you mad, you reach the caves. After the first immense chamber, where sunlight illuminates tropical plants and the singing, swooping birds, it's pure obscurity and silence, except for the sound of water dripping from stalactites and the occasional chirping of a bat or two. A lantern reveals formations in the multi-colored rock and the remnants of ancient visitors. Don't explore these endless, narrow caves on your own unless you're an expert. At the adobe house adjacent to the bus stop you'll find Roger and his sons, who have been leading tours of the caves for three generations. Tours last about two hours, at about $7 an hour. Ropes and ladders, mud, bees, and lots of bat guano are involved in a cave trip—it's not for the weak of heart nor for the less than agile. A flashlight of your own is also helpful.

On the road back to the village of Calcehtok is the turnoff for the ruins of **Oxkintok,** a few miles away. The ruins are badly preserved and seldom visited. The enormous site, about 2 kilometers square, was probably the largest of all Puuc cities and was populated during the late Classic period. The central area features three large pyramids, as well as the pitiful remains of small pyramid temples, palace-like buildings, a ball court, and a variety of houses. Ringing the central area like suburbs are three other sets of ruins, each connected by a system of sacbés. Despite the relative isolation of the site, once you get to the ruins an informally dressed state official emerges from his VW to charge you the $3.50 admission.

Oxkintok was once a huge and important city, but you have to strain to make something out of the badly restored piles of rubble here. Of particular interest are the three carved anthropomorphs (stylized human figures) that stand in their original places in front of a slightly better preserved temple.

COMING AND GOING Getting to Calcehtok and Oxkintok by public transport is tiring and time-consuming. Take a Maxcanú-bound bus from the main bus station in Mérida—they make the one-hour trip every hour or so. The detour for Calcehtok is a few hundred yards before Maxcanú—just tell the driver you want to get off at the grutas or ruinas. From there, either hitchhike or catch a minitruck taxi to the village. From Calcehtok, it's 5 kilometers to Oxkintok and 3 kilometers to the caves. You may be able to arrange transport in the village; otherwise you'll have to walk or hitch. To try both on foot would be an exhausting endeavor. If you can't make a good deal in advance with the only taxi driver in town, then forget the ruins and go to the caves. The closest hotels are in Ticul and Mérida.

MAYA RUINS

MAYAPAN A day trip to Mayapán, about 52 kilometers southeast of Mérida, is a must for every amateur archaeologist. The ruins, dismissed by many as cheap imitations of Chichén Itzá, are nevertheless impressive. Even more impressive is the fact that so few tourists come this way. Mayapán was built during the post-Classic period and inhabited by the Cocam, a tribe of Mexican origin. The Cocam, along with the Xiú of Uxmal and the Itzá of Chichén Itzá, formed part of a power-

In Mayapán you're likely to be the only living thing in sight, apart from the giant iguanas admiring the ruins.

Maya Civilizations: Time Periods

The Maya first settled in lowland areas of Guatemala, Mexico, and Belize and then moved north onto the Yucatán Peninsula. Hence, the height of the Classic Period in the northern settlements occurred at about the same time the southern centers were being abandoned. The history of Maya civilization is traditionally broken down into the following eras. These divisions are not absolute, and archaeologists often differ on the criteria used to designate them.

Pre-Classic Period (1500 BC–AD 300, also called the Formative Period): During this time, agriculture replaced the hunter/gatherer, nomadic lifestyle. Toward the end of this era, monumental buildings with corbeled arches and roof combs (typical of Classic Maya architecture) appeared, as did the first hieroglyphics and early calendric notation.

Classic Period (AD 300–900): During this period, the Maya developed a strong self-identity, and their architecture shows few traces of outside influence. Inspiration for the Maya's art, language, science, and architecture came from a unified way of thinking about the world. Temples and pyramids built with precise relation to one another illustrate the close tie between religion and aesthetics. Buildings were placed on superstructures atop stepped platforms and were often decorated with bas-reliefs and ornate frescoes. The architectural styles of the Puuc, Chenes, and Río Bec regions were among the most elaborate. The population's growing dependence on agriculture inspired the creation of the highly accurate Maya calendar, which is based on planting cycles. Economy and trade flourished, and the Maya began to observe class distinctions and live extremely lavish lifestyles around great ceremonial centers. Toward the end of this period, more palaces were constructed on top of or in place of temples, evidence of the growth of secular authority and centralized political rule.

Post-Classic Period (900–1520): Maya civilization declined during this period, which is marked by increased military activity and the growth of conquest states. The Toltecs of Mexico invaded the Yucatán during this time, greatly influencing the Maya architecture and lifestyle. The invasion ultimately led to a more warlike society, more elaborate temples and palaces, and a greater number of human sacrifices. Architectural techniques involved less detailed and careful craftsmanship. For example, carved-stone building facades were replaced at this time by carved stucco.

ful alliance which lasted from about 1000 to 1200, when Mayapán broke the alliance and established its hegemony over the already weakened Mayan empire. The city's dominance lasted only a couple of centuries, however—a coup d'état by a noble family ousted the rulers, leading to the city's demise some time before 1450. The buildings of Mayapán have not fared as well as those of Chichén, in part due to the poorer quality of the construction. The most interesting building is the **Great Pyramid,** similar to El Castillo at Chichén Itzá but without the temple chamber at the summit. **The Temple of Chaac,** next to the pyramid, is a long, low building decorated with carved masks of the rain god. A few banana trees grow in the center of the small cenote between the Great Pyramid and the Temple of Chaac, and you need a flashlight to explore the moldy caves and reach the water. **Telchaquillo,** about a kilometer from the ruins, is the closest pueblo to Mayapán and is a good place to cool off after an excursion to the ruins. A well-maintained **cenote** in the park next to the bus stop is used mostly for swimming by local teenagers, but they won't mind if you share in the fun. *Admission to ruins and cenote: $2.50, free Sun. and holidays. Open daily 8–5.*

➢ COMING AND GOING • Buses from Mérida travel down Road 18 to Telchaquillo and the Mayapán turnoff every hour from the station at Calles 50 and 67. Ask the driver to drop you off at las ruinas. There are no hotels anywhere in the area, so you'll probably have to go back to Mérida for the night.

DZIBILCHALTÚN Dzibilchaltún is one of the most visited archaeological sites in the region, perhaps because of its proximity to Mérida. As popular as it is, Dzibilchaltún will not impress most visitors. Most of its archaeological riches lie underground, and the two remaining buildings cannot compare with the grandeur of the ruins of Uxmal and the Puuc Hills or even Mayapán (*see above*). Still, Dzibilchaltún's location, within a natural park just 20 kilometers north of Mérida, makes it an accessible half-day trip. The site was first inhabited in about 2000 BC, reaching its apogee during the Classic Period, from AD 600 to 900, when it became a major ceremonial and residential center. The main building is the **Temple of the Seven Dolls,** noteworthy for its structural elegance and for the fact that it is the only known Maya temple with windows. The temple received its name from the seven clay dolls found under the floor.

Near the ruins is the **Cenote Xlacah,** a natural, fresh-water pool that supplied the population of Dzibilchaltún with drinking water and now provides visitors to the ruins with a refreshing dip. It was also used for religious ceremonies, judging from the bones of sacrificial victims found inside. The small **museum** at the entrance to the ruins has some samples of the pottery found in the cenote as well as the original seven dolls from the temple. Unless you are a real ceramics aficionado, it will take you about two minutes to see everything. *Admission to ruins and museum: $3.50, free Sun. and holidays. Open daily 8–5.*

➢ COMING AND GOING • Buses to Dzibilchaltún leave Mérida from the station at Parque San Juan every couple of hours. During the week, the last bus returns to Mérida around 4 PM, and on weekends the last bus returns an hour earlier. Otherwise, you can catch a bus or combi heading north along Highway 261 to Progreso. Buses drop you at the turnoff to the ruins, which lie about 3 kilometers down a side road. To get back to Mérida or Progreso, flag down a passing bus.

THE GULF COAST

The Gulf Coast has a look all its own, quite different from the azure perfection of the Caribbean coast. The coast road between Progreso and Dzilam de Bravo passes by marshes and savannas to one side, and grassy dunes, palm trees, and the dark sea on the other. Birds fly in patterns overhead or float in the waters, seemingly oblivious to the awesome summer storms that fill the moody skies with dramatic clouds and flashes of lightning, but most of the time it remains dry, peaceful, and deserted. Modern beach houses belong to wealthy residents of Mérida, who use them only in July and August. During the rest of the year, you can share miles of white beaches and the sea with a few fishermen. In most of these villages accommodations are limited or nonexistent, but don't despair. If you look respectable enough, it's easy to convince a local family to rent you hammock hooks.

PROGRESO The largest town on the Gulf Coast is one of those curious hybrids that is increasingly common in Mexico. On the one hand, Progreso is a growing tourist resort, catering mainly to residents of Mérida who make the 32-kilometer pilgrimage to its beaches during the latter half of summer. On the other hand, Progreso maintains a small-town atmosphere, and locals live their lives independently of the tourists. During the low season (September–June), Progreso is the ideal destination for those looking to enjoy mostly deserted beaches but who aren't yet ready to abandon the comforts of city life. During July and August everything is crowded, so be prepared to wait for restaurants, to have difficulty finding a room (at higher prices), and to share the beach with countless others. Progreso's beaches are nice enough, although you can walk for hundreds of meters before the water becomes deep enough to cover your belly button, and seaweed can be a nuisance.

➤ COMING AND GOING • In Mérida, Progreso buses leave from the station on Calle 62 between Calles 65 and 67. Buses depart every hour and cost $1.50. The Progreso bus station is on Calle 29, between Calles 80 and 82. Buses leave for Mérida ($1) every 15 minutes between 5 AM and 9:30 PM. Buses for **Telchac Puerto** (*see below*) leave at 7 AM and 2 PM and cost $2.50.

➤ WHERE TO SLEEP AND EAT • During the low season, you should have no problem getting a room in one of Progreso's several hotels. Prices fluctuate, but never get dirt cheap. Each of the large rooms at **Playa Linda** (Av. Malecón, near Calle 26, tel. 993/5–13–57) has a small pseudo-kitchen with a table, chairs, and a burner; rooms on the second floor have balconies. Both singles and doubles cost $17. **Hotel Progreso** (Calle 78, at Calle 29, tel. 993/5–00–39) offers immaculate rooms and the nicest bathrooms you'll see in the Yucatán. It's sort of far from the beach, but the added comfort is worth the walk. Singles are $17, doubles $20 ($25 and $28 with air-conditioning).

Progreso is a port town surrounded by fishing villages, so it's no surprise that seafood is a staple at the town's restaurants. If cheap food is what you're looking for, head for the market at the corner of Calles 27 and 80. You can buy fresh fruits and vegetables or eat in one of the many fondas and loncherías. For fresh bread and drinks, try the supermarkets and bakeries on Calle 27. **Sol y Mar** (Av. Malecón, at Calle 80, no phone) is a great place to hang out with a beer and nachos or some fish *botanas* (snacks). The management provides changing rooms for clients who want to swim on a full stomach. For a real splurge, try **Capitán Marisco** (Calle 19, btw Calles 60 and 62, tel. 993/5–06–39), with terrace dining overlooking the sea; main courses are $8 and $10.

TELCHAC PUERTO Few tourists ever get to Telchac Puerto, yet the town is lovely. Several tire-track "roads" lead through grassy dunes, past a few small restaurants, and down to a quiet beach. As on the rest of the Gulf Coast of the Yucatán, the beaches aren't spectacular, but they are peaceful. Telchac Puerto has few places to eat and no hotels, but not for much longer—a new government project called Nuevo Yucatán is developing the area. Four buses make the trip daily from Progreso (1 hr) and Mérida (1½ hrs). Buses drop you off on the side of the road, about 400 meters south of the beach. If you miss the afternoon bus for Progreso, you may be able to arrange lodgings with a local family—ask at the police station.

SISAL A quiet fishing village on the western Gulf Coast, Sisal remains almost undiscovered by tourists. Some Americans come here during hunting season (November through March) to shoot game, but the hunters generally stick to the Club de Patos (Duck Club). The beaches are deserted during most of the year, and they are much broader and whiter than those on the northern Gulf Coast. From here, you can visit **Puerto de Abrigo**, a fishing *refugio* (refuge) 2 kilometers west of the pier; just walk along the beach. The lighthouse, reconstructed in 1909, is still in use and occupied by a family. For a tip, a girl named Wendy will lead you up the stairs for a terrific view of the town. **Balneario Las Felicidades** (Av. 6 No. 104, about 700 meters east of main street) has small rooms on the beach with clean private baths. If you're a light sleeper, ask the owner if they'll be playing music at the disco that night. Singles with private bath are $13.50, doubles $17 (he'll let two sleep in a single). **Hotel Marea Roja** (Av. 6 No. 72, about 300 meters east of main street, no phone) has fairly clean rooms with no hot water. A room for up to three people costs $13.50. Several good, cheap restaurants line Sisal's main street.

Buses leave Mérida hourly during the day for Sisal from the **Autobuses de Occidente** bus station (Calles 50 and 67). The last bus back to Mérida ($2, 2 hrs) leaves Sisal at 6:30 PM. If you want to go from Sisal to Celestún, change buses in Hunucmá, and take the opportunity to explore the magnificent colonial church there.

CELESTÚN On the tip of a narrow strip of land that separates the estuaries of Río Esperanza from the Gulf of Mexico, Celestún is one of the most-visited places around Mérida, and with good reason. Set in the middle of the Parque Natural Ría Celestún, the town has beaches and large colonies of exotic birds. Star billing goes to the flamingos, thousands of whom stand quietly in the waters of the estuary in pink formations. Although it is illegal to approach them closely enough to make them fly, they might give you a show anyway if you wait long enough. You can rent a boat from the dock under the bridge that spans the river about a kilometer out of town. The two-hour trip to see the flamingos costs $30–$40. Bargaining doesn't work, but you can share the cost with other tourists, of which there are plenty in high season and on weekends. The beaches at Celestún are broad and fairly clean, but afternoon winds can kick up clouds of sand.

There's free flamingo-watching from Celestún's dock in the afternoon. The birds take to the sky all at once, creating a bright pink cloud.

There are plenty of restaurants on the main street between the zócalo and the beach, and on the beach itself. Most serve only seafood, but **Restaurant La Playita** on the beach always has one non-seafood dish for about $3.50. The few budget accommodations on the beach fill up during July and August and on weekends. **Hotel María del Carmen** (Calles 12 and 15, tel. 993/28–69–78) offers clean new rooms, some with great sun decks. Singles are $10, doubles $13.50. Prices go up by a few dollars during in high season. **Hotel San Julio** (Calle 12 No. 93-A, no phone), also on the beach, has the cheapest rooms, which are still pretty clean and even have hot water. Singles cost $8, doubles $13. Free camping on the beach in front of the Hotel María del Carmen is allowed.

Buses for Celestún leave Mérida every two hours from the Autobuses del Occidente bus station (Calles 50 and 67) and cost about $3.

DZILAM DE BRAVO Seventy-five kilometers northeast of Mérida is Dzilam de Bravo, a birdwatcher's paradise. Unfortunately, sand flies make the beach a sun-bather's nightmare. A thin strip of land just off shore serves as a resting place for birds nesting in the nearby savannas. This "island" is just a five minute boat ride from shore, and you can get a fisherman to bring you out there for a few dollars. If you're feeling rich or traveling with a fairly large group, consider a day trip to the **Bocas de Dzilam**, about 40 kilometers away. The bocas are freshwater springs flowing from the sea floor. The whole region is an avian extravaganza, with colonies of pelicans, albatrosses, and seagulls. The one-day excursion, including stops at various beaches and islets, costs about $60–$75 for up to six people. Dzilam has one decent hotel: The **Hotel y Restaurant Los Flamencos** (Calle 11 No. 120, btw Calles 18 and 20, no phone) offers clean, basic rooms, some with great sea views, but the bathrooms are tiny and lack hot water. You can fit up to four people in one room for $10. The other option is to stay at the **Cabañas Totolandia,** on the beach 2 kilometers west (toward Progreso) of town. A cabana for with private bath costs $10 a night for up to four people. The palapa restaurant here, however, is only open July and August.

From Mérida, take one of the nine daily buses ($3, 1½ hrs) from the Autobuses del Noreste station (Calle 50, btw Calles 65 and 67). To return to Mérida, catch the bus outside the store at the southern end of the park. The last bus to Mérida leaves around 6 PM. Two buses that travel along the gorgeous coastal road leave from Progreso ($2.50, 2 hrs) at 7 AM and 2 PM.

IZAMAL

Tourism boosters often point to Izamal, 70 kilometers east of Mérida, as *the* colonial city in the Yucatán. The well-kept buildings around the main plaza do indeed recall the peninsula's colonial past, but most actually weren't built until the 19th century. There isn't really any reason to spend a great deal of time in Izamal, but it breaks up the long bus trip between Mérida and

Valladolid or Cancún. Check out the magnificent **Convento de San Antonio de Padua,** an impressive example of colonial architecture. Built in 1549 by Franciscan monks, the convent is the largest of its kind in the Yucatán and looms above the surrounding buildings. The convent complex is built on the ancient ruins of the Maya temple Popol-Chac and contains a church, a chapel, a sacristy, and an enormous atrium surrounded by arched galleries. *Admission free. Open daily 6 AM–8 PM. Mass held daily at 6:30 AM and 7:30 PM.*

Two blocks from the main plaza are the remains of the **Pyramid of Kinichkakmo,** whose summit is the highest point for miles around. The large pyramid and six other scarcely discernible structures are all that remain of the ancient Maya city of Itzamal, founded in AD 500 and named after the great Maya sun god Itzamná. The site has deteriorated but remains interesting both for its proximity to the colonial city and the fact that it is of pure Maya design, free of Toltec or Aztec influence. *Admission free. Open daily 8–5.*

COMING AND GOING You can reach Izamal from either Mérida ($2, 2 hrs) or Valladolid (2½ hrs). From Mérida, there are 10 buses daily from the station at Calle 62, between Calles 65 and 67. Five buses make the trip daily to Izamal from Valladolid's bus station. The best way to see Izamal is en route from one city to another. Take an early bus to Izamal and store your luggage for free at the station. In an hour or two, you can see everything and be on the next bus out of town.

WHERE TO SLEEP AND EAT Izamal is not well-prepared for visitors. Rooms in the two hotels here are small, dark and bug-infested. The **Hotel Kabul** (Calle 31 No. 301, tel. 995/4–00–08) has rooms with bathrooms (no hot water) that cost between $13.50 and $17. The **Hotel Canto** (next door, no phone), has a nice courtyard, but the rooms ($10–$17) look like jail cells. Restaurants and loncherías are plentiful around the zócalo, and the market in front of the convent is also a cheap source of nourishment. **Restaurant Wayné Né** (Calle 30, at Calle 33, tel. 995/4–01–67), open Wednesday–Monday 10–10, has pollo pibil and enchiladas de mole for $4. Fresh juices are 50¢.

Chichén Itzá

Chichén Itzá is probably the most complex and interesting archaeological site on the peninsula. It is also the most crowded. People come from all over the world to admire the remains of this great city, and then are grossly misinformed by dorky tourist guides who try to titillate rather than inform. Chichén is only 120 kilometers east of Mérida and 157 kilometers southwest of Cancún, and can be hurriedly explored on a day trip from either town. A better idea, though, is to stay in the nearby village of Pisté or even in Valladolid, and save yourself the two- or three-hour bus ride to the ruins. Another advantage of staying nearby is that you can avoid the crowds. Around midday literally scores of tour buses arrive, and the mass of humanity completely changes the feel of the place. It's much better to arrive early in the morning, when relatively few people are around and the sun isn't as intense.

Chichén Itzá is Mayan for "opening of the wells," a reference to the area's cenotes, around which the Maya first settled. Humans lived on this site centuries before Mayan tribes emigrated from northern Guatemala and built it into a major metropolis around AD 520. The city was abandoned as early as two centuries later, and it was not until around AD 1000 that the Maya occupied it again, building several new structures in a very different style. The new occupants also modified many of the existing buildings, creating an eclectic architecture. For this reason, visiting Chichén is like being at several sites at one time, and trying to make "sense" of everything can be exhausting. Those who have been to Uxmal (and other Puuc and Chenes ruins) will notice similarities between them and the buildings clustered around the observatory—choza motifs, Chaac masks, and elaborate latticework on the upper facades. Added features such as columns and carvings of serpents, jaguars, and eagles are typical of a later Toltec-Maya style. The buildings surrounding El Castillo, the great pyramid of Kukulcan, were constructed from scratch by the Toltec-Maya, and have a more definitive style, with exquisite stone carvings glorifying human sacrifice, and images of Chac Mool, whose semi-reclining figure waits everywhere, ready to receive offerings from the high priests.

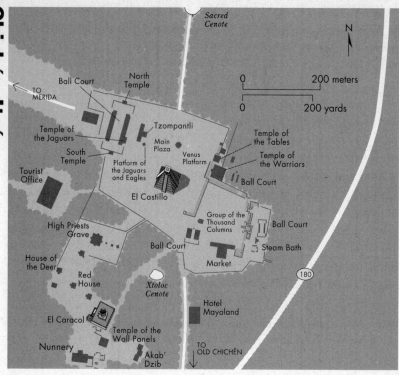

COMING AND GOING

First- and second-class buses leave Mérida ($3, 2½ hrs), Cancún ($3.50, 3 hrs), and Valladolid ($1.50, 40 min) on the hour for Chichén Itzá; there are also five daily buses from Playa del Carmen. Most buses stop at the ruins, the bus station in the nearby village of Pisté (about 700 meters from the zócalo), and downtown Pisté. If you have luggage in the storage compartment, you'll have to get off at the bus station. Catching a bus out of Chichén is more difficult. First-class buses to Cancún, Playa del Carmen, or Mérida are often full, so you may have to settle for second-class. Most of the restaurants, hotels, and handicraft stores line Calle 15, the road leading from Pisté's zócalo to the ruins. You can walk between the two easily (it's only 2½ kilometers), or take a taxi for about $2.

WHERE TO SLEEP

Accommodations and food near Chichén Itzá are geared toward wealthy tourists; budget travelers will do much better in the small village of Pisté, 3 kilometers to the west. Pisté is a characterless town, but it's cheap. If you can't get into either of the places below, try **Posada Maya** (Calles 41 and 42, no phone), about half a kilometer west of the bus station. Campers can pitch a tent at the expensive **Pirámide Inn Hotel and Trailer Park** (Calle 15, next to bus station, no phone) for $5, or you can string a hammock in one of their filthy shacks next to a clunky generator that runs all night. Either way, you get access to the hotel pool.

Posada Chac Mool. These are clean, stereotypical budget hotel rooms with beds and hammock hooks and hot water. The bathrooms are very clean. Singles are about $19 and doubles $20. *Calle 15, a short walk toward town from the Pisté bus station, no phone. 6 rooms, all with bath. Kitchen, laundry, luggage storage, wheelchair access.*

Posada Olalde. Run by a friendly family, this hotel offers clean, spartan rooms with fans and occasional hot water. Singles go for $13.50, doubles $17, and triples $20. *Calle 6 No. 49, no phone. Walk toward town from the bus station, left at the Carrousel restaurant, continue down the dirt road 150 meters. 4 rooms, all with bath. Kitchen, laundry, luggage storage, wheelchair access.*

FOOD

Eating in Pisté is affordable as long as you avoid tourist-oriented restaurants. For drinks and snacks, head to the small stores along the main road. The **market,** open each morning, is just east of downtown Pisté. In front of the plaza are three **loncherías,** where you can get tortas for $1, salbutes and panuchos for 65¢, and main dishes for about $4.50.

Restaurant El Parador Maya. Mama serves up daily specials and a few other menu items, while neighbors drop in for cervezas. Main dishes of *pac chuc* (grilled pork) and pollo pibil cost $5, but you can get a big plate of rice and beans with tortillas for just $2. It's open only when there are customers—just knock if the door isn't open between 8 AM and 9 PM, or inquire across the street at the Posada Maya. *Calle 15, no phone.*

Restaurante Los Pájaros. This restaurant seems to be popular among baby lizards waiting out the rain under the festive thatch roof. Sandwiches and veggie soup are both $2. If you're up for something more substantial, try the pac chuc for $4. Beers are $1.50. *Calle 15, no phone.*

Restaurant Sayil. This four-table restaurant serves good Yucatecan food, although the menu is limited. Main dishes cost about $3, sodas 65¢. They don't serve alcohol. *Calle 15 No. 57, west of bus station, no phone. Open 7 AM–9 PM.*

WORTH SEEING

Exploring Chichén Itzá can take a whole day, or two if you're moving at a leisurely pace. It's a large site so bring plenty of water. There are bathrooms, as well as an expensive refreshment stand serving cold drinks and snacks. During the rainy season the vegetation and muddy paths reaching some of the ruins get sloppy. Guided tours are—of course—available. If you take the tour, make sure the guide is certified. Around noon, you'll probably be able to tag along with one of the many tour groups. The sound-and-light show in Spanish at 7 PM costs $1.50; in English at 9 PM it costs $2. *Admission: $6.50, free Sun. and holidays. Parking $3.50. Open daily 8–5.*

EL CASTILLO The first building you see when you enter the site is this awe-inspiring step-pyramid. It's 27 meters tall and has four stairways, one on each side in traditional Toltec style. Ninety-one steps up the pyramid is a temple to Kukulcan, the feathered serpent deity. El Castillo is fraught with symbolism—the four stairways face the cardinal directions and the steps total 365, the number of days in the year. Fifty-two panels on the sides stand for the 52 years in the secular Maya calendar, and the 18 terraces symbolize the 18 months in the Maya year. By the base of one balustrade is the carved head of a giant serpent. At the spring and fall equinox (March 20/21 and September 20/21), the afternoon light hitting the balustrade forms a shadow that resembles the slithering form of Kukulcan descending the pyramid toward the Sacred Cenote. Northeast of El Castillo is the **Group of a Thousand Columns,** a large plaza surrounded by intricately carved columns that probably supported arches and a roof. Some archaeologists speculate that this plaza was the town market.

TEMPLE OF THE JAGUARS This temple, appended to the eastern side of the ball court, faces El Castillo. If you don't want to spend your *whole* day at Chichén squinting at stone carvings, put your maximum effort into this building. The columns that support the lower enclosure are thought to depict the cosmogony, or creation of the world and all of its beings—from plants, fish, and fowl to serpents and men—springing from the head of a god. Inside the enclosure, a detailed mural of a village scene depicts soldiers and townspeople.

BALL COURT The court is similar to others found at ancient centers in Mexico, but this one is bigger and more elaborate. The long, rectangular stadium featured two stone circles embedded high in the walls, into which players tried to shoot a large, rubbery ball using every bodily appendage except their hands. On either side of the ball court are two small temples decorated with images of warriors and Kukulcan. From the north temple you can clearly hear the voice of anyone in the south temple—the sound travels along the walls of the ball court. For more information about the religious significance of the game played here, *see box* Ball Courts, *above.*

THE TZOMPANTLI Tzompantli means "place of the skulls" in Toltec, and the T-shaped platform is indeed decorated with the carved images of hundreds of human skulls. Tribes from the west used to display the heads of defeated captains on stakes, and some think that the Maya-Toltecs used this platform for similar purposes.

THE PLATFORM OF JAGUARS AND EAGLES Immediately southeast of the Tzompantli is a small rectangular structure with a staircase on each side. Supposedly both the eagles and jaguars carved here represent the kings or captains of certain tribes. Scroll-like designs coming out of their mouths suggest that they may be discussing the plight of the sacrifical victims whose hearts they clutch.

SACRED CENOTE Many sacrifices took place at the Sacred Cenote, a well about 1 kilometer from the main ceremonial area. It was once believed that virgins were hurled into these waters to appease the rain gods, but diving archaeologists have since discovered skeletons belonging to individuals of all ages. The slippery walls were impossible to climb, and most sacrificial victims could not swim well enough to survive until noon, when the survivors were fished out to relate the stories of what they had learned from the spirits in the water. Thousands of gold-and-jade artifacts, highly precious to the Maya, have also been found in the murky depths of the cenote, which undoubtedly holds more treasures. Since the pool is fed by a network of underground rivers, it cannot be drained.

TEMPLE OF THE WARRIORS Carved warriors adorning the rectangular columns in front of this temple stand in perfect file guarding the staircase. The upper facade of the temple features gruesome masks of Chaac, as well as an eagle with a serpent head projecting itself fearsomely out of the stone surface. A closer look reveals the head of a human being emerging from the serpent's mouth.

STEAM BATH Steam baths were popular for hygiene and therapy all over pre-Columbian Mesoamerica. In Chichén's steam bath, you can still see the stone benches on which bathers waited their turn. A narrow doorway leads to a room containing two benches and a hearth where stones were heated, then sprinkled with water to produce steam.

MARKET There is no evidence to suggest that this building was used as a market—the decorations on the altar are human figures, not avocados—but some have speculated that the columns supported a palapa-style roof under which vendors sold their merchandise.

HIGH PRIEST'S GRAVE Following the road southwest of El Castillo you'll reach the High Priest's Grave, with its succession of underground chambers. The last of the seven humans buried there appeared to be the most important, possibly an important priest.

The Reptilian Bogeyman

Superstition and magic still have a tenacious hold on the hearts of modern yucatecos. One story common in the villages to the south and east of Mérida tells of a venomous snake whose hiss sounds just like a crying child. At night, the snake visits the houses of newborns. It sits by the cradle and cries in the dark, until the mother comes to comfort the child. What she encounters, of course—to her horror—is a deadly snake bite.

RED HOUSE AND HOUSE OF THE DEER Farther along the road past the High Priest's Grave is the small House of the Deer, a Puuc-style building from the late Classic period. The house owes its name to the mural of a deer that once decorated a wall. Next door is a similar building known as the Red House, after the red border painted around the doorway. The building is pure Puuc style, and hieroglyphs on its frieze date to AD 870.

EL CARACOL El Caracol is the second most famous building in Chichén Itzá, after El Castillo. It was enlarged and renovated several times, making it a truly weird hybrid of shape and style. Astronomers used this building to observe the motion of the sun and stars in order to plan festivals, ceremonies, planting cycles, and other important events. A spiral staircase (hence the Spanish name, referring to the shape of a snail or a conch) leads to a small observation chamber. Square windows or slits are oriented toward key astronomical points. Southeast of the Caracol is **Akab-Dzib**, a 9th-century building. Akab-Dzib means "obscure writing" in Mayan, and if you look at the lintel of the southern doorway you'll notice a carving of a priest sitting on a throne surrounded by hieroglyphics.

LA IGLESIA This building stands behind the less interesting **Temple of the Wall Panels,** just southeast of El Caracol. It is a beautiful example of Puuc architecture, adorned with masks of Chaac and other geometrical motifs. In between the masks are animal gods—four in all—which represent the four Bacabes, the beings that hold up the heavens. The animals related to these gods are the bee, snail, turtle, and armadillo.

NUNNERY COMPLEX Next door to La Iglesia is the Nunnery Complex, a strange cluster of buildings named by Spaniards who thought it resembled a European convent. Chenes designs adorn the east building, whose doorway is the gaping mouth of Chaac. The form of the central building, with its classic corbeled arches, seems to suffer a bit from several additions. The building was probably a palace.

OLD CHICHEN Two kilometers down a path from the Nunnery Complex is group of poorly preserved ruins known as the **date group**. A carved black block here contains Maya dates going back to AD 879. The **Temple of the Phallic Symbols**, whose cornice shows phallic reliefs, is in the best condition. About 20 minutes further into the jungle is another group of ruins, most badly decayed, with the exception of the **Temple of the Three Lintels**, a beautiful Puuc-style building similar to the buildings at Uxmal. Unless you're a real bushwhacker, it is *not* recommended that you visit these ruins on your own. Instead, strike up a deal with an official guide. Groups of four or five may end up paying $10 or $15 each for the excursion. Bring lots of water.

Near Chichén Itzá

BALANKANCHE CAVES

A mere 6 kilometers from Chichén Itzá are the immense Balankanché caves, thought to have been a Maya ceremonial center in the 10th and 11th centuries. In 1959 a local tour guide stumbled upon the stalactite-filled caves and discovered a number of ceramic and carved artifacts inside. The images engraved on some of the artifacts are thought to be that of Tlaloc, the Toltec god of rain. No one knows why the site was abandoned so abruptly some 800 years ago. The caves are open daily 9–5, but you have to take an organized tour ($5, $2 on Sunday), which includes a sound-and-light show. Tours in English are supposed to leave at 11, 1, and 3, but they're canceled unless there are at least five participants. To get to Balankanché, take any second-class bus running between Chichén Itzá and Valladolid and ask the driver to drop you "en las grutas." From the road it's a couple hundred yards to the caves. On the way back, flag down a bus on the road.

Valladolid

Much slower-paced than Mérida or Cancún, Valladolid (which lies smack-dab between the two) is a pleasant colonial town, and an ideal base from which to visit Chichén Itzá. The ruins are just 40 minutes away by bus, so you can arrive early and beat the heat and swarms of tourists. Many travelers stay in Valladolid to soak up ambience that hasn't been packaged for tourists.

Valladolid was originally the Maya ceremonial site of Zací. The Spanish conquistador Francisco de Montejo was driven off by the indomitable Maya in 1543, but his son, Montejo the Younger, succeeded where his father failed. He laid out Valladolid in the classic Spanish colonial style and built six churches. The Maya, who had been banned from the city, constantly raided the city and besieged it for two months during the Caste War of 1847–48, sending many a tail-tucked Mexican fleeing back to Mérida.

BASICS

CASA DE CAMBIO **Bancomer** (Calle 40, facing the zócalo, tel. 985/6–32–95) is open weekdays 9–1:30. The ATM accepts Visa and Mastercard.

EMERGENCIES The **police** are at Calle 41 No. 156-A, between Calles 22 and 20, and you can reach them by phone at 985/6–21–00.

MEDICAL AID **Clínica Santa Anita** offers 24-hour medical service. *Calle 40 No. 221, at Calle 47, tel. 985/6–28–11.*

Farmacia Canto is half a block from the zócalo. *Calle 41, btw Calles 42 and 44, tel. 985/4–32–17. Open 8 AM–10 PM.*

PHONES AND MAIL The **post office** (Calle 40, facing the zócalo) is open weekdays 8–7, Saturdays 9–1. They'll hold mail sent to you at the following address for up to 10 days: Lista de Correos, Valladolid, Yucatán, CP 97780, México. Card- and coin-operated **phones** are located just outside the bus terminal and near the zócalo. For privacy and air-conditioning try the **Computel** either in the bus terminal or next door to the Hotel San Clemente on Calle 42, at Calle 41. Both are open daily 7 AM–10 PM.

COMING AND GOING

Valladolid is a major crossroads for buses to almost anywhere on the peninsula. **Autobuses del Norte** and **Autobuses del Centro del Estado de Yucatán** share the same terminal (Calle 37, at Calle 54, tel. 985/6-34-49). All buses listed below are second class. Buses to and from Cancún ($4, 3 hrs) run hourly between 5 AM and 10 PM, and to Mérida ($4, 2½ hrs) hourly from 5 AM to 11 PM. There is also service to Cobá ($3, 45 min), Tulum ($4, 1 hr), and Playa del Carmen ($6, 1 hr). Buses bound for Tizimín ($1.50, 1 hr) depart five times daily between 7:30 AM and 9 PM. Four buses leave for Izamal ($2.50, 2 hrs), and all of the Mérida-bound buses stop there, too. To reach Isla Holbox, take a bus to the ferry port at Chiquilá ($4, 3 hrs); departure time is 3 AM.

WHERE TO SLEEP

The few budget hotels in Valladolid are conveniently located between the bus station and the zócalo. You get a lot more for your money here than in Mérida and Cancún. If you want to stay cheaply and close to the zócalo, the **Hotel Lily** (Calle 44 No. 190, btw Calles 39 and 41, tel. 985/6–21–63) has functional accommodations. Singles with rather grimy shared baths are $7 and doubles are $10. A private bathroom costs an extra $2. The rooms at the **Hotel Maya** (Calle 41 No. 231, btw Calles 48 and 50, tel. 985/6–20–69) receive more attention than in other hotels; the sheets are changed daily, and each room has a private bath with soap and towels provided. Make sure you don't get a room with a clanky fan. Singles and doubles cost $10 ($15 with air-conditioning). The **Hotel San Clemente** (Calle 42 No. 206, btw Calles 39 and 41, tel. 985/6–22–08) borders on dee-luxe. To get the most for your pesos, avoid the rooms with pigeons nesting outside—they're noisy. Singles are $20, doubles are $24, and triples are $28. Rooms with TVs and air-conditioning are $5 more.

FOOD

Valladolid's restaurants don't offer the variety that Merida does, but you can still sample Yucatecan food at reasonable prices. **Casa de los Arcos** (Calle 39 No. 200-A, btw Calles 38 and 40, tel. 985/6–24–67) is set beneath pink-and-white arches, and offers lime soup ($2), pac chuc ($5.50) and *queso relleno* (stuffed cheese; $6). Sweet papaya with cheese ($3) is a good note to end on. It's open daily 7 AM–10 PM. The local hangout is **El Bazar** (Calle 39, at Calle 40, NE cnr of the zócalo, no phone), a plaza shared by several small *comedores* (sit-down food stands). Great comidas corridas with soup, a meat dish, tortillas, and a drink will run you about $4. Tacos and panuchos are readily available for about 65¢ each. At least one of the shops is open from about 6:30 AM until midnight. **Restaurant del Parque** (Calle 42, at Calle 41, no phone) has daily specials ($4–$5) and an excellent shrimp cocktail ($3), both served daily 7 AM–10 PM. If you're just looking to soothe your sweet tooth, try the corn ice cream at **Paletería La Flor de Michoacán** (Calle 41, btw Calles 42 and 44, tel. 985/6–20–52).

WORTH SEEING

Valladolid's churches are more impressive from the exterior, since interiors were looted during the Caste War. Nonetheless, the **Iglesia de San Bernardino de Siena** and the **Convento de Sisal** (about 1½ kilometers southwest of the park) deserve mention. Built in 1552, the buildings are rumored to be the oldest Spanish churches on the peninsula.

CENOTES Within walking distance of anywhere in town, the **Cenote Zací** (Calle 36, between Calles 37 and 39) is well worth a visit on a hot afternoon. Though it glows an eerie green, the water is cool and fresh. The admission price of $1.50 includes access to the cenote, a visit to the modest museum, and a peek at a few cooped-up animals in a haphazard zoo. You can swim there daily 8–6. Though not as convenient as Cenote Zací, **Cenote Dzitnup** will enlighten you as to why the Maya regarded these pools as sacred. If you haven't been paralyzed by awe, have a swim with the blind fish in the brilliant blue water. If you arrive early, enjoy the magic of having the place to yourself. Don't let the rain dissuade you from coming—it's underground. The admission price is $1.50, and it's open daily 7–5. *To get to Cenote Dzitnup, take a west-bound bus, ask to be let off at the crossroads, and walk 2 kilometers along the pleasant country road. Otherwise, you can rent a bicycle for $1 an hour in town. Look for the sign marked* ALQUILER Y VENTA BICICLETAS *on Calle 44, between Calles 39 and 41. The rental shop is open daily 7:30–2 and 5–8.*

Near Valladolid

RÍO LAGARTOS

The creatures that gave "Alligator River" its name have long since been sacrificed to fashion— flamingos steal the show here now. The people of this small fishing village 103 kilometers north of Valladolid are especially friendly and appreciate the peace and tranquility of their home. You won't find much in the way of nightlife here, but Río Lagartos outdoes itself during its festival in mid-July, with folk dances, bullfights, and processions. On the first of July, all the boats get decked-out and parade about the lagoon in celebration of Día de Marina.

Río Lagartos is a bird-watcher's heaven. Pelicans stand by the side of the road like old men, looking as if they'd strike up a conversation at any moment. The flamingos supposedly inhabit the area throughout the year, but May through August is the time to catch them in great numbers. Laws prohibit approaching the nesting areas too closely, for fear the birds will suddenly take flight and disturb the eggs. You might also see snowy egrets, red egrets, snowy white ibis, and great white herons, among other winged creatures. Arrangements for a boat trip to the flamingos' favorite hangout can be made at the Hotel Nefertiti or at the Restaurant Isla Contoy. The cost for the three- to five-hour trip, including a stop for a swim, averages about $20 per person, but fluctuates according to the size of the group. If you are only interested in swimming, the gulf off the Río Lagartos Peninsula is more pleasant than the lagoon. You can get a boat to take you across to the beach for about $3 per person. Otherwise, head to Chiquilá, a natural freshwater pool (*ojo de agua dulce*) 1 kilometer from the Hotel Nefertiti.

COMING AND GOING The 2½ hour excursion from Valladolid could be staged as a day trip if you live by a rigid itinerary. Otherwise, plan to spend at least one night. Five buses leave Valladolid daily for Tizimín, where you will have to transfer to a second bus to Río Lagartos. Twelve second-class buses leave Tizimín roughly every hour betwen 5:15 AM and 7 PM for Río Lagartos ($2, 1 hr). The last bus back to Tizimín from Río Lagartos leaves at 6 PM.

WHERE TO SLEEP AND EAT The **Hotel Nefertiti** (Calle 14, tel. 986/3-26-68, ext. 14-26) is the sole hotel in town, and its bare, blockish appearance isn't exactly inviting. The extra-large rooms have big bathrooms with clean towels. Singles are $13.50 and doubles go for $20. The hotel is currently adding 20 rooms (at a snail's pace), so don't be surprised if their prices rise to cover expenses. **Cabañas Los Dos Hermanos** (Calle 19, 50 meters from the bus station, no phone) rents two cabanas, complete with private baths and mosquito netting, for $17 a night. The drawback is that the cabanas themselves aren't very private. If you have your own tent, try camping on the seashell-laden gulf beaches and hike the 14 kilometers to see the flamingos. Bring all the supplies you'll need, including anti-mosquito paraphernalia. Bargain with a fisherman to take you across the lagoon. You should be able to get him down to $5 for two people.

Behind the Hotel Nefertiti, **Restaurant Los Flamingos** serves excellent fresh fish dinners for $5, and lobster, when in season, for $10–$13. The outdoor tables on the sand sit beside the "alligator pit," where a lone reptile sadly sloshes about. **Restaurant Los Negritos** (2 blocks from the bus station, no phone) serves good ceviches ($2–$4) and fried fish for $5 daily 9–8. **Restaurant Isla Contoy** (next to Hotel Nefertiti, no phone) is owned by a friendly family. Fish fillets are $5 and make a plentiful meal. Generous cerviches go for $4 daily 7:30 AM–9 PM.

Cancún
The only reason for budget travelers to go to Cancún is to catch a plane out. Paradise it may be for unadventurous vacationers, but it has little to offer the rest of us. The city is a giant mass of five-star hotels, shopping malls, and overpriced restaurants. A 22-kilometer, elbow-shape sandbar, Cancún overlooks the Caribbean Sea on one side and two lagoons on the other. The resort has no coherence or personality—it is a city without a soul. Sure. it has beautiful beaches, but so do Playa del Carmen, Isla Mujeres, and Cozumel.

The removal of coral from reefs causes thousands of species to lose their habitat. Although stores all over Mexico's Caribbean coast sell black coral jewelry, buying it contributes to the destruction of this fragile ecosystem.

The story of how Cancún was created is fairly well known. Looking for a new location for a money-making resort, the Mexican government asked a computer to come up with the answer. A computer knows a good stretch of silicon when it sees one. Cancún's setting on the northern coast of Quintana Roo is ideal, with white-sand beaches, warm Caribbean waters, and coral reefs. Construction in Cancún began in 1972 and hasn't stopped since.

All in all, Cancún is better avoided. The city lacks the charm that might justify its high prices. Whether you want to snorkel or check out Maya ruins, your best bet is to head for the nearby budget paradises of Isla Mujeres or Playa del Carmen.

BASICS

AMERICAN EXPRESS As well as providing all the services of a travel agent, the AmeEx office here replaces lost cards and traveler's checks, cashes personal checks, changes cash

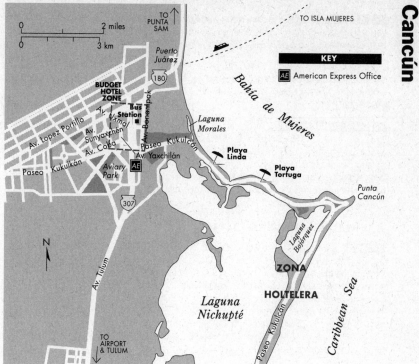

TO
PUNTA
SAM

TO ISLA MUJERES

Puerto
Juárez

KEY

AE American Express Office

and traveler's checks, and holds customers' mail for up to 30 days. *Av. Tulum and Brisas A, near Hotel América, tel. 988/4–19–99. Open weekdays 9–6, Sat. 9–1.*

CASAS DE CAMBIO The many casas de cambio here are open until around 9 or 10 PM. Rates at banks are better, but the lines are long. **Banamex** (tel. 988/4–37–59) and **Bancomer** (tel. 988/4–35–08) downtown on Avenida Tulum change money weekdays 9:30–1:30. Banamex has an ATM machine that accepts Plus and Cirrus system cards, and you can also get cash advances with a Visa or Mastercard.

CONSULATES **Canada.** *Plaza México 312, 2nd floor, tel. 988/4–37–16. Open weekdays 10–2.*

United States. This is not an official consulate, but an impotent representative office. For any real help you'll have to go to Mérida. *Edificio Marruecos 31, Av. Náder 40, tel. 988/4–24–11. Open weekdays 9–2 and 3–5:30.*

EMERGENCIES The **police** station (tel. 988/4–12–02) is downtown, on Avenida Tulum next to the banks. **Cruz Roja** (Labná 2, at Yaxchilán, tel. 988/4–16–16) has 24-hour ambulance service.

LAUNDRY **Lavandería ELA** (Supermanzana 28, near Mercado 28, tel. 988/4–96–02) has do-it-yourself laundry service for $1.50; it's $2 if you want them to do it.

MEDICAL AID The **Hospital Americano** (Viento 15, at Av. Tulum, tel. 988/4–61–33) has 24-hour service. The tourist information booklet *Cancun Tips* also has a list of English-speaking doctors.

Farmacia París (Yaxchilán 32, in the Edificio Marrufo, tel. 988/4–01–64) is open 24 hours. **425**

PHONES AND MAIL The **post office** will hold mail sent to you at the following address for up to 10 days: Lista de Correos, Cancún, Quintana Roo, CP 77500, México. *Av. Sunyaxchen, Supermanzana 28, tel. 988/4–14–18. Open weekdays 8–7, Sat. 9–noon.*

Public telephones abound in the downtown area; for international collect calls dial 09, or **01 to get an AT&T operator. You can place collect calls from **Computel** (Av. Tulum, near the bus terminal, tel. and fax 998/7–42–24) between 7 AM and 10 PM; the service charge for five minutes is $2.

VISITOR INFORMATION Open daily 9–9, the main office of the **Secretaría Estatal de Turismo** (Av. Tulum 26, tel. 988/4–80–73) has a knowledgeable, English-speaking staff that will assail you with brochures. However, the best resource is *Cancun Tips*, a booklet you can pick up at the airport, the mall at Playa Caracol, or the tourist office. Or visit the publication's frank and helpful staff at Avenida Tulum 29, near the bus station. They're a valuable resource for the most recent discounts offered by local sport and tour companies.

COMING AND GOING

BY BUS The bus station is downtown, on Uxmal near Avenida Tulum. Two major bus companies, **Autotransportes del Oriente (ADO)** and **Autotransportes del Caribe,** serve most points in Quintana Roo and Yucatán, as well as other important cities in the republic. Buses leave frequently for Mérida ($9), Valladolid ($5), Chichén Itzá ($6), Chetumal ($11), and points in between. Minibuses depart every 15 minutes for Playa del Carmen and Puerto Morelos ($2). The bus stop for Puerto Juárez is on the east side of Avenida Tulum near the Monument to History. To get to the Zona Hotelera, cross Avenida Tulum and catch a HOTELES bus. The budget hotels are within walking distance of the station, and you can store luggage at the Caribe terminal for $2 per day.

BY CAR If you've got the money to rent a car, the drive to Tulum is a pleasant one: There are no tolls, and Highway 307 is well maintained. Watch out for speeding tour buses. The road to the ruins via Valladolid and Mérida, however, is another story. Many an unsuspecting driver has paid through the teeth after taking the *carretera de cuota* (toll road) to Mérida, which costs $24 (they charge $12 at X-Can and $12 at Pisté). The toll is charged in both directions. You can really cruise on the toll road, but you can't get off it until Valladolid, so you won't see much more than the painted lines. The *carretera libre* (free road, otherwise known as Highway 180) takes the same route as the toll road but passes through small towns. To avoid the toll road, take the highway out of Cancún and keep going straight—a CUOTA sign on your right will try to lure you in, but don't bite.

BY BOAT Boats leave Puerto Juárez and Punta Sam (both north of Cancún) for Isla Mujeres every hour. The fare is about $1.50 for the 40-minute trip, and $3.50 for the "express" trip (30 min). To reach the ports from Avenida Tulum, take a bus marked PUERTO JUAREZ for 50¢. Unless you're using the Punta Sam ferry to bring a car across to Isla Mujeres, you're better off leaving from Puerto Juárez.

BY PLANE The Cancún airport is the largest and busiest on the peninsula and is a frequent destination for many U.S. airlines (*see* Coming and Going in Chapter 1, Basics). Domestic airlines include **Aeroméxico** (tel. 988/4–10–97) and **Mexicana** (tel. 988/7–44–44). The casa de cambio at the airport, humorously named $EXCHANGE, is open during the day, but avoid changing a lot of money there as rates are better in town.

➤ AIRPORT TRANSPORT • Unfortunately, taxi and combi drivers monopolize the transport situation, and no public buses serve the airport. A taxi from the airport to Cancún costs about $16; the only other option is to take a combi for $7. You'll see the station wagons lined up outside as you leave the terminal. If you refuse to spend that much, there is an alternative. Take a bus heading to Playa del Carmen and get off at the detour for the airport; from there, the 1½-kilometer walk can be excruciating on a hot day.

GETTING AROUND

Cancún is divided into two sections: the Zona Hotelera (Hotel Zone), home to monstrous resorts, and the *centro*. Only one street, Paseo Kukulcan, goes through the Zona Hotelera, and there are no cross streets. Buses marked HOTELES or CENTRO travel from downtown to the Zona every few minutes from 5 AM to 1 AM. Starting at the intersection of Paseo Kukulcan and Avenida Tulum, the Zona Hotelera is marked off by kilometers; the numbered signs are visible in the center of the boulevard.

The centro is on the mainland at the base of the elbow-shape sandbar that is the Zona Hotelera. It's divided into dozens of numbered zones—some only one block long—called supermanzanas. A good map will have the numbers superimposed on it. Addresses are often signified by the initials "S.M." followed by a number. Avenida Tulum is the main drag, where you will find most of the restaurants and shopping centers selling expensive Mexican crafts.

BY TAXI There's a taxi glut in Cancún, so they're cheaper than in other Mexican cities. Fare within downtown should be around $1.50, from downtown to the youth hostel $2.50, and $3.50 to Puerto Juárez. Still, you'll probably have to bargain for these prices.

WHERE TO SLEEP

You got it—staying in Cancún is expensive. This city was built not for budget travelers but as a getaway for well-to-do foreigners on their annual vacation. Unfortunately, sleeping on the beach is out of the question. If you want to stay near the beach, your only option is the youth hostel (*see below*). Otherwise, you'll have to stay downtown, where hotels are a little more affordable.

➢ UNDER $25 • **Hotel María Isabel Cancún.** Just off Avenida Uxmal and near the cheap eateries, the tiny rooms in this hotel all have air-conditioning and TVs, and there's a nice little terrace for hanging out. The management takes great pride in their monthly fumigation ritual. Singles and doubles are both $23.50, and triples are $27. *Palmera 59, Supermanzana 23, tel. 988/4–90–15. 2½ blocks west of bus station. 10 rooms, all with bath. Luggage storage.*

Hotel Villa Rossana Cancún. This is the best deal for solo travelers. It's a long walk from the bus station, but close to cheap restaurants. The large, clean rooms have fans, and some have great decks. Singles are $15, doubles $22. Each additional person pays $5. *Yaxchilán 68, just north of Sunyaxchen, tel. 988/4–19–43. 10 rooms, all with bath. Luggage storage.*

➢ UNDER $30 • **Hotel Alux.** Large, airy rooms with air-conditioning, new furniture, telephones, TVs, and impeccable bathrooms with hot water make this a great place to stay. But you'll pay for it: Singles are $22, doubles $30 (with one bed $25). *Uxmal 21, tel. 988/4–05–56. ½ block north of the bus station. 32 rooms, all with bath. Luggage storage, laundry.*

Hotel Canto. This hotel offers clean, air-conditioned rooms with large bathrooms, TVs, comfortable beds, and all the *agua purificada* you can swallow. If you get lonely, you can hang out in the lobby and watch cartoons with the kids. Singles are $23.50, doubles $27, and triples $30. *Yaxchilán 22, at Sunyaxchen, tel. 988/4–12–67. 23 rooms, all with bath. Luggage storage. MC, V.*

➢ UNDER $40 • **Hotel El Rey del Caribe.** If you want to splurge in Cancún, and atmosphere is more important than proximity to the beach, this is the place. Set in a gorgeous jungle-like garden, with tropical plants, a pool, and Jacuzzi, this small hotel has spacious, comfortable rooms with kitchens and clean bathrooms. It's a place people come back to again and again. Singles and doubles cost $35, plus $5 for each additional person. *Uxmal, at Náder, tel. 988/4–20–28. 23 rooms, all with bath. Luggage storage, wheelchair access. Reservations advised.*

➢ HOSTEL • **Villa Deportiva Juvenil Cancún.** Still known to the bus drivers as the **CREA** hostel, this is the cheapest place in town and the only budget lodging on the beach. The enormous youth hostel has separate wings for men and women, with dorm rooms equipped with bunks and lockers. Some of the dorms have views of the sea. The place is fairly clean (except on weekends), although bathrooms lack toilet paper and hot water. During rainy season this place leaks pretty badly, and ants and mice seek refuge here. The beaches out front are terrible, but the hostel has Ping-Pong tables, a volleyball net, and a decent, albeit crowded, swimming pool. Beds cost $10 plus a $10 deposit. *Paseo Kukulcan Km. 3.2, tel. 988/3–13–37. 300 beds. Luggage storage, meal service, wheelchair access.*

➤ CAMPING • **Villa Deportiva Juvenil Cancún** (*see above*) lets travelers camp on the grassy lawns and use the hostel facilities for $5 per person.

FOOD

Food isn't cheap in Cancún, but if you're willing to walk a few extra blocks and stick to typical Mexican fare, it's affordable. In the Zona Hotelera the pickings are extremely slim—guests at the youth hostel can choose between the acceptable though meager fare offered there and at **Superdeli**, a 24-hour minimarket 250 meters east of the hostel. Downtown, look for cheaper options on Avenidas Uxmal and Cobá, and on nearby streets. Even the supermarkets in Cancún are expensive, but **Comercial Mexicana** (Av. Tulum, at Uxmal) serves ready-made food by weight, from spaghetti dishes for about $5 a kilo to black beans and rice for $2.35 a kilo—300 grams should suffice. **Mercado 28,** a fake-colonial shopping mall, has an array of loncherías serving cheap, homemade meals and antojitos. Most offer breakfast for under $3, comidas corridas for about $4 and antojitos for $1. Fruit vendors also swamp the market in the morning. Take a bus marked RUTA 5 and get off at the post office. The market is right behind it.

La Parrilla. This Mexican grill is a favorite among locals. The busy bar is big on reggae, and restaurant specialties *sopa azteca* (tortilla soup; $3) and five different kinds of quesadillas for $4. Beers are $2 and cocktails are $4. *Yaxchilán 51, tel. 988/4–53–98. Open daily 6 PM–3 AM.*

La Peña Taurino. If you're willing to walk a bit out of your way, hang here with a crowd of locals on the industrial end of town. Songs of long-lost loves and pictures of Hollywood couples of the past provide the ambience, and you can drown your sorrows at the fully stocked bar. Surprisingly good mariachi bands liven up the mood. Carne asada is $7, seafood (when they have it) is $8. *Chichén Itzá 48, btw Uxmal and Ceibo, no phone. Open Mon.–Sat. noon–midnight.*

Restaurant Tlaquepaque. Hidden from the street by a lovely little maze of vines and a thatched canopy roof, this place offers a cheap breakfast (all the usual fare for $3.50). Steak and chicken dishes are more expensive ($8), and the menu includes lots of seafood. *Yaxchilán 59, tel. 988/4–44–41. Next to the Hotel Villa Rossana. Open Thurs.–Tues. 6 AM–10 PM.*

Rincón Yucateco. The prices are more than reasonable, and the place is just up the street from the bus station. Huevos rancheros go for $2.50, quesadillas are $3.50. Eat and go elsewhere for coffee—they only serve instant. *Uxmal 24, no phone. Next to the Hotel Alux. Open daily 7:30 AM–9:30 PM.*

WORTH SEEING

People come to Cancún for one reason: beaches (*see* Outdoor Activities, *below*). Most travelers expect a flawless turquoise sea, tropical palms, and immaculate white-sand beaches. And, for the most part, Cancún delivers. But what is truly mind-blowing is the little universe of consumer gluttony packed onto this thin stretch of land. If you're stuck here, one of the more amusing things to do is watch the package-tour crowd go on vacation. Plush malls like the **Plaza Caracol** provide well-heeled gringos with the air-conditioned, sanitized bubble they require to indulge that greatest of passions, shopping. At the resorts, a grumpy underclass serves icy daiquiris to sunburn victims on manicured beaches. The most amazing thing is that no one seems to wonder how this pasteurized paradise descended to earth.

AFTER DARK

The great advantage that Cancún has over most Caribbean coastal towns is the abundance of its nightlife, but it's generally what you'd expect. Huge discos with pseudo-Mayan motifs and flashing lights, and bars offering every drink imaginable, are easy to find both in the Zona Hotelera and downtown. Cover charges are high (about $10), but many set aside one day a week, usually Monday, when admission is free. Check also in *Cancún Tips* for special offers. The discos here are known for their discriminatory policies. In many places Mexicans are prohibited from entering, lest they offend gringos by their presence or behavior. You should consider whether you want to support this blatant discrimination against Mexicans in their own country.

If you are in downtown Cancún on a Friday night at about 8, head to the park behind Tulipanes. A special show called **Noche Caribeña** (Caribbean Night) features songs, dances, poetry readings, and raffles. Best of all, it's for locals, so it'll give you a chance to escape the tourist crowd.

CINEMAS If you're craving some reel fun, try one of the several cinemas downtown that show fairly recent American movies. **Cine Royal,** on Avenida Tulum, and **Cine Cancún,** on Avenida Cobá, show English-language and Mexican films.

DANCING The super-hip discos in the Zona Hotelera are the characterless cousins of tourist-oriented clubs you'd find in many towns in Mexico. **La Boom** (tel. 988/3–14–58), a short distance from the hostel, opens nightly at 10:30 PM. Downtown along Avenida Tulum, try **Risky Business** or **Mary Juana.** There's salsa at **Batachá** (Hotel Miramar in the Zona Hotelera) after 11 PM. **Cat's** on Avenida Yaxchilán has live reggae music, and is free with a *Cancún Tips* card. For a more mellow atmosphere, head to the bar **La Palapa,** at Hotel Club Lagoon Caribe, where you can listen to live music and dance after 9 PM.

OUTDOOR ACTIVITIES

BEACHES Beaches in Cancún face the Caribbean Sea or the calmer Bahía de Mujeres. Since Hurricane Gilbert barreled through, those on the Caribbean side have become very narrow. Many of the best beaches are backed by luxury hotels but all are public. If you're discreet, you can make easy use of hotel facilities such as hammocks, lounges, huge pools, bars (watch out—a Coke could set you back $3.50), and showers. The best Caribbean beaches are those in front of the **Hyatt Cancún** and **Sheraton** hotels and **Playa Chac Mool,** all just around Punta Cancún, the northeast point of the Zona. Calm Playa Linda, near the youth hostel, is just 10 minutes by bus from town, and **Playa Tortugas,** another mile further along Paseo Kukulcan, has some of Cancún's clearest water.

There are lifeguards on the beaches as well as flags indicating the the water's danger level. A green or blue flag means calm, a yellow flag means caution, and a red or black flag signifies danger. Buses (80¢) run to the beaches in the Zona Hotelera all day long. Just tell the driver where you're going. If you want to take it all off, head for the **nude beaches** near Club Med, at the southern end of the Zona Hotelera. Buses don't make it all the way out there, so take a taxi or hitchhike.

WATER SPORTS Water sports can be arranged at almost any hotel or through one of the independent vendors lining the streets downtown. Activities include (with ballpark prices): diving ($70 for two tanks), parasailing ($35 for a 15-minute ride), sailwaving ($15 for 15 minutes strapped to the sail of a catamaran), windsurfing ($15 per hour), waverunners ($40 for half-hour ride on a Jet-Ski-like machine), fishing ($300–$600 a day), and snorkeling ($25 per hour). Don't expect to pay much less to do this stuff, but check out *Cancún Tips* (*see* Visitor Information, *above*) for discounts.

➤ SNORKELING • Despite the incredible clarity of the water, snorkeling off the beaches around Cancún is not as rewarding, or as affordable, as at some other Caribbean resorts. It's usually cheaper to snorkel from Isla Mujeres, because most of the reefs are closer to the island than to the Zona Hotelera. You can go on snorkeling trips from any of the many marinas in town for about $25, or simply rent snorkeling equipment. Many of the agencies require a minimum number of people to make the trip (usually four to six).

➤ SCUBA DIVING • Don't come to Cancún if your main motive is scuba diving: The underwater scene at Cozumel is far superior. Unfortunately, in Cancún you can only rent diving equipment if you're certified, and most of the three-day certification courses offered by marinas will set you back as much as $350. Some marinas, such as **Marina Aqua Ray** (tel. 988/3–30–07), in front of Villas Plaza Hotel, offer short resort courses and easy dives for about $80. Diving trips to the reefs in Bahía de Mujeres cost about $45 for one-tank dives and $75 for two-tank dives. Another good place to dive is **Punta Nizuc**, next to Club Med.

Near Cancún

ISLA HOLBOX

Mosquitoes and flies keep less tolerant tourists away from this tiny island north of Cancún. Not only is this a great place to get away from the tourist swarms in Cancún and meet the people who live here, it's also an excellent place to buy a nylon hammock. Several of the locals make them here by hand, so just poke your head into an open doorway when you see a loom. However, fishing is the main economic activity, and green turtles waddle ashore to deposit their eggs from late May through June. The eggs begin to hatch in August and September. Nearby Isla Contoy, a national reserve, and Isla de Pájaros are home to flamingos, pelicans, camachos, and wild ducks. Trips to Contoy don't cost more than $10 per person for a small group. You can also rent a motor scooter ($15 per half-day) and drive around Holbox.

BASICS Tiny Isla Holbox has a **general store** open daily 9–9. A **telephone caseta** (½ block west of zócalo) is open 8–1 and 4–8 every day. To call Holbox, dial 998/7–14–62, 998/7–16–68, or 998/7–29–83 and then ask for the person, place, or extension you want. **Farmacia Pepes** is open 8 AM–10 PM (tel. ext. 182). The two doctors at the **Centro de Salud** (main drag, just before the water tower) are on call round the clock.

COMING AND GOING Ferries leave Chiquilá ($3, ½ hr) at approximately 8 AM and 2 PM; they leave Holbox at 5 AM and 1 PM. To get to Chiquilá, take a direct bus from Cancún or from Valladolid ($4, 3 hrs; the only direct bus from there leaves at 3 AM, en route from Mérida). There's a bus from Tizimín at 11:30, and the ferry in Chiquilá waits until it arrives.

WHERE TO SLEEP AND EAT **Posada Amapola** (on the zócalo) rents nice rooms with clean baths for $7 (single) and $8 (double). Also on the zócalo is **Posada Los Arcos,** where doubles go for $10. The owner also has five cabanas on the beach near town, each one with a private bathroom. Kitchen units are $17; without a kitchen, they're $10. Inquire at the Tienda Dinora on the zócalo. Other posadas in town are **Hotel Flamingo's** ($10 for a double) and **Posada Playa Bonita** ($13.50 for a double). In addition, the island offers unlimited camping possibilities. The ocean side is the best place to look for a camping spot, but bring your mosquito net!

Lonchería El Parque (on the zócalo) serves whopping portions of local fish for $3–$4. Beers are 65¢. Otherwise, the supermarket sells fruit and cookies, and you can buy fresh bread at the bakery.

PUERTO MORELOS

South of Cancún is the tranquil fishing town of Puerto Morelos, a welcome change from the resort frenzy up north. It's fairly upscale, benefiting from the overflow of tourists on country drives in rented 4x4s. There isn't much to do in town, and the beaches aren't great—if you want to bake in the sand, walk a couple of kilometers south to more secluded, attractive areas. Puerto Morelos's main draw is an offshore reef where you can snorkel or dive. A small dive shop, on the beach in front of Restaurant Los Pelícanos, rents equipment and arranges boat excursions to more distant reefs. If you're staying overnight, consider the **Posada Amor** (Javier Rojo Gómez, tel. 987/71–00–33), a great little hotel just south of the zócalo that offers singles for $22 and doubles for $25. A private bath costs about $5 extra. **Restaurant Las Palmeras** and **Restaurant Los Pelícanos,** both on Avenida Rafael Melgar, serve typical seafood dishes for about $7.50. At **Restaurant Zac-be,** in front of the zócalo, you can get chicken tacos for $3 and pork sandwiches for $2. To get to Puerto Morelos take one of the five daily minibuses from the bus station in Cancún. You can also take a second-class bus for $1 and ask to be let off at the road to Puerto Morelos. From there cab drivers charge $1.50 for the 2-kilometer ride into town. Minibuses also leave occasionally from Playa del Carmen ($2, 25 min). Three ferries depart Puerto Morelos daily for Cozumel. The 2½-hour ride costs $7 per person and $45 per car. At these rates, you are much better ditching your car and taking one of the frequent ferries from Playa del Carmen.

Isla Mujeres

At first sight, Isla Mujeres, just 10 kilometers east of Cancún, is a stereotypical resort. The carefully arranged souvenir and artesanía stores jostle for space with a handful of expensive restaurants and charmless hotels. Still, Isla Mujeres is sweet and simple, with a subtle attraction that draws budget travelers from all over the world and lulls them into staying much longer than they had planned. This small island, just 8 kilometers long, is part of the established shoestring itinerary, which includes such places as Goa in India, Koh Samet in Thailand, and Bali in Indonesia. You will meet the same people in all these places, literally and figuratively, stretching their money as far as possible.

Isla Mujeres has what it takes: The white beaches are quiet and peaceful, perfect for reading, walking, and playing ball. Snorkeling and diving opportunities abound, including trips into the Cave of Sleeping Sharks, a natural phenomenon straight out of *National Geographic*. Still, the main reason people come (and return) to the island is to relax, read a couple of books, make new friends, and avoid doing much of anything. It's a way of life that's becoming endangered, however, as day-trippers from Cancún pour onto the island and elbow one another for room over the coral reefs.

The Cave of the Sleeping Sharks

A series of underwater caverns off Isla Mujeres are a crash pad for a dangerous species of shark. The sharks are not actually sleeping but are in a state of relaxed nonaggression not seen anywhere else. They are usually reef sharks, a species normally responsible for the largest number of attacks on humans. These sharks may come to the caves for two reasons.

One explanation is that the water inside the caves is chemically different from the water outside. It contains more oxygen, more carbon dioxide, and less salt. The decrease in salinity causes the parasites that plague sharks to loosen their grip and allows the remora fish (the sharks' personal vacuum cleaner) to eat the parasites more easily.

Because of the deep state of relaxation of these sharks, it's also suspected that they come to the caves to get high. Fresh water seeps up into the caves from the ground, and the combination of fresh and salt water may produce an effect on sharks akin to that of humans' smoking marijuana.

The sharks inside the caves must continuously pump water over their gills to breathe, which requires more energy than does swimming. Whatever they experience while "sleeping" in the caves must be well worth the extra effort. If you dive in this area, be cautious. The sharks may appear to sleep, but they're still a potential nightmare.

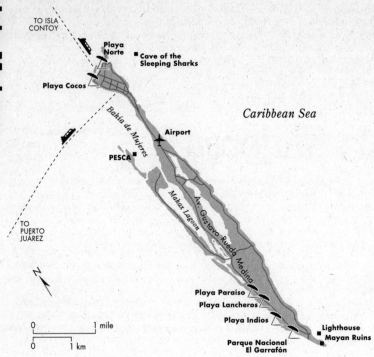

TO ISLA
CONTOY

Playa
Norte

■ Cave of the
Sleeping Sharks

Playa Cocos

Bahía de Mujeres

Caribbean Sea

Airport

PESCA ■

Makax Lagoon

Av. Gustavo Rueda Medina

TO
PUERTO
JUÁREZ

Playa Paraíso

Playa Lancheros

Playa Indios

Lighthouse
■ Mayan Ruins

Parque Nacional
El Garrafón

0 _____ 1 mile

0 _____ 1 km

How the island got its alluring name is open to debate. One fanciful story says pirates stashed their women here while they went off for a good plunder. A more plausible explanation is that the island is named after some Maya female figurines found here by Francisco Hernández de Córdoba, the commander of a Spanish expedition, who "discovered" the island in 1517. The subsequent history of the island is common to the Caribbean: It was a hideaway for pirates and later became a fishing village. During the late '60s and '70s, the island became an ideal hammock haven for hippie castaways, but that's pretty much faded with the movement.

BASICS

BANK **Banco del Atlántico,** on your right as you come off the ferry, offers good exchange rates. *Rueda Medina 3, btw Morelos and Bravo, tel. 987/7–00–05. Money exchange weekdays 10–noon.*

LAUNDRY **Tim Phó** does your laundry for $7. *Juárez, at Abasolo, two blocks from the zócalo, tel. 987/7–05–29. Open Mon.–Sat. 7 AM–9 PM.*

MEDICAL AID The **Centro de Salud** (Guerrero 5, tel. 987/7–01–17) offers 24-hour emergency service. The English-speaking doctor, **Antonio Salas** (Hidalgo, next to Farmacia Lily, tel. 987/7–04–77) makes house calls round the clock.

Farmacia Lily is open daily 8:30 AM–9:30 PM. *Madero, at Hidalgo, no phone.*

PHONES AND MAIL The **post office** will hold mail sent to you at the following address for up to ten days: Lista de Correos, Isla Mujeres, Quintana Roo, CP 77400, México. *Guerrero, at Mateos, tel. 987/7–00–85. Open weekdays 8–7, Sat. 9–1.*

The long-distance **telephone office** (Rueda Medina 9-B, near the ferry terminal) is open daily 9–9. You can also find coin and card-operated phones scattered about the town. Buy phone cards at the tourist information office (*see below*). For collect calls to the United States, dial 09 to talk to an operator.

VISITOR INFORMATION Although the staff at the **tourist office** is knowledgeable, they speak little English. Make sure to pick up a copy of the *Islander*, a monthly publication with good maps of the island and general tourist information. *Hidalgo 6, near zócalo, tel. 987/2–03–16. Open weekdays 8–2 and 5–8.*

COMING AND GOING

You can get to Isla Mujeres from Puerto Juárez or Punta Sam. Ferries and water taxis make the trip from Puerto Juárez at 6 AM, 7 AM, and every hour on the half hour after that. The fare is $1.50 for the 40-minute ride, unless you take the luxury, air-conditioned ferries for $3.50, which only take 15 minutes. Puerto Juárez is 15 minutes from Cancún by bus—catch a bus (65¢) from any of the bus stops on Avenida Tulum. You could also organize a small group of people to split the taxi ride ($2.50).

You don't need a car to travel aboard the car ferries from Punta Sam, but unless you're bringing a car over, you might as well cross from Puerto Juárez, which is closer. Ferries leave every two to three hours, and the fare is $1.50. The cost of transporting a car starts at about $7. Water taxis make the crossing in 10–15 minutes for about $3.50 per person (if you have four people or more, you should be able to bargain). The taxis run at amazing speeds, and the ride is exhilarating, if bumpy—if you get seasick, take the ferry. To get to Punta Sam from Cancún, take a PUERTO JUAREZ bus from Avenida Tulum, and ask the driver if he continues to Punta Sam.

GETTING AROUND

Isla Mujeres is only about 8 kilometers long and 810 meters wide. It's easy to get around, and the public transport is adequate. The town of Isla Mujeres, where most travelers stay, is at the northern tip of the island. Almost completely surrounded by water, the town is connected to the rest of the island by a narrow neck. Most of the shops and restaurants are in the southern part of town, and the northern part is more residential. You should consider renting a bicycle or moped to explore the rest of the island. It gives you a chance to see the "other" Isla of locals' houses and some unspoiled coastal vistas.

BY BUS One bus makes its way from Avenida Rueda Medina in the center of town to the *colonias*, neighborhoods where the *isleños* (islanders) live. It goes as far south as Playa Paraíso, on the west coast. From there it's a 3-kilometer walk to El Garrafón, at the southern end of the island.

BY MOPED AND BIKE Isla Mujeres has beautiful rides and the terrain is quite flat. Several places around town rent mopeds for about $5 an hour, but you should try bargaining if you rent them for several hours. You need to leave a deposit or let them hold your ID. Renting a bicycle is only $2 an hour, $7 for eight hours. **Sport Bike** (Juárez and Morelos, just below the zócalo, tel. 987/2–00–36) rents bikes with locks overnight for $7.

WHERE TO SLEEP

Most of the hotels are in town. Prices, which have skyrocketed over the last few years, rise even more during high season (November–April and July–August), but you can still find an affordable place to sleep. Prices listed below reflect the low season range. If you're looking for something more luxurious than the hotels reviewed below, try the charming **Cabañas María del Mar** (Av. Carlos Lazol, in front of Playa Cocos, tel.

If you don't mind the wind, wet sand, and the occasional rain shower, you can sleep on the beach. Officially, you're not supposed to do it, but the police tend to look the other way.

987/7–02–13). These clean rooms are definitely worth the heavy investment if you're on a lover's holiday. However, loud music from the disco down the beach can be heard until 3 AM. Romantic cabañas, towers, and castles run $25–$65 a double.

➤ UNDER $10 • **Poc-Na.** This is *the* place for budget travelers, not only because it's cheap and near the beach, but because of the atmosphere. Come here to meet travelers from all over the world and make instant friends. Hang out on the rooftop under the stars, or spend your time playing chess or backgammon under the large palapa that doubles as dining room and living area. The coed dorm rooms have bunks or hammock hooks and lockers for your things. They rent towels, sheets, and pillows. A $7 deposit (or a passport) is required. Showers are cold but clean, and laundry facilities include sinks and clotheslines. The small restaurant serves mediocre food and the prices are better in town, so eat elsewhere. The price, including hammock rental, is $5 per person. *Matamoros, tel. 987/7–00–90. From ferry, left on Rueda Medina to Matamoros. Luggage storage, meal service, wheelchair access.*

➤ UNDER $15 • **Hotel Osorio.** This hotel in a tacky turquoise building is typical of budget hotels here—comfortable but bare. Bathrooms are clean and have hot water. Singles and doubles cost $13.50 and triples go for $17. *Madero 10, tel. 987/7–00–18. From ferry dock, 1 block left and right on Madero. 18 rooms, all with bath. Luggage storage, wheelchair access. Reservations advised Dec. and Jan.*

Hotel Posada San Jorge. Close to the beach, this hotel is comfortable, albeit ugly. Rooms are reasonably clean, and some have mini-refrigerators. During the summer, watch out for the humongous insects—you could mistake them for vultures. The hot water runs only intermittently. Singles are $10 and doubles cost around $13.50. This place was up for sale when we checked it out, so prices may change. *Juárez, btw Mateos and Matamoros, tel. 987/7–01–55. From the ferry, left on Rueda Medina, right on Matamoros and left on Juárez. 17 rooms, all with bath. Laundry, luggage storage, wheelchair access.*

➤ UNDER $20 • **Hotel Caribe Maya.** Close to the zócalo, the Caribe Maya has small, depressing rooms lacking light and ventilation. Some are air-conditioned, though, and the bathrooms are clean and have hot water. Singles cost about $12 ($20 with air-conditioning), doubles about $15 ($20 with air-conditioning). They also rent mopeds for $5 an hour and offer tours to Isla Contoy for $30. *Madero 9, tel. 987/7–01–90. From ferry dock, 1 block left and right on Madero. 25 rooms, all with bath. Laundry, luggage storage, wheelchair access. Reservations advised Dec.–Apr.*

Hotel Carmelina. Roaches and other bugs check into this pink motel and don't check out, but there's plenty of space for everybody—the rooms are large and sunny and have clean bathrooms and fans. The friendly management will let you use their refrigerator and stove during the slow season. They also rent bicycles. Singles cost $10, doubles $17, and triples $18. *Guerrero 4, tel. 987/7–00–06. Up Morelos from ferry and left on Guerrero. 18 rooms, all with bath, 2 with air-conditioning. Laundry, luggage storage, wheelchair access.*

Hotel Xul-Ha. Very close to the beach, this hotel has basic, whitewashed rooms and immaculate bathrooms and shower stalls. Singles cost about $13, doubles $17, and triples $20. *Hidalgo 23, tel. 987/7–00–75. Left from ferry terminal to last street, then right to Hidalgo, and right again. 11 rooms, all with bath. Laundry, luggage storage, wheelchair access. MC, V.*

➤ UNDER $30 • **Hotel Francis Arlene.** This hotel offers a little bit of luxury for a reasonable price. The rooms, all with terraces, are individually decorated, and there's even art on the walls. The roof is beautifully tiled, and you can sunbathe on chaise lounges up there. Singles start at $20, doubles are $25, and triples are $30. *Guerrero 7, tel. 987/7–03–10. 12 rooms, all with bath, 3 with air-conditioning.*

➤ CAMPING • You can sleep on the beach with little worry. Technically, they don't allow it, so if the police want to make your life difficult, they can. At El Faro, the lighthouse keeper doesn't mind if you want to camp at the small ruins nearby. It's beautiful, but stake your tent well and prepare for a windy night.

FOOD

Inexpensive loncherías are scattered throughout town, including four on Avenida Guerrero, between Matamoros and Mateos, which serve typical fare. Small sandwiches cost about $1, a plate of tacos $3, and main dishes, such as fish, about $4.50. An especially good one is the tiny nameless lonchería on Guerrero between Matamoros and Abasolo. If you have your own stove or are staying at a hotel with cooking facilities, buy your food at the **market** on Guerrero at Mateos. **Panadería La Reina** (Madero, at Juárez) sells fresh pastries and great banana bread.

➤ UNDER $5 • **Cafecito.** Sitting beside a stained-glass wave at a table decorated with seashells, you may decide that you've fallen into a tourist trap. As you sip a cappuccino ($1.50) or hover over a huge banana split ($4), you probably won't care. This is the place to hook up with tarot card and palm readers. It's an excellent place for breakfast, which costs about $3.50. *Matamoros 42, at Juárez, no phone. Open daily 8–noon and 6–10.*

Chen Huaye. With Silvio Rodríguez tapes in the stereo and pink flamingos on the wall, this is the path to enlightened eating. The name of the place means "always here," which describes where you might be after you discover *chaya* ($2), a green drink made from a tropical plant resembling spinach. Popeye never had it so good. The chicken tortas, at $1.50 each, make the wallet happy as well as the soul. *Hidalgo 17, no phone. Near zócalo, behind the basketball courts. Open daily 9 AM–11 PM.*

Lonchería La Lomita. South of the zócalo, this unpretentious lonchería is well worth the walk from your hotel. The food is terrific and servings are large. Wonderful panuchos and salbutes cost $1 each (you'll probably eat three or four), and the great lentil-vegetable soup is $4. Huge, yummy daily specials with soup, rice, and tortillas are an amazing $3.50. *Juárez 25-B, tel. 987/7–04–66. From the south end of zócalo, 1 block toward western shore, turn left, and go uphill. Open daily 8 AM–11 PM.*

➤ UNDER $10 • **El Cuba Ron.** The Cuban owner of this restaurant likes to party. Come here for a late dinner and live music, from salsa to reggae to a guy who sounds frighteningly like Lou Rawls when he sings "Bésame Mucho." The service isn't great, but you'll be too busy making friends to notice. Carne asada is $7, seafood meals are $9. Ask for a stiff Cuba libre (rum and Coke). *Guerrero, at Morelos, no phone. Open daily 11 AM–late.*

Restaurant La Palapa. Housed in the largest palapa in Playa Norte, this place is very popular with beach-goers. It's not fancy, but it's convenient. Seafood is the specialty—fish costs about $6 and shrimp about $8.50. *Playa Norte, near Hidalgo, no phone. Open daily 9–6. Closed during bad weather.*

Restaurant Las Flores. This small place has whitewashed walls, an outdoor grill, and live music. If you want to ignore mom's perennial advice, plunge into their pool after taking advantage of the $8.50 all-you-can-eat lunch buffet. *Juárez 32, btw Mateos and Matamoros, tel. 987/7–05–06. Open daily 12:30–3:30.*

WORTH SEEING

HACIENDA MONDACA The mansion of reputed pirate Fermín Mondaca de Marechaja, Hacienda Mondaca is just a ruin now, and not really a mansion by our standards. After the British began their antislavery campaign in the 1860s, Mondaca moved to Isla Mujeres, where he supposedly fell in love with a local woman. She married another man and Mondaca went mad. In the local cemetery you can still see his tombstone, inscribed with the phrase, "As you are, I was. As I am, you will be." *From town, walk or take a bus going south; get off at HACIENDA MONDACA sign and walk 5 min east.*

MAYA RUINS The island's Maya ruins are just that—ruins—and visitors today see little. A small sandstone building at the southern tip of the island was once a temple to Ixchel, the Maya goddess of fertility. Female figurines, believed to be votive offerings, were found here by Hernández de Córdoba and provide the most plausible explanation of the island's name. Despite the temple's disrepair, the striking effect of the waves breaking on the steep cliffs beneath it is spectacular. *From town, follow the road as far south as possible, then walk up the dirt path. Or, take the bus to Playa Paraíso and walk 2 km.*

PESCA None of the island brochures mentions this biological research station in the less populated area of the island. It's worth visiting for a lesson in native fish, and the scientists here can tell you a lot about marine conservation. It's best to visit before 3 PM. *Take a bike out of town and make a hairpin right turn at the Hacienda Mondaca and continue north; or take the bus and ask them to drop you off at Mondaca, then walk.*

Apart from Carnaval, Isla Mujeres's most important event is the Regata del Sol al Sol, celebrated yearly in late April, when boats leave St. Petersburg, Florida, and arrive at Isla amid much partying. The event is concluded by a basketball game between Mexican and American teams, which the Mexicans always win.

AFTER DARK

Whenever something big is going down, usually on the weekends, you'll hear about it through flyers passed out along the beaches or posted at Poc-Na (*see* Where to Sleep, *above*). For the best in techno/house head for **La Peña** (Guerrero 5, tel. 987/7–03–09), a restaurant by day and a steamy (touristy) disco after 11 PM. There's no cover, and beers are under $2. Kick up the sand at **Las Palapas** (Hidalgo, at Playa Cocos, no phone), a huge palapa complex with a bar and dance floor right on the beach. Here you'll find a younger, more Mexican crowd dancing to salsa and disco. There's no cover, and drinks are two-for-one between 9 and midnight. If you just want to mellow out and listen to some live music, try **Cocos Fríos** (Hidalgo, no phone), a restaurant/bar with a pretty good menu. For live music from all over the Caribbean, check out **El Cuba Ron** (*see* Food, *above*). The **zócalo** is also a fun place hang out at night, with music, games, fried plaintain stands, and basketball under the lights.

Travelers on the island (especially the Poc-Na crew) tend to make their own parties. The most common source of weeknight fun is a fiesta on the beach—you can buy tequila and cold beer at any liquor store in town. The "green scene" remains more laid-back here than in many other parts of Mexico, and pretty much any fisherman can hook you up (no pun intended). Smoking on the beach is fairly common—still, be subtle. Skinny-dipping in the warm Caribbean waters is also a thrill, but don't kid yourself into believing your idea is original. When 3 AM rolls around and the bars and discos begin to close, starry-eyed couples trickle down to the beach to smooch, and you might have to wait out the crowd before wading back to your lonely lump of clothes. During July and August the beach can be a real slumber party at night, with inebriated visitors crashed out on the sand.

OUTDOOR ACTIVITIES

BEACHES Northwest of town is **Playa Norte**, a wide, white-sand beach. It's the traditional topless beach, but until the Europeans arrive in July and August, mammary toasting is not all that common. For the best swimming, head for the eastern corner of the beach, where the water is deeper. A plethora of water sports is available at Playa Norte, including snorkeling, water cycling, sailing, and water skiing (*see* Snorkeling, *below*). You can use the bathrooms and showers on the beach, close to Hidalgo, for $1.

The three modest beaches on the west coast of the island—**Playa Paraíso, Playa Lancheros, and Playa Indios**—don't have the fine white sand you'd expect from a Caribbean island, and Hurricane Gilbert was not kind to them. The shallow sea is rocky and full of seaweed, making it a less-than-ideal place to swim and snorkel. Playa Paraíso, in particular, is a popular harbor for tourist boats from Cancún that deliver tired guests for an expensive lunch or dinner after a day of snorkeling at El Garrafón. The beach has quite a few restaurants, a number of small stands selling souvenirs, and clean bathrooms. Someone may ask you to pay an entrance fee, but the beaches are government-owned and the fee is a scam. From town, take a bus, bicycle, or moped south down the main road about 4 kilometers.

ISLA CONTOY Isla Contoy, 45 minutes by boat north of Isla Mujeres, is a bird sanctuary where you can see brown pelicans, cormorants, frigate birds, herons, and flamingos. The island is lush and inviting, with a thin strip of white-sand beach. The quality of snorkeling depends on the weather—if it's windy, sand can make visibility close to zero. You can visit the island as part of a day trip offered by most of the travel agencies in town. **Poc-Na** (*see* Where to Sleep, *above*) arranges trips to the island on a sailboat. The day-long trips cost $20 (minimum of 10 people, $25 if fewer than 10) and include snorkeling and fishing equipment as well as food and drink. **La Isleña** (Morelos, at Juárez, tel. 987/7–05–78) arranges tours for $30 per person. Usually they require a six-person minimum, but you may be able to talk them down to four. The tours consist of a boat ride, a stop on the beach to snorkel and eat lunch, and bird-watching on the island.

SCUBA DIVING Isla Mujeres offers one of the world's most exciting and unusual diving trips. Aside from the obvious attraction of the coral reefs, divers have a chance to explore the **Cave of the Sleeping Sharks** (*see* box *above*). Diving trips to the coral reefs around the island cost between $27 and $75, depending on whether or not you need gear and how many tanks you use. If you're not certified, you must take the $25, three-hour introductory course before diving with an instructor. Carlos Gutiérrez at **Mexico Divers** on Rueda Medina near the ferry (tel. 987/7–02–74) is a good person to talk to and his prices are reasonable.

Only certified divers can visit the Cave of Sleeping Sharks. But, if you're gung-ho and loaded, you can get a PADI certificate for $350 in one week's time. **Bahía Dive Shop** (Rueda Medina, near the ferry, tel. 987/7–03–40) has all the equipment and instructors for snorkeling, diving, and fishing. What makes them different from the other dive shops is their two-person minimum, six-person maximum policy.

SNORKELING The island is fringed by coral reefs, and in many places you can just wade in and start snorkeling. Remember that coral is a living organism—walking on or just touching the coral can easily damage or kill it. **Marina Amigos del Mar,** under a small palapa on Playa Norte near Hidalgo, will rent you almost any kind of water equipment you want: snorkels, masks, water cycles, sailboats, banana boats, and water skis. If you want to snorkel close to town, the best spot is on the northern corner of the island, across from the bridge connecting the town to a small peninsula and a luxury hotel.

A few years ago the **Parque Nacional El Garrafón,** at the southern tip of the island, was a paradise for snorkelers. There's still a lot to see here, but unfortunately much of the coral has died, and many of the fish have found new homes. What remains are hundreds of day-trippers from Cancún, floating on the surface of the water like a fat, white, algal bloom. The park complex itself is geared to tourists and includes a gallery of shops, a diving center, a restaurant, a snack bar, bathrooms, showers, and lockers. The dive shop rents snorkels, masks, and fins for about $5; lockers (too small for a backpack) are $2. However, the snorkeling is better at Playa Norte. You can easily bike to El Garrafón, or take the bus to Playa Paraíso and walk the rest of the way. *Admission: $2. Open daily 8–4.*

You can take a 1½- to three-hour snorkeling trip to the huge coral reef of **Manchones.** You could also try **El Farrito Reef,** which is supposed to be the best snorkeling experience off Isla Mujeres. The trip usually includes a visit to a couple of small coral reefs as well. All agencies in town, as well as the one at El Garrafón, offer almost identical versions of this trip for $18 per person. Poc-Na (*see* Where to Sleep, *above*) offers a particularly good trip; try asking them for a discount. All trips should include a loan of snorkeling gear. If you want to rent snorkeling gear and hit the beach by yourself, La Isleña, on Morelos at Juárez (*see* Isla Contoy, *above*), rents the snorkel, mask, and fins for $4 per day.

Playa del Carmen

Don't kid yourself into believing that Playa del Carmen is a quaint little seaside fishing village— tourism is the main industry here. Increasingly, herds of tourists are lured by the empty white-sand beaches stretching for miles in each direction. Nonetheless, it's affordable, with many hotels and restaurants geared toward the budget travelers that come here from all corners of the world. Although this may not be the best place to practice your Spanish, you'll have the opportunity to improve your French, German, and Italian. The warm, clear waters are all you've dreamt about and are free of the seaweed common to other Caribbean resorts. And if cavorting on the beautiful beaches has lost its thrill, the Maya ruins of Tulum and Cobá are both an easy day trip away.

The word from the beach is that Playa del Carmen may soon be a "little Cancún." The developers are building like mad, and in the off-season the noise of hammers drowns out the sounds of the birds. Depending on when you go, you'll find two different types of visitors here. The Playa of July, August, and December through April is a destination for package tourists. Hotel prices skyrocket, and even the roach motels are full. The beaches are packed and gasoline from the boats pollutes the water in the harbor. The rest of the year, Playa is relatively peaceful, with a group of hip, young travelers taking advantage of the empty hotels offering great deals.

BASICS

CASAS DE CAMBIO The **money-exchange center** at 5a Avenida and Juárez offers lousy rates, but it's open Monday–Saturday 8–8. **Banco del Atlántico** (Juárez, 1 block from bus station) changes cash and traveler's checks weekdays 8–noon. **Bancomer** (Juárez, 4 blocks from 5a Av.) offers the same services and keeps the same hours.

LAUNDRY **Maya Laundry** washes clothes for $2 per kilo and underwear and socks for 15¢ each. *Calle 2, at 5a Av., tel. 987/2–12–11, ext. 165. Open Mon.–Sat. 8–8.*

MEDICAL AID The **clinic** (tel. 987/3–03–14) on Avenida Juárez, three blocks up from 5a Avenida, is open 24 hours.

Farmacia Yoli's, on 5a Avenida between Calles 4 and 6, is open daily 8:30–8.

PHONES AND MAIL The **post office** (Juárez, 2 blocks from bus station) is open weekdays 8–7, weekends 9–1. They will hold mail sent to you at the following address for up to 10 days: Lista de Correos, Playa del Carmen, Quintana Roo, CP 77710, México. Public card-operated **phones** are located near the post office on Juárez and across from the bus station on 5a Avenida and Juárez. The **telephone caseta** (Juárez, about 1 block from bus station, tel. 987/2–12–11) is supposed to be open Monday–Saturday 7–2 and 3–9, but don't count on it.

COMING AND GOING

BY BUS Playa del Carmen has two adjacent bus stations. **Autotransportes del Caribe** (Juárez, at 10a Av.) offers frequent bus and minibus service to Cancún; the 62-kilometer ride takes about 45 minutes and costs $2.50. First- and second-class buses serve Chetumal five times daily ($10, 4 ½ hrs). Several buses also leave daily for Mérida via Ticul ($13.50, 5 hrs). **ADO**, the large bus station on the corner of 5a Avenida and Juárez, also operates regular first- and second-class buses on the Cancún–Valladolid–Chichén Itzá–Mérida route, and on the Tulum–Cobá–Valladolid route. The one-hour ride to Tulum costs about $2.

BY FERRY The second-class ferry to Cozumel departs 11 times daily ($5 one way, $8.50 round trip, 45 min). If you negotiate, you can get a ticket for the earliest ferry (5 AM) for $3.50. The first-class ferry departs 13 times daily for Cozumel ($7 one way, 20 min; $10 round trip). The earliest trip is at 5:30 AM and you may be able to shave off some money off the price if you haggle. The ferry leaves from the pier just in front of Plaza Marina Playacar.

GETTING AROUND

The avenues run parallel to the beach and are numbered in multiples of 5. Quinta (5a) Avenida, one block from the beach, is the malecón (pedestrian walkway) and the social center of town. The main street is Avenida Juárez, also known as Avenida Principal, which runs perpendicular to the beach. Calles are numbered in multiples of 2 and are also perpendicular to the beach.

WHERE TO SLEEP

Playa del Carmen is affordable for the budget traveler during the off-season. But in July, August, and December, prices can really soar, depending on how crowded it is. Usually prices go up $5–$10 more than the prices listed here. Most budget hotels are on 5a Avenida close to the beach, or on Juárez, near the bus station.

➤ UNDER $15 • **La Ruina.** This is the cheapest and by far the most fun place to stay in Playa, as long as you don't mind a little grit in your backpack. Right on the beach, it's more like an international hippie commune than a hotel. You'll hook up with Playa's semi-permanent subculture here, and it's a good place to find out where the parties are. Hang your hammock in a huge, open-air palapa/dormitory for $5 and stash your stuff in a sandy locker, or rent a cabaña for $12 for two or three people. You can also pitch a tent in the grass for $5. The shared bathrooms are passable. A little secret: The women's shower furthest to the east usually has hot water, and no one will hassle guys if they use it. *Calle 2, on beach, no phone. From bus station, 1 block left on 5a Av. and take first right. 21 huts, 32 palapa spaces. Laundry, luggage storage.*

➤ UNDER $20 • **Casa Tucán.** In the off-season, the manager charges the ridiculously low price of $17 for a single or double. The hotel is a quiet, clean building with dark wood beams and whitewashed walls. The whole place is surrounded by lush trees and has a rooftop with a dining room and lounge chairs. Rooms have fans, excellent bathrooms, and nice wall hangings. *Calle 4, btw 10a and 15a Avs., tel. 987/3–02–83. 10 rooms, all with bath. Laundry, wheelchair access.*

Posada Lily. This blue motel-like place is near the bus station—convenient if you arrive in town late. Rooms are fairly clean and have hot water. Ask for one in the back, since they're quieter, and some have balconies. Singles are $12, doubles $13.50, and triples $17. *Juárez, tel. 987/91–9–87. 24 rooms, all with bath.*

Posada Marinelly. People and ants *can* live together in harmony. The family that owns the place is friendly, and has a watchful German shepherd and kittens carrying cute little fleas. The small, vine-encircled courtyard is a nice place to sit and relax. Rooms have cement bed frames, but comfortable mattresses, good fans, and hot water. Ask for a room upstairs. Singles are $13.50, doubles $15. *Juárez, at 10a Av., tel. 987/3–01–40. Next to Hotel Playa del Carmen. 10 rooms, all with bath. Wheelchair access.*

Hotel Posada Sian-Ka'an. Large iguanas crawl around this place, supposedly to entertain guests. The clean rooms with shared bath cost $13.50 for a double. Singles with private bath run $20, doubles $22.50. Two rooms have a kitchen, and the upper-floor deck overlooks the sea. *5a Avenida, tel. 987/3–02–03. 1 block north of bus station. 17 rooms. Reservations advised July and Dec.*

➤ UNDER $25 • **Banana Cabañas.** The cabanas here consist of simple, bare rooms with beds, mosquito nets, and small decks where you can read, write, or drink the night away. The jungle-like decor makes them interesting, but the shared bathrooms could be cleaner. Doubles are $20, $22 for two beds and hammock hooks, and $23.50 with private bath. *5a Av., 3½ blocks from Juárez, no phone. 15 cabañas. Laundry, luggage storage, wheelchair access.*

Hotel Playa del Carmen. About three blocks from the beach, this place resembles a motel, with clean rooms facing a small, central patio. Light sleepers beware—it can get noisy here. Singles are $17, doubles $20. *Juárez, at 10a Avenida, 1½ blocks from bus station, tel. 987/3–02–92. 17 rooms, all with bath. Laundry, luggage storage, wheelchair access.*

➤ HOSTEL • **Villa Deportiva Juvenil Playa del Carmen.** This hostel is way out in the boonies, about a kilometer from any semblance of civilization and (more importantly) far from the beach. If you stay here, be prepared for long treks into town. You can get a bunk in a crowded dormitory room and a locker without a lock for $5. Rooms are strictly segregated by sex. The bathrooms are clean enough but lack toilet paper, hot water, and shower walls. If dorm life doesn't appeal to you, you can get a bare double room with private bath for $15, but at these rates you might as well get something closer to the beach. An $8 deposit is required of all guests. Guests receive a 10% discount with a Hostelling International card. *Calle 8, at 35a Av., no phone. From bus station, 4 blocks north on 5a Av., left until you see sign. 198 beds. Laundry, luggage storage, wheelchair access.*

➤ CAMPING • You can pitch your tent in the yard of La Ruina (*see above*) and have access to their facilities for $5 per tent. Otherwise, pick a spot and crash on the beach. To the northeast of town you'll have a little more privacy, but with that comes greater risk of theft. You might try the beach right in front of La Ruina if you're inconspicuous.

FOOD

An array of restaurants and loncherías makes it easy to eat cheaply in Playa del Carmen. **El Huerto de Chapo** (5a Av., btw Calles 4 and 6) sells fruits and vegetables daily 7:30–1 and 5–9:30. Other supermarkets and stores on 5a Avenida cater to most needs. The liquor store in town closes at 9 or 10 and doesn't open on Sunday, so make sure to buy what you want early. Most restaurants are on 5a Avenida, with a few on Juárez and 10a Avenida. Restaurants on the zócalo are expensive and should be avoided.

➤ UNDER $5 • **Media Luna.** Playa del Carmen's vegetarian restaurant serves tofu with vegetables for $3.50, and soyburgers with cheese for $2. Fettuccine with shrimp and salsa is about $5. *5a Av., 4 ½ blocks from Juárez, no phone. Open daily 7:30–3 and 6–10.*

Nuestra Señora del Carmen. This is one of the least expensive good restaurants on the malecón, though the food is a bit greasy. Prices for chicken and meat dishes average $4. *5a Av., ½ block from bus station. No phone.*

Pollo Caribe. This chicken-only joint is where local people gather at lunch time to stuff themselves. The food is cheap, but the options are limited. Chicken with rice, salad, tortillas, and salsa will run you $3, or $6 if you want a whole chicken. Beers are $1. *10a Av., no phone. Btw Calle 2 and Juárez, near bus station. Open daily 10–9.*

Sabor. This restaurant, just two blocks from Juárez, serves good scrambled eggs ($2.50), yogurt and fruit smoothies ($2.50), and chaya ($1). It's a great place to hang out. They also have good cakes and pastries. *5a Av., no phone. Open daily 8 AM–10 PM.*

➤ UNDER $10 • **Restaurant Bar El Chine.** Under this great palapa, a live band plays on Friday, Saturday, and Sunday nights. Just when you're almost full of the best fresh chips, salsa, and guacamole, and beginning to wonder if you should have even ordered at all, a huge scrumptious meal arrives. Any of the fish dishes here ($4.50) are good, and the ceviche is amazing. There's also a decent breakfast menu. *Calle 4 Norte, btw 10a and 15a Avs., no phone. Open daily 7:30 AM–11 PM.*

Restaurant Bar Tarraya. A popular watering hole for locals during low season, this restaurant serves typical seafood dishes for around $5 and chicken for $3. Try ceviche ($7) if you haven't yet. There's a huge liquor selection. *Playa 2 Norte, no phone. On the beach across from La Ruina. Open daily noon–9.*

OUTDOOR ACTIVITIES

Playa del Carmen is a beach town and little else. If you don't like swimming and sand, keep on going. The beaches here are spectacular—certainly better than Cozumel's. The white sand shaded by palms is largely free of seaweed, and the water is liquid crystal. The best section of beach in town is near La Ruina hotel, although litter and the lack of trees may turn some people off. If you walk south along the beach a couple of kilometers you'll find yourself on deserted (but narrow) beaches backed by thick vegetation. The beaches more than 1 kilometer north of Playa are the least populated. The water is cleaner in the series of protected lagoons, and you'll see few people besides the occasional fisherman.

El Albatraz, a dive shop on the beach near La Ruina hotel, rents snorkeling and windsurfing equipment for about $5. To snorkel off the beach, head around the point north of the Blue Parrot Inn to a small coral reef. It's also possible to organize snorkeling, diving, and fishing trips on charter boats. A fishing trip should cost about $120 for four people, and snorkeling is $100 for six people, including lunch and drinks. There are several other dive shops along the beach and 5a Avenida. Scuba diving tours go to a number of reefs lying just off the shore. **Playacar Divers** (in front of the Plaza Marina Playacar, just south of the ferry dock, tel. 987/3–04–49) and **Yax Ha Dive Shop** (on the beach, btw Calles 10 and 12, no phone) offer comparable prices and a professional dive staff. A two-tank dive is $55, and a snorkeling trip to the shallower reefs costs $25 per person, with a minimum of two people.

AFTER DARK

During tourist season the bars along the beach are open late. But the only place that is consistently happening is the **Blue Parrot** (on the beach, 6 blocks north of Juárez). The clientele at this hotel bar are mostly travelers, who get shnockered while sitting on stools that hang by ropes from the ceiling and listening to classic rock.

Near Playa del Carmen

PUNTA BETE Punta Bete, at least the southern end of it, is idyllic—kilometers of pristine white sand, coconut palms, and gentle waves curling in from the sea. The only thing missing is naked dancers singing "Bali Hai." If you can't arrange that, try the snorkeling, which is excellent just 20 or 40 meters offshore. Schools of fantastically-colored fish, octopus, and stingrays are within wading distance. Fishing and snorkeling trips can be arranged at the cabanas at the northern end of the beach for about $20 per person all day, and you can rent snorkeling gear from the local dive shop. Not surprisingly, hotels are beginning to appear on the 4-kilometer stretch of beach, and none of them is particularly cheap. But you can still hang your hammock under a palapa roof for about $5, or rent a cabana big enough for three people for $20. Hammock sleeping is recommended, but it can get chilly at night here, so bundle up. Tent camping is $3 per person and includes use of clean showers. Fix a price and pay in advance, so you won't be surprised by overnight rate changes. The elderly people who run the palapa restaurants are hard of hearing, and the food is mediocre, but they're your only option. If you've got the energy, the 12-kilometer walk from Playa del Carmen to Punta Bete takes you along a gorgeous stretch of beach. The walk takes about an hour and a half, so start early in the morning, before the sun gets too high. You can lock your things up at La Ruina if you're just going for the day. If you can't face the trek, take a bus along the main highway, get off at the sign for Punta Bete, and walk 4 kilometers down the dirt road.

XCARET No more than 10 kilometers south of Playa lies Xcaret, where the Maya used to come for bathing rituals before setting sail for Cozumel. Today, the site is about as authentically Maya as any ride in Disneyland. The main attraction is an underground river, which you can float down with scores of screaming kids. Snorkeling equipment rental is $9. Admission to the park and underground caves is (gasp) $18, but save your money. Take a bus from anywhere along the main road and ask to be let off at Xcaret; there's a free "folk bus" shuttle from the crossroads to the park entrance. *Open Oct.–Mar., daily 8–5.*

PAAMUL About 15 kilometers south of Xcaret is Paamul, famous as the nesting site of the giant turtle, a behemoth that weighs upward of 200 pounds. Now an endangered species, the turtles emerge from the ocean on June and July nights to lay as many as 200 eggs each. The turtles may like the beach, but you probably won't—Paamul's beach doesn't have the white sandy expanses found in tourist brochures. It's a great spot for beachcombing, though, since shells and dead coral wash ashore in abundance. Snorkeling over the reef, about 375 meters offshore, is excellent. Get on any bus going to Tulum and ask to be dropped off at Paamul.

Cozumel

If you want to dive, come to Cozumel—it's as simple as that. Even jaded Jacques Cousteau raved about the coral reefs that ring this island 19 kilometers from Playa del Carmen. While Cozumel is not the snorkling paradise it once was (tourism has killed a lot of the coral), it's still the best site on the Yucatán Peninsula. Most famous of all the reefs is **Palancar Reef,** where underwater visibility extends more than 67 meters; divers can experience the whole gamut of underwater excitement at other reefs, too, including plunging walls, passages, caves, and even a phony airplane wreck left behind by a film crew. For those who don't want to go through the expense and trouble of hiring a boat, the snorkeling and diving off the beach are also good. However, most people come to Cozumel prepared to drop a bundle on diving and accommodations, so it's not exactly budget paradise. Consider staying in Playa del Carmen and taking the ferry to Cozumel, especially if you're more a beach bum than a dive enthusiast.

San Miguel de Cozumel, the small town on the western coast of the island, is geared to cruise-ship passengers: Expensive shops and tourist restaurants abound. If you walk a few blocks inland you'll find the Mexican part of the city, where the locals live. Although it's not so picturesque, it has less of the artificial gloss of the tourist sections of town.

During Mayan times Cozumel was a sacred island covered with temples and shrines to Ixchel, the goddess of fertility. Maya peoples from all over what is now Central America and southern Mexico made pilgrimages here to pray and leave votive offerings. Unfortunately, many of the temples were destroyed by Cortés in 1519, and the U.S. military destroyed others while constructing an airstrip during World War II. If you're not going to some of the major archaeological sites on the mainland, it's worth heading to Cozumel's interior for a look at the ruins. Otherwise, forget it.

BASICS

AMERICAN EXPRESS The AmEx representative here is **Fiesta Cozumel.** They cash and issue traveler's checks, but do not give cash advances. *Calle 11 Sur, at Coldwell, tel. 987/2–09–74. Follow Rafael Melgar south to Calle 11, take a left, and walk 6½ blocks. Open weekdays 8–1 and 4–8.*

CASAS DE CAMBIO Most banks are in downtown San Miguel. You can get cash with a Visa card from **Bancomer** (5a Av. Sur 51, at Calle 1 Sur, tel. 987/2–05–50). **Banco del Atlántico** (Calle 1 Sur 11, tel. 987/2–01–42), at the southern corner of the zócalo, has ATM machines that accept MasterCard and Cirrus cards. You can change cash or traveler's checks at either bank weekdays 10–1:30. American dollars are accepted all over the island.

CONSULATES Cozumel has no consulates, but citizens of all nations can get help from **Bryan Wilson** (Calle 13 Sur, at 15a Av. Sur, tel. 987/2–06–54), who works as an unofficial ombudsman and interpreter. On call 24 hours a day, he speaks perfect Spanish, is well acquainted with Mexican law, and can help you out of sticky situations. His services are free unless they result in considerable savings for you, in which case he'll take a commission.

EMERGENCIES Police (tel. 987/2–00–92) and ambulance (tel. 987/2–06–39).

LAUNDRY Margarita Laundromat charges $2.50 per load to wash and $2 per 10 minutes of drying. They also sell detergent. *20a Av. Sur, at Calle 3 Sur, tel. 987/2–28–65. Open Mon.–Sat. 7 AM–9 PM, Sun. 9–5.*

MEDICAL AID Round the clock emergency service is available at the **Centro de Especialidades Médicas.** *20a Av. Norte, at Calle 8 Norte, tel. 987/2–14–19 or 987/2–29–19.*

Farmacia Kiosco (zócalo, tel. 987/2–24–85) is open daily 9 AM–10 PM.

PHONES AND MAIL The **post office** (Rafael Melgar, at Calle 7 Sur, tel. 987/2–01–06) is open weekdays 8–8, Saturday 9–5, and Sunday 9–1. They will hold mail sent to you at the following address for up to 10 days: Lista de Correos, Cozumel, Quintana Roo, CP 77600, Méx-

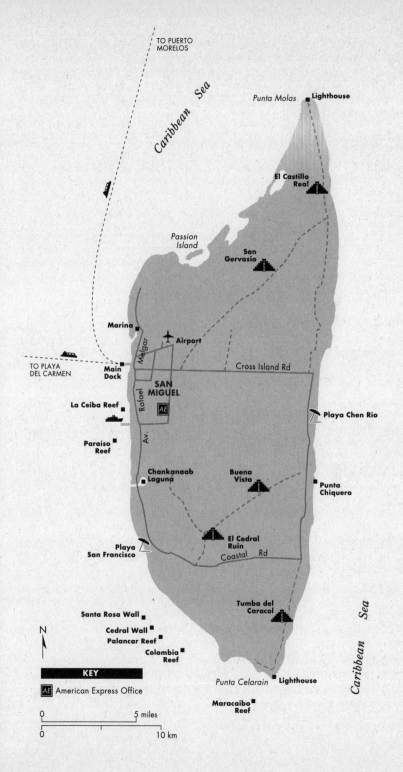

Cozumel

TO PUERTO
MORELOS

Caribbean Sea

Punta Molas • Lighthouse

El Castillo
Real

*Passion
Island*

San
Gervasio

Marina

✈ Airport

Malgar

TO PLAYA
DEL CARMEN

Main
Dock

Cross Island Rd

**SAN
MIGUEL**

Rafael

AE

La Ceiba Reef

Playa Chen Rio

Av.

Paraiso
Reef

Chankanaab
Laguna

Buena
Vista

Punta
Chiquero

El Cedral
Ruin

Playa
San Francisco

Coastal Rd

Tumba del
Caracol

Santa Rosa Wall

N
↑

Cedral Wall
Palancar Reef

Colombia
Reef

KEY

Punta Celarain • Lighthouse

Caribbean Sea

AE American Express Office

Maracaibo
Reef

0   5 miles
0   10 km

443

ico. **Computel** (Calle 1 Sur 165, btw 5a and 10a Avs., tel. 987/2–40–87, fax 987/2–41–54) allows you to make local and long-distance calls. It's open daily 7 AM–10 PM.

VISITOR INFORMATION The **tourist office** has a very friendly though somewhat uninformed staff. The best reason to come here is to kick back with one of their many newspapers and enjoy the air-conditioning. *Rafael Melgar, at Calle 11 Sur, tel. 987/2–43–79. Open weekdays 8–1 and 4–7.*

COMING AND GOING

BY FERRY Ferries between Cozumel and the mainland leave from **Playa del Carmen,** with about 10 departures in each direction daily (for prices, *see* Coming and Going, in Playa del Carmen, *above*).

BY PLANE Cozumel has a small international airport, with flights to and from the States on **American** and **Continental**. **Mexicana** (tel. 987/2–02–63), **Aero Cozumel** (tel. 987/2–09–28 or 2–08–77), and **Aerocaribe** (tel. 987/2–09–28) offer service to cities all over Mexico, including Cancún, Mérida, and Mexico City. From Playa del Carmen, you can fly to Cozumel on **Aero Saab** for $17—ask at the information booth on Playa del Carmen's zócalo. Collective taxis take passengers the 2 kilometers into town from the airport for about $2 each. A taxi to the airport costs about $7.50.

GETTING AROUND

Cozumel is the largest of Mexico's islands, 53 kilometers long and 14 kilometers wide. It's easy to get around the town of San Miguel on foot, since the streets are laid out in a grid, and run either parallel or perpendicular to the coast. Apart from the main avenues, all streets have numerical designations. The avenue running along the *malecón* (seawall) is Rafael Melgar; parallel avenues are numbered in multiples of five (5a Avenida is followed by 10a Avenida and 15a Avenida). Avenida Benito Juárez, the main drag, runs directly inland from the ferry dock and cuts the town in two. Streets and avenues north of Avenida Juárez receive the appellation Norte; those to the south, Sur. To further confuse the situation, streets north of Avenida Juárez have even numbers, and those to the south have odd numbers. You'll need transport to reach other parts of the island.

The western coastline is the most developed, with resort hotels spreading north and south from San Miguel. This is the leeward side of the island, where the water is calm. The water off the eastern and northern coasts is much rougher and the gorgeous coastline almost deserted. A road circles the island, making it easy to explore, and several other roads and trails cut through the flat jungle.

BY SCOOTER The most popular way to see the island is by scooter—rental agencies abound. You should be able to get one for $17 for the whole day, although bargaining is not out of the question.

BY BIKE The island is a bit large to explore fully on a bicycle. If you plan on riding, make sure you take enough water. Taxis constantly circle the island, so bring enough money to take one back if you get stranded. **Rentadora Águila** (Rafael Melgar, btw Calles 3 and 5 Sur, tel. 987/2–07–29) rents bikes for $5 a day. They're open Monday through Saturday 8–8, Sunday 8–7.

BY BUS Buses run around the perimeter of the city every day. They are there mainly to take locals to the residential areas, and they do not go beyond the urban area.

WHERE TO SLEEP

After Cancún, Cozumel is the most expensive place on the peninsula. Budget travelers should choose between camping and staying in a hotel in San Miguel, most of which are within a few blocks of the central plaza. If you plan to camp out, get permission in the morning at the Palacio Municipal or the Sector Naval. Both are on Rafael Melgar near Calle 11 Sur. Playa del Sol and Playa Casita, both just south of town (walking distance) are fine campsites. Better, though, are the secluded places on the southern and eastern portions of the island. Try the 4-kilometer stretch of dirt road that follows the beach to the Punta Celarain. Also, several spots along the paved road parallel to the eastern shore are sequestered by dunes or scrub. Authorities will warn you to be careful of thieves because the beaches are not patrolled, but there have been few incidents recently.

➢ UNDER $20 • **Hotel Flores.** Right downtown, Hotel Flores offers large, clean rooms. Ask for Room 103 or 107; they have gorgeous bathrooms. Singles cost $15, doubles $17 ($20 with air-conditioning), and triples $18.50. The hotel also rents bicycles ($3 a day) and scooters ($20 a day). *Rosado Salas, btw Rafael Melgar and 5a Av., tel. 987/2–14–29. 30 rooms, all with bath. Luggage storage.*

Hotel Pepita. The friendly owner serves complimentary coffee and cookies in the morning in a courtyard filled with big cages of scruffy-looking cardinals. The rooms are small but sunny and quiet, with refrigerators and adequate bathrooms. Doubles are $16.50. *15a Av. sur, at Calle 1 Sur, 3 blocks from main pier, tel. 987/2–00–98. 30 rooms with bath. Wheelchair access.*

Hotel Posada Edén. This place has about as much character as Cheez Whiz, but these practical rooms are well kept and the cheapest in town. You can also rent scooters here or hang out with the housecats and shoot pool. Doubles are $13.50, plus $3.50 for air-conditioning or extra people. *Calle 2 Norte 12, btw 5a and 10a Avs. Norte, tel. 987/2–11–66. 14 rooms, all with bath. Luggage storage. MC, V.*

Posada del Zorro. This place has unpretentious rooms with faded, drooping posters on the walls and some furniture. The bathrooms could stand a cleaning, but the place is okay for the price. Singles start at $14 ($17 with air-conditioning). Doubles are $17 and $20, triples $20 and $23. *Juárez 30, at Coldwell, 8 blocks east of ferry dock, tel. 987/2–07–90. 8 rooms, all with bath. Luggage storage.*

➢ UNDER $25 • **Hotel Kary.** After trudging the seven blocks from the ferry dock, you'll be overjoyed to see these impeccable rooms. The gorgeous pool and patio will make you feel pampered, especially after a couple of margaritas under the poolside palapa. Singles and doubles are about $22 ($25 with air-conditioning). Suites with kitchenettes are more expensive. *25a Av. Sur, at Rosado Salas, tel. 987/2–20–11. From ferry dock, 2 blocks south (right) and 5 blocks east. 17 rooms and 2 suites, all with bath. Luggage storage. MC, V.*

Hotel Cozumel Inn. These small rooms have clean bathrooms and occasionally hot water. Check to make sure your ceiling fan works before you move in. Some of the rooms have tiny balconies, and there's a nice patio and a small pool overseen by a giant ceramic frog. Singles are $17, doubles $22 ($27 with air-conditioning). *Calle 4 Nte. 3, at Rafael Melgar, tel. 987/2–03–14. 30 rooms, all with bath. Luggage storage.*

➢ UNDER $30 • **Hotel Marycarmen.** The well-kept rooms at this downtown hotel have wood furniture, air-conditioning, and great bathrooms. A small atrium is ideal for sunbathing. Singles and doubles cost $25, triples $30. *5a Av. Sur 4, btw Calle 1 Sur and Rosado Salas, tel. 987/2–05–81. From ferry dock, 1 block inland and 1½ blocks to the right. 27 rooms, all with bath. Luggage storage, wheelchair access. MC, V.*

FOOD

If you're willing to walk a little, you can eat quite cheaply in Cozumel. The **mercado** (Rosado Salas, at 25a Avenida) sells fresh fruits and vegetables daily 7–5. Several **loncherías** in the market also offer breakfast deals and main dishes for a mere $3.

➢ UNDER $5 • **Casa Denis.** This place has an eclectic mix of food. Wander through five different eating areas and choose from the huge menus. They've got everything from cheeseburgers and fries ($2) to fruit salad with yogurt and granola ($2). Carnivores can indulge in mighty steak lunches for $3.50. *Calle 1 Sur, btw 5a Av. and 1a Av., tel. 987/2–00–67. ½ block east of zócalo. Open Mon.–Sat. 7 AM–11 PM.*

Lonchería Rogers. The amiable owners of this food stand sell salbutes and tacos for 65¢, tortas for $2, and milkshakes and orange juice for about $2. Everything is fresh, and the food is great. No alcohol is served. *Rosado Salas, ½ block west of market. Open Mon.–Sat. 8–2 and 6–10.*

Restaurant Toñita. You shouldn't have any problem with flies on your food here—strategically placed fans protrude from the walls and ceiling. This simple, clean restaurant serves cheap food from a menu that changes daily. Great meals including soup, a meat dish, veggies, rice, and tortillas will run you about $4. Bring your own beer. *Rosado Salas, btw 10a and 15a Avs., 2½ blocks east of zócalo, tel. 987/2–04–01. Open Mon.–Sat. 8–6.*

➢ UNDER $10 • **La Casa del Waffle.** A bunch of surfers got together and formed this waffle joint to finance their aquatic habits. They've got waffles rancheros, waffles benedict (both $5), an obscenely sweet waffle special with fruit, syrup, and whipped cream ($5.50), and just plain waffles for $3.50. The waffles aren't actually the best you'll ever have, but the draw here is the bottomless coffee cup policy. *Juárez, btw Calles 20 and 25, no phone. Open daily 8–1 and 6–9.*

Costa Brava. A roof of shellacked wood and a huge tree growing out of a green astroturf carpet give this place an outdoorsy feel—sort of. It's worth the walk out of town to free yourself from the grease of the loncherías. Excellent fillets of tuna are $6.50, chicken fajitas $5. Ceviche with tender conch morsels goes for $5.50. Try the guacamole, too. *Rafael Melgar, across from Sector Naval, no phone. Open daily 6:30 AM–11:30 PM.*

DESSERT/COFFEEHOUSE **Cafe Caribe.** A welcome relief for travelers in a serious Nescafé rut, this place has more character than the sports bars and Texas-style grills that prevail in San Miguel. It's a European coffee house where quiet jazz and classical music plays. Enjoy a cappuccino ($2) and a bran muffin ($2) or a homemade pastry ($3.50), or stock up on coffee beans from southern Veracruz. *10a Av. Sur, btw Rosado Salas and Calle 3 Sur, tel. 987/2–36–21. Open Mon.–Sat. 8–1 and 6–9:30.*

WORTH SEEING The eastern coast of Cozumel is well worth exploring: It's still wild, despite the paved road that runs along the shoreline. The rocky coast is beautiful, and many areas are deserted. You can swim in some places, especially **Punta Chiquero, Chen Río,** and the beach at the **Punta Morena Hotel.** At other points, however, the strong undertow makes it dangerous to swim. A lighthouse sits on Punta Celarain at the southern tip of the island. At the end of a 4-kilometer dirt road, the lighthouse looks out over pounding surf that hurls spray high over the rocks. You can get a great view of the island from the top of the lighthouse. If you clamber over the sand dunes, you'll find some great empty beaches where you can swim nude without hassle. The ruins at **El Cedral, Buena Vista,** and **Tumba El Caracol** are easy to get to, but not really worth the effort, consisting mostly of sad piles of rubble.

➢ EL CASTILLO REAL AND SAN GERVASIO • The most important of the island's ruins, El Castillo Real is poorly preserved, but it's large and hard to miss. The ruin is on the northeast side of the island and is very hard to get to without a four-wheel drive. You can make it on a scooter, but be prepared for a long ride. Take the eastern road about 17 kilometers past the point where it meets the cross-island road; a dirt track leads to the ruins. On your way back from El Castillo you can stop to see the equally uninspiring ruins of San Gervasio, in the middle of Cozumel's jungle. To get here, go south on the eastern road and take the trail inland that originates at Playa Bonita. *Admission: $3.50, free Sun. and holidays.*

➢ MUSEO DE LA ISLA DE COZUMEL • The museum on Rafael Melgar between Calles 4 and 6 Norte has a floor devoted to natural history, geology, and biology, and a second floor with displays covering the island's history. It includes a lot of artifacts found on the island, including an excellent stone carving of the island's matron goddess, Ixchel. You may find them more interesting than visiting the ruins themselves. Another plus: the building is air-conditioned and the café on the second floor overlooks the harbor. *Admission: $3, free Sun. Open daily 10–6.*

OUTDOOR ACTIVITIES

Come to Cozumel for the underwater sights and beaches, and leave the cultural stuff for another time and place. Although you can see some Maya ruins here, the business at hand is exploring the island's magnificent coral reefs. If you don't dive or snorkel, consider taking a glass-bottom boat to see the biodiversity in the watery depths below. Boats leave the San Miguel docks every couple of hours from morning until early afternoon, and trips cost around $20.

SNORKELING SITES Snorkeling is a cheap and relatively painless way to explore Cozumel's sea life. Particularly good is snorkeling off the beach on the western coast, especially in the area between Hotel Sol Caribe and Playa Maya. Equipment rental costs about $5 at any of the dive shops in town; a snorkeling trip to the shallow reefs is about $15. **Bel Mar Aquatics** (Hotel La Ceiba, 1 km south of ferry dock on Rafael Melgar, tel. 987/2–16–65), **Blue Bubble Divers** (5a Av. Sur and Calle 3 Sur, tel. 987/2–18–65), and **Diving Adventures** (Calle 5 Sur, at Melgar, tel. 987/2–30–09) all offer snorkeling trips.

➤ LAGUNA CHANKANAB • The most popular snorkeling spot in Cozumel is off Laguna Chankanab, a national park 9 kilometers south of San Miguel. At the center of the park is a lagoon separated from the beach and fed by an underwater cave. A large botanical garden with a replica of Maya housing surrounds the lagoon. It's no longer possible to swim in the lagoon (the mass of paddling tourists was slowly killing it, so swimming is now prohibited), but snorkeling in the clear waters of the adjacent bay is spectacular, as is diving on the offshore reef. Underwater you can see interesting coral heads, myriad tropical fish, and a large statue of Christ, sunk for the entertainment of divers. Chankanab is, unfortunately, a little too crowded: Head elsewhere if you want to snorkel on your own. Four dive shops on the premises rent snorkeling and diving equipment. *To get to Chankanab, take a taxi ($5) or rent a scooter or bike. Admission: $4. Open daily 9–5:30.*

➤ LA CEIBA REEF • La Ceiba Reef, in front of La Ceiba Hotel, is another good place to snorkel or dive. A 120-meter trail has been marked out on the reef, starting at a fake airplane wreck (it was sunk during the filming of a movie) and continuing past several interesting coral formations. *4 km south of San Miguel; walk or take a scooter or taxi ($5). Admission free.*

DIVE SITES Diving is the raison d'être of tourism in Cozumel. Dozens of dive shops offer instruction, as well as a wide range of boat trips to shallow and deep reefs; anybody, from beginner to expert, can find a suitable dive. The water is among the clearest in the world, and the coral and marine life is abundant, to say the least. Some of the main reefs are discussed below, but it's impossible to include them all. Beginners hone their skills over shallow **Yocab**

Coral Reefs

If diving is your thing, the Yucatán offers some of the most beautiful reefs in the world, but some of these areas have paid a high price for their popularity. Coral reefs are the undersea equivalent of rain forests: They're one of the most complex ecosystems on earth. Like rain forests, they're severely threatened and underprotected. Once damaged, coral reefs repair themselves slowly, growing at a rate of just one centimeter every 10 years. They're endangered by divers, boat anchors, overfishing, severe storms and hurricanes, and pollution. The following are a few tips for environmentally aware travelers: When diving in reef areas, do not break off a piece of coral for a keepsake of your trip to Mexico—it may be beautiful, but it is also home to thousands of species of tropical fish, plants, and crustacea and is itself a living organism.

Coral is often used to create souvenirs and jewelry. Do not purchase these items. Like the trade in elephant ivory and tortoise shells, each purchase you make supports exploitation and is detrimental to the coral's survival. If you're mooring a boat, be careful where you drop anchor—a 30-pound weight can do a lot of damage.

Reef, close to shore and just south of Laguna Chankanab. Expert divers will want to head for the more challenging (and thrilling) reefs, such as **Maracaibo, San Juan, Santa Rosa Wall,** and **Colombia.** You must be certified to rent diving gear and take diving trips. At the more reputable agencies, the staff will test your diving ability before letting you attempt advanced dives. Good agencies are more expensive, but they're safer. **Aqua Safari** (Rafael Melgar 429, btw Calles 5 and 7 Sur, tel. 987/2–01–01) **Cozumel Equalizers** (Rosado Salas 72, at 5a Av. Sur, tel. 987/2–35–11), and **Dive Paradise** (Rafael Melgar 601, tel. 987/2–10–07) are among the most reputable. Four-day certification courses cost about $300. Two-tank dive trips cost about $50 (usually with a six-diver minimum), and night dives are $30.

➢ PALANCAR REEF • The most famous of Cozumel's reefs, Palancar lies about 1½ kilometers offshore. The reef stretches intermittently for about 5 kilometers and offers divers a range of underwater experiences. Best known of the formations is **Horseshoe,** a collection of coral heads that form a horseshoe curve right at the drop off. A 4½-meter bronze statue of Christ, intentionally sunk here in 1985, is a startling sight amid the reef life. The visibility—about 85 meters in places—is extraordinary.

➢ PARAISO REEF • The northern part of Paraíso is accessible from the beach. The reef lies 12–22 meters deep and has excellent star and brain coral formations. The southern part is farther offshore, but it's worth taking a boat out to see the extensive marine life. *Just north of the Stouffer Presidente Hotel, near San Miguel.*

HORSEBACK RIDING This is a great way to see the jungle and some of the inland ruins. A handful of stables on the island offer tours on horseback. The best package can be arranged at the **Acuario Restaurant,** south on Rafael Melgar next to the Sector Naval, an easy walk from town. Go in person or contact Kelly at 987/2–15–37. The four-hour, $18 tour includes transportation, a bilingual guide, and soft drinks or beer.

Tulum

The setting of the ancient Maya city of Tulum is breathtaking. A backdrop of talcum-powder beaches, rocky cliffs, and clear Caribbean waters gives the crumbling gray ruins a unique aura. Tourists generally come here on organized day trips from Cancún to admire the ruins, take a few pictures, buy some souvenirs, and get back to their air-conditioned hotel rooms. Budget travelers, on the other hand, have made Tulum one of their favorite hangouts. The beaches (with people in various stages of undress) south of the ruins are the setting of a series of campgrounds and cabanas and attract a friendly, low-budget crowd. Young Europeans come here to let their hair grow, peel off their tie-dyed shirts, and make jewelry. The beaches at Tulum are secluded and relatively untouched compared with those at Playa del Carmen.

Tulum was built sometime between AD 700 and 1300 by the Putún-Maya, the same people associated with Mayapán. Intended as a fortress and trading center, the city was protected by cliffs on one side and a large wall surrounding the other three sides. The 7-meter walls were a wise insurance policy, since Tulum appears to have been involved in several wars with other Maya states. Juan de Grijalva sighted the city in 1518 when his Spanish expedition sailed past the coast. Grijalva compared Tulum, whose buildings were painted red, white, and blue, with Seville. The city was still occupied by Maya at the time of the Spanish conquest: One of the images in the Temple of the Frescoes depicts Chaac riding a horse, an animal introduced by the Spanish.

COMING AND GOING

The ancient city of Tulum is 63 kilometers from Playa del Carmen and 127 kilometers from Cancún. From Cancún, buses leave every couple of hours for Playa del Carmen, continuing on to Tulum. Each stage of this two-part journey takes about an hour and costs $2.50, or you can do it in one shot. Frequent service is also available from Chetumal. From Valladolid and Cobá, two buses a day pass Tulum on their way to Playa. A bus schedule is posted at the dining room in Camping Santa Fe (*see* Where to Sleep, *below*). Hitchhiking along the main highway is common and relatively easy.

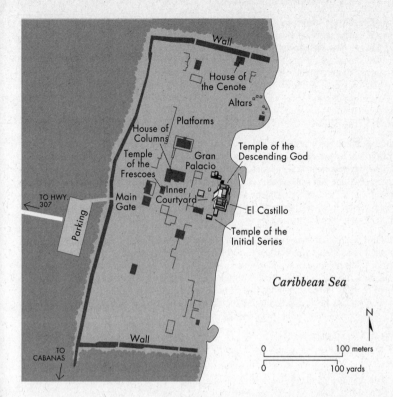

GETTING AROUND

The *crucero* (turnoff) for the ruins and budget lodging is about 4 kilometers north of the modern town of Tulum. Ask the driver to let you off at the crucero, then walk about a kilometer east to the coast. South of the ruins a road runs parallel to the beach; off the road lie various cabanas, a popular lodging option. The town of Tulum is very small and has one hotel, a handful of restaurants and grocery stores, a pharmacy, a post office, and a telephone office. Taxi rides between town and the ruins and campgrounds cost about $3.50. A minibus runs between the ruins and the town between 6 AM and 5 PM.

WHERE TO SLEEP

The various cabanas that lie along the beach south of the ruins are the best lodging alternative if you don't mind the lack of electricity (bring a flashlight) and the primitive bathroom facilities that accompany this style of living. The only good reason to stay in town is if you plan to catch the 6 AM bus to Cobá (the next one leaves at 11 AM and only gives you about three hours at Cobá). In that case, bed down at the clean **Hotel Maya** (Av. Tulum 32), which has singles for $15 and doubles for $23.50.

➢ UNDER $10 • **Camping Santa Fe.** This place is very popular with budget travelers, especially earthy types who get a primal thrill from sand floors, lack of electricity, and grungy huts. For $8 you can cram as many people as you want into a small, bare hut. For $10 you can get one with a bed. The bathrooms are repugnant and lack running water (the sinks are purely aesthetic). The showers lack walls and hence privacy. Campers don't mind joining you naked and self-conscious people are out of luck. Camping on the grass costs $2 per person. *On beach, 1 km south of ruins. 15 cabanas. Laundry, luggage storage, meals.*

➤ UNDER $20 • **Cabañas Don Armando.** Next to Camping Santa Fe, these well-constructed cabanas are more comfortable and more expensive. They have beds on cement platforms, hammock hooks, sand floors, and windows. The bathrooms are clean and locked (you get a key) to keep marauding guests from Camping Santa Fe away. If you intend to turn in at twilight, rocking your hammock to the gentle sound of Caribbean surf, go elsewhere: The disco nearby plays the same loud, obnoxious music every night until about 2. It's a shame, because the grounds and facilities really are some of the nicest here. Cabanas cost $13.50 with one bed and one hammock, $15 with two beds, and $17 for a beachfront hut with one bed and one hammock. Camping costs $3 per person. *1 km south of ruins. 24 cabanas. Laundry, luggage storage, meals.*

Cabañas El Mirador. This place is quieter and more isolated than Santa Fe and Don Armando and attracts fewer people because unlike the other two establishments, El Mirador offers no nighttime entertainment. The cabanas are well constructed but expensive ($16.50, hammocks only, no beds—you can fit two hammocks in each one). There is no shower and the bathrooms are primitive, but discrete guests can use the bathing facilities at Santa Fe. Dine and party elsewhere, and come back to peace. *On the beach, 1 km from the ruins. 20 cabanas. Laundry, luggage storage, meals (high season only).*

➤ UNDER $30 • **Cabañas Los Gatos.** This place is romantic and frequented by an older, European crowd. Behind beautifully carved doors, the rooms have comfortable beds hanging from ropes. The huge showers under a lush palapa structure are fit for entertaining. You'll have to walk down the road a bit to swim, but the rocky shoreline here is breathtaking and leads to deserted beaches. Smaller cabanas that fit two are $13.50. Three people fit in a cabana with one hammock and a king-size bed for $27, or hang your hammock in a large communal palapa for $3.50. *2 km south of ruins. Meals, wheelchair access.*

FOOD

The restaurants outside the ruins and at the crucero are nothing spectacular and ridiculously expensive. Instead, go to the village or eat at one of the cabana sites. **Don Armando** and **Santa Fe** (*see* Where to Sleep, *above*) offer main dishes for about $4–$5 and beer for $1. The food is particularly good at Sante Fe, and they always have at least one vegetarian dish. If you go to town you can buy groceries, or you can eat at **Restaurant El Paradero,** where *chuletas* (pork chops) are $4 and carne asada is $4.50, or the more expensive **Restaurant Ambrosia** (open 24 hours), which serves tasty salbutes for $3.50 and quesadillas for $4.

WORTH SEEING

MAYA RUINS The ruins are open daily 8–5, and admission is $5.50, free Sunday and holidays. If you're determined not to pay, it's fairly easy to climb over the city wall where it runs along the road. Tagging along with the guided tours is easy.

Tulum is the product of a war-troubled, declining Mayan empire. Those who built and fortified it were probably pushed eastward to the coast—from inland cities such as Cobá—by Toltec invaders. Thick walls enclose the city on three sides, and watchtowers enabled the inhabitants to know about invasions in advance.

Tulum's builders abandoned the laborious technique of smoothing and polishing each fitted stone to perfection. Instead, they slathered the stones together with troughs of mortar and covered the uneven surfaces with stucco. There are some reliefs carved into the stucco walls of the buildings, but fresco painting was the most prevalent form of decoration in Tulum.

➤ TEMPLE OF THE FRESCOES • Large stucco masks, probably representing the god Quetzalcoatl, stare from the corners of the **Temple of the Frescoes.** The mask on the southern corner has one eye open and one closed, symbolizing the duality underlying the Mayan world view. In the Maya belief system, darkness (the closed eye) and evil were not understood as the absence of light and good, but as equally important aspects of nature.

Inside the temple are murals divided into three sections, symbolizing the realms of the universe: the underworld, the mortal world, and the heavens. The middle realm depicts a figure riding a horse-like animal, which indicates that the paintings were completed or reworked after the Spaniards arrived.

➤ EL CASTILLO • The most impressive structure at Tulum, El Castillo is a small two-chamber temple built atop a tall pyramid. A staircase on the western side leads to the temple, from which you get an extensive view of the sea, the jungle, and the surrounding ruins. At some point, the columns supporting the doorway were modified to look like feathered serpents, the symbol of Kukulcan, and are further evidence of the strong Toltec influence in Tulum.

➤ TEMPLE OF THE DESCENDING GOD • Immediately north of El Castillo, the Temple of the Descending God is a small elevated structure that received its name from the beautiful relief above the doorway. The stucco carving depicts a deity diving head-first from the sky. This deity is thought to represent Quetzalcoatl—it has wings and a strange pointed tail, and carries what seems to be a flower. Some say the figure is a honey-bee, of central significance in Yucatecan Maya religion, medicine, and commerce.

OUTDOOR ACTIVITIES

Near the ruins is a small beach that's clean and free of seaweed. The beach continues south, but a wall divides it in two at the ruins. To reach the rest of the beach, you have to enter through a campground just south of the ruins. Nude bathing is allowed at the beaches in front of the cabanas, and you can snorkel over a reef about 500 yards offshore. The water is not as clear as at Playa del Carmen, but the sea life is just as abundant. Tulum's only dive shop is at Camping Santa Fe. A snorkeling trip to the reef and a few inland cenotes costs $12, while scuba diving trips cost $35 for one tank and $70 for two.

Near Tulum

BEACHES AND LAGOONS

The coast road (Highway 307) running north to Playa del Carmen passes some of the most spectacular beaches in the Caribbean, as well as a variety of lagoons that support an incredible array of wildlife and fish. Hop on the bus from Tulum to Playa del Carmen and tell the driver where you want to get off. Otherwise, it shouldn't be too difficult to hitch a ride, particularly during the day. For information about towns and beaches north of Akumal, *see* Near Playa del Carmen, *above*.

XEL-HA LAGOON Now a national park, Xel-Ha ("clear water" in Mayan) is home to tropical fish, including parrotfish and angelfish. Underwater caverns filled with coral (and, in one case, a Maya altar) make for interesting snorkeling. Unfortunately, tourism and tanning oil have polluted this lagoon. Hordes of day-trippers from Cancún, Playa, and Cozumel jostle for space in the water, dramatically reducing the lagoon's visibility. If you're determined, make sure you come early in the morning, before the rush starts. Snorkeling equipment can be rented for $9. *15 km north of Tulum; hitch along the main road, or ask the bus driver to let you off here.*

XCACEL About 3 kilometers north of Xel-Ha, this beach is everything a traveler could want—most of the time. As beautiful as other beaches along the coast, Xcacel has no hotels and is usually fairly empty. Except, of course, when cruise ships from Playa or Cancún arrange shore excursions to the expensive little restaurant here, and their buses disgorge loads of passengers. The fishing is great from the sandy part of the shore. Admission for the day costs $1.50, and camping costs about $3.50 a night.

CHEMUYIL The sign at the intersection on Highway 307, 4 kilometers north of Xcacel, calls Chemuyil the most beautiful beach in the world, but this place ain't what it used to be. Most of the palm trees here have succumbed to disease, leaving gray stumps littering the landscape. The palapa bar and little round cabanas have been abandoned, and on the northern end of the beach are some ugly condominiums. Still, the snorkeling in the small coves is said to be the best on the coast. Camping costs $3.50, and the best place is at the south end of the beach, far from visitors.

AKUMAL An upscale resort 7 kilometer north of Chemuyil, Akumal has some riches everyone can afford—a coral reef, a long white crescent beach, and crystal-clear water. The name means "Place of the Turtle" in Mayan, and giant green turtles lurch ashore in October to lay their eggs before returning to the sea. Budget travelers probably can't afford to stay here (there is no camping), but it's worth coming just for the beach and the sea, and only 7 kilometers north of Chemuyil. You can rent snorkeling gear at the dive shops for about $7.

SIAN KA'AN BIOSPHERE RESERVE Twenty-five kilometers south of Tulum are the ruins of **Muyil.** The six structures here are far from spectacular, but may merit a stop if you've got a car. Otherwise, continue south into the Sian Ka'an Biosphere Reserve. This expanse of quiet bays, deserted beaches, mangrove swamps, and jungle is populated with birds, crocodiles, jaguars, and boars, as well as wild orchids. Within the reserve, the marshy area around **Laguna Chunyaxche** is an ideal spot for bird-watching. This is a popular rest stop and habitat for over 300 species of birds, including flamingos, herons, and egrets. **Isla Pájaros** is equally popular with our feathered friends, and crocodiles lurk around as well. Small canals believed to have been built by the Maya and used as ceremonial sites are also of interest. Wade, swim, or haggle with a fisherman for a boatride. Sian Ka'an is only affordable if you're going to camp out. Cabanas at the northern entrance start at about $60, and lodging in the fly-fishing resort of **Boca Paila** are even steeper. You can camp along the beach: If there are people around, ask permission just to be polite. Restaurants are few and far between, and those that exist are expensive, so bring your own provisions. During the tourist season (December–April and July and August), pickup trucks sometimes depart from the intersection about 3 kilometers south of the Tulum ruins (just past Cabañas Los Gatos). From here, it's a 50-kilometer trip. Drivers should fill up at the gas station in Tulum before making the trip. **Amigos de Sian Ka'an** in Cancún (tel. 988/4–95–83) may also be able to get you aboard one of their tour buses.

COBA

This site, covering more than 50 square kilometers, has been largely ignored by archaeologists and the Mexican government. Jungle envelops much of it, and visitors will feel like pioneers stumbling onto something unknown and exotic. You can't help becoming excited at the sight of mounds and mounds of unexcavated ruins. Distances between the structures are all 1–2 kilometers, so be prepared to walk and bring some water and *lots* of insect repellent. The jungle that surrounds the ruins is no less an attraction. If you're adventurous and not afraid of snakes, follow any of the paths into undergrowth.

Cobá is one of the oldest sites on the peninsula. Built around several shallow lakes and marshes, it was settled about 400 BC but didn't develop into a city until around AD 500. The city's inhabitants died out mysteriously 600 years before the arrival of the Spanish, and no one discovered the ruins until the late 19th century.

The remains of more than 30 roads, once paved with smoothed stones, indicate that Cobá was a large commercial center. The two huge pyramids that archaeologists have unearthed here bear more resemblance to the structures at Tikal, Guatemala, than to local architecture, suggesting royal ties with the wealthy Maya of the Petén jungle. More than 6,500 structures here remain to be excavated.

Closest to the entrance is a group of temples known as the **Cobá Group,** the first of which is the enormous pyramid called the **Iglesia.** It's a vigorous climb up the pyramid, the second-largest on the peninsula (26 meters high), but you'll be rewarded with a fantastic view of two lakes, the jungle surrounding the ruins, and Nohoch Mul, the peninsula's tallest pyramid. In front of the pyramid is a small shrine where local Maya occasionally leave offerings to the gods.

Walk a short way back down the main trail to **Las Pinturas** (The Paintings). Unfortunately, the pyramidal temple bears only scant remnants of frescoes on its walls. It's an ideal place to rest, though, and many travelers find it tranquil enough for meditation. On your way back to the entrance is a 3-kilometer side trip to the **Stelae Group.** More than 30 carved stelae have been found at Cobá, some with intricate hieroglyphs telling the city's history. They show tyrannical rulers standing imperiously on the backs of captives, subjects, or slaves. Most of the carvings have deteriorated, and you can barely see the images.

Back on the main trail, follow the signs to **Nohoch Mul,** the Yucatán's largest Maya structure. It's a 2-kilometer trek, but you really should see this pyramid, which soars 41 meters from the jungle floor. The climb is not for the weak of heart, but the view from the top is superb. Chances are you'll have the summit to yourself, a rarity in this region. The temple on top of the pyramid is thought to have been constructed long after the pyramid itself was finished. Note the carvings of diving gods on the front wall.

Admission to Cobá is $6, but the adventurous can enter clandestinely. Remember, the admission price pays workers and the upkeep of the ruins, which may or may not matter to you. Here goes: Across from the Restaurant Isabel, a dirt road passes by a white-and-blue water tower. Take the road straight through the village and keep following it past the small pharmacy and a square thatched home with a red roof. There the road turns into a trail and enters the jungle. Stay on the main trail for about 15 minutes and when you come to a wider, well-trod road, take a left. The hulking Nohoch Mul pyramid is 100 meters ahead.

COMING AND GOING Getting to Cobá is not too difficult. Three buses go from Tulum to Cobá daily at 6 AM, 11 AM, and 6 PM. If you catch the last bus you'll have to stay the night in Cobá. The last bus to Tulum leaves at 3 PM. Large groups can negotiate with a taxi driver, but the fare is still likely to be $20–$25.

WHERE TO SLEEP AND EAT Hotel El Bocadito (main road, no phone) has eight dusty rooms with beds on cement bases and private bathrooms for $11.50, single or double. Even cheaper are the grungy rooms at **Cabañas Isabel** (main road, no phone). The huts, which feature one or two beds and hammock hooks, cost a desperate $2 for a single, $3.50 for a double, and $5 for a triple. There's electricity, and the management might even offer to sweep the room for you. If those places are full, look for SE RENTAN CUARTOS signs or ask in the stores about places to stay.

Eating in Cobá doesn't have to be expensive, but it certainly costs more than in other places. **Restaurant El Bocadito,** next to the hotel, serves main dishes for around $5 and will prepare a cooked vegetable dish for $4. Behind the basketball court, **Lonchería La Amistad** is a cheaper option, where you can get tacos for 50¢ and great licuados with fresh fruit for 65¢.

Chetumal
Travelers come to Chetumal, at the southern tip of Quintana Roo, for two reasons: to use the city as a springboard for trips to Belize and Guatemala, and to take advantage of duty-free bargains. Architecturally, this state capital has little to offer: Its modern block-style buildings are boring at best. Chetumal survives today only because its duty-free status attracts people in search of cheap foreign goods. They tote off stereos, refrigerators, and every other kind of electronic gadget. Avenida Héroes is lined with dozens of stores selling imported junk. If you can't find what you're looking for here, try the old market on Héroes at Avenida Gandhi.

BASICS

BANKS Several banks in the city change money. **Bancomer** (tel. 983/2–12–31) and **Banamex** (tel. 983/2–10–44), both on Juárez at Obregón, change money weekdays 10:30–1:30. Both have ATMs that accept Mastercard, Visa, and Cirrus cards.

CROSSING THE BORDER

➤ TO BELIZE • American and British Commonwealth citizens do not need visas to enter Belize, but they do need passports. Travelers pay nothing to enter Belize.

➤ TO GUATEMALA • For information on visas and tourist cards, see box Going to Guatemala, Chapter 10. For paperwork, visit the **Guatemalan Consulate.** Obregón 342, at Cecilio Chi, tel. 983/2–13–65. Open Mon.–Sat. 8–6, but try knocking after hours.

MEDICAL AID There are a number of hospitals near the budget hotels. The cleanest one is **Hospital Morelos,** at Juárez and Aguilar, with 24-hour emergency ambulance service. Tel. 983/2–45–99.

Farmacia Canto (Héroes, at Gandhi, tel. 983/2–04–83) is open 7 AM–10 PM.

PHONES AND MAIL The **post office** (Plutarco Elías and Calle 2a, 2 blocks east of Héroes, tel. 983/2–25–78) is open weekdays 8–7, Saturday 9–1. They will hold mail sent to you at the following address for up to 10 days: Lista de Correos, Chetumal, Quintana Roo, CP 77000, México. **Teléfonos de México** (Cárdenas, at Juárez, tel. 983/2–35–44) sells telephone cards. They're open weekdays 8–1:30. Card- and coin-operated phones are common throughout town. Dial 09 for the Mexican international operator and **01 for AT&T USA Direct. There is also a **Computel** at the bus station open daily 7 AM–10 PM.

VISITOR INFORMATION The **Secretaría de Turismo** has a helpful staff that speaks English. *Palacio Municipal, 1 block west of Héroes on Bahía, tel. 983/2–36–63. Open weekdays 8–1 and 5–8.*

COMING AND GOING

BY BUS There are three bus terminals along Insurgentes, the main drag. The farthest one from downtown is **Peninsulares,** at Palermo. First- and second-class buses leave frequently for Mérida ($16 1st class, $13 2nd class) all day long. Two first-class buses leave for Cancún, and five leave for Playa del Carmen.

The second station (Insurgentes, at Belice) as you approach town has first- and second-class service on **Autotransportes del Caribe,** serving all points in the Yucatán and some destinations in other states. This station is quite large and has a restaurant, stores, and luggage storage. Destinations with second-class service include Tulum ($7, 3½ hrs), Playa del Carmen ($10, 5½ hrs), and Cancún ($12, 6½ hrs); the same bus goes to all three five times a day. First-class buses go to Palenque ($18, 7 hrs) once a day; Cancún ($15, 6 hrs) six times a day; Mérida ($15, 5 hrs), twice daily; and Mexico City ($60, 22 hrs) three times a day.

Venus Bus Lines goes to Belize City ($5, 4 hrs) from the *mercado nuevo* (new market) on Insurgentes at Héroes. They leave every hour on the hour starting at 4 AM. **Batty's** buses leave for Belize City several times a day from the same place, and continue on to Melchor de Mencos ($3, 4 hrs) and Flores ($3, 3 hrs).

To reach Kohunlich, Bacalar, Cenote Azul, Laguna Milagros, El Palmar, or other points on the Río Hondo, take one of the small buses that leaves from the station at Hidalgo and Francisco Primo de Verdad. Buses for Xcalak ($7) leave from Avenida 16 de Septiembre at Gandhi at 7 AM.

BY PLANE The small airport 2 kilometers outside of Chetumal handles only domestic flights and flights to Guatemala and Belize. Carriers serving the airport include **Aeroméxico** (tel. 983/2–15–76) and **Aerocaribe** (tel. 983/2–66–75). A taxi downtown costs about $2, or walk east on Revolución (the main street north of the airport), which becomes Aguilar.

GETTING AROUND

It's easy to get around Chetumal on foot, and almost everything you need is in the downtown area. The most important street running north–south is Avenida Héroes. Boulevard Bahía runs west–east and then north around the coast, hugging the shoreline. Buses and minibuses run around town on fixed routes, but they rarely pass anything of interest, and you're better off taking a taxi. Taxis in Chetumal are amazingly cheap and abundant.

WHERE TO SLEEP

There are plenty of budget hotels in Chetumal, catering to shoppers who come for the cheap wares the city offers. The best place to start looking is the plaza, around the intersection of Héroes and Aguilar, where you can also take advantage of the cheap loncherías and bookstores in the area.

➢ UNDER $15 • **Hotel María Dolores.** These small, drab rooms are at least clean and have fans. The prices make it popular. Singles go for $11, doubles $13, and triples $18. *Obregón 206, ½ block west of Héroes, tel. 983/2–05–08. 41 rooms, all with bath. Laundry, meal service.*

Hotel Tulum. This noisy hotel in the center of the downtown action is as cheap as it gets in Chetumal. Spartan singles are $10, doubles $13.50, and triples $17. The place is often full, so come early. *Héroes 164, btw Gandhi and Aguilar, tel. 983/2–05–18. 17 rooms, all with bath. Luggage storage. Reservations advised in summer.*

Hotel Ucum. The rooms in this rambling hotel tend to be large, bright, and very clean. Sometimes there's hot water in the afternoons. Laundry facilities consist of a clothesline on the roof. Singles and doubles are $13.50, and triples are $16.50. *Gandhi 167, btw Héroes and 16 de Septiembre, tel. 983/2–07–11. 56 rooms, all with bath. Luggage storage.*

➢ UNDER $25 • **Hotel Real Azteca.** The rooms at this pleasant hotel have wood closets, air-conditioning, and clean bathrooms decorated with black and white tile. Singles go for $17, doubles $20, and triples $25. *Belice 186, btw Aguilar and Gandhi, tel. 983/2–07–20. 25 rooms, all with bath. Luggage storage, restaurant.*

HOSTEL **Albergue Juvenil CND.** It's the cheapest place to stay in Chetumal, but so few people come here that you may have a dorm room to yourself. Tiny rooms are segregated by sex, and each has four bunks. The cleaning lady does not believe in dusting hidden corners, but open areas are fairly clean. However, biologists may find the strange slime and mold in the women's bathroom worthy of a dissertation. Bunks rent for $4.50 a night; you have to leave a $7 deposit if you want a towel, sheet, and pillow. You can camp on the lawn for $2 a night. Bring your own toilet paper. *Obregón, at Veracruz, about 5 blocks east of Héroes, tel. 983/2–34–65. 66 beds. Luggage storage, meal service.*

CAMPING You can tent-camp on the lawn of the youth hostel (*see above*) for $2.50 per person. A more scenic option is **Laguna Milagros** (*see* Near Chetumal, *below*), 12 kilometers west of town, for $5 per person per night.

FOOD

In Chetumal you'll find Yucatecan food, sometimes with a Belizean influence, including Yucatecan lime soup and *tikinchic* (fried fish seasoned with sour orange). If you're trying to save money, pick up some fruit at **Frutería La Merced** (Héroes, at Cristóbal Colón). There's a convenient bakery, **Pan La Terminal,** right on Avenida Héroes.

El Vaticano. This place serves large dishes of fresh fish for a lot less than they charge in Cancún or Playa. Ceviche is $7, fillets are $5. Nestled in a corner across from the market, it's a nice place to sit outside and sip a beer. *Belice, at Gandhi, no phone. Open Mon.–Sat. 10–5, Sun. 10–3.*

Restaurant Pandoja. Popular with tourists, this place still maintains a local atmosphere. You can eat well here for $5. Try the chicken in mole sauce for $3.50. No alcohol is served. *Gandhi, at 16 de Septiembre, tel. 983/2–39–57. Open daily 7 AM–9 PM.*

Restaurant Ucum. This is probably the only color-coordinated place in Chetumal—too bad they chose mint green. Fortunately, there's more variety in terms of food. Extremely hearty breakfast dishes cost $3 and include eggs, rice, beans, salad, and tortillas. Try the comida corrida (the chicken dishes are especially hearty) for $3. *Gandhi 167, btw 16 de Septiembre and Héroes, tel. 983/2–21–88. Open daily 7:30 AM–9 PM.*

Near Chetumal

Calderitas, 8 kilometers north of town, has the best swimming. To get here, take a minibus from the bus stop in back of the market on Belice between Colón and Gandhi. They leave every half hour and cost about 20¢. Divers head for **Banco Chincorro,** a 42-kilometer coral atoll two hours offshore that's littered with shipwrecks. There is one bus daily at 7 AM from the station at 16 de Septiembre and Gandhi. Chetumal's major water attractions, however, are inland. The **Río Hondo,** filled with alligators and manatees, runs along the borders of Mexico, Belize, and Guatemala. Travelers to Belize must pass through customs at the border.

Laguna Milagros, Cenote Azul, and Laguna de Bacalar (*see below*) can all be reached easily by taking a combi ($1) from the corner of Hidalgo and Primo de Verdad in Chetumal.

LAGUNA MILAGROS

Laguna Milagros is a good place to pitch your tent or hang your hammock (beware of falling coconuts). The lagoon is nothing special, but the warm water is inviting and peaceful. If you want to explore the land around the lagoon, it's best to swim to your chosen spot: You can't walk through the thick vegetation without destroying it. Camping costs $5 per person. The 12-kilometer trip here by minibus takes 15 minutes. The lake is about 110 meters from the main road. To return to Chetumal, stand at one of the bus stops on the main road.

CENOTE AZUL

If you have time to visit only one place near Chetumal, it should be Cenote Azul. The largest cenote in the world, it's 89 meters deep and 220 meters across and is surrounded by thick jungle. It takes its name from the intense blue of its waters, which are home to an array of beautiful fish. The cenote is a popular watering hole, so come early or late in the day to avoid crowds. From Chetumal, take any minibus to Bacalar and ask the driver to let you off at the cenote. To get back, stand on the roadside and flag down a passing bus or minibus.

LAGUNA DE BACALAR

About 40 kilometers north of Chetumal is the Laguna de Bacalar, a favorite destination for day tripping locals. Also known as the Laguna de Siete Colores, the lagoon changes color according to the light and the depth of the water. The warm, calm waters are a safe swimming spot that attracts families on holidays and weekends. The lagoon is surrounded by private property and the neighboring town of Bacalar. You can camp for $2 at Ejidal, and use the toilet and shower facilities. To get to Ejidal, walk away from the central square toward the water. Turn left on the road that runs along the water and walk about 800 meters. You'll have to move out at daybreak, though, because the restaurant/bar is open all day with people passing through. While in Bacalar, take a look at the perfectly preserved **Fuerte San Felipe Bacalar**. The fort has an impressive view of the area, and the main room serves as the town museum. The fort is open Tuesday–Sunday 10–6; admission is 50¢.

KOHUNLICH RUINS

You may have difficulty getting to these Maya ruins, but you can be sure of one thing—no one will disturb your reverie. Located 60 kilometers west of Chetumal, off Highway 186, Kohunlich is one of the more recently discovered Maya settlements, and its 200 or so mounds have yet to be excavated. Here you'll find the **Pyramid of the Masks,** with huge images of the Maya sun god, and a ball court, one of the oldest in Quintana Roo. The pyramid is thought to contain the tomb of a Maya ruler. Archaeologists believe Kohunlich was built and occupied from AD 300 to 600. No public transport stops here, but you can get a bus headed toward Escárcega (from the small terminal at Hidalgo and Primo de Verdad in Chetumal), get off at the crossroads to the ruins, and walk 9 kilometers. Taxis and buses back to Chetumal are hard to find, so you're better off renting a car or hitching.

VERACRUZ 12

By Ariana Mohit

The state of Veracruz, a long, skinny crescent of land bordering the Gulf of Mexico, is often ignored by travelers, many of whom do no more than glimpse the state through the window of a bus barreling toward the Yucatán Peninsula. But while Veracruz's ruins and beaches can't compare with those on the Yucatán, life is more than rocks and rays, and the state is popular with vacationing Mexicans, drawn to the cool hill towns of the Sierra de Los Tuxtlas and the liveliness of Veracruz city.

Descending from the volcanic Sierra, the Veracruz coast consists of flat lowlands characterized by terrible heat and swamps and pockmarked by noisome oil refineries. As you head inland a ways—Veracruz is only 140 kilometers across at its widest point—the land rises to meet the Sierra Madre Oriental range, with its 5,610-meter Pico de Orizaba (also called Citlaltépetl), Mexico's highest mountain. In the foothills of this range, you'll find the university town and state capital of of Jalapa, where long-haired students share the colonial streets with local farmers who have come to town to market their crops. The state does have some good beaches along the coast, particularly around the northern city of Tuxpán, but the real reasons to come are the atmosphere, the history, and the people. All of these are to be found at their best in the raffish city of Veracruz, a working port with so many marimba bands in the *zócalo* (main square) on weekend evenings that they must compete to be heard.

Olmec civilization thrived in Veracruz long before the rise of the Maya. The state's best-preserved ruins, at El Tajín near Papantla, are thought to have been the work of yet another civilization, which had its heyday later, between AD 550 and AD 1100. By the time Hernán Cortés landed in Veracruz in 1519, the Aztecs held sway, but within a very short time the Indian population was decimated by disease and war. To meet their labor needs, the Spanish then brought a large number of Africans to Veracruz as slaves, and their presence has had a profound influence on the character of the place. In modern times, the discovery of oil here prompted a population explosion that saw the number of Veracruzanos go from about a million at the beginning of the century to more than six million today. For most foreign travelers, the sulfurous stench of a coastal oil refinery is an unpleasant intrusion on their tropical reverie, but for many of the state's residents, it's their lifeblood.

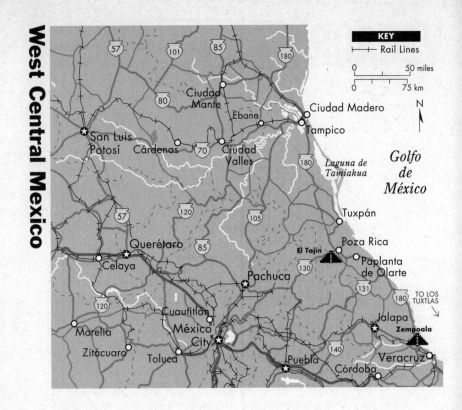

Veracruz

Veracruz is a hot, raucous port town. With its Caribbean flavor, lively music, and diverse population, the city holds a special place in the hearts of many Mexicans who admire the welcoming, ready-to-celebrate attitude of the *jarochos,* as the city's residents are known. People come here for the seafood, the marimba music, and the breezes off the Caribbean, though—not to frolic in the ocean. Since Good Friday, 1519 (the day Hernán Cortés and his men landed here), Veracruz has been one of Mexico's most important ports, and more than five centuries of heavy traffic has taken its toll on the area's beaches.

The principal entry point for both people and goods headed to Mexico City, Veracruz has been a bitterly contested prize in many of the conflicts of Mexico's stormy history. An array of forts and walls, originally built as protection against pirates, failed to save the city from a succession of foreign attacks. Pirates sacked the city a number of times, most viciously in 1683, when a Frenchman known as Lorenzillo held the town hostage for three days and carried off enormous quantities of loot. The French invaded in 1838, and the United States seized the town twice, first in 1847 and again in 1914. The most dramatic of the fortifications—the castle at San Juan de Ulúa—still stands testament to Veracruz's volatile past and is one of the city's most popular attractions.

BASICS

AMERICAN EXPRESS The AmEx office is in **Viajes Olymar.** The agency provides the usual services for cardholders, including personal check cashing and mail holding. They also deliver MoneyGrams and sell traveler's checks, but they do not change money. *Ávila Camacho 2221,*

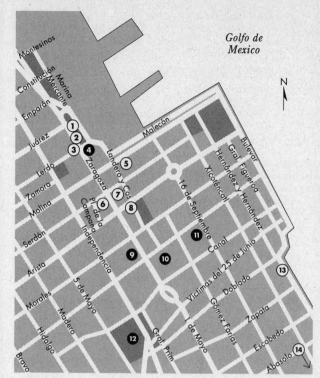

*Golfo de
Mexico*

N

Sights ●

Baluarte de
Santiago, **11**

Instituto
Veracruzano de
la Cultura, **10**

Museo de
la Ciudad, **9**

Parque Zamora, **12**

Plaza de Armas, **4**

Lodging ○

Casa de
Huéspuedes
La Tabasqueña, **1**

La Concha
Dorada, **3**

Gran Hotel
Balneario
Royalty, **14**

Hotel Amparo, **6**

Hotel Mallorca, **7**

Hotel Santander, **5**

Hotel Santillana, **8**

Hotel Sevilla, **2**

Hotel Villa Rica, **13**

Veracruz, Veracruz, CP 91910, México, tel. 29/31–34–06. Open weekdays 9–1 and 4–6, Sat. 9–noon.

CASAS DE CAMBIO The best rates in town are available at **Bancomer** (Juárez, at Independencia). Unfortunately, they only change money weekdays 9 AM–11:30 AM, so you'll have to arrive early to make it through the lines. For later hours, try **Casa de Cambio Puebla** (Juárez 112, tel. 29/31–24–50), open weekdays 9–6, or use the ATM at **Banamex** (also on Juárez, at Independencia).

CONSULATE United States. Víctimas del 25 del Julio 384, btw Gómez Farias and 16 de Septiembre, tel. 29/31–58–21. Open weekdays 9–1.

EMERGENCIES Oficinas Para La Seguridad del Turista (tel. 91/800–90–392) operates a 24-hour toll-free hotline to provide legal and medical help for tourists in Veracruz.

LAUNDRY Lavandería Mar y Sol charges $3.50 per three-kilo load. Same-day service is $4.50. Madero 600, btw Arista and Serdán, tel. 31–77–34. Open Mon.–Sat. 9–2 and 4–8, Sun. 9–2.

MAIL The central post office, a magnificent building dating from the Porfirio Díaz era, offers the usual services. They will hold mail sent to you at the following address for up to 10 days: Lista de Correos, Administración No. 1, Veracruz, Veracruz, CP 91700. María Mercante 210, tel. 29/32–20–38. Open weekdays 8–8, Sat. 9–1.

MEDICAL AID Benavides (Independencia 1291, at Serdán tel. 29/31–89–29) is a big, convenient drugstore downtown, but it closes at 10 PM daily. For 24-hour service, try **Farmacia San Francisco** (5 De Mayo 1634 , tel. 29/32–27–88).

In addition to its renowned jarocho and marimba music, Veracruz is also the birthplace of the famous song "La Bamba," and of Yuri, Mexico's answer to Madonna.

PHONES The pay phones on the zócalo accept Ladatel phone cards. If you don't mind shelling out big bucks, you can also make long-distance phone calls at **Teléfonos Mirna** (Molina 127, tel. 29/31–40–07), behind the cathedral.

VISITOR INFORMATION The bilingual staff at the **Subdelegación Federal de Turismo** has some helpful pamphlets and a lot of enthusiasm. *Palacio Municipal, on zócalo, tel. 29/32–19–99. Open daily 9–9.*

COMING AND GOING

BY BUS The main bus terminal (Díaz Mirón 1698, tel. 29/37–57–44) is about 4 kilometers south of the zócalo. The main bus company is **Autobuses del Oriente (ADO)** (tel. 29/37–57–88), with daily service to Jalapa ($5, 3 hrs) every 15–30 minutes between 5:30 AM and 11 PM and round-the-clock departures for Mexico City ($20, 9 hrs). ADO also offers first- and second-class service to Reynosa ($48–$57, 17 hrs), on the Texas border. For those headed south, **Cristobal Colón** (tel. 29/35-03-17) and **Cuenca** (tel. 29/35–54–05) run to Oaxaca and Chiapas. Luggage storage costs $4 a day, but if you lose the key, they'll charge you $33. Public phones and a *caseta de larga distancia* (long-distance phone office) are available in the station. **Autobuses Unidos** (tel. 29/37–57–32) and **Transportes Los Tuxtlas** (tel. 29/37–28–78) operate from another station on the same block and offer frequent second-class service to Jalapa ($3.50, 3½ hrs) and Los Tuxtlas ($4, 3 hrs).

Any city bus marked DIAZ MIRON on Avenida Zaragoza near the zócalo will stop right by both terminals. A taxi between the zócalo and the terminal should cost you no more than $2.

BY TRAIN The train station (tel. 29/32–25–69) is in a romantic 19th-century building, five long blocks from the zócalo. The **Jarocho** train departs nightly at 9:30 for Mexico City (10 hrs). Classes of service include: second-class (no guaranteed seating; $6.50), first-class (assigned seats; $11), first-class *especial* (assigned seats and air-conditioning; $15), and sleeper-car (bed, sink, chair, and air-conditioning; $38). All tickets are sold at the same window. If you're traveling first class during peak tourist seasons (July, August, and holidays), buy your tickets in advance—they are available as much as a month before the departure date. Second-class-only trains also run to Mexico City at 8 AM and 9 PM daily. They are somewhat slower (the trip takes 12 hours), but tickets are a mere $5. Tickets can be purchased Monday–Saturday 6–11 and 2–9. To reach the station, follow María Mercante until it ends, then turn right

BY PLANE **Mexicana** (tel. 29/34–15–34) has three direct flights a day to Mexico City for about $110 one way. The airline also has flights to other major cities, including Cancún and Monterrey. No city bus serves the airport, and a cab costs $12. Alternatively, you can ride the $10 minivan that runs between the office of **Transportación Terrestre Aeropuerto** (Hidalgo 826, btw Canal and Morales, tel. 29/32–32–50) and the airport.

GETTING AROUND

Downtown Veracruz centers around two plazas: the **Plaza de Armas,** also known as the zócalo, and **Parque Zamora,** with its old trolley car. The two are connected by Avenida Independencia, the city's busiest shopping street. Just as important to the visitor is the *malecón,* the boardwalk that runs along the seashore. Called Molina in the downtown area, the malecón makes a 90-degree turn and becomes Boulevard Ávila Camacho, referred to by everyone as *el bulevard.* This winding street follows the southern coast of Veracruz, passing Playa de Hornos and Playa Mocambo before arriving in Boca del Río. Fortunately, most other streets adhere to a grid system.

WHERE TO SLEEP

There are over 60 hotels scattered throughout this relatively small city, so finding a place to stay should be simple. Prices are based on the hotel's proximity to the beach and the efficiency of its cooling system. The area near the zócalo is safe, clean, and well lit, or you can stay right on the water for very little money, as long as you're willing to forgo a certain amount of luxury. Lodging in the the older, more urban, center of town is plentiful and cheap, but the room quality is low, and the area is unsafe at night.

NEAR THE ZOCALO

➤ UNDER $25 • **Casa de Huéspedes La Tabasqueña.** The other five *casas de huéspedes* (rooming houses) in the city should either be destroyed or used as insect farms, but this one is okay. Rooms are small and a bit musty, but the exposed beams and colored floor tiles give the place some character. Singles are $12, doubles $20. *Morelos 325, btw Lerdo and Juárez, tel. 29/32–05–60. 26 rooms, all with bath. Luggage storage, wheelchair access. AE, MC, V.*

Hotel Amparo. Big rooms, plenty of hot water, and enough little soaps to open a store make this hotel one of the best deals in town. The blaring TV in the lobby is *always* on, and the same old crowd of *cuates* (buddies) are slouched on its uncomfortable chairs day in and day out—especially during soccer season. Ask for a room on the main courtyard—they tend to be cleaner and cooler than interior rooms. Singles are a steal at $11, and doubles are only $16.50. *Serdán 478, btw Zaragoza and Independencia. tel. 29/32–27–38. 64 rooms, all with bath. Luggage storage.*

Hotel Santillana. A chattering parrot greets visitors in the otherwise gloomy lobby of this hotel, which charges $16.50 for a single and $20 for a double. The rooms are all decent, and all have fans and clean bathrooms. *Landero y Cos 209, tel. 29/32–31–16. 42 rooms.*

Hotel Sevilla. Everything in this small, otherwise nondescript hotel is light blue—the walls, the tiles, the sheets—everything. The rooms tend to be noisy, especially those that open onto Zaragoza, but all have ceiling fans, TVs, and clean bathrooms with plenty of hot water. The hotel itself is two-second walk from the zócalo. *Morelos 359, btw Lerdo and Juárez tel. 29/32–42–46. 30 rooms. Luggage storage.*

➤ UNDER $30 • **La Concha Dorada.** The cheapest rooms on the zócalo are at this small hotel whose name—the Golden Shell—can be vaguely obscene in colloquial language. The place is cramped but clean, with phones and sturdy beds in every room. Singles and doubles with ceiling fans will cost you $20 and $26, respectively. An air-conditioned double will cost you a wallet-thinning $34. *Lerdo 77, on zócalo, tel. 29/31–29–96. 35 rooms, all with bath. Luggage storage. AE, MC, V.*

Hotel Mallorca. If you're unlucky enough to be carrying a lot of luggage, reaching the second floor of this hotel requires a painfully long, steep climb. You'll probably want to drag yourself up, though, because second-floor rooms are breezier, and the rickety ceiling fans that are the hotel's only cooling system are about as effective as a pair of soccer cleats on an ice rink. Still, the bathrooms are clean and the tiny rooms comfortable enough. Singles are $15, doubles $25. *Serdán 424, tel. 29/32–75–49. 34 rooms, all with bath.*

Hotel Santander. Once called the Hotel Vigo, this place is perhaps the only hotel in town with any character. Colored tiles, high ceilings, breezy balconies, and the most temperamental key holes in all of Mexico make it interesting. Singles with narrow beds are a manageable $16.50, and doubles run $25. *Molina 56, tel. 29/32–86–59. 2 blocks from zócalo. 42 rooms, all with bath. Luggage storage.*

NEAR THE BEACH

➤ UNDER $25 • **Gran Hotel Balneario Royalty.** Known to locals as "El Royalty," this hulking gray building is one of the largest budget hotels in the city. Many of the rooms have breezy balconies with nice views of the bay, and all have phones and TVs. Singles and doubles with ceiling fans are $20 and $23, respectively. Air-conditioning bumps up the prices considerably, to $33 for a single, $40 for a double. *Abasolo 34, at Ávila Camacho, tel. 29/32–39–88. 270 rooms, all with bath. Garage, restaurant. MC, V.*

Hotel Playa. The building is musty and the plaster has a tenuous hold on the walls, but if you want a truly cheap hotel right off the water, this your only choice. Rooms are dark and nondescript, but the bathrooms are bearable and the water gets hot quickly. Single rooms with fans are $15; doubles are $20. With air-conditioning, the price goes up $5. *Ávila Camacho 28, at Valencia, tel. 29/37–25–10. 33 rooms, all with bath. Luggage storage.*

Hotel Villa Rica. You'll have to look hard to find this innocuous hotel about a block south down the malecón from the massive, multicolored Mar y Tierra hotel. The cats that live at the reception desk are decidedly unamused (i.e. no amount of gurgling and cooing will tempt them to come and play), as is the robust señora in charge. But the rooms ($20 single, $23.50 double) are decent, if bare, and all have tiny bathrooms. Some oceanside rooms have balconies. *Ávila Camacho 165, tel. 29/32–48—54. 33 rooms. Luggage storage.*

HOSTEL Except for a few food stands, Veracruz's **Villa Juvenil** stands alone on the beach, about 30 kilometers north of the city. Plan to stay for a few days, because getting here through cane fields, villages, and flooded roads can take hours. The good news is that beds ($3 a night) are almost always available; the beach is among the cleanest in the area; there's great fishing off a nearby reef; and a 45-minute walk in either direction will bring you to isolated, virgin dunes bordered by jungle. The bad news is that after a major hassle to get here, you may find the place temporarily closed. They have no phone, so the only way to find out for sure if they're open (barring just going yourself) is to ask around, or call the main Villas Juveniles office in Mexico City (tel. 5/525–29–16). When the hostel is in operation, the friendly family that runs it also cooks up cheap and filling meals. To get here, catch an **Autobuses Teziutecos** bus to the town of Villa Cardel from Veracruz's second-class bus terminal, behind the main station. From the station in Villa Cardel, walk toward town and to the left, where you'll find dilapidated blue buses running to Paso Doña Juana, where the hostel is located (just tell the driver to let you off at the Villa Juvenil, or CREA, as it used to be known). *Paso Dona Juana, Municipio de Úrsulo Galván, Villa Cardel.*

FOOD

Veracruz offers a mind-boggling array of culinary choices, from tempura to lasagna, but seafood is the star attraction. People drive miles to Boca del Río for the *robalo al mojo de ajo* (sea bass in garlic sauce; $10) at **Pardiño's** (Zamora 40, on zócalo, tel. 29/86–01–35). There's no real need to leave the city, though: Veracruz's **municipal fish market,** a block south of the zócalo, has scores of stands where vendors cook up just about every kind of seafood until late into the night. The stretch of Calle Serdán between Zaragoza and Madero also offers plenty of good, cheap eats. Picnic supplies, such as fresh vegetables, fruits, nuts, and cheeses, are available at the outdoor market on Guerrero between Juan Soto and Serdán.

➢ UNDER $5 • **Pizza Palace.** The buffet here is an extravagant, all-you-can-eat affair in air-conditioned surroundings. You can gorge yourself on pizza (which goes fast, so jump when it comes out) and an array of vegetables and other goodies, including fresh fruit for dessert, all for a reasonable $4.50. Don't come here for the atmosphere, though—it's pretty sterile. *Zamora, btw Independencia and 5 de Mayo, tel. 29/31–71–42. Open Mon.–Sat. 9 AM–1 AM. Buffet served weekdays noon–5.*

Tacoyote. Set back from the street on a little fountain-filled plaza near the zócalo, this taquería serves a filling plate of beef tacos with *horchata* (a cool drink made with milk, rice, water, and cinnamon) for $4. Vegetarians can go for the quesadillas (five for $4) or cheese *empanadas* (turnovers; $2.50). *Plazuela de la Campana 55-A, at Arista, no phone. Open Sun.–Wed. 2 PM–1 AM, Thurs.–Sat. 2 PM–3 AM. Wheelchair access.*

The Nevería Amparito on Landero y Cos and Serdán, makes its own ice cream, with different flavors served every day. On Wednesday, try the cacahuate (peanut) flavor.

➢ UNDER $10 • **Café La Catedral.** This sizeable café is usually crowded with locals intent on their coffee and animated conversations. For a splurge, try the house specialty, *pescado relleno con camarones* (fish stuffed with shrimp) for $10. The comida corrida is a more affordable option at $6. *Ocampo 202, near Parque Zamora, tel. 29/32–52–06. Open daily 8 AM–10 PM. Wheelchair access.*

La Concha Dorada. This unpretentious bar/restaurant is right off the zócalo, adjacent to the hotel of the same name. It gets busy around lunch time, when people flock in for an afternoon drink and some fragrant chicken soup, which is served here in small, plastic tea cups. Beef tacos ($3) and other simple fare are also available. *Lerdo 77-B, tel. 29/31–29–96. Open daily noon–1 AM. Wheelchair access.*

Gran Café La Parroquia. Veracruz's most venerable and busiest café serves mostly coffee, sandwiches, and eggs. When you want some *café con leche* (coffee with milk), bang your glass with your spoon and a waiter armed with pitchers of hot milk and coffee will scurry over. The *tortilla parroquín* (chile-and-onion omelet cooked in chicken broth; $5) makes a filling meal, as do the various other egg dishes and crêpes on the menu. *Independencia 1187, near zócalo, tel. 29/82–25–84. Open daily 6 AM–1 AM.*

WORTH SEEING

Most main attractions are either near the zócalo and easily accessible on foot or served by convenient public transporatation. The malecón is lively day and night, with men hawking boat rides, boys diving for coins, and scores of tacky souvenir shops. If you plan on cruising around here at night (a popular weekend activity among young jarochos in the throes of puppy love), watch out for the street brawls that break out all too frequently.

The malecón is lined with artesanía (crafts) vendors hawking everything from ugly plastic souvenirs to polished seashells. If you'd like your own white jarocho apparel, try looking here or in the huge municipal market near Parque Zamora.

ACUARIO The aquarium, located in a shopping plaza on Playa de Hornos, a quick bus ride from the center, is extremely popular with locals, who flock here on weekends. It contains a round tank with 3,000 different species of marine life native to the Gulf of Mexico, including nurse sharks, manta rays, barracudas, and sea turtles. Shark movies, of the make-you-never-want-to-set-foot-in-the-ocean-again variety, are shown near the exit. If that doesn't do the trick, check out the enormous shark-shaped outline on the far wall, above the caption: "This is the actual size of a great white shark caught off the coast of Tuxpán, Veracruz." *Plaza Acuario, tel. 29/34—79–84. Take* VILLA DEL MAR *or* BOCA DEL RIO *bus from cnr of Molina and Zaragoza. Admission: $5. Open Mon.–Thurs. 10–7, Fri.–Sun. 10–7:30.*

BALUARTE DE SANTIAGO The Baluarte de Santiago is all that remains of the ramparts that once stood sentinel over the port of Veracruz. The colonial bulwark is impressively solid from the outside and romantically lit at night. Inside is a small museum that displays temporary art exhibits. None of it is worth the $4.50 admission fee, so come on Sunday when it's free. *Canal, at 16 de Septiembre. Open Tues.–Sun. 10–4:30.*

FUERTE DE SAN JUAN DE ULUA A miniature city in itself, the island fort of San Juan de Ulua is a maze of moats, ramparts, and drawbridges smack in the middle of the busy port area. Now connected to the mainland by a causeway, this island was witness to some of the most momentous events in Mexican history. Cortés landed here in 1519, establishing Veracruz as a major gateway for Spanish settlement of Mexico. Fortification of the island began in 1535 under the direction of Antonio de Mendoza, the first viceroy of New Spain. Ground coral, sand, and oyster shells were used for the original walls. A few centuries later, the fort was used as a prison, housing such figures as Benito Juárez, who was held prisoner here by conservative dicatator Santa Anna before being exiled to Louisiana in 1853. *Take* SAN JUAN DE ULUA *bus from zócalo. Admission: $4.50, free Sun. and holidays. Open Tues.–Sun. 9–4.*

INSTITUTO VERACRUZANO DE LA CULTURA The bright blue Veracruz Cultural Institute building was a hospital until health authorities closed it in 1975. The massive 18th-century structure, with its long, arched hallways and green tree-filled garden, now hosts cultural events and rotating art exhibits. *Canal, at Zaragoza. Admission free. Open daily 10–8.*

MUSEO DE LA CIUDAD If you've just arrived in Veracruz, the city museum is a good place to start exploring. The region's history is narrated via artifacts and displays, and scale models of the city give you a sense of the lay of the land. Also exhibited are copies of pre-Columbian statues and contemporary indigenous art. A $1 donation pays for a guided tour by a bilingual student. *Zaragoza, at Morelos. Admission: $3. Open Mon.–Sat. 9–4.*

CHEAP THRILLS

Boat tours of the bay leave from the malecón daily 7–7. Boats leave whenever they're full, and the $4, half-hour ride includes a (Spanish-language) talk on Veracruz history.

Longer trips to nearby **Isla Verde** (Green Island) and **Isla de Enmedio** (Middle Island) leave daily from the shack marked PASEO EN LANCHITA near the Plaza Acuario. Boats leave whenever they're full, so it's best to come in a big group. The cost should be about $5–$7 per person, but feel free to bargain. Make sure your guide will give you time to enjoy the island beaches—some guides may try to hasten your trip by claiming that the beaches are restricted, but don't believe it. (This is, however, true of Isla de los Sacrificios, to the south). Some of the boats from the malecón will also take you to the islands.

Those who prefer their leisure activities landlocked can stop by **Bicicentros Lezama** (Ávila Camacho 2775, tel. 29/31–04–32) and rent a bicycle ($2.50 per day) for a breezy ride along the broad sidewalks of the malecón. Motor scooters ($33 a day) are also available.

AFTER DARK

To get away from the zócalo and soak in some of the grittier port atmosphere, try one of the traditional bars south of the plaza, such as **Bella Epoca** on Lagunilla, an alley cordoned off for pedestrians. The bar serves seafood, and drink prices here are lower than what you'll find on the square. Bella Epoca's clientele is mostly male, so unaccompanied women can count on getting lots of attention here.

Every Tuesday and Friday night after 8 PM, the Plaza de Armas is the scene of open-air dances, with a dressed-up crowd and live marimba music. Sunday nights the dancing moves to Parque Zamora.

Discos and video bars are plentiful along the malecón. Both **Ocean** (Ruíz Cortines 8, at Ávila Camacho, tel. 29/37–63–27), a flashy, modern discotheque, and **Blue Ocean** (Ávila Camacho 9, tel. 29/22–03–66), a video bar with a light show, are packed on Friday and Saturday nights with a young, largely local crowd. Both play a wide variety of music and are open Thursday–Saturday only. Ocean charges cover ($10) on Saturdays only. The more relaxed Blue Ocean charges $7 at the door and has a small dance floor and some pool tables.

OUTDOOR ACTIVITIES

Veracruz's beaches are much less inviting than you might expect: Most are somewhat dirty, and the water is fairly polluted. If you are determined to get a glimpse of the Gulf marine life anyway, you can rent snorkel or scuba gear from **Tridente** (Ávila Camacho 165-A, tel. 29/31–79–24) and venture into the murky depths. **Villa del Mar** is the beach closest to downtown, about 2 kilometers south along the malecón, but the noticeable filth will dissuade all but the most avid fans of hepatitis. A little better, though quite built up and still a bit dirty and shallow, is **Playa Mocambo**, 8 kilometers further south. The **Hotel Playa Mocambo** will let you use their pool for about $5 a day.

Better beaches are farther from town. About 4 kilometers south of Playa Mocambo is **Boca del Río,** a small fishing village at the mouth of the Río Jamapa that is getting quickly sucked into greater Veracruz. While Boca's beach gets dirtier as you move closer to the center, it's uncrowded, and the water is relatively unpolluted. Boca del Río has a number of open-air restaurants that sell fantastic seafood at high prices. Don't expect a charming little seaside village, though: Boca is basically a suburb that happens to be by the water. These beaches can all be reached via any of the BOCA DEL RIO buses that run along the malecón, leaving from Calle Serdán, a block east of the zócalo.

If you have more time to kill and are determined to find really nice beaches, you can head to **Villa Cardel,** where a youth hostel operates sporadically (*see* Where to Sleep, *above*), or 20 kilometers south of town, to the village of **Anton Lizardo,** where a number of small islands and coral reefs just offshore offer some of the best scuba diving in the area. You can rent overpriced snorkel gear ($7 an hour) or scuba equipment ($35) at the local branch of **Tridente** (Pino Suárez, at Av. de la Playa, tel. 29/34–08–44), where you can also arrange boat rides out to the islands. Three-hour boat trips are $17 per person (with an eight-person minimum), and it's a good idea to call ahead and reserve at least a day in advance. **Autobuses Unidos** buses serve the town from the main station in Veracruz city.

Los Tuxtlas

The Sierra de Los Tuxtlas is a small volcanic mountain range that meets the sea some 140 kilometers south of Veracruz. Simply known as Los Tuxtlas, the area has lakes, waterfalls, rivers, mineral springs, and access to beaches, making it a popular stopover for travelers heading east from Mexico City to the Yucatán. The region's three principal towns—Santiago Tuxtla, San Andrés Tuxtla, and Catemaco—are carved into the mountainsides more than 200 meters above sea level, lending them a coolness even in summer that's the envy of the perspiring masses on the coastal plain.

The Tuxtlas gain an air of mystery from the cool, gray fog that slips over the mountains and lakes and the whisperings among the townspeople about the brujos (witches), also called curanderos (healers), who read tarot cards, prescribe herbal remedies, and cast spells here.

While much of the architecture here is of the 1960s school of looming cement, all three towns are laid out in the colonial style around a main plaza and a church, and all retain a certain amount of charm. The region was also a center of Olmec culture, and Olmec artifacts and small ruins abound, especially around the town of Santiago Tuxtla. Today, the economic life of Los Tuxtlas depends on cigar manufacturing and tourism. The largest of the three towns is San Andrés, which is also the local transport hub. With plenty of hotels, it serves as a good base from which to explore the entire region. From Santiago, you can check out the ruins at Tres Zapotes; the town also has an informative museum where you can learn about the region's indigenous heritage and contemporary local cultures. Lake Catemaco is popular among Mexicans as a summer and Christmas resort and is also the place to go for a *consulta* (consulation) with a brujo or curandero, should you have any problems or questions that require some spiritual clarity or supernatural intervention.

BASICS

CASAS DE CAMBIO The only place in the Tuxtlas to change money is San Andrés, where both **Bancomer** (Madero 20) and **Banamex** change cash and traveler's checks weekdays 9 AM–11:30 AM. The latter has an ATM that accepts Plus, Cirrus, MasterCard, and Visa. **Hotel de Los Pérez** (*see* Where to Sleep, *below*) will also change money at all hours, but their rates are lousy.

EMERGENCIES The **Cruz Roja** (González Boca Negra 242, tel. 294/2–05–00) in San Andrés provides emergency care only. The phone number for the **police** in San Andrés is 294/2–02–35. In Santiago, the police police can be reached at 294/7–00–92; the number for the police in Catemaco is 294/3–00–55.

PHONES AND MAIL The largest **post office** in the region is in San Andrés, on 20 de Noviembre and La Frauga, a block down the hill from the main square. They will hold mail sent to you at the following address for up to 10 days: Lista de Correos, San Andrés Tuxtla, Veracruz, CP 95701, México. There are no Ladatel international phones in the Tuxtlas, but there are a number of small **phone offices** in all three towns—just look for the blue-and-white signs marked LARGA DISTANCIA. One of the most convenient is in San Andrés, at Madero 6-B.

COMING AND GOING

The transport hub for Los Tuxtlas is San Andrés's **Autobuses del Oriente (ADO)** terminal (Juárez 762, tel. 294/2–08–71), about six blocks from the zócalo. Buses for Veracruz city ($7, 2½ hrs) **465** leave hourly 5 AM–8 PM. One bus leaves daily at 1:30 PM for Mexico City ($27, 9 hrs). There are also frequent departures for Villahermosa ($15, 5 hrs) and Jalapa ($17, 8 hrs).

Second-class buses based in San Andrés connect the three towns. Buses for Santiago leave the **Terminal de los Rojos** station (Juárez, 1 block past ADO) in San Andrés every 10 minutes and cost less than $1.50. You don't have to go to the station to get the bus for Catemaco, however—just wait on the highway near the ADO terminal for one of the Rojos CATEMACO buses that pass every 10–15 minutes. In Catemaco, the second-class company operates a small station two blocks from the main square. In Santiago, the bus stop is at the corner of Morelos and Ayuntamiento, three blocks from the plaza.

San Andrés Tuxtla

Spotless San Andrés Tuxtla is the largest and most modern town in Los Tuxtlas. The city has two good movie theaters, and cafés line the central plaza. The pleasant atmosphere combined with the town's central location and cool nights make it an ideal stopover for travelers feeling abused by too many hours on buses. Those in need of more than just relaxation can try some of the curative teas and medicinal herbs at the **Farmacia Homeopática La Esperanza** (Juárez 264, at Hidalgo), two blocks from the zócalo.

Saltos de Eyipantla is a spectacular waterfall and popular picnic spot. Bring a friend and frolic in the pools at the bottom of the falls. Take a bus marked SALTOS from either Catemaco or San Andrés.

If you're more interested in polluting your body than purifying it, there's always the **Fábrica de Puros Santa Clara** (5 de Febrero 10, tel. 294/2–12–00), a huge cigar factory where you can see experts making fine cigars that cost $60 for a box of 24. If you buy a box, they'll print your name or slogan on each cigar at no extra charge. Also for sale are cartons of five for $13 and super-deluxe cigars that come in lovely, handmade wooden boxes and cost more than you can afford.

WHERE TO SLEEP On a quiet side street near the cathedral is the spotless **Hotel Catedral** (Pino Suárez 3, tel. 294/2–02–37). A night here costs $7 for one person, $9 for two, and most rooms have large, comfortable beds and lovely, wrought-iron window frames. All have clean bathrooms with cranky plumbing. If the Catedral is full, try **Hotel San Andrés** (Madero 6, tel. 294/2–04–22), where exterior rooms have balconies that look out onto the lively street below, and all have private bathrooms. Singles are $18, doubles $21.50. **Hotel de Los Pérez** (Rascón 2, tel. 294/2–07–77) is your best bet at the high end. Carpeted rooms on the third floor go for about $28 for a single and $35 for a double, but they tend to be mustier than their uncarpeted counterparts ($26 and $33, respectively) on the first and second floors. All rooms have phones, TVs, blissfully quiet air conditioners, and spotless bathrooms, and the hotel has a decent restaurant.

FOOD The cafés by the zócalo on Madero serve cappuccino and fixed-price breakfasts. In the afternoons, the restaurant at **Hotel del Parque**, also on the zócalo, serves a filling comida corrida for about $6. Otherwise, stop off at **Caperucita Roja** (Juárez 108) for a sandwich or taco at rock-bottom prices. A favorite of local teenagers on dates, this small restaurant is outside under a bamboo roof, with meat for the tacos slowly turning over an open flame in one corner. Folks trying to beat the heat on summer afternoons head to **Restaurante Tortacos** (tel. 294/2–32–66) in the cool, quiet La Fuente shopping center on the corner of Juárez and Argudín. The daily comida corrida is $4, but the most popular item on the menu is *papas a la francesa* (french fries). This is also the place to satisfy late-night cravings—it's open daily 7 AM–2 AM.

Catemaco

On the western shore of huge Lake Catemaco, the town of Catemaco is now almost entirely devoted to tourism but has lost little of its bizarre personality. Populated by people of Spanish, African, and Indian descent, Catemaco is dotted with *consultorios* (consulting rooms) where brujos ply their trade. If you'd like to sample their services, the best way to avoid being scammed is to ask the locals to recommend someone—outward skepticism notwithstanding, most residents have snuck off for a *limpieza* (spiritual cleansing) once or twice themselves.

Catemaco is the local center for brujería (witchcraft). Practicioners of traditional medicine and magic come here from all over Mexico during the first eight days of March for a yearly convention.

Catemaco's lakeside walkway, or malecón, bustles with seafood vendors, souvenir stands, small restaurants, and men hawking boat rides, all set against a gorgeous backdrop of lake and mountains. The fauna, too, is spectacular: You can see *changos* (monkeys), parakeets, and white herons without leaving the shore. For a better look at the local wildlife, take a ride in a *lancha* (flat-bottom boat) to **Isla de los Changos** (Monkey Island), thickly populated with the aggressive, screaming brutes, and to **La Nanciyaga**, an ecological reserve. At La Nanciyaga you can pay $2 for a tour of the island and a mud facial. If you're there on a weekend night, you can also sweat it out in an adobe sweat house. With a full boat (about six people) the tours are $7–$8 per person. Back on shore, you can cavort for free on the lakeside beaches, but they are unspectacular, and the only sandy one, **Playa Hermosa**, is about 2 kilometers south of town.

The town's other attractions include the gaudy church on the zócalo, dedicated to Catemaco's patron saint, the Virgen del Carmen, who appeared in 1714 to Juan Catemaxca, a local fisherman for whom the town is named. Every year, on May 30, locals descend upon the malecón, where lanchas await to take them out to the **Monumento a Juan Catemaxca** (a tall statue of Catemaxca planted right off the coast) to leave offerings of fish, flowers, and fruit in honor of their city's namesake.

WHERE TO SLEEP It's possible to camp out by the lake, but it's probably unsafe; nice campsites are hard to find, anyway. If you really want to plop down in the sand, you're better off taking a bus down to the Gulf Coast (*see* Near Catemaco, *below*). **Hotel Los Arcos** (Madero 7, at Mantilla, tel. 294/3–00–03) is the place to go if you find a few forgotten pesos stuffed deep in your pocket. The rooms are pricey ($23 single, $26 double) but as comfy as they come and have phones, TVs, air-conditioning, private bathrooms, and balconies that overlook the lake. There's even a small pool in the courtyard. The cheapest rooms on the waterfront are to be found at the tiny **Hotel y Restaurant La Julita** (Playa 10, 2 blocks from plaza, tel. 294/3–00–08). Clean, well-furnished rooms here are only $5 per person, and the manager is unusually easygoing. **Posada Koniapan** (Revolución, at malecón, tel. 294/3–00–63) also offers a fair deal for the price. Air-conditioned rooms on the ground floor cost $27 for one person, $30 for two. Upstairs rooms have ceiling fans instead of air-conditioning and run $20 and $25, respectively. In off season (August–November), it's possible to bargain a bit, and students (or non-students who look studious) get a 10% discount year-round.

FOOD The malecón is lined with small restaurants overlooking the lake. **Las 7 Brujas** (tel. 294/3–01–57) is the best-known and most expensive, but many others, including **El Pescador** (tel. 294/3–06–25), are equally inviting. For a cheaper meal or seafood appetizers, go to the **mercado** (market) just off the malecón, where *comedores* (sit-down food stands) sell well-rounded meals for less than $2, and a cocktail of shrimp, oysters, or octopus won't cost you more than $2.50.

NEAR CATEMACO

The Gulf Coast beaches, about 1½ bumpy hours by bus out of Catemaco, are one of Los Tuxtlas's great secrets. Foreign tourists rarely venture down this far, unless they're staying at one of the few isolated resorts dotted among the tiny fishing villages. The bus ride itself takes you through some beautiful ranching country before it stops at **Sontecomopan**, a resort on the shore of a picturesque lagoon framed by green hills. About 10 kilometers farther is the stop for **Playas Jicacal** and **Escondida**, two of the best beaches in the region. When you get off the bus, follow the marked trail downhill for about a kilometer to the sandy expanse of Playa Jicacal. Playa Escondida lies on the other side of the promontory at the far end of the beach. (Keep your eyes open in the water here: Locals claim the area is frequented by sharks.) Buses leave the stop at the top of the trail for the return trip to Catemaco as late as 8 PM, but you'd be crazy to try hiking back up the hill after nightfall. On top of the promontory, the basic **Hotel Playa Escondida**, where double rooms rent for $20 a night, is your best overnight option.

Santiago Tuxtla and Tres Zapotes

With its winding streets, red-tile roofs, and small market, Santiago Tuxtla has managed to retain more of its colonial character than the other two Tuxtla towns. Although it was founded in 1525, most visitors come here to see the even older traces of Olmec civilization, centered at the nearby ruins of **Tres Zapotes.** A huge stone Olmec head dominates the town's zócalo, and the **Museo Tuxteco,** also on the plaza, displays a collection of neolithic pieces, including detailed clay sculptures, black obsidian blades, and a skull showing evidence of ritual deformation. Dr. Fernando Bustamante, the museum's director, is an expert on local indigenous cultures and more than willing to answer (in Spanish) any question you may have. He usually hangs around the museum weekday mornings.

The ruins themselves are about 21 kilometers west of town. Tres Zapotes, now decidedly unspectacular, was once an important Olmec ceremonial center; it is believed to have been occupied as early as AD 100. Little remains of the original site, except for **La Camila,** a burial mound that rises from the corn fields outside town. Over 15 meters tall, this large mound is rumored to be an important nexus of spritualism and cosmic energy. More edifying is the **museum** to the left of the taxi stand in the village of Tres Zapotes, 1 kilometer from the ruins. Here you can see Stela C, a stone relief dated to 31 BC that features a series of bars and dots relating to the Maya calendar. The only way to make the bumpy, 25-minute trip from town to the ruins is by collective taxi (about $1.50 per person). Taxis leave from **Los Pozitos** bar (just over bridge from Hidalgo) whenever they're *very* full.

WHERE TO SLEEP Casa de Huéspedes Morelos (Morelos 12, tel. 294/7–04–74) is the cheaper of the town's two lodging options and feels like what it is: someone's cramped but comfy and welcoming home. There's no air-conditioning, but each room has a fan, and the owner doesn't mind if you use her washboard and clothesline. Rooms are $10 per person. The wheelchair-accessible **Hotel Castellanos** (5 de Mayo, at Comonfort, tel. 294/7–03–00), right off the main square, is the only real hotel in town. Because the hotel forms a circle and each room has a balcony, you can pick a room overlooking whichever part of the city you prefer. The comfortable, even fancy, rooms have TVs, rugs, air-conditioning, and spotless bathrooms. The price, however, is a stiff $27–$34 a night.

FOOD Santiago is not noted for its restaurants. If you decide to stay here, head for the area near the bus terminal, which has several inexpensive *fondas* (covered food stands). For a little more atmosphere (and better-tasting food) try **Parrilla la Ribera** (Castellanos Quinto 43, tel. 294/7–06–73). The chicken tacos are a steal at $2 for an order of five, and the owner, Señor Gutierrez, is super-friendly. To get here, walk down Morelos to Victoria and go left over the bridge.

Jalapa

Jalapa is perched on the side of a mountain, between the coastal lowlands of Veracruz and the high central plateau. A little more than 1,400 meters above sea level, the city has an enviable climate that will come as a pleasant surprise to perspiration-soaked escapees from Veracruz city, which swelters on the coast some 100 kilometers to the southeast. The capital of the state of Veracruz and a university town, Jalapa boasts the finest archaeological museum outside Mexico City, as well as hills that pose intriguing engineering problems—in some places you'll find the twisting, cobblestone streets bordered by six-foot high sidewalks built to compensate for sudden, sharp inclines. The presence of the university makes for a diverse population as well, and you are as likely to see long-haired young people sitting around in cafés as you are wizened campesinos walking to work. The town is also home to a symphony orchestra and a state theater that attracts big-name performers.

BASICS

AMERICAN EXPRESS The travel agency **Viajes Xalapa** functions as the local AmEx representative from its office about a block from Parque Juárez. They do not exchange money but provide all other AmEx services, including emergency check cashing and mail holding for cardholders, MoneyGram delivery, and replacement of lost or stolen AmEx cards or traveler's checks. *Carillo Puerto 24, Jalapa, Veracruz, CP 91000, México, tel. 28/17–87–44. Open weekdays 9–1:30 and 4–7, Sat. 9–1.*

If you find yourself in "Xalapa," wondering if you may have taken a wrong turn somewhere, don't panic. Jalapa and Xalapa are one and the same: The first is the Hispanicized version of the latter, a Nahuatl word.

CASAS DE CAMBIO One block from Parque Juárez, **Casa de Cambio Jalapa** offers good rates. *Zamora 36, tel. 28/18–68–60. Open weekdays 9–1:30 and 4:30–6.*

You can also change money in the mornings at several banks on Parque Juárez. **Bancomer** (Lucío 1, tel. 28/14–43–22), right next to the cathedral, has better rates than the casa de cambio, but only changes traveler's checks—no cash. **Banamex** (Xalapeños Ilusores 3, tel. 18–03–74) has similar rates, changes both cash and traveler's checks, and has an ATM that accepts Cirrus, Plus, Visa, and MasterCard.

EMERGENCIES The number for the **police** is 28/17–63–10. For an ambulance, call the **Cruz Roja** (tel. 28/14–45–00).

LAUNDRY **Lavandería Diamante** gets your clothes so clean you won't recognize them. Not only will they wash, fabric-soften, dry, and neatly fold a 3-kilo load for $4—they'll even pick it up and drop it off at your hotel. *Ferrocarril Interoceánico 11, tel. 28/12–63–91. Open Mon.–Sat. 9–2 and 3:30–8:30.*

MAIL The full-service post office will hold mail sent to you at the following address for up to 10 days: Lista de Correos, Administración No. 1, Jalapa, Veracruz, CP 91000, México. You can send telegrams and faxes at the office next door. *Diego Lenyo, at Zamora, tel. 28/18–52–83. Open weekdays 8–8, Sat. 9–noon.*

MEDICAL AID Calle Enríquez is lined with pharmacies. For 24-hour service, the pharmacy in **Super Tiendas Ramón** (Revolución 171, at Sagayo, tel. 28/18–09–35) is your best option.

PHONES There are Ladatel phones in front of the Palacio del Gobierno. If you'd rather go to a caseta de larga distancia, **Caseta Victoria** doesn't charge outrageous commissions. *Guadalupe Victoria 74, tel. 28/17–42–32. Open Mon.–Sat. 9–9.*

SCHOOLS The **Escuela Para Estudiantes Extranjeros** of the Universidad Veracruzana offers language programs for foreign students. They offer fixed, six-week programs, but will also tailor a course to your needs. Family stays can be arranged by the department. The director is Maestra Berta Cecilia Murrieta Cervantes, and she's more than willing to answer questions (in English) over the phone. *Sebastián Camacho 5, at Zaragoza, tel. 28/17–86–87, fax 29/17–64–13. In center of town, near Cine Variedades.*

VISITOR INFORMATION You can get information (in Spanish only) as well as maps and pamphlets from the helpful folks at the municipal tourist office. *Ávila Camacho 191, tel. 28/18–70–75. Open weekdays 9–4.*

COMING AND GOING

BY BUS Jalapa's modern **Central Camionera** (20 de Noviembre Ote. 571, tel. 28/18–92–29) is served by the first-class **Autobuses del Oriente (ADO)** line (tel. 28/18–99–22), as well as the second-class **Autobuses Unidos (AU)** (tel. 28/18–70–77). ADO has frequent departures to Veracruz city ($5, 3 hrs), Mexico City ($13, 5 hrs), and Catemaco ($10, 4 hrs). AU has equally frequent service and slightly lower prices. The terminal has a 24-hour pharmacy, a long-distance phone office, and luggage storage.

BY TRAIN The small **Estación Nueva Miguel Alemán** (tel. 28/15–17–64) is in the northern part of Jalapa. Two painfully slow trains creep to Mexico City and Veracruz daily. The eight-hour trip to Mexico City costs about $5, whether you ride in first or second class, but first-class seats are limited. The train to Veracruz has only second-class seats, costs $3, and arrives in four hours. A cab from downtown to the train station will run you less than $2.

GETTING AROUND

Jalapa's streets are twisty and confusing. Orient yourself around **Parque Juárez,** the city's emotional, if not geographic, heart. Uphill from the park on Calle Revolución are the markets. Downhill you'll find the more elegant shops on busy Calle Zamora, which runs past the park, becoming Enríquez as it passes the purple Banamex building. Uphill, Zamora turns into Ávila Camacho and passes the **Teatro del Estado** (state theater). Revolución begins at Zamora and runs north past Juárez and the markets on Altamirano.

The most important city buses originate in front of the **3 Hermanos** shoe store on Zamora, two blocks down the hill from Parque Juárez. Vans called *minis* work the same routes. Taxis, which wait for passengers on Enríquez by the park and on most of the main streets, are also relatively cheap and extremely convenient. They don't have meters—just get in, name your destination, and don't pay more than $2.

WHERE TO SLEEP

Because of its triple function as the seat of state government, a university town, and the only big city in a poor, thickly settled rural area, Jalapa offers plenty of lodging choices. In general, the cheaper hotels are on the winding streets near the market, above Parque Juárez. These, unfortunately, seem to economize on insecticide, however. Don't despair, however; not every place in Jalapa is a roach motel, and if you shop around a bit, you shouldn't have to pay too much for a bug-free room.

➢ UNDER $15 • **Hotel Continental.** The Continental as a whole is beautiful, with gloriously high ceilings and a pretty, covered courtyard, but its rooms ($11 single and $14 double) are anticlimactic: They're big and roomy and have relatively clean bathrooms and large, wooden doors, but the musty odor is overwhelming and the hot water only works between 6 AM and noon. The courtyard restaurant serves cheap, satisfying lunches. *Zamora 4, tel. 28/17–35–30. 22 rooms, all with bath. Luggage storage, wheelchair access. MC, V.*

Hotel Plaza. You'll have to look carefully for this place—the reception desk is hidden at the top of a flight of stairs at the end of a long, yellow-tiled hallway next to Enrico's restaurant. All rooms are tidy and fan-cooled and have bathrooms with hot water, complimentary soap, and clean towels. They lack TVs and phones, but all feature a shiny, white spittoon for your expectorating pleasure. A single here will cost you $10, a double $14. *Enríquez 4, tel. 28/117–33–10. 36 rooms, all with bath. Luggage storage.*

Hotel San Bernardo. The downstairs lobby of this hotel is gloomy and dark, and the rooms are bare except for small, lopsided desks, rickety chairs, and the occasional six-legged visitor. On the upside, the price is right: Singles are $10, doubles $11. Be sure to ask for a room facing away from the street, or the screeching brakes of the lumbering buses that stop nearby will have you batty by morning. *Altamirano 18, 2 blocks uphill from Parque Juárez, tel. 28/17–35–50. 39 rooms, all with bath. Laundry, luggage storage.*

➢ UNDER $20 • **Hotel Limón.** Set back from the busy traffic of Revolución under a pretty, tiled archway, the Limón is a great bargain, with hand-painted tiles and bright-colored floors to lend it a great deal of character. Ask to see a few rooms before you choose: The management charges solo travelers $10, couples $15, regardless of room size, so you might as well take the biggest one available. *Revolución 8, behind cathedral, tel. 28/17–22–04. 45 rooms, all with bath. Laundry, luggage storage.*

Hotel Principal. This aging but immaculate hotel is smack in the center of town. Get an interior room, or the traffic will set your teeth rattling. The rooms (singles $15, doubles $17) are big and comfy, with phones and ceilings high enough to accommodate a small herd of giraffes. The clean bathrooms are, oddly enough, configured to allow you to use the toilet and sink while showering. *Zaragoza 28, tel. 28/17–64–00. 40 rooms, all with bath. Laundry, luggage storage, wheelchair access.*

➤ UNDER $25 • **Hotel Citlalli.** You may have to trudge up Clavijero—one of Jalapa's steeper streets—to get to this hotel, but it merits the effort. The entire place is spotless and well lit, and every room has a phone and a private bathroom; the showers even have nice stay-in-one-place sliding doors instead of the grimy, float-towards-you-and-stick-to-your-bottom curtains you'll find in many other hotels. *Clavijero 43, tel. 28/18–34–58. 42 rooms, all with bath. Luggage storage. Reservations advised.*

FOOD

Like everything else in Jalapa, even the better restaurants are affordable. A big comida corrida at an elegant place on Enríquez will fill you up for less than $10. For tacos and vendor food, including delicious "hot cakes" topped with sweet condensed milk, head to the market area.

Jalapa is home to the jalapeño pepper. With almost every bite of the city's spicy food, you'll be reminded of where you are.

➤ UNDER $5 • **El Balcon de la Ágora.** This excellent café is set on the edge of a cliff in Parque Juárez, overlooking the city and the mountain peaks beyond. It's a favorite hangout among both local students and the foreigners who are here in town for the summer language program. Consequently, the management is accustomed to having young people with very little money linger over a soda or a small sandwich for hours. You probably couldn't spend more than $5 here if you tried, though the genuinely good coffee is not so cheap at $1.50. *Bajos del Parque Juárez, tel. 28/18–57–30. Down stairs at south end of park. Open daily 8:30 AM–10 PM.*

La Sopa. You won't find better food at cheaper prices anywhere in town. Homemade tortillas, refreshing *agua de fruta* (fruit juice), and terrific garbanzo-bean soup come with the $2 comida corrida that is served daily 1 PM–5 PM. The place is usually packed, but once you get a table the service is prompt and polite. *Antonio M. de Rivera (a.k.a. Callejón del Diamante) 3-A, tel. 28/17–80–69. Open Mon.–Sat. 1 PM–11 PM. Wheelchair access.*

➤ UNDER $10 • **La Fonda.** Multicolored *papel picado* (traditional Mexican cut paper) hangs from the brightly painted walls of this little fonda, and the upstairs balcony, complete with pink-and-blue linen tablecloths and stenciled awnings, is a great place to relax over coffee. The comida corrida ($5) goes well with the unusual *tepache*, a drink made of fermented pineapples, that is sold here for less than $1. *Antonio M. de Rivera (a.k.a. Callejón del Diamante) 1, tel. 28/18–45–20. Open Mon.–Sat. 8–6:30. Wheelchair access.*

Restaurant/Bar Terraza Jardín. This restaurant, set under the colonnade in Parque Juárez, serves standard, northern Veracruzan fare. Seafood and spicy meat dishes are about $8, and vegetarians can choose from a fair selection of soups and salads, all of which cost about $2. The clientele, largely consisting of university types, is drawn as much by the alcohol as the food. *Edificio Nachita, in front of Parque Juárez, tel. 28/17– 48–64. Open daily 8 AM–11 PM.*

WORTH SEEING

The terraced gardens of **Parque Juárez** should be the starting point for your exploring. Aside from offering gorgeous views of both the 5,610-meter Pico de Orizaba (or Citlaltépetl, as it was originally known), Mexico's highest peak, and the city sprawling below, they are within walking distance of almost everything. Just off the park are the 19th-century **Palacio del Gobierno** and the **Cathedral,** whose bell-tower chimes hourly.

CASA DE ARTESANIAS Jalapa's state-run handicrafts center is housed in a beautifully renovated colonial mansion that sits on a hill overlooking the lakes of the **Parque Paseo de los Lagos.** Inside the center is a studio with rotating exhibits and an enormous shop selling locally produced crafts and typical clothing. Fruit wines ($3 a bottle) are also sold. *Paseo de los*

Lagos, tel. 28/17–08–04. From Parque Juárez, straight down Herrera, right on Dique, left on Carranza. Open weekdays 9–3 and 4–7, Sat. 9–1.

CENTRO DEL ARTE This small cultural center hosts exhibitions of everything from photography and sculpture to finger painting. A billboard on the wall by the entryway provides the scoop on current cultural events. *Xalapeños Ilusores, at Insurgentes, no phone. Admission free. Open Mon.–Sat. 11–8, Sun. 11–6.*

GALERIA UNIVERSITARIA RAMON ALVA DE LA CANAL This two-story university gallery, with its polished wood floors and clean, white walls, houses rotating exhibits of art and photography, almost all of which is produced by university students. *Zamora 27, tel. 28/17–75–79. Admission free. Open weekdays 9–2 and 5–8, Sat. 10–noon.*

JARDIN BOTANICO FRANCISCO JAVIER CLAVIJERO These well-kept botanical gardens about 2 kilometers outside town contain more than 1,500 varieties of flora from throughout the state of Veracruz. A small arboretum houses a slew of palm species, and a large pond showcases a vast array of aquatic plants. Hilly stone walkways and narrow steps guide you into the woods, where most plants bear placards giving both their Spanish and scientific names and explaining any useful properties they possess. *Carretera Antigua a Coatepec Km. 2.5, tel. 28/18–60–09 ext. 253. COATEPEC BRIONES buses come here from stop in front of Teatro del Estado, at cnr of Ignacio de la Llave and Ávila Camacho. Open Tues.–Sun. 10–5.*

MUSEO DE ANTROPOLOGIA DE JALAPA With more than 29,000 pieces on display, Jalapa's archaeological museum is second only to Mexico City's (*see* Worth Seeing in Chapter 2). The building is divided into three sections focusing on the Huastec, Totonac, and Olmec cultures of the state of Veracruz. Highlights include stone Olmec heads, small statues with smiling faces, jade jewelry, and a burial mound complete with bones, ritually deformed skulls, and ceremonial statuettes. There is also an exhibit on the contemporary clothing and customs of the Indians of Veracruz state. Out back, a garden features examples of local flora. Guided tours by English-speaking students are available Tuesday–Sunday 11 AM–4 PM, but you may want to call in advance and make an appointment, as the tour schedule is unpredictable. *Av. Jalapa s/n, tel. 28/15–49–52. Take ALVARIO PANTEON or MERCADO TESORARIA from Revolución, just beside market. Admission $3, $2 students. Open Tues.–Sun. 10–5.*

MUSEO DE CIENCIA Y TECNOLOGIA Jalapa's newest major attraction, the Museum of Science and Technology was inaugurated in November 1992 by then-president Salinas de Gortari. All exhibits here are interactive—nothing is off limits. Even the planes, trains, tanks, and tractors that dot the tree-lined park at the museum's entry are equipped with ladders for climbing. *Rafael Murillo Vidal s/n, tel. 28/12–50–88. Admission $5, $2.50 students. Open Tues.–Sun. 10–4.*

AFTER DARK

Despite its student population, Jalapa is relatively quiet at night. On weekends, Parque Juárez becomes the meeting place for the city's young, and the bars nearby are a good place to start looking for some action. **Video Bar Terraza,** above the Restaurant/Bar Terraza Jardín (*see* Food, *above*), is a crowded lounge popular with students and young professionals. The upscale **Café El Escorial** purveys beer, coffee, and live music to a well-heeled crowd. The Escorial is hidden off Pasaje Enríquez; turn off Enríquez at the Banco de Comercio. **La 7a Estación** (20 de Noviembre, near Central Camionera) is a well-known dance place that is packed with salsa dancers on Wednesday nights. Thursday–Saturday, rock and alternative music are featured. There's no cover before 10 PM, but it's $5 after that. The club is a little out of the way on the east side of town, so it's most easily reached by taxi. **Tortilla Flats** (Díaz Mirón 23, off Parque Los Berros), a small restaurant near the university, features rock music on Saturday nights, starting about 9; admission is free.

The **Ágora** (Parque Juárez) is a cultural center that stages art exhibits and the occasional folk-music performance and shows classic and avant-garde films in its cinema club. Stop by during the day to see what's planned. The **Teatro del Estado** (Ignacio de la Llave s/n, tel.

28/17–41–77 ext. 38) is the big, modern, state theater of Veracruz. The Orquesta Sinfónica de Jalapa performs here, often giving free concerts here during its off-season (early June to mid-August). Check *El Diario de Jalapa* (the Jalapa city newspaper, available at newsstands) for dates and times of performances, or stop by the Ágora (*see above*) in Parque Juárez.

Near Jalapa

COATEPEC

Just 8 kilometers of major highway from Jalapa, the colonial city of Coatepec is a center for coffee and orchid cultivation. You can see how orchids grow at the **Invernadero María Cristina** (Miguel Rebolledo 4, tel 28/16–03–79), right by the main square. Fruit wines are sold (and free samples offered) at **Licores Finos Bautista Gálvez** (Hernández y Hernández 5, tel. 28/16–01–35).

You can camp or play amidst the hills at **Agualegre** (5 blocks NW of plaza, tel. 28/17–07–21), a 13-hectare ecotourism wonderland on Río La Marina complete with a water slide, four swimming pools, stables, a restaurant, and trails for horseback riding or hiking. Admission is $2.50, and campsites are an additional $3. An hour of horseback riding through the verdant reserve is $8. Longer trips to sites as far off as Xico (*see below*) can be arranged with advance notice.

➢ COMING AND GOING • Buses marked TERMINAL that leave from the stop in front of the **3 Hermanos** shoe store on Enríquez in Jalapa will let you off at a bunch of bus stands. Look for the rusty, white TERMINAL EXCELSIOR sign. From here, blue buses marked COATEPEC leave every 5–10 minutes for the short journey to Coatepec.

The arts department of the university frequently opens dress rehearsals of upcoming presentations. Performances run the gamut from modern dance to Shakespeare and take place on campus and in the Teatro del Estado. Check El Diario de Jalapa for details.

In a small park north of the plaza on Hernandez y Hernandez sits a big cement structure called el hongo (the mushroom). Walk silently to the center, then speak softly, and see what happens.

XICO

Xico (pronounced He-koe), a tiny town at the base of the Perote foothills, 19 kilometers from Jalapa, is one of the few places left on planet Earth where donkeys are the major mode of transportation. Influenced by the heavy Spanish presence in the 16th century (Hernán Cortés passed through Xico on his way to the Aztec capital of Tenochtitlán), the very traditional town holds bullfights and *pamplonadas* (running of the bulls) each year as part of the **Feria de Santa María Magdalena** (July 22). The town's year-round selling point is the **Cascada de Texolo,** 3 kilometers outside town. A cobblestone path leads through banana plantations to the falls, but it's not easy to find: From the entrance to town on the main street (there's a sign marked ENTRADA), go up the hill, bearing left at the fork, and follow the CASCADA TEXOLO sign down the unpaved road. At the next fork, take the high road. There's a restaurant near the waterfall that serves a cheap comida corrida for $3; the owner moonlights as a taxi driver and will take you back to Xico for about $3 if you're too beat to walk.

Be sure to head back to Jalapa before nightfall, as there are no hotels here. The food is great, though, and almost all the restaurants near the plaza serve excellent dishes with *mole* (chile and chocolate sauce). Another local specialty is *verde*, a liqueur made with herbs.

➢ COMING AND GOING • Buses marked TERMINAL that leave from the stop in front of the **3 Hermanos** shoe store on Enríquez in Jalapa will let you off at a bunch of bus stands; look for the TERMINAL EXCELSIOR sign. From here, blue buses marked XICO leave every 5–10 minutes for the 40-minute journey to Xico.

Papantla de Olarte

Papantla de Olarte sits amid tropical hills about 250 kilometers northwest of Veracruz on Highway 180. The town's character is distinctive largely because of the mix of Spanish colonial and indigenous influence that is so visible here: Totonac men in flowing white pants lead their donkeys through the crowded streets; palm trees shade the traditional, tiled zócalo; and a site next to the ornate cathedral is set up for a Totonac ritual in which four voladores dive off a 25-meter pole (*see box, below*). Papantla is also the town nearest the ruins of El Tajín (*see* Near Papantla, *below*). Nevertheless, some travelers prefer to visit Papantla as part of a day trip from Tuxpán (*see below*), which has a much better lodging scene.

BASICS

CASAS DE CAMBIO Papantla lacks a casa de cambio, but the **Banamex** (Enríquez 102), just past Andy's Cadillac Bar, changes both cash and traveler's checks weekdays 9–noon and has an ATM that digests Cirrus, Plus, Visa, and Mastercard and regurgitates pesos.

EMERGENCIES **Police** (tel. 784/2–01–93); **Cruz Roja** (784/2–01–01).

MAIL The post office is just down the hill from the Mercado Juárez. No address is visible—just go up the stairs where you see SERVICIO POSTAL MEXICANO written in blue on the wall. They will hold mail sent to you at the following address for up to 10 days: Lista de Correos, Azueta 198 Altos, Papantla, Veracruz, CP 93400, México. *Azueta 198, tel. 784/2–00–73. Open weekdays 9–1 and 3–6, Sat. 9–noon.*

MEDICAL AID **Farmacia Médico** is the biggest pharmacy in Papantla. The staff doesn't speak English but is good at charades. *Gutierrez Zamora 3, tel. 784/2–19–41. Open daily 7:30 AM–10 PM.*

PHONES The three Ladatel phones in town are down the hill from the **Teléfonos de México** caseta (5 de Mayo 201, tel. 784/2–05–35). **Farmacia Médico** (*see* Medical Aid, *above*) also has a caseta de larga distancia.

VISITOR INFORMATION The tourist office has an attentive staff, but you'll have a tough time getting information if you don't speak Spanish. *Palacio Municipal, on zócalo, tel. 784/2–01–77. Open weekdays 9–3, Sat. 9–1.*

Voladores of Papantla

The ritual of the voladores was originally performed as a tribute to the god of sun and rain—the tree or pole used in the ceremony was meant to bring the dancers (or "fliers") closer to him. The four fliers begin the dance on a platform at the top of the ceremonial pole, each facing one of the cardinal directions. They begin their descent from the side of the platform facing east—where the sun rises and the world awakes—twisting left for 13 full rotations each. Between them, the four fliers circle the pole 52 times, once for each year of the cycle of the Totonac calendar. A fifth man, the prayer giver, sits atop the pole and plays a small flute while keeping rhythm on a drum as the fliers descend. Originally, the ceremony was held on the spring equinox, but Catholicism and tourism have changed all that. Now the voladores fly for the crowds every Saturday and Sunday at 12:45 PM and give special performances during Corpus Christi.

COMING AND GOING

The first-class **Autobuses del Oriente (ADO)** station (Juárez 207, tel. 784/2–02–18) is a five-minute walk downhill from the zócalo. Eight buses leave daily for Jalapa ($12, 4 hrs); five for both Veracruz city ($15, 4 hrs) and Mexico City ($12, 5 hrs). One bus also leaves at 7:30 PM daily for Villahermosa ($36, 12 hrs). A taxi between the zócalo and the station will cost you about $1.50. The ADO station in the nearby town of Poza Rica, which can be reached via a Transportes Papantla bus (*see below*), has a much more extensive schedule, so if you want a direct ride to some far-flung destination, you may want to try your luck there.

Second-class **Transportes Papantla** (20 de Noviembre s/n, tel. 784/2–00–15) buses serve the surrounding villages and a few major cities in Veracruz. There are frequent departures for Veracruz city ($8.50, 7 ½ hrs) and Jalapa ($9, 6 ½ hrs); buses to Poza Rica ($1, 20 min) run every 20 minutes between 4 AM and 11:30 PM. The station is straight downhill from the zócalo.

WHERE TO SLEEP

Hotels in Papantla are either cheap and lousy or expensive and passable. Just about all, however, are within a block or two of the zócalo. If you've got cash to burn, the pretentious and overpriced **Hotel Premier** has balconies overlooking the square. Penny-pinchers will prefer one of the places listed below.

Hotel Pulido. If the rickety fans at this hotel don't fall from the ceiling and decapitate you, the carbon monoxide fumes from the parking lot are sure to finish you off. The rooms, however, are decent, though they do vary in size, so ask to see a few before you commit yourself. They cost $13 for a single, $18 for a double, and those on the second floor offer more peace and somewhat fresher air. *Enríquez 205, tel. 784/2–00–36. 23 rooms, all with bath. Luggage storage.*

Hotel Tajín. Given your other options in Papantla, this place may be worth the price. Its hilltop perch makes for beautiful views of the city, and the hotel itself features an upscale restaurant and clean rooms with big bathrooms. Singles and doubles with air-conditioning cost $31 and $36, respectively; *económico* (budget) rooms have a fan instead of an air conditioner and cost $21 for a single and $26 for a double. *Nuñez y Domínguez 104, tel. 784/2–06–44. 60 rooms, all with bath. Laundry, luggage storage.*

Hotel Trujillo. The Trujillo is the cheapest hotel in town, and it feels like it. There's no hot water, the bathrooms are less than pristine, and each sparsely furnished room is illuminated by a single, naked light bulb. Rooms with one bed are $10; with two beds, they jump to $15. *5 de Mayo 401, tel. 784/2–08–63. 30 rooms, all with bath.*

FOOD

Papantla does not offer many culinary options, but you'll be hard-pressed to blow more than $5 on a meal anywhere in town. As usual, the fondas in the market (between Azueta and 20 de Noviembre) are your cheapest option. The restaurant at **Hotel Tajín** (*see* Where to Sleep, *above*) is one of the classiest places in town, and the prices here aren't significantly higher than those in the dives near the second-class bus station. You can stock up on souvenirs while you wait for your meal at **Restaurante Plaza Pardo** (Enríquez 105, tel. 784/2–00–59), which serves delicious chicken tacos ($3.50) and sweet aguas de fruta ($1) and doubles as a store. Just next door is the cheapest place in town, **Restaurante Sorrento** (Enríquez 104,

There's not much nightlife in Papantla, but those who want to get down with the pueblo can head over to Pulquería La Rosita on Serdán and sample their pulque, a viscous, whitish liquid made from the same succulent as tequila.

no phone). This small restaurant by the zócalo serves satisfying egg breakfasts and a $2 comida corrida, which includes a hearty entrée such as the spicy *bistec a la mexicana* (steak with tomatoes, chiles, and onion).

Near Papantla

EL TAJIN

Just 15 minutes outside Papantla is **El Tajín,** the ruins of what is thought to have been a religious complex dating as far back as AD 100. Although much of the site has been excavated and restored, many structures remain hidden under thick jungle growth; some archaeologists speculate that more than 400 buildings remain to be excavated.

Tajín is a Totonac word meaning "thunder."

Little is known about the people who built El Tajín. Early theories attributed the complex to a settlement of either Totonacs or Huastecas, the two most important cultures of the Veracruz area. Given the immense size and unique architecture and art that characterizes the complex, however, scholars are now talking about a distinct El Tajín cultural group.

Guided tours of the site are not available: The plaque at the entrance tells some of what little is known about the site in Spanish, English, and French, but the rest is up to your imagination. Evidence suggests that the southern half of the uncovered ruins—the area around the lower plaza—was reserved for ceremonial purposes, while the northern areas were administrative and residential. There is a dumbbell-shaped **ball court** just south of the pyramid (structure 5) near the lower plaza. Most archaeologists agree that the main object of the games played on these courts (found in most major Mesoamerican cities) the was to shoot a ball through the stone hoop-shaped outcroppings placed high on the walls of the court—without using hands. The absence of graded seating for spectators here may mean that this particular court was for special matches that were seen by only a few priests. Intricate carvings in the corners of the court and at midfield illustrate aspects of the game, including the post-game sacrifice of one of the players. Whether the sacrificial victim was the winner or loser of the match is still a subject of debate.

On the far side of structure 5 is the **Pyramid of the Niches.** This impressive seven-level pyramid has more than 300 cubby-like indentations, which appear to have once been painted blue and red. **El Tajín Chico,** to the north, is thought to have been the secular part of the city. The most important structure here is the **Building of the Columns.** The columns once held up stone ceilings, but early home builders from Papantla removed the ceiling stones to construct the first houses in the town. If the "killer beast" exhibit in the museum at the entrance (*see box, below*) didn't dissuade you, and you're prepared to work your way through the thick jungle, you can see some more recent finds along the dirt paths that lead over the nearby ridges.

Admission to the ruins is $4.50, except on Sunday, when it's free. Don't worry about finding food—the entrance is lined with fondas that sell cheap eats and mountains of tacky souvenirs, and there's even a big cafeteria-style restaurant at the site. El Tajín is also a good place to see the voladores (*see box, above*) perform. Their pole is near the entrance, just past the museum. Performances take place on weekends, usually around 2 PM, and during the week if enough people show up. Donations are the only wages the fliers receive.

Killer Beasts

The museum at the entrance to El Tajín has a rather disturbing exhibit of the various poisonous creatures that have killed workers here. Jars contain coral snakes and centipedes that, according to the blurb, "latch onto the skin and don't let go. When you tear them off, the claws remain embedded in your skin, where the venom is released." Needless to say, the exhibit is supposed to keep tourists from venturing off the marked paths.

COMING AND GOING Both the EL TAJIN and CHOTE buses that run along 16 de Septiembre in Papantla will get you to the ruins. A round-trip ticket to the ruins costs about $1. The last bus back to Papantla leaves at 5:45 PM.

Tuxpán

Tuxpán is a peaceful riverside town about an hour north of Papantla. The city's main attraction is the miles of beaches that begin just 7 kilometers to the east. Few tourists ever enjoy them, however, perhaps because the town lacks impressive sights and has not been developed for roving herds of souvenir hunters. So much the better for you: The white sandy beaches, beautiful green river, and tranquil setting make Tuxpán a prime destination for anyone wanting to play tropical beach bum in relative solitude.

The **Río Tuxpán** passes through town on its way to the sea at **Playa Tuxpán.** The surf isn't huge here, but there's enough action to warrant breaking out your surf- or boogieboard. Landlubbers can groove to the tropical tunes that drift out of the seafood and beer stands in the pine grove behind the beach.

Tuxpán itself is a pleasant town, with winding streets lined with two-story buildings. Juárez, the main street, runs parallel to the river and is lined with diners, hotels, and shops. The **Parque Reforma** is the center of social activity in town, with more than a hundred tables set around a hub of cafés and fruit stands, and the river is clean enough for swimming. *Lanchas* (flat-bottom boats) shuttle passengers across the river to the **Casa de Fidel Castro,** where Castro lived for a time while planning the overthrow of dictator Fulgencio Batista. A replica of the *Granma,* the ship that carried Fidel's freedom fighters from Tuxpán to battle in Cuba, rots outside. Inside, the casa is bare save some black-and-white photos of Fidel and Mexican President Lázaro Cárdenas.

BASICS

CASA DE CAMBIO Bancomer (Juárez, at Escuela Médico Militar, tel. 783/4–00–09) changes cash and traveler's checks weekdays 9:30–noon.

EMERGENCIES Police (tel. 783/4–02–52); **Cruz Roja** (tel. 783/4–01–58).

PHONES AND MAIL The full-service **post office** (Clavijero 28) is two long blocks east of Parque Reforma. They will hold mail sent to you at the following address for up to 10 days: Lista de Correos, Administración 1, Tuxpán, Veracruz, CP 92801, México. You can make both long-distance and local calls from the pay phones on Parque Reforma and at the ADO station (*see* Coming and Going, *below*).

VISITOR INFORMATION The small tourist office is across the street from the cathedral. The friendly staff only speaks Spanish, and maps are in chronic short supply. *Juárez 65, tel. 783/4–01–77. Open daily 10–3 and 5–7.*

COMING AND GOING

Tuxpán doesn't have a central first-class bus terminal; instead, each line has its own depot. The **Autobuses del Oriente (ADO)** station (Rodríguez 1, tel. 783/4–01–02), half a block off the river at the foot of Juárez, is the most convenient, with 10 buses a day to Mexico City ($13, 6 hrs), and four buses a day to Papantla ($3, 1½ hrs). If you can't get a ticket at the ADO terminal, try **Omnibus de México** (tel. 783/4–11–47), which has a depot 1 kilometer further down the river, near the bridge. Their service is similar to ADO's.

Bus tickets are a prized commodity in Tuxpán during such holidays as Christmas, Semana Santa, and the entire month of July. To avoid getting stuck here, it's best to buy your ticket out at least two days before you want to leave.

Second-class buses operate from the outdoor **Terminal ABC** (tel. 783/4–20–40) on Cuauhtémoc. Service is available to Tampico ($9, 6 hrs), Nuevo Laredo ($33, 16 hrs), Monterrey ($28, 12 hrs), and Reynosa ($28, 12 hrs), among other destinations.

GETTING AROUND

Central Tuxpán is small and easily covered on foot. Juárez, the main street, runs parallel to the river, one block inland. You can walk down Juárez from the ADO station to Parque Reforma in about five minutes. Boat rides across the river will set you back only pennies. Buses marked PLAYA run frequently along the river's edge to and from the beach and cost less than $1.

WHERE TO SLEEP

Hotels tend to be expensive, but you'll find a few moderately priced establishments near the center. If the places below are full, try the bare but passable **Hotel del Parque** (Humboldt 11, tel. 783/4–08–12), where both singles and doubles cost $15.

Hotel El Huasteco. Just a block east of Parque Juárez, the Huasteco is one of the better deals in Tuxpán and tends to fill up fast. The rooms are basic, but clean and air-conditioned. Singles go for $14, doubles for $17. *Morelos 41, tel. 783/4–18–59. 40 rooms, all with bath. Laundry, luggage storage.*

Hotel Posada San Ignacio. Potted plants fill the small central courtyard of this pretty hotel, and the rooms, while small, are spotless. Marbled bathrooms have plenty of hot water and freshly laundered towels. Rooms are $11 for one bed, $15 for two. *Melchor Ocampo 29, tel. 783/4–29–05. 17 rooms, all with bath. Laundry, luggage storage, wheelchair access.*

Hotel Tuxpán. Also near Parque Juárez, this hotel is a bit overpriced considering the mediocre accommodations it offers: Rooms are relatively clean but small and stuffy, and bathrooms are long, skinny, awkward affairs, though they do have hot water. Singles cost $13, doubles $15. *Mina 2, at Juárez, tel. 783/4–41–10. 43 rooms, all with bath. Luggage storage.*

CAMPING It's free and legal to pitch a tent on **Playa Tuxpán,** and hammocks, bathrooms, and showers cost less than a beer (though you may have to smile sweetly to talk someone into letting you use a hammock overnight—they're usually rented for day use only). It's also possible to camp on **Isla Lobos** (*see* Outdoor Activities, *below*), but you must first obtain a permit from the Coast Guard office (tel. 783/4–03–43), about 3 kilometers from the center, on the way to Playa Tuxpán. Permits can take up to four days to process, so plan ahead.

FOOD

Restaurants congregate on Juárez in the center of town. There are also several good, cheap taco stands up the street from the ADO depot, near the Cafetería Kon Tiki. Midnight munchies can be satisfied at the 24-hour **Cafetería Monte** (Rodríguez 17, tel. 783/4–19–61), where locals hang out, watch TV, and eat basic Mexican dishes till all hours.

Antonio's. This elegant, air-conditioned restaurant has prompt, polite service and a menu that runs the gamut from prohibitively expensive to happily budget-friendly. The *desayuno americano* (American breakfast) includes eggs, toast, jam, juice, and tea for $5.50, and a plate of chicken or cheese enchiladas is $4. There's also a full bar here. Friday and Saturday nights see live music beginning at 9 PM. *Juárez s/n, at Garizurieta, tel. 783/4–16–02. Open daily 7 AM–midnight.*

The beaches in Tuxpán are lined with cheap palapa (thatched-hut) restaurants selling everything from crab burritos to ice-cold coconuts.

Cafetería el Mante. This place is almost always packed with hungry locals and is especially popular for breakfast. The most popular dish is *bocoles con huevo* (fried dough filled with egg; $2). *Piplan 8, at Juárez, tel. 783/4–57–36. Open daily 6 AM–midnight.*

Cafetería Kon Tiki. If plastic patio chairs are your thing, you'll love this coffee shop. Try the *empanadas* (turnovers) filled with meat or cheese for about $2. *Rodríguez 19, tel. 783/4–72–04. Open daily 8 AM–11 PM.*

Pizza Cats. This (more-or-less) Italian restaurant serves tasty spaghetti, pizza with tuna, mushrooms, jalapeños, onions, and olives, and *queso fundido* (cheese fondue). A full meal here should cost you no more than $10. *Juárez 44, at Mina, tel. 783/4–44–73. Open daily 3 PM–11 PM.*

OUTDOOR ACTIVITIES

Playa Tuxpán is the most accessible beach in the area, about 7 kilometers from downtown. Pick up a PLAYA bus near the dock where the lanchas leave to cross the river. For scuba diving, head to **Tamiaula,** a small village just north of Tuxpán, where you can hire a fishing boat for the 45-minute journey to the prime diving around **Isla Lobos** (Wolf Island). There are a military outpost and a lighthouse on the island. In the shallow water offshore you'll find a few shipwrecks and colorful reefs that are home to a large variety of sealife, including pufferfish, parrotfish, damselfish, and barracuda. Buses to Tamiaula ($3, 30 min) leave from the **Terminal ABC** (*see* Coming and Going, *above*).

The last bus back to town leaves Playa Tuxpán at about 8:30 PM. If you miss it, rent a hammock for the night—it costs about the same as the ride back to the city

If you didn't bring your own equipment, you can rent gear from **Aquasport** (tel. 783/7–02–59), just before Playa Tuxpán, where they also arrange trips to Isla Lobos ($100 a day) that include all permits, scuba gear, food, and transportation. No scuba classes are offered, however, so non-experts are stuck with snorkeling.

NORTHEASTERN MEXICO   13

By Ariana Mohit

Few travelers go out of their way to visit northeastern Mexico. Near the border, the landscape is dry, uninviting, and increasingly industrial, as increasing numbers of multinational companies establish *maquiladoras* (foreign-owned factories in duty-free zones) along the border. Those who do visit typically come from Texas for the day or weekend, seeking what border towns like Nuevo Laredo, Matamoros, and Reynosa are known for—relatively cheap food and drink, flashy discos, and Mexican handicrafts. Yet those who venture beyond the border will discover a lot more than hot, empty deserts and tacky tourist towns: Just 230 kilometers south of the U.S. border is Monterrey, a fast-paced city that's home to excellent museums and one of Latin America's finest universities. If you need a break from Mexico's third-largest city, in Monterrey you can arrange horseback and camping treks into the pine forests of the nearby Sierra Madre mountains.

The northeast is not famous for its food and drink, but caffeine addicts will get a serious buzz from café de olla, a blend of coffee, chocolate, and cinnamon brewed slowly in a clay pot.

Two hours south of Monterrey lies Saltillo, the slow-paced capital of Coahuila state. You won't find many tourists here, only locals relaxing in the shadow of the city's magnificent Catedral de Santiago. If you're a serious nature-loving type, the Parque Nacional Cumbres de Monterrey, an hour beyond Monterrey, offers dozens of hiking, spelunking, camping, and swimming opportunities, although you may have to resort to hitchhiking and second-class buses to get here.

The weather in this area can be fickle. In winter expect daytime temperatures in the low 50s and nighttime temperatures in the low 40s. During summer, sweltering heat is the norm, punctuated by powerful surprise rainstorms. Also remember that while it's easy to drive across the border for a day trip, things get more complicated if you're planning a prolonged trek (*see* Chapter 1, Basics).

Matamoros
Matamoros is the easternmost border crossing between the United States and Mexico. The city hugs the Río Bravo (or Rio Grande, as it's known in the States) 38 kilometers west of the Gulf Coast and is connected to Brownsville, Texas, by a 100-meter bridge. Matamoros has the high prices and hordes of souvenir-hungry tourists you'd expect to find in a border town, but it also has a number of historic buildings; during the U.S. Civil War, Brownsville/Matamoros prospered as the "back door to the Confederacy," the South's only open port. The city may be crowded, but it's a lot more inter-

esting than Brownsville; and, while some parts of town look rough at the edges, Matamoros's tourist quarters are surprisingly clean.

BASICS

AMERICAN EXPRESS **Viajes Axial** operates the AmEx office. They offer good exchange rates, with no commission on cash and traveler's checks. Cardholders can also pick up mail and cash personal checks here. *Morelos 94–107, Centro, CP 87300, Matamoros, Tamaulipas, México, tel. 88/13–69–69. Open weekdays 8–6, Sat. 9–1.*

CASA DE CAMBIOS **Banamex** (Calle 7, at Morelos, tel. 88/13–60–35) changes cash and traveler's checks weekdays 9–11:30. They also have an ATM that accepts Plus, Cirrus, Mastercard, Visa, and, surprisingly, American Express.

CONSULATE The **American Consulate** is a madhouse. To avoid standing in line, show the guard your passport. *Calle 1 No. 2002, at Azaleas, tel. 88/12–44–02. 11 long blocks from Plaza Hidalgo; take CONSULADO bus. Open weekdays 8–10 and 1–4.*

CROSSING THE BORDER If you're only staying in Matamoros a couple of days, simply show the scowling border guard your passport or another picture ID. If you plan to go more than 22 kilometers into Mexico, get a tourist card (*see* Chapter 1, Basics) at the crossing.

EMERGENCIES For minor medical emergencies, the well-stocked **Benavides** pharmacy is the most convenient to downtown. *Guerrero s/n, tel. 88/16–69–58. Open daily 8 AM–9 PM.*

PHONES AND MAIL At the main **post office** (Calle 6 No. 214), they'll hold mail sent to you at the following address for up to 10 days: Lista de Correos, Matamoros, Tamaulipas, CP

87300, México. There's also a convenient branch at the Matamoros bus depot. It's open daily 9–8, but closes for a long siesta between noon and 3 PM. For faster delivery, mail your correspondence at the Brownsville post office (1001 East Elizabeth, at Calle 10, tel. 210/546–9462).

You can make collect and credit-card international calls from the shiny aluminum Ladatel **pay phones** (not the orange ones) are in the Plaza Hidalgo, Plaza Allende, and in the bus and train stations.

VISITOR INFORMATION A few blocks from the international bridge is a small white building marked **Tours-Transport** (Tamaulipas and Obregón, tel. 88/12–21–18), where friendly older men answer questions and try to sell you a two-hour tour of Matamoros (it's not worth it). They're open daily 8–6. The **Brownsville Chamber of Commerce** has excellent street maps of Brownsville and Matamoros. *1600 E. Elizabeth, Brownsville, tel. 210/542–4341. 1 block from international bridge. Open daily 9–5.*

COMING AND GOING

BY BUS The **Central de Autobuses** (Calle 1, at Canales) is 25 blocks south of the international bridge. To get here, flag down a CENTRAL *pesero* (mini-bus) at the international bridge or in the Plaza Hidalgo. First-class **ADO** (tel. 88/12–01–81) serves Veracruz twice daily; the 16-hour trip costs about $43. Other destinations include Mexico City ($40, 15 hrs), and Guadalajara ($38, 18 hrs). **Omnibus de México** (tel. 88/13–27–68) has first- and second-class service (cheaper, but takes about an hour longer and lacks air-conditioning) to most major cities; several buses a day make the trip to Monterrey ($11 1st class, $8 2nd class; 5 hrs), Reynosa ($6 1st class, $3 2nd class; 2 hrs), and Nuevo Laredo ($12 1st class, $10.50 2nd class; 6 hrs). Inside the terminal you'll find a post office; plenty of Ladatel phones; a 24-hour, air-conditioned cafeteria; and luggage lockers ($4 per day).

BY TRAIN The *primera especial* (special first-class) train, **El Tamaulipeco,** crawls from Matamoros to Monterrey via Reynosa in six hours. There's one departure per day at 9:20 AM, and tickets ($15) usually sell out early. *Hidalgo, btw Calles 9 and 10, tel. 88/16–67–06. Ticket counter open daily 8–5, but subject to change.*

BY PLANE Aeroméxico (tel. 88/12–24–60) offers one flight per day to Mexico City; cost at press time was $235 one way. The airport is 17 kilometers south of town, toward Ciudad Victoria. You can take a blue *pesero* (minibus) from Independencia and Calle 10, which drops you off a kilometer from the airport; or, take a taxi (about $5).

GETTING AROUND

The *puente internacional* (international bridge) over the Río Bravo connects Matamoros and Brownsville. Walking is the easiest and fastest way to cross the border; it costs about 50¢ each way; drivers pay $2. Numbered *calles* (streets) run north–south, from the river to the bus station and beyond. Peseros are the best way to get downtown; they run until 9 PM. A taxi can deliver you anywhere in town for about $3.

WHERE TO SLEEP

Rooms are expensive in Matamoros, but they're still half the price of those in Brownsville. The budget hotels, most nearly identical, are clustered on or near Abasolo. Keep in mind that Matamoros is not the safest city in Mexico, and the cheaper hotels are more accessible to an occupationally varied clientele. Stay inside with the door shut after 10 PM.

➢ UNDER $15 • **Hotel Majestic.** If the slimy, lime-green hallway didn't lead to a reception desk staffed by one of the nicest old ladies in Matamoros, this hotel wouldn't be worth a mention. Only cold water comes from the tap, and drab rooms have peeling paint and roaches, but the señora is an able cucaracha-crusher. Singles are $10, doubles $13. *Abasolo 89, btw Calles 8 and 9, tel. 88/13–36–80. Across from Mercado Juárez. 29 rooms, all with bath.*

➤ UNDER $20 • **Casa de Huéspedes Margarita.** Rooms here look like they were painted by the Easter Bunny, but they're clean in a dusty, deserted way. The water takes its time getting warm, but, on the plus side, the roaches seem to be smaller here than in other hotels. Singles and doubles are $13 ($20 and $23, respectively, with air-conditioning). *Calle 4, btw Abasolo and Matamoros, no phone. 1 block west and 2 blocks north of Plaza Allende. 10 rooms, all with bath.*

Hotel Alameda. Two blocks south of Plaza Allende, this hotel has a great air-conditioned central patio complete with a lofty dome. The comfortable, cable TV-equipped rooms have fans. Felipe, the guy at the desk at night, is very cool and allows guests to use the fridge. Rates are a good deal at $14 for a single and $17 a double. *Victoria 91, btw Calles 10 and 11, tel. 88/16–77–90. 2 blocks south of Plaza Hidalgo. 24 rooms, all with bath. Luggage storage, wheelchair access.*

ROUGHING IT Matamoros can be a risky place to sleep in public, but desperate travelers have been know to try the bustling and thoroughly uncomfortable bus station (*see above*).

FOOD

Head to the Mercado Juárez for taco stands and other cheap eats. The heat may be unbearable, but if you're on a tight budget, remember there's a direct correlation between air-conditioning and high prices. Across from the public bathrooms on Plaza Allende is **Los Panchos Café y Pan,** a large and deliciously air-conditioned bakery and coffeehouse.

Café California. Factory workers stop in here at all hours for good food and gossip. Pull up a bar stool and have a 50¢ taco or a bowl of hot, spicy *menudo* (tripe soup) for $2.50. The lack of clear signs can make it tough to find this joint; it's right off the Mercado Juárez, and just north of the coffee roastery on the corner. *Calle 9 No. 24, at Matamoros, no phone. Open 24 hrs.*

La Canasta. Local kids pack this diner in search of the famous double burger with cheese ($3), but good Mexican food is also served. The $1 burritos and 50¢ tacos with cheese are as cheap as they come. *Abasolo s/n, btw Calle 7 and 8, tel. 88/12–29–00. Open daily 9–7. Wheelchair access.*

El Chinchonal. This little restaurant fills up around lunchtime. Steaming flour tortillas are filled with everything from scrambled eggs to shredded beef ($1.50). *Calle 9 s/n, next to Café California, no phone. Open Mon.–Sat. 7–6, Sun. 7–noon.*

Las Dos Repúblicas. This strange half-restaurant, half-store has air-conditioning and tables suitable for Munchkins. But at $4 an entrée, the flautas (six fried, meat-filled tortillas with beans, chips, guacamole, and sour cream) or quesadillas (six tortillas with white Chihuahua cheese and hot sauce) are a great deal. Wash it all down with an 18-ounce margarita. *Calle 9 s/n, at Matamoros, tel. 88/16–68–94. Open daily 9–8. Wheelchair access.*

WORTH SEEING

Matamoros has two squares: the original center of town, **Plaza Allende,** and the newer one, **Plaza Hidalgo.** Both are typical Mexican zócalos with a cathedral, fountains, benches full of elderly men, and local kids darting about. Loudly colored serapes, bullwhips, and mounds of silver jewelry are sold at the **Mercado Juárez** and at **Pasaje Juárez** (the old market) on Calle 8 across from the Hotel Roma. Nearby **Abasolo** is closed to traffic, making it an ideal spot to grab a bench and watch the pedestrian traffic ebb and flow through the shops.

Air-conditioning adds to the appeal of the small stone fortress of the **Casa Mata,** which was established in 1845 to defend the city against an expected American invasion. It wasn't completed in time, however, and American troops under Zachary Taylor were able to capture Matamoros easily in 1846. Casa Mata is now a museum housing photos and artifacts, mainly from the Mexican Revolution. *Guatemala and Santos Degollado. Admission free. Open Tues.–Sat. 9:30–5:30, Sun. 9:30–3:30.*

CHEAP THRILLS

When the energy-zapping heat becomes too much, head to the swimming pool at the **Centro Deportivo Eduardo Chávez,** across from the Casa Mata. This clean 50-meter pool is filled with jumping, splashing local kids by midday, so do your laps early. There are dressing rooms and showers, but you must bring your own towel. The pool closes from September 15 to March 21. *Guatemala, near Laura Villar, tel. 88/16–28–37. Admission: $3, $1.50 with student ID. Open daily 8–noon and 2–6.*

Near Matamoros

PLAYA BAGDAD

During the U.S. Civil War, this beach was the site of the Confederacy's only open harbor. Freighters skirting the Union naval blockade unloaded their war supplies and loaded up with Confederate cotton destined for Europe. Today, palapas run the length of the shore, and dozens of restaurants offer fresh seafood at reasonable prices. A large, green water slide rises above the shore, and all sorts of tacky T-shirts and seashell ashtrays are available at the stands. Showers and bathrooms are free, but drivers pay $8 to park. Camping is perfectly free and legal, but be careful—the beach is deserted at night and far from civilization. To get here, take a blue pesero marked PLAYA ($1.50, 1½ hrs) from Independencia and Calle 10 in Matamoros. The last pesero back to town leaves at 7 PM.

Reynosa

Because of its manageable size and mellow attitude, Reynosa, across the border from McAllen, Texas, is one of the most pleasant points of entry into Mexico, and a convenient starting point if you're bound for Mexico City, Monterrey, or the Bajío. That said, Reynosa is still an industrial border town of limited charm, driven economically by the petrochemical industry, agriculture, and the ever-present tourist trade. If you're looking for something to do, the open-air market on Hidalgo and the area south of the central plaza bustle with activity; the smells of fruit, sweat, leather, and tamales intertwine as they waft through the streets. The **Zona Rosa** is home to raucous nightlife, but unless you're in a large group or write detective stories, stay off the streets after 11 PM.

BASICS

AMERICAN EXPRESS **Erika Viajes**, eight blocks from the plaza, provides limited American Express services: They will not cash a personal check, though they will replace lost traveler's checks and hold mail for cardmembers. You can also buy traveler's checks here. *Ávila Camacho 1325, at Lázaro Cárdenas, tel. 89/22–60–16. Open weekdays 9–6, Sat. 9–1.*

CASAS DE CAMBIO You'll pass several casas de cambio on Zaragoza as you head downtown from the international border, but most won't change traveler's checks. However, they do offer excellent rates for American dollars. If you've only got traveler's checks, bite the bullet and pray that the manager is on duty at **Casa de Cambio Sogo**—he has to approve the transaction. *Juárez 610 Nte., no phone. Open weekdays 9–6 and Saturday 9–2.*

CROSSING THE BORDER You can stay in Reynosa up to 72 hours without getting a tourist card, but if you stay longer or venture more than 22 kilometers into Mexico, you'll need one (they're free) at the border crossing. Requirements for the tourist card include either an original birth certificate and picture ID or your passport (*see* Passports, Visas, and Tourist Cards in Chapter 1).

EMERGENCIES You can also call the **police** (tel. 89/22–00–08); **fire** department (tel. 89/24–39–99); or **Cruz Roja** (tel. 89/22–13–14) for an **ambulance**.

MEDICAL AID **Farmacia Regis** has a good selection of medications and sells Ladatel phone cards. *Hidalgo s/n, at Madero, tel. 89/12–05–83. Open daily 7 AM–9:30 PM.*

PHONES AND MAIL There's a cluster of pay **phones** in the plaza, where you'll also find a *caseta de larga distancia* (long-distance phone office) and public fax office (Hidalgo 990, tel. 89/22–85–93) that's open daily 8 AM–10 PM. The main **post office** is on the corner of Díaz and Colón, near the train station. It's open weekdays 8–8 and Saturday 9–1. They'll hold mail sent to you at the following address for up to 10 days: Lista de Correos, Reynosa, Tamaulipas, CP 88620, México.

COMING AND GOING

A bridge over the Río Bravo connects Reynosa with McAllen, Texas. Reynosa is small and the downtown area, laid out in a grid, can be crossed in less than 15 minutes. **Hidalgo** is the main north–south axis, and **Morelos** the principal east–west axis. Peseros run from the bridge to the plaza, the train station, and the bus depot.

BY BUS The **Central Camionera** (tel. 89/22–33–07) is behind the huge Gigante supermarket, five blocks south and 10 blocks east of the central plaza. Catch a C. CAMIONERA/OBRERO pesero from the bridge or the center of town. There's frequent first- and second-class service to Matamoros ($5, 2 hrs 1st class; $3, 3 hrs 2nd class), Monterrey ($9.50, 4 hrs 1st class; $7, 5½ hrs 2nd class), and Saltillo ($13, 6 hrs 1st class; $10.50, 7 hrs 2nd class). First-class **Omnibus de México** (tel. 89/22–33–27) runs routes east to Chihuahua ($37, 14 hrs) and south to Mexico City ($40, 15 hrs). **Transportes del Norte** (tel. 89/22–41–87) goes daily to Guadalajara ($38, 18 hrs), and Mexico City ($43, 15 hrs). **Autobuses del Oriente (ADO)** (tel. 89/22–17–19) has first-class buses that travel along the Gulf Coast twice a day to Tampico ($21, 6 hrs), Tuxpan ($26, 8½ hrs), and Veracruz city ($45, 17½ hrs). There have been a few thefts in and around the station, so be extra careful, especially at night. Luggage storage is available in the station from 6 AM to 10 PM. There is also a caseta de larga distancia that is open round the clock.

BY TRAIN The train station (tel. 89/22–00–85) is south of the town plaza, at the end of Hidalgo. The special first-class **El Tamaulipeco** departs at 11:25 AM daily for Monterrey ($10, 4½ hrs). The train to Matamoros leaves at 2:40 PM ($3, 2½ hrs). Tickets go on sale daily at 10:30 AM until they're gone or until Margarita, the cashier, gets tired of sitting around. For points farther south, transfer in Monterrey. The station is served by peseros from the bridge and bus depot. *7 blocks down Hidalgo from central square.*

WHERE TO SLEEP

Hotels in the Zona Rosa and around the central plaza cater to businesspeople and vacationers and are priced accordingly. For a budget room, head toward the train station; the cheapest rooms are found just north of the tracks.

Hotel Avenida. Look closely for the neatly lettered white sign—this is one of Reynosa's best-kept secrets. A beautiful, grassy patio borders the spotless rooms on the ground floor. The rooms are small but luxurious, with carpets, phones, TVs, and quiet air-conditioning. Bathrooms are immaculate. Singles and doubles are just $20. *Zaragoza 885 Ote., tel. 89/22–05–92. 26 rooms, all with bath. Luggage storage, wheelchair access.*

Hotel Estación. The "Station," just across the tracks from the train depot and a few blocks south of downtown, couldn't be more convenient. If you're tired enough, you won't even hear the roar of passing trains. Rooms are small but relatively clean, and rickety air-conditioners do a surprisingly good job. Bathrooms have hot water. The daytime reception guy, Marcelino Córdova, is helpful and trustworthy. Singles are $10, doubles $14. *Hidalgo 305, tel. 89/22–73–02. 40 rooms, all with bath. Luggage storage.*

Hotel Nuevo León. The clean, western-style lobby of this hotel has a charm that is conspicuously absent in the staff. Rooms are fan-cooled and clean, with screen doors. Bathrooms have drippy faucets, but at least there's hot water. Singles are $15 on weekdays, $13 on Friday, Saturday, Sunday. Doubles are $18 weekdays, $15 on weekends. *Díaz 580, tel. 89/22–13–10. 28 rooms, all with bath. Laundry, luggage storage.*

FOOD

The stands at the market on Hidalgo offer economical meals. Across the street from the bus depot is the extremely hygienic **Paleterín,** serving standard Mexican fare. Have a grilled torta (sandwich) and watch the crowds drift by.

Café París. This mirror-lined place is always full, so you may have to loom in the doorway until someone leaves a paisley-cushioned booth. The delicious *comida corrida* (pre-prepared lunch special) is served noon–2 and is a steal at $3; a filling breakfast omelet is $2. In the evening, the bar is a good place to hang out, with two-for-one White Russians ($2.50) and potent margaritas. *Hidalgo 815, tel. 89/22–55–35. Open daily 7 AM–10 PM. Wheelchair access.*

La Fogata. This elegant, air-conditioned restaurant/piano bar is the place for a splurge. Royal-blue linen tablecloths are draped over wood tables, and there is live music 2–6 and 7–midnight daily. Vegetarians won't find much here beside the *queso flameado* (fondue) for $6. *Cabrito* (grilled baby goat) is $11, and beers are just $1. *Matamoros 750, tel. 89/12–47–72. Open 10 AM–midnight. Wheelchair access.*

AFTER DARK

The weekend nightlife in the **Zona Rosa** may be the highlight of a visit here. Most of the action centers around Ocampo and Allende. Forget the discos for tourists and head to where Reynosan youth descend in force: At **Rodeo** (Allende 910), open Friday–Sunday 6 PM–4:30 AM, you can salsa or cumbia in a huge western-style dance hall for $2.50. Friday and Saturday there's a mechanical-bull riding contest. **Fiesta Mexicana** (Ocampo 1140, at Allende, tel. 89/22–01–11) has a mellower atmosphere and an older crowd. The house band plays everything from *baladas* (ballads) to salsa Friday–Sunday 8 PM–3 AM. There's no cover Friday and Sunday, and Saturday it's only $5, including one free drink.

Nuevo Laredo

Of all the eastern border towns, Nuevo Laredo, just over the international bridge from Laredo, Texas, receives the largest onslaught of American souvenir-seekers. Shopping is the primary pursuit here, and you'll find a warren of stalls and shops concentrated on Avenida Guerrero in a seven-block stretch that extends from the international bridge to the main plaza. In addition to the standard border town schlock, Nuevo Laredo shops stock a good selection of high-quality handicrafts imported from all over Mexico, at somewhat inflated prices. Wander a few blocks off the main drag in any direction for better prices and smaller crowds. There's also a large crafts market on the east side of Avenida Guerrero, just north of the plaza.

Nuevo Laredo was founded after the Treaty of Guadalupe Hidalgo in 1848, which ended the Mexican-American War. The treaty established the Río Bravo (or Rio Grande) as the border between the two countries, and forced Mexico to give up a substantial amount of territory. Many of Laredo's Mexican residents, who suddenly found themselves living in the United States, crossed the river and founded Nuevo Laredo on what had been the outskirts of town. Today, Nuevo Laredo's economy depends greatly on gringos who head south for a few days of drunken revelry, returning home with a bottle of tequila, suitcases full of souvenirs, and a mean hangover.

Nuevo Laredo's vibrant commercialism takes the form of overflowing stalls, street vendors parading meter-high stacks of straw hats, and little kids standing against shaded walls with cheap photos of the latest lucha libre (wrestling) heroes.

BASICS

AMERICAN EXPRESS You can replace lost AmEx traveler's checks, cash personal checks, receive mail, and buy traveler's checks at **Lozano Viajes Internacionales.** They'll even change a few traveler's checks for you—a rarity around here. *Paseo Reforma 3311, Col. Jardín, Nuevo Laredo, Tamaulipas, CP 88260, tel. 87/15–44–55. Open weekdays 9–5:30.* **487**

CASAS DE CAMBIO Change cash at one of several **casas de cambio** on Guerrero, just below the international bridge. To change traveler's checks, try **Divisas Terminal** in the bus station. They're open Monday–Saturday 6 AM–10 PM, Sunday 6 AM–8 PM. **Banamex** (Guerrero, btw Canales and Madero, tel. 87/12–30–01) has an ATM that accepts Cirrus, Plus, Visa and Mastercard.

CROSSING THE BORDER Souvenir seekers who just want to stay a day or two (72 hours maximum) need only show a passport or other form of ID at the border. To go more than 22 kilometers from the border, you'll have to get a tourist card (*see* Passports, Visas, and Tourist Cards in Chapter 1).

EMERGENCIES You can also call the **police** (tel. 87/12–21–46); **fire** department (87/12–21–24); or **Cruz Roja** (tel. 87/12–09–49) for an **ambulance**.

MEDICAL AID The **Cruz Roja** (Independencia 1619, at San Antonio, tel. 87/12–09–49) offers emergency and routine medical care.

Benavides pharmacy (Guerrero s/n, at Dr. Mier, tel. 87/12–21–60) is the biggest pharmacy in town. They're open daily 8 AM–10 PM. For 24-hour service, head to **Farmacia Calderón** (Guerrero 704, tel. 87/12–55–63) next door.

PHONES AND MAIL The main **post office** (Reynosa, at Dr. Mier, tel. 87/12–23–50), right behind the Palacio Municipal, is open weekdays 8–7 and Saturday 9–1. They'll hold mail sent to you at the following address for up to 10 days: Lista de Correos, Nuevo Laredo, Tamaulipas, CP 88000, México. It's quicker and cheaper to drop foreign mail at the U.S. post office, about six blocks north of the border. Next door to the Nuevo Laredo post office you can send faxes and telegrams daily 9–7.

Ladatel pay **phones** can be found on Plaza Hidalgo, but it's cheaper to place international calls from the States; pay phones are over the international bridge, just past U.S. customs.

TOURIST INFORMATION The **tourist office** is near the international bridge on Guerrero. The friendly folks here aren't very helpful, but they've got maps of the city. *Puente Internacional s/n, tel. 87/12–01–04. Open daily 8:30–8.*

COMING AND GOING

BY BUS The **Terminal Central Maclovio Herrera** (J. R. Romo 3800) is a 15-minute bus ride south of the bridge. Take a PUENTE/CENTRAL CAMIONERA/CARRETERA bus from the corner of Juárez and Victoria, or from Galeano on the east side of the square. **Transportes Frontera** (tel. 87/14–08–29) runs nonstop buses every three hours to Mexico City ($34, 15 hrs 1st class; $30, 16½ hrs 2nd class). Buses also leave hourly for Saltillo ($10, 5 hrs 1st class; $7.50, 7 hrs 2nd class) and San Luis Potosí ($23, 12 hrs 1st class; $20, 15 hrs 2nd class). First class **Omnibus de México** (tel. 87/14–06–17) serves nearby cities as well as Zacatecas ($25, 10 hrs) and Guadalajara ($40, 14 hrs). **Tres Estrellas de Oro** (tel. 87/14–00–91) serves Monterrey, San Luis Potosí, Mexico City, and Manzanillo. A caseta de larga distancia is open 24 hours a day, and the casa de cambio here changes traveler's checks. Luggage storage is available in the station Monday–Saturday 7 AM–10 PM, Sunday 7–5.

BY TRAIN The train station is on Avenida López de Lara, at the west end of Gutiérrez, about a dozen short blocks west of the main plaza. It's a 15-minute walk from the border to the station; otherwise, take an ARTEGA GONZALEZ bus from Juárez and Victoria. The first-class train to Mexico City ($32, 25 hrs) leaves daily at 6:55 PM, with stops at Monterrey ($8, 3½ hrs), Saltillo ($11, 7½ hrs), San Luis Potosí ($21, 15½ hrs), San Miguel de Allende ($24, 18½ hrs), and Querétaro ($26, 19½ hrs), among others. First-class tickets cost about $40, second-class $24. For another $6, you can get a larger seat on an air-conditioned car. Tickets go on sale daily at 5:30 PM.

BY PLANE Mexicana (tel. 87/12–22–11) flies to Guadalajara and Mexico City. Cost at press time for a one-way ticket to either city was $118. The airport is 15 kilometers south of town, so you'll need a car or taxi to get there.

WHERE TO SLEEP

Hotels tend to be either too expensive for the budget traveler or dreadfully run down; your best bet for something in between is the area around Avenida Guerrero, between the bridge and central square. The streets stay lit until about 9 or 10 PM, and Guerrero is almost always busy. Nevertheless, be careful, because tourists are targeted by thieves.

Hotel Calderon. This is the cheapest but most dilapidated option. The showers barely trickle, and the management seems to have trouble distinguishing mattresses from box springs, but you can't beat the $10 price for singles or doubles. There's no sign out front, but it's the only four-story, brown brick building on the block. *Juárez 313, at Victoria, tel. 87/12–00–04. 16 rooms, all with bath. Luggage storage.*

Hotel La Finca. Large, comfy rooms with air-conditioning and color TVs are standard here. Expect clean, fluffy towels in the bathrooms, and hot water day and night. Singles are $20, doubles $23. *Reynosa 811, tel. 87/12–04–70. 25 rooms, all with bath. Luggage storage. AE, MC, V.*

Hotel Romanos. This is by far the best budget hotel in town, complete with wooden shutters and frosty air-conditioning. Rooms are spacious and clean. Spotless bathrooms have plenty of hot water and carefully wrapped soaps. Singles and doubles are only $13, $18 with a color TV. *Dr. Mier 2420, tel. 87/12–23–91. 35 rooms, all with bath. Luggage storage, wheelchair access.*

FOOD

The dining scene includes everything from cheap taco stands and fast-food joints on the first few blocks of Guerrero to exponentially overpriced eateries, like the **Cadillac Bar and Grill,** which cater primarily to touring Texans. For moderately priced restaurants, explore the side streets south of the main plaza.

Cafetería Modelo. This restaurant/caseta de larga distancia is a favorite among locals. Atmosphere is lacking, but the cheap, delicious breakfasts (ham and eggs for $2) can't be beat. Avoid the donuts. *Dr. Mier s/n, at Ocampo, tel. 87/12–15–66. Open daily 7 AM–3 AM. Wheelchair access.*

El Pollo Loco. This fast-food chicken chain serves consistently good chow at reasonable prices. Try the *platillo de pollo* (half a chicken, six tortillas, and salsa) for $4.50. *Matamoros 702, at Dr. Mier, tel. 87/12–87–00. Open daily 10 AM–11 PM. Wheelchair access.*

Restaurant Hotel Reforma. This 24-hour restaurant at one of the classier hotels in town isn't much to look at but it's always packed at lunchtime. Folks from the hotel and families crowd in to eat one of the best comidas corridas ($5.50) around. *Guerrero 806, tel. 87/12–34–88.*

Monterrey

In this metropolis of four million people, decadence and absolute poverty coexist side by side, a jarring reminder that Monterrey is the country's unchallenged industrial giant. In juxtaposition to the city's grand buildings and luxurious suburbs is the ring of squalid huts and smoke-belching factories known as the *cinturón de miseria* (belt of misery). Pollution is a serious problem here, and unless you confine yourself to Monterrey's sprawling but manageable center, it's likely you'll end up with a serious case of the urban-industrial blues.

Monterrey was founded by the Spanish in the late 1500s. To encourage settlement in the region, the Spanish Crown granted vast tracts of land to a handful of families. The success of these sheep ranchers quickly created a small, wealthy elite, who, following the construction of a railroad in the 1880s, decided to invest in industry. Monterrey's first iron and steel mill was built at the turn of the century, as was the **Cuauhtémoc Brewery,** now the largest in the country. The powerful Garza Sada family refined the art of mass-produced beer, and religiously reinvested the profits. They established glass factories and cardboard mills, and even produced their own barrels and delivery wagons. To ensure proper training for the future leaders of this vast industrial empire, the Garza Sadas founded the **Instituto Tecnológico de Monterrey,** now considered one of the best universities in Latin America.

Life in Monterrey, also known as "the Pittsburgh of Mexico," is hectic, and staying here can be quite expensive. Even so, those who take the time to wander Monterrey's busy streets will encounter the region's best museums, good examples of colonial and modern civic architecture, and a spectacular central plaza that gives great views of the Sierra Madre, which forms a semicircle around the southern edge of town. These pine-forested mountains are home to the **Parque Nacional Cumbres de Monterrey** (The Summits of Monterrey National Park), known for several beautiful caves and waterfalls, as well as **La Silla,** a saddle-shaped rock formation that is the symbol of Monterrey.

BASICS

AMERICAN EXPRESS Rather inconveniently located 2 kilometers from the Zona Rosa, the local AmEx office is staffed with friendly English-speaking folks. They cash personal checks, but at a crappy exchange rate, and you must pay in cash when buying traveler's checks. Other services include holding cardmembers' mail and replacing lost or stolen traveler's checks. *Padre Mier 1424 Pte., tel. 8/343–09–10. Open weekdays 9–6, Sat. 9–3. Take RUTA 4 bus from Pino Suárez in the Zona Rosa.*

BOOKSTORE The **American Bookstore** (Garza Sada 2404-A, near the Pemex station, tel. 8/387–08–38) has a great selection of books in English.

CASAS DE CAMBIO **Base Internacional** (Pino Suárez 1217, tel. 8/372–86–22), just north of Avenida Colón and the Cuauhtémoc metro station, changes traveler's checks; they're open weekdays 9–6 and Saturday 9–1. **Casa de Cambio Euromex** (Juárez, at Padre Mier, tel. 8/318–17–73) changes cash only Monday–Saturday 9–1:30 and 3–5. **Banamex** (Pino Suárez 933 Nte.) has an ATM that accepts Cirrus, Plus, Mastercard, and Visa.

CONSULATES **Canada.** *Edificio Kalos, Zaragoza 1300 Sur, Suite 108, tel. 8/344–32–00. Open weekdays 9–5:30.*

United States. *Constitución Pte. 411, tel. 8/345–21–20. Open weekdays 8–2.*

EMERGENCIES In an emergency, contact the **police** (tel. 8/342–91–88); **fire** department (tel. 8/342–00–53); or, for an **ambulance**, the **Cruz Roja** (tel. 8/342–12–12).

LAUNDRY At **Lavandería Automática Express**, you can get 3 kilos of clothes washed for about $4. *Garza Sada 3022, no phone. Open Mon.–Sat. 9:30–8:30.*

MEDICAL AID For non-emergency consultations, try the **Cruz Roja** clinic (Alfonso Reyes, Col. del Prado, tel. 8/342–12–12), near the Plaza de Toros.

Benavides pharmacy (Morales 499, tel. 8/345–02–57) is open every day 7 AM–10 PM. For 24-hour service, try **Farmacia Medix** (Pino Suárez 510 Sur, tel. 8/342–90–02).

PHONES AND MAIL The main **post office** is in the basement of the Palacio Federal building, at the north end of the Macroplaza. They'll hold mail sent to you at the following address for up to 10 days: Lista de Correos, Administración 1, Monterrey, Nuevo León, CP 64000, México. *Washington, at Zaragoza, tel. 8/342–40–03. Open weekdays 8–7, Sat. 9–1.*

Phone calls from casetas are unjustifiably expensive here, so use the shiny Ladatel phones throughout the city. You can buy cards that give you phone credit at **El Niagara** (Morelos 359 Ote., Zona Rosa, tel. 8/342–40–23), open daily 9:30–8. Or you can just use cash or your credit card.

VISITOR INFORMATION **Infotour,** under the Macroplaza, is one of Mexico's best tourist offices. In addition to its great brochures and maps, the office has a friendly English-speaking staff. *Zaragoza, at Matamoros, tel. 8/345–08–70. Open daily 10–5.*

COMING AND GOING

BY BUS The huge **Central de Autobuses** is an impressive transport hub with scores of bus companies serving virtually the entire country. Buses leave frequently for the border towns of Nuevo Laredo ($12 1st class, $8.50 2nd class; 5 hrs), Reynosa ($9 1st class, $8 2nd class; 3½ hrs), and Matamoros ($13 1st class, $11 2nd class; 3 hrs). Numerous first-class buses head down the coast to Tampico ($20, 8 hrs), and inland to Saltillo ($3, 1½ hrs) and Mexico City ($34, 12 hrs). Major first-class bus lines include **Omnibus de México** (tel. 8/374–07–16), which serves Chihuahua ($32, 12 hrs) and Juárez ($48, 18 hrs); **Transportes del Norte** (tel. 8/318–37–45), which, in conjunction with **Greyhound,** goes to San Antonio ($41), Dallas ($66), and Houston ($54); **Transportes Zua Zua** (tel. 8/374–04–20); and the ever-present **Tres Estrellas de Oro** (tel. 83/74–24–10). The terminal has a post office, 24-hour pharmacy, luggage lockers ($4 a day), Ladatel phones, a basement medical center, and an upstairs porn theater.

The terminal is on Colón near Cuauhtémoc in the northwestern part of the city. The easiest way to get here is by metro: take Line 1 to the CENTRAL stop. From downtown you can catch the RUTA 39 bus, which runs from the Macroplaza north along Juárez to the bus station. From the bus station to downtown, catch the bus labeled RUTA 45 at Bernardo Reyes and Colóna or a RUTA 206 PERIFERICA bus on Suárez.

BY TRAIN Three trains pass through Monterrey's station (tel. 8/375–46–04) daily. The first-class **El Regiomontano,** with seats and sleeping berths, runs from Monterrey to Saltillo, San Luis Potosí, and Mexico City. The 14-hour trip from Monterrey to Mexico City costs $40 ($80 for a sleeping berth); the train leaves at 7:50 PM. **El Tamaulipeco,** a special first-class train from Monterrey to Matamoros via Reynosa, costs $12 and takes 6½ hours. The Mexico City–Monterrey–Nuevo Laredo train is also first-class only. The trip from Monterrey to Mexico City ($23) is 17 hours long, with stops in Saltillo, San Luis Potosí, San Miguel de Allende, and Querétaro. The trip to Nuevo Laredo ($8) is direct and takes five hours. Buy tickets for all trains the day of departure from the TAQUILLA window 8:30–12:30 and 4–8.

The train depot is six blocks northwest of the bus station and Central metro stop. To reach downtown, hoof it to the bus station and catch a bus there (*see* By Bus, *above*).

BY PLANE The **Aeropuerto Internacional Mariano Escobedo** (tel. 8/345–44–32), equipped with luggage storage ($4 a day), and a money exchange booth, is 6 kilometers northeast of downtown. The only way to get here is by taxi, which will cost about $12. **Aeroméxico** (tel. 8/344—77–30) and **Mexicana** (tel. 8/344–77–10) are domestic airlines serving the airport. **American Airlines** (tel. 8/340–30–31) has five flights a day to Dallas ($105 one way).

GETTING AROUND

Monterrey is a sprawling monstrosity, and very few places are within walking distance of one another. Luckily, the extensive public transit system makes it easy to get around. Downtown, also called the **Zona Rosa,** is the city's luxury hotel and shopping area, bordered on the east by the **Macroplaza** and on the west by **Avenida Juárez.** The intersection of Juárez and Armberri marks the official center of town, and addresses to the west of this intersection are followed by "Poniente" or "Pte."; to the east, by "Oriente" or "Ote."; to the north, by "Norte" or "Nte."; and to the south, by "Sur." Street numbers become larger the farther you move from the intersection.

BY METRO The new Monterrey metro is a modern and efficient system that runs along elevated tracks across the city. There are only two lines, but a third is in the works. Magnetic cards are used to enter the station; buy them from station vending machines in units of one, three, or five rides; each ride costs less than 50¢. The metro runs every day from 4:45 AM to 11:45 PM.

BY BUS Monterrey's loud, rickety, smoke-belching buses go everywhere. The buses on each route are color-coded, and the names of major stops are often painted across the windshield—sometimes they're even legible. There are few fixed bus stops, each marked by a blue PARADA sign, but buses will stop anywhere; just wave madly at any corner along a route.

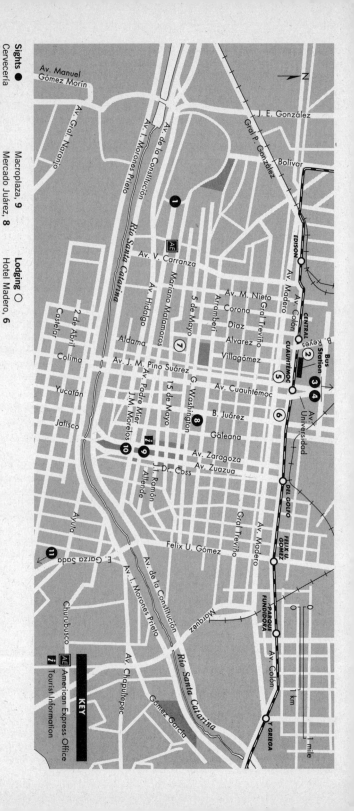

Monterrey

Sights ●
Cervecería
Cuauhtémoc, **3**
El Obispado, **1**
Instituto
Tecnológico de
Monterrey, **11**
Macroplaza, **9**
Mercado Juárez, **8**
Museo de Arte
Contemporáneo
(MARCO), **10**
Parque de los
Niños Héroes, **4**

Lodging ○
Hotel Madero, **6**
Hotel Posada, **5**
Hotel Posada de
los Reyes, **7**
Hotel Victoria, **2**

KEY
AE American Express Office
i Tourist Information

WHERE TO SLEEP

Monterrey's relative wealth, combined with a steady flow of business travelers, keeps hotel prices high, though there are some shoestring fleabags clustered by the obnoxiously loud bus station. Avoid hotel hunting at night. Even if you have a place to crash, it's unwise to wander around the city after 10 PM. A reasonably priced hotel near the Zona Rosa is the **Hotel Posada de los Reyes** (Aldama 446 Sur, tel. 8/343–18–80). The rooms are big, with two queen-size beds, and the bathrooms won't make you cringe. Things get real quiet around here late at night, so avoid traipsing around alone. Singles and doubles are $26, and you can also store luggage here. The hotels listed below are near the bus and train stations, in neigborhood that aren't the safest at night; on the other hand, 24-hour cheap eats are plentiful.

Hotels become cheaper and neighborhoods less secure as you move away from the Zona Rosa.

Hotel Estación. The hotel's stern management keeps things clean and quiet and charges $18 for spartan rooms with fans (single or double). Bathrooms are small but decent, and hot water flows readily. The primary draw, however, is the hotel's proximity to the train station. *Victoria 1450, tel. 8/375–07–55. From train station, across Nieto and to right. 25 rooms, all with bath. Luggage storage, wheelchair access.*

Hotel Madero. The owner's daughter must be dating the health inspector—otherwise, this place would have been shut down long ago. It's noisy and the rooms are matchbox-like, but there is hot water. Your sheets may be cleanish, but you'll have to ignore the affectionate cockroaches who want to share your bed. Singles and doubles with bath are $12 and $17, respectively. *Madero 418, tel. 8/375–54–71. 43 rooms, all with bath. Luggage storage.*

Hotel Posada. Small, brown-tiled, fan-cooled rooms with double beds await you at the Posada. The bathrooms are decent and there's hot water, but you may have to put up with the occasional cucaracha. The management usually blames their presence on the hotel next door. Singles and doubles are $23. *Amado Nervo 1138 Nte., tel. 8/372–39–08. 32 rooms, all with bath. Luggage storage, wheelchair access.*

Hotel Victoria. Clean, tiled rooms with fans and recently washed sheets make this hotel the best deal near the bus terminal. Other than the somewhat erratic toilets, the bathrooms are fine. Singles here cost $19, doubles $21. Ask for a room on the right side—they're more pleasant. *Bernardo Reyes 1205 Nte., tel. 8/375–69–19. 1 block NW of bus depot. 75 rooms, all with bath. Luggage storage.*

FOOD

Food stands in all major markets offer the best meal deals in town—grilled meats and rice-and-bean platters are less than $2. Get here early because popular dishes usually run out by 2–3 PM. The fast-food chain **El Pollo Loco** (open daily 10 AM–11 PM) has several branches around

How to Bus It in Monterrey

• *Ruta 1 runs between the Instituto Tecnológico de Monterrey and the Universidad Autónoma along Garza Sada and Cuauhtémoc, and returns along Pino Suárez. The buses are green with a yellow stripe.*

• *Ruta 15 loops around the Macroplaza before heading west along Padre Mier to the foot of the Obispado.*

• *Ruta 39's red and black buses connect the Central de Autobuses and the Macroplaza.*

• *Ruta 45 runs from the Central de Autobuses (stopping at the corner of Bernardo Reyes and Colón) to the Macroplaza along Villagran, Matamoros, Juárez, and Ocampo.*

town that serve large chicken combination plates for about $4. Most of the good, moderately priced restaurants are in the Zona Rosa.

➤ UNDER $5 • **Café Sevilla.** For that late-night snack, this somewhat grungy 24-hour coffee shop serves taco plates, burgers, and surprisingly good coffee ($1). It's a favorite with bus drivers—always an encouraging sign. The enchiladas ($3) are tasty. *Colón, at Villagran, just west of the bus depot, no phone.*

Las Monjitas. If you can stop laughing at the waitresses' nun outfits long enough to take a bite, you'll enjoy this taquería chain's very tasty food. Try the house specialty: bite-size pieces of steak sautéed with peppers, onions, mushrooms, sausage, and bacon, served with a huge platter of tortillas for about $4.50. *Morelos 240 Ote., at Galeana, tel. 8/342–85–67. Open daily 8 AM–10:30 PM.*

Torta 'n Go. Despite the cheesy name, this is the place to go for great *tortas calientes* (warm sandwiches). Delicious steak sandwiches with cheese, onion, tomato, chile, and avocado cost about $3.50, and breakfasts are about $2.50. *Padre Mier 402 Ote., at Carranza, no phone. Open Mon.–Sat. 9 AM–10 PM, Sun. 1–10.*

Restaurant El Palmito. If you're on your way to the "Tec" (Instituto Tecnológico), make sure to stop by here for some of the best tacos in town. Three carne asada tacos and a Coke are just $4. Vegetarians won't find much here, but the baked potatoes are big, buttery affairs ($1.50). The place gets packed around 9 PM, when service can be slow. *2 de Abril 2902, 3 blocks from Garza Sada, tel. 8/359–96–50. Open daily 12:30 PM–midnight.*

➤ UNDER $10 • **Restaurante Vegetariano Superbom.** Come to this Zona Rosa hangout for good, moderately priced veggie platters. Unfortunately, the place is completely lacking in atmosphere. The all-you-can-eat lunch buffet ($8), offered between noon and 4 PM, is recommended only for people with serious appetites. *Padre Mier, at Galeana, tel. 8/345–26–63. Open Mon.–Thurs. 8–5, Fri. and Sun. 8–4.*

WORTH SEEING

Architecturally distinguished buildings—some colonial, some modern—make a walk around town interesting in itself, but there are also a number of museums worth visiting. The many parks and plazas are great for relaxing, but if you just want to check the scene out, the Zona Rosa is usually the place to be.

For frosty mugs of beer, head to the beer garden at Cuauhté-moc Brewery, where the drinks are free.

CERVECERIA CUAUHTEMOC Named after the famous Aztec ruler, **Cuauhtémoc Brewery** is the heart of an industrial empire producing a number of brands of beer. Brewery tours are offered Tuesday–Friday at 11, noon, and 3. One of the complex's older buildings has been converted into a collection of hodgepodge museums, but the unlimited free beer in the tree-lined **beer garden** is the biggest draw and definitely makes the trip worthwhile. The **Museo de Monterrey** houses some fairly unimportant works of art, though its brick-walled upstairs café offers a quiet place to pass the afternoon. The **Salon de la Fama** (Hall of Fame) is full of memorabilia from Mexico's baseball legends. The **Museo Deportivo** (Sports Museum) contains exhibits on Mexican boxing, bullfighting, and American college football. *Universidad 2202, about 10 blocks north of bus station. Take RUTA 1 bus. Admission free. Open Tues.–Fri. 9:30–5:30, weekends 10:30–6:30.*

INSTITUTO TECNOLOGICO DE MONTERREY One of the top business and technical schools in Latin America, the Institute was founded by Monterrey's industrial elite to train future managers and engineers. The school's modern, geometric campus, built around a central patio, is a great place to hang out and meet locals and exchange students. The dorms are not coed, so most socializing starts here on the patio. The Tec, as it is known, lies in the far southeast corner of Monterrey; from downtown, take RUTA 1 bus from Pino Suárez.

MACROPLAZA At the heart of Monterrey is one of the world's largest public squares. Extending over 40 acres, the plaza begins on Washington, runs past the Palacio del Gobierno (city hall), and ends at the Santa Catarina riverbank. The southernmost boundary is marked by a beautiful Rufino Tamayo sculpture entitled *Homage to the Sun*. The sound of gushing fountains and the pleasant aromas of the trees and shrubs in the square's gardens offer a needed respite from the deafening roar of Monterrey's traffic. Stop in at **Infotour** (*see* Visitor Information, *above*) for a detailed guide to this central plaza.

MUSEO DE ARTE CONTEMPORANEO (MARCO) Near the southeast corner of the Macroplaza, the museum has 14 exhibition halls and a beautiful water-filled marble patio. Wednesdays and Sundays 5:30 PM–7:30 PM there is live music on the patio, and the candlelit tables fill with boho types who sip coffee ($1.50) and nibble on pieces of pie ($3.50). *Zuazua s/n, at Ocampo, tel. 8/342–48–20. Admission: $3.50, $2 students, free Wed. Open Tues. and Thurs.–Sat. 11–7, Wed. and Sun. 11–9.*

EL OBISPADO The old Bishop's Palace affords great views of Monterrey. Constructed in 1788, it served as a fort during the Mexican-American War and the French Intervention. Today, it houses a museum that is a necessary stop with an interest in Nuevo León's history. *At far west end of Padre Mier, tel. 8/346–04–04. Take RUTA 15 from Macroplaza. Admission: $3.50. Open Tues.–Sun. 10–5.*

PARQUE DE LOS NINOS HEROES This extensive stretch of green between Avenidas Alfonso Reyes and Manuel Barragan, 2 kilometers (1½ miles) north of the bus depot, has pleasantly landscaped paths weaving in and out of lovely gardens and a small artificial lake where people rent rowboats. Monterrey's **Museo del Automóvil** (Automobile Museum), **Museo de la Fauna** (Fauna Museum), **Museo de la Pinacoteca** (Regional Art Museum), and **Casa de la Tecnología** (Science Museum) are also here. The park is open daily 10–6. The 50¢ admission includes everything but the rowboat rentals and a $1 donation for the upkeep of the animals at the Fauna Museum. Make sure to get a map from the ticket booth. *From downtown, catch a RUTA 17 bus on Pino Suárez. To return to town, cross park and catch the same bus on Barragan.*

AFTER DARK

Nightlife is varied and lively but spread out across the city. **Kaos** (Garza Sada, at Revolución) is a dark, split-level club playing modern Mexican and American dance music. The cover is $8, drinks are $4; take a RUTA 1 bus to the main entrance of the university (known as the Tec), then transfer to a SATELITE bus. All this transferring can be pretty difficult after 1 AM; a cab to most of the budget hotels is about $6. West of the Zona Rosa, try **Koko Loco** (Pino Suárez, at Padre Mier), a bar on Thursday that also becomes a disco playing modern dance tunes on Friday and Saturday. They're open 9:30 PM–2 AM, and cover is $6.50. If you're tired of techno, go to **Pachanga** (Pino Suárez 849 Sur, tel. 8/340–15–23) around the corner, where you can cumbia for free on Fridays 7 PM–2 AM. On Saturday, women pay $1.50, men pay $3, and Sunday everyone gets in for $3. **El Mesón del Gallo** (Padre Mier 943 Pte., tel. 8/342–12–87), three blocks east of the Macroplaza, is the place to dance to live music—everything from salsa to nueva canción. They're open Monday–Saturday 7:30 PM–2 AM. Cover is $5.

Skip That Trip to the Louvre

In the Museo de la Pinacoteca in the Parque de los Niños Héroes is a collection of artwork created almost exclusively by artists from Nuevo León. The first painting on the right side is El Nacionalista, by Carlos Saenz. Stand to the left of the painting and notice how the subject's body—his feet, shoulders, and even his eyes—seem to be oriented to your left. Then slowly move to your right, noting how the fixed stare of the poncho-clad gentleman shifts magically as you move. This technique, mastered by Saenz, is the same that Leonardo da Vinci used for his smirking Mona Lisa.

Near Monterrey

LA CASCADA COLA DE CABALLO

An hour northwest of Monterrey, in the Sierra Madre mountains just off Highway 85, is the **Parque Nacional Cumbres de Monterrey.** One of the highlights of a trip here is a view of **La Cascada Cola de Caballo** (Horse Tail Falls), a dramatic waterfall that tumbles down from the pine-forested heights. The fall is spectacular, but it's hardly a secret; peseros from Monterrey regularly take visitors almost to the base. Entrance to the falls (open daily 8–7) will set you back $3. The waterfall is about 1 kilometer from the entrance, up a cobblestone road. You can rent a docile horse from the local kids who hang out by the ticket booth for about $3, or hop on a horse-pulled carriage for $2.50.

Ice-cream vendors selling paletas (popsicles) in the square offer the best way to beat the midday heat. Flavors include guanábana, guava, and mango.

COMING AND GOING Horse Tail Falls lies 6 kilometers up a winding road from the small town of **El Cercado.** Autobuses Amarillos buses leave every 15 minutes between 4:30 AM and 11:45 PM, and the 45-minute ride costs $2. From the stop in El Cercado, walk two blocks to the town plaza and take a pesero (blue or orange van) to the foot of the falls; the fare ($1 part-way, $5 to the entrance) is higher on weekends. The last pesero heads back to the plaza at 7:15 PM sharp, and it's a long, mosquito-ridden walk back to town.

CAMPING About 1 kilometer up the road past the entrance to the falls, climb the ridge to the left of the road. The river forms small, clear pools up on the ridge. Get the park administrator's okay before pitching your tent in this perfect spot. His office is some 200 meters toward the falls from the **Hacienda Cola de Caballo.** There are toilets and sinks with nonpotable water near the entrance to the falls.

GRUTAS DE GARCIA

The awe-inspiring subterranean caverns of García have, sadly, been transformed into an overdone tourist attraction, the sort of place where stalagmites carry names such as Christmas Tree and the Hand of Death. But don't run screaming, because the caves' impressive natural beauty somehow survives the thick crowds and glittering signs.

For $7 you can ride a tram to the cave entrance. Alternatively, make the steep, 20-minute hike up a gorgeous mountain path (bring some water) from Villa de García on foot. A one-hour guided tour of the caves is included in the entrance fee. The tram leaves two or three times per hour from 10 AM to 4 PM and often sells out, so come early. You may also want to bring a picnic, though there is a small restaurant here.

COMING AND GOING The Grutas de García are just outside Villa de García. From Monterrey, catch one of the frequent Monterrey–Villa de García buses ($2.50, 1 hr) from the corner of Colón and B. Reyes, opposite the Hotel Victoria (*see* Where to Sleep, *above*). Monterrey's **Infotour** office (*see* Visitor Information, *above*) organizes its own cave tours in English and Spanish on Thursdays and Saturdays at 1:30 PM.

Saltillo

Set 1,600 meters up in the mountains, about an hour southwest of Monterrey, the capital of Coahuila state is a great place to take a deep breath and relax after the pollution and bustle of Monterrey. The city's industrial complexes, including Chrysler and GM plants, are relegated to the suburbs, leaving the downtown plazas and parks clean and tranquil.

Saltillo grew up around the **Plaza de Armas,** bordered by the elegant **Palacio de Gobierno** (Government Palace) and the **Catedral de Santiago,** the elaborately carved stone facade of which is one of the finest in Mexico. The ground level of the **Mercado Juárez** is full of handicrafts, and an upstairs level has cheap places to eat a filling meal. For a great view of the city, walk from the cathedral south along Hidalgo to the Plaza de México.

From late July through mid-August, the entire town meets at the fairgrounds for the **Feria Anual** (Annual Fair), with games, dancing, regional foods, roller coasters, crafts, and bloody *palenques* (cockfights).

BASICS

CASAS DE CAMBIO Serfin (tel. 84/12–31–73), on the corner of Allende and Lerdo de Tejada, changes cash and traveler's checks weekdays 9:30–1. For 24-hour instant cash gratification, use the ATM at **Banamex** (Allende, at Ocampo, tel. 84/14–49–17), which accepts Cirrus, Plus, Mastercard, and Visa.

EMERGENCIES You can reach the **police** round the clock at 84/16–21–83.

PHONES AND MAIL At the main post office (Victoria 453, btw Acuña and Padre Flores, tel. 84/14–90–97), they'll hold mail sent to you at the following address for up to 10 days: Lista de Correos, Saltillo, Coahuila, CP 25280, México. They're open weekdays 8–8 and Saturday 9–1. There's a small cluster of Ladatel **phones** in Plaza Acuña near the Mercado Juárez and a few more sprinkled in Plaza San Francisco (Juárez, behind the cathedral). Otherwise, you can make international calls (though no collect calls) from Café Victoria (*see* Food, *below*) for $3 a minute.

VISITOR INFORMATION If you just want a couple of maps, check out the small **tourist office** (tel. 84/12–40–50) on the corner of Francisco Coss and Acuña, open weekdays 9–5 and Saturday 9–2. A bigger office (tel. 84/30–05–10) is in the extremely inconvenient Centro de Convenciones (convention center), about 6½ kilometers out of town toward Arteaga (*see* Near Saltillo, *below*). They're open Monday–Saturday 9–3 and 6–9.

COMING AND GOING

BY BUS Saltillo's **Central de Autobuses** is about 2 kilometers southwest of the centro. Most smaller second-class lines have service to obscure places, but the biggest one, **Transportes Frontera** (tel. 84/17–00–76), goes to Monterrey every half-hour ($3.50, 2 hrs), Ciudad Juárez ($39, 18 hrs) and Mexico City ($30, 12 hrs). Six first-class lines, among them the ubiquitous **Omnibus de México** (tel. 84/17–03–15) and **Transportes del Norte** (tel. 84/17–09–02), have frequent service to Guadalajara ($29, 10 hrs), Mazatlán ($34, 16 hrs), Ciudad Juárez ($44, 15 hrs), and Matamoros ($16, 5 hrs). **Greyhound** tickets to destinations in the U.S. and Canada via Texas are sold by Transportes del Norte (tel. 84/17–09–02). A 24-hour long distance/fax office is open every day, and the station's Ladatel phones accept credit cards and coins. Luggage storage is available daily from 6 AM to 9 PM. RUTA 9 buses run between the station and downtown.

BY TRAIN The **Estación de Ferrocarril** is a large, impressive building a few blocks southwest of Parque Zaragoza on Emilio Carranza. Three trains a day connect Saltillo to eight other cities

Stop and Smell the Roses

If you want to come to a halt and simply exist for an afternoon, head out to the tranquil village of Arteaga, 20 kilometers east of Saltillo on the San Luis Potosí–México City highway. You can daydream by the quiet stream that meanders through town, or search out the waterfall on the outskirts for an afternoon picnic. From Saltillo, second-class buses marked ARTEAGA make the one-hour trek daily for less than $1.

in the Republic. The first-class **Regiomontano** train heads south to San Luis Potosí ($14 1st class, $37 sleeper car; 6 hrs), and Mexico City ($33 1st class, $67 sleeper car; 12 hrs) and north to Monterrey (sleeper car only $25, 3 hrs).

The **Coahuilense** leaves for Piedras Negras. Tickets are $8 for second-class, $11 for an assigned seat, and $13 for an assigned seat in an air-conditioned train. The first-class only **México–Monterrey–Nuevo Laredo** train heads south to Mexico City ($23, 17 hrs) and north to Nuevo Laredo ($11, 16 hrs), stopping in Monterrey ($3, 9 hrs).

WHERE TO SLEEP AND EAT

Most budget hotels are clustered near the bustling Plaza Acuña. The **Hotel Bristol** (Aldama 405 Pte., tel. 84/12–91–20) is Saltillo's best-kept secret. Rooms are small but clean, with bathrooms marred only by peeling paint and the conspicuous absence of hot water. Singles and doubles are a low $15 each. Probably the cheapest place in town is the **Hotel Hidalgo** (Padre Flores 217, tel. 84/14–98–53). It's a bit rough around the edges, but tolerable. Rooms are gloomy and the beds sag, but the bathrooms are fairly clean and the showers drool a tepid, water-like substance. Rooms are reasonable at $10 for a single, $13 for a double.

Saltillo does not offer fabulous cuisine, but you can grab a taco or slurp down homemade soup at the *fondas* (covered food stands) in the Mercado Juárez in Plaza Acuña. **Taquería El Pastor** (Aldama 340 Pte., tel. 84/12–21–12) is always filled with locals wolfing down corn tortillas filled with carne asada and *carne al pastor* (marinated pork). It's open Sunday–Thursday 8 AM–midnight, Friday–Saturday 8 AM–1 AM. The unofficial house specialty at the **Café Victoria** (Padre Flores 221, tel. 84/14–98–00), open daily 7 AM–11 PM, are the *palomas con aguacate* (flour tortillas filled with shredded beef and avocado) for $3.50. A good comida corrida is available daily 11–4.

WORTH SEEING

Saltillo's winding streets may be colonial and quaint, but they're also confusing. Fortunately, most sights in Saltillo are within walking distance of the **Plaza de Armas** (the central plaza) at Hidalgo and Juárez and the **Plaza Acuña** at Aldama and Padre Flores. The Plaza de Armas contains the churrigueresque (ultra baroque) **Catedral de Santiago**. Opposite the cathedral is the **Palacio del Gobierno,** an immense, rose-colored building that houses government offices as well as beautiful murals illustrating the political history of Coahuila by Spanish painter Salvador Almaraz y Tarazona.

CULTURAL CENTERS/GALLERIES Saltillo has an abundance of artists who show their works in spaces throughout the city. There are a few larger, more established museums and galleries, such as the free **Centro Cultural Universitario**, where you'll find arrowheads, stone figures, and a "hoop" from a pre-Columbian ball court. *Aldama s/n, at G. Cepeda, tel. 84/12–68–57. Open Tue.–Sun. 10–7. Wheelchair accessible.*

Also free is the **Centro de Arte Contemporáneo**, which houses everything from paintings to sculpture. *Behind cathedral, tel. 84/10–09–32. Open weekdays 10–1 and 4 –7, Sat. 10–1.*

Finally, the **Instituto Coahuilense de Cultura** exhibits sculpture, *artesanía* (crafts), painting, woodwork, and photography. *Juárez s/n, at Hidalgo, tel. 84/14–22–45. Open Tue.–Sun. 9–7.*

EL SARAPE DE SALTILLO A small, rusting yellow sign swinging rythmically in the afternoon breeze is the only marker for this fabulous serape factory/artesanía store. Everything from silver earrings and chocolate beaters to tea cups and cured tree bark is for sale in the tiny store. But the real draw is watching nimble-fingered craftspeople make the serapes. The store itself is open Monday–Saturday 9–1 and 3–7, but the serape makers only work during the week. *Hidalgo 305 Sur, no phone.*

Tampico

Just north of the Veracruz-Tamaulipas border, Tampico is a bustling port town with what the locals call *mucha movida*. The city itself is beautiful, although there isn't much to do except check out the French-inspired architecture that prompts many to call Tampico the "Mexican New Orleans." Although the humid, salty air has taken a toll on the city's older buildings, some well-preserved structures still line the Plaza de la Libertad on Avenida Juárez. On the east side of the Plaza de Armas (central plaza) is the **Catedral de Tampico,** covered in a fine layer of pink firestone, with an intricate mosaic of Jesus along the front facade. Profit-wise *tampiqueños* have lined the Plaza de Armas with tall, gleaming hotels, resulting in prohibitively high prices for both accommodations and food. If you're in town over the weekend, don't miss the **domingo cultural** (cultural Sunday), with performances in front of the Plaza de Arma's Palacio Municipal. On Monday and Friday afternoons, a live band plays classical music 4 PM–7 PM in the plaza's beautiful kiosk.

Surrounded by water—the Gulf of Mexico and Playa Miramar to the east, the Río Panuco to the south, and the lagoons formed by the Río Tamesi to the west—Tampico offers an overwhelming array of aquatic sports and activities. The long, white sandy expanse of Playa Miramar is also a good place to pitch a tent and save a fortune.

BASICS

AMERICAN EXPRESS The AmEx office is in **Viajes Pozos,** a travel agency about 10 minutes from downtown. The staff begrudgingly cashes personal checks, holds client mail, and sells and replaces traveler's checks. *Zapote 106, Colonia Águila, tel. 12/13–72–00 or 12/17–14–76. Open weekdays 9–2 and 4–6, Sat. 10–1.*

CASAS DE CAMBIO Casa de Cambio (tel. 12/14–06–57), on the corner of Madero and Juárez, has long hours and competitive rates. They change both cash and traveler's checks weekdays 9–6 and Saturdays 9–1:30. **Banamex** (Madero, at Aduana) has an ATM that digests Cirrus, Plus, Visa, and Mastercard and regurgitates pesos.

EMERGENCIES Dial 12/12–10–32 for the **police;** 12/12–12–22 for the **fire** department; or 12/12–13–33 for the **Cruz Roja** or an **ambulance**.

MEDICAL AID **Benavides** is a big, well-equipped pharmacy right off the Plaza de Armas. *Olmos, at Carranza, tel. 12/19–25–28. Open Mon.–Sat. 8 AM–11 PM, Sun. 8 AM– 10 PM.*

PHONES AND MAIL The **post office** (Madero 309, tel. 12/12–19–27) is three blocks from the Plaza de Armas. They'll hold mail sent to you at the following address for up to 10 days: Lista de Correos, Tampico, Tamaulipas, CP 89000, México. Right outside the post office are some shiny new Ladatel **phones,** but they're almost always in use. More can be found on the Plaza de Armas. Purchase Ladatel cards at Refresquería La Victoria at Colón and Carranza on the Plaza de Armas (*see* Food, *below*).

VISITOR INFORMATION The **tourism office** does little more than hand you a map or two and send you on your merry way. Look for a small, dark stairway squeezed next to a *refresquería* (drink stand). *Carranza, at Olmos, above Benavides pharmacy, tel. 12/12–26–78. Open weekdays 9–7.*

COMING AND GOING

BY BUS Tampico's **Central de Autobuses** has both first- and second-class terminals that are divided by a small verdant courtyard, making comparing ticket prices a breeze. **ADO** (tel. 12/13–43–39) and **Transportes Futura/Transportes del Norte** (tel. 12/13–46–55) are major first-class carriers with service to Matamoros ($19, 7 hrs), Nuevo Laredo ($35, 12 hrs), and Mexico City ($26, 10 hrs). Second-class lines include: **Transportes Frontera** (tel. 12/13–48–67), **Blancos** (tel. 12/13–42–35), and **Oriente Golfo** (tel. 12/13–44–96). Destinations include Monterrey ($16, 6 hrs), Reynosa ($19, 8 hrs), and Mexico City ($24, 11½hrs).

Each terminal is equipped with Ladatel phones and casetas de large distancia. Storage lockers in the first-class terminal swallow your gear for $4 a day. To get downtown, catch a *micro* (minibus) marked CENTRAL CAMIONERA PERIMETRAL in front of the station; to get to the terminal, take the same micro from the corner of Madero and Colón.

BY TRAIN Once a bustling doorway to the northeast, the **Estación de Ferrocarriles de Tampico** has all but been forgotten. Three lonely trains a day still lumber to San Luis Potosí ($7, 10 hrs), Ciudad Victoria ($4, 5½ hrs), and Monterrey ($8, 10 hrs). Tickets are sold only between 6 AM and 8 AM. *Aduana and Héroes de Nacozari, tel. 12/12–03–34.*

BY PLANE The **Aeropuerto Francisco Javier Mina** (Universidad 700, tel. 12/28–21–95) is a small airport in the northwest corner of town. **Mexicana** (tel. 12/13–97–59), **Aeroméxico** (tel. 12/17–08–02), and **Aerolitoral** (tel. 12/28–08–57) serve both domestic and international destinations. To get downtown, catch an AVIACION POR BULEVARD micro to Carranza and walk four blocks to the Plaza de Armas.

WHERE TO SLEEP

Rooms here tend to be extremely overpriced and mediocre. There are a few hotels with more reasonable rates a few blocks from the Plaza de Armas, but the neighborhoods tend to be unsafe and poorly lit late at night. Downtown, you'll find the **Hotel Posada Don Francisco** (Díaz Mirón 710, tel. 12/19–25–34), one of your cleaner budget options. *Económico* rooms, cooled with fans, are roomy, clean, and a real bargain at $14 for a single or double with a phone and TV. Bathrooms are clean and have plenty of hot water. The aging but clean **Hotel Imperial** (López de Lara, at Carranza, tel. 12/14–13–63) is the cheapest budget hotel near the plaza. Dingy carpeting in every room gives the place the feel of a dusty attic and the air-conditioners—standard in every room—shudder and wheeze so hard you almost feel sorry for them. Singles and doubles, all with phones and TVs, cost $23, and Mastercard and Visa are accepted.

Hotels along the beach tend to be pricey and a tad run down. The bright red-and-white **Hotel Orinoco** (Playa Miramar s/n, no phone) tends to fill up fast, so get here early in the day to stake your claim. Rooms are carpeted and cooled by a noisy but relatively effective floor fan. Singles and doubles are $20, and four people can crash here for under $10 each. If the great outdoors calls you, pitch a tent for free on **Playa Miramar,** where hammocks, bathrooms, and showers cost less than a taco. It's relatively safe at night, but let the beach patrol (behind Restaurant and Bar Icacos) know you're here.

FOOD

Like almost everything else in Tampico, food is overpriced. It's possible to eat cheaply, but only if you're not scared that eating at street stands will send you running for the bathroom. The food at the **mercado** on Juárez is cheap, cooked to order, and delicious. Try the *milanesa* (thinly sliced, breaded beef) with tortillas, beans, rice, salad, and a soft drink for $3. Most people come to the **Restaurant y Cafetería Emir** (Olmos 207, tel. 12/12–51–39) for the delicious $1 tamales. Strong coffee and sweet rolls will run you about $2.50, but stay away from the stale corn flakes. Emir's is open daily 6 AM–midnight. **Refresquería La Victoria** (south side of Plaza de Armas, tel. 12/12–08–89), serves a mean chocolate shake for $1.50 daily 7 AM–11 PM. The central location and *licuados* (smoothies; $1) keep the place packed, especially on Friday and Saturday nights.

CHEAP THRILLS

The newly remodeled **Unidad Deportiva Tampico** (Tampico Sports Center) has two Olympic-size pools, providing a great way to beat the humid Tampico heat. *Blvd. López Mateos s/n. Take micro marked MADERO from the plaza. Open Mon.–Sat. 9–6. Admission: $5.*

OUTDOOR ACTIVITIES

Ten kilometers of white sand and blue-green waters make Playa Miramar a popular stretch of the Gulf of Mexico. Straw huts and lounge chairs dotting the shore can be rented all day for $5.50, and you can also rent showers, bathrooms, and towels from hotels and restaurants along the beach. **Restaurant/Bar Los Icacos** (2 km south of micro stop) has a small water slide and great seafood. Catch a PLAYA micro from in front of Hotel Mundo on Díaz Mirón.

AFTER DARK

Avenida Universidad, the long, winding street that borders the university, is the best place to start the evening. Most clubs luring the student population don't have a cover before 11 PM, and beers are about $2.50. To shake your booty to techno, head to **Eclipse** (Universidad 2004, tel. 12/13–14–95), open daily 9 PM–3 AM. **Restaurante/Bar Santa Fe 1900,** on the corner of Universidad and Francita, has a mellower atmosphere but more expensive drinks.

NORTH CENTRAL MEXICO AND THE COPPER CANYON

14

By Jamie Davidson and Ariana Mohit

Tourists in the states of Chihuahua and Durango are largely limited to border town thrill-seekers and travelers who are just passing through on the way to Mexico City. Those who are just passing by, however, miss the chance to ride the Chihuahua al Pacífico Railroad—one of the most awe-inspiring iron rooster trips in the world—as well as the enigmatic pre-Columbian ruins at Paquimé and the lively, historic town of Durango.

Chihuahua, which means "dry sandy place" in the Tarahumara language, is—you guessed it—predominantly a wasteland of windswept sand. However, it also encompasses part of the massive Sierra Madre mountain range and Copper Canyon country, which is characterized by a wildly fluctuating climate, pine forests, tropical vegetation, and fertile farmland. Miguel Hidalgo and Pancho Villa, two founding fathers of contemporary Mexico, called this region home, and today Chihuahua remains at the forefront of popular dissent, being a longstanding bastion of support for the PAN, Mexico's leading opposition party. You'll see a lot of cowboy types here sporting brimmed hats and boots, but the state is also home to Tarahumara and Mennonite communities. The Mennonites produce some of Mexico's tastiest cheese and are known for their austere lifestyle. The Tarahumara maintain many of their traditional religious practices, still honoring the gods of the sun and moon.

The dusty landscape around the capital city of the state of Durango is what many people picture when they think of Mexico—probably because it's been used as the setting for a number of Hollywood westerns. The city of Durango itself comes to most travelers as a pleasant surprise: Once you get past the urban sprawl at the outskirts, you'll find a friendly colonial city with a number of attractions, not the least of which are pretty streets perfect for aimless wandering.

Ciudad Juárez

If you find yourself in Ciudad Juárez, leave fast. Only hang around if: (1) you are in need of an inexpensive root canal; (2) you collect velvet Elvis paintings and require a lot of time to find the perfect example of the genre; or (3) you are wanted by the law on both sides of the border and want to be able to hop jurisdictions easily. Ciudad Juárez exhibits the worst aspects of both Mexico and the United States. U.S. companies set up plants here to capitalize on cheap Mexican labor, and a majority of Juárez's population currently works in *maquiladoras* (foreign-owned factories in duty-free zones). Many Mexicans are injured or killed as they try to cross the border illegally; intense heat and cold in the workers' settlements not served by public utilities

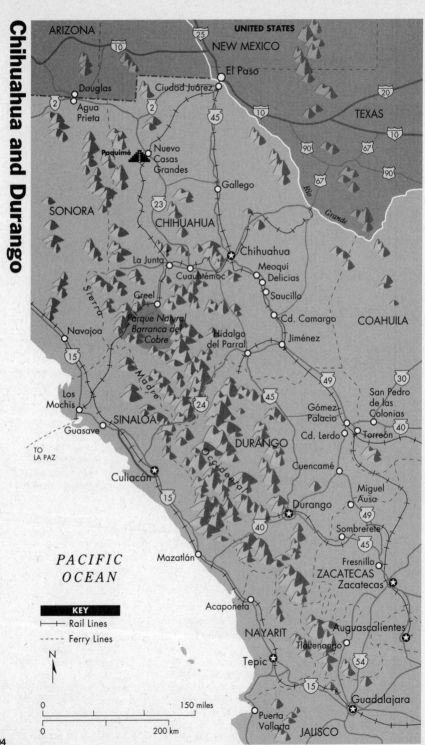

ARIZONA

UNITED STATES

NEW MEXICO

El Paso

Douglas

Ciudad Juárez

Agua
Prieta

TEXAS

Paquimé

Nuevo
Casas
Grandes

SONORA

Gallego

CHIHUAHUA

Rio
Grande

La Junta

Chihuahua

Meoqui
Delicias

Cuauhtémoc

Greel

Saucillo

Parque Natural
Barranca del
Cobre

Cd. Camargo

COAHUILA

Navojoa

Hidalgo
del Parral

Jiménez

Sierra

Los
Mochis

Madre

San Pedro
de las
Colonias

Guasave

SINALOA

Gómez
Palacio

TO
LA PAZ

Cd. Lerdo

Torreón

DURANGO

Occidental

Cuencamé

Culiacán

Miguel
Ausa

Durango

PACIFIC
OCEAN

Sombrerete

Mazatlán

KEY

Rail Lines

Ferry Lines

Fresnillo

ZACATECAS

Zacatecas

Acaponeta

N

Aguascalientes

NAYARIT

Tlaltenango

0   150 miles

Tepic

0   200 km

Guadalajara

Puerta
Vallarta

JALISCO

claim more lives; and toxic dumping, often by U.S. companies unwilling to pay hazardous-waste disposal fees in the States, exacts an additional health toll.

If you are stranded in Ciudad Juárez, consider it a sociological exercise, and try not to get too depressed. Make the best of it by admiring the city's turn-of-the-century architecture or stocking up on weird trinkets at the Plaza de las Américas, Juárez's best attempt at a tourist trap. The city's more dubious offerings include a sleazy bar scene and a flourishing sex trade. If you're passing through during the last two weeks of June, however, you lucked out, because this is when the **Feria Juárez** is in full swing in the Parque del Chamizal on Colegio Militar, with amusement-park rides and arts-and-crafts displays. Other special events include the **Festival de la Raza**, celebrated during the first week of May with dancing, films, theater, and music, all culminating in a big **Cinco de Mayo** bash along Avenida Juárez.

BASICS

AMERICAN EXPRESS The AmEx representatives at **Sun Travel**, across the border in El Paso, can help with lost or stolen checks, insurance, and transportation arrangements. The office also sells traveler's checks, offers MoneyGram service, and holds mail for cardholders. *3100 North Mesa, Suite B, El Paso, Texas 79902, U.S.A, tel. 915/532–8900. Open weekdays 7:30–5:30.*

CASAS DE CAMBIO More money-exchange places than you can shake a stick at line Avenida Juárez near the bridge, but rates are slightly better in El Paso. After business hours, try **Banamex's** *cajas permanentes* (ATMs) on the corner of Avenidas Juárez and 16 de Septiembre, in Ciudad Juárez.

CONSULATE United States. *López Mateos Nte. 924, tel. 16/13–40–50.*

CROSSING THE BORDER When entering Mexico, pick up a tourist card at the immigration office (open 24 hours) near the Stanton Street bridge, or at the **Mexican Consulate** in El Paso (tel. 915/533–3644). If you travel further than 32 kilometers from the border, you will be asked to show the card at checkpoints. Bringing a car into Mexico is possible, but complicated (*see* Coming and Going, *below*). For more information, *see* Passports, Visas, and Tourist Cards in Chapter 1, or call the customs office at the border (tel. 16/16–08–25).

EMERGENCIES For emergency assistance (including **ambulance** service) call the **police** (tel. 16/15–15–98) in Ciudad Juárez, or dial 911 from any phone on the U.S. side of the border.

MEDICAL AID The **Hospital General** (Paseo Triunfo de la República 2401, tel. 16/13–15–71) offers emergency care. **Farmacia Iris** (Villa, at Corona, tel. 16/12–81–90), one block north of 16 de Septiembre, is small but stays open until midnight Monday—Saturday. Dental offices abound on 16 de Septiembre and side streets near the border crossing.

PHONES The public phones here are dependable for cash, credit (Visa, Mastercard, and calling cards), and even collect calls. For Mexican long distance, dial **01; to call El Paso, dial 08; for other international calls, dial 09 or your long-distance carrier's access number.

VISITOR INFORMATION Ciudad Juárez's tourist office is on the ground floor of the Palacio Municipal, just west of the Stanton Street Bridge. The friendly staff speaks English. *Villa, at malecón, tel. 16/15–23–01. Open Mon.–Sat. 8–7.*

The El Paso Tourism Office also provides information for travelers crossing into Mexico. *1 Civic Center Plaza, tel. 800/351–6024. Open weekdays 8–5.*

COMING AND GOING

BY BUS The bus terminal is way out of Juárez, at the junction of Highways 2 and 45. The monstrous building has two long-distance telephone offices, a money-changing booth, cafeterias, and 24-hour luggage storage. **Estrella Blanca** (tel. 16/10–62–82) has hourly service to Chihuahua ($13, 4½ hrs), Nuevo Casas Grandes ($9, 4 hrs), Mazatlán ($51, 21 hrs), and Durango ($40, 14 hrs). Four buses also depart daily to Mexico City ($55, 26 hrs). **Transportes**

Chihuahuenses and **Tres Estrellas de Oro** serve the same routes, and **Turistar** and **Futura** charge a few dollars more for *especial* first class with air-conditioning, bathrooms, and on-board movies. **Greyhound** bus tickets can also be purchased here for trips to Los Angeles ($35), Albuquerque ($20), and Denver ($69), as well as other U.S. destinations. To get to the bus station from downtown, take a bus marked CENTRAL CAMIONERA and ask the bus driver where to get off; allow at least an hour.

BY TRAIN The train station (tel. 16/12–31–88) is 12 blocks down the tracks from the Stanton Street bridge. Two trains daily leave Ciudad Juárez headed south to Mexico City ($50 1st class, $30 2nd class) with stops in Chihuahua ($9 1st class, $5.50 2nd class), Zacatecas ($32 1st class, $19 2nd class), and Aguascalientes ($35 1st class, $23 2nd class). The second-class train leaves at 7 AM, so if you want to bail out of this border town at dawn's light, you have to line up early to buy a ticket (they go on sale at 6 AM). Tickets for the 10 PM first-class departure can be purchased in advance Monday–Saturday 9 AM–noon. Tickets usually sell out, so plan ahead. If you're looking for a taxi, it's better to walk a block or two toward downtown and hail one there, where prices are less likely to be inflated.

BY CAR You are allowed to bring a car into Mexico for a period of up to 180 days. To cross the border with your car you need to present the title (in your name) and a current driver's license. You also have to provide a guarantee that you'll bring the car back across once your permit expires. You can accomplish this by giving them your credit-card number, so they can charge you a fine if you fail to comply with the rules. If you don't have a credit card, you'll have to buy a bond from one of the bond sellers close to the border. The cost will depend on the value of your car. The customs officials don't care if you buy Mexican insurance or not, but a cop further south (or the 'other party' in case of an accident) might. If you choose to buy some, it's available from a number of companies near the border.

BY PLANE The international airport is far from the center of town, just off Highway 45. **Aeroméxico** (tel. 16/13–80–89 or 800/237–6639 from the U.S.) is the main carrier, with daily flights to Chihuahua ($105 one way), Mexico City ($144 one way), and Mazatlán ($191 one way). A taxi from downtown to the terminal costs about $10. It's cheaper to grab a bus marked CENTRAL CAMIONERA, get off at the bus station, and take a taxi the rest of the way.

GETTING AROUND

Juárez is very spread out and the transport terminals are all far from each other. Fortunately, budget accommodations and restaurants cluster downtown along Avenida Juárez between the Stanton Street Bridge and Avenida 16 de Septiembre. The downtown area is also fairly easy to navigate on foot.

Finding local buses that travel to outlying points can be confusing because of the number of one-way streets. Buses generally arrive and depart from Avenidas Lerdo and Vicente Guerrero, south of Avenida 16 de Septiembre. Though not cheap, taxis are plentiful and their drivers generally knowledgeable. Settle on a price before you get in and don't hesitate to negotiate. Fares should run $1–$2 per kilometer. Bus 34 goes from the town square in El Paso (within walking distance of the border) to the El Paso airport.

WHERE TO SLEEP

Most tourists stay in El Paso rather than Juárez, so lodging options here are limited. The real cheapies are fairly run-down and often charge by the hour, but there are several reasonable places to stay on or near Avenida Juárez. Plan on arriving during the day, however, because this area is not safe after dark. If you do arrive in Juarez's bus terminal in the middle of the night, your best bet is to stay put. The station is brightly lit and staying here is probably safer than lugging your bags down some dark street.

➤ UNDER $20 • **Hotel Génova.** This small hotel is a bit out of the way, but at least you won't be kept awake all night by the noise from downtown discos. Air-conditioning and telephones in each room are also a plus. Singles are $12, doubles $15. *Moctezuma 569 Nte., off Colón, tel. 16/15–01–43. 30 rooms, all with bath. Wheelchair access.*

➤ UNDER $25 • **Bombin Café Bary Hotel.** This hot and noisy hotel just east of Avenida Juárez has lots of Formica, Naugahyde, and chrome furniture. The rooms are actually quite decent, though, and have private bathrooms with hot water. The musty bar is usually empty, but the staff is helpful and friendly. Singles are $10, doubles $20. *Colón, at Manuel Doblado, tel. 16/14–23–20. 32 rooms, all with bath.*

Hotel Juárez. This four-story building is straight down from the Stanton Street Bridge on Lerdo. The rooms are a bit larger than average but are sparsely furnished, and the bathrooms need scrubbing. Singles are $15 and doubles $19. *Lerdo 143 Nte., tel. 16/15–02–98. 46 rooms, all with bath.*

Hotel Moran. On the east side of Juárez, the Hotel Moran is a favorite with families. The small, basic rooms have comfortable beds, but the baths have cranky plumbing. Singles and doubles are $22; rooms with TV cost a few dollars more. *Juárez 264 Nte., tel. 16/15–08–02. 31 rooms, all with bath.*

Hotel Sevilla. So it's a bit loud, you might get the heebie-jeebies in the bathroom, and there's a loose tile here and there, but all in all, the place really isn't that bad. Singles and doubles are $12, triples $17. *Juárez 544, tel. 16/12–08–10. 56 rooms, all with bath. Luggage storage.*

HOSTEL **Gardner Hotel/Youth Hostel.** Upon meeting the owner of this place (which is in El Paso, not Juárez), you may find yourself wondering how it came about that such a traveling-youth hater should find himself running a hostel. Karma, perhaps? The hostel itself, however, is conveniently situated near the Mexican Consulate, the Greyhound bus station, and the border. You must be a member either of the AYH or the HI hostel associations to stay here, and prices begin at $14 for a dorm bed with a shared bath and communal kitchen privileges. Linen rental is an extra $2. Prices for rooms start at $24 for a single with shared bath. *311 East Franklin St., tel. 915/532-3661.*

FOOD

Restaurants and taco stands serving decent grub line Avenida Juárez. The **mercado municipal** on Avenida 16 de Septiembre offers fresh fruits, vegetables, and cheeses. If you are a recent arrival to Mexico, be kind to your stomach: Wait a few days before diving mouth first into every facet of the local menu. **Antojitos La Herradura** (González 184, tel. 16/12–09–32) serves a $5 *comida corrida* (pre-prepared lunch special) to satisfy even the hungriest traveler. For late-night cravings, **El Coyote Inválido** (Juárez 910, at Colón, tel. 16/14–27–27) is basic and economical. The $5 comida corrida and the *pollo en mole* (chicken in chile and chocolate sauce; $4.50) are the most popular dishes. Juárez's most tradition-steeped eatery, **Restaurant La Sevillana** (González 140 Pte., tel. 16/12–05–58), behind the old bullring, has been churning out the same dishes for close to 40 years. Pancakes and coffee ($3) and the *picadillo con chile verde* (shredded beef with green chile sauce; $5) are sure to please. More adventurous eaters may be tempted by the kidneys in wine sauce ($6.50).

WORTH SEEING

Most of the city's main attractions are downtown, within easy walking distance of Avenida Juárez. Getting to the few sights farther out will take some planning, but if you're stuck here anyhow, it's worth the extra hours to visit them. Bullfights occur on Sundays at the **Plaza de Toros Monumental** from April to August. The best time to catch a *charreada* (rodeo) is from April to October at the **López Mateos Arena** on Avenida del Charro.

The **Plaza de las Americas** is Juárez's gringo shopping area, about 3 kilometers from the border crossing at Lincoln and 16 de Septiembre. The **Centro Artesanal,** a huge adjoining warehouse, has high-quality, somewhat expensive *artesanía* (crafts) from all over Mexico and is open daily 10–6. The free **Museo de Arte y Historia** (tel. 16/16–74–13), open Tuesday–Sunday 11–7, displays indigenous artifacts and contemporary local art. To get here from downtown, take a trolley, or take a bus marked 8A or PRONAF from Avenida 16 de Septiembre.

ANTIGUA ADUANA The Mexican Revolution officially ended in Ciudad Juárez with the signing of the Tratado de Ciudad Juárez (Juárez Treaty), which provided for the stepping down of Porfirio Díaz and his administration. The 19th-century customs building now houses the **Museo de Historia.** The museum's small collection includes Madero's 1910 Mercedes Benz and Benito Juárez's carriage. *Near border crossing. Admission free. Open Mon.–Sat. 9–1 and 3–5.*

AFTER DARK

Every storefront not open during the day on Avenida Juárez magically transforms after dark into a disco or bar, as teenagers from both sides of the border throw themselves into mass consumption of alcohol. Since you won't get a wink of sleep amidst the train whistles and rock bands, you might as well paint on your acid-washed jeans and join the debauchery. Heavy-metal fans will like **Spanky's** (Juárez 887), where the beer is served in *yardas* (literally, yards). **Alive** is a popular dance spot half a block from the Stanton Street bridge, where the latest hip-hop is played in a cave-like den. Most places charge a cover between $3 and $8, but if you go before 10 PM or on a slow night, you can often get in free. To avoid this scene and enjoy a well-crafted mixed drink, head to the **Kentucky Club** (Juárez 629), a haven of Naugahyde couches and decades-old sports memorabilia. You can also listen to strolling musicians at the **Plaza del Mariachi,** farther south on the east side of Avenida Juárez.

Nuevo Casas Grandes and Paquimé

Some 260 kilometers southwest of Ciudad Juárez lie the twin towns of Nuevo Casas Grandes and Casas Grandes. Nearby are the ruins of Paquimé, a settlement thought to have been occupied by Pima, Concho, and Jolima peoples as early as AD 700 and to have served as a center for trade between the indigenous civilizations of Mexico and the Pueblo peoples of the southwest United States around AD 1100. Note the mixture of architectural styles here: T-shaped doors similar to those of pueblo dwellings coexist here with Mesoamerican masonry techniques. Paquimé was a sophisticated settlement, with fortified heat-shielding walls and indoor plumbing. Its residents raised fowl and manufactured jewelry and pottery. The finest of the site's artifacts are now on display at the Museo Nacional de Antropologia in Mexico City (*see* Worth Seeing, in Chapter 2).

The ruins are currently undergoing restoration. Keep this in mind as you explore the ruins, and try not to add to the natural disintegration of the structures. Bring along plenty of sun block, water, and a hat—the former inhabitants of the settlement raised their birds in cool adobe pens for a reason. Admission is about $3, but if the caretaker's not there, you can cruise in free. In any case, it's always free on Sundays. The ruins are open every day from 10 to 5 in summer, but winter hours are limited and unpredictable.

BASICS

CASAS DE CAMBIO Several banks and money-exchange places can be found at the intersection of 5 de Mayo and Constitución. Both **Serfin** and **Banamex** change cash and traveler's checks weekdays 9–1:30 and have ATMs that accept Visa, MasterCard, Cirrus, and Plus.

Cambios California has better hours but changes cash only. *Constitución 207, tel. 169/ 4-32-32. Open weekdays 9–2 and 3:30–7, Sat. 9–6.*

MEDICAL AID The English-speaking **Dr. Amaro Prieto Saldovar** works in association with the **Farmacia de la Clínica.** *5 de Mayo 404, tel. 169/4–01–70. Open daily 9 AM–1 PM.*

PHONES AND MAIL The full-service **post office** is on 16 de Septiembre, one block east of Obregón. You can find public phones in **Cambios California** (*see above*) and in **Denni's** and

Dino's (*see* Where to Sleep and Eat, *below*). **Regalos Albas** has a *caseta de larga distancia* (long-distance phone office), which allows collect and credit-card calls. *Obregón, near 5 de Mayo, across from Estrella Blanca bus terminal. Open Mon.–Sat. 8:30 AM–10:30 PM.*

COMING AND GOING

Most visitors use Nuevo Casas Grandes, a two-horse town 8 kilometers from Casas Grandes and the ruins, as a stopover between Juárez and Chihuahua, and then visit Paquimé as a day excursion.

BY BUS Nuevo Casas Grandes has two terminals adjacent to one another on Obregón at 5 de Mayo. **Estrella Blanca** is most convenient, with ten buses daily to Juárez ($10, 4 hrs) and six a day to Chihuahua ($13, 5½ hrs). To get to Casas Grandes and Paquimé from Nuevo Casas Grandes, grab an orange bus marked either COL JUAREZ or CASAS GRANDES on Juárez, Nuevo Casas's main drag. After a 15-minute ride you will be deposited at the zócalo in Casas Grandes. A 10-minute walk—just follow the sign—will take you to the ruins.

WHERE TO SLEEP AND EAT

Unfortunately, the few hotels in town are rather expensive. Your best hope is the comfortable and friendly **Hotel Juárez** (Obregón 110, next to Estrella Blanca, tel. 169/4–02–33), where the English-speaking Mario Pérez will set you up in a clean single for $10 or double for $13. There's also a room that will hold up to five people for $17. **Motel Piñon** (Juárez 605, tel. 169/4–01–66), has a swimming pool and is everybody's favorite. Be sure to check out their private mini-museum of *ollas* (clay pots) from Paquimé. Singles are $30, doubles are $33, and they accept Visa and MasterCard, as does the wheelchair-accessible **Hotel Paquimé** (Juárez 401, tel. 169/4–13–20). Singles here are $28, doubles $32. You're just as well off at **Hotel California** (Constitución 209), where air-conditioned singles will run you $22 and doubles $25.

Cheap food is scarce in Casas Grandes, so shoestring travelers will want to eat their fill in Nuevo Casas Grandes, where plenty of taquerías and restaurants can be found near the bus station or along Juárez. For a good sit-down meal in Nuevo Casas Grandes try **Denni's** (Juárez 412, at Urueta, tel. 169/4–10–75), which bears no relation to the cheesy U.S. chain. A juicy T-bone steak is $10. **Dino's Pizza** (Constitución, near 5 de Mayo, tel. 169/4–02–40) makes a decent pie starting at about $5, but their $4 comida corrida is the way to go. **Nevería Chuchy** (Constitución 202, tel. 169/4–07–09) is a fun soda fountain with sandwiches ($1), burgers ($1.50), and ice cream cones ($1); all the kids in town wind up here at some point during the day.

Chihuahua

The city of Chihuahua, capital of Chihuahua state, lies on a high hilly plain some 375 kilometers south of Ciudad Juárez. Agriculture and lumber are the primary money makers here, so you won't get the feeling that you are a big, walking peso, as you may in its much poorer and more tourism-dependent neighbor to the north.

Chihuahua has long played a leading role in Mexican history: Founded in 1709, the city witnessed the execution of Independence leaders Padre Miguel Hidalgo and Ignacio Allende, fell to U.S. forces in 1847, and was occupied by Pancho Villa's army during the Mexican Revolution. The days of invading hordes are long over, however, and the primary reason visitors come here today is the Copper Canyon train that passes through town. There's no reason to hurry to the train, however: A day or two can happily be spent wandering through the city's cathedral, historical museums, and various other sights close to downtown. You may also be surprised by the occasional Mennonite in somber dress, a strange counterpoint to Mexicans in cowboy clothes and the traditional dress of the Tarahumaras—the Mennonite community of Cuauhtémoc is just a short train ride away.

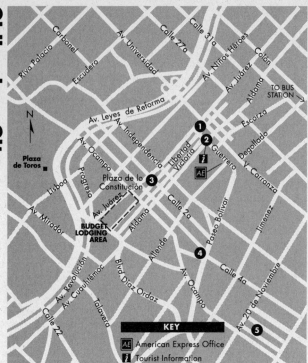

Catedral
Metropolitana
de Chihuahua, **3**

Palacio del
Gobierno, **2**

Palacio Federal, **1**

Museo de la
Revolución
Mexicana, **5**

Quinta Gameros, **4**

KEY

AE American Express Office

ℹ Tourist Information

Special events here include the **Feria de Santa Rita** (held in late May), when Chihuahuenses pay homage to their patron saint with food, music, and regional crafts at the fairgrounds on the Carretera al Aeropuerto. You might catch a rodeo during the second week of October, when **ExpoGan,** basically a state fair, is held at the Unión Gandera, just outside town. People come from all over the state on the eve of September 15 to celebrate **Mexican Independence** with a fireworks display at the Palacio del Gobierno. Holidays are also marked by bullfights, which are held at the **Plaza de Toros** (Lisboa, at Reforma).

BASICS

AMERICAN EXPRESS The AmEx representative in the full-service **Rojo y Casavantes** travel agency sells traveler's checks, replaces lost or stolen checks and AmEx cards, and offers MoneyGram service, but doesn't do traveler's-check exchange or emergency check cashing. Cardholders can, however, have their mail held here. *Guerrero 1207, Chihuahua, Chihuahua, CP 31000, México, tel. 14/15–58–58. Open weekdays 9 –6, Sat. 9–noon.*

AUTO PARTS/SERVICE **Centro Automotriz** has an English-speaker on duty who can sell you parts or refer you to a mechanic. *Libertad 1106, btw Calle 13a and Carranza, tel. 14/10–00–10. Open Mon.–Sat. 9–7.*

CASAS DE CAMBIO Several banks with ATMs line Avenida Independencia. **Serfin's** ATM (Independencia, at Juárez) accepts Visa, MasterCard, Cirrus, and Plus. Most banks change money weekdays 9:30 to noon or 1. The best rates for cash (and shortest lines), however, are at the **Centro de Cambio Rachasa.** Rachasa changes traveler's checks as well as cash, but charges a 2% commission. *Independencia 401, at Victoria, tel. 14/15–14–14. Open Mon.– Sat. 9–9.*

EMERGENCIES As in the United States, in the state of Chihuahua you can dial 911 from any phone for emergency assistance.

MAIL The post office is in the Palacio Federal, just opposite the old Palacio del Gobierno. They offer all the usual services and will hold mail sent to you at the following address for up to 10 days: Lista de Correos, Libertad, Chihuahua, Chihuahua, CP 31000, México. *Libertad, btw Carranza and Guerrero, tel. 14/15–14–17. Open weekdays 8–7, Sat. 9–1.*

MEDICAL AID Two clinics near downtown offer 24-hour emergency service and English-speaking doctors: **Clínica del Parque** (Calle de la Llave, at Calle 12a, tel. 14/15–74–11) and **Central Médico Dental** (Niños Héroes 606, tel. 14/15–55–70). About three blocks from the Palacio del Gobierno is the **Farmacia Mendoza** (Aldama 1901, tel. 14/16–44–14), also open 24 hours. Many pharmacies, though not technically open, advertise *servicio nocturno* (night service); you can ring their buzzer at any hour of the night and wake somebody if necessary.

PHONES You'll find Ladatel public phones on the main square. For cash calls, the Central Camionera (*see* Coming and Going, *below*) has a caseta de larga distancia, but it doesn't allow collect or credit-card calls. Downtown, the staff of the **Servicio de Larga Distancia** (Independencia 608, near Morelos) may be persuaded to place a collect or credit-card call for a small fee (and a big smile).

VISITOR INFORMATION The state tourism office is in the Palacio de Gobierno. There's usually someone on duty who speaks English, and maps and brochures are plentiful. *Calle 11a, at Libertad, tel. 14/10–10–77. Open weekdays 9–7, weekends 10–2.*

COMING AND GOING

BY BUS Chihuahua is a main hub for bus transportation, and the companies serving its **Central Camionera** run routes all over Mexico. The modern terminal is complete with a phone office, 24-hour luggage storage, and a cafeteria. Regular first-class service is available to Creel ($11, 4½ hrs), Ciudad Juárez ($15.50, 4½ hrs), Mexico City ($60, 22 hrs), Guadalajara ($50, 18 hrs), Monterrey ($28.50, 12 hrs), and Nuevo Casas Grandes ($14, 3 hrs). To get here, take a city bus marked CENTRAL CAMIONERA from the corner of Avenidas Ocampo and Juárez, downtown. If you arrive in town at night, your only choice is to take a taxi from the station to downtown: Don't let the driver charge you more than $5.

BY TRAIN The **Chihuahua al Pacífico** (Méndez, at Calle 24a, tel. 14/12–04–13) is the famous Copper Canyon train. Two trains run daily to Los Mochis ($36 1st class, $10 2nd class) via Creel ($16.50 1st class, $5 2nd class), Divisadero ($19.50 1st class, $5.50 2nd class), Bahuichivo ($22 1st class, $6 2nd class), and Sufragio ($34 1st class, $28 2nd class). Leaving at 7 AM, the first-class *Vista* train passes through Creel around noon and arrives in Los Mochis about 9 PM. The second-class *Mixto* train leaves Chihuahua at 8 AM and arrives in Los Mochis anytime between midnight and 5 AM. As a rule, second-class trains always lollygag and arrive late but, all in all, they aren't really that bad. The windows open (they don't on the first-class trains) and the crowd includes food vendors, musicians, and colorful characters of all sorts. To be absolutely certain of a first-class seat, you may consider buying your ticket in advance from **Mexico by Train** (tel. 800/321–1699 in the U.S.), but you'll pay more. This is, for the most part, only necessary during Semana Santa, the first week in July (when schools let out), and from late September through mid-November. To get to the terminal, take a bus marked COL. ROSALIA or STA. ROSA down Ocampo.

The station for the **Juárez–Chihuahua–Mexico** (tel. 14/12–22–84) route is at at the north entrance to town, just off Avenida Tecnológico. From here you can catch second-class trains to Ciudad Juárez ($5) and Mexico City ($15, 30 hrs), but they are notoriously slow. To get here, hop on a COLON bus from downtown.

BY PLANE The international airport is about 14 kilometers out of town. Any bus marked COL. AEROPUERTO will get you here for about 35¢; a taxi will do the same for about $6. **Aeroméxico** (tel. 14/15–63–03), **Taesa** (tel. 14/16–51–46), **SAM** (tel. 14/16–28–28), and **Leo López** (tel. 14/16–24–01) all serve Chihuahua's airport with flights to El Paso ($108 one way) and Dallas

($236 one way) in the United States, and destinations throughout Mexico such as Mazatlán ($174 one way) and Mexico City ($86 one way).

GETTING AROUND

The downtown area, roughly 10 blocks by three, contains virtually all the town's points of interest, including the **Plaza de la Constitución** (Chihuahua's zócalo) and the cathedral, as well as budget rooms and eateries. Odd-numbered streets lie north of Avenida Independencia, the core of the downtown area, and even-numbered streets are to the south. Buses for points all around the city leave from the corner of Avenidas Ocampo and Juárez during the day; after dark, unfortunately, they vanish. Taxi service (usually consisting of a sorry-looking Subaru with a helpful driver) is relatively cheap, and, unless you're headed to the airport or have just stepped out of an expensive hotel, you can get practically anywhere for a couple of dollars.

WHERE TO SLEEP

Most hotels here are well maintained and clean, and since they are clustered together in the area just southwest of the Plaza de la Constitución, you can easily take a look at them all before deciding which suits you best. The places listed below are the best of the cheapies, and all have hot water. Keep in mind, however, that water is rationed in Chihuahua, and availability is often limited in the evenings.

Hotel Carmen. The rooms here are small, but the hotel itself is centrally located, clean, comfortable, and equipped with spotless bathrooms. Single are $10, doubles $13. Be sure to check out the closed-circuit TV that monitors, strangely enough, the nearby Hotel Roma's lobby. Who do you think the people at the Roma are watching? *Juárez, at Calle 10a, tel. 14/15–70–96. 28 rooms, all with bath.*

Hotel del Cobre. Clean and comfy, this hotel tends to fill fast. The main draws are the air-conditioning, the quirkily decorated lounge, and the satellite TV. Singles are $17, doubles $20. *Calle 10a, at Progreso, tel. 14/15–17–60. 26 rooms, all with bath. Cafeteria, pharmacy.*

Hotel Turista. The three-story Turista has long been undergoing renovation, and cement bags and hardware often line the carpeted halls. The rooms, however, are air-conditioned and freshly painted, and the bathrooms have only a slight case of mildew. Singles are about $9, doubles $12, and one double without bath is available for $8.50. *Juárez 817, btw Calle 10a and Ocampo, tel. 14/10–04–00. 22 rooms, 21 with bath.*

Posada Aida. Close to downtown, this hotel is without a doubt the best deal in Chihuahua. The sheets are always fresh, the bathrooms are clean, the staff is friendly, and the pleasant courtyard is a good place to unwind if you're prepared to chat—the owner loves company. You'll pay $8.50 for a single and $10 for a double, and all rooms have private baths. *Calle 10a 105, btw Juárez and Doblado, tel. 14/15–38–30. 21 rooms.*

FOOD

Seafood stalls and hot-dog stands sprout from almost every downtown corner in Chihuahua. There are also two excellent vegetarian restaurants in town (*see below*); and the **market** (just north of Calle 4a, btw Niños Héroes and Juárez) is always stocked with fresh fruits, vegetables, meats, and cheeses. For luxury fare, the pricier hotels in town have fine dining, including the **Victoria** in the Palacio del Sol and **La Mansión** in Hotel Mirador.

➢ UNDER $5 • **Naturaleza Casa de Nutrición.** This health-food store runs a kitchen for those looking for a quick vegetarian burrito or salad bar. They serve a variety of tofu dishes for about $3, and the generous comida corrida will set you back $4. *Libertad 1910-A, about 5 blocks north of downtown, tel. 14/15–96–74. Open daily 8 AM–9 PM.*

➢ UNDER $10 • **Café Merino.** Late-night noshers sit in chrome and beige-vinyl booths here downing standard diner grub: eggs, sausage, toast, pancakes . . . you get the idea. Breakfast here should run you about $4 with coffee and juice. The $1.50 hamburgers and $5 *enchiladas de pollo en mole* (enchiladas with chicken in a chile and chocolate sauce) are popular lunch items. *Ocampo, at Juárez, tel. 14/12–87–42. Open Wed.–Mon. 8 AM–midnight. Wheelchair access.*

Dino's Pizza. This place makes a passable pie fairly quickly, and the cheese is good, even if it's not mozzarella. The salads ($3.50–$6) are acceptable, too. Dino's jumbo special pizza runs about $13; a plain medium costs about $7.50. *Doblado 301 at Calle 3a, a few blocks west of Plaza de la Constitución, tel. 14/16–57–07. Open daily 8 AM–midnight. Wheelchair access.*

Restaurant El Delfin. This comfortable place feels a bit like the social club of some large corporation, but the staff is all smiles and will try their darndest to lure you into their downstairs bar. The tasty food is affordable if you stick with the specialties, such as the shrimp cocktail ($2.50), T-bone steak ($6), and black bass with veggies ($5). *Juárez, at Calle 3a, no phone. Open daily noon–11.*

Restaurant Los Olivos. This excellent little vegetarian eatery serves organic fruits and vegetables, soy-based entrées, and egg dishes in a smoke-free environment polluted only by New Age Muzak. Whole-wheat pancakes are about $3; a fruit plate smothered with yogurt, granola, and honey is $2.50; and the huge lunch buffet is $7. *Calle de la Llave 202, btw Calles 2a and 4a, tel. 14/10–01–61. Open daily 8–4:30.*

WORTH SEEING

Once you've got your bearings and realized that Chihuahua is not just an evil cinderblock sprawl, you'll find that there's a good deal of culture and history to be absorbed, much of which is free. The town's main church, the baroque **Catedral Metropolitana de Chihuahua,** is on the **Plaza de la Constitución,** also called the Plaza de Armas. The cathedral is dedicated to St. Francis of Assisi, and its exterior is adorned with statues of Francis and the 12 Apostles. Inside, the **Museo de Arte Sacro** (Museum of Sacred Art) houses a collection of 18th-century religious art. Admission to the museum is $1, and it's open weekdays 10–2 and 4–6.

The **Palacio del Gobierno** and the **Palacio Federal** face each other on Juárez, between Guerrero and Carranza. The Palacio Federal contains the tower in which Padre Miguel Hidalgo was held prisoner before being executed for his role in the independence movement. Today, lights shining through the glass ceiling of the basement illuminate the tower, which holds Hidalgo's Bible, crucifix, and pistol. The Palacio del Gobierno (also home to the state tourism office) is where Hidalgo was actually executed—a plaque on the inner courtyard wall marks the spot. The Palacio del Gobierno also houses a set of historical murals painted by Aarón Piña Mora.

MUSEO DE LA REVOLUCION MEXICANA Quinta Luz, as the former home of the legendary Francisco "Pancho" Villa is sometimes called, is Chihuahua's biggest attraction. One of his many wives, Luz Corral, gave personal tours of the building until her death. The mansion was built by Pancho himself and, in its current incarnation, is dedicated to telling the history of the Mexican Revolution through photographs, treaties, maps, and artifacts, including weapons and and the 1922 Dodge Villa driving when he was assassinated. See if you can count the bullet holes. Most Chihuahuenses are familiar with the museum; don't hesitate to ask for directions. *Calle 10a No. 3014, about 1½ km from downtown, tel. 14/16–29–68. Take bus marked COL. DALES or OCAMPO. Admission: $1. Open daily 9–1 and 3–7.*

QUINTA GAMEROS This turn-of-the-century manor was built in French Nouveau style by one Manuel Gameros to impress his fiancée, who nevertheless turned her affection to another. It is now home to a museum displaying the mansion's original furniture, gilt-framed paintings, and ornate chandeliers, as well as the works of local art students, an exhibit on the ruins at Paquimé, and several rotating exhibits. Look for the reclining, headless nude on the outside upper reaches of the building, as well as the Little Red Riding Hood motif of the child's room, complete with a snarling wolf on the headboard of the bed. *Paseo Bolívar 401, at Calle 4a, tel. 14/16–66–84. Admission: $2. Open Tues.–Sun. 10–2 and 4–7.*

AFTER DARK

Chihuahua is not a big after-hours party town. Movies are a popular evening diversion: **Sala 2001** (Guerrero, at Escorza) and **Cine Olimpia Vistrana** (Escorza, at Carranza) both show Hollywood films with Spanish subtitles and the occasional Latin American or Spanish flick for about $4. The disco **Robin Hood** (Cuauhtémoc 2207) charges $5 at the door and is the only dance place around where gay couples are tolerated: Public displays of affection remain an exclusively heterosexual privilege in these parts. Because the disco is quite a walk south of downtown, you're better off taking a taxi. Weekend nights you can go watch music videos and drink at **Boeing 747** (tel. 14/13–25–16), in the Hotel Nieves on Avenida Tecnológico. **Hobbet** (Reforma 103, tel. 14/14–31–52) is a piano bar similar to those found in the the nicer hotels in town, but the drink prices and upscale dress code are prohibitive.

Creel and Las Barrancas del Cobre

It has often been said that there are five Grand Canyons in the Barrancas del Cobre, or Copper Canyons. This is an understatement. A series of canyons cut by rivers, this is a region of extremes, with mountains more than 3,600 meters high and gorges deeper than a kilometer. One of the last truly wild areas in North America, the Barrancas only became accessible to the general public with the completion of the Chihuahua al Pacífico railroad in 1961. The line, which runs between Chihuahua and Los Mochis, took nearly 100 years to complete and boasts some 87 tunnels and 37 bridges. The canyon's climate varies dramatically with elevation and season. In the uppermost regions you'll see lodgepole and ponderosa pines and Douglas firs, while the lower regions sprout wild oranges, bamboo, and berry vines. Long before it was discovered by the miners who brought the trains, and the tourists who brought the hotels and guided tours, the area was home to Tarahumara people. Those who remain tenaciously maintain one of the most traditional indigenous cultures in North America. Once occupying most of the state, the Tarahumara have dwindled to about 50,000, but continue to live in and around the canyons, farming and weaving pine-needle baskets, the majority of which are sold to tourists.

The train ride through the canyon region has become famous over the years, but the view from the observation car should not be considered the last word on the Barranca country. Creel, Divisadero, and Bahuichivo, all stops on the rail line, offer almost unlimited opportunities to strike out on your own or with a guide into the wilds of the canyon country. The best time to visit is after the rainy season, in early fall, when the waterfalls and rivers are at their best, and temperatures have settled to a comfortable level. Unless you're camping, however, afternoon thunderstorms during summer months can be spectacular in their own right.

If you pay an extra 15% for your Chihuahua al Pacífico train ticket, you can hop on and off the train at any of the Copper Canyon stops over a period of several days.

GETTING AROUND

BY BUS Trains are the primary mode of transportation through the canyons, but you can shorten the train ride in either direction by taking an **Estrella Blanca** bus, eight of which run daily between Creel and Chihuahua ($11). If you attempt this, board at either Chihuahua or Creel; boarding at intermediate points may leave you standing, due to lack of seats, for many leg-numbing hours.

BY TRAIN Two trains in each direction run daily between Chihuahua and Los Mochis: the first-class *Vista* and the second-class *Mixto*. The Vista is faster and more comfortable, with climate control and bathrooms; however, at $36 for the entire journey, it's almost four times the price of the second-class ride. The first-class train is very popular during the summer and fall, so try to book ahead if you're traveling during this time. Bring toilet paper and, for the moun-

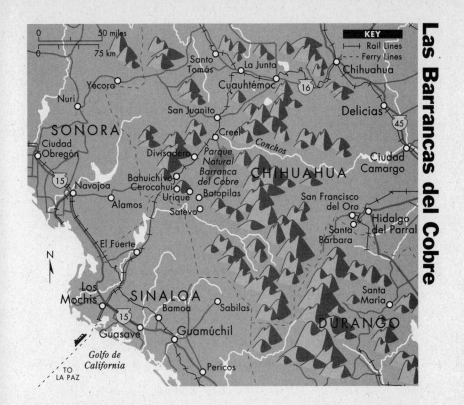

tainous areas, warm clothing. (In first class you'll probably need a sweater even in the low-lands—the air-conditioning is somewhat overenthusiastically used.) Tickets for the *Mixto* are only available the morning of departure—be prepared to fight tooth and nail for both tickets and seats during Semana Santa and September–October. For specific information on prices and departures, *see* Coming and Going, in Chihuahua, *above*; Creel, *below;* and Los Mochis in Chapter 7. Starting in Los Mochis is recommended, especially since the *Mixto* leaving from Chihuahua will probably pass the Barrancas in the dark. If you're heading out of Chihuahua, the best view is on the right until you pass Creel and on your left from Creel to Los Mochis.

The second-class train has an unpredictable schedule and no reserved seating, but it provides the best opportunity to meet local campesinos (peasants) and their poultry.

HIKING Extreme temperatures, lack of resupply points, and a wide range of altitudes make hiking in the Copper Canyon a challenge. However, if you know where you're going and have the proper equipment, overnight trips are undoubtedly the best way to see the Barrancas. Pick up hiking supplies in Los Mochis or Chihuahua. Rather unhelpful topographical maps are available in Creel, as is the best book on the region, *Mexico's Copper Canyon Country,* by M. John Fayhee. The best jumping-off points for hikes within the canyons are Creel and Bahuichivo, and it's easy to find a guide in either of these places. Use your head, though—holdups have been reported by tourists. Get someone moderately trustworthy—i.e. a hotel owner, rather than the guy hanging out on the corner—to refer you to a reputable guide.

HITCHING Barring walking for days, hitchhiking is the only way to reach some points off the rail line. It's fairly safe and common in rural areas, but some days you'll wait so long you can actually feel yourself getting older. Sundays are the worst, as nobody's off to work. Trucks often pick up groups of people and charge a few dollars, depending on the length of the journey.

Creel

Set in a shallow valley high in the Sierra Madre, about halfway between Los Mochis and Chihuahua, the medium-size town of Creel is rapidly becoming the favorite stop for travelers on the Chihuahua al Pacífico line who wish to explore the Barrancas without too much hassle. There's not much to keep you hanging around Creel per se, but the surrounding area is beautiful. The locals are accustomed to tourists, friendly, and knowledgeable.

Hiking is the best way to enjoy the area. Even if you don't want to join a group from one of the hotels, it's a good idea to ask around for tips on trails. Some of the most popular destinations are **Cusárare**, a waterfall 22 kilometers away; **Lake Arareco**, some 7 kilometers south of Creel; and **San Ignacio,** about 4 kilometers south, past the town cemetery and various Tarahumara caves. San Ignacio is a modest mission built in 1744, where masses are still held each Sunday at 11 AM in the Tarahumara language. Try hitching a ride just outside town, or ask about rides to these sights, and to the nearby attractions of **Batopilas** and **Basaseachic Falls** in the few small grocery stores on Avenida López Mateos, the main drag that parallels the train tracks.

As an alternative to the ubiquitous mariachi bands, a local Jesuit priest in Creel blasts classical music for the whole town to enjoy every evening from 7 to 10. Head down to the zócalo for the best acoustics. The padre has a couple hundred CDs and claims he can play music for three months without a repetition.

BASICS

CASA DE CAMBIO **Serfin** (tel. 145/6–02–50), just east of the tracks, changes money weekdays 10:30–noon and charges a hefty commission on traveler's checks. A better idea is changing money in Chihuahua or Los Mochis.

BOOKSTORE The nameless book and cassette shop on López Mateos has some excellent books in Spanish and a small selection of English-language materials on the Tarahumara and the region. *Near tourist office. Open Mon.–Sat. noon–9 PM.*

LAUNDRY The local lavandería charges $3 a load. *Villa 112. Open daily 8–8.*

MEDICAL AID For pharmaceuticals and advice about minor medical problems, look for **Farmacia Rodríguez.** *López Mateos 43. Open Mon.–Sat. 9–2 and 3–8, Sun. 10–1.*

PHONES AND MAIL López Mateos has several casetas de larga distancia that charge less than $1 for collect phone calls. The **post office** (tel. 145/6–02–58) is in the Presidencia Municipal, south of the zócalo, and will hold mail sent to you at the following address for up to 10 days: Lista de Correos, Presidencia Municipal, Creel, Chihuahua, CP 33200, México.

VISITOR INFORMATION The **Complejo Turístico Arareco** on López Mateos has a rough map of the area and provides information on tours. They arrange boat rentals for Lake Arareco ($7 an hour) and rent bicycles ($2 an hour). *Tel. 145/6–01–26. Open daily 9–6.*

Information in English is available at **Artesanías Misión** (tel. 145/6–01–80), next to the bank. They also sell maps of Creel ($2) and topographical maps of the Barrancas ($6). The latter, while interesting, are virtually useless for hiking unless you're a cartography expert. Groovy, dreadlocked Arturo, who works at **Café del Sol** (next to Margarita's), can answer just about any travel-related question in perfect English.

COMING AND GOING

BY BUS The **Estrella Blanca** terminal (tel. 145/6–00–73) is on the west side of the train tracks, opposite the zócalo. Eight buses depart Creel every 1½ hours between 7 AM and 5:30 PM for Chihuahua ($11, 4½ hrs), stopping at most of the towns along the way. The terminal for Batopilas (*see Near Creel, below*) is behind the main terminal.

BY TRAIN First-class trains from Los Mochis pull into Creel at about 3:15 PM, second-class at 5:30 PM (more or less). First- and second-class trains heading in the opposite direction from Chihuahua arrive in Creel about 12:30 PM and 2 PM, respectively. The first-class trains are rarely late; the second-class trains show up when they feel like it, so be prepared to wait. You can buy tickets on the train.

WHERE TO SLEEP

As soon as you step off the train you will be assailed by a horde of children beckoning you to **Margarita's** (Mateos 11, tel. 145/6–00–45). Make the kids happy and jump on the hotel's courtesy shuttle, as you will inevitably end up there anyhow. The owner, Margarita, provides whatever type of accommodation you can afford, from a $3 mattress on the floor to a $5 bunk to a $20 double room with private bath. She even rents an elegant suite ($10 per person) and has recently opened another place with more upscale rooms ($40 a double). And as if that's not enough, yummy communal meals are included in the price. The place is very well known—summer finds it packed with groups of oh-so-cosmopolitan international travelers—and Margarita's staff leads guided tours when there's demand. If you prefer to avoid the highly social scene at Margarita's, the hotels listed below are solid alternatives.

Casa Valenzuela. This single-story hotel is ususally semi-vacant, and the proprietor is pleased to accommodate your needs and budget. The communal bathroom is tiny but fairly clean, though the ceiling sags. Well, okay, the beds sag, too. Singles are $8.50, doubles $17. *López Mateos, tel. 145/6–01–04. 13 rooms, 5 with bath.*

Hotel Tarahumara. This quiet hotel a few blocks from the zócalo has a very helpful staff and few guests, and the rooms and bathrooms are fairly clean. Rooms are $10, regardless of how many people you stuff in them. *López Mateos 48, tel. 145/6–02–52. 15 rooms, all with bath.*

FOOD

Cheery **Café Manzano**, just off the train tracks, is a favorite of rail crews. Basic Mexican dishes run about $4, and the service is fast and friendly. Come early; they close at 8 PM daily. **Café El Tungar**, across from the bus station, serves a filling bowl of *menudo* (tripe soup) for less than $4, but closes even earlier (7 PM). Open latest (a daring 9 PM) is **Restaurant Lupita**, also on López Mateos. Morning hotcakes are just $2. Later, try *bistec ranchero* (steak cooked with tomatoes and onions) or fish fillet, both $4. You can purchase fresh fruits and vegetables from the grocery stores along López Mateos.

OUTDOOR ACTIVITIES

Creel is a convenient base from which to explore the natural beauty of the canyons and the rivers that tumble through them. While river-rafting is strictly for those adventurers who bring their own equipment (and come with the rains), you can rent horses and mountain bikes in Creel or set off on hikes that last anywhere from one hour to several days. Remember to take it easy for a while to let your body get used to changes in altitude. You can rent mountain bikes at **Margarita's** (*see* Where to Sleep, *above*), as well as at the **Complejo Turístico Arareco** (*see* Visitor Information, *above*), which also arranges boat and horse rentals.

Guided tours are available to virtually any place in the area. You can go to the Complejo Turístico Arareco or join a group from Margarita's. You can also arrange your own tour by asking around at the main plaza; many residents own trucks, are quite knowledgeable, and will take you anywhere, as long as the price is right.

HIKING Topographical maps and guidebooks are available at **Artesanías Misión** (*see* Visitor Information, *above*), but most of what you'll find is pretty useless. You're better off with a live guide—ask at Margarita's or the adjacent **Café del Sol.** Creel is the base for long treks to Basaseachic Falls and Batopilas (*see* Near Creel, *below*), but those with less time or less ambition may prefer to meander over to the statue of Jesus in the hills west of town, where you'll find a nice picnic spot. You can ask anyone in Creel to point you in the right direction. You can also head to the **Valle de las Monjas** (Valley of the Nuns), so named for the rocks said to resemble a huddle of nuns. Also close by is the **Valle de los Hongos** (Valley of the Mushrooms), where, after rains, Tarahumara people go to pick mushrooms.

NEAR CREEL

Two nice swimming spots are within easy hitching distance of Creel, past cold, muddy Lake Arareco. The first of these is **Recohuata,** where you'll find bubbling hot springs. Once your driver drops you off, you'll probably need to hike about an hour to the pools. The return trip is strenuous, so bring water. The whole trip will take you five to seven hours. A bit further out (22 kilometers south of Creel) is the Tarahumara town of **Cusárare,** where a 35-meter waterfall cascades into a natural pool. Once you arrive in town, you'll have to take a quick 3-kilometer hike to the waterfall and pay $1 to get in. If you don't want to hitch, you can always pay someone to take you to either of these places, or join a tour.

BASASEACHIC FALLS About a four-hour drive northwest from Creel brings you to the magnificent Basaseachic Falls, which plunge a sheer 250 meters into a pool below. The area, recently made a national park, is magnificent after the rainy season (July–August). Tours can be arranged in Creel for groups of four or more (the ones from Margarita's are about $27 per person), or you can hitch from **San Juanito** or **La Junta,** both on the rail line. If you do hitch, however, plan to stay overnight somewhere in the park—good camping spots abound. Hiking trails are a dime a dozen, and there's an excellent swimming hole at the waterfall's edge. Bring your own supplies because there are no shops at all.

BATOPILAS About 140 kilometers south of Creel, in the heart of the canyon lands, is the small mining town of Batopilas, which sits alongside the river of the same name. The town is hard to reach, so it doesn't see many tourists, but it provides great access to the canyons. An easy 4-kilometer hike south takes you to the tiny town of **Satevo,** where a spooky abandoned mission is worth exploring; about 6 kilometers north is **La Bufa,** a forgotten gold mine. You can swim and camp by the river, but it's not advised in the summer months when the creepy-crawlies are out in legion. Deforestation upstream has also made flash floods frequent and dangerous, so exercise caution near the river. A few small eateries provide the calories to keep you going. Rooms are available at the **Hotel Batopilas**, just about the only establishment that's clearly marked, for about $10 per person, or occasionally at the Tarahumara artesanía shop for a little less. Buses depart Creel at 7 AM on Tuesdays, Thursdays, and Saturdays and cost $10. The return bus departs Batopilas at 4 AM (yes, AM) on Mondays, Wednesdays, and Fridays, and the trip takes eight hours. The road has been called the best and worst in North America: The scenery is magnificent, but switchbacks are stomach-wrenching.

When the Batopilas mines were in full operation, they produced chunks of silver as big as basketballs—the profits of which would be used, in part, to throw lavish high-society parties in the town's grand haciendas.

Batopilas is also accessible by trail from both Urique and Cerocahui, off the Bahuichivo rail stop (*see below*), though most people make the three-day trip in the other direction. Ask around for guides and more information.

Divisadero

Divisadero is the first significant stop on the rail line after Creel. Most visitors stop for 15 minutes to snap pictures, buy baskets, and gawk over the canyon rim. The expensive **Posada del Cobre** arranges guided tours into the canyon, or you can hire a guide on your own for overnight trips down to the **Río Urique.** Less formidable is the 2-kilometer hike from the north side of the hotel to an abandoned Tarahumara cliff dwelling. If you want to hang out and do some hiking, it is possible to catch a later train for a small surcharge, but all the hotels here are out of budget range. Your alternatives are hiking a ways from town and camping (ask permission before pitching a tent on someone's land), or renting a room from a local family (up to $10 a night). Ask around at the artesanía stands about either option.

Bahuichivo and Around

A day or so in Bahuichivo will convince you that you've been transplanted to the Old West. It consists of a few dusty hotels, dirt roads, and farm animals. The town hugs the railroad tracks 260 kilometers north of Los Mochis and, from a traveler's point of view, is not much more than a departure point for exploring the towns of Cerocahui and Urique, or hiking down into the canyon's hot belly. If you're foraging for food, cross the railroad tracks heading east and walk up the hill to two nameless restaurants. Another restaurant, **La Amistad,** 100 meters uphill from the train station, is recommended by travelers. A shabby, white building on your left as you come up the hill reads SE RENTAN CUARTOS (rooms rented). A dark room here for one or two people is $10. You're better off at **Hotel el Camino Real** (mid-hill on your right, no phone), which has decent rooms with private baths for $7.50 a single and $10 a double. For medical help in Bahuichivo, see the English-speaking and reputable Dr. Leyva. His office is labeled FARMACIA and is near Abarrotes Gabby.

To make the three-hour trip to Urique from Bahuichivo, hop on the white van marked TRANSPORTES CAÑON URIQUE that comes to meet the trains—the charge to Urique is $8.50. The bus will pass through Cerocahui, charging about $3 for that leg of the journey. It's also easy to hitch between Cerocahui and Bahuichivo.

Cerocahui

This teeny town about 17 kilometers southeast of Bahuichivo is probably one of the best places in Mexico for stargazing: Cerocahui has no electricity after 10 PM (although solar panels are becoming increasingly popular for after-hours light and hot water), and the air is pristine. A Jesuit mission, founded here in 1680 and restored in 1940, still operates a boarding school for Tarahumara children, but its *iglesia* (church) is eerily vacant most of the time. If you're fortunate enough to be here during Semana Santa, be sure to catch the *matachines* (Tarahumara dances) at the old mission. On June 24, locals douse each other with water in homage to John the Baptist.

You can explore the nearby waterfalls or the abandoned **Sangre de Cristo** gold mines, about 3 kilometers from town on horse or on foot. You can also set out on a two- to three-day trek/horseback ride to Batopilas (*see* Near Creel, *above*) from here, but you'll need a guide. Information is available from the knowledgeable and trustworthy Eduardo Muños, who can be found at the small artesanía shop at the entrance of town.

Paraíso el Oso

Twelve kilometers from Bahuichivo is Paraíso el Oso, a small hotel/retreat run by a Mexican/American couple. Fantastic rooms for two with solar-heated water and sparkling-clean private bathrooms run $35 a night, but you can pitch a tent on the premises and use all the facilites for about $10 a night per tent. (Bring your own food, because meals can be expensive.) In the morning, bilingual staff members lead spectacular hikes (or horseback rides) up streams and over mesas to a cave filled with crosses, each commemorating an Indian that died, probably during a cholera epidemic introduced by Pancho Villa's troops. Another hike will take you to a cave filled with bones, tools, and bedrock mortars for grinding corn strewn under a smoke-stained ceiling. Mario, the hotel's driver, meets the trains daily to pick up guests and will approach you to see if you're interested. For reservations (a good idea in September and October), write to Doug (Diego) Rhodes, P.O. Box 31089, El Paso, TX 79931, U.S.A.

While in Cerocahui, be sure to check out the action at the crude, two-cell jail, which is exposed to the street. Weekend borrachos (drunks) are about all that keeps the pen in business. After a particularly wild (by Copper Canyon standards) weekend, townspeople congregate, some to console and some to heckle their unfortunate neighbors.

WHERE TO SLEEP AND EAT Rooms with private baths and hot water are available at **Posada Cerocahui** for $10 (single) and $17 (double). It's a white house at the entrance to town—in case he hasn't put up a sign yet, ask for Enrique. A woman known as Fea (yup, that's really what they call her) has a house next to the mission with a few crude rooms that fit up to three people for $7. Let her show you the nifty new solar lights of which she's so terribly proud. There is only one restaurant in town, and it's more a living room than anything else. The menu changes daily, but meals are always less than $5. To find it, continue west past the hotel; it's diagonally across from the small park.

Urique

Thirty-eight kilometers southeast of Cerocahui, the village of Urique offers places to play in the gushing **Río Urique** and fantastic views of the surrounding canyon. You can also walk down the dirt road at the edge of town and explore **Chiflón**, an abandoned mine near the foot of a hanging footbridge. As long as heavy rains haven't got the water raging, this is a great spot for a swim. Vans leave Urique in time to meet the first-class train in Bahuichivo and return to Urique after the arrival of second-class passengers.

WHERE TO SLEEP AND EAT Urique boasts three hotels, but your best bet is the **Hotel Cañon Urique**, on the main drag beneath the huge ceiba tree. The hotel has its own mini-zoo. Singles with private bath are $8.50, doubles are $13, and the rooms in the rear are quieter. If you've brought camping equipment, ask for Tom and Keith's house (a couple of friendly expatriates from the States). They've got a great camping area under the mesquite trees by the river. A $1 donation is requested for use of the squat toilet and fresh water. Chiggers can get really bad here during the rainy season. The best eats in town are found at the **Restaurant Plaza** (actually someone's home), down the street from the Cañon Urique. About $4 will get you the meal of the day between 6 AM and 11 PM. Travelers have complained about the town's other main restaurant, the **Zulema**—don't risk it.

Durango

The modern, industrialized city of Durango sits in the Valle del Guadiana. The city's downtown area is built on a series of hills and retains some superb colonial architecture. If the dusty landscape and exceptionally clear light you see on the bus ride into town strike a familiar chord, you're not crazy. You probably *have* seen the place before, as the area was used in a number of major Hollywood productions, including *Big Jake,* starring John Wayne. Proud of its contribution to the film industry, the tourism office often organizes weekend trips to two "western" towns used as film sets. Of these, **Villa del Oeste** (Village of the West) is the only one still used for moviemaking. Another set is known as **Chupaderos,** and although its been forgotten by film, it has become a refuge for destitute people who live in the sets.

Every July, Durango wraps two weeks of **Feria Nacional** around two significant dates: July 4, the day of the Virgen del Refugio; and July 22, the anniversary of Durango's 1563 founding by Francisco de Ibarra. The festival has taken on national status, and people come from all around to hear the music, eat the food, ride the rides, bid on cows, and bet on cock fights.

BASICS

AMERICAN EXPRESS AmEx services are provided by friendly, English-speaking representatives in the travel agency **Touris Viajes,** a few long blocks west of the Plaza de Armas. You can buy or change traveler's checks here and have lost or stolen traveler's checks or AmEx cards replaced. Cardholders can also have their mail held or cash a personal check here. *20 de Noviembre 810 Ote., tel. 18/17–00–23. Take orange bus from stop marked NARANJA on cnr of Victoria and 20 de Noviembre. Open weekdays 9–7, Sat. 10–5.*

CASAS DE CAMBIO Serfin (20 de Noviembre 400 Ote., tel. 18/1–15–03) changes traveler's checks only weekdays 9–12:30. **Mundinero**, next door to the AmEx office, changes both cash and traveler's check and has decent hours; unfortunately, the rates here are lousy. *20 de Noviembre 806 Ote., tel. 18/17–03–44. Open weekdays 9:30–2 and 4–6:30, Sat. 10–2.*

EMERGENCIES The number for the **police** is 18/17–54–06. For an ambulance, call the **Cruz Roja** (tel. 18/17–34–44).

LAUNDRY The friendly guys at **Lavanderia Automatica Ale** will wash, dry, fold, and even deliver your clothes (up to 3 kilos) for $5 a load. *Lázaro Cárdenas 232 Nte., tel. 18/17–22–20. Take orange bus from stop marked NARANJA on cnr of Victoria and 20 de Noviembre. Open Mon.–Sat. 9–7.*

MAIL The full-service post office will hold mail sent to you at the following address for up to 10 days: Lista de Correos, Administración No. 1, 20 de Noviembre 500-B Ote., Durango, Durango, CP 34001, México. *20 de Noviembre, btw Cuauhtémoc and Roncal, tel. 18/ 11–41–05. Open weekdays 8–7, Sat. 9–noon.*

MEDICAL AID Two 24-hour clinics are: **Hospital San Jorge** (Libertad 249, tel. 18/ 17–22–10) and **Hospital de La Paz** (5 de Febrero 903, tel. 18/18–95–41). **Farmacia el Fénix** (20 de Noviembre, at Victoria, tel. 18/11–40–41) has a knowledgeable staff and carries a lot of U.S. brands, but closes daily at 9:30 PM. For 24-hour service, go to **Farmacia del Ahorro** (20 de Noviembre 100 Ote., no phone).

PHONES Several casetas de larga distancia line 5 de Febrero. For some reason, most resent being asked to place collect calls, so you might have to plug your ears and scream into the public phones on the street corners and in the Plaza de Armas.

VISITOR INFORMATION The staff of the state tourism office is multilingual, friendly, and thoroughly helpful. Stop by for the great city maps and informative pamphlets (in English) about Durango. *Hidalgo 408 Sur, tel. 18/11–21–39. West of plaza on 20 de Noviembre, left on Hidalgo. Open weekdays 8–3 and 5–8, Sat. 10–2.*

COMING AND GOING

BY BUS The **Central Camionera** is about 4 kilometers east of the town center, but regular city buses and cheap taxis (about $3 to the central plaza) make it fairly accessible. The station is served by a number of national lines, including **Omnibus de México** (tel. 18/18–33–61) and **Transportes del Norte** (tel. 18/18–32–41), which shares a phone with **Estrella Blanca, Transportes Chihuahuenses**, and **Futura**. First-class buses run daily to points all over Mexico, including Mexico City ($38, 12 hrs), Chihuahua city ($26, 9 hrs), Ciudad Juárez ($40, 12 hrs), Mazatlán ($13, 7 hrs), Monterrey ($27, 9 hrs), and Saltillo ($23, 7½ hrs). Estrella Blanca also provides limited second-class service. A small pharmacy and long-distance telephone service are available at the station.

BY TRAIN Durango's train station (tel. 18/11–22–94) is right below the Cerro del Mercado, off Avenida Felipe Pescador, about nine blocks north of the plaza. A first-class train to Mexico City ($12, 15 hrs) departs at 6 AM. Another leaves for Ciudad Juárez ($13, 11 hrs) at 7 AM, with a stop in Chihuahua ($8, 8 hrs). Other destinations include Saltillo ($7, 9 hrs), Monterrey ($8, 11 hrs), and Zacatecas ($4, 16 hrs). The ticket office is only open from 5 AM to noon. To get here, take the bus marked FERR.

GETTING AROUND

The main thoroughfare, 20 de Noviembre, runs east–west. Juárez, Constitución, and Victoria are the main streets that intersect 20 de Noviembre in the heart of the downtown area. The main square, called the **Plaza de Armas,** is off 20 de Noviembre, between Juárez and Victoria. Addresses in the city contain cardinal directions—Nte. for north, Sur for south, Ote. for east, and Pte. for west—which indicate where they are in relation to the plaza. City buses congregate near the plaza, and taxis charge a little less than $1 per kilometer.

WHERE TO SLEEP

There are a few decent places near the center of town, but, in general, budget hotels in Durango tend to be bottom-of-the-barrel. Around festival time (the first two weeks in July) make reservations, or expect to stay far away from downtown, pay a lot, and get little. The cheapest place downtown is the scruffy, none-too-clean **Hotel Gallo** (5 de Febrero 117, tel. 18/11–52–90), where singles are $10, doubles $12.

Hotel María del Pilar. The María del Pilar is the best of the cheapies: Rooms are drab and have peeling paint, but they're clean and relatively comfy, and all have spotless, lime-green tiled bathrooms with plenty of hot water. Singles are a steal at $11, and doubles are $15. *Pino Suárez 410 Pte., tel. 18/11–54–71. 20 rooms, all with bath. Luggage storage, phone, wheelchair access.*

Hotel Posada Durán. Everybody's favorite, this colonial building just across from the cathedral has large wooden doors, a bar, and a courtyard with a fountain. The rooms are impeccable and have wood floors, and some have big glass doors that open onto balconies. Bathrooms are spotless and have plenty of scalding water. Singles are $15, doubles $19. *20 de Noviembre 506 Pte., tel. 18/11–24–12. 15 rooms, all with bath. Luggage storage. Reservations advised. MC, V.*

Hotel Reyes. The Reyes smells a bit like disinfectant but is clean and has good (if tiny) bathrooms and an amiable staff. Singles are $13, doubles $16. *20 de Noviembre 220 Ote., tel. 18/13–02–03. 56 rooms, all with bath. Laundry, luggage storage, wheelchair access.*

Posada San Jorge. A good bet for your money, this downtown hotel is popular with traveling businesspeople. The covered inner courtyard is massive, airy, and filled with green, leafy life. The rooms, all of which have telephones, are tiled throughout, and the bathrooms are clean and have generous hot water. Singles cost about $19, doubles $22. *Constitución 102 Sur, tel. 18/13–32–57. 25 rooms, all with bath. Luggage storage. MC, V.*

FOOD

There are virtually no outstanding budget places to eat downtown: A few small places serve almost identical comidas corridas, and there are hot-dog stands galore, but few places distinguish themselves. The **mercado** on 20 de Noviembre, right near the Hotel Reyes (*see above*), is a good place to get fresh fruits and vegetables; *fondas* (covered food stands) toward the back serve standard meals for about $2.50.

➤ UNDER $5 • **Restaurant Vegetariano Samadhi.** The only meatless place in town is tiny and located a block off 20 de Noviembre. The menu changes daily, except for the yogurt with fruit and honey ($2). *Negrete 403 Pte., tel. 18/11–62–27. Open daily 8 AM–10 PM.*

Rincón Taurino. Even if you're not hungry, stop by this small, dark restaurant to check out the collection of bullfighting memorabilia that adorns the walls. The enchiladas are excellent and only about $3; a variety of soups costing about $2 is also served. Economical breakfasts are about $3. *Constitución 106 Nte., tel. 18/11–29–34. Open daily 8 AM–midnight.*

➤ UNDER $10 • **La Bohemia.** If you're sick of tacos, try this Mexican-German restaurant just east of the Parque Guadiana. Lime green and deep purple give the place an eclectic elegance, and the staff is attentive. A German sausage-and-cabbage dinner costs about $7.50; a breakfast of hotcakes is less than $4; and an excellent comida corrida ($6) is available 2–4. *Negrete 1314 Pte., tel. 18/11–00–45. Open daily 8 AM–midnight.*

Pizzaly. Thin-crust pizzas with lots of cheese and a thin layer of tomato sauce are served with a smile at this popular pizzeria. One-topping *chicas* (enough for one person) and *medianas* (serving two or three) cost $6 and $9 respectively. Best of all, Pizzaly will deliver a pizza to your hotel room free of charge. *20 de Noviembre 1004, Pte., tel. 12–13–81, Open daily 1–10:30. Wheelchair access.*

Sloan's. This small restaurant/bar is almost always full of young people and music, as well as a bizarre clutter of plane propellers, drum sets, and other random junk. Both roast beef and Italian-style spaghetti cost $7; a monster-size piña colada is $3.50. *Negrete 1003 Pte., tel. 18/12–21–99. Open daily 1 PM–11:30 PM. Wheelchair access.*

WORTH SEEING

Fortunately, most of Durango's most interesting sites are well within walking distance of the main **Plaza de Armas**; the huge, baroque **Catedral Basílica Menor**, Durango's main church, faces the plaza. The best of the outlying sights is the **Parque Guadiana** (on Carretera Durango–Mazatlán). Fourteen long blocks from the main plaza, this park is a favorite spot for sports-minded locals. Miles of dirt paths make it an ideal for runners and bicyclists alike, and the huge public swimming pool is a great place to beat the afternoon heat. Free aerobics classes are held daily at 7 AM in the little clearing behind the pool. Just across the highway is the **Zoológico Sahuatoba** (tel. 18/12–44–57), where a gawk at the lions, panthers, hippos, and snakes is free of charge.

CASA DE LOS CONDES DE SUCHIL Once an aristocratic residence, this churrigueresque (ultra-baroque) palace is now inhabited by pricey shops. Come here to browse or to admire the arched courtyard and well-preserved masonry and stone carvings. *5 de Febrero, at Madero.*

MUSEO REGIONAL DE DURANGO Built in the second half of the 19th century by architect Stanislaus Slonecky, the Regional Museum of Durango was originally a residence. Today, the two-story building houses fossilized remains dating to the Paleozoic era. A mummified set of child-size human remains is also on display; their discovery in nearby El Mezquital has led some archaeologists to believe that a colony of pygmies once lived in Durango. The museum also houses paintings, textiles, and sculptures. *Victoria 100 Sur, tel. 18/12–53–11. Admission: $1.50. Open Tues.–Sat. 10–3.*

PALACIO DE GOBIERNO This impressive 18th-century baroque palace houses the offices of various state officials, including that of the governor of Durango state. The reason to visit, however, is the impressive murals on the top floor, depicting Durango's indigenous population's struggle for survival (which continues for many in the southernmost portion of the state). On the ground floor, you'll find an unfinished mural abandoned by painter Manuel Guerrero Lourdes in 1936. The state of Durango never got around to paying the master his salary. In protest, he refused to finish the painting. *5 de Febrero, at Zaragoza, 4 blocks west of plaza.*

AFTER DARK

Nightlife isn't exactly hip-hoppin' in Durango, but there are a few clubs such as **La Covacha** (Pino Suárez, at Madero) where young Durango youth and older couples dance to the latest pop/rock tunes Wednesday–Saturday night for a $6.50 cover charge. **Buchagas Pool and Snack Bar** (20 de Noviembre 310 Ote., tel. 18/12–40–64) is a respectable place to play eight ball (tables are $5 per hour) and down a few pricey beers. They stay open into the wee hours, but do not admit patrons after 10 PM.

Spanish Glossary

In Spanish, what you see is what you get: Every letter is pronounced, and the accent usually falls on the second-to-last syllable, unless there is an accent mark. Of course, there are exceptions to both rules. And, to confound matters, you'd be hard pressed to find a Mexican who actually pronounces everything clearly. Still, if you learn a few rules, you should be able to pronounce almost any Spanish word; figuring out what it means may take a little more effort. The following letters are pronounced as follows:

a like the **a** in ah	**e** like the **a** in make
i like the **ee** in beet	**o** like the **o** in cold
u like the **oo** in loot	**y** like the **ea** in eat
ñ like the **ni** in senior	**ll** like the **y** in kayak

The **h** is silent in Spanish. **G** before **a**, **o**, **u**, or a consonant is hard (like in gate); when before **e** or **i**, it's soft, sounding just slightly harder than the **h** in hay. When g is paired with u (**gu**), it sounds like the English **w**. For all practical purposes, **b** and **v** sound the same—roughly like a **b** in English.

Spanish	English
Basics	
Hola	Hello
Buenos días	Good morning
Buenas tardes	Good afternoon
Buenas noches	Good night
Cómo está?	How are you?
Estoy bien, gracias	I'm fine, thanks
Adiós	Goodbye
Perdóneme	I'm sorry
Con permiso	Excuse me
Habla inglés?	Do you speak English?
No hablo español	I don't speak Spanish
Soy estadounidense	I'm from the United States
Soy australiano(a)	I'm Australian
Soy canadiense	I'm Canadian
Soy inglés(a)	I'm English
Soy escocés(a)	I'm Scottish
Bésame, soy irlandés	Kiss me, I'm Irish
No entiendo	I don't understand
Cómo se dice . . .	How do you say . . .
Más despacio, por favor	More slowly, please
No sé	I don't know
Por favor	Please
Gracias	Thank you

Barato	Cheap
Caro	Expensive
De nada	You're welcome
No	No
Sí	Yes
Dónde está(n)	Where is (are)
Baño, sanitario	Bathroom
Mochila	Backpack
Oficina de correos	Post office
Caseta de larga distancia	Long-distance telephone office
Llamada al cobrar	Collect call
Lavandería	Laundromat
Banco/casa de cambio	Bank/money exchange place
Abierto(a)	Open
Cerrado(a)	Closed
Ayer	Yesterday
Hoy	Today
Mañana	Tomorrow
Qué horas son?	What time is it?
Entrada	Entrance
Salida	Exit
Piso	Floor/story
Colonia, barrio	Neighborhood

Emergencies and Medical Aid

La policía	Police
Déjame en paz!	Leave me alone!
Socorro!	Help!
Estoy enfermo(a)	I'm sick
Necesito a un médico	I need a doctor
Me duele la cabeza	I have a headache
Me duele el estómago	I have a stomachache
Fiebre	Fever
Receta	Prescription
Remedio	Medicine
Aspirina	Aspirin
Preservativo	Condom
SIDA	AIDS

Coming and Going

Ida	One-way
Ida y vuelta	Round-trip
A pie	On foot
Seguro	Insurance
Hacer dedo	Hitchhike
Aventón	Ride
A dónde va?	Where are you going?
Derecha	Right
Izquierda	Left
Derecho/recto	Straight
Taquilla	Ticket window
Un boleto para . . .	A ticket for . . .
Cuántos kilómetros?	How many kilometers?
Me voy a . . .	I'm going to . . .
Quiero bajar en . . .	I want to get off at . . .
Mapa	Map
Aeropuerto	Airport

Estación de ferrocarril	Train station
Autobús, camión	Bus
Terminal de autobuses	Bus station
Parada	Bus stop
Gasolina	Gas
Llanta	Tire
Semáforo	Stoplight
Motocicleta	Motorcycle
Carretera	Highway
El camino a . . .	The road to . . .
Puente	Bridge
Estación de Metro	Metro stop
Tarifa	Fare
Cruzar	To cross
Bicicleta	Bicycle

Where to Sleep

Casa de huéspedes	Guest house
Llave	Key
Gerente	Manager
Habitación, cuarto	Room
Para dos personas	For two people
Con	With
Sin	Without
Ducha	Shower
Agua caliente	Hot water
Ventilador	Fan
Aire acondicionado	Air-conditioning
Cama matrimonial	Double bed
Sábanas	Sheets
Incluido	Included
Camping	Campground
Hamaca	Hammock

Food

Comida	Food
Panadería	Bakery
Supermercado	Supermarket
Abarrotes	Groceries
Tengo hambre	I'm hungry
Mesero(a)	Waiter (waitress)
Desayuno	Breakfast
Almuerzo	Lunch
Cena	Dinner
Soy vegetariano(a)	I'm a vegetarian
Menú del día	Daily special
Comida corrida	Pre-prepared lunch special
Cuenta	Bill/check
Pan (integral)	(Wheat) bread
Pan tostado	Toast
Agua (purificado)	(Purified) water
Trago	Cocktail
Té/café	Tea/coffee
Refresco	Soda
Leche	Milk
Jugo	Juice
Manzana	Apple

Naranja	Orange
Piña	Pineapple
Limón	Lemon
Coconut	Coco
Fresa	Strawberry
Papa	Potato
Papas fritas	French fries
Arroz	Rice
Huevo	Egg
Pimiento	Pepper
Sal	Salt
Azúcar	Sugar
Carne	Meat
Bistec	Steak
Pollo	Chicken
Puerco	Pork
Pescado	Fish
Mariscos	Shellfish
Tenedor	Fork
Cuchara	Spoon
Cuchillo	Knife
Servilleta	Napkin
Helado	Ice cream

Numbers

Uno/una	One
Dos	Two
Tres	Three
Cuatro	Four
Cinco	Five
Seis	Six
Siete	Seven
Ocho	Eight
Nueve	Nine
Diez	Ten
Once	Eleven
Doce	Twelve
Veinte	Twenty
Treinta	Thirty
Cuarenta	Forty
Cincuenta	Fifty
Sesenta	Sixty
Setenta	Seventy
Ochenta	Eighty
Noventa	Ninety
Cien	One hundred
Mil	One thousand

Days and Months

Domingo	Sunday
Lunes	Monday
Martes	Tuesday
Miércoles	Wednesday
Jueves	Thursday
Viernes	Friday
Sábado	Saturday
Enero	January

Febrero	February
Marzo	March
Abril	April
Mayo	May
Junio	June
Julio	July
Agosto	August
Septiembre	September
Octubre	October
Noviembre	November
Diciembre	December

Conversions

Mexico, like most of the world, uses the metric system of weights and measures.

1 kilo = 2.205 pounds	1 pound = .454 kilos
1 meter = 3.281 feet	1 foot = .305 meters
1 liter = .264 U.S. gallons	1 U.S. gallon = 3.785 liters
$°C = 5/9(°F-32)$	$°F = 9/5(°C+32)$

Index

Notes

Escape to ancient cities and exotic

islands *with CNN Travel Guide, a*

wealth of valuable advice. Host Valerie Voss will take you

to all of your favorite destinations,

including those off the beaten path.

Tune into your passport to the world.

CNN TRAVEL GUIDE
SATURDAY 10:00 PMPT   SUNDAY 8:30 AMET

THE BERKELEY GUIDES

1995 "Big Bucks and a Backpack" Contest

Four lucky winners will receive $2,000* cash and a Jansport® World Tour backpack to use on the trek of a lifetime!

HOW TO ENTER:

Complete the official entry form on the opposite page, or print your name, complete address, and telephone number on a 3" x 5" piece of paper and mail it, to be received by 1/15/96, to: "Big Bucks and a Backpack" Contest, PMI Station, P.O. Box 3562, Southbury, CT 06488-3562, USA. Entrants from the United Kingdom and the Republic of Ireland may mail their entries to: Berkeley Guides Backpack Contest, Random House Group, P.O. Box 1375, London SW1V 2SL, England.

You may enter as many times as you wish, but mail each entry separately.

* One Grand Prize — £1,000 and a Jansport® World Tour backpack — will also be awarded to entrants from the United Kingdom and the Republic of Ireland.

Prizes: On or about 2/1/96, Promotions Mechanics, Inc., an independent judging organization, will conduct a random drawing from among all eligible entries received, to award the following prizes:

(4) Grand Prizes—$2,000 cash and a Jansport® World Tour backpack, approximate retail value $2,180, will be awarded to entrants from the United States and Canada (except Quebec).

(1) One Grand Prize — £1,000 and a Jansport® World Tour backpack, approximate retail value £1,090, will be awarded to entrants from the United Kingdom and the Republic of Ireland.

Winners will be notified by mail. Due to Canadian contest laws, Canadian residents, in order to win, must first correctly answer a mathematical skill testing question administered by mail. Odds of winning will be determined from the number of entries received. Prize winners may request a statement showing how the odds of winning were determined and how winners were selected.

To receive a copy of these complete official rules, send a self-addressed, stamped envelope to be received by 12/15/95 to: "Big Bucks and a Backpack" Rules, PMI Station, P.O. Box 3569, Southbury, CT 06488-3569, USA.

Eligibility: No purchase necessary to enter or claim prize. Open to legal residents of the United States, Canada (except Quebec), the United Kingdom, and the Republic of Ireland who are 18 years of age or older. Employees of The Random House, Inc. Group, its subsidiaries, agencies, affiliates, participating retailers, and distributors and members of their families living in the same household are not eligible to enter. Void where prohibited.

General: Taxes on prizes are the sole responsibility of winners. By participating, entrants agree to these rules and to the decisions of judges, which shall be final in all respects. Winners must complete an Affidavit of Eligibility and Liability/Publicity Release, which must be returned within 15 days or prize may be forfeited. Each winner agrees to the use of his/her name and/or photograph for advertising and publicity purposes without additional compensation (except where prohibited by law). Sponsor is not responsible for late, lost, stolen, or misdirected mail. No prize transfer or substitution except by sponsor due to unavailability. All entries become the property of the sponsor. One prize per household.

Winners List: For a list of winners, send a self-addressed, stamped envelope to be received by 1/15/96 to: "Big Bucks and a Backpack" Winners, PMI Station, P.O. Box 750, Southbury, CT 06488-0750 ,USA.

Random House, Inc., 201 East 50th Street, New York, NY 10022

Complete this form and mail to:
"Big Bucks and a Backpack" Contest, PMI Station, P.O. Box 3562, Southbury, CT 06488-3562.

Entrants from the United Kingdom and the Republic of Ireland, mail to: Berkeley Guides Backpack Contest, Random House Group, P.O. Box 1375, London SW1V 2SL, England.

Mail coupon to be received by 1/5/96.

NAME _____

ADDRESS _____

_____

COUNTRY _____   TELEPHONE _____

WHERE I BOUGHT THIS BOOK _____

A T-SHIRT FOR YOUR THOUGHTS . . .

After your trip, drop us a line and let us know how things went. People whose comments help us most improve future editions will receive our eternal thanks as well as a Berkeley Guides T-shirt. Just print your name and address clearly and send the completed survey to: The Berkeley Guides, 515 Eshleman Hall, U.C. Berkeley, Berkeley, CA 94720.

Your Name _____

Address _____

_____ Zip _____

Where did you buy this book? City _____ State _____

How long before your trip did you buy this book? _____

Which Berkeley Guide(s) did you buy? _____

Which other guides, if any, did you purchase for this trip? _____

Which other guides, if any, have you used before? (Please circle)
Fodor's   Let's Go   Real Guide   Frommer's   Birnbaum   Lonely Planet
Other _____

Why did you choose Berkeley? (Please circle as many as apply)
Budget information   More maps   Emphasis on outdoors/off-the-beaten-track
Design   Attitude   Other _____

_____

If you're employed: Occupation _____

If you're a student: Name of school _____ City & state _____

Age _____ Male _____ Female _____

How many weeks was your trip? (Please circle) 1 2 3 4 5 6 7 8 More than 8 weeks

After you arrived on your trip, how did you get around? (Please circle one or more)
Rental car   Personal car   Plane   Bus   Train   Hiking   Biking   Hitching
Other _____

When did you travel? _____

Where did you travel? _____

_____

The features/sections I used most were (please circle as many as apply):
Basics   Where to Sleep   Food   Coming and Going   Worth Seeing   Other

The information was (circle one):
Usually accurate   Sometimes accurate   Seldom accurate

I would _____ would not _____ buy another Berkeley Guide.

These books are brand new, and we'd really appreciate some feedback on how to improve them. Please also tell us about your latest find, a new scam, a budget deal, whatever—we want to hear about it.

For your comments:

_____

_____